Exploring Education

D1308867

This much-anticipated fourth edition of *Exploring Education* offers an alternative to traditional foundations texts by combining a point-of-view analysis with primary source readings. Pre- and in-service teachers will find a solid introduction to the foundations disciplines—history, philosophy, politics, and sociology of education—and their application to educational issues, including school organization and teaching, curriculum and pedagogic practices, education and inequality, and school reform and improvement. This edition features substantive updates, including the addition of discussion on the neo-liberal educational policy and recent debates about teacher evaluation, updated data and research, and new readings by leading researchers, such as Diane Ravitch, Robert Dreeben, and Helen F. Ladd.

At a time when foundations of education are marginalized in many teacher education programs and teacher education reform pushes scripted approaches to curriculum and instruction, *Exploring Education* helps teachers to think critically about the "what" and "why" behind the most pressing issues in contemporary education.

Alan R. Sadovnik is Board of Governors Distinguished Service Professor of Education, Sociology, and Public Administration and Affairs at Rutgers University, USA.

Peter W. Cookson, Jr. teaches at Teachers College, Columbia University, USA, and is President of Ideas without Borders in Washington, DC, USA.

Susan F. Semel is Professor of Education and Chair of the Department of Secondary Education at the City College of New York, USA.

Exploring Education

An Introduction to the Foundations of Education

Fourth Edition

Alan R. Sadovnik, Peter W. Cookson, Jr., and Susan F. Semel
With the assistance of Ryan W. Coughlan

Routledge
Taylor & Francis Group

NEW YORK AND LONDON

Fourth edition first published 2013
by Routledge
711 Third Avenue, New York, NY 10017

Simultaneously published in the UK
by Routledge
2 Park Square, Milton Park, Abingdon, Oxon OX14 4RN

Routledge is an imprint of the Taylor & Francis Group, an informa business

First edition published by Pearson Education, Inc. 1994
Third edition published by Pearson Education, Inc. 2006

Library of Congress Cataloging in Publication Data
Sadovnik, Alan R.
    Exploring education: an introduction to the foundations of education/
    by Alan R. Sadovnik, Peter W. Cookson, Jr. and Susan F. Semel.—4th ed.
    p. cm.
    Includes bibliographical references and index.
    1. Education—United States. 2. Educational sociology—United States.
    3. Education—United States—Philosophy. I. Cookson, Peter W. II. Semel,
    Susan F., 1941– III. Title.
    LA217.2.S23 2012
    370.973—dc23
    2012026851

ISBN: 978-0-415-80862-0 (hbk)
ISBN: 978-0-415-80861-3 (pbk)

Typeset in Goudy
by Florence Production, Stoodleigh, Devon

Printed and bound in the United States of America by Sheridan Books, Inc. (a Sheridan Group Company).

Contents

Preface

The first three editions of *Exploring Education: An Introduction to the Foundations of Education* were published by Allyn & Bacon. After they decided not to publish a fourth edition, Routledge generously offered to publish this fourth edition. It originally developed out of our dissatisfaction with the textbooks available for foundations of education courses. None of us is a strong advocate of traditional textbooks, as they often simplify complex material to the point of distortion, and, more importantly, they do too much work for students. One of the reasons many undergraduate and graduate students cannot read in a critical and analytical mode is that they have been educated, in part, through reading textbooks that summarize everything for them. As firm believers in the use of primary sources, we have written a book that will provide students with material that will encourage them to read, write, and think critically.

Originally, we wanted to compile a reader on the foundations of education. Once we began, however, the project evolved into a combined text/reader in a number of ways. First, in testing the readings in our classes, we found that many of our students required a context to help them make sense of the readings. Thus, we concluded that a book that combined our own text with illustrative readings made more pedagogical sense. As we moved along, we began to realize that our writings should not simply be an introduction to the readings; rather, each chapter should include our own analysis of the material, with a set of readings at the end of each chapter to illuminate the major concepts. This formula, we believed, would provide the necessary balance between text and primary sources.

Moreover, in thinking about our own textual material, we concluded that we wanted to present our point of view about the value of the foundations of education and their application to understanding education. Further, we wanted to argue that a "foundations perspective," as we call it, is a useful tool in helping to improve schools and schooling.

Thus, the final product is the result of considerable thinking about the importance of the foundations of education for teachers and prospective teachers and about how best to present the foundations of education to students. Our book is nontraditional in that it combines our own analysis with primary source readings. We have chosen to include a smaller number of complete or near-complete readings, rather than a larger number of shorter, excerpted readings. We believe strongly that students need to read complete sources to develop their critical reading, writing, and thinking skills.

The purpose of *Exploring Education* is to provide prospective and practicing teachers with an introduction to the foundations of education: history, philosophy, politics, and sociology of education. We also draw on the research of anthropologists of education in a number of places. Chapters 1 through 5 provide a basic introduction to the value of the foundations perspective and to the politics, history, sociology, and philosophy of education. Chapters 6 through 10 apply the foundations of education to particular educational issues, including school organization and teaching, curriculum and pedagogic practices, education and inequality, and school reform and improvement. Our approach is not meant to be exhaustive. Rather, we have attempted to provide a research- and theory-based approach that demonstrates the usefulness of the foundations lens for thinking critically about and, hopefully, solving educational problems.

This fourth edition continues to reflect these goals. We have eliminated some readings and added others based on responses from faculty, students, and reviewers. Additionally, the new readings often reflect more updated perspectives and data. At a time when foundations of education are marginalized in many teacher education programs and teacher education reform standards in favor of putatively more practical approaches in curriculum and instruction, we hope this book helps teachers and prospective teachers to think critically about the what and why as well as the how.

Exploring Education has truly been a collaborative effort. Although each of us was responsible for writing a number of chapters (Sadovnik: Chapters 2, 7, and 9; Cookson: Chapters 4, 6, and 8; Semel: Chapters 3 and 5; Sadovnik, Cookson, and Semel: Chapter 1; Semel, Cookson, and Sadovnik: Chapter 10), each of us edited all of the chapters, and the final product is the outcome of our joint efforts. We have attempted to create a consistency in style throughout.

Finally, we hope this book provides teachers and prospective teachers with a tool for understanding schools and a belief in their ability to help improve schooling. Although this book conveys a realistic portrayal of the societal and institutional factors that inhibit meaningful educational change, we believe that teachers, long the forgotten voice in educational reform, need to be part of such change. We believe that the foundations perspective is an important tool in school improvement and change, and hope our book provides its readers with both a realistic picture of educational problems and a sense of hope that they can contribute to change.

Acknowledgments

A number of individuals have contributed to the publication of the fourth edition. First and foremost, our editor Catherine Bernard, who has been Sadovnik's editor on two previous books and Semel's on one, has provided exemplary support, guidance and friendship throughout. She has kept us on task in a firm, but supportive manner. Second, her editorial assistants, Georgette Enriquez (now an acquisitions editor at Routledge), and Allison Bush have been instrumental in the revision and production processes. Ms. Bush has been especially effective in the detailed and difficult permissions process.

A number of individuals at Rutgers University provided research assistance for the fourth edition: Peijia Zha, Research Associate at the Newark Schools Research Collaborative, graduate assistants T.K. Kim and Elizabeth Rivera Rodas, Jean Sung, Camille Ferguson, Joyvin Benton and Ryan Coughlan, and intern Kelly Post. Ms. Post provided essential assistance in updating references, tables, charts and figures. Mr. Coughlan provided exemplary research assistance, editing, writing, and updating of tables, charts, and figures. Without his technical expertise the final manuscript could not have been prepared to meet our deadline.

In addition, Rosie Stewart and Diana Chambers of Florence Production offered invaluable assistance in copy-editing the final manuscript and guiding us through the production process. We believe this is a better book because of their input.

The Limits and Promises of Education

Toward Reflective Practitioners

Americans have always placed a great deal of faith in education. Schools have been viewed as providers of opportunities for social mobility, as places that nurture and develop the hearts and minds of children, as antidotes for ignorance and prejudice, and as solutions to myriad social problems. Throughout this country's history, countless Americans have regarded schools as a symbol of the American dream—that each successive generation, through hard work and initiative, could achieve more than their parents' generation.

This is not to say that Americans have not been critical of their educational system—quite the contrary! Throughout history, schools have been the subject of intense controversy and debate. Questions concerning teaching methods, politics, curricula, racial desegregation, equality of educational opportunity, and countless other issues have constantly defined the educational arena. It is precisely because Americans believe so passionately in education and expect so much from their schools that the educational system has never been free of disagreements and, at times, heated disputes.

Throughout the twentieth century, educational leaders, teachers, parents, and students disagreed about the fundamental goals of education and the educational practices occurring within classrooms. As the educational system steadily expanded and as the society of which it is a part became more complex, the role of schools also became more diverse, if not more diffuse. As prospective teachers, you are about to enter a profession that has both exciting possibilities and serious challenges. It is also a profession that is constantly subject to criticism and reform efforts. A look at the last 30 years provides a small but poignant glimpse of some of these reform movements.

Once again, today, there is a crisis in education. To historians of education, however, the existence of a crisis is by no means new and the meaning of *crisis* is by no means clear. In the early 1970s, *crisis in education* referred to the inequalities of educational opportunity, the allegedly authoritarian and oppressive nature of the schools, and the way in which classroom practices thwarted the personal development of students. The phrases of the day emphasized *relevance*, *equity*, *freedom*, and *individualism*. In the 1980s and 1990s, however, the emphasis shifted and the crisis was attributed to the decline of standards and authority, which was thought to be linked to the erosion of U.S. economic superiority in the world. The phrases of the day talked about *excellence*, *standards*, *back to basics*, and *cultural literacy*.

In these cycles of educational reform, teachers are often seen as both scapegoats and saviors. They are scapegoats in that if students do not know enough, it is because their teachers have not taught them enough or, worse still, do not know enough to teach them. Or, if children are not developing their individual creative abilities, it is because their teachers may have been more concerned with classroom control than individualized instruction. Teachers are saviors, on the other hand, in that they are mandated to implement the recommendations of each new wave of reforms.

As prospective teachers, you are thinking about a career in education for a variety of reasons. Some of them may include your love of children, the effects your own teachers had on you, the desire to make a difference and contribute to society, and your desire to help children develop both emotionally and intellectually. Some of you may have some less noble reasons, including the perception—however inaccurate—that teachers have easy schedules (home by 3:00 and summers off). Whatever your specific motives, we are sure that you are entering the profession to make a positive contribution to the lives of children and to gain internal satisfaction from witnessing educational success. Although we strongly believe that teachers can and do make a difference, we also recognize that you will be entering an educational system that has many problems. These problems often limit teachers in the fulfillment of their goals.

It is not our intention to depress you with pictures of educational problems nor to create an unrealistic portrait of an educational panacea that does not exist. Rather, we wish to produce a balanced tapestry of the world of schools—a world filled with both promise and limits, hope and despair. But most important, the purpose of this book is to help you understand this world of education: how it works, the factors that affect it, and your role as a teacher in making it better.

The following vignettes present the two poles of the teaching experience. The first, the poignant story of a teacher in an urban public school system, represents the underside of this country's schools and the frustration of a teacher caught in the middle of political, social, and educational problems that she alone cannot possibly solve:

My experience as a school teacher, both as a high school English teacher and an elementary school teacher, has been one of disappointment, frustration, anger and anxiety. I chose secondary English for a number of reasons, two primary ones being my love of literature and my comfortable familiarity with the school setting. Nothing in my college training gave me even an inkling that literature would not be the focus of my teaching, or that my future students would have values, outlooks and attitudes that were totally unfamiliar to me . . . .

Imagine my shock, then, when I walked into a classroom the following fall as a newly licensed teacher, and encountered surly, hostile, disinterested, below-grade-level students! . . . They had been reared on failure and low expectations, and consequently regarded school and teachers as enemies . . . .

As shocked and repulsed as I was initially, I was still determined to make a difference in the lives of my students. I thought I could plough through the poverty, illness, abuse, neglect and defeatism of their lives and get them to respond to Shakespeare's language, to Hawthorne's characters, to Hardy's themes. How foolishly unrealistic I was. My successes were scant and infrequent, my failures numerous and daily. I rarely knew the feeling that some teachers profess to experience when they "reach even one child." I was too numbed by a sense of futility to feel any sense of success . . . .

Over the years, I became cynical and resentful and even contemptuous of some of my students. When colleagues praised my teaching and my management ability, I felt as though I were fooling the world—a guilty feeling. Why would people think I was a good teacher when I knew that most of my students were bored, that they were making little if any progress and that I was not being dynamic or even enthusiastic in my approach? The answer is that none of those things mattered. As long as there was order in the room and notes on the chalkboard, everyone was satisfied. Record-keeping and keeping control of the kids were all that seemed important to administrators. You clocked in and clocked out and got paid, regardless of what you did in the intervening hours. Good teachers got no more recognition than poor ones, and poor ones could not be weeded out once they were tenured. It all seemed so pointless and hopeless.

. . . My current school has classrooms that are converted closets, lacks paper and other integral supplies, employs an assistant principal whose job was given to him by a politician, allows hoards of children to simply watch cartoons in the auditorium and calls that a "media lesson," is overrun with mice and roaches, has gaping holes in ceilings and walls, has toilets and water fountains that are nonfunctioning, and promotes children who are practically illiterate. Security breeches abound, with intruders walking in and out of the building at will; instruction is interrupted sometimes ten or fifteen times in one hour by announcements blaring over the intercom; innovative ideas that certain teachers toil to create in an effort to improve the school are almost always ignored by a principal who is resistant to change. Teachers live for 3 o'clock dismissals, for holidays, for summer vacations. A snow storm that closes the school for a day is viewed as one of nature's blessings.

What happened to the joys and rewards of teaching and learning? After eighteen years of seeking the answer and trying to buck the system, I've given up. It's been said that one good teacher can influence a child's entire life. I've never seen that happen personally. I've seen students come back to visit favorite teachers, I've heard students thank and praise helpful teachers, and I've known students who'll work harder for one teacher than he has for others. But I've never met an inner-city student who claimed that the course of his life had been shaped by one particular teacher, or who was inspired enough by that teacher's values and ideals to rethink his own. Maybe I expected too much from the profession; maybe I should be satisfied when one or two children out of thirty improve their reading comprehension or math skills each year. But I'm not; it isn't enough for me! (Katz, 1988)

The difficulties experienced by this teacher are not representative of what all or even most teachers face, but they do indicate that the educational systems that you will enter are often beset with problems that are not solely educational.

On the other hand, this second vignette speaks passionately and lovingly about the positive effects of teachers and describes the kind of teacher we all want to be. Written by Fred Hechinger in the *New York Times* and entitled "Gift of a Great Teacher," this tribute captures the ways in which teachers make a significant difference in the lives of students:

Tessie is different from the other teachers, a 9-year-old boy told his parents. . . . When he was asked how she was different, he replied, "Tessie knows how we children think."

Tessie, the boy's fourth-grade teacher at [a school in New York City], was Theresa Ross, who taught elementary and middle school classes for nearly 60 years. . . . Last June Tessie, who was affectionately known by that name to children and adults alike, died at the age of 83 . . . .

The only way to describe great teaching, a rare art, is to study great teachers like Tessie. When her pupils recognized that she knew how they thought, it did not mean that she herself thought childishly or indulgently about them. To write about her is not to celebrate a person but to try to define some qualities of exceptional teaching.

It has been said that education is what you remember when you have forgotten what you learned. Often, that means remembering one's great teachers more vividly than any particular lesson. Anyone who has never had at least one such teacher is truly deprived. To expect many is unreasonable. . . . As a teacher, [Tessie's] only doctrine was to make education come to life. When she taught history, her favorite subject, she took the children back with her into antiquity. She believed that even fourth-graders could deal with the universe.

[A former student teacher] in Tessie's class . . . recalls how Tessie used all the children's experiences to teach them—street games, the previous night's television programs, great myths.

She would do "weird" things. . . . To make children understand the evil consequences of a hostile invasion, she once had her pupils "invade" another classroom. As expected, the result was often bedlam, and she asked the children to report on the experience.

Great teachers are strong enough to dare being unconventional, even controversial, and this was an example. Actually, . . . Tessie had second thoughts about the experiment and never repeated it. Still, both she and the children had learned from the experience.

. . . Great teachers develop their own ways, without relying on prescribed lesson plans. Tessie said: "The child needs a framework within which to find himself; otherwise, he is an egg without a shell. The adult is there to guide and teach. If a child asks how to do something, you don't tell him just to go and find out; you say, 'Come, let's work it out together.'"

. . . Once, a picnic in the park that she and her fourth-graders had prepared was rained out, to universal groans. Tessie's response was to have the desks and chairs pushed aside, turning the classroom floor into a substitute picnic ground.

Tessie tried to get children to understand the nature of leadership without lecturing about it. She might start with baseball or with the news, and then move on to Julius Caesar.

. . . When Tessie died, even the youngest children who had known her sensed a sharp loss. Some felt guilty, said one teacher who met with them to talk about Tessie's life and to help them cope with her death. Perhaps, the teacher thought, as Tessie got older and a little forgetful, the children thought they might not have been sufficiently thoughtful and appreciative. A more plausible explanation may be that the children instinctively recognized an extraordinary teacher, and mourned the loss. (Hechinger, 1987)

How do you balance the extremes of these portraits? On one hand, you see an educational system beset with insurmountable problems; on the other hand, you see a world in which individual teachers have the power to influence countless children in a positive way. Moreover, what is the relationship between the two? That is, how do the problems within schools limit teachers' abilities to make a difference? And how do teachers who do make a difference help solve some of the problems? Teacher number 1 was not a less effective teacher than teacher number 2. Rather, the social, political, and economic problems she encountered in her school made it almost impossible to be effective. Teacher number 2 worked in a setting without these problems and one far more conducive to teaching excellence. The important point is that teachers work within organizational contexts that have a profound impact on their lives in classrooms.

As a person entering the teaching profession, you will ultimately find yourself in a curious quandary—responsible for educational problems and their solutions, but often without the necessary knowledge and perspective for understanding the complexity of these problems and the intricacies of their solutions. Furthermore, although teacher education programs do a respectable job at providing teachers with teaching methods, research on teacher education as well as a number of reform proposals indicates that programs are less effective in providing teachers with a social and intellectual context for understanding the educational world in which these methods will be employed. This understanding is crucial to the development of teachers, who must be an integral part of the problem-solving process if schools are to fulfill their promise.

In his classic book, *The Sociological Imagination*, C. Wright Mills (1959) outlined the value of a sociological perspective for understanding society. The sociological imagination, according to Mills, allows individuals to transcend the often narrow boundaries of their lives and to see the world from the broader context of history and society. Adopting the sociological imagination permits the user to connect his or her own life with the social, cultural, and historical events that have affected it, and ultimately enables the individual to understand how and why these forces are instrumental in shaping human existence. The promise of sociology, then, is its ability to provide a powerful understanding of society and oneself (Sadovnik, Persell, Baumann & Mitchell, 1987, p. 3). In light of the significant social, political, economic, and moral questions of his time, Mills argued that "the sociological imagination [is] our most needed quality of mind" (Mills, 1959, p. 3).

In a similar vein, contemporary American education, as we have argued, is beset by problems. The following section provides a brief overview of some of these.

Educational Problems

During the 1980s and 1990s, educational problems became the focus of national attention, and they continue to be today. The issues of educational standards, excellence, and the decline of

U.S. educational superiority in the international arena became central concerns. To a lesser extent, although of equal importance, the topic of equity, with particular attention to the crisis in urban education and the plight of children in the United States, received significant discussion. Although subsequent chapters will look at these issues more completely, this section briefly outlines a few of the significant educational problems today and some of the policies and programs aimed at treating them.

The Achievement Gaps

Since the 1960s, the achievement gaps based on social class, race, ethnicity, and gender have been the focus of educational policy. These gaps include group differences in achievement based on standardized tests and grades; attainment based on the number of years of schooling, high school and college attendance and graduation, dropout rates, and completion of honors and advanced placement courses; and opportunity based on access to qualified teachers, challenging curriculum, placement in special education, and investments in education, including state and local funding. Beginning with the Elementary and Secondary Education Act of 1965 through President George W. Bush's reauthorization of the act, the No Child Left Behind Act of 2001, federal educational policy has attempted to reduce these gaps (Cross, 2004). Under President Obama, Race to the Top (RTT) has continued many of the policies initititated under NCLB. In addition, beginning with the Coleman Report (1966), educational research has focused on the causes of inequalities of educational achievement, with a variety of factors both inside and outside schools seen as responsible for the gaps.

Trends

The gaps include higher academic achievement by high-income students compared to low-income students; white and Asian-American students compared to African-American and Hispanic students, even when controlling for socioeconomic level; and male students compared to female students. There have been some improvements since the 1960s, with the gender gap closing dramatically and in some cases, women outperforming men. Until 1988, social class, race, and ethnic differences decreased, but since then these gaps have widened, despite continued educational policies aimed at reducing them. Data from the National Assessment of Education Progress (NAEP) illustrate these achievement gaps.

- From 1970 to 1988, the gaps between African-Americans and Hispanic-Americans, as a group, and whites narrowed on the NAEP Reading for 17-year-olds; from 1973 to 1986, it narrowed on the NAEP Math for 13-year-olds. Between 1988 and 1990, this progress halted and gaps began to widen. In 1990, the gap between white and African-American 17-year-olds on the NAEP Math was 20 points, and in 1999, it was 32 points; in 1988, the gap between white and African-American 17-year-olds in NAEP Reading was 21 points, and in 1999, it was 31 points (U.S. Department of Education, National Center for Educational Statistics, NAEP Trends in Academic Progress, 2000). In 2009, the gap between white and African-American 17-year-olds slightly contracted to 27 points on the NAEP Reading and 30 points on the NAEP Math (U.S. Department of Education, National Center for Educational Statistics, The Condition of Education 2012a).
- On grade 4 Reading Achievement, 31 percent of all students were proficient or above, and 65 percent of all students scored basic or above. Disaggregated by group, the scores are African-American: 2 percent advanced, 12 percent proficient, 32 percent basic, and 54 percent below basic; Asian-American: 14 percent advanced, 30 percent proficient, 32 percent basic, and

24 percent below basic; Hispanic-American: 3 percent advanced, 14 percent proficient, 32 percent basic, and 51 percent below basic; Native American: 4 percent advanced, 16 percent proficient, 31 percent basic, and 49 percent below basic; white: 10 percent advanced, 31 percent proficient, 36 percent basic, and 23 percent below basic (Education Trust, 2009, www.edtrust.org).

- On grade 8 Mathematics Achievement, 31 percent of all students were proficient or above, and 70 percent of all students were basic or above. Disaggregated by group, the scores are African-American: 1 percent advanced, 10 percent proficient, 36 percent basic, and 53 percent below basic; Asian-American: 17 percent advanced, 32 percent proficient, 33 percent basic, and 18 percent below basic; Hispanic-American: 2 percent advanced, 13 percent proficient, 39 percent basic, and 46 percent below basic; Native American: 2 percent advanced, 15 percent proficient, 38 percent basic, and 44 percent below basic; white: 9 percent advanced, 32 percent proficient, 41 percent basic, and 19 percent below basic (Education Trust, 2009, www.edtrust.org).

- With respect to social class differences, on grade 4 Reading Achievement, the average scale score of poor students was approximately 207, and for nonpoor students approximately 235. On grade 8 Mathematics Achievement, the average scale score for poor students was approximately 269, and for nonpoor students approximately 296 (U.S. Department of Education, National Center for Educational Statistics, The Condition of Education, 2012a).

- Based on 2009 NAEP data, African-American and Hispanic-American 17-year-olds did math at the same levels as white 13-year-olds, and African-American and Hispanic-American 17-year-olds read at the same levels as white 13-year-olds (Education Trust, 2009, www.edtrust.org).

- With respect to attainment, four-year high school graduation 2006 rates, by group, were: all students: 73 percent; African-American: 59 percent; Asian-American: 90 percent; Hispanic-American: 61 percent; Native American: 62 percent; white: 82 percent (Education Trust, 2009, www.edtrust.org). Four-year college graduation 2004 rates for students who began college as freshmen were: all students: 29 percent; African-American: 18 percent; Asian-American: 34 percent; Hispanic-American: 19 percent; white: 31 percent. Based on longer term graduation rates of six years or more, in 2006, group graduation rates were African-American: 41 percent; Asian-American: 64 percent; Hispanic-American: 46 percent; white: 57 percent (Education Trust, 2009, www.edtrust.org).

- With respect to opportunity, in 2007–2008, 15.6 percent of all secondary classes were taught by teachers without a major or minor in their teaching field. In low-poverty schools it was 10.9 percent; in high-poverty schools it was 21.9 percent (U.S. Department of Education, National Center for Education Statistics, 2008).

- With respect to opportunity, in 2000, African-Americans comprised 17 percent of all public school K–12 enrollment. They comprised 8 percent of enrollment in gifted and talented classes; 22 percent of enrollment in special education classes; and 34 percent of suspensions. Asian-Americans comprised 4 percent of all public school K–12 enrollment. They comprised 7 percent of enrollment in gifted and talented classes; 2 percent of enrollment in special education classes; and 2 percent of suspensions. Hispanic-Americans comprised 16 percent of all public school K–12 enrollment. They comprised 10 percent of enrollment in gifted and talented classes; 15 percent of enrollment in special education classes; and 15 percent of suspensions. Native Americans comprised 1 percent of all public school K–12 enrollment. They comprised 1 percent of enrollment in gifted and talented classes; 1 percent of enrollment in special education classes; and 1 percent of suspensions. Whites comprised 61 percent of all public school K–12 enrollment. They comprised 74 percent of enrollment in gifted and talented classes; 60 percent of enrollment in special education classes, and 48 percent of suspensions (U.S. Department of Education, National Center for Education Statistics, 2004). These data have not changed significantly since 2000.

- With respect to investments, in 2006, the nation had an effective funding gap between highest and lowest poverty districts of $773 per student, $19,325 for a typical classroom of 25 students, and $309,200 for a typical elementary school of 400 students. These gaps vary by state, with some (e.g., Illinois, New York, and Pennsylvania) having large gaps and some (e.g., Delaware, Massachusetts, Minnesota, and New Jersey) providing more funding to high-poverty districts (Education Trust, 2009, www.edtrust.org).

Policy Issues

There is little agreement about the causes of the achievement gap or solutions aimed at eliminating it. Some researchers point to factors inside schools, including school funding, teacher quality, curriculum tracking, and teacher expectations; others blame outside-school factors, including poverty, parental involvement, cultural differences, genetic differences in intelligence, and lack of economic opportunities. The policy issues aimed at reducing the achievement gap are discussed more fully in the next section on improving urban schools, where the various achievement gaps are most pronounced.

Programmatic Issues

Consequently, there is also little agreement about programs aimed at eliminating the gaps. Some advocate programs that are aimed at reducing the school-based gaps in opportunity, including teacher quality and experience, unequal funding, access to rigorous curricula, and comprehensive whole-school reforms (Education Trust, 2004b, www.edtrust.org). No Child Left Behind (NCLB) and Race to the Top (RTT) are this type of programmatic reform. Others advocate programs that are aimed at reducing economic and cultural disadvantage as well as social, economic, and health disparities related to poverty (Anyon, 1997, 2005a; Rothstein, 2004b). The programmatic issues aimed at reducing the achievement gap are discussed more fully in the next section on improving urban schools, where the programmatic debates have been most heated.

The Crisis in Urban Education

This nation's urban public schools continue to be in crisis. Over the past 40 years, as central cities have become increasingly poor and populated by minorities, the schools have come to reflect the problems endemic to urban poverty. Although there are similar problems in rural schools and in many suburban schools, urban educational problems represent perhaps the nation's most serious challenge. A high proportion of urban schools are ineffective by most measures of school quality, a large percentage of urban students perform below national standards, and high school dropout rates in many large cities are over 40 percent. Despite these dismal data, there are policies and programs—including school restructuring programs, effective school models, and school choice and magnet programs—that many believe display significant potential for improvement. Clear national, state, and local policies are needed that emphasize excellence with equity and funding for programs.

Trends

Urban schools reflect the demographic characteristics of the urban environment. As large cities have become increasingly poor and populated by minorities, their schools have come to reflect the problems of urban poverty. Low student achievement, high dropout rates, and high levels of school ineffectiveness characterize many urban school districts.

- The United States has witnessed a significant increase in the percentage of poor and minority children and youth living in the central cities of the country. In 1971, 17 percent of the children and youth between the ages of 6 and 17 in large central cities were both poor and minority; by 1983, this percentage increased to 28 percent and continued to increase throughout the 1980s, the 1990s, and persists today (Anyon, 1997, 2005a; Levine & Havighurst, 1989, p. 75; Reardon, Arshan, Atteberry, & Kurlaender, 2010).
- Urban schools reflect social stratification and segregation. Due to the concentration of poor and minority populations in large urban areas, urban public schools have significantly higher percentages of low socioeconomic status (SES) and minority students than neighboring suburban school districts. In 2011, 78.2 percent of the children in New York City were from low-income families eligible for free or reduced lunch; 85.8 percent were black, Hispanic, or Asian. Increasingly, affluent white families in cities send their children to private schools (New York State Council on Children and Families, 2012, www.nyskwic.org/). This pattern continues in the 21st century.

In 2010, the enrollments of the six largest city school districts in the United States were:

1. New York: Asian-American: 13.7 percent; African-American: 32.2 percent; Hispanic-American: 39.4 percent; white: 14.2 percent.
2. Los Angeles: Asian-American: 6.4 percent; African-American: 10.2 percent; Hispanic-American: 73.4 percent; white: 9.5 percent.
3. Chicago: Asian-American: 3.6 percent; African-American: 45.0 percent; Hispanic-American: 41.0 percent; white: 9.0 percent.
4. Miami: Asian-American: 1.0 percent; African-American: 26 percent; Hispanic-American: 62 percent; white: 9 percent.
5. Houston: Asian-American: 2.9 percent; African-American: 26.5 percent; Hispanic-American: 61.7 percent; white: 7.8 percent.
6. Philadelphia: Asian-American: 7.0 percent; African-American: 58.3 percent; Hispanic-American: 18.0 percent; white: 13.8 percent.

- In urban schools, the relationship between socioeconomic status (SES) and academic attainment and achievement reflects overall national patterns. Students from lower SES families attain lower levels of academic attainment and performance than students from higher SES backgrounds. For example, in New York City districts with 50 percent or more students from low-income families, less than 40 percent are reading at or above grade level; in districts with less than 50 percent of students from low-income families, almost 60 percent are reading at or above grade level (New York City Department of Education, 2003). In addition, urban school dropout rates reflect this pattern. For example, the dropout rate in East Los Angeles is 60 percent; Boston, 50 percent; and Washington, DC, 45 percent. In other cities, such as Detroit, Pittsburgh, Chicago, New York, Cleveland, and Baton Rouge, high school dropout rates are also very high (between 30 and 45 percent) (Levine & Havighurst, 1989, pp. 55–58). Again, these patterns continue in the 21st century (Anyon, 1997, 2005a).
- Many urban public schools do not provide their students with a minimally adequate education. In 2011, only 24 percent of eighth grade students in New York City performed at or above the proficient level on the NAEP mathematics test and the reading test.

Furthermore, only 25 percent of eighth grade students in New York City performed at or above the proficient level on the NAEP writing test and only 13 percent performed at or above the proficient level on the NAEP science test. These data reflect national patterns for public schools in large urban areas (U.S. Department of Education, National Center for Educational Statistics, Trial Urban District Assessment, 2012).

Policy Issues

There is considerable disagreement among researchers and policy makers about how to improve urban schools. There is little consensus about school choice (giving parents the right to choose their children's schools), desegregation, and school financing policies. What is clear, however, is that policies that are aimed at the schools alone, without addressing the significant social and economic problems of urban areas, are doomed to failure (Anyon, 1997, 2005a; Ravitch, 2010; Rothstein, 2004b).

- Inequities in school financing exacerbate the problems faced by urban school systems. Because school financing is based on state funding formulas and local property taxes, most urban districts spend significantly less per pupil than wealthier suburban districts. Recent lawsuits in New Jersey, New York, and other states have sought to remedy these inequalities with varying degrees of success. For example, *Abbott* v. *Burke* in New Jersey has provided funding for its 31 urban Abbott districts, equal to its highest socioeconomic districts, although the School Finance Reform Act (SFRA) of 2008 has replaced Abbott as the New Jersey funding formula. The new formula has maintained additional funding for all low-income districts in the state. Also, the Campaign for Fiscal Equity lawsuit in New York resulted in the state's highest court mandating an additional $5.6 billion per year for New York City students.
- Demographic realities make urban schools increasingly segregated both by race and social class. Although the evidence on the effects of school desegregation on academic achievement is not conclusive, much research indicates significant positive effects of racial and economic integration (Grant, 2009; Mickelson, 2008; Frankenberg & Orfield, 2007; Schwartz, 2010) and many policy makers argue that there are moral imperatives requiring school desegregation (see UCLA Civil Rights Project, 2012).
- The difficult problems within urban schools have, in part, resulted in a crisis in staffing. Many urban school systems face a continual teacher shortage and witness significant teacher turnover. Most important, in many cities there is a crucial shortage of minority teachers to serve as role models for the increasingly minority student population (Educational Priorities Panel, 1987; Ingersoll, 2004; Ingersoll & Perda, 2010; Khalil, 2012; New York State Board of Regents, 1999).
- Policy makers disagree about how to improve urban schools. Some studies propose a radical overhaul of public education, including a voucher system, a free market competition between public and private schools, and unlimited parental choice in school selection (Chubb & Moe, 1990). Other studies suggest that such policies will increase the ability of high-income families to improve their children's education and ultimately continue to penalize low-income families. From the 1990s onward, charter schools (public schools that are independent of local school districts) became increasingly popular (Bulkley & Wohlstetter, 2004; Wells et al., 1998, Sadovnik, 2011b). There is significant diagreement about whether or not charter schools outperform traditional public schools (Baker, 2012; CREDO, 2009a, 2009b; Hoxby, 2009; Sadovnik, 2011b).

Programmatic Issues

Research suggests that there are programs that will improve urban schools. Effective school models, magnet programs (specialized schools), school choice programs, and parental community involvement all indicate promise. Funding for successful programs is needed to encompass a larger urban population.

- Effective school research has indicated that there are programmatic ways to improve urban schools. For example, the following characteristics have been identified with unusually effective schools in general and in urban settings: a safe and orderly environment; a clear school mission; instructional leadership by a principal or school head; a climate of high expectations; a concentration on instructional tasks; monitoring of student progress; and positive home-school relations (cited in Gartner & Lipsky, 1987, p. 389). School restructuring efforts based on these principles suggest promise (New Jersey Assessment of Knowledge and Skills, 2011). For instance, the work of Deborah Meier, former principal of Central Park East Secondary School in New York City, and James Comer, at Yale Medical School, in the New Haven Schools, are striking examples. Meier successfully implemented progressive school restructuring in an urban school with a mostly black and Latino population. Although CPESS closed in the early 2000s, years after Meier left, the school under Meier's leadership remains an example of an effective urban school (Semel & Sadovnik, 2008). Comer sucessfully implemented a school–university cooperative program for mostly low-income black students.
- Compensatory education programs (programs aimed at providing equality of opportunity for disadvantaged students) have resulted in academic improvement for children from low SES and disadvantaged backgrounds. Although the overall research on the effects of compensatory programs is mixed, there are studies that indicate that effective compensatory programs result in positive academic and social results (Natriello, McDill, & Pallas, 1990). Many policy makers believe that programs such as Head Start (a preschool program for children from low-income families), dropout prevention programs, and many bilingual education programs need to be funded, not eliminated (Lynch, 2004/2005).
- School choice programs may help to improve the education of urban children. Although there is disagreement about the extent of parental choice, many researchers believe that some combination of school choice and magnet school programs will improve urban education problems. In a number of urban settings, such as Minneapolis and District 4 in New York City, there have been significant improvements. In addition, studies of magnet and charter schools indicate significant educational possibilities (Grant, 2009; Lubienski, Weitzel, & Lubienski, 2009; Miron, Evergreen, & Urschel, 2008; Powers & Cookson, Jr., 1999; Tractenberg, Sadovnik, & Liss, 2004; Sadovnik, 2011b).
- The paucity of minority teachers and the lack of multicultural curricula are significant problems in urban school systems. Many experts believe that, given the student populations of most urban schools, it is imperative that programs are developed to attract and train minority teachers and to develop more multicultural curriculum projects.

The Decline of Literacy

Critics of U.S. public education have pointed to the failure of schools to teach children basic literacy skills in reading, writing, and mathematics, and basic knowledge in history, literature, and the arts. Although there has been significant controversy over the value of such skills and knowledge, and whether such a decline is related to the decline in U.S. economic superiority, it is apparent that schools have become less effective in transmitting skills and knowledge.

Trends

During the 1990s and into the twenty-first century, educational reforms stressed standards and accountability. Goals 2000, an educational bill passed under the Clinton administration, and state-mandated curriculum standards and assessments resulted in some increases in educational achievement. Although there are some problems with using standardized tests, and despite some achievement increases of the 1990s, comparisons of U.S. students to students from other countries, SAT scores, and other data indicate continuing problems in literacy.

- U.S. high school students performed less well than their counterparts in other industrialized nations in mathematics, science, history, and literature. Studies by the International Association for the Evaluation of Educational Achievement (IAEEA) reflect this trend. In 2009, students in the U.S. scored about average in comparison to other OECD countries on measures of reading literary. U.S. students had significantly lower reading literacy scores than 6 countries and higher reading literacy scores than 13 countries. Students in the U.S. scored below the OECD average in mathematics. Overall, U.S. students scored significantly lower than 17 countries and higher than 5 countries in mathematics. Students in the U.S. scored close to the average of OECD countries in science. U.S. students scored significantly lower than 12 countries and higher than 9 countries in science (U.S. Department of Education, National Center for Education Statistics, 2010).

  The belief that U.S. public schools are mediocre was not universally supported. David Berliner and Bruce Biddle argued in *The Manufactured Crisis* (1995) that the literacy and achievement crisis was largely a myth perpetuated by conservatives who supported tuition vouchers, school choice, and charter schools. They stated that the real crisis in education in the United States is the large achievement gap between affluent and poor students. Data from the Third International Mathematics and Science Study (TIMSS) indicated general improvement by U.S. students in science. The performance of U.S. students in mathematics remains a little below the international average (Baker & Smith, 1997). Recent TIMSS data in 2010 support those conclusions (U.S. Department of Education, National Center for Education Statistics, Trends in International Mathematics and Science Study, 2012).

- U.S. high school students scored lower on the SAT verbal and mathematic tests in the 1980s than in previous decades. For example, in 1967–1968, the average verbal SAT score was 466 and the average mathematics score was 492. In 1977–1978, the average scores were 429 and 468, respectively; in 1987–1988, the average scores were 428 and 476, respectively; in 1994–1995, the average scores were 428 and 482, respectively; in 2002–2003, the average scores were 507 and 519, respectively; and in 2009–2010, the average scores were 501 and 516, respectively (U.S. Department of Education, National Center for Education Statistics, 1989a, 1989b, 1997a, 1997b; U.S. Department of Education, Office of the Under Secretary and Office of Elementary and Secondary Education, 2004). Again, the validity of these scores is questionable, since more students attended college and thus took the SATs in the 1980s (therefore, a larger number of students from the lower achievement tracks in high school took the SATs), and the scores were recentered, creating higher scores in the post-1998 period, but these data point to problems in the U.S. schools. In addition, U.S. high school students do not score particularly well on standardized tests of culturally valued knowledge in history and literature. For example, in *What Do Our Seventeen Year Olds Know?* Ravitch and Finn (1987) argued that 17-year-old high school students have abysmal knowledge of basic information in history and literature. Although there is general controversy over the intrinsic value of such knowledge, New York State high school performance on these tests may indicate a problem in U.S. schools in transmitting this form of cultural knowledge to its students.

- In the 1980s, critics argued that the curriculum in many public and private high schools was "watered down" and provided far too many elective courses of suspect value and too little of substance. The National Commission on Excellence report (*A Nation at Risk*) and other reports pointed to the absence of a core curriculum of required courses for all students. In addition, critics suggested that, because most states require only the fulfillment of credit hours (that is, four years of English, three years of mathematics, etc.), specific knowledge in curriculum areas is rarely uniformly required. In addition, some critics pointed to the absence of a national curriculum and standards, commonplace in many countries (e.g., France), as a major shortcoming in U.S. education. Although there was significant controversy over many of these claims, there was agreement that the curriculum in most U.S. high schools needs significant attention.

  In the 1990s, although national curriculum standards did not emerge, curriculum standards set by national associations, such as the National Council of Teachers of Mathematics (NCTM) and the National Council of Social Studies (NCSS), as well as standards mandated by individual states often based on these, resulted in an increase in curriculum standards ("Quality Counts, 1999," 1999). Over the past few years, voluntary Common Core standards have been adopted in most states, moving the U.S. closer to a national curriculum.

- The U.S. literacy rate (and illiteracy rate) is shocking. According to the National Assessment of Adult Literacy, 30 million Americans have below basic literacy levels. An additional 60 million Americans function at a basic level and are only able to perform simple, everyday literacy activities. These data are well below the literacy rates of other indutrialized nations and are a serious indictment of the nation's educational system.

Policy Issues

There is little agreement about policy regarding standards and curriculum. Given the constitutional authority granted to states and localities for educational policies, many people argue against any federal governmental role. Others, such as Chester Finn, Jr., continue to propose the adoption of national standards in curriculum, knowledge, and skills (Finn, 1989). Finally, many are concerned with the need to balance higher standards with the guarantee that all students are given an equal opportunity to meet these standards.

- The adoption of national standards in curriculum, knowledge, and skills is a controversial proposal. The creation of nationally prescribed norms of what should be taught, what students should learn and know, and what students should be able to do is favored by some and opposed by others. Those in opposition believe that such norms should be locally determined or that such norms are impossible to develop.
- The balancing of higher standards and the ability of all students, particularly disadvantaged students, to meet these standards is an important issue. With dropout rates over 50 percent in many urban school districts, many fear that simply raising standards will exacerbate an already problematic situation.
- The development of core curriculum for graduation from high school, which would include the same academic subjects and knowledge for all students, poses significant issues about what the curriculum would include. Proponents of core curriculum, such as Diane Ravitch, Chester Finn, Jr., and E. D. Hirsch, suggest that the curriculum should include the canons of Western civilization as its starting point. Critics of this view suggest that a more multicultural curriculum needs to be developed.
- Policies aimed at raising standards and improving curriculum need to look at the effects of curriculum tracking policies. Curriculum tracking at the high school level and ability grouping

(with the same or different curricula) at the K–12 level is a controversial policy. Proponents point to the functional necessity and benefits of homogeneous groups; critics, such as Jeannie Oakes (1985), point to the inequities of such arrangements. Because research is inconclusive, policies concerning tracking need to be carefully addressed.

Programmatic Issues

In the past few years, all 50 states and most localities have implemented programs to raise academic achievement. At the federal level, the Goals 2000 legislation defined a national set of learning goals for all students, NCLB mandated state testings in grades 3 through 8, and RTT pushed Value Added Models (VAM) of assessment of schools and teachers based on student test scores.

- Programs at the state and local levels to define what students should know and be able to do were implemented in the 1990s. Taking their initial cue from the National Commission on Excellence report, *A Nation at Risk* (1983), many states and districts increased curriculum requirements for graduation and instituted core curriculum requirements. One fear is that such programmatic reforms may be artificial and raise scores simply by having teachers teach to tests. Another concern is that such standardization of curriculum may reduce innovation.
- States initiated minimum performance requirements for promotion (grades 4, 8, 10) and graduation (grade 12). NCLB initiated mandated state testing as well as required states to label schools that did not meet standards, as In Need of Improvement. Schools labeled this way face significant sanctions, including restructuring or closure. There is a concern with the use of standardized tests as the inclusive evaluation tool, and many states and local districts are experimenting with portfolios and other more qualitative evaluations. However, NCLB has made such assessments difficult, if not impossible.
- Effective school research indicates that schools that place student learning as the most important school goal are effective in improving learning. The application of effective school models, especially in urban areas, is necessary to ensure equity.
- Compensatory education programs and dropout prevention programs are essential if higher standards are not to become one more barrier for disadvantaged students. With literacy rates lowest with at-risk children and poor adults, both in urban and rural settings, literacy programs aimed at these populations are required.
- There have been increases in achievement due to these reforms. For example, from 1982 to 2012, the percentage of high school students taking the challenging academic courses recommended in *A Nation at Risk* increased significantly. Enrollments in Advanced Placement (AP) courses also increased significantly, and the number of students passing AP exams nearly tripled between 1982 and 2012. National Assessment of Educational Progress (NAEP) scores also increased. The average performance in mathematics improved substantially on the NAEP between 1978 and 2012. Among 9- and 13-year-olds, the improvement was the equivalent of at least one grade level. Performance in science was also higher in 2012 than in 1978 among all age groups, especially in general science knowledge and skills. These gains in academic performance, while significant, are not sufficient. The NAEP results in reading performance remain relatively unchanged, and the narrowed gap in performance between white and minority students remains unacceptably large (U.S. Department of Education, National Center for Education Statistics, 1998, 2000, 2003, 2012a, 2012b).

Assessment Issues

For both educational problems—the crisis in urban education and the decline of literacy—there are a number of assessment issues that need to be addressed. More empirical evidence on school effectiveness, especially qualitative studies on school processes, is needed. New assessment measures that eliminate class, racial, gender, and cultural bias must be developed.

- Large-scale educational studies have provided important data on school and student outcomes. More studies on the process of schooling, including ethnographic studies, are needed to understand the factors within schools that affect student achievement.
- Effective school research has provided significant understanding of the relationship between school organization and processes, and academic achievement. Research that assesses the implementation of effective school models based on this research is needed.
- More research on the relationship between family, culture, community, and school is needed. Although there are many theoretical analyses of these issues, far more empirical research is needed.
- New assessment techniques are needed to evaluate teacher and student performance and curriculum design. Studies indicate that traditional assessment devices may be culturally and racially biased. In addition to different quantitative measures, many researchers and educators believe that qualitative approaches such as portfolios should be considered (Martin-Kniep & Kniep, 1992; "Quality Counts, 1999," 1999). More recently, value added models (VAM) of teacher quality based on student growth on standardized achievement tests have been part of the federal Race to the Top (RTT) policies. More research is needed to ensure that such measures are valid and reliable (B. Baker, 2011).

The preceding discussion is a brief overview of a few of the many problems addressed more fully in this book. The presentation of trends, policy issues, programmatic issues, and assessment issues provides only a glimpse into the complexity of the problems and their solutions. In subsequent chapters, the specific issues will be explored in greater detail. For our purposes here, it is important to recognize that, as teachers, you will face many of these problems and will need a perspective for grappling with them. We believe that the foundations perspective is an important tool in understanding and solving such difficult educational dilemmas.

Understanding Education: The Foundations Perspective

As you can see, there is no shortage of critiques and there are a plethora of reform proposals. New teachers need a quality of mind—the kind of perspective that the sociological imagination advocated by Mills (1959) offers—in order to place the educational system in a context. Such a context or framework is necessary to understand the schools and the teacher's place within them, to understand how the schools relate to other aspects of society, and to see how educational problems are related to larger societal dilemmas. Finally, seeing the schools in their context will enhance your understanding of how the schools today reflect the historical evolution of reform efforts as well as how current debates frame what the schools will look like for each successive generation of teachers and students.

What do we propose that you, as prospective teachers, need in order to understand and answer these questions? Quite simply, we call it a *foundations perspective*. The foundations perspective is a lens for viewing the schools analytically from a variety of approaches that, taken together, provide the viewer with an understanding of the connections between teacher, student, school, and society. The foundations perspective also serves to relate educational organization and processes, and educational theory and practice. Most important, it links the understanding of these relationships to meaningful activity—the improvement of this nation's schools.

The foundations perspective consists of four interrelated approaches: historical, philosophical, political, and sociological. Through the use of the insights of the history of education, the philosophy of education, the politics of education, and the sociology of education, you will be better able to comprehend the educational system you are about to enter as teachers.

The history, philosophy, politics, and sociology of education, or what are commonly referred to as the *foundations of education*, are by no means separate and distinct perspectives. On one hand, they represent the unique vantage points of the separate disciplines of history, philosophy, political science, and sociology. On the other hand, historians, philosophers, political scientists, and sociologists rarely write from their own disciplines alone; more often than not, they tend to view the world from interdisciplinary and multidisciplinary perspectives. Therefore, although the following discussion presents the insights of each as a separate entity, please keep in mind that ultimately the foundations perspective seeks to combine all four disciplinary approaches and to look at the relationships between their central areas of concern. What, then, are the central areas of concern? And what is their value for teachers? We begin with the first question.

The History of Education

In *The Culture of Narcissism*, Christopher Lasch (1983) bemoaned what he termed the "waning of a sense of history." Lasch argued that contemporary Americans had lost their understanding of the past and therefore could neither understand the complexities of the present nor look to a better future. For Lasch, the historical perspective is essential not only because it gives one a grasp of one's heritage but also because it empowers one to envision the possibilities of the future.

All of you will enter an educational system that looks the way it does today because of historical processes and events. The debates, controversies, and reforms of the past are not unimportant footnotes for historians to mull over in their scholarly work. Rather, they are the pieces in the historical puzzle that comprise the educational world that you, as teachers, will inherit. Likewise, you in turn will become the next generation to place its stamp and have an impact on what the schools of tomorrow will be like.

In *The Eighteenth Brumaire of Louis Bonaparte*, Karl Marx (1963) wrote, "Men make their own history, but they do not make it just as they please; they do not make it under circumstances chosen by themselves, but under circumstances directly encountered, given, and transmitted from the past." History, then, provides people not only with a chronicle of the past but with a deep understanding of how and why the world has come to be. Such an understanding helps individuals to see both the limits and the possibilities for the future.

The schools look and work the way they do because of complex historical events and processes. To understand the educational problems of today, you must first have a perspective from which to comprehend these historical processes. This is the value and purpose of the history of education.

It is often said that people who do not understand history are doomed to repeat the mistakes of the past. Although we do not claim that the study of the history of education will make educators capable of eliminating mistakes altogether, and although the history of education suggests that people indeed tend to repeat some mistakes, we nonetheless believe that an ignorance of the past is a major barrier to educational improvement. Thus, the insights of the history of education are crucial to a foundations perspective.

This book will introduce you to the events that have defined the evolution of the U.S. educational system and to the significant debates between historians of education regarding the meaning of these events. First, you will look at the major historical periods in U.S. educational history: the colonial period, the common school era, the progressive era, and the modern era. Through an examination of what historians have written about each period, you will come to understand the relationship between each period and the debates and issues that characterized it, and you will be able to see how each educational reform set the stage for successive reform and reaction. Second, the readings in this book will also explore the controversies in the history of education about the interpretation of these events. That is, even when historians agree about the facts of educational development, they often passionately disagree about why things happened as they did. Over the past 30 years, for example, democratic liberal historians, who believe the history of U.S. education represents the increasing success of the schools in providing equality of opportunity for all citizens, and revisionist historians, who believe that the history of U.S. education represents a series of broken promises and the triumph of social and economic elites, have raised significant questions about the role of schools and the groups that have power to shape the educational system. Through an exploration of the views of historians from both of these perspectives, you may see that our schools are indeed the product of a variety of related factors and that the present debates are inherited from the past and influenced by its triumphs and defeats. To understand this is to understand the complexity of the present.

The Philosophy of Education

In order to comprehend fully the world of schooling, you, as future teachers, must possess a social and intellectual context (the foundations perspective). An understanding of the philosophy of education is essential in building this perspective.

Students often wonder why philosophy is considered to be an integral part of the foundations perspective, arguing that education is shaped by practice rather than by theory. They argue that teachers are called on to make situational decisions and that the methods employed by teachers at any given moment are based on their instincts or feelings. Students object to the study of philosophy on the grounds that it is an elite discipline that has little practical value. Why, then, do we contend that philosophy is an important component of both comprehending and negotiating the world of schooling?

We begin to answer this question by establishing the relationship between educational practices and philosophy. As is customary in the discipline of philosophy, issues are often resolved by posing questions and offering answers, which in turn usually lead to more questions. This method, established centuries ago by the ancient Greeks, is known as the *dialectic method*. Thus, we begin by posing the first of two questions to our students: What is your practice?—that is, What will you do with your own classes when you become practitioners? After our students describe, define, or clarify what they intend, we pose a second question: Why will you do what you have just described? By asking you to reflect on the "what" and "why" as you go about teaching in your classrooms, we may help you realize that your decisions and actions are shaped by a host of human experiences firmly rooted in our culture.

For example, why do some of you prefer informal classroom settings to formal ones? Why might some of you lean toward the adoption of the project method—an interdisciplinary curriculum approach developed during the progressive era? We suggest that your feelings might be articulated in the work of John Dewey, or that a preference for adopting the spiral curriculum may best be articulated through Jerome Bruner's work on curriculum. In other words, the choices that you, as prospective teachers, make and the preferences you have may best be clarified and expressed through the study of the philosophy of education.

As educators, we believe certain fundamentals exist within the human experience that color the choices we make as human beings and as teachers in the classroom. We suggest that as prospective teachers, you begin your reflective quest for these fundamentals by examining thought patterns and ideas within the discipline of philosophy.

This brings us to our second point: the uniqueness of the study of the philosophy of education, as distinct from philosophy. An interdisciplinary approach is called for in order to seek out the theoretical foundations upon which practice will be built. As students of the philosophy of education, it is important that you read selections from literature, psychology, sociology, and history, as well as philosophy. Through a thorough examination of thought patterns within the different disciplines, you will be sufficiently empowered to affect your own personal syntheses of the human experience, reflect on your world views, and make your own intensely personal choices as to what sort of practitioners you will be. Ultimately, the philosophy of education will allow you to examine *what ought to be* and thus enable you to envision the type of teachers you want to be and the types of schools that ought to exist.

The Politics of Education

Throughout history, schools have been the subject of considerable conflict about goals, methods, curriculum, and other important issues. Decisions about educational policies are rarely made in a smooth consensual manner, but rather are often the result of battles between various interest groups. U.S. schools are a contested terrain in which groups attempt to use political strategies to shape the educational system to best represent their interests and needs.

Political science helps educators understand power relations and the way interest groups use the political process to maximize their advantages within organizations. A political science perspective focuses on the politics of education—on power relations; on the relationship between the local, state, and federal governments and education; on school financing and law; and on the question of who controls the schools.

One of the major questions political scientists ask is How democratic are our schools?—that is, To what extent are educational policies shaped by the pluralistic input of many groups, or To what extent are they the result of domination by political elites? The political science approach to education will allow you to examine the complexities of questions such as these, while also providing important insights into education policy and change.

Another issue of importance, especially for teachers, is the organizational politics within schools. How do educational interest groups within schools—including administrators, teachers, students, and parents—arrive at policy? Which groups have the power to shape educational decisions for their own benefit? What are the patterns of political conflict and consensus? How do the relationships between these groups help define the educational debates of today? Through a close look at the politics of education, you will become aware of how these group interactions are essential for understanding schools and, more importantly, the ability of teachers to shape and change the educational system.

The Sociology of Education

The discipline of sociology developed at the end of the nineteenth century amid the turmoil and promise of industrialization, urbanization, and a growing faith in democracy and education. As more and more children were required to attend schools, questions arose about the relationship between school and society. As the institution of education grew, there was a perception among many thinkers that schools would help usher in a modern era in which merit and effort would replace privilege and inheritance as the criteria for social and occupational success.

Sociologists of education generally shared in this optimism. They began to explore the ways in which students were socialized for adult status, they examined the school as a social system, and they analyzed the effects of education on students' life chances. They believed that they could improve education through the application of social scientific theory and research. Because of their scientific orientation, sociologists of education are more apt to ask *what is* rather than *what ought to be*. They want to know what really goes on in schools and what the measurable effects of education are on individuals and on society. The hallmark of the sociological approach to education is empiricism, or the collection and analysis of social facts within a theoretical context that allows researchers to build a coherent set of findings. Thus, sociologists of education are interested in collecting data, and they try to avoid abstract speculation.

The sociological method is particularly useful when educational practices are related to educational outcomes. For example, in a study of public, Catholic, and other private schools, sociologists Coleman, Hoffer, and Kilgore (1982) were able to compare learning outcomes in these three types of schools by using survey analysis techniques. A practitioner or policy maker interested in school improvement can have some confidence that these results are valid and generalizable, and not simply opinion or wishful thinking. Of course, results are always subject to interpretation because all knowledge is, in a sense, the result of competing interpretations of events and ideas.

In sum, the methods of sociology are useful tools for understanding how schools actually interact with society. Although social science has no monopoly on wisdom or knowledge, it is based on an honest attempt to be objective, scientific, and empirical. Like history, sociology grounds us in the social context and tempers our educational inquiries by contrasting the real with the ideal. The sociological approach is fundamental to the foundations perspective because it keeps one's observations focused and testable. Without knowing *what is*, one cannot make the *ought to be* a reality.

The Foundations Perspective: A Multidisciplinary and Interdisciplinary Approach

The history, philosophy, politics, and sociology of education are separate disciplines; they are rarely used in isolation and are most often combined to ask the type of questions we have discussed. Although the selections in this book are often written from one of the perspectives, they generally use more than one of the disciplinary approaches. In fact, they are usually multidisciplinary and/or interdisciplinary (i.e., integrating more than one discipline). Moreover, the foundations perspective is a way of viewing schools that uses each of the approaches—the historical, the philosophical, the political, and the sociological—in an integrative manner. Therefore, although Chapters 2 through 5 of this book are organized around each discipline, the remainder is thematically arranged. Each theme is looked at through a variety of foundations approaches, each reflecting the critical applications of a foundations perspective to education.

Critical Literacy and Empowerment: Toward the Active Voice of Teachers

In the past few years, teacher accountability has become a centerpiece of educational reform debates. On one hand, those who have been termed the new educational reformers, have argued that teacher quality is among the most important factors in effective schools and that strong accountability measures are required to ensure that every child has a high quality teacher. Arguing that teacher unions have protected ineffective teachers through tenure, dismissal, and layoff policies, these reformers have called for a number of policies to ensure teacher quality. These include the evaluation of teachers through value added models (VAM) linked to their students' achievement on standardized tests, the end of tenure and last in, first out seniority (LIFO), rather than merit based layoff policies, and streamlined policies for removing teachers deemed to be ineffective (Ravtich, 2010). These policies have become cornerstones of President Obama's Race to the Top policy.

On the other hand, critics of these policies argue that the new reformers overstate dramatically the number of incompetent teachers and that value added models are extremely flawed in evaluating teacher quality (B. Baker, 2011). Further, they argue that while teacher quality is an important factor in school and student achievement, the new reformers' "no excuses" perspective ignores the many factors outside of schools, especially poverty, as central to explaining the achievement gap (Ravitch, 2010; Sadovnik, 2011b). Teacher unions, such as the American Federation of Teachers (AFT) and the National Education Association (NEA) have responded to these criticisms by saying that teachers are being scapegoated for problems often beyond their control.

Although these vociferous debates between the new reformers and teacher unions and other policymakers have highlighted important differences about the causes of the achievement gap, for the most part the voices of teachers have been left out of policy decisions. Teachers' voices have long been silent in discussions of educational reform. On one hand, administrators, college professors, politicians, and other educational experts all write about what is wrong with schools, but often without the practical experiential foundation of what it is like in the classroom. On the other hand, teachers often criticize these writings because the experts lack an understanding of what is termed "life in the trenches." However, many teachers show the same kind of oversight when they criticize the experts—they sometimes believe that the voice of experience is sufficient to describe, understand, and change schools. What is needed is a perspective that relates theory and practice so that teachers can combine their experiential knowledge with a broader, more multidimensional analysis of the context in which their experiences occur. The foundations perspective provides a theoretical and empirical base, but it alone is similarly insufficient as a tool for optimal understanding and effective change. When combined with the experiential voice of teachers, however, the foundations perspective becomes a powerful tool for teachers in the development of their active voice about educational matters.

In the view of C. Wright Mills (1959), the individual does not have the ability to understand the complex social forces that affect him or her and make up a society simply by virtue of living in the society. Likewise, teachers, solely by virtue of their classroom experiences, do not have the tools to make sense of the world of education. In fact, some teachers are too close and subjectively involved to have the emotional distance that is required for critical analysis. We are not suggesting that a teacher's experience is unimportant. We are saying that the theoretical and empirical insights of the foundations of education must comprise a crucial part of a teacher's perspective on education and thereby contribute to critical literacy. *Critical literacy* in education is simply the ability to connect knowledge, theory, and research evidence to the everyday experiences of teaching. Through the use of a foundations perspective, teachers can develop this essential ability and become, in Donald Schön's (1983) words, "reflective practitioners."

Criticisms of teacher education programs suggest that teachers do not receive a sufficiently intellectually rigorous education. Reports by the Carnegie Task Force (1986), the Holmes Group (1986, 1995), and the National Commission on Teaching and America's Future (1996) stated that teacher education programs, especially those at the undergraduate level, place too much emphasis on methodology and do not provide a solid knowledge base in the traditional disciplines that education students will eventually teach. The overemphasis on process at the expense of depth and breadth of knowledge and intellectual demands has, according to these critics, resulted in teachers who do not possess the intellectual tools needed to educate their students successfully. Thus, the cycle of educational decline in terms of knowledge and skills is reproduced. These reports propose the elimination of undergraduate education programs. In their place, the Commission recommends the requirement that prospective teachers complete professional training at the graduate level after attaining a liberal arts baccalaureate degree. Since these reports, a number of alternatives to traditional university-based teacher education have emerged that have sought to fast track the "best and brightest" into teaching. These include Teach For America (www.teachforamerica.org/), the New York City Teaching Fellows (www.nycteachingfellows.org), and the New Teacher Project (http://tntp.org/). There has been considerable debate about the effectiveness of such programs and the degree to which they may threaten teacher professionalism (Darling-Hammond & Snowden, 2005; Darling-Hammond & Bransford, 2005).

Although these criticisms are somewhat simplistic in that they often scapegoat teachers for educational problems that go well beyond the shortcomings of teacher education programs, we do believe that teachers should be more liberally and critically educated. The emphasis on knowledge, however, is not sufficient. The cultural literacy envisioned by the educational reformers of the 1980s and championed by writers such as E. D. Hirsch, Allan Bloom, and Diane Ravitch will not by itself provide teachers with the analytical and critical tools needed for understanding the schools. Although cultural literacy is important (even though the question of what constitutes the knowledge that teachers and students ought to have is a crucial dilemma), teachers need critical literacy in their ongoing attempt to make their voices heard and to effect meaningful change.

Students and teachers often ask us how critical literacy will help them solve problems. Are we suggesting that teachers equipped with the ability to understand the educational system will improve it easily? Of course not! Understanding the schools and improving them are two different matters. Without changes in the factors that affect the schools, as well as changes in the structure and processes within the schools, it is highly unlikely that large-scale change or even significant improvement will take place. What we are saying, however, is that teachers must be part of the ongoing dialogue focused on improving schools, and in order to contribute meaningfully to this dialogue they need more than their own experiences. They need the knowledge, confidence, and authority that are products of critical literacy.

Developing critical literacy is a first and necessary step toward bringing the active voice of teachers into the educational debates so that, together with other professionals, teachers can become intimately involved in the development of a better educational world. It will not be easy. As sociologists, philosophers, and historians of education, we do not pretend that the record suggests that we should be overly optimistic; neither does it suggest, however, that we should lose hope. It is our profound desire that the readings in this book will give you the tools to become part of this ongoing effort—the quest for better schools, better teachers, and a more humane and intelligent society!

2 The Politics of Education

Conservative, Liberal, Radical, and Neo-liberal Perspectives

Too often, teachers and prospective teachers look at educational issues within the narrow context of schools. That is, they treat what goes on inside classrooms and in the school at large as unrelated to the larger society of which it is a part. Schools are institutions that are rarely immune from external influences such as the economy, the political system, the family, and so on. Moreover, schools in every society exist for specific reasons, not all of which are educational. It is essential, then, that you understand the diverse and often conflicting purposes of schooling, as these goals are often at the heart of disagreements about education.

The terms *education* and *schooling* are sometimes used interchangeably when, in fact, they refer to somewhat different but related processes. Lawrence A. Cremin, the distinguished historian of U.S. education, defined *education* as

> the deliberate, systematic, and sustained effort to transmit, evoke, or acquire knowledge, attitudes, skills, or sensibilities, as well as any outcomes of that effort . . . . The definition projects us beyond the schools and colleges to the multiplicity of individuals and institutions that educate—parents, peers, siblings, and friends, as well as families, churches, synagogues, libraries, museums, summer camps, benevolent societies, agricultural fairs, settlement houses, factories, publishers, radio stations, and television networks. (1977, pp. 135–136)

Cremin's definition looks at education in the broadest possible sense to include all processes in a society that transmit knowledge, skills, and values, and educational institutions as all the places in which these activities occur.

Schooling is a more narrow process, as it is concerned with the activities that occur in schools. Therefore, where education is the most general societal activity, schooling is a particular example of the ways in which education occurs within the schools. Clearly from these definitions, schools are educational institutions. Why do they exist and what are their purposes?

In the broadest sense, schools have political, social, economic, and intellectual purposes. On a philosophical level, however, the purposes of education speak to what the political scientist Amy Gutmann refers to as

> that portion of education most amenable to our influence; the conscious efforts of men and women to inform the intellect and to shape the character of less educated men and women. And we naturally begin by asking what the purposes of human education should be—what kind of people should human education create. (1987, p. 19)

Therefore, the purposes of education, in general, and schooling, in particular, are concerned with the type of society people wish to live in and the type of people we wish to live in it. Ultimately, the purposes of education are directed at conceptions of what constitutes the "good life" and a "good person"—questions that have been at the center of philosophical inquiry from Plato to Aristotle, Marx, Freud, and Dewey.

As you will read throughout this book, there is little agreement about these difficult questions. Although men and women have different ideas about what society and individuals ought to look like, every society attempts to transmit its conception on these matters to its citizens. Education is crucial to this process.

The Purposes of Schooling

The specific purposes of schooling are intellectual, political, social, and economic (Bennett & LeCompte, 1990, pp. 5–21). These purposes refer to their role within any existing society—for our purposes, U.S. society. As you will read later in this chapter and in Chapter 4, one often must make the distinction between what the purposes of schooling are and what they ought to be. For example, those who support the goals of a society believe that schools should educate citizens to fit into that society; those who disagree with its goals believe that schools should educate citizens to change the society. As you can see, differing visions of education relate back to differing conceptions of what constitutes a good society.

The *intellectual* purposes of schooling are to teach basic cognitive skills such as reading, writing, and mathematics; to transmit specific knowledge (e.g., in literature, history, the sciences, etc.); and to help students acquire higher-order thinking skills such as analysis, evaluation, and synthesis.

The *political* purposes of schooling are to inculcate allegiance to the existing political order (patriotism); to prepare citizens who will participate in this political order (e.g., in political democracies); to help assimilate diverse cultural groups into a common political order; and to teach children the basic laws of the society.

The *social* purposes of schooling are to help solve social problems; to work as one of many institutions, such as the family and the church (or synagogue) to ensure social cohesion; and to socialize children into the various roles, behaviors, and values of the society. This process, referred to by sociologists as *socialization*, is a key ingredient to the stability of any society.

The *economic* purposes of schooling are to prepare students for their later occupational roles and to select, train, and allocate individuals into the division of labor. The degree to which schools directly prepare students for work varies from society to society, but most schools have at least an indirect role in this process.

As you will read in Chapter 4, these purposes sometimes contradict each other. For example, the following question underscores the clash between the intellectual and political purposes of the school: If it is the intellectual purpose of the school to teach higher-order thinking skills, such as critical thinking and evaluation, then can it simultaneously engender patriotism and conformity to society's rules? Lawrence A. Cremin pointed out:

> Schooling—like education in general—never liberates without at the same time limiting. It never empowers without at the same time constraining. It never frees without at the same time socializing. The question is not whether one or the other is occurring in isolation but what the balance is, and to what end, and in light of what alternatives. (1977, p. 37)

This dialectic, or the tension between schooling's role in maintaining the status quo and its potential to bring about change, is at the heart of differing conceptions of education and schooling. As we pointed out earlier, those who support the society tend to stress the school's role in helping to maintain it; those who believe the society is in need of improvement or change stress its role in either improving or transforming it. In the following sections, you will read about how different political perspectives on education view not only the purposes of schooling but a variety of related issues.

Political Perspectives

Debates about educational issues often focus on different views concerning the goals of schools and their place within society. From the inception of the U.S. republic through the present, there have been significantly different visions of U.S. education and the role of schools in society. Although many of the views are complex, it is helpful to simplify them through the use of a political typology. In its most simple form, the different visions of U.S. education can be discussed in terms of conservative, liberal, and radical perspectives. Although the nature of these approaches has changed over time, what follows is a contemporary model of how each perspective views a number of related educational issues. In the following sections, we will explore each perspective in terms of its view of U.S. society, its view of the role of the school in relation to equality and the "American dream," its explanation of student failure and under-achievement in schools, its definition of educational problems at the turn of the twenty-first century, and its educational policy and reform proposals.

General Issues: Conservative, Liberal, Radical, and Neo-liberal Perspectives

Political perspectives on education have rarely been used consistently. One of the problems in using labels or typologies is that there is often little agreement about what constitutes the basic principles of any particular perspective. Furthermore, there have been historical changes in the meanings of each of the approaches under consideration: the conservative, the liberal, and the radical. In addition, as many educators have used the terms *traditional* and *progressive* to denote similar approaches, there is often considerable confusion over matters of terminology. In this section, we will define each of the perspectives and relate them to progressive and traditional perspectives. In subsequent sections, the specific features of the conservative, liberal, radical, and neo-liberal perspectives will be delineated.

A *perspective* is a general model for looking at something—in this case, a model for understanding, analyzing, and solving educational problems. As you will see throughout this book, there has been and continues to be little agreement about the nature, causes, and solutions to educational problems. In order to understand the ways in which various authors look at educational issues, it is necessary to understand how they approach the problems—that is, to understand where they are coming from (their perspective, its assumptions, etc.).

The conservative, liberal, and radical perspectives all look at educational issues and problems from distinctly different, although at times overlapping, vantage points. Although there are areas of agreement, they each have distinctly different views on education and its role in U.S. society. Moreover, they each have fundamentally different viewpoints on social problems and their solution in general, and their analysis of education is a particular application of this more general world view. Finally, the neo-liberal perspective supports some of the tenets of both the liberal and conservative positions. The following sections first summarize the conservative, liberal, and radical perspectives and then present the neo-liberal perspective in relation to these.

The Conservative Perspective

The conservative view has its origins in nineteenth-century social Darwinist thought (see Gordon, 1977) that applied the evolutionary theories of Charles Darwin to the analysis of societies. This perspective, developed originally by the sociologist William Graham Sumner, looks at social evolution as a process that enables the strongest individuals and/or groups to survive, and looks at human and social evolution as adaptation to changes in the environment. From this point of view, individuals and groups must compete in the social environment in order to survive, and human progress is dependent on individual initiative and drive.

A second feature of the conservative viewpoint is the belief that the free market or market economy of capitalism is both the most economically productive economic system and the system that is most respectful of human needs (e.g., for competition and freedom). Based in part on the eighteenth-century writings of the British political economist Adam Smith and applied to twentieth-century economic policy by the Nobel laureate economist Milton Friedman, conservatism argues that free market capitalism allows for the maximization of economic growth and individual liberty with competition ensuring that potential abuses can be minimized. Central to this perspective is the view that individuals are rational actors who make decisions on a cost-benefit scale.

Thus, the conservative view of social problems places its primary emphasis on the individual and suggests that individuals have the capacity to earn or not earn their place within a market economy, and that solutions to problems should also be addressed at the individual level. The presidency of Ronald Reagan represented the political ascendancy of this viewpoint. Reagan championed a free market philosophy and argued that welfare state policies (government intervention in the economy) were at the heart of an American malaise. His presidency (1980–1988) was characterized by supply-side economics (a form of free market capitalism), the elimination of many governmental regulations, and the curtailment of many social programs. The Reagan philosophy stressed individual initiative and portrayed the individual as the only one capable of solving his or her own problems. Whereas conservatives lauded Reagan's policies and credited him with restoring U.S. economic growth, both liberals and radicals were very critical.

The Liberal Perspective

The liberal view has its origins in the twentieth century, in the works of the U.S. philosopher John Dewey, and, historically, in the progressive era of U.S. politics from the 1880s to the 1930s. Perhaps more important, the liberal view became politically dominant during the administration of Franklin Delano Roosevelt (1933–1945) and what is often referred to as the *New Deal era*.

The liberal perspective, although accepting the conservative belief in a market capitalist economy, believes that the free market, if left unregulated, is prone to significant abuses, particularly to those groups who are disadvantaged economically and politically. Moreover, the liberal view, based on the economic theories of John Maynard Keynes, believes that the capitalist market economy is prone to cycles of recession that must be addressed through government intervention. Thus, the liberal perspective insists that government involvement in the economic, political, and social arenas is necessary to ensure fair treatment of all citizens and to ensure a healthy economy. The impact of such liberal policies is evident throughout the twentieth century, from the New Deal initiatives of FDR (including the Social Security Act and the Works Progress Administration, a federally funded jobs program) to the New Frontier proposals of John F. Kennedy, to the Great Society programs of Lyndon Baines Johnson to (although he probably would take issue with this) George H. W. Bush's savings and loan bailout.

The liberal perspective, then, is concerned primarily with balancing the economic productivity of capitalism with the social and economic needs of the majority of people in the United States. Because liberals place a heavy emphasis on issues of equality, especially equality of opportunity, and because they believe that the capitalist system often gives unfair advantages to those with wealth and power, liberals assert that the role of the government is to ensure the fair treatment of all citizens, to ensure that equality of opportunity exists, and to minimize exceedingly great differences in the life chances and life outcomes of the country's richest and poorest citizens. Moreover, liberals believe that individual effort alone is sometimes insufficient and that the government must sometimes intercede on behalf of those in need. Finally, the liberal perspective on social problems stresses that groups rather than individuals are affected by the structure of society, so solutions to social problems must address group dynamics rather than individuals alone.

The Radical Perspective

The radical perspective, in contrast to both the conservative and liberal perspectives, does not believe that free market capitalism is the best form of economic organization, but rather believes that democratic socialism is a fairer political-economic system. Based on the writings of the nineteenth-century German political economist and philosopher Karl Marx (1818–1883), the radical viewpoint suggests that the capitalist system, although undeniably the most productive form of economic organization, also produces fundamental contradictions that ultimately will lead to its transformation into socialism.

Although the economic analysis of these contradictions is complex and unnecessary to the level of understanding required here, it is important to note that the central contradiction pointed out by radicals is between the accumulation laws of capitalism (i.e., that wealth is both accumulated and controlled privately) and the general social welfare of the public. That is, radicals (Gordon, 1977; Bowles & Gintis, 1976, 1986) assert that, at this stage in capitalist development, U.S. society has the productive capacity to ensure a minimally acceptable standard of living, including food, shelter, and healthcare for all its citizens. Thus, radicals believe a socialist economy that builds on the democratic political system (and retains its political freedoms) would more adequately provide all citizens with a decent standard of living. What is essential to the radical perspective is the belief that social problems such as poverty and the educational problems of the poorest citizens are endemic to capitalism and cannot be solved under the present economic system. Rather, radicals assert that only a transformation of capitalism into democratic socialism will ensure that the social problems that disproportionately affect the disadvantaged in U.S. society will be addressed.

Radicals believe that the capitalist system is central to U.S. social problems. They also recognize that the capitalist system is not going to change easily and, furthermore, that most Americans fervently support it. Therefore, most radicals place their primary emphasis on the analysis of inequality under capitalism, the economic and power relationships that are central to the perpetuation of inequalities, and policies that seek to reduce these inequities under the existing capitalist system. Thus, while theoretically and politically supporting change, the radical perspective often agrees with those liberal programs aimed at issues concerning equity.

Finally, the radical perspective believes that social problems are structural in nature—that is, that they are caused by the structure of U.S. society and therefore the solutions must be addressed to this structure, not at individuals. To argue that social problems are caused by deficits in individuals or groups is to "blame the victim," according to the radical perspective (Ryan, 1971).

The collapse of the communist (state socialism) world in Eastern Europe and the former Soviet Union has resulted in serious challenges in the United States to the claims of the radical perspective. Conservatives and many liberals argue that the events in the former Soviet Union and Eastern Europe signal the death of communism, as well as socialism, and denote historical evidence for the superiority of capitalism. Although it is clear that state socialism as practiced in the former Soviet Union and Eastern Europe has failed, radicals do not agree that its failure denotes either the bankruptcy of socialism or the final moral victory of capitalism. Rather, radicals suggest that socialism failed in these cases for a number of reasons.

First, without a capitalist economic base to build on (a prerequisite for socialism in Marx's original theory), socialist economies in communist societies could not efficiently produce sufficient goods and services. Second, without a democratic political base, communist societies denied the necessary human freedoms essential to a healthy society. Furthermore, radicals suggest that the collapse of state socialist economies does not preclude the ability of socialism to succeed in democratic-capitalist societies. Finally, radicals argue that the collapse of communism in no way eliminates the problems endemic to Western capitalist societies, particularly those related to extremes of inequality. Therefore, although conservatives view these events with great satisfaction, radicals point to the social problems in U.S. society. Liberals, to some degree, believe that these events point to the power of their point of view: that the collapse of socialist economies in communist societies indicates the strength of the capitalist economy, while the significant social problems that remain in U.S. society suggest the importance of further liberal responses.

The three perspectives, then, have overlapping but distinctly different views on the nature of U.S. society and its social problems. The conservative perspective is a positive view of U.S. society and believes that capitalism is the best economic system, as it ensures maximum productivity with the greatest degree of individual freedom. Social problems, from its vantage point, are caused by individuals and groups, and it must be individuals and groups that solve them on their own, with little or no direct government intervention.

The liberal perspective is also positive about U.S. society, albeit with reservations. Liberals also believe that capitalism is indeed the most productive economic system, but they suggest that, if left unrestrained, capitalism often creates far too much political and economic disparity between citizens. Thus, liberals believe the state (government) must intercede to ensure the fair treatment of all and that social problems are often the result of societal rather than individual or group forces.

Finally, the radical perspective, unlike the other two, is negative about U.S. society. It recognizes the productive capacity of its capitalist economic system, but it argues that the society structurally creates vast and morally indefensible inequalities between its members. Radicals, who favor significantly greater equality of outcomes between citizens, believe that U.S. social problems cannot be solved under the existing economic system. They favor a movement toward democratic socialism: a society that, according to radicals, would combine democratic political principles (including representative government, civil liberties, and individual freedom) with a planned economic system—one that is planned for the satisfaction of the human needs of all of its citizens.

In the United Kingdom, under Tony Blair's and Gordon Brown's New Labour party, which was in power from 1997 to 2010, the government supported a blend of liberal and radical policies. Based on British sociologist Anthony Giddens's (the director of the London School of Economics) concept of *the third way* (1999), New Labour believed that the strengths of market capitalism, combined with welfare state socialism, reflected the goals of social democracy. After the election of Conservative Party Prime Minister David Cameron in 2010, the country returned to consertative and neo-liberal policies.

Traditional and Progressive Visions of Education

Discussions of education often refer to *traditional* and *progressive* visions. Although these terms have a great deal in common with the conservative, liberal, and radical perspectives discussed earlier, they are sometimes used interchangeably or without clear definitions, and therefore there is often confusion concerning terminology. For our purposes, we will use the terms *traditional* and *progressive* as the most general representations of views about education. Traditional visions tend to view the schools as necessary to the transmission of the traditional values of U.S. society, such as hard work, family unity, individual initiative, and so on. Progressive visions tend to view the schools as central to solving social problems, as a vehicle for upward mobility, as essential to the development of individual potential, and as an integral part of a democratic society.

In a nutshell, traditionalists believe the schools should pass on the best of what was and what is, and progressives believe the schools should be part of the steady progress to make things better. In relation to the conservative, liberal, and radical perspectives, there is significant overlap. If we use a political continuum from left to right, with the left signifying the radical pole and the right the conservative pole (mirroring the political terminology of *left* and *right wing*), we suggest the following relationship:

Thus, progressive visions encompass the left liberal to the radical spectrums; traditional visions encompass the right liberal to the conservative spectrums. Obviously, as with all typologies, this is somewhat of a simplification. Although many theories that we will discuss and illustrate in subsequent chapters may have significantly more overlap, this typology is, nonetheless, a useful tool for understanding different visions about education.

The discussion so far has concentrated on the general approach to U.S. society and social problems taken by each perspective. The next section looks specifically at how each perspective analyzes education and educational problems.

The Role of the School

The role of the school is a central focus of each of the perspectives and is at the heart of their differing analyses. The school's role in the broadest sense is directly concerned with the aims, purposes, and functions of education in a society.

The conservative perspective sees the role of the school as providing the necessary educational training to ensure that the most talented and hard-working individuals receive the tools necessary to maximize economic and social productivity. In addition, conservatives believe that schools socialize children into the adult roles necessary to the maintenance of the social order. Finally, they see the school's function as one of transmitting the cultural traditions through what is taught (the curriculum). Therefore, the conservative perspective views the role of the school as essential to both economic productivity and social stability.

The liberal perspective, while also stressing the training and socializing function of the school, sees these aims a little differently. In line with the liberal belief in equality of opportunity, it stresses the school's role in providing the necessary education to ensure that all students have an equal opportunity to succeed in society. Whereas liberals also point to the school's role in socializing children into societal roles, they stress the pluralistic nature of U.S. society and the school's role in teaching children to respect cultural diversity so that they understand and fit into a diverse society. On the political level, liberals stress the importance of citizenship and participation in a democratic society and the need for an educated citizenry in such a society. Finally, the liberal perspective stresses individual as well as societal needs and thus sees the school's role as enabling the individual to develop his or her talents, creativity, and sense of self.

Therefore, the liberal perspective sees the role of education as balancing the needs of society and the individual in a manner that is consistent with a democratic and meritocratic society. That is, liberals envision a society in which citizens participate in decision making, in which adult status is based on merit and achievement, and in which all citizens receive a fair and equal opportunity for economic wealth, political power, and social status.

Diane Ravitch, historian of education, eloquently summarizes the liberal view of education:

> To believe in education is to believe in the future, to believe in what may be accomplished through the disciplined use of intelligence, allied with cooperation, and good will. If it seems naively American

to put so much stock in schools, colleges, universities, and the endless prospect of self-improvement and social improvement, it is an admirable, and perhaps even a noble flaw. (1983, p. 330)

The radical perspective, given its vastly differing view on U.S. society, likewise has a significantly different view of what the school's role is. Although radicals believe schools ought to eliminate inequalities, they argue that schools currently reproduce the unequal economic conditions of the capitalist economy and socialize individuals to accept the legitimacy of the society. Through what radicals term *social and cultural reproduction*, the school's role is to perpetuate the society and to serve the interests of those with economic wealth and political power. Most important, through a vastly unequal educational system, radicals believe that schools prepare children from different social backgrounds for different roles within the economic division of labor. The radical perspective, unlike the liberal, views equality of opportunity as an illusion and as no more than an ideology used to convince individuals that they have been given a fair chance, when in fact they have not. Therefore, the radical perspective argues that schools reproduce economic, social, and political inequality within U.S. society.

In Chapter 1, we discussed the U.S. belief in education and the view that schooling is an essential component of the American dream of social mobility and equality of opportunity. Conservatives, liberals, neo-liberals and radicals have differing views on the role of the school in meeting these goals.

The conservative perspective believes that schools should ensure that all students have the opportunity to compete individually in the educational marketplace and that schools should be meritocratic to the extent that individual effort is rewarded. Based on the belief that individuals succeed largely on their own accord, conservatives argue that the role of the school is to provide a place for individual merit to be encouraged and rewarded.

Liberals believe that schools should ensure that equality of opportunity exists and that inequality of results be minimized. Based on the historical record, the liberal perspective indicates that although schools have made a significant difference in the lives of countless Americans and have provided upward mobility for many individuals, there remain significant differences in the educational opportunities and achievement levels for rich and poor.

Radicals believe that schools should reduce inequality of educational results and provide upward social mobility, but that historically the schools have been ineffective in attaining these noble goals. Moreover, the radical perspective argues that under capitalism schools will remain limited, if not wholly unsuccessful, vehicles for addressing problems of inequality—problems that radicals suggest are structurally endemic to capitalism.

Explanations of Unequal Educational Performance

If, as radicals and many liberals suggest, schooling has not sufficiently provided a reduction in inequality of results, and as educational achievement is closely related to student socioeconomic backgrounds (as was indicated in Chapter 1), then the explanation of why certain groups, particularly from lower socioeconomic backgrounds, perform less well in school is a crucial one. Conservatives argue that individuals or groups of students rise and fall on their own intelligence, hard work, and initiative, and that achievement is based on hard work and sacrifice. The school system, from this vantage point, is designed to allow individuals the opportunity to succeed. If they do not, it may be because they are, as individuals, deficient in some manner or because they are members of a group that is deficient.

The liberal perspective argues that individual students or groups of students begin school with different life chances and therefore some groups have significantly more advantages than others. Therefore, society must attempt through policies and programs to equalize the playing field so that students from disadvantaged backgrounds have a better chance.

Radicals, like liberals, believe that students from lower socioeconomic backgrounds begin school with unequal opportunities. Unlike liberals, however, radicals believe that the conditions that result in educational failure are caused by the economic system, not the educational system, and can only be ameliorated by changes in the political-economic structure.

Definition of Educational Problems

Until this point, we have focused on the role of the school and, in particular, its relationship to equality of opportunity and results. Although these are certainly significant issues, the ways in which each perspective addresses specific educational problems at the close of the twentieth century, and consequently how each sees solutions to these, is of the utmost importance. We will begin with a discussion of the definition of educational problems.

The conservative perspective argues the following points:

1. In their response to liberal and radical demands for greater equality in the 1960s and 1970s, schools systematically lowered academic standards and reduced educational quality. Conservatives often refer to this problem as the *decline of standards*.
2. In their response to liberal and radical demands for multicultural education (i.e., education that responds to the needs of all cultural groups), schools watered down the traditional curriculum and thus weakened the school's ability to pass on the heritage of American and Western civilizations to children. Conservatives often define this problem as the *decline of cultural literacy*.
3. In their response to liberal and radical demands for cultural relativism (i.e., that every culture's values and ideas are equally valid), schools lost their traditional role of teaching moral standards and values. Conservatives often refer to this problem as the *decline of values or of civilization*.
4. In their response to liberal and radical demands for individuality and freedom, schools lost their traditional disciplinary function and often became chaotic. Conservatives often refer to this problem as the *decline of authority*.
5. Because they are state controlled and are immune from the laws of a competitive free market, schools are stifled by bureaucracy and inefficiency. Liberals have significantly different viewpoints on the major educational problems of our times.

The liberal perspective argues the following points:

1. Schools have too often limited the life chances of poor and minority children and therefore the problem of underachievement by these groups is a critical issue.
2. Schools place too much emphasis on discipline and authority, thus limiting their role in helping students develop as individuals.
3. The differences in quality and climate between urban and suburban schools and, most specifically, between schools with students of low socioeconomic backgrounds and high socioeconomic backgrounds is a central problem related to inequalities of results.
4. The traditional curriculum leaves out the diverse cultures of the groups that comprise the pluralistic society.

The radical perspective, although often similar in its analysis to the liberal viewpoint, is quite different in its tone. The radical perspective argues the following points:

1. The educational system has failed the poor, minorities, and women through classist, racist, sexist, and homophobic policies.

2. The schools have stifled critical understanding of the problems of American society through a curriculum and teaching practices that promote conformity.
3. The traditional curriculum is classist, racist, sexist, and homophobic and leaves out the cultures, histories, and voices of the oppressed.
4. In general, the educational system promotes inequality of both opportunity and results.

Educational Policy and Reform

Defining educational problems is the first step toward the construction of solutions. From the 1980s to the 2000s, proponents of each perspective supported specific educational reform and policy recommendations. The following brief discussion outlines the policies and programs of each without going into any detail. (A more detailed analysis will be provided in Chapters 3, 6, and 10.)

Conservatives support the following:

1. Return to basics (often referred to as *back to basics*), including the strengthening of literacy skills, such as reading and writing, and other forms of traditional learning.
2. Return to the traditional academic curriculum, including history, literature, and the canons of Western civilization.
3. Introduce accountability measures for students and schools, including minimum standards of performance and knowledge—that is, create minimum standards for what students should know and for the skills they should possess at specific grade levels (e.g., fourth, eighth, and twelfth grades).
4. Introduce free market mechanisms in the educational marketplace, including tuition tax credits and vouchers for parents who wish to send their children to private schools and public school choice programs, including charter schools (allowing parents to choose among different public schools). This is often referred to as *school privatization*.

Liberals support the following:

1. Policies should combine a concern for quality for all students with equality of opportunity for all. This is sometimes referred to as *quality with equality*.
2. Policies should lead to the improvement of failing schools, especially urban schools. Such programs should include school-based management and teacher empowerment (decentralized control of individual schools with teachers having a significant voice in decision making), effective school programs (programs that are based on what is called the *effective school research*—research that indicates "what works"), and public school choice programs. Whereas liberals support parental choice of public schools, they rarely support conservative proposals for complete privatization, tuition tax credits, and vouchers, as these are seen as threatening public education and creating increasingly unfair advantages for parents who are already economically advantaged.
3. Programs should enhance equality of opportunity for disadvantaged groups, including Head Start (a preschool program for students from lower socioeconomic backgrounds), affirmative action programs, compensatory higher education programs (college programs for disadvantaged students), and so forth.
4. A curriculum should balance the presentation of the traditions of Western civilization with the treatment of other groups within the culturally diverse society.
5. A balance should be maintained between setting acceptable performance standards and ensuring that all students can meet them.

Radicals support the following:

1. On a general level, radicals do not believe that educational reform alone will solve educational problems, as they see their causes outside the purview of the educational system. Short of what most radicals see is necessary but unrealistic largescale societal change—they support most liberal reform programs as long as they lead to greater equality of educational results.
2. Programs should result in greater democratization of schools—that is, give teachers, parents, and students a greater voice in decision making. Examples of these are teacher empowerment, school-based management, school decentralization, and school-community cooperation efforts.
3. Curriculum and teaching methods should involve "critical pedagogy" (Giroux, 1988; Kincheloe & Steinberg, 1998)—that is, radicals support educational programs that enable teachers and students to understand social and educational problems and to see potential solutions (radical) to these.
4. Curriculum and teaching methods should be multicultural, antiracist, antisexist, anticlassist, antihomophobic—that is, radicals support educational programs that include curricular treatment of the diverse groups that comprise U.S. society and that are pedagogically aimed at sensitizing students to classism, racism, sexism, and homophobia.

Radicals, although often supporting many of the liberal educational reform proposals, are less sanguine about their potential effectiveness. In fact, as Samuel Bowles pointed out, the failure of liberal reforms may prove successful in a very different political context:

> Educational equality cannot be achieved through changes in the school system alone. Nonetheless, attempts at educational reform may move us closer to that objective if, in their failure, they lay bare the unequal nature of our school system and destroy the illusion of unimpeded mobility through education. Successful educational reforms—reducing racial and class disparities in schooling, for example, may also serve the cause of equality of education, for it seems likely that equalizing access in schooling will challenge the system to make good its promise of rewarding educational attainment or find ways of coping with mass disillusionment with the great panacea. (1977, p. 149)

Education and the American Dream

The next chapter will focus directly on the ways in which educational reform evolved in U.S. history. Although our discussion thus far has looked at the last 50 years, it is essential to understand that the present debates and crises are outcomes of a much longer historical time span in which the disagreements about educational issues helped shape the present educational system. It is also important to note that all three perspectives have different views on U.S. educational history, especially with regard to the school's success in living up to the democratic promise discussed in Chapter 1.

Conservatives argue that the U.S. schools have succeeded in providing a quality education for those who are capable and have taken advantage of it, and that, until the 1960s and 1970s, schools were responsible for U.S. superiority in economic and technological realms. On one hand, conservatives argue that the system has provided a meritocratic selection process that has ensured that the most talented and motivated individuals are rewarded by the schools and later in life. This mechanism historically has successfully guaranteed that the important roles and occupations are filled with those individuals capable of handling them. On the other hand, conservatives believe that the progressive reforms of the twentieth century (to be discussed in Chapter 3), especially those occurring in the 1960s and 1970s, eroded the quality of the schools, their curriculum, and what students learned. Thus, the U.S. educational system, from this point of view, is found wanting, especially in relation to its role in economic development and competitiveness.

The liberal perspective is more concerned with the social and political functions of schooling than the economic. As such, liberals believe that schools have been successful in extending public education to the masses and providing more opportunity for mobility than any other system in the world. Moreover, liberals believe that U.S. education has been essential in the long, slow, and flawed march toward a more democratic and meritocratic society—a society where one's individual achievement is more important than one's family background, a society that is more just and humane, and a society where tolerance of others who are different is an important value. Despite these successes, liberals argue that the educational system has been an imperfect panacea (Perkinson, 1995) and has yet to provide sufficient access, opportunity, and success for all citizens, and thus must continue to improve.

The radical perspective is far less optimistic about the historical success than either the liberal or conservative viewpoints. According to radicals, the U.S. schools have been unsuccessful in providing equality of opportunity or results to the majority of citizens. Although it is true that the United States has educated more people for longer periods of time than any other nation in the world, radicals believe the overall outcomes have reproduced rather than reduced social and economic inequalities. According to this perspective, the historical record suggests that, although educational opportunities expanded throughout the twentieth century, students from different class backgrounds were offered different types of education (e.g., middle- and upper middle-class students in an academic program in the public high school and poor students in a vocational program; middle- and upper middle-class students in a four-year baccalaureate college education and poor students in a two-year community college education). Therefore, according to radicals, the history of U.S. education has been the story of false promises and shattered dreams.

In the next chapter, you will have the opportunity to explore the events, conflicts, debates, and reforms that comprise this history and to judge for yourself the extent to which the history of U.S. education supports one or more of these political interpretations.

The Neo-liberal Perspective

During the past decade, neo-liberal reforms have received significant attention as the latest solutions in policy discussions of urban school reform and efforts to reduce the achievement gap. Neo-liberal reform is often a synthesis of conservative and liberal perspectives. Neo-liberal reformers have critiqued failing traditional urban public schools and attribute their failures to teacher unions and their support of teacher tenure and layoffs based on seniority and the absence of student, teacher and school accountability to ensure improvement. This critique has been part of an over two-decade conservative and neo-liberal celebration of market based choice reforms, with reformers arguing that school choice through charters and vouchers is necessary to destroy the public school monopoly and to provide the competition required to improve urban schools. Borrowing from the logic of Diane Ravitch's Left Back (2000), neo-liberals turned the progressive left's argument about equity on its head, suggesting that traditional public schools, rather than providing equality of opportunity for low-income children, have systematically reproduced inequalities through failing schools for these students, a claim reminiscent of Bowles and Gintis's Schooling in Capitalist America (1976).

This neo-liberal agenda has become an important feature of official federal, state, and local policy. At the federal level, President Bush's No Child Left Behind (2001) mandated the use of student achievement tests to measure school quality, and President Obama's Secretary of Education Arne Duncan's signature program, Race to the Top (RTT), requires states to expand the number of charter schools and to implement Valued Added Models (VAM) of teacher evaluations based on student achievement to qualify for RTT funding. At the state level, Republican New Jersey Governor Chris Christie has pledged to eliminate teacher tenure and seniority based layoffs, increase the number of charter schools, and pass voucher legislation. At the local level, Democratic Newark Mayor, Cory Booker, with the influx of a $100 million dollar gift from Facebook Founder Mark Zuckerberg and another $100 million in matching funds, has initiated a school reform process that includes an expansion of charter schools. Also in Newark, the two-year-old Newark Charter School Fund, with over $20 million in funding from among others the Walton, Broad, and Gates Foundations, has embarked on increasing the number of charter schools in Newark.

Neo-liberal reforms stress five areas for educational policy: 1. Austerity; 2. The market model; 3. Individualism; 4. State intervention; and 5. Economic prosperity, race and class. They have synthesized both conservative and liberal perspectives to provide a critique of traditional public education.

First, austerity involves cutting public spending on education. Like conservatives, they argue that the enormous increases in federal, state and local education spending has not resulted in concomitant increases in student achievement, especially in urban schools and that efficiency can reduce costs and improve quality. They argue that urban parochial schools perform at higher levels than their traditional counterparts at much lower costs, although the evidence on this is extremely mixed at best (B. Baker, 2011).

Second, neo-liberals, like conservatives, believe that the free market solves social problems better than governmental policy. Based on this belief, neo-liberals support charter schools, vouchers for private school attendance, especially for low-income children, and privatization of schooling through for-profit educational management companies (Lipman, 2011).

Third, like conservatives, neo-liberals believe that educational success or failure is the result of individual effort rather than of social and economic factors. The only factors outside the individual responsible for educational success are school quality, which is better addressed by a market model, and the culture of students and their families, which are better addressed through the promotion of middle-class educational attitudes, values and behaviors (Mosovitch et al., 2010).

Fourth, like liberals, neo-liberals believe that state intervention in the educational system is at times necessary to ensure equality of opportunity. Whereas conservatives believe that the market is capable of "raising all boats," neo-liberals believe that state intervention is sometimes required to ensure that failing schools or districts improve. Therefore, neo-liberal policies include state intervention into failing districts and schools, the closing of failing schools, and, as in No Child Left Behind and Race to the Top, federal measures to support and reward successful educational policies, and negative sanctions to punish failing policies (Sadovnik, 2011b).

Fifth, like liberals, neo-liberals believe that race and social class are important factors in the achievement gap and that African-American and Hispanic students and lower income students are more likely to achieve and attain at lower levels than White, Asian and higher income students. While neo-liberals have made the elimination of these race and socio-economic achievement gaps as a central part of their reform policies, they do not see poverty as an excuse for educational inequality. Rather, neo-liberals blame failing schools and ineffective teachers as the primary causes of school and student failures. Moreover, they argue that education is the key to global economic competitiveness, so that improving education is fundamental to United States global economic superiority (Apple, 2004; Lipman, 2011).

Ironically, Diane Ravitch (2010) herself has attacked these neo-liberal reforms as betraying their promise of improving public schools because the new reformers have attempted to privatize public education, have championed closing schools rather than fixing them, have supported charter schools over traditional public schools, and narrowed the curriculum through the overreliance on standardized testing in reading, writing and mathematics.

From Political Perspectives to the Politics of Education

As you have read, there is considerable disagreement among the four perspectives. In the world of education, these disagreements play themselves out in conflicts. These conflicts involve different groups, parents, teachers, administrators, legislators, business people, and so on, and are central to understanding educational decision making. As you will read in Chapter 3, the history of education in the United States has rarely been a smooth one. It has involved the conflict between groups with opposing values and interests, groups all seemingly interested in the same thing—the best education for the nation's children—but with significantly different perceptions of what that constitutes and how to go about it.

Sometimes these conflicts have been about curriculum and pedagogy (e.g., the conflicts about vocational versus academic education in the 1930s and 1940s or traditional versus child-centered teaching at the turn of the twentieth century); sometimes they have been about values and morality (e.g., as in the textbook and book-banning controversies of the last 20 years or over the question of prayer in schools); and sometimes they have been about civil rights and racial issues (e.g., the violent battles over school desegregation in Little Rock, Arkansas, in the late 1950s and in Boston, Massachusetts, in the 1970s).

Sometimes these conflicts are external to the school and involve the federal, state, and local governments, the courts, and the business community. Sometimes they are internal to the schools and involve parents, teachers, and teacher unions or organizations, students, and administrators.

Whatever the specific nature of the conflicts, they all involve power and power relationships. Political scientists are concerned with understanding how power relationships (i.e., which groups have power and which do not) affect educational decision making and organizational outcomes. As our discussion in Chapter 3 about the history of education will reveal, struggles about education rarely involve equals, but rather involve groups with disparate degrees of power. Therefore, these struggles often involve the attempts to maximize political advantage and to minimize that of opposing groups.

Whereas political scientists are concerned with who controls our schools (Kirst, 1984), political philosophers are concerned with who ought to control them and for what end. In her brilliant book *Democratic Education*, Gutmann (1987) outlined the philosophical dimensions of this political question. She argued that there are four different conceptions of who should have the authority to determine educational matters: the family state, the state of families, the state of individuals, and the democratic state (pp. 19–47). Each perspective answers the question, Who should have the authority over educational decisions in a different manner?

The family state viewpoint is derived from Plato's theories of education (to be discussed more fully in Chapter 5). This approach sees the purpose of education as creating a socially stable society committed to the good life and justice. The definition of a just society, however, is determined by an elite—what Plato referred to as the *philosopher kings* (or in Gutmann's gender equal terminology, *philosopher queens*). It is this elite that defines the just society, and it is through education that citizens learn to accept this view of society and are thereby able to contribute to its smooth functioning. In terms of educational authority, it is a small and hopefully just elite that should determine educational decisions.

The second viewpoint, the state of families, is derived from the eighteenth-century English political philosopher John Locke. Based on the Lockean view that parents are the best guardians of their children's rights and interests, it suggests that families should have the final authority in educational decision making.

The third position, the state of individuals, is derived from the work of the nineteenth-century British philosopher John Stuart Mill. Based on the nineteenth-century liberal notion that the state should not impose its will on individuals nor threaten their individual liberties, it suggests that educational authorities should not "bias the choices of children toward some disputed or controversial ways of life and away from others" (Gutmann, 1987, p. 34). Thus, educational authority ought to provide opportunity for choice among competing conceptions of the good life and neutrality among them (Gutmann, 1987, p. 34). In this manner, individuals have authority over educational matters to the extent that they are given the freedom to choose among the widest possible options about the kind of lives they wish to live.

Gutmann provided an exhaustive criticism of these three perspectives, suggesting that the family state leaves one at the tyranny of the state, the state of families at the tyranny of families, and the state of individuals without a clear way to reproduce what a society believes is responsible for its citizens. Each perspective, she argued, is flawed because it fails to provide a compelling rationale for either its view of a good society or who should define it.

Gutmann proposed a fourth perspective: the democratic state of education. In this view,

> Educational authority must be shared among parents, citizens, and professional educators even though such sharing does not guarantee that power will be wedded to knowledge (as in the family state), that parents can successfully pass their prejudices on to their children (as in the state of families), or that education will be neutral among competing conceptions of the good life (as in the state of individuals). (1987, p. 42)

Recognizing that a democratic state has built-in problems, including the tyranny of the many over the few, Gutmann argued that there must be two limitations on such a state: nonrepression and nondiscrimination. Nonrepression does not permit the state or groups to use the educational system for eliminating choice between different alternatives of a just society; nondiscrimination requires that all children receive an adequate education—one that will enable them to participate in the democratic deliberations of their society (1987, p. 46).

As you can see, the question of educational authority is a complex one and has been at the center of educational conflict. Throughout this book, you will read about different educational viewpoints and different recommendations for solutions to educational problems. In this chapter, we have tried to make you aware that such conflicts rest on different assumptions about society, the purposes of education, and who should determine these important matters.

In the following readings, the perspectives on education are illustrated. In the first article, "Hijacked! How the Standards Movement Turned into the Testing Movement," historian of education and former Assistant Secretary of Education under George H.W. Bush, Diane Ravitch, argues the standards movement she once supported has become dominated by standardized testing.

The second article, "What 'Counts' as Educational Policy? Notes Toward a New Paradigm," by educational researcher Jean Anyon, argues that these types of conservative and liberal educational policies have had little impact on reducing the achievement gap. Anyon's article outlines a radical perspective in which she argues that liberal educational reforms must be tied to larger political, social, and economic reforms to be successful. Her article combines a radical critique of the excesses of free market capitalism with a view that liberal educational reforms are necessary under capitalism.

Hijacked! How the Standards Movement Turned into the Testing Movement

Diane Ravitch

In the first decade of the twenty-first century, the leading reform ideas in American education were accountability and choice. These ideas were at the heart of President George W. Bush's No Child Left Behind program, which he signed into law in January 2002. No Child Left Behind—or NCLB—changed the nature of public schooling across the nation by making standardized test scores the primary measure of school quality. The rise or fall of test scores in reading and mathematics became the critical variable in judging students, teachers, principals, and schools. Missing from NCLB was any reference to what students should learn; this was left to each state to determine.

I was initially supportive of NCLB. Who could object to ensuring that children mastered the basic skills of reading and mathematics? Who could object to an annual test of those skills? Certainly not I. Didn't all schools test their students at least once annually?

As NCLB was implemented, I became increasingly disillusioned. I came to realize that the law bypassed curriculum and standards. Although its supporters often claimed it was a natural outgrowth of the standards movement, it was not. It demanded that schools generate higher test scores in basic skills, but it required no curriculum at all, nor did it raise standards. It ignored such important studies as history, civics, literature, science, the arts, and geography. Though the law required states to test students eventually in science, the science scores didn't count on the federal scorecard. I saw my hopes for better education turn into a measurement strategy that had no underlying educational vision at all. Eventually I realized that the new reforms had everything to do with structural changes and accountability, and nothing at all to do with the substance of learning. Accountability makes no sense when it undermines the larger goals of education.

How did testing and accountability become the main levers of school reform? How did our elected officials become convinced that measurement and data would fix the schools? Somehow our nation got off track in its efforts to improve education. What once was the standards movement was replaced by the accountability movement. What once was an effort to improve the quality of education turned into an accounting strategy: Measure, then punish or reward. No education experience was needed to administer such a program. Anyone who loved data could do it. The strategy produced fear and obedience among educators; it often generated higher test scores. But it had nothing to do with education.

Tests should follow the curriculum. They should be based on the curriculum. They should not replace it or precede it. Students need a coherent foundation of knowledge and skills that grows stronger each year. Knowledge and skills are both important, as is learning to think, debate, and question. A well-educated person has a well-furnished mind, shaped by reading and thinking about history, science, literature, the arts, and politics. The well-educated person has learned how to explain ideas and listen respectfully to others.

In the 1980s and early 1990s, efforts to revive liberal education in the schools seemed to be gaining ground; many states were reviewing their academic expectations with an eye to strengthening them in all grades. In 1991 and 1992, the agency that I headed in the U.S. Department of Education awarded grants to consortia of professional groups of teachers and scholars to develop voluntary national standards in history, English language arts, science, civics, economics, the arts, foreign languages, geography, and physical education.[1] I acted at the direction of Secretary Lamar Alexander, who believed as I did that all children should have access to a broad education in the arts and sciences.

The efforts to establish voluntary national standards fell apart in the fall of 1994, when Lynne V. Cheney attacked the not-yet-released history standards for their political bias. As chairperson of the National Endowment for the Humanities, Cheney had funded their development along with the Department of Education. Cheney's scathing critique in the *Wall Street Journal* opened up a bitter national argument about what history, or rather, *whose* history, should be taught.[2]

Cheney lambasted the standards as the epitome of left-wing political correctness, because they emphasized the nation's failings and paid scant attention to its great men. The standards document, she said, mentioned Joseph McCarthy and McCarthyism nineteen times, the Ku Klux Klan seventeen times, and Harriet Tubman six times, while mentioning Ulysses S. Grant just once and Robert E. Lee not at all. Nor was there any reference to Paul Revere, Alexander Graham Bell, Thomas Edison, Jonas Salk, or the Wright brothers. Cheney told an interviewer that the document was a "warped and distorted version of the American past in which it becomes a story of oppression and failure."[3]

Editorialists and radio talk shows across the country weighed in on the dispute, some siding with Cheney, others defending the standards. Every major newspaper and newsmagazine covered the story of the angry ideological conflict. The controversy quickly became a debate about the role of minority groups and women in American history, which was placed in opposition to the role of great white men. Radio host Rush Limbaugh said the standards should be "flushed down the toilet," but they were endorsed by many editorial boards and historians.[4]

Unfortunately, the historians at the University of California at Los Angeles who supervised the writing of the history standards did not anticipate that their political views and their commitment to teaching social history through the lens of race, class, and gender would encounter resistance outside the confines of academe. They insisted that their critics were narrow-minded conservatives who opposed the standards' efforts to open American history to a diversity of cultures.

Meanwhile, in D.C., the administration changed from George H. W. Bush to Bill Clinton, and in the turnover, there was no provision for oversight of the standards, no process by which they might be reviewed and revised, again and again, to remove any hint of political bias. After Cheney raised a ruckus about the history standards, elected officials in Washington wanted nothing to do with them. The Clinton administration disowned them, pointing out that it had not commissioned them. In January 1995, the U.S. Senate passed a resolution condemning them by a vote of 99–1 (the lone dissenter, a senator from Louisiana, thought the resolution was not strong enough).[5] After the vitriolic front-page battle over the history standards, the subject of standards, curriculum, and content became radioactive to political leaders.

I was disappointed by the national history standards, but unlike Cheney I thought they could be fixed by editing. When the controversy first exploded into public view, I told *Education Week* that the document was a very good start, but "they should keep working on it, make it more parsimonious, and get out whatever seems to be biased in terms of politics. It shouldn't have a whiff of political partisanship from the left or the right." I wrote a letter to the *New York Times*, which had editorially supported the standards, warning that the history standards had to be "depoliticized," because they were jeopardizing the bipartisan movement to set voluntary national standards.[6] In the *Chronicle of Higher Education*, I argued that the history standards should be revised, not abandoned. I worried that the controversy would "lead to the demise of the entire effort to set national standards, even in less contentious fields, such as mathematics and science." I insisted that national standards would succeed only as long as they were voluntary and nonpartisan and avoided "any effort to impose 'correct' answers on disputed questions." I concluded that the project to develop national standards was at a crossroads; either we as a nation would recognize that much more time was needed to do it right, or the entire effort would be abandoned. I predicted, "The questions that will soon be answered are: Will we learn from our mistakes and keep trying? Or will we give up?"[7]

In hindsight, it is clear that we gave up, in reaction to the media firestorm. The politicians whose leadership and endorsement were needed to establish national standards lost interest. Senators, congressmen, and governors watched the spectacle and determined that it was political suicide to get involved in the contretemps. To Republicans, national standards were anathema, a policy that would turn our education system over to leftist academics, a point that Lynne Cheney drove home again and again in her newspaper articles and public appearances. To Democrats, national standards sounded like a good idea—after all, Bill Clinton had run for office with a promise to establish national standards and assessments[8]—but after the debacle associated with the history standards, the Clinton administration backed away from national standards.

Even as the history standards came into disrepute, the Clinton administration was writing its own legislation to promote standards and accountability. Having seen the political disaster that erupted around the national history standards, administration strategists concluded that it would be politically impossible to forge federally directed academic standards, even voluntary ones. So they punted: The law they wrote said that every state should write its own standards, pick its own tests, and be accountable for achievement. The task of identifying what students should learn—the heart of curriculum standards—was left to each state.

The Clinton administration's Goals 2000 program gave the states federal money to write their own academic standards, but most of the state standards were vague when it came to any curriculum content. It seemed that the states had learned from the battle over the history standards that it was better to say nothing than to provoke controversy by setting out any real curriculum standards. Most state standards were windy rhetoric, devoid of concrete descriptions of what students should be expected to know and be able to do. One exception was Massachusetts, which produced stellar state standards in every subject area. But most states wrote social studies standards in which history was mentioned tangentially with few or no references to names, events, or ideas. The states seemed to understand that avoiding specifics was the best policy; that standards were best if they were completely noncontroversial; and that standards would survive scrutiny only if they said nothing and changed nothing.

A few examples should suffice. A typical middle-school history standard says that "students will demonstrate an understanding of how ideas, events, and conditions bring about change." A typical high school history standard says that "students will demonstrate an understanding of the chronology and concepts of history and identify and explain historical relationships." Or, "explain, analyze, and show connections among patterns of change and continuity by applying key historical concepts, such as time, chronology, causality, change, conflict, complexity, and movement."[9] Since these statements do not refer to any actual historical event, they do not require students to know any history. They contain no historical content that students might analyze, debate, or reflect on. Unfortunately, they are typical of most state standards in history. The much-maligned voluntary national history standards of 1994, by contrast, are intellectually challenging, because they expected students to discuss the causes and consequences of the American Revolution, the Great Depression, world wars, and other major events in American history. Without specificity and clarity, standards are nothing more than vacuous verbiage.

State standards for the English language arts are similarly vapid. Few states refer to a single significant work of literature that students are expected to read. In most states, the English standards avoid any mention of specific works of fiction or nonfiction or specific major authors. Instead, they babble about how students "interact with text," apply "word analysis and vocabulary skills to comprehend selections," "relate reading to prior knowledge and experience and make connections to related information," "make text-to-text, text-to-self, and text-to-world connections," use "language processes" as "meaning-making processes," engage in "meaningful literacy activities," and "use effective reading strategies to achieve their purposes in reading." Students should certainly think about what they read, but they should read something worth thinking about.[10]

The standards movement died in 1995, when the controversy over the national history standards came to a high boil. And the state standards created as a substitute for national standards steered clear of curriculum content. So, with a few honorable exceptions, the states wrote and published vague documents and called them standards. Teachers continued to rely on their textbooks to determine what to teach and test. The tests and textbooks, written for students across the nation, provided a low-level sort of national standard. Business leaders continued to grouse that they had to spend large amounts of money to train new workers; the media continued to highlight the mediocre performance of American students on international tests; and colleges continued to report that about a third of their freshmen needed remediation in the basic skills of reading, writing, and mathematics.

When Governor George W. Bush of Texas was elected president in 2000, he decided that education reform would be his first priority. He brought with him the Texas plan: testing and accountability. Bush's No Child Left Behind program melded smoothly with a central feature of the Clinton administration's Goals 2000 program: namely, leaving it to the states to set their own standards and pick their own tests. Under the terms of NCLB, schools that did not demonstrate adequate progress toward the goal of making every student proficient in math and English by 2014 would be subject to increasingly onerous sanctions. But it was left to each state to decide what "proficiency" meant. So the states, most of which had vague and meaningless standards, were left free to determine what children should learn and how well they should learn it.[11] In effect, they were asked to grade themselves by creating tests that almost all children could eventually pass. NCLB was all

sticks and no carrots. Test-based accountability—not standards—became our national education policy. There was no underlying vision of what education should be or how one might improve schools.

NCLB introduced a new definition of school reform that was applauded by Democrats and Republicans alike. In this new era, school reform was characterized as accountability, high-stakes testing, data-driven decision making, choice, charter schools, privatization, deregulation, merit pay, and competition among schools. Whatever could not be measured did not count. It was ironic that a conservative Republican president was responsible for the largest expansion of federal control in the history of American education. It was likewise ironic that Democrats embraced market reforms and other initiatives that traditionally had been favored by Republicans.

Nothing better portrayed the new climate than a charged battle during and after the 2008 presidential campaign over the definition of the term "reformer." During the campaign, the *New Republic* chided Democratic candidate Barack Obama for waffling on education reform. A real reformer, said this usually liberal magazine, was someone who supports competition between schools, charter schools, test-based accountability, performance pay for teachers, and No Child Left Behind, while being ready to battle the teachers' unions. This agenda, the article asserted, was shared by influential center-left think tanks in Washington, D.C., such as the Center for American Progress.[12]

After Obama's election, the media vigorously debated the new president's likely choice for secretary of education. For a brief time, it appeared that the new president might pick his main campaign adviser on education, scholar Linda Darling-Hammond of Stanford University. This prospect alarmed the champions of corporate-style reform, because Darling-Hammond was known as an advocate of teacher professionalism and a critic of Teach for America; the new breed of reformers thought she was too friendly with the teachers' unions. Consequently, writers in the *New York Times*, the *Washington Post*, the *Chicago Tribune*, and other publications warned President-elect Obama not to choose Darling-Hammond, but to select a "real" reformer who supported testing, accountability, and choice. True reformers, said the pundits and editorialists, fought the teachers' unions and demanded merit pay based on student test scores. True reformers closed low-performing schools and fired administrators and teachers. True reformers opposed teacher tenure. Never mind that these had long been the central tenets of the Republican approach to education reform.[13]

This rhetoric represented a remarkable turn of events. It showed how the politics of education had been transformed. The same views might as well have appeared in conservative journals, such as *National Review* or the *Weekly Standard*. Slogans long advocated by policy wonks on the right had migrated to and been embraced by policy wonks on the left. When Democratic think tanks say their party should support accountability and school choice, while rebuffing the teachers' unions, you can bet that something has fundamentally changed in the political scene. In 2008, these issues, which had been the exclusive property of the conservative wing of the Republican Party since Ronald Reagan's presidency, had somehow managed to captivate education thinkers in the Democratic Party as well.

Where did education reform go wrong? Ask the question, and you'll get different answers, depending on whom you ask. But all roads eventually lead back to a major report released in 1983 called *A Nation at Risk*.

It is important to understand A *Nation at Risk* (ANAR), its role in the rise and fall of the standards movement, and its contrast with No Child Left Behind. ANAR encouraged states and the nation to craft genuine curriculum standards in many subjects; this movement foundered when the history standards came under attack. Consequently, education leaders retreated into the relative safety of standardized testing of basic skills, which was a poor substitute for a full-fledged program of curriculum and assessments. In the trade-off, our education system ended up with no curricular goals, low standards, and dumbed-down tests.

A *Nation at Risk* was a response to the radical school reforms of the late 1960s and early 1970s. Whoever remembers that era fondly is sure to dislike ANAR; conversely, whoever was skeptical toward the freewheeling reforms of those years is likely to admire ANAR. No one who lived in that time will forget the proliferation of experiments and movements in the nation's schools. Reformers differed mainly in terms of how radical their proposals were. The reforms of the era were proffered with the best of intentions; some stemmed from a desire to advance racial equity in the classroom and to broaden the curriculum to respect the cultural diversity of the population. Others were intended to liberate students from burdensome requirements. Still others proceeded in the spirit of A. S. Neill's *Summerhill*, where any sort of adult authority was strictly forbidden. Tear down the walls between the classrooms, said some reformers. Free the children, free the schools, abolish all rules and requirements. Let the English teacher teach math, and the math teacher teach English. Let students design their own courses and learn whatever they feel like learning whenever (or if ever) they feel like learning. Get rid of graduation requirements, college entrance requirements, grades, tests, and textbooks. Down with the canon. On it went, with reformers, radicals, and revolutionaries competing to outdo one another.[14]

And then one day in 1975, the *New York Times* reported on its front page that scores on the SAT—the nation's premier college entrance examination—had fallen steadily for over a decade.[15] The College Board, which sponsors the SAT, appointed an august commission to consider the likely causes of the score decline. The SAT commission in 1977 found plenty of reasons, including the increased numbers of minority students taking the test, whose test scores on average were lower than those of traditional test takers. But, said the commission, the test score decline was not entirely explained by the changing ethnic composition of the test takers. Some erosion in academic learning had probably been caused by large social forces, such as increased television viewing and the rising divorce rate, as well as political upheavals, such as the Vietnam War and Watergate. Significantly, the commission also concluded that changes in the schools' practices had contributed to the steady slippage of SAT scores, especially in the verbal portion. Students were taking fewer basic academic courses and more fluffy electives; there was less assignment of homework, more absenteeism, and "less thoughtful and critical reading"; and, the commission noted, "careful writing has apparently about gone out of style."[16] The SAT report was soon followed by doleful federal reports about the state of the nation's schools, documenting falling enrollments in math and science and in foreign language study.[17]

Then in 1983 came *A Nation at Risk*, the all-time blockbuster of education reports. It was prepared by the National Commission on Excellence in Education, a group appointed by President Reagan's secretary of education, Terrel Bell. Bell was a subversive in the Reagan cabinet, a former school superintendent and a bona fide member of the education establishment. Whenever the president launched into a lecture about his desire to restore school prayer or to promote vouchers, Secretary Bell was notably silent.[18]

The report was an immediate sensation. Its conclusions were alarming, and its language was blunt to the point of being incendiary. It opened with the claim that "the educational foundations of our society are presently being eroded by a rising tide of mediocrity that threatens our very future as a Nation and a people. What was unimaginable a generation ago has begun to occur—others are matching and surpassing our educational attainments." The nation, it warned, has "been committing an act of unthinking, unilateral educational disarmament." Beset by conflicting demands, our educational institutions "seem to have lost sight of the basic purposes of schooling, and of the high expectations and disciplined effort needed to attain them."[19]

In the years since *A Nation at Risk* was published, academics, educators, and pundits have debated whether the report was an accurate appraisal of academic standards or merely alarmist rhetoric by the Reagan administration, intended to undermine public education. The language was flamboyant, but that's how a report about education gets public attention. If it had been written in the usual somber, leaden tones of most national commissions, we would not be discussing it a generation later. *A Nation at Risk* was written in plain English, with just enough flair to capture the attention of the press. Its argument and recommendations made sense to nonspecialists. People who were not educators could understand its message, which thoughtfully addressed the fundamental issues in education. The national news media featured stories about the "crisis in education." The report got what it wanted: the public's attention.

A Nation at Risk was notable for what it did not say. It did not echo Reagan's oft-expressed wish to abolish the U.S. Department of Education. It did not support or even discuss his other favorite education causes: vouchers and school prayer. It did not refer to market-based competition and choice among schools; it did not suggest restructuring schools or school systems. It said nothing about closing schools, privatization, state takeover of districts, or other heavy-handed forms of accountability. It referred only briefly, almost in passing, to testing. Instead, it addressed problems that were intrinsic to schooling, such as curriculum, graduation requirements, teacher preparation, and the quality of textbooks; it said nothing about the governance or organization of school districts, because these were not seen as causes of low performance.

Far from being a revolutionary document, the report was an impassioned plea to make our schools function better in their core mission as academic institutions and to make our education system live up to our nation's ideals. It warned that the nation would be harmed economically and socially unless education was dramatically improved for *all* children. While it did not specifically address issues of race and class, the report repeatedly stressed that the quality of education must improve across the board. What was truly at risk, it said, was the promise that "all, regardless of race or class or economic status, are entitled to a fair chance and to the tools for developing their individual powers of mind and spirit to the utmost."[20] To that end, the report recommended stronger high school graduation requirements; higher standards for academic performance and student conduct; more time devoted to instruction and homework; and higher standards for entry into the teaching profession and better salaries for teachers.

The statistics it cited showed declining SAT scores from 1963 to 1980, as well as a decline in the number and proportion of high-scoring students on that test; lowered scores on standardized achievement tests; poor performance on international assessments; large numbers of functionally illiterate adults and seventeen-year-olds; the expansion of remedial courses on college campuses; and the cost of remedial training to the military and businesses.[21]

The primary cause of this inadequate academic performance, the commission said, was the steady erosion of the *content* of the curriculum: "Secondary school curricula have been homogenized, diluted, and diffused to the point that they no longer have a central purpose. In effect, we have a cafeteria-style curriculum in which the appetizers and desserts can easily be mistaken for the main courses. Students have migrated from vocational and college preparatory programs to 'general track' courses in large numbers." The proportion in this general track—neither academic nor vocational—had grown from 12 percent in 1964 to 42 percent in 1979. This percentage exceeded that of enrollment in either the academic or the vocational track. This "curricular smorgasbord," combined with extensive student choice, led to a situation in which only small proportions of high school students completed standard, intermediate, and advanced courses. Second, the commission cited data to demonstrate that academic expectations had fallen over time—that students were not doing much homework, that high school graduation requirements were minimal, that college entry requirements had fallen, and that students were not taking as many courses in math and science as their peers in other nations.[22]

Although the report offered many recommendations, the most consequential, listed first in the report, was that high school graduation requirements should be strengthened. All high school students, the commission urged, should study what it called "The Five New Basics." This was to consist of four years of English, three years of mathematics, three years of science, three years of social studies, and one-half year of computer science. In addition, college-bound students should study at least two years of a foreign language. The commission proposed that foreign language study begin in elementary school and that schools include courses in the arts and vocational education in addition to the new basics.[23]

The commission did not just list the subjects to be studied; it succinctly defined the essential goals of each subject, without using jargon. For example, the commission said that the teaching of English "should equip graduates to: (a) comprehend, interpret, evaluate, and use what they read; (b) write well-organized, effective papers; (c) listen effectively and discuss ideas intelligently; and (d) know our literary heritage and how it enhances imagination and ethical understanding, and how it relates to the customs, ideas, and values of today's life and culture." The teaching of mathematics "should equip graduates to: (a) understand geometric and algebraic concepts; (b) understand elementary probability and statistics; (c) apply mathematics in everyday situations; and (d) estimate, approximate, measure, and test the accuracy of their calculations." In addition to the traditional course of study for college-bound students, the commission recommended that "new, equally demanding mathematics curricula" be developed "for those who do not plan to continue their formal education immediately."[24] Again, none of this was revolutionary; the commission called on schools to educate all students well and to prepare them for whatever path they chose after high school.

A *Nation at Risk* proposed that four-year colleges and universities raise their admissions requirements. It urged scholars and professional societies to help upgrade the quality of textbooks and other teaching materials. It called on states to evaluate textbooks for their quality and to request that publishers present evidence of the effectiveness of their teaching materials, based on field trials and evaluations.

A *Nation at Risk* urged "significantly more time" for learning. High school students, it said, should receive more homework. *ANAR* called on school districts and states to lengthen the school day (to seven hours) and the school year (from the current 180 days to as many as 200 or 220 days). It called for firm, fair codes of conduct and for special classes or schools for children who were continually disruptive.

Those preparing to teach, said the commission, should be expected to meet high educational standards, by demonstrating not only their aptitude for teaching but also their competence in an academic discipline. Teachers' salaries should be increased and should be "professionally competitive, market-sensitive, and performance-based." Decisions about salary, tenure, promotion, and retention should be tied to peer review "so that superior teachers can be rewarded, average ones encouraged, and poor ones either improved or terminated."[25] The report recommended differential pay for teachers in relation to their quality, but proposed that judgments about teacher quality include peer review.

The commission correctly observed that "learning is the indispensable investment required for success in the 'information age' we are entering."[26] And it was right to say that those who are uneducated or poorly educated would be effectively excluded from material rewards and the chance to participate fully in our shared political and civic life. It was right to point to the curriculum as the heart of the matter, the definition of what students are expected to learn. When the curriculum is incoherent and insubstantial, students are cheated.

A *Nation at Risk* was certainly not part of a right-wing plot to destroy public education or a precursor to the privatization movement of the 1990s and early twenty-first century.[27] Nor did it offer simple solutions to complex problems or demand the impossible. Every one of its recommendations was within the scope of the schools as they existed then and as they exist now, and none had any potential to harm public education. The report treated public education

as a professional, purposeful enterprise that ought to have clear, attainable goals.

Some critics complained that the commission should have paid more attention to social and economic factors that affect educational outcomes, such as poverty, housing, welfare, and health.[28] That's a fair criticism. But the commission was asked to report on the quality of education in the nation's schools, so it focused on the academic aspects of education. When critics said *ANAR* unfairly blamed the nation's economic woes in the early 1980s on the schools, they took their argument too far, as if schools have nothing at all to do with a nation's economic health. When the economy subsequently improved, the critics asked, "Why aren't the schools getting credit for the upturn?" The critics confused the relationship between schools and the economy. Of course schools create human and social capital. Of course they are not the immediate cause of good times or bad times. Schools did not cause the Great Depression, nor can they claim credit for boom times. But economists have long recognized that good schools are important for a nation's future economic, civic, social, and cultural development.

The one consequential error of A *Nation at Risk* was its implication that the fundamental problems of American education resided solely in the nation's high schools and could be corrected by changes to that institution. The report assumed that elementary schools and junior high schools or middle schools were in fine shape and needed no special attention. But a closer look might have persuaded the commission that many students arrived in high school without the foundation of basic skills and knowledge essential to a good high school education. If the high school curriculum was a smorgasbord, the curriculum in the early grades was equally haphazard, lacking in coherence or content. This meant that students began their freshman year of high school with widely varying levels of preparation many without even the most rudimentary knowledge of history, science, literature, or other subjects. The commission blamed the high schools for the undereducated students who arrived at their doors. Whatever its deficiencies, the high school was not the cause of the poor preparation of its first-year students.

Today, when we contrast the rhetoric of A Nation at Risk with the reality of the No Child Left Behind legislation of 2002, A Nation at Risk looks positively idealistic, liberal, and prescient. A Nation at Risk was a report, not a legal mandate; if leaders in states and school districts wanted to implement its recommendations, they could; but they were also free to ignore the report and its recommendations. No Child Left Behind, however, was a federal law; any state or district that refused to comply with its mandates risked losing millions of dollars targeted to its neediest students. A Nation at Risk envisioned a public school system that offered a rich, well-balanced, and coherent curriculum, similar to what was available to students in the academic track in successful school districts. No Child Left Behind, by contrast, was bereft of any educational ideas. It was a technocratic approach to school reform that measured "success" only in relation to standardized test scores in two skill-based subjects, with the expectation that this limited training would strengthen our nation's economic competitiveness with other nations. This was misguided, since the nations with the most successful school systems do not impose such a narrow focus on their schools.

Whereas the authors of A Nation at Risk concerned themselves with the quality and breadth of the curriculum that every youngster should study, No Child Left Behind concerned itself only with basic skills. A Nation at Risk was animated by a vision of good education as the foundation of a better life for individuals and for our democratic society, but No Child Left Behind had no vision other than improving test scores in reading and math. It produced mountains of data, not educated citizens. Its advocates then treated that data as evidence of its "success." It ignored the importance of knowledge. It promoted a cramped, mechanistic, profoundly anti-intellectual definition of education. In the age of NCLB, knowledge was irrelevant.

By putting its emphasis on the importance of a coherent curriculum, A Nation at Risk was a precursor to the standards movement. It recognized that what students learn is of great importance in education and cannot be left to chance. When the standards movement collapsed as a result of the debacle of the national history standards the reform movement launched by ANAR was left without a strategy. To fill the lack, along came the test-based accountability movement, embodied by the No Child Left Behind law.

So, the great hijacking occurred in the mid-1990s when the standards movement fell apart. The passage of No Child Left Behind made testing and accountability our national education strategy. The controversies over national standards showed that a national consensus would be difficult to achieve and might set off a political brawl. State education departments are averse to controversy. Most states settled for "standards" that were bland and soporific to avoid battles over what students should learn. Education reformers in the states and in the federal government endorsed tests of basic skills as the only possible common ground in education. The goal of testing was higher scores, without regard to whether students acquired any knowledge of history, science, literature, geography, the arts, and other subjects that were not important for accountability purposes.

Whereas A Nation at Risk encouraged demands for voluntary national standards, No Child Left Behind sidestepped the need for any standards. In spirit and in specifics, they are not closely related. ANAR called for sensible, mainstream reforms to renew and repair our school system. The reforms it recommended were appropriate to the nature of schools: strengthening the curriculum for all students; setting clear and reasonable high school graduation requirements that demonstrate students' readiness for postsecondary education or the modern workplace; establishing clear and appropriate college entrance requirements; improving the quality of textbooks and tests; expecting students to spend more time on schoolwork; establishing higher requirements for new recruits into the teaching profession; and increasing teacher compensation.

These recommendations were sound in 1983. They are sound today.

Notes

1. The National Council of Teachers of Mathematics had already written mathematics standards.
2. Lynne V. Cheney, "The End of History," *Wall Street Journal*, October 20, 1994.
3. Karen Diegmueller, "Panel Unveils Standards for U.S. History," *Education Week*, November 2, 1994.
4. *Los Angeles Times*, "Now a History for the Rest of Us," October 27, 1994; Gary B. Nash, Charlotte Crabtree, and Ross E. Dunn, *History on Trial: Culture Wars and the Teaching of the Past* (New York: Knopf, 1997).
5. U.S. Congress, Senate, *Congressional Record* (January 18, 1995), S1026–S1040.
6. Diegmueller, "Panel Unveils Standards"; Diane Ravitch, "Standards in U.S. History: An Assessment," *Education Week*, December 7, 1994; Ravitch, letter to the editor, *New York Times*, February 14, 1995.
7. Diane Ravitch, "Revise, but Don't Abandon, the History Standards," *Chronicle of Higher Education*, February 17, 1995.
8. Bill Clinton and Al Gore, *Putting People First: How We Can All Change America* (New York: Times Books, 1992), 85–86.
9. Diane Ravitch, "Social Studies Standards: Tune for a Decisive Change," in *Reforming Education in Arkansas: Recommendations from the Koret Task Force, 2005* (Stanford, CA: Hoover Press, 2005), 69–74. The standards cited here are similar to those in most other states.
10. Diane Ravitch, *The Language Police: How Pressure Groups Restrict What Students Learn* (New York: Knopf, 2003), 124–125. For this book, I read the standards in English language arts and history/social studies in every state in the nation.
11. The law said that the state plans must include challenging academic standards, and that state plans had to win the approval of the U.S. secretary of education. However, by June 2003 every state plan was approved, even though many did not have challenging academic standards. Lynn Olson, "All States Get Federal Nod on Key Plans," *Education Week*, June 18, 2003.
12. Josh Patashnik, "Reform School: The Education (On Education) of Barack Obama," *New Republic*, March 26, 2008, 12–13.
13. David Brooks, "Who Will He Choose?" *New York Times*, December 5, 2008; *Washington Post*, "A Job for a Reformer," December 5, 2008; *Chicago Tribune*, "Obama and Schoolkids," December 9, 2008. Republicans recognized that President Obama was embracing some of the GOP's core beliefs, including school choice, merit pay, and accountability. Richard N. Bond, Bill McInturff, and Alex Bratty, "A Chance to Say Yes: The GOP and Obama Can Agree on School Reform," *Washington Post*, August 2, 2009.
14. Diane Ravitch, *The Troubled Crusade: American Education, 1945–1980* (New York: Basic Books, 1983), 228–266.
15. Edward B. Fiske, "College Entry Test Scores Drop Sharply," *New York Times*, September 7, 1975.
16. College Entrance Examination Board, *On Further Examination: Report of the Advisory Panel on the Scholastic Aptitude Test Score Decline* (New York: College Entrance Examination Board, 1977), 26–31.
17. Presidents Commission on Foreign Language and International Studies, *Strength Through Wisdom: A Critique of U.S. Capability* (Washington, D.C.: U.S. Government Printing Office, 1979); National Science Foundation and U.S. Department of Education, *Science and Engineering Education for the 1980s and Beyond* (Washington, D.C.: U.S. Government Printing Office, 1980).
18. For his perspective on *A Nation at Risk*, see Terrel H. Bell, *The Thirteenth Man: A Reagan Cabinet Memoir* (New York: Free Press, 1988), 114–143.
19. National Commission on Excellence in Education, *A Nation at Risk: The Imperative for Educational Reform* (Washington, D.C.: U.S. Government Printing Office, 1983), 5–6.
20. Ibid., 8.
21. Ibid., 8–9.
22 Ibid., 18–22.
23. Ibid., 24–27.
24. Ibid., 25.
25. Ibid., 30.
26. Ibid., 7.
27. David C. Berliner and Bruce J. Biddle, *The Manufactured Crisis: Myths, Fraud, and the Attack on America's Public Schools* (Reading, MA: Addison-Wesley, 1995), 3–5, 139–140, 184.
28. See, for example, Richard Rothstein, "'A Nation at Risk' Twenty-five Years Later," Cato Unbound, April 7, 2008, www.cato-unbound.org/2008/04/07/richard-rothstein/a-nation-at-risk-twenty-five-years-later/.

What "Counts" as Educational Policy? Notes Toward a New Paradigm

Jean Anyon

In my first article as a young PhD, which was published in the *Harvard Educational Review*, I argued that high school U.S. history curriculum, as represented in widely used textbooks, excises and thereby defines out of existence radical responses American workers have had to the problems they face on the job and in their communities (Anyon, 1979). This educational excision is one way that schooling mitigates against the development of working-class consciousness.

In empirical and theoretical work since then, I have investigated knowledge and pedagogical experiences made available to students in different social-class contexts (1980, 1981), and have attempted to understand the consequences of ways we conceptualize urban education, urban school reform, and neighborhood poverty. Recent arguments have aimed at unseating simplistic notions of the causes of urban poverty and low achievement in city districts, and explicating unexplored relations between urban education and movements for social change (e.g., 1995, 1997, 2005).

In this article I think about education policy over the seventy-five years of *Harvard Educational Review* publication. During these decades, many K–12 policies have been written and implemented by federal, state, and local governments. Some of these have aimed at improving education in America's cities and are my primary focus. Over the years, dominant strategies called upon to improve urban schools have included curricular, administrative, and funding reforms, as well as increases in educational opportunity and district/school accountability.

A historical examination of policies can inform decisions we make today. Policy failures, for example, may demonstrate that we need to rethink strategies we choose in our long-term attempts to solve the problems of school and student achievement in urban districts. Indeed, I will argue that the quality of education in city schools is a complex problem, and education policy as historically conceived has not been adequate to the task of increasing urban school achievement to acceptable levels. Academic learning in city schools is undoubtedly higher than in, say, 1900, yet there is still no large urban district that can demonstrate high achievement in even half its students or schools. Noting this failure of educational policy to render most urban schools high-quality institutions, I ask, what *should* count as educational policy? As in any attempt to resolve complex issues, workable solutions can only be generated by an understanding of underlying causes.

The diagnosis I provide is based on analyses completed for my book, *Radical Possibilities: Public Policy, Urban Education, and a New Social Movement* (Anyon, 2005). In this book I examine federal and regional mandates that affect economic and social opportunities available to the urban poor. I find that despite stated intentions, federal and metropolitan policies and arrangements generally restrict opportunities available to city residents and neighborhoods. I show how job, wage, housing, tax, and transportation policies maintain minority poverty in urban neighborhoods, and thereby create environments that overwhelm the potential of educational policy to create systemic, sustained improvements in the schools. For example, policies such as minimum wage statutes that yield full-time pay below the poverty level, and affordable housing and transportation policies that segregate low-income workers of color in urban areas but industrial and other job development in far-flung suburbs where public transit routes do not reach, are all culpable.

In order to solve the systemic problems of urban education, then, I argue in the book—and will argue here—that we need not only better schools but also the reform of these public policies. Rules and regulations regarding teaching, curriculum, and assessment certainly are important, but policies to eliminate poverty-wage work and housing segregation (for example) should be part of the educational policy panoply as well, for these have consequences for urban education at least as profound as curriculum, pedagogy, and testing.

In the sections that follow I describe major K–12 education policies that have been implemented over the years to attempt to improve urban education, and then discuss several federal and metro-area policies and practices that limit the potential and success of these strategies. I also report hopeful new research suggesting that even modest income and other family supports typically improve low-income students' academic achievement. I end by arguing that, given this power of economic access to influence educational outcomes, strategies to support economic opportunity and development for urban residents and neighborhoods should be among the policies we consider in our attempts to improve urban schools and districts. Just as in affluent suburban districts where economic strength is the engine of educational reform, so it would be in urban districts where resident and neighborhood affluence would support and retool the schools. I begin with an overview of education policy as typically conceived.

Education Policies

Over the last seventy-five years or so, federal policies have attempted various strategies to improve city education. The first federal policy aimed at working-class populations was the Smith-Hughes Act of 1917, which provided funds to prepare students in industrialized areas for working-class jobs through vocational programs. Variants of this policy continued throughout the twentieth century, in the Vocational Education Acts of 1963, 1984, and 1998, and in the School-to-Work Opportunity Act of 1994 and the later federal legislation in which it was subsumed.

Some federal education policies have attempted to improve urban education by making funding available for increased curriculum materials and libraries, early childhood classes, and various types of programmatic innovations in city schools. Head Start in 1965, Follow Through in 1967, and, to a lesser extent, Title IX, which banned sex discrimination in 1972, brought and instigated new curricula and programs into city districts.[1] These policies were intended to increase student access and/or achievement by upgrading curricular resources and experiences.

Other federal K–12 policies have aimed specifically at increasing educational equity. The 1954 *Brown* decision (which committed the federal government to desegregation as a policy stance), the Elementary and Secondary Education Act of 1965 (ESEA), the Bilingual Act in 1968, Title IX in 1972, and the Education for All Handicapped Children Act in 1975 opened doors to academic experiences for previously under-served K–12 students. These policies are generally thought to have expanded urban students' educational opportunities.

More recent federal education policies to improve schooling—with urban students and teachers often a target—have called for increased academic standards and requirements, standardized testing, and professional development of teachers. These policies were recommended by the influential report *A Nation at Risk*, commissioned by President Ronald Reagan and published in 1983. The emphasis on increased academic standards was part of an effort to support business needs for well-prepared workers and employees. The report's recommendations for higher standards and increased testing were introduced as policy in 1994 and 1996 as part of the Goals 2000 legislation. In 2001 these goals were instantiated as federal mandates in the No Child Left Behind Act (NCLB). Privatization of education via nonpublic providers when K–12 schools fail is a subtextual education policy in NCLB (Conley, 2003; Cross, 2004; Stein, 2004).

It is important to note that federal education policies intended to improve urban schools did not take aim at the economic arrangements and practices that themselves produced the poverty in which city schools were embedded. Despite increases in educational opportunity, the effects of almost a century of educational policies on urban school and student achievement have, by most accounts, been disappointing.

The first state policies regarding the education of America's urban (and rural) poor emerged earlier than federal ones. What has counted as state education policy regarding poor students can be said to have begun with mid- to late-nineteenth century insertions into state constitutions of the right of all students to a free, "thorough," "efficient," or "useful" education (Odden & Picus, 1992). Following these insertions and until the 1970s, however, most state education policies did not focus specifically on urban education. State mandates typically set regulations and requirements for school systems, teacher and administrator preparation, and school funding (through property taxes). During the 1970s and 1980s, lawsuits challenging state education funding systems brought increased attention to city schools and districts. State urban education policy in these decades involved various kinds of efforts, including school-based management and basic skills mandates. In the 1990s, state policies attempted to align education standards and regulations with federal ones, mandated curriculum and teacher licensure reform, and closely monitored urban districts. As legal challenges to state systems have led to increased funding of city schools, states have imposed stricter academic and graduation requirements, as well as multigrade and multi-subject standardized testing. Quasi-privatization policies supporting charter schools, vouchers, and other school choice programs have also been a state strategy to attempt to improve the education of urban children by offering them a choice of schools to attend (Conley, 2003).

Over the decades, federal and state policies codified an increasing number of requirements that urban schools and districts must meet. Local governments and educational bureaucracies have undertaken a plethora of programs to attempt to meet those guidelines. Local districts have also mounted school reform projects in response to local social conditions and political pressure from parents and communities. Most local initiatives have been curricular, pedagogical, and administrative.

During the Progressive Era, cities consolidated and professionalized their school systems and personnel, introduced programs like the Gary Plan to prepare students for the industrial experience, increased access to high school, organized educational opportunities for immigrant parents, and sometimes fed, bathed, and clothed poor children. During the decade of the Great Depression, most large cities retrenched and severely cut educational social service and academic programs, as local tax receipts plummeted and banks that offered loans demanded broad cuts in education. During the 1960s, many urban districts were weakened further as most remaining businesses and jobs moved to the suburbs, decimating the urban property tax base (Anyon, 1997; Ravitch, 2000; Tyack, 1974; Wrigley, 1982).

Since the 1970s, in response to federal, judicial, and state mandates, urban districts have bused students to meet racial integration guidelines, decentralized authority to increase community participation, and created magnet schools to attempt to attract middle-class parents. Other local policies that have been attempted to improve achievement are a multitude of reform programs or "school improvement projects," student retention services, privatization of educational offerings, vouchers and magnets, mayoral control, small schools, and curriculum standardization and evaluation through testing. The social context of these policies has included pressure to be accountable in the wake of increased funding, as well as community and corporate demands for better schools. None of the local policies has focused on the poverty of families or neighborhoods.

One way to evaluate this long run of education policy is to compare the achievement of urban students at the beginning of the twentieth and twenty-first centuries. Although achievement is higher now in that larger percentages of students remain in school past the elementary years than in 1900, I would argue that the improvement is relative and illusory. That is, while in the early twentieth century relatively few urban poor students went beyond fifth grade, the vast majority did not require further education to find employment in industries that could lead to middle-class income (Anyon, 1997; Ayres, 1909). Currently, relatively few urban poor students go past ninth grade: The graduation rates in large comprehensive inner-city high schools are abysmally low. In fourteen such New York City schools, for example, only 10 percent to 20 percent of ninth graders in 1996 graduated four years later (Fine, 2001; Greene, 2001; Miao & Haney, 2004).[2] Despite the fact that low-income individuals desperately need a college degree to find decent employment, only 7 percent obtain a bachelor's degree by age twenty-six (Education Trust, 2001; Mishel, Bernstein, & Schmitt, 2001). So, in relation to the needs of low-income students, urban districts fail their students with more egregious consequences now than in the early twentieth century.

Given the plethora of federal, state, and local education policies aimed at urban schools and the current widely acknowledged necessity of high-quality education for all, why have most urban schools and districts not been able to provide such an education for their students?

Barriers to High-Quality Public Education in Cities

There are multiple causes of low-quality schooling in urban areas, and education policies as heretofore conceived address only a few. Education policy has not addressed the neighborhood poverty that surrounds and invades urban schools with low expectations and cynicism. Education policy has not addressed the unemployment and joblessness of families who will have few if any resources for the further education of their children, even if they excel in K–12 classes.

And education policy—even in response to state financial challenges—has not addressed the political economy that largely determines low levels of city district funding. Taxes on wealthy families and corporations are among the lowest on record (Phillips, 2002). Business and government investment in affluent suburban job centers

rather than urban areas continues to deprive poor neighborhoods of entry-level jobs and a tax base, and residents' poverty wages further diminish available funding sources (Anyon, 2005; Orfield, 2002; Rusk, 1999). These political-economic constraints on quality schooling are not challenged by current or past education policy. In most U.S. cities, the political leverage of urban parents has not been sufficient to force the funding necessary to overcome outdated buildings, broken computer labs, and overcrowded classrooms.

These economic and political conditions are the building blocks of formidable barriers to systemic, sustainable school quality. Indeed, even when urban school reform succeeds, it fails— when there are no decent jobs a diploma from a successfully reformed school or district will attract, and there is no government or familial funding sufficient for the vast majority of low-income graduates of even good urban high schools to obtain a bachelors degree.

Individual and neighborhood poverty builds walls around schools and classrooms that education policy does not penetrate or scale. In the following section I describe some of the federal and metro-area policies and arrangements that sustain these barriers.

Federal Policy

Analysts typically do not link federal policies to the maintenance of poverty, to the lack of jobs that bedevils American workers, or to the increasingly large portion of employment that pays poverty and near-poverty wages. Yet federal policy is determinative. To take a blatant example, Congress set the first minimum wage in 1938 at $3.05 (in 2000 dollars); it stands in 2005 at $5.15—a mere two dollars more. (Yearly income at this wage is $10,712.) This sum ensures that full-time, year-round, minimum-wage work will not raise people out of poverty (Mishel, Bernstein, & Boushey, 2003). Analysis in 2004 found that minimum-wage standards directly affect the wages of 8.9 percent of the workforce (9.9 million workers); when we include those making one dollar more an hour than the minimum wage, this legislation affects the wages of as much as 18 percent of the workforce (Economic Policy Institute, 2004). Contrary to the claims of those who oppose raising the minimum wage (that an increase will force employers to fire, or hire fewer of those affected by the increase), studies of the 1990–1991 and 1996–1997 minimum-wage increases failed to find any systematic, significant job losses associated with the increases and found no evidence of negative employment effects on small businesses (Economic Policy Institute, 2004).

Almost half the workforce earns what some economists call poverty-zone wages (and what I define as up to and including 125% of the official poverty level; Anyon, 2005). I analyzed figures provided by the Economic Policy Institute to calculate the overall percentage of people who work full-time year round yet make wages up to and including 125 percent of the official poverty threshold needed to support a family of four at the poverty level. The analysis demonstrates that in 1999, during a very strong economy, almost half of the people at work in the United States (41.3%) earned poverty-zone wages—in 1999, $10.24/hour ($21,299/ year) or less, working full-time year round (Mishel et al., 2001). Two years later, in 2001, 38.4 percent earned poverty-zone wages working full-time year round (in 2001, 125% of the poverty line was a $10.88 hourly wage; Mishel et al., 2003). This suggests that the federal minimum-wage policy is an important determinant of poverty for many millions of U.S. families.

There are other macroeconomic policies that produce hardship. These especially penalize Blacks and Latinos, the majority of whom live in segregated, low-income urban neighborhoods. These policies include the following: job training as a predominant federal antipoverty policy when there have been too few jobs for graduates; ineffective federal implementation of policies that outlaw racial discrimination in hiring and housing; regressive income taxes that charge wealthy individuals less than half the rate charged the rich during most of the first sixty years of the twentieth century, yet substantially raise the payroll taxes paid by the working poor and middle class; and corporate tax policies in recent years that allow 60 percent of large U.S. corporations to pay no federal taxes at all (and in some cases to obtain millions in rebates; Citizens for Tax Justice, 2002; Lafer, 2002; Orfield, 2002; Rusk, 1999).

These federal policies and practices contribute to personal, neighborhood, and educational poverty because they lead to the following problems: There are not enough jobs for poor families who need them; low-income families of color are concentrated in low-resourced urban neighborhoods; and when the wealthy do not contribute equitably to public expenses, funding for services like education declines and the quality of the services tends to be low.

The effects of these policies are compounded by harsh union laws and lack of federal protection for labor organizing; Federal Reserve Bank pronouncements that ignore the portion of its mandate to maintain a high level of employment; and free-trade agreements that send thousands of corporations, and their job opportunities, to other countries. These policies hurt workers of all colors—and in most sectors of the economy—as existing jobs disappear and those remaining pay lower wages, in part because they are not unionized (Anyon, 2005; Citizens for Tax Justice, 2002; Economic Policy Institute, 2002, 2004; Galbraith, 1998; Lafer, 2002; Mishel et al., 2001).

However, there are federal policies we could create that would lower poverty by important margins—including a significantly raised minimum wage, comparable worth laws, and policies to enforce existing regulations that outlaw discrimination in hiring. A raise in the minimum wage that brought workers above poverty would improve the lives of at least a fifth of U.S. workers (Economic Policy Institute, 2004). Paying women the same amount men are paid for comparable work would, according to one analysis, reduce poverty by 40 percent, as such a large percentage of poor people are women in low-wage jobs (Lafer, 2002). And requiring employers to hire without discriminating against Blacks and Latinos would further open opportunities currently denied.

In addition, policies that worked against U.S. poverty in the past could be reinstated: U.S. government regulation of the minimum wage, which kept low-paid workers' income at the median of highly paid unionized workers in the decades after World War II; federal support for union organizing; a federal program of job creation in cities, as during the Great Depression of the 1930s; and federal programs for urban youth that would support further education, as such policies did for eight million men and women after World War II (Anyon, 2005; Galbraith, 1998). These national policies were important supports of the widespread prosperity of the United States' working and middle classes in the quarter century following 1945 (Galbraith, 1998).

Metropolitan Policy and Practice

Like current federal mandates, there are metro-area policies and practices that increase the problems of urban residents and neighborhoods. Metro areas are shaped by regional markets—for jobs, housing, investment, and production. Metro areas account for over 80 percent of national output and drive the economic performance of the nation as a whole. Each metro area is anchored by one or more cities (Dreier, Mollenkopf, & Swanstrom, 2001).

Today, metropolitan regions are characterized by population growth, extensive inequality, and segregation (Orfield, 2002; Rusk, 1999). The percentage of racial minorities in large metro areas who live in the suburbs jumped from 19 percent to 27 percent during the 1990s. However, a growing share of these families lives in fiscally stressed suburbs, with an increasing number of neighborhoods having poverty levels over 30 percent (Kingsley & Petit, 2003; Orfield, 2002). As in areas of concentrated poverty in the central city, low levels of taxable resources in these "urbanized" segregated suburbs leave services like education lacking in funds.

U.S. metropolitan areas are characterized by the following problems, all of which disadvantage urban minority families and communities: Most entry-level jobs for which adults with low to moderate education levels are qualified are increasingly located in suburbs, rather than in central cities, but public transit systems do not connect these suburban job centers to urban areas, where most low-income minorities live—thus preventing them from access to jobs there. State-allowed local zoning on the basis of income prevents affordable housing in most suburbs where entry-level jobs are located, which means there is little if any housing for low-income families near the suburban job centers. Indeed, as I have mentioned, the failure to enforce antiracial discrimination statutes in housing confines most Blacks and Latinos to housing sites in central cities and segregated suburbs. Finally, even though federal and state taxes are paid by residents throughout metro regions (including inner cities), most tax-supported development takes place in the affluent suburbs rather than in low-income areas. Thus, few jobs exist in most low-income urban neighborhoods (Anyon, 2005; Dreir et al., 2001; Orfield, 2002; Rusk, 1999). These inequitable regional arrangements and policies exacerbate federal wage and job mandates and contribute in important ways to joblessness and poverty in cities and urbanized suburbs, and to the low quality of investment in services such as education there.

Poverty

One consequence of federal and regional policies regarding work, wages, housing segregation, and transportation is that the numbers of poor people approach the figures of 1959—before massive urban poverty became a national issue. Although the percentages are lower now, the numbers are still staggering: There were about as many people officially poor in 1993 (39.2 million) as in 1959 (39.4 million; Harrington, 1963). And in 2003, 35.8 million were officially poor, only 3.5 million fewer than in 1959 (Mishel et al., 2003).

A more realistic measure of poverty than federal guidelines is that those earning incomes up to 200 percent of the official levels are considered poor (Bernstein, Brocht, & Spade-Aguilar, 2000; Citro & Michael, 1995; Short, Iceland, & Garner, 1999). This revised threshold is used by increasing numbers of social scientists. A calculation of the individuals who earned less than 200 percent of the poverty level in 2001 ($17.40/hour, or $36,192/year), demonstrates a much larger percentage of poor employees than is commonly acknowledged: 84 percent of Hispanic workers, 80 percent of Black workers, and 64.3 percent of White workers made wages at or under 200 percent of the official poverty line (Mishel et al., 2001).

A calculation of *families* living with earnings up to 200 percent of the poverty line reveals that Black and Latino families face the greatest financial hurdles. More than 50 percent of Black and Latino families earn less than 200 percent of the poverty level, compared to only 20.3 percent of White families, even though White families constitute a slight majority (50.5%) of families that fall below 200 percent of the poverty level (Mishel et al., 2001). In sum, poverty in the United States is higher than commonly perceived and is maintained in urban areas by federal and metro-area policies and distributions.

Effects of Poverty on Urban Students

Macroeconomic policies that set wages below poverty levels, that train inner-city hopefuls for jobs that do not exist, that do not extract from the wealthy a fair share of social expenses, and that rarely enforce laws that would substantially decrease the economic discrimination of people of color all support persistent poverty and near-poverty among minority urban populations. This economic and social distress can prevent children from developing their full potential and can certainly dampen the enthusiasm, effort, and expectations with which urban children and their families approach K-12 education.

As I will report, a recent national study of young children confirms the potential of impoverished circumstances to prevent students' full cognitive growth before they enroll in kindergarten. Of countervailing power, however, is research demonstrating that when parents obtain better financial resources or better living

conditions, the educational achievement of the children typically improves significantly. These findings empirically support the argument that for the urban poor, even with the right educational policies in place, school achievement may await a family's economic access.

I already presented adult poverty figures at the official threshold and noted the alarming increase in numbers when a more realistic assessment is made. The same disparities exist between federal and alternative counts of poor children. Sixteen percent of American children—almost 12 million—lived below the *official* federal poverty line in 2001. Almost half of those children (44%, or a little over 5 million) lived in *extreme* poverty (less than half the poverty line, or $7,400 for a family of three in 2001)—including nearly a million African American children. This was a 17 percent increase in the number of children in extreme poverty from 2000, at the end of the economic boom (Cauthen & Lu, 2001; Dillon, 2003; Lu, 2003).

When the more appropriate alternative poverty threshold criterion is applied, however, a full *38 percent* of American children are identified as poor—27 million who lived in families with income up to 200 percent of the official poverty line. These children live in poverty as well—although official statistics do not designate them as such. However, these families experience hardships that are almost as severe as those who are officially poor (Cauthen & Lu 2001; Lu, 2003). *By the revised measure —200 percent of the official poverty cutoff—a full 57 percent of African American children, 64 percent of Latino, and 34 percent of White children were poor in the United States in 2001* (Lu, 2003; Mishel et al., 2003).

It is only in the 1990s that empirical studies focused on why and how poverty affects cognitive development and school achievement. Researchers began to document the specific effects of poverty environments on children's development (Brooks-Gunn, Duncan, Leventhal, & Aber, 1997; Goering & Feins, 2003; Sampson, Morenoff, & Gannon-Rowley, 2002). This body of work documents the correlations between low income, child development, and educational achievement (see Duncan & Brooks-Gunn, 1997, for an overview of studies). For example, poverty has been found to have consistently negative effects on children's cognitive development (Duncan & Brooks-Gunn, 1997; Duncan, Brooks-Gunn, & Klebanov, 1994; McLoyd, 1998). Longitudinal studies that have been carried out also demonstrate that "family income consistently predicts children's academic and cognitive performance, even when other family characteristics are taken into account" (Duncan & Brooks-Gunn, 1997). Persistent and extreme poverty has been shown to be more detrimental to children than temporary poverty (Bolger & Patterson, 1995; Duncan et al., 1994). Family income may influence children through both lack of resources and parental emotional stress (Bradley, 1984; McLoyd & Jartayne, 1994; Smith, Brooks-Gunn, & Klebanov, 1997; Sugland, Zaslow, Brooks-Gunn, & Moore, 1995). Poor children have more health and behavior difficulties than those from more affluent families, which mitigates against educational success (Duncan & Brooks-Gunn, 1997; Houser, Brown, & Prosser, 1997; Klerman, 1991/ 2003; Korenman & Miller, 1997). Studies collected by Duncan and Brooks-Gunn teased out some of the variables within the effects of income. In summarizing research reported in their 1997 volume *Consequences of Growing up Poor*, they point out the following:

1. Income matters for the cognitive development of preschoolers "because it is associated with the provision of a richer learning environment" (p. 601). This is true in part because family income is a "significant determinant of child care environments, including center-based childcare (p. 601). . . . Income allows parents to provide their children with safer, more stimulating home environments; to live in communities with better schools, parks, and libraries and more challenging peers; to afford tuition and other expenses associated with higher education; to purchase or otherwise gain access to higher-quality health care; and in many other ways to buy the things that promote the health

and development of their children" (p. 14).

2. "A variety of income measures—income [relative to needs] . . . income loss, the ratio of debts to assets, and unstable work—are associated with family economic pressure" (p. 602). Economic pressure has been found to be associated with depression (and stress) in parents, which can affect parenting, and thus school achievement.

3. "Family income is usually a stronger predictor of ability and achievement outcomes than are measures of parental schooling or family structure [e.g., single parenthood]" (p. 603). Many studies have shown that children raised in low-income families score lower than children from more affluent families do on assessments of health, cognitive development, and positive behavior. "In general, the better the measure of family income and the longer the period over which it is measured, the stronger the association between the family's economic well-being and children's outcomes" (p. 14).

It is important to understand that these findings do not suggest that poor students are of low intelligence; rather, the studies point to the power of the economy—and of economic hardship—to place extremely high hurdles to full development in front of children who are poor. It is of course possible—although it is not the norm—that education over time mitigates the effects of SES (Hout, 1988; Jencks & Phillips, 1998).

In 2002, Valerie Lee and David Burkham published the results of a large-sample assessment of the effects of poverty on cognitive development. They utilized data from the United States Department of Education's early childhood longitudinal kindergarten cohort, which is a comprehensive dataset that provides a nationally representative portrait of kindergarten students. Lee and Burkham (2002) explored differences in young children's achievement scores in literacy and mathematics by race, ethnicity, and socioeconomic status (SES) as they began kindergarten. They also analyzed differences by social background in an array of children's homes and family activities.

The study demonstrates that inequalities in children's cognitive ability by SES are substantial even before children begin kindergarten and that poverty has a detrimental impact on early intellectual achievement. Importantly, it demonstrates that the disadvantages of being poor outweigh by far the race or family structure of children as causes of the cognitive disadvantages.

Details of the national assessment include the following:

1. Before children enter kindergarten, the average cognitive scores of children in the highest SES group are 60 percent above the scores of the lowest SES group.
2. Cognitive skills are much *less* closely related to race/ethnicity after accounting for SES. After taking racial differences into account, children from different SES groups achieve at different levels—before they begin kindergarten.
3. The impact of family structure on cognitive skills (e.g., being in a single-parent family) is much less than either race or SES.
4. Socioeconomic status is very strongly related to cognitive skills; SES accounts for more of the variation in cognitive scores than any other factor by far.

Lee and Burkham (2002) also found that disadvantaged children not only enter kindergarten with significantly lower cognitive skills than their advantaged peers, but also that low-SES children begin school (kindergarten) in systematically lower-quality elementary schools than their more advantaged counterparts. "However school quality is defined—in terms of higher student achievement, more school resources, more qualified teachers, more positive teacher attitudes, better neighborhood or school conditions, private vs. public schools—the least advantaged United States children begin their formal schooling in consistently lower-quality schools. This reinforces the inequalities that develop even before children reach school age" (p. 3; see also Entwistle & Alexander, 1997;

Phillips, Brooks-Gunn, Duncan, Klevanov, & Crane, 1998; Phillips, Crouse, & Ralph, 1998; Stipic & Ryan, 1997; White, 1982).

In their review of studies of poverty's effects on individual development, Duncan and Brooks-Gunn (1997) conclude, "Taken together, [these studies] suggest that programs that raise the incomes of poor families will enhance the cognitive development of children and may improve their chance of success in [education and] the labor market during adulthood. Most important appears to be the elimination of deep and persistent poverty during a child's early years" (p. 608). I now turn to research suggesting that familial financial and other supports do indeed lead to increased educational achievement in children.

Evidence That Familial Supports Raise Educational Achievement

I have been examining relationships among education policy, the economy, and achievement in urban schools. First, I critiqued education policy for its lack of attention to urban poverty, which, I argued, is maintained by policies and decisions made at the federal and metropolitan levels. I provided evidence of some of the egregious consequences of federal and regional policies and practices for urban families, neighborhoods, students, and schools. In particular, I demonstrated that child poverty creates obstacles to full development and educational achievement, especially when low-income minority children attend low-resourced schools—which most do. In this section I provide indirect and direct research evidence that increased family supports such as financial resources and less segregated neighborhoods raise educational achievement.

Indirect evidence is present in a longitudinal study completed in 2003 that found that improving family income reduces the negative (aggressive) social behavior of children, which in turn is likely to lead to better school behavior and performance. For eight years, researchers studied a representative population sample of 1,420 children ages nine to thirteen in rural North Carolina. A quarter of the children were from a

Cherokee reservation. Psychological tests were given at the start of the study and repeated each year (Costello, Compton, Keeler, & Angold, 2003; O'Connor, 2003).

When the study began, 68 percent of the children were living below the official poverty line. On average, the poorer children engaged in more vandalism, stealing, bullying, stubbornness, and outbursts of anger than those who were not poor. But halfway through the study, a local casino began distributing a percentage of its profits to tribal families. Given to each tribal member over eighteen and put in a trust fund for younger members, the payment increased slightly each year, reaching about $6,000 per person for the year 2001. Psychiatric tests administered by researchers for the four years that the funds were being distributed demonstrated that the negative behaviors of children in families who were no longer poor dropped to the same levels found among children whose families had never been poor (decreasing by 40%). Parents who moved out of poverty reported having more time to spend with their children, and researchers identified better parenting behavior. Researchers also identified the psychological benefits of not being poor as important to both parents and children. Poverty puts stress on families, which can increase the likelihood of children developing behavioral problems. One parent in the study told researchers that "the jobs [produced by the casino] give people the chance to pull themselves up by their bootstraps and get out of poverty. That carries over into less juvenile crime, less domestic violence, and an overall better living experience for families" (O'Connor, 2003, p. 2).

Other research demonstrates that urban low-income parents are also able to practice more effective parenting strategies when some of the stress of poverty is eased by a higher income. And the reduction in stress in turn may positively affect the behavior and achievement of low-income children (see information below; also Jackson, Brooks-Gunn, Huang, & Glassman, 2000; Jeremiah, 2003; Seitz, Rosenbaum, & Apfel, 1985).

Direct evidence that income supports improved educational achievement is also available. In March 2001, the Manpower Demonstration Research Corporation (MDRC) published a synthesis of research on how welfare and work policies affect the children of single mothers (Morris, Huston, Duncan, Crosby, & Bos, 2001). This synthesis reviewed data from evaluations of five programs that provided income supplements to poverty-wage workers (Florida's Family Transition Program, the Minnesota Family Investment Program, the National Evaluation of Welfare-to-Work Strategies, Milwaukee's New Hope for Families and Children Program, and the Self-Sufficiency Project). These programs offered supports of differing kinds to poverty-wage workers— income supplements, earnings disregards (rules that allow working welfare recipients to keep more of their income when they go to work), subsidized health care, employment services, counseling, supervised afterschool activities for children and youth, and informal get-togethers with project staff.

MDRC's review of the studies found that even relatively small income supplements to working parents (amounting to about $4,000 per year) improved children's elementary school achievement by about 10 to 15 percent of the average variation in the control groups. These improvements were seen on test scores as well as on ratings by parents and/or teachers. The earning supplements had "consistently positive impacts on children's [school] achievement" (Morris et al., 2001, p. 63). The positive effects were small, but were statistically significant.

Longitudinal studies have found that the achievement and behavior problems of young children can have important implications for their well-being in adolescence and adulthood (Caspi, Wright, Moffit, & Silva, 1998; Masten & Coatsworth, 1995). Moreover, even small differences between children in school achievement early on can translate into larger differences later (Entwistle & Alexander, 1997). Therefore, as the authors of the research synthesis state, "a program's effects on children, even if the effects are small, may continue to have implications over the course of their lives" (Caspi et al., 1998, p. 25).

The earning supplements provided by four of these programs did not, however, bring the families above the poverty level. The improvements in children's school achievement and behavior from even these relatively meager cash supplements for working families suggest that if we were to increase family resources substantially, we could probably improve educational and social outcomes for children substantially.

Indeed, one program that did provide an earning supplement that brought the families above poverty level showed particularly impressive results for children's behavior and achievement. New Hope for Families and Children was run between 1994 and 1998 in two inner-city areas in Milwaukee. Candidates had to live in one of two targeted areas, be eighteen or older, be willing and able to work at least thirty hours per week, and have a household income at or below 150 percent of the federal poverty level (Huston et al., 2001). Almost 90 percent of the adults in the sample were single or separated mothers with children when they entered the study, and 80 percent were receiving public assistance. The program was conceived by a nonprofit community-based organization and provided several benefits: the earnings supplement, subsidized health insurance, and subsidized child care. The program offered help in obtaining a job and provided a community-service job for up to one year for those not able to find work elsewhere, the advice and support of project staff were made available. The annual cost of providing these benefits was $5,300 per family.

New Hope was evaluated at two-year and five-year intervals using a random assignment research design. After conducting outreach in the communities to identify eligible people, the study enrolled over 1,300 low-income adults. Half the applicants were randomly assigned to a program group that received New Hope's benefits, and the other half were randomly assigned to a control group that was not eligible for the benefits.

Both evaluations showed positive results (Bos, Huston, Duncan, Brock, & McLoyd, 1996; Huston et al., 2001). Financial supplements in the New Hope program did reduce the number of families in poverty, but both program and control groups reported similar levels of hardship, such as food insecurity and financial insufficiency. Yet the program had positive effects on parents' well-being and coping skills. As Huston et al. (2003) explain:

> Parents in the New Hope group were more aware of available "helping" resources in the community, such as where to find assistance with energy costs or housing problems. More of them also knew about the [Earned Income Tax Credit] and its support, an important source of support for low-income workers. Ethnographic data suggest that a significant number of families intentionally used the Earned Income Tax Credits as a savings plan for making major purchases, reducing debt, and stabilizing rent and other payments. Parents in New Hope also reported better physical health and fewer symptoms associated with depression than did parents in the control group. At the two-year point, New Hope parents reported reduced stress, increased feelings of social support, and increased time pressure. The ethnographic study found that many parents had children with disabilities or behavioral difficulties; New Hope helped the parents achieve a difficult balance among work, services, and parenting. . . . The New Hope parents did report fewer problems controlling their children, and parents of adolescents reported more effective management (better control and less need for punishment). (p. 9)

New Hope improved children's school performance. "At both the two-year and the five-year points, children in the program performed better than control group children on several measures of academic achievement, particularly on reading and literacy tests. After five years, they scored higher on a standardized test of reading skills and their parents reported that they got higher grades in reading skills" (Huston et al., 2001, p. 13). These effects were slightly more pronounced for boys than for girls. Compared with their control group counterparts, boys in New Hope also received higher ratings of academic performance from their teachers and were more likely to expect to attend college at both the two-year and the five-year assessments. "New Hope adolescents reported more engagement with schools, feelings of efficacy, and expectations to finish college than did their control group counterparts" (pp. 13–14). New Hope's effects are consistent with the results of other programs that have improved children's outcomes by providing wage supplements and subsidized child care (Michalopoulos et al., 2002; Morris et al., 2001).

Indeed, the New Hope findings are in line with the increased educational achievement of students that has been identified in large-scale programs that assist low-income minority families by helping them move from inner-city neighborhoods to more affluent and/or less segregated metropolitan areas. The first of these "mobility programs" was the Gautreaux program in the Chicago metropolitan area.

As a result of a victorious lawsuit charging the Chicago Housing Authority with segregation in public housing, the court ordered the housing authority to move families who wanted to live in less segregated areas of the city and suburbs. The Gautreaux program moved over 7,000 families to higher-income areas of the Chicago metropolitan region between 1976 and 1998 (Rubinowitz & Rosenbaum, 2002). Although at first a disproportionate number of the children who moved were placed in classes for the learning disabled by their suburban schools, they ultimately were significantly more likely than their urban counterparts to be in college-bound tracks, in four-year colleges, and were subsequently more likely to be employed in jobs with higher pay and with benefits than children who stayed in the city (Rubinowitz & Rosenbaum, 2002).

The success of the Gautreaux program led to more than fifty other mobility programs, including the Moving To Opportunity program (MTO) begun by the U.S. Department of Housing and Urban Development (HUD) in 1994. The Housing and Community Development Act of 1992 authorized HUD to "assist very low-income families with children who reside in public housing or housing receiving project-based assistance under Section 8 of the Housing

and Community Development Act of 1937 to move out of areas with high concentrations of persons living in poverty (40% or more) to areas with low concentrations of such persons (less than 10% in poverty)" (Goering & Feins, 2003, p. 6). Moving To Opportunity projects were carried out in five cities: Baltimore, Boston, Chicago, Los Angeles, and New York. Congress stipulated that HUD conduct evaluations of the program to determine its effects (Goering & Feins, 2003).

Overall, roughly 5,300 families volunteered to move within the metropolitan area of the city in which they lived. In total, 4,608 families were eligible. They were divided into three groups: the MTO "treatment" or experimental group, which received Section 8 certificates or vouchers that could only be used in areas where 10 percent or less of the residents lived below official poverty levels; they also received counseling assistance in finding private rental units. A second group was given Section 8 certificates with no special restrictions on where they were to move, and no counseling (Section 8-only group). An in-place control group continued to receive housing project assistance in the inner-city neighborhoods where they lived. The families in all three groups of the MTO program tended to be young single mothers (under age 35), African American, with a median income of $8,200. Most stated that their main reason for wanting to move was fear of gangs and violence in the neighborhoods in which they lived.

Social scientists conducted research at all five sites, using HUD data, baseline surveys, follow-up surveys of families, qualitative interviews, and data on juvenile crime, labor-market outcomes, and school performance. Among their findings are the following.

One to three years after the families in the experimental group moved, they lived in significantly more affluent and more racially mixed communities than families in the other two groups. In addition, those who were in the experimental group had median incomes that were 73 percent higher than the median incomes for the control group and 53 percent higher than the Section 8-only group. In 1997, three years after the program began, the MTO experimental group families in all five metropolitan areas lived in less-segregated neighborhoods than either of the other two groups.

Studies of adults in the experimental groups in New York and Boston reported significantly better health and emotional well-being than the Section 8-only and control groups in those cities. Mothers in both the experimental groups were much less likely to report being depressed or stressed. The parents provided more structure for their children's activities and used less restrictive parenting styles. By the third year, 10 percent fewer of the experimental group in New York City were receiving welfare. In Boston, public assistance for MTO families dropped by half, and employment in all MTO sites increased from 27 percent at the beginning of the program to 43 percent three years later. Employment in Boston increased by more than one-half.

The outcomes for children in these experimental groups were also encouraging. They attended schools that had higher pass rates, more affluent student bodies, and more resources than the schools attended by control group children. Ludwig, Duncan, and Ladd (2003) hypothesize that the peer groups in the new schools had more positive attitudes toward school than in the inner city, and this may also have contributed to good outcomes for the children.

Ludwig, Duncan, and Ladd report that young children in the experimental and Section 8-only groups "achieved higher test scores than the controls, and experienced fewer arrests for violent criminal behavior" (2003, p. 164). The authors report in some detail the assessments in Baltimore, and state that they are "largely consistent with evidence from the other MTO sites" (p. 163). Young children in the experimental and Section 8-only groups had Comprehensive Test of Basic Skills (CTBS) reading scores that were on average six to seven percentage points higher than those in the control group (i.e., in low-income urban schools). "This large effect is equal to around one-quarter of the control group mean of 25 percentile points and one-quarter of a standard deviation in the national CTBS math distribution" (p. 165). Children in the experimental

group also raised their CTBS math scores about the same amount, and their pass rates on the Maryland Functional Tests' (MFT) reading test were almost double those in the inner-city schools.

High school students in the Baltimore experimental group had a more difficult transition. In the first three years of MTO, they had higher rates of grade retention, disciplinary action, and school dropout rates than the children of families in the other two groups. The authors suggest that these differences may be due to the enforcement of higher behavioral and/or educational standards in more affluent schools (Ludwig et al, 2003).

However, teens who moved from high- to low-poverty neighborhoods were arrested less often than teens in the other groups. For example, 2.7 percent of control group adolescents were arrested during an average three-month period, compared with only 1.4 percent of teens in the experimental group during the same period. Furthermore, there was a 50 percent reduction in the proportion of juveniles in the experimental group who were arrested for violent offenses. For example, in a given quarter, 3 percent of adolescents in the control group were arrested for violent crimes, compared with only 1.4 percent among the experimental group (Ludwig et al., 2003).

Research in the Boston MTO found significantly fewer behavioral and mental health problems among boys in both the experimental and Section 8-only groups, and experimental-group children were less likely to be injured or to experience asthma attacks. Among children with asthma, the number of attacks requiring medical attention fell significantly (Goering & Feins, 2003). Additionally, the children in the experimental group in Boston were less likely to engage in antisocial behavior (Ludwig et al., 2003).

In sum, these results are in general agreement with evaluations of other mobility programs, which have generally led to "substantial improvements in ... neighborhood conditions, physical and mental health, safety, housing conditions, adult labor-market outcomes (although the findings here are mixed)"

(Johnson, Ladd, & Ludwig, 2002, p. 185) and improvements in the children's behavior and educational outcomes of families who moved.

The success of even small family supports and of a move to places of increased opportunity suggests that we should provide a financial and opportunity base for urban families. This in itself will lay the foundation for fuller child development and educational achievement.

A New Education Policy Paradigm

I have outlined a number of federal and regional polices and practices that undermine urban school quality and potential by maintaining large poverty populations in urban neighborhoods. I have also provided evidence that this poverty works against the development and achievement of urban students. Importantly, however, we also see that even modest financial and social supports for poor families enable the children to achieve at higher levels in school. This suggests that policies to counter the devastating effects of macroeconomic and regional mandates and practices should "count" as policies we call on to create equity and quality in urban districts and schools.

As education policymakers and practitioners, we can acknowledge and act on the power of urban poverty, low-wage work, and housing segregation to dwarf most curricular, pedagogical, and other educational reforms. The effects of macroeconomic policies continually trump the effects of education policies.

To remove economic barriers to school quality and consequence, we can legislate a significantly higher living wage; we can create jobs in cities that offer career ladders and prepare low-income residents to fill them. And, like a number of European countries, we can tax wealthy families and corporations to pay for these and other investments. We should enforce federal antidiscrimination measures to integrate segregated housing and create public transit routes so low-income urban residents without cars are not denied access to jobs in the suburbs. Policies like these would create a social foundation on which high-quality schooling would rest. As has been the case in affluent

suburbs, economic access creates the financial and political conditions in families and communities for educational commitment and reward.

In this new paradigm, education policies for which we press would take on the larger issues: Education funding reform would include the companion need for financing neighborhood jobs and decent wages. New small schools would be created as an important part of coordinated efforts at neighborhood revitalization for low-income residents. Vocational offerings in high school would link to living-wage campaigns and employers who support them. College graduation would be understood as a continuation of government's financial responsibility for public education. And lawsuits to racially integrate districts would acknowledge housing segregation as fundamental and target legal challenges accordingly.

Policies that set the standards schools must meet would identify the money, materials, teachers, courses, and neighborhood needs that must be filled in order to provide opportunities to learn at high levels. Educational accountability would be conceived as a public undertaking, centrally involving families, communities, and students, in consultation with district and government officials.

In this approach to urban school reform, "policy alignment" would not refer to the fit between education mandates issued by various levels of government and bureaucracy. The fit we would seek is between neighborhood, family, and student needs and the potential of education policies to contribute to their fulfillment.

However, economic strength and political leverage is not all that is required to transform urban education. Good schools require not only good neighborhoods, but—as equity-seeking educational reforms have promised—also the detracking of minority and working-class youth, a culture responsive to students, and assistance to teachers in their struggle to surmount the wall of resignation and defiance that separates many students from the educational enterprise.

A new paradigm of education policy is possible—one that promotes equity-seeking school change and that includes strategies to create conditions that will allow the educational improvements to take root, grow, and bear fruit in students' lives.

Harvard Educational Review, Vol. 75, No. 1, Spring 2005. Copyright © by the President and Fellows of Harvard College.

Notes

1. The 1958 National Defense Education Act (NDEA) funded and promoted curriculum materials, primarily in science, math, and foreign languages (e.g., the "New Math"), and some of these probably found their way into city districts and classrooms. But the NDEA was aimed at increasing the security and technological prowess of the United States, not at improving urban schools.

2. Graduation rates in large urban high schools are lower than is commonly believed. Jay P. Greene, senior fellow at the Manhattan Institute for Policy Research, calculated graduation rates in all states and large cities for major racial groups. For this calculation he first identified the eighth-grade public school enrollment for each jurisdiction and for each subgroup from the 1993 fall semester, adjusting for student movement into or out of an area. He then obtained counts of the number of regular high school diplomas awarded in the spring of 1998 when the eighth graders should have been graduating. (In calculating the 1998 graduation rate, he did not include later GED or other alternative diplomas, as the federal government does.) He found that the national graduation rate for the class of 1998 was 71 percent. For White students the rate was 78 percent, for African American students it was 56 percent, and for Latinos, 54 percent. In fifteen of forty-five large (mostly urban) districts for which there were data, fewer than 50 percent of African American students graduated; and in twenty-one of thirty-six large, mostly urban districts for which there were data, fewer than 50 percent of Latino students graduated (Greene, 2001, pp. 1–5).

References

Anyon, J. (1979). Ideology and U.S. history textbooks. *Harvard Educational Review, 49*, 361–386.

Anyon, J. (1980). Social class and the hidden curriculum of work. *Journal of Education, 162*, 7–92.

Anyon, J. (1981). Social class and school knowledge. *Curriculum Inquiry, 11*, 3–42.

Anyon, J. (1995). Race, social class, and educational reform in an inner city school. *Teachers College Record, 97*, 69–94.

Anyon, J. (1997). *Ghetto schooling: A political economy of urban educational reform.* New York: Teachers College Press.

Anyon, J. (2005). *Radical possibilities: Public policy, urban education, and a new social movement.* New York: Routledge.

Ayres, L. (1909). *Laggards in our schools: A study of retardation and elimination in city school systems.* New York: Russell Sage.

Bernstein, J., Brocht, C., & Spade-Aguilar, M. (2000). *How much is enough? Basic family budgets for working families.* Washington, DC: Economic Policy Institute.

Bolger, K., & Patterson, C. (1995). Psychosocial adjustment among children experiencing persistent and intermittent family economic hardship. *Child Development, 66*, 1107–1129.

Bradley, R. (1984). One hundred, seventy-four children: A study of the relation between the home environment and early cognitive development in the first 5 years. In A. Gottfried (Ed.), *The home environment and early cognitive development* (pp. 5–56). Orlando, FL: Academic Press.

Brooks-Gunn, J., Duncan, G., Leventhal, T., & Aber, L. (1997). Lessons learned and future directions for research on the neighborhoods in which children live. In J. Brooks-Gunn, G. Duncan, & L. Aber (Eds.), *Neighborhood poverty, volume 1: Contexts and consequences for children* (pp. 279–298). New York: Russell Sage.

Bos, J., Huston, A. C., Duncan, G. J., Brock, T., & McLoyd, V. (1996). *New hope for people with low incomes: Two-year results of a program to reduce poverty and reform welfare.* New York: Manpower Demonstration Research Corporation.

Caspi, A., Wright, B., Moffit, E., & Silva, T. (1998). Early failure in the labor market: Childhood and adolescent predictors of unemployment in the transition to adulthood. *American Sociological Review, 63*, 424–451.

Cauthen, N., & Lu, H. (2001, August). *Living on the edge: Employment alone is not enough for America's low-income children and families* (Research Brief No. 1, Mailman School of Public Health, National Center for Children in Poverty). New York: Columbia University.

Citizens for Tax Justice. (2002). *Surge in corporate tax welfare drives corporate tax payments down to near record low.* Washington, DC: Author.

Citro, C., & Michael, R. (Eds.). (1995). *Measuring poverty: A new approach.* Washington, DC: National Academy Press.

Conley, D. (2003). *Who governs our schools? Changing roles and responsibilities.* New York: Teachers College Press.

Costello, J., Compton, S., Keeler, G., & Angold, A. (2003). Relationships between poverty and psychopathology: A natural experiment. *Journal of the American Medical Association, 290*, 2023–2029.

Cross, C. (2004). *Political education: National policy comes of age.* New York: Teachers College Press.

Dillon, S. (2003, April 30). Report finds number of black children in deep poverty rising. *New York Times,* p. 18A.

Dreier, P., Mollenkopf, J., & Swanstrom, T. (2001). *Place matters: Metropolitics for the 21st century.* Lawrence: University Press of Kansas.

Duncan, G., & Brooks-Gunn, J. (Eds.). (1997). *Consequences of growing up poor.* New York: Russell Sage.

Duncan, G., Brooks-Gunn, J., & Klebanov, P. (1994). Economic deprivation and early childhood development. *Child Development,* 65, 296–318.

Economic Policy Institute. (2002). *Economic snapshots.* Washington, DC: Author.

Economic Policy Institute. (2004). *EPI issue guide: Minimum wage.* Washington, DC: Author.

Education Trust. (2001). *The funding gap: Low-income and minority students receive fewer dollars.* Washington, DC: Author.

Entwistle, D., & Alexander, K. (1997). *Children, schools, and inequality.* Boulder, CO: Westview Press.

Fine, M. (2001, May). *Comparative analysis of the organization of high schools 1996–97, NYC Board of Education.* Findings presented at the Spencer Conference, New York. Document available at www.nysed.gov.80/emsc/docs4-99NYStrategy. ppt.3.

Galbraith, J. (1998). *Created unequal: The crisis in American pay.* New York: Free Press.

Goering, J., & Feins, J. (Eds.). (2003). *Choosing a better life? Evaluating the Moving To Opportunity social experiment.* Washington, DC: Urban Institute Press.

Greene, J. (2001). *High school graduation rates in the United States.* Washington, DC: Black Alliance for Educational Options and the Manhattan Institute.

Harrington, M. (1963). *The other America: Poverty in the United States.* Baltimore: Penguin.

Houser, R. M., Brown, B. V., & Prosser, W. R. (1998). *Indicators of children's well-being.* New York: Russell Sage.

Hout, M. (1988). More universalism, less structural mobility: The American occupational structure in the 1980s. *American Journal of Sociology,* 93, 1358–1400.

Huston, A. C., Duncan, G. J., Granger, R., Bos, J., McLoyd, V. C., Mistry, R., Crosby, D. A., Gibson, C., Magnuson, K., Romich, J., & Ventura, A. (2001). Work-based anti-poverty programs for parents can enhance the school performance and social behavior of children. *Child Development,* 72, 318–336.

Huston, A. C., Miller, C., Richburg-Hayes, L., Duncan, G. J., Eldred, C. A., Weisner, T. S., Lowe, E., McLoyd, V. C., Crosby, D. A., Ripke, M. N., & Redcross, C. (2003). *Summary report, New Hope for families and children: Five-year results of a program to reduce poverty and reform welfare.* New York: Manpower Demonstration Research Corporation.

Jackson, A., Brooks-Gunn, J., Huang, C., & Glassman, M. (2000) Single mothers in low-wage jobs: Financial strain, parenting, and preschoolers' outcomes. *Child Development,* 71, 1409–1423.

Jencks, C., & Phillips, M. (1998) *The Black/White test score gap.* Washington, DC: Brookings Institution Press.

Jeremiah, L. (2003). *Family support programs and academic achievement: Lessons for Seattle.* Unpublished manuscript. Available online at www.evans. washington.edu/research/psclinic/pdf/02-03dp/ Jeremiahdp.pdf.

Johnson, M., Ladd, H., & Ludwig, J. (2002). The benefits and costs of residential mobility programs. *Housing Studies,* 17, 125–138.

Kingsley, T., & Petit, K. (2003). *Concentrated poverty? A change in course.* Neighborhood change in urban America series. Washington, DC: Urban Institute.

Klerman, L. (1991; 2003 Reprint edition). The health of poor children: Problems and programs. In A. C. Huston (Ed.), *Children and poverty: Child development and public policy* (pp. 136–157). New York: Cambridge University Press.

Korenman, S., & Miller, J. (1997). Effects of long-term poverty on physical health of children in the national longitudinal survey of youth. In G. Duncan & J. Brooks-Gunn (Eds.), *Consequences of growing up poor* (pp. 70–99). New York: Russell Sage.

Lafer, G. (2002). *The job training charade.* Ithaca, NY: Cornell University Press.

Lee, V., & Burkham, D. (2002). *Inequality at the starting gate: Social background and achievement at kindergarten entry.* Washington, DC: Economic Policy Institute.

Lu, H. (2003). *Low-income children in the United States.* New York: Columbia University, Mailman School of Public Health.

Ludwig, J., Duncan, G., & Ladd, H. (2003). The effects of moving to opportunity on children and parents in Baltimore. In J. Goering & J. Feins (Eds.), *Choosing a better life?* (pp. 153–177). Washington, DC: Urban Institute Press.

Masten, A., & Coatsworth, D. (1995). The structure and coherence of competence from childhood through adolescence. *Child Development,* 66, 1635–1659.

McLoyd, V. (1998). Socioeconomic disadvantage and child development. *American Psychologist,* 53, 185–204.

McLoyd, V., & Jartayne, T. (1994). Unemployment and work interruption among African-American single mothers: Effects on parenting and adolescent socio-emotional functioning. *Child Development*, 65, 562–589.

Miao, J., & Haney, W. (2004). High school graduation rates: Alternative methods and implications. *Education Policy Analysis Archives*, 12(55). Available online at http://epaa.asu.edu/epaa/v12n55.

Michaloupolos, C., Tattri, D., Miller, C., Robins, P. K., Morris, P., Gyarmati, D., Redcross, C., Foley, K., & Ford, R. (2002). *Making work pay: Final report on the self-sufficiency project for long-term welfare recipients.* New York: Manpower Demonstration Research Corporation.

Mishel, L., Bernstein, J., & Boushey, H. (2003). *The state of working America: 2002/2003.* Ithaca, NY: Cornell University Press.

Mishel, L., Bernstein, J., & Schmitt, J. (2001). *The state of working America: 2000/2001.* Ithaca, NY: Cornell University Press.

Morris, P., Huston, A.C., Duncan, G.J., Crosby, D., & Bos, J. (2001). *How welfare and work policies affect children: A synthesis of research.* Washington, DC: Manpower Demonstration Research Corporation.

O'Connor, A. (2003, October 21). Rise in income improves children's behavior. *New York Times*, p. F5.

Odden, A., & Picus, L. (1992). *School finance: A policy perspective.* New York: McGraw-Hill.

Orfield, M. (2002). *American metropolitics: The new sub-urban reality.* Washington, DC: Brookings Institute.

Phillips, K. (2002). *Wealth and democracy: A political history of the American rich.* New York: Broadway Books.

Phillips, M., Brooks-Gunn, J., Duncan, G., Klevanov, P., & Crane, J. (1998). Family background, parenting practices, and the Black/White test score gap. In C. Jencks & M. Phillips (Eds.), *The Black/White test score gap* (pp. 103–145). Washington, DC: Brookings Institution Press.

Phillips, M., Crouse, J., & Ralph, J. (1998). Does the Black/White test score gap widen after children enter school? In C. Jencks & M. Phillips (Eds.), *The Black/White test score gap* (pp. 229–272). Washington, DC: Brookings Institution Press.

Ravitch, D. (2000). *The great school wars: A history of the New York City public schools.* Baltimore: Johns Hopkins University Press.

Rubinowitz, L., & Rosenbaum, J. (2002). *Crossing the class and color line: From public housing to White suburbia.* Chicago: University of Chicago Press.

Rusk, D. (1999). *Inside game/outside game: Winning strategies for saving urban America.* Washington, DC: Brookings Institution.

Sampson, R., Morenoff, J., & Gannon-Rowley, T. (2002). Assessing "neighborhood effects": Social processes and new directions in research. *Annual Review of Sociology*, 28, 443–478.

Seitz, V., Rosenbaum L., & Apfel, N. (1985). Effects of family support intervention: A ten-year follow-up. *Child Development* 56, 376–391.

Short, K., Iceland, J., & Garner, T. (1999). *Experimental poverty measures: 1998.* Washington, DC: U.S. Census Bureau.

Smith, J., Brooks-Gunn, J., & Klebanov, P. (1997). Consequences of living in poverty for young children's cognitive and verbal ability and early school achievement. In G. Duncan & J. Brooks-Gunn (Eds.), *Consequencs of growing up poor* (pp. 132–189). New York: Russell Sage Foundation.

Stein, S. (2004). *The culture of educational policy.* New York: Teachers College Press.

Stipic, D., & Ryan, R. (1997). Economically disadvantaged preschoolers: Ready to learn but further to go. *Developmental Psychology*, 33, 711–723.

Sugland, B., Zaslow, M., & Brooks-Gunn, J. (1995). The early childhood HOME inventory and HOME short form in differing socio-cultural groups: Are there differences in underlying structure, internal consistency of subcases, and patterns of prediction? *Journal of Family Issues*, 16, 632–663.

Tyack, D. (1974). *The one best system: A history of American urban education.* Cambridge, MA: Harvard University Press.

White, K. (1982). The relationship between socio-economic status and academic achievement. *Psychological Bulletin*, 91, 46–81.

Wrigley, J. (1982). *Class politics and public schools: Chicago 1900–1950.* New Brunswick, NJ: Rutgers University Press.

I would like to thank my colleague Tony Picciano for his thoughts.

3 The History of Education

Our discussion of the history of education in the United States begins with the introduction of schooling in colonial America when Europeans settled in the colonies and began to devise systematic and deliberate forms of education for their children. Other forms of education existed in North America prior to European settlement. Native Americans educated their children within the structure of their communities and acculturated them into the rituals, obligations, and roles necessary for the maintenance and continuity of community life. Although such forms of education were extremely important, the development of U.S. schooling was heavily influenced by the European colonists as they adapted to life in North America.

There are many interpretations as to why education was so important to the early settlers and why it continues to be an important issue in contemporary society. Historians, such as Bernard Bailyn (1960), have attributed the use of the school to the failure of particular institutions such as the family, church, and community to provide the necessary tools demanded by the conditions of the new emerging society. Historian Merle Curti (1959/1971) attributed the use of formal schooling to the interests of the colonists in protecting freedoms such as thought, religion, and press—freedoms necessary for the maintenance of a democratic society. Regardless of the motives and intentions, it is important to look at the early versions of schools in order to understand how the present-day school evolved. What will become increasingly apparent are three ideas:

1. From its very inception, the school was charged with assuming roles that once were the province of family, church, and community.
2. The school continues to serve as a focal point in larger issues of societal needs.
3. There is little consensus on the motives for school reforms.

Old World and New World Education: The Colonial Era

Our discussion of the history of U.S. education begins with the settlers who brought their ideas about education to the New World. In general, the society of the Old World was highly stratified, and the view most Europeans held was that only the sons of the rich required an education since they would be the future ruling class. Thus, early affluent settlers such as planters and townsmen, particularly in the southern colonies, hired tutors for their sons and sent their sons back to England, if they could afford it, for their university educations.

It is interesting to note, however, that many of the wealthy colonists' sons did remain in the United States for their higher education, since nine institutions of higher learning were founded prior to the American Revolution. These were Harvard University (1636), College of William and Mary (1693), Yale University (1701), University of Pennsylvania (1740), Princeton University (1746), Columbia University (1754), Brown University (1764), Rutgers University (1766), and Dartmouth College (1769). However, the colleges themselves were not at all revolutionary. They taught most of the same subjects found at Oxford or Cambridge, and Greek and Latin were required subjects.

What becomes increasingly apparent in the history of U.S. education is that even before education began to formalize and acquire certain specific patterns, there emerged distinctly different themes regarding the purpose of education. For example, as just noted, the upper-class planter aristocracy and wealthy merchants saw education as a means of perpetuating the ruling class. Religious, utilitarian, and civic motives also emerged over time.

The religious impetus to formalize instruction can best be exemplified by the Puritans in New England who, early in 1642 and 1647, passed school laws commonly referred to as the *Old Deluder Laws*. The first law chastised parents for not attending to their children's "ability to read and understand the principles of religion and capital laws of this country" and fined them for their children's "wanton" and "immodest" behavior. Thus, the first law pointed to a problem among the young to which the parents failed to attend.

The second law was far more specific regarding formalized schooling. To keep the "old deluder" Satan away, the Massachusetts School Law of 1647 provided that every town that had "50 household" would appoint one person to teach all children, regardless of gender, to read and write. Furthermore, the town was required to pay the wages of the teacher. Towns that numbered "100 families or household" had to set up a grammar school (equivalent to a secondary school today) to prepare students for university studies. Towns that failed to comply were subject to fines. Thus, early in the nation's history, the theme of literacy as a means of teaching a Christian life was articulated.

The *Old Deluder Law* was not very popular throughout New England. Often, towns simply neglected to provide the education for their youth as dictated by law. However, it remains a landmark in the history of U.S. education, for it established a precedent for public responsibility for education.

The theme of utilitarianism as the purpose of education can best be seen through an examination of the ideas of Benjamin Franklin, who, in 1749, published "Proposals Related to the Education of Youth in Pennsylvania." Franklin called for an education for youth based on secular and utilitarian courses of study rather than on the traditional studies of religion and classics. However, as Bailyn (1960) pointed out, Franklin did not define education along narrowly defined utilitarian principles. Rather, Franklin believed that "the purpose of schooling was to provide in systematic form what he had extemporized, haphazardly feeling his way" (p. 35). Thus, Franklin believed that students should pursue a course of study that would allow them mastery of process rather than rote learning. Reading, writing, public speaking, and art as a means of understanding creative expression would be integral components of the curriculum.

Utilitarian components of the curriculum would be practical aspects of mathematics, such as accounting and natural history (biology). Additionally, students would study history, geography, and political studies. Languages such as Latin and Greek would be available to students who wished to enter the ministry. Others, who sought commerce and trade as careers, might study more modern languages such as French, Italian, German, and Spanish.

Perhaps because of his own life experience, Benjamin Franklin fervently believed in the ability of people to better themselves. His faith in self-improvement through education and in an education that reflected practical concerns was not explored again until the nineteenth century. Franklin's proposal for an academy became the prototype for private secondary education in the United States. It was not until the second half of the nineteenth century, however, that public support for Franklin's ideas became a reality.

The civic motive for education is best illustrated through the ideas of the prominent American statesman, Thomas Jefferson, who fervently believed that the best safeguard for democracy was a literate population. It was Jefferson who proposed to the Virginia Legislature in 1779, a "Bill for the More General Diffusion of Knowledge," which would provide free education to *all* children for the first three years of elementary school. Jefferson, a product of enlightenment thinking, was optimistic enough to think that if citizens possessed enough education to read newspapers and thus inform themselves of pressing public issues, they would make intelligent, informed decisions at the polls.

Jefferson's bill also provided for a limited meritocracy within the educational structure. After the initial three years of reading, writing, and "common arithmetic," all students could advance to 1 of 20 grammar schools within the state of Virginia, contingent on their payment of tuition. However, Jefferson proposed that each elementary school send one scholarship student to a grammar school. After two to three years of rigorous, classical studies (Latin, Greek, English grammar, geography, mathematics), the most promising scholarship student from among this group of 20 students would be selected for another funded four years of study, while the remaining group would be dismissed.

Finally, each grammar school would have the task of selecting 10 of its best students who would receive three-year scholarships to the College of William and Mary. Thus, Jefferson set forth in his bill a proposal for an aristocracy of talent, which would be nurtured and supported through a statewide educational structure. Unfortunately, Jefferson was ahead of his time; the majority of the state legislators agreed that the state should not be involved in educating its inhabitants and that, in any event, Jefferson's proposal required funds far beyond those possessed by the state of Virginia at that time.

The schools that were established in the United States during the colonial period varied greatly in the quality of instruction. In Puritan New England, often an elderly housewife (usually a widow) heard lessons, which consisted of recitations. These schools became known as *dame schools*. Elementary education, in the New England *town school*, established by the *Old Deluder Law*, consisted of such basic subjects as reading, writing, and religion. Students were taught by learning the alphabet: letters first, syllables and words next, and then sentences. There were few supplies and textbooks, except for the famous *New England Primer*. This book, sometimes referred to as the "Little Bible of New England," combined the teaching of reading with religious education, obedience, and citizenship. For example, in teaching the first letter of the alphabet, children would be treated to an illustration of Adam and Eve, the latter holding an apple given to her by a serpent, wrapped around a tree that was separating the couple, with the accompanying words: "A: In Adam's Fall/We Sinned, All." This book, which appeared about 1690, sold more than 3 million copies during the 1700s (Gutek, 1991).

Students were taught content mastery through memorization. They were taught writing skills by copying directly from the printed page or by taking dictation from the schoolmaster. Classes were ungraded; all students were housed in the same room and taught by a teacher who might have been either an indentured servant, a divinity student, or a village preacher. Strict disciplinary methods prevailed, which might be considered overly harsh by today's standards, perhaps influenced by the Puritan predilection to the "authoritarian temperament" of leadership (Button & Provenzano, 1989).

Secondary education, as it evolved in New England, was not coeducational, as was the elementary school; rather, it was for the sons of the elite who were usually tutored at home rather than receiving their primary schooling at the local town school. This school was called the *Latin Grammar School*, as the curriculum emphasized the teaching of Latin and Greek—languages of the educated elite in Europe. Ultimately, it served as a sorting device through which the newly formed Puritan elite in the United States could reproduce itself. Male students entered the Latin Grammar School at eight years of age and studied there for another eight years. They read classical texts such as Cicero and Caesar in Latin and Homer and Hesiod in Greek. Clearly, the emphasis here was not on a utilitarian education as later articulated by Franklin; rather, students were being "taught by example" from classical literature, which hopefully would enable them to function effectively as leaders in the Puritan oligarchy.

Education in the middle colonies was far more diverse than in Puritan New England, as the schools that emerged there reflected the vast religious and cultural differences of the region. Generally, education was the province of the colonies' numerous religious denominations, such as Dutch Reformed, Quaker, Roman Catholic, and Jewish. New York was dominated by the Dutch Reformed Church, which, like the Puritans, espoused the importance of literate congregations. When the English took over New York, they established charity schools, which were controlled by the Anglican Church. These schools emphasized reading, writing, arithmetic, catechism, and religion. In Pennsylvania, where English Quakers dominated the political and economic life of the colony, they also controlled education. However, in keeping with their humane attitude toward human life, the Quakers rejected the harsh treatment of children prevalent in the other colonies and paid more attention to individual children as they mastered reading, writing, arithmetic, and religion (Gutek, 1991).

Education in the South was largely confined to the upper class and took place at home on the plantation, since the vastness of these economic units made the construction of formal schools virtually impossible. Education was provided by tutors who might have been indentured servants, divinity students, impoverished second sons of European aristocrats, or convicts. Indeed, before the American Revolution, one observer reported that "two-thirds of the schoolmasters in Maryland were either indentured servants or convicts" (Wright, 1957, p. 101).

Both male and female children were educated on an aristocratic model: Classical studies were emphasized for boys, whereas dancing and music lessons were emphasized for girls. Although some Southern women may have shared their brothers' tutors, learning to master the social graces took precedence over Caesar in aristocratic Southern households. Occasionally, boys were sent away to school, most likely to England. Plantation management was learned by both sexes according to gender-specific roles. Girls were expected to master the domestic side of plantation management from their mothers, while boys learned the practical aspects from their fathers. Southern planters often sent their sons north to colonial colleges or to Europe to complete their education. However, by 1817, Jefferson wrote the "Rockfish Gap Report," the report of the Commission to establish a public university in Virginia, leading to the establishment of the University of Virginia in Charlottesville. The university was based on Jefferson's model of a natural aristocracy based on talent, or what later was called a *meritocracy*.

On the eve of the American Revolution, almost all of the African-American population of one-half million were slaves. As Gutek (1991) observed,

> In being uprooted from their native Africa, the blacks were torn from their own culture and thrust into an environment not merely inhospitable, but completely alien. As slaves the African blacks were undergoing induction into a society vastly different from that of their homeland. (p. 10)

Few members of this group could read or write. Those who could, more often than not, had received their instruction outside of existing formal schools, for "it appears that only a handful attended school along with the whites" (Cremin, 1972, pp. 194–195). Schools that did exist for African-Americans were usually sponsored by church groups, in particular Anglicans and Quakers (Button & Provenzano, 1989). Few slave owners were willing to support formal education for their slaves, since literacy was not directly connected to their work. Moreover, many feared that literate slaves would be more likely to lead insurrections. Although African-Americans were kept illiterate as part of their subordinate position both on plantations and in the cities, some managed to learn skills as artisans, working as carpenters, coopers, wainwrights, farriers, coachmen, and skilled domestics.

Formal schooling for Native Americans was largely confined to missionary activities. In Virginia, the colonists at first attempted to establish "friendly" relations with their Native American neighbors. However, after hostilities broke out in 1622, they decided that "the way of conquering them is much more easy than of civilizing them by fair means" (Cremin, 1972, p. 194). There were some mildly successful educative endeavors in New England, particularly in Cambridge and Roxbury, which were directed by individual schoolmasters to prepare Native Americans for the Indian College that was established at Harvard University in approximately 1653. This Indian College, as Wright (1957) noted, was brought about largely due to the misguided belief held by some educated whites that "Indians were merely awaiting the opportunity to embrace classical scholarship and learn Cicero's orations" (p. 116). Ultimately, this experiment resulted in failure and was the first example of attempting to educate Native Americans by assimilating them into European culture. As in the case of African-Americans, this period represents the beginning of the marginalization of Native Americans with respect to formal schooling.

The Age of Reform: The Rise of the Common School

Historians point to the period from 1820 to 1860 in the United States as one in which enormous changes took place with unprecedented speed. The Industrial Revolution, which began in the textile industry in England, crossed the Atlantic Ocean and brought its factory system with its new machinery to urban areas, particularly in the North. Urban clusters grew more dense as migrants from agricultural areas and immigrants from Europe flocked to the factories, looking for work. By 1850, these immigrants included a significant group of Roman Catholics who were escaping starvation in Ireland. Westward expansion, aided in part by the revolution in transportation and in part by the land hunger of pioneers, extended to settlements in Oregon and California by 1850.

By 1828, when Andrew Jackson was elected president, all men (except slaves and emotionally disturbed persons) had obtained the right to vote. Thus, the founding fathers' visions of a political democracy were increasingly becoming a reality.

In the decades following 1815, groups of reformers—quite different from such archetypes of rationalism as Franklin and Jefferson—emerged. These men and women often lacked higher education and did not hold public office but often articulated their ideas with the fervor of evangelical Christianity. However, their ultimate goals were secular in nature. America, once seen as the New Jerusalem by the Puritans, would become a secular paradise created by the new reformers.

Ralph Waldo Emerson, a New England essayist and philosopher, wrote of this age, "We are all a little wild here with numberless projects of social reform." Although the reform movement attempted to address such diverse societal problems as slavery, mental illness, intemperance, and pacifism, many reformers generally believed that the road to secular paradise was through education.

By 1820, it had become evident to those interested in education that the schools that had been established by the pre-war generation were not functioning effectively. Webster's *New England Primer* had been secularized so that the first line "In Adam's Fall/We Sinned, All" was replaced by "A was an Apple Pie made by the Cook" (Malone & Rauch, 1960, p. 491), but few children had access to the reader. The vast majority of Americans were, not surprisingly, illiterate. Even in New England, with its laws specifying common schools, towns neglected or evaded their duties. In other parts of the country, charity schools provided the only opportunities for disadvantaged children to obtain an education.

The struggle for free public education was led by Horace Mann of Massachusetts. Abandoning a successful career as a lawyer, Mann lobbied for a state board of education, and when the Massachusetts legislature created one in 1837, Horace Mann became its first secretary, an office he occupied for 11 years. His annual reports served as models for public school reforms throughout the nation, and, partly due to Mann's efforts, the first state *normal school* (from the French *école normale*), or teacher training school, was established in Lexington, Massachusetts, in 1839.

Mann's arguments for the establishment of the *common school*, or free publicly funded elementary schools, reflects both the concern for stability and order and the concern for social mobility—both of which were to be addressed through free public education. Admittedly, Mann could not have been immune to the waves of different immigrant groups that were changing the cultural composition of the cities. Nor could he fail to be immune to the goals of his audiences, often the wealthy factory owners, who had to be convinced to support public education. Thus, he spoke of school as a preparation for citizenship as well as the "balance wheel"—"the great equalizer of the conditions of men."

Although many historians, particularly liberals and conservatives, view Mann as one of America's greatest educational reformers, radicals take issue with his arguments, pointing to the common school as a pernicious device for teaching skills such as hygiene, punctuality, and rudimentary skills that would create docile, willing workers. Whatever interpretation one chooses, Mann's belief that schools can change the social order and that education can foster social mobility are beliefs responsible for the faith and support many people give to U.S. public schools.

Opposition to Public Education

Not all groups subscribed to the idea of the common school. The same arguments made today by people without children or people who send their children to private schools in opposition to public support of schools were articulated against the common school Horace Mann envisioned. For example, taxation for public education was viewed as "unjust" by nonrecipients. Roman Catholics, who viewed the common school as dominated by a Protestant ethos, founded their own schools. However, by 1860, public support of elementary schools was becoming prevalent throughout the United States. Education beyond the elementary level, however, was primarily a province of private academies. Nonetheless, in 1862, Congress passed the Morrill Act, which authorized the use of public money to establish public land grant universities, resulting in the establishment of large state universities, espcially in the Midwest.

Education for Women and African-Americans

Traditionally, the role of a woman in Western society has been that of helpmate or homemaker to the male, who assumed the role of provider. This role for women was vividly described by Jean-Jacques Rousseau in *Émile*, written in the eighteenth century. Rousseau, in his tract on education, created the female character, Sophie, who was to be the companion of the central male character, Émile, the recipient of a nontraditional but rigorous education. Sophie was encouraged to eat sweets, learn womanly arts, and be a supportive, loving helpmate to Émile.

This prescriptive role for women held sway throughout the nineteenth century and, for some, into the twentieth century as well. Generally, education for women was viewed as biologically harmful or too stressful. Thus, through the first half of the nineteenth century, educational opportunities for women were severely limited. Few females achieved an education other than rudimentary literacy and numeracy.

By the middle of the nineteenth century, however, a significant number of girls attended elementary schools and many were admitted to private academies, which functioned as secondary schools. By 1820, the movement for education for women in the United States was making important inroads.

In 1821, Emma Hart Willard opened the Troy Female Seminary in Troy, New York. The curriculum at this female seminary included so-called serious subjects of study, such as mathematics, science, history, and geography. Modeled on the curriculum of single-sex male academies, Troy Female Seminary sought to deliver an education to females that was similar to that of their male counterparts. In subsequent years, other female reformers dedicated to education for women, such as Catharine Esther Beecher and Mary Lyon, opened schools for females. A pioneer in postsecondary education for women, Mary Lyon founded Mount Holyoke Seminary in 1837. Entry requirements (with the exception of a foreign language) and level of instruction were the same for women as for men at their institutions of higher learning.

Higher education for women did not remain the exclusive domain of Eastern reformers; the movement for female education spread quickly through the Midwest. In 1833, Oberlin Collegiate Institute in Ohio opened its doors to women as well as African-Americans. In 1856, the University of Iowa became the first state university to admit women. In 1865, Vassar College, the first of the Seven Sisters women's colleges, was founded in Poughkeepsie, New York. Shortly after, Wellesley College and Smith Colleges in Massachusetts were founded, and Mount Holyoke and Bryn Mawr Seminaries became colleges.

Although educational opportunities for women were expanding during the period preceding the Civil War, education for African-Americans was severely limited. After Nat Turner's Revolt in 1831, Southerners believed more than ever that literacy bred both insubordination and revolution. Thus, they forbade the teaching of reading and writing to the slave population. In the North, education for African-Americans was usually of inferior quality and separate from the mainstream public school, if provided at all by the public.

This dismal picture of schooling for African-Americans prompted African-American Benjamin Roberts to file a legal suit in Boston in 1846 over the requirement that his daughter attend a segregated school. In a precedent-setting case, *Roberts* v. *City of Boston*, the court ruled that the local school committee had the right to establish separate educational facilities for whites and blacks. As a result of this ruling, African-Americans were encouraged to establish their own schools. These were usually administered by their churches and aided in part through funds from abolitionists. During the Civil War, President Abraham Lincoln issued the Emancipation Proclamation in 1863, which announced the end of slavery in all states in rebellion against the Union. In 1865, several months after the end of the Civil War, Congress passed the Thirteenth Amendment to the Constitution, which freed four million slaves. In 1868, the Fourteenth Amendment to the Constitution was ratified, giving full citizenship to ex-slaves. Although this amendment and the Freedman's Bureau attempted to reconstruct the South's economy and include blacks as full citizens, the Ku Klux Klan continued to spread racial hatred, and Jim Crow Laws and Black Codes in the South continued discrimination against Blacks. Its equal protection clause, however, has been applied to important legal decisions regarding education. In 1868, the Freedman's Bureau helped to establish historically Black Colleges, including Howard University in Washington, D.C., and Hampton Institute in Virginia. However, the problem of equality of opportunity, in general, and school segregation, in particular, continued to be a significant issue throughout the remainder of the nineteenth and twentieth centuries (Andersen, 1988).

Urbanization and the Progressive Impetus

The beginning of the nineteenth century ushered in the First Industrial Revolution—immigration and urbanization of unprecedented proportions. Accordingly, the conditions created by these events were met with responses from social reformers whose concerns were far reaching and who attempted to address and redress the evils in U.S. life.

If the beginning of the nineteenth century seemed problematic to Americans, the close of the century must have been even more so. Again, there was a revolution in industry, referred to as the Second Industrial Revolution, this time involving steam-driven and electric-powered machinery. Factories had given way to gigantic corporations, under the control of such captains of industry as Andrew Carnegie, John D. Rockefeller, and Cornelius Vanderbilt. Significantly, immigrant labor played an essential role in this revolution.

At the beginning of the nineteenth century, the largest number of immigrants to the United States came from the northwestern part of Europe—namely, Great Britain, Scandinavia, Germany, and the Netherlands. After 1890, an increasingly large number of immigrants came from southern and eastern Europe. These immigrants' languages, customs, and living styles were dramatically different from those of the previous group. They settled in closely crowded substandard living quarters in urban areas and found work in factories. Thus, by the turn of the century, U.S. cities contained enormous concentrations of both wealth and poverty. Indeed, the gap between rich and poor had never been as great as it was at the close of the nineteenth century.

Thus far in this chapter, we have argued that the purpose of education has been seen in a variety of ways: religious, utilitarian, civic, and, with Mann, social mobility. The common school was born of an age of reform in this country that was unprecedented until the period between 1900 and 1914 in which a new reform movement, the Progressive Movement, would sweep the country. Progressive reformers insisted on government regulation of industry and commerce, as well as government regulation and conservation of the nation's natural resources. Moreover, progressive reformers insisted that government at national, state, and local levels be responsive to the welfare of its citizens rather than to the welfare of corporations. Significantly, progressive reforms had a sweeping agenda, ranging from secret ballot to schooling. As reformers, such as Horace Mann, in the nineteenth century had looked to schools as a means of addressing social problems, so reformers once again looked to schools as a means of preserving and promoting democracy within the new social order.

An important U.S. philosopher whose influence on schooling is still very much with us today was John Dewey (1859–1952). Dewey was a contemporary of such reformers as "Fighting Bob La Follette," governor of Wisconsin and architect of the "Wisconsin Idea," which harnessed the expertise of university professors to the mechanics of state government; settlement workers, such as Jane Addams and Lillian Wald; and municipal reformers and labor leaders, such as Henry Bruere and John Golden. Thus, progressive education, the movement with which John Dewey has become associated, can best be understood, as both historians Lawrence Cremin and Richard Hofstadter remind us, as part of "a broader program of social and political reform called the Progressive Movement" (Cremin, 1961, p. 88).

Just as the schools today are undergoing a transformation due in part to rapidly changing technology, altered life-styles, and new, massive waves of immigrants, it could be argued that the schools at the turn of the twentieth century were undergoing a similar transformation in their time. In 1909, for example, 57.8 percent of the children in schools in 37 of the largest cities in the United States were foreign born (Cremin, 1961, p. 72). Suddenly, teachers were faced with problems of putative uncleanliness (bathing became part of the school curriculum in certain districts), and teachers began to teach basic socialization skills. Just how these socialization skills have come to be interpreted, whether malevolently by radical historians or benevolently by liberal and conservative historians, is of little concern here. What is important is to consider how Dewey proposed to meet these challenges through education and how his ideas were interpreted by progressive disciples in such a way as to alter the course of schooling in this country.

John Dewey was born and raised in Vermont. By 1894, he had become thoroughly enmeshed in the problems of urbanization as a resident of Chicago and Chair of the Department of Philosophy, Psychology, and Pedagogy at the University of Chicago. Distressed with the abrupt dislocation of families from rural to urban environments, concerned with the loss of traditional ways of understanding the maintenance of civilization, and anxious about the effects unleashed individualism and rampant materialism would have on a democratic society, Dewey sought answers in pedagogic practice (see Westbrook, 1991, for an in-depth biography).

Dewey argued in *My Pedagogic Creed* (1897), *The School and Society* (1899), and *The Child and the Curriculum* (1902) for a restructuring of schools along the lines of "embryonic communities."

He advocated the creation of a curriculum that would allow for the child's interests and developmental level while introducing the child to "the point of departure from which the child can trace and follow the progress of mankind in history, getting an insight also into the materials used and the mechanical principles involved" (Dworkin, M.S., 1959, p. 43).

Dewey believed that the result of education was growth, which was firmly posited within a democratic society. Thus, school for Dewey was "that form of community life in which all those agencies are concentrated that will be most effective in bringing the child to share in the inherited resources of the race, and to use his own powers for social ends" (Dworkin, M.S., 1959, p. 22).

To implement his ideas, Dewey created the Laboratory School at the University of Chicago. There, children studied basic subjects in an integrated curriculum, since, according to Dewey, "the child's life is an integral, a total one" and therefore the school should reflect the "completeness" and "unity" of "the child's own world" (Dworkin, M.S., 1959, p. 93). Dewey advocated active learning, starting with the needs and interests of the child; he emphasized the role of experience in education and introduced the notion of teacher as facilitator of learning rather than the font from which all knowledge flows. The school, according to Dewey, was a "miniature community, an embryonic society" (Dworkin, M.S., 1959, p. 41) and discipline was a tool that would develop "a spirit of social cooperation and community life" (Dworkin, M.S., 1959, p. 40).

That John Dewey made important contributions to both philosophy of education and pedagogic practice is undisputable, especially if one examines what happened to education in the wake of Dewey's early work. It is important to keep in mind just how rapidly education had expanded in this period. For example, in 1870, about 6.5 million children from ages 5 through 18 attended school; in 1880, about 15.5 million children attended school—a significant increase, indeed. No fewer than 31 states by 1900 had enacted compulsory education laws. Thus, what occurred in schools throughout this nation was to influence large numbers of Americans.

Although few can dispute Dewey's influence on educational reformers, many believe that Dewey was often misread, misunderstood, and misinterpreted. Thus, Dewey's emphasis on the child's impulses, feelings, and interests led to a form of progressive education that often became synonymous with permissiveness, and his emphasis on vocations ultimately led the way for "life adjustment" curriculum reformers.

Psychologists as well as philosophers became actively involved in educational reform. In fact, two distinctly different approaches to progressive educational reforms became apparent: the child-centered pedagogy of G. Stanley Hall and the social efficiency pedagogy of Edward L. Thorndike.

G. Stanley Hall (1844–1924), once referred to as "the Darwin of the mind" (Cremin, 1961, p. 101), believed that children, in their development, reflected the stages of development of civilization. Thus, according to Hall, schools should tailor their curriculums to the stages of child development. Hall argued that traditional schools stifled the child's natural impulses, and he suggested that schools individualize instruction and attend to the needs and interests of the children they educate. This strand of progressive reform became known as *child-centered* reform.

On the opposite side of child-centered reform *was social engineering reform*, proposed by Edward L. Thorndike. Thorndike (1874–1949) placed his emphasis on the organism's response to its environment. Working with animals in the laboratory, he came to the conclusion that human nature could be altered for better or worse, depending on the education to which it was subjected. Ultimately, Thorndike came to believe that schools could change human beings in a positive way and that the methods and aims of pedagogy to achieve this would be scientifically determined (Cremin, 1961, p. 114).

Thorndike's work, Frederick Winslow Taylor's work in scientific management, and that of other progressive thinkers encouraged educators to be "socially efficient" in the ways they went about educating students. In particular, this thinking led to a belief that schools should be a meaningful experience for students and that schools should prepare students to earn a living. It also suggested that schools might begin to educate students based on their abilities or talents. In particular, a leading proponent of this view was educational reformer Franklin Bobbitt. An issue of particular importance, although never resolved, was Bobbitt's scientific approach to curriculum design (a curriculum designer, according to Bobbitt, was like a "great engineer"). The purpose of curriculum design was to create a curriculum that would include the full range of human experience and prepare students for life.

Education for All: The Emergence of the Public High School

Prior to 1875, fewer than 25,000 students were enrolled in public high schools. Most adolescents who were engaged in some form of secondary education attended private academies that were either traditional, college preparatory schools, or vocational schools (such as Franklin had proposed a century earlier). These academies taught not only academic subjects but also vocational ones. Yet, between 1880 and 1920, 2,382,542 students attended public high schools (Gutek, 1991, p. 122), probably outnumbering those who attended academies, and by 1940, about 6.5 million students attended public high school (U.S. Department of Education, National Center for Education Statistics, 1989b, p. 45). In a scant 40 years or so, a structure for the high school had to be put in place and debates had to be resolved regarding the purpose of secondary education.

One of the great changes that has affected high school attendance is that "whereas once it was altogether voluntary, and for this reason quite selective, it is now, at least for those sixteen and under, compulsory and unselective" (Hofstadter, 1966, p. 326). Compulsory school laws grew steadily. In 1890, 27 states had them; by 1918, all states followed suit, encouraged by court cases, such as the one in Kalamazoo, Michigan, in 1874, which paved the way for the school districts' right to levy taxes to support public high schools.

In examining the evolution of the high school, what becomes immediately apparent is the tension in society over the meaning and purpose of education—a debate that began with the ideas of Jefferson and Franklin, that was augmented by the arguments of Horace Mann, and that was made even more complex with the ideas of progressive educators.

Historian Diane Ravitch has pointed to four themes in particular that were troubling high school educators at the turn of the century. The first was the tension between classical subjects, such as Latin and Greek, and modern subjects, such as science, English literature, and foreign languages. The second was the problem of meeting college entrance requirements, since different colleges required different courses of study. The third involved educators who believed that students should study subjects that would prepare them for life, as opposed to traditional academic subjects. And the fourth, inextricably linked to the other three, was whether all students should pursue the same course of study or whether the course of study should be determined by the interests and abilities of the students (Ravitch, 1983, pp. 136–137).

In order to address the reality that by the 1890s "the high school curriculum had begun to resemble a species of academic jungle creeper, spreading thickly and quickly in many directions at once" (cited in Powell, Farrar, & Cohen, 1985, p. 240) and to clarify the purpose of a high school education, a Committee of Ten was formed by the National Education Association, headed by Harvard University President Charles Eliot. The committee issued its report in 1893, supporting the academic purpose of secondary education and dismissing curricula differentiation. It argued that the purpose of secondary education was to prepare students for "the duties of life" (quoted in Ravitch, 1983, p. 138). Furthermore, the committee recommended that modern academic subjects be awarded the same stature as traditional ones. It proposed five model curricula, including classical and modern languages, English, mathematics, history, and science—in essence, a liberal arts curriculum. Finally, the committee recommended that all students should be taught in the same manner; it was conspicuously silent on the subject of vocational education.

The Committee of Ten's recommendations were subsequently reinforced in two ways. The first was through the National Education Association's (NEA's) newly established committee on college entrance requirements, which recommended that all high school students study a core of academic subjects. The second was through the Carnegie Foundation for the Advancement of Teaching's adoption of the same core courses, which became known as *Carnegie units* and which were implemented in high schools throughout the country.

Not to be ignored was the progressive response to the Committee of Ten. In 1918, the NEA's Commission on the Reorganization of Secondary Schools made its report, which became known as the *Cardinal Principles of Secondary Education*. These principles, harkening back to the work of men such as G. Stanley Hall and supported by the "neutral measurement" work of Edward F. Thorndike, opened the door to a curriculum less academically demanding and far more utilitarian than the one proposed by Charles Eliot's Committee of Ten. Essentially, the Cardinal Principles, or the main goals of secondary education, were:

1.   Health
2.   Command of fundamental processes
3.   Worthy home-membership
4.   Vocation
5.   Citizenship
6.   Worthy use of leisure
7.   Ethical character (Ravitch, 1983, p. 146)

For many educators, these Cardinal Principles helped to resolve the difficulty of educating students who were not college bound (at this time, only a small group of students in U.S. high schools expected to attend college). Educational historian David Cohen stated, "Americans quickly built a system around the assumption that most students didn't have what it took to be serious about the great issues of human life, and that even if they had the wit, they had neither the will nor the futures that would support heavy-duty study" (cited in Powell, Farrar, & Cohen, 1985, p. 245).

The final curriculum reform and a logical conclusion to the direction educational reform took during the period preceding the Second World War was the "Education for Life Adjustment" movement, first proposed in a lecture at Harvard University by Charles Prosser in 1939. Concerned with the failure of educators to enact any meaningful changes during the Depression years, Prosser proposed a curriculum for the nation's high schools, which addressed the practical concerns of daily living. Prosser's ideas were not entirely new; in fact, they could be said to be the logical conclusion of educators who believed, in the final analysis, that not all students were able to master serious academic subject matter.

However, Prosser and his apostles sought life adjustment courses, not just for those at the bottom of the educational ladder but for all high school students. As Hofstadter (1966) aptly observed, "American utility and American democracy would now be realized in the education of all youth" (p. 353). Students who once studied chemistry might study "the testing of detergents; not physics, but how to drive and service a car; not history, but the operation of the local gas works" (p. 356). As historians, Richard Hofstadter and David Cohen are quick to point out that this phase in educational reform exemplifies both the unbridled faith Americans have in education and the ambivalent feelings they harbor toward the life of the mind.

The Post-World War II Equity Era: 1945–1980

During the post-World War II period, the patterns that emerged during the Progressive Era were continued. First, the debate about the goals of education (i.e., academic, social, or both) and whether all children should receive the same education remained an important one. Second, the demand for the expansion of educational opportunity became perhaps the most prominent feature of educational reform. Whereas the Common School era opened access to elementary education and the Progressive Era to secondary education, the post-World War II years were concerned with expanding opportunities to the post-secondary level. They were also directed at finding ways to translate these expanded opportunities into more equal educational outcomes at all levels of education. As in the first half of the twentieth century, so too in the second half, the compatibility of expanded educational opportunity with the maintenance of educational standards would create significant problems. Thus, the tensions between equity and excellence became crucial in the debates of this period.

Cycles of Reform: Progressive and Traditional

The post-World War II years witnessed the continuation of the processes that defined the development of the comprehensive high school. The debates over academic issues, begun at the turn of the twentieth century, may be defined as the movement between pedagogical progressivism and pedagogical traditionalism. This movement focuses not only on the process of education but on its goals. At the center of these debates are the questions regarding the type of education children should receive and whether all children should receive the same education. Although many of these debates focused on curriculum and method, they ultimately were associated with the question of equity versus excellence.

Perhaps these debates can be best understood by examining reform cycles of the twentieth century that revolved between progressive and traditional visions of schooling. On one hand, traditionalists believed in knowledge-centered education, a traditional subject-centered curriculum, teacher-centered education, discipline and authority, and the defense of academic standards in the name of excellence. On the other hand, progressives believed in experiential education, a curriculum that responded to both the needs of students and the times, child-centered education, freedom and individualism, and the relativism of academic standards in the name of equity. Although these poles and educational practices rarely were in only one direction, the conflicts over educational policies and practices seemed to move back and forth between these two extremes. From 1945 to 1955, the progressive education of the previous decades was critically attacked.

These critics, including Mortimer Smith, Robert Hutchins, and Arthur Bestor, assailed progressive education for its sacrificing of intellectual goals to social ones. They argued that the life adjustment education of the period, combined with an increasingly anti-intellectual curriculum, destroyed the traditional academic functions of schooling. Arthur Bestor, a respected historian and a graduate of the Lincoln School (one of the early progressive schools in New York City) argued that it was "regressive education," not progressive education, that had eliminated the school's primary role in teaching children to think (Ravitch, 1983, p. 76). Bestor, like the other critics, assailed the schools for destroying the democratic vision that all students should receive an education that was once reserved for the elite. He suggested that the social and vocational emphasis of the schools indicated a belief that all students could not learn academic material. In an ironic sense, many of the conservative critics were agreeing with the radical critique that the Progressive Era distorted the ideals of democratic education by tracking poor and working-class children into nonacademic vocational programs.

Throughout the 1950s, the debate between progressives who defended the social basis of the curriculum and critics who demanded a more academic curriculum raged on. What was often referred to as "the great debate" (Ravitch, 1983, p. 79) ended with the Soviet launching of the space satellite *Sputnik*. The idea that the Soviets would win the race for space resulted in a national commitment to improve educational standards in general and to increase mathematical and scientific literacy in particular. From 1957 through the mid-1960s, the emphasis shifted to the pursuit of excellence, and curriculum reformers attempted to redesign the curricula in ways that would lead to the return of academic standards (although many doubted that such a romantic age ever existed).

By the mid-1960s, however, the shift in educational priorities moved again toward the progressive side. This occurred in two distinct but overlapping ways. First, the Civil Rights movement, as we will discuss, led to an emphasis on equity issues. Thus, federal legislation, such as the Elementary and Secondary Education Act of 1965, emphasized the education of disadvantaged children. Second, in the context of the antiwar movement of the times, the general criticism of U.S. society, and the persistent failure of the schools to ameliorate problems of poverty and of racial minorities, a "new progressivism" developed that linked the failure of the schools to the problems in society. Ushered in by the publication of A. S. Neill's *Summerhill* in 1960— a book about an English boarding school with few, if any, rules and that was dedicated to the happiness of the child—the new progressivism provided an intellectual and pedagogical assault on the putative sins of traditional education, its authoritarianism, its racism, its misplaced values of intellectualism, and its failure to meet the emotional and psychological needs of children.

The new progressivism developed during one of the most turbulent decades in American history (Cavallo, 1999). Colleges and universities became sites of protests by the anti-Vietnam War and Civil Rights movements. In 1964, Students for a Democratic Society (SDS), a radical group of students headed by Tom Hayden at the University of Michigan, issued the *Port Huron Statement*, a radical critique of U.S. society and a call for action by U.S. students. In the same year, the University of California, Berkeley, Free Speech Movement, led by Mario Savio, protested university rules limiting assembly and demonstrations on campus. In 1968, African-American students went on strike at San Francisco State University, resulting in the resignation of its president. Its new president, S. I. Hiyakawa, a law and order advocate, threatened to suspend anyone who interfered with the college. The strike ended after a number of months, with each side declaring victory. At the same time, African-American students took over Willard Straight Hall at Cornell University. Faced with threats to take over the entire university by the African-American Society (AAS) and SDS, President James Perkins agreed to consider their demands without reprimands. Downstate, New York City police were called in to end a takeover of the Columbia University library. SDS-led students protesting the Vietnam War and the university's plan to build a gymnasium in the neighboring Morningside Heights section of Harlem were removed forcefully. Finally, on May 4, 1970, four students at Kent State University, protesting the U.S. invasion of Cambodia, were killed by the Ohio National Guard called in by Governor James Rhodes after protestors burned down the Army ROTC building. These killings, memorialized by Crosby, Stills, Nash, and Young's haunting words, "four dead in Ohio, four dead in Ohio" in their song *Ohio*, resulted in mass demonstrations at colleges and universities throughout the United States, but also in the beginning of the end of the antiwar movement. When students recognized that the government would kill them, the protests began to slowly subside.

Throughout the 1960s and early 1970s, a variety of books provided scathing criticism of U.S. education. These included Jonathon Kozol's *Death at an Early Age* (1967), which assailed the racist practices of the Boston public schools; Herbert Kohl's *36 Children* (1967), which demonstrated the pedagogical possibilities of open education; and Charles S. Silberman's *Crisis in the Classroom* (1969), which attacked the bureaucratic, stultifying mindlessness of U.S. education. These books, along with a series of articles by Joseph Featherstone, and Beatrice and Ronald Gross on British progressive education (or open education), resulted in significant experimentation in some schools. Emphasis on individualism and relevant education, along with the challenge to the unquestioned authority of the teacher, resulted in alternative, free (or open) education—schooling that once again shifted attention away from knowledge (product) to process.

Although there is little evidence to suggest that the open classroom was a national phenomenon, and as the historian Larry Cuban noted in his history of teaching, *How Teachers Taught* (1984), there was surprisingly little variation in teaching methods during the twentieth century—that is, despite the cycles of debate and reform, most secondary teachers still lectured more than they involved students. Nonetheless, the period from the mid-1960s to the mid-1970s was a time of great turmoil in the educational arena. The time was marked by two simultaneous processes: (1) the challenge to traditional schooling and (2) the attempt to provide educational opportunity for the disadvantaged. In order to understand the latter, one must look back to the origins of the concerns for equity.

Equality of Opportunity

The demand for equality of opportunity, as we have noted, has been a central feature of U.S. history. From the Jeffersonian belief in a meritocratic elite, to Mann's vision of schooling as a "great equalizer," to Dewey's notion that the schools would be a "lever of social progress," U.S. reformers have pointed to the schools as capable of solving problems of inequality. More importantly, as Lawrence Cremin (1990) pointed out, Americans have expected their schools to solve social, political, and economic problems, and have placed on the schools "all kinds of millennial hopes and expectations" (p. 92). While this has been true throughout America's history, the translation of this view into concrete policy has defined the postwar years and has helped explain the increasing politicization of the educational conflicts.

Immediately following the Second World War, the issue of access to educational opportunity became an important one. The GI Bill of Rights offered 16 million servicemen and women the opportunity to pursue higher education. Ravitch (1983, pp. 12–13) pointed out that the GI Bill was the subject of considerable controversy over the question of access and excellence. On one hand, veterans' groups, Congress, and other supporters believed the bill provided both a just reward for national service and a way to avoid massive unemployment in the postwar economy. Further, although aimed at veterans, it was part of the growing policy to provide access to higher education to those who, because of economic disadvantage and/or poor elementary and secondary preparation, had heretofore been denied the opportunity to attend college. On the other hand, critics such as Robert Maynard Hutchins, chancellor at the University of Chicago, and James Conant, president of Harvard University, feared that the policy would threaten the traditional meritocratic selection process and result in the lowering of academic standards (Ravitch, 1983, p. 13).

Despite these criticisms, the GI Bill, according to Ravitch (1983), was "the most ambitious venture in mass higher education that had ever been attempted by any society" (p. 14). Furthermore, she noted that the evidence does not suggest a decline in academic standards but rather a refreshing opening of the elite postsecondary education system. Historians and policy makers may disagree about the success of the GI Bill, but it is clear that it represented a building block in the post-World War II educational expansion. This expansion was similar to previous expansions, first in the Common School Era to compulsory elementary education, second in the Progressive Era to the high school, and in the post-World War II years to postsecondary education. The same types of questions left unresolved, especially from the Progressive Era, as to whether mass public education was possible, would become central points of controversy in the coming years.

Although the GI Bill set an important precedent, the issue of educational inequality for the poor and disadvantaged, in general, and for African-Americans in particular, became the focus of national attention and debate during this period. From the years immediately following the Second World War to the present, the questions of equality of opportunity at all levels have been significant areas of concern. In the late 1940s and 1950s, the relationships between race and education, and the question of school segregation were at the forefront of political, educational, and moral conflicts.

Race, as much as any other single issue in U.S. history, has challenged the democratic ethos of the American dream. The ideals of equality of opportunity and justice have been contradicted by the actual practices concerning African-Americans and other minorities. Although legally guaranteed equal protection by the Fourteenth Amendment, African-Americans continue to experience vast inequities. Nowhere was this more evident than in education.

The post-Civil War Reconstruction period, despite the constitutional amendments enacted to guarantee equality of treatment before the law, had little positive effect on African-Americans, especially in the South. During the latter years of the nineteenth century, the Supreme Court successfully blocked civil rights legislation. In the famous 1896 decision relating to education, *Plessy v. Ferguson*, the Court upheld a Louisiana law that segregated railway passengers by race. In what is commonly referred to as its "separate but equal" doctrine, the Court upheld the constitutionality of segregated facilities. In his famous dissenting opinion, Justice John Marshall Harlan stated:

> In view of the Constitution, in the eye of the law, there is in this country no superior, dominant, ruling class of citizens. There is no caste here. Our constitution is color blind, and neither knows nor tolerates classes among citizens. In respect of civil rights, all citizens are equal before the law. The humblest is the peer of the most powerful. The law regards man as man, and takes no account of his surroundings or of his color when his civil rights guaranteed by the supreme law of the land are involved . . . (cited in Ravitch, 1983, p. 120)

Despite Justice Harlan's interpretation that the Constitution guaranteed a colorblind treatment of all citizens, the *Plessy v. Ferguson* decision remained the precedent through the first half of the twentieth century. In the 1930s and 1940s, the National Association for the Advancement of Colored People (NAACP) initiated a campaign to overthrow the law, with school segregation a major component of its strategy.

The proper education of African-Americans became a controversial subject for African-American leaders. In 1895, Alabama Tuskegee Institute's Booker T. Washington gave his "Atlanta Compromise Speech" at the Atlanta Exposition, arguing that blacks should be more thrifty and industrious, and should pursue vocational education to prepare them for work in the new Southern industrial economy. In 1903, W. E. B. DuBois, a Harvard Ph.D. and professor at Atlanta University, published *The Souls of Black Folk*, which criticized Booker T. Washington's vocational approach to education as assimilationist. DuBois called for academic education and Civil Rights protest against institutional racism.

The unequal and separate education of African-Americans in the South became a focal point of the civil rights movements of the 1930s, 1940s, and 1950s. Although the *Plessy* decision supported separate and equal, it was apparent to civil rights advocates that the schools were anything but equal. Furthermore, in terms of both educational opportunities and results, African-Americans in both the North and South received nothing approximating equal treatment.

After a series of victories, the advocates of civil rights won their major victory on May 17, 1954, when, in its landmark decision in *Brown v. Topeka Board of Education*, the Supreme Court ruled that state-imposed segregation of schools was unconstitutional. Chief Justice Earl Warren wrote,

> It is doubtful that any child may reasonably be expected to succeed in life if he is denied the opportunity of education. Such an opportunity, where the state has undertaken to provide it, is a right that must be made available to all on equal terms. (cited in Ravitch, 1983, p. 127)

Thus, the Supreme Court reversed the "separate but equal" doctrine enshrined in the *Plessy* case, and stated that separate educational institutions are unequal in and of themselves.

Although there would be considerable conflict in the implementation of the ruling, and although many legal scholars criticized both the basis and scope of the decision, the *Brown* decision marked both a symbolic and concrete affirmation of the ethos of democratic schooling. Although a compelling victory, *Brown* served to underscore the vast discrepancies between what Myrdal (1944) pointed to as the American belief in equality and the American reality of inequality. In the coming years, the fight for equality of opportunity for African-Americans and other minorities would be a salient feature of educational reform. The *Brown* decision may have provided the legal foundation for equality, but the unequal results of schooling in the United States did not magically change in response to the law.

In the years following the 1955 *Brown II* decision, which ordered desegregation "with all deliberate speed," the battle for equality of opportunity was fought on a number of fronts with considerable conflict and resistance. The attempt to desegregate schools in the South first, and later in the North, resulted in confrontation and, at times, violence. For example, in Little Rock, Arkansas, President Eisenhower sent federal troops to enforce desegregation in 1957. When Arkansas Governor Orval Faubus responded to the Supreme Court's refusal to delay desegregation by closing Little Rock's high schools, the federal courts declared the Arkansas school closing laws unconstitutional. Thus, events in Little Rock made it clear that the federal government would not tolerate continued school segregation. Although protests continued in the South into the 1960s, it was apparent that the segregationists would lose their battle to defend a Southern tradition.

The issue of school desegregation, however, was not an exclusively Southern matter. In the Northern cities and metropolitan area suburbs, where housing patterns resulted in segregated schools, the issue of de jure (segregation by law) segregation was often less clear. Where de facto segregation existed (that is, the schools were not segregated intentionally by law but by neighborhood housing patterns), the constitutional precedent for desegregation under *Brown* was shaky. Nonetheless, the evidence in the North of unequal educational opportunities based on race was clear. Thus, civil rights advocates pressed for the improvement of urban schools and for their desegregation.

The desegregation conflicts in Boston, every bit as embittered as in the South, demonstrated the degree to which the issue divided its citizens. As recently as the 1970s and early 1980s, the Boston School Committee was under judicial mandate to desegregate its schools. Judge Arthur Garrity ruled that the school committee knowingly, over a long period of time, conspired to keep schools segregated and thus limited the educational opportunity of African-American children. For a period of over five years, the citizens of Boston were torn apart by the Garrity desegregation order. Groups of white parents opposed, sometimes violently, the forced busing that was imposed. As J. Anthony Lukas, in his Pulitzer prize-winning account *Common Ground* (1986) noted, the Boston situation became a symbol of frustration as it signified how a group of families, all committed to the best education for their children, could have such significantly different visions of what that meant. Judge Garrity stood resolute in his interpretation of the Constitution. Over time, the violence subsided. Many white Bostonians who could afford to do so either sent their children to private schools or moved to the suburbs. Thus, the Boston school system moved into an uneasy "cease-fire" and committed, at least publicly, to the improvement of education for all.

The Boston desegregation wars, like the conflicts a decade earlier in the South, revealed that U.S. society, although moving to ameliorate problems of racial inequality, was nonetheless a society in which racist attitudes changed slowly. Moreover, the Boston schools were a microcosm of the U.S. educational system—a system in which inequalities of race and class were salient features. The educational reforms of the 1960s and 1970s were directed at their elimination.

An important concurrent theme was the question of unequal educational outcomes based on socioeconomic position. From the late 1950s, the findings of social scientists, including James Coleman, author of the 1966 report *Equality of Educational Opportunity*, focused national attention on the relationship between socioeconomic position and unequal educational outcomes. Furthermore, as part of the social programs of Presidents John F. Kennedy and Lyndon Baines Johnson, Americans were sensitized to the idea of ameliorating poverty. Since schools were, in Horace Mann's vision, the lever of social reform, it was only natural that schools once again became the focal point.

During the 1960s and 1970s, a series of reform efforts were directed at providing equality of opportunity and increased access at all levels of education. Based on the Coleman report findings that unequal minority student educational achievement was caused more by family background than differences in the quality of schools attended, federally funded programs, such as Project Head Start, were aimed at providing early preschool educational opportunities for the disadvantaged. Although many radicals criticized the assumption of cultural deprivation implicit in these efforts, many reform efforts were aimed at the family and the school rather than the school itself.

In 1974, the U.S. Supreme Court in a 5–4 vote in *Milliken v. Bradley* ruled that the Detroit interdistrict city-suburb busing plan was unconstitutional. Based on this ruling and continuing opposition to forced busing for desegregation, educational reformers shifted their attention to improving education for often segregated inner-city school districts. From the 1970s on, school finance litigation attempted to equalize spending between high-income suburban and low-income urban and rural districts. In 1971, in *Serrano v. Priest*, the California Supreme Court ruled the state's system of unequal funding unconstitutional. However, in 1973, the U.S. Supreme Court ruled 5–4 in *San Antonio (Texas) Independent School District v. Rodriguez* that there was no constitutional guarantee to an equal education. In subsequent years, school finance cases had to be filed at the state level based on individual state constitutional provisions for equal education. Examples of successful cases are *Robinson v. Cahill* (1973) and *Abbott v. Burke* (1990) in New Jersey, *The Campaign for Fiscal Equity v. New York State* (2004), and *Williams v. The State of California* (2004). The Kentucky Education Reform Act (1988) represented one of the landmark legislative reforms to provide equal education.

Although these cases provided increased funding for low-income students, they did little to eliminate the de facto segregation in most Northern urban districts, which by the fiftieth anniversary of *Brown* in 2004 were almost as segregated as Southern districts before desegregation (Orfield & Lee, 2004; Harvard Civil Rights Project, 2004). Furthermore, court decisions such as the long-standing *Swann v. Charlotte-Mecklenberg (NC) School District* (2002), which ruled that busing was no longer necessary to achieve racial balance, resulted in the resegregation of many formerly integrated districts (Frankenberg & Lee, 2002; Frankenberg, Lee, & Orfield, 2003; Mickelson, 2002). Paul Tractenberg, founder of the Education Law Center in Newark, New Jersey, which has represented the state's low-income children in *Robinson* and in *Abbott*, noted that *Abbott* is more consistent with the separate but equal doctrine of *Plessy* than the separate but never equal doctrine of *Brown* (Tractenberg et al., 2002).

The fiftieth anniversary of *Brown v. Board of Education* in 2004 was marked by disagreements over whether the decision should be celebrated or commemorated. Advocates of celebration argued that the decision ended legally sanctioned segregation, marked the end of Jim Crow, and ushered in the Civil Rights movement. Advocates of commemoration argued that U.S. schools are still overwhelmingly segregated and that the continuing black–white achievement gap indicates that the decision never lived up to its promise. Further, Supreme Court decisions on desegregation in Charlotte Mecklenburg, Seattle, and Louisville ruled that these districts had accomplished their goals for desegregation and were now termed "unified." In the Seattle case, in particular, the court ruled that school placement could not be based on race (see UCLA Civil Rights Project, 2012, for details of these cases). The result of these and other housing patterns in both cities and suburbs has been an ongoing resegregation of U.S. schools (Reardon et al., forthcoming; UCLA Civil Rights Project, 2012).

Nowhere was the conflict over these liberal reforms more clearly demonstrated than in the area of higher education. During the 1960s, educational reformers placed significant emphasis on the need to open access to postsecondary education to students who were traditionally underrepresented at colleges and universities—namely, minority groups and the disadvantaged. Arguing that college was a key to social mobility and success, reformers concluded that college was a right rather than a privilege for all (see Lavin, Alba, & Silberstein, 1981). Defenders of the traditional admissions standards argued that postsecondary education would be destroyed if admissions standards were relaxed (see Sadovnik, 1994).

By the late 1960s, many colleges and universities adopted the policy of open enrollment. The City University of New York, long a symbol of quality education for the working class and poor, guaranteed a place for all graduating New York City high school students in either its four-year colleges (for students with high school averages of 80 and above) or its community college system (for students with averages below 80). Similar open admissions systems were introduced in other public university systems. Furthermore, federal financial aid funds were appropriated for students from low-income families. The results were a dramatic increase in the numbers of students participating in U.S. higher education and a growing debate over the efficacy of such liberal reforms.

Conservatives bemoaned the decline of standards and warned of the collapse of the intellectual foundations of Western civilization. Radicals suggested that more often than not students were given "false hopes and shattered dreams" as they were sometimes underprepared, given their unequal educational backgrounds, for the rigors of college education. Liberals, agreeing that the new students were often underprepared, suggested that it was now the role of the college to provide remedial services to turn access into success (see Sadovnik, 1994).

During the 1970s, colleges took on the task, however reluctantly, of providing remediation for the vast number of underprepared students, many of whom were first-generation college students. The City University of New York (CUNY) became perhaps the largest experiment in compensatory higher education. Its efforts symbolized both the hopes and frustrations of ameliorating unequal educational achievement. Although there is significant disagreement as to the success of these higher-education reforms (which we will examine more closely later in this book), it is important to recognize that this period did result in the significant expansion of higher education. By the late 1990s, CUNY abolished remediation at its four-year colleges, thus ending open admissions. Chancellor Matthew Goldstein argued that remediation should occur at two-year colleges and that this represented the necessary first step in restoring CUNY's reputation as an elite public university system, which provided meritocratic access to generations of low-income students. Critics argued that the end of open admissions would have a deleterious effect on access for these students in general and African-American and Hispanic students in particular (Attewell & Lavin, 2008). A recent New York Times article indicated that while the academic profiles in terms of selectivity of incoming students at CUNY's five selective four-year colleges continues to rise, the number of African-American and Hispanic students continues to decline (New York Times, 2012).

During the late 1960s and early 1970s, the coeducation movement at elite colleges and universities began. In 1969, all-male Ivy League Universities (Harvard, Yale, Princeton, Columbia, Brown, Pennsylvania, and Dartmouth) began to admit women. In response, in 1970, Vassar College became coeducational, leading to other women's colleges such as Connecticut College for Women and Skidmore College admitting men. Coeducation became the rule, with only some of the elite Seven Sisters (Smith, Mount Holyoke, Wellesley, and Bryn Mawr) and a few others still women's colleges in the year 2012 (Miller-Bernal & Poulson, 2006).

We have looked at two related processes that define the post-World War II history of education. The first is the continued debate between progressives and traditionalists about the proper aims, content, and methods of schooling. The second is the struggle for equality of opportunity and the opening of access to higher education. The educational history of the 1980s and 1990s, as you will see, was characterized by the perceived failure of the reforms of this period, most particularly those of the 1960s and 1970s.

Educational Reaction and Reform and the Standards Era: 1980s–2012

By the late 1970s, conservative critics began to react to the educational reforms of the 1960s and 1970s. They argued that liberal reforms in pedagogy and curriculum, and in the arena of educational opportunity had resulted in the decline of authority and standards. Furthermore, the critics argued that the preoccupation with using the schools to ameliorate social problems, however well-intended, not only failed to do this but was part of an overall process that resulted in mass mediocrity. What was needed was nothing less than a complete overhaul of the U.S. educational system. While radical critics also pointed to the failure of the schools to ameliorate problems of poverty, they located the problem not so much in the schools but in the society at large. Liberals defended the reforms of the period by suggesting that social improvement takes a long time, and a decade and a half was scarcely sufficient to turn things around.

In 1983, the National Commission on Excellence (1983), founded by President Reagan's Secretary of Education, Terrel Bell, issued its now famous report, A *Nation at Risk*. This report provided a serious indictment of U.S. education and cited high rates of adult illiteracy, declining SAT scores, and low scores on international comparisons of knowledge by U.S. students as examples of the decline of literacy and standards. The committee stated that "the educational foundations of our society are presently being eroded by a rising tide of mediocrity that threatens our very future as a Nation and a people" (p. 5). As solutions, the commission offered five recommendations: (1) that all students graduating from high school complete what was termed the "new basics"—four years of English, three years of mathematics, three years of science, three years of social studies, and a half year of computer science; (2) that schools at all levels expect higher achievement from their students and that four-year colleges and universities raise their admissions requirements; (3) that more time be devoted to teaching the new basics; (4) that the preparation of teachers be strengthened and that teaching be made a more respected and rewarded profession; and (5) that citizens require their elected representatives to support and fund these reforms (cited in Cremin, 1990, p. 31).

The years following this report were characterized by scores of other reports that both supported the criticism and called for reform. During the 1980s and 1990s, and into the twenty-first century, significant attention was given to the improvement of curriculum, the tightening of standards, and a move toward the setting of academic goals and their assessment. A coalition of U.S. governors took on a leading role in setting a reform agenda; business leaders stressed the need to improve the nation's schools and proposed partnership programs; the federal government, through its Secretary of Education (under Ronald Reagan), William Bennett, took an active and critical role but continued to argue that it was not the federal government's role to fund such reform; and educators, at all levels, struggled to have a say in determining the nature of the reforms.

As we have pointed out in Chapter 2, the politics of the reform movement were complex and multidimensional. Conservatives wanted to restore both standards and the traditional curriculum; liberals demanded that the new drive for excellence not ignore the goals for equity; radicals believed it was another pendulum swing doomed to failure (one that sought to reestablish *excellence* as a code word for *elitism*).

In the 1990s and in the early part of the twenty-first century, the reforms initiated in the 1980s continued and expanded (see Tyack & Cuban, 1995). There are a number of reforms, including President Clinton's Goals 2000 in 1994, President G. W. Bush's No Child Left Behind (NCLB) in 2001, and President Obama's Race to the Top (RTT) in 2009, that have the most visibility. Although they all purport to balance equity and excellence as their goal, it is not clear how effective they have been. In Chapter 10, we will discuss them more fully; in this section, we will describe them briefly.

First, the school choice movement seeks to give parents the right to choose the public school to send their children, rather than the traditional method in which one's school was based on neighborhood zoning patterns (Cookson, 1994; Fuller, El-more, & Orfield, 1996; Wells, 1993a, 1993b; Tractenberg, Sadovnik, & Liss, 2004; Sadovnik, 2011b). The choice movement is divided into those who support public school choice only (that is, giving parents the right to choose from public schools) to those who would include intersectional choice policies, including private schools. Such an intersectional choice program has been employed in Milwaukee where low-income parents receive tuition vouchers to send their children to private schools. There has been significant controversy over this plan, with supporters stating it is the key to equity and critics arguing that it means the death of public education. The most important reform in this area is charter schools, which are independent of local district control, but receive public funding. By 1998, 33 states passed charter school legislation, resulting in more than 1,000 charter schools (Wells et al., 1998, p. 6). As of 2012, 41 states had charter school legislation, resulting in more than 5,700 charter schools (Consoletti, 2012). Second, Race to the Top, while enlarging the federal support of charter schools, has also enhanced NCLB's accountability mechanisms. In this regard, RTT has supported Value Added Models (VAM) of teacher quality linked to standardized tests of student achievement and negative sanctions, including school closings (B. Baker, 2012). In addition, the Obama Administration has provided waivers from NCLB to numerous states if they provide alternatives consistent with RTT.

It is perhaps too early to assess these reforms, but it is apparent that they are part of the recurring debate in U.S. educational history about the efficacy of mass public education and the compatibility of excellence and equity. Throughout history, these themes have been crucial as the preceding historical discussion delineates; the answer to the questions is a matter of both historical interpretation and empirical investigation.

Understanding the History of U.S. Education: Different Historical Interpretations

The history of education in the United States, as we have illustrated, has been one of conflict, struggle, and disagreement. It has also been marked by a somewhat ironic pattern of cycles of reform about the aims, goals, and purpose of education on one hand, and little change in actual classroom practice on the other (Cuban, 1984). Moreover, as we pointed out in Chapter 2, one's view of U.S. educational history and the effectiveness of the schools in meeting their democratic aspirations depends on one's interpretation of the historical trends and events. In the following sections, we outline the different schools of historical interpretation.

The different interpretations of U.S. educational history revolve around the tensions between equity and excellence, between the social and intellectual functions of schooling, and over differing responses to the questions, Education in whose interests? Education for whom? The U.S. school system has expanded to serve more students for longer periods of time than any other system in the modern world. This occurred, first, by extending primary school to all through compulsory education laws during the Common School Era; second, by extending high school education to the majority of adolescents by the end of the Progressive Era; and third, by extending postsecondary education to the largest number of high school graduates in the world by the 1990s. However, historians and sociologists of education disagree about whether this pattern of increased access means a pattern of educational success. Moreover, these disagreements concern the questions of the causes of educational expansion (that is, who supported the reforms), who benefited from them, and which types of goals have been met and/or sacrificed.

The Democratic-Liberal School

Democratic-liberals believe that the history of U.S. education involves the progressive evolution, albeit flawed, of a school system committed to providing equality of opportunity for all. Democratic-liberal historians suggest that each period of educational expansion involved the attempts of liberal reformers to expand educational opportunities to larger segments of the population and to reject the conservative view of schools as elite institutions for the meritorious (which usually meant the privileged). Historians such as Ellwood Cubberly, Merle Curti, and Lawrence A. Cremin are representative of this view. Both Cubberly (1934) and Curti (1959/1971) have portrayed the Common School Era as a victory for democratic movements and the first step in opening U.S education to all. Furthermore, both historians, in varying degrees, portray the early school reformers such as Horace Mann and Henry Barnard as reformers dedicated to egalitarian principles (Curti is more critical than Cubberly).

Lawrence A. Cremin, in his three-volume history of U.S. education (1972, 1980, 1988) and in a study of the Progressive Era (1961), portrays the evolution of U.S. education in terms of two related processes: popularization and multitudinousness (Cremin, 1988). For Cremin, educational history in the United States involved both the expansion of opportunity and purpose. That is, as more students from diverse backgrounds went to school for longer periods of time, the goals of education became more diverse, with social goals often becoming as or more important than intellectual ones. Although Cremin does not deny the educational problems and conflicts, and he notes the discrepancies between opportunity and results—particularly for the economically disadvantaged—he never relinquished his vision that the genius of U.S. education lies with its commitment to popularization and multitudinousness. In his final book, *Popular Education and Its Discontents* (1990), Cremin summarized this democratic liberal perspective as follows: "That kind of organization [referring to U.S. higher education] is part of the genius of American education—it provides a place for everyone who wishes one, and in the end yields one of the most educated populations in the world" (p. 46).

Although democratic-liberals tend to interpret U.S. educational history optimistically, the evolution of the nation's schools has been a flawed, often conflictual march toward increased opportunities. Thus, historians such as Cremin do not see equity and excellence as inevitably irreconcilable, but rather as the tensions between the two, resulting in necessary compromises. The ideals of equality and excellence are just that: ideals. Democratic-liberals believe that the U.S. educational system must continue to move closer to each, without sacrificing one or the other too dramatically.

The Radical-Revisionist School

Beginning in the 1960s, the optimistic vision of the democratic-liberal historians began to be challenged by radical historians, sociologists, and political economists of education. The radical-revisionist historians of education, as they have come to be called, revised the history of education in a more critical direction. These historians, including Michael Katz (1968), Joel Spring (1972), and Clarence Karier (1976), argue that the history of U.S. education is the story of expanded success for very different reasons and with very different results. Radical historians do not deny that the educational system has expanded; rather, they believe it expanded to meet the needs of the elites in society for the control of the working class and immigrants, and for economic efficiency and productivity. In addition, radicals suggest that expanded opportunity did not translate into more egalitarian results. Rather, they point out that each period of educational reform (the Common School Era, the Progressive Era, the post-World War II Era) led to increasing stratification within the educational system, with working-class, poor, and minority students getting the short end of the stick.

Let us examine the radical view on educational expansion and the question of whose interests it served. Michael Katz (1968) argued that it was the economic interests of nineteenth-century capitalists that more fully explain the expansion of schooling and that educational reformers stressed the ability of schools to train factory workers, to socialize immigrants into U.S. values, and to create stability in the newly expanding urban environments. Likewise, historians Joel Spring (1972) and Clarence Karier (1976) both advanced the thesis that the expansion of the schools in the late nineteenth and early twentieth centuries was done more so in the interests of social control than in the interests of equity. Spring argued that this perspective

> advances the idea that schools were shaped as instruments of the corporate liberal state for main streaming social control. . . . The public schools were seen as an important instrument used by the government to aid in the rationalization and minimization of conflict by selecting and training students for their future positions in the economy and by imbuing the population with a sense of cooperation and national spirit. (1986, p. 154)

One of the problems with this view, pointed out by radicals who generally agree with this interpretation, is that it views the expansion of education as imposed on the poor and working class from above and often against their will. Other radical historians, including David Hogan (1978) and Julia Wrigley (1982), suggest that the working class and labor unions actively supported the expansion of public education for their own interests. Thus, the explanation of educational expansion is a more conflictual one rather than a simplistic tale of elite domination.

Despite these historiographical disagreements, radical historians agree that the results of educational expansion rarely met their putative democratic aspirations. They suggest that each new expansion increased stratification of working-class and disadvantaged students within the system, with these students less likely to succeed educationally. For example, political economists Samuel Bowles and Herbert Gintis (1976) noted that the expansion of the high school resulted in a comprehensive secondary system that tracked students into vocational and academic curriculums with placement, more often than not, determined by social class background and race. Furthermore, the expansion of higher education in the post-World War II period often resulted in the stratification between community colleges that stressed vocational education and four-year colleges and universities that stressed the liberal arts and sciences. Once again, radicals argue that placement in the higher education system is based on social class and race. Studies by Kevin Dougherty (1987, 1994) and Steven Brint and Jerome Karabel (1989) give ample evidence to support the view that the expansion of higher education has not resulted in equality of opportunity.

Thus, the radical interpretation of U.S. educational history is a more pessimistic one. While acknowledging educational expansion, they suggest that this process has benefited the elites more than the masses, and has not produced either equality of opportunity or results. Further, they view the debates about equity and excellence as a chimera, with those who bemoan the decline of standards seeking to reimpose excellence with little regard for equality.

Conservative Perspectives

In the 1980s, as we noted in Chapter 2, a rising tide of conservative criticism swept education circles. Although much of this criticism was political and, at times, ahistorical, it did have an implicit historical critique of the schools. Arguing that U.S. students knew very little and that U.S. schools were mediocre, the conservative critics such as William Bennett, Chester Finn, Jr., Diane Ravitch, E. D. Hirsch, Jr., and Allan Bloom all pointed to the failure of so-called progressive education to fulfill its lofty social goals without sacrificing academic quality. Although critics such as Ravitch and Hirsch supported the democratic-liberal goal of equality of opportunity and mobility through education, they believed that the historical pursuit of social and political objectives resulted in significant harm to the traditional academic goals of schooling.

Diane Ravitch (1977) provided a passionate critique of the radical-revisionist perspective and a defense of the democratic-liberal position. Yet, in the 1980s, Ravitch moved from this centrist position to a more conservative stance. In a series of essays and books, including *The Troubled Crusade* (1983), Ravitch argued that the preoccupation with using education to solve social problems has not solved these problems and, simultaneously, has led to the erosion of educational excellence. Although Ravitch remains faithful to the democratic-liberal belief that schools have expanded opportunities to countless numbers of the disadvantaged and immigrants, she has argued that the adjustment of the traditional curriculum to meet the needs of all of these groups has been a violation of the fundamental function of schooling, which is to develop the powers of intelligence (1985, p. 40). According to Ravitch, the progressive reforms of the twentieth century denigrated the traditional role of schools in passing on a common culture and produced a generation of students who know little, if anything, about their Western heritage. Although she believes the curriculum ought to be fair and nonracist, she has also argued that efforts at multiculturalism are often historically incorrect and neglect the fact that the heritage of our civilization, from a conservative vantage point, is Western. In 2010, Ravitch again moved back to a more liberal position, as she provided a scathing critique of neo-liberal education reforms, like charter schools, vouchers, privatization, and standardized testing. Ravitch has argued that these reforms that she once supported have resulted in a corporate takeover of public schooling and threaten the democratic nature of public schooling (Ravitch, 2010).

Ravitch's perspective over the past three decades has been far more complex than that of other conservative critics such as Bennett, Bloom, Finn, and Hirsch. Where these authors, like Bloom in *The Closing of the American Mind* (1987) and Hirsch in *Cultural Literacy* (1987), never fully capture the complex relationship between educational reform and social and political milieu, Ravitch's *The Troubled Crusade* (1983) points to the putative decline of educational standards within the context of political movements to move us closer to a fair and just society. In fact, Ravitch has argued that the belief that all students learn a rigorous curriculum is not conservative, but rather consistent with her earlier liberal belief that all students be given an equal opportunity to succeed (Ravitch, 1994). Ravitch understands the conflictual nature of U.S. educational history and simultaneously praises the schools for being a part of large-scale social improvement while damning them for losing their academic standards in the process. Bloom blames the universities for watering down their curriculums; Hirsch blames the public schools for valuing skills over content; and Bennett, in his role as Secretary of Education during the Reagan administration, called for a return to a traditional Western curriculum. None of these conservatives has analyzed, as Ravitch has (perhaps because she is the only historian among them), the historical tensions between equity and excellence that are crucial to understanding the problem. Nonetheless, what they all have in common is the vision that the evolution of U.S. education has resulted in the dilution of academic excellence. Over the past few years, Ravitch has passionately argued that the conservative and neo-liberal pursuit of academic excellence has neither improved the schools or moved us closer to a fair and just society. In fact, she accuses conservatives and neo-liberals of ignoring the pernicious effects of poverty on student achievement, a position closer to liberals, if not radicals.

Conclusion

As students of educational history, you may well be perplexed by the different interpretations of the history of U.S. education. How is it possible, you may ask, that given the same evidence, historians reach such vastly different conclusions? As we pointed out in Chapter 2, the interpretation of educational issues, including the interpretation of its history, depends to a large extent on one's perspective. Thus, each school of historical interpretation sees the events, data, and conflicts in different ways. We do not propose that there is one unified theory of the history of education, nor do we believe that the historical and sociological data support only one theory. Rather, we believe that there are patterns in the history of education and that the foundations perspective is a lens for looking at these patterns.

The history of U.S. education has involved a number of related patterns. First, it has been defined by the expansion of schooling to increasingly larger numbers of children for longer periods of time. Second, with this expansion has come the demand for equality of opportunity and ways to decrease inequality of results. Third is the conflict over goals, curriculum, and method, and the politicization of these issues. Fourth is the conflict between education for a common culture, or a "distinctively American paideia, or self-conscious culture" (Cremin, 1990, p. 107) and education for the diversity of a pluralistic society. And fifth are the tensions between popularization and educational excellence. All of these processes speak to the fact that Americans have always asked a great deal, perhaps too much, from their schools, and that conflict and controversy are the definitive features of the evolution of the school.

The history of U.S. education is a complex story of conflict, compromise, and struggle (see Table 3.1). The disagreements over this history are summed up well by Diane Ravitch, defending the democratic-liberal tradition, and David Nassaw, arguing for a more radical interpretation. Ravitch (1977) stated:

> Education in a liberal society must sustain and balance ideals that exist in tension: equity and excellence. While different generations have emphasized one or the other, in response to the climate of the times, schools cannot make either ideal a reality, though they contribute to both. The schools are limited institutions which have certain general responsibilities and certain specific capacities; sometimes they have failed to meet realistic expectations, and at other times they have succeeded beyond realistic expectations in dispersing intelligence and opportunity throughout the community. In order to judge them by reasonable standards and in order to have any chance of improving their future performance, it is necessary to abandon the simplistic search for heroes and devils, scapegoats and panaceas. (p. 173)

Nassaw (1979), in a very different vein, stated:

> The public schools emerge in the end compromised by reform and resistance. They do not belong to the corporations and the state, but neither do they belong to their communities. They remain "contested" institutions with several agendas and several purposes. The reformers have not in the past made them into efficient agencies for social channeling and control. Their opponents will not, on the other hand, turn them into truly egalitarian institutions without at the same time effecting radical changes in the state and society that support them. The public schools will, in short, continue to be the social arena where the tension is reflected and the contest played out between the promise of democracy and the rights of class division. (p. 243)

Text continues on page 90.

Table 3.1   Timeline of Historical Events in U.S. Education

Date	Event
1636	The first college in the American colonies, Harvard College, is founded in Newtown (later renamed Cambridge, MA). Its dual function was educating civic leaders and preparing a learned clergy.
1779	Thomas Jefferson writes his *Bill for a More General Diffusion of Knowledge*, outlining his views on the popularization of elementary and grammar school education.
1789	The Tenth Amendment to the U.S. Constitution provides for public education and delegates authority to the states. This has resulted in the absence of a national system of education or national curriculum, as exists in many other liberal-democratic societies.
1817	Thomas Jefferson writes the "Rockfish Gap Report," the report of the Commission to establish a public university in Virginia, leading to the establishment of the University of Virginia in Charlottesville. The university is based on Jefferson's model of a natural aristocracy based on talent, or what later was called a *meritocracy*.
1821	Troy Female Seminary in New York is founded by Emma Willard.
1833	Oberlin College in Ohio admits women, becoming the first coeducational college in the United States.
1837	Horace Mann becomes Secretary to the Massachusetts Board of Education, ushering in the Common School Era of compulsory primary education.
1837	Mount Holyoke Female Seminary (later, Mount Holyoke College) in Massachusetts is founded by Mary Lyon.
1848	Horace Mann, in his Twelfth (and final) Report to the Massachusetts Board of Education, states that "education is the great equalizer of the conditions of men . . . the balance wheel of the social machinery," which becomes the basis of an American democratic ideology of education.
1862	The Morrill Act is passed, authorizing the use of public money to establish public land grant universities, resulting in the establishment of large public universities, especially in the Midwest.
1863	During the Civil War, President Abraham Lincoln issues the Emancipation Proclamation, announcing the end of slavery in all states in rebellion against the Union.
1865	Several months after the end of the Civil War, Congress passes the Thirteenth Amendment to the Constitution, which freed four million slaves.
1865	Vassar College, the first of the Seven Sisters women's colleges, is founded in Poughkeepsie, NY. Shortly after, Wellesley College and Smith College in Massachusetts are founded, and Mount Holyoke and Bryn Mawr (PA) Seminaries become colleges.
1868	The Fourteenth Amendment to the Constitution is ratified, giving full citizenship to ex-slaves. Although this amendment and the Freedman's Bureau attempted to reconstruct the South's economy and include Blacks as full citizens, the Ku Klux Klan continued to spread racial hatred, and Jim Crow Laws and Black Codes in the South continued discrimination against Blacks. Its equal protection clause has been applied to important legal decisions regarding education.
1868	The Freedman's Bureau helps establish historically Black Colleges, including Howard University in Washington, D.C., and Hampton Institute in Virginia.
1891	Jane Addams founds Hull House in Chicago, a settlement house that provided cultural and educational programs for Chicago's immigrants and poor.
1893	The National Education Association's Committee of Ten, chaired by Harvard University President Charles Eliot, issues its report on secondary education, which reasserts the college-preparatory function of the high school. Eliot is to become one of the leaders of the social efficiency strand of progressive education.
1895	Alabama Tuskegee Institute's Booker T. Washington gives his "Atlanta Compromise Speech" at the Atlanta Exposition, arguing that Blacks should be more thrifty and industrious and should pursue vocational education to prepare them for work in the new southern industrial economy.

Continued

Date	Event
1896	The Laboratory School at the University of Chicago is founded by John and Alice Chipman Dewey, ushering in the child-centered, developmental democratic strand of progressive education.
1896	In *Plessy v. Ferguson*, the U.S. Supreme Court rules that separate but equal facilities are constitutional. Justice John Marshall Harlan, the lone dissenter, argued that the Constitution is color-blind and that all citizens are equal before the law.
1903	W. E. B. DuBois, a Harvard Ph.D. and professor at Atlanta University, publishes *The Souls of Black Folk*, which criticizes Booker T. Washington's vocational approach to education as assimilationist. DuBois called for academic education and Civil Rights protest against institutional racism.
1918	The NEA's *Cardinal Principles of Secondary Education* argues for the broadening of the functions of the high school to include civic, vocational, and social responsibilities ushering in the life-adjustment period of U.S. education.
1920	The Nineteenth Amendment to the Constitution is ratified, giving women the right to vote.
1931	Jane Addams is the first woman recipient of the Nobel Peace Prize for her work, including founding the Women's Peace Party in 1915 and the Women's International League for Peace and Freedom in 1919.
1945	The GI Bill of Rights is passed, authorizing college tuition assistance for soldiers.
1950	After two years, Superintendent Willard Goslin is fired by the Pasadena (CA) School Board, after conservative forces protest his progressive policies and accuse him of being a Communist. The Goslin firing was part of the larger attack on "subversives" during the McCarthy Era, named after Wisconsin Joseph McCarthy, who led a congressional investigation of alleged Communists that resulted in blacklisting.
1950	In *Sweatt v. Painter* and in *McLaurin v. Board of Regents of the University of Oklahoma*, the U.S. Supreme Court rules that blacks must be admitted to segregated state law schools in Texas and Oklahoma, respectively.
1954	In *Brown v. The Topeka Board of Education*, the U.S. Supreme Court rules that separate but equal schools for black and white children is unconstitutional. The case consisted of separate cases in four states, *Briggs v. Elliot* (South Carolina), *Brown v. Board of Education of Topeka* (Kansas), *Davis v. School Board of Prince Edward County* (Virginia), *Belton v. Gebhart* and *Bulah v. Gebhart* (Delaware), and *Bolling v. Sharpe* (District of Columbia).
1956	Critics of progressive education, historians Arthur Bestor and Mortimer Smith establish the Council for Basic Education, committed to making intellectual training the primary focus of public education and the elimination of separating students by ability into different tracks.
1957	Arkansas Governor Orval Faubus sends in the state National Guard to prevent the desegregation of Little Rock Central High School; President Dwight D. Eisenhower sends in federal troops to implement the court order.
1957	The Soviet Union launches the first space satellite, *Sputnik*, resulting in U.S. efforts to improve mathematics and science education.
1958	The National Defense Education Act is passed, authorizing millions of dollars to mathematics, science, and gifted education.
1960	A. S. Neill's *Summerhill*, about a progressive English boarding school, begins the revival of child-centered progressive education in the United States.
1964	Congress passes the Civil Rights Act.
1964	Students for a Democratic Society (SDS) issue the *Port Huron Statement*, a radical critique of U.S. society and a call for action by U.S. students.
1964	The University of California, Berkeley, Free Speech Movement, led by Mario Savio, protests university rules limiting assembly and demonstrations on campus.
1965	The Elementary and Secondary School Act is passed.
1967	Criticism of schools, and urban schools in particular, reaches a crescendo, with the publication of Jonathan Kozol's *Death at an Early Age* and Herbert Kohl's *36 Children*.

Date	Event
1968	African American students go on strike at San Francisco State University, resulting in the resignation of its president. Its new president, S. I. Hiyakawa, a law and order advocate, threatened to suspend anyone who interfered with the college. The strike ended after a number of months, with each side declaring victory.
1968	African American students take over Willard Straight Hall at Cornell University. Faced with threats to take over the entire university by the African-American Society (AAS) and SDS, President James Perkins agrees to consider their demands without reprimands.
1968	New York City police are called in to end the takeover of the Columbia University library. SDS-led students protesting the Vietnam War and the university's plan to build a gymnasium in the neighboring Morningside Heights section of Harlem are removed forcefully.
1969	City University of New York (CUNY) adopts its Open Admissions Policy, which offers a place for all New York City high school graduates in one of its senior colleges (for students with a high school average of above 80) or community colleges (for students with a high school average below 80). This policy results in the development of the largest remediation effort in U.S. higher education. Critics argue that it represents the downfall of the meritocratic ideal of higher education; proponents argue it represents higher education for all and the triumph of the democratic ideal of higher education.
1969	All-male Ivy League universities (Harvard, Yale, Princeton, Columbia, Brown, Pennsylvania and Dartmouth) begin to admit women.
1970	Charles Silberman publishes *Crisis in the Classroom*, a radical critique of U.S. public schools as "grim, joyless places," preoccupied with "order and control" and characterized by "banality and triviality."
1970	On May 4, four students at Kent State University, protesting the U.S. invasion of Cambodia, are killed by the Ohio National Guard called in by Governor James Rhodes after protestors burned down the Army ROTC building.
1970	Vassar College becomes coeducational, leading to other women's colleges such as Connecticut College for Women and Skidmore College admitting men. Coeducation will become the rule, with only some of the elite Seven Sisters (Smith, Mount Holyoke, Wellesley, and Bryn Mawr) and a few others remaining women's colleges in the year 2000.
1974	U.S. Federal Judge W. Arthur Garrity rules Boston School Committee is in violation of *Brown* v. *Board*, resulting in Boston school desegregation wars.
1975	During the New York City fiscal crisis, City University of New York initiates tuition, ending its more than century-long policy of free tuition.
1983	The National Commission for Excellence in Education, headed by U.S. Secretary of Education Terel Bell, releases *A Nation at Risk*, which argues that U.S. education is mediocre. The report results in the beginning of the education excellence movement and a repudiation of progressive education.
1986	National Governors Conference, headed by Governors Clinton of Arkansas, Alexander of Tennessee, and Riley of South Carolina, issues its report *A Time for Results*, calling for higher state standards in education.
1987	Chester Finn and Diane Ravitch's *What Do Our Seventeen Year Olds Know?* and E. D. Hirsch, Jr.'s *Cultural Literacy* provide a critique of U.S. students' lack of liberal arts and sciences knowledge and proposes the Core Curriculum movement.
1988	Minnesota becomes the first state to pass school choice legislation. As of 1992, 37 states have passed choice legislation.
1992	California becomes the second state (after Minnesota) to pass charter school legislation, allowing for state funding of schools independent of the public school system. By 1998, it has over 50,000 students in charter schools—the most in the nation—and the second most charter schools (130), second only to Arizona (241).
1994	President William Jefferson Clinton's *Goals 2000: Educate America Act* becomes law, establishing national goals for content and performance; opportunity to learn standards; school-to-work opportunities; school, parent, and community support; teacher professional development; and safe and drug-free schools.

Continued

Date	Event
1995	Social psychologists David Berliner and Bruce D. Biddle publish *The Manufactured Crisis*, which argues that the empirical evidence does not support the conservative attack on U.S. public schools.
1998	The New Jersey Supreme Court issues the fifth of its historic decisions in *Abbott v. Burke* (1990), a landmark state school finance case.
2002	President George W. Bush signs into law the No Child Left Behind Act of 2001, the reauthorization of the Elementary and Secondary Education Act of 1965, aimed at eliminating student achievement gaps by 2014.
2002	In *Zelman v. Simmons-Harris*, the U.S. Supreme Court rules that the Constitution does not prohibit public funding of religious schools, at least in the form of Cleveland's school voucher program.
2003	In *Grutter v. Bollinger*, the U.S. Supreme Court rules that the University of Michigan Law School's use of racial preferences in student admissions did not violate the Equal Protection Clause of the Fourteenth Amendment or Title VI of the Civil Rights Act of 1964. In *Gratz v. Bollinger*, the Court adopts the same standard and finds that the university's undergraduate admissions system used race too mechanically and therefore did violate the Equal Protection Clause of the Fourteenth Amendment or Title VI of the Civil Rights Act of 1964.
2004	In *Williams v. State of California*, the plaintiffs argue that the state has failed to provide a minimally adequate education for low-income children. Governor Arnold Schwarzenegger settles the four-year-old case by agreeing to provide new state standards to ensure an adequate education for all children.
2004	A three-member panel appointed by New York Supreme Court Justice Leland DeGrasse recommends that the New York State legislature provide an additional $5.6 billion per year to the New York City public schools. As part of the final ruling in the decade-long Campaign for Fiscal Equity lawsuit, the Court rules that the state's funding formulas discriminated against New York City.
2007	In *Parents Involved in Community Schools v. Seattle School District No. 1*, the U.S. Supreme Court rules that districts cannot assign students to public schools for the sole purpose of racial integration.
2009	President Barack Obama's *Race to the Top* initiative is included in the American Recovery and Reinvertment Act of 2009. The initiative awards funding to states that demonstrate plans to adopt high academic standards, build data systems to improve assessment, recruit and retain quality school staff, and turn around low-achieving schools.
2011	President Barack Obama and Secretary of Education Arne Duncan begin to grant NCLB waivers to states that propose acceptable alternatives to specific provisions of the No Child Left Behind Act and the Elementary and Secondary Education Act.

Thus, from their very different vantage points, Ravitch and Nassaw agree that schools are imperfect institutions with conflicting goals that have been the center of struggle throughout our history. There have been no easy answers to the complex questions we have examined. As teachers, you will become a part of this ongoing history, and we believe only through reflective consideration of the issues will you be able to understand the many conflicts of which you will be a part, let alone resolve these conflicts and make a difference.

In order to evaluate the issues raised in this chapter, one must look at empirical evidence, including, but not limited to, the historical record. That is, to analyze the extent to which schools have provided opportunity and mobility or the extent to which standards have fallen requires data. As you will see, the sociological approach to education has been central to this endeavor. In the next chapter, we will explore this sociological approach in depth.

The following articles illustrate some of the major historical periods, writers, and reforms discussed in this chapter. The first selection, "Popular Schooling," written by the late historian of education

Lawrence A. Cremin, discusses the historical dissatisfaction with U.S. education and the possibility of achieving the American dream of a quality education for all. This liberal version of education is illustrated through an historical analysis of popularization of the U.S. educational system.

The second selection, "Capital Accumulation, Class Conflict, and Educational Change," by radical political economists Samuel Bowles and Herbert Gintis, provides a radical-revisionist interpretation of the history of American education, one that is quite different than Cremin's.

Popular Schooling

Lawrence A. Cremin

> Every nation, and therefore every national system of education, has the defects of its qualities.—Sir Michael Sadler, "Impressions of American Education"

The popularization of American schools and colleges since the end of World War II has been nothing short of phenomenal, involving an unprecedented broadening of access, an unprecedented diversification of curricula, and an unprecedented extension of public control. In 1950, 34 percent of the American population twenty-five years of age or older had completed at least four-years of high school, while 6 percent of that population had completed at least four years of college. By 1985, 74 percent of the American population twenty-five years of age or older had completed at least four years of high school, while 19 percent had completed at least four years of college. During the same thirty-five year period, school and college curricula broadened and diversified tremendously, in part because of the existential fact of more diverse student bodies with more diverse needs, interests, abilities, and styles of learning; in part because of the accelerating growth of knowledge and new fields of knowledge; in part because of the rapid development of the American economy and its demands on school systems; and in part because of the transformation of America's role in the world. The traditional subjects could be studied in a greater range of forms; the entry of new subjects into curricula provided a greater range of choice; and the effort to combine subjects into

new versions of general education created a greater range of requirements. Finally, the rapid increase in the amount of state and federal funds invested in the schools and colleges, coupled with the rising demand for access on the part of segments of the population traditionally held at the margins, brought a corresponding development of the instruments of public oversight and control—local community boards, state coordinating boards, court-appointed masters and monitors, and federal attorneys with the authority to enforce federal regulations. In the process, American schools became at the same time both more centralized and more decentralized.[1]

It was in many ways a remarkable achievement, of which Americans could be justifiably proud. Yet it seemed to bring with it a pervasive sense of failure. During the 1970s, there was widespread suspicion that American students were falling behind in international competition, that while more people were going to school for ever longer periods of time, they were learning less and less. And in the 1980s, that suspicion seemed to be confirmed by the strident rhetoric of the National Commission on Excellence in Education. Recall the commission's charges in *A Nation at Risk:*

> We report to the American people that while we can take justifiable pride in what our schools and colleges have historically accomplished and contributed to the United States and the well-being of its people, the educational foundations

of our society are presently being eroded by a rising tide of mediocrity that threatens our very future as a Nation and a people. What was unimaginable a generation ago has begun to happen—others are matching and surpassing our educational attainments.

If an unfriendly power had attempted to impose on America the mediocre educational performance that exists today, we might well have viewed it as an act of war. As it stands, we have allowed this to happen to ourselves.[2]

Now, there have always been critics of the schools and colleges. From the very beginning of the public school crusade in the nineteenth century, there were those who thought that popular schooling was at best a foolish idea and at worst a subversive idea. The editor of the Philadelphia *National Gazette* argued in the 1830s that free universal education was nothing more than a harebrained scheme of social radicals, and claimed that it was absolutely illegal and immoral to tax one part of the community to educate the children of another. And beyond such wholesale opposition, even those who favored the idea of universal education thought that the results were unimpressive. The educator Frederick Packard lamented that the schools were failing dismally in even their most fundamental tasks. He charged on the basis of personal visits to classrooms that nine out of ten youngsters were unable to read a newspaper, keep a simple debit and credit account, or draft an ordinary business letter. The writer James Fenimore Cooper was ready to grant that the lower schools were developing a greater range of talent than was the case in most other countries, but he pointed to what he thought was the superficiality of much of the work of the colleges and bemoaned the absence of genuine accomplishment in literature and the arts. And the French commentator Alexis de Tocqueville, echoing the English critic Sydney Smith, observed that America had produced few writers of distinction, no great artists, and not a single first-class poet. Americans were a practical people, he concluded, but not very speculative. They could boast many lawyers but no jurists, many good workers but few imaginative inventors.[3]

By the early years of the twentieth century, as some elementary education was becoming nearly universal and as secondary education was beginning to be popularized, the criticism became broader and sharper. A writer in *Gunton's Magazine* charged that as schooling had spread it had been made too easy and too entertaining. "The mental nourishment we spoonfeed our children," he observed, "is not only minced but peptonized so that their brains digest it without effort and without benefit and the result is the anaemic intelligence of the average American schoolchild." And a Maryland farmer named Francis Livesey became so outraged at the whole idea of free universal education that he organized a society called the Herbert Spencer Education Club with two classes of membership—one for those seeking the complete abolition of public schooling and one for those willing to settle for the repeal of all compulsory attendance laws.[4]

With respect to secondary and higher education, critics such as Irving Babbitt, Abraham Flexner, and Robert Hutchins leveled blast after blast against the relaxation of language requirements, the overcrowding of curricula with narrow technical courses, and the willingness to permit students to work out their own programs of study. The spread of educational opportunity in the United States, they observed, reflected less a spirit of democratic fairness than a willingness to prolong adolescence. The result was an inferior educational product at every level—high school programs were too watered down and fragmented; the colleges were graduating men and women unable to write and spell a decent English and pitifully ignorant of mathematics, the sciences, and modern languages; and the graduate schools were crowded with students of mediocre ability who lacked the slightest appreciation of higher culture.[5]

Even those foreign observers who were prone to admire the American commitment to popular schooling wrung their hands at what they saw as the widespread absence of high intellectual expectations, particularly at the high school and college levels. Thus, Sir Michael Sadler, the director of the Office of Special Inquiries and Reports of the British government, and a great friend of the United States, noted an absence of intellectual discipline and rigor in American schools—too much candy and ice cream, he liked to say, and not enough oatmeal porridge. And Erich Hylla, a member of the German ministry of education who had spent a year in residence at Teachers College, Columbia University, and who translated Dewey's *Democracy and Education* into German, lamented what he perceived as the disjointedness and superficiality of secondary and undergraduate study and the resultant poor achievement of American students.[6]

As popularization advanced at every level of schooling after World War II, the drumbeat of dissatisfaction grew louder. Arthur Bestor and Hyman Rickover argued during the 1950s and 1960s that popular schooling had been literally subverted by an interlocking directorate of education professors, state education officials, and professional association leaders; they charged that the basics had been ignored in favor of a trivial curriculum parading under the name of Life Adjustment Education and that as a result American freedom was in jeopardy. Robert Hutchins continued his mordant criticisms of the 1930s, contending that the so-called higher learning purveyed by the colleges and universities was neither higher nor learning but rather a collection of trade school courses intended to help young people win the material success that Americans prized so highly. And again, even those foreign observers who were disposed to admire the American commitment to popular education now made it something of a litany to comment on what they perceived to be the low standards and mediocre achievements of American students. The English political economist Harold Laski noted the readiness of American parents to expect too little of their youngsters and the readiness of the youngsters to see interest in abstract ideas as somewhat strange at best, with the result that American college graduates seemed to him to be two to three years less intellectually mature than their English or French counterparts. And the Scottish political scientist D. W. Brogan was quite prepared to grant that the American public school had been busy Americanizing immigrants for several generations at least—he liked to refer to the

public school as "the formally unestablished national church of the United States"—but he saw the price of that emphasis on social goals as an insufficient attention to intellectual goals. For all their talk of preparing the young for life, Brogan maintained, Americans were not being realistic about what life would actually demand during the second half of the twentieth century.[7]

Within such a context, Paul Copperman's allegations of the late 1970s that Americans of that generation would be the first whose educational skills would not surpass or equal or even approach those of their parents, which the National Commission on Excellence in Education quoted approvingly in *A Nation at Risk*, and Allan Bloom's assertions of the late 1980s that higher education had failed democracy and impoverished the souls of American students were scarcely surprising or even original. Why all the fuss, then? How, if at all, did the criticisms of the 1980s differ from those that had come before? I believe they differed in three important ways: they were more vigorous and pervasive; they were putatively buttressed by data from cross-national studies of educational achievement; and, coming at a time when Americans seemed to be feeling anxious about their place in the world, they gave every indication of being potentially more dangerous and destructive.[8] . . .

The 1980s brought another shift in the climate of educational opinion, this one exemplified by the two reports that have already been alluded to, the reports of the National Commission on Excellence in Education entitled *A Nation at Risk*, and of the Study Group on the State of Learning in the Humanities in Higher Education entitled *To Reclaim a Legacy*.

The National Commission had been created in 1981 by President Reagan's first secretary of education, Terrel Bell—the same Terrel Bell, incidentally, who in the 1970s had introduced the report of the USOE's National Panel on High School and Adolescent Education with a glowing foreword referring to the report as a major contribution to the public discussion of secondary education. The membership of the commission included educators, scientists, business-people, and politicians, with David P.

Gardner, president of the University of Utah, as chair (Gardner subsequently became president of the University of California) and Yvonne W. Larsen, immediate past president of the San Diego school board, as vice-chair. The commission held hearings, took testimony, and visited schools in various parts of the country through much of 1982 and then reviewed various quite different drafts of the report during the first months of 1983. The final report—terse, direct, and unqualified in its assertions—was largely the work of the scientists on the panel. In effect, it put forward a severe indictment of American education and proposed a fundamental set of reforms. The report cited rates of adult illiteracy (as many as 23 million functionally illiterate Americans), declining scores on the Scholastic Aptitude Test (an almost unbroken decline from 1963 to 1980), and deficiencies in knowledge on the part of seventeen-year-olds as revealed by international tests of achievement (American students never ranked first or second on any of nineteen academic tests). From this and other "dimensions of the risk before us," the commission concluded that "the educational foundations of our society are presently being eroded by a rising tide of mediocrity that threatens our very future as a Nation and a people."[9]

As remedies, the commission put forward five recommendations: (1) that, as a minimum, all students seeking a high school diploma be required to complete during the four years of high school the following work in the "new basics"—four years of English, three years of mathematics, three years of science, three years of social studies, and a half year of computer science; (2) that schools, colleges, and universities adopt higher expectations of their students and that four-year colleges and universities raise their requirements for admission; (3) that significantly more time be devoted to teaching and learning the new basics, and that this be achieved through more effective use of the existing school day, a lengthened school day, or a lengthened school year; (4) that the preparation of teachers be strengthened and teaching be made a more rewarding and more respected profession; and (5) that citizens throughout the nation require

their elected officials to support these reforms and to provide the money necessary to achieve them. Interestingly, the report mentioned a role for the federal government in defining the national interest in education, but it assigned to state and local officials the primary responsibility for initiating and carrying out the recommendations. Beyond that, it ended with a word to parents and students, asking the parents to raise their expectations of their children, and asking students to work harder in school.[10]

During the next few years there followed in the wake of A Nation at Risk a score of reports on the problems of the schools, each putting forth its own particular agenda for reform. A task force organized by the Twentieth Century Fund stressed the need for English as the language of schooling, through the grades and across the country. A commission organized by the National Science Board stressed the need for all young Americans to have a firm grounding in mathematics, science, and technology. A task force organized by the Education Commission of the States stressed the relationship of more intense schooling to the maintenance of America's economic competitiveness in the world. A panel organized by the National Academy of Sciences stressed the need for academic competence in the kind of workplace that was coming into being in the United States. A task force organized by the Committee for Economic Development stressed the need for businesspeople to be interested and involved in the work of the schools. And Ernest Boyer, writing on behalf of the Carnegie Foundation for the Advancement of Teaching, stressed the need for a coherent curriculum core at the heart of any worthy secondary education. All in one way or another re-sounded the themes of A Nation at Risk—the need for emphasis on a new set of basics, the need for a more intensive school experience for all young people, and the need for a better trained teaching profession in the nation's schools.[11]

In addition, several major reports dealing with higher education also followed the publication of A Nation at Risk, notably, William J. Bennett's report on behalf of the National Endowment for the Humanities Study Group, entitled

To Reclaim a Legacy; the report of a Select Committee of the Association of American Colleges, entitled *Integrity in the College Curriculum*; and a report of Ernest Boyer, again writing on behalf of the Carnegie Foundation for the Advancement of Teaching, entitled *College: The Undergraduate Experience in America*. All three lamented the absence of a clear vision of the educated person at the heart of undergraduate education, one that would call for all students to undertake fundamental studies in the humanities (Bennett), the natural sciences, and the social sciences (the AAC Select Committee and Boyer); all three lamented the concentration on research and the inattention to teaching in the preparation and careers of college professors; all three called for a renewed effort to develop an integrated core of required subjects that would be taught to all candidates for the bachelor's degree, whatever their majors or professional goals; and all three called for a new emphasis on imaginative and informed teaching in the nation's colleges and universities.[12]

Yet again, let us examine the grand story implicit and explicit in these reports, the ideas they present about how education works, why it goes wrong, and how it can be set right. For the various commissions of the early 1980s, the popularization of education has been an utter and complete failure, because popularization has brought with it declension and degradation. For the National Commission on Excellence in Education, the educational foundations of society are being eroded by a rising tide of mediocrity; in the National Commission's view, Paul Copperman is correct in his assertion that for the first time in the history of the United States the educational achievement of the present generation will not surpass, equal, or even approach the educational achievement of its parents. For the AAC Select Committee, a century-long decline of undergraduate education into disarray and incoherence has accompanied the rise of academic specialization associated with the research universities, and that decline has been accelerated by the upsurge of higher education enrollments since World War II. In effect, the decline and degradation have occurred because education is essentially the study of

the liberal arts—what Conant called general education, what the National Commission called the new basics, what Ernest Boyer called the integrated core. The liberal arts were at the heart of education during the nineteenth and early twentieth centuries, and popularization has brought a vitiation of their formative power in favor of narrow specialization and crass vocationalism. How can education be set right? By requiring study of the liberal arts of all students, and by popularizing education without permitting it to be vulgarized, that is, by universalizing precisely the education that was formerly preserved for the few and making it mandatory for all. The popularization of education involves an increase in the size of the clientele, not a transformation in the nature of the curriculum.

Nowhere was the grand story of the early 1980s more dramatically presented than in Allan Bloom's *The Closing of the American Mind*. The educational and political crisis of twentieth-century America is essentially an intellectual crisis, Bloom asserted. It derives, he continued, from the university's lack of central purpose, from the students' lack of fundamental learning, from the displacement of the traditional classical humanistic works that long dominated the curriculum—the works of Plato and Aristotle and Augustine and Shakespeare and Spinoza and Rousseau—by specialized electives and courses in the creative arts, and from the triumph of relativism over perennial humanistic values. How can the crisis be resolved? Clearly, by a restoration of true learning in the schools and colleges through the traditional disciplines and the works of the Western canon. Could that restoration be compatible with further popularization of higher education? Almost certainly not!

My friend Richard Heffner once asked me on his television program, *The Open Mind*, whether the ideal of popular education was not an impossible ideal, whether it not only was not working but in the end could not work. I maintained that no ideal is ever completely achievable; if it is, it is not an ideal. What an ideal does hold out is a goal, which people can then approach more or less successfully. And I argued that the ideal of popular education, at least as it had developed in the United States, was one of the most radical ideals in the Western world, that we had made great progress in moving toward the ideal, but that the attainment had been wanting in many domains, and that the institutions we had established to further that attainment had been flawed in many respects. We had, to be blunt, a long way to go, but it was worth trying to get there.

After we were off the air, I asked Heffner if he was not really asking whether the phrase popular education is an oxymoron, a contradiction, in its very nature flawed and unachievable. He protested not. But I think many people believe that the contradiction is there, that education in its true meaning is an elite phenomenon, just as such people would argue that culture in its true meaning is an elite phenomenon, and that as soon as education begins to be transformed by popularization—by popular interest, popular demand, popular understanding, and popular acceptance—it is inevitably vulgarized. In essence, these people would argue that there is no more possibility of a popular education than there is of a popular culture. What results when education is popularized is an educational version of what the critic Dwight Macdonald once labeled "masscult" or "midcult." I believe this is the explicit message of Allan Bloom's book. And I would trace the most fundamental and abiding discontent with popular education in the United States to the sense that it is not only an impossible ideal but in the end a hopeless contradiction.[13]

To argue in favor of popular education is not to deny the tremendous difficulties inevitably involved in achieving it. On the one side, there are the inescapable political problems of determining the nature, content, and values of popular education. Legislators want the schools to teach the advantages of patriotism and the dangers of substance abuse; parents want the schools to teach character and discipline; employers want the schools to teach diligence and the basic skills; arts advocates want the schools to teach painting, drama, music, and dance; academics want the schools to teach more of what they know—historians want more

history, mathematicians more mathematics, and economists more economics; students want the schools to equip them to go on to college if they wish, to prepare them to obtain and hold a job with a future, and to offer them opportunities to enjoy sports, hobbies, and a decent social life; and a host of organized citizens' groups want the schools to attend to their special concerns, which range from civil liberties to fire prevention. Out of a process that involves all three branches of government at the state and federal levels as well as thousands of local school boards, a plethora of private interests ranging from publishers to accrediting agencies, and the variety of professionals who actually operate the schools emerges what we call the curriculum, with its requirements, its electives, its informal activities, and its unacknowledged routines. It is that curriculum, in various versions, that is supposed to be offered to all the children of all the people. On the other side, there are the demands of the children, with their almost infinite variety of needs, wants, and values, deriving from extraordinary differences in their family backgrounds, their rates and patterns of development, their learning styles, and their social, intellectual, and vocational aspirations.

The resulting dilemmas are as difficult philosophically as they are insistent politically. Will the increased stringency of academic requirements stimulated by the report of the National Commission on Excellence in Education create a rise in the dropout rate at the same time that it encourages more capable students to higher levels of academic performance? The dropout rate has indeed gone up, but we do not know whether that testifies to the inability (or unwillingness) of students to master the newly required material or the difficulties teachers face in teaching the newly required material with sufficient versatility, or both. However that may be, the loss to the American polity, economy, and society, and to the individual youngsters who drop out, is prodigious. Meanwhile, the Japanese, though admittedly a less heterogeneous people than the Americans, are mandating even more difficult material for their high school students, with a lower dropout rate. Will the effort to advance racial integration by insisting upon comprehensive high schools cause white flight that in the end leads to increased segregation and lower academic performance? There are those who say that it will, and there are communities where the effort to maintain comprehensive high schools has been correlated with white flight, increased segregation, and lower academic performance. Meanwhile, the Swedes seem to be managing to maintain comprehensive high schools in an increasingly heterogeneous society without lowering academic performance. Do the traditions of competitive individualism lead American parents, teachers, and students to assume that some young people must inevitably fall? The data from John Goodlad's study of schooling provide evidence that such assumptions are rampant. Yet there have long been experimental schools in the United States and abroad in which the school class as a whole has been made responsible for the performance of individual members, with the result that students end up helping one another to succeed. In sum, does the success of popular education ultimately depend upon the values of the society it is meant to nurture and sustain, which in the American case involves a penchant for utility, an ambivalence toward book learning, and a preoccupation with individual success? Do such values by their very nature compromise the success of popular education?[14]

Furthermore, there are the patent flaws in the system of institutions Americans have created to realize the ideal of popular education. One might note in the first place the undetermined number of children in the United States who are simply not in school at any given time for one reason or another and who are not even known to be not in school. When the Children's Defense Fund did its pioneering study of *Children Out of School in America* during the early 1970s, it found, quite beyond the United States census statistic of nearly two million children between the ages of seven and seventeen out of school, thousands of children who had been expelled or suspended for disciplinary reasons, countless truants who had managed to elude census enumerators and attendance officers, and undetermined numbers of children who had

fallen through the cracks of the system for reasons of pregnancy, poverty, mental retardation, or emotional disability. In addition, it found even greater numbers of children who were technically in school but who might just as well have been counted as out of school—youngsters of recent immigrant families sitting uncomprehendingly in classrooms conducted in English, youngsters misdiagnosed as retarded who were really deaf, youngsters so alienated by real or perceived indifference, condescension, or prejudice that they had long since stopped profiting from anything the schools had to offer.[15]

One might go on to note the flaws in individual institutions—elementary schools where children do not learn to read because they are not taught; high schools where young men and women from working-class backgrounds are denied access to the studies of languages and mathematics that would make it possible for them to become engineers or scientists; junior colleges where recent immigrants with aspirations to undergraduate degrees cannot find the guidance they require to choose the proper academic courses and hence end up locked into narrow occupational programs; and four-year colleges where students graduating with a melange of "gut" courses find themselves with a worthless credential and few prospects of decent employment. One might note, too, the flaws in whole systems of schooling, especially the overbureaucratized and underfinanced systems of many of our central cities, heavily populated by the poor, the non-white, and the recently arrived, those most in need of carefully and expertly delivered educational services and least likely to receive them.

Popular education, then, is as radical an ideal as Americans have embraced. It is by its very nature fraught with difficulty, and the institutions we have established to achieve it are undeniably flawed. Yet it is important to be aware of what has been accomplished in the movement toward popular education and of the possibilities for the future. I believe the predicament of American schooling during the early 1980s was not nearly so dire as the report of the National Commission suggested. As Lawrence Stedman and Marshall Smith pointed out in a detailed examination of the evidence cited in the report, the academic achievement of young Americans in the early 1980s was far more mixed than the commission alleged. There were definite improvements in the performance of younger children, reflecting, I believe, the additional educational services made available by Title I/ Chapter I federal funds. These were coupled with a patently uneven performance on the part of adolescents, a performance marked by relatively good showings in literature and the social studies and rather poor showings in foreign languages, mathematics, and the natural sciences as well as in the development of the higher order skills associated with critical thinking. Everyone agreed that the results should have been better—in fact, there were data in John Goodlad's study of schooling suggesting that significant numbers of the students themselves believed they might have been working harder and more effectively. Moreover, given the extraordinary percentage of young Americans who were continuing on to postsecondary education, the results would likely have been better in comparison with other countries had the tests been administered at age nineteen or twenty instead of seventeen or eighteen. However that may be, there was surely no evidence to support the commission's affirmation of Paul Copperman's claim that the present generation would be the first in American history whose educational skills would not equal or even approach those of its parents.[16]

Furthermore, we know that standardized tests measure at best only a fraction of what young people have learned in school, and they measured that imperfectly, so that if one were to venture past the test scores to examine what was actually happening in the schools of the early 1980s, a cluster of studies by scholars such as John Goodlad, Philip Jackson, Sara Lawrence Lightfoot, Mary Haywood Metz, Vito Perrone, Arthur Powell, and others revealed a far more complex picture of what was going on. They indicated that, overall, there was strong emphasis in school curricula on the English language and literature; that considerable importance was being placed on social studies, mathematics, the natural sciences, the arts, physical education,

and, in the upper grades, so-called career education but that foreign languages were receiving limited attention at best; that teachers were mindful of their responsibility to inculcate discipline and nurture civic and social skills; that most schools were orderly places where teachers and students went about the diurnal business of education in a systematic and mutually respectful fashion; that many schools were contending thoughtfully and effectively with the prodigious problems of integrating vastly diverse clienteles into the American polity and economy; that students in general were learning what their parents and teachers thought it was important for them to learn; and that there were significant numbers of students who excelled, by any reasonable standard, in literature, the sciences, the fine and performing arts, and athletics. But they also indicated that students spent less time in school each year and less time at home doing schoolwork than their counterparts in a number of other countries; that teachers, particularly at the elementary level, were poorly trained in mathematics and the natural sciences and that their poor training was a key factor in the relatively low achievement of students in those subjects; that far too much teaching was uninspired and unimaginative, with consistent overreliance on lectures, drills and workbooks and underreliance on a wide range of alternative pedagogies and technologies; that teachers felt severely constrained in their daily work by bureaucratic rules and procedures; and, most important, that the greatest failures and most serious unsolved problems of the system were those relating to the education of poor children from minority populations in the schools of the central cities.[17]

The reports on higher education during the 1980s, with their emphasis on the loss of an integrated core in undergraduate education and the deleterious effects of that loss, were also at best distorted in their diagnosis of the current situation. Whatever core there might have been in the liberal arts institutions of the seventeenth and eighteenth centuries had already begun to disintegrate in the nineteenth century in the face of rising enrollments and expanding commitments, and with the exception of its presence in a few elite colleges and universities, that core as traditionally defined has not been much seen in the twentieth century. The explosion of knowledge that marked the rise of the research university necessitated not only the extensive choice embodied in the elective system but also the kind of continuing redefinition of any integrated core by college and university faculties that would inevitably lead to various versions of general and liberal education. Allan Bloom's Western canon is one of those versions, but only one. There are other versions that derive from different definitions of the educated person.

That variety of definitions holds the key, it seems to me, to the current situation in American education. Americans have traditionally assigned a wide range of responsibilities to their schools and colleges. They want the schools and colleges to teach the fundamental skills of reading, writing, and arithmetic; to nurture critical thinking; to convey a general fund of knowledge; to develop creativity and aesthetic perception; to assist students in choosing and preparing for vocations in a highly complex economy; to inculcate ethical character and good citizenship; to develop physical and emotional well-being; and to nurture the ability, the intelligence, and the will to continue on with education as far as any particular individual wants to go. And this catalogue does not even mention such herculean social tasks as taking the initiative in racial desegregation and informing the population about the dangers of drug abuse and AIDS. Americans have also maintained broad notions of the active intellect and informed intelligence required to participate responsibly in the affairs of American life. One associates these notions with the inclusive definitions of literacy that make the role of literacy in everyday life central and with the plural definitions of intelligence that embrace musical and kinesthetic intelligence as well as logical, linguistic, and mathematical intelligence—the sorts of definitions that Howard Gardner has advanced in *Frames of Mind* (1983). And they have not only countenanced but urged a wide-ranging curriculum that goes far beyond the "new basics" or the "integrated core" or the "Western canon" of the recent policy reports—

those are at best somewhat narrow, academicist versions of American education. As with all latitudinarianism, such definitions can permit triviality to enter the curriculum, and triviality is not difficult to find in American schools and colleges. But on balance I believe such broad definitions have served the American people well.[18]

If there is a crisis in American schooling, it is not the crisis of putative mediocrity and decline charged by the recent reports but rather the crisis inherent in balancing this tremendous variety of demands Americans have made on their schools and colleges—of crafting curricula that take account of the needs of a modern society at the same time that they make provision for the extraordinary diversity of America's young people; of designing institutions where well-prepared teachers can teach under supportive conditions, and where *all* students can be motivated and assisted to develop their talents to the fullest; and of providing the necessary resources for creating and sustaining such institutions. These tough problems may not make it into the headlines or onto television, and there is no quick fix that will solve them; but in the end they constitute the real and abiding crisis of popular schooling in the United States.

In thinking about the search for solutions, it is well to bear in mind that there remain some 15,000 school districts in the United States that sponsor about 59,000 elementary schools and 24,000 secondary schools, and that there are also almost 21,000 private elementary schools and 8,000 private secondary schools. In addition, there are around 3,000 institutions of higher education, of which fully a third are two-year community colleges. Given this multitude of institutions organized into fifty state systems—some highly centralized, some loosely decentralized—programs of education will differ, and local as well as cosmopolitan influences will prevail. For all the centralizing tendencies in American schooling—from federal mandates to regional accrediting association guidelines to standardized tests and textbooks—the experience students have in one school will differ from the experience they have in another, whatever the formal curriculum indicates might be going on; and the standards by which we judge those experiences will derive from local realities, clienteles, faculties, and aspirations as well as from cosmopolitan knowledge, norms, and expectations. The good school, as Sara Lightfoot has argued, is good in its context.[19]

It is that point, I believe, that the high school reports of the 1970s were trying to make, when they recommended the further differentiation of curricula and the brokering by the schools of educational opportunities for youngsters in libraries, museums, workplaces, government agencies, and community organizations. It is that point, too, that the Carnegie Commission was trying to make when it recommended a vast expansion of enrollments and a further diversification of curricula in the first two years of postsecondary education. Where I would quarrel with the Carnegie Commission (and later the Carnegie Council on Policy Studies in Higher Education) would be in its insistence on confining the expansion and diversification to the junior college and on protecting the four-year colleges from the demands and effects of popularization. In my own view, the commission drew far too great a distinction between the programs of two-year and four-year colleges and invested far too much energy in trying to preserve the imagined distinctions. For one thing, there is tremendous overlap in the character of the two kinds of institutions. For another, both need adjustment to facilitate the easy transfer of students from the former to the latter, which was envisioned by President Truman's Commission on Higher Education, but which has not come to pass.

More important, however, I believe there is need for a far greater sense of unity in the American school system, one that envisions the system whole, extending from nursery schools through the so-called doctorate-granting institutions, with individuals making their way through the system according to their own lights and aspirations and institutions creating their clienteles competitively, much as they do today. I would abandon the constraint the Carnegie Commission preached when it expressed the hope that the two-year colleges would be discouraged from trying to become four-year

undergraduate institutions. Sir Eric Ashby, who prepared the immensely incisive monograph *Any Person, Any Study* for the Carnegie Commission—the title bespoke Sir Eric's sense of the openness of American higher education —observed that while the Soviet Union maintained a diversity of higher education institutions stratified according to subjects the United States maintained a diversity of higher education institutions stratified according to quality. He defined quality, of course, in terms of what Martin Trow had called the "autonomous" functions of higher education—with the elite universities devoted primarily to research at the top, with the comprehensive universites dividing their efforts between research and teaching at a somewhat lower status, and with the colleges and universites devoting their efforts primarily to teaching occupying an even lower status. I would alter Ashby's aphorism to argue that while the Soviet Union maintains a diversity of higher education institutions stratified according to subjects the United States maintains a diversity of higher education institutions organized according to missions, missions that vary considerably. And I think that kind of organization is part of the genius of American education —it provides a place for everybody who wishes one, and in the end yields one of the most educated populations in the world.[20]

Excerpts from *Popular Education and Its Discontents* by Lawrence A. Cremin. Copyright © 1990 by Lawrence A. Cremin. Reprinted by permission of HarperCollins Publishers, Inc.

Notes

1. Thomas D. Snyder, *Digest of Education Statistics, 1987* (Washington, D.C.: Government Printing Office, 1987), 13.
2. National Commission on Excellence in Education. *A Nation at Risk: The Imperative for Educational Reform* (Washington, D.C.: GPO, 1983), 5.
3. Philadelphia *National Gazette*, July 10, 1830, 2; [Frederick Adolphus Packard], *The Daily Public School in the United States* (Philadelphia: Lippincott, 1866), 10–11; J. F. Cooper, *Notions of the Americans* (2 vols.; London: Henry Colburn, 1828), 2:122, 127; and Alexis de Tocqueville,

Democracy in America, edited by Phillips Bradley (2 vols.; New York: Knopf, 1945), 1:315.

4. Lys d'Aimée, "The Menace of Present Educational Methods," *Gunton's Magazine*, 19 (September 1900):263; and Lawrence A. Cremin and Robert M. Weiss, "Yesterday's School Critic," *Teachers College Record*, 54 (November 1952): 77–82.

5. Irving Babbitt, *Literature and the American College: Essays in Defense of the Humanities* (Boston: Houghton Mifflin, 1908), chap. 3; Abraham Flexner, *A Modern College and a Modern School* (Garden City, N.Y.: Doubleday, 1923); *Do Americans Really Value Education?* (Cambridge, Mass.: Harvard University Press, 1927); and *Universities: American, English, German* (New York: Oxford University Press, 1930); and Robert Maynard Hutchins, *The Higher Learning in America* (New Haven: Yale University Press, 1936).

6. Michael E. Sadler, "Impressions of American Education," *Educational Review*, 25 (March 1903):228; and Erich Hylla, *Die Schule der Demokratie, Ein Aufriss des Bildungswesens der Vereinigten Staaten* (Langensalza: Verlag von Julius Beltz, 1928), chap. 3.

7. Arthur Bestor, *The Restoration of Learning: A Program for Redeeming the Unfulfilled Promise of American Education* (New York: Knopf, 1955); H. G. Rickover, *Education and Freedom* (New York: Dutton, 1959); Hutchins, *Higher Learning in America*; Harold J. Laski, *The American Democracy: A Commentary and an Interpretation* (New York: Viking, 1948), chap. 8; and D. W. Brogan, *The American Character* (New York: Knopf, 1944), 137.

8. Paul Copperman, *The Literacy Hoax: The Decline of Reading, Writing, and Learning in the Public Schools and What We Can Do About It* (New York: Morrow, 1978), and "The Achievement Decline of the 1970's," *Phi Delta Kappan*, 60 (June 1979): 736–739; National Commission on Excellence in Education, *A Nation at Risk*, 11; and Allan Bloom, *The Closing of the American Mind* (New York: Simon and Schuster, 1987).

9. National Commission on Excellence in Education, *A Nation at Risk*, 8–11, 5.

10. Ibid., 24–33.

11. Twentieth Century Fund Task Force on Federal Elementary and Secondary Education Policy, *Making the Grade* (New York: The Twentieth Century Fund, 1983); National Science Board Commission on Precollegiate Education in Mathematics, Science, and Technology, *Educating Americans for the 21st Century: A Plan of Action for Improving Mathematics, Science, and Technology Education for All American Elementary and Secondary Students So That Their Achievement Is the Best in the World by 1995* (Washington, D.C.: National Science Foundation, 1983); *Education Commission of the States, Task Force on Education for Economic Growth, Action for Excellence: A Comprehensive Plan to Improve Our Nation's Schools* (Washington, D.C.: Education Commission of the States, 1983); National Academy of Sciences, Committee on Science, Engineering, and Public Policy, Panel on Secondary School Education for the Changing Workplace, *High Schools and the Changing Workplace: The Employers' View* (Washington, D.C.: National Academy Press, 1984); Committee for Economic Development, Research and Policy Committee, *Investing in Our Children: Business and the Public Schools* (New York: Committee for Economic Development, 1985); and Ernest L. Boyer, *High School: A Report on Secondary Education in America* (New York: Harper & Row, 1983).

12. William J. Bennett, *To Reclaim a Legacy: A Report on the Humanities in Higher Education* (Washington, D.C.: National Endowment for the Humanities, 1984); Association of American Colleges, Project on Defining the Meaning and Purpose of Baccalaureate Degrees, *Integrity in the College Curriculum: A Report to the Academic Community* (Washington, D.C.: Association of American Colleges, 1985); and Ernest L. Boyer, *College: The Undergraduate Experience in America* (New York: Harper & Row, 1987).

13. Dwight Macdonald, *Against the American Grain* (New York: Random House, 1962), part 1.

14. With respect to the prodigious costs of continuing high dropout rates, one might note the argument of Margaret D. LeCompte and Anthony Gary Dworkin: "Given the indirect link between education and poverty, we believe that a significant measure of the success of an educational innovation, whether enriching or compensatory, is not whether the student test scores rise, but whether it improves the retention of an entire cohort of students and faculty," in "Educational Programs: Indirect Linkages and Unfulfilled Expectations," in Harrell R. Rodgers, Jr., ed., *Beyond Welfare: New Approaches to the Problem of Poverty in America* (Armonk, N.Y.: Sharpe, 1988), 136. For some of the Goodlad evidence, see Kenneth A. Tye, *The Junior High: School in Search of a Mission* (Lanham, Md.: University Press of America, 1985), 1–2.

15. Children's Defense Fund, *Children out of School in America* (Washington, D.C.: Children's Defense Fund, 1974).

16. Lawrence C. Stedman and Marshall S. Smith, "Recent Reform Proposals for American Education," *Contemporary Education Review*, 2 (Fall 1983): 85–104. See also Ralph W. Tyler, "The U.S. vs. the World: A Comparison of Educational Performance," *Phi Delta Kappan*, 62 (January 1981): 307–310; Gilbert R. Austin and Herbert

Garber, eds., *The Rise and Fall of National Test Scores* (New York: Academic Press, 1982); and, for a later summary of the test data, U.S. Congress, Congressional Budget Office, *Trends in Educational Achievement* (April 1986) *and Educational Achievement: Explanations and Implications of Recent Trends* (August 1987); John I. Goodlad, *A Place Called School Prospects for the Future* (New York: McGraw-Hill, 1984), chap. 3 and passim; and Barbara Benham Tye, *Multiple Realities: A Study of 13 American High Schools* (Lanham, Md.: University Press of America, 1985), chap. 4 and passim.

17. Goodlad, *A Place Called School*; Stephen R. Graubard, ed., "America's Schools: Portraits and Perspectives." *Daedalus*, 110 (Fall 1981); Sara Lawrence Lightfoot, *The Good High School: Portraits of Character and Culture* (New York: Basic Books, 1983); Mary Haywood Metz, *Different by Design: The Context and Character of Three Magnet Schools* (New York: Routledge & Kegan Paul, 1986); Jeannie Oakes, *Keeping Track: How Schools Structure Inequality* (New Haven: Yale University Press, 1985); Vito Perrone et al., *Portraits of High Schools* (Princeton, N.J.: The Carnegie Foundation for the Advancement of Teaching, 1985); Barbara Benham Tye, *Multiple Realities*; Kenneth A. Tye, *The Junior High*, and Arthur G. Powell, Eleanor Farrar, and David K. Cohen, *The Shopping Mall High School: Winners and Losers in the Educational Marketplace* (Boston: Houghton Mifflin, 1985).

For an early warning against using the international studies of education achievement as some kind of "international contest," see Torsten Husen, ed., *International Study of Achievement in Mathematics: A Comparison of Twelve Countries* (2 vols.; New York: Wiley, 1967), 2:288, and passim. For a review of the uses and limitations of standardized paper-and-pencil tests as instruments for assessing what is learned in school, see Bernard R. Gifford, ed., *Test Policy and Test Performance: Education, Language, and Culture* (Boston: Kluwer, 1989), Bernard R. Gifford and M. Catherine O'Connor, eds., *New Approaches to Testing: Rethinking Aptitude, Achievement, and Assessment* (Boston: Kluwer, 1990), and other publications reporting the work of the National Commission on Testing and Public Policy.

18. The list of responsibilities assigned to the schools and colleges is based on John I. Goodlad's study of schooling, as reported in *What Schools Are For* (Bloomington, Ind.: Phi Delta Kappa Educational Foundation, 1979) and *A Place Called School* and Ernest L. Boyer's study of the undergraduate experience, as reported in *College*.

19. Lightfoot, *The Good High School*.

20. Eric Ashby, *Any Person, Any Study: An Essay on Higher Education in the United States* (New York: McGraw-Hill, 1971); and Martin Trow, "Reflections on the Transition from Mass to Universal Higher Education," *Daedalus*, 99 (Winter 1970):1–7.

Capital Accumulation, Class Conflict, and Educational Change

Samuel Bowles and Herbert Gintis

> The school is to fit us for the world, and life is more a season of discipline than of amusement Discipline is the role, pleasure the exception . . .
> (From a statement by the Boston School Masters, 1844)

Not surprisingly, historians and other students of the subject offer different—and often sharply contrasting—interpretations of the process of educational change.

Some, like the prominent educational historian, R. Freeman Butts, have described the development of U.S. education as an ". . . unflagging search for freedom."[1] According to Butts, the question dominating U.S. educational history is: "What kind of education will best develop the free citizen and the free person?" As the leaders of the new nation ". . . set up and operated a republican form of government dedicated to equality, democracy, and freedom, they found that they needed an educational system appropriate to such a government."[2] The problem of control of the schools was settled in favor of democracy: "The only institution of a free society which serves everyone equally and is controlled by everyone is the government. So the government should control the common schools."[3] The shift from the mid-nineteenth-century common school ideology to the class stratification of education at the turn of the present century fits neatly into this analysis. While the contribution of the early educators to freedom was significant, it was not, according to Butts, complete:

> Their primary concern was to design a universal, free, public school that would promote free institutions and free citizenship. For the first one hundred years of the Republic, the need for creating the common bonds and loyalties of a free community was paramount.
>
> Less attention was given to the claims of diversity and difference as the essence of freedom for individuals. This came later when the Union had been established, made secure against internal opposition, defended against outside invaders, and preserved despite a war between the states themselves.[4]

Ordinarily troublesome for libertarian thinkers is the problem of compulsory attendance. But not for Butts:

> A smaller freedom must be limited in the interests of a greater freedom. And to guarantee the larger freedom, the state must exert its authority to see to it not only that schools were available to all but that all children actually attended school. Massachusetts led the way by passing its compulsory attendance law in 1852. The solution was a genuinely creative one.[5]

This widely held view, which we refer to as the "democratic imperative" interpretation, does not so much explain educational change as posit for the school system an evolutionary process by which it progressed along some unexplained and predetermined, but evidently universally endorsed path, toward freedom. The only role for

conflict in this theory is in the pace of movement, not the direction of change.

Other writers, stressing the role of conflict in the development of U.S. schooling, have seen the present system as the monument to the triumph of the little people over the powerful. Typical of this view is that expressed by Ellwood Cubberly. "The second quarter of the nineteenth century may be said to have witnessed the battle for tax-supported, publicly controlled and directed, and non-sectarian common schools. Excepting the battle for the abolition of slavery, perhaps no question has ever been before the American people for settlement which caused so much feeling or aroused such bitter antagonism."[6]

Naturally, such a bitter discussion of a public question forced a division of the people for or against publicly supported and controlled schools. This ". . . alignment of interests . . . ," according to Cubberly, saw ". . . philanthropists, humanists, public men of large vision, New England men and intelligent working men in the cities . . ." pitted against the forces of reaction— ". . . politicians of small vision, the ignorant, narrow-minded and penurious, the old aristocratic class and the non-English speaking classes . . ."—in a battle for progress.[7]

Frank Tracy Carleton, a historian, stressed, in particular, the role of labor in the struggle:

> Practically every workingmen's meeting . . . took up the cry. Horace Mann, Henry Barnard, James G. Carter, Robert Dale Owen, George H. Evans, and others directed the movement, but the potent push came from the firm demand of an aroused and insistent wage earning class armed with the ballot.
>
> The rural districts, employers, and men of wealth were rarely favorable to the tax-supported schools; and often their voices were raised against it in bitter protest or stinging invective. A careful study of the development of a free school system in the different states— and the utter lack of a free school system in the slaveholding South, confirm these general statements.[8]

We refer to Cubberly and Carleton's view as the "popular demand for education" interpretation, recently espoused by S. M. Lipset as the "democratic class struggle theory."[9]

Others have put forward a view at once less inspiring than that of Butts and less exciting than that of Cubberly and Carleton: This is what may be called the technological interpretation. According to this interpretation, the growth and structure of U.S. education has represented an accommodation to the labor-training needs generated by the growth and structure of skill requirements in the economy. Typical of this view is the following statement by Martin Trow:

> The mass public secondary school system as we know it has its roots in the transformation of the economy and society that took place after the Civil War. . . . The growth of the secondary school system after 1870 was in large part a response to the pull of the economy for a mass of white collar employees with more than an elementary school education.[10]

These three interpretations—the democratic imperative, the popular demand for education, and the technological—were, until very recently, dominant theories of the rise of U.S. mass education. The reader will not be surprised to find that we hold them to be fundamentally deficient. We present them not simply because they are standard academic arguments which must be considered, but also because we feel that many readers, upon reflection, will find they subscribe to one of them.

Both the democratic imperative and the technological perspectives fail because they are based on false premises. The inspirational interpretation of historians such as Butts is confounded by the fact that the history of the structure, content, and control of U.S. education reveals a striking constancy in its self-conscious repression of youth. Control, not liberation, is the word on the lips of our most influential educational leaders.[11] While secondary education has promoted tolerance, broad-mindedness, and cosmopolitan values to a significant extent, and while the elite remnants of U.S. higher education have fostered an increased social awareness on the part of many students, these seem like oases of freedom in a desert of authoritarianism. Writers of the democratic imperative persuasion are in the unenviable position of having explained the historical genesis of something that never occurred!

The technological perspective finds little support in the history of mass elementary education. There is no evidence of a growth of skill requirements in the nineteenth-century economy.[12] Nor did the proponents of mass education embrace the notion that schools would teach occupationally relevant skills. Indeed, the fragmentary evidence available, while suggesting that educated workers may have been "better behaved" in the eyes of the employers, suggests that, in a technical sense, they were no more productive than unschooled workers.[18] It is particularly difficult to make the case that the objective of early school reform movements was mass literacy in view of the fact that literacy was already very high—about 90 percent of adult whites—prior to the common school revival.[14] For secondary and higher education, the occupational skills perspective explains the need for an educational system to foster cognitive development, but leaves untouched the really crucial issue as to why the resulting school system took the form that it did. For we have shown in previous chapters that the social relations of today's schools cannot be deduced from the technical requisites of imparting cognitive skills. Moreover, we have shown that cognitive skills imparted do not account for the association between educational attainment and economic success.[15]

The evidence in favor of Carleton's and Cubberly's "popular demand" interpretation of educational progress appears, at first glance, rather more convincing. Workers' organizations and citizens' groups often demanded more schooling and, in due course, the school system expanded. A closer look, however, reveals a number of difficulties with this view. First, working people's organizations made a large variety of demands throughout the periods we have studied. Educational reform and expansion tended to be a rather minor concern compared to more direct economic demands—for land reform, co-ops, job security, and the like. Accepting for the moment the view that they were responsible for the expansion in enrollments, what explains their ability to achieve a larger school system when their other demands were not met with such conspicuous success? The answer, we believe, is that the expansion of public education was supported by employers and other powerful people as well as by organized labor. Where the educational demands of organized labor diverged from that of business elites—as in the turn-of-the-century struggle for control of vocational education—labor generally lost. (But not always, as the successful battle against vocational tracking by the Chicago Federation of Labor reveals.)

A second problem with this interpretation is that the evidence of working-class support for educational expansion is not altogether persuasive. Educational demands by working people's organizations are hardly indicative of the perspectives of the majority of workers. In the nineteenth and twentieth centuries alike, only a small minority of workers have been in unions. The nineteenth-century unions whose educational demands provided the prime evidence for Carleton's view were comprised primarily of relatively well-off skilled workers. The educational demands of unorganized common people—farmers and workers—are almost impossible to discover. Nonetheless, the available evidence is hardly supportive of the popular-demand approach. Substantial opposition to educational consolidation and expansion is evident both in the rural small farmers' opposition to the demise of the district school and in the widespread nonattendance, and later truancy, of Irish children as well as rural children generally. The evidence from the turn of this century is similarly ambiguous. Opposition to the school reformers came primarily from popular urban machines and, to some extent, from teachers. Educational reform in rural areas was almost always imposed from the outside.[16]

Third, Carleton's interpretation prompts us to ask: Did working people get what they wanted from education? This is an impossible question to answer satisfactorily. However, the available evidence on the timing and content of educational change does not support an affirmative answer. The periods of pre-Civil War educational ferment in New England and New York most likely were prompted in large measure by the growing militance of workers and other less well-off people.

Workers spoke out for universal education and local control. What they got was quite a different matter: Taking New England as a whole, the percentage of all children attending school fell slightly from 1840 to 1860.[17] Local control was gradually undermined by the formation of centralized school systems, by professionalization of teaching, and the gradual assertion of state government authority over education. In New York City, the available evidence suggests that neither the level of enrollment nor class composition changed much between 1795 and 1860.[18] The antebellum period in the Northeast was one of educational reorganization, not expansion. Other regions—the upper Midwest, in particular—witnessed substantial educational expansions. But these were not areas of working-class organization or strength.

Enrollment did expand in New England, New York, and throughout the country after the Civil War. We do not question the important role of popular pressure in opening up the school system. Particularly in recent years, widespread demands for open enrollments in college have further propelled the development of a mass educational system. But here again, we see a familiar pattern in the relationship between popular demands and educational change. Working-class and poor families have demanded and, to some extent, gained access to postsecondary education. But did they ask to be channeled into dead-end community college programs? Did they ask for "high schools with ashtrays?" Was theirs the vision of stratification in higher education?

We find little support for the view that our educational system took its shape from the demands of common people. There can be little doubt that popular demands have had an important influence on the evolution of U.S. schools and colleges. Yet we are struck by the fact that working people have managed, over the years, to get more education. However, they have, by and large, managed to get the kind of education demanded only when their needs coincided with those of economic elites. We doubt that even the most generous treatment of evidence can invoke popular pressure as an explanation of the structure of control—from the classroom to the school board to the private foundation—of U.S. education. Nor can the popular-pressure argument deal effectively with the extensive need for truancy officers, nor the nearly universal tracking and labeling of working-class and minority youth.

Even the more limited analysis of the popular-pressure interpretation—that focusing on political mechanisms involved in educational change—has recently been shown to be largely incorrect. A "revisionist" viewpoint of educational history has challenged the putative importance of working-class pressure as an agent in educational change. In the course of less than a decade, the path-breaking work of Michael Katz, Clarence Karier, Marvin Lazerson, Carl Kaestle, Joel Spring, David Tyack, Colin Greer, and others has offered a dramatically different picture of educational history.[19] With painstaking care, these and other authors have gone back to the early school-committee reports, the personal letters of the major reformers, the relevant business and foundation reports. Employing both traditional historical arguments and sophisticated statistical treatments they have put forward a new view—too diverse to be called a "school" but coherent enough to loosely summarize. The expansion of mass education and the evolution of its structural forms, they have argued, was sparked by demographic changes associated with the industrialization and urbanization of economic and social activity. The main impetus for educational change was not, however, the occupational skills demanded by the increasingly complex and growing industrial sector, nor was it primarily the desire for the elimination of urban squalor. Rather, in their view, schools were promoted first and foremost as agents for the social control of an increasingly culturally heterogeneous and poverty-stricken urban population in an increasingly unstable and threatening economic and political system. Katz, perhaps the most prominent of the revisionists, suggested that

schools, far from being won by workers over the opposition of capitalists and other entrenched interests, were imposed upon the workers.[20]

As our footnotes amply testify, we have learned much from the revisionist historians. Yet our reading of the history of U.S. education has led us to an alternative interpretation—one which, while generally supportive of the revisionist view, differs in essential respects from theirs as well.

Contradiction and Educational Change: An Overview

> . . . The whole battle with the slum is fought out around the public school . . .
>
> (Jacob Riis, *How the Other Half Lives*, 1902)

> The clash of cultures in the classroom is essentially a class war, a socio-economic and racial warfare being waged on the battleground of the schools . . . This is an uneven balance, particularly since, like most battles, it comes under the guise of righteousness.
>
> (Kenneth Clark, *Dark Ghettos*, 1965)

Our interpretation of the process of educational change is a straightforward extension of our analysis of the the capitalist economy. The role of education in legitimizing the class structure and in fostering forms of consciousness consistent with its reproduction also figure prominently in our analysis.

Capital accumulation has been the driving force behind the transformation and growth of the U.S. economy. Labor is combined in production with increasing amounts of machinery and other capital goods. At the same time, labor power is itself augmented by schooling and training. Two important aspects of the process of capital accumulation may be identified. The first is the expansion of the forces of production with a consequent rapid and sustained increase in the output of goods and services per worker.[21] The second is an equally dramatic transformation of the social relations of production. The sphere of capitalist control over production is widened through the reduction of ever-increasing segments of the population to the status of wage labor. At the same time, capitalist control has deepened through the gradual extension and refinement of the hierarchical division of labor in the enterprise.

The accumulation of capital and the associated extension of the wage-labor system are essential aspects of the expanded reproduction of the capitalist system. The capitalist economy and bicycle riding have this in common: stability requires forward motion. Yet the accumulation of capital and the widening of capitalist control over production also undermines the reproduction of the capitalist order. It inevitably involves the creation of a growing class of wage laborers and the growth of a reserve army of unemployed or marginally employed workers. The antagonistic relationship between capital and labor, and the increased potential for working-class action against capital afforded by the agglomeration of workers into large enterprises and urban areas have threatened the perpetuation of the capitalist system. We refer to this tension between growth and stability as the contradiction between the accumulation of capital and the reproduction of the capitalist relations of production.[22] This basic contradiction has constituted one of the major underlying forces propelling U.S. history for the past century and a half.

At times, the contradiction between accumulation and reproduction has been expressed in militant class struggle and other forms of political activity—examples are the mass strikes which paralyzed the economy in the last quarter of the nineteenth century and again following the First World War, in the Populist revolt of the 1880s and 1890s, in the sit-down strikes and mass labor organizing drives of the late 1930s, and in the urban uprisings of the 1960s. Equally important, however, is the fact that, through much of U.S. history, dominant elites have successfully confined class conflict to the isolated daily struggles of workers in the factories, offices, and shops across the country. The ever-present contradiction between accumulation and reproduction has been submerged or channeled into demands which could be contained within the outlines of capitalist society. The contradiction has been temporarily resolved or suppressed in

a variety of ways: through ameliorative social reforms; through the coercive force of the state; through racist, sexist, ageist, credentialist, and other strategies used by employers to divide and rule; and through an ideological perspective which served to hide rather than clarify the sources of exploitation and alienation of the capitalist order. The expansion of mass education, embodying each of the above means, has been a central element in resolving—at least temporarily—the contradiction between accumulation and reproduction.

It is thus hardly accidental that many of the manifestations of this contradiction in the U.S. economy have appeared in the state sector, and particularly in the educational system. Reformers have consistently believed that our most pressing social problems could be solved, or at least significantly attenuated, through the benign offices of the state. Yet the types of social distress which excite the reformers' conscience result from the most basic workings of the capitalist economy. They are not readily alleviated through a strategy of reforms which leaves untouched the property and market institutions that characterize capitalism as a system. The problem of inequality provides a telling example. The intervention of the state in the income-distribution process—through welfare assistance, social security, unemployment insurance, and progressive taxation, for example—has probably helped to forestall the outbreak of open class conflict in the economic sphere. Yet the problems to which they are addressed are not solved. Rather, we observe a welfare crisis, or a conflict over taxes; or a struggle within the school system over resource transfers. Increasingly, the classroom and the admissions office, as well as the factory floor and the office, are arenas in which basic social conflicts are fought out.

The reformers' optimism has not been rewarded: The problem of inequality is not solved. Rather, its form is changed. But the reform strategy can hardly be considered a failure from the standpoint of the capitalist class. The displacement of social problems into the state sector plays a central role in the reproduction of the capitalist order. The form in which a social problem manifests itself and the arena in which the resulting conflicts are fought out are matters of no small importance. Conflicts within the state sector, even if bitter and enduring, appear to be much less threatening to capital and less disruptive to profits than those which take place on the shop floor or in the office. The class nature of social problems is often obscured when the manifestations of the underlying contradictions are displaced into the state sector.

The overarching role of the state in social reproduction is a relatively recent development. Prior to the expansion of capitalist production in the era of commercial capitalism extending into the early decades of the nineteenth century, the nuclear family successfully unified the functions of accumulation and reproduction. The demise of the family as the primary unit of production, the growing preponderance of wage labor, and the evolution of large-scale business organizations posed problems which shattered the unity of accumulation and reproduction. Both the expansion of capitalist production and the reproduction of the capitalist relations of production required a radically new nexus of social institutions. The school was increasingly looked to by the capitalist class as an institution which could enhance the labor power of working people and at the same time reproduce the social conditions for the transformation of the fruits of labor into capitalist profits. We have attempted to show that the main periods of educational reform coincided with, or immediately followed, periods of deep social unrest and political conflict. The major reform periods have been preceded by the opening up of a significant divergence between the ever-changing social organization of production and the structure of education. Lastly, each major reform period has been associated with the integration into the dynamic capitalist wage-labor system of successive waves of workers. These workers have emerged from the relatively stagnant sectors of the economy or from abroad. More concretely, the uneven expansion of the school system has played the role alternatively of recruiter and of gatekeeper—depending on the level of labor needs—of the dynamic sectors. Schools at once supply labor to the dominant

enterprises and reinforce the racial, ethnic, sexual, and class segmentation of the labor force.

The evolving social relationships of the classroom and school, too, were a response to the pattern of capitalist development primarily as manifested in the ever-changing social organization of work in enterprises of the dynamic sectors of the economy. The system of class, race, and sex relations which was continually shaped and reshaped by the evolving structure of production plus the uneven development of the capitalist economy has been reflected in the segmented, hierarchically structured, racist, sexist, and nativist structure of U.S. education. The emergence and evolution of this educational system, we contend, represented an outgrowth of the political and economic conflict arising from this continued widening and deepening of capitalist control over production, and the contradictions inherent in this process.

The three turning points in U.S. educational history which we have identified all correspond to particularly intense periods of struggle around the expansion of capitalist production relations. Thus the decades prior to the Civil War—the era of the common school reform—was a period of labor militancy associated with the rise of the factory system, growing economic inequality, and the creation and vast expansion of a permanent wage-labor force. The Progressive education movement—beginning at the turn of the present century—grew out of the class conflicts associated with the joint rise of organized labor and corporate capital. At least as much so, Progressive education was a response to the social unrest and dislocation stemming from the integration of rural labor—both immigrant and native—into the burgeoning corporate wage-labor system. The particular concerns of the Progressives—efficiency, cooperation, internalization of bureaucratic norms, and preparation for variegated adult roles—reflect the changing social organization of production in the giant corporate enterprises. The Progressive reforms represented in their implementation little more than an echo of the corporate managers' growing commitment to scientific-management and the control of production and personnel.

The recent period of educational change and ferment—covering the Sixties to the present—is, in large measure, a response to the post-World-War-II integration of three major groups into the wage-labor system: uprooted Southern blacks, women, and the once-respectable, "solid" members of the precorporate capitalist community—the small business people, independent professionals, and other white-collar workers.

The Process of Educational Reform: Conflict and Accommodation

> Education is the property of no one. It belongs to the people as a whole. And if education is not given to the people, they will have to take it.
>
> (Che Guevara, 1964)

The idea that the dynamics of the capitalist economy and the pattern of change in the educational system are intimately related will not strike the reader as either novel or particularly controversial. Nor will the proposition that educational change is the product of intense social conflict provoke adverse comment from any but the most committed advocate of a consensus view of history. A more likely reaction to our overview will be frustration. We have described the process of educational change without identifying the mechanisms whereby economic interests are translated into educational programs. We turn now to this critical last step in our interpretation.

We have argued that the moving force behind educational change is the contradictory nature of capital accumulation and the reproduction of the capitalist order. Conflicts in the educational sphere often reflect muted or open conflicts in the economic sphere. Thus, analysis of the process of educational reform must consider the shifting arenas of class conflict and the mechanisms which the capitalist class has developed to mediate and deflect class conflict. This is a tall order. Indeed, a thorough treatment would require—as a bare minimum—an extended investigation of the bureaucratization and professionalization of education, the role of the major private foundations and quasi-public institutions, the composition of major public decision-making bodies, the crucial process of educational finance and resource allocation, the impact of parental and student opinion, and the role of teachers' associations. Historical and contemporary research into these areas is at best rudimentary. Our interpretation is necessarily somewhat tentative.

First, the economic and educational systems possess fairly distinct and independent internal dynamics of reproduction and development. The process of incessant change within the economic system is a basic characteristic of capitalism. The educational system is rather less dynamic: Our schools and colleges, foundations and schools of education tend to promote a set of cultural values and to support an educational elite which reproduces and stabilizes these institutions through time.

Second, the independent internal dynamics of the two systems present the ever-present possibility of a significant mismatch arising between economy and education. We have seen in the previous three chapters that the educational system acquires its economic importance and contributes to the reproduction of the class structure through a correspondence of its social relationships with the social relations of economic life. Yet the historical dynamic of the capitalist economy involves continual change in the social relations of production and transformation of the class structure. Thus, the relatively static educational system periodically falls out of correspondence with the social relations of production and becomes a force antithetical to capitalist development. This disjunction between an economic dynamic which extends the wage-labor system and incessantly alters the organization of work and the class structure on the one hand, and the educational system which tends to stabilize it in a given form on the other, is, we believe, an essential aspect of the process of educational change.

Third, the accommodation of the educational system to new economic conditions proceeds by two distinct but parallel processes. One operates through the relatively uncoordinated pursuit of interests by millions of individuals and groups as mediated by local school boards, the market for private educational services, and other decentralized decision-making arenas. This process, which we shall call "pluralist accommodation," involves a more or less automatic re-orientation of educational perspectives in the face of a changing economic reality. Historical experience exhibits the strong tendency of educators, in periods of economic change, to alter their educational values and goals in progressive directions—i.e., directions conforming to the new economic rationality emerging in the social relations of production.[23] Parents desirous of a secure economic future for their children often support moves toward a more "vocationally relevant education."[24] The several governmental inputs into the educational decision-making process seek to tailor education to the perceived needs of their various political constituencies. These elements of pluralist accommodation in education provide a strong latent force for re-establishing a "natural" correspondence between the social relations of education and production. Periodic financial crisis can play an important role in this process of educational rationalization. When budgets are ample and the demand by employers for the products of the school system is high, educators have a relatively independent hand in developing new programs and approaches to instruction. Students, also, are freer to pursue their own interests. This was certainly the case for higher education during the late 1960s. But a budget squeeze and the threat of unemployment serve to weed out both the opportunity and the student demand for educational experiences that do not contribute directly to employ ability. Financial hardship thus operates in educational evolution somewhat as famine or drought does in Darwin's "survival of the fittest."

The day-to-day operations of these pluralist forces—the "free market" choices of students, the school bond-issue referenda, the deliberations of elected school boards and the like—reinforce the image of an educational system whose open and decentralized structure defies control or even significant influence by an elite. Indeed, it is absolutely essential for the school system to appear to be democratically controlled if it is

successfully to contribute to the legitimation and reproduction of the U.S. capitalist order.

What is less often noted is that the accommodation by the educational system to a changing economic reality, however pluralistic, is, in essence, a process led by a changing structure of production. The evolution of the structure of production is governed by the pursuit of profit and class privilege by the small minority of capitalists and managers who dominate the dynamic sectors of the economy. The process of pluralist accommodation thus operates within an economic framework determined almost entirely outside of the democratic political arena. Decentralized administration, democratically elected and representative school boards, and local control over school finance thus do not inhibit the process of establishing and continually re-establishing the correspondence between school structure and the social relations of production.

It is only during the crisis periods—which appear in retrospect as the major turning points in U.S. educational history—that control over the relevant decision-making institutions makes a major difference. It is here that our second process of adjustment—concrete political struggle along the lines of class interest—comes to the fore. Particularly in periods of serious disjuncture between the school system and the economy—the 1840s and the 1850s, the first two decades of the present century, and the 1960s and early 1970s—the school system appears less as a cipher impartially recording and tallying the choices of millions of independent actors and more as an arena for struggle among major social groups. The response of forward-looking capitalists to popular unrest is typically dual: material amelioration and educational expansion or reform. Thus the response to the strikes of the 1840s was higher wages for organized workers and the consolidation of the common school. The fruits of Populism as a political movement were somewhat higher farm incomes and the development of agricultural extension and education. The response to the Civil Rights Movement and black urban rebellions of the 1960s was an attempt to ameliorate the economic condition of blacks and a massive program in so-called compensatory education.

In each case, the capitalist class—through its use of the police power of the state in suppressing anticapitalist alternatives, through more generalized political power naturally attending its control over production and investment, and through its extensive control over the financial resources for educational research, innovation, and training—has been able to loosely define a feasible model of educational change, one which has appeared reasonable and necessary in light of the "economic realities" of the day. Forces for educational reform can coalesce only around a common and forcefully articulated social philosophy and program of action. Yet the ideological framework for educational reform is determined in what, with embarrassing accuracy, is called the "free marketplace in ideas." In a relatively decentralized decision-making framework, this preponderant control over information, educational values, and the articulation of programatic ideas—exercised by the capitalist class in large measure through its foundations—has played a crucial role in directing the process of educational accommodation to economic change.

In the absence of any clearly spelled out alternative to the evolving capitalist system, and lacking a political vehicle for the transformation of social life, those who have proposed school reforms which would have significantly undermined the profitability or stability of the economy have been more or less easily swept aside as Utopians. The only feasible counterforce to the capitalist domination of the educational reform process would have been—indeed is today—a party representing all working people and articulating both concrete educational reforms and a general ideological and programatic alterative to capitalism. Only the Socialist Party during the second decade of this century came remotely close to providing such a real alternative. In general, then, popular forces have had no recourse from the capitalist dominated strategy of educational reforms save chaos.

Partly as a result, the accommodation of working people's educational objectives to changing economic conditions has tended to betray a partially regressive character. Groups have struggled against a change in economic status—for instance, proletarianization—that they are more or less powerless to prevent, rather than against the system imposing the change. Thus struggle has frequently taken the form of attempts to restore the irretrievable past. Such has been the case with farmers in the 1840s, workers' organizations in the mid-nineteenth century, craft unions in the early twentieth century, and the student movement of the 1960s.

Conclusion

> By the infirmity of human nature, it happens that the more skillful the workman, the more self-willed and intractable he is apt to become, and of course the less fit a component of a mechanical system in which . . . he may do great damage to the whole.
>
> (Andrew Ure, *The Philosophy of Manufactures*, 1835)

The development of mass education—now extending up through the college level—was, in many respects, a genuinely progressive development. A larger fraction of U.S. youth is now enrolled in college than was enrolled in elementary school 135 years ago. Illiteracy has been virtually eliminated: In 1870, one-tenth of whites and four-fifths of blacks could not read or write.[25] This massive expansion of schooling and the structural forms which it assumed were not simply an imposition on the working class, though workers and their children did sometimes resist attendance. Less still was it a victory for the working class, though the benefits of literacy, access to more advanced learning, custodial care of children and the like are real enough. Rather, the spread of mass education can best be seen as an outcome of class conflict, not class domination. The impetus for educational reform and expansion was provided by the growing class consciousness and political militancy of working people. While working people's groups have, at least for the past hundred and fifty years, demanded more and better education for their children, demands for economic reform and material betterment have been both more urgent and more strongly pressed. In supporting greater access to education, the progressive elements in the capitalist class were not so much giving workers what they wanted as giving what would minimize the erosion of their power and privilege within the structure of production. Educational change has historically played the role not of a complement to economic reform, but as a substitute for it.

The evolution of U.S. education over the last century and a half was the result of a compromise—granted an unequal one—between the capitalist class and the very social classes it had unintentionally but nonetheless inexorably created. Though the business interests often struck their compromise under severe duress, and—as we have seen in numerous cases—did not always prevail, they were highly successful in maintaining ultimate control over the administration of educational reform. Working people got more schooling, but the form and content of schooling was more often than not effectively out of their hands.

The liberal professionals and enlightened school reformers—from Horace Mann and Henry Barnard, John Dewey and Ellwood Cubberly to Clark Kerr and Charles Silberman—were essential mediators of this compromise. These professional educators developed and propagated its ideological rationale, articulated its objectives, and helped shape its programs. Always involved in the implementation of educational change but never independent of its ultimate financial dependence on the business elite, the educational elite has not been able to mount an independent and sustained movement for overall reform.

The major actors with independent power in the educational arena were, and continue to be, labor and capital. We conclude that the structure and scope of the modern U.S. educational system cannot be explained without reference to both the demands of working people—for literacy, for the possibility of greater occupational mobility, for financial security, for personal growth, for social respect—and to the imperative of the capitalist class to construct an institution which would both enhance the labor power

of working people and help to reproduce the conditions for its exploitation. To a major extent the schools did successfully weld together the functions of accumulation and reproduction. By obscuring the underlying contradiction between accumulation and reproduction, the school system has played an important role in preserving the capitalist order; within that order, it has also brought tangible, if limited, benefits to the working people of the United States.

The expansion of schooling, like the expansion of the wage-labor system, has had consequences not only unanticipated by the capitalist and professional elites, but unwanted as well. The schools have been used to smother discontent. By embracing potentially radical elements in the society, the school system has helped to extract the political sting from fundamental social conflicts. Yet the basis for these conflicts continues in the underlying contradictions of the capitalist economy. Educational reformers have partially succeeded in displacing these conflicts out of the workplace and into the classroom. Thus, the contradictions of capitalism frequently surface as contradictions within the educational system. And what Charles Silberman has labeled the "crisis in the classroom" has opened up a host of educational alternatives.

Notes

1. Butte, in John E. Sturm and John A. Palmer, eds., *Democratic Legacy in Transition* (New York: Van Nostrand, 1971), p. 50.
2. *Ibid.*, p. 18.
3. *Ibid.*, pp. 27–29.
4. *Ibid.*, pp. 27–29.
5. *Ibid.*, p. 30.
6. Elwood P. Cubberly, *Public Education in the US.* (Boston: Houghton-Mifflin, 1934), pp. 164–165. Cubberly's writings on educational history are, in fact, difficult to categorize. Though clearly influenced by the conflict theory originally proposed by Carleton, Cubberly also expressed the evolutionary idealism represented by Butts. At times, he appears to espouse the technological perspective which we also discuss.
7. *Ibid.*
8. Frank Tracy Carleton, *History and Problems of Organized Labor* (Boston: D. C. Heath, 1911), p. 46.

9. S. M. Lipset, *Political Man: Social Bases of Politics* (New York: Doubleday and Co., 1960).

10. Trow, in Reinhard Bendix and Seymour Lipset, eds., *Class, Status and Power* (New York: The Free Press, 1966), p. 438.

11. See Michael Katz, *The Irony of Early School Reform* (Cambridge, Massachusetts: Harvard University Press, 1968); and Clarence J. Karier, Joel Spring, and Paul C. Violas, *Roots of Crisis* (Chicago: University of Illinois Press, 1973).

12. See Alexander J. Field, "Skill Requirements in Early Industrialization: The Case of Massachusetts," working paper in Economics, University of California at Berkeley, December 1973.

13. Hal Luft, "New England Textile Labor in the 1840's: From Yankee Farmgirl to Irish Immigrant," mimeo, January 1971.

14. Albert Fishlow, 'The American Common School Revival: Fact or Fancy?" in Henry Rosovsky, ed., *Industrialization in Two Systems* (New York: John Wiley & Sons, 1966); and M. Vanovskis and R. Bernard. "Women and Education in the Anti-Bellum U.S." (Madison, Univ. of Wisconsin Center for Demography and Ecology, working paper 73–7, 1973).

15. See Chapter 4.

16. David Tyack, *The One Best System: A History of American Urban Education* (Cambridge, Massachusetts: Harvard University Press, 1974).

17. Vanovskis and Bernard, *op. cit.* The figure refers to whites aged 5–19 years.

18. C Kaestle, *The Evolution of an Urban School System: New York City, 1750–1850* (Cambridge, Massachusetts: Harvard University Press, 1973).

19. Representative works are: Katz (1968), *op. cit.*; Michael Katz, *Class, Bureaucracy and Schools* (New York: Praeger Publishers, 1971a); Michael Katz, ed., *School Reform Past and Present* (Boston: Little, Brown and Company, 1971b); Karier, Spring, and Violas (1973), *op. cit.*; Marvin Lazerson, *Origin of Urban Schools: Public Education in Massachusetts* (Cambridge, Massachusetts: Harvard University Press, 1971); Kaestle (1973), *op. cit.*; Tyack (1974), *op. cit.*; Colin Greer, *The Great School Legend* (New York: Viking Press, 1973); Clarence J. Karier, *Shaping the American Educational State: 1900 to the Present* (New York: The Free Press, 1975).

20. Katz (1968), *op. cit.*

21. James O'Connor develops a related, but not identical, concept—the contradiction between accumulation and legitimation—in his *Fiscal Crisis of the State* (New York: St. Martin's Press, 1973).

22. Raymond Callahan, *Education and the Cult of Efficiency* (Chicago: University of Chicago Press, 1962); Joel H. Spring, *Education and the Rise of the Corporate State* (Boston: Beacon Press, 1972); Clarence J. Karier, "Ideology and Evaluation: In Quest of Meritocracy," Wisconsin Conference on Education and Evaluation at Madison, April 1973; Katz (1968), *op. cit.*; and Field (1973), *op. cit.*

23. Binstock (1970), *op. cit.*; Burton E. Rosenthal, "Educational Investments in Human Capital: The Significance of Stratification in the Labor Market," unpublished thesis, Harvard University, 1972.

24. U.S. Bureau of the Census, *Historical Statistics of the U.S.—Colonial Times to 1957* (Washington, D.C.: U.S. Government Printing Office, 1960).

25. Idem.

4 The Sociology of Education

Many years ago, the famous philosopher Alfred North Whitehead was asked, "Which is more important, facts or ideas?" He reflected for a while and said, "Ideas about facts." At its very core, sociological inquiry is about ideas and how they shape people's understandings of society. The desire to know and to transform society is not unique to sociologists; in fact, social curiosity has played a key role in humans' adaptive capacity. In one sense, sociology is simply a method for bringing social aspirations and fears into focus by forcing people to ask sharp and analytic questions about the societies and cultures in which they live. The tools of sociology can be thought of as empirical and conceptual. Sociology is empirical because most sociologists gather facts about society. Facts, however, do not speak for themselves; without arranging them into meaningful patterns, facts are virtually useless. Trying to uncover the underlying patterns that give larger meaning to facts is the purpose of making social theories. Often, teachers think that social theories are of little use in teaching children. Nothing could be further from the truth.

Without some idea of how the major elements in society fit together, teachers are at a loss in understanding the relation between school and society, how their own profession has evolved, and why students behave the way they do in school and outside of school. An understanding of society is essential if teachers are to develop as reflective practitioners. In a society that is becoming increasingly multiethnic and multiracial, the need for a sociological perspective among educators is urgent. In this chapter, we will explore some of the main elements of the sociology of education; these elements include theories about the relation between school and society, whether or not schooling makes a significant difference in individuals' lives, how schools influence social inequalities, and an examination of how school processes affect the lives of children, teachers, and other adults who are involved in the educational enterprise.

In her book *Education and Inequality* (1977), Persell provided a model for analyzing the relationship between school and society through four interrelated levels of sociological analysis (see Figure 4.1). The *societal* level includes the most general structures of a society, including its political and economic systems, its level of development, and its system of social stratification (or institutionalized levels of inequality). The *institutional* level includes a society's major institutions, such as the family, school, churches and synagogues, business and government, and the media, all of which play an important role in socialization. The *interpersonal* level includes the processes, symbols, and interactions that occur within such institutional settings. These include language, dress, face-to-face interactions, gestures, and rituals, all of which comprise everyday life. The *intrapsychic* level includes individual thoughts, beliefs, values, and feelings, which are to a large degree shaped by the society's institutions and interactions.

For sociologists, the issue of whether the individual actions are determined by external forces (*determinism*, called *behaviorism* in psychology) or whether individuals are capable of freely shaping the world (*voluntarism*, called *existentialism* in philosophy) is a crucial one. A sociological perspective, while recognizing human capacity for free will, emphasizes the power that external forces have on individual choices and how these are often related to group differences within the social stratification system.

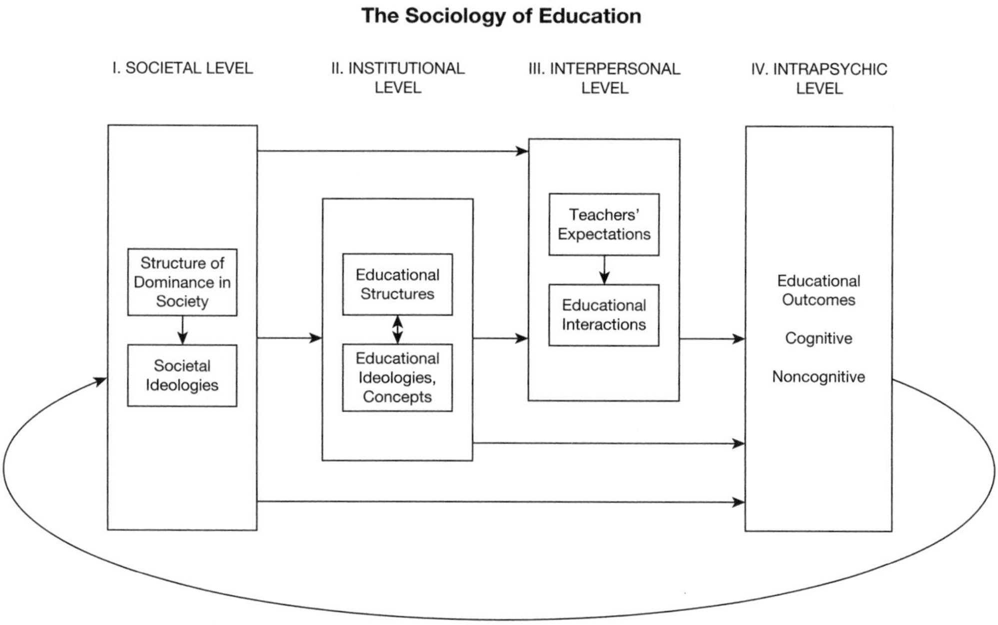

The Sociology of Education

Figure 4.1 Theoretical Model of Relevant Variables and Their Interrelationships.

Source: Reprinted with the permission of The Free Press, a division of Simon & Schuster Adult Publishing Group, from *Education and Inequality: A Theoretical Empirical Synthesis* by Caroline Hodges Persell. Copyright © 1977 by The Free Press. All rights reserved.

As you will see, functionalism is concerned with the ways that societal and institutional forces create, in Durkheim's terms, a collective conscience (society internalized in the individual) based on shared values. Conflict theory is concerned with the ways in which differences among groups at the societal level produce conflict and domination that may lead to change.

The Uses of Sociology for Teachers

How can people create schools that are more effective environments in which children can grow and learn? What is the relation between school and the larger society? Can schools produce more social and economic equality? These questions and many more have sparked the imaginations of generations of educators and those noneducators who have a deep interest in academic achievement, the welfare of children, and a more just, more open society. The kind of answers that are found to these questions will shape education and society for years. Without clear thinking, good information, and honest assessments, education as an institution is bound to move into the future like a ship without a rudder, floundering, directionless, and in danger of sinking. Before better educational programs can be designed, educators must know what works and what does not. The empirical and conceptual tools of sociology are ideally suited to this task because they guide one toward systematic thinking and realism about what is actually possible. There are those who would argue that sociology is not fully scientific, but compared to other ways of problem solving, sociology utilizes the principles and methods of science and, moreover, sociologists are self-critical. Because of the standards of the discipline, the work of sociologists must bear the scrutiny of other sociologists and the public at large.

Sociologists, then, are in a good position to view schools with a dispassionate eye and a critical awareness that simple solutions to complex educational problems are almost bound to fail and can be counterproductive. From these observations, it should be evident that teachers can learn a great deal from the sociology of education; for example, sociological research helps pinpoint the characteristics of schools that enable them to become effective learning environments. These characteristics include vigorous instructional leadership; a principal who makes clear, consistent, and fair decisions; an emphasis on discipline and a safe and orderly environment; instructional practices that focus on basic skills and academic achievement; collegiality among teachers who believe that students can and will learn; and frequent review of student progress.

To take another example, it is known that interactions in the classroom shape the learning experiences of the child. Sociologists have developed many techniques for understanding classroom interactions. One of the best known is Ned Flanders's Interaction Analysis Scale (Amidon & Flanders, 1971). This method involves the use of observers who watch classroom interactions and note these interactions on a standard scale. This process gives observers a thorough and objective measure of what really goes on in classrooms. Flanders hypothesized that student performance and learning is greatest when teacher influence is indirect—that is, when there were other classroom interactions besides "teacher talk." The hypothesis was upheld when observations showed that students in indirect teacher classrooms learned more and were more independent than students in classrooms where most, if not all, instructional activities were directed by the teacher.

As teachers, sociology provides you with a special analytic lens on education and school that, when you learn to use it, will give you greater insight and coherence in your approach to studying education. We hope that this clarity will help you improve your pedagogical practices and promote your professional growth. Part of becoming a professional is developing an intellectual and experiential frame of reference that is sufficiently sophisticated. It is our belief that this intellectual sophistication will help you integrate the world of education into its larger social context. This last observation leads to our first major issue in exploring how sociology can help us understand education in the "big picture." What is the relation between school and society?

The Relation between School and Society

Have you ever wondered why schools are the way they are? Why do teachers teach what they teach in the way they do? Can schools change society, or must society change if schools are to become different? Obviously, there are no simple answers to these questions; yet struggling to find answers, even for complex questions, is in itself a process of clarification. Sociologists of education often ask big questions about the relation between school and society because they believe that educators cannot really understand how schools operate, or why they operate as they do, without a working idea of how schools and society interact. To help them in this complex intellectual and empirical process, sociologists almost always have a theory about the organization of society and how it shapes the education of children. In particular, sociologists take an interest in how schools act as agents of cultural and social transmission.

Schools—as well as parents, churches and synagogues, and other groups—shape children's perceptions of the world by processes of *socialization*. That is, the values, beliefs, and norms of society are internalized within children so that they come to think and act like other members of society. In this sense, schools socially and culturally reproduce the existing society through the systematic socialization of its youngest members. Think of such a simple ritual as pledging allegiance to the flag. Through this culturally approved ritual, young children learn something about citizenship and patriotism.

Socialization processes can shape children's consciousness profoundly. Schools, for instance, wittingly or unwittingly, promote gender definitions and stereotypes when they segregate learning and extracurricular activities by gender, or when teachers allow boys to dominate class discussions and activities. Not only do schools shape students' perceptions and consciousness but they also act as important, perhaps the most important, sorters and selectors of students. Schools, through such practices as tracking, academically stratify students by curricular placement, which, in turn, influences the long-term social, economic, and cultural destinies of children. In effect, schools play a major role in determining who will get ahead in society and who will not.

How do schools select some students for educational mobility? Is it on the basis of merit or is it primarily on the basis of students' ascriptive characteristics, such as class, race, or gender? Or is it a combination of merit and social position that explains who gets into the educational "fast track" and who gets "cooled out"? The concept of equal educational opportunity is a key element in the belief system that maintains that the United States is a land of opportunity where hard work is rewarded. Is this belief based on real social facts or is it simply a myth that confuses people and leads them to believe that their relative social and economic failure is caused by personal inadequacies?

At an even deeper level, one might wonder why people study the subjects and materials they do. Who selects what people teach and learn, and why? Is knowledge value free or socially constructed? Can ideas ever be taken out of their contexts? For instance, history texts have traditionally overlooked the role of minorities and women in shaping U.S. society. How has this influenced people's perceptions of what is really historically significant and what is not?

Theoretical Perspectives

From these remarks, it should be apparent to you that the sociology of education is a contentious field and that the questions sociologists ask about the relation between school and society are fundamental and complex. Because the scope of these questions is so large, sociologists usually begin their studies with an overall picture of how society looks in its most basic form. This is where theory comes in. A good definition of *theory* is "an integration of all known principles, laws, and information pertaining to a specific area of study. This structure allows investigators to offer explanations for relative phenomenon and to create solutions to unique problems" (Woolfolk, 1990, p. 585). Theory is like an X-ray machine; it allows one to see past the visible and obvious, and examine the hidden structure. Unlike X-ray pictures, however, theoretical pictures of society are seldom crystal clear or easy to interpret. Why is this? Partly this is because people are members of society (i.e., people have been socialized by society) and it is very difficult to be objective or disinterested in the analysis of people. Theoretical pictures of society are created by human beings and interpreted by them. Thus, knowledge of the social world cannot be totally separated from one's personal and social situation. Still, should you let the fact that all knowledge is socially generated and interpreted discourage you from exploring those issues that shape your life? Obviously not. Without the struggle for objectivity and honesty, there is little hope that people can create a productive and just society.

Theory, then, as inadequate as it is, is one's best conceptual guide to understanding the relation between school and society because it gives one the intellectual scaffolding from which to hang empirical findings. Essentially, there are three major theories about the relation between school and society: functional, conflict, and interactional (for a full discussion of these theories, see Sadovnik, 2011b).

Functional Theories

Functional sociologists begin with a picture of society that stresses the *interdependence* of the social system; these researchers often examine how well the parts are integrated with each other. Functionalists view society as a kind of machine, where one part articulates with another to produce the dynamic energy required to make society work. Perhaps the earliest sociologist to embrace a functional point of view about the relation of school and society was Emile Durkheim (1858–1917), who virtually invented the sociology of education in the late nineteenth and early twentieth centuries. His major works include *Moral Education* (1962), *The Evolution of Educational Thought* (1977), and *Education and Sociology* (1956). While Durkheim recognized that education had taken different forms at different times and places, he believed that education, in virtually all societies, was of critical importance in creating the moral unity necessary for social cohesion and harmony. For Durkheim, moral values were the foundation of society.

Durkheim's emphasis on values and cohesion set the tone for how present-day functionalists approach the study of education. Functionalists tend to assume that consensus is the normal state in society and that conflict represents a breakdown of shared values. In a highly integrated, well-functioning society, schools socialize students into the appropriate values, and sort and select students according to their abilities. Educational reform, then, from a functional point of view, is supposed to create structures, programs, and curricula that are technically advanced, rational, and encourage social unity. It should be evident that most U.S. educators and educational reformers implicitly base their reform suggestions on functional theories of schooling. When, for example, *A Nation at Risk* was released in 1983, the argument was made by the authors of the report that schools were responsible for a whole host of social and economic problems. There was no suggestion that perhaps education might not have the power to overcome deep, social, and economic problems without changing other aspects of U.S. society.

Conflict Theories

Not all sociologists of education believe that society is held together by shared values alone. Some sociologists argue that the social order is not based on some collective agreement, but on the ability of dominant groups to impose their will on subordinate groups through force, cooptation, and manipulation. In this view, the glue of society is economic, political, cultural, and military power. Ideologies or intellectual justifications created by the powerful are designed to enhance their position by legitimizing inequality and the unequal distribution of material and cultural goods as an inevitable outcome of biology or history. Clearly, conflict sociologists do not see the relation between school and society as unproblematic or straightforward. Whereas functionalists emphasize cohesion in explaining social order, conflict sociologists emphasize struggle. From a conflict point of view, schools are similar to social battlefields, where students struggle against teachers, teachers against administrators, and so on. These antagonisms, however, are most often muted for two reasons: the authority and power of the school and the achievement ideology. In effect, the achievement ideology convinces students and teachers that schools promote learning, and sort and select students according to their abilities and not according to their social status. In this view, the achievement ideology disguises the real power relations within the school, which, in turn, reflect and correspond to the power relations within the larger society (Bowles & Gintis, 1976).

Although Karl Marx (1818–1883) did not write a great deal about education specifically, he is the intellectual founder of the conflict school in the sociology of education. His analytic imagination and moral outrage were sparked by the social conditions found in Europe in the mid-nineteenth century. Industrialization and urbanization had produced a new class of workers—the proletariat—who lived in poverty, worked up to 18 hours a day, and had little, if any, hope of creating a better life for their children. Marx believed that the class system, which separated owners from workers and workers from the benefits of their own labor, made class struggle inevitable. He believed that, in the end, the proletariat would rise up and overthrow the capitalists, and, in doing so, establish a new society where men and women would no longer be alienated from their labor.

Marx's powerful and often compelling critique of early capitalism has provided the intellectual energy for subsequent generations of liberal and leftist thinkers who believe that the only way to a more just and productive society is the abolition or modification of capitalism and the introduction of socialism. Political economists Bowles and Gintis, in their book *Schooling in Capitalist America* (1976), used a Marxist perspective for examining the growth of the U.S. public school. To their minds, there is a direct correspondence between the organization of schools and the organization of society, and, until society is fundamentally changed, there is little hope of real school reform. It has been argued by other conflict sociologists of education, however, that traditional Marxism is too deterministic and overlooks the power of culture and human agency in promoting change.

An early conflict sociologist who took a slightly different theoretical orientation when viewing society was Max Weber (1864–1920). Like Marx, Weber was convinced that power relations between dominant and subordinate groups structured societies, but, unlike Marx, Weber believed that class differences alone could not capture the complex ways human beings form hierarchies and belief systems that make these hierarchies seem just and inevitable. Thus, Weber examined status cultures as well as class position as an important sociological concept, because it alerts one to the fact that people identify their group by what they consume and with whom they socialize.

Weber also recognized that political and military power could be exercised by the state, without direct reference to the wishes of the dominant classes. Moreover, Weber had an acute and critical awareness of how bureaucracy was becoming the dominant type of authority in the modern state and how bureaucratic ways of thinking were bound to shape educational reforms. Weber made the distinction between the "specialist" and the "cultivated" man. What should be the goal of education—training individuals for employment or for thinking? Or are these two goals compatible?

The Weberian approach to studying the relation between school and society has developed into a compelling and informative tradition of sociological research. Researchers in this tradition tend to analyze school organizations and processes from the point of view of status competition and organizational constraints. One of the first U.S. sociologists of education to use these concepts was Willard Waller. In *The Sociology of Teaching* (1965), Waller portrayed schools as autocracies in a state of "perilous equilibrium." Without continuous vigilance, schools would erupt into anarchy because students are essentially forced to go to school against their will. To Waller's mind, rational models of school organization only disguise the inherent tension that pervades the schooling process. Waller's perspective is shared by many contemporary conflict theorists who see schools as oppressive and demeaning, and portray student noncompliance with school rules as a form of resistance.

Another major research tradition that has emerged from the Weberian school of thought is represented by Randall Collins (1971, 1979), who has maintained that educational expansion is best explained by status group struggle. He argued that educational credentials, such as college diplomas, are primarily status symbols rather than indicators of actual achievement. The rise of credentialism does not indicate that society is becoming more expert, but that education is increasingly used by dominant groups to secure more advantageous places for themselves and their children within the occupation and social structure.

A variation of conflict theory that has captured the imagination of some U.S. sociologists began in France and England during the 1960s. Unlike most Marxists who tend to emphasize the economic structure of society, cultural reproduction theorists, such as Bourdieu and Passeron (1977), examined how "cultural capital"—knowledge and experiences related to art, music, and literature—and "social capital"—social networks and connections—are passed on by families and schools. The concepts of cultural and social capital are important because they suggest that, in understanding the transmission of inequalities, one ought to recognize that the cultural and social characteristics of individuals and groups are significant indicators of status and class position. More recently, Lareau (2003, 2011) provided an application of Bourdieu to the understanding of how social class differences in social capital within family and their relationship to child rearing and schooling contributes to the reproduction of social and educational inequalties. Finally, the work of Basil Bernstein (1977, 1990, 1996) analyzed how communication, family, and educational codes (patterns and processes that create meaning and understanding) also contribute to social and educational inequalities.

A growing body of literature suggests that schools pass on to graduates specific social identities that either enhance or hinder their life chances. For example, a graduate from an elite prep. school has educational and social advantages over many public school graduates in terms of college attendance and occupational mobility. This advantage has very little to do with what prep. school students learn in school, and a great deal to do with the power of their schools' reputations for educating members of the upper class. The theories of Bourdieu and Passeron extend the work of other sociologists who have argued persuasively that human culture cannot be understood as an isolated and self-contained object of study but must be examined as part of a larger social and cultural structure. To understand the impact of culture on the lives of individuals and groups, one must understand the meanings that are attributed to cultural experiences by those who participate in them (Mannheim, 1952).

The conflict perspective, then, offers important insights about the relation between school and society. As you think about schools and education, we hope that you will utilize functional and conflict theoretical perspectives as a way of organizing your readings and perceptions. Before we turn from theory to more empirical issues about students and schools, there is a theoretical perspective that ought not to be overlooked.

Interactional Theories

Interactional theories about the relation of school and society are primarily critiques and extensions of the functional and conflict perspectives. The critique arises from the observation that functional and conflict theories are very abstract, and emphasize structure and process at a very general (macrosociological) level of analysis. Although this level of analysis helps in understanding education in the "big picture," macrosociological theories hardly provide an interpretable snapshot of what schools are like on an everyday level. What do students and teachers actually do in school? Interactional theories attempt to make the commonplace strange by turning on their heads everyday taken-for-granted behaviors and interactions between students and students, and between students and teachers. It is exactly what one does not question that is most problematic at a deep level. For example, the processes by which students are labeled gifted or learning disabled are, from an interactional point of view, important to analyze, because such processes carry with them many implicit assumptions about learning and children. By examining the microsociological or the interactional aspects of school life, people are less likely to create theories that are logical and eloquent, but without meaningful content.

Some of the sociology of education's most brilliant theorists have attempted to synthesize the macro- and microsociological approaches. Basil Bernstein (1990), for instance, has argued that the structural aspects of the educational system and the interactional aspects of the system reflect each other and must be viewed wholistically. He has examined how speech patterns reflect students' social class backgrounds and how students from working-class backgrounds are at a disadvantage in the school setting because schools are essentially middle-class organizations. Bernstein has combined a class analysis with an interactional analysis, which links language with educational processes and outcomes.

In this section, we have tried to give you a sense of how theory can be used to explain the relation between school and society. These theories provide background metaphors and analytic focuses for the work of sociologists. We turn now to some specific areas of research that have interested sociologists of education for many years.

Effects of Schooling on Individuals

Do schools matter? This provocative question is one that most people feel they have already answered. It is safe to say that most Americans believe that schools have a significant impact on learning and on social and economic mobility. In this section, we examine some of the effects of schooling on individuals to see what the relative importance of schooling is in terms of what people learn, employment, job performance, income, and mobility.

Knowledge and Attitudes

It may be surprising to learn that sociologists of education disagree strongly about the relative importance of schooling in terms of what knowledge and attitudes young people acquire in school. Nobody argues that schools have no impact on student development, but there are sharp divisions among researchers about how significant school effects are, when taking into account students' social class background. Generally, it is found that the higher the social class background of the student, the higher his or her achievement level. According to such researchers as Coleman and colleagues (1966) and Jencks and colleagues (1972), differences between schools account for very little of the differences in student achievement. Is this true? Does this finding make sense of the world as we know it? Does it make no difference whether a student attends a school in a wealthy suburb or an underfinanced, overcrowded school in the inner city?

Actually, other research indicates that differences between schools in terms of their academic programs and policies do make differences in student learning. One of the first researchers to show that differences in schools are directly related to differences in student outcomes was Ron Edmonds (1979a, 1979b), the pioneer of the effective schools movement. As mentioned earlier, the effective schools research demonstrates that academically oriented schools do produce higher rates of learning. More recent research, which compares public and private schools, also indicates that in schools where students are compelled to take academic subjects and where there is consistent discipline, student achievement levels go up. An important study by Heyns (1978) found that sixth- and seventh-grade students who went to summer school, used the library, and read a great deal in the summer made greater gains in knowledge than pupils who did not study in the summer. Moreover, it has been found that the actual amount of time students spend in school is directly related to how much they learn.

Other research has indicated that the more education individuals receive, the more likely they are to read newspapers, books, and magazines, and to take part in politics and public affairs. More highly educated people are also more likely to be liberal in their political and social attitudes. Education is also related to individuals' sense of well-being and self-esteem. Thus, it is clear that, even taking into account the importance of individual social class background when evaluating the impact of education, more years of schooling leads to greater knowledge and social participation.

Employment

Most students believe that graduating from college will lead to greater employment opportunities, and they are right. In 1986, about 54 percent of the 8 million college graduates in the United States entered professional and technical jobs. Research has shown that large organizations, such as corporations, require high levels of education for white-collar, managerial, or administrative jobs (Collins, 1971). In fact, as we discussed earlier, credential inflation has led to the expectation among employers that their employees will have an ever-increasing amount of formal education. But do well-educated employees actually do a better job? Surprisingly, most research has shown that the amount of education is only weakly related to job performance. Berg (1970), for instance, studied factory workers, maintenance workers, department store clerks, technicians, secretaries, bank tellers, engineers, industrial research scientists, military personnel, and federal civil service employers and found that the level of education was essentially unrelated to job performance. From this evidence, it seems clear that schools act as gatekeepers in determining who will get employed in high-status occupations, but schools do not provide significant job skills for their graduates. People learn how to do their jobs by doing them, which is not so surprising.

The economic and social worth of an academic credential, however, cannot be fully measured by examining its effects on job performance. Perhaps because academic credentials help individuals to obtain higher-status jobs early in their careers, possession of a college degree is significantly related to higher income. In 2011, high school graduates earned, on average, $32,552; college graduates earned $53,976 (U.S. Bureau of the Census, 2003a). Among household heads at all levels of education, women earned less than men. Women with professional degrees, on average, earned considerably less than men with college degrees. These differences are due to occupational segregation by sex, pay discrimination, and the fact that women, more than men, take time off or work part-time due to family commitments.

These general findings, however, mask a great deal of variation when examining the relation between educational level and income level. According to some research, young African-American males who are highly educated earn as much as their white male counterparts, but whether this remains true across the life course remains to be seen. Many other factors besides education affect how much income people earn in their lifetimes; these include type of employer, age, union membership, and social class background. In fact, even the most thorough research cannot demonstrate that more than one-third of income is directly attributable to level of education. So, getting a college and professional degree is important for earning more money, but education alone does not fully explain differences in levels of income.

Education and Mobility

The belief that occupational and social mobility begin at the schoolhouse door is a critical component of the American ethos. As part of what might be termed *civil religion*, there is an abiding faith among most Americans that education is the great equalizer in the "great status race." Of course, not everybody subscribes to this faith. In a fascinating study, MacLeod (1995) found that working-class boys often reject the prevailing "attainment through education" ethos by emphasizing their relative lack of economic and social mobility through cultural values that glorify physical hardness, manual labor, and a certain sense of fatalism. In general, however, most Americans believe that more education leads to economic and social mobility; individuals rise and fall based on their merit. Turner (1960) called this *contest* mobility. He compared *contest* mobility in the United States to *sponsored* mobility in the United Kingdom, where students are selected at an early age for academic and university education and where social class background is very important in determining who will receive academic or vocational training.

In this regard, keep in mind another important distinction when thinking of education and mobility. Hopper (1971) has made the point that there is a difference between educational *amount* and educational *route*. That is, the number of years of education is one measure of educational attainment, but *where* people go to school also affects their mobility. Private and public school students may receive the same amount of education, but a private school diploma may act as a "mobility escalator" because it represents a more prestigious educational route (Cookson & Persell, 1985).

The debate as to whether the public school is really the great equalizer has not been resolved. For some groups, such as the middle class, increased education may be directly linked to upward occupational mobility; for the poor and rich, education may have little to do with mobility. An educational degree alone cannot lift many people out of poverty, and upper-class individuals do not lose their social class position if they fail to achieve a high-status educational degree. In general, the data do not support the belief that education alone provides individuals with great amounts of economic and social mobility.

Rosenbaum (1976) has offered one suggestion as to why this may be the case. He likened mobility to *tournament selection*, where winners are allowed to proceed to the next round of competition, and losers are dropped from the competition. Players (students) can be eliminated, but winners must still continue to compete. The problem with this tournament, however, is that the criteria for winning and losing include a great many variables that are related to students' social class, race, and gender characteristics, as well as merit variables, such as grade-point average and SAT scores. The complex interplay between merit and privilege creates a tournament where the rules are not entirely even-handed and not everyone has the opportunity to set the rules. Without a doubt, the relation between education and mobility will continue to be debated among scholars and policy makers. The popular belief that education opens the doors of opportunity, however, is likely to remain firmly embedded in the American ethos.

Inside the Schools

How can the sociology of education help one to understand schools in terms of their objectives, cultures, and how they shape students' perceptions and expectations? In other words, how do sociologists look at schools from an organizational point of view? How do such organizational characteristics as curricula, teacher behaviors, and student peer groups shape learning and social growth? Since most people are apt to think about learning and growth from a psychological perspective, it is illuminating to stand back and speculate how school structures can also influence student outcomes. Think of something as simple as school size. Larger schools can offer students more in the way of facilities, but large schools are also more bureaucratic and may restrain initiative. Smaller schools may allow more student and teacher freedom, but small schools often lack resources. In general, schools are getting larger, if for no other reason than they are cost-effective. Whether schools are large or small, however, the content of what they teach is a topic of important study.

Curriculum expresses culture. The question is, Whose culture? For some time, sociologists of education have pointed out that curricula are not value free; they are expressions of certain groups' ideas, beliefs, and prejudices. Knowing something about the bias and viewpoints of those who write curricula awakens one to the relativity of knowledge, and its social and cultural context.

As you know, not all students study the same curriculum. It is also a fact that curriculum placement within schools has a direct impact on the probabilities of students attending college. In 2000, approximately 47 percent of public high school students took what is called a college preparatory course of study, which includes such subjects as English, history, science, math, and foreign language; 10 percent took a vocational program and approximately 43 percent enrolled in a general program, which combines such courses as English with accounting and clerical courses (U.S. Department of Education, National Center for Education Statistics, 2000a). In private schools, virtually all students are enrolled in an academic curriculum. Research has shown that curricular placement is the single biggest determinant of college attendance (Lee & Bryk, 1989; Bryk, Lee, & Holland, 1993). For example, in 1992, there were significant differences among white, African-American, Hispanic-American, and Asian-American high school students with regard to track placement. Some 46 percent of white students were in the college track, compared to 35 percent of African-American students, 31 percent of Hispanic-American students, 51 percent of Asian-American students, and 23 percent of American-Indian students. Some 11 percent of white students were in the vocational track; compared to 15 percent of African-American students, 13 percent of Hispanic-American students, 9 percent of Asian-American students, and 17 percent of American-Indian students. Some 43 percent of white students were in the general track, compared to 49 percent of African-American students, 56 percent of Hispanic-American students, 40 percent of Asian-American students, and 61 percent of American-Indian students (U.S. Department of Education, National Center for Educational Statistics, 1997a). In 2010, 16.9 percent of all students in the United States scored a 3 or higher on an AP exam; however, only 3.9 percent of African-American students scored a 3 or higher on at least one AP exam (Collegeboard, 2012). We will have a great deal to say about curriculum later in this book, but for now, it may be useful to underscore the importance of curriculum when studying schools from a sociological perspective, especially in terms of cultural transmission and the selective channelling of opportunity.

Teacher Behavior

It may seem obvious, but teachers have a huge impact on student learning and behavior. Jackson (1968) found that teachers have as many as 1,000 interpersonal contacts each day with children in their classrooms. Teachers are extremely busy people; they must also wear many different occupational hats: instructor, disciplinarian, bureaucrat, employer, friend, confidant, educator, and so on. Ingersoll (2004) supports these findings. These various roles sometimes are compatible with each other, and sometimes they are not. This can lead to *role strain*, where such conflicting demands are placed on teachers that they cannot feel totally comfortable in any role. Could this be a cause of teacher burnout?

Clearly, teachers are models for students and, as instructional leaders, teachers set standards for students and influence student self-esteem and sense of efficacy. In a fascinating study conducted by Rosenthal and Jacobson (1968), teachers' expectations of students were found to directly influence student achievement. The researchers told some teachers in a California elementary school that children in their classes were likely to have a mental growth spurt that year. In reality, the intelligence test that the children had taken revealed nothing about their potential achievement level. The students had been placed in their classes randomly. At the end of the year, the researchers returned to school and gave another test to see which children had improved. Although all the children improved somewhat, those labeled "spurters" made significantly greater achievement gains than other children, especially in the first and second grades. Thus, the labels that teachers apply to children can influence actual performance. This form of *self-fulfilling prophecy* indicates that teachers' expectations play a major role in encouraging or discouraging students to work to their full potential.

Persell (1977) found that when teachers demanded more from their students and praised them more, students learned more and felt better about themselves. Research indicates that many teachers have lower expectations for minority and working-class students; this suggests that these students may be trapped within a vicious cycle of low expectation–low achievement–low expectation. In part, this cycle of failure may be responsible for high dropout rates and failure to achieve at grade level. Of course, teachers cannot be held responsible for all the failures of education; there are many nonpedagogic reasons why U.S. schools are failing to educate so many children. Teachers should not be scapegoated for society's problems, but the findings on teacher expectations do indicate that the attitudes of teachers toward their students may have a significant influence on student achievement and perceptions of self. Also, it is important not to overlook the fact that there are many outstanding teachers who are dedicated and inspirational, and who have helped motivate students to do their best.

Student Peer Groups and Alienation

When you reflect on your high school and junior high experiences, you undoubtedly have strong memories of your fellow students and the various social groups that they created. Almost nobody wants to be labeled a "nerd," and in most schools, the student culture idealizes athletic ability, looks, and that detached style that indicates "coolness." In a sense, the adult culture of the teachers and administrators is in conflict with the student culture. This conflict can lead to alienation and even violence.

Stinchcombe (1964) found, for instance, that students in vocational programs and headed toward low-status jobs were the students most likely to join a rebellious subculture. In fact, student violence continues to be a problem. Students are not only attacking each other in increasing numbers but they are also assaulting teachers. The number of beatings, rapes, and even murders that are perpetrated against teachers has become something of a national scandal, but compared to what students do to each other, the danger for teachers is minimal. Some argue that school violence is increasing because teachers are underpaid and classes are too large. This may explain some of the violence, but it certainly does not explain all of it. A hundred years ago, teachers taught for little money and had class sizes double or triple present-day standards and there was little school violence. In today's culture, violence is far more acceptable, even glorified in the popular media. Being "bad" is misconstrued as being tough and smart. School children are bombarded with imaginary and actual violence in their homes, in their schools, and on the streets. It has been estimated that by the time the average child is 12 years old, he or she has been exposed to 18,000 television murders.

Student subcultures continue to be important after high school. There are four major types of college students: careerists, intellectuals, strivers, and unconnected. *Careerists* generally came from middle- and upper middle-class backgrounds, won few academic honors, lost confidence during college, and were not intellectually motivated by their experience. *Intellectuals* usually came from highly educated families, studied in the humanities, were politically involved, and earned many academic honors. *Strivers* very often had a working-class background, came from ethnic or racial minorities, worked hard, often did not have a high grade-point average, but graduated with a real sense of accomplishment. The *unconnected* came from all backgrounds, participated in few extracurricular activities, and were the least satisfied among all the groups with their college experience.

It should be evident, then, that student cultures play an important role in shaping students' educational experiences. We also hope that it is evident to you that looking within school from a sociological perspective can be very illuminating. Schools are far more than mere collections of individuals; they develop cultures, traditions, and restraints that profoundly influence those who work and study within them. They socialize and sort and select students and, in doing so, reproduce society. In the next section, we examine an issue of critical importance: How do schools reproduce social, cultural, and economic inequalities?

Education and Inequality

Suppose we asked you to draw a picture of American society. How would it look? Like a circle? A square? A shapeless blob? Let's rephrase this question a bit. In terms of the distribution of income, power, and property, would you say that the shape of American society is flat? Probably not. Most of us know that income, power, and property are unevenly distributed in society. There are the "haves" and the "have-nots." Thinking figuratively again, most of us would agree that the economic and social structure of the U.S. population resembles a triangle where most of the people can be found at the base.

In the United States, there are essentially five classes: the *upper class*, with 1–3 percent of the total U.S. population; the *upper middle class*, with 10–15 percent of the population; the *lower middle class*, with 25 percent of the population; the *working class*, with 40 percent of the population; and the *lower* or *underclass*, with 20 percent of the population. The distribution of income, power, and property among these classes is highly uneven. The top fifth of the U.S. population owns three-fourths of the nation's wealth, whereas the remaining four-fifths own only one-fourth of the wealth (U.S. Bureau of the Census, 1998, 2003a). The bottom fifth own less than 0.2 percent of the nation's wealth. In 1987, the top fifth of U.S. families earned 43.7 percent of all income, whereas the bottom fifth earned 4.6 percent of the income. Moreover, by 1998, income differences became wider and the United States increasingly became a bipolar society of great wealth, great poverty, and an ever-shrinking middle class (U.S. Bureau of the Census, 1998, 2003a). In 2009, the top fifth of U.S. families earned 50.3 percent of all income, whereas the bottom fifth earned 3.4 percent of the income (U.S. Bureau of the Census, 2012).

Social class differences are not only reflected in differences in income but in other social characteristics such as education, family and child-rearing practices, occupation, place of residence, political involvement, health, consumer behavior, and religious belief. In short, if you know a family's or individual's class position, you have a good idea about their life-style and life chances. Moreover, class influences what people think, by shaping the way in which they think. Class position creates selective perception which, in turn, creates a world view that "explains" inequalities. Ideology, then, grows out of the class system and reinforces the class system through beliefs that justify or condemn the status quo. Those who are oppressed by the class system may resist and revolt, and those who benefit usually cooperate with and defend the current form of *social stratification*.

People, however, are not just stratified by class; they are also stratified by race, ethnicity, age, and gender. In short, Americans live in a hierarchical society where mobility is blocked because of structural inequalities that have little or nothing to do with individuals' merits or abilities.

For some time, sociologists have speculated and argued about whether schools mitigate social inequalities by providing opportunities for those who would not normally have them. Can schools create a more open society? This is a topic of immense importance and complexity. In later chapters, we will examine this issue in depth; for now, however, it might be useful to review some of the major ways that schools help transmit social and economic inequalities.

Inadequate Schools

Perhaps the most obvious way that schools reproduce inequalities is through inadequate schools. We have already discussed the crisis in U.S. education and how numerous critics of contemporary schooling have pointed out that the way in which children are educated today will not prepare them for productive and fulfilling lives in the future. Urban education, in particular, has failed to educate minority and poor children. Moreover, differences between schools and school systems reinforce existing inequalities. Students who attend suburban schools and private schools get a better educational experience than other children (Coleman, Hoffer, & Kilgore, 1982). Students who attend the most elite private schools obtain substantial educational benefits, both in terms of their actual educational experience and the social value of their diplomas (Cookson & Persell, 1985).

Tracking

There is compelling evidence that within-school tracking has a critical impact on student mobility (Lucas, 2002; Oakes, 1985, 2005; Tyson, 2011). In principle, *tracking* refers to the placement of students in curricular programs based on students' abilities and inclinations. In reality, it has been found in many thorough studies that tracking decisions are often based on other criteria, such as students' class or race. By and large, working-class students end up in vocational tracks and middle-class students in academic tracks. Studies have shown that students placed in "high-ability" tracks spend more time on actual teaching and learning activities; are able to use more interesting materials; and consistently receive better teachers, better laboratory facilities, and more extracurricular activities than do their lower-track peers (Oakes, 1985; Goodlad, 1984). Moreover, track placement directly affects cognitive development (Rosenbaum, 1976). Students in lower tracks experience more alienation and authoritarian teachers than high-track students.

De Facto Segregation

Another important way that schools reinforce (even create) inequalities, particularly racial and ethnic inequalities, is through de facto segregation. In the previous chapter, we discussed in some depth the effects of segregated schools on student achievement, not to mention the issue of basic rights and equities. Although this issue is far from resolved, most of the evidence indicates that racially mixed schools benefit minorities and do *not* suppress white achievement. One study found that African-Americans from low-income communities who attended racially mixed schools were more likely to graduate from high school and college than similar African-American children who attended segregated schools. Moreover, African-American students who attended integrated schools were less likely to be arrested by the police, more likely to live in desegregated neighborhoods, and women were less likely to have a child before the age of 18. Thus, racial integration at the school level seems to be beneficial to minority students, and there is no conclusive evidence that majority students are harmed by integration.

The issue of segregation, or resegregation, will be with society for a long time, if for no other reason than most people live in racially segregated neighborhoods. Groups and individuals who believe that students should be allowed to choose the schools they wish to attend argue that school choice will break down the barriers to integration created by racially segregated neighborhoods. Whether school choice would really end segregation is still very debatable; certainly, the historical evidence from the South during the 1960s and 1970s is not reassuring. During this period, white families set up their own academies in order to avoid racially integrated public schools. More recent evidence indicates that following a number of court decisions, including *Swan* v. *Charlotte Mecklenburg* and *Parents Involved in Community Schools* v. *Seattle School District No. 1*, have resulted in significant resegregation, a pattern representative of the country (UCLA Civil Rights Project, 2012). In addition, the evidence on school choice indicates that it has often resulted in segregated rather than integrated schools (UCLA Civil Rights Project, 2012).

Gender

Another way that schools reproduce inequalities is through gender discrimination. Men and women do not share equally in U.S. society. Men are frequently paid more than women for the same work, and women, in general, have fewer occupational opportunities than men. Although this gender gap has been somewhat reduced for middle- and upper-middle-class women in the last decade, inequalities persist, particularly for working-class and lower-class women. How do schools perpetuate this problem?

Although girls usually start school cognitively and socially ahead of boys, by the end of high school, girls have lower self-esteem and lower aspirations than do boys. Somewhere during the high school years, in particular, girls begin to show signs of not living up to their potential. Is it the gender composition of the faculty and staff that influences girls to lower their aspirations?

Most teachers are female, whereas most administrators are male; could this be sending a subliminal message to girls that they are somehow subordinate to men? Do teachers treat boys and girls differently by stereotyping them by behavior? Are girls supposed to be "nice" and "feminine" while boys are allowed to act out and gain the center of attention? Studies do show that boys get more teacher attention (good and bad) than girls.

Traditionally, textbooks have been biased against women by ignoring their accomplishments and social contributions. Until very recently, there was little discussion in textbooks of sexism or gender bias. Discrimination need not always be overt. Often, gender bias is subtle; for instance, women go to college at higher rates than men, but they often go to two-year colleges or to less academically prestigious institutions.

Over the past two decades, however, the gender gap in academic achievement has all but disappeared, with female students outperforming males in language arts and social studies, and closing the gap significantly in mathematics, sciences, and having higher college attendance rates, albeit much lower participation in science, technology, engineering, and mathematics (STEM) disciplines (Arnot, David, & Weiner, 1999; Borman, Tyson, & Halperin, 2010; Buchmann, 2009; Buchmann, DiPrete, & McDaniel, 2008).

Thus, schools are active organizational agents in recreating gender inequalities. However, schools alone should not be held accountable for gender discrimination. This form of social stratification is rooted in the values and organization of society; schools in some ways only reflect these societal problems. This is not to say that educators *intend* to reproduce class, ethnic, racial, and gender inequalities, but the *consequences* of certain school policies and processes may reproduce these inequalities. Moreover, there is some evidence that for middle-class students, schooling does provide a "channel of attainment." In the main, however, the best evidence indicates that schools, despite educators' best intentions, tend to reproduce social inequalities. A major aspect of any meaningful reform movement must address this issue if schools are really to open doors to equal opportunity.

Sociology and the Current Educational Crisis

To grasp the magnitude of the current crisis in U.S. education, it is essential to recognize that at least one-third of the nation's children are at risk at failing in school, even before they enter kindergarten. Demographer Harold Hodgkinson (1991) described the condition of U.S. children in stark and poignant terms. Since 1987, one-fourth of all preschool children in the United States live in poverty. In 1990, approximately 350,000 children were born to mothers who were addicted to cocaine during pregnancy. Some 15 million children are being reared by single mothers whose family income averages about $11,400 a year. At least 2 million school-age children have no adult supervision after school, and every night between 50,000 and 200,000 children have no home. By 2009, these figures indicated an increase in these measures of poverty. As of 2009, there were 15.5 million children from families living in poverty and an additional 31.9 million children from low-income families. How can schools help children to become productive and happy adults when so many children begin life with such severe disadvantages?

The sociological imagination helps one understand what is and what can be when one tries to imagine schools and school systems that meet the challenges that are facing today's children and young adults. The current educational crisis is complex, and solutions to the pressing problems are difficult to find. But people should not despair; we need to begin the work of reconstructing U.S. education. Sociologists ask the tough questions about schools and they search for answers by collecting data. Sometimes the data support preconceived beliefs, sometimes they do not. In either case, sociologists are committed to finding out the truth about the relationship between school and society, and it is this truth-seeking activity that is most likely to lead to meeting the challenges facing education today.

The following selections illustrate the sociological imagination applied to educational problems. The articles address important issues concerning the relationship between school and society and illustrate Persell's model of the levels of sociological analysis. The first article, "The Contribution of Schooling to the Learning of Norms," by sociologist Robert Dreeben, illustrates the functionalist theory of education through an analysis of how the schools socialize children into the norms of society.

The second selection, written by sociologist Ray C. Rist, "On Understanding the Processes of Schooling: The Contributions of Labeling Theory," provides an illustration of the interpretive or interactionist perspective. Rist demonstrates how labeling theory provides a useful tool for understanding what goes on inside schools. The interactionist perspective, as Rist suggests, is an alternative to the more structural approaches of functionalism and conflict theory.

The third selection, "The Politics of Culture: Understanding Local Political Resistance to Detracking in Racially Mixed Schools," written by sociologists Amy Stuart Wells and Irene Serna, examines how affluent parents resist detracking policies. This article illustrates the ways in which conflict theory and interaction theory, used together, help us understand how power and privilege affect school practices and policies.

The Contribution of Schooling to the Learning of Norms

Robert Dreeben

This paper is concerned with the familiar phenomenon known as schooling. It departs from the usual approaches to education in that the problems of instruction and its direct outcomes are of peripheral interest. The main argument is based on the observation that schools and the classrooms within them have a characteristic pattern of organizational properties different from those of other agencies in which socialization takes place and on the contention that what children learn derives as much from the nature of their experiences in the school setting as from what they are taught.

Traditional approaches to understanding the educational process usually deal with the explicit goals of schools as expressed in curriculum content: the cognitive skills involved in reading, arithmetic, and the like; subject matter content; national tradition; vocational skills; and a multitude of good things such as citizenship, self-confidence, tolerance, patriotism, cooperation, and benevolent attitudes of various kinds. They are also concerned with pedagogy: methods of instruction considered broadly enough to include motivation and quasi-therapeutic activities as well as didactics more narrowly conceived. One indication that curriculum and pedagogy occupy a central place in educational thinking is the existence of a massive literature reporting research devoted overwhelmingly to problems in these two areas and to evaluations of instructional effectiveness in bringing about curricular outcomes.[1]

There is no question but that schools are engaged in an instructional enterprise, but the preoccupation with instruction has been accompanied by the neglect of other equally important problems. It is my contention that the traditional conception of schooling as an instructional process, primarily cognitive in nature, is at best only partially tenable. That is, what pupils learn is in part some function of what is taught; but what *is* learned and from what experiences remain open questions. Doubtless the dissemination of knowledge is high on the school's agenda; but does such dissemination represent its peculiar contribution?

Instruction and knowledge, even at a high level, are made available to children outside the school: through the family, the mass media, travel, museums, libraries, and personal contacts with a variety of people. Perhaps the inconclusiveness of research designed to measure the impact of teaching on learning is attributable in part to the fact that many social agencies other than schools contribute to the acquisition of similar knowledge generally thought to fall largely within the school's jurisdiction.

Even though other agencies may resemble schools in their instructional impact, schools do have structural characteristics that distinguish them sharply from other settings—most particularly the family—contributing to the socialization of children, characteristics whose obviousness and familiarity probably account for their neglect. For example:

1. Responsibility for the control of schools and for instruction in the classroom rests in the hands of adults who are not the kinsmen of pupils.
2. Children leave the household daily to attend school but return at the close of the day; that is, they continue their active membership and participation in the family.
3. Schools are distinguished structurally according to level; despite the similarities between elementary and secondary levels, there are conspicuous differences involving:
    a. variation in the heterogeneity of the student body related to school district size;
    b. degree of differentiation of the teaching staff based upon subject matter specialization;
    c. presence or absence of formal provision for tracking pupils based largely on past academic achievement;
    d. variation in the number of pupils that each teacher confronts daily.
4. Pupils progress through school grade-by-grade at yearly intervals, each time severing associations with one set of teachers and establishing associations with a new set (unlike the family where children's relationships with parents do not follow a sequential pattern of severance and re-establishment).
5. Pupils move through school as members of age-equal cohorts (unlike the family in which the age dispersion of children is characteristically larger than that of the classroom).
6. Classrooms, like families, consist of adult and non-adult positions, but the former have a much larger non-adult membership.

Whatever pupils learn from the didactic efforts of teachers, they also learn something from their participation in a social setting some of whose structural characteristics have been briefly identified. Implicit in this statement are the following assumptions: (a) the tasks, constraints, and opportunities available within social settings vary with the structural properties of those settings; (b) individuals who participate in them derive principles of conduct based on their experiences coping with those tasks, constraints, and opportunities; and (c) the content of the principles learned varies with the nature of the setting. To the question of what is learned in school, only a hypothetical answer can be offered at this point: pupils learn to accept social norms, or principles of conduct, and to act according to them.[2]

Social Norms

The concept of social norm has long been important in sociological thinking where it has been treated primarily as a determinant, a prior condition accounting in part for some pattern of behavior: a rule, expectation, sanction, or external constraint; an internal force, obligation, conviction, or internalized standard. Given some pattern of conduct or rate of behavior, sociologists characteristically ask, among other things, whether it represents conformity to or deviation from a norm or whether it is a phenomenon emerging from a situation in which several norms operate. Comparatively little attention has been paid to the question of how norms originate in social settings and how individuals learn them.

Norms are situationally specific standards for behavior: principles, premises, or expectations indicating how individuals in specifiable circumstances *ought* to act. For example, pupils are expected to arrive at school on time. To say that they accept this norm means that: (a) there is such a standard whose existence can be determined independently of pupils' conduct (in this case, the hour they arrive at school); and (b) pupils adhere to the standard in the sense they consider that their actions should be governed by it. Acceptance, then, refers to a self-imposed, acknowledgeable obligation of variable intensity. The content of the norm must be in somebody's mind and communicable by gesture, spoken word, written rule, or sanction.

There are both logical and empirical problems in using the concept "norm."[3] First, norm and behavior must be distinguished analytically, for there is a logical circularity in inferring norms from behavior and then using them to account for variations in behavior. Second, norm acceptance and related behavior are empirically distinct; that is, there is a range of behavioral alternatives relative to any norm. Conduct varies, for example, relative both to a given norm and to prevailing conditions, and some norms explicitly acknowledge permissible variation in conduct.[4]

The Functions of Schooling

Schooling contributes to pupils' learning what the norms are, accepting them, and acting according to them; norm content, acceptance, and behavior can, however, all vary independently. This ostensibly straightforward assertion, however, conceals complexities behind obvious facts. Children leaving the household each day to attend school is an event so familiar that one tends to forget how problematic it is. Herskovits reminds us that "the significance of the distinction between 'schooling' and 'education' is to be grasped when it is pointed out that while every people must train their young, the cultures in which any substantial part of this training is carried on outside the household are few indeed."[5] The separation of schooling from the household is most characteristic of industrial

societies (though not restricted to them) where economic, political, and religious institutions also tend to be independent of the family—independent, that is, in the sense that dominant principles of conduct (social norms) governing relations among kin differ from those governing the conduct of persons in non-familial institutions.

Even though the norms of family life have an important and complex relationship to conduct in non-familial settings, I am concerned here not with that relationship but with aspects of the process by which individuals learn new norms; for when other social institutions in industrial societies have replaced the family as the predominant economic, political, and religious unit and differ from it structurally, principles of conduct appropriate among kin cannot be generalized to them. Since schooling follows a period of life when children are largely dependent on kin, and precedes the period of adulthood when individuals participate as economic producers and citizens, one naturally looks to the school to discover how the addition of new principles of behavior to the psychological repertoire takes place.

Four norms have particular relevance to economic and political participation in industrial societies; those of independence, achievement, universalism, and specificity. I have selected these, not because they form an exhaustive list, but because they are central to the dominant, non-familial activities of adults in American society.[6] In school, pupils participate in activities where they are expected to act as if they were conforming to these norms whether they actually accept them at a particular time or not. Through such participation, it is my belief, pupils will in time know their content,[7] accept them as binding upon themselves, and act in accordance with them in appropriate situations. How schooling contributes to the acquisition of these norms will be discussed in the following pages.

In speaking of independence, achievement, universalism, and specificity as norms, I mean that individuals accept the obligations, respectively: to act by themselves (unless collaborative effort is called for) and accept personal responsibility and accountability for their conduct and its consequences (independence); to perform tasks actively and master the environment according to standards of excellence (achievement); and to acknowledge the right of others to treat them as members of categories often based on a few discrete characteristics rather than on the full constellation of them representing the whole person (universalism and specificity).

In one sense, full adult status, at least for men, requires occupational employment; and one of the outcomes of schooling is employability. The ability to hold a job involves not only adequate physical capacities but the appropriate psychological skills to cope with the demands of work. The requirements of job-holding are multifarious; most occupations, for example, require among other things that individuals assume personal responsibility for the completion and quality of their work and individual accountability for its shortcomings and that they perform their tasks to the best of their ability. Public life, however, extends beyond occupational employment. Although people work in their occupational capacities and in association with others (as clients, patients, customers, parishioners, students, and so on in *their* occupational capacities), they also have non-occupational identities as voters, communicants, petitioners, depositors, applicants, and creditors, to name a few, in which people are classified similarly as members of the same category based on a small number of specific characteristics irrespective of how they differ in other respects.

"The prime social characteristic of modern industrial enterprise," Goode observes, "is that the individual is ideally given a job on the basis of his ability to fulfill its demands, and that this achievement is evaluated universalistically; the same standards apply to all who hold the same job."[8] Societies in which industrial enterprise is the primary form of economic organization tend to have occupational systems characteristically organized around normative principles different from those of kinship units. Some observers, recognizing that individuals must undergo psychological changes of considerable magnitude in order to make the transition from family to economic employment,[9] have

noted yet understated the contribution of schooling. Eisenstadt, for example, in an otherwise penetrating analysis of age-grouping, restricts his treatment of the school's contribution to "adapting the psychological (and to some extent also physiological) learning potential of the child to the various skills and knowledges which must be acquired by him;"[10] his emphasis is too narrowly limited to the cognitive outcomes of schooling. Furthermore, while stressing the transition between family and occupation, most writers have largely ignored the contribution of schooling to the development of psychological capacities necessary for participating in other (non-economic) segments of society. It is my contention that the social experiences available to pupils in schools, by virtue of the nature and sequence of their structural arrangements, provide opportunities for children to learn norms characteristic of several facets of adult public life, occupation being but one.

In the early grades, a formal and prolonged process of separating children from the family begins. It does not involve severing or renouncing kinship ties nor relinquishing the normative principles of family life since most members of society, after all, remain part of some kinship unit throughout most of their lives. Schooling does, however, put demands on pupils to adopt principles of conduct different from those they have come to accept as family members— more precisely, to restrict the premises governing family life to conduct among kinsmen, and to learn new premises that apply to settings outside the family. It is a process in which children learn both to generalize principles of conduct from one setting to another and at the same time to specify what principles are appropriate to which setting.

The Structural Basis of Sanctions

Learning to accept norms and act according to them, like other forms of learning, requires the use of sanctions. In both family and school, patterns of action appropriate to each setting are encouraged and discouraged by rewards and punishments taking the form of both specific, momentary acts and more elaborate patterns of action over time.

I assume that in encouraging and discouraging enduring patterns of behavior, a sustained relationship between the parties involved must exist, one that involves more than the reward and punishment of specific acts on a *quid pro quo* basis. In the family, the basis for encouraging and discouraging children's behavior lies in their dependence on parents from earliest childhood and in mutual affection—in effect, the maintenance of a continuous and diffuse relationship based on goodwill. Although rewards for specific acts can replenish the bank of goodwill, it is maintained by gratuitous expressions of concern, friendliness, support, sympathy, encouragement, and the like, not simply as responses to specific acts, but as indications of a more enduring solidarity. Punishment, even if severe, will then mean one thing if administered in the context of sustained affection and another where such feeling is absent.

Problems of reward and punishment confront teachers as well as parents, but the problems differ. First, since children in classrooms outnumber those in families, teachers, because of the limitations on their time and energy, can neither attend to nor sanction each child in the same ways that parents can; they must control a class without sacrificing the school's agenda to the imperatives of keeping order. Second, pupils' school work is customarily sanctioned by means of grades based on the quality of assignments completed. Grades, however, are not inherently rewarding or punishing, at least not at the outset. One critical problem of early elementary schooling is for teachers to establish grades *as* sanctions; and to the extent that pupils do not learn to accept them as such, grades cannot serve to reward good performance and punish poor. Secondary schools operate on the assumption—not always correct—that pupils have already come to accept the sanctioning quality of grades.

Teaching in the early grades presents a classic problem in the creation of goodwill—finding some appropriate equivalent in the classroom of affection in the family. That is, gratuitous pleasure not tied to specific acts in a relationship of exchange must be created in order to develop in pupils a diffuse and positive attachment both to the teacher and to the school. But the problem of sanctioning does not end with the creation of goodwill and the assignment of grades. The demands of schooling, particularly in the early years, can prove difficult, taxing, and often alien when contrasted with the more protective and indulgent environment of the home. The school day is long; there is much sitting in one place, following orders, completing assigned and not necessarily enjoyable tasks on time; teachers devote less time and interest to each child than parents do—this despite whatever intrinsic pleasures children may find in the school environment. Yet the school must convey to the pupil that certain forms of conduct acceptable at home will be held unacceptable at school, that certain rights he may legitimately claim from the household will not be honored in the classroom, that however alien they may seem, the tasks that school presents must be confronted and will hopefully come to represent new sources of gratification. To effect such changes, the school must have more resources than grades and goodwill in its kit of sanctions.

Resources available for sanctioning derive initially from two structural characteristics of classrooms: the visibility of pupils and their homogeneity of age. Classrooms are public places in that their membership is collective and visible. Many activities are carried on out loud and in front of everybody (reports, recitations, replies to questions, discussions, praise, chastisement, laughter); pupils perform publicly and are judged openly by the teacher and by other members of the class.[11]

The similarity of pupils in age is important for at least three reasons. First, age represents an index (even if inexact) of developmental maturity, and by implication, of capacity;[12] and even though children of the same age vary greatly in what they can do, age is still used as a common shorthand to gauge the assignment of tasks, responsibilities, privileges, and the like. Second, it provides classrooms with a built-in standard for comparison, a fixed point indicative of the level of those capacities directly relevant to the activities in which pupils are engaged. Each pupil, then, can be compared and compare himself with all others because the comparisons can be anchored to the standard. Third, it allows each pupil the experience of finding himself in the same boat with others in terms of the characteristics of their social surroundings and in the way they are treated by teachers.

Since many classroom activities are in effect judged in public, the pupil is bombarded with messages telling him how well he has done and—with a short inferential leap—how good he is. If he doesn't take the teacher's word for it, he need only look at the performance of others of the same age and in the same circumstances. The school, in effect, plays on his self-respect. Each pupil is exposed and vulnerable to the judgments of adults in authority and of his equals—those who resemble him in many respects.[13] If the child at home wonders whether he is loved, the pupil in school wonders whether he is a worthwhile person. In both settings, he can find some kind of answer by observing how others treat him and what they think of him.

Given the standards for and the patterns of behavior that children learn from their family experiences, the schools, in preparing them for adult public life, must effect changes of considerable magnitude, changes that require giving up certain patterns of conduct found gratifying in other settings and adopting new patterns whose gratifications may at best take the form of promissory notes. If knowledge about other forms of socialization is applicable to schooling—and there is no reason in principle why it should not be—the sanctions required must affect people's emotions deeply as is true in some of the most demanding and stressful social situations involving psychological change: psychotherapy, religious conversion, brain-washing, deracination. It is my contention that the emotions aroused in schooling derive from events in which the pupil's sense of self-respect is either supported or threatened and that school classrooms permitting the public exposure and judgment of performance against a reasonably fixed reference point (age-adapted tasks) are organized so that the pupil's sense of personal adequacy or self-respect, becomes the leverage for sanctioning.

Not all sanctions employed in school settings have the potentiality for arousing intense emotions, nor are they similarly diffuse in character. Some, like grades, compliments, admonitions, and chastisements, are contingent upon desirable and undesirable conduct; others, like friendly greetings, gentleness, sympathy, sarcasm, bitchiness, and so on through the whole gamut of words and gestures indicating approval, disapproval, and general attitude are non-contingent. All represent resources at the teacher's disposal—used consciously or unconsciously—and influence whether or not pupils will find their early experiences at school enjoyable enough to act according to its standards.

As suggested earlier, the school provides constraints and opportunities related to its structural properties, the behavior of its members, and its resources available for sanctioning. I have argued that pupils infer principles of conduct on the basis of their experiences in school, that they learn principles underlying the alternative ways of coping with a social situation having a particular set of properties. Over a period of years, they discover which patterns of conduct permit them to cope with the school's constraints and opportunities; and, to the extent that they find that certain patterns of action lead to the successful accomplishment of tasks and bring gratifications, they adopt those patterns as the right ways to act—that is, they value them.[14]

The Learning of Social Norms

The social properties of schools are such that pupils, by coping with the sequence of classroom tasks and situations, are more likely to learn the principles—social norms—of independence, achievement, universalism, and specificity than if they had remained full-time members of the household.

Independence

Pupils learn to acknowledge that there are tasks to be done by them alone and to do them that way. Along with this self-imposed obligation goes the idea that others have a legitimate right to expect such independent behavior under certain circumstances.[15] Independence has a widely acknowledged though not unequivocal meaning. In using it here I refer to a cluster of meanings: doing things on one's own, being self-reliant, accepting personal responsibility for one's behavior, acting self-sufficiently;[16] and to a way of approaching tasks in whose accomplishment *under different circumstances* one can rightfully expect the help of others. The pupil, when in school, is separated from family members who have customarily provided help, support, and sustenance—persons on whom he has long been dependent.

A constellation of classroom characteristics and both teacher and pupil-actions shape experiences in which the norm of independence is learned. In addition to the fact that school children are removed from persons with whom they have already formed strong relationships of dependency, the sheer size of a classroom assemblage limits each pupil's claim to personal contact with the teacher, and more so at the secondary levels than at the elementary.[17] This numerical property of classrooms reduces pupils' opportunities for establishing new relationships of dependency with adults and for receiving help from them.

Parents expect their children to act independently in many situations but teachers are more systematic in expecting pupils to adhere to standards of independence in performing academic tasks. There are at least two additional aspects of classroom operation, however, that bear directly on learning the norm of independence: rules about cheating and formal testing. First, as to cheating. The word itself is condemnatory in its reference to illegal and immoral acts. Most commonly, attention turns to how much cheating occurs, who cheats, and why. But these questions are of no concern here (though obviously they are elsewhere). My interest is in a different problem: to what types of conduct is the pejorative "cheating" assigned?

In school, cheating usually refers to acts in which two or more parties participate when the unaided action of only one is expected and pertains primarily to instructional activities. Illegal and immoral acts such as stealing and vandalism, whether carried out by individuals or groups, are not considered cheating because they have no direct connection with the central academic core of school activities. Nor is joint participation categorically proscribed; joint effort is called cooperation or collusion depending upon the teacher's prior definition of the task.

Cheating takes many forms, most of which involve collective effort. A parent and a child may collaborate to produce homework; two pupils may pool their wisdom—or ignorance, as the case may be—in the interest of passing an examination. In both cases, the parties join deliberately; deliberateness, however, is not essential to the definition. One pupil can copy from another without the latter knowing; nor need the second party be a person, as in the case of plagiarism. The use of crib notes, perhaps a limiting case, involves no collusion; it consists, rather in an illegitimate form of help. These are the main forms of school cheating of which there are many variations, routine to exotic. Thus, actions called cheating are those closely tied to the instructional goals of the school and usually involving assisted performance when unaided performance is expected.

The irony of cheating *in school* is that the same kinds of acts are morally acceptable and even commendable in other situations. One friend assisting another in distress, a parent helping a child—both praiseworthy; if one lacks the information to do a job, the resourceful thing is to look it up. In effect, many school activities called cheating are those in which customary forms of support and assistance in the family and among friends are expected.

In one obvious sense, school rules against cheating are designed to establish the content of moral standards. In another sense, the school attaches the stigma of immorality to certain types of behavior for social as distinct from ethical reasons; namely, to change the character of prevailing social relationships in which children are involved. In the case of homework, the school, in effect, attempts to redefine the relationship between parents and children by proscribing one form of parental support, unproblematic in other circumstances. The teacher has no direct control over parents, but tries to influence them at a distance by asking their adherence to a principle clothed in moral language whose violations are punishable. The line between legitimate parental support (encouraged when it takes the form of parents stressing the importance of school and urging their children to do well) and collusion is unclear; but by morally proscribing parental intervention beyond a certain point, the teacher attempts to limit the child's dependence upon family members in doing his school work. He expects the pupil, in other words, to work independently. The same argument applies to pupils and their friends: the teacher attempts to eliminate those parts of friendship that make it difficult or impossible for him to discover what a pupil can do on his own. In relationships with kin and friends, the customary sources of support in times of adversity, the school intervenes by restricting solidarity and, in the process determines what the pupil can accomplish unaided. The pupil, for his part, discovers which of his actions he is held accountable for individually within the confines of tasks set by the school.

The comparison between schooling and occupational employment for which school is intended as preparation provides indirect support for this argument. The question here is the sense in which school experience is preparatory. Usually workers are not restricted in seeking help on problems confronting them; on the contrary, many occupations provide resources specifically intended to be helpful: arrangements for consultation, libraries, access to more experienced colleagues, and so on. Only in rare situations are people expected not to enlist the aid of family and friends in matters pertaining to work where that aid is appropriate. In other words, activities on the job analogous to school work do not carry comparable restrictions. Required, however, is that people in their occupational activities accept individual responsibility and accountability for the performance of assigned and self-initiated tasks. To the extent that the school contributes to the development of independence, the preparation lies more in the development of a frame of mind to act independently than in a vocationalism consisting of the capacity to perform a certain range of tasks without help.

Second, as to testing, and particularly the use of achievement tests. Most important for

independence are the social conditions designed for the *administration* of tests, not their content or format. By and large, pupils are tested under more or less rigorously controlled conditions. At one end of the spectrum, formal, standardized tests are administered most stringently: pupils are physically separated, and the testing room is patrolled by proctors whose job is to discover contraband and to guarantee that no communication occurs—these arrangements being designed so that each examination paper represents independent work. At the other end, some testing situations are more informal, less elaborately staged, although there is almost always some provision that each pupil's work represents the product of only his own efforts.[18]

Testing represents an approach to establishing the norm of independence different from the proscription against cheating even though both are designed to reduce the likelihood of joint effort. Whereas the rules against cheating are directed more toward delineating the form of appropriate behavior, the restrictions built into the testing situation provide physical constraints intended to guarantee that teachers will receive samples of work that pupils do unassisted; the restrictions, that is, bear more on the product than on the motive. Actually, unless they stipulate otherwise, teachers expect pupils to do most of their everyday work by themselves; daily assignments provide opportunities for and practice in independent work. Tests, because they occur at less frequent intervals than ordinary assignments cannot provide comparably frequent opportunities; by the elaborate trappings of their administration, particularly with college entrance exams, and the anxiety they provoke, they symbolize the magnitude of the stakes.

It may be objected that in emphasizing independence I have ignored cooperation since an important item on the school agenda is instructing pupils in the skills of working with others. Teachers do assign work to groups and expect a collaborative product—and to this extent require the subordination of independent to collective efforts; judging the product according to collective standards, however, is another question.

To evaluate the contribution of each member of a working team, the teacher must either judge the quality of each one's work, in effect relying on the standard of independence, or rate each contribution according to the quality of the total product. The latter procedure rests on the assumption that each member has contributed equally, an untenable assumption if one has carried the rest or if a few have carried a weak sister. That occurrences of this kind are usually considered "unfair" suggests the normative priority of independence and the simple fact of life in industrial societies that institutions of higher learning and employers want to know how well each person can do and put constraints on the schools to find out. Thus, although the school provides opportunities for pupils to gain experience in cooperative situations, in the last analysis it is the individual assessment that counts.

Achievement

Pupils come to accept the premise that they should perform their tasks the best they can, and act accordingly. The concept of achievement, like independence, has several referents. It usually denotes activity and mastery, making an impact on the environment rather than fatalistically accepting it, and competing against some standard of excellence. Analytically, the concept should be distinguished from independence since, among other differences, achievement criteria can apply to activities performed collectively.

Much of the recent literature treats achievement in the context of child-rearing within the family, as if achievement motivation were primarily a product of parental behavior.[19] Even though there is reason to believe that early childhood experiences in the family do contribute to its development, classroom experiences also contribute through teachers' use of resources beyond those ordinarily at the command of family members.

Classrooms are organized around a set of core activities in which a teacher assigns tasks to pupils and evaluates and compares the quality of their work. In the course of time, pupils differentiate themselves according to how well they perform a variety of tasks, most of which require the use of symbolic skills. Achievement standards are not limited in applicability to the classroom nor is their content restricted to cognitive areas. Schools afford opportunities for participation in a variety of extra-curricular activities, most conspicuously, athletics, but also music, dramatics, and a bewildering array of club and small group activities appealing to individual interests and talents.

The direct relevance of classroom work to learning achievement standards is almost self-evident; the experience is built into the assignment-performance-evaluation sequence of the work. Less evident, however, is that classroom activities force pupils to cope with various degrees of success and failure both of which can be psychologically problematic. Consistently successful performance requires that pupils deal with the consequences of their own excellence in a context of peer-equality in non-academic areas. For example, they confront the dilemma inherent in surpassing their age-mates in some respects but depending on their friendship and support in others, particularly in out-of-school social activities. The classroom thus provides not only the achievement experience itself but by-products of it, taking the form of the dilemma just described.

Similarly, pupils whose work is consistently poor not only must participate in activities leading to their academic failure but also experience living with that failure. They adopt various modes of coping with this, most of which center around maintaining personal self-respect in the face of continuing assaults upon it. Probably a minority succeed or fail consistently; a large proportion, most likely, do neither one consistently, but nonetheless worry about not doing well. Schooling, then, affords most pupils the experiences of both winning and losing; and to the extent that they gain some modicum of gratification from academic activities they learn to accept the general expectation of approaching their work with an achievement frame of mind. At the same time, they learn how to cope in a variety of ways, and more or less well, with success and failure.

Failure is perhaps the more difficult because it requires acknowledgement that the premise of achievement, to which failure itself can be attributed in part, is a legitimate principle for governing one's actions. Yet, endemic to industrial societies in which many facets of public life are based on achievement principles are situations that constrain people to live with personal failure; political defeat and occupational non-promotion being two cases in point.

As already suggested, the school provides a broader range of experiences than those restricted to the classroom and academic in nature; these experiences are based similarly on achievement criteria but differ in several important respects. The availability of alternatives to academic performance means that a pupil can experience success in achievement-oriented activities even if he lacks the requisite talents for doing well in the classroom.

How these alternative activities differ from those of the classroom is as important as the fact that they do, as evidenced by the case of athletics. Competitive sports resemble classroom activities in that both provide participants with the chance to demonstrate individual excellence; however, the former—and this is more true of team than individual sports—permit collective responsibility for defeat whereas the latter by and large allow only individual responsibility for failure. That is to say, the chances of receiving personal gratification for success are at least as great in sports as in the classroom, while the assault on personal self-respect for failure is potentially less intense. Athletics should not be written off as a manifestation of mere adolescent non-intellectualism as several recent writers have so treated it.[20]

A similar contention holds for music and dramatics; both provide the potentiality for individual accomplishment and recognition but without the persistent, systematic, and potentially corrosive evaluation typical of the classroom. Finally, in various club activities based on interest and talent, a pupil can do the things he is good at in the company of others who share an appreciation for them. In all these situations, either the rigors of competition and judgment characteristic of the classroom are

mitigated; or the activity in question has its own built-in sources of support and personal protection, not to the same extent as in the family, but more than is available in the crucible of the classroom.

The school provides a wider variety of achievement experiences than does the family but at the same time has fewer resources for supporting and protecting pupils' self-respect in the face of failure. As pupils proceed through successive school levels, the rigors of achievement increase at least for those who continue along the main academic line. Moreover, at the secondary levels the number of activities governed according to the achievement principle increases as does the variety of these activities. As preparation for adult public life in which the application of this principle is widespread, schooling contributes to personal development in assuring that the majority of pupils not only will have performed tasks according to the achievement standard but will have had experience in an expanding number of situations in which activities are organized according to it.

Universalism and Specificity

Unlike independence and achievement, universalism and specificity are not commonly regarded as good things. Parents and teachers admonish children to act independently and to do their work well; few of them support the idea that people should willingly acknowledge their similarity to others in specifically categorical terms while ignoring obvious differences—denying, in a sense, their own individuality.

Ideologically, social critics have deplored the impersonal, ostensibly dehumanizing aspects of categorization, a principle widely believed to lie at the heart of the problem of human alienation—the attachment of man to machine, the detachment of man from man. Often ignored, however, is the connection between this principle and the idea of fairness, or equity. Seen from this vantage point, categorization is widely regarded as a good thing, especially when contrasted to nepotism, favoritism and arbitrariness. People resent the principle when they think they have a legitimate reason to receive special consideration or when their individuality appears to vanish by being "processed." Yet when a newcomer breaks into a long queue instead of proceeding to the end of the line, they usually condemn him for acting unfairly (for not following the standard rule for all newcomers to a line) and do *not* express any sense of their own alienation (for abiding by the same categorical principle). The contrasts between individuality and dehumanization, fairness and special privilege, are similarly predicated on universalism and specificity; they differ in the ideological posture of the observer, and, more cynically, in his conception of self-interest.

The concepts of universalism and specificity have been formulated most comprehensively by Parsons, though only part of his formulation pertains directly to this discussion. As part of his concern with social systems, Parsons views universalism as one horn of a dilemma—the other being particularism—in role definition; under what circumstances does the occupant of one social position govern his actions by adopting one standard or the other in dealing with the occupant of another position? My concern, however, is not with a selection among alternative, conflicting standards but with the conditions under which individuals learn to accept the obligation to impose the standards of universalism and specificity upon themselves and to act accordingly.

Defining the central theme of universalism raises problems because the term has various meanings, not all of them clear.[21] The relevant distinction here is whether individuals are treated as members of categories or as special cases. In one respect or another, an individual can always be viewed as a member of one or more categories; he is viewed particularistically if, notwithstanding his similarity to others in the same category or circumstances, he still receives special treatment.[22]

The norm of specificity is easily confused with universalism despite its distinctiveness. It refers to the scope of one person's interest in another; to the obligation to confine one's interest to a narrow range of characteristics and concerns, or

to extend them to include a broad range.[23] Implicit is the notion of relevance; the characteristics and concerns that should be included in the range, whether broad or narrow, are those considered relevant in terms of the activities in which the persons in question are involved. Doctors and storekeepers, for example, differ in the scope of their interest in persons seeking their services, but the content of their interests also varies according to the nature of the needs and desires of those persons.

It is my contention that the school's contribution to children's accepting these norms that penetrate so many areas of public life is critical because children's preschool experience in the family is weighted heavily on the side of special treatment and parental consideration of the whole child.

To say that children learn the norm of universalism means that they come to accept being treated by others as members of categories (*in addition to* being treated as special cases, as in the family). Schools provide a number of experiences that families cannot readily provide because of limitations in their social composition and structure, one of which is the systematic establishment and demarcation of membership categories. First, by assigning all pupils in a classroom the same or similar tasks to perform, teachers in effect make them confront the same set of demands; and even if there are variations in task content, class members still confront the same teacher and the obligations he imposes. Second, parity of age creates a condition of homogeneity according to developmental stage, a rough equalization of pupil capacities making it possible for teachers to assign similar tasks. Third, through the process of yearly promotion from grade to grade, pupils cross the boundaries separating one age category from another. With successive boundary crossings comes the knowledge that each age-grade category is associated with particular circumstances (e.g., teachers, difficulty of tasks, subject matter studied); moreover, pupils learn the relationship between categories and how their present positions relate to past and future positions by virtue of having experienced the transitions between them. In these three ways, the grade—

more specifically, the classroom within the grade—with its age-homogeneous membership and clearly demarcated boundaries provides a basis for categorical grouping that the family cannot readily duplicate. Most important, as a by-product of repeated boundary-crossing, pupils acquire a relativity of perspective, a capacity to view their own circumstances from other vantage points, having themselves occupied them.[24]

Although each child holds membership in the category "children" at home, parents, in raising them, tend to take age differences into account and thereby accentuate the uniqueness of each child's circumstances and to belie in some measure the categorical aspects of "childhood." However, even if the category "children" breaks into its age-related components within the family, it remains intact when children compare themselves with friends and neighbors of the same age. In typical situations of this kind, children inform their parents that friends of the same age have greater privileges or fewer responsibilities than they. Parents, if they cannot actually equalize the circumstances, often explain or justify the disparity by pointing to the special situation of the neighbor family: they have more money, fewer children, a bigger house—whatever the reason; that is, parents point out the uniqueness of family circumstances and thereby emphasize the particularities of each child's situation The school, in contrast, provides the requisite circumstances for making comparisons among pupils in categorical rather than particular terms.

The second school experience fostering the establishment of social categories is the re-equalization of pupils by means of the high-school track system after they have differentiated themselves through academic achievement in the lower grades, a mechanism that reduces the likelihood that teachers will have to deal with special cases.[25] Teachers with a variegated batch of pupils must adopt more individualized methods of instruction than those whose pupils are similar in their level of achievement, and who in so doing would partially recreate a kinship-type of relationship with pupils, treating segments of the class differently according to differences in capacity much as parents treat their children differently according to age-related capacities.

As far as level is concerned, the high school is a better place to learn the principle of universalism than the lower school levels because pupils within each track, and therefore of roughly similar capacity, move from classroom to classroom, in each one receiving instruction in a different subject area from a different teacher. They discover that over a range of activities they are treated alike and that relatively uniform demands and criteria of evaluation are applied to them. That is to say, by providing instruction from different teachers in different subject matter areas and by at the same time applying criteria for judging performance and task difficulty which remain roughly constant within each track and across subjects, the school makes it possible for pupils to learn which differences in experience are subordinated to the principle of categorization. The elementary classroom, oriented more to instruction in different subjects by a single teacher, does not provide the necessary variations in persons and subjects for a clear-cut demonstration of the categorical principle.

Although the idea of categorization is central to the norm of universalism, there are additional and derivative aspects of it. One is the crucial distinction, widely relevant in industrial society, between the person and the social position he occupies. A frequent demand made on individuals is to treat others and be treated by them according to the identity that their positions confer rather than according to who they are as people. Schooling contributes to the capacity to make the distinction (and the obligation to do so) by making it possible for pupils to discover that different individuals can occupy a single social position but act in ways that can be discovered as attached to the position rather than to the different persons filling it. Even though all members of a given classroom find themselves in the same circumstances, are about equal in age, and resemble each other, roughly, in social characteristics related to residence, they still differ in many respects—sex, race, ethnicity, and physical characteristics being among the most obvious.

Their situation, therefore, provides the experience of finding that common interests and shared circumstances are assigned a priority that submerges obvious personal differences. The same contention holds for adults. Male and female adults are found in both school and family settings; in school, pupils can discover that an increasingly large number of different adults of both sexes can occupy the same position, that of "teacher." This discovery is not as easily made in the family because it is not possible to determine definitively whether "parent" represents two positions, one occupied by a male, the other by a female, or a single position with two occupants differing in sex.[26] The school, in other words, makes it possible for pupils to distinguish between persons and the social positions they occupy—a capacity crucially important in both occupational and political life—by placing them in situations where both the similarities between persons in a single position are made evident and the membership of each position is varied in its composition.

Regarding the norm of specificity, again the school provides structural arrangements more conducive to its acquisition than does the family. First, since the number of persons and the ratio of non-adults to adults is much larger in classrooms than in the household, the school provides large social aggregates in which pupils can form many casual associations (in addition to their close friendships), in which they invest but a small portion of themselves. As both the size and heterogeneity of the student body increase at each successive level, the opportunities for these somewhat fragmented social contacts increase and diversify. The relative shallowness and transiency of these relationships increase the likelihood that pupils will have experiences in which the fullness of their individuality is *not* involved as it tends to be in their relationships among kin and close friends.

Second, upon leaving the elementary school and proceeding through the departmentalized secondary levels, pupils form associations with teachers who have a progressively narrowing and specialized interest in them. (This comes about both because of subject matter specialization itself and because the number of pupils each teacher faces in the course of a day also grows larger.) Although it is true that children, as they grow older, tend to form more specific relationships with their parents—symptomatically, this trend manifests itself in adolescents' complaints of parental invasions of privacy—the resources of the school in providing the social basis for establishing relationships in which only narrow segments of personality are invested far exceed those of the family.

A second facet of universalism is the principle of equity, or fairness (I use the terms interchangeably). When children compare their lot—their gains and losses, rewards and punishments, privileges and responsibilities—with that of others and express dissatisfaction about their own, they have begun to think in terms of equity; their punishments are too severe, chores too onerous, allowance too small compared, for example, to those of siblings and friends. Children's comparisons with siblings, who are almost always different in age, usually prompt parents to resolve the sensed inequities by equalizing age hypothetically. "If you were as young as he, you wouldn't have to shovel the walk either." "He is only a child and doesn't know any better." The pained questions to which these statements are replies are familiar enough.

Among children in a family, age is critical in determining what is fair and unfair.[27] In a sense, it is the clock by which we keep developmental time, changing constantly though not periodically. The personal significance of age is heightened among children because any given age difference between them is "larger" the younger they are. Thus, the difference between a four-year-old and an eight-year-old is "greater" than that between a fourteen-year-old and an eighteen-year-old because, on the average, there are greater developmental changes occurring during the earlier four-year span than during the later one. When life's circumstances change rapidly, when one is still in the process of learning what is one's due and what is due others, and when younger children do not have to fight the battles that older ones have already won, determining whether one is being treated fairly on any given occasion can be difficult.

Among young children, then, age provides a variable standard for judging questions of equity, a more fixed standard among older ones.[28] In the context of the transition between childhood and adulthood, two children *within the same family* (except if they are twins), cannot easily settle a question of equity by referring to their ages—they may acknowledge that the older child is entitled to more, but not how much more—because they differ in age, because the meaning of age differences changes, and because there can be disagreement over the coefficient for converting age units into units of gain and loss.

In school classrooms, the age of children is nearly constant; the problem of settling equity questions attributable to age variations found in families does not arise. Teachers cannot treat all pupils identically, but they can use age similarity as a guide for assigning similar instructional tasks to all members of a class and to communicate, implicitly or explicitly, that they all share the same situation together.

Even though age differences found in the family (and their associated problems of equity) are not present, problems of fairness and unfairness do arise in classrooms; they originate when pupils who are supposed to be treated similarly are not so treated. Grades, for example, according to the usual procedure, must be assigned according to the quality of work completed; equivalent products should receive the same grade. Marking similar work differently, or unequal work the same, represents unfair grading; a similar principle holds for the punishment of offenses—the punishment should fit the crime, and similar forms of misbehavior should be treated alike—and for the assignment of tasks and responsibilities according to difficulty and onerousness. But there are secondary considerations that enter the process of evaluating performance: how hard pupils work and how much they have improved. These criteria cannot readily replace quality of performance unless teachers, pupils, and parents are willing to acknowledge the justice of various anomalies (so defined at least, within the scope of American values): for example, pupils who do excellent work with little effort receiving lower grades than those who produce mediocre work through feverish activity.

The contrast between classroom and family is pronounced. Equity in the former is based by and large on how well pupils perform and how they are treated in a setting whose characteristics are alike for all. From the vantage point of an outside observer, objective conditions within the classroom are similar for each pupil as are the tasks assigned; pupils, in other words, find themselves in the same boat. Within the family, on the other hand, each child rides his own boat, and judgments about equity derive from that fact.

As argued earlier, equity involves a comparative assessment of one's circumstances: gains and losses, rewards and punishments, rights and duties, privileges and responsibilities. To determine whether his circumstances in a given situation are equitable, an individual must learn to make comparisons by which he can discover whose circumstances resemble his own and whose do not, who is treated like him and who is not; he must also discover the relationships between his circumstances and the way he is treated.

Schooling, then, through the structural properties of classrooms at each school level and through teachers' treatment of pupils, provides opportunities for making the comparisons relevant for defining questions of equity far more effectively than does the family. The process is similar to that (above described) of learning the norm of universalism in general. Both within the classroom and within each grade, age and, to a lesser extent, other personal and social characteristics provide a basis for discovering both similarities and differences in categorical terms. The existence of grade levels, distinguished primarily by the demandingness of work and demarcated by the device of yearly promotion, and the progression of pupils through them year by year make it possible for children to learn that *within the context of the school* certain qualities that determine their uniqueness as persons become subordinated to those specific characteristics in which they are alike. Thus, fourth and fifth graders, despite their individuality, are judged according to specific criteria of achievement; and the content and difficulty of their assigned tasks are regulated according to the developmental considerations symbolized by grade. The fourth grader having completed the third grade can grasp the idea that he belongs to a category of persons whose circumstances differ from those of persons belonging to another.

Family relationships are not organized on a cohort basis nor do they entail anything comparable to the systematic, step-by-step progression of grades in which the boundaries between one category and another are clearly demarcated. Although a child knows the difference between family members and non-members and can distinguish even the categorical distinctions within his own family, his experiences in a kinship setting do not allow him to find as clear an answer to the question of whether his circumstances are uniquely his own or whether they are shared. In other words, these relationships are not structured in such a way as to form a basis for making the categorical comparisons basic to the universalistic norm. Specifically, they provide little or no basis for the repeated experience of crossing boundaries from one category to another so important for learning to make the comparisons involved in judgments of equity. Moreover, since parents treat their children more in terms of the full range of personal characteristics—that is, according to the norm of diffuseness rather than that of specificity—the family setting is more conducive to the special rather than the categorical treatment of each child (since the boundaries of a category are more clearly delineated if one characteristic, not many, constitutes the basis of categorization).

A Conceptual Caveat

The argument of this paper rests on the assumption that schools, through their structural arrangements and the behavior patterns of teachers, provide pupils with certain experiences unavailable in other social settings and that these experiences, by virtue of their peculiar characteristics, represent conditions conducive to the acquisition of norms. I have indicated how pupils learn the norms of independence,

achievement, universalism, and specificity as outcomes of the schooling process. A critical point, however, is how the relationship between experience and outcome is formulated.

There is no guarantee that pupils will come to accept the four norms simply because these experiences are available;[29] for example, they may lack the necessary social and psychological support from sources outside of school or sufficient inner resources to cope with the demands of schooling. These are reasons external to the school situation and may be sufficient to preclude both instructional and normative outcomes. Forces internal to the schooling process itself, however, may be equally preclusive since the same activities and sanctions from which some pupils derive the gratification and enhancement of self-respect necessary for both types of outcome may create experiences that threaten the self-respect of others. Potentialities for success *and* failure inhere in tasks performed according to achievement criteria. Independence manifests itself as competence and autonomy in some, as a heavy burden of responsibility in others. Universalistic treatment represents fairness to some, cold impersonality to others. Specificity may be seen as situational relevance or personal neglect.

Within industrial societies, where norms applicable to public life differ markedly from those governing conduct among kin, schools provide a sequence of experiences in which individuals, during the early stages of personality development, acquire new principles of conduct, principles instituting additions to those already accepted during early childhood. The family, as a social setting with characteristic social arrangements, lacks the resources and the "competence"[30] to effect the psychological transition for reasons earlier enumerated in detail. This is not to say that only the school can produce these changes. Of those institutions having some claim over the lives of children and adolescents in industrial societies—the family, child labor, job apprenticeship, mass media, tutoring, the church—only the schools at the present time provide adequate, though not always effective, task experiences, sanctions, and arrangements for the generalization and specification of normative principles throughout the many spheres of public life.

It is conceivable, of course, that families (and these other institutions as well as some yet to be invented) can provide the experiences necessary for the acquisition of these norms; family life provides opportunities for achievement, for assuming individual responsibility, and for categorical and specific treatment, yet it is more likely than schools to provide experiences that also undermine the acquisition of these norms. The crucial consideration is the relationship between structural arrangements and activities in determining whether one setting or another is more conducive to producing a given outcome, for if two activities interfere with each other or if the situation is inappropriate to the performance of an activity, the outcome is unlikely to appear.

An Ideological Caveat

Although I construe them as norms, independence and achievement have been regarded by many observers of the American scene as dominant cultural themes or values—general standards of what is desirable.[31] In view of this, it is important that the argument of this paper not be taken as a defense of national values, although it should not surprise anyone that the normative commitments of individuals who have passed through American schools are generally though not invariably consistent with national values. The main purpose of this analysis was to present a formulation, hypothetical in nature, of how schooling contributes to the emergence of certain psychological outcomes, not to provide an apology or justification for those outcomes on ideological grounds. I have avoided calling universalism and specificity cultural values, even though both are norms, since few if any observers include them among the broad moral principles desirable in American life. Their exclusion from the list of values should further confirm the analytic and non-apologetic intent of this discussion.[32]

Having the means to produce a desired result is not the same thing as an injunction to use them in producing it. Of the many considerations entering into the decision to employ available resources in creating even widely valued outcomes, the probable costs involved should give pause. For the norms in question here, whose desirability can be affirmed either on ideological grounds or in terms of their relevance to public life in an industrial society, conditions conducive to their development are also conducive to the creation of results widely regarded as undesirable. Thus, a sense of accomplishment and mastery, on the one hand, and a sense of incompetence and ineffectualness, on the other, both represent psychological consequences of continually coping with tasks on an achievement basis. Similarly with independence: self-confidence and helplessness can each derive from a person's self-imposed obligation to work unaided and to accept individual responsibility for his actions. Finally, willingness to acknowledge the rightness of categorical and specific treatment may mean the capacity to adapt to a variety of social situations in which only a part of one's self is invested, or it may mean a sense of personal alienation and isolation from human relationships.

From the viewpoint of ideological justification, the process of schooling is problematic in that outcomes morally desirable from one perspective are undesirable from another; and in the making of school policy the price to be paid must be a salient consideration in charting a course of action.

Notes

*   I wish to thank Barrie D. Bortnick, Andrew Effrat, Michael B. Katz, Larry A. Weiss, and Charlene A. Worth for their invaluable help. The research and development reported herein was performed pursuant to a contract (OE 5–10–239) with the

United States Department of Health, Education, and Welfare, Office of Education, under the provisions of the Cooperative Research Program, as a project of the Harvard University Center for research and Development on Educational Differences, Copyrighted © 1967, Dreeben; reproduction in whole or in part permitted for any purposes by the United States Government.

This paper is adapted from Part IV of *On What is Learned in School*, to be published in 1968 by Addison-Wesley Publishing Company, Inc. The volume is in a series on The Foundations of Education, under the editorship of Byron Massialas. Used by permission of Robert Dreeben and the publisher.

1. In one near-encyclopedic volume on educational research, the instructional emphases are most clearly illustrated. Nine of twenty-three long chapters are devoted to "Research on Teaching Various Grade Levels and Subject Matters." Six deal with measurement: both problems of measurement *per se*, and of measuring particular types of educational outcomes (cognitive and non-cognitive). Two deal with the characteristics of teachers, two with methods and media; one with social interaction in classrooms. The major preoccupations of educators and educational researchers are summarized in the following statement from Benjamin S. Bloom "Testing Cognitive Ability and Achievement" in N. L. Gage (ed.), *Handbook of Research on Teaching* (Chicago: Rand McNally, 1963), p. 379:

   While it may or may not be true that the most important changes in the learner are those which may be described as cognitive, i.e., knowledge, problem-solving, higher mental processes, etc., it is true that these are the types of changes in students which most teachers do seek to bring about. These are the changes in learners which most teachers attempt to gauge in their own tests of progress and in their final examinations. These, also, are the changes in the learners which are emphasized in the materials of instruction, in the interaction between teachers and learners, and in the reward system which the teachers and the schools employ.

   There is a brief treatment of the characteristics of learning environments but with primary emphasis on teaching techniques in George G. Stern, "Measuring Non-cognitive Variables in Research on Teaching," (*Ibid.*, pp. 425–433).

2. Several questions pertaining to the connection between the acquisition of norms and the structural properties of social settings are beyond the scope of this paper, and so in places the argument must remain elliptical. For a more detailed discussion, see the writer's forthcoming book: *On What is Learned in School* (Reading, Mass.: Addison-Wesley).

3. The empirical problems of identifying norms in a given situation are beyond the scope of this discussion. Suffice it to say that identifying them requires that one consider at least the following: verbal statements behavior, situation, and emotional expressions—none of which when taken alone is sufficient—and the connections among them.

4. A variety of conditions can affect the relationship between norm acceptance and behavior. (a) There may be disagreements among persons about what norm applies in a particular situation; behavior where consensus is lacking may not represent conformity to any of the conflicting norms. (b) Behavioral conformity may depend on the explicitly or implicitly conditional nature of norms. For example, although lying is proscribed in principle, there are widely-acknowledged situations in which telling "white lies" is acceptable. (c) People vary in their desire to conform; they calculate the likelihood and severity of punishment if they do not; they judge the opportunities to conform or deviate; and they determine where their interests lie.

5. Melville J. Herkovits, *Man and His Works* (New York: Alfred A. Knopf, 1949), p. 311.

6. For technical discussions of the relevance of these norms to industrialism, see Talcott Parsons. *The Social System* (Glencoe: Free Press, 1951) and S. N. Eisenstadt, *From Generation to Generation* (Glencoe: Free Press, 1956).

7. I do not imply that accepting a norm as binding upon oneself implies the ability to formulate its underlying general principle verbally.

8. William J. Goode, *World Revolution and Family Patterns* (New York: Free Press of Glencoe, 1963), p. 11.

9. See, for example, Ruth Benedict, "Continuities and Discontinuities in Cultural Conditioning," in Glyde Kluckhohn, Henry A. Murray, and David M. Schneider, (eds.), *Personality* (New York: Alfred A. Knopf, 1953), pp. 522–31; Eisenstadt, *op. cit.*, pp. 115–85. An important exception to this neglect of the importance of schooling is Talcott Parsons' paper, "The School Class as a Social System," *Harvard Educational Review*; XXIX No. 4, 297–318.

10. Eisenstadt, *op. cit.*, p. 164.

11. Formal grades, both for assigned work and for general evaluation of performance over several months' time, are customarily given in some degree of privacy; once pupils receive them, whatever confidentiality the teacher maintains in assigning grades usually tends to be short-lived. Pupils themselves turn private into public knowledge, and parents have been known to do the same.

12. Perhaps the social expectations for and beliefs about the capacities of similar-aged children are

narrower than their actual capacities (however these are measured). If so, age is an exaggeratedly "good" index of equal capacity even if the "goodness" represents a self-fulfilling prophesy. There is some controversy about the usefulness of the term "capacity" among psychometricians, but for present purposes, it is beside the point since people often think in terms of children's capacities and act accordingly.

13. "Remember that you are as good as any man—and also that you are no better. . . . [But] the man who is as good as his neighbors is in a tough spot when he confronts all of his neighbors combined." Louis Hartz, *The Liberal Tradition in America* (New York: Harcourt, Brace and Co., 1955), p. 56. The opinions of massed equals are not negligible.

14. For empirical confirmation of the fact that experience in the performance of particular tasks can produce changes in preferences, beliefs, and most importantly in values (norms) and their generalization from one situation to another without verbal instruction in the content of those outcomes, see Paul E. Breer and Edwin A. Locke, *Task Experience as a Source of Attitudes* (Homewood: Dorsey Press, 1965), especially chapter 6. A statement of the argument of how the actual performance of a task can effect changes in norms—how it *should* be performed— is beyond the scope of this paper.

15. My emphasis here differs from Parsons' in that he views independence primarily as a personal resource: ". . . It may be said that the most important single predispositional factor with which the child enters the school is his level of independence" (Parsons, *op. cit.*, p. 300). Although independence is very likely such a predisposition—whether it is the most important single one is moot—it is part of the school's agenda to further the development of independence to a point beyond the level at which family resources become inadequate to do so.

16. Winterbottom, for example, lumps independence and mastery together; the indices she uses to measure them involve ostensibly distinct phenomena in that the mastery items refer to tendencies toward activity rather than independence. Marian R. Winterbottom, "The Relation of Need for Achievement to Learning Experiences in Independence and Mastery," in John T. Atkinson (ed.), *Motives in Fantasy, Action, and Society* (Princeton, N.J.: D. Van Nostrand Co., 1958), pp. 453–78. As a definitional guideline for this discussion, I have followed the usage of Bernard C. Rosen and Roy D'Andrade, "The Psychosocial Origins of Achievement Motivation," *Sociometry*, XXII No. 3, 1959, 186, in their discussion of achievement training; also, David C. McClelland, A. Rindlisbacher, and Richard

DeCharms, "Religious and Other Sources of Parental Attitudes toward Independence Training," in David C. McClelland (ed.), *Studies in Motivation* (New York: Appleton-Century-Crofts, Inc., 1955), pp. 389–97.

17. Thus, the ratios of children per adult in households are 0.5, 1.0, 2.0, and 3.0 in one-, two-, four-, and six-child families, respectively, with two parents present; comparatively few families have more than six children. In classrooms, the ratios of different children per adult at the elementary and secondary levels are approximately 28.1 and 155.8, respectively; *The American Public School Teacher 1960–61*, Research Monograph 1963–M2, Research Division, National Education Association, April, 1963, p. 51.

18. By describing the conditions surrounding the administration of tests, I do not thereby attempt to justify these procedures; other means might accomplish the same ends.

19. See, for example, Winterbottom, *op. cit.*, pp. 453–78; Rosen and D'Andrade, *op. cit.*, pp. 185–218; and Fred L. Strodtbeck, "Family Interaction, Values, and Achievement," in David C. McClelland et al., *Talent and Society* (Princeton: D. Van Nostrand Co., Inc., 1958), pp. 135–91.

20. For one attempt to treat athletics condescendingly as anti-intellectualism, see James S. Coleman, *The Adolescent Society* (New York: Free Press of Glencoe, 1961). I do not suggest that athletics has an as yet undiscovered intellectual richness; rather, that its contribution should not be viewed simply in terms of intellectuality.

21. Although Parsons, in *The Social System*, p. 62, considers universalism and particularism to form a dichotomy, he distinguishes them on at least two dimensions: cognitive and cathectic:

    The primacy of cognitive values may be said to imply a *universalistic* standard, while that of appreciative values implies a *particularistic* standard. In the former case the standard is derived from the validity of a set of existential ideas, or the generality of a normative rule, in the latter from the particularity of the cathectic significance of an object or of the status of an object in a relational system.

22. The treatment of others does not become more particularistic as an increasing number of categories is taken into account. If age, sex, religion, ethnicity, and the like—all examples of general categories—are considered, treatment is still categorical in nature because it is oriented to categorical similarities, even if they number more than one, and not to what is special or unique about the person or about a relationship in which he is involved.

23. In the case of specificity, "the burden of proof rests on him who would suggest that ego has obligations vis-à-vis the object in question which transcend this specificity of relevance" (Parsons, *The Social System*, p. 65). In the case of diffuseness, "the burden of proof is on the side of the exclusion of an interest or mode of orientation as outside the range of obligations defined by the role-expectation" (*Ibid.*, p. 66).

24. For a discussion of relativity of perspective, empathy, and parochialism in the context of the economic and political development of nations, see Daniel Lerner, *The Passing of Traditional Society* (New York: Free Press of Glencoe, 1958), pp. 43–75 and *passim*.

25. The secondary school track system by which pupils are segregated according to academic achievement has conventionally been interpreted as a distributive device for directing pupils toward one or another broad segment of the occupational hierarchy. Although the distributive or allocative function of the track system has pre-empted most discussions, it should not be regarded as the only function; in fact, a very different view of it is taken here.

26. Children are not left completely without clues in this matter since they do have other adult relatives who can be seen as distinct persons occupying the same position. Yet, families, even of the extended variety, do not provide the frequent and systematic comparisons characteristic of schooling.

27. There are, of course, events in family life where the explanation that renders inequities fair lies not in age but in circumstances—"Your brother could stay home from school and watch television because he was sick (and you weren't)"—and in other personal characteristics besides age, such as sex—"It isn't safe for girls to walk home alone at that hour (but it's O.K. for your brother)."

28. The contrast between age as a constant and as a variable in questions of equity is evident by comparison with Homans' treatment of age: "One of the ways in which two men may be 'like' one another is in their investments [age being one]. Accordingly the more nearly one man is like another in age, the more apt he is to expect their net rewards to be equal and to display anger when his own are less." In the context of this statement, age is the fixed criterion for assessing the fairness of rewards as one man compares his gain with that of another. George C. Homans, *Social Behavior: Its Elementary Forms* (New York: Harcourt, Brace & World, 1961.) p. 75.

29. Nor should one conclude that these experiences contribute to the learning of only the four norms discussed here and no others.

30. For a discussion of competence as an organizational characteristic, see Philip Selznick, *Leadership in Administration* (Evanston, Ill.: Row, Peterson, and Co., 1957), pp. 38–56.

31. For a general discussion of the concept of "value" and of major American cultural themes, see Robin M. Williams, Jr., *American Society* (New York: Alfred A. Knopf, 1960), pp. 397–470.

32. The hypothetical nature of this discussion should be kept in mind especially since there has been no empirical demonstration of the relationships between schooling and the acceptance of norms.

On Understanding the Processes of Schooling

The Contributions of Labeling Theory

Ray C. Rist

There have been few debates within American education which have been argued with such passion and intensity as that of positing causal explanations of success or failure in schools.[1] One explanation which has had considerable support in the past few years, particularly since the publication of *Pygmalion in the Classroom* by Rosenthal and Jacobson (1968), has been that of the "self-fulfilling prophecy." Numerous studies have appeared seeking to explicate the mechanisms by which the teacher comes to hold certain expectations of the students and how these are then operationalized within the classroom so as to produce what the teacher had initially assumed. The origins of teacher expectations have been attributed to such diverse variables as social class, physical appearance, contrived test scores, sex, race language patterns, and school records. But from the flurry of recent research endeavors, there has emerged a hiatus between this growing body of data and any larger theoretic framework. The concept of the self-fulfilling prophecy has remained simply that—a concept. The lack of a broader conceptual scheme has meant that research in this area has become theoretically stymied. Consequently, there has evolved instead a growing concern over the refinement of minute methodological nuances.

The thrust of this [article] is to argue that there is a theoretical perspective developing in the social sciences which can break the conceptual and methodological logjam building up on the self-fulfilling prophecy. Specifically, the emergence of *labeling theory* as an explanatory framework for the study of social deviance appears to be applicable to the study of education as well. Among the major contributions to the development of labeling theory are Becker, 1963, 1964; Broadhead, 1974; Lemert, 1951, 1972, 1974; Douglas, 1971, 1972; Kitsuse, 1964; Loffland, 1969; Matza, 1964, 1969; Scheff, 1966; Schur, 1971; Scott and Douglas, 1972; and Rubington and Weinberg, 1973.

If the labeling perspective can be shown to be a legitimate framework from which to analyze social processes influencing the educational experience and the contributions of such processes to success or failure in school, there would then be a viable *interactionist* perspective to counter both biological and cultural determinists' theories of educational outcomes. While the latter two positions both place ultimate causality for success or failure *outside* the school, the labeling approach allows for an examination of what, in fact, is happening *within* schools. Thus, labeling theory would call our attention for example, to the various evaluative mechanisms (both formal and informal) operant in schools, the ways in which schools nurture and support such mechanisms, how students react, what the outcomes are for interpersonal interaction based on how these mechanisms have evaluated individual students, and how, *over time*, the consequences of having a certain evaluative tag influence the options available to a student within a school. What follows first is a summary of a number of the key aspects of labeling theory as it has been most fully developed in the sociological literature; second is an attempt to integrate the research on the self-fulfilling prophecy with the conceptual framework of labeling theory. Finally, the implications of this synthesis are explored for both future research and theoretical development.

I. Becoming Deviant: The Labeling Perspective

Those who have used labeling theory have been concerned with the study of *why* people are labeled, and *who* it is that labels them as someone who has committed one form or another of deviant behavior. In sharp contrast to the predominant approaches for the study of deviance, there is little concern in labeling theory with the motivational and characterological nature of the person who committed the act.

Deviance is understood, not as a quality of the person or as created by his actions, but instead as created by group definitions and reactions. It is a social judgment imposed by a social audience. As Becker (1963:9) has argued:

> The central fact of deviance is that it is created by society. I do not mean this in the way it is ordinarily understood, in which the causes of deviance are located in the social situation of the deviant, or the social factors, which prompted his action. I mean, rather, that social groups create deviants by making the rules whose infraction constitute deviance, and by applying those rules to particular people and labeling them as outsiders. From this point of view, *deviance is not the quality of the act the person commits, but rather a consequence of the application by others of rules and sanctions to an "offender." This deviant is one to whom the label has been successfully applied. Deviant behavior is behavior that people so label.* (emphasis added)

The labeling approach is insistent on the need for a shift in attention from an exclusive concern with the deviant individual to a major concern with the *process* by which the deviant label is applied. Again citing Becker (1964:2):

> The labeling approach sees deviance always and everywhere as a process and interaction between at least two kinds of people: those who commit (or who are said to have committed) a deviant act, and the rest of the society, perhaps divided into several groups itself. . . . One consequence is that we become much more interested in the process by which deviants are defined by the rest of the society, than in the nature of the deviant act itself.

The important questions, then, for Becker and others, are not of the genre to include, for example: Why do some individuals come to act out norm-violating behavior? Rather, the questions are of the following sort: Who applied the deviant label to whom? Whose rules shall prevail and be enforced? Under what circumstances is the deviant label successfully and unsuccessfully applied? How does a community decide what forms of conduct should be singled out for this kind of attention? What forms of behavior do persons in the social system consider deviant, how do they interpret such behavior, and what are the consequences of these interpretations for their reactions to individuals who are seen as manifesting such behavior? (See Akers, 1973.)

The labeling perspective rejects any assumption that a clear consensus exists as to what constitutes a norm violation—or for that matter, what constitutes a norm—within a complex and highly heterogeneous society. What comes to be determined as deviance and who comes to be determined as a deviant is the result of a variety of social contingencies influenced by who has the power to enforce such determinations. Deviance is thus problematic and subjectively given. The case for making the societal reaction to rulebreaking a major independent variable in studies of deviant behavior has been succinctly stated by Kitsuse (1964:101):

A sociological theory of deviance must focus specifically upon the interactions which not only define behaviors as deviant, but also organize and activate the application of sanctions by individuals, groups, or agencies. For in modern society, the socially significant differentiation of deviants from the nondeviant population is increasingly contingent upon circumstances of situation, place social and personal biography, and the bureaucratically organized activities of agencies of social control.

Traditional notions of who is a deviant and what are the causes for such deviance are necessarily reworked. By emphasizing the processual nature of deviance, any particular deviant is seen to be a product of being caught, defined, segregated, labeled, and stigmatized. *This is one of the major thrusts of the labeling perspective—that forces of social control often produce the unintended consequence of making some persons defined as deviant even more confirmed as deviant because of the stigmatization of labeling. Thus, social reactions to deviance further deviant careers.* Erikson (1966) has even gone so far as to argue that a society will strive to maintain a certain level of deviance within itself as deviance is functional to clarifying group boundaries, providing scapegoats, creating out-groups who can be the source of furthering in-group solidarity, and the like.

The idea that social control may have the paradoxical effect of generating more of the very behavior it is designed to eradicate was first elaborated upon by Tannenbaum. He noted (1938:21):

> The first dramatization of the "evil" which separates the child out of his group . . . plays a greater role in making the criminal than perhaps any other experience. . . . He now lives in a different world. He has been tagged. . . . The person becomes the thing he is described as being.

Likewise, Schur (1965:4) writes:

> The societal reaction to the deviant, then, is vital to an understanding of the deviance itself

and a major element in—if not the cause of—the deviant behavior.

The focus on outcomes of social control mechanisms has led labeling theorists to devote considerable attention to the workings of organizations and agencies which function ostensibly to rehabilitate the violator or in other ways draw him back into conformity. Their critiques of prisons, mental hospitals, training schools, and other people-changing institutions suggest that the results of such institutions are frequently nearly the opposite of what they were theoretically designed to produce. These institutions are seen as mechanisms by which opportunities to withdraw from deviance are sealed off from the deviant, stigmatization occurs, and a new identity as a social "outsider" is generated. There thus emerges on the part of the person so labeled a new view of himself which is one of being irrevocably deviant.

This movement from one who has violated a norm to one who sees himself as a habitual norm violator is what Lemert (1972:62) terms the transition from a primary to a secondary deviant. A primary deviant is one who holds to socially accepted roles, views himself as a nondeviant, and believes himself to be an insider. A primary deviant does not deny that he has violated some norm, and claims only that it is not characteristic of him as a person. A secondary deviant, on the other hand, is one who has reorganized his social-psychological characteristics around the deviant role. Lemert (1972:62) writes:

> Secondary deviation refers to a special class of socially defined responses which people make to problems created by the societal reaction to their deviance. These problems ... become central facts of existence for those experiencing them. ... Actions, which have these roles and self-attitudes as their referents make up secondary deviance. The secondary deviant ... is a person whose life and identity are organized around the facts of deviance.

A person can commit repeated acts of primary deviation and never come to view himself or have others come to view him as a secondary deviant. Secondary deviation arises from the feedback whereby misconduct or deviation initiates social reaction to the behavior which then triggers further misconduct. Lemert (1951:77) first described this process as follows:

> The sequence of interaction leading to secondary deviation is roughly as follows: 1) primary deviation; 2) societal penalties; 3) further primary deviation; 4) stronger penalties and rejections; 5) further deviations, perhaps with hostilities and resentments beginning to focus upon those doing the penalizing; 6) crisis reached in the tolerance quotient, expressed in formal action by the community stigmatizing of the deviant; 7) strengthening of the deviant conduct as a reaction to the stigmatizing and penalties; and 8) ultimate acceptance of deviant social status and efforts at adjustment on the basis of the associated role.

Thus, when persons engage in deviant behavior they would not otherwise participate in and when they develop social roles they would not have developed save for the application of social control measures, the outcome is the emergence of secondary deviance. The fact of having been apprehended and labeled is the critical element in the subsequent construction of a deviant identity and pursuit of a deviant career.

II. The Origins of Labeling: Teacher Expectations

Labeling theory has significantly enhanced our understanding of the process of becoming deviant by shifting our attention from the deviant to the judges of deviance and the forces that affect their judgment. Such judgments are critical, for a recurrent decision made in all societies, and particularly frequent in advanced industrial societies, is that an individual has or has not mastered some body of information, or perhaps more basically, has or has not the capacity to master that information. These evaluations are made periodically as one moves through the institution of school and the consequences directly affect the opportunities to remain for an additional period. To be able to remain provides an option for mastering yet another body of information, and to be certified as having done so. As Ivan Illich (1971) has noted, it is in industrial societies that being perceived as a legitimate judge of such mastery has become restricted to those who carry the occupational role of "teacher." A major consequence of the professionalization of the role of teacher has been the ability to claim as a near exclusive decision whether mastery of material has occurred. Such exclusionary decision-making enhances those in the role of "teacher" as they alone come to possess the authority to provide certification for credentials (Edgar, 1974).

Labeling theorists report that in making judgments of deviance, persons may employ information drawn from a variety of sources. Further, even persons within the same profession (therapists, for example) may make divergent use of the same material in arriving at an evaluative decision on the behavior of an individual. Among the sources of information available to labelers, two appear primary: first-hand information obtained from face-to-face interaction with the person they may ultimately label, and second-hand information obtained from other than direct interaction.

The corollary here to the activities of teachers should be apparent. Oftentimes, the evaluation by teachers (which may lead to the label of "bright," "slow," etc.) is based on first-hand information gained through face-to-face interaction during the course of the time the teacher and student spent together in the classroom. But a goodly amount of information about the student which informs the teacher's evaluation is second-hand information. For instance, comments from other teachers, test scores, prior report cards, permanent records, meetings with the parents, or evaluations from welfare agencies and psychological clinics are all potential informational sources. In a variation of the division between first-hand and second-hand sources of information, Johnson (1973) has suggested that there are three key determinants of teacher evaluations: student's prior performance, social status characteristics, and present performance. Prior performance would include information from cumulative records (grades, test scores, notes from past teachers or counselors, and outside evaluators) while social status and performance would be inferred and observed in the ongoing context of the classroom.

What has been particularly captivating about the work of Rosenthal and Jacobson (1968) in this regard is their attempt to provide empirical justification for a truism considered self-evident by many in education: School achievement is not simply a matter of a child's native ability, but involves directly and inextricably the teacher as well. Described succinctly, their research involved a situation where, at the end of a school year, more than 500 students in a single elementary school were administered the "Harvard Test of Inflected Acquisition." In actuality this test was a standardized, relatively nonverbal test of intelligence, Flanagan's (1960) Test of General Ability (TOGA). The teachers were told that such a test would, with high predictive reliability, sort out those students who gave strong indication of being intellectual "spurters" or "bloomers" during the following academic year. Just before the beginning of school the following fall, the teachers were given lists with the names of between one and nine of their students. They were told that these students scored in the top twenty percent of the school on the test, though, of course, no factual basis for such determinations existed. A twenty percent subsample of the "special" students was selected for intensive analysis. Testing of the students at the end of the school year offered some evidence that these selected children did perform better than the nonselected. The ensuing debate as to the validity and implications of the findings from the study will be discussed in the next section.

The findings of Deutsch, Fishman, Kogan, North, and Whiteman (1964); Gibson (1965): Goslin and Glass (1967); McPherson (1966); and Pequignot (1966) all demonstrate the influence of standardized tests of intelligence and achievement on teacher's expectations. Goaldman (1971), in a review of the literature on the use of tests as a second-hand source of information for teachers, noted: "Although some of the research has been challenged, there is a basis for the belief that teachers at all levels are prejudiced by information they receive about a student's ability or character." Mehan (1971, 1974) has been concerned with the interaction between children who take tests and the teachers who administer them. He posits that testing is not the objective use of a measurement instrument, but the outcome of a set of interactional activities which are influenced by a variety of contingencies which ultimately manifest themselves in a reified "test score." Mehan suggests (1971):

> Standardized test performances are taken as an unquestioned, non-problematic reflection of the child's underlying ability. The authority of the test to measure the child's real ability is accepted by both teachers and other school officials. Test results are accepted without doubt as the correct and valid document of the child's ability.

Characteristics of children such as sex and race are immediately apparent to teachers. Likewise, indications of status can be quickly inferred from grooming, style of dress, need for free lunches, information on enrollment cards, discussion of family activities by children, and visits to the school by parents. One intriguing study recently reported in this area is that by two sociologists, Clifford and Walster (1973:249). The substance of their study was described as follows:

> Our experiment was designed to determine what effect a student's physical attractiveness has on a teacher's expectations of the child's intellectual and social behavior. Our hypothesis was that a child's attractiveness strongly influences his teachers' judgments; the more attractive the child, the more biased in his favor we expect the teachers to be. The design required to test this hypothesis is a simple one: Teachers are given a standardized report card and an attached photograph. The report card includes an assessment of the child's academic performance as well as of his general social behavior. The attractiveness of the photos is experimentally varied. On the basis of this information, teachers are asked to state their expectations of the child's educational and social potential.

Based on the responses of 404 fifth grade teachers within the state of Missouri, Clifford and Walster concluded (1973:255):

> There is little question but that the physical appearance of a student affected the expectations of the teachers we studied. Regardless of whether the pupil is a boy or girl, the child's physical attractiveness has an equally strong association with his teacher's reactions to him.

The variables of race and ethnicity have been documented, by Brown (1968), Davidson and Lang (1960), Jackson and Cosca (1974), and Rubovits and Maehr (1973), among others, as powerful factors in generating the expectations teachers hold of children. It has also been documented that teachers expect less of lower-class children than they do of middle-class children (cf. Becker, 1952; Deutsch, 1963; Leacock, 1969; Rist, 1970,1973; Stein, 1971; Warner, Havighurst, and Loeb, 1944; and Wilson, 1963). Douglas (1964), in a large scale study of the tracking system used in British schools, found that children who were clean and neatly dressed in nice clothing, and who came from what the teachers perceived as "better" homes, tended to be placed in higher tracks than their measured ability would predict. Further, when placed there they tended to stay and perform acceptably. Mackler (1969) studied schools in Harlem and found that children tended to stay in the tracks in which they were initially placed and that such placement was based on a variety of social considerations independent of measured ability. Doyle, Hancock, and Kifer (1971) and Palardy (1969) have shown teacher expectations for high performance in elementary grades to be stronger for girls than boys.

The on-going academic and interpersonal performance of the children may also serve as a potent source of expectations for teachers. Rowe (1969) found that teachers would wait longer for an answer from a student they believed to be a high achiever than for one from a student they believed to be a low achiever. Brophy and Good (1970) found that teachers were more likely to give perceived high achieving students a second chance to respond to an initial incorrect answer, and further, that high achievers were praised more frequently for success and criticized less for failure.

There is evidence that the expectations teachers hold for their students can be generated as early as the first few days of the school year and then remain stable over the months to follow (Rist, 1970, 1972, 1973; Willis, 1972). For example, I found during my three-year longitudinal and ethnographic study of a single, *de facto* segregated elementary school in the black community of St. Louis, that after only eight days of kindergarten, the teacher made permanent seating arrangements based on what she assumed were variations in academic capability. But no formal evaluation of the children had taken place. Instead, the assignments to the three tables were based on a number of socio-economic criteria as well as on early interaction patterns in the classroom. Thus, the placement of the children came to reflect the social class distinctions in the room—the poor children from public welfare families all sat at one table, the working class children sat at another and the middle class at the third. I demonstrated how the teacher operationalized her expectations of these different groups of children in terms of her differentials of teaching time, her use of praise and control, and the extent of autonomy within the classroom. By following the same children through first and second grade as well, I was able to show that the initial patterns established by the kindergarten teacher came to be perpetuated year after year. By second grade, labels given by another teacher clearly reflected the reality each of the three groups experienced in the school. The top group was called the "Tigers," the middle group the "Cardinals," and the lowest group, the "Clowns." What had begun as a subjective evaluation and labeling by the teacher took on objective dimensions as the school proceeded to process the children on the basis of the distinctions made when they first began.

Taken together, these studies strongly imply that the notion of "teacher expectations" is multi-faceted and multi-dimensional. It appears that when teachers generate expectations about their students, they do so not only for reasons of academic or cognitive performance, but for their classroom interactional patterns as well. Furthermore, not only ascribed characteristics such as race, sex, class, or ethnicity are highly salient, interpersonal traits are also. Thus, the interrelatedness of the various attributes which ultimately blend together to generate the evaluation a teacher makes as to what can be expected from a particular student suggests the strength and tenacity of such subsequent labels as "bright" or "slow" or "trouble-maker" or "teacher's little helper." It is to the outcomes of the student's having one or another of these labels that we now turn.

III. An Outcome of Labeling: The Self-Fulfilling Prophecy

W. I. Thomas, many years ago, set forth what has become a basic dictum of the social sciences when he observed, "If men define situations as real, they are real in their consequences." This is at the core of the self-fulfilling prophecy. An expectation which defines a situation comes to influence the actual behavior within the situation so as to produce what was initially assumed to be there. Merton (1968:477) has elaborated on this concept and noted: "The self-fulfilling phase is, in the beginning, a *false* definition of the situation evoking a new behavior which makes the originally false conception come true." (emphasis in the original)

Here it is important to recall a basic tenet of labeling theory—that an individual does not become deviant simply by the commission of some act. As Becker (1963) stressed, deviance is not inherent in behavior *per se*, but in the application by others of rules and sanctions against one perceived as being an "offender." Thus, the only time one can accurately be termed a "deviant" is after the successful application of a label by a social audience. Thus, though many persons may commit norm violations, only select ones are subsequently labeled. The contingencies of race, class, sex, visibility of behavior, age, occupation, and who one's friends are all influence the outcome as to whether one is or is not labeled. Scheff (1966), for example, demonstrated the impact of these contingencies upon the diagnosis as to the severity of a patient's mental illness. The higher one's social status, the less the willingness to diagnose the same behavioral traits as indicative of serious illness in comparison to the diagnosis given to low status persons.

The crux of the labeling perspective lies not in whether one's norm violating behavior is known, but in whether others decide to do something about it. Further, if a label is applied to the individual, it is posited that this in fact causes the individual to become that which he is labeled as being. Due to the reaction of society, the change in the individual involves the development of a new socialized self-concept and social career centered around the deviant behavior. As Rubington and Weinberg (1973:7) have written:

> The person who has been typed, in turn, becomes aware of the new definition that has been placed upon him by members of his groups. He, too, takes this new understanding of himself into account when dealing with them. When this happens, a social type has been ratified, and a person has been socially reconstructed.

As noted, Rosenthal and Jacobson's *Pygmalion in the Classroom* (1968) created wide interest in the notion of the self-fulfilling prophecy as a concept to explain differential performance by children in classrooms. Their findings suggested that the expectations teachers created about the children randomly selected as "intellectual bloomers" somehow caused the teachers to treat them differently, with the result that the children really did perform better by the end of the year. Though the critics of this particular research (Snow, 1969; Taylor, 1970; Thorndike, 1968, 1969) and those who have been unsuccessful in replicating the findings (Claiborn, 1969) have leveled strong challenges to Rosenthal and Jacobson, the disagreements are typically related to methodology, procedure, and analysis rather than to the proposition that

relations exist between expectations and behavior.

The current status of the debate and the evidence accumulated in relation to it imply that teacher expectations are *sometimes* self-fulfilling. The early and, I think, overenthusiastic accounts of Rosenthal and Jacobson have obscured the issue. The gist of such accounts have left the impression, as Good and Brophy (1973:73) have noted, that the mere existence of an expectation will automatically guarantee its fulfillment. Rather, as they suggest:

> The fact that teachers' expectations can be self-fulfilling is simply a special case of the principle that any expectations can be self-fulfilling. This process is not confined to classrooms. Although it is not true that "wishing can make it so," our expectations do affect the way we behave in situations, and the way we behave affects how other people respond. In some instances, our expectations about people cause us to treat them in a way that makes them respond just as we expect they would.

Such a position would be borne out by social psychologists who have demonstrated that an individual's first impressions of another person do influence subsequent interactions (Dailey, 1952; Newcomb, 1947) and that one's self-expectations influence one's subsequent behavior (Aronson and Carlsmith, 1962; Brock and Edelman, 1965; and Zajonc and Brinkman, 1969).

The conditionality of expectations related to their fulfillment is strongly emphasized by labeling theorists as well. Their emphasis upon the influence of social contingencies on whether one is labeled, how strong the label, and if it can be made to stick at all, points to a recognition that there is a social process involved where individuals are negotiating, rejecting, accepting, modifying, and reinterpreting the attempts at labeling. Such interaction is apparent in the eight stages of the development of secondary deviance outlined above by Lemert. Likewise, Erikson (1964:17), in his comments on the act of labeling as a rite of passage from one side of the group boundary to the other, has noted:

The common assumption that deviants are not often cured or reformed, then, may be based on a faulty premise, but this assumption is stated so frequently and with such conviction that it often creates the facts which later "prove" it to be correct. If the returning deviant has to face the community's apprehensions often enough, it is understandable that he, too, may begin to wonder whether he has graduated from the deviant role—and *so respond to the uncertainty by resuming deviant activity.* In some respects, this may be the only way for the individual and his community to agree as to what kind of person he really is, for it often happens that the community is only able to perceive his "true colors" when he lapses, momentarily into some form of deviant performance, (emphasis added)

Explicit in Erikson's quote is the fact of the individual's being in interaction with the "community" to achieve some sort of agreement on what the person is "really" like. Though Erikson did not, in this instance, elaborate upon what he meant by "community," it can be inferred from elsewhere in his work that he sees "community" as manifesting itself in the institutions persons create in order to help organize and structure their lives. Such a perspective is clearly within the framework of labeling theory, where a major emphasis has been placed upon the role of institutions in sorting, labeling, tracking, and channeling persons along various routes depending upon the assessment the institution has made of the individual.

One pertinent example of the manner in which labeling theory has been applied to the study of social institutions and their impact upon participants has been in an analysis of the relation of schooling to juvenile delinquency. There have been several works which suggest as a major line of argument that schools, through and because of the manner in which they label students, serve as a chief instrument in the creation of delinquency (Hirschi, 1969; Noblit and Polk, 1975; Polk 1969; Polk and Schafer, 1972; Schafer and Olexa, 1971). For example, Noblit and Polk (1975:3) have noted:

> In as much as the school is the primary institution in the adolescent experience—one that promises not only the future status available to the adolescent, but also that gives or denies status in adolescence itself—it can be expected that its definitions are of particular significance for the actions of youth. That is, the student who has been reported from success via the school has little reason to conform to the often arbitrary and paternalistic regulations and rules of the school. In a very real sense, this student has no "rational constraints" against deviance. It is through the sorting mechanisms of the school, which are demanded by institutions of higher education and the world of work, that youth are labeled and thus sorted into the situation where deviant behavior threatens little while providing some alternative forms of status.

It is well to reiterate the point—interaction implies behavior and choices being made by both parties. The person facing the prospect of receiving a new label imputing a systemic change in the definition of his selfhood may respond in any of a myriad number of ways to this situation. Likewise, the institutional definition of the person is neither finalized nor solidified until the end of the negotiation as to what precisely that label should be. But, in the context of a single student facing the authority and vested interests of a school administration and staff, the most likely outcome is that over time, the student will increasingly move towards conformity with the label the institution seeks to establish. Good and Brophy (1973:75) have elaborated upon this process within the classroom as follows:

1. The teacher expects specific behavior and achievement from particular students.
2. Because of these different expectations, the teacher behaves differently toward the different students.
3. This teacher treatment tells each student what behavior and achievement the teacher expects from him and affects his self-concept, achievement motivation, and level of aspiration.
4. If this teacher treatment is consistent over time, and if the student does not actively resist or change it in some way, it will tend to shape his achievement and behavior.

High-expectation students will be led to achieve at high levels, while the achievement of low-expectations students will decline.

5. With time, the student's achievement and behavior will conform more and more closely to that originally expected of him.

The fourth point in this sequence makes the crucial observation that teacher expectations are not automatically self-fulfilling. For the expectations of the teacher to become realized, both the teacher and the student must move towards a pattern of interaction where expectations are clearly communicated and the behavioral response is consonant with the expected patterns. But as Good and Brophy (1973:75) also note:

> This does not always happen. The teacher may not have clear-cut expectations about a particular student, or his expectations may continually change. Even when he has consistent expectations, he may not necessarily communicate them to the student through consistent behavior. In this case, the expectation would not be self-fulfilling even if it turned out to be correct. Finally, the student himself might prevent expectations from becoming self-fulfilling by overcoming them or by resisting them in a way that makes the teacher change them.

Yet, the critique of American education offered by such scholars as Henry (1963), Katz (1971), Goodman (1964), or Reimer (1971) suggests the struggle is unequal between the teacher (and the institution a teacher represents) and the student. The vulnerability of children to the dictates of adults in positions of power over them leaves the negotiations as to what evaluative definition will be tagged on the children more often than not in the hands of the powerful. As Max Weber himself stated, to have power is to be able to achieve one's ends, even in the face of resistance from others. When that resistance is manifested in school by children and is defined by teachers and administrators as truancy, recalcitrance, unruliness, and hostility,

or conversely defined as a lack of motivation, intellectual apathy, sullenness, passivity, or withdrawal, the process is ready to be repeated and the options to escape further teacher definitions are increasingly removed.

Postscript: Beyond the Logjam

This paper has argued that a fruitful convergence can be effected between the research being conducted on the self-fulfilling prophecy as a consequence of teacher expectations and the conceptual framework of labeling theory. The analysis of the outcomes of teacher expectations produces results highly similar to those found in the study of social deviance. Labels are applied to individuals which fundamentally shift their definitions of self and which further reinforce the behavior which had initially prompted the social reaction. The impact of the self-fulfilling prophecy in educational research is comparable to that found in the analysis of mental health clinics, asylums, prisons, juvenile homes, and other people-changing organizations. What the labeling perspective can provide to the study of educational outcomes as a result of the operationalization of teacher expectations is a model for the study of the *processes* by which the outcomes are produced. The detailing over time of the interactional patterns which lead to changes in self-definition and behavior within classrooms is sadly lacking in almost all of the expectation research to date. A most glaring example of this omission is the study by Rosenthal and Jacobson themselves. Their conclusions are based only on the analysis of a pre- and post-test. To posit that teacher expectations were the causal variable that produced changes in student performances was a leap from the data to speculation. They could offer only suggestions as to how the measured changes in the children's performance came about, since they were not in the classrooms to observe how assumed teacher attitudes were translated into subsequent actual student behavior.

To extend the research on the educational experiences of those students who are differentially labeled by teachers, what is needed is a theoretical framework which can clearly isolate the influences and effects of certain kinds of teacher reactions on certain types of students, producing, certain typical outcomes. The labeling perspective appears particularly well-suited for this expansion of both research and theoretical development on teacher expectations by offering the basis for analysis at either a specific or a more general level. With the former, for example, there are areas of investigation related to 1) types of students perceived by teachers as prone to success or failure; 2) the kinds of reactions, based on their expectations, teachers have to different students; and 3) the effects of specific teacher reactions on specific student outcomes. At a more general level, fruitful lines of inquiry might include 1) the outcomes in the post-school world of having received a negative vs. a positive label within the school; 2) the influences of factors such as social class and race on the categories of expectations teachers hold; 3) how and why labels do emerge in schools as well as the phenomenological and structural meanings that are attached to them; and 4) whether there are means by which to modify or minimize the effects of school labeling processes on students.

Labeling theory provides a conceptual framework by which to understand the processes of transforming attitudes into behavior and the outcomes of having done so. To be able to detail the dynamics and influences within schools by which some children come to see themselves as successful and act as though they were, and to detail how others come to see themselves as failures and act accordingly, provides in the final analysis an opportunity to intervene so as to expand the numbers of winners and diminish the numbers of losers. For that reason above all others, labeling theory merits our attention.

Endnote

1. The preparation of this paper has been aided by a grant (GS-41522) from the National Science Foundation—Sociology Program. The views expressed here are solely those of the author and no official endorsement by either the National Science Foundation or the National Institute of Education is to be inferred.

References

Akers, R. L. *Deviant Behavior: A Social Learning Approach.* Belmont, Cal.: Wadsworth, 1973.

Aronson, E., and Carlsmith, J. M. "Performance Expectancy as a Determinant of Actual Performance." *Journal of Abnormal and Social Psychology* 65 (1962): 179–182.

Becker, H. S. "Social Class Variations in the Teacher-Pupil Relationship." *Journal of Educational Sociology* 25 (1952):451–465.

Becker, H. S. *Outsiders.* New York: The Free Press, 1963.

Becker, H. S. *The Other Side.* New York: The Free Press, 1964.

Broadhead, R. S. "A Theoretical Critique of the Societal Reaction Approach to Deviance." *Pacific Sociological Review* 17 (1974):287–312.

Brock, T. C., and Edelman, H. "Seven Studies of Performance Expectancy as a Determinant of Actual Performance." *Journal of Experimental Social Psychology* 1 (1965):295–310.

Brophy, J., and Good, T. "Teachers' Communications of Differential Expectations for Children's Classroom Performance: Some Behavioral Data." *Journal of Educational Psychology* 61 (1970): 365–374.

Brown, B. *The Assessment of Self-Concept among Four Year Old Negro and White Children: A Comparative Study Using the Brown IDS Self-Concept Reference Test.* New York: Institute for Developmental Studies, 1968.

Claiborn, W. L. "Expectancy Effects in the Classroom: A Failure to Replicate." *Journal of Educational Psychology* 60 (1969): 377–383.

Clifford, M. M., and Walster, E. "The Effect of Physical Attractiveness on Teacher Expectations." *Sociology of Education* 46 (1973):248–258.

Dailey C. A. "The Effects of Premature Conclusion upon the Acquisition of Understanding of a Person." *Journal of Psychology* 33 (1952):133–152.

Davidson, H. H., and Lang, G. "Children's Perceptions of Teachers' Feelings toward Them." *Journal of Experimental Education* 29 (1960): 107–118.

Deutsch, M. "The Disadvantaged Child and the Learning Process," in *Education in Depressed Areas,* edited by H. Passow. New York: Teachers College Press, 1963.

Deutsch, M.; Fishman, J. A.; Kogan, L.; North, R.; and Whiteman, M. "Guidelines for Testing Minority Group Children." *Journal of Social Issues* 20 (1964): 129–145.

Douglas, J. *The Home and the School.* London: MacGibbon and Kee, 1964.

Douglas, J. *The American Social Order.* New York: The Free Press, 1971.

Douglas, J. (ed.). *Deviance and Respectability.* New York: Basic Books, 1972.

Doyle, W.; Hancock, G.; and Kifer, E. "Teachers' Perceptions: Do They Make a Difference?" Paper presented at the meeting of the American Educational Research Association, 1971.

Edgar, D. E. *The Competent Teacher.* Sydney, Australia: Angus & Robertson, 1974.

Erikson, K. T. "Note on the Sociology of Deviance," in *The Other Side,* edited by H. S. Becker. New York: The Free Press, 1964.

Erikson, K. T. *Wayward Puritans.* New York: Wiley, 1966.

Flanagan, J. C. *Test of General Ability: Technical Report.* Chicago: Science Research Associates, 1960.

Gibson, G. "Aptitude Tests." *Science* 149 (1965): 583.

Goaldman, L. "Counseling Methods and Techniques: The Use of Tests," in *The Encyclopedia of Education,* edited by L. C. Deighton. New York: Macmillan, 1971.

Good, T., and Brophy, J. *Looking in Classrooms.* New York: Harper and Row, 1973.

Goodmam, P. *Compulsory Mis-Education.* New York: Random House, 1964.

Goslin, D. A., and Glass, D. C. "The Social Effects of Standardized Testing on American Elementary Schools." *Sociology of Education* 40 (1967): 115–131.

Henry, J. *Culture Against Man.* New York: Random House, 1963.

Hirschi, T. *Causes of Delinquency.* Berkeley: University of California Press, 1969.

Illich, I. *Deschooling Society.* New York: Harper and Row, 1971.

Jackson, G., and Cosca, C. "The Inequality of Educational Opportunity in the Southwest: An Observational Study of Ethnically Mixed Classrooms." *American Educational Research Journal* 11 (1974):219–229.

Johnson, J. *On the Interface between Low income Urban Black Children and Their Teachers during the Early School Years: A Position Paper.* San Francisco: Far West Laboratory for Educational Research and Development, 1973.

Katz, M. Class, *Bureaucracy and Schools.* New York: Praeger, 1971.

Kitsuse, J. "Societal Reaction to Deviant Behavior: Problems of Theory and Method," in *The Other Side,* edited by H. S. Becker. New York: The Free Press, 1964.

Leacock, E. *Teaching and Learning in City Schools.* New York: Basic Books, 1969.

Lemert, E. *Social Pathology.* New York: McGraw-Hill, 1951.

Lemert, E. *Human Deviance, Social Problems and Social Control.* Englewood Cliffs, N.J.: Prentice-Hall, 1972.

Lemert, E. "Beyond Mead: The Societal Reaction to Deviance." *Social Problems* 21 (1974):457–468.

Lofland, J. *Deviance and Identity.* Englewood Cliffs, N.J.: Prentice-Hall, 1969.

Mackler, B. "Grouping in the Ghetto." *Education and Urban Society* 2 (1969):80–95.

Matza, D. *Delinquency and Drift.* New York: Wiley, 1964.

Matza, D. *Becoming Deviant.* Englewood Cliffs, N.J.: Prentice-Hall, 1969.

McPherson, G. H. *The Role-set of the Elementary School Teacher: A case study.* Unpublished Ph.D. dissertation, Columbia University, New York, 1966.

Mehan, H. B. *Accomplishing Understanding in Educational Settings.* Unpublished Ph.D. dissertation, University of California, Santa Barbara, 1971.

Mehan, H. B. *Ethnomethodology and Education.* Paper presented to the Sociology of Education Association conference, Pacific Grove, California, 1974.

Merton, R. K. "Social Problems and Social Theory," in *Contemporary Social Problems,* edited by R. Merton and R. Nisbet. New York: Harcourt, Brace and World, 1968.

Newcomb, T. M. "Autistic Hostility and Social Reality." *Human Relations* 1 (1947):69–86.

Noblit, G. W., and Polk, K. *Institutional Constraints and Labeling.* Paper presented to the Southern Sociological Association meetings, Washington, D.C., 1975.

Palardy, J. M. "What Teachers Believe—What Children Achieve." *Elementary School Journal,* 1969, pp. 168–169 and 370–374.

Pequignot, H. "L'équation Personnelle du Juge." In *Semaine des Hopitaux* (Paris), 1966.

Polk, K. "Class, Strain, and Rebellion and Adolescents." *Social Problems* 17 (1969):214–224.

Polk, K., and Schafer, W. E. *Schools and Delinquency.* Englewood Cliffs, N.J.: Prentice-Hall, 1972.

Reimer, E. *School Is Dead.* New York: Doubleday, 1971.

Rist, R. C. "Student Social Class and Teachers' Expectations: The Self-fulfilling Prophecy in Ghetto Education." *Harvard Educational Review* 40 (1970):411–450.

Rist, R. C. "Social Distance and Social Inequality in a Kindergarten Classroom: An Examination of the 'Cultural Gap' Hypothesis." *Urban Education* 7 (1972):241–260.

Rist, R. C. *The Urban School: A Factory for Failure.* Cambridge, Mass.: The M.I.T. Press, 1973.

Rosenthal, R., and Jacobson, L. "Teachers' Expectancies: Determinants of Pupils' IQ Gains." *Psychology Reports* 19 (1966):115–118.

Rosenthal, R., and Jacobson, L. *Pygmalion in the Classroom.* New York: Holt, Rinehart and Winston, 1968.

Rowe, M. "Science, Silence and Sanctions." *Science and Children* 6 (1969):11–13.

Rubington, E., and Weinberg, M. S. *Deviance: The Interactionist Perspective.* New York: Macmillan, 1973.

Rubovits, P., and Maehr, M. L. "Pygmalion Black and White." *Journal of Personality and Social Psychology* 2 (1973):210–218.

Schafer, W. E., and Olexa, C. *Tracking and Opportunity.* Scranton, Pa.: Chandler, 1971.

Scheff, T. *Being Mentally Ill.* Chicago; Aldine, 1966.

Schur, E. *Crimes without Victims.* Englewood Cliffs, N.J.: Prentice-Hall, 1965.

Schur, E. *Labeling Deviant Behavior.* New York: Harper and Row, 1971.

Scott, R. A., and Douglas, J. C. (eds.). *Theoretical Perspectives on Deviance.* New York: Basic Books, 1972.

Snow, R. E. "Unfinished Pygmalion." *Contemporary Psychology* 14 (1969):197–199.

Stein, A. "Strategies for Failure." *Harvard Educational Review* 41 (1971):158–204.

Tannenbaum, F. *Crime and the Community.* New York: Columbia University Press, 1938.

Taylor, C. "The Expectations of Pygmalion's Creators." *Educational Leadership* 28 (1970): 161–164.

Thorndike, R. L. "Review of Pygmalion in the Classroom." *Educational Research Journal* 5 (1968): 708–711.

Thorndike, R. L. "But Do You Have to Know How to Tell Time?" *Educational Research Journal* 6 (1969):692.

Warner, W. L.; Havighurst, R.; and Loeb, M.B. *Who Shall be Educated?* New York: Harper and Row, 1944.

Willis, S. *Formation of Teachers' Expectations of Student Academic Performance.* Unpublished Ph.D. dissertation, University of Texas, Austin, Texas, 1972.

Wilson, A. B. "Social Stratification and Academic Achievement," in *Education in Depressed Areas,* edited by H. Passow. New York: Teachers College Press, 1963.

Zajonc, R. B., and Brinkman, P. "Expectancy and Feedback as Independent Factors in Task Performance." *Journal of Personality and Social Psychology* 11 (1969):148–150.

The Politics of Culture

Understanding Local Political Resistance to Detracking in Racially Mixed Schools

Amy Stuart Wells and Irene Serna

Research on tracking, or grouping students into distinct classes for "fast" and "slow" learners, has demonstrated that this educational practice leads to racial and socioeconomic segregation within schools, with low-income, African American, and Latino students frequently placed in the lowest level classes, even when they have equal or higher test scores or grades (see Oakes, 1985; Oakes & Welner, 1995). Furthermore, being placed in the low track often has long-lasting negative effects on these students, as they fall further and further behind their peers and become increasingly bored in school. Partly in response to this research and partly in response to their own uneasiness with the separate and unequal classrooms created by tracking, educators across the country are beginning to respond by testing alternatives to tracking, a reform we call "detracking."

Over the last three years, our research team studied ten racially and socioeconomically mixed schools undergoing detracking reform, and attempted to capture the essence of the political struggles inherent in such efforts.[1] We believe that an important aspect of our qualitative, multiple case study is to help educators and policymakers understand the various manifestations of local political resistance to detracking—not only who instigates it, but also the ideology of opposition to such reforms and the political practices employed (see Oaken & Wells, 1995).

This article focuses on how forces outside the school walls shaped the ability of educators to implement "detracking reform"—to question existing track structures and promote greater access to challenging classes for all students. More specifically, we look at those actors whom we refer to as the "local elite"—those with a combination of economic, political, and cultural capital that is highly valued within their particular school community.[2] These elites are most likely to resist detracking reform because their children often enjoy privileged status in a tracked system. The capital of the elites enables them to engage in political practices that can circumvent detracking reform.

In order to understand the influence of local elites' political practices on the tracking reform, we examine their ideology of entitlement, or how they make meaning of their privilege within the educational system and how others come to see such meanings as the way things "ought to be." According to Gramsci (cited in Boggs 1984), insofar as ruling ideas emanating from elites are internalized by a majority of individuals within a given community, they become a defining motif of everyday life and appear as "common sense"—that is, as the "traditional popular conception of the world" (p. 161).

Yet we realize that the high-status cultural capital—the valued tastes and consumption patterns—of local elites and the resultant ideologies are easily affected by provincial social contexts and the particular range of class, race, and culture at those sites (Bourdieu, 1984). In a study of social reproduction in postmodern society, Harrison (1993) notes that "the task is not so much to look for the global correspondences between culture and class, but to reconstruct the peculiarly local and material micrologic of investments made in the intellectual field" (p. 40). Accordingly, in our study, we particularize the political struggles and

examine the specific ideologies articulated at each school site. Because we were studying ten schools in ten different cities and towns, we needed to contextualize each political struggle over detracking reform within its local school community. These local contexts are significant because the relations of power and domination that affect people most directly are those shaping the social contexts within which they live out their everyday lives: the home, the workplace, the classroom, the peer group. As Thompson (1990) states, "These are the contexts within which individuals spend the bulk of their time, acting and interacting, speaking and listening, pursuing their aims and following the aims of others" (p. 9).

Our research team used qualitative methods to examine technical aspects of detracking—school organization, grouping practices, and classroom pedagogy—as well as cultural norms and political practices that legitimize and support tracking as a "commonsense" approach to educating students (Oakes & Wells, 1995). Our research question was, What happens when someone with power in a totally mixed secondary school decides to reduce tracking? Guided by this question, we selected ten sites—six high schools and four middle schools—from a pool of schools that were undergoing detracking reform and volunteered to be studied. We chose these particular schools because of their diversity and demonstrated commitment to detracking. The schools we studied varied in size from more than three thousand to less than five hundred students. One school was in the Northeast, three were in the Midwest, one in the South, two in the Northwest, and three in various regions of California. Each school drew from a racially and socioeconomically diverse community and served significant but varied mixes of White, African American, Latino, Native American/Alaska Native, and/or Asian students. We visited each school three times over a two-year period. Data collection during our site visits included in-depth, semi-structured tape-recorded interviews with administrators, teachers, students, parents, and community leaders, including school board members. In total, more than four hundred participants across all ten schools were interviewed at least once. We also observed classrooms, as well as faculty, PTA, and school board meetings. We reviewed documents and wrote field notes about our observations within the schools and the communities. Data were compiled extensively from each school to form the basis of cross-case analysis. Our study ran from the spring of 1992 through the spring of 1995.[3]

Descriptions of "Local Elites"

The struggles over tracking and detracking reforms are, to a large extent, concerned with whose culture and life-style is valued, and, thus, whose way of knowing is equated with "intelligence." Traditional hierarchical track structures in schools have been validated by the conflation of culture and intelligence. When culturally biased "truths" about ability and merit confront efforts to "detrack," political practices are employed either to maintain the status quo or to push toward new conceptions of ability that would render a rigid and hierarchical track structure obsolete (see Oakes, Lipton, & Jones, 1995).

While we acknowledge that many agents contribute to the maintenance of a rigid track structure, this article examines the political practices of local elites in the school communities we studied. The elites discussed here had children enrolled in the detracking schools and thus constitute the subgroup of local elites active in shaping school policies. Their practices were aimed at maintaining a track structure, with separate and unequal educational opportunities for "deserving" elite students and "undeserving" or non-elite students. Our analysis of elite parents' ideology of privilege and the resultant political practices therefore includes an examination of "corresponding institutional mechanisms" (Bourdieu & Wacquant, 1992, p. 188) employed to prevent structural change that would challenge their status and privilege.

Our intention is not to criticize these powerful parents in an unsympathetic manner. Yet, we believe that too often the cultural forces that shape such parents' agency as they try to do what is best for their children remain hidden from view

and thus unquestioned. Our effort to unpack the "knapsack" of elite privilege will expose the tight relationship between the "objective" criteria of the schools and the cultural forces of the elite (McIntosh, 1992).

Detracking, or the process of moving schools toward a less rigid system of assigning students to classes and academic programs, is a hotly contested educational reform. In racially mixed schools, the controversy surrounding detracking efforts is compounded by beliefs about the relationship among race, culture, and academic ability. In virtually all racially mixed secondary schools, tracking resegregates students, with mostly White and Asian students in the high academic tracks and mostly African American and Latino students in the low tracks (Oakes, 1985; Oakes, Oraseth, Bell, & Camp, 1990). To the extent that elite parents have internalized dominant, but often unspoken, beliefs about race and intelligence, they may resist "desegregation" within racially mixed schools—here defined as detracking—because they do not want their children in classes with Black and Latino students.

Efforts to alter within-school racial segregation via detracking, then, are generally threatening to elites, in that they challenge their position at the top of the hierarchy. The perceived stakes, from an elite parent's perspective, are quite high. They argue, for instance, that their children will not be well served in detracked classes. And while these stakes are most frequently discussed in academic terms—for example, the dumbing down of the curriculum for smart students—the real stakes, we argue, are generally not academics at all, but, rather, status and power. For example, if a school does away with separate classes for students labeled "gifted" but teachers continue to challenge these students with the same curriculum in a detracked setting, the only "losses" the students will incur are their label and their separate and unequal status. Yet in a highly stratified society, such labels and privileged status confer power.

In looking at the ability of the upper strata of society to maintain power and control, Bourdieu (1977) argues that economic capital—that is, income, wealth, and property—is not the only form of capital necessary for social reproduction. He describes other forms of capital, including political, social, and cultural (Bourdieu & Wacquant, 1992). In our analysis of resistance to detracking reforms, we focus on cultural capital and its relationship to dominant ideologies within our school communities because of the explicit connections between cultural capital and educational achievement within Bourdieu's work. According to Bourdieu (1984), cultural capital consists of culturally valued tastes and consumption patterns, which are rewarded within the educational system. Bourdieu discusses "culture" not in its restricted, normative sense, but rather from a more anthropological perspective. Culture is elaborated in a "taste" for refined objects, which is what distinguishes the culture of the dominant class or upper social status from that of the rest of society. In order for elites to employ their cultural capital to maintain power, emphasis must be placed on subtleties of taste—for example, form over function, manner over matter. Within the educational system, Bourdieu argues, students are frequently rewarded for their taste, and for the cultural knowledge that informs it. For instance, elite students whose status offers them the opportunity to travel to other cities, states, and countries on family vacations are often perceived to be more "intelligent" than other students, simply because the knowledge they have gained from these trips is reflected in what is valued in schools. When high-status, elite students' taste is seen as valued knowledge within the educational system, other students' taste and the knowledge that informs it is devalued (Bourdieu & Passeron, 1979). In this way, high-status culture is socially constructed as "intelligence"— a dubious relationship that elites must strive to conceal in order to legitimize their merit-based claim to privileged status. In other words, what is commonly referred to as "objective" criteria of intelligence and achievement is actually extremely biased toward the subjective experience and ways of knowing of elite students. Similarly, Delpit (1995) describes the critical role that power plays in our society and educational system, as the worldviews of those in privileged positions are "taken as the only

reality, while the worldviews of those less powerful are dismissed as inconsequential" (p. xv). The education system is the primary field in which struggles over these cultural meanings take place and where, more often than not, high-status cultural capital is translated into high-status credentials, such as academic degrees from elite institutions (Bourdieu & Passeron, 1977).

Thus, socially valuable cultural capital—form and manner—is the property many upper class and, to a lesser extent, middle-class families transmit to their offspring that substitutes for, or supplements, the transmission of economic capital as a means of maintaining class, status, and privilege across generations (Bourdieu, 1973). Academic qualifications and high-status educational titles are to cultural capital what money and property titles are to economic capital. The form and manner of academic qualifications are critical. Students cannot simply graduate from high school; they must graduate with the proper high-status qualifications that allow them access to the most selective universities and to the credentials those institutions confer.

Through the educational system, elites use their economic, political, and cultural capital to acquire symbolic capital—the most highly valued capital in a given society or local community. Symbolic capital signifies culturally important attributes, such as status, authority, prestige, and, by extension, a sense of honor. The social construction of symbolic capital may vary from one locality to another, but race and social class consistently play a role, with White, wealthy, well-educated families most likely to be at the top of the social strata (Harrison, 1993).

Because the cultural capital of the elite is that which is most valued and rewarded within the educational system, elite status plays a circular role in the process of detracking reform: parents with high economic, political, and cultural capital are most likely to have children in the highest track and most prestigious classes, which in turn gives them more symbolic capital in the community. The elite parents can then employ their symbolic capital in the educational decision-making arena to maintain advantages for their children. Educational reforms that, like detracking, challenge the advantages bestowed upon children of the elite are resisted not only by the elites themselves, but also by educators and even other parents and community members who may revere the cultural capital of elite families. The school and the community thus bestow elite parents with the symbolic capital, or honor, that allows them political power.

The status of the local elites in the ten school communities we studied derived in part from the prestige they and their children endowed to public schools simply by their presence. The elite are the most valued citizens, those the public schools do not want to lose, because the socially constructed status of institutions such as schools is dependent upon the status of the individuals attending them. These are also the families most likely to flee public schools if they are denied what they want from them. For example, at Grant High School, an urban school in the Northwest, the White, upper-middle-class parents who sent their children to public schools held tremendous power over the district administration. Many of them were highly educated and possessed the economic means to send their children to private schools if they so chose.

While the elites at each of the schools we studied held economic, social, and political capital, the specific combination of these varied at each site in relation to the cultural capital valued there. Thus, who the elites were and their particular rationale for tracking varied among locations, based on the distinctive mix of race, class, and culture. For instance, at Liberty High School, located in a West Coast city, many of the White parents were professors at a nearby university. As "professional intellectuals," they strongly influenced the direction of Liberty High; although they were generally not as wealthy as business executives, they were nevertheless imbued with a great deal of high-status cultural capital. Meanwhile, educators and White parents at Liberty noted that most of the Black and Latino students enrolled in the school came from very low-income families. Many of the people we interviewed said there was a sizable number of middle-class Black families in this community, but that they did not send their children to public schools. This school's social class divide, which some educators and Black students argued was a caricature, allowed White parents to blame the school's resegregation through tracking on the "family backgrounds" of the students, rather than on racial prejudice.

In the midwestern town of Plainview, the local White elites worked in private corporations rather than universities. Here, the high-status cultural capital was, in general, far more conservative, pragmatic, and less "intellectual" than at Liberty. Nonetheless, the elite parents here and at each of the schools we studied strove for the same advantages that the elite parents at Liberty High demanded for their children.

The African American students in Plainview comprised two groups—those who lived in a small, working-class Black neighborhood in the district and those who transferred into Plainview from the "inner city" through an inter-district desegregation plan. At this site, however, the social class distinctions between the two groups of Black students were blurred by many White respondents, particularly in their explanations of why Black students from both groups were consistently found in the lowest track classes. For instance, teachers could not tell us which Black students lived in Plain-view and which rode the bus in from the city. Some teachers also spoke of Black students'—all Black students'—low levels of achievement as the result of their families culture of poverty, and not the result of what the school offered them. Despite the relative economic advantages of many African American students who lived in the Plainview district as compared to those who lived in the city, all Black students in this mostly White, wealthy suburban school were doing quite poorly. While African Americans constituted 25 percent of the student population, less than 5 percent of the students in the highest level courses were Black. Furthermore, a district task force on Black achievement found that more than half of the Black students in the high school had received at least one D or F over the course of one school year.

In other schools, the interplay between race and class was more complex, especially when the local elite sought to distinguish themselves from other, lower income Whites. For instance, in the small midwestern Bearfield School District, which is partly rural and partly suburban, wealthy, well-educated, White suburban parents held the most power over the educational system because they possessed more economic and highly valued cultural capital than rural Whites or African Americans. When a desegregation plan was instituted in the 1970s, it was Black and poor rural White children who were bused. As the Bearfield Middle School principal explained, "As our business manager/superintendent once told me, the power is neither Black nor White; it's green—as in money. And that's where the power is. Rich people have clout. Poor people don't have clout."

Still, the less wealthy and less educated rural Whites in Bearfield, while not as politically powerful as the suburban Whites, remained more influential than the African American families. When the two middle schools in the district were consolidated in 1987, Whites—both wealthy suburban and poor rural—were able to convince the school board to close down the newly built middle school located in the African American community and keep open the older middle school on the White side of the town.

Although the interplay between class and culture within a racially mixed community is generally defined along racial lines, we found that was not always the case. For example, King Middle School, a magnet school in a large north-eastern city, was designed to attract students of many racial groups and varied socioeconomic status. A teacher explained that the parents who are blue-collar workers do not understand what's going on at the school, but the professional and middle-class parents frequently call to ask for materials to help their children at home. Educators at King insisted that middle-class and professional parents were not all White, and that there was very little correlation between income and race at the school, with its student body composed of more than twenty racial/ethnic groups, including Jamaican, Chinese, Armenian, Puerto Rican, African American, and various European ethnic groups. While we found it difficult to believe that there was no correlation between race/ethnicity and income in the city with relatively poor African American and

Latino communities, it is clear that not all of the local elites at King were White.

Thus, the layers of stratification in some schools were many, but the core of the power elite in all ten communities consisted of a group of parents who were more White, wealthy, and well-educated relative to others in their community. They were the members of the school communities with the greatest economic and/or high-status cultural capital, which they have passed on to their children. The schools, in turn, greatly rewarded the children of these elite for their social distinctions, which were perceived to be distinctions of merit (DiMaggio, 1979).

The Political Ideology of Tracking and Detracking: "Deserving" High-Track Students

Bourdieu's concepts of domination and social reproduction are particularly useful in understanding the education system, because education is the field in which the elite both "records and conceals" its own privilege. Elites "record" privilege through formal educational qualifications, which then serve to "conceal" the inherited cultural capital needed to acquire them. According to Harrison (1993), "What is usually referred to as equality of opportunity or meritocracy is, for Bourdieu, a 'sociodicy'; that is, a sacred story that legitimates the dominant class' own privilege" (p. 43).

The political resistance of the local elite to de-tracking reforms cannot, therefore, be understood separately from the "sociodicy" or ideology employed to legitimize the privileged place elites and their children hold in the educational system. Ideology, in a Gramscian sense, represents ideas, beliefs, cultural preferences, and even myths and superstitions, which possess a certain "material" reality of their own (Gramsci, 1971). In education, societal ideas, beliefs, and cultural preferences of intelligence have found in tracking structures their own material reality. Meanwhile, tracking reinforces and sustains those ideas, beliefs, and cultural preferences.

According to Thompson (1990), ideology refers to the ways in which meaning serves, in particular circumstances, to establish and sustain relations of power that are systematically asymmetrical. Broadly speaking, ideology is *meaning in the service of power*. Thompson suggests that the study of ideology requires researchers to investigate the ways in which meaning is constructed and conveyed by symbolic forms of various kinds, "from everyday linguistic utterances to complex images and texts; it requires us to investigate the social contexts within which symbolic forms are employed and deployed" (p. 7).

The ideology of the local elites in the schools we studied was often cloaked in the "symbolic form" that Thompson describes. While the symbols used by politically powerful people to express their resistance to detracking differed from one site to the next, race consistently played a central, if not explicit, role. Although local elites expressed their dissatisfaction with detracking reform in overtly racial terms, their resistance was couched in more subtle expressions of the politics of culture that have clear racial implications. For example, they said they liked the concept of a racially mixed school, as long as the African American or Latino students acted like White, middle-class children, and their parents were involved in the school and bought into the American Dream. At Central High, a predominately Latino school on the West Coast with a 23 percent White student body, the local elite consisted of a relatively small middle class of mostly White and a few Latino families. No real upper middle class existed, and most of the Latino students came from very low-income families; many were recent immigrants to the United States. A White parent whose sons were taking honors classes explained her opposition to detracking efforts at Central, exposing her sense of entitlement this way:

> I think a lot of those Latinos come and they're still Mexicans at heart. They're not American. I don't care what color you are, we're in America here and we're going for this country. And I think their heart is in Mexico and they're with that culture still. It's one thing to come over and bring your culture and to use it, but it's another thing to get into that . . . and I'm calling it the American ethic. They're not into it and that's why they end up so far behind. They get in school, and they are behind.

This construct of the "deserving minority" denies the value of non-White students' and parents' own culture or of their sometimes penetrating critique of the American creed (see Yonesawa, Williams, & Hirshberg, 1995), and implies that only those students with the cultural capital and underlying elite ideology deserve to be rewarded in the educational system. Yet because the political arguments put forth by powerful parents in the schools we studied sounded so benign, so "American," the cultural racism that guided their perspective was rarely exposed. Consequently, both the racial segregation within the schools and the actions of parents to maintain it were perceived as natural.

We found many instances in which elite parents attempted to distance their children from students they considered to be less deserving of special attention and services. For instance, at Rolling Hills Middle School, located in a southeastern metropolitan area with a large, county-wide desegregation plan, one wealthy White parent said she and her husband purchased a home in the nearby neighborhood because Rolling Hills and its feeder high school are two of the handful of schools in the district that offer an "advanced program." She said several people had told her that in the advanced program the curriculum was better, fewer behavior problems occurred in the classes, and students received more individualized attention from teachers. She also said that had her children not been accepted into the advanced program, she and her family would not have moved into this racially mixed school district, but would have purchased a home in one of the Whiter suburbs east of the county line. Interestingly enough, this parent did not know whether or not the White suburban schools offered an advanced program. Also of interest in this district is the creation of the advanced program in the same year as the implementation of the desegregation plan.

The White, well-educated parents at Grant High School often stated that the racial diversity of the student body was one characteristic they found most appealing about the school; They said that such a racially mixed environment better prepared their children for life in "the real world." One parent noted that "the positive mixing of racial groups is important to learning to live in society." But some teachers argued that while these parents found Grant's diversity acceptable—even advantageous—their approval was conditioned by their understanding that "their children [would] only encounter Black students in the hallways and not in their classrooms." Grant's assistant principal noted that "many upper class, professional parents hold occupational positions in which they work toward equity and democracy, but expect their children to be given special treatment at Grant."

This ideology of "diversity at a distance" is often employed by White parents at strategic moments when the privileged status of their children appears to be threatened (Lareau, 1989). In our study, the parents of honors students at Grant successfully protested the school effort to eliminate the "tennis shoe" registration process by which students and teachers jointly negotiated access to classes.[4] Some of the faculty had proposed that the school switch to a computer registration program that would guarantee Black and Latino students greater access to high-track classes. The parents of the honors students stated that they were not protesting the registration change because they were opposed to having their children in racially mixed classes, but because "they [felt] that their children [would] learn more in an environment where all students are as motivated to learn as they are—in a homogeneous ability classroom."

Respondents at Grant said that parents assumed that if any student was allowed into an honors class, regardless of his or her prior track, it must not be a good class. The assumption here was that if there was no selectivity in placing students in particular classes, then the learning and instruction in those classes could not be good. Parents of the most advanced students "assumed" that since the language arts department had made the honors and regular

curriculum the same and allowed more students to enroll in honors, the rigor of these classes had probably diminished, despite the teachers' claims that standards had remained high.

At Liberty High School, where the intellectual elite were more "liberal" than the elite in most of the other schools, parents also frequently cited the racial diversity of the school as an asset. For instance, one parent commented that it was the racial and cultural mix—"the real range of people here"—that attracted her to Liberty High. She liked the fact that her daughter was being exposed to people of different cultures and different socioeconomic backgrounds: "We took her out of private school, where there's all these real upper middle-class White kids." Yet, despite this espoused appreciation for diversity among White liberal parents at Liberty, they strongly resisted efforts to dismantle the racially segregated track system. According to another White parent of a high-track student at Liberty:

> I think the one thing that really works at Liberty High is the upper track. It does. And to me, I guess my goal would be for us to find a way to make the rest of Liberty High work as well as the upper track. But it's crucial that we not destroy the upper track to do that, and that can happen . . . it really could. . . . I feel my daughter will get an excellent education if the program continues the way it is, if self-scheduling continues so that they aren't all smoothed together.

In all of the schools we studied, the most interesting aspect of elites' opposition to detracking is that they based their resistance on the symbolic mixing of high "deserving" and low "undeserving" students, rather than on information about what actually happens in detracked classrooms. For instance, an English teacher at Plainview High School who taught a heterogeneous American Studies course in which she academically challenged all her students said that the popularity of the Advanced Placement classes among the elite parents was in part based upon a "myth" that "they're the only classes that offer high standards, that they're the only courses that are interesting and challenging. And the myth is that that's where the best learning takes place. That's a myth."

At Explorer Middle School, located in a mid-sized northwestern city, the identified gifted students—nearly all White, despite a school population that was 30 percent American Indian—were no longer segregated into special classes or teams. Rather, "gifted" students were offered extra "challenge" courses, which other "non-gifted" students could choose to take as well. The day after a grueling meeting with parents of the "gifted" students, the designated gifted education teacher who works with these and other students in the challenge classes was upset by the way in which the parents had responded to her explanation of the new challenge program and the rich educational opportunities available in these classes:

> And they didn't ask, "well what are our kids learning in your classes?" Nobody asked that. I just found that real dismaying, and I was prepared to tell them what we do in class and here's an example. I had course outlines. I send objectives home with every class, and goals and work requirements, and nobody asked me anything about that ... like they, it's ... to me it's like I'm dealing with their egos, you know, more than what their kids really need educationally.

What this and other teachers in our study told us is that many elite parents are more concerned about the labels placed on their children than what actually goes on in the classroom. This is a powerful illustration of what Bourdieu (1984) calls "form over function" and "manner over matter."

Notions of Entitlement

Symbols of the "deserving," high-track students must be juxtaposed with conceptions of the undeserving, low-track students in order for strong protests against detracking to make sense in a society that advocates equal opportunity. Bourdieu argues that "impersonal domination"— the sociocultural form of domination found in

free, industrial societies where more coercive methods of domination are not allowed—entails the rationalization of the symbolic. When symbols of domination are rationalized, the *entitlement* of the upper strata of society is legitimized, and thus this impersonal domination is seen as natural (Harrison, 1993, p. 42).

In our study, we found that elite parents rationalized their children's entitlement to better educational opportunities based upon the resources that they themselves brought to the system. For instance, parents from the White, wealthy side of Bearfield Middle School's attendance zone perceived that the African American students who attended the school and lived on the "other" side of town benefited from the large tax burden shouldered by the White families. One White parent noted, "I don't feel that our school should have, you know, people from that far away coming to our school. I don't think it's right as far as the taxes we pay.... They don't pay the taxes that we pay, and they're at our schools also. Um, I just don't feel they belong here, no." According to the superintendent of the school district, this statement reflects the widely held belief among Whites that they are being taxed to pay for schools for Black students, "and therefore the White community ... should make the decisions about the schools ... because they are paying the bill." These perspectives explain in part why the consolidation of the district's two middle schools resulted in the closing of the mostly Black but much more recently built school, and favored the old, dilapidated Bearfield building as the single middle school site.

At the same time, these parents balked at the suggestion that their own social privilege and much of their children's advantages had less to do with objective merit or intellectual ability than it had to do with their families' economic and cultural capital. Harrison (1993) expands upon Bourdieu's notion that culture functions to deny or disavow the economic origins of capital by gaining symbolic credit for the possessors of economic and political capital. Harrison argues that the seemingly legitimate and meritocratic basis upon which students "earn" academic credentials is an important aspect of the dominant class's denial of entitlement as a process in which inherited economic and political power receives social consecration. In other words, the elite parents must convince themselves and others that the privileges their children are given in the educational system were earned in a fair and meritocratic way, and are not simply a consequence of the parents' own privileged place in society. "The demonstration that the belief of merit is a part of the process of social consecration in which the dominant class's power is both acknowledged and mis-recognized, is at the core of Bourdieu's analysis of culture" (Harrison, 1993, p. 44).

There is strong evidence from the schools we studied that students frequently end up in particular tracks and classrooms more on the basis of their parents' privilege than of their own "ability." A school board member in the district in which Rolling Hills Middle School is located explained that students are placed in the advanced program depending on who their parents happen to know. Because the advanced program was implemented at the same time as the countywide desegregation plan, it has become a sophisticated form of resegregation within racially mixed schools supported by conceptions of "deserving" advanced students. The school board member said that parents of the advanced students are very much invested in labels that their children acquire at school. When children are labeled "advanced" it means their parents are "advanced," as well. In fact, said the board member, some of these parents refer to themselves as the "advanced parents": "There is still an elitist aspect as far as I am concerned. I also think it is an ego trip for parents. They love the double standard that their children are in Advanced Placement programs."

Similarly, several elite parents of students in the advanced program at Grant High School expressed regret that the school had such a poor vocational education department for the "other" students—those who were not advanced. Their lament for vocational education related to their way of understanding the purpose of the high school in serving different students. One of these parents, for example, stated that the role of the honors classes was to groom students to become "managers and professionals" and that something else should be done for those kids who would grow up to be "workers."

According to Harrison (1993), the elite seek to deny the arbitrary nature of the social order that culture does much to conceal. This process, which he calls "masking," occurs when what is culturally arbitrary is "essentialized, absolutized or universalized" (p. 45). Masking is generally accomplished via symbols—culturally specific as opposed to materially specific symbols (Bourdieu & Wacquant, 1992). For example, standardized test scores become cultural symbols of intelligence that are used to legitimize the track structure in some instances while they are "masked" in other instances.

An example of this "masking" process was revealed to us at Grant High School, where elite parents of the most advanced students approved of using test scores as a measure of students' intelligence and worthiness to enroll in the highest track classes. But when children of the elite who were identified as "highly able" in elementary school did not make the test score cutoffs for high school honors classes, the parents found ways to get their children placed in these classes anyway, as if the tests in that particular instance were not valid. The educators usually gave in to these parents' demands, and then cited such instances as evidence of a faulty system. The so-called faults within the system, however, did not lead to broad-based support among powerful parents or educators to dismantle the track structure.

Similarly, at Explorer Middle School, where the wealthy White "gifted" students were all placed in regular classes and then offered separate challenge classes along with other students who chose to take such a class, the principal collected data on the achievement test scores for the identified gifted students and other students in the school. She found huge overlaps in the two sets of scores with some identified "non-gifted" students scoring in the 90th percentile and above, and some "gifted" students ranking as low as the 58th percentile. Yet, when the mostly White parents of children identified by the district as "gifted" were presented with these data, they attributed the large number of low test scores among the pool of gifted students to a handful of non-White students participating in that program, although the number of non-White "gifted" students was far lower than the number of low test scores within the gifted program. The White parents simply would not admit that any of their children did not deserve a special label (and the extra resources that come with it). According to the teacher of the challenge classes, one of the most vocal and demanding "gifted" parents was the mother of a boy who was not even near the top of his class: "I still can't figure out how he got in the gifted program; he doesn't perform in any way at that high a level. . . . She is carrying on and on and on. . . ."

Despite evidence that the "gifted" label may be more a form of symbolic capital than a true measure of innate student ability, the parents of students who had been identified as gifted by this school district maintained a strong sense of entitlement. For instance, a Whiter upper middle-class father of two so-called gifted boys told us he was outraged that the "gifted and talented" teacher at Explorer spent her time teaching challenge classes that were not exclusively for gifted students. This father was adamant that the state's special funding for gifted and talented (G/T) programs should be spent exclusively on identified G/T students. He noted that at the other middle school in the district, the G/T teacher worked with a strictly G/T class, "whereas at Explorer, the G/T teacher works with a class that is only 50 percent G/T." In other words, "precious" state resources for gifted and talented students were being spent on "non-deserving" students—many of whom had higher middle school achievement test scores than the students who had been identified by the school district as gifted many years earlier.

At Plainview High School, the English teacher who created the heterogeneous American Studies class began reading about the social science research on intelligence, and concluded that our society and education system do not really understand what intelligence is or how to measure it. When the principal asked her to present her research to parents at an open house, her message was not well received, particularly by those parents whose children were in the Advanced Placement classes. According to this teacher, "If you were raised under the system that said you were very intelligent and high achieving, you don't want anyone questioning that system, OK? That's just the way it is." She said that what some of the parents were most threatened by was how this research on intelligence was going to be used and whether the high school was going to do away with Advanced Placement classes. She recalled, "I used the word 'track' once and debated whether I could weave that in because I knew the power of the word, and I didn't want to shut everyone down. It was very interesting."

Political Practices: How the Local Elite Undermined Detracking

The ideology and related symbols that legitimate local elites' sense of entitlement are critical to educational policy and practice. As Harrison (1993) and Harker (1984) note, Bourdieu's work is ultimately focused on the strategic practices employed when conflicts emerge. In this way, Bourdieu identifies "practices"—actions that maintain or change the social structures—within strategically oriented forms of conflict. These strategic actions must be rooted back into the logic or sense of entitlement that underlies these practices. In other words, we examined political practices that are intended to be consistent with an ideology of "deserving" high-track students. These practices were employed by elite parents when educators posed a threat to the privileged status of their children by questioning the validity and objectivity of a rigid track structure (Useem, 1990).

According to Bourdieu, when seemingly "objective" structures, such as tracking systems, are faithfully reproduced in the dispositions or ways of knowing of actors, then the "arbitrary" nature of the existing structure can go completely unrecognized (Bourdieu & Wacquant, 1992). For instance, no one questions the evidence of the separate and unequal "gifted and talented" or "highly advanced" program for children of the local elites, despite the fact that the supposedly "objective" measures that legitimize these programs—standardized tests scores—do not always support the somewhat "arbitrary" nature of student placement. This arbitrary placement system is more sensitive to cultural capital than academic "ability."

In the case of tracking, so-called objective and thus non-arbitrary standardized tests are problematic on two levels. First, the tests themselves are culturally biased in favor of wealthy, White students, and therefore represent a poor measure of "ability" or "intelligence." Second, scores on these exams tend to count more for some students than others. Elite students who have low achievement test scores are placed in high tracks, while non-White and non-wealthy students with high test scores are bound to the lower tracks (see Oakes et al., 1995; Welner & Oakes, 1995). Still, test scores remain an undisclosed and undisputed "objective" measure of student track placement and thus a rationale for maintaining the track structure in many schools.

When these undisclosed or undisputed parts of the universe are questioned, conflicts arise that call for strategic political practices on the part of elites. As Harrison (1993) states, "Where the fit can no longer be maintained and where, therefore, the arbitrary nature of the objective structure becomes evident, the dominant class must put into circulation a discourse in which this arbitrary order is misrecognized as such" (p. 41). When the arbitrary nature of the "objective" tracking structure becomes evident, detracking efforts are initiated, often by educators who have come to realize the cultural basis of the inequalities within our so-called meritocratic educational system.

Within each of our ten schools, when educators penetrated the ideology that legitimizes the track structure (and the advantages that high-track students have within it), elite parents felt that their privileges were threatened. We found that local elites employed four practices to undermine and co-opt meaningful detracking efforts in such a way that they and their children would continue to benefit disproportionately from educational policies. These four overlapping and intertwined practices were threatening flight, co-opting the

institutional elites, soliciting buy-in from the "not-quite elite," and accepting detracking bribes.

Threatening Flight

Perhaps nowhere in our study was the power of the local elite and their ideology of entitlement more evident than when the topic of "elite flight" was broached, specifically when these parents threatened to leave the school. Educators in the ten schools we studied were acutely aware that their schools, like most institutions, gain their status, or symbolic capital, from the social status of the students who attend (Wells & Crain, 1999). They know they must hold onto the local elites in order for their schools to remain politically viable institutions that garner broad public support. As a result, the direct or indirect threat of elite flight can thwart de-tracking efforts when local elite parents have other viable public or private school options.

At Liberty High School, the liberal ideals and principles that are the cornerstone of this community were challenged when local elites were asked to embrace reforms that they perceived to be removing advantages held by their children. In fact, discussions and implementation of such reforms—for example, the creation of a heterogeneous ninth-grade English/social studies core—caused elite parents to "put into circulation a discourse" that legitimized their claim to something better than what other students received. Without this special attention for high-track students, elite parents said, they had little reason to keep their children at Liberty. As one parent of a high-track student noted in discussing the local elite's limits and how much of the school's equity-centered detracking reforms they would tolerate before abandoning the school:

> I think it happens to all of us; when you have children, you confront all your values in a totally different way. I mean, I did all this work in education, I knew all these things about it, and it's very different when it's your own child cause when it's your own child your real responsibility is to advocate for that child.

I mean, I might make somewhat different decisions about Liberty High, though probably not terribly different, because as I say, I would always have in mind the danger of losing a big chunk of kids, and with them the community support that makes this school work well.

The power of the threat of elite flight is evident in the history of the creation of tracking structures in many of our schools, where advanced and gifted programs began to appear and proliferate at the same time that the schools in these districts were becoming more racially mixed, either through a desegregation plan or demographic shifts. This shift toward more tracking as schools became increasingly racially mixed follows the long history of tracking in the U.S. educational system. Tracking became more systematized at the turn of the century, as non-Anglo immigrant students enrolled in urban high schools (Oakes, 1985). At Grant High School, which is located in a racially diverse urban school district surrounded by separate Whiter and more affluent districts, the highly advanced and "regular" advanced programs were started shortly after desegregation at the insistence of local elite parents who wanted separate classes for their children. One teacher noted that the advanced programs were designed to respond to a segment of the White community that felt, "Oh, we'll send our kids to public school, but only if there's a special program for them."

At Grant, the chair of the language arts department, an instigator of detracking reforms efforts, said that the parents of the "advanced" students run the school district:

> They scare those administrators the same way they scare us. They're the last vestiges of middle-class people in the public schools in some sense. And they know that. And they flaunt that sometimes. And they scare people with that. And the local media would spit [the deputy superintendent] up in pieces if she did something to drive these parents out of the school district. So, yeah, I'm sure she's nervous about anything we're doing.

Similarly, at Rolling Hills Middle School, where the Advanced Program began in the late 1970s, shortly after the county-wide desegregation plan was implemented, the mother of two White boys in the program noted, "If I heard they were going to eliminate the Advanced Program, I would be very alarmed, and would seriously consider if I could afford a private school." She indicated that she thought that most parents of students at Rolling Hills felt this way.

At Central High School, White flight consistently paralleled the influx of Latino immigrant students into the school. Administrators said they hoped that the relocation of the school to a new site in a more middle-class area of the district would allow Central to maintain its White population. But many educators said they felt that what keeps White students at Central is the honors program, which would have been scaled back under detracking reform. This reform effort has been almost completely derailed by political roadblocks from both inside the school and the surrounding community.

Suburban, midwestern Plainview High School was the school in which we perhaps noted the *perceived* threat of elite flight to be most powerful. There, the concept of "community stability" was foremost on the minds of the educators. Many of the teachers and administrators in the Plainview district, particularly at the high school, came to Plainview from the nearby Hamilton School District, which experienced massive White flight two decades earlier. Essentially, the population of the Hamilton district shifted from mostly White, upper middle class to all Black and poor in a matter often years—roughly between 1968 and 1978. According to these educators and many other respondents in Plainview, the status of the Hamilton district and its sole high school plummeted, as each incoming freshman class became significantly darker and poorer. Once regarded as the premier public high school in the metropolitan area, Hamilton suddenly served as a reminder of the consequences of White flight. The large numbers of White residents and educators who came to Plainview after fleeing Hamilton kept the memory of White flight alive, and used Hamilton as a symbol of this threat.

Of all the educators in the district, it was the Plainview High School principal, Mr. Fredrick, who appeared most fixated on issues of community "stability" and the role of the schools in maintaining it:

> Here's my problem, what I'm doing at Plainview High School is essentially trying to make it stable enough so that other people can integrate the neighborhood. Now if other people aren't integrating the neighborhood, I'm not doing it either. I'm not out there working on that, I don't have time to be out there working on that, I've got to be making sure that what we're doing in Plainview High School is strong, we're strong enough, and have the reputation of, so that as we integrate, which I'm hoping is happening, that Whites won't get up and flee . . . when they come in and say, I hope you're here in eight years, that is a commitment those White people are gonna be there in eight years.

Fredrick argues that an academically strong high school led by a principal who maintains a good relationship with the community will help stabilize the whole community. As he explains, "I believe we can keep stability in Plainview while still being out in front of education. Now that's what I feel my job is." Frederick's goal of maintaining racial stability in the community is noble in many respects, but we learned during our visits to Plainview that his focus on White flight has resulted in intense efforts to please the elite White parents. These efforts to cater to elite parents have consistently worked against detracking reform in the school. While some of the teachers and other administrators continued to push for more innovative grouping and instructional strategies, Fredrick has advocated more Advanced Placement courses and encouraged more students to take these classes. In this way, the threat of White elite flight has helped maintain the hierarchical track structure and an Advanced Placement curriculum that many teachers, students, and less elite parents argue is not creative or instructionally sound.

Co-opting the Institutional Elites

The threat of flight is one of the ways in which local elites provoke responses to their institutional demands. This threat, and the fear it creates in the hearts of educators, is related to the way in which the "institutional elites" —that is educators with power and authority within the educational system—become co-opted by the ideology of the local elites. Both Domhoff (1983, 1990) and Mills (1956) write about institutional elites as "high-level" employees in institutions (either private corporations or governmental agencies, such as the U.S. Treasury Department) who see their roles as serving the upper, capitalist-based class. At a more micro or local level, we find that the institutional elites are the educational administrators who see their roles as serving the needs and demands of the local elites. Indeed, in most situations, their professional success and even job security depend on their ability to play these roles.

For instance, in small-town Bearfield, the new superintendent, who is politically very popular with elite parents and community members, has developed a less than positive impression of detracking efforts at the middle school. Yet his view is based less on first-hand information about the reform through visits to the school or discussions with the teachers than on the input he has received from White parents who have placed their children in private schools. To him, the educators at Bearfield Middle School have "let the academics slide just a little bit." Because of the superintendent's sense of commitment to the powerful White, wealthy parents, the principal of Bearfield indicated that he feels intense pressure to raise standardized test scores and prove that academics are not sliding at the school. Thus, some degree of "teaching to the test" has come at the expense of a more creative and innovative curriculum that facilitates detracking efforts by acknowledging, for example, different ways of knowing material. In a symbolic move, the teaching staff has rearranged the Black History Month curriculum to accommodate standardized test prepping in the month of February.

The relationship among the institutional elites at urban Grant High School, its school district office, and the local elite parents, however, demonstrates one of the most severe instances of "co-optation" that we observed. At the district's main office and at the high school, many of the educational administrators are African American. Still, these administrators frequently have failed to push for the kinds of reforms that would benefit the mostly African American students in the lowest track classes. Several respondents noted that Black educators who have been advocates for democratic reform have not survived in this district, and that those who cater to the demands of powerful White parents have been promoted within the system.

At the end of the 1993–1994 school year, the African American principal of Grant, Mr. Phillips, rejected the language arts department's proposal to detrack ninth-grade English by putting "honors" and "regular" students together in the same classes and offering honors as an extra credit option for all students. The principal claimed that it was not fair to do away with separate honors classes when the proposal had not been discussed with parents. His decision, he explained, was based on frequent complaints he received from the mostly White parents of high-track students that changes were being made at the school, particularly in the language arts department, without their prior knowledge or consent. According to the language arts department chair, when her department detracked twelfth-grade electives, it "really pissed people off." Also, when these elite parents were not consulted about the proposal to change the school schedule to an alternative four-period schedule, they protested and were successful in postponing the change.

Furthermore, a recent attempt by Grant's history department to do away with separate honors classes at the request of some students was thwarted by the parents of honors students, who, according to one teacher, "went through the roof." Some of the teachers in other departments indicated that they suspected the history department's move to eliminate honors classes was not sincere, but rather a political tactic designed to generate support among powerful elite parents for the honors program. In fact, the history department chair, who opposes detracking, noted that his only recourse to stop the detracking reform was to go to the parents and get them upset "because they had the power to do things at school."

At Grant, administrators at the district office have historically been very responsive to the concerns of White parents, and thus regularly implement policies designed to retain the White students. For instance, the district leadership convened an all-White "highly capable parent task force" to examine issues surrounding the educational advanced programs for "highly capable" students. The task force strongly recommended self-contained classrooms for advanced students, making detracking efforts across the district more problematic. According to one of the teachers at Grant, school board members would not talk about the elitism around this program because they were "feeling under siege."

At several schools in our study, educational administrators, especially principals, have lost their jobs since detracking efforts began, in part because they refused co-optation and advocated detracking. At Liberty High School, despite the principal's efforts to make de-tracking as politically acceptable to the elite parents as possible, in the end he was "done in" by the institutional elites at the district office who would not give him the extra resources he needed to carry out detracking in a manner local elites would have considered acceptable.

Buy-In of the "Not-Quite Elite"

In an interesting article about the current political popularity of decentralized school governance and growth of school-site councils with broad decision-making power, Beare (1993) writes that the middle class is a very willing accomplice in the strategy to create such councils and "empower" parents to make important decisions about how schools are run. He notes that it is the middle-class parents who put themselves forward for election to such governing bodies. Yet he argues that in spite of this new-found participatory role for middle-class parents, they actually have little control over the course of their children's schools, because such courses are chartered by a larger power structure. As Beare states, "In one sense, then, participative decision-making is a politically diversionary tactic, a means of keeping activist people distracted by their own self-inflicted, busy work. The middle class are willing accomplices, for they think they are gaining access to the decision-making of the power structures" (p. 202).

The ideology of the local elite's entitlement is so pervasive and powerful that the elites do not necessarily have to be directly involved in the decision-making processes at schools, although they often are. But between the local elites' threats to flee, co-optation of institutional elites, and ability to make their privilege appear as "common sense," such school-site councils will most likely simply reflect, as Beare (1993) points out, the broader power structure. In this way, the "self-inflicted busy work" of the not-quite elites, which, depending on the context of the schools, tend to be the more middle- or working-class parents, is just that— busy work that helps the schools maintain the existing power relations and a highly tracked structure. This is what Gramsci (1971) would refer to as the "consensual" basis of power, or the consensual side of politics in a civil society (see Boggs, 1984; Gramsci, 1971).

We saw a clear example of how this co-optation plays out at Plainview High School, where a group of about thirty predominantly White parents served on the advisory board for the most visible parent group, called the Parent-Teacher Organization, or PTO (even though there were no teachers in this organization). The PTO advisory board met with the principal once a month to act as his "sounding board" on important school-site issues, particularly those regarding discipline. We found through in-depth interviews with many of the parents on the PTO Board that these parents were not the most powerful or most elite parents in the one-high-school district. In fact, as the former president of the advisory board and the mother of a not-quite-high-track student explained, "The Advanced Placement parents don't run the president of the PTO. As a matter of fact, I'm trying to think when the last time [was] we had a president of the PTO whose kids were on the fast track in Advanced Placement. I don't think we've had one in quite a few years."

She did note, however, that there were "a lot of parents on the [district-wide] school board whose kids are in the Advanced Placement classes." Interestingly, in the Plainview school district, the school board, and the central administration, and not the school-site councils such as the PTO advisory board, have the power to change curricular and instructional programs—the areas most related to detracking reform—in the schools.

Furthermore, despite the past president's assertion that the Advanced Placement parents do not run the PTO advisory board, the board members we interviewed told us they were unwilling to challenge the pro-Advanced Placement stance of the principal. Still, several of the PTO board members said they believed there was too much emphasis on Advanced Placement at Plainview, and that they were at times uncomfortable with the principal's constant bragging about the number of Advanced Placement classes the school offers, the number of students taking Advanced Placement exams, and the number of students who receive 3's, 4's, or 5's on these exams. Some of these parents said that, in their opinion, a heavy load of Advanced Placement classes is too stressful for high school students; others said the curriculum in the Advanced Placement classes is boring rote memorization: But none of these parents had ever challenged the principal in his effort to boost the number of Advanced Placement classes offered and students enrolling in them. According to one mother on the PTO board:

> I think parents have seen that there are so many pressures in the world, they realize that this is a high school and they're fed up with all the competition. At the same time they know you have to play the game, you know. . . . And again, it's hard to evaluate with some of the top, top students, you know, what's appropriate. . . . I think a lot of this has to do with Plainview as a community, too. Now, for example, where I live right here is in Fillburn, and that is a more upscale community [within the Plainview district]. Two houses from me is the Doner school district, which is a community of

wealthier homes, wealthier people, many of whom have children in private schools.

During interviews, most of the not-quite-elite parents at all of the schools in our study discussed their awareness of the demands that families with high economic and cultural capital placed on the schools. They cited these demands as reasons why they themselves did not challenge the push for more Advanced Placement or gifted classes and why they were not supporters of detracking efforts—even when they suspected that such changes might be beneficial for their own children. For instance, at Grant High School, the chair of the language arts department formed a parent support group to focus on issues of tracking and detracking. This group consisted mostly of parents of students in the regular and honors classes, with only a handful of parents of very advanced students in the highest track. The department chair said she purposefully postponed "the fight" with more of the advanced parents. "We thought if we could get a group of parents who are just as knowledgeable . . . as we were, they should be the ones that become the advocates with the other parents. So that's probably our biggest accomplishment this year is getting this group of parents that we have together." But one of the few parents of advanced students left the group because she said her concerns were not being addressed and the advisory group disbanded the following spring.

We saw other examples of "not-quite-elite" buy-in at schools where middle-class minority parents had become advocates of tracking practices and opponents of detracking efforts, despite their lament that their children were often the only children of color in the high-track classes. For instance, a Black professional parent at Rolling Hills Middle School, whose two children were in the advanced program, noted that a growing number of African American parents in the district were upset with the racial composition of the nearly all-White "advanced" classes and the disproportionately Black "comprehensive" tracks within racially mixed schools. He said, "So you have segregation in a supposedly desegregated setting. So what it is, you have a growing amount of dissatisfaction within the African American community about these advanced programs that are lily White." Despite his dissatisfaction, this father explained that he is not against tracking per se. "I think tracking has its merits. I just think they need to be less rigid in their standards."

Similarly, at Green Valley High School, a rural West Coast school with a 43 percent White and 57 percent Latino student population, a professional, middle-class Latino couple who had sent their children to private elementary and middle schools before enrolling them in the public high school said that the students at Green Valley should be divided into three groups: those at the top, those in the middle, and those at the bottom. The father added that those students in the middle should be given more of a tech prep education, and that an alternative school might be good for a lot of kids who won't go to college.

Detracking Bribes

Another political practice employed by local elites in schools that are attempting detracking reforms is their use of symbolic capital to bribe the schools to give them some preferential treatment in return for their willingness to allow some small degree of detracking to take place. These detracking bribes tend to make detracking reforms very expensive and impossible to implement in a comprehensive fashion.

Bourdieu (in Harrison, 1993) would consider such detracking bribes to be symbolic of the irreversible character of gift exchange. In exchange for their political buy-in to the detracking efforts, elite parents must be assured that their children are still getting something more than other children. In the process of gift exchange, according to Bourdieu, gifts must be returned, but this return represents neither an exchange of equivalents nor a case of cash on delivery:

> What is returned must be both different in kind and deferred in time. It is within this space opened up by these two elements of non-identity [of the gifts] and temporality [deferred time] that strategic actions can be deployed

through which either one actor or another tries to accumulate some kind of profit. The kind of profit accumulated is, of course, more likely to be either symbolic or social, rather than economic, (p. 39)

In the case of the detracking bribes, the elite parents tend to profit at the expense of broad-based reform and restructuring. Yet, detracking bribes take on a different shape and character in different schools, depending upon the bargaining power of the local elite parents and the school's resources. As Bourdieu notes, in the case of the gift exchange, it is the agent's sense of honor that regulates the moves that can be made in the game (Harrison, 1993).

For instance, at King Middle School, located in a large northeastern city, the bribe is the school itself—a well-funded magnet program with formal ties to a nearby college and a rich art program that is integrated into the curriculum. Because King is a school of choice for parents who live in the surrounding area of the city, it is in many ways automatically perceived to be "better than" regular neighborhood schools, where students end up by default. Still, an administrator noted that King must still work at getting elite parents to accept the heterogeneous grouping within the school: "The thing is to convince the parents of the strong students that [heterogeneous grouping] is a good idea and not to have them pull children out to put them in a gifted program. It is necessary to really offer them a lot. You need parent education, along with offering a rich program for the parents so that they don't feel their children are being cheated."

At Rolling Hills Middle School, where African American students are bused to this otherwise White, wealthy school, the detracking bribe comes in the form of the best sixth-grade teachers and a "heterogeneous" team of students, which is skewed toward a disproportionate number of advanced program students. For instance, the heterogeneous team is comprised of 50 percent "advanced" students, 25 percent "honors" students, and 25 percent "regular" students, while the sixth grade as a whole is only about one-third "advanced" students and about one-half "regular" students. Thus, detracking at

Rolling Hills is feasible when it affects only one of four sixth-grade teams, and that one team enrolls a disproportionate number of advanced students and is taught by the teachers whom the local elite consider to be the best. The generosity of the "gifts" that the school gives the elite parents who agree to enroll their children in the heterogeneous team are such that this team has become high status itself. The "parent network" of local elites at this school now promotes the heterogeneous team and advises elite mothers of incoming sixth-graders to choose that team. According to one wealthy White parent, "the heterogeneous team is 'hand-picked'." Another White parent whose daughter is on the heterogeneous team noted, "It's also been good to know that it's kind of like a private school within a public school. And that's kind of fair, I hate to say that, but it's kind of a fair evaluation."

Of course, Rolling Hills does not have enough of these "gifts" to bribe all of the local elite parents to place their children on a heterogeneous team. In other words, Rolling Hills will never be able to detrack the entire school as long as the cost of the bribe remains so high and the elite parental profit is so great. By definition, the "best" teachers at any given school are scarce; there are not enough of them to go around. In addition, the number of Advanced Placement students in the school is too small to assure that more heterogeneous teams could be created with the same skewed proportion of advanced, honors, and comprehensive tracks.

At Grant High School, the bribe for detracking the marine science program consists of this unique science offering, coupled with the school's excellent science and math departments and one of the two best music programs in the city. These are commodities that elite parents cannot get in other schools—urban or suburban. As one teacher explained, "So what options do these parents have? Lift their kids out of Grant, which they love? They can't get a science program like this anywhere else in the city." Although the school itself is highly tracked, especially in the history department, the marine science classes enroll students from all different tracks. A marine science teacher noted that parents of the advanced students never request that their kids be placed in separate classes because curricula in this program are both advanced and unique.

Interestingly, the detracking bribe at Liberty High, as the school moved toward the ninth-grade English/ social studies core classes, was to be smaller class sizes and ongoing staff development. Unfortunately, the district administration withheld much of the promised funding to allow the school to deliver these gifts to the parents of high-track students. Whether or not these parents were ever committed to this bribe— whether they thought the school was offering them enough in return–is not really clear. What we do know is that the principal who offered the gift was, as we mentioned, recently "let go" by the district. His departure may have been the ultimate bribe with the local elites, because, as Bourdieu (in Harrison, 1993) argues, the kind of profit accumulated is, of course, more likely to be either symbolic or social, rather than economic.

Conclusions

When our research team began this study in 1992, we initially focused on what was happening *within* the racially mixed schools we were to study. Yet as we visited these schools, it became increasingly evident to us that the parents had a major impact on detracking reform efforts. Over the course of the last three years, we came to appreciate not only the power of this impact but its subtleties as well. In turning to the literature on elites and cultural capital, we gained a deeper understanding of the barriers educators face in their efforts to detrack schools.

As long as elite parents press the schools to perpetuate their status through the intergenerational transmission of privilege that is based more on cultural capital than "merit," educators will be forced to choose between equity-based reforms and the flight of elite parents from the public school system.

The intent of this article is not simply to point fingers at the powerful, elite parents or the educators who accommodate them at the ten schools we studied. We understand that these parents are in many ways victims of a social system in which the scarcity of symbolic capital creates an intense demand for it among those in their social strata. We also recognize the role that the educational system—especially the higher education system—plays in shaping their actions and their understanding of what they must do to help their children succeed.

Still, we hope that this study of ten racially mixed schools undertaking detracking reform is helpful to educators and policymakers who struggle to understand more clearly the political opposition to such reform efforts. Most importantly, we have learned that in a democratic society, the privilege, status, and advantage that elite students bring to school with them must be carefully deconstructed by educators, parents, and students alike before meaningful detracking reforms can take place.

From Amy Stuart Wells and Irene Serna, "The Politics of Culture: Understanding Local Political Resistance in Racially Mixed Schools," *Harvard Educational Review*, 66:1 (Spring 1996), pp. 93–118.

Endnotes

1. Our three-year study of ten racially mixed secondary schools that are detracking was funded by the Lilly Endowment. Jeannie Oakes and Amy Stuart Wells were coprincipal investigators. Research associates were Robert Cooper, Amanda Datnow, Diane Hirshberg, Martin Lipton, Karen Ray, Irene Serna, Estella Williams, and Susie Yonezawa.
2. By "school community," we mean the broad and diverse network of students, parents, educators, and other citizens who are connected to these schools as institutions.
3. For a full description of the study and its methodology, see Oakes & Wells (1995).
4. During the "tennis shoe" registration, teachers set up tables in the gymnasium with registration passes for each of the classes they will be offering. Students have an allocated time slot in which they are allowed into the gym to run from teacher to teacher and ask for passes for classes they want. Under this system, teachers are able to control who gets into their classes, and the children of the elite, who hold more political power in the school, are more likely to get the high-track classes that they want.

References

Beare, H. (1993). Different ways of viewing school-site councils: Whose paradigm is in use here? In H. Beare & W. L. Boyd (Eds.), *Restructuring schools: An international perspective on the movement to transform the control and performance of schools* (pp. 200–214). Washington, DC: Falmer Press.

Boggs, C. (1984). *The two revolutions: Gramsci and the dilemmas of western Marxism.* Boston: South End Press.

Bourdieu, P. (1973). Cultural reproduction and social reproduction. In R. Brown (Ed.), *Knowledge, educations, and cultural change* (pp. 487–501). New York: Harper & Row.

Bourdieu, P. (1977). *Outline of a theory of practice.* Cambridge, Eng.: Cambridge University Press.

Bourdieu, P. (1984). *Distinction: A social critique of the judgement of taste.* Cambridge, MA: Harvard University Press.

Bourdieu, P., & Passeron, J. C. (1977). *Reproduction in education, society and culture.* Beverly Hills, CA: Sage.

Bourdieu, P., & Passeron, J. C. (1979). *The inheritors: French students and their relation to culture.* Chicago: University of Chicago Press

Bourdieu, P., & Wacquant, I. J. D. (1992). *An invitation to reflexive sociology.* Chicago, IL: University of Chicago Press.

Delpit, L. (1995). *Other people's children: Cultural conflict in the classroom.* New York: New Press.

DiMaggio, P. (1979). Review essay: On Pierre Bourdieu. *American Journal of Sociology, 84,* 1460–1472.

Domhoff, W. G. (1983). *Who rules America now? A view for the 80s.* Englewood Cliffs, NJ: Prentice-Hall.

Domhoff, W. G. (1990). *The power elite and the state: How polity is made in America.* New York: A. de-Gruyter.

Gramsci, A. (1971). *Selections from the prison notebooks.* New York: International Publishers.

Harker, K. (1984). On reproduction, habitus and education. *British Journal of Sociology of Education, 5*(2), 117–127.

Harrison, P. R. (1993). Bourdieu and the possibility of a postmodern sociology. *Thesis Eleven, 35,* 36–50.

Lareau, A. (1989). *Home advantage.* London: Falmer Press.

McIntosh, P. (January/February, 1992). White privilege: Unpacking the invisible knapsack. *Creation Spirituality,* pp. 33–35

Mills, C. W. (1956). *The power elite.* London: Oxford University Press.

Oakes, J. (1985). *Keeping track: How schools restructure inequalities.* New Haven, CT: Yale University Press.

Oakes, J., Oraseth, T., Bell, R., & Camp, P. (1990). *Multiplying inequalities: The effects of race, social class, and tracking on opportunities to learn mathematics and science.* Santa Monica, CA: Rand.

Oakes, J., Lipton, M., & Jones, M. (1995, April). *Changing minds: Deconstructing intelligence in detracking schools.* Paper presented at the annual meeting of the American Educational Research Association, San Francisco.

Oakes, J., & Wells, A. S. (1995, April) *Beyond sorting and stratification: Creative alternatives to tracking in racially mixed secondary schools.* Paper presented at the annual meeting of the American Educational Research Association, San Francisco.

Thompson, J. B. (1990). *Ideology and modern culture.* Stanford, CA: Stanford University Press.

Useem, E. (1990, April). *Social class and ability group placement in mathematics in transition to seventh grade: The role of parental involvement.* Paper presented at the annual meeting of the American Educational Research Conference, Boston.

Wells, A. S., & Crain, R. L. (1992). Do parents choose school quality or school status? A sociological theory of free-market education. In P. W. Cookson (Ed.), *The choice controversy* (pp. 65–82). Newbury Park, CA: Corwin Press.

Welner, K., & Oakes, J. (1995, April). *Liability grouping: The new susceptibility of school tracking systems to legal challenges.* Paper presented at the annual meeting of the American Educational Research Association, San Francisco.

Yonesawa, S., Williams, E., & Hirshberg, D. (1995, April). *Seeking a new standard: Minority parent and community involvement in detracking schools.* Paper presented at the annual meeting of the American Educational Research Association, San Francisco.

An earlier version of this article was presented at the American Educational Research Association's 1995 Annual Meeting in San Francisco.

5 The Philosophy of Education and Its Significance for Teachers

In Chapter 1, we argued that Americans place a great deal of faith in education, and particularly that Americans view schools as the great panacea for the multitude of problems that plague both individuals and society as a whole. In this chapter, we point out that the study of the philosophy of education as an integral part of the foundations perspective will allow prospective teachers to reflect on educational issues from a particular perspective—the perspective of philosophy. This perspective encourages logical, systematic thinking. It stresses the importance of ideas and allows—indeed, encourages—the act of reflection on every aspect of practice. Thus, philosophy acts as the building block for the reflective practitioner.

The Perspective of Philosophy of Education

Practitioners often argue, as do students in schools of education, that although philosophy of education may add another dimension to the way in which they view schools, nevertheless, they haven't the time for a discipline that does not offer tangible results. Rather, they wish to learn *what* to do, not *why* to do it. For too many practitioners and students of education, the practice of teaching is reduced to action devoid of a rationale or justification.

We believe that the practice of teaching cannot be separated from a philosophical foundation. Philosophy, as applied to education, allows practitioners and prospective practitioners to apply systematic approaches to problem solving in schools and illuminates larger issues of the complex relationship of schools to the social order.

What Is Philosophy of Education?

Philosophy of education differs from philosophy, as we have stated in Chapter 1. Philosophy of education is firmly rooted in practice, whereas philosophy, as a discipline, stands on its own with no specific end in mind. Given this difference, it is necessary to consider for a moment how a particular philosophy might affect practice.

All teachers, regardless of their action orientation, have a personal philosophy of life that colors the way in which they select knowledge; order their classrooms; interact with students, peers, parents, and administrators; and select values to emphasize within their classrooms. Engaging in philosophy helps teachers and prospective teachers to *clarify* what they do or intend to do and, as they act or propose to act, to *justify* or explain why they do what they do in a logical, systematic manner. Thus, the activity of doing philosophy aids teachers in understanding two very important notions: (1) who they are or intend to be and (2) why they do or propose to do what they do. Furthermore, through the action of clarification and justification of practice, teachers and prospective teachers think about practice and acquire specific information, which lends authority to their decision making.

The Meaning of Philosophical Inquiry

Although people exist as individuals, they also exist within the greater context of their culture. Through interactions with the norms common to the culture, people form attitudes, beliefs, and values, which are then transmitted to others. As people go about this process of acquiring cultural norms, they may accept norms wholeheartedly, accept norms partially, or, in certain instances, totally reject them. Whatever people choose to embrace, if their choices are made in a logical, rational manner, they are engaged in the process of "doing philosophy."

To proceed in doing philosophy, certain key questions are posed that can be divided into three specific areas of philosophical inquiry. The first is called *metaphysics*, a branch of philosophy that concerns itself with questions about the nature of reality. The second is called *epistemology*, a branch of philosophy that concerns itself with questions about the nature of knowledge. Last is *axiology*, a branch of philosophy that concerns itself with the nature of values.

We believe that these distinctions in philosophy are important for prospective teachers to know, since ideas generated by philosophers about education usually fall under a particular branch of philosophy, such as epistemology. Furthermore, the ideas generated by philosophers interested in particular questions help people to clarify their own notions of existence, knowledge, and values—in sum, one's personal philosophy of life. Moreover, this philosophy of life, as one comes to understand it, becomes the foundation upon which people construct pedagogic practice.

Particular Philosophies of Education

In the following pages, we will discuss several leading schools of philosophy that have influenced and continue to influence the way people view educational practice. We have included both classical philosophies and modern philosophies which, in our opinion, have made the most impact on the ways in which people think about schools. Many of the ideas overlap; many of the distinctions we make are artificial and, at times, arbitrary. Most important, we hope that you will appreciate the fact that all successful practitioners borrow from many schools of thought.

Idealism

We begin our discussion of particular schools of philosophy that have influenced educational thought with *idealism*, the first systematic philosophy in Western thought. Idealism is generally thought to be the creation of the Greek philosopher, Plato (427–347 B.C.), the pupil of Socrates, a famous Greek teacher and philosopher who lived in Athens (c.469–399 B.C.). Socrates did not write anything down; rather, he taught through establishing oral dialogues with his students or those he wished to engage in philosophical questions. Socrates saw himself, as Plato stated in *The Apology (The Defense)*, as "the gadfly of Athens." Through questioning, he forced his fellow Athenians to consider their life choices, and, in many instances, made them uncomfortable or often provoked them to anger. In 399 B.C., Socrates was executed for his beliefs. He was officially charged with corrupting the minds of the youth of Athens.

Plato wrote down Socrates' ideas and his method, which was the dialogue. While doing so, he probably added to Socrates' ideas, since he was only 28 years old when Socrates was executed, and he continued to write Socratic dialogue long after Socrates' death. Scholars concur with the idea that Plato augmented Socrates' beliefs, since it is generally held that Plato was far more sophisticated in his thinking than Socrates (Guthrie, 1969). Nevertheless, it is difficult for the uninitiated to distinguish between Socrates' and Plato's work. Thus, we will refer to this combination as *Platonic philosophy*.

Generic Notions

Philosophers often pose difficult, abstract questions that are not easily answered. Plato helped to initiate this tradition through his concern for the search for *truth*.

Plato distrusted the world of matter; he believed that it was in a constant state of flux. Therefore, matter was an inaccurate measurement of truth since it was constantly changing. Plato also believed that the senses were not to be trusted, as they continually deceive us. Because truth for Plato was perfect and because truth is eternal, it was not to be found in the world of matter: "The unchanging realities we can apprehend by the mind only: the senses can show us only transient and imperfect copies of reality" (Kitto, 1951, p. 194).

The only constant for Plato was the field of mathematics, since $1 + 1 = 2$ will never change. In fact, it is eternal. The problem, however, with all of this is that mathematics is only one field of inquiry and so individuals must look to other modes of inquiry in the quest for truth. For Plato, this was the task of the philosopher.

Plato's method of doing philosophy was to engage another individual in a dialogue and, through the dialogue, question that individual's point of view. This questioning was done in a systematic, logical examination of both points of view. Ultimately, both parties would reach a synthesis of viewpoints that would be acceptable to both. This approach, called the *dialectic*, was used by Plato to move individuals from the world of matter to the world of ideas. Perhaps, as some philosophers suggest, Plato's philosophy should be called "ideaism" rather than idealism, since, for Plato, ideas were what mattered above all.

Plato thought that education, in particular, was important as a means of moving individuals collectively toward achieving the *good*. He believed that the state should play an active role in education and that it should encourage the brighter students to follow a curriculum that was more abstract and more concerned with ideas rather than with concrete matter. Thus, brighter students would focus on ideas, and data collecting would be assigned to the less able. Plato's "tracking system" was gender free; however, he proposed that those students who functioned on a more concrete level should assume roles necessary for maintaining the city-state, such as craftsmen, warriors, and farmers. Those who functioned on a more abstract level should rule. In fact, Plato put forth the idea of a philosopher-king: an individual who would lead the state to discover the ultimate *good*. Thus, Plato believed that rulers were individuals of thought, action, and obligation.

Since Plato's time, people have seen the state become a major force in determining the system of education. People have also witnessed how increasingly the school and tracking, in particular, determine the life chances of students. Additionally, people still cling to the importance that Plato attached to education as the instrument that will enlighten rulers and aid them in achieving the highest *good*. Perhaps naively, people still believe that evil comes through ignorance, and that if only the rulers are educated, evil will be obliterated. Unfortunately, modern history has yet to validate this view.

Modern Idealists

Since Plato, there has been a series of philosophers who have augmented his original notions. For example, St. Augustine (354–430 A.D.) added religion to classical idealism; later philosophers, such as René Descartes (1596–1650), Immanuel Kant (1724–1804), and George Wilhelm Friedrich Hegel (1770–1831), added their particular visions to Platonic idealism.

Goal of Education

Educators who subscribe to idealism are interested in the search for truth through ideas rather than through the examination of the false shadowy world of matter. Teachers encourage their students to search for truth as individuals. However, with the discovery of truth comes responsibility—responsibility of those who achieve the realization of truth to enlighten others. Moreover, idealists subscribe to the notion that education is transformation: Ideas can change lives.

Role of the Teacher

It is the teacher's responsibility to analyze and discuss ideas with students in order for students to move to new levels of awareness so that ultimately they can be transformed. Teachers should deal with abstract notions through the dialectic method but should aim to connect analysis with action as well.

In an idealist's classroom, the teacher plays an active role in discussion, posing questions, selecting materials, and establishing an environment, all of which ensure the teacher's desired outcome. An idealist teacher subscribes to the doctrine of *reminiscence*, described in the *Meno*, an important Platonic dialogue, which states that the role of the teacher is to bring out that which is already in the student's mind. Additionally, an idealist teacher supports moral education as a means of linking ideas to action. Last, the idealist teacher sees herself or himself as a role model in the classroom, to be emulated by students.

Methods of Instruction

Idealist teachers take an active part in their students' learning. Although they lecture from time to time, perhaps to fill in background material not covered in the reading, they predominately use the dialectic approach described by Plato. Through questioning, students are encouraged to discuss, analyze, synthesize, and apply what they have read to contemporary society. Students are also encouraged to work in groups or individually on research projects, both oral and written.

Curriculum

Idealists place great importance on the study of classics (i.e., great literature of past civilizations that illustrated contemporary concerns). For idealists, all contemporary problems have their roots in the past and can best be understood by examining how previous individuals dealt with them. A good example of an idealist curriculum would be the Great Books curriculum at Saint John's University, in Annapolis, Maryland. During their four years in college, students read, analyze, and apply the ideas of classical works to modern life. For elementary school-age children, there is a Great Books course promoted by individuals in the private sector and there exists as well a grass-roots movement to institute a core curriculum in elementary and junior high schools throughout the nation.

An interesting proposal that has not taken root is Mortimer Adler's *Paideia Proposal* (1982), which advocates great literature for children of all abilities. Adler proposed that elementary school children read great literature that would contain issues of relevance to all. Adler emphasized both content and process through the actual readings, much like the current whole-language movement.

Many idealists also support a back-to-basics approach to education, which emphasizes the three Rs. Such an approach became popular among educational conservatives, such as President Reagan's Secretary of Education, William Bennett, in the 1980s.

Realism

Realism is a philosophy that follows in the same historical tradition as idealism. Realism is associated with both Plato and Aristotle, although philosophers tend to view Aristotle as the leading proponent of realism. Aristotle (384–322 B.C.), a student of Plato's, was the son of a physician. He studied at Plato's Academy in Athens until Plato's death in 347 B.C. Aristotle also lived in Asia Minor and in Macedonia, where he was tutor to King Philip of Macedonia's son, Alexander. Aristotle's pupil later became Alexander the Great and a lover of all things Greek, thanks to Aristotle's influence.

In 355 B.C., Aristotle returned to Athens and started a school in the Lyceum, a public grove. Aristotle's career as a great teacher was cut short by the death of Alexander, his protector. The Athenians charged Aristotle with "impiety" and thus Aristotle was forced to leave Athens and settle in Euboea, where he remained until his death. Aristotle is particularly important because he was the first philosopher who developed a systematic theory of logic.

Generic Notions

In our discussion of idealism, we noted that Plato argued for the centrality of ideas. Aristotle, however, believed that only through studying the material world was it possible for an individual to clarify or develop ideas. Thus, realists reject the Platonic notion that only ideas are real, and argue instead that the material world or matter is real. In fact, realists hold that matter exists, independent of ideas. Aristotle, in fact, might have argued that a triangle exists whether or not there is a thinking human being within range to perceive it.

If Plato were to study the nature of reality, he would begin with ideas, since he believed that the world of matter was shadowy and unreliable (see *The Allegory of the Cave*). Aristotle, however, in his quest for the nature of reality, would begin with the world of matter. It is important to note that both Plato and Aristotle subscribed to the importance of ideas but each philosopher dealt with them very differently.

Since the classical realism of Aristotle, many forms of realism have evolved. These range from the religious realism of Thomas Aquinas (1225–1274) to the modern realism of individuals such as Francis Bacon (1561–1626) and John Locke (1632–1704) to the contemporary realism of Alfred North Whitehead (1861–1947) and Bertrand Russell (1872–1970).

Aristotle's Systematic Theory of Logic

Aristotle is particularly important because he was the first philosopher to develop a rational, systematic method for testing the logic of statements people make. Aristotle began his process with empirical research; then, he would speculate or use dialectic reasoning, which would culminate in a syllogism. A *syllogism* is a system of logic that consists of three parts: (1) a major premise, (2) a minor premise, and (3) a conclusion. A famous example of a syllogism, used by many philosophers is as follows:

> All men are mortal
> Socrates is a man
> therefore, Socrates is mortal. (Ozmon & Craver, 1990, p. 43)

For a syllogism to work, all of the parts must be correct. If one of the premises is incorrect, the conclusion will be fallacious. Basically, Aristotle used syllogisms to systematize thinking. The problem, however, with this method is that Aristotle never made it clear where the syllogism was to be placed in his schema or framework. Thus, subsequent philosophers may have misinterpreted Aristotelian logic, grossly misusing the syllogism.

As you may have concluded by now, philosophers have been posing questions concerned with "the good life" or "the importance of reason" from the Greeks through the present (and probably long before the Greeks, considering that recorded history began in 3500 B.C. in Sumer). Aristotle, as did his contemporaries, stressed the importance of moderation in all things—the importance of achieving balance in leading one's life. Reason, concluded Aristotle, was the instrument that individuals could employ to achieve the proper balance or moderation in their lives. Education, therefore, became particularly important in achieving moderation since education would introduce individuals to the process of systematic, rigorous thought. Through education, individuals would learn to reason and thus become able to choose the path of moderation in their lives. Since Aristotle, there have been important subsequent developments in this school of philosophy.

Neo-Thomism

Aristotle was never clear about the place of the syllogism in his schema, although classical scholars believe that the syllogism was to be the culmination of his system rather than the starting point (Bowder, 1982). Many medieval thinkers, however, used Aristotle's syllogism to begin their logical proofs and *deduced* from generalizations to specific conclusions.

Thomas Aquinas (1225–1274) was an important medieval authority on the works of Aristotle. A school of philosophy, Neo-Thomism, is derived from Aquinian thought based on Aristotle. Basically, Aquinas affected a synthesis of pagan ideas and Christian beliefs, employing reason as a means of ascertaining or understanding truth. Aquinas thought that God could be understood through reasoning but reasoning based on the *material world*. Thus, Aquinas and Aristotle both emphasized matter and ideas in their particular philosophical investigations.

Aquinas's philosophy became known as Neo-Thomism in the latter part of the nineteenth century when it was revived by the Vatican as a way of resolving the conflict between the natural sciences and the Catholic Church. In particular, the Church, through Neo-Thomism, could argue that there was no conflict between science and religion since scientific inquiry ultimately led to belief in God. Aquinas's influence on contemporary educational practice is especially profound in Catholic schools, that base their educational goals on balancing the world of faith with the world of reason.

Modern Realism

Modern realism dates from the Renaissance, particularly with the work of Francis Bacon (1561–1626), who developed the inductive or scientific method of learning. Bacon was troubled by the reliance of classical realists on a prior or preconceived notion upon which thinkers deduced truths. Based on Aristotle's use of observable data, Bacon was able to develop a method starting with observations, that might culminate in a generalization, which then might be tested in specific instances for the purpose of verification.

John Locke (1632–1704), continuing in the scientific tradition established by Bacon, attempted to explain how people know things from the *empirical* point of view. He, too, chafed at the notion of a priori *ideas*, stating that the mind was a blank page, or *tabula rasa*, and what humans know is based on information gathered through the senses and through experience. Locke thought that the human mind ordered sense data and experience and then *reflected* on it.

Contemporary Realists

Contemporary realists, or realists in modern times, have tended to focus on science and philosophy—in particular, on scientific issues that have philosophical dimensions. For example, Alfred North Whitehead came to philosophy through the discipline of mathematics and was concerned with the search for "universal patterns" (Ozmon & Craver, 1990, p. 50).

Bertrand Russell studied both mathematics and philosophy as a student at Trinity College and Cambridge University, and coauthored with Whitehead the important book, *Principia Mathematica*. Both men believed that the universe could be characterized through universal patterns; however, Russell proposed that these patterns could be verified and classified through mathematics. Both were interested in education. Whitehead confined his interests to writing about education—in particular, advocating (like Plato) the primacy of ideas. Nevertheless (like Aristotle), he recognized the necessity of grounding ideas within the context of the living world. Russell actually founded a school called Beacon Hill, in which he sought to put into practice some of his notions of education, particularly the idea of employing knowledge to social problems in order to create a better world.

Goal of Education

Both Plato and Aristotle believed that important questions concerning such notions as the good life, truth, beauty, and so on could be answered through the study of ideas, using the dialectical method. They differed, however, in their studying points. Plato emphasized only the study of ideas to understand ideas. Aristotle believed that it was possible to understand ideas through studying the world of matter. For Plato, the real world was shadowy and deceptive; for Aristotle, the real world was the starting point in the quest for understanding philosophical concerns.

For contemporary realists, the goal of education is to help individuals understand and then apply the principles of science to help solve the problems plaguing the modern world. Again, the leading notion of realists is that through basic disciplines—and in particular, science—individuals will be able to fathom what philosophers have been debating since the beginning of their discipline: existence of the good life, but thanks to Aristotle, how it can be encouraged through science.

Role of the Teacher

Teachers, according to contemporary realists, should be steeped in the basic academic disciplines in order to transmit to their students the knowledge necessary for the continuance of the human race. They should have a solid grounding in science, mathematics, and the humanities. Additionally, teachers must present ideas in a clear and consistent manner, and demonstrate that there are definitive ways to judge works of art, music, poetry, and literature. From this point of view, it is the role of the teacher to enable students to learn objective methods of evaluating such works (Ozmon & Craver, 1990, p. 63).

Methods of Instruction

Realists would support a number of methods—in particular, lecture, and question and answer. Additionally, since realists believe in objective criteria for judging the value of artistic and literary works, they would support the lecture as a method of instruction in order to give students the knowledge necessary to make these evaluations. Finally, many realists support competency-based assessment as a way of ensuring that students learn what they are being taught (Ozmon & Craver, 1990, p. 63). Remember that realists believe that the material world holds the key to the ideal world; therefore, realists would encourage questions that would help students in the classroom grasp the ideal through specific characteristics of particular manifestations.

Curriculum

Curriculum for realists would consist of the basics: science and math, reading and writing, and the humanities. Realists believe that there is a body of knowledge that is essential for the student to master in order to be part of society. Indeed, as stated previously, this body of knowledge is viewed as being essential for the survival of society.

Recent debates have centered on various groups questioning whether, in fact, there is an essential core of knowledge and, if so, what it might consist of. In particular, the debate about cultural literacy, sparked by the work of E. D. Hirsch, and the championing of the primacy of history and geography in social studies curricula proposed by Diane Ravitch, Chester Finn, and Paul Gagnon (see the Bradley Commission, 1988, for a detailed discussion of these proposals) support the notion of specific knowledge that helps students better understand their culture. Those who might question just what "culture" consists of and support a curriculum that truly reflects the multiplicity of U.S. society are scholars of curriculum, such as James Banks (1988).

Pragmatism

Pragmatism is generally viewed as an American philosophy that developed in the latter part of the nineteenth century. Generally speaking, the founders of this school of thought are George Sanders Peirce (1839–1914), William James (1842–1910), and John Dewey (1859–1952). However, there are European philosophers from earlier periods who might also be classified as pragmatists, such as Frances Bacon, John Locke, and Jean-Jacques Rousseau.

Pragmatism comes from the Greek word *pragma*, meaning work. Both George Sanders Peirce and William James are credited with having described pragmatism in part through the biblical phrase, "By their fruits ye shall know them." James specifically makes such a reference in his book, *Varieties of Religious Experience* (James, 1978). That is, pragmatism is a philosophy that encourages people to find processes that work in order to achieve their desired ends. Although pragmatists do study the past, they generally are more interested in contemporary issues and in discovering solutions to problems in present-day terms. Pragmatists are action oriented, experientially grounded, and will generally pose questions such as "What will work to achieve my desired end?" A pragmatic schema might look like this:

$$\text{problem} \rightarrow \text{speculative thought} \rightarrow \text{action} \rightarrow \text{results}$$

Pragmatists might then ask "Do the results achieved solve the problem?" If the question is answered in the affirmative, then the solution may be judged as valid.

Pragmatism's roots, as well as modern realism's roots, may be traced to the English philosopher and scientist, Francis Bacon (1561–1626), who we have previously discussed. Troubled with the Aristotelian legacy of deductive reasoning through the syllogism, Bacon sought a way of thinking in which people might be persuaded to abandon the traditions or "idols" of the past for a more experiential approach to the world. Because Bacon emphasized experience posited firmly within the world of daily existence, he can be thought of as a pioneer in the pragmatic school of philosophy. Furthermore, the method of reasoning he emphasized was *inductive*, which became the foundation of observational method in educational research.

Another modern realist, political philosopher John Locke (1632–1704), also followed in the pragmatic tradition. Locke was particularly interested in the ways in which people come to know things. He believed that the mind was a *tabula rasa*, a blank tablet, and that one acquires knowledge through one's senses (in opposition to Plato who, centuries earlier, had supported the notion of innate ideas). Locke believed that people can have ideas, that people can obtain these ideas through their senses but that they never verify them through the material or natural world. Locke's emphasis on the world of experience is particularly important for later developments in the philosophy of education.

Jean-Jacques Rousseau (1712–1778), a French philosopher, wrote mainly in France during the years preceding the French Revolution. Rousseau believed that individuals in their primitive state were naturally good and that society corrupted them. Society was harmful, for it led people away from pure existences. For Rousseau, the good life meant, simply stated, "back to nature." Thus, the Queen of France, Marie Antoinette, and her court at Versailles, influenced by Rousseau's ideas, attempted to return to nature by dressing as milkmaids, shepherds, and shepherdesses.

Rousseau placed an important emphasis on *environment* and *experience*, which makes him important to subsequent pragmatic thinkers. He is mainly known to educators for his book *Émile*, which centers on a young boy who is removed from society to the country and learns experientially, through his environment, with the help of a tutor. Two points of interest are (1) Émile does not read books until he reaches 12 years of age and (2) there is little regard for the education of women in Rousseau's scheme other than two chapters on Sophie, who eats sweets and cakes and plays with dolls, and whose *raison d'être* is to be Émile's companion.

Rousseau is thought to be a romantic due to his preoccupation with individuals in their natural state. Nevertheless, his emphasis on experience and on the child in a state of nature, constantly growing and changing, paved the way for thinkers such as John Dewey.

John Dewey (1859–1952), intellectually, was heir to Charles Darwin, the British naturalist, whose theory of natural selection emphasized the constant interaction between the organism and its environment, thus challenging the Platonic and Aristotelian notions of fixed essences. Unlike the static, ordered world of the eighteenth-century philosophers, nineteenth-century pragmatists saw the world as dynamic and developing. Although Dewey acknowledged his intellectual debt to Hegel, an early nineteenth-century idealist, the idea of the dynamic quality of life was, to Dewey, of overriding importance. It could not have existed without the work of Charles Darwin.

Dewey, originally from Vermont, taught philosophy at the Universities of Minnesota, Michigan, Chicago, and Columbia. During this time, he formulated his own philosophy, introducing the terms *instrumentalism* and *experimentalism*. Instrumentalism refers to the pragmatic relationship between school and society; experimentalism refers to the application of ideas to educational practice on an experimental basis. While at the University of Chicago, he opened the Laboratory School (with his wife Alice Chapman Dewey), in which his ideas about education were applied.

Dewey's philosophy of education was the most important influence on what has been termed *progressive education*. Actually, progressive education from Dewey to the present has included a number of different approaches. Historically, the two most important have been child-centered progressivism, influenced by Dewey, and social reconstructionism, a radical interpretation of Dewey's work. Social reconstructionists, such as George Counts (1932) and Theodore Brameld (1956), viewed the schools as vehicles for improving and changing society. As we will suggest in Chapter 7, although social reconstructionists had some effect on curriculum, it has been Dewey's work that had the most profound intellectual and practical influence on U.S. progressive education. Our discussion of the progressive educational philosophy based on pragmatism therefore concentrates on Dewey's work.

Dewey's Pragmatism: Generic Notions

Dewey's form of pragmatism—instrumentalism and experimentalism—was founded on the new psychology, behaviorism, and the philosophy of pragmatism. Additionally, his ideas were influenced by the theory of evolution and by an eighteenth-century optimistic belief in progress. For Dewey, this meant the attainment of a better society through education. Thus, the school became an "embryonic community" where children could learn skills both experientially as well as from books, in addition to traditional information, which would enable them to work cooperatively in a democratic society.

Dewey's ideas about education, often referred to as *progressive*, proposed that educators start with the needs and interests of the child in the classroom, allow the child to participate in planning his or her course of study, employ project method or group learning, and depend heavily on experiential learning.

Dewey's progressive methodology rested on the notion that children were active, organic beings, growing and changing, and thus required a course of study that would reflect their particular stages of development. He advocated both freedom and responsibility for students, since those are vital components of democratic living. He believed that the school should reflect the community in order to enable graduating students to assume societal roles and to maintain the democratic way of life. Democracy was particularly important for Dewey. He believed that it could be more perfectly realized through education that would continually reconstruct and reorganize society.

Goal of Education

Dewey's vision of schools was rooted in the social order; he did not see ideas as separate from social conditions. He fervently believed that philosophy had a responsibility to society and that ideas required laboratory testing; hence, he stressed the importance of the school as a place where ideas can be implemented, challenged, and restructured, with the goal of providing students with the knowledge of how to improve the social order. Moreover, he believed that school should provide "conjoint, communicated experience"—that it should function as preparation for life in a democratic society.

In line with the progressive political atmosphere of the turn of the century, Dewey viewed the role of the school within the larger societal conditions of which it was a part. As such, Dewey's vision of schooling must be understood as part of the larger project of social progress and improvement. Although Dewey was certainly concerned with the social dimensions of schooling, he also was acutely aware of the school's effects on the individual. Thus, Dewey's philosophy of education made a conscious attempt to balance the social role of the school with its effects on the social, intellectual, and personal development of individuals. In other words, Dewey believed that the schools should balance the needs of society and community on one hand and the needs of the individual on the other. This tension, or what the philosopher of education Maxine Greene (1988) termed the "dialectic of freedom," is central to understanding Dewey's work.

Dewey, like his contemporary, the French sociologist Émile Durkheim, saw the effects of modernization and urbanization on the social fabric of Western society. The rapid transformation in the nineteenth century from a traditional, agrarian world to a modern industrial one shattered the traditional bonds of solidarity and cohesion that held people together. Combined with the mass immigration to the United States in the late nineteenth century, the urban worlds of Chicago and New York City where Dewey spent his adult life were often fragmented and, in Durkheim's words, *anomic* (without norms). For both Durkheim and Dewey, the schools had to play a key role in creating a modern form of cohesion by socializing diverse groups into a cohesive democratic community.

The key to Dewey's vision is his view that the role of the school was to integrate children into not just any type of society, but a democratic one. Therefore, Dewey's view of integration is premised on the school as an embryonic democratic society where cooperation and community are desired ends. Dewey did not believe, however, that the school's role was to integrate children into a non-democratic society. Rather, he believed that if schools instilled democratic and cooperative values in children, they would be prepared as adults to transform the social order into a more democratic one. Although he located this central function of schools, he never adequately provided a solution to the problem of integrating diverse groups into a community without sacrificing their unique characteristics. This is a problem still hotly debated.

For Dewey, the primary role of education was growth. In a famous section of *Democracy and Education*, Dewey (1916) stated that education had no other goals than growth—growth leading to more growth. As Lawrence Cremin (1990) noted:

> John Dewey liked to define the aim of education as growth, and when he was asked growth toward what, he liked to reply, growth leading to more growth. That was his way of saying that education is subordinate to no end beyond itself, that the aim of education is not merely to make parents, or citizens, or workers, or indeed to surpass the Russians or Japanese, but ultimately to make human beings who will live life to the fullest, who will continually add to the quality and meaning of their experience and to their ability to direct that experience, and who will participate actively with their fellow human beings in the building of a good society. (p. 125)

Historian of education Diane Ravitch (1983, pp. 43–80) noted that Dewey's philosophies of education were often misunderstood and misapplied. As we discussed in Chapter 3, it was often misapplied as "life adjustment education" and learning through experience as vocational education; it was often misapplied with regard to freedom, with individual freedom often confused with license and becoming far more important than other processes; and it was often totally distorted by providing social class appropriate education (i.e., vocational education for the poor). Despite these distorted applications, Dewey's philosophy of education, often referred to as *progressive education*, was central to all subsequent educational theory. For Dewey, the role of the school was to be "a lever of social reform"—that is, to be the central institution for societal and personal improvement, and to do so by balancing a complex set of processes.

Role of the Teacher

In a progressive setting, the teacher is no longer the authoritarian figure from which all knowledge flows; rather, the teacher assumes the peripheral position of facilitator. The teacher encourages, offers suggestions, questions, and helps plan and implement courses of study. The teacher also writes curriculum and must have a command of several disciplines in order to create and implement curriculum.

Methods of Instruction

Dewey proposed that children learn both individually and in groups. He believed that children should start their mode of inquiry by posing questions about what they want to know. Today, we refer to this method of instruction as the *problem-solving* or *inquiry method*. Books, often written by teachers and students together, were used; field trips and projects that reconstructed some aspect of the child's course of study were also an integral part of learning in Dewey's laboratory school. These methods in turn became the basis for other progressive schools founded in the Deweyan tradition.

Formal instruction was abandoned. Traditional blocks of time for specific discipline instruction were eliminated. Furniture, usually nailed to the floor, was discarded in favor of tables and chairs that could be grouped as needed. Children could converse quietly with one another, could stand up and stretch if warranted, and could pursue independent study or group work. What at first glance to the visitor used to formal pedagogy might appear as chaotic was a carefully orchestrated classroom with children going about learning in nontraditional yet natural ways. Lockstep, rote memorization of traditional schools was replaced with individualized study, problem solving, and the project method.

Curriculum

Progressive schools generally follow Dewey's notion of a core curriculum, or an integrated curriculum. A particular subject matter under investigation by students, such as whales, would yield problems to be solved using math, science, history, reading, writing, music, art, wood or metal working, cooking, and sewing—all the academic and vocational disciplines in an integrated, interconnected way. Progressive educators support starting with contemporary problems and working from the known to the unknown, or what is now called in social studies education, "the curriculum of *expanding environments.*" Progressive educators are not wedded to a fixed curriculum either; rather, curriculum changes as the social order changes and as children's interests and needs change.

There is some controversy over Dewey's ideas about traditional discipline-centered curriculum. Some contemporary scholars (Egan, 1992, pp. 402–404) have stated that Dewey's emphasis on the need for the curriculum to be related to the needs and interests of the child suggests he was against traditional subject matter and in favor of a child-centered curriculum based on imagination and intuition. Others, including Howard Gardner (1992, pp. 410–411), felt that Dewey proposed a balance between traditional disciplines, and the needs and interests of the child. We concur with Gardner's reading of Dewey and believe that Dewey thought that an integrated curriculum provided the most effective means to this balance.

Existentialism and Phenomenology

Like pragmatism, existentialism is a rather modern philosophy. Although its roots can be traced back to the Bible, as a philosophy that has relevance to education, one may date existentialism as beginning with the nineteenth-century European philosopher Soren Kierkegaard (1813–1855). More recent philosophers who work in this school include Martin Buber (1878–1965), Karl Jaspers (1883–1969), Jean Paul Sartre (1905–1986), and the contemporary philosopher Maxine Greene.

Phenomenology was primarily developed by Edmund Husserl (1859–1935), Martin Heidegger (1889–1976), and Maurice Merleau-Ponty (1908–1961). Since both existentialism and phenomenology have much in common, and since many phenomenologists are existentialists as well, we have chosen to combine our discussion of these two schools here.

Generic Notions

Because existentialism is an individualistic philosophy, many of its adherents argue that it is not a particular school of philosophy at all. However, there are certain notions to which a majority of existentialists adhere. So, for our purposes, we will consider it as a particular philosophical movement that has important implications for education.

Unlike traditional philosophers, such as Plato and Aristotle, who were concerned with posing questions about epistemology, axiology, and metaphysics, existentialists pose questions as to how their concerns impact on the lives of individuals. Phenomenologists focus on the phenomena of consciousness, perception, and meaning, as they arise in a particular individual's experiences.

Basically, existentialists believe that individuals are placed on this earth alone and must make some sense out of the chaos they encounter. In particular, Sartre believed that "existence precedes essence"—that is, people must create themselves, and they must create their own meaning. This is done through the choices people make in their lives. Thus, individuals are in a state of constantly becoming, creating chaos and order, creating good and evil. The choice is up to the individual. The amount of freedom and responsibility people have is awesome, since they can, according to Sartre, make a difference in a seemingly absurd world. Although Sartre rejected the idea of the existence of God, other existentialists, especially its founder Soren Kierkergaard, were devout

Christians who, while attacking contemporary Christianity, proposed "a great leap to faith" through which individuals might accept the existence of God. Whereas Kierkegaard was rallying against the scientific, objective approach to existence, Sartre was attempting to sort out meaning in a world that supported gross inhumane behavior—in particular, World War II and the Holocaust.

Phenomenologists are concerned with the way in which objects present themselves to people in their consciousness, and how people order those objects. Hermeneutics, an outgrowth of phenomenology, seeks to discover how people give objects meaning. Language is important here, since language is used to describe the various phenomena in life.

Goal of Education

Existentialists believe that education should focus on the needs of individuals, both cognitively and affectively. They also believe that education should stress individuality; that it should include discussion of the non-rational as well as the rational world; and that the tensions of living in the world—in particular, anxiety generated through conflict—should be addressed. Existential phenomenologists go further; they emphasize the notion of *possibility*, since the individual changes in a constant state of becoming. They see education as an activity liberating the individual from a chaotic, absurd world.

Role of the Teacher

Teachers should understand their own "lived worlds" as well as that of their students in order to help their students achieve the best "lived worlds" they can. Teachers must take risks; expose themselves to resistant students; and work constantly to enable their students to become, in Greene's (1978) words, "wide awake." Introspection is useful in order to enable students to become in touch with their worlds and to empower them to choose and to act on their choices. Thus, the role of the teacher is an intensely personal one that carries with it a tremendous responsibility.

Methods of Instruction

Existentialists and phenomenologists would abhor "methods" of instruction as they are currently taught in schools of education. They view learning as intensely personal. They believe that each child has a different learning style and it is up to the teacher to discover what works for each child. Martin Buber, an existentialist, wrote about an I–thou approach, whereby student and teacher learn cooperatively from each other in a nontraditional, nonthreatening, "friendship." The teacher constantly rediscovers knowledge, the student discovers knowledge, and together they come to an understanding of past, present, and future, particularly a future ripe with possibilities. Thus, the role of the teacher is to help students understand the world through posing questions, generating activities, and working together.

Curriculum

Existentialists and phenomenologists would choose curriculum heavily biased toward the humanities. Literature especially has meaning for them since literature is able to evoke responses in readers that might move them to new levels of awareness, or, in Greene's (1978) words, "wide awakeness." Art, drama, and music also encourage personal interaction. Existentialists and phenomenologists believe in exposing students at early ages to problems as well as possibilities, and to the horrors as well as accomplishments humankind is capable of producing.

Neo-Marxism

Neo-Marxist philosophies of education are those approaches that trace their intellectual roots and theoretical assumptions to the nineteenth-century economist and philosopher Karl Marx (1818–1883). Based on the radical critique of capitalism, these theories argue that the role of education in capitalist society is to reproduce the ideology of the dominant class and its unequal economic outcomes; and conversely, that the role of education ought to be to give students the insight to demystify this ideology and to become agents of radical educational and social change.

The neo-Marxist perspective is more an overall theory of society than a particular philosophy of education. That is, while its proponents suggest specific philosophical approaches to educational issues, they are a part of the longer critique of capitalist society and capitalist education. The neo-Marxist approach includes the political–economic analysis of education, such as the works of Samuel Bowles and Herbert Gintis (1976), the curriculum theories of Michael Apple (1978, 1979a, 1982a, 1982b), the pedagogical work of Paulo Freire (1972), and the critical educational theory of Henry Giroux (1983b). To understand the neo-Marxist philosophy of education, it is important first to understand some basic background issues.

Generic Notions

The intellectual, theoretical, and methodological foundations of neo-Marxism are all found in the works of Karl Marx. Marx was an economist, sociologist (before the discipline of sociology was officially founded), and philosopher who left his native Germany in 1842, first for Paris and then to London, where he spent the remainder of his life. Marx is usually associated with the worldwide movement he inspired—communism—but his writings were the foundation for a radical critique of capitalism throughout the twentieth century.

Although critics have pointed to problems with his theories (e.g., that socialism always proceeds out of the collapse of capitalism, which it has not; that capitalism is destined to collapse, which it has not), it is unfair to blame the problems and apparent failures of communist and socialist societies (e.g., in the former Soviet Union and Eastern Europe) on Marx himself, for he wrote very little on what socialism would look like. Rather, the bulk of his voluminous life's work concerned the understanding of capitalism.

Marx's works may be divided into two periods. The early philosophical works, including *The Economic and Philosophical Manuscripts of 1844* (1844), *The German Ideology* (1846), and *The Communist Manifesto* (1848) (the later two written with his lifelong friend and collaborator Frederick Engels), were concerned with philosophical and political issues such as alienation, freedom, ideology, and revolution. His later economic works, including the three volumes *of Das Kapital* (1867–1894), are concerned with the economic laws of capitalism and the contradictions (a Marxian term meaning "irreconcilable differences") that make its collapse inevitable.

Marx's theories are far too complex to do justice to in these brief pages. However, it is necessary to understand those parts of his theories that form the basis of neo-Marxist philosophies of education. Simply stated, Marx believed that the history of civilization was defined by class struggle—the struggle between the dominant economic group and subordinate economic groups. Although every society defined such groups according to its own economic system (e.g., under feudalism, the serfs and the nobility; under capitalism, the proletariat (workers) and the bourgeoisie (the capitalist owners), it was the domination of subordinate economic groups by those who controlled the economy (or means of production) that marked each historical period and the revolution by subordinate groups that marked the collapse of an outmoded economic system and its replacement by a new and superior one.

For Marx, each new economic system moved civilization closer to his ideal: a society that would produce sufficient economic resources to allow all of its citizens to live productive and decent lives. Capitalism, for Marx, with its vast productive capacity, would have the potential to render economic scarcity and human misery obsolete. The problem, however, is that Marx believed that the laws of capitalist accumulation that give the bulk of its productive resources to those who own the means of production (capitalists) would make such a just society impossible. Therefore, Marx asserted that it was necessary for those who produced the resources (the workers) to recognize that it is in their collective interest to change the system to what he saw as the next logical stage in history: socialism, a society where the means of production are owned by the state in trust for the entire public. Marx believed that the laws of capitalism would lead to increasing economic crises (e.g., inflation, recession, depression), increasing poverty of the working class side by side with increasing wealth on the part of the small capitalist class. Thus, Marx believed that the working class would unite (class consciousness) and rebel (class struggle) to create a more just socialist society.

Numerous historical problems are evident with this theory. For instance, Marx did not foresee the rise of the welfare state to partially ameliorate such social problems, nor the success of labor unions in working within the system to gain significant economic rewards for workers. Theoretical problems also abound, such as the view of dominant and subordinate groups in narrow economic terms, rather than in broader social, political, and cultural terms. However, the general conflict theory of society (discussed more fully in Chapter 4) is central to understanding modern neo-Marxist philosophies of education.

The key component to this conflict theory is Marx's theory of social order and change. Although Marx indeed believed that economic laws are the foundation of any society, it is people, through conflict and struggle, who make history. Thus, the dominant group in any society must preserve order either through force and coercion, that is inherently unstable, or by convincing the subordinate groups that the system is fair and legitimate. For Marx, this is accomplished through *ideology*, or the ideas or belief system of the ruling class (Marx & Engels, 1848). Conversely, in order for change to take place, the subordinate group must see through this ideology and become conscious of its own interests (to change society). Thus, the subordinate groups must demystify the illusions of the dominant ideology and work toward change. It is education's role in transmitting this dominant ideology and its potential in allowing students to demystify it that is the main thrust of neo-Marxist philosophies of education.

Goal of Education

Modern neo-Marxist theories include what may be termed *reproduction theories* (Bowles & Gintis, 1976) and *resistance theories* (Freire, 1978; Giroux, 1983b). Reproduction theories argue that the role of education in capitalist societies is to reproduce the economic, social, and political status quo. More specifically, the school, through its ideology and curriculum (Apple, 1978, 1979a, 1982a, 1982b) and pedagogic practices (McLaren, 1989), transmits the dominant beliefs to children and serves to legitimate the capitalist order. Resistance theories, while agreeing that schools often reproduce the dominant ideology, state they also have the potential to empower students to question it.

Therefore, resistance theories question the overly deterministic view of reproduction theories and state that such approaches deny what they call "human agency"—that is, the power of individuals to shape their own world and to change it. In this respect, resistance theories have a great deal in common with existentialists, as they believe that the process of education contains the tools to enable individuals both to understand the weaknesses in the dominant ideology and to construct alternative visions and possibilities. Further, what are termed *postmodernist* (Cherryholmes, 1988; Giroux, 1991) and *feminist* (Ellsworth, 1989; Laird, 1989; Lather, 1991; Martin, 1987) theories of education are closely related to this aspect of neo-Marxism, although not all postmodernists and feminists are neo-Marxists.

What all of these theorists have in common is the view that education should transform the dominant culture (for a complete discussion of postmodernism and feminism, see Giroux, 1991, and Sadovnik, 1995b). Postmodernists and feminists disagree with neo-Marxists about who exactly comprises the dominant culture. Feminists argue that male domination is the problem; postmodernists are skeptical of any one theory that explains domination and therefore rejects the neo-Marxist emphasis on economic domination as too one-dimensional (Lyotard, 1984).

The Role of the Teacher

The neo-Marxist philosophy of education concentrates on the teacher and student as part of a critical pedagogical process. The teacher, from this vantage point, must become a "transformative intellectual" (Giroux, 1988) whose role is to engage his or her students in a critical examination of the world. The student thus becomes part of an educational process that seeks to examine critically the society and its problems and to seek radical alternatives.

In some respects, this view of education is similar to the existential phenomenology of Greene (1978, 1988) in that it views the purpose of education as "wide awakeness." The difference is that Greene is less committed to an objective truth that constitutes such a state (that is, one reality that is true), whereas neo-Marxists believe that "wide awakeness" requires an objective truth that includes a critique of capitalism. Such a conclusion is open to considerable debate, even among those sympathetic to neo-Marxism. However, its idea that education ought to result in critical awareness of self and society is a view that goes well beyond neo-Marxist philosophy and is shared by many of the other philosophies discussed here, including pragmatism, existentialism, phenomenology, postmodernism, and feminism.

Methods of Instruction

Given their emphasis on education as transformation, neo-Marxists favor a dialectical approach to instruction, with the question-and-answer method designed to move the student to new levels of awareness and ultimately to change. Through rigorous analysis of the taken-for-granted aspects of the world, the goal of instruction is to reveal underlying assumptions of society and to help students see alternative possibilities.

Curriculum

The neo-Marxist view of curriculum is that the curriculum is not objective or value free but is socially constructed (Apple, 1978, 1979a, 1982a, 1982b; Young, 1971). This view suggests that the curriculum is the organized and codified representation of what those with the power to shape it want the children to know. Such a critical stance requires that teachers understand the ways in which curriculum represents a particular point of view and to become critical curriculum constructors—that is, individuals who can reshape the curriculum to represent a fairer view of the world (although for neo-Marxists, this fairer view of the world means a curriculum that is critical of capitalism).

As we will discuss in Chapter 7, this view of the curriculum is shared by feminist curriculum theorists (Macdonald & Macdonald, 1981; Miller, 1982; Mitrano, 1979) and postmodern theorists (Giroux, 1991). The difference, however, is that feminists and postmodernists often disagree about whose interests the curriculum represents. Feminists, for example, argue that it is patriarchal interests rather than capitalist interests that affect the curriculum. The view of curriculum shared by these theorists leads them to support more multicultural and feminist curricula, which emphasize those social groups who are not in power.

Postmodernist and Critical Theory

Generic Notions

Postmodernism developed out of a profound dissatisfaction with modernism. Beginning with the poststructural writings of Derrida (1981, 1982) and Baudrillard (1981, 1984), social theorists, particularly in France, questioned the appropriateness of modernist categories for understanding what they saw as a postmodern world—a world that transcended the economic and social relations of the industrial world that modernist thought sought to understand. In particular, the work of Lyotard (1984) rejected the Marxist project, as well as the Enlightenment and modernist assumptions underlying Marxist theory, and sought to create a different theory of the late twentieth century.

There is a vast body of literature on the definition of *postmodernist theory* (Aronowitz & Giroux, 1991; Giroux, 1991; Harvey, 1989; Jameson, 1982; Jencks, 1987; Lyotard, 1984), as well as a growing body of literature on postmodern approaches to education (Aronowitz & Giroux, 1991; Cherryholmes, 1988; Ellsworth, 1989; Giroux, 1988, 1991; Lather, 1991; McLaren, 1991; McLaren & Hammer, 1989; Wexler, 1987).

Modernist social theory, in both sociology and philosophy, traces its intellectual heritage to the Enlightenment. From the classical sociological theory of Marx (1971), Marx and Engels (1846/1947), and Durkheim (1938/1977, 1947), to the pragmatist philosophy of Dewey (1916, 1927/1984), and to the social theory of Habermas (1979, 1981, 1982, 1983, 1987), what is usually referred to as modernist theories had a number of things in common. First, the theories were based on the belief in progress through science and technology, even if they were skeptical of positivist social science. Second, they emphasized the Enlightenment belief in reason. And third, they stressed Enlightenment principles such as equality, liberty, and justice.

Postmodernist thought consists of many interrelated themes:

1. Postmodernism insists on what Lyotard (1984) has labeled the rejection of all metanarratives. By this, Lyotard meant that the modernist preoccupation with grand, total, or all-encompassing explanations of the world needs to be replaced by localized and particular theories.
2. Postmodernism stresses the necessary connection between theory and practice as a corrective to the separation of them in much modernist thought.
3. Postmodernism stresses the democratic response to authoritarianism and totalitarianism. In particular, Aronowitz and Giroux (1991), Giroux (1991), and McLaren and Hammer (1989) call for a democratic, emancipatory, and antitotalitarism theory and practice, with schools seen as sites for democratic transformation.
4. Postmodernism sees modernist thought as Eurocentric and patriarchal. Giroux (1991), Lather (1991), Ellsworth (1989), and others provide an important critique of the racism and sexism in some modernist writings and the failure of modernism to address the interests of women and people of color.
5. Postmodernist theorists believe that all social and political discourse is related to structures of power and domination.
6. Postmodernism stresses what Burbules and Rice (1991) term "dialogue across differences." Recognizing the particular and local nature of knowledge, postmodern theorists call for the attempt to work through differences, rather than to see them as hopelessly irreconcilable.

Thus, postmodern theories of education call for teachers and students to explore the differences between what may seem like inherently contradictory positions in an effort to achieve understanding, respect, and change.

Although much of postmodern theory developed as a critical theory of society and a critique of modernism, it quickly became incorporated into critical writings on education, often called *critical theory*. Educational theory—which over the past two decades has involved an interdisciplinary mixture of social theory, sociology, and philosophy—has been profoundly affected by postmodernist thought. In particular, critical theories of education, which, from the late 1970s, attempted to provide an antidote to the overdeterminism of Bowles and Gintis (1976), by the 1980s regularly incorporated postmodern language and concerns. There have been numerous postmodern theories of education or applications of postmodernism to education. Critical and postmodern theories of education often draw heavily on the work of the Brazilian educator Paolo Freire (1972, 1985, 1987), whose influential work *Pedagogy of the Oppressed* (1972) became the foundation for critical educational theory in the United States (Kincheloe & Steinberg, 1998; Macedo, 1990).

The Role of the Teacher, Methods of Instruction, and Curriculum

Postmodern and critical theories of education are similar to neo-Marxist theory with respect to curriculum and pedagogy. Critical pedagogy (Kincheloe & Steinberg, 1998, Chapter 1) stresses the classroom as a site for political action and teachers as agents of change.

Of all the postmodern writing in the United States, Henry Giroux's represents the most sustained effort to develop a postmodern theory of education and to connect it to previous critical theories, including neo-Marxism, critical theory, and resistance theory. Giroux (1991, pp. 47–59) outlined principles of critical pedagogy, which he stated are based on the insights of modernism, postmodernism, and feminism. Thus, he provided a synthesis of three of the important theoretical systems in the twentieth century, and from these he developed a critical pedagogy, whose function is to transform teachers, schools, and ultimately society:

1. Giroux has argued that education must be seen not only as producing knowledge, but political subjects as well (1991, p. 47). Thus, schooling must be linked to a critical pedagogy aimed at the development of democratic education.
2. Giroux has indicated that ethics need to be a central concern of postmodern theories of education and critical pedagogy.
3. Critical pedagogy should focus on postmodern concerns with difference in a politically transformative manner. According to Giroux, students need to understand the social construction of different voices and identities, how these are related to historical and social forces, and how they can be used as the basis for change. The incorporation of different voices into the curriculum and student reflection on these voices need to be connected to the conception of a democratic community.
4. The concern for difference needs to be translated into a critical language that allows for competing discourses and that rejects any master narratives or curriculum canons.
5. Critical pedagogy needs to create new forms of knowledge out of analysis of competing discourses and from voices historically absent from traditional canons and narratives. Thus, pedagogic practice is seen as a political activity, with curriculum development no longer a technocratic exercise concerned with educational goals and objectives, but rather with providing students with new forms of knowledge rooted in a pluralistic and democratic vision of society.
6. Building on his earlier work, Giroux suggested that a postmodern critical pedagogy must provide a sense of alternatives through a "language of critique and possibility" (1991, p. 52). Critical pedagogy as a critique of what exists and a development of what is possible is central to a project of social transformation.

7. Critical pedagogy must be related to a view of teachers as transformative intellectuals. In his work on postmodernism, Giroux developed a theme that was central to his earlier work and has connected it to a view of democratic public life. Giroux calls for teachers to be involved not only within schools, but to connect their voices to democratic politics in their communities and within society, in general. Critical pedagogy needs to engage students and teachers in the systematic discovery of alternatives to institutional racism, classism, and sexism through the inclusion of the voices of marginalized groups. Such an enterprise should not be, Giroux has warned, merely exercises in giving voice to the voiceless, but needs to connect their voices to political strategies aimed at social change.

Sadovnik (1995b) has pointed out a number of problems with postmodern and critical theories of education. First, postmodern theories of education are often written in a language that is difficult to understand. While this is problematic for all academic work, it is more so for a theory that purports to provide an agenda for critique and change in the school. Second, postmodern theories usually eschew empirical methods to study schools. Thus, they are sometimes long on assertion and short on evidence. Finally, and most importantly, postmodernist theories of education often fail to connect theory to practice in a way that practitioners find meaningful and useful. Although this does not suggest that postmodernists write exclusively for practitioners, if one of the stated aims of theorists such as Giroux is to develop teachers as transformative intellectuals and to provide a critical pedagogy for school transformation, then the problem of language use is of central importance. How can there be dialogues across difference if teachers are excluded from the dialogue?

Conclusion

In this chapter, we have presented some of the major philosophies of education. Through a discussion of how each school of philosophy views the goal of education, the role of the teacher, methods of instruction, and the curriculum, we have presented how philosophers of education view important educational issues. These schools of philosophy often overlap. As a teacher, you will, more often than not, make use of several approaches. It is important that you develop, clarify, and justify your own particular philosophical approach to teaching, as it will form the foundation of your practice. Moreover, as we suggest in Chapter 10, the successful school reforms at schools such as Central Park East in New York City are based on a sound philosophical foundation. Thus, school improvement depends on both teachers and schools having a clear sense of purpose, and a philosophy of education provides the basis for such a purpose.

The following selections illustrate some of the philosophies of education discussed in this chapter. In the first selection, "My Pedagogic Creed," John Dewey presents the central aspects of the "new" or progressive education. Written in 1897, Dewey discusses his definition of education, the school, the curriculum, pedagogy, and the role of the school in social progress, and proposes a pragmatist philosophy of education.

In the second selection, "Wide-Awakeness and the Moral Life," philosopher of education Maxine Greene presents an existentialist philosophy of education. Greene passionately argues for teachers to become critically aware of the world around them and to help students better understand their own lives. This understanding, according to Greene, is a necessary condition for social improvement.

"The Ideal of the Educated Person," written by feminist philosopher of education Jane Roland Martin, examines what an educated person ought to be. Martin argues that traditional conceptions of the "educated man" have been gender-biased.

My Pedagogic Creed

John Dewey

Article I—What Education Is

I believe that all education proceeds by the participation of the individual in the social consciousness of the race. This process begins unconsciously almost at birth, and is continually shaping the individual's powers, saturating his consciousness, forming his habits, training his ideas, and arousing his feelings and emotions. Through this unconscious education the individual gradually comes to share in the intellectual and moral resources which humanity has succeeded in getting together. He becomes an inheritor of the funded capital of civilization. The most formal and technical education in the world cannot safely depart from this general process. It can only organize it or differentiate it in some particular direction.

I believe that the only true education comes through the stimulation of the child's powers by the demands of the social situations in which he finds himself. Through these demands he is stimulated to act as a member of a unity, to emerge from his original narrowness of action and feeling, and to conceive of himself from the standpoint of the welfare of the group to which he belongs. Through the responses which others make to his own activities he comes to know what these mean in social terms. The value which they have is reflected back into them. For instance, through the response which is made to the child's instinctive babblings the child comes to know what those babblings mean; they are transformed into articulate language and thus the child is introduced into the consolidated wealth of ideas and emotions which are now summed up in language.

I believe that this educational process has two sides—one psychological and one sociological; and that neither can be subordinated to the other or neglected without evil results following. Of these two sides, the psychological is the basis. The child's own instincts and powers furnish the material and give the starting point for all education. Save as the efforts of the educator connect with some activity which the child is carying on of his own initiative independent of the educator, education becomes reduced to a pressure from without. It may, indeed, give certain external results, but cannot truly be called educative. Without insight into the psychological structure and activities of the individual, the educative process will, therefore, be haphazard and arbitrary. If it chances to coincide with the child's activity it will get a leverage; if it does not, it will result in friction, or disintegration, or arrest of the child nature.

I believe that knowledge of social conditions, of the present state of civilization, is necessary in order properly to interpret the child's powers. The child has his own instincts and tendencies, but we do not know what these mean until we can translate them into their social equivalents. We must be able to carry them back into a social past and see them as the inheritance of previous race activities. We must also be able to project them into the future to see what their outcome and end will be. In the illustration just used, it is the ability to see in the child's babblings the promise and potency of a future social intercourse and conversation which enables one to deal in the proper way with that instinct.

I believe that the psychological and social sides are organically related and that education cannot be regarded as a compromise between the two, or a super-imposition of one upon the other. We are told that the psychological definition of education is barren and formal—that it gives us only the idea of a development of all the mental powers without giving us any idea of the use to which these powers are put. On the other hand, it is urged that the social definition of education, as getting adjusted to civilization, makes of it a forced and external process, and results in subordinating the freedom of the individual to a preconceived social and political status.

I believe that each of these objections is true when urged against one side isolated from the other. In order to know what a power really is we must know what its end, use, or function is; and this we cannot know save as we conceive of the individual as active in social relationships. But, on the other hand, the only possible adjustment which we can give to the child under existing conditions, is that which arises through putting him in complete possession of all his powers. With the advent of democracy and modern industrial conditions, it is impossible to foretell definitely just what civilization will be twenty years from now. Hence it is impossible to prepare the child for any precise set of conditions. To prepare him for the future life means to give him command of himself; it means so to train him that he will have the full and ready use of all his capacities; that his eye and ear and hand may be tools ready to command, that his judgment may be capable of grasping the conditions under which it has to work, and the executive forces be trained to act economically and efficiently. It is impossible to reach this sort of adjustment save as constant regard is had to the individual's own powers, tastes, and interests—say, that is, as education is continually converted into psychological terms.

In sum, I believe that the individual who is to be educated is a social individual and that society is an organic union of individuals. If we eliminate the social factor from the child we are left only with an abstraction; if we eliminate the individual factor from society, we are left only with an inert and lifeless mass. Education, therefore, must begin with a psychological insight into the child's capacities, interests, and habits. It must be controlled at every point by reference to these same considerations. These powers, interests, and habits must be continually interpreted—we must know what they mean. They must be translated into terms of their social equivalents—into terms of what they are capable of in the way of social service.

Article II—What the School Is

I believe that the school is primarily a social institution. Education being a social process, the school is simply that form of community life in which all those agencies are concentrated that will be most effective in bringing the child to share in the inherited resources of the race, and to use his own powers for social ends.

I believe that education, therefore, is a process of living and not a preparation for future living.

I believe that the school must represent present life—life as real and vital to the child as that which he carries on in the home, in the neighborhood, or on the playground.

I believe that education which does not occur through forms of life, or that are worth living for their own sake, is always a poor substitute for the genuine reality and tends to cramp and to deaden.

I believe that the school, as an institution, should simplify existing social life; should reduce it, as it were, to an embryonic form. Existing life is so complex that the child cannot be brought into contact with it without either confusion or distraction; he is either overwhelmed by the multiplicity of activities which are going on, so that he loses his own power of orderly reaction, or he is so stimulated by these various activities that his powers are prematurely called into play and he becomes either unduly specialized or else disintegrated.

I believe that as such simplified social life, the school life should grow gradually out of the home life; that it should take up and continue the activities with which the child is already familiar in the home.

I believe that it should exhibit these activities to the child, and reproduce them in such ways that the child will gradually learn the meaning of them, and be capable of playing his own part in relation to them.

I believe that this is a psychological necessity, because it is the only way of securing continuity in the child's growth, the only way of giving a background of past experience to the new ideas given in school.

I believe that it is also a social necessity because the home is the form of social life in which the child has been nurtured and in connection with which he has had his moral training. It is the business of the school to deepen and extend his sense of the values bound up in his home life.

I believe that much of present education fails because it neglects this fundamental principle of the school as a form of community life. It conceives the school as a place where certain information is to be given, where certain lessons are to be learned, or where certain habits are to be formed. The value of these is conceived as lying largely in the remote future; the child must do these things for the sake of something else he is to do; they are mere preparation. As a result they do not become a part of the life experience of the child and so are not truly educative.

I believe that the moral education centers upon this conception of the school as a mode of social life, that the best and deepest moral training is precisely that which one gets through having to enter into proper relations with others in a unity of work and thought. The present educational system, so far as they destroy or neglect this unity, render it difficult or impossible to get any genuine, regular moral training.

I believe that the child should be stimulated and controlled in his work through the life of the community.

I believe that under existing conditions far too much of the stimulus and control proceeds from the teacher, because of neglect of the idea of the school as a form of social life.

I believe that the teacher's place and work in the school is to be interpreted from this same basis. The teacher is not in the school to impose certain ideas or to form certain habits in the child, but is there as a member of the community to select the influences which shall affect the child and to assist him in properly responding to these influences.

I believe that the discipline of the school should proceed from the life of the school as a whole and not directly from the teacher.

I believe that the teacher's business is simply to determine on the basis of larger experience and riper wisdom, how the discipline of life shall come to the child.

I believe that all questions of the grading of the child and his promotion should be determined by reference to the same standard. Examinations are of use only so far as they test the child's fitness for social life and reveal the place in which he can be of the most service and where he can receive the most help.

Article III—The Subject-Matter of Education

I believe that the social life of the child is the basis of concentration, or correlation, in all his training or growth. The social life gives the unconscious unity and the background of all his efforts and of all his attainments.

I believe that the subject-matter of the school curriculum should mark a gradual differentiation out of the primitive unconscious unity of social life.

I believe that we violate the child's nature and render difficult the best ethical results, by introducing the child too abruptly to a number of special studies of reading, writing, geography, etc., out of relation to this social life. I believe, therefore, that the true center of correlation on the school subjects is not science, nor literature, nor history, nor geography, but the child's own social activities. . . .

I believe that literature is the reflex expression and interpretation of social experience; that hence it must follow upon and not precede such experience. It, therefore, cannot be made the basis, although it may be made the summary of unification.

I believe once more that history is of educative value in so far as it presents phases of social life and growth. It must be controlled by reference to social life. When taken simply as history it is thrown into the distant past and becomes dead and inert. Taken as the record of man's social life and progress it becomes full of meaning. I believe, however, that it cannot be so taken excepting as the child is also introduced directly into social life.

I believe accordingly that the primary basis of education is in the child's powers at work along the same general constructive lines as those which have brought civilization into being.

I believe that the only way to make the child conscious of his social heritage is to enable him to perform those fundamental types of activity which make civilization what it is. . . .

I believe that there is, therefore, no succession of studies in the ideal school curriculum. If education is life, all life has, from the outset, a scientific aspect, an aspect of art and culture, and an aspect of communication. It cannot, therefore, be true that the proper studies for one grade are mere reading and writing, and that at a later grade, reading, or literature, or science, may be introduced. The progress is not in the succession of studies but in the development of new attitudes towards, and new interests in, experience.

I believe finally, that education must be conceived as a continuing reconstruction of experience; that the process and the goal of education are one and the same thing.

I believe that to set up any end outside of education, as furnishing its goal and standard, is to deprive the educational process of much of its meaning and tends to make us rely upon false and external stimuli in dealing with the child. . . .

From "My Pedagogic Creed" by John Dewey. In Martin Dworkin (ed.), *Dewey on Education*. New York: Teachers College Press, 1959. Reprinted by permission.

Wide-Awakeness and the Moral Life

Maxine Greene

"Moral reform," wrote Henry David Thoreau, "is the effort to throw off sleep." He went on:

> Why is it that men give so poor an account of their day if they have not been slumbering? They are not such poor calculators. If they had not been overcome with drowsiness they would have performed something. The millions are awake enough for physical labor; but only one in a million is awake enough for effective intellectual exertion, only one in a hundred million to a poetic or divine life. To be awake is to be alive. I have never yet met a man who was quite awake. How could I have looked him in the face? We must learn to reawaken and keep ourselves awake, not by mechanical aids, but by an infinite expectation of the dawn, which does not forsake us in our soundest sleep. I know of no more encouraging fact than the unquestionable ability of man to elevate his life by a conscious endeavor.[1]

It is of great interest to me to find out how this notion of wide-awakeness has affected contemporary thought, perhaps particularly the thought of those concerned about moral responsibility and commitment in this difficult modern age. The social philosopher Alfred Schutz has talked of wide-awakeness as an achievement, a type of awareness, "a plane of consciousness of highest tension originating in an attitude of full attention to life and its requirements."[2] This attentiveness, this *interest* in things, is the direct opposite of the attitude of bland conventionality and indifference so characteristic of our time.

We are all familiar with the number of individuals who live their lives immersed, as it were, in daily life, in the mechanical round of habitual activities. We are all aware how few people ask themselves what they have done with their own lives, whether or not they have used their freedom or simply acceded to the imposition of patterned behavior and the assignment of roles. Most people, in fact, are likely to go on in that fashion, unless—or until—"one day the 'why' arises," as Albert Camus put it, "and everything begins in that weariness tinged with amazement." Camus had wide-awakeness in mind as well; because the weariness of which he spoke comes "at the *end* of the acts of a mechanical life, but at the same time it inaugurates the impulse of consciousness."[3]

The "why" may take the form of anxiety, the strange and wordless anxiety that occurs when individuals feel they are not acting on their freedom, not realizing possibility, not (to return to Thoreau) elevating their lives. Or the "why" may accompany a sudden perception of the insufficiencies in ordinary life, of inequities and injustices in the world, of oppression and brutality and control. It may accompany, indeed it may be necessary, for an individual's moral life. The opposite of morality, it has often been said, is indifference—a lack of care, an absence of concern. Lacking wide-awakeness, I want to argue, individuals are likely to drift, to act on impulses of expediency. They are unlikely to identify situations as moral ones or to set themselves to assessing their demands. In such cases, it seems to me, it is meaningless to talk of obligation; it may be futile to speak of consequential choice.

This is an important problem today in many countries of the world. Everywhere, guidelines are deteriorating; fewer and fewer people feel themselves to be answerable to clearly defined norms. In many places, too, because of the proliferation of bureaucracies and corporate structures, individuals find it harder and harder to take initiative. They guide themselves by vaguely perceived expectations; they allow themselves to be programmed by organizations and official schedules or forms. They are like the hero of George Konrad's novel, *The Case Worker*. He is a social worker who works with maltreated children "in the name," as he puts it, "of legal principles and provisions." He does not like the system, but he serves it: "It's law, it works, it's rather like me, its tool. I know its ins and outs. I simplify and complicate it, I slow it down and speed it up. I adapt myself to its needs or adapt it to my needs, but this is as far as I will go."[4] Interestingly enough, he says (and this brings me back to wide-awakeness) that his highest aspiration is to "live with his eyes open" as far as possible; but the main point is that he, like so many other clerks and office workers and middle management men (for all their meaning well), is caught within the system and is not free to choose.

I am suggesting that, for too many individuals in modern society, there is a feeling of being dominated and that feelings of powerlessness are almost inescapable. I am also suggesting that such feelings can to a large degree be overcome through conscious endeavor on the part of individuals to keep themselves awake, to think about their condition in the world, to inquire into the forces that appear to dominate them, to interpret the experiences they are having day by day. Only as they learn to make sense of what is happening, can they feel themselves to be autonomous. Only then can they develop the sense of agency required for living a moral life.

I think it is clear that there always has to be a human consciousness, recognizing the moral issues potentially involved in a situation, if there is to be a moral life. As in such great moral presentations as *Antigone*, *Hamlet*, and *The Plague*, people in everyday life today have to define particular kinds of situations as moral and to identify the possible alternatives. In *Antigone*, Antigone defined the situation that existed after her uncle forbade her to bury her brother as one in which there were alternatives: she could indeed bury her brother, thus offending against the law of the state and being sentenced to death, or (like her sister Ismene) submit to the men in power. In *Hamlet*, the Danish prince defined the situation in Denmark as one in which there were alternatives others could not see: to expose the murderer of his father and take the throne as the true king or to accept the rule of Claudius and his mother and return as a student to Wittenberg. In *The Plague*, most of the citizens of Oran saw no alternative but to resign themselves to a pestilence for which there was no cure; but Dr. Rieux and Tarrou defined the same situation as one in which there were indeed alternatives: to submit—or to form sanitary squads and, by so doing, to refuse to acquiesce in the inhuman, the absurd.

When we look at the everyday reality of home and school and workplace, we can scarcely imagine ourselves taking moral positions like those taken by a Hamlet or a Dr. Rieux. One reason has to do with the overwhelming ordinariness of the lives we live. Another is our tendency to perceive our everyday reality as a given—objectively defined, impervious to change. Taking it for granted, we do not realize that reality, like all others, is an interpreted one. It presents itself to us as it does because we have learned to understand it in standard ways.

In a public school, for instance, we scarcely notice that there is a hierarchy of authority; we are so accustomed to it, we forget that it is man-made. Classroom teachers, assigned a relatively low place in the hierarchy, share a way of seeing and of talking about it. They are used to watching schedules, curricula, and testing programs emanate from "the office." They take for granted the existence of a high place, a seat of power. If required unexpectedly to administer a set of tests, most teachers (fearful, perhaps, irritated or sceptical) will be likely to accede. Their acquiescence may have nothing at all to do with their convictions or with what they have previously read or learned. They simply see no alternatives. The reality they have constructed and take for granted allows for neither autonomy nor disagreement. They do not consider putting their objections to a test. The constructs they have inherited do not include a view of teachers as equal participants. "That," they are prone to say, "is the way it is."

Suppose, however, that a few teachers made a serious effort to understand the reasons for the new directive. Suppose they went out into the community to try to assess the degree of pressure on the part of parents. Suppose that they investigated the kinds of materials dispatched from the city or the state. Pursuing such efforts, they would be keeping themselves awake. They might become increasingly able to define their own values with regard to testing; they might conceivably see a moral issue involved. For some, testing might appear to be dehumanizing; it might lead to irrelevant categorizing; it might result in the branding of certain children. For others, testing might appear to be miseducative, unless it were used to identify disabilities and suggest appropriate remedies. For still others, testing might appear to be a kind of insurance against poor teaching, a necessary reminder of what was left undone. Discussing it from several points of view and within an understood context, the teachers might find themselves in a position

to act as moral agents. Like Dr. Rieux and Tarrou, they might see that there are indeed alternatives: to bring the school community into an open discussion, to consider the moral issues in the light of overarching commitments, or to talk about what is actually known and what is merely hypothesized. At the very least, there would be wide-awakeness. The members of the school community would be embarked on a moral life.

Where personal issues are concerned, the approach might be very much the same. Suppose that a young person's peer group is "into" drugs or alcohol or some type of sexual promiscuity. Young persons who are half asleep and who feel no sense of agency might well see no alternative to compliance with the group, when the group decides that certain new experiences should be tried. To such individuals, no moral situation exists. They are young; they are members; whether they want to particularly or not, they can only go along.

Other young persons, just as committed to the group, might be able to realize that there are indeed alternatives when, say, some of their comrades go out to find a supply of cocaine. They might be able to ponder those alternatives, to play them out in their imagination. They can accompany their friends on their search; they might even, if they are successful, get to sniff a little cocaine and have the pleasure such sniffs are supposed to provide. They can, on the other hand, take a moment to recall the feelings they had when they first smoked marijuana—the nervousness at losing touch with themselves, the dread about what might happen later. They can consider the fact that their friends are going to do something illegal, not playful, that they could be arrested, even jailed. They can confront their own reluctance to break the law (or even to break an ordinary rule), imagine what their parents would say, try to anticipate what they would think of themselves. At the same time, if they decide to back away, they know they might lose their friends. If they can remember that they are free, after all, and if they assess their situation as one in which they can indeed choose one course of action over another, they are on the way to becoming moral agents. The more considerations they take into account, the more they consider the welfare of those around, the closer they will come to making a defensible choice.

A crucial issue facing us is the need to find ways of educating young persons to such sensitivity and potency. As important, it seems to me, is the matter of wide-awakeness for their teachers. It is far too easy for teachers, like other people, to play their roles and do their jobs without serious consideration of the good and right. Ironically, it is even possible when they are using classroom manuals for moral education. This is partly due to the impact of a vaguely apprehended relativism, partly to a bland carelessness, a shrugging off (sometimes because of grave self-doubt) of responsibility, I am convinced that, if teachers today are to initiate young people into an ethical existence, they themselves must attend more fully than they normally have to their own lives and its requirements; they have to break with the mechanical life, to overcome their own submergence in the habitual, even in what they conceive to be the virtuous, and ask the "why" with which learning and moral reasoning begin.

"You do not," wrote Martin Buber, "need moral genius for educating character; you do need someone who is wholly alive and able to communicate himself directly to his fellow beings. His aliveness streams out to them and affects them most strongly and purely when he has no thought of affecting them . . . ."[5] This strikes me as true; but I cannot imagine an aliveness streaming out from someone who is half-asleep and out of touch with herself or himself. I am not proposing separate courses in moral education or value clarification to be taught by such a teacher. I am, rather, suggesting that attentiveness to the moral dimensions of existence ought to permeate many of the classes taught, that wide-awakeness ought to accompany every effort made to initiate persons into any form of life or academic discipline.

Therefore, I believe it important for teachers, no matter what their specialty, to be clear about how they ground their own values, their own conceptions of the good and of the possible. Do they find their sanctions in some supernatural reality? Are they revealed in holy books or in the utterances of some traditional authority? Do they, rather, depend upon their own private intuitions of what is good and right? Do they decide in each particular situation what will best resolve uncertainty, what works out for the best? Do they simply refer to conventional social morality, to prevailing codes, or to the law? Or do they refer beyond the law—to some domain of principle, of norm? To what extent are they in touch with the actualities of their own experiences, their own biographies, and the ways in which these affect the tone of their encounters with the young? Teachers need to be aware of how they personally confront the unnerving questions present in the lives of every teacher, every parent: What shall we teach them? How can we guide them? What hope can we offer them? How can we tell them what to do?

The risks are great, as are the uncertainties. We are no longer in a situation in which we can provide character-training with the assurance that it will make our children virtuous and just. We can no longer use systems of rewards and punishments and feel confident they will make youngsters comply. We recognize the futility of teaching rules or preaching pieties or presenting conceptions of the good. We can no longer set ourselves up as founts of wisdom, exemplars of righteousness, and expect to have positive effects. Children are active; children are different at the various stages of their growth. Engaged in transactions with an environment, each one must effect connections within his or her own experience. Using whatever capacities they have available, each one must himself or herself perceive the consequences of the acts he or she performs. Mustering their own resources, each one must embark—"through choice of action," as Dewey put it[6]—upon the formation of a self.

Moral education, it would seem, must be as specifically concerned with self-identification in a community as it is with the judgments persons are equipped to make at different ages. It has as much to do with interest and action in concrete situations as it does with the course of moral reasoning. It has as much to do with consciousness and imagination as it does with principle. Since it cannot take place outside the vital contexts of social life, troubling questions have to be constantly confronted. How can indifference be overcome? How can the influence of the media be contained? How can the young be guided to choose reflectively and compassionately, even as they are set free?

The problem, most will agree, is not to tell them what to do—but to help them attain some kind of clarity about how to choose, how to decide what to do. And this involves teachers directly, immediately—teachers as persons able to present themselves as critical thinkers willing to disclose their own principles and their own reasons as well as authentic persons living in the world, persons who are concerned—who care.

Many teachers, faced with demands like these, find themselves in difficult positions, especially if they are granted little autonomy, or their conceptions of their own projects are at odds with what their schools demand. Today they may be held accountable for teaching predefined competencies and skills or for achieving objectives that are often largely behavioral. At once, they may be expected to represent both the wider culture and the local community, or the international community and the particular community of the individual child. If teachers are not critically conscious, if they are not awake to their own values and commitments (and to the conditions working upon them), if they are not personally engaged with their subject matter and with the world around, I do not see how they can initiate the young into critical questioning or the moral life.

I am preoccupied, I suppose, with what Camus called "the plague"—that terrible distancing and indifference, so at odds with commitment and communion and love. I emphasize this because I want to stress the connection between wide-awakeness, cognitive clarity, and existential concern. I want to highlight the fact that the roots of moral choosing lie at the core of a person's conception of herself or himself and the equally important fact that choosing involves action as well as thought. Moral action, of course, demands choosing between alternatives, usually between two goods, not between good and bad or right and wrong. The problem in teaching is to empower persons to internalize and incarnate the kinds of principles that will enable them to make such choices. Should I do what is thought to be my duty and volunteer for the army, or should I resist what I believe to be an unjust war. Should I steal the medicine to save my mother's life, or should I obey the law and risk letting her die?

These are choices of consequence for the self and others; and they are made, they can only be made in social situations where custom, tradition, official codes, and laws condition and play upon what people think and do. We might think of Huck Finn's decision not to return Jim to his owner or of Anna Karenina's decision to leave her husband. These are only morally significant in relation to a particular fabric of codes and customs and rules. Think of the Danish king's wartime decision to stand with Denmark's Jewish citizens, Daniel Ellsberg's decision to publish the Pentagon Papers, or Pablo Casals' refusal to conduct in fascist Spain. These decisions too were made in a matrix of principles, laws, and ideas of what is considered acceptable, absolutely, or conditionally good and right. To be moral involves taking a position towards that matrix, thinking critically about what is taken for granted. It involves taking a principled position of one's own (*choosing* certain principles by which to live) and speaking clearly about it, so as to set oneself on the right track.

It is equally important to affirm that it is always the individual, acting voluntarily in a particular situation at a particular moment, who does the deciding. I do not mean that individuals are isolated, answerable only to themselves. I do mean that individuals, viewed as participants, as inextricably involved with other people, must be enabled to take responsibility for their own choosing, must not merge themselves or hide themselves in what Soren Kierkegaard called "the crowd."[7] If individuals act automatically or conventionally, if they do only what is expected of them (or because they feel they have no right to speak for themselves), if they do only what they are told to do, they are not living moral lives.

Indeed, I rather doubt that individuals who are cowed or flattened out or depressed or afraid can learn, since learning inevitably involves a free decision to enter into a form of life, to proceed in a certain way, to do something because it is right. There are paradigms to be found in many kinds of teaching for those interested in moral education, since teaching is in part a process of moving people to proceed according to a specified set of norms. If individuals are wide-awake and make decisions consciously to interpret a poem properly, to try to understand a period in English history, or to participate in some type of social inquiry, they are choosing to abide by certain standards made available to them. In doing so, they are becoming acquainted with what it means to choose a set of norms. They are not only creating value for themselves, they are creating themselves; they are moving towards more significant, more understandable lives.

Consider, with norms and self-creation in mind, the case of Nora in Ibsen's *The Doll's House*. If she simply ran out of the house in tears at the end, she would not have been engaging in moral action. Granting the fact that she was defying prevailing codes, I would insist that she was making a decision in accord with an internalized norm. It might be called a principle of emancipation, having to do with the right to grow, to become, to be more than a doll in a doll's house. If asked, Nora might have been able to generalize and talk about the right of *all* human beings to develop in their own fashion, to be respected, to be granted integrity.

Principles or norms are general ideas of that kind, arising out of experience and used by individuals in the appraisal of situations they encounter as they live—to help them determine what they ought to do. They are not specific rules, like the rules against stealing and lying and adultery. They are general and comprehensive. They concern justice and equality, respect for the dignity of persons and regard for their points of view. They have much to do with the ways in which diverse individuals choose themselves; they are defined reflectively and imaginatively and against the backgrounds of biography. When they are incarnated in a person's life, they offer him or her the means for analyzing particular situations. They offer perspectives, points of view

from which to consider particular acts. The Golden Rule is such a principle, but, as Dewey says, the Golden Rule does not finally decide matters just by enabling us to tell people to consider the good of others as they would their own. "It suggests," he writes, "the necessity of considering how our acts affect the interests of others as well as our own; it tends to prevent partiality of regard. . . . In short, the Golden Rule does not issue special orders or commands; but it does clarify and illuminate the situations requiring intelligent deliberation."[8] So it was with the principle considered by Ibsen's Nora; so it is with the principle of justice and the principles of care and truth-telling. Our hope in teaching is that persons will appropriate such principles and learn to live by them.

Now it is clear that young people have to pass through the stages of heteronomy in their development towards the degree of autonomy they require for acting on principle in the way described. They must achieve the kind of wide-awakeness I have been talking about, the ability to think about what they are doing, to take responsibility. The teaching problem seems to me to be threefold. It involves equipping young people with the ability to identify alternatives, and to see possibilities in the situations confront. It involves the teaching of principles, possible perspectives by means of which those situations can be assessed and appraised, *as well as* the norms governing historical inquiry, ballet dancing, or cooperative living, norms that must be appropriated by persons desiring to join particular human communities. It also involves enabling students to make decisions of principle, to reflect, to articulate, and to take decisive actions in good faith.

Fundamental to the whole process may be the building up of a sense of moral directedness, of oughtness. An imaginativeness, an awareness, and a sense of possibility are required, along with the sense of autonomy and agency, of being present to the self. There must be attentiveness to others and to the circumstances of everyday life. There must be efforts made to discover ways of living together justly and pursuing common ends. As wide-awake teachers work, making principles available and eliciting moral judgments, they must orient themselves to the concrete, the relevant, and the questionable. They must commit themselves to each person's potentiality for overcoming helplessness and submergence, for looking through his or her own eyes at the shared reality.

I believe this can only be done if teachers can identify themselves as moral beings, concerned with defining their own life purposes in a way that arouses others to do the same. I believe, you see, that the young are most likely to be stirred to learn when they are challenged by teachers who themselves are learning, who are breaking with what they have too easily taken for granted, who are creating their own moral lives. There are no guarantees, but wide-awakeness can play a part in the process of liberating and arousing, in helping people pose questions with regard to what is oppressive, mindless, and wrong. Surely, it can help people—all kinds of people— make the conscious endeavors needed to elevate their lives.

Camus, in an essay called "The Almond Trees," wrote some lines that seem to me to apply to teachers, especially those concerned in this way. He was talking about how endless are our tasks, how impossible it is to overcome the human condition—which, at least, we have come to know better than ever before:

We must mend "what has been torn apart, make justice imaginable again—give happiness

a meaning once more. ... Naturally, it is a superhuman task. But superhuman is the term for tasks men take a long time to accomplish, that's all. Let us know our aims, then, holding fast to the mind. ... The first thing is not to despair.[9]

Notes

1. Henry David Thoreau, *Walden* (New York: Washington Square Press, 1963), pp. 66–67.
2. Alfred Schutz, ed. Maurice Natanson, *The Problem of Social Reality*, Collected Papers I (The Hague: Martinus Nijhoff, 1967), p. 213.
3. Albert Camus, *The Myth of Sisyphus* (New York: Alfred A. Knopf, 1955), p. 13.
4. George Konrad, *The Case Worker* (New York: Harcourt Brace Jovanovich, 1974), p. 168.
5. Martin Buber, *Between Man and Man* (Boston: Beacon Press, 1957), p. 105.
6. John Dewey, *Democracy and Education* (New York: Macmillan Company, 1916), p. 408.
7. Soren Kierkegaard, "The Individual," in *The Point of View for My Work as an Author* (New York: Harper & Row, 1962), pp. 102–136.
8. Dewey, *Theory of the Moral Life* (New York: Holt, Rinehart and Winston, 1960), p. 142.
9. Camus, "'The Almond Trees," in *Lyrical and Critical Essays* (New York: Alfred A. Knopf, 1968), p. 135.

From "Wide-Awakeness and the Moral Life" by Maxine Greene. In *Landscapes for Learning*. New York: Teachers College Press, 1978. Reprinted by permission.

The Ideal of the Educated Person

Jane Roland Martin

R. S. Peters calls it an ideal.[1] So do Nash, Kazemias and Perkinson who, in their introduction to a collection of studies in the history of educational thought, say that one cannot go about the business of education without it.[2] Is it the good life? the responsible citizen? personal autonomy? No, it is the educated man.

The educated man! In the early 1960s when I was invited to contribute to a book of essays to be entitled *The Educated Man*, I thought nothing of this phrase. By the early 1970s I felt uncomfortable whenever I came across it, but I told myself it was the thought not the words that counted. It is now the early 1980s. Peters's use of the phrase "educated man" no longer troubles me for I think it fair to say that he intended it in a gender-neutral way.[3] Despite one serious lapse which indicates that on some occasions he was thinking of his educated man as male, I do not doubt that the ideal he set forth was meant for males and females alike.[4] Today my concern is not Peters's language but his conception of the educated man—or person, as I will henceforth say. I will begin by outlining Peters's ideal for you and will then show that it does serious harm to women. From there I will go on to argue that Peters's ideal is inadequate for men as well as women and, furthermore, that its inadequacy for men is intimately connected to the injustice it does women. In conclusion I will explore some of the requirements an adequate ideal must satisfy.

Let me explain at the outset that I have chosen to discuss Peters's ideal of the educated person here because for many years Peters has been perhaps the dominant figure in philosophy of education. Moreover, although Peters's ideal is formulated in philosophically sophisticated terms, it is certainly not idiosyncratic. On the contrary, Peters claims to have captured our concept of the educated person, and he may well have done so. Thus, I think it fair to say that the traits Peters claims one must possess to be a truly educated person and the kind of education he assumes one must have in order to acquire those traits would, with minor variations, be cited by any number of people today if they were to describe their own conception of the ideal. I discuss Peters's ideal, then, because it has significance for the field of philosophy of education as a whole.

I. R. S. Peters's Educated Person

The starting point of Peters's philosophy of education is the concept of the educated person. While granting that we sometimes use the term "education" to refer to any process of rearing, bringing up, instructing, etc., Peters distinguishes this very broad sense of "education" from the narrower one in which he is interested. The concept of the educated person provides the basis for this distinction: whereas "education" in the broad sense refers to any process of rearing, etc.,

"education" in the narrower, and to him philosophically more important, sense refers to the family of processes which have as their outcome the development of an educated person.[5]

Peters set forth his conception of the educated person in some detail in his book, *Ethics and Education*.[6] Briefly, an educated person is one who does not simply possess knowledge. An educated person has a body of knowledge and some kind of conceptual scheme to raise this knowledge above the level of a collection of disjointed facts which in turn implies some understanding of principles for organizing facts and of the "reason why" of things. Furthermore, the educated person's knowledge is not inert: it characterizes the person's way of looking at things and involves "the kind of commitment that comes from getting on the inside of a form of thought and awareness"; that is to say, the educated person cares about the standards of evidence implicit in science or the canons of proof inherent in mathematics. Finally, the educated person has cognitive perspective. In an essay entitled "Education and the Educated Man" published several years later, Peters added to this portrait that the educated person's pursuits can be practical as well as theoretical so long as the person delights in them for their own sake, and that both sorts of pursuits involve standards to which the person must be sensitive.[7] He also made it clear that knowledge enters into his conception of the educated person in three ways, namely, depth, breadth and knowledge of good.

In their book, *Education and Personal Relationships*, Downie, Loudfoot and Telfer presented a conception of the educated person which is a variant on Peters's.[8] I cite it here not because they too use the phrase "educated man," but to show that alternate philosophical conceptions of the educated person differ from Peters's only in detail. Downie, Loudfoot and Telfer's educated person has knowledge which is wide ranging in scope, extending from history and geography to the natural and social sciences and to current affairs. This knowledge is important, relevant and grounded. The educated person understands what he or she knows,

knows how to do such things as history and science, and has the inclination to apply this knowledge, to be critical and to have curiosity in the sense of a thirst for knowledge. Their major departure from Peters's conception—and it is not, in the last analysis, very major—is to be found in their concern with knowledge by acquaintance: the educated person must not merely have knowledge *about* works of art—and, if I understand them correctly, about moral and religious theories—but must know these as individual things.

Consider now the knowledge, the conceptual scheme which raises this knowledge above the level of disjointed facts and the cognitive perspective Peters's educated person must have. It is quite clear that Peters does not intend that these be acquired through the study of cooking and driving. Mathematics, science, history, literature, philosophy—these are the subjects which constitute the curriculum for his educated person. In short, his educated person is one who has had—and profited from—a liberal education of the sort outlined by Paul Hirst in his famous essay, "Liberal Education and the Nature of Knowledge." Hirst describes what is sought in a liberal education as follows:

> first, sufficient immersion in the concepts, logic and criteria of the discipline for a person to come to know the distinctive way in which it "works" by pursuing these in particular cases; and then sufficient generalization of these over the whole range of the discipline so that his experience begins to be widely structured in this distinctive manner. It is this coming to look at things in a certain way that is being aimed at, not the ability to work out in minute particulars all the details that can be in fact discerned. It is the ability to recognize empirical assertions or aesthetic judgments for what they are, and to know the kind of consideration on which their validity will depend, that matters.[9]

If Peters's educated person is not in fact Hirst's liberally educated person, he or she is certainly its identical twin.

Liberal education, in Hirst's view, consists in an initiation into what he calls the forms of knowledge. There are, on his count, seven of them. Although he goes to some lengths in his later writings on the topic to deny that these forms are themselves intellectual disciplines, it is safe to conclude that his liberally educated person, and hence Peters's educated person, will acquire the conceptual schemes and cognitive perspectives they are supposed to have through a study of mathematics, physical science, history, the human sciences, literature, fine arts, philosophy. These disciplines will not necessarily be studied separately: an interdisciplinary curriculum is compatible with the Peters-Hirst ideal. But it is nonetheless their subject matter, their conceptual apparatus, their standards of proof and adequate evidence, their way of looking at things that must be acquired if the ideal is to be realized.

II. Initiation into Male Cognitive Perspectives

What is this certain way in which the educated person comes to look at things? What is the distinctive manner in which that person's experience is structured? A body of literature documenting the many respects in which the disciplines of knowledge ignore or misrepresent the experience and lives of women has developed over the last decade. I cannot do justice here to its range of concerns or its sophisticated argumentation. Through the use of examples, however, I will try to give you some sense of the extent to which the intellectual disciplines incorporate a male cognitive perspective, and hence a sense of the extent to which Hirst's liberally educated person and its twin—Peters's educated person—look at things through male eyes.

Let me begin with history. "History is past politics" was the slogan inscribed on the seminar room wall at Johns Hopkins in the days of the first doctoral program.[10] In the late 1960s the historian, Richard Hofstadter, summarized his field by saying: "Memory is the thread of personal identity, history of public identity." History has defined itself as the record of the public and political aspects of the past; in other words, as the record of the productive processes—man's sphere—of society. Small wonder that women are scarcely mentioned in historical narratives! Small wonder that they have been neither the objects nor the subjects of historical inquiry until very recently! The reproductive processes of society which have traditionally been carried on by women are excluded *by definition* from the purview of the discipline.

If women's lives and experiences have been excluded from the subject matter of history, the works women have produced have for the most part been excluded from literature and the fine arts. It has never been denied that there have been women writers and artists, but their works have not often been deemed important or significant enough to be studied by historians and critics. Thus, for example, Catherine R. Stimpson has documented the treatment accorded Gertrude Stein by two journals which exert a powerful influence in helping to decide what literature is and what books matter.[11] Elaine Showalter, pursuing a somewhat different tack, has documented the double standard which was used in the nineteenth century to judge women writers: all the most desirable aesthetic qualities—for example, power, breadth, knowledge of life, humor—were assigned to men; the qualities assigned to women, such as refinement, tact, precise observation, were not considered sufficient for the creation of an excellent novel.[12]

The disciplines are guilty of different kinds of sex bias. Even as literature and the fine arts exclude women's works from their subject matter, they include works which construct women according to the male image of her. One might expect this tendency to construct the female to be limited to the arts, but it is not. Naomi Weisstein has shown that psychology constructs the female personality to fit the pre-conceptions of its male practitioners, clinicians either accepting theory without evidence or finding in their data what they want to find.[13] And Ruth Hubbard has shown that this tendency extends even to biology where the stereotypical picture of the passive female is projected by the male practitioners of that field onto the animal kingdom.[14]

There are, indeed, two quite different ways in which a discipline can distort the lives, experiences and personalities of women. Even as psychology constructs the female personality out of our cultural stereotype, it holds up standards of development for women to meet which are derived from studies using male subjects.[15] Not surprisingly, long after the source of the standards is forgotten, women are proclaimed to be underdeveloped and inferior to males in relation to these standards. Thus, for example, Carol Gilligan has pointed out that females are classified as being at Stage 3 of Kohlberg's six stage sequence of moral development because important differences in moral development between males and females are ignored.[16]

In the last decade scholars have turned to the study of women. Thus, historical narratives and analyses of some aspects of the reproductive processes of society—of birth control, childbirth, midwifery, for example—have been published.[17] The existence of such scholarship is no guarantee, however, of its integration into the mainstream of the discipline of history itself, yet this latter is required if initiation into history as a form of knowledge is not to constitute initiation into a male cognitive perspective. The title of a 1974 anthology on the history of women, *Clio's Consciousness Raised*, is unduly optimistic.[18] Certainly, the consciousness of some historians has been raised, but there is little reason to believe that the discipline of history has redefined itself so that studies of the reproductive processes of society are not simply tolerated as peripherally relevant, but are considered to be as central to it as political, economic and military narratives are. Just as historians have begun to study women's past, scholars in literature and the fine arts have begun to bring works by women to our attention and to reinterpret the ones we have always known.[19] But there is still the gap between feminist scholarship and the established definitions of literary and artistic significance to be bridged, and until it is, the initiation into these disciplines provided by a liberal education will be an initiation into male perspectives.

In sum, the intellectual disciplines into which a person must be initiated to become an educated person *exclude* women and their works, *construct* the female to the male image of her and *deny* the truly feminine qualities she does possess. The question remains of whether the male cognitive perspective of the disciplines is integral to Peters's ideal of the educated person. The answer to this question is to be found in Hirst's essay, "The Forms of Knowledge Revisited."[20] There he presents the view that at any given time a liberal education consists in an initiation into *existing* forms of knowledge. Hirst acknowledges that new forms can develop and that old ones can disappear. Still, the analysis he gives of the seven distinct forms which he takes to comprise a liberal education today is based, he says on our present conceptual scheme. Thus, Peters's educated person is not one who studies a set of ideal, unbiased forms of knowledge; on the contrary, that person is one who is initiated into whatever forms of knowledge exist in the society at that time. In our time the existing forms embody a male point of view. The initiation into them envisioned by Hirst and Peters is, therefore, one in male cognitive perspectives.

Peters's educated person is expected to have grasped the basic structure of science, history and the like rather than the superficial details of content. Is it possible that the feminist critique of the disciplines therefore leaves his ideal untouched? It would be a grave misreading of the literature to suppose that this critique presents simply a surface challenge to the disciplines. Although the examples I have cited here may have suggested to you that the challenge is directed at content alone, it is in fact many pronged. Its targets include the questions asked by the various fields of inquiry and the answers given them: the aims of those fields and the ways they define their subject matter; the methods they use, their canons of objectivity, and their ruling metaphors. It is difficult to be clear on precisely which aspects of knowledge and inquiry are at issue when Hirst speaks of initiation into a form of knowledge. A male bias has been found on so many levels of the disciplines, however, that I think we can feel quite confident that it is a property also of the education embodied in Peters's ideal.

III. Genderized Traits

The masculinity of Peters's educated person is not solely a function of a curriculum in the intellectual disciplines, however. Consider the traits or characteristics Peters attributes to the educated person. Feelings and emotions only enter into the makeup of the educated person to the extent that being committed to the standards of a theoretical pursuit such as science, or a practical one such as architecture, counts as such. Concern for people and for interpersonal relationships has no role to play: the educated person's sensitivity is to the standards immanent in activities, not to other human beings; an imaginative awareness of emotional atmosphere and interpersonal relationships need be no part of this person's makeup, nor is the educated person thought to be empathic or supportive or nurturant. Intuition is also neglected. Theoretical knowledge and what Woods and Barrow—two more philosophers who use the phrase "educated man"—call "reasoned under-standing" are the educated person's prime characteristics:[21] even this person's practical pursuits are to be informed by some theoretical perspectives; moreover, this theoretical bent is to be leavened neither by imaginative nor intuitive powers, for these are never to be developed.

The educated person as portrayed by Peters, and also by Downie, Loudfoot and Telfer, and by Woods and Barrow, coincides with our cultural stereotype of a male human being. According to that stereotype men are objective, analytic, rational; they are interested in ideas and things; they have no interpersonal orientation; they are neither nurturant nor supportive, empathetic or sensitive. According to the stereotype, nurturance and supportiveness, empathy and sensitivity are female attributes. Intuition is a female attribute too.[22]

This finding is not really surprising. It has been shown that psychologists define moral development, adult development and even human development in male terms and that therapists do the same for mental health.[23] Why suppose that philosophers of education have avoided the androcentric fallacy?[24] Do not misunderstand! Females can acquire the traits and dispositions which constitute Peters's conception of the educated person; he espouses an ideal which, if it can be attained at all, can be by both sexes.[25] But our culture associates the traits and dispositions of Peters's educated person with males. To apply it to females is to impose on them a masculine mold. I realize that as a matter of fact some females fit our male stereotype and that some males do not, but this does not affect the point at issue, which is that Peters has set forth an ideal for education which embodies just those traits and dispositions our culture attributes to the male sex and excludes the traits our culture attributes to the female sex.

Now it might seem that if the mold is a good one, it does not matter that it is masculine; that if the traits which Peters's educated person possesses are desirable, then it makes no difference that in our society they are associated with males. Indeed, some would doubtless argue that in extending to women cognitive virtues which have long been associated with men and which education has historically reserved for men, Peters's theory of education strikes a blow for sex equality. It does matter that the traits Peters assigns the educated person are considered in our culture to be masculine, however. It matters because some traits which males and females can both possess are *genderized*; that is, they are appraised differentially according to sex.[26]

Consider aggressiveness. The authors of a book on assertive training for women report that in the first class meetings of their training courses they ask their students to call out the adjectives which come to mind when we say "aggressive woman" and "aggressive man." Here is the list of adjectives the women used to describe an aggressive man: "masculine," "dominating," "successful," "heroic," "capable," "strong," "forceful," "manly." Need I tell you the list of adjectives they used to describe an aggressive woman?: "harsh," "pushy," "bitchy," "domineering," "obnoxious," "emasculating," "uncaring."[27]

I submit to you that the traits Peters attributes to the educated person are, like the trait of aggressiveness, evaluated differently for males and females. Imagine a woman who is analytical

and critical, whose intellectual curiosity is strong, who cares about the canons of science and mathematics. How is she described? "She thinks like a man," it is said. To be sure, this is considered by some to be the highest accolade. Still, a woman who is said to think like a man is being judged to be masculine, and since we take masculinity and femininity to lie at opposite ends of a single continuum, she is thereby being judged to be lacking in femininity.[28] Thus, while it is possible for a woman to possess the traits of Peters's educated person, she will do so at her peril: her possession of them will cause her to be viewed as unfeminine, i.e., as an unnatural or abnormal woman.

IV. A Double Bind

It may have been my concern over Peters's use of the phrase "educated man" which led me to this investigation in the first place, but as you can see, the problem is not one of language. Had Peters consistently used the phrase "educated person" the conclusion that the ideal he holds up for education is masculine would be unaffected. To be sure, Peters's educated person can be male or female, but he or she will have acquired male cognitive perspectives and will have developed traits which in our society are genderized in favor of males.

I have already suggested that Peters's ideal places a burden on women because the traits constituting it are evaluated negatively when possessed by females. The story of Rosalind Franklin, the scientist who contributed to the discovery of the structure of DNA, demonstrates that when a woman displays the kind of critical, autonomous thought which is an attribute of Peters's educated person, she is derided for what are considered to be negative unpleasant characteristics.[29] Rosalind Franklin consciously opted out of "woman's sphere" and entered the laboratory. From an abstract point of view the traits she possessed were quite functional there. Nonetheless she was perceived to be an interloper, an alien who simply could not be taken seriously in relation to the production of new, fundamental ideas no matter what her personal qualities might be.[30]

But experiencing hostility and derision is the least of the suffering caused women by Peters's ideal. His educated person is one who will know nothing about the lives women have led throughout history and little if anything about the works or art and literature women have produced. If his educated person is a woman, she will have been presented with few female role models in her studies whereas her male counterpart will be able to identify with the doers and thinkers and makers of history. Above all, the certain way in which his educated man and woman will come to look at the world will be one in which men are perceived as they perceive themselves and women are perceived as men perceive them.

To achieve Peters's ideal one must acquire cognitive perspectives through which one sex is perceived on its own terms and one sex is perceived as the Other.[31] Can it be doubted that when the works of women are excluded from the subject matter of the fields into which they are being initiated, students will come to believe that males are superior and females are inferior human beings? That when in the course of this initiation the lives and experiences of women are scarcely mentioned, students will come to believe that the way in which women have lived and the things women have done throughout history have no value? Can it be doubted that these beliefs do female students serious damage? The woman whose self-confidence is bolstered by an education which transmits the message that females are inferior human beings is rare. Rarer still is the woman who, having been initiated into alien cognitive perspectives, gains confidence in her own powers without paying the price of self-alienation.

Peters's ideal puts women in a double bind. To be educated they must give up their own way of experiencing and looking at the world, thus alienating themselves from themselves. To be unalienated they must remain uneducated. Furthermore, to be an educated person a female must acquire traits which are appraised negatively when she possesses them. At the same time, the traits which are evaluated positively when possessed by her—for example, being nurturant and empathetic—are excluded from the ideal. Thus a female who has acquired the traits of an educated person will not be evaluated positively for having them, while one who has acquired those traits for which she will be positively evaluated will not have achieved the ideal. Women are placed in this double bind because Peters's ideal incorporates traits genderized in favor of males and excludes traits genderized in favor of females. It thus puts females in a no-win situation. Yes, men and women can both achieve Peters's ideal. However, women suffer, as men do not, for doing so.

Peters's masculine ideal of the educated person harms males as well as females, however. In a chapter of the 1981 NSSE Yearbook I argued at some length that Hirst's account of liberal education is seriously deficient.[32] Since Peters's educated person is to all intents and purposes Hirst's liberally educated person, let me briefly repeat my criticism of Hirst here. The Peters-Hirst educated person will have knowledge about others, but will not have been taught to care about their welfare, let alone to act kindly toward them. That person will have some understanding of society, but will not have been taught to feel its injustices or even to be concerned over its fate. The Peters Hirst educated person is an ivory tower person: a person who can reason yet has no desire to solve real problems in the real world; a person who understands science but does not worry about the uses to which it is put; a person who can reach flawless moral conclusions but feels no care or concern for others.

Simply put, quite apart from the burden it places on women, Peters's ideal of the educated person is far too narrow to guide the educational enterprise. Because it presupposes a divorce of mind from body, thought from action, and reason from feeling and emotion, it provides at best an ideal of an educated *mind*, not an educated *person*. To the extent that its concerns are strictly cognitive however, even in that guise it leaves much to be desired.

V. Education for Productive Processes

Even if Peters's ideal did not place an unfair burden on women it would need to be rejected for the harm it does men, but its inadequacy as an ideal for men and the injustice it does women are not unconnected. In my Yearbook essay I sketched in the rough outlines of a new paradigm of liberal education, one which would emphasize the development of persons and not simply rational minds; one which would join thought to action, and reason to feeling and emotion. I could just as easily have called it a new conception of the educated person. What I did not realize when I wrote that essay is that the aspects of the Peters-Hirst ideal which I found so objectionable are directly related to the role, traditionally considered to be male, which their educated person is to play in society.

Peters would vehemently deny that he conceives of education as production. Nonetheless, he implicitly attributes to education the task of turning raw material, namely the *un*educated person, into an end product whose specifications he sets forth in his account of the concept of the educated person. Peters would deny even more vehemently that he assigns to education a societal function. Yet an examination of his conception of the educated person reveals that the end product of the education he envisions is designed to fit into a specific place in the social order; that he assigns to education the function of developing the traits and qualities and to some extent the skills of one whose role is to use and produce ideas.[33]

Peters would doubtless say that the production and consumption of ideas is everyone's business and that an education for this is certainly not an education which fits people into a particular place in society. Yet think of the two parts into which the social order has traditionally been divided. Theorists have put different labels on them, some referring to the split between work and home, others to the public and private domains and still others to productive and reproductive processes.[34] Since the public/private distinction has associations for educators which are not germaine to the present discussion while the work/home distinction obscures some important issues, I will speak here of productive and reproductive processes. I do not want to make terminology the issue, however. If you prefer other labels, by all means substitute them for mine. My own is only helpful, I should add, if the term "reproduction" is construed broadly.

Thus I use it here to include not simply biological reproduction of the species, but the whole process of reproduction from conception until the individual reaches more or less independence from the family.[35] This process I take to include not simply childcare and rearing, but the related activities of keeping house, running the household and serving the needs and purposes of all the family members. Similarly, I interpret the term "production" broadly to include political, social and cultural activities and processes as well as economic ones.

Now this traditional division drawn within the social order is accompanied by a separation of the sexes. Although males and females do in fact participate in both the reproductive and productive processes of society, the reproductive processes are considered to constitute "woman's sphere" and the productive processes "man's sphere." Although Peters's educated person is ill-equipped for jobs in trades or work on the assembly line, this person is tailor-made for carrying on certain of the productive processes of society, namely those which require work with heads, not hands. Thus his educated person is designed to fill a role in society which has traditionally been considered to be male. Moreover, he or she is not equipped by education to fill roles associated with the reproductive processes of society, i.e., roles traditionally considered to be female.

Once the functionalism of Peters's conception of the educated person is made explicit, the difficulty of including it in the ideal feelings and emotions such as caring and compassion, or skills of cooperation and nurturance, becomes clear. These fall under our culture's female stereotype. They are considered to be appropriate for those who carry on the reproductive processes of society but irrelevant, if not downright dysfunctional, for those who carry on the productive processes of society. It would therefore be irrational to include them in an ideal which is conceived of solely in relation to productive processes.

I realize now, as I did not before, that for the ideal of the educated person to be as broad as it should be, the two kinds of societal processes which Peters divorces from one another must be joined together.[36] An adequate ideal of the educated person must give the reproductive processes of society their due. An ideal which is tied solely to the productive processes of society cannot readily accommodate the important virtues of caring and compassion, sympathy and nurturance, generosity and cooperation which are genderized in favor of females.

To be sure, it would be possible in principle to continue to conceive of the educated person solely in relation to the productive processes of society while rejecting the stereotypes which produce genderized traits. One could include caring and compassion in the ideal of the educated person on the grounds that although they are thought to be female traits whose home is in the reproductive processes of society, they are in fact functional in the production and consumption of ideas. The existence of genderized traits is not the only reason for giving the reproductive processes of society their due in an ideal of the educated person, however. These processes are themselves central to the lives of each of us and to the life of society as a whole. The dispositions, knowledge, skills required to carry them out well are not innate, nor do they simply develop naturally over time. Marriage, childrearing, family life: these involve difficult, complex, learned activities which can be done well or badly. Just as an educated person should be one in whom head, hand and heart are integrated, he or she should be one who is at home carrying on the reproductive processes of society, broadly understood, as well as the productive processes.

Now Peters might grant that the skills, traits, and knowledge necessary for carrying on reproductive processes are learned—in some broad sense of the term, at least—but argue that one does not require an education in them for they are picked up in the course of daily living. Perhaps at one time they were picked up in this way, and perhaps in some societies they are now. But it is far from obvious that, just by living, most adults in our society today acquire the altruistic feelings and emotions, the skills of childrearing, the understanding of what values are important to transmit and which are not, and the ability to put aside one's own projects and enter into those of others which are just a few of the things

required for successful participation in the reproductive processes of society.

That education is needed by those who carry on the reproductive processes is not in itself proof that it should be encompassed by a conception of the educated person however, for this conception need not be all-inclusive. It need not be all inclusive but, for Peters, education which is not guided by his ideal of the educated person scarcely deserves attention. Moreover, since a conception of the educated person tends to function as an ideal, one who becomes educated will presumably have achieved something worthwhile. Value is attached to being an educated person: to the things an educated person knows and can do; to the tasks and activities that person is equipped to perform. The exclusion of education for reproductive processes from the ideal of the educated person thus carries with it an unwarranted negative value judgment about the tasks and activities, the traits and dispositions which are associated with them.

VI. Redefining the Ideal

An adequate ideal of the educated person must give the reproductive processes of society their due, but it must do more than this. After all, these processes were acknowledged by Rousseau in Book V of *Emile*.[37] There he set forth two distinct ideals of the educated person, the one for Emile tied to the productive processes of society and the one for Sophie tied to the reproductive processes. I leave open here the question Peters never asks of whether we should adopt one or more ideals of the educated person.[38] One thing is clear, however. We need a conception which does not fall into the trap of assigning males and females to the different processes of society, yet does not make the mistake of ignoring one kind of process altogether. We all participate in both kinds of processes and both are important to all of us. Whether we adopt one or many ideals, a conception of the educated person which is tied only to one kind of process will be incomplete.

An adequate ideal of the educated person must also reflect a realistic understanding of the limitations of existing forms or disciplines of knowledge. In my Yearbook chapter I made a case for granting them much less "curriculum space" than Hirst and Peters do. So long as they embody a male cognitive perspective, however, we must take into account not simply the amount of space they occupy in the curriculum of the educated person, but the hidden messages which are received by those who are initiated into them. An ideal of the educated person cannot itself rid the disciplines of knowledge of their sex bias. But it can advocate measures for counteracting the harmful effects on students of coming to see things solely through male eyes.

The effects of an initiation into male cognitive perspectives constitute a hidden curriculum. Alternative courses of action are open to us when we find a hidden curriculum and there is no reason to suppose that only one is appropriate. Let me say a few words here, however, about a course of action that might serve as at least a partial antidote to the hidden curriculum transmitted by an education in male biased disciplines.[39] When we find a hidden curriculum we can show it to its recipients; we can raise their consciousness, if you will, so that they will know what is happening to them. Raising to consciousness the male cognitive perspective of the disciplines of knowledge in the educated person's curriculum is no guarantee, of course, that educated females will not suffer from a lack of self-confidence and from self-alienation. Yet knowledge can be power. A curriculum which, through critical analysis, exposes the biased view of women embodied in the disciplines and which, by granting ample space to the study of women shows how unjust that view is, is certainly preferable to a curriculum which, by its silence on the subject, gives students the impression that the ways in which the disciplines look at the world are impartial and unbiased.

Now it might seem to be a relatively simple matter both to give the reproductive processes of society their due in an ideal of the educated person and to include in that ideal measures for counteracting the hidden curriculum of an education in the existing disciplines of knowledge. Yet given the way philosophy of education conceives of its subject matter today, it is not. The productive-reproductive dualism is built

not simply into Peters's ideal but into our discipline.[40] We do not even have a vocabulary for discussing education in relation to the reproductive processes of society, for the distinction between liberal and vocational education which we use to cover the kinds of education we take to be philosophically important applies within productive processes: liberal and vocational education are both intended to fit people to carry on productive processes, the one for work with heads and the other for work with hands. The aims of education we analyze—critical thinking, rationality, individual autonomy, even creativity—are also associated in our culture with the productive, not the reproductive, processes of society. To give the reproductive processes their due in a conception of the educated person we will have to rethink the domain of philosophy of education.

Given the way we define our subject matter it is no more possible for us to take seriously the hidden curriculum I have set before you than the reproductive processes of society. Education, as we conceive of it, is an intentional activity.[41] Teaching is too.[42] Thus, we do not consider the unintended outcomes of education to be our concern. Moreover, following Peters and his colleagues, we draw a sharp line between logical and contingent relationships and treat the latter as if they were none of our business even when they are the *expected* outcomes of educational processes.[43] In sum, we leave it to the psychologists, sociologists and historians of education to worry about hidden curricula, not because we consider the topic unimportant—although perhaps some of us do—but because we consider it to fall outside our domain.

The redefinition of the subject matter of philosophy of education required by an adequate ideal of the educated person ought not to be feared. On the contrary, there is every reason to believe that it would ultimately enrich our discipline. If the experience and activities which have traditionally been considered to belong to women are included in the educational realm, a host of challenging and important issues and problems will present themselves for study. If the philosophy of education tackles questions about childrearing and the transmission of values, if it develops accounts of gender education to inform its theories of liberal education, if it explores the forms of thinking, feeling and acting associated with childrearing, marriage and the family, if the concepts of coeducation, mothering and nurturance become fair game for philosophical analysis, philosophy of education will be invigorated.

It would also be invigorated by taking seriously contingent as well as logical relationships. In divorcing educational processes from their empirical consequences and the mental structures which are said to be intrinsically related to knowledge from the empirical consequences of having them, we forget that education is a practical endeavor. It is often said that philosophy of education's concerns are purely conceptual, but the conclusion is inescapable that in analyzing such concepts as the educated person and liberal education we make recommendations for action. For these to be justified the contingent relationships which obtain between them and both the good life and the good society must be taken into account. A redefinition of our domain would allow us to provide our educational theorizing with the kind of justification it requires. It would also allow us to investigate the particularly acute and very challenging value questions that arise in relation to hidden curricula of all kinds.

Conclusion

In conclusion I would like to draw for you two morals which seem to me to emerge from my study of Peters's ideal of the educated person. The first is that Plato was wrong when, in Book V of the *Republic*, he said that sex is a difference which makes no difference.[44] I do not mean by this that there are inborn differences which suit males and females for separate and unequal roles in society. Rather, I mean that identical educational treatment of males and females may not yield identical results so long as that treatment contains a male bias. There are sex differences in the way people are perceived and evaluated and there may well be sex differences in the way people think and learn and view the world. A conception of the educated person must take these into account. I mean also that the very nature of the ideal will be skewed. When sex or gender is thought to make no difference, women's lives, experiences, activities are overlooked and an ideal is formulated in terms of men and the roles for which they have traditionally been considered to be suited. Such an ideal is necessarily narrow for it is rooted in stereotypical ways of perceiving males and their place in society.

For some time I assumed that the sole alternative to a sex-biased conception of the educated person such as Peters set forth was a gender-free ideal, that is to say an ideal which did not take sex or gender into account. I now realize that sex or gender has to be taken into account if an ideal of the educated person is not to be biased. To opt at this time for a gender-free ideal is to beg the question. What is needed is a *gender-sensitive* ideal, one which takes sex or gender into account when it makes a difference and ignores it when it does not. Such an ideal would truly be gender-just.

The second moral is that *everyone* suffers when an ideal of the educated person fails to give the reproductive processes of society their due. Ideals which govern education solely in relation to the productive processes of society will necessarily be narrow. In their failure to acknowledge the valuable traits, dispositions, skills, traditionally associated with reproductive processes, they will harm both sexes although not always in the same ways.[45]

Notes

1. R. S. Peters, "Education and the Educated Man," in R. F. Dearden, P. H. Hirst, and R. S. Peters, eds., *A Critique of Current Educational Aims* (London: Routledge & Kegan Paul, 1972), pp. 7, 9.
2. Paul Nash, Andreas M. Kazemias, and Henry J. Perkinson, eds., *The Educated Man: Studies in the History of Educational Thought* (New York: John Wiley & Sons, 1965), p. 25.
3. For a discussion of "man" as a gender neutral term see Janice Moulton, "The Myth of the Neutral 'Man,'" in Mary Vetterling-Braggin, Frederick A. Elliston, and Jane English, eds., *Feminism and Philosophy* (Totowa, NJ: Littlefield, Adams, 1977), pp. 124–137. Moulton rejects the view that "man" has a gender-neutral use.
4. Peters, "Education and the Educated Man," p. 11. Peters says in connection with the concept of the educated man: "For there are many who are not

likely to go far with theoretical enquiries and who are unlikely to develop much depth or breadth of understanding to underpin and transform their dealings as workers, *husbands* and *fathers*" (emphasis added).

5. Ibid., p. 7.
6. R. S. Peters, *Ethics and Education* (London: George Allen & Unwin, 1966).
7. Peters, "Education and the Educated Man," pp. 9–11.
8. R. S. Downie, Eileen M. Loudfoot, and Elizabeth Telfer, *Education and Personal Relationships* (London: Methuen & Co., 1974), p. 11ff.
9. In Paul Hirst, *Knowledge and the Curriculum* (London: Routledge & Kegan Paul, 1974), p. 47.
10. Nancy Schrom Dye, "Clio's American Daughters," in Julia A. Sherman and Evelyn Torton Beck, eds., *The Prism of Sex* (Madison: University of Wisconsin Press, 1979), p. 9.
11. Catherine R. Stimpson, "The Power to Name," in Sherman and Beck, eds., *Prism*, pp. 55–77.
12. Elaine Showalter, "Women Writers and the Double Standard," in Vivian Gornick and Barbara Moran, eds., *Women in Sexist Society* (New York: Basic Books, 1971), pp. 323–343.
13. Naomi Weisstein, "Psychology Constructs the Female" in Gornick and Moran, eds., *Women in Sexist Society*, pp. 133–146.
14. Ruth Hubbard, "Have Only Men Evolved?" in Ruth Hubbard, Mary Sue Henifin, and Barbara Fried, eds., *Women Look at Biology Looking at Women* (Cambridge: Schenkman Publishing Co., 1979), pp. 7–35.
15. Carol Gilligan, "Women's Place in Man's Life Cycle," *Harvard Educational Review* 49, 4 (1979): 431–446.
16. Carol Gilligan, "In a Different Voice: Women's Conceptions of Self and of Morality," *Harvard Educational Review* 47, 4 (1979): 481–517.
17. See, for example, Linda Gordon, *Woman's Body, Woman's Right: A Social History of Birth Control in America* (New York: Viking, 1976); Richard W. Wertz and Dorothy C. Wertz, *Lying-in* (New York: Free Press, 1977); Jean Donnison, *Midwives and Medical Men: A History of Interprofessional Rivalries and Women's Rights* (New York: Schocken Books, 1977).
18. Mary Hartman and Lois W. Banner, eds., *Clio's Consciousness Raised* (New York: Harper & Row, 1974).
19. See, for example, Carolyn G. Heilbrun, *Toward a Recognition of Androgyny* (New York: Alfred A. Knopf, 1973); Patricia Meyer Spacks, *The Female Imagination* (New York: Avon, 1975); Ellen Moers, *Literary Women* (New York: Anchor Books, 1977); Elaine Showalter, *A Literature of Their Own: British Women Novelists from Bronte to Lessing* (Princeton: Princeton University Press, 1977); Ann Sutherland Harris and Linda Nochlin,

Women Artists: 1550–1950 (New York: Alfred A. Knopf, 1976); Elsa Honig Fine, *Women and Art: A History of Women Painters and Sculptors from the Renaissance to the Twentieth Century* (Montclair and London: Allanheld & Schram/Prior, 1978); and Karen Peterson and J. J. Wilson, *Women Artists: Recognition and Reappraisal from the Early Middle Ages to the Twentieth Century* (New York: New York University Press, 1976).
20. In Paul Hirst, *Knowledge and the Curriculum*, p. 92.
21. R. G. Woods and R. St. C. Barrow, *An Introduction to Philosophy of Education* (Methuen & Co., 1975), Ch. 3.
22. For discussions of our male and female stereotypes see, e.g., Alexandra G. Kaplan and Joan P. Bean, eds., *Beyond Sex-role Stereotypes* (Boston: Little, Brown, 1976); and Alexandra G. Kaplan and Mary Anne Sedney, *Psychology and Sex Roles* (Boston: Little, Brown, 1980).
23. Carol Gilligan, "Women's Place"; I. Broverman, D. Broverman, F. Clarkson, P. Rosencrantz and S. Vogel, "Sex-role Stereotypes and Clinical Judgements of Mental Health," *Journal of Consulting and Clinical Psychology* 34 (1970): 1–7; Alexandra G. Kaplan, "Androgyny as a Model of Mental Health for Women: From Theory to Therapy," in Kaplan and Bean, eds., *Beyond Sex-role Stereotypes*, pp. 353–362.
24. One commits the androcentric fallacy when one argues from the characteristics associated with male human beings to the characteristics of all human beings. In committing it one often commits the naturalistic fallacy because the traits which are said to be natural to males are held up as ideals for the whole species.
25. I say *if* it can be attained by all, because it is not entirely clear that the ideal can be attained by *anyone* insofar as it requires mastery of Hirst's seven forms of knowledge.
26. See Elizabeth Beardsley, "Traits and Genderization," in Vetterling-Braggin, et al., eds., *Feminism and Philosophy*, pp. 117–123. Beardsley uses the term "genderization" to refer to language while I use it here to refer to traits themselves.
27. Lynn Z. Bloom, Karen Coburn, Joan Pearlman, *The New Assertive Woman* (New York: Delacorte Press, 1975), p. 12.
28. For discussion of the assumption that masculinity-femininity is a bipolar dimension see Anne Constantinople, "Masculinity-Femininity: An Exception to a Famous Dictum"; and Sandra L. Bem, "Probing the Promise of Androgyny" in Kaplan and Bean, eds., *Beyond Sex-role Stereotypes*.
29. Anne Sayre, *Rosalind Franklin & DNA* (New York: W. W. Norton & Co., 1975). See also James D. Watson, *The Double Helix* (New York: Atheneum, 1968); and Horace Freeland Judson, *The Eighth*

Day of Creation (New York: Simon and Schuster, 1979).

30. It is important to note, however, that some colleagues did take her seriously as a scientist; see Sayre, ibid. Adele Simmons cites historical evidence of the negative effects of having acquired such traits on women who did not opt out of "woman's sphere" in "Education and Ideology in Nineteenth-Century America: The Response of Educational Institutions to the Changing Role of Women," in Berenice A. Carroll, ed., *Liberating Women's History* (Urbana, IL: University of Illinois Press, 1976), p. 123. See also Patricia Meyer Spacks, *The Female Imagination* (New York: Avon Books, 1976), p. 25.

31. See Simone de Beauvoir, *The Second Sex* (New York: Bantam Books, 1961) for an extended discussion of woman as the Other.

32. Jane Roland Martin, "Needed: A Paradigm for Liberal Education," in Jonas F. Soltis, ed., *Philosophy and Education* (Chicago: National Society for the Study of Education, 1981), pp. 37–59.

33. For an account of education as production see Jane Roland Martin, "Sex Equality and Education: A Case Study," in Mary Vetterling-Braggin, ed., *"Femininity," "Masculinity," and "Androgyny"* (Totowa, N. J.: Littlefield, Adams, 1982). It should be noted that an understanding of the societal role for which Peters's educated person is intended illuminates both the sex bias and the class bias his ideal embodies.

34. For an interesting discussion and criticism of the two-sphere analysis of society, see Joan Kelly, "The Doubled Vision of Feminist Theory: A Postscript to the 'Women and Power' Conference," *Feminist Studies* 5, 1 (1979): 216–227. Kelly argues that a two-sphere analysis distorts reality and that feminist theory should discard it. I use it here as a convenient theoretical device.

35. I am indebted here to Lorenne M. G. Clark, "The Rights of Women: The Theory and Practice of the Ideology of Male Supremacy," in William R. Shea and John King-Farlow, eds., *Contemporary Issues in Political Philosophy* (New York: Science History Publications, 1976), pp. 49–65.

36. In saying that an adequate conception of the educated person must reject a sharp separation of productive and reproductive processes I do not mean that it must be committed to a specific philosophical theory of the relationship of the two. An adequate conception of the educated person should not divorce mind and body, but it does not follow from this that it must be committed to a specific view of the mind-body relationship; indeed, the union of mind and body in a theory of education is quite compatible with a dualistic philosophical account of the relationship between the two. Similarly, a theory of the educated person must not divorce one kind of societal process from the other even if the best account of the relationship of productive to reproductive processes should turn out to be dualistic.

37. Jean-Jacques Rousseau, *Emile* (New York: Basic Books, 1979, Allan Bloom, trans.). See also Lynda Lange, "Rousseau: Women and the General Will," in Lorenne M. G. Cark and Lynda Lange, eds., *The Sexism of Social and Political Theory* (Toronto: University of Toronto Press, 1979), pp. 41–52; Susan Moller Okin, *Women in Western Political Thought* (Princeton: Princeton University Press, 1979); and Jane Roland Martin, "Sophie and Emile: A Case Study of Sex Bias in the History of Educational Thought," *Harvard Educational Review* 51, 3 (1981): 357–372.

38. I also leave open the question of whether any ideal of the educated person should guide and direct education as a whole.

39. For more on this question see Jane Roland Martin, "What Should We Do with a Hidden Curriculum When We Find One?" *Curriculum Inquiry* 6, 2 (1976): 135–151.

40. On this point see Jane Roland Martin, "Excluding Women from the Educational Realm."

41. See, for example, Peters, *Ethics and Education.*

42. See, for example, Israel Scheffler, *The Language of Education* (Springfield, IL: Charles C. Thomas, 1960), Chs. 4, 5.

43. For a discussion of this point see Jane Roland Martin, "Response to Roemer," in Jerrold R. Coombs, ed., *Philosophy of Education 1979* (Normal, IL: Proceedings of the 35th Annual Meeting of the Philosophy of Education Society, 1980).

44. This point is elaborated on in Jane Roland Martin, "Sex Equality and Education: A Case Study."

45. I wish to thank Ann Diller, Carol Gilligan, Michael Martin and Janet Farrell Smith for helpful comments on earlier versions of this address which was written while I was a Fellow at the Mary Ingraham Bunting Institute of Radcliffe College.

6 Schools as Organizations and Teacher Professionalization

In this chapter, we explore the organizational characteristics of U.S. elementary and secondary education, school cultures, and the vocation of teaching. These topics are tied together by one underlying issue—the parameters and possibilities inherent in creating better schools. How can schools be distinguished organizationally, and why are some schools more effective learning environments than others? You undoubtedly have strong memories of the schools you attended, but have you ever wondered why these memories are so vivid? Why is it that schools create such powerful organizational cultures that deeply influence one's life and one's approach to learning? The schools that an individual attends shape not only his or her life chances but his or her perceptions, attitudes, and behaviors. Of course, schools operate in conjunction with families and society. No school is an island unto itself. Still, schools are powerful organizations that profoundly affect the lives of those children and adults who come in contact with them. It seems logical, therefore, that knowing more about schools' organizational characteristics is a first step in understanding their impact on students, teachers, and the society at large.

Education in the United States is one of the nation's largest businesses. According to the U.S. Department of Education (U.S. Department of Education, National Center for Educational Statistics, 2012a), elementary and secondary education was a $650 billion enterprise, serving 55.4 million students in 50 states and the District of Columbia. Understanding the complexity and enormity of the educational enterprise is a difficult task because it contains so many different elements. Just feeding all the youngsters who attend school every day is a substantial undertaking. The New York City Board of Education, for instance, serves more meals per day than Friendly's Restaurants. Supplying schools with equipment, textbooks, and such consumable items as paper and pencils is in itself a big business. Obviously, one could go on in this vein, but the point should be clear. To understand education, one must look beyond the classroom itself and the interaction between teachers and pupils to the larger world where different interest groups compete with each other in terms of ideology, finances, and power.

Clearly, any one of the preceding topics would be worthy of a book itself. In this chapter, we provide an overview of some of the basic elements of the organization of U.S. education so that you will be able to make increasingly informed decisions about the nature of education and how you as a teacher can grow professionally. In that sense, the purpose of this chapter is to create a broad frame of reference that grounds the perceptions of education in their organizational and social realities. To this end, we have included a section of this chapter that deals with the structure of U.S. education and compares that structure briefly to the structure of education in Great Britain, France, the former Soviet Union, Japan, Germany, and Finland.

We then turn to what is often called *school processes*; that is, we examine the way in which school cultures are created and maintained. Accordingly, we discuss such elements of school culture as authority structures and the significance of bureaucracy. These observations naturally lead to questions concerning the nature of teaching and the need for greater teacher professionalization. Good teaching will always be at the core of learning. Creating the conditions where teachers can use and improve their craft should be a major objective of those who believe that education is a cornerstone for a better society.

The Structure of U.S. Education

The organization of U.S. schools is complex on several levels. In this section, we examine the nation's elementary and secondary school system from the point of view of governance, size, degree of centralization, student composition, and its relative "openness." We also examine the duality of the U.S. school system; that is, in the United States, we have public and private educational systems that sometimes work in tandem and sometimes in opposition. The purpose of discussing the organization of schools should be clear—without a sense of structure, one has little way of grasping it as a whole. If one was to paint a landscape of elementary and secondary education in the United States, it would require a picture of almost infinite complexity and subtlety. It is the product of ideology, pragmatism, and history. It is unlike virtually any other educational system because the U.S. system is so decentralized and so dedicated to the concept of equal educational opportunity. We turn now to the issue of who is legally responsible for education in the United States.

Governance

When the Constitution of the United States was written, its authors indicated that those powers that were not mentioned explicitly as belonging to the federal government were retained by individual states. Because the federal government made no claims concerning its authority relative to education, the states retained their authority and responsibility for education. Thus, the United States has 50 separate state school systems. This picture is made even more complex by the fact that there is also a private school system within each state. There are few countries with this degree of decentralization. But this is just the beginning of the story, because most U.S. public schools are paid for by the revenue that is raised by local property taxes. As a consequence, taxpayers within particular school districts have a substantial stake in the schools within their districts and are able to make their voices heard through community school boards.

What this means, in effect, is that the U.S. public school system is, in large part, decentralized right down to the school district level. It is true that the state may mandate curriculum, qualifications for teaching, and safety codes, but the reality is that these mandates must be carried out not by agents of the state but by citizens of a particular school district. Is it any wonder that top-down reform in the United States is difficult to achieve?

Since the Civil Rights movement of the 1960s, the federal government has entered the educational policy field originally through the enforcement of students' civil rights. The role of the federal government in creating educational policy has increased since that time. This expansion of the federal role in education is perhaps best symbolized by the founding of the United States Department of Education in the late 1970s. During the era of Presidents Reagan and Bush, the U.S. Department of Education served primarily as a "bully-pulpit" for Secretaries of Education who helped to define the crisis in U.S. education and to provide blueprints for the resolutions of these crises. In actual fact, however, the Secretary of Education has relatively little authority when it comes to the governance of public schools.

Size and Degree of Centralization

As indicated earlier, the elementary and secondary school system in the United States is extremely large. It is estimated that more than 55 million youngsters are enrolled in kindergarten through the twelfth grade and that the cost of educating these children is over $650 billion annually. Interestingly enough, at the same time that the school system has been growing, it has been simultaneously becoming more centralized, presumably for reasons of efficiency. For instance, in the early 1930s, there were approximately 128,000 public school districts in the United States.

By the late 1980s, this number had been reduced to slightly fewer than 16,000. In 2010, there were 13,709 school districts. Part of this consolidation process has been by virtue of elimination of single-teacher schools. At the turn of the twentieth century, there were approximately 200,000 such schools and by 1998, there were 380 (Muse, 1998).

As a consequence of this consolidation, the average number of pupils per elementary public school rose from 91 in the early 1930s to 450 in the late 1980s. Public high schools expanded from 195 students per school in the early 1930s to 513 in the late 1980s (Witte, 1990, p. 15). In 2009–2010, the average number of pupils per school in the United States was 450 at the elementary level and 856 at the secondary level (National Center for Education Statistics, NCES). At the same time schools are becoming larger, the number of pupils per teacher is decreasing. Today, the average public elementary school classroom averages 16 students, whereas 80 years ago, there were nearly 34 students per teacher. At the high school level, the average number of pupils per teacher is 16, whereas 80 years ago, it was 22.

What these statistics reveal is that there has been a considerable amount of consolidation and centralization in the last 80 years in U.S. public education. Although this trend may be cost-effective, it may also have a negative impact on the diversity of schools that students may attend. Usually, large institutions are more bureaucratic than smaller ones and a high degree of centralization diminishes the amount of democratic participation. For example, because school districts have become larger, superintendents have become more powerful, and as a consequence teachers have had fewer opportunities to make decisions regarding curriculum, conditions of employment, and school policy.

Student Composition

In 2010, 53.5 percent of the students in primary and secondary public schools were white. This percentage, however, masks a great deal of variation in terms of racial composition between states and school districts. Of the 50 states and the District of Columbia, 16 have less than 50 percent of white students, and 10 states have almost no minority students. Some large states such as California, Texas, and New York are extremely mixed racially. Many urban school districts enroll mostly minority students. For instance, in 2009, in New York City, 85.6 percent of the students were nonwhite; in Los Angeles, the figure was 91.3 percent; and in Detroit, 97.4 percent of the system's students were from minority backgrounds (U.S. Department of Education, National Center for Education Statistics, Characteristics of the 100 Largest Public Elementary and Secondary School Districts in the United States: 2008–09, 2010). In effect, nonminority families have moved out of the cities and into the suburbs, leading to a high degree of residential segregation. In some cities, less than 5 percent of the suburban population is minority.

What this means is that the student composition of U.S. schools is becoming more diverse at the same time that there has been a trend toward increasing residential segregation. Another way of expressing this is that de jure segregation has been replaced by de facto segregation (see Harvard Civil Rights Project, 2004). Student composition can also be viewed along other dimensions such as gender, class, ethnicity, and even ability. Later on, we will discuss how these characteristics of students can affect not only the student composition of schools but are related to educational and life outcomes. For example, we might wonder why it is that although approximately half the students in U.S. education are female, so few of them choose to pursue technological or scientific careers. Schools are also segregated or stratified according to the wealth and income of their student bodies. Students who attend schools in wealthy school districts, for instance, are more likely to have more curriculum options, better teachers, and more extracurricular activities than are students who attend relatively poor school districts. We will have a great deal more to say about these issues in subsequent chapters.

Degree of "Openness"

Public schools in the United States are organized as elementary, junior high or middle school, and high school. Elementary school usually encompasses kindergarten through grades 5 or 6; junior high, grades 7 through 9; middle school, grades 6 through 8; and high school, grades 9 through 12. Usually, children enter kindergarten at age 5 and graduate from high school at age 18. A key element to understanding the U.S. school system is that relatively few academic impediments are placed before students if they choose to graduate from high school. Indeed, there may be many social and personal impediments that keep students from graduating from high school, but the school system is designed to give students many opportunities for advancement.

In this sense, the U.S. school system is quite open. All youngsters are entitled to enroll into public schools and to remain in school until they graduate. There is a powerful democratic ethos underlining the belief in the "common school." From a structural point of view, this means that there are multiple points of entry into the school system and there are few forced exits. When this openness is compared to other school systems, you will see that this is unusual, although most Americans would agree that schools should be as democratic as possible.

Private Schools

Private schools tend to attract students from families that are relatively affluent and have a commitment to education. There are approximately 28,220 elementary and secondary private schools in the United States, enrolling 5.5 million students. Private schools constitute 25 percent of all elementary and secondary schools and educate 10 percent of the student population. The mean student enrollment of private schools is 193; only 7 percent of private schools enroll more than 600 students. Unlike the public sector, which has been consolidating over the last 50 years, there has been a remarkable growth of private schools. In the early 1930s, for instance, there were fewer than 10,000 private elementary schools in the United States; 50 years later, there were nearly 17,000 such schools. In 2009, there were 21,870 private elementary schools in the United States (U.S. Department of Education, National Center for Education Statistics, 2010).

There is a tremendous amount of diversity in the private sector, although most private schools are affiliated with religious organizations. Private school researcher Donald Erickson (1986, p. 87) has noted 15 major categories of private schools: Roman Catholic, Lutheran, Jewish, Seventh Day Adventist, Independent, Episcopal, Greek Orthodox, Quaker, Mennonite, Calvinist, Evangelical, Assembly of God, Special Education, Alternative, and Military. It should also be mentioned that in the United States there is very little regulation of private education by state authorities. The separation of Church and State ensures the relative autonomy of private schools as long as they do not violate safety regulations and the civil rights of students. Each state has slightly different regulations, but in the main, it is safe to say that the autonomy of private schools is protected by a series of decisions made by the United States Supreme Court.

Most private schools are located on the East and West Coasts. Connecticut has the highest percent of private school students and Wyoming has the lowest. Even though the percent of students who attend private schools has remained relatively steady when compared to the public sector, there has been a significant shift in the private sector in terms of enrollment patterns. Clearly, Roman Catholic schools are experiencing a decline in enrollment. In the period between 1965 and 1983, there was a 46 percent drop in the number of students who attended Roman Catholic schools. During the same period, virtually every other type of private school experienced a great growth in terms of students and number of schools. Other religious schools doubled and tripled in size. This trend continued throughout the early twenty-first century.

Throughout the 1980s and 1990s, numerous studies seemed to indicate that private schools were more effective learning environments than were public schools. Various researchers claimed that private schools are communities and, because they compete for students, they are less bureaucratic than public schools, and as a consequence, they are more innovative. As you will see, there has been growing movement among some educational reformers to allow students to choose between public and private schools. It is difficult to know whether, in fact, this kind of school choice will lead to school improvement or whether allowing students to choose private schools will lead to increased educational and social stratification. Many of these issues will be discussed in future chapters.

Conclusion

As this overview indicates, describing the U.S. elementary and secondary school system requires viewing the organization of schools from a variety of points of view. There is considerable diversity in the system despite the fact that there has been a trend toward centralization in the public sector. The authority structure of the public school system is diffuse; ultimately, it is the people who are responsible for the schools. This fact should not be minimized. Individuals, families, and groups are able to influence education by voting, by attending school district board meetings, and by paying for schools through taxes. This democratization gives the U.S. school system an unique egalitarian ethos. How does the U.S. system compare to other education systems? This is an important question to ask, because it is through comparison that one can see the unique features of the U.S. school system and those features that the U.S. system shares with the other national systems. This broadening frame of reference gives one greater understanding about the relationship between educational structure, processes, and outcomes.

International Comparisons

Countries vary considerably by how they organize their school systems. Few school systems are as complex as that in the United States; for instance, most countries have a National Ministry of Education or a Department of Education that is able to exert considerable influence over the entire educational system. Educational reforms can start from the top down with relative success because the state has the authority to enforce its decisions right down to the classroom level. Another dimension apparent in comparative analysis is the relative selectivity of systems. Education in the United States is fundamentally inclusive in its purposes; most other educational systems are not as inclusive. Individuals in other systems undergo a very rigorous academic rite of passage that is designed to separate the "academically talented" from the less gifted. The relative selectivity of a school system is an excellent indicator of its exclusiveness or inclusiveness.

What is the major purpose of the system? Is it to train an academic elite or to provide a broad-based educational experience for a wide segment of the population? Clearly, the relative openness of an educational system is related to the culture from which it originates. In this sense, educational systems are the expression of the values of the larger society. Educational systems can be located relative to each other by examining their degree of openness and the amount of authority that is exercised over the educational system by the national government. For instance, as we will see, France is a highly centralized educational system compared to the system in the United States. Moreover, the educational system in France is designed to produce an academic elite compared to the system in the United States, where equality of educational opportunity for all children is a strong normative value.

Great Britain

Before the nineteenth century, the education of children in Great Britain was considered to be a responsibility of parents. All schools were private. For the children of very wealthy families, parents often hired tutors. For poor children, there was no schooling. During the nineteenth century, there was a system of charity schools for the poor. Most of these schools were operated by religious organizations. The establishment of a national educational system for all children in the early nineteenth century was opposed by the Church of England and Roman Catholics. The 1870 Education Act led to the beginnings of a national system, although the Church of England continued to maintain its own schools. This compromise between Church and State led to the dual system of education that still exists in Great Britain, whereby State-run schools are controlled by Local Education Authorities (LEAs), while Church schools continue to operate, often funded by the State through the LEAs.

Although there were many attempts to reform this system, it was not until the 1944 Education Act that a truly national system of education was established as part of an "integrated public service welfare state" (Walford, 1992b). Free primary and secondary education was provided for all children. Despite the fact that the 1944 Education Act was designed to democratize Great Britain's school system, on the whole, the system re-created the class system by channeling students into different kinds of schools. Children from wealthy homes received academic training in grammar schools, and children from working-class homes received vocational training. In short, Great Britain had a decentralized educational system that was fundamentally elitist.

During the 1960s, there was an effort to democratize Great Britain's educational system. When Margaret Thatcher was elected prime minister in 1979, however, she promised to reform the educational system. Throughout the 1980s, the Conservative Government, led by Thatcher, attempted to reform the educational system by privatizing public education, by encouraging greater parental choice, and by reorganizing the administrative structure of the State educational system. There were a series of legislative changes, culminating in the 1988 Reform Act. This reform established a national curriculum and set national assessment goals. Governing bodies of all secondary schools and many primary schools were given control over their own budgets. Parental choice was encouraged and a pilot network of City Technology Colleges was established. Also, State schools were given the right to opt out of local educational authority control. Thus, the 1988 Educational Reform Act was a radical challenge to the education system that had been established in 1944.

Since 1988, England and Wales have implemented a highly centralized national curriculum and system of national assessment. Although teachers have been critical of the overly bureaucratic nature of these reforms, and the number of key curriculum areas has been narrowed, nonetheless, the 1988 Educational Reform Act has led to significant change (Walford, 1999).

The educational system in Great Britain is more open and less class stratified than it was a quarter century ago. However, despite a decrease in the school leaving rate to under 30 percent (from over 60 percent) (Brint, 2006) and an increase in university attendance to approximately 30 percent from under 10 percent, the educational system remains class stratified. It is also increasingly becoming race and ethnic stratified as Great Britain, especially London, has become increasingly multiracial and multiethnic, with a dramatic influx of immigrants from former colonial countries in Africa, the Caribbean, and Asia, including India and Pakistan. The inner-London schools are as multicultural as any urban school system in the United States, with some of the same problems experienced in U.S. urban schools.

The British educational system is no longer the highly stratified system in which students are sorted and selected by age 11 by examination, with achievement highly correlated to social class background. The national curriculum has also eliminated the comprehensive secondary school, which offered noncollege curriculum for its mostly working-class students. Nonetheless, critics of the 1988 Education Reform Act argue that it has not significantly reduced educational stratification and to some degree has exacerbated it (Walford, 1999). Although some believe that with the election of Labour Party Prime Minister Tony Blair in the late 1990s, educational reform would become more concerned with equity than standards, to date this does not appear to have happened.

France

The educational system in France is quite centralized compared to the United States and Great Britain. The central government in France controls the educational system right down to the classroom level. Traditionally, there have been two public school systems—one for ordinary people and one for the elite. Efforts to end this dual system have been only partially successful, although throughout the last three decades, there has been an attempt to create one comprehensive system. The French educational system is highly stratified. For the academically talented, who usually come from the upper classes, there is a system of elementary, secondary, and postsecondary schools that is highly selective, highly academic, and socially elite. At the top of the system are the *grandes écoles*, which are small specialized institutions that produce members of the country's governmental and intellectual elite.

According to a noted authority on French education, George Male (1992), the French educational system is "excessively verbal." That is, French students are taught to frame ideas almost as an end unto itself, even as a matter of aesthetics. This sense of using language aesthetically is closely related to the importance placed on intellectual attainment within the French system. At one level, the objective of the French system is to produce a small number of highly qualified intellectuals. To identify this small group, the government has instituted a set of examinations that effectively, and one might even say ruthlessly, sort out the academically talented from the less academically gifted. The French believe, by and large, that this system of examinations is meritocratic, even though it is common knowledge that the system stratifies students by social class background. The French educational system is frankly competitive.

Efforts to democratize the system have not succeeded. Despite a number of reforms associated with particular Ministers of Education, the French system continues to be centralized, competitive, and stratified. In 1984, the socialist government proposed to reduce State grants to private Catholic schools. The opposition to this proposal was so fierce that the plan was dropped, and since that time there have been few reform efforts, especially at the structural level.

In the past decade, the French educational system has become a little more democratic. Approximately a third of 17- and 18-year-olds enroll in some form of higher education, although only about 15 percent graduate from university. The majority complete some form of postsecondary occupational education. The top 10 percent of secondary students compete for the rare opportunity to enter the *grandes écoles*, which prepare students for prestigious civil service (Brint, 1998, p. 50). Entrance into the *grandes écoles*, although based on meritocratic selection, remains highly correlated with social class background.

The Former Soviet Union

In 1991, the Soviet Union as a single geographical and national entity dramatically and abruptly ceased to exist. The importance of this event cannot be underestimated. The end of the Soviet Union has affected the education of children in Russia and the other countries that have reemerged since the collapse of the Soviet system. It is interesting from a historical perspective how the Soviet educational system was organized, if for no other reason than as an example of how the best-planned educational policies will fail if they are unsupported by other cultural institutions.

The educational system that was established after the Bolshevik Revolution of 1917 was highly centralized, stratified, and deeply ideological. The purpose of the educational system was to create the "new Soviet man and woman." These new men and women were to become the leaders of the proletarian revolution that would transform the Soviet Union into a socialist paradise. Communist values were to be unquestioned and the educational system was conceived as being part of a planned economy that would produce a society where scarcity was virtually unknown. In reality, the Soviet system was quite stratified; that is, the children of high party members attended schools that taught foreign languages and prepared their students for university entrance, whereas the children of workers attended schools that were often underfunded and underequipped, and produced graduates who took jobs in the Soviet factory system.

In the 1980s, it became increasingly clear to Soviet leaders and the Soviet people that the educational system was failing to educate Soviet students in the new skills that were required by technological change and international competition. Moreover, the system had become so rigid that it no longer provided significant opportunities for upward mobility. This situation led to a wave of educational reform in the Soviet Union. In the period between 1980 and 1985, a series of minor reforms attempted to change the system by finetuning it. For example, the age at which children were to start the first grade went from 7 years to 6 years. Teachers were paid slightly more and there was more emphasis on technical training. After the assent to power of Mikhail Gorbachev, the Soviet educational system was transformed by a vision of education that allowed for decentralization, teacher initiative, and curriculum reform. As part of the policy of restructuring Soviet society (*perestroika*), education was to become more open, flexible, and responsive to the needs of students, parents, and communities. Naturally, such a huge change was difficult to implement. After all, teachers and administrators in the system had been trained under wholly different sets of values. The idea of creating an experimental school, more or less free of government control, was profoundly radical within the Soviet context.

Educational reform was made even more complex as the decade of the 1980s drew to a close and the 1990s began, because the Soviet Union's economy virtually collapsed and the very nature of the Soviet Union was in transition. Because the Soviet Union was composed of so many nationalities, there was little consensus between national groups, except that which had been imposed by the Soviet government. As the power of the Soviet government diminished, the demand for nationalistic autonomy increased. Social change exceeded the pace in which schools could be reformed. There is little doubt that education in the former Soviet Union has dramatically changed. Former Soviet citizens are still experimenting with new curricula, privatization, school choice, and new educational philosophies. Certainly, education in the former Soviet Union is dramatically different today than the education system that was established by the Bolshevik Party at the beginning of the twentieth century.

Japan

During the late twentieth century, some experts thought that the educational system in Japan was exemplary when compared to the educational system in the United States (White, 1987). The Japanese educational system seemed to produce skilled workers and highly competent managers. In fact, Japan's economic rise in the 1980s represented a serious challenge to the international economic position of the United States. What is it about the Japanese system that makes it so distinctive?

The first national system of education in Japan was established in the 1880s under the central authority of the Ministry of Education, Science, and Culture. After World War II, the structure of schooling was changed when compulsory education was extended from 6 to 9 years and the democratic principles of equality of opportunity were suffused throughout the system. Parallel to the public system is a large and thriving private sector that plays an important role in providing educational opportunities at all levels of education. The Japanese system of education is highly competitive. To be admitted to a prestigious university, students are required to pass examinations that are extremely competitive. This emphasis on achievement and attainment is exemplified by the fact that Japanese students excel in every measured international standard up to the age of 17, both for the top students and for the 95 percent of students who graduate from high school.

What distinguishes the Japanese educational system from other educational systems in terms of its efficiency and effectiveness? Certainly, the educational system benefits by the work ethic that is so deeply entrenched in Japanese culture. Japanese parents have a high regard for the importance of education. The belief in education in Japan is so strong that it has led to the "double-schooling" phenomenon. In effect, many Japanese students are exposed to two educational systems. The first system is the traditional public schools and the second system is the nonformal schools that act as a national system of tutorial opportunities for students. The largest nonformal school system in Japan is the "study institution" (*Juku*). It is estimated that there are over 10,000 *Jukus* in Japan.

This love of education has made Japan a nation of strivers, but not without its own drawbacks. The Japanese have always placed a high value on moral education. Ethical dimensions of a moral education are not always easily compatible with the values inherent in competition. Thus, the debate over education in Japan has more to do with national character than it does with structural reform. Reconciling the cultural values of achievement and competition with those of cooperation and mutuality will be the hallmark of Japanese educational reform in the coming years.

Germany

The German educational system is significantly different from that of the United States. Through examinations, Germany selects and sorts its children at a relatively young age and tracks them into a tripartite system of secondary education (Mitter, 1992). The *Hauptschule* is designed for those destined for blue-collar and lower-level service positions; the *Realschule* is for lower-level white-collar and technical positions; the *Gymnasium* is for academic preparation for university and the intellectual and management professions (Brint, 1998, p. 41).

By the end of the lower secondary years, students from the *Hauptschule* and *Realschule* enter the distinctive dual system of apprenticeship, where students spend part of the day working in apprenticeships in businesses and the other part in school. The close connection between business and schools in the training of workers is viewed as a model by many advocates of vocational educational reform in the United States. Students in the *Gymnasium* complete a rigorous academic curriculum that prepares them to take *Abitur*, the college entrance examination. About 25 percent qualify for university attendance, which is State supported and tuition free. Of these, more than half enroll in *Fachhochschulen*, or technical colleges. The remainder enter a four-year rigorous academic education in the arts and sciences, in universities that are similar to one another. Therefore, the rigid secondary school tracking system leads into a somewhat equal and undifferentiated system of higher education (Brint, 1998, p. 42). Less than 15 percent of German students complete this university education.

The German system is almost the opposite of the U.S. system. Primary schools in the United States are relatively untracked, and secondary schools, although tracked, provide a relatively high degree of access to higher education. Higher education is open to large numbers of students, but also highly unequal and stratified, with technical and vocational programs and liberal arts and sciences in two-year community colleges, and a system of nonelite and elite four-year public and private colleges and universities. About 40 percent of U.S. students enter colleges and universities, and another 35 percent enter community colleges, with approximately 30 percent completing a baccalaureate degree (U.S. Department of Education, National Center for Education Statistics, 2008).

German primary education sorts and selects students for a highly stratified and tracked secondary system, marked by a rigorous university preparatory track and two vocational and technical tracks, with a State-supported apprenticeship system. Although the system appears meritocratic, as placement is based on achievement, academic achievement is related to social class background (Mitter, 1992).

German reunification took place on October 3, 1990. Since then, the former East German system of communist education has been completely altered and replaced by the system of the Federal Republic of Germany (West Germany). Radical transformation of the curriculum to reflect a capitalist rather than communist ideology, and the transition to the highly stratified system just described, have taken place. Although it is too early to assess this transformation, some preliminary indications are that former East Germans may be having some difficulty adjusting to the more competitive system. Moreover, it will be interesting to see how those students who were socialized in the primary grades in the 1980s under communism and schooled in the 1990s in unified secondary schools are faring. The reunification of the German educational system is currently a fruitful avenue of educational research in Germany.

Finland

In recent years, education experts have focused their attention on the high level of student achievement in Finland. Throughout the first decade of the twenty-first century, Finland has had some of the highest scores on the math, science and literacy exams administered by PISA (Program for International Student Assessment). Even more impressive than their overall scores on the PISA exams is the fact that there is little variation in student outcomes on the exams across all populations of racial, ethnic, and socioeconomic groups in Finland. Many other countries that participate in PISA, including the United States, have large gaps in the performance of the highest scoring students and the lowest scoring students. In an effort to learn from Finland's experience and replicate its successes, education experts have been looking at the organization and implementation of education in Finland.

How has Finland's education system achieved such dramatic results? During the past 40 years, Finland has undertaken a major overhaul of its education system by focusing on equal access to curriculum, the provision of wrap-around services for students, and teacher education. Finland eliminated all forms of tracking and instead turned it focus to ensuring that all students attain a high level of academic success. Unlike many other countries, Finland has abolished almost all forms of standardized testing. Instead, Finland places an emphasis on formative evaluation, and relies on oral and narrative dialogues between teachers and students to track progress. The one standardized exam that Finland does administer is a college entrance exam that includes between 6 and 10 items that evaluate students' problem-solving skills, analysis, and writing (Darling-Hammond, 2010).

Perhaps the most remarkable characteristic of the Finnish education system is the way in which it recruits, educates, retains, and respects the professionalism of classroom teachers. Only 15 percent of college graduates who apply for teacher education programs are admitted. People who are accepted into these well-respected programs receive a stipend and free tuition as they complete a three-year graduate program preparing them to be classroom teachers. As graduate students, aspiring teachers develop research skills that aid them in honing their own teaching practice throughout their careers. Upon entering the teaching profession, Finnish teachers receive competitive wages, are treated with a high degree of professionalism, and maintain a large amount of autonomy over their teaching practice. Teachers oversee small classes of students and are alotted significant periods of time to collaborate with co-workers, develop curriculum, and review student work. As a result of these teaching conditions, Finnish teachers are able to develop innovative practices that meet the specific needs of their students. Furthermore, Finnish teachers have a high degree of work satisfaction, making teacher retention and teacher shortages non-issues across the country (Darling-Hammond, 2010). Education reform in Finland has taken a decidedly different path than education reform in the United States and has achieved markedly better results. As the United States works towards improving its education system and eliminating achievement gaps, it might be able to learn from the Finnish experience with education reform.

Conclusion

In sum, it is apparent from the preceding examples that educational systems and structures are in the process of change on an almost continuous basis. Educational systems are difficult to change because they are deeply embedded in their respective cultures. The values of a culture become institutionalized in an educational system. Every system is confronted with the same kinds of challenges. How many children shall be educated and what shall they learn? Every educational system attempts to select and sort students by their academic talent. The ethics and efficacy of any system is difficult to evaluate outside of its cultural context. Culture not only shapes structure but it also shapes school processes. Knowing the organization of a school or school system is a bit like knowing the architectural plans for a house. From a set of plans, one knows a house's dimensions and its form, but one does not know what it feels like to live in that structure. In the next section, we examine some of the key elements that underlie school processes.

School Processes and School Cultures

When you think back over your educational experiences, you undoubtedly have strong memories of the schools that you attended. You may remember particular teachers (for better or for worse), you may recall the students in your classes, and perhaps particular incidences stand out in your mind. Certainly, you remember the cafeteria. If you have strong powers of recall, you may remember the schools you attended more globally in terms of atmosphere, culture, and even smells. When one walks into a school, it is obvious that one is in a very particular place. Schools are unlike other organizations and because of this, they remain etched in one's memories for a lifetime. Thus, when one speaks of school processes, what we really are identifying are the powerful cultural qualities of schools that make them so potent in terms of emotional recall, if not in terms of cognitive outcomes.

Explaining school cultures is not easy because culture, by definition, is exactly that which one takes most for granted. Roughly 60 years ago, a sociologist of education, Willard Waller, attempted to understand the culture of schools. He later wrote:

> The school is a unity of interacting personalities. The personalities of all who meet in the school are bound together in an organic relation. The life of the whole is in all its parts, yet the whole could not exist without any of its parts. The school is a social organism. (1965, p. 146)

According to Waller (p. 147), schools are separate social organizations because:

1. They have a definite population.
2. They have a clearly defined political structure, arising from the mode of social interaction characteristics of the school, and influenced by numerous minor processes of interaction.
3. They represent the nexus of a compact network of social relationships.
4. They are pervaded by a "we feeling."
5. They have a culture that is definitely their own.

Waller went on to describe schools as despotisms in a state of perilous equilibrium (1965, p. 150). What is meant by this is that schools have authority structures that are quite vulnerable and that a great deal of political energy is expended every day, thus keeping the school in a state of equilibrium. In other words, school cultures are extremely vulnerable to disruption and that continuity is often maintained by the use of authority. Curiously, without the compliance of students, the exercise of authority within schools would be virtually impossible. Metz (1978) examined the use of authority in public schools and discovered that there was chronic tension within schools, in part because of conflicting goals. The teachers often have pedagogic goals that are difficult to reconcile with the social goals of the students. Administrators often have organizational goals that are shared neither by the teachers nor by the students. Communities can exert tremendous pressure on schools and thus aggravate tensions within schools.

It is ironic that organizations that are formally dedicated to the goals of learning should be riddled with so many tensions and competing interests. However, this is the social reality within which many real schools operate. Schools are political organizations in which there are numerous competing interests. Thus, the culture of any one particular school is the product of the political compromises that have been created in order for the school to be viable. As a student, you experience these political compromises from a particular point of view. Individually, students generally have little power, but collectively they have a great deal of power in terms of whether they will accept the school's authority. Very often, this authority is represented in terms of the principal. Studies show that it is the principal who establishes the goals for the school, the level of social and academic expectations, and the effectiveness of the discipline (Persell & Cookson, 1982; Semel, 1992).

Because schools are so deeply political, effecting change within them is very difficult. Groups and individuals have vested interests. For example, teachers, represented through their unions, have a great deal to say about the conditions of their employment. Local school board members often struggle with the teachers in terms of pay, productivity, and professional standards. Many of these conflicts are resolved through negotiation. This is possible because schools, especially public schools, are bureaucracies.

Sociologist Max Weber (1976) suggested that bureaucracies are an attempt to rationalize and organize human behavior in order to achieve certain goals. In theory, bureaucracies are characterized by explicit rules and regulations that promote predictability and regularity in decision making and minimize the significance of personal relationships. Rules of procedure are designed to enforce fairness. As one knows, however, bureaucracies can become so complex, so rule oriented, and so insensitive that they suppress individualism, spontaneity, and initiative. Bureaucratic rationality can often suppress the creativity required for learning. Is it reasonable to suppose that learning best takes place in 40- or 50-minute segments that are marked by the ringing of bells or the mechanical rasp of buzzers? Is it reasonable to suppose that learning best takes place when every student reads the same textbook? Is it reasonable to suppose that learning is best measured by multiple-choice tests? In short, the demands of the bureaucracy can often be destructive to the very spontaneity and freedom that is required by teachers and students if they are to develop intellectually and personally.

Schools, as they are now organized, are shaped by a series of inherent contradictions that can develop cultures that are conflictual and even stagnant. Changing the cultures of schools requires patience, skill, and good will. Research on the effects of school-based management, for instance, indicate that it is not an easy task for teachers, administrators, parents, community members, and students to arrive at consensus.

An interesting example of how complex the restructuring of schools was is the "Schools of Tomorrow . . . Today" project, run by the New York City Teachers Center Consortium of the United Federation of Teachers. The purpose of this project was to create schools that were "more centered on learner's needs for active, experiential, cooperative, and culturally-connected learning opportunities supportive of individual talents and learning styles" (Lieberman, Darling-Hammond, & Zuckerman, 1991, p. ix). The aim of this project was to create schools that are "energized by collaborative inquiry, informed by authentic accountability, and guided by shared decision making." It was discovered that despite the best efforts of the restructuring participants within the schools, reform was difficult to achieve. Each of the 12 schools participating in the project had strikingly different approaches to change and experienced significantly different outcomes in terms of achieving the stated objectives.

The evaluators of this project identified four elements of change that applied to all the schools:

> Conflict is a necessary part of change. Efforts to democratize schools do not create conflicts, but they allow (and to be successful, *require*) previously hidden problems, issues, and disagreements to surface. Staff involvement in school restructuring must be prepared to elicit, manage, and resolve conflicts.
>
> New behaviors must be learned. Because change requires new relationships and behaviors, the change process must include building communication and trust, enabling leadership and initiative to emerge, and learning techniques of communication, collaboration, and conflict resolution.
>
> Team building must extend to the entire school. Shared decision making must consciously work out and give on-going attention to relationships within the rest of the school's staff. Otherwise, issues of exclusiveness and imagined elitism may surface, and perceived "resistance to change" will persist.
>
> Process and content are interrelated. The process a team uses in going about its work is as important as the content of educational changes it attempts. The substance of a project often depends upon the degree of trust and openness built up within the team and between the team and the school. At the same time, the usefulness and the visibility of the project will influence future commitments from and the relationships among the staff and others involved. (Lieberman et al., 1991, pp. ix–x)

As these quotes indicate, changing the culture of a school in order to make the school more learner centered requires time, effort, intelligence, and good will. Reflecting on the observations of Willard Waller, one can see that altering a particular school's culture is similar to diverting a river as it flows to the sea. Just as change is institutionalized, the institution itself changes. School processes are elusive and difficult to define, but all powerful nonetheless. This does not mean that planned change is not possible. It does mean that planned change requires new ways of thinking. It is our contention that teachers must be at the forefront of educational change and, therefore, the very definition of the profession must be redefined.

Teachers, Teaching, and Professionalization

In the prologue to his engaging and important book, *Horace's Compromise* (1984), Theodore Sizer describes Horace Smith, a 53-year-old, 28-year veteran of high school classrooms. Horace is an "old pro." He gets up at 5:45 a.m. in order to get to school before the first period of the day, which begins at 7:30 a.m. Horace puts in a long day, teaching English to high school juniors and seniors. In all, he will come in contact with 120 students. His days are long and demanding. Horace figures that by judiciously using his time, he is able to allot 5 minutes per week of attention on the written work of each student and an average of 10 minutes of planning for each 50-minute class. For this, he is paid $27,300. He earns another $8,000 a year working part-time in a liquor store. Horace's daughter just graduated from law school and has her first job in a law firm. Her starting salary is $32,000 a year.

The story of Horace is by no means unusual. His loyalty, dedication, and hard work is repeated thousands of times by thousands of teachers every day. As this story indicates, there are numerous paradoxes related to the teaching profession. Teachers are expected to perform miracles with children but are seldom given the respect that professionals supposedly deserve. Teachers are asked to put in 60-hour weeks but are paid relatively small salaries. Teachers are expected to reform education, but are left out of the educational reform process. In short, teachers are the key players in education but their voices are seldom heard and their knowledge is terribly underutilized, and even devalued.

In this section we will briefly examine the nature of the teaching profession and the possibilities for further teacher professionalization. This topic is of utmost importance because we believe, as do John Goodlad and others, that teachers will be key players in educational reform in the future. After all, teachers are responsible for student learning. If they cannot assume responsibility for school improvement, how likely is it that schools will improve in terms of students learning?

Who Becomes a Teacher?

In 2008, 75.2 percent of all public school teachers in the United States were women. Their median age was 46; 73.1 percent were married, 13.2 percent were single, and 13.8 percent were widowed, divorced, or separated. Some 37.2 percent had a bachelor's degree, 60.4 percent had a master's degree, and 1.4 percent had a doctorate. Also, 38.2 percent would certainly teach if they had to do it over again; 27.3 percent probably would teach again; 16.1 percent said the chances were about even; 12.7 percent said they probably would not teach again; and 5.8 percent certainly would not teach again (U.S. Department of Education, National Center for Education Statistics, 2006, 2012b). With the aging of the teaching force and an attrition rate of approximately 40 percent in the first five years (Ingersoll, 2004), there will be increased demand for new teachers in the first decade of the twenty-first century.

Recently, there has been a great deal of discussion about the qualifications of those entering the teaching profession. In 1982, for instance, the national average Scholastic Aptitude Test (SAT) score was 893; the average score among students intending to major in education was 813 (Walker, Kozma, & Green, 1989, p. 26). Although SAT scores may not be accurate predictors of professional development, they do indicate that, on average, students entering the teaching profession are relatively weak academically. When top high-school seniors are asked to indicate their future professions, less than 10 percent indicate that they are interested in becoming teachers. These data did not significantly change in the 1990s (National Commission on Teaching and America's Future, 1996). What is perhaps even more alarming is that the best students who enter the teaching profession are the ones that are most likely to leave the profession at an early date. Another concern is that there are few minority teachers. The United States is becoming an increasingly multicultural society. One wonders about the educational effectiveness of an aging white teaching force in the context of increasing racial and ethnic diversity.

Given the concerns about teacher qualifications and quality, and the positive relationship between teacher quality and student achievement, especially in high-poverty schools (Education Trust, 1998), the No Child Left Behind Law mandates that states require all teachers to be highly qualified. According to NCLB, teachers are "highly qualified" when they meet three conditions:

1. A college degree.
2. Full certification or licensure, which specifically does not include any certification or licensure that has been "waived on an emergency, temporary, or provisional basis."
3. Demonstrable content knowledge in the subject they're teaching, or in the case of elementary teachers, in at least verbal and mathematics ability. This demonstration can come in various forms:

   – New elementary teachers must pass a state test of literacy and numeracy;
   – New secondary teachers must either pass a rigorous test in the subject area or have a college major;
   – Veteran teachers may either pass the state test, have a college major, or demonstrate content knowledge through some other uniformly applied process designed by the state. (Education Trust, 2003)

Most states require that both elementary and secondary teachers pass a test in their subject area, such as the Educational Testing Services Praxis II examinations, which are given in each subject area. Although these processes have raised the entry-level qualifications of teachers, advocates for increased teacher quality, such as the Education Trust, argue that many states have set the bar for passing these examinations so low that teacher subject-level knowledge still needs improvement (Education Trust, 2003). Some states, such as New York, require that new teachers pass examinations in general liberal arts knowledge, teaching pedagogy, and pedagogical content knowledge and subject matter knowledge; other states, such as New Jersey, only test subject matter knowledge, permitting new teachers to enter the classroom with no examinations of teaching competence.

The majority of new teachers enter the profession after completing a university or college teacher education program, where they student teach for a semester prior to entering the classroom. Many states permit alternate route certification, where new teachers who pass subject matter examinations enter the classroom with little or no teacher education or student teaching. Teach for America (TFA), a national teacher corps that recruits liberal arts graduates for teaching in high-poverty urban and rural school districts, is an example of such an alternate route program. Although proponents of high-quality traditional teacher education, such as Linda Darling-Hammond, have been critical of TFA, saying that no other profession allows people to practice without years of training, defenders of TFA argue that their teachers are among the best and brightest in the country, are dedicated to teaching in areas that most new teachers do not want to teach, and have a positive effect on student achievement (Darling Hammond, Holtzman, Gatlin, & Vasquez, 2005; Decker, Mayer, & Glazerman, 2004).

The Nature of Teaching

Few professions are as demanding as teaching. Teachers must be skilled in so many areas of technical expertise and human relations. In their book, *The Complex Roles of the Teacher: An Ecological Perspective* (1984), Heck and Williams described the many roles that teachers are expected to play in their professional lives. These roles include colleague, friend, nurturer of the learner, facilitator of learning, researcher, program developer, administrator, decision maker, professional leader, and community activist. This is a daunting list and it leaves out the most important role of the teacher: the caring, empathetic, well-rounded person that can act as a role model to students, parents, and other professionals. Thus, on any single day, a teacher will be expected to wear many personal and professional "hats." This role switching is extremely demanding and may be one of the reasons for teacher burnout (Johnson, 2004). It takes a great deal of emotional energy and imagination to maintain a sense of personal equilibrium in the face of meeting the needs of so many diverse groups.

Lieberman and Miller (1984) have explored what they call "the social realities of teaching." Through their research, they have been able to identify elements of the teaching experience that give it its unique flavor. According to Lieberman and Miller, the central contradiction of teaching is that

> teachers have to deal with a group of students and teach them something and, at the same time, deal with each child as an individual. The teachers, then, have two missions: one universal and cognitive, and the other particular and affective. (p. 2)

In order to reconcile this contradiction, teachers develop all kinds of classroom strategies that become highly personal and that evolve into a teaching style that is more akin to an artistic expression than it is to a technocratic or scientific resolution. Teachers, according to Lieberman and Miller, are best viewed as craftspeople and most of the craft is learned on the job. Teaching is a somewhat messy and personal undertaking.

There are other social realities of teaching that are significant. For instance, rewards are derived from students. Very often, the greatest and perhaps the only positive feedback that teachers receive is from their students. Seymour Sarason has written that teaching is a lonely profession. By this, he means that teachers get few opportunities to have professional interactions with their peers, and administrators seldom take the time or make the effort to give the kind of positive feedback teachers need.

Another element that gives teaching its unique characteristics is that very little is known about the links between teaching and learning. Researchers have only a marginal knowledge of whether or not what is taught is what is learned and what the nature of learning is. This means that the knowledge base of teaching is relatively weak compared to the knowledge base of other professions. Few teachers are experts in learning theory and many are only minimally qualified in some of the content areas they teach. What is key in teaching is the exercise of control. Control precedes instruction. Without control, there are few opportunities for learning, and yet control can stifle learning. Walking the razor's edge between social claustrophobia in the classroom and chaos in the classroom requires a high degree of self-understanding and understanding of group behavior. This is made more difficult by the fact that the goals of teaching are not always clear. There is a great deal of talk about holding teachers accountable for student learning. But the fact is that classrooms are communities, where many needs must be met. To be an effective teacher requires a sensitivity to individual and group dynamics.

Lieberman and Miller (1984) devoted a great deal of time discussing the "dailiness of teaching." There is a rhythm to the teacher's day. Thinking back to Horace in *Horace's Compromise* (Sizer, 1984), one can see that his day is punctuated by a set of rules, interactions, and feelings that are played out on a day-to-day basis with a certain predictability. Each day has a rhythm, weeks have rhythms, months have rhythms, and seasons have rhythms. For instance, fall is a time of high hopes and promise. As the fall winds down, energy winds down. By Thanksgiving, there is a great need for a break from the routine. Between Thanksgiving and Christmas, there is a frantic round of activities that culminate with the Christmas break. January can be brief, but February can seem never to end. It is in February that most teachers begin to think of other professions. By March, spirits begin to rise. This is accelerated by the spring break and the last-minute rush to fulfill the promises made in September by the closing of school in June. And then one day in June, school ends: No more routines, no more rituals, just memories of the year past.

Few professions are as simultaneously routinized and creative as teaching. Good teachers are creators. They take the dailiness of teaching and turn each day into a special event. A great teacher can turn a mundane lesson into an exciting intellectual voyage, and a poor teacher can make students reject learning altogether. There are few rules about what it takes to be a good teacher. Certainly, most good teachers genuinely like their students, have a commitment to their subject matter, are reasonably orderly in terms of their classroom organization, and have at least a working sense of humor. But these qualities are not professional qualities per se. How can one ensure that the teaching force will be staffed by people who are academically sound and pedagogically artistic? Given the condition of education today, it is important, even critical, that teachers be trained in new ways and redefine the nature of their professionalism.

Underqualified Teachers

A requirement of the No Child Left Behind (NCLB) Act is that all schools have highly qualified teachers in every classroom. This criterion highlighted the problem of unqualified teachers, many of whom were teaching out of their field of expertise. In the 1999–2000 school year, just prior to the enactment of NCLB, 99 percent of public school teachers held at least a bachelor's degree and almost half held a master's degree or higher. Moreover, about 92 percent of public school teachers held a regular or full teaching certificate.

Most teachers today meet the highly qualified standards of NCLB; however, the data indicate that significant numbers of classrooms are staffed by teachers who are not highly qualified in the particular subject taught. This is the result of the practice called *out-of-field teaching*—teachers being assigned to teach subjects that do not match their training or education. This is a crucial practice because highly qualified teachers may actually become highly unqualified if they are assigned to teach subjects for which they have little training or education. At the secondary school level, about one-fifth of classes in each of the core academic subjects (math, science, English, social studies) are taught by teachers who do not hold a teaching certificate in the subject taught. The data also show that some kinds of schools and classes have more out-of-field teaching than others. For example, low-income public schools have higher levels of out-of-field teaching than do schools in more affluent communities, and lower-track classes are more often taught by out-of-field teachers than are higher-track classes (Ingersoll, 2004).

According to Richard Ingersoll, a leading expert on issues relating to teacher staffing, the reasons for underqualified teachers have less to do with teacher shortages and more to do with organizational issues inside schools. Principals often find it easier to hire unqualified teachers than qualified ones, and the absence of status and professionalism in teaching leads to high dropout rates in the first five years of teaching. Therefore, districts are constantly replacing teachers on an ongoing basis, which has significant consequences, because it takes years to become an expert teacher. Rates of teacher attrition and misassignment are more prevalent in urban and high-poverty schools (Ingersoll, 1999, 2003, 2004). Ingersoll's research suggests that programs aimed at solving school staffing problems at the supply level through alternative teacher education programs—such as Teach for America, the New York City Teaching Fellows Program, and New Jersey's Alternative Certification Program (all of which allow college graduates with majors in their teaching field to enter teaching without traditional certification through a college teacher education program)—fail to address the organizational problems within schools that are responsible for high turnover rates (Ingersoll, 2004).

Teacher Professionalization

Sociologist Dan Lortie (1975) argues that teaching, particularly elementary school teaching, is only partially professionalized. When he compared elementary school teachers to other professionals, he found that the prerequisites for professionalism among elementary school teachers were vaguely defined or absent altogether. For example, doctors have many clients, which means that they are not economically dependent on any single individual. This economic independence provides professional autonomy so that doctors need not always comply with the wishes of the client. Teachers are in a very different market situation. They receive their income from "one big client." There is little opportunity for teachers to teach independently of their school, and thus there is little opportunity for teachers to gain a reputation for excellence outside of their school or their school district. There is, in Lortie's words, "an incomplete subculture." Teacher socialization is very limited compared to other professions and there is little evidence that the socialization processes associated with becoming a teacher are highly professionalized or represent standards of behavior congruent with other professions. Lortie (1975, p. 213) concluded: "The general status of teaching, the teacher's role and the condition and transmission arrangements of its subculture point to a truncated rather than fully realized professionalization."

Educational researcher Linda M. McNeil (1988b) has written about what she calls the contradictions of control. She pointed out that "in theory, the bureaucratic design of schools frees teachers to teach by assigning to administrators and business managers the duties of keeping the school 'under control'" (p. 433). But, as McNeil indicated, when so much attention is placed on keeping things under control, the educational purposes of the school can diminish in importance and teachers can begin to be part of a controlling process rather than an instructional one.

As a result, teachers begin to take on the characteristics of the workers whose craft was splintered and recast when they became factory workers. When teachers see administrators emphasizing compliance with rules and procedures, rather than long term educational goals, teachers begin to structure their courses in ways that will elicit minimum participation from their students. When they see administrators run the schools according to impersonal procedures aimed at credentialing students, teachers begin to assert in their classrooms the authority they feel they are lacking in their schools as a whole. And when the complicated and often unpredictable task of educating a wide range of students is less valued than having quiet halls and finishing paperwork on time, teachers try to create in their own classrooms the same kind of efficiencies by which they are judged in the running of their schools. (McNeil, 1988b, p. 433)

Clearly, Lortie and McNeil are pointing to a set of conditions within the teaching profession that makes genuine professional autonomy a difficult goal to attain. On one hand, teachers are expected to be autonomous, thoughtful experts in education. On the other hand, the conditions of their employment leave little scope for autonomy, thoughtfulness, or expertise. Perhaps none of this would really matter if the compromise between the norms of professionalism and the norms of bureaucracy did not lead to a kind of intellectual and moral paralysis among many teachers. Trying to be a professional and a bureaucrat, while at the same time trying to fulfill the many roles of a teacher, is a task that cannot be reasonably fulfilled by most people. Thus, in the teaching profession there is a tendency toward malaise, a lack of self-worth, and even cynicism. A visit to a teachers' lounge can be bracing and challenging to the idealist because teachers' lounges are notorious sites for gossip and back-stabbing. This is not to say that teaching is an impossible profession. There are many incredible teachers who overcome these obstacles and are inspirational to their students and even to their colleagues.

It is difficult to think of ways of educating inspirational teachers. After all, teaching is so personal. For educators such as John Goodlad, however, the time has come when society must find ways of better educating teachers. In the mid-1980s, Goodlad and two colleagues created the Center for Educational Renewal at the University of Washington. Using the Center as a base, they conducted a number of studies about teacher education in the United States. Goodlad's (1991, p. 5) findings included the following: "(1) A debilitating lack of prestige in the teacher education enterprise, (2) Lack of program coherence, (3) Separation of theory and practice, and (4) A stifling regulated conformity." These findings underscore what many already know. There is a crisis in teacher education. Goodlad suggested that there is a need for a complete redesign of teacher education programs and that a share of this redesign be conducted by policy makers, state officials, university administrators, and faculty members in the arts and sciences as well as in the schools of education. He also suggested that the redesign of teacher education include input from parents, teachers in schools, and the community at large.

Goodlad believes that a teacher education program should include a clearly articulated relationship between education and the arts and sciences. He believes that students should stay together with teams of faculty members throughout their period of preparation and that universities should commit enough resources to ensure first-rate teacher education programs. He is a strong believer that schools and universities should collaborate to operate joint educational projects as a way of preparing teachers for the real world of schools and as a way of revitalizing schools themselves. In short, Goodlad wants to raise the level of academic preparation for teachers, create a more cohesive curriculum, and professionalize teacher education by enlarging its clinical component.

Goodlad's ideas are far from radical. Many of them were incorporated into the recommendations of the National Commission on Teaching and America's Future (1996), which are summarized in Chapter 10. But if they are to be implemented, the way most teachers are prepared would have to be fundamentally altered. Clearly, there is a relationship between a higher level of preparation and professionalization. However, if teachers are to be truly professional, they must be able to share in the important decisions within the schools. School-based management, if it is to succeed, must empower teachers in terms of their decision-making capacities about curriculum, discipline, and other academic areas of importance. Whether or not school-based management will succeed as a reform will determine in no small degree the level of professionalization achieved by teachers. As one looks to the future, one can only hope that educational reformers will listen to teacher advocates such as John Goodlad who argue that without creating a new generation of teacher-leaders, there is little hope that schools will become more productive and just.

In this chapter we have discussed schools as organizations and teacher professionalization. Clearly, the many topics covered in this chapter deserve further discussion. The readings for this chapter touch on critical issues related to schools and teachers. The first selection, "Contradictions of Reform," written by educational researcher Linda M. McNeil, discusses the conflicting goals of U.S. high schools. The bureaucratic structure of the high schools is designed to control large numbers of students, while at the same time nurturing each student as an individual. Teachers are at the very center of this contradiction. McNeil argues that "standardized generic education" limits teachers' abilities to be creative and to take risks. Without true collaboration between teachers, administrators, and students, there is little hope for genuine reform.

The second selection, "Rich Land, Poor Schools," by sociologists David Baker and Gerald LeTendre provides a comparative and international analysis of schooling.

The third selection, "Is the Supply of Mathematics and Science Teachers Sufficient?" written by sociologists Richard M. Ingersoll and David Perda, discusses whether or not there is a teacher shortage in mathematics and sciences, two of the hardest to staff fields, as it relates to the high turnover rate in teaching.

Contradictions of Reform

Linda M. McNeil

> If you can't teach at this school, you can't teach.
> Magnet high school teacher (spring 1984)

> We're not teachers any more. We're workers now.
> Magnet high school teacher (spring 1986)

Ms. Watts is an extraordinary science teacher. She is one of the teachers who come to my mind when I think of Patricia Graham's recommendation that we recruit into the profession people who have a "passion for teaching," a passionate love of their subject and a deep commitment to bringing it to their students.

Ms. Watts' academic background includes degrees in science and engineering; she represents the level of professional knowledge and training for which schools are accustomed to being outbid by industry. She has taught in a predominately Hispanic high school, and she now teaches in an integrated magnet school in which black students are the majority.

Ms. Watts begins her physics course with the reading of a play about the ethics of physics. Right from the start, her students learn that science is full of emotions, moral dilemmas, and personal involvement. She tries to organize all her courses around the concepts and processes that help students see science in the world around them. Ms. Watts is the kind of teacher who is both willing and expertly able to expend the time to build her lessons in ways that will involve her students in the scientific questions and procedures she finds so exciting.

Although she was very reluctant to leave her previous teaching position, Ms. Watts welcomed the chance to teach in a magnet program whose official purpose is to engage students in active learning. Within such a program, she knew she would not only be allowed but required to create distinctive curricula in physics and physical science that would draw on her own "best" knowledge in these fields. In the company of other teachers developing active, engaging courses, she would be able to work on ways to structure classroom activities to link her students to the concepts and processes of the physical sciences.[1]

During Ms. Watts' first year of teaching, the district had pilot-tested a system of proficiency exams that, over a two-year period, would take both the choices of curriculum-building and the testing of students away from teachers like Ms. Watts and place them in the hands of consultants who design standardized tests. The content of Ms. Watts' courses would be divided into closely sequenced, numbered sections of factual content—"proficiencies." All of her lesson plans would need to be coded by number to show which element of the curriculum students were becoming "proficient" in during each lesson. The district office would supply her with a computer-gradable, multiple-choice final examination composed of the proficiencies recast as questions.

From her first year in the district, then, Ms. Watts' physical science course was proficiency-based. She was convinced that this format did a disservice to her students and an even greater disservice to science. "You have to spend a month on [the physics of] machines," she says. "You get to the end of it and the students hate it, and you hate it for what it does to them. They may be able to figure out the right answer on the proficiency test, but they don't know anything about machines."

The curriculum mandated by the district is heavily computational and assumes background in algebra that many students do not have (and are not required to have) when they enroll in the course. The curriculum (like the tests from which

it derives) is not about machines and how they work; it is about calculation, about using formulas to describe the mechanics of machines. "The students aren't going to remember those formulas—never. They are only going to remember that it was a pain," Ms. Watts says. "And this will add to the general population of people out there who say, 'Science is hard. I don't want to do science.' This is not a conceptual course; it is an introductory course. It's a calculation and manipulation course. I'm not allowed and don't have time to give them a conceptual basis—to say, 'You can make a better machine.'" In her physics class, Ms. Watts has tried to preserve the links between student and content, links that she has seen the proficiencies severing in the freshman physical science course. "If the district makes a proficiency test for physics," she says, "I will quit. That's it, period. I will not do it."

If Ms. Watts bases her physical science course on the district's numbered proficiencies and if 70% of her students make scores of 70% or better on the proficiency exams handed down from the district office, the district's reforms will be said to have worked. Ms. Watts' students will have "covered" the same chapter each week and will have worked the same computational problems as other high school freshmen in the district. They will have attained a minimum standard of knowledge in physical science.

In the process, according to Ms. Watts, they will have learned very little about what science is, about how to "do" science, about how science can be a part of their thinking. Her professional knowledge of science and her students' personal curiosities about the way the world works will have been set aside, while she and they meet in an exchange of "school science" that neither finds very meaningful. The institutional requirements will have been met, but Ms. Watts is fairly sure that any chance to learn real science will have been lost for her students.

The first two articles in this series suggested that behind the overt symptoms of poor quality in our schools lie very complicated organizational dynamics. The quality of the curriculum, the range of teaching styles, and the level of student commitment may not be what is "wrong" with schools. Each of these is an indication of the health (or lack of health) of the fundamental structure of the school. But an attempt to reform any one "problem" without giving attention to the underlying structural flaws may, as in the proficiencies imposed on Ms. Watts' courses, inadvertently make matters worse.

In Part 1 of this series, "Administrators and Teachers," I suggested that the American high school today embodies conflicting goals: educating individual students and at the same time processing large groups of students through to their credentials. The structure of the high school reflects this contradiction: school administration has evolved bureaucratic procedures to organize and control large numbers of students to insure that they are in the appropriate physical "place" and in the appropriate "place" on the path to a diploma. At the same time, the public expectation is that teachers will carry on the legacy of educating and caring for individual students—teaching course content and promoting learning.

As the most vulnerable of school employees, teachers stand at the point of conflict and must resolve the tension between these two contradictory purposes. The extensive classroom observations discussed in *Contradictions of Control: School Structure and School Knowledge* demonstrated that, when teachers feel that the administration and the school's reward structure subordinate educational goals to procedural controls, they will begin to treat their students in a similarly controlling manner. Feeling little sense of efficacy in the school as a whole, teachers will create their own efficiencies and establish their own authority in their classrooms by tightly controlling course content.

In Part 2, "Teachers, Students, and Curriculum," I described teachers who taught *defensively*, deliberately presenting simplified, fragmented bits of information to their students in the hope that students would comply with minimum requirements and leave the teacher in charge of the pacing of the course. These teachers often taught their most important content in the form of easily tested lists, they mystified complex topics, and they frequently omitted controversial or current material that

might generate student discussion and thus disrupt the efficient "coverage" of the material.

Interviews with both students and teachers revealed that the "school knowledge" they dealt with in class bore little resemblance to the much more complex and sophisticated personal knowledge of the teachers. Students (and many school reformers) misread the dullness of lectures as a lack of teacher knowledge, and teachers mistook students' disappointment with this diluted content for apathy and a lack of curiosity. Although the students in the schools I studied did comply with course requirements in most cases, ironically they came to devalue what they learned at school. It seemed too divorced from the "real world" they knew from home and jobs and television. Indeed, "school knowledge" held little credibility for them.[2]

In my study of teachers' treatment of course content in a variety of school settings, one school demonstrated that, when the procedures, resources, and structures of the school are organized in support of academics (rather than in conflict with them), teachers feel supported to bring their best knowledge to their students.[3] In Chapter 6 of *Contradictions of Control* I describe Nelson High School's educational priorities, which helped encourage teachers to bring their best professional knowledge into their classrooms. Finding that one school, where knowledge did not seem artificial, where teachers allowed their students to see them learning and asking questions (rather than tightly controlling all discussion), where scarce resources went first to instruction in a variety of imaginative ways, caused me to wonder what other structural arrangements might support the educational purposes of schools and overcome the organizational tendencies that reinforce defensive teaching.

Magnet Schools: Structured for Excellence

Nelson High School was an exception to the pervasive pattern of defensive teaching, student disengagement, and administrative attention to minimal compliance. This one school's building-level support for teaching and learning raised the issue of the difference that district level support might make in promoting the quality of education. More resources and policies originate at the district level than at the building level. If at the district level the tension between educating students and controlling them could be resolved in favor of the educational purposes of schooling, perhaps teachers would be even freer to bring their knowledge into the classroom.

A large urban district's system of magnet schools provided an opportunity to investigate this possibility. The district touts its magnet schools as "the best schools money can't buy." Organized as the district's response to court-ordered desegregation, the system of magnet schools promotes racial diversity by offering specialized curricula and excellent instruction. The district established specialized schools for such programs as engineering, fine arts, the health professions, gifted and talented students, law enforcement, aviation, computer science, and business. Teachers were hired according to their willingness and ability to create new courses and to work with colleagues to design distinctive programs. They were expected to teach so well that students all over the city would be willing to ride buses for an hour or more each day in order to attend these special schools.[4]

The federal court required reports on the programs and on student enrollments. District-level support for the magnet school program began with the efforts of the research and evaluation office in documenting enrollment statistics by race, but it also included the efforts of staff members in newly created administrative offices who worked with program development and provided support services in such areas as pupil transfers, transportation, and student recruitment. Although these supports centered first on equity, building-level magnet school co-ordinators were added as quasi-administrative staff to play leading roles in program development and daily oversight. In addition, some schools found added resources through corporate and foundation donations, state vocational funds for equipment purchases, and in participation from volunteers and school/community partnerships.

Months of daily classroom observations and interviews with teachers and students showed conclusively that teaching is very different in settings in which teachers do not have to choose between meeting minimum bureaucratic standards and teaching their students. When teachers do not have to teach in conflict with administrative policies, they are more likely to demand the best of their students, to learn along with their students, and to place few barriers between their professional knowledge and their classroom treatment of their subject.

Watching excellent, engaging teaching thrive in the supportive structures of these magnet schools and seeing the resulting engagement of students of widely ranging abilities affirmed the possibility that school organization need not stand in the way of "real teaching." These very positive observations and their implications for non-magnet schools were to have been the sole subject of my research.

However, my study took an unexpected turn when these teachers, who had been hired to specialize; came under the influence of centralized policies of "reform" that aimed to standardized teaching and the content of lessons. The contrast between their work as professionals in magnet schools and the new directives that required conformity to a centralized model of practice provides a dramatic story of the dangers of centralized school reforms and their power to create the very mediocrity that they are intended to eliminate.

Before the reforms, these magnet school teachers exhibited a high degree of professionalism in their work with colleagues and students. Several mentioned that they had chosen to work in the magnet schools not only because they cared about school integration but because the specialization of the magnet schools would permit them to function as curriculum developers in a state otherwise known for its statewide adoption of textbooks.

Teachers in the few magnet schools that required high entrance standards said that they felt ambivalent about teaching in "elite" public schools. They chose to remain because of their belief that "all students should be taught this way"—though in their district it was impossible to have the freedom to design courses anywhere except in a magnet school. "Teaching this way" meant first having the opportunity to collaborate with other teachers in developing the overall plan for the school. In a district in which faculty governance, even in the form of lively discussion in faculty meetings, is generally absent, magnet schools offer teachers a voice in shaping the program and a sense that a coherent educational program exists. Teachers in the magnet schools tended to develop a strong faculty culture, built around their commitment to desegregation, their participation in a specialized program, and their roles as professionals in schools aimed at excellence.

The magnet schools were not luxurious places in which to teach. In one school, teachers worked under asbestos-laden ceilings. Even at the science-specialty magnet school, science teachers rarely had adequate equipment for simple laboratory experiments. School libraries across the district were sparse, and they were no less so in most of the magnet schools. Some magnet schools had been placed as school-within-a-school programs in inner-city buildings whose declining enrollments needed a boost. Many of the school grounds were treeless, asphalt deserts that had long histories of neglect.

While more cheerful, better-equipped buildings and libraries would have made their teaching easier (and strained their personal pocketbooks less), these teachers found that the organizational support present in their magnet schools was a resource critical to their teaching. They managed to develop interesting courses and engaging teaching styles; they upheld a standard of excellence in a district historically known for the excellence of only a few schools in wealthier neighborhoods. They brought minority students into programs that would give them an opportunity to prepare for college, and they made science and engineering attractive fields for minority students and for girls. Their students spent hours riding buses and more hours reading literature, composing poetry, entering engineering design contests, discovering public and university libraries, and even asking questions in class.

The teaching in these magnet schools differed from school to school and from teacher to teacher. The common element seemed to be the teacher's ability to bring their "passion for teaching" into the classroom and to make classroom knowledge credible to students by making students participants in shaping it.

The teachers I reported on in *Contradictions of Control* had trivialized content by using it as a means of controlling students and by teaching defensively in order to gain at least minimal compliance from students and avoid unnecessary inefficiencies. The teachers in the magnet schools, on the other hand, did not feel that they were teaching in opposition to student apathy or administrative passion for efficiency. Their treatment of course content was almost exactly the opposite of defensive teaching.[5]

The midwestern teachers who taught defensively presented their most important course content in the form of lists of facts and fragments of information. They covered much material quickly, and their students knew what would be tested. The unintended consequence of their actions was the lack of credibility that such oversimplified, decontextualized information had for the students.

By contrast, teachers in the magnet schools tended to integrate rather than to fragment course content. They made—and allowed students to make—connections between lectures, readings, personal experience, current events, information from mentors in the community, and independent projects. Unlike the defensive presentation of the history of labor as a list of labor leaders and the dates of strikes, one teacher in a magnet school had her students stage a trial of robber barons. Through careful research and role-playing each student became a resource for the rest of the class on such matters as the competing interests of laborers, the survivors of workplace accidents, and the politicians, industrialists, journalists, and legal experts of the period. Her students debated "their" positions with fervor and were able to refer to issues and events they had studied long after the names and dates in a list-based lecture would have been forgotten.

The defensive practice of mystifying complex information rather than explaining it would itself have mystified most of these magnet school teachers. Rather than keep their lecture moving quickly by avoiding complex or controversial material, many of these teachers felt a direct commitment to demystify the world for their students. Exit polling after a federal election sent racially integrated teams of students into black, working-class white, and upper-class white neighborhoods to poll voters. Such terms as *interest group* and *social class* were no longer just vocabulary words in the government text.

A biology teacher knew that city children rarely think of being surrounded by nature. He required each student to build a collection of insects or leaves over the course of the semester, so that they could begin to appreciate the hundreds species around them and the purposes of scientific classification. The students also began to think about environments and habitats and to see themselves as gathers of information.

Mystification teaches children to "trust the experts" not to bother learning difficult things. Demysti-fication begins to make the world theirs. When school knowledge incorporates personal dimensions, tools of inquiry—whether specialized vocabulary, steps in measurement in the laboratory, or ways of thinking—become useful to students for their own ends, rather than disconnected parts of "skill" units that teachers are compelled to teach.

The defensive teaching strategy that most offended the students I talked with in the *Contradictions of Control* study was the tendency of teachers to omit topics that were extremely current or controversial. Whether in sciences or in the humanities, limiting classroom knowledge to things about which experts had reached consensus maintained the teacher's authority over content and kept the students in the role of passive recipients.

The teachers in the magnet schools were much more likely to bring current issues and their own current reading and learning into their courses. A biology teacher attended summer institutes to learn more about biology and studied microbiology with a professor at a medical college. As a result, her courses were enriched, and she contributed to the districtwide curriculum in those areas. More important, her excitement for learning was never hidden from her students. The week a scientific journal carried dramatically new information about DNA, this teacher brought the journal—and her own genuine excitement—to her biology students.

When the time came for students to choose a subject and a teacher/advisor for their independent projects, many selected this teacher and a biological topic. Some even found mentors in the medical and industrial research communities as an additional resource. These students were willing to be fumbling amateurs in the company of experts because they had seen their teacher take similar risks and achieve good results. "School science" and the continually developing field of biology were not separate in the minds of these students. Similarly, two teachers developed active assignments for bringing students into the study of the stock market, and a history teacher skirted no controversies when she allowed a Hispanic student to talk to the class about proposed immigration laws in light of his own parents' status as undocumented aliens.

These magnet school teachers and others like them offered no apologies for the work they demanded of students; few settled for minimal, passive compliance. High school teachers whose courses were related to the health professions felt a special imperative to keep their courses up to date by dealing with the personal, scientific, and ethical demands that the students would face in their rotations through the labs and practice areas of local hospitals. In doing so, they demonstrated what both Fred Newmann and Theodore Sizer have termed *authentic* evaluation: the assessment of students' performance for a purpose beyond generating grades for the grade book.[6] To have made the work easy merely to avoid student complaints and potential resistance would have been to lay the groundwork for serious incompetence once these students reached the hospital. Instead, the students wore their lab coats and their new skills with great pride, as participants in their own learning, participants whose knowledge mattered.

These magnet school teachers rarely had the physical materials that they needed for their teaching. Many subsidized classroom resources out of their own pockets and taught in inelegant city schools, when they would have been in great demand in more comfortable suburban settings. They chose the magnets because in them they could work as professionals, empowered by the structure of the school to place their students and their subjects at the center of their teaching. They had avoided school settings in which they would be de-skilled by state-adopted lists of textbooks and prescribed curricula. The results of their choice showed in teaching that kept school knowledge integrated with their personal knowledge, with their professional knowledge of their subjects, with the growing information and changing events around them, and with their students' capacities to become engaged in learning.

Meanwhile Downtown. . .

My study of magnet schools was to have ended with the documentation of the kinds of teaching and the resulting course content and levels of student involvement that characterized schools in which the tension between administrative controls and educational purposes was clearly resolved in favor of the latter. Many of the teachers in the magnet schools would be prime candidates for certification by the Carnegie Forum's National Board or for positions as "lead teachers." The magnet schools in which they taught would have demonstrated within a traditional school structure excellent models of variations that empowered teachers.

However, when the school district and the state moved to enact "school reforms," these strong teachers were not distinguished from their weaker colleagues. They fell under the jurisdictions of two levels of reform, both of which aimed to improve teaching through tighter management of teachers. Both the state and the district aimed to bring up the lowest levels of educational quality, and both aimed to standardize teaching. *Both levels of reform significantly shifted the structural conditions of teaching and placed these engaging teachers squarely in conflict with new administrative controls over teaching and curriculum*. The district-level reforms removed the design of curriculum and of student

assessments from the teachers' control. The state-level reforms dictated the teachers' role in the classroom and redefined teaching style as "teacher behaviors."

Proficiency-Based Curricula

The district-level reforms took the form of a proficiency system. Partly in response to the superintendent's anticipation that the state would soon impose a set of standardized tests on the schools and partly from genuine concern over such factors as the uneven quality of education, grade inflation in weak schools, and wide variations in teacher competence, the district staff sought a means for raising the quality of education in the schools most severely at risk.

Such an effort might have taken a very different direction had it arisen as a curriculum issue, an issue of oversight of principals, or even a staff development matter. In this district, however, the problem arose in the research and evaluation office, and the solution was thought to lie in better *testing*.

The research staff borrowed a test model previously used for assessing minimum levels of mastery of basic skills in an at-risk school. For reasons of cost and ready availability, the minimum competency test, rather than a "yardstick" of academic excellence from, for example, the district's stronger schools, became the model for the assessment of teaching.

Under this reform plan, the quality of teaching was to be assessed through the testing of students. Curriculum was to be reformed to achieve not academic quality but ease of testing. Staff members recall that curriculum was criticized as lacking "clarity," in the words of the testing office, the goals and purposes needed to be made "measurable." Up-to-dateness, comprehensibility for various groups of students, rigor of thought, use of high-quality resources, coherence of information, and variety of instructional activities were subordinated to measurability.

Curriculum committees (and this process remains mystified for the teachers) consisting of central office staff members, local graduate students, some teachers, and apparently some clerical assistants selected aspects of each course on which students were to become "proficient." The curriculum components were taken apart, sequenced, numbered, and sub-numbered in a manner reminiscent of the transformation of factories by "efficiency experts" early in the century.[7]

For each semester's work, a private testing firm designed tests of student outcomes that were multiple-choice and computer-gradable. A teacher who followed the prescribed curriculum in sequence, keeping pace with the district's guide, would "cover" the material in time for the test. All lesson plans were to be numbered to match appropriate proficiencies, and some principals required that the day's proficiencies be posted for students to see. Teacher merit pay, building principals' bonuses, and newspaper comparisons of school scores were all linked to student performance on the proficiencies.

A subject such as English, with an enormous range of content, was limited to proficiencies in the form of reading comprehension selections and grammar. Other subjects, such as social studies and science, were transformed into fragments of fact and bits of jargon, similar to the lectures typical of the defensive teaching I found in my earlier study. Although central office curriculum staff members were concerned about critical thinking and conceptual content, the reductionist format of the proficiency tests and related curriculum material reinforced convergent, consensus-based thinking, with the student in the role of recipient and rote learner rather than active participant. The teacher's role was reduced to that of monitor.

To blunt the effects of the proficiency-based curricula—which official district policy claimed to be the minimum standard, not the entire curriculum, but which in fact overwhelmed class time—the magnet school teachers began to deliver "double-entry" lessons. The biology teacher who was working with medical college researchers refused to dumb down her lessons to match the proficiencies: one day she wrote a simplified formula for photosynthesis on the board, telling students to write it in their notebooks and learn it for the proficiency test. For the remaining two weeks' lessons, the teacher provided another, more complex version of the formula that the students helped derive through lab activities.

Frequently, the magnet school teachers would have to put their "real" lessons on hold for a few days in order to lecture on the proficiencies, or they would have to continually point out proficiencies during each lesson, so that students could keep them separate from the "real" information. The students were not unaware that often the "official" content contradicted the complicated interpretations and reflected only partial information and oversimplified processes.

It was ironic that the teachers in these magnet schools, whose teaching embodied an integration of their personal knowledge, their professional knowledge, their students' developing knowledge, and the knowledge they arrived at jointly in the classroom, were being required to cordon off their knowledge of their students and of their subject from the official "school knowledge."

Rather than call on these "best" teachers as models and resources the district reformers placed measurability ahead of substance. Like the administrators described in Part 1 of this series, they subordinated the educational purposes of the institution to the procedural ones. Unlike the defensive teachers, however, the magnet school teachers generally refused to be de-skilled by the proficiencies. Either they went to great lengths to overcome the inadequacies of the new system and took time out to "cover" proficiency material at the expense of other course activities (rather than transform the whole course into fragments and facts), or they helped students keep parallel sets of notes.

When proficiency scores began to be tied to teacher assessment and merit pay, these teachers began to talk of leaving the profession or at least the school district. When Ms. Watts said that she would refuse to teach physics under the proficiency system, she was speaking for many of her colleagues. When ways to work around the proficiencies and the administrative controls with which they were aligned became too confining, the magnet school teachers would not acquiesce in the de-skilling that these approaches represented.

Teacher Assessment

The state mechanism for assessing the classroom practice of teachers paralleled the district prescriptions for curriculum and student testing. Measurability was paramount, and the wisdom of teachers was discounted. Again, in the name of reform and in an effort to even out the quality of teaching across the state, an instrument was developed to standardize practice and hold teachers accountable to central management.

The assessment instrument, modeled perhaps unwittingly on the activity-analysis efficiency procedure for pacing assembly lines, transforms the tasks of the teacher into a set of *generic behaviors*. Derived from the language of classroom management and the narrowest applications of cognitive psychology, the list of 45 behaviors (55 in the first year it was used) enumerates such teacher actions as varying activities and waiting for student responses to questions. Providing "closure" at the end of class and using praise words are also among the behaviors that assessors look for.

The behaviors are meant to be scientifically derived from "research" on effective teachers (such studies are listed in a bibliography at the end of the teacher's guide to the assessment process). These "objective" measures include just three evaluation levels for the observer: "satisfactory," "needs improvement," and "exceptional quality"—the last a very subjective term for which little guidance is given either to the teachers or to the administrator/assessors.

The teacher assessment instrument is directly tied to teachers' progress through the career ladder and in fact was the cost teachers paid politically to have the state legislature approve a career ladder system of salary advancement. The assessment system leaves little to chance regarding its implementation: the frequency of the observations, the number of hours of training for assessors, the scores needed to advance on the career ladder are all carefully specified.

However, the educational aspects of teacher practice are not specified. The latest edition of the assessment form does have a place for the teacher's signature, but it still does not have a place for a teacher to explain *why* certain classroom activities were undertaken or how the teacher's role in the class that day related to his or her knowledge of the students' needs or to the purposes of the lesson.

Administrator/assessors are not required to have subject-matter expertise in the courses they observe. (After all, these behaviors are supposed to be generic.) Worst of all, the assessment instrument reinforces the extreme of teacher centered classroom practice. Many of the teachers described in Part 2 of this series as teaching defensively could have earned high scores on the assessment instrument, even though their students found teacher controlled knowledge boring and trivial.

Decades of research on child development and the entire movement toward enhancing teachers' knowledge are ignored by this mandatory, statewide assessment system. Most teachers feel that to do the items listed on the form (enough of them to produce a high score) during one 50-minute class period would be to perform more as a marionette than as a teacher.

The teachers who want to hold onto a more personalized, professional teaching style must work around the assessment instrument, just as they must work around the proficiencies. Their students figure out quickly that class will be different on assessment days. A teacher who has developed writing workshops and is known for creative ways to relate writing assignments to literature says that when the assessor is due, she teaches a very traditional grammar lesson. "They would never understand our literature lesson," she asserts.

A 25-year veteran second-grade teacher reports that she has never felt politically motivated by a school policy before. But now "they have taken away my ability to do what I know my students need." A teacher of Advanced Placement courses reported using praise words during the class his assessor observed; later, the students who were accustomed to the teacher's probing questions and impatience with glibness, asked, "What were you *doing* in there today? Are you feeling all right?"

Teachers' views of administrative inability to link their best practice with the assessment instrument are not overstated. In a workshop devoted to placing students in the role of active workers in the classroom, a teacher asked how this could be reconciled with the teacher centered system of assessment. A principal stood up and said, "That's easy to figure out. When I go to assess a teacher and see the kids are working on projects or group activities, I just leave and come another day. It's like being there when the projector is running—you just come back some other time."

That principal and the designers and implementers of the assessment system have mistaken technique for teaching, classroom management for pedagogy. They are supported by a body of reductionist research and by political pressure for placing quality controls on public expenditures for education. It is little wonder that the magnet school teachers, who had chosen schools in which they could integrate their teaching style and course content and could continue developing their courses and their expertise, now feel like workers on assembly lines.

The Contradiction

The contradictions of control evident in these two reforms, the proficiencies and the generic assessment system, are even more serious than those I discussed in Parts 1 and 2 of this series. First, by leaping from symptoms (some weak teaching, some low achievement scores) to remedies, these top-down reforms not only ignore many of the dynamics that produce low-quality instruction, but they actually reinforce them. By applying across-the-board generic remedies, they are dumbing down the best teaching even as they try to raise the bottom. Disclaimers that these efforts establish "minimums" have little credibility when the best teachers are the ones who feel most alienated and who are talking of leaving the profession (several have done so since this research began).

Good teaching can't be engineered into existence. But an engineering approach to schooling can crowd out good teaching. Instead of holding up a variety of models for practice and learning from their strengths, these reforms continue our historically flawed search for "one best way" to run our schools. These reforms take a cynical view of teachers' ability to contribute constructively to schooling; they choose to make the content, the assessment of students, and the decisions about pedagogy all teacher-proof, so that a standardized model will become the norm.

Such reforms render teaching and the curriculum inauthentic. If we are to engage students in learning, we must reverse this process. When school knowledge is not credible to students, they opt out and decide to wait until "later" to learn "what you really need to know." Mechanical teaching processes knowledge in a way that guarantees it will be something other than credible. Centralized curricula, centralized tests of outcomes, and standardized teacher behaviors can only frustrate those teachers whose "passion for teaching" has shown students (and the rest of us) what education should be about.

The teachers in the magnet schools I studied now have a superintendent who thinks that teachers should participate in curriculum development. That superintendent is working with the school board to dismantle the proficiency system, perhaps in favor of a system of diagnostic tests (that will help teachers learn more about their students rather than control the curriculum) and in favor of new curricula produced by groups of teachers.

Meanwhile, the state assessment system has been ratcheted into place in exchange for increased teacher pay. The resources for pay increments along the career ladder have dissolved with the state's economic problems, but the system remains in place nevertheless. The state school chief has deflected criticism by suggesting that critics who oppose the system may not understand school reform; he has also implied that only the weakest teachers would oppose it.

Despite a national effort to professionalize and board-certify teachers and to increase their latitude for leadership within schools, outcomes testing is now on the national agenda, in the form of congressional approval for extending the reach of the National Assessment of Educational Progress. Before the federal government increases its role in outcomes testing and before a centralized curriculum inevitably evolves, this experience in this state should serve as an example that, educationally speaking, the emperor of standardized, generic education wears no clothes. The effects of such standardized reforms contradict the rhetoric of their purpose and leave us more educationally impoverished than when we began. Genuine reform will have to address the structural tensions within schools and seek, not minimum standards, but models of excellence. Reforms that make schools educational will require not adversarial relations between administrators and teachers, but the best collaborative efforts of all who work in and for our schools.

From "The Contradictions of Control, Part 3: Contradictions of Reform" by Linda M. McNeil, *Phi Delta Kappan*, March 1988. Reprinted by permission.

Notes

1. Ms. Watts is a fictitious name, but the teacher I am describing is a very real, dedicated teacher who consented to be interviewed and quoted for my study of magnet schools.

2. See "Contradictions of Control, Part 1: Administrators and Teachers." *Phi Delta Kappan*, January 1988, pp. 333–39; and "Contradictions of Control, Part 2: Teachers, Students, and Curriculum," *Phi Delta Kappan*, February 1988, pp. 432–38.

3. See Linda M. McNeil, *Contradictions of Control-School Structure and School Knowledge* (New York: Methuen/Routledge & Kegan Paul, 1986), Ch. 6.

4. This ethnographic study of magnet high schools was funded by a grant from the National Institute of Education. See Linda M. McNeil, *Structuring Excellence and Barriers to Excellence* (Washington, DC: National Institute of Education/Office of Educational Research and Improvement, 1987).

5. See *Contradictions of Control*, Ch. 7.

6. Fred Newmann's project on alternative, "authentic" assessments has been profiled in a fall 1987 *Newsletter* of the National Center for Effective Secondary Schools, University of Wisconsin-Madison. Theodore Sizer's Coalition of Essential Schools aims for "exhibitions" of students' work, as advocated in his book, *Horace's Compromise* (New York: Houghton Mifflin, 1984).

7. See Raymond Callahan, *Education and the Cult of Efficiency* (Chicago: University of Chicago Press, 1962), which reminds us that school reforms are always born of good intentions and always have unintended consequences.

Rich Land, Poor Schools

Inequality of National Educational Resources and Achievement of Disadvantaged Students

David Baker and Gerald LeTendre, with Brian Goesling

Using broad strokes, one could paint the theme of the politics of schooling in many wealthy nations in the 1960s and 1970s as trying to create school systems with equal educational resources, or what is called "educational equality." The main objective was expanding access to roughly equal educational opportunities for children who were underrepresented in education at the time: females, minorities, and rural children. Gradually shifting away from educational equality, the political agenda in many nations over the past twenty years has been and continues to be on educational quality, where the main objective is raising the basic level of educational achievement. Of course, international information has intensified many nations' focus on international educational competitiveness.

The preceding two chapters explored how a deepening institutionalization of schooling and rising resources in many nations shape how families invest their resources in their children's mathematics and science achievement. In this chapter, we shift attention from differences among families to those among schools in terms of resources dedicated to teaching and learning these two subjects. As we noted in the discussion of the Coleman and Heyneman/Loxley effects in Chapter 3, even though there has been an observable effect of a rising level of quality in many nations, there are still significant differences in access to resources among schools within a given country. Further, as we will show here, nations vary in how much resource inequality among schools their system produces; such educational inequality can have severe negative consequences for the school achievement of poor and disadvantaged students.

Unequal resources among schools can be a result of both intentional education policy and an unintentional consequence of the system. For the most part, modern national systems have tended to reduce both types—the latter as a reflection of greater institutionalization of the idea of the universality of education, and the former as a consequence of political action aimed at alleviation of poverty and social disadvantage. Of course, both kinds of inequality still exist in many nations.

Many national systems intentionally sort children into different kinds of schools, sometimes leading to differences in secondary credentials and rights vis-à-vis higher education. For example, as early as age ten in some parts of Germany or around age fifteen in Japan children are sorted by the kind of school. In Germany, the most academic stream, the Gymnasium, has teachers with more advanced training, accepts only academically talented students, and prepares these students for university entrance. Such a system deliberately creates distinct school types with differing goals and specific resources out tries to equalize resources within each type, thereby legitimizing differences. Similarly in many nations, by law basic physical resources and teacher pay scales are equal; it is rare for a school system to intentionally distribute resources unequally, but there are a number of mechanisms by which this can happen (Oakes, 1985). Sometimes unintended inequalities occur

because of variation in the level of educational expenditures across regions, provinces, or state. In the United States, for example, tying local property tax revenues to educational finance has led to discernible differences in resources across school districts in everything from the physical condition of the school to the quality of the teachers (LeTendre, Hofer, and Shimizu, 2003).

Unintended differences in resources continue to frustrate national and local education administrators who hope to attain equality of educational opportunity. By implementing compulsory education for all children over the past century, nations eliminated one major historical source of inequality in access to education, but successful expansion of mass schooling has created a new problem. Implementing mass schooling in most nations meant the rise of expectations about national academic outcomes, and the related goal of lowering (and even doing away with) any unintentional gross differences in the quality of schooling from one school to the next. As schooling becomes more central to so many facets of the future of children and youth, the public's expectations for more equality rise as its tolerance of unintended inequality plummets. The logic of modern schooling emphasizes the general principle that among schools of similar types there should be similar curricula, a similar level of student attainment, and similar basic educational resources. If this is not achieved, it increasingly becomes a political concern and even sometimes a national crisis. We focus here on the amount of unintended resource inequality among schools across nations.

Comparative Savage Inequalities

Twelve years ago, in a richly descriptive and aptly titled book, *Savage Inequalities*, Jonathan Kozol (1993) presented haunting stories of the failure of U.S. public schools to educate the nation's most socially and economically disadvantaged students. The American case of educational inequality is particularly telling about how institutional values of universalism and considerable inequalities coexist in one national context.

Public education in America, as elsewhere, has always been held up as one of the key paths to a socially just and prosperous society. As we have seen, wealthy nations invest considerably in education, and in general this pays off in a higher average level of achievement. Yet the United States, economically dynamic and the most politically powerful nation in the world, has a poor record in establishing a fair and level educational playing field. Evidence continues to show a disproportionately high number of educational problems (low achievement, low attainment, and premature ending of schooling) among economically, racially, and ethnically disadvantaged youths (Farkas, 1996). At the same time, there is growing evidence that the human costs of educational failure for both individuals and society continue to increase over time (Rubinson and Browne, 1994). Simply put, educational inequality creates problems that drain social resources over a long period of time.

Scholars and reformers in the United States have been aware of this problem for quite a while. Over the last thirty years, unequal distribution of basic educational resources has garnered considerable attention and significant academic studies and policy ideas (see, for example, Coleman and others, 1966; Hanusek, 1994; Hedges, Laine, and Greenwald, 1994; Mosteller and Moynihan, 1972). Much of the empirical work centers on the large differences in per-pupil expenditures that appear when comparing schools, districts, and states. These funding disparities have been linked with differences in the quality of schools and instruction; political attempts to change resource inequalities between schools have resulted in litigation challenging school finance systems within almost all U.S. states and have even been linked to vigorous debate on tracking and social inequality (Lucas, 1999; Loveless, 1999).

The ongoing debates and failed attempts to eliminate between-school resource inequality led us to explore what the situation in the United States looked like from a comparative perspective. Is this really an "American" problem, or can we identify global patterns and factors that might help us clarify the situation in the United States? We asked two questions about how

savage inequalities look from a global perspective. First, are American disadvantaged students comparatively more at risk of educational failure than similarly disadvantaged students in other wealthy nations? Second, what is the consequence of educational performance among disadvantaged students for the overall international educational competitiveness of the nation?

With the TIMSS data, we examine how well American schools educate students with several types of disadvantaged background and compared these results with findings from other nations. For this chapter, we focus only on high schools, but readers can find the results of an analysis of the eighth grade in Baker (2002). We used two indicators of social and economic disadvantage: low education of the student's mother and living in a single-parent home. The proportion of students with mothers having less than a high school degree and single-parent homes in the U.S. twelfth grade TIMSS sample is 11 percent and 15 percent respectively; international averages for students in all wealthy nations are 29 percent and 11 percent.[1] Although these family characteristics do not create a disadvantaged home in every case, they significantly increase the risk that children will have a disadvantaged home life, which can lead to less-than-full academic achievement for a number of reasons.

Are disadvantaged American students more at risk of educational failure? As shown in Table 6.1, the answer is clearly yes. American disadvantaged students learn considerably less general mathematics than similarly disadvantaged students in other nations. Among the thirteen wealthiest nations in the TIMSS twelfth grade sample, the average American mathematics knowledge for both students with mothers having less than a high school education and from single-parent homes is strikingly low. Overall, American twelfth graders did not perform well, so on the one hand it is not a surprise that disadvantaged students in the United States also performed poorly. But on the other hand, it is true that although the American overall eighth grade sample did as well as that in a number of other wealthy nations, American

Table 6.1 Comparative Analysis of Educating Disadvantaged Students

Students with Mothers Without a High School Degree (x Proportion in Nation = 29%)	Mean Math Achieve- ment	Students from Single-Parent Homes (x Proportion in Nation = 11%)
Netherlands	560	Netherlands
Sweden		
Denmark	550	Iceland
Iceland	540	Sweden
New Zealand		
Austria, Norway	530	Switzerland
Switzerland		Australia
International mean	520	Norway, Denmark
France, Australia		
Canada	510	New Zealand
	500	
	490	
	480	
	470	Germany
Germany	460	
	450	
United States	440	
	430	**United States**
	420	

Source: TIMSS 12th 1995.

eighth grade disadvantaged students also finished last compared to similar students in other wealthy nations (Baker, LeTendre, and Goesling, 2002). This suggests that the most disadvantaged students in the United States are not just affected at one level of the school system; they fail to achieve across the span of compulsory schooling.

The consequences of low educational performance in human terms are pervasive and complex, and we can judge the impact of low educational performance by recalculating the overall American mean mathematics knowledge to see what would happen if the United States educated its disadvantaged students as well as

other wealthy nations do. If the United States were as successful as, say, Sweden in educating youths with mothers without a high school degree, then it would improve its overall national mean by fourteen points in twelfth grade mathematics. If we add doing as well as Sweden does with youths whose mothers have just a high school degree, the improvement in the U.S. TIMSS mathematics average score would place the country above five wealthy nations that currently outperform it.[2]

This is a simple exercise that can be done with any proportion of a distribution, but the message is clear. Because the United States (as well as other nations) fails to educate its most disadvantaged students, it lowers the overall cross-national standing. Receiving a subpar education significantly adds to the risk of entering the ranks of the underclass, and coming from a disadvantaged home in the United States places a youth at greater risk of poor educational performance than in many other wealthy nations.

These findings should also be disturbing for American policy makers because they show that school systems in other nations somehow have found ways to lessen the impact of disadvantaged background on school achievement. This is not to say that what is done in these nations is perfect, or that the negative impact of disadvantaged families has been completely ameliorated, but these findings suggest there may be social and educational policies at work in other nations that might serve as a model for the United States in meeting the educational challenge of students from disadvantaged families. We know that disadvantaged students are more at risk of lower educational performance, and that in nations like the United States the overall effect substantially lowers the national mean achievement.

But what have nations done to address this issue? The school has been the central institution used to prevent social problems in most nations, and it is often thought that reducing resource inequality across schools is a key to lessening the impact of disadvantaged families on achievement. Has any country devised a mass education system that significantly lowers, or even eradicates, differences in basic educational resources across schools?

Educational Resource Inequality Among Schools Worldwide

To answer this question, we analyzed how well national school systems distribute basic educational resources equitably across schools. With our colleague Brian Goesling, we estimated the degree of resource inequality among schools with eighth graders in fifty-two nations by combining the 1994 and 1999 TIMSS data (Baker, LeTendre, and Goesling, 2002). We developed a measure of inequality for basic educational resources, including instructional resources such as budget for teaching materials, supplies, libraries, heating and lighting, and other physical plant resources; instructional space; computer hardware and software; professional experience of teachers; and student-to-teacher ratio (class size). We also restricted the analysis to middle grade schools in order to lessen the chance of including some intentional resource differences across curricular streams in upper secondary schools.

When we estimated the degree of inequality of educational resources across schools, we found that all TIMSS nations have some level of between-school resource inequality (*between-school* is the research shorthand for saying resource differences among schools). As shown in Table 6.2, although mass schooling is predicated on equality in basic resources in practice this is just not the case. There is considerable cross-national variation in educational resource inequality, and like cross-national differences in mathematics and science achievement the national level of between-school inequality clusters into three distinct groups. The first, with the highest estimated level of between-school inequality, includes South Africa, the Philippines, Latvia, Chile, and sixteen other nations. The seventeen nations in the second group are roughly equal to the international mean; notable in this group are Greece, France, the United States, and South Korea. The nineteen nations with less between-school inequality include Sweden, Germany, Japan, and

Kuwait. Most wealthy nations have less inequality in basic resources across schools than the United States does, and this surely has some consequences for its overall educational competitiveness as well as persistent poverty across generations.

When we examined which nations had high and low levels of between-school inequality, the results were as we expected, with one surprise. First, wealthier nations tend to have less inequality in resources across schools, although there are a few interesting exceptions, among them the United States. Second, nations with a lower level of inequality tend to produce a higher

Table 6.2 Basic Resource Inequality Across Nations

Nations with Significant Levels of Inequality	Nations with Average Levels of Inequality	Nations with Low Levels of Inequality
South Africa	Moldova	Sweden
Philippines	Greece	Hong Kong
Colombia	Malaysia	Italy
Macedonia	Bulgaria	Germany
Morocco	Lithuania	Iceland
Iran	Slovenia	Australia
Romania	Israel	Spain
Portugal	France	Cyprus
Turkey	Chinese Taipei	New Zealand
Russian Federation	Slovak Republic	Japan
	Canada	Finland
Latvia	Ireland	Singapore
Thailand	*International average*	Norway
Denmark	Tunisia	Austria
Jordan	United States	Netherlands
Chile	Korea	Czech Republic
Indonesia	England	Belgium (Flemish)
	Hungary	Switzerland
		Kuwait

Source: TIMSS 1995.

Note: Within boxes, national levels of inequality are not statistically different from one another.

level of overall mathematics and science achievement. The positive impact of having more equal resources among schools is about the same in magnitude as the impact of national wealth on average national achievement, discussed in Chapter 3. Last, contrary to what many think, the degree to which education governance is centralized is not associated with less or more resource inequality.

The first two findings make sense intuitively. Wealthier nations have more to spend on education, more sophisticated consumers of education (that is, better-educated parents), more professionalized administration, and better-trained teachers; these are all factors that go into the political process to reduce gross inequality in distributing resources across a set of schools in the nation. Also, as we have already shown, education resource inequality deprives socially disadvantaged students, which in turn causes considerable damage to a nation's overall efforts to raise the national level of achievement. In other words, in a highly inequitable system it is probably the case that those students who most need instructional resources (to make up for the detrimental effects of a poorer family background) do not receive them.

This compounds educational disadvantage, leading to potentially severe and lasting social disadvantage. Although wealthier nations have, on average, lower resource inequality, academic failure in these nations probably has more dire ramifications because of their complex labor markets and the domination of educational credentials. Compared to individuals in developing economies, less-educated individuals in highly developed economies have few ways to compete in the labor market, and since that fact is compounded by attending schools with lower resources this can result in large communities of impoverished, undereducated adults.

The lack of association between administrative style in nations and level of resource inequality is not so surprising in light of the rather ambiguous state of centralized versus decentralized government structures that many nations now find themselves in as a reaction to the "devolution revolution" in educational governance (see Chapter 9).

The numbers behind Table 6.2 representing educational resource inequality within these mass systems of education are abstract compared to the tragic human stories of educational failure in the United States found in Kozol's book. But they are in reality one and the same, and they give us a way to measure the extent to which poorly implemented mass education can contribute to the creation of savage inequalities in some nations (see early estimates of inequality in Heyneman, 1982). Similar to what we find about school violence in Chapter 6, these results show that resource inequality is not only an "American" problem; it occurs in other nations as well. How can our institutional perspective of the widespread strength of schooling take into account persistent inequality in school resources within a nation?

National Politics and Educational Inequality

These results show problems in many nations in the implementation of mass schooling. Returning to some basic institutional assumptions, we know that around the world mass schooling is legitimated by (among other values) the commonly held ideal that schooling should operate in a meritocratic fashion with achievement as its main currency. This means opportunity should be linked primarily to performance, not social status, family background, or other nonacademic aspects of the student. It also means that one's ability to learn specific curricula is connected to the opportunities with which one is presented at school. So to orchestrate a meritocratic process, schools should have at least equal resources. Some would argue that schools serving disadvantaged communities should even have more resources to compensate for poor family background, to put each student at the same starting line academically; as an example, this is what Japan actually implements.[3]

But why doesn't this happen in more nations? Why can't a country like the United States, which seems to value mass education so highly and spends a substantial amount on schooling, do away with its resource differences that reproduce across generations an unfair amount of low achievement and limited future educational opportunities, and all the concomitant social problems faced by children of poor families?

The usual answers to this question are particularistic and mechanical, not institutional. One such answer goes that U.S. governmental policy and its resulting programs aimed at poverty are comparatively weaker than social and economic welfare systems in many other wealthy nations. In other words, the United States has comparatively less progressive income transfer policies in its tax system, which combined with the variation in state-to-state policies and resources to assist families in poverty both add up to making the American disadvantaged experience a greater economic deprivation than that for similar people in other developed nations.

Another frequent answer concerns the uniquely American practice of running public schooling through its system of locally administered, property-tax-funded school districts (some fourteen thousand of them). This, the argument goes, causes many districts in poorer urban and rural communities serving a geographically concentrated population of students from disadvantaged families to suffer severely deficient financial and managerial support for schools.

But politically neither factor is insurmountable; there are obvious ways to fix them toward more educational equity. In fact, they really are such flimsy barriers to more educational equality that many frustrated advocates for American disadvantaged children turn to almost paranoiac images of planned, sustained, systematic racism and social classism in educational policy. Kozol's otherwise moving account of educational inequality in the United States is a classic example of this, suffering from an unrealistic image of an officially unstated yet systematic and oppressive educational policy presumably blessed by an uncaring American majority.

Certainly racism and social classism have had some influence on education inequality in the United States, but as the preceding chapters have shown the production of inequality of educational outcomes such as mathematics and science achievement in many nations is more a product of informal forces acting through the family. For example, some U.S. states have tried to equalize resources among numerous local districts that heretofore were captives (or winners) of differing property values (tax base) between communities. As welcome as this expression of equal resources is in some quarters, stories abound about how upper-middle-class families conspire to provide direct financial support to enhance school resources beyond a state-imposed limit. Probably on the whole these families do not see themselves in some grand social-class or racial struggle, but rather as families with considerable resources attempting to improve their own kids' school for all the obvious benefits.

The same is true in nations such as Chile, where all of the upper and middle class buy out of the public system with its generally lower resources level and uses private schooling directly because of a belief in higher educational quality (among other benefits). For the same reasons given in Chapter 4 about the growth in consumption of shadow education, as schooling becomes the main (and virtually only) game by which to pass on social status to children, pressure for better implementation of meritocratic processes in schools is met by counterpressure from families competing to secure better education for their own children.

But in and of itself this does not explain the persistence of resource inequality among schools in so many nations. Undoubtedly, as we have just done for the United States and Chile, we could pick through each national case and piece together particular mechanisms that lead to some degree of inequality within the system. But that does not really get to the question at hand of why so many nations implement mass public schooling with some degree of resource inequality present that has a detrimental effect on disadvantaged students. What is missed in much discussion of educational inequality is that organizational barriers to more equity in most nations are by themselves relatively easily overcome, but at the same time the institutional values that education weaves into modern society strongly reinforce even the weakest technical barriers to more equity.

Toward an Institutional Explanation of Educational Inequalities

Among scholars of social inequality, the most popular image of schooling holds that unequal resources and unequal access to quality schools reflect (and hence reproduce in the next generation) underlying social power differences among groups within a society. Wealthier groups demand and find ways to secure the best schooling for their children regardless of children's ability to achieve, and in some systems this comes at a price of lower school quality for less wealthy and less politically powerful families.

Correspondence between schooling and its role in social inequality has been a central notion in social stratification research at least since the late 1920s, when sociologist Pitirim Sorokin and others first wrote about "social mobility," a term meaning how easy or difficult it is for children to attain a higher social position than their parents. This image also motivated some of the earliest comparative analysis of schooling and national patterns of social mobility, as found in Turner's now-classic article (1960) about how "sponsored" and "contest" mobility processes differentiate the education systems of England and the United States.

In the same spirit, sociologist Richard Rubinson (1986) argues, in an award-winning article, that implementation of mass schooling is shaped by the specific social class struggles within a nation. So, for example, the nineteenth-century American working class won greater access to public schooling from a fragmented capitalist class that was more involved in internecine competition than consolidating its own power, compared to the working class in Western Europe at the same time. His larger point is that schooling is porous and penetrable to political interests; the relative power of these political interests shapes educational access and inequalities. In this image of schooling and society, institutionalization of mass schooling and its organizational implementation is constrained by national politics (see also Buchmann and Hannum, 2001).

We don't disagree with the basic idea of mass schooling being porous to political interests, or that those interests can be motivated by social class competition or even racial or ethnic bigotry. There have been many sad chapters in the development of schooling in which it was used for bad purposes by political interests. Also, mass schooling's long-term development by national governments certainly attests to the major role of political action in the organization of schooling. But we would add that now, in many nations, the holes through which political interests of specific groups seep into schooling are small, and probably becoming even smaller with greater incorporation of common values about education that the world culture seems to interweave so thoroughly into national systems of schooling.

We predict this first of all because of the impression the TIMSS data give of the relatively modest absolute amount of inequality in mass education found across nations. Even though inequalities persist in real systems of schooling, in a matter of minutes anyone can dream up a far more effective *elite-serving* inequitable education system than is actually operating in most developed nations in the world today, including the United States (Werum and Baker, 2004). Indeed, there is historical evidence that although many nations initially constructed schooling with intentional resource inequalities built in, from the early part of the nineteenth century onward they systematically dismantled such intentional inequalities to a significant degree. There are, of course, nations such as Germany with remnants of a highly stratified nineteenth-century secondary system still operating with unequal educational secondary school degrees built in. But also in Germany (as in other nations of Western Europe) basic resource equality among schools is legally prescribed and organizationally achieved to a large degree (see Table 6.2). The point is, even with clear cross-national differences as we describe here, mass public systems in developed nations are not hugely unequal in resource distribution, certainly not to the degree implied by more conspiratorial images of the role of schooling in social reproduction.

Secondly, we predict a lessening of inequality of resources in the future because as an institution mass schooling gains considerable legitimation from developing and maintaining a meritocracy process based on achievement, even though this is rarely, if ever, perfectly implemented. Mass schooling works to spread the belief that individuals should be evaluated and promoted on the basis of merit, which is reflected in their achievement. (Chapter 2 describes the impact that this institutional value has had on gender and achievement.) Further, for a number of reasons outlined in the introductory chapter, national governments have bought into this idea to a considerable degree. Of course, state apparatuses are open to group political interests, but the ideas of human capital investment and its universal acceptance have proven powerful enough for the development of schooling generally to occur with little partisan difference in beliefs in these basic institutional values. This is reflected in the public expectation of mass schooling as a way to break the cycle of enduring poverty and social disadvantage across generations. Of course, implementation of these ideas can be on a partisan level, as is seen in the divergent emphasis that political parties of the left and right put on certain educational policies, but the point is they all think mass formal education is the key.

The ideas of merit and cognitive achievement are attractive to the modern mind; compared to a century or so ago, now highly schooled populations in many nations help to create and maintain these ideals. Even overt differentiation of future educational opportunity at a relatively young age in national systems such as in Germany and Japan are legitimated by the same basic ideal of meritocracy that pervades schooling throughout the world. The ideas of merit and academic achievement may even trump more local cultural beliefs about when and to what degree school performance should result in differing opportunities, and even about what causes ability in students (LeTendre, Hofer, and Shimizu, 2003). They certainly have already trumped more traditional conservative ideologies about schooling as maintaining a "natural, hierarchical" social order, or confirming the individual's natural place in that order.

Perhaps, then, the best way to think about the origin of educational inequality in mass schooling is as a result of two institutional characteristics that mass schooling itself simultaneously produces: meritocratic opportunities to learn and the increased social and economic relevance of school performance and credentials for adult status and well-being. These institutional characteristics per se are not contradictory; they are highly complementary and together increase the overall institutional stature of schooling (Meyer, 1977). But they lead to differing behavior on the part of school systems and families. The former (the school) attempts to ratchet up meritocratic functions on the basis of cognitive performance within schooling, while the latter (the family) is highly motivated to create as much educational opportunity for children as it can. This not only includes things done within families but also more collective action taken by similar families acting as interest groups. Schooling as an institution increases the motivation for successful cognitive achievement, particularly in subjects such as mathematics that are deemed highly applicable to further achievement; at the same time it attempts better and better implementation of meritocratic processes around such achievement.

Certainly not every individual school does this, but for better or worse the overall trend in the operation of mass schooling in many nations increasingly turns on cognitive achievement and the idea of merit according to mastery of a few highly valued academic subjects. On top of this is the fact that the prominence of schooling in society as the main avenue to adult success makes this a powerful set of values. Therefore in the United States the problem is not a socially uncaring upper-middle class of families; instead the problem is that as a group the upper-middle class have supercharged motivations and significant resources to assist their own children to better educational achievement. The paradox is that, as an institution, schooling produces both forces. The holes that make schooling porous to political interests may indeed become smaller in the future, but the pressure behind the political interests attempting to find those holes intensifies as education determines more and more of children's future.

Of course, the government in many nations mediates raw political interests in the education arena, and nations differ partly in the degree to which the government is a buffer. The United States, compared to France, has less governmental buffering of local interests, for example. This is also not to say that since inequality always tends to exist national systems can do nothing to address it. Our simple yet compelling evidence here about cross-national differences in achievement among socially disadvantaged students suggests that some nations buffer students from social inequalities educationally more than others. A nation like the United States, with its considerable wealth, certainly can and should do far more for its disadvantaged students.

But our larger point is that the powers unleashed by institutionalization of the belief in merit and the primacy of educational achievement for attaining a successful future inevitably create a dynamic tension between the efforts of schools to focus on more equity in the conditions for achievement and private interests to focus on educational advantages for their children.

By and large, our discussion about educational resource inequality has been limited to wealthier nations, but what about poorer ones? As our results showed, they tend to produce greater inequality than in wealthier nations. What is happening on the level of schools and families of the students who attend them also happens on an international level as well. Educational inequality among nations, as well as within them, is a major challenge to national economic and social development. In a world increasingly dominated by the drive for human capital enrichment, substandard education systems that produce large inequality along the lines of social disadvantage are at risk of national disadvantage as well. Continued educational expansion and its

recent revolution in quality (and, we would add, the growing trend toward less unintended inequality of educational resources) ups the human-capital stakes for poorer nations.

Particularly troubling are nations that—through poverty, internal corruption, and external exploitation—have in recent times failed to develop effective systems of mass education, public health delivery, and economic development. Called "failed states" by some scholars, these countries (notably Angola, Afghanistan, and the Congo) have been beset by civil war and a host of terrifying social problems. In such nations, expansion of mass schooling is effectively disrupted and the equalizing effects are lost. We know very little about how severe the impact has been in these states, but it is clear that significant international resources are needed to stabilize such nations or regions and restart mass schooling. Many other nations are still struggling with basic educational and developmental issues (examples are Cameroon and Niger). If these nations and regions continue to find themselves stalled in equalizing access to education and developing quality schooling for at least a large portion of children, then their inhabitants will be forced to endure long-term deprivation and social instability—a scenario that has serious implications for all nations.

Notes

1. Although the United States has a high dropout rate by age eighteen, it offers a number of other ways to obtain a high school diploma such that it has one of the highest high school completion rates in the world in cohorts aged twenty-four to twenty-eight.
2. Similar results are found for other indicators of student disadvantage.
3. Our technical measures of resource inequality could not pull out this kind of ameliorative distribution, so for some nations the overall measure of inequality is a bit inflated.

Is the Supply of Mathematics and Science Teachers Sufficient?

Richard M. Ingersoll and David Perda

Few education issues have received more attention in the past few decades than the challenge of staffing the nation's classrooms with qualified mathematics and science teachers. Recent high-profile reports from organizations such as the John Glenn Commission (National Commission on Mathematics and Science Teaching for the 21st Century, 2000), the National Research Council (2002), and the National Academy of Sciences (2007) have directly tied mathematics and science teacher staffing problems to a host of educational and societal problems—to the inability to meet student achievement goals, to low U.S. educational performance compared to other nations, to the minority achievement gap, to national economic competitiveness, and even to the security of the nation.

There are a number of competing explanations concerning the sources of, and solutions to, these mathematics and science teacher staffing problems. One of the most prominent explanations focuses on teacher shortages. The primary root of the problem, in this thesis, is insufficient production of new mathematics and science teachers in the face of two demographic trends: increasing student enrollments and increasing teacher retirements. Subsequent shortages, this view continues, force many school systems to lower standards to fill teaching openings, in turn inevitably leading to high levels of under-qualified mathematics and science teachers and lower student performance (e.g., Blank & Langesen, 2003; Liu, Rosenstein, Swann, & Khalil, 2008; National Commission on Teaching and America's Future, 1996, 1997; U.S. Department of Education, 2002).

Researchers and policy analysts hold, moreover, that these shortfalls affect some locations and groups more than others. Some argue that teacher shortages are geographically based, vary by region and state, and result from

an uneven production of new teachers across locales (e.g., Curran, Abrahams, & Clarke, 2001; Murphy, DeArmond, & Guin, 2004; National Commission on Teaching and America's Future, 1997). Others focus on issues of equity and argue that shortages fall disproportionately on schools in high-minority and high-poverty communities and contribute to unequal educational and, ultimately, occupational outcomes (e.g., National Commission on Teaching and America's Future, 1996, 1997; Oakes, 1990; Oakes, Franke, Quartz, & Rogers, 2002; Quartz et al., 2008).

Concerns over teacher shortages, especially for mathematics and science, are not new to the education system. For example, in the 1980s, a series of highly publicized reports trumpeted a similar series of concerns (see, e.g., Darling-Hammond, 1984; National Academy of Sciences, 1987; National Commission on Excellence in Education, 1983). Indeed, teacher shortages historically have been a cyclic concern in the educational system, and references to teacher shortages have long been ubiquitous in both education research and policy (Lortie, 1975; Tyack, 1974; Weaver, 1983).

The prevailing policy response to these school staffing problems, both now and in the past, has been to attempt to increase the quantity of new teachers supplied (see Darling-Hammond, 2007; Fowler, 2008; Hirsch, Koppich, & Knapp, 2001; Liu et al., 2008; Lortie, 1975; Rice, Roellke, Sparks, & Kolbe, 2008; Theobald, 1990; Tyack, 1974). In recent decades, a wide range of initiatives has been implemented to recruit new candidates into teaching—especially targeted to the fields of mathematics and science. Among these are midcareer-change programs, such as "troops-to-teachers," alternative certification programs, overseas teacher recruiting initiatives, and financial incentives, such as scholarships, signing bonuses, student loan forgiveness, housing assistance, and tuition reimbursement.

Research on the Adequacy of Teacher Supply

Despite the long-standing prominence of this issue as a national policy concern, empirical research on the adequacy of the quantity of the supply of teachers has been surprisingly limited—in data, methods, and measures. There are few sources of comprehensive data, especially at a nationally representative level, on the new supply of qualified teachers. The most readily available data focus on perhaps the most obvious source of new hires: the "pipeline" of college students who have recently completed a teacher preparation program in a school of education and obtained an education degree and teaching certificate (e.g., Darling-Hammond, 1984; Grissmer & Kirby, 1997; National Commission on Teaching and America's Future, 1997). But data are less readily available on several other important sources of new hires in schools, such as those entering teaching with noneducation degrees and those entering through alternative, mid-career, and nontraditional routes. In addition to those in these pipelines of newly qualified candidates, there is the "reserve pool" of those who completed teacher preparation in prior years but delayed teaching, as well as former teachers who left teaching to later return. Finally, a third and large source of new entrants to particular schools is, of course, other schools—those who are already employed as teachers who move from one school to another. Accurately assessing the quantity of teacher supply requires data on all of the major sources of new hires.

Related to these data limits have been limitations of measures and methods. Empirically measuring inadequacies and shortfalls in teacher supply is difficult (see Behrstock, 2009, for a detailed review). One possible indicator used to assess the extent of shortages is the vacancy rate, that is, unfilled teaching positions in schools (e.g., Blank & Langesen, 2003; U.S. Department of Education, 2009). But national data have long shown that in any given school year, there are very few teaching openings left vacant or withdrawn because suitable candidates could not be found (Ingersoll, 1999). In reality, for legal reasons, schools often simply cannot, and do not, leave teaching positions unstaffed, regardless of the quantity and quality of supply.

An alternative indicator used to assess shortages is the number of positions filled by underqualified teachers (e.g., Blank & Langesen, 2003; National Academy of Sciences, 2007; National Center for Education Statistics, 1997; National Commission on Teaching and America's Future, 1996, 1997; Rumberger, 1987; U.S. Department of Education, 2009). However, the problem of underqualified and out-of-field teaching has multiple sources, and is often tied to the management of teachers in schools independent of supply shortages (Ingersoll, 2004). Shortages, for instance, cannot explain high levels of underqualified and out-of-field teaching that exist in fields such as social studies and English, long held to have surpluses (Ingersoll, 1999).

Another commonly used empirical measure to assess shortages focuses on teacher recruitment and hiring difficulties (e.g., American Association for Employment in Education, 2008; National Academy of Sciences, 2007; National Center for Education Statistics, 1997; National Commission on Teaching and America's Future, 1996, 1997). Data from school administrators on the degree of difficulty they encounter filling their teaching job openings are probably the most grounded and accurate measures available of the extent of actual staffing problems at the school level. But data on hiring difficulties themselves do not indicate the sources of these difficulties, and they do not themselves allow us to evaluate the magnitude, or sufficiency, of the quantity of supply.

Because of these data limitations, much of the research and policy commentary on teacher shortages have not been empirically well grounded. Researchers have rarely specified how to empirically evaluate whether teacher supply and demand are, or are not, in balance and how to empirically determine at what point the new supply of teachers is, or is not, sufficient to meet the demand for new teachers. It is difficult to find any research, especially with representative data, that empirically tests either of the two main claims of the teacher shortage thesis: that the production of new teachers has not kept pace either with student enrollment increases or with teacher losses from retirement. Addressing these gaps is the objective of this study.

The Study

This study builds on our prior research on teacher supply and demand. In this earlier work, we have offered an alternative hypothesis and perspective to the contemporary teacher shortage thesis to explain the staffing problems encountered by many schools (see Figure 6.1; for summaries, see Ingersoll, 2001, 2003). Our analyses revealed that preretirement teacher turnover—the departure of teachers from their schools—is a significant factor behind the need for new hires and the accompanying difficulties that schools encounter staffing classrooms with qualified teachers. In turn, we documented that teacher turnover varies greatly between different kinds of schools serving different student populations and is closely tied to the organizational characteristics and working conditions of those schools. Unlike research on employee turnover in other industries, until recently, there has been little empirical investigation of the types and amounts of costs and benefits, advantages, and disadvantages of teacher turnover.[1] Our alternative perspective revealed that one negative consequence of teacher turnover is its connection to the larger staffing problems that plague the educational system. Hence, from a policy perspective, the data suggest that improving teacher retention could be an important antidote to school staffing problems.

However, this earlier work did not include any analysis, or evaluation, of the quantity of the supply of teachers and did not investigate field-to-field differences in the adequacy of supply. Teacher turnover may be a significant factor, but remaining empirically unaddressed is the question of the extent to which particular fields, such as mathematics and science, do indeed suffer from an insufficient supply in the production of new teachers. In this new study, we build on this previous work by combining, analyzing, and comparing comprehensive national data on the actual quantity of qualified teachers supplied from different sources, the quantity of student enrollment, and the quantities of teacher retirement, attrition, and migration. We also build on this prior work by disaggregating the data and comparing different fields. Specifically, we focus on and compare the

The teacher shortage thesis:

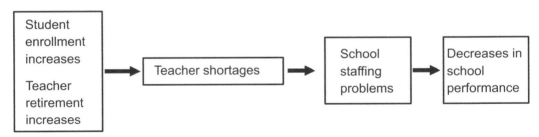

An organizational perspective:

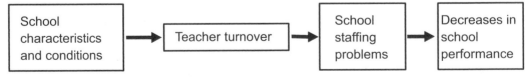

Figure 6.1 Two perspectives on the consequences of school staffing problems.

data for mathematics and science, considered shortage fields, with the data for other kinds of teachers, especially English, typically considered a surplus field. The objectives of this new study are to empirically ground the debate over mathematics and science teacher shortages; to evaluate the extent to which there is, or is not, sufficient supply of teachers in these fields; and to test our alternative perspective for the fields of mathematics and science and English.

Research Questions

There are four sets of specific research questions we seek to address:

1. What is the magnitude of demand for new teacher hires and the magnitude of school staffing problems? Have student enrollments and teacher retirements increased? Has teacher hiring increased? To what extent do schools suffer from teacher hiring difficulties, especially for mathematics and science, in comparison with English?
2. Is the new supply of teachers sufficient? What are the main supply sources of new teacher hires for mathematics, science, and English? What are the magnitudes of these sources? Has the new supply of qualified teachers kept pace with student enrollments and with teacher retirements? What portion of the new supply of qualified teachers is willing to teach?
3. Do school staffing problems vary by location? Are school staffing problems geographically based or concentrated in particular states, districts, or locales?
4. What is the role of teacher turnover in school staffing problems? What portion of the need for new mathematics and science teachers is accounted for by teachers moving between schools or leaving teaching altogether?

The theoretical perspective we adopt in our research is drawn from organizational theory and the sociology of organizations, occupations, and work. Our operating premise is that in order to fully understand the causes and consequences of

school staffing problems, it is necessary to "put the organization back" into the analysis (cf. Stolzenberg, 1978) and to examine these issues from the perspective of the schools and districts where these processes happen and within which teachers work. Employee supply, demand, and turnover are central issues in organizational theory and research (e.g., Hom & Griffeth, 1995; Price 1977, 1989). However, there have been few efforts to apply this theoretical perspective to understanding staffing problems in education. By adopting this perspective, we seek to discover the extent to which staffing problems in schools can be usefully reframed from macrolevel issues, involving inexorable societal demographic trends, to organizational-level issues, involving policy-amenable aspects of particular districts and schools.

In the next section, we describe our data sources and define key terms and measures. In the following sections of this article, we present our results sequentially for each of our four research questions. We then conclude by discussing the implications of these findings for understanding and addressing the math and science staffing problems of schools.

Data and Methods

Data

To try to provide a more complete and comprehensive understanding of teacher supply, demand, and staffing problems, this study utilizes three different nationally representative data sets. All three are based on surveys undertaken by the National Center for Education Statistics (NCES), the statistical arm of the U.S. Department of Education. Fortuitously, these three data-bases were collected during the same year, allowing us to utilize them in conjunction and, hence, to gain a more comprehensive portrait of teacher supply and demand.

The first source of data for this study is the Schools and Staffing Survey (SASS) and its supplement, the Teacher Follow-Up Survey (TFS), collected by the Census Bureau for NCES. SASS/TFS is the largest and most comprehensive data source available on teacher staffing in elementary and secondary schools. SASS administers questionnaires to a random sample of about 50,000 teachers, 12,000 principals, and 4,500 districts, representing all types of teachers, schools, districts, and all 50 states. NCES has administered SASS on a regular basis; to date, six cycles have been completed: 1987–1988, 1990–1991, 1993–1994, 1999–2000, 2003–2004, and 2007–2008 (see NCES, 2005). We analyze the SASS data items on the numbers of students; the sources, numbers, ages, and qualifications of the teaching force; and the degree of difficulty school administrators report when filling teaching job openings. Our analysis uses data from all cycles of SASS, but we focus in particular on the 1999–2000 SASS. Our data represent all teachers for grades prekindergarten through 12, working part-time and full-time, and from all types of schools, including public, charter, and private.

In addition, all those teachers in the SASS sample who departed from their schools in the year subsequent to the administration of the initial survey questionnaire were contacted to obtain information on their departures. This nationally representative supplemental sample, the TFS, contains about 7,000 teachers. The TFS distinguishes between two general types of turnover. The first, often (and hereafter) called teacher attrition, refers to those who leave teaching altogether. The second type, often (and hereafter) called teacher migration, refers to those who transfer or move to different teaching jobs in other schools. We analyze TFS data items on the rates and magnitude of teacher movements between schools and of attrition from teaching altogether. Our analysis uses data from all cycles of the TFS available, but we focus in particular on the 2000–2001 TFS.

The SASS/TFS data are useful for understanding the existing teaching force; however, these data sources do not provide much information on the new supply of teachers. To obtain data on the latter, we utilize two additional NCES databases. One of these is the Integrated Postsecondary Educational Data System (IPEDS). IPEDS is a comprehensive source of data collected annually from the universe of postsecondary education providers (see NCES, 2003). For our purposes, we focus on the IPEDS data on those who complete both undergraduate and graduate degrees in education (e.g., mathematics education, biology education). We utilize data from the 1999–2000 IPEDS cycle to coincide with data from the 1999–2000 SASS data.

Data on recipients of noneducation degrees (e.g., mathematics, engineering, biology, English) in the teacher supply pipeline come from our final data source, the 2000–2001 Baccalaureate and Beyond Survey (B&B). This survey collected data from a nationally representative sample of 10,030 new recipients of undergraduate bachelor's degrees who graduated during or at the end of the 1999–2000 academic year (see NCES, 2004). This cohort sample was interviewed at the end of senior year in college and a year later, in July 2001. We utilize data from this source to examine new recipients of noneducation undergraduate degrees who entered the teacher supply pipeline to become teachers within 1 year after their graduation. We count these degree completers as being in the pipeline if they met one or more of the following criteria: (a) They obtained a teaching certificate during their senior year or immediately after their graduation; (b) within a year of graduation, they took a national or state teacher certification exam; (c) within a year of graduation, they applied for a teaching job; or (d) within a year of graduation, they actually began teaching.

From the SASS, TFS, and B&B databases, we used data weighted to compensate for the over and undersampling of the complex stratified design of the surveys. To obtain unbiased estimates of the national population of schools, students, and teachers in the year of the survey, we weighted observations by the inverse of their probability of selection.

Methods and Measures

As indicated, our emphasis in this study is on the comparison between mathematics, science, and English teachers. We define a teacher as qualified in a given field if he or she holds an undergraduate or graduate degree in that or a related field. We define qualified mathematics teachers as those who indicated they had completed an undergraduate or graduate major in mathematics, statistics, mathematics education, or engineering. We define qualified science teachers as those who indicated they had completed an undergraduate or graduate major in science education, biology, physics, chemistry, geology, or another natural science. We define qualified English teachers as those who indicated they had completed an undergraduate or graduate major in English literature, English composition, English education, or language arts education.

The theory of supply and demand defines the labor supply as the number of individuals both able and willing to offer their services in a particular line of work, depending on wages and conditions. In this study, we attempt to distinguish and quantify the main sources of teacher supply. We focus in particular on the new supply of teachers, which we define as the pool of those qualified individuals who had not taught the previous year and from which schools can draw potential new hires. The new supply includes two components: first, the pipeline of newly qualified candidates or those actively seeking to be qualified who have not had prior teaching experience; and second, the reserve pool, which includes delayed entrants, who completed their preparation in a prior year but have not previously held regular teaching jobs, and reentrants, who taught previously, stopped for a while, and then returned. We also attempt to examine both those able to teach and those willing to teach, separately and together, by examining both those who are qualified, as defined above, and those qualified who actually seek employment as teachers. This distinction is useful to discern different sources of staffing problems; for instance, is the problem an insufficient quantity of qualified candidates produced or an insufficient quantity of qualified candidates willing to teach?

From the perspective of the teacher shortage thesis, the term shortage is typically assumed to be a result of insufficient production of new teachers in the face of increasing student enrollments and teacher retirements (Figure 6.1). This is a narrower definition than typically used in supply-and-demand theory, which defines a shortage as any imbalance where the quantity of labor demanded is greater than the quantity supplied given the prevailing wages and conditions. In supply-and-demand theory, such imbalances can result from a variety of factors, including those hypothesized by both perspectives in Figure 6.1. Here we use the term in the context of examining the teacher shortage thesis. Our focus is on empirically distinguishing and evaluating the magnitude and sources of staffing problems underlying the labels and terms used. From our data sources, we have been able to create several indicators and criteria to empirically evaluate the extent to which the new supply of teachers is, or is not, sufficient.

The first of our indicators, trends in the pupil-teacher ratio, examines changes over time in the number of qualified and employed teachers compared to changes in the number of students enrolled, by field. This addresses the question, Has the quantity of qualified math and science teachers employed kept pace with increases in student enrollments?

Our second criterion is the replacement rate, the ratio of the quantity of new supply of teachers to the quantity of those leaving teaching, for instance, because of retirement. This addresses the question, Has the new supply of qualified math and science teachers been sufficient to replace losses due to retirement and other factors?

A third indicator we use is the employment rate, the proportion of new qualified candidates in the pipeline who seek teaching jobs and enter employment as teachers. This addresses the question, How much of the new supply has been willing to teach and has been successful in finding a teaching job?

Limitations of Data and Measures

Our objective is to empirically test the two main tenets of the teacher shortage thesis: whether the quantity of new supply has been sufficient to keep up with student enrollment and with teacher retirement increases. But we do not address the question of whether the quantity of teacher supply is ideal or optimal or whether it is sufficient to meet an ideal or optimal level of demand. Determining these would entail first defining desired class sizes, desired teacher-pupil ratios, desired graduation requirements, and so on. In this study, we define demand in a typical sense as schools' need for teachers, based on the number of teachers actually hired and employed.

This study also does not focus on, or distinguish, the quality, character, fit, effectiveness, or performance of teachers. Our data cannot indicate whether there is, or is not, a sufficient supply of highly effective or high-quality math and science teachers. Nor do the data indicate whether there are, or are not, sufficient numbers of qualified math and science teachers who have the unique characteristics to be effective in particular settings, such as urban schools or private religiously oriented schools. All of the latter are, of course, crucial issues from both a practical and a policy perspective. But parallel to most analyses of labor supply and demand, we focus on the quantity of qualified and willing candidates.

It is unclear whether our data sources (IPEDS, B&B, and SASS) allow us to reliably estimate the numbers of qualified teachers for each of the separate disciplines within the multidisciplinary field of science. This limitation is especially pertinent for physics, because the latter is a numerically smaller discipline than either biology or chemistry and is often cited as having the most severe shortages (e.g., National Academy of Sciences, 2007; U.S. Department of Education. 2009). Some of those who prepare to become science teachers obtain a degree in science education. Often, these degrees require recipients to concentrate or major in one or two of the several specific science disciplines. However, our data sources (IPEDS, B&B, and SASS) do not indicate in which of the science discipline(s) these science education degree holders were qualified.

As mentioned, because of the necessity of utilizing three data sources in conjunction, we focus on the 1999–2000 school year because our databases were all, fortuitously, collected during that year. But this raises the question of whether such data are outdated and no longer relevant. For several reasons, we do not think this is a problem. Teacher shortages, especially for mathematics and science, are not new, and indeed, almost identical concerns have been voiced periodically for decades. Moreover, as we will show, the 1999–2000 data are especially useful for testing the teacher shortage thesis because the data reveal that the 1999–2000 school year was the high point in the proportion of secondary schools that reported hiring difficulties in mathematics or science over the 20-year period from the late 1980s to 2008. In addition, one of the major factors driving demand—the growth rate of student enrollments—was fastest in the late 1990s, slowing since 1999–2000—again, making that year especially useful for testing the teacher shortage thesis.

Finally, it is important to clarify that for several reasons, our data on the new supply of teachers are biased downward and provide underestimates. Our B&B and IPEDS data on the qualified pipeline do not include those who, while they did not have a major in a field, are qualified because they had passed a subject area test, held a teaching certificate, or had taught in a field. Our pipeline data do not include new recipients of noneducation degrees at the graduate level who entered the pipeline to become teachers. Our pipeline data do not include most midcareer switchers who came into teaching through nondegree, nontraditional routes. In addition, and most importantly, we do not have data on the number of qualified and willing candidates in the reserve pool of delayed entrants and former teachers. In our analyses, we use data from SASS on the number of teachers actually hired from the reserve pool—most likely an underestimate of the total number of those in the reserve pool who are qualified and willing to teach. The implications of this overall downward bias, however, will differ according to what we find in our analyses to follow. Given our underestimates, a finding that the new supply of teachers is sufficient would be strengthened, while a finding that the new supply of teachers is insufficient would be weakened.

Results

What Is the Magnitude of Demand for New Teacher Hires and the Magnitude of School Staffing Problems?

After declining through the 1970s, total elementary and secondary public and private student enrollments have increased. Data from SASS in Table 6.3 show that since the late 1980s, student enrollments have increased by almost one fifth (row 1). The data in Table 6.3 also document that there has been an aging of the teaching force. The percentage of teachers 50 years or older has greatly increased (row 3a), as has the number of teacher retirements (row 4a). Our background analyses of the SASS/TFS data indicate that the modal age of retirement for teachers is 59 and the modal age of the teaching force in 2007–2008 was 55. This suggests that the number of teachers retiring will probably continue to increase until about the 2011–2012

school year, the point at which it will probably be at an all-time high and after which the number retiring will probably begin to decline.

Given increases in both enrollments and retirements, not surprisingly, the SASS data also show that for any given year, most schools have had job openings for which teachers were recruited and interviewed, and the number of teachers hired annually has increased by almost two thirds over the past two decades (row 2). Interestingly, the size of the teaching workforce has increased at a faster rate than the student population (row 3), a point to which we will return in the next section.

In addition to this increase in teacher hiring, and importantly for our analysis, the SASS data indicate that a substantial number of school principals have reported that they have experienced difficulties finding candidates to fill their teaching job openings for the upcoming school year. Overall, the data show that for the

Table 6.3 Trends in Student Enrollments, the Teaching Force, and Teacher Flows In and Out of Schools

Variable	School Year 1987–1988	1990–1991	1993–1994	1999–2000	2003–2004	2007–2008	Increase 1987–1988 to 2007–2008
I. Total student enrollment (K–12)	45,220,953	44,777,577	46,592,207	50,629,075	52,375,110	53,644,872	19%
2. Total teacher hires at beginning of school year	361,649	387,807	377,135	534,861	537,001	589,786	63%
3. Total teaching force during school year	2,630,335	2,915,774	2,939,659	3,451,316	3,717,998	3,894,230	48%
a. Teachers age 50 or older	527,562	660,434	724,754	1,009,731	1,230,049	1,270,959	141%
4. Total teacher turnover after end of school year	390,731	382,879	417,588	546,247	621,427	NA	59%a
a. Retirees	35,179	47,178	50,242	66,788	87,271	NA	148%a

Note. The data in rows 2 and 4 are calculated at the level of the school. Hires and turnover refer to those newly entering or departing a particular school. Cross-school transfers within districts are counted as hires or as turnover. Within-school reassignments are not counted as either hires or turnover. NA = not available.

a Increase in percentage is for period from 1988–1989 to 2004–2005.

1999–2000 school year, 74% of all secondary schools reported that it was at least "somewhat difficult" filling one or more teaching job openings in one or more of 11 fields, and 49% indicated that it was either "very difficult" or they "could not fill" one or more openings.[2]

Moreover, as expected, the data also show large field-to-field differences in hiring difficulties (see Figure 6.2). For instance, in the field of English, 54% of secondary schools had job openings at the beginning of the 1999–2000 school year, but only about one tenth of these —representing 5% of all secondary schools— indicated that it was "very difficult" or they "could not fill" these openings. On the other hand, for science, 56% of secondary schools had job openings for teachers in this field, and about 35% of these indicated serious difficulties filling these openings, representing 18% of secondary schools. Of the fields represented in Figure 6.2, mathematics experienced among the most serious hiring and recruitment problems: 54% of secondary schools had job openings for mathematics teachers, and about 41% of these indicated serious difficulties filling these openings, representing about 22% of all secondary schools.

In sum, over the past two decades, student enrollments and teacher retirements have increased, as have demand for and hiring of teachers. In any given year, a sizable minority of secondary schools reported hiring difficulties in mathematics or science. Our analyses of the other cycles of SASS, from the early 1990s to 2008, reveal that the 1999–2000 school year was the high point in the proportion of secondary schools that reported serious hiring difficulties in mathematics or science (see 6.3). This makes the 1999–2000 data especially useful for testing the teacher shortage thesis. What is not clear, thus far, are the sources of, and reasons for, both the need for new teacher hires and the accompanying difficulties filling those positions, a question to which we turn in the next several sections.

Is the New Supply of Teachers Sufficient?

While student enrollments, teacher retirements, and the demand for new hires have all increased and, moreover, many principals have reported hiring difficulties, what do the data indicate about whether there is a sufficient supply of teachers? Table 6.4 provides data from all three of our sources to address this question. It is similar to Table 6.3 but focuses in more detail on the school year 1999–2000, when hiring problems were at a high point, and focuses on three specific

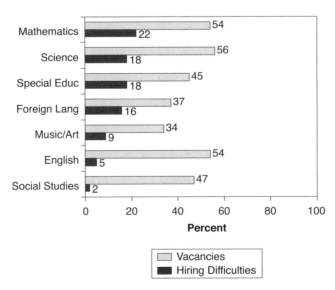

Figure 6.2 Percentage of secondary schools with teaching vacancies and with serious difficulties filling those vacancies, by field (1999–2000).

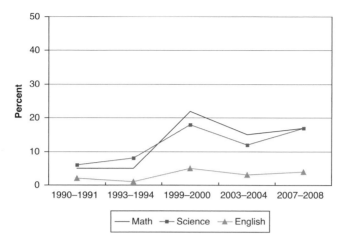

Figure 6.3 Trends in percentage of secondary schools reporting serious difficulties filling teaching vacancies, by field (1990–2008).

Table 6.4 Teaching Hires, Turnover, and Supply, 1999–2000

Variable	All	English	Science	Math	Source
1. Total teacher hires at beginning of 1999–2000 year	534,862	50,920	35,382	29,188	SASS
(i) Newly qualified entrants: from programs, with no experience	100,377	10,827	6,831	5,230	SASS
(i) Delayed entrants: with no teaching experience	52,103	4,847	4,339	1,649	SASS
(ii) Reentrants: with prior teaching experience	79,751	6,703	5,505	4,416	SASS
c. Movers from other schools	302,630	28,534	18,577	17,891	SASS
2. Total teaching force during 1999–2000 year	3,451,316	308,632	223,080	182,456	SASS
3. Total teacher turnover after end of 1999–2000 year	546,247	48,450	39,979	28,166	TFS
a. Migration: movers to other schools	268,642	25,003	18,352	14,416	TFS
b. Attrition: leavers from occupation (including retirees)	277,605	23,447	21,627	13,750	TFS
(i) Retirees	66,788	7,100	3,935	3,915	TFS
4. Total new supply of teachers in pipeline at end of 1999–2000 year	347,138	21,372	12,413	7,969	IPEDS/ B&B
a. With education bachelor's and master's	189,554	3,313	2,390	2,173	IPEDS
b. With noneducation bachelor's and exam, certified, applied, or taught	157,584	18,059	10,023	5,796	B&B

Note. SASS 5 Schools and Staffing Survey; TFS 5 Teacher Follow-Up Survey; IPEDS 5 Integrated Postsecondary Educational Data System; B&B 5 Baccalaureate and Beyond Survey.

fields: mathematics, science, and English. It presents data on the flows of new hires into schools at the beginning of that school year, the size of the teaching force at midpoint in the school year, the departures of teachers from schools after the end of that school year, and the new supply of teachers produced in the pipeline by the end of that same year.

Reading down the first column, for all teachers, Table 6.4 indicates that there were just under 3.5 million teachers in the K–12 education system in the 1999–2000 school year (row 2). About 535,000 of these teachers entered their schools at the beginning of the school year (row 1). Of these, 302,630 of the total hires to schools were movers—that is, they moved from another school (row 1[c]). Another 232,231 were entrants from the new supply who had not taught the prior year. This latter group includes those from the pipeline of newly qualified entrants from preparation programs (row 1a[i]) and entrants from the reserve pool (rows 1b[i] and 1b[ii]).[3] By the following school year, 546,247 teachers had moved from their school jobs or left teaching (row 3). Just under half of these total departures—268,642— moved to other schools to teach (row 3a). Another 277,605 left teaching altogether (row 3b). Of the latter, 66,788 were

retirees. Simultaneously, at the end of the 1999–2000 academic year, there were 189,554 new recipients of education degrees at either the undergraduate or graduate level (row 4a) and 157,584 new recipients of noneducation degrees at the undergraduate level in the pipeline (row 4b).

Figure 6.4 illustrates two important points from Table 6.4 about these sources of newly hired math and science teachers. First, those with education degrees are not the sole or even primary source of the new supply of teachers in the pipeline. Second, the pipeline is not the sole or even main source of new teacher hires; more new hires come from the reserve pool than directly from preparation programs and higher education institutions.

How can we use the data to empirically evaluate whether the teacher supply is or is not sufficient? Our first criterion, trends in the pupil-teacher ratio, examines changes in the number of qualified and employed math and science teachers compared to changes in the number of enrolled students.

As shown in Figure 6.5, the total number of K-12 students increased by 19% during the past two decades. Overall, the teaching force increased at over twice the rate—by 48%—of

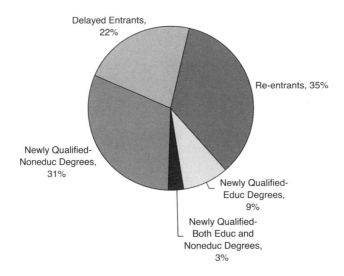

Figure 6.4 Percentage of math and science teachers newly hired in the school system, by supply source (1999–2000).

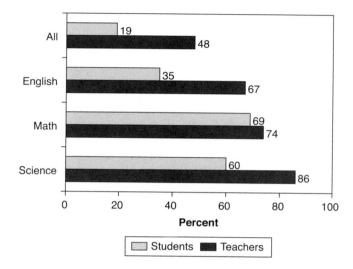

Figure 6.5 Percentage increase in students and qualified employed teachers, by field, from 1987–1988 to 2007–2008.

overall student enrollments. Elsewhere, we present a closer examination of the reasons behind this relatively dramatic growth in the teaching force in the past two decades (see Ingersoll & Merrill, 2010); our focus here is on examining whether the employment of English, math, and science teachers has kept pace with student enrollment growth.

The SASS data show that during this same period, the average number of years of English course work required by public schools for high school graduation increased slightly, from 3.7 to 3.9 years of instruction; English course taking by students increased by 35%; and the number of qualified English teachers employed went up by 67%.[4]

The number of courses required for high school graduation has been smaller for both math and for science than for English, and also there have been proportionately fewer math or science teachers employed than English teachers (see Table 6.4). In 1987–1988 the ratio of math to English required courses was about .6, and the ratio of math to English teachers employed was about the same. However, during the 20-year period from 1987–88 to 2007–08, average high school graduation requirements for mathematics and science increased at a faster rate than for any other core academic field—by .7 years of instruction. The number of students enrolled in mathematics and science courses also increased—by 69% and 60%, respectively. The number of qualified mathematics and science teachers employed in schools even more dramatically increased. Math teachers rose by 74%, from about 120,000 to 208,000. Science teachers rose by 86%, from about 127,000 to 237,000. Interestingly, the data also show that the fastest rate of increase in the employment of qualified math and science teachers occurred during the 1990s, before the advent of the No Child Left Behind Act (2001). Moreover, our analyses of the IPEDS data also show that growth in the employment of math and science teachers has also outstripped growth in the production of those completing undergraduate or graduate degrees in science education, math education, math, or the sciences. We also disaggregated the science data by discipline especially to examine physics. We found that student enrollments in physics courses increased by 28% during that same period, and the number of employed teachers with degrees in physics also increased by the same amount. But as mentioned earlier, such within-science estimates must be interpreted with caution.

During this period, average class sizes at the middle and secondary level changed little, while there was a slight increase in the number of class periods teachers taught per day. Math class sizes have been just slightly less than the average for all subject-area courses at the middle and secondary levels. Science class sizes have been about average, with the exception of physics class sizes, which have been 25% smaller on average than others.

In sum, the data indicate that despite a rapid increase in math and science graduation requirements and student course taking over the past two decades, the number of qualified math and science teachers employed has more then kept pace. The numbers of math and science teachers have increased at a rate far greater than the average for all teachers. Math and science class sizes are close to the average and have changed little over the past two decades. This, of course, does not mean the math and science teacher supply is ideal—that would depend on defining desired pupil-teacher ratios and class sizes and so on. But the data do suggest that math and science teacher production and recruitment efforts have been more than successful in keeping pace.

Our second evaluative criterion is the replacement rate, the ratio of the quantity of new qualified candidates being supplied to the quantity of those permanently leaving teaching, for instance, because of retirement. The All column in Table 6.4 appears to suggest that overall, there are more than enough prospective teachers produced in the pipeline to replace the loss of existing teachers through attrition. While over 347,000 new candidates were produced in the pipeline at the end of the 1999–2000 year (row 4), only about 277,000 left teaching at the end of that same year (row 3b), and of these, only about 67,000 did so because of retirement (row 3b[i]). But is there a sufficient quantity of teachers supplied each year in specific fields, such as English, mathematics, and science, to replace losses?

The English column in Table 6.4 shows that at the end of the 1999–2000 year, there were just over 21,000 degree holders produced in the pipeline who were eligible to teach English (row 4). This includes about 3,000 language arts education and English education majors and a much larger number of English majors (18,059) who pursued teaching. This new supply of 21,372 English teachers was 3 times the number of English teachers who retired (7,100) (row 3b[i]) but slightly less than the total number of those who left teaching at the end of that same year (23,447) (row 3b).

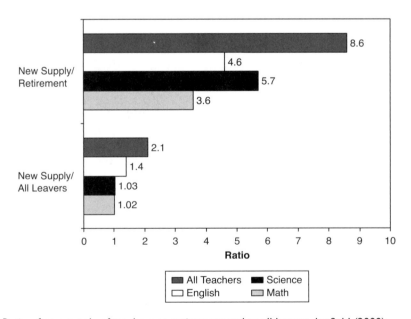

Figure 6.6 Ratio of new supply of teachers to retirement and to all leavers, by field (2000).

Table 6.4 shows that in contrast to English, significantly fewer potential science teachers were produced in the pipeline at the end of the 1999–2000 academic year: 12,413. This pipeline supply of new science teaching candidates was, as in the case of English, over 3 times as large as the number of science teachers who retired that same year (3,935) but was far smaller than the total number of leavers (21,627). A similar portrait holds for mathematics. The 7,969 new mathematics teachers produced by the pipeline at the end of the 1999–2000 year was about twice the number of mathematics teachers who retired (3,915) but was much smaller than the number of all mathematics teachers who left classroom teaching that year (13,750).

The above comparisons, however, leave out the other major source of new supply, the reserve pool. As mentioned, we do not know the total magnitude of the reserve pool, but as shown in rows 1b(i) and 1b(ii) in Table 6.4, we do know how many were actually hired from that pool for the 1999–2000 year. Derived from the table, Figure 6.6 presents a variant of the replacement rate that adds to the pipeline the portion of the reserve pool that ended up employed as teachers that year. Using this estimate of new supply, the figure displays the ratios of the quantity of new supply to the quantity of retirement and also the ratios of the new supply to the quantity of all those leaving teaching.

Adding this portion of the reserve pool to the pipeline shows that the overall new supply of teachers was not only more than sufficient to replace retirees but was also sufficient to replace all attrition. This, however, varies by field, and for mathematics and science, there was a very close balance.

For instance, while there were several times the number of new mathematics or science teachers for every one who retired, there was only about one math or science teacher supplied for every one math or science teacher to leave teaching.

The Figure 6.6 ratios for English, math, and science are not precise and must be interpreted with some caution. As we will next document, some of those in the pipeline delay their entrance into teaching and, by definition, shift from the pipeline to become part of the reserve pool. However, in Figure 6.6, delayed entrants are unavoidably counted twice (in both pipeline and reserve pool), hence overestimating the ratio of new supply to attrition. On the other hand, our ratios also underestimate supply to attrition, because as discussed in the Data and Methods section, our data in the numerators on the new supply of teachers do not include several supply sources, such as midcareer entrants in the pipeline and all qualified and willing candidates in the reserve pool.

We also disaggregated the science data displayed in Figure 6.6 by discipline. For physics, the data show that the variants of the replacement rate were 2.7 for the new supply to retirement and 1.16 for the new supply to all attrition. In other words, the data suggest that as with science as a whole, there was a sufficient supply of qualified physics teachers to replace losses. However, as mentioned earlier, limitations to our estimates of the total numbers of qualified teachers within the science disciplines could introduce error into both the numerators and denominators of our ratios.

Our third indicator assessing the sufficiency of the new supply is the employment rate, the portion of the new supply of qualified candidates in the pipeline who seek teaching jobs and enter employment as teachers. Supply-and-demand analysts often interpret significant numbers of qualified but unemployed candidates as an indicator of a labor surplus. Here we primarily analyze the employment data to discern what portion of the qualified supply is willing, or not willing, to enter the teaching occupation.

To accurately examine the actual employment rates of those in the pipeline, we analyzed the 2000–2001 B&B data on the teaching employment status 1 year after graduation for all of those who completed a bachelors degree at the end of the 1999–2000 year and who entered the pipeline. We focused on a key group and major component of the pipeline: those with noneducation degrees in math, English, or any one of the science disciplines in the teaching pipeline (6.2, row 4b).

As shown in Figure 6.7, the data indicate that large proportions of those in the teaching

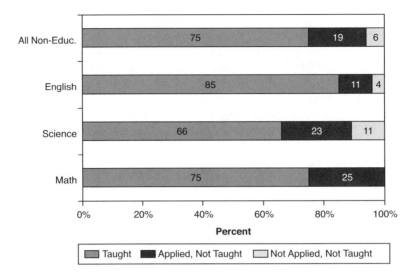

Figure 6.7 Of total new supply of teachers in pipeline with a noneducational bachelor's degree, percentage who taught or applied within one year after graduation, by field (2000–2001).

pipeline who completed degrees in math, science, or English had taught within only 1 year of their graduation (the left portion of the bars). Another significant portion of those with such degrees had applied for teaching jobs but had not taught within a year (the middle portion of the bars). A far smaller portion of those with such degrees had neither applied for a teaching job nor taught within 1 year (the right portion of the bars). Notably, none in the sample of those in the pipeline with math degrees had neither taught nor applied, but it must be cautioned that the math pipeline sample was small ($n = 58$).

Of those in the middle portion of the bars (who had applied for teaching jobs but had not taught within a year), 42% had received an offer for a teaching position. Of these, about half accepted their offers but had not yet begun their teaching job as of the month of the survey (July). Of those who did not accept offers, about half indicated that this was because of dissatisfaction with salary, safety, or location of the school (representing about one tenth of the middle portion of the bar).

Of those in the right portion of the bars (who had neither applied for a teaching job nor taught), less than 1% indicated that a "lack of interest in teaching" was the reason that they

had not applied to teach during their 1st year out of college. In contrast, a far larger number indicated that their reason for not teaching was that they had not passed required tests or obtained proper certification. These breakdowns were generally similar for each of the separate fields, but small sample sizes (30) suggest caution for disaggregating the data within portions of the bars for each field.

Comparable data on the employment rates of those who completed education degrees in math education, English education, and science education (Table 6.4, row 4a) are not available, but the 2000–2001 B&B data do show similar patterns for those with secondary-level subject area education degrees as a whole. Furthermore, our analyses of the earlier 1993 B&B survey data also show that of those in the pipeline who did not teach immediately after finishing their degree, within a decade, almost all had sought teaching jobs at one point or another and over 90% had been employed as teachers.[5]

In sum, the data show that there is a sufficient number of new math and science teachers supplied to keep pace with enrollment and retirement increases. Moreover, the data indicate that of the new supply of teachers in the pipeline, the majority entered teaching right after finishing college, and another portion were delayed entrants who spent a period of time in the reserve pool. Of those few qualified candidates who never taught, some may have been willing to teach but were never hired, and only a very few indicated they were not interested in ever teaching.

Do School Staffing Problems Vary by Location?

Of course, a sufficient or insufficient national supply does not necessarily mean there is a sufficient or insufficient local supply. Indeed, educational analysts have long held that elementary and secondary teaching has a highly localized labor market in contrast to, for instance, the national labor market for professors in higher education. In turn, a widely believed variant of the teacher shortage thesis holds that teacher shortages are not national but vary by location and are geographically based. From this view, shortages are a result of an uneven production of new teachers across states and locales (e.g., Murphy et al., 2004; National Commission on Teaching and America's Future, 1997). Moreover, in this view, barriers to cross-state and cross-district movement, such as a lack of pension portability, nontransferability of certification across states, and little coverage of moving expenses, exacerbate these geographically based shortages (e.g., Curran et al., 2001; State Higher Education Executive Officers Association, 2004). In addition to these structural barriers, a number of studies have shown that those entering teaching tend to prefer to teach in schools like those they themselves attended and, hence, seek teaching jobs close to home (e.g., Boyd, Lankford, Loeb, & Wyckoff, 2005; Loeb & Reininger, 2004). The result of all these factors, analysts argue, is that the teacher supply is unevenly distributed, and the supply available for one district or state is not necessarily available for others.

However, data from various sources raise several questions for this geographically based teacher shortage thesis. First, the IPEDS data do show that the production of new teachers varies across state and region. But it should be recognized that this is not due to a lack of teacher-training programs. The United States is unusual because of its large numbers of accessible, nonselective, low-cost, widely dispersed teacher preparation programs—an average of 25 per state (Lortie, 1975). China, with about 4 times the number of students as the United States, has less than half the number of teacher-training programs (Ingersoll, 2007).

Second, the data show that there are, in fact, large cross-state flows of teachers, and the degree to which the teacher labor market is local, regional, or national varies. Federal data collected under the federal Higher Education Act's Title II (1998 Amendments to the Higher Education Act) indicate that in 2003–2004, over a quarter of applicants for teaching jobs across the nation were from out-of-state candidates. In almost one third of the states, more than one third of the teaching job applications were from candidates certified in other states (Barnes, 2006).

Third, requirements impacting cross-state mobility are not unique to teaching, and the degree to which they are deemed overly burdensome barriers is relative. For example, bar exams in the law profession are partly state based and attorneys moving out of state usually are required to pass an exam in the new state before being allowed to practice. It is unclear to what extent these requirements decrease cross-state mobility of attorneys. However, the law profession in general does not suffer from labor supply shortages; indeed, it is often referred to as a surplus field. At issue is the ratio between requirement and rewards, between costs and benefits, in a given occupation. Even time-consuming and financially costly requirements for cross-state occupational mobility could be deemed acceptable by candidates if the job and occupation are sufficiently attractive. The data suggest that this ratio varies in the teaching occupation. The above Title II data indicate that some schools and school districts in some states clearly have been successful in attracting candidates from a regional or national labor market; others, less so.

Fourth, the largest variations in hiring difficulties and in staffing problems by location are those between different schools, even within the same district. As shown in Figures 6.2 and 6.3, only a minority of schools have serious math and science hiring difficulties in any given year. Our analysis of variance of these data found that variation in reported school hiring difficulties is far greater within, than between, states, and moreover, such variation is far greater between schools than between districts.[6] In other words, within the same state and locale, the same teacher labor market, and the same licensure and pension system, the extent of staffing problems varies greatly among different types of schools. In the same metropolitan area in the same year, some schools could have extensive waiting lists of qualified candidates for their teaching job openings while other nearby schools may have great difficulty filling their teaching job openings with qualified candidates (see, e.g., Liu et al., 2008; National Commission on Teaching and America's Future, 1997).

In sum, discussion of shortages and staffing problems at a national level masks an important part of the diagnosis, which is revealed by disaggregation. The data show that both the production of new teachers through teacher preparation programs and hiring problems are not evenly distributed across different locations. But the largest source of difference in hiring problems is not between regions or states but between schools, even within the same district.

Moreover, that some locations have staffing problems does not necessarily mean they suffer from shortages in the sense that too few new teachers are produced in their particular pipeline. Rather, the data suggest that staffing problems are due to the relative ability, or inability, of particular schools, even within the same district, to ensure that their classrooms are all staffed with qualified teachers drawn from the available supply, whether from the pipeline, the reserve pool, or in state or out of state. All of this suggests that school staffing problems, and apparent imbalances between supply and demand, must be examined from a school and organizational-level perspective to be fully understood. The next section turns to an examination of an alternative source of these school staffing problems.

What Is the Role of Teacher Turnover in School Staffing Problems?

In addition to the level and adequacy of the new supply of teachers, the data in Table 6.4 illuminate several other important points. Because teaching is one of the largest occupations (U.S. Bureau of the Census, 2008), the flows of teachers in and out of schools are numerically large. As shown in Table 6.4, over 64,000 qualified math and science teachers newly entered schools at the beginning of the 1999–2000 school year; by the following year, a larger number—about 68,000 math and science teachers—moved from or left their schools. In other words, during that period, there were over 100,000 job transitions by mathematics and science teachers, representing almost one third of the mathematics and science teaching force. Large outflows, in particular, of teachers likely incur a variety of different costs and benefits and advantages and disadvantages (for a detailed discussion, see Ingersoll & Perda, 2010). Here we focus on one consequence: their connection to math and science staffing problems.

The data in Table 6.4 suggest that the attrition of math and science teachers is linked to the increasing need for new hires and accompanying staffing problems. For instance, at the beginning of the 1999–2000 year, about 16,675 science teachers entered, or reentered, teaching (rows 1a[i], 1b[i], and 1b[ii]), but by the following school year, about 21,627 (row 3b)—equivalent to 130% of those just hired—left teaching altogether. For mathematics, at the beginning of the 1999–2000 year, about 11,300 new mathematics teachers entered teaching, but by the following school year, 13,750—equivalent to about 120% of those just hired—left teaching.

Moreover, although teacher retirements have increased in recent years, as shown in both Tables 6.3 and 6.4, they account for only a portion of attrition. For example, at the end of the 1999–2000 year, there were about 7,850 math and science retirees, accounting for only 22% of all those math and science teachers leaving teaching and 12% of the total math and science teacher turnover during that period. This has been fairly consistent across the five cycles of SASS/TFS from 1988 to 2004 (see Table 6.3, row 4a).

In addition, the data suggest that math and science teacher migration is also linked to staffing problems. Teacher migration between schools, of course, does not decrease the overall net supply of teachers, as does attrition due to retirement and career changes. Hence from a systemwide level of analysis, migration does not contribute to overall shortages. However, from an organizational level of analysis, teacher migration and attrition have the same effect: Both result in a decrease in staff in that particular organization that usually must be replaced, at times with difficulty.

A similar impact holds for temporary attrition—those who leave teaching for a year or more and then return. The latter, of course, do not represent a permanent loss of human capital from the teacher supply; as shown in Table 6.4, the reentrance of former math and science teachers is a major source of new supply. However, from an organizational perspective, temporary attrition, like migration, also results in a decrease in staff that usually must be replaced.

We further empirically tested our alternative hypothesis of a link between math and science teacher turnover and school staffing problems (Figure 6.1) using a school-level of measure of turnover (obtained from principals in the 1990–1991 SASS). Turnover, of course, is one factor leading to job openings and hiring. And in any given year, as shown earlier in Figure 6.2, the majority of secondary schools have job openings in math and science, but only a minority of these reported experiencing serious difficulties filling their openings. The latter schools were almost twice as likely, and at a statistically significant level, to have had above-average turnover rates the prior year as those schools reporting no difficulties. This held true for both teachers leaving and teachers moving.

In sum, the data show that the majority of the hiring of new mathematics and science teachers is simply to fill spots vacated by other math and science teachers who departed their schools at the end of the prior school year. And the majority of these departures are not a result of a

"graying workforce." Rather, math and science migration and preretirement turnover are primary factors behind the need for new hires and the accompanying difficulties some schools have adequately staffing math and science classrooms with qualified teachers. In other words, our alternative organizational perspective reveals that one negative consequence of math and science teacher turnover is its connection to the larger math and science staffing problems that exist in a significant minority of the school population.

In a companion study, we followed up by more closely focusing on the rates, destinations, variations, and determinants of mathematics and science teacher turnover in public schools (see Ingersoll & May, 2010). Here we briefly summarize our main findings. Average annual total turnover rates for math and science teachers increased slightly since the early 1990s to 2005, but notably, mathematics and science teachers have not had, on average, significantly higher rates of turnover than other teachers. The data also show that there are large differences in rates of math and science turnover between different schools, even within the same district. The data showed that the bottom quartile of schools had an average annual turnover rate of 8% in 2004–2005. In contrast, the top 25% of public schools had an average annual turnover rate of 32% and accounted for 45% of all turnover. High-poverty, high-minority, urban and rural public schools have among the highest rates of both attrition and migration of math and science teachers. Moreover, in the case of those moving between schools, there is a large annual asymmetric reshuffling of a significant portion of the math science teaching force, with a net loss on the part of poor, minority rural and urban schools and a net gain to nonpoor, nonminority suburban schools. Over half of math and science teachers who departed reported that the reason was primarily to pursue another or better job or because of dissatisfaction with some aspect of the teaching job—many times the number of teachers who departed because of retirement. In detailed multivariate, multilevel analyses, we found that among the strongest school predictors of mathematics and science teacher turnover in public schools were the degree of student discipline problems in schools, the degree of individual classroom autonomy held by teachers, the provision of useful content-focused professional development, and professional development concerning student discipline and classroom management; for science teachers, an additional predictor was salary levels.

Conclusions and Implications

Contemporary educational thought holds that one of the pivotal causes of inadequate student performance is the inability of schools to staff classrooms with adequately qualified teachers, especially in mathematics and science. One of the most prominent explanations holds that the root of these staffing problems are shortages primarily resulting from an insufficient supply of math and science teachers in the face of increasing student enrollments and increasing teacher retirements (e.g., Liu et al., 2008; U.S. Department of Education, 2002). What do the data in our analysis indicate?

The data show that in any given year, a significant number of schools experience difficulties filling their classrooms with qualified candidates; that there are large school-to-school variations in the extent of these hiring difficulties, even within the same school district; and that math and science are the most severely effected fields. In 1999–2000, when hiring difficulties were at a 20-year high point, about 7,200, or 31%, of secondary schools reported that they had serious difficulty finding qualified teachers to fill either their mathematics or science teaching openings. The data also show that the reasons for these math and science school staffing problems are more complex and varied than simply an insufficient production of new teachers.

There are multiple sources of the new supply of math and science teachers. A relatively minor source was the pipeline of the newly qualified with education degrees. Far larger sources were those in the pipeline with non-education degrees in math and science, and the reserve pool.

The data show that the math and science teacher supply, from all of the above sources combined, has been more than sufficient to cover both student enrollment and teacher retirement increases. Despite an increase over the past two decades in graduation requirements for math and science, and a subsequent dramatic rise in math and science course taking by students, the data show that the employment of qualified math and science teachers has more than kept pace, while class sizes have remained stable. Moreover, the number of newly qualified mathematics and science teachers produced in the pipeline has been more than sufficient to cover increases in mathematics and science teacher retirements. These findings are further reinforced because our data sources are downward biased and provide underestimates of the new supply of math and science teachers.

Nevertheless, a significant number of schools each year report serious problems filling their math and science teaching openings. An important source of these problems is preretirement losses of teachers—a figure that is many times larger than losses due to retirement— and a primary factor behind the need for new hires. Mathematics and science teachers have had about the same annual rates of attrition as other teachers. But unlike, for instance, the case of English teachers, the educational system does not enjoy a surplus of new mathematics and science teachers relative to losses. For mathematics and science, there was a much tighter balance between the new supply and total attrition. Moreover, an annual migration of math and science teachers from some schools to others also contributes to the difficulties the former schools face in ensuring that their mathematics and science classrooms are staffed.

The data also show that there are large differences in rates of math and science turnover between different schools, even within the same district. There are many factors behind these school differences in teacher turnover. A major set of factors involves the attractiveness of the teaching job and teachers' dissatisfaction with aspects of their schools.

It is useful to reiterate some limitations to our study, introduced earlier in the Data and

Methods section. While the data indicate that there is sufficient new supply of qualified math and science teachers to cover increases in student enrollments and increases in teacher retirements, our study does not address the question of whether the supply of math and science teachers is ideal or optimal—that would depend on defining desired pupil-teacher ratios, class sizes, and graduation requirements. Moreover, our study focuses on qualified teachers; we do not address the issue of the quality, character, fit, performance, or effectiveness of such teachers. In addition, our data may not accurately indicate whether there is sufficient new supply for each of the separate disciplines with the larger field of science. Finally, our study indicates that teacher turnover contributes to staffing problems. Our study does not suggest that all teacher turnover is negative or that 100% retention could, or should be, a goal of schools.

From the framework of supply-and-demand theory, any imbalance between labor demand and supply can technically be referred to as a shortage, in the sense that there is an inadequate quantity of individuals able and willing to offer their services under given wages and conditions.

From this framework, the situation we find— math and science staffing problems in a significant portion of schools significantly driven by migration and preretirement attrition—can technically be referred to as a shortage. However, in the context of teachers and schools, the term shortage is typically given a narrower connotation: an insufficient production of new teachers in the face of increasing student enrollments and increasing teacher retirements. These terminological and diagnostic differences have crucial implications for prescription and policy.

Where the quantity of teachers demanded is greater than the quantity of teachers supplied given the prevailing wages and conditions, there are numerous possible policy responses. Recruiting new qualified mathematics and science candidates has long been a dominant strategy, and nothing in this study suggests that this is not worthwhile. Indeed, our data appear to show that this approach has yielded results; in the past two decades, there has been a disproportionately large increase in the employment of qualified mathematics and science teachers. Of the many examples of recruitment approaches, one strategy that has been less emphasized—yet is suggested by our data analysis—is to further tap into the large reserve pool of former teachers.

But the data indicate that teacher production and recruitment strategies alone do not directly address a major root source of mathematics and science teacher staffing problems—turnover. This analysis suggests that recruiting more teachers, while an important first step, will not fully solve school staffing inadequacies if large numbers of such teachers then depart in a few years (see, e.g., Fowler, 2008; Liu, Johnson, & Peske, 2004). Again, the turnover of mathematics and science teachers is especially important to address because these fields do not have the same large "cushion" of new supply enjoyed by fields such as English. To illustrate, President Bush pledged in his 2006 State of the Union speech to recruit 30,000 new mathematics and science teachers across the nation. However, the data indicate that over 35,000 mathematics and science public and private school teachers left teaching just after the 1999–2000 school year alone. Only about 8,000 of these left because of retirement. Over twice as many indicated that job dissatisfaction was a major factor in their decision to leave. Decreasing the attrition of those recruited by such initiatives could lessen losses of the investment and also lessen the ongoing need for creating new recruitment initiatives. Moreover, production and recruitment strategies alone do not address the role of school-to-school teacher migration in mathematics and science staffing problems.

What alternative policy prescriptions are suggested by this analysis? From the organizational perspective of this analysis, schools are not simply victims of external demographic trends, and there is a significant role for the management of particular schools in both the genesis of and solution to school staffing problems. This analysis suggests the efficacy of improving teacher recruitment and teacher retention simultaneously by improving the attractiveness of the teaching job in those settings that suffer from staffing problems.

Notes

This research was supported by a grant (No. 0455744) from the Teacher Professional Continuum Program of the National Science Foundation. Opinions in this article reflect those of the authors and do not necessarily reflect those of the granting agency. This article draws from earlier papers presented at the Teacher Supply and Demand Symposium at the National Center for Education Statistics, March 2007, Washington, D.C., and the National Commission on Teaching and America's Future Symposium on the Scope and Consequences of K12 Science and Mathematics Teacher Turnover, October 2006, Wingspread Conference Center, Racine, Wisconsin. Thanks are due to Dan McGrath, Tom Carroll, and especially Ellen Behrstock for helpful comments on earlier drafts. Henry May and Elizabeth Merrill provided assistance with the data analyses.

1. In a related study, we closely examine data and research on teacher turnover compared to employee turnover in other occupations and the benefits and costs of teacher turnover. See Ingersoll and Perda (2010).

2. The Schools and Staffing Survey (SASS) school questionnaires asked school administrators, "Were there teaching vacancies in this school for this school year, that is—teaching positions for which teachers were recruited and interviewed?" and "How difficult or easy it was to fill the vacancies for this school year?" in each field. Answers were on a 4-point scale: *easy*, *somewhat difficult*, *very difficult*, and *could not fill*. In Figures 6.2 and 6.3, we counted as having "serious" difficulty those schools reporting either *very difficult* or *could not fill*.

3. In Table 6.4, because of limitations in the SASS teacher questionnaire, many of those enrolled in alternative certification programs during their 1st year of teaching are unavoidably classified as delayed entrants (row 1b[i]) rather than newly qualified entrants from the pipeline (row 1a[i]). Hence, Table 6.4 underestimates the number of those hired from the pipeline.

4. The data in Figure 6.5 for math, science, and English represent students enrolled in and teachers instructing departmentalized subject area courses, predominant at the middle and secondary school levels.

5. Note that our findings in Figure 6.7 showing that most qualified candidates end up teaching at some point appear to contradict the findings of other analyses (e.g., Henke, Chen, & Geis, 2000). Once disaggregated, we found large differences across fields in employment rates.

6. Using a one-way random effects ANOVA model, the data show that the variance component within states is 44 times the size of the variance component between states, and between schools, it is 84 times that between districts.

References

1998 Amendments to the Higher Education Act of 1965. (1998). Available at http://ed.gov/policy/highered/leg/hea98/index.html

American Association for Employment in Education. (2008). *Educator supply and demand in the United States*. Columbus, OH: Author.

Barnes, N. (2006). *Promoting teacher mobility through license reciprocity: What is being done* (Unpublished master's thesis). University of Pennsylvania, Philadelphia, PA.

Behrstock, E. (2009). *Teacher shortage in England and Illinois: A comparative history* (Unpublished dissertation). Oxford University, Oxford, UK.

Blank, R., & Langesen, D. (2003). *State indicators of science and mathematics education 2001–2002: State-by-state trends and new indicators from the 2001–2002 school year*. Washington, DC: Council of Chief State School Officers.

Boyd, D., Lankford, H., Loeb, S., & Wyckoff, J. (2005). The draw of home: How teachers' preferences for proximity disadvantage urban schools. *Journal of Policy Analysis and Management*, 24(1), 113–132.

Curran, B., Abrahams, C., & Clarke, T. (2001). *Solving teacher shortages through license reciprocity*. Denver, CO: State Higher Education Executive Officers Association.

Darling-Hammond, L. (1984). *Beyond the commission reports: The coming crisis in teaching*. Santa Monica, CA: RAND Corporation.

Darling-Hammond, L. (2007). *Recruiting and retaining teachers: What matters most and what can government do?* Washington, DC: Forum for Education and Democracy.

Fowler, C. (2008). The heralded rise and neglected fall of the Massachusetts signing bonus. *Phi Delta Kappan*, 89, 380–385.

Grissmer, D., & Kirby, S. (1997). Teacher turnover and teacher quality. *Teachers College Record*, 99, 45–56.

Henke, R., Chen, X., & Geis, S. (2000). *Progress through the pipeline: 1992–93 college graduates and elementary/secondary school teaching as of 1997*. Washington, DC: National Center for Education Statistics.

Hirsch, E., Koppich, J., & Knapp, M. (2001). *Revisiting what states are doing to improve the quality of teaching: An update on patterns and trends*. Seattle: University of Washington, Center for the Study of Teaching and Policy.

Hom, P., & Griffeth, R. (1995). *Employee turnover*. Cincinnati, OH: South-Western.

Ingersoll, R. (1999). The problem of underqualified teachers in American secondary schools. *Educational Researcher*, 28(2), 26–37.

Ingersoll, R. (2001). Teacher turnover and teacher shortages: An organizational analysis. American *Educational Research Journal*, 38(3), 499–534.

Ingersoll, R. (2003). *Is there really a teacher shortage?* Philadelphia: University of Pennsylvania, Consortium for Policy Research in Education.

Ingersoll, R. (2004). Why some schools have more underqualified teachers than others. In D. Ravitch (Ed.), *Brookings papers on education policy* (pp. 45–88). Washington, DC: Brookings Institution.

Ingersoll, R. (2007). *A comparative study of teacher preparation and qualifications in 6 nations*. Philadelphia: University of Pennsylvania, Consortium for Policy Research in Education.

Ingersoll, R., & May, H. (2010). *The magnitude, destinations and determinants of mathematics and science teacher turnover*. Philadelphia: University of Pennsylvania, Consortium for Policy Research in Education.

Ingersoll, R., & Merrill, E. (2010). Six trends: How the teaching force has changed over the past two decades. *Educational Leadership*. May, 67(8), 14–20.

Ingersoll, R., & Perda, D. (2010). *How high is teacher turnover and is it a problem?* Philadelphia: University of Pennsylvania, Consortium for Policy Research in Education.

Liu, E., Johnson, S., & Peske, H. (2004). New teacher and the Massachusetts signing bonus: The limits of inducements. *Educational Evaluation and Policy Analysis*, 26(3), 217–236.

Liu, E., Rosenstein, J., Swann, A., & Khalil, D. (2008). When districts encounter teacher shortages? The challenges of recruiting and retaining math teachers in urban districts. *Leadership and Policy in Schools*, 7(3), 296–323.

Loeb, S., & Reininger, M. (2004). *Public policy and teacher labor markets*. East Lansing: Michigan State University, Education Policy Center.

Lortie, D. (1975). *School teacher*. Chicago, IL: University of Chicago Press.

Murphy, P., DeArmond, M., & Guin, K. (2004). A national crisis or localized problems? Getting perspective on the scope and scale of the teacher shortage. *Education Policy Analysis Archives*, 11 (23). Retrieved from http://epaa.asu.edu/epaa/v11n23/

National Academy of Sciences. (1987). *Toward understanding teacher supply and demand*. Washington, DC: National Academies Press.

National Academy of Sciences. (2007). *Rising above the gathering storm*. Washington, DC: National Academies Press.

National Center for Education Statistics. (1997). *America's teachers: Profile of a profession, 1993–94*. Washington, DC: Author.

No Child Left Behind Act of 2001. (2001). Available at http://ed.gov/nclb/landing.jhtml

National Center for Education Statistics. (2003). *Integrated postsecondary educational data system* (IPEDS) [Data file]. Washington, DC: U.S. Department of Education.

National Center for Education Statistics. (2004). *2000–2001 Baccalaureate and Beyond Survey* (B&B) [Data file]. Washington, DC: U.S. Department of Education.

National Center for Education Statistics. (2005). *Schools and Staffing Survey (SASS) And Teacher Follow-Up Survey (TFS)* [Data file]. Washington, DC: U.S. Department of Education.

National Commission on Excellence in Education. (1983). *A nation at risk: The imperative for educational reform*. Washington, DC: Government Printing Office.

National Commission on Mathematics and Science Teaching for the 21st Century (the Glenn Commission). (2000). *Before it's too late*. Washington, DC: Government Printing Office.

National Commission on Teaching and America's Future. (1996). *What matters most: Teaching for America's future*. New York, NY: Author.

National Commission on Teaching and America's Future. (1997). *Doing what matters most: Investing in quality teaching*. New York, NY: Author.

National Research Council. (2002). *Learning and understanding: Improving advanced study of mathematics and science in U.S. schools*. Washington, DC: National Academies Press.

Oakes, J. (1990). *Multiplying inequalities: The effects of race, social class, and tracking on opportunities to learn mathematics and science*. Santa Monica, CA: RAND Corporation.

Oakes, J., Franke, M. L., Quartz, K. H., & Rogers, J. (2002). Research for high quality urban teaching: Defining it, developing it, assessing it. *Journal of Teacher Education*, 53(3), 228–234.

Price, J. (1977). *The study of turnover*. Ames: Iowa State University Press.

Price, J. (1989). The impact of turnover on the organization. *Work and Occupations*, 16, 461–473.

Quartz, K. H., Thomas, A., Anderson, L., Masyn, K., Lyons, K. B., & Olsen, B. (2008). Careers in motion: A longitudinal retention study of role changing patterns among urban educators. *Teachers College Record*, 110(1), 218–250.

Rice, J., Roellke, C., Sparks, D., & Kolbe, T. (2008). Piecing together the teacher policy landscape: A policy-problem typology. *Teachers College Record*. Retrieved from www.tcrecord.org/Content.asp?ContentId=15223

Rumberger, R. W. (1987). The impact of salary differentials on teacher shortages and turnover: The case of mathematics and science teachers. *Economics of Education Review*, 6(4), 389–399.

State Higher Education Executive Officers Association. (2004). *Teacher quality initiative*. Denver, CO: Author.

Stolzenberg, R. (1978). Bringing the firm back in: Employer size, employee schooling and socioeconomic achievement. *American Sociological Review*, 43, 813–828.

Theobald, N. (1990). An examination of the influence of personal, professional and school district characteristics on public school teacher retention. *Economics of Education Review*, 9, 241–250.

Tyack, D. (1974). *The one best system*. Cambridge, MA: Harvard University Press.

U.S. Bureau of the Census. (2008). *The statistical abstract* (137th ed.). Washington, DC: U.S. Department of Commerce.

U.S. Department of Education. (2002). *Meeting the highly qualified teachers challenge: The secretary's annual report on teacher quality*. Washington, DC: Author.

U.S. Department of Education. (2009). *Teacher shortage areas nationwide listing 1990–91 to 2009–10*. Washington, DC: Author.

Weaver, T. (1983). *America's teacher quality problem: Alternatives for reform*. New York, NY: Praeger.

7 Curriculum, Pedagogy, and the Transmission of Knowledge

In Chapter 6, we looked at the organization and structure of U.S. schools. In this chapter, we will examine what goes on inside of the schools by focusing on curriculum and teaching practices. As we argued in Chapter 4, sociologists of education suggest that schools produce important cognitive and noncognitive results and affect students' lives in significant ways. The important question, however, is how do the schools do this? The answer, in part, lies in what the schools teach and how they teach it. This chapter explores these issues in detail.

What Do the Schools Teach?

Teachers and students in teacher education programs too often think in very simplistic terms about what the schools teach. Their answer to the question is that the schools teach a specific curriculum, one that is mandated by the state education department and implemented in an organized manner within the schools. This view defines the curriculum as an objective and organized body of knowledge to be transmitted to students. Unfortunately, such a view simplifies the complexity of the curriculum and ignores the social and political dimensions of what is taught in schools.

Traditional approaches to the curriculum have been concerned with the science of the curriculum. These approaches view the curriculum as objective bodies of knowledge and examine the ways in which this knowledge may be designed, taught, and evaluated. Using a technical-rational model, traditional curriculum theorists and curriculum planners are not concerned with why the curriculum looks as it does, but rather with how it can be effectively designed and transmitted to students. Students in teacher education programs, from this perspective, are taught to design curriculum using goals and objectives, and to evaluate it in terms of the effectiveness of student learning. Although there may be some practical merit for prospective teachers to understand how to develop curriculum strategies, these traditional approaches eschew important political, sociological, historical, and philosophical questions about what is taught in schools. The effects of such teacher education practices is that teachers look at the curriculum from this "objectivist" perspective and therefore seldom question critically the central component of what they do on a daily basis: transmit knowledge and values to students.

Beginning in the 1960s and 1970s, sociologists of education and curriculum began to challenge the traditional theories of curriculum. Rather than viewing curriculum as an objective body of knowledge, they suggested that the curriculum is an organized body of knowledge that represents political, social, and ideological interests. The "new sociology of education" ushered in by the works of Michael F. D. Young (1971) and Basil Bernstein (1973a, 1973b, 1977) in Britain looked critically at the curriculum as a reflection of the dominant interests in society and suggested that what is taught in schools is a critical component of the effects of schooling.

Drawing on the insights of the sociology of knowledge (Berger & Luckmann, 1967; Durkheim, 1947, 1954; Mannheim, 1936; Marx & Engels, 1846/1947), the new sociology did not view the curriculum as value neutral, but rather as the subject for critical and ideological analysis. Although the new sociology certainly had a radical flavor to it and inspired what has been labeled "critical curriculum theory" (Apple, 1978, 1982a, 1982b; Giroux, 1981, 1983a, 1983b), the insights of the sociology of curriculum do not always have a radical perspective. What is important about the sociological approach to the curriculum is that it rejects the view that the curriculum is objective and instead insists that the curriculum be viewed as subjectively reflecting particular interests within a society. What these interests are and how the curriculum reflects them is a question of ideological debate as well as for empirical investigation.

We will return to sociological studies of the curriculum later in this chapter. First, we will examine the historical and philosophical dimensions of the curriculum. Whereas the sociology of curriculum analyzes what is taught in schools, the history of the curriculum examines what was taught, the politics of the curriculum examines the battles and conflicts over what is and should be taught, and the philosophy of the curriculum examines what ought to be taught and why.

The History and Philosophy of the Curriculum

The history of the curriculum helps explain why the curriculum looks as it does today. Kliebard (1986), in his book *The Struggle for the American Curriculum: 1893–1958*, outlines four different types of curriculum in the twentieth century: humanist, social efficiency, developmentalist, and social meliorist, each of which had a different view of the goals of schooling.

The *humanist curriculum* reflects the idealist philosophy that knowledge of the traditional liberal arts is the cornerstone of an educated citizenry and that the purpose of education is to present to students the best of what has been thought and written. Traditionally, this curriculum focused on the Western heritage as the basis for intellectual development, although some who support this type of curriculum argue that the liberal arts need not focus exclusively on the Western tradition. This curriculum model dominated nineteenth-century and early twentieth-century U.S. education and was codified in the National Education Association's Committee of Ten report issued in 1893, "which recommended that all secondary students, regardless of whether they intended to go to college, should be liberally educated and should study English, foreign languages, mathematics, history, and science" (Ravitch, 1983, p. 47).

Although the view that a Western liberal arts curriculum for all secondary students did not remain the dominant model of secondary schooling in the twentieth century, conservative critics have called for a return to the humanist curriculum. As we noted earlier, critics such as Bennett (1988), Hirsch (1987), and Ravitch and Finn (1987) have argued that U.S. students do not know enough about their cultural heritage because the school curriculum has not emphasized it for all students. They have proposed that schools should return to a traditional liberal arts curriculum for all students and that this curriculum should focus, although not necessarily exclusively, on the Western tradition. Bennett (1988), as Secretary of Education during the Reagan administration, took an activist posture in promoting such curriculum reform. In his proposals for a model elementary and secondary curriculum, he emphasized the need for a traditional core of subjects and readings that would teach all students a common set of worthwhile knowledge and an array of intellectual skills.

From a functionalist perspective, the conservative curriculum reformers of the 1980s and 1990s believed that the purpose of schooling was to transmit a common body of knowledge in order to reproduce a common cultural heritage. As we noted earlier, the problem with this view, from a conflict perspective, is that it assumed a common culture. It is this disagreement about the role of schools in transmitting a common culture that was at the heart of disagreements over curriculum in the twentieth century.

The *social efficiency curriculum* was a philosophically pragmatist approach developed in the early twentieth century as a putatively democratic response to the development of mass public secondary education. As we suggested in Chapter 3, the introduction of the comprehensive high school was marked by the processes of differentiated curriculum, scientific management of the schools and the curriculum, and standardized testing of students for placement into ability groups and/or curriculum tracks (Oakes, 1985, Chapter 2; Powell, Farrar, & Cohen, 1985, Chapter 5). Rather than viewing the need for a common academic curriculum for all students, as with the humanist tradition, the social efficiency curriculum was rooted in the belief that different groups of students, with different sets of needs and aspirations, should receive different types of schooling. Although this perspective emerged from the progressive visions of Dewey about the need for individualized and flexible curriculum, many critics (Cremin, 1961; Hofstadter, 1966; Sadovnik, 1991a; Tyack, 1974) believe that the social efficiency curriculum was a distortion of his progressive vision.

The publication of the *Cardinal Principles of Secondary Education* in 1918 by the National Education Association's Commission on the Reorganization of Secondary Schools represented a direct contrast to the humanist tradition of the Committee of Ten. This report ushered in what Ravitch (1983, p. 48) termed *pedagogical progressivism* and stressed the relationship between schooling and the activities of adults within society. Given the stratified nature of adult roles, the school curriculum was tailored to prepare students for these diverse places in society. The result, as we argued in Chapter 3, was that students often received very different curricula, based on their race, class, and gender. In criticizing the distortion of early progressivism, Ravitch (1983, p. 48) wrote, "The social efficiency element of the *Cardinal Principles*, which inverted Dewey's notion of the school as a lever of social reform into the school as a mechanism to adjust the individual to society, became the cornerstone of the new progressivism." It is important to note the distinction made between this new progressivism and its social efficiency bent and the principles of Dewey, which we believe were profoundly distorted by this view of curriculum.

The development of the social efficiency curriculum in the twentieth century was related to the scientific management of the schools. Based on the writings of Frederick Taylor about the management of the factory system, the administration of schools began to mirror this form of social organization, with its emphasis on efficiency, time on task, and a social division of labor (see Callahan, 1962; Tyack, 1974; Tyack & Hansot, 1982). The scientific management of the curriculum involved both the division of knowledge into strictly defined areas and its transmission into scientifically defined goals and objectives, as well as the division of students into different aspects of the curriculum, based on ability. Beginning in the early twentieth century, the definition of ability became increasingly based on performance on standardized tests.

The development of standardized testing was inextricably related to the differentiation of the curriculum. At the elementary school level, intelligence tests and reading tests were used to assign students to ability groups and ability-grouped classes. At the secondary level, standardized tests, as well as previous school achievement (and other factors not related to ability), were used to place students into different curriculum tracks: academic, for college-bound students; vocational, to prepare students directly for the postsecondary world of work; and general, which usually was an academic curriculum taught at a lower level. These practices, which will be discussed later in this chapter, became a defining characteristic of U.S. education. The important point, however, is that the development of standardized testing became the process by which students were placed in different curriculum tracks, putatively in a fair and meritocratic manner. The extent to which such placement has been meritocratic (i.e., based on ability) has been a controversial and hotly debated issue. It will be discussed in Chapter 9.

Putting the fairness of curriculum placement aside for the moment, the basic assumption of the social efficiency curriculum that different groups of students should receive different curricula has come increasingly under criticism from both conservatives and radicals. Conservatives argue that the separation of the curriculum into different tracks has led to the denigration of the traditional purpose of schooling—to pass on a common culture to all citizens. Radicals argue that the placement into curriculum tracks has been based on race, class, and gender, and thus has limited the life chances of minority, working class, and female students, who, because they are often more likely to elect or wind up in general or vocational tracks, are less likely to go on to college. These are empirical questions that will be discussed in Chapter 9.

The important point is that the curriculum tracking associated with the social efficiency curriculum is a subject of considerable research and debate. Moreover, many critics question the moral basis of providing different students with such radically different school experiences. This issue returns us to the very nature and purpose of schooling in a complex and diverse society: Should it be the same for everyone or should it be variable and flexible, given the diverse nature of the social division of labor?

The *developmentalist curriculum* is related to the needs and interests of the student rather than the needs of society. This curriculum emanated from the aspects of Dewey's writings related to the relationship between the child and the curriculum (Dewey, 1902), as well as developmental psychologists such as Piaget, and it emphasized the process of teaching as well as its content. This philosophically progressive approach to teaching was student centered and was concerned with relating the curriculum to the needs and interests of each child at particular developmental stages. Thus, it stressed flexibility in both what was taught and how it was taught, with the emphasis on the development of each student's individual capacities. Moreover, the developmental curriculum stressed the importance of relating schooling to the life experiences of each child in a way that would make education come alive in a meaningful manner. The teacher, from this perspective, was not a transmitter of knowledge but rather a facilitator of student growth.

Although school and curriculum historians (Kliebard, 1986; Spring, 1989) pointed out that the developmental curriculum model was not very influential in the U.S. public schools, they also noted that it has been profoundly influential in teacher education programs, as well as an important model in independent and alternative schools. It was in the private, independent sector that this view of curriculum and pedagogy first became dominant, with Dewey's progressive principles implemented in a number of independent progressive schools, such as Bank Street (Antler, 1987), City and Country (Pratt, 1924), Dalton (Semel, 1992), Putney (Lloyd, 1987), and Shady Hill (Yeomans, 1979).

Furthermore, in the 1960s and 1970s, the reemergence of what Ravitch (1983, pp. 239–256) called *romantic progressivism* occurred, placing its philosophical allegiance squarely within this form of curriculum and pedagogy. Among its most radical proponents was the British psychoanalyst and educator A. S. Neill, whose boarding school, Summerhill, had no required curriculum and became a prototype of the "open" and "free" schools of the period.

Although the influence of the developmental curriculum has been marginal in public schools (Cuban, 1984) and its advocacy waned in the conservative era of the 1980s and 1990s, there are still remnants of it in both the public and private sectors. In the private sector, many of the early progressive schools still exist and in varying degrees still reflect their early progressive character. Some, such as Bank Street, and City and Country, remain faithful to their founders' visions; others, such as Dalton, have been transformed considerably into a more traditional humanist model (Semel, 1992). In the public sector, the whole-language movement for teaching reading and writing is developmental in its approach. Rather than teaching reading and writing through traditional basal readers, it relates literacy instruction to the experiences and developmental stages of children (Bennett & LaCompte, 1990, p. 186).

The *social meliorist curriculum*, which was philosophically social reconstructionist (the radical wing of progressive education), developed in the 1930s, both out of the writings of Dewey, who was concerned with the role of the schools in reforming society (James, 1995; Semel & Sadovnik, 1999), as well as a response to the growing dominance of the social efficiency curriculum. Two of the most influential of the social meliorists were two Teachers College (Columbia University) professors, George Counts and Harold Rugg, who radicalized Dewey's philosophy into an explicit theory that the schools should change society, or, at the least, help solve its fundamental problems. In books such as Counts's *Dare the Schools Build a New Social Order?* (1932) and Rugg's writings on curriculum, these critics proposed that the school curriculum should teach students to think and help solve societal problems, if not to change the society itself.

Although this view of curriculum never challenged the dominance of the social efficiency model, it has continued to influence curriculum theory in the United States and elsewhere. The social meliorist tradition is the precursor to what is called *contemporary critical curriculum theory*, with Apple and Giroux's work the most important examples. Additionally, philosophers such as Maxine Greene and Paulo Freire, discussed in Chapter 5, adopt a consciously social meliorist view of curriculum, which stresses the role of the curriculum in moving students to become aware of societal problems and active in changing the world. Although these writings are sometimes presented to prospective teachers in teacher education programs, the effects of the social meliorist model in public schools is minimal. For the most part, it has been the social efficiency curriculum, much more than the other three models, that is responsible for what is taught in U.S. schools.

The social efficiency curriculum resulted in the organization of the curriculum into distinct tracks. Although we will discuss the stratification of the curriculum later in this chapter, it is important to note that the degree of overlap between various segments of the curriculum varied according to the type of school and its philosophy of curriculum. Bernstein (1977) argued that curriculum may be either strongly classified (i.e., where there is a strong distinction between academic subjects such as mathematics, science, history, literature, music, art, etc.) or weakly classified (i.e., where there is integration and overlap between academic subjects, such as mathematics and science, social studies, humanities—including history, literature, art, music, etc.). Additionally, in the social efficiency curriculum there may be strong classification between academic and vocational curricula, with students taking the majority of their courses in one area or the other, or weak classification, with students taking courses in both areas. There have been both philosophical and sociological factors in the organization of the curriculum.

From a philosophical vantage point, traditionalists (conservatives) supported the humanist curriculum model and the strong classification between academic subjects. This was necessary, they argued, to properly transmit the traditional cultural knowledge. Progressives tended to support a more integrative curriculum, discouraging the separation of subjects. In many of the early progressive schools, such as the Lincoln School in New York City, an integrative core curriculum revolving around common themes rather than subjects was favored. This approach reappeared in the 1990s in the contemporary whole-language movement and in the thematic core curriculum at New York City's now closed Central Park East Secondary School, Urban Academy, and other public progressive schools.

From a sociological vantage point, the organization of the curriculum has been stratified according to the social class composition of the school. Elite private schools, for example, have always had a humanist curriculum with strong classification between academic subjects. Public high schools have had a social efficiency curriculum with strong classification between academic and vocational subjects. Within the public system, the degree to which the academic track has mirrored the humanist curriculum has varied, often in relation to the social class composition of the students. Progressive private and public schools have had a weakly classified academic curriculum that reflected their particular philosophy of education, but, as Bernstein (1977) suggested, this philosophy reflected their particular middle- and upper middle-class preferences. Thus, the organization of the curriculum has not been and is not now a simple matter. It relates to philosophical, sociological, and political factors. We now turn to the sociological and political dimensions.

The Politics of the Curriculum

The politics of curriculum analyzes the struggles over different conceptions of what should be taught. As we have noted, the history of the U.S. curriculum may be understood in terms of different models of school knowledge. Throughout the twentieth century, various groups, both inside and outside schools, fought to shape and control the schools' curriculum. Labeling these groups and determining their degree of control is still the subject of debate. For example, functionalists, subscribing to a pluralist democratic model of schooling, believe that the curriculum represents a democratic consensus about what should be taught. Neo-Marxist conflict theorists believe that the dominant capitalist class controls what is taught in school. Non-Marxist conflict theorists believe that many groups struggle over the curriculum, with different groups winning and losing at different historical periods.

Ravitch (1983) has documented the long and conflictual struggles that have marked U.S. educational history. Her history of education in the twentieth century reveals a pattern of conflict between various groups about the purpose and goals of the schools. Within this context, the curriculum became contested terrain—the subject of heated controversy and disagreements. Earlier in this chapter, we presented the four curriculum models that predominated in the twentieth century; in this section, we will discuss the politics of curriculum and how various groups attempt to shape the curriculum to reflect their own interests and ideologies.

The central question in the politics of the curriculum is: *Who shapes the curriculum?* As the new sociology of education suggests, the curriculum is not a value-neutral, objective set of information to be transmitted to students; rather, it represents what a culture wants its students to know. From this perspective, curriculum represents culturally valued knowledge. The question remains, however: Whose values are represented and how do groups manage to translate their values into the subjects that are taught in school?

These questions are first and foremost related to power. The ability to shape the curriculum requires that groups have the power to affect the selection of instructional materials and textbooks. There are two models of political power used by political scientists. The first, the pluralist model (Dahl, 1961), argues that the political system in the United States is not controlled by any one group; rather, the decisions are made through the input of many groups, each attempting to exercise influence and control. The second, the political elite model (Domhoff, 1967, 1983; Mills, 1956), argues that a small number of powerful groups (i.e., those with wealth and political influence) dominate the political landscape and have disproportionate control over political decision-making.

Although the controversy over which of the two views is correct has not been settled, we believe that the reality, as in most controversies, lies somewhere in the middle. The U.S. political system allows for participation from many groups, but it also requires a great deal of money and power to successfully affect political decisions. On this level, the political elite model finds considerable support. Nonetheless, the evidence does not support the view that less powerful groups cannot win some of the time or that a ruling elite manages to control the political arena. For example, the ability of a coalition of community groups in New York City to defeat the proposed Westway Project (to rebuild the collapsed West Side Highway), which was supported by the most powerful and wealthy interests in the city, is an example of the ability of the less powerful to sometimes emerge victorious. Thus, political decision-making is a complex, conflictual process in which many groups vie for advantage, with those with more wealth and power having distinct advantages but not total domination. In the educational arena, these conflicts are certainly apparent.

Conflicts over curriculum are more likely to occur in public schools than in private ones. The reason for this is fairly clear. Parents who send their children to private or parochial schools do so, in part, because they support the particular school's philosophy. Where there are conflicts in the private sector, it is usually about disagreements within a particular philosophical or religious tradition, as opposed to between two or more different philosophies. In the public sector, however, there is rarely agreement about educational matters, and thus the curriculum, like other aspects of the educational system, is the focus of considerable debate. In a society with diverse cultural groups, it is inevitable that what the schools teach will not be the product of consensus. The questions are: How do all of the groups affect what is taught in classrooms, and which groups are successful in accomplishing this task?

Kirst (1984, p. 114) has outlined the different levels of influence on the school curriculum in Table 7.1. As the table indicates, there are multiple factors that influence curriculum policy making at the national, state, and local levels. Curriculum decisions occur through a number of different channels, including the legislative and executive branches of government; the levels of the school system; and other interests, including professional associations, bureaucratic interests, and private interests (such as business and parent groups). As we discussed in Chapter 6, unlike many countries where there is governmental control of education and thus a national curriculum, education in the United States is controlled at the state and local levels. Therefore, curriculum policy making is, for the most part, a state and local matter, although in the last decade the federal government has taken an increasingly activist role in education. Nonetheless, the federal government, through its Department of Education or through the president himself, is one part of the process, not the determining factor.

Although each of these political actors just listed has input into the curriculum, it is evident that all do not have equal input. If there is any one group with more influence than the others, it is the education profession itself, consisting of state-level educational bureaucrats, administrators at the district and school levels, and teachers. The traditional humanist curriculum and the social efficiency curriculum, which have dominated U.S. education to a large degree, reflect the values

Table 7.1 Influences on Curriculum Policy Making

	National	State	Local
General Legislative	Congress	State Legislature	City Council (usually has no influence)
Educational Legislative	U.S. House Committee on Education & Labor	State School Board	Local School Board
Executive	President	Governor	Mayor (usually has no influence)
Administrative School	U.S. Department of Education	State Department of Education	Superintendent
Bureaucratic	National Science Foundation (Division of Curriculum Improvement)	State Department of Education (Division of Instruction)	Department Chairmen, Teachers
Professional Association	National Testing Agencies such as Educational Testing Services (ETS)	Accrediting Association; State Subject Matter Affiliates, National Education Association	County Association of Superintendents
Private Interests	Foundations & Business Corporations, Political & Service Organizations		

Source: Wirt and Kirst (1972).

and interests of professional educators. Moreover, as Ravitch (1983) and Kliebard (1986) noted, the struggle over the U.S. curriculum has involved primarily educators and revolved around different philosophies of education.

Although there is no denying that there have been influences from outside the educational establishment—including students, parents, and politicians—their influence has not been nearly as significant. The U.S. curriculum has reflected the professional values of educators. Additionally, it mirrored the increased power of expertise in the twentieth century. As Collins (1979) argued, the rise of professions has led to the use of professional expertise as a means of influence. In the case of the curriculum, professional educators have made valuable use of their expertise as a means to legitimate their control over the curriculum.

Despite the dominance of professional educators in determining the curriculum, other groups have sought control with varying degrees of success. More often than not, conflicts over the curriculum have symbolized significant political and cultural conflicts. For example, in 1925, amid the fundamentalist religious movements of the period, the Scopes Trial reflected the tensions between schooling and particular groups opposed to the official curriculum. More importantly, the trial represented the role of the school in reflecting the values of a modern society and the opposition of those still faithful to traditional societal values.

This trial involved the prosecution of a Tennessee biology teacher, John Scopes, who violated the state law prohibiting the teaching of evolution and requiring the teaching of creationism. In the decades following the publication of Darwin's *On the Origin of Species* (1859), conflict between secular theories of evolution and religious theories of creationism raged on. Backed by the American Civil Liberties Union, Scopes used a biology textbook that taught evolution and was arrested. The trial, which literally became a circus and a symbol of the conflict between the old and the new, involved two important individuals in U.S. political and legal history: William Jennings Bryan, the populist leader and fundamentalist crusader, who assisted the prosecution, and Clarence Darrow, the liberal legal crusader, who represented the defendant. In Tennessee, where fundamentalism was widely accepted, and with a judge who was clearly biased against Scopes (Garraty, 1985, p. 430), the defendant was found guilty and fined $100.

This case represented the battle between the values of the secular modern world and the values of the traditional religious world. Despite the belief of the majority of educators that evolution was the correct scientific interpretation, the power of a conservative state legislature to shape the curriculum won out, at least temporarily. Over the years, however, the professional expertise of scientists has been dominant. Today, fundamentalists are still trying to eliminate the teaching of evolution or to include creationism as a viable alternative theory.

In the 1940s and 1950s, controversies over curriculum were widespread. As part of the intellectual attack on progressive education, a number of educational and cultural critics argued that progressivism had watered down the traditional curriculum and replaced it with a social efficiency curriculum. Critics such as Arthur Bestor (1953) called for a return to the classical humanist curriculum and to an emphasis on the intellectual functions of schooling.

Whereas many of these critiques were based on academic and intellectual grounds, some of the conflicts revolved around blatantly political issues. With the rise of anticommunism during the McCarthy Era (where alleged Communists were brought before the House on an Un-American Activities Committee and a Senate Investigative Committee chaired by Senator Joseph McCarthy of Wisconsin), the school curriculum became the subject of political turmoil. Anti-Communist groups pressured school districts to eliminate textbooks and instructional materials that they believed to be Communist. Moreover, progressive education, as a whole, was seen as part of a Communist conspiracy and labeled REDucation (Ravitch, 1983, p. 105). During this period, books by noted progressive educators such as Harold Rugg were banned in many districts, teachers at both the K–12 and university levels were required to take loyalty oaths, and many teachers and professors were dismissed as Communists or Communist sympathizers. This was a period in which conservatives actively sought to control what was taught in school, both by controlling the curriculum and the faculty.

One of the best examples of the politics of schooling during this period occurred in Pasadena, California. In 1948, Willard Goslin, a celebrated progressive educator, was hired as superintendent. As Cremin (1990, pp. 87–88) noted, for the next two years, a strongly organized group of conservatives attacked the superintendent's policies, the school curriculum, and its teaching methods. In 1950, under considerable pressure and amid continual conflict, Superintendent Goslin was forced to resign. Cremin has suggested that this case is a prime example of the historical tendency for Americans to use politics as a means for controlling education, with political disagreements often a key aspect of the fight for control.

Although this period was a shameful era in U.S. history, Ravitch (1983) pointed out that the incidents of book banning were by no means the rule. Many districts successfully battled the book-banning activists. Moreover, by the 1950s, the tide began to turn, with both the legislative and judicial branches reacting against McCarthyism. However, during this time, conscious efforts were made to control what was taught in schools, and the wounds inflicted did not easily heal.

During the past 20 or so years, new controversies surrounding the curriculum have emerged. In the 1970s through the 1990s, conservative groups argued that many books—including Ken Kesey's (1977) *One Flew Over the Cuckoo's Nest*, Richard Wright's (1969) *Native Son*, and Joseph Heller's (1985) *Catch 22*—were unsuitable for use in public schools. In some districts, books were banned and taken off reading lists and library shelves. Recently, the state of Arizona has implemented legislation banning ethnic studies curricula.

Although the cases of book banning are the most sensational examples of the attempt to control curriculum, the struggle over what is conveyed to students occurs in more routine ways, such as in the selection of textbooks. Kirst (1984, pp. 118–122) provided an illuminating discussion of the factors affecting textbook adoptions. He suggested that a number of forces—including the economics of publishing, the dominance of those states such as Texas and California with statewide adoption policies, the clout of political pressure groups, the guidelines of professional associations, and the input of educators—all combine to create a complex and politically charged process. The attempt to meet the demands of such a complex and often contradictory set of pressure groups leads to what many critics suggest are textbooks with little controversy and less life (Sewall, 1991). According to Kirst, although textbook publishers are constantly concerned with which group they will offend and thus risk losing market share, they are unfortunately less concerned with such significant issues as content and presentation.

The difficulties in textbook publishing are part of a larger curricular issue—that is: What is the appropriate content of the curriculum? In the 1980s, the question of what should be taught became a difficult and controversial subject. Beginning with the conservative claim that U.S. students know very little because the schools have abandoned their traditional role in transmitting the nation's cultural heritage, questions about the definition of the cultural heritage became central to curriculum debates. While conservatives such as Finn and Hirsch argued that the school curriculum should consist largely of the Western tradition, liberals and radicals countered that this tradition unfairly ignored the important traditions of non-Western groups, people of color, women, and other minority groups.

This controversy affected both the K–12 level and the postsecondary level. At the K–12 level in New York state, a commission was appointed in 1990 by Commissioner of Education Thomas Sobel to revise the social studies curriculum in light of the demands of some groups for a more multicultural curriculum and the counterclaims by other groups that such demands were both racist and encouraged historical inaccuracies. On the one hand, supporters of multicultural curriculum charged that the traditional curriculum was ethnocentric and reinforced the low self-esteem of minority groups because they rarely were presented with historical role models. On the other hand, conservative critics responded that in order to give equal time to all groups, the teaching of history would be revised in a distorted and inaccurate manner (Ravitch, 1989).

The conflict between parental values and the curriculum was clearly illustrated in New York City in 1992 when District 24 in Queens objected to the New York City Board of Education's new multicultural curriculum. This curriculum was titled "Children of the Rainbow" and it called for the teaching of tolerance for homosexual families to elementary school children. Outraged parents and community leaders, first in District 24 and then throughout New York City, challenged the curriculum, arguing that schools do not have the right to teach "immoral" values to children. Proponents of the curriculum argued that the intent behind the curriculum was to foster tolerance and respect for all groups and that the schools were the appropriate place for such an education.

Some of the curriculum's optional teaching materials, including "Heather Has Two Mommies" and "Daddy Has a Roommate," became the focus of heated conflict between New York City Chancellor Joseph Fernandez and a number of local school boards. The Chancellor suspended the District 24 Community School Board for refusing to comply with the curriculum or to offer a suitable alternative; the Board of Education reinstated the community school board and called on all parties to reach a compromise that would maintain the integrity of the multicultural curriculum. Although the conflict has yet to be resolved fully, the issue has revealed strong feelings about homosexuality and the fact that significant numbers of parents are strongly opposed to schools teaching what parents consider values to their children. It also underscores the political dimension of the curriculum and how the often moral aspects of such political conflict become educational issues. In the aftermath of this conflict, the New York City Board of Education did not renew Fernandez's contract. Although attitudes have liberalized since then, with many states passing laws permitting gay civil unions and/or marriage, the backlash has also been considerable with many states, such as North Carolina, passing constitutional amendments banning such unions and marriages. These differences continue to manifest them in heated curricular debates.

At the postsecondary level, debates about the need for a core curriculum for all students and what that core should be have raged from campus to campus. At Stanford University, for example, the requirement that all undergraduates take a core curriculum stressing Western civilization was abolished after considerable controversy and was replaced with requirements stressing multiculturalism. At Columbia University, where undergraduates have for decades taken a core curriculum stressing Western civilization, the curriculum has been retained despite vigorous criticism. However, the University of Chicago has decided to revise its curriculum.

By the early 1990s, the term *politically correct* became part of the popular culture. It referred to definitions of what is construed as acceptable language, curriculum, and ideas. It was initially coined by campus conservatives who argued that universities were dominated by radicals who conspired to alter the traditional curriculum and who "censor" all ideas that they deem offensive (e.g., see D'Souza, 1991; Kimball, 1990). Critics responded that the university has always reflected the dominant interests of society and that the curriculum is in dire need of revision in a more democratic and representative manner. In the 2000s these debates have continued on campuses throughout the United States.

Although there have been serious debates on many campuses on the important philosophical issues underlying these disagreements—such as the purpose of higher education and the nature of a literary canon, or whether one exists—to a large degree, the media has simplified the issue of political correctness in such a way that it has become a symbol not for the critical questions it raises but for the putative silliness of university life. More importantly, the conflicts over curriculum correctness and free speech (that is, whether individuals have the right to say offensive things, and who decides what is and what is not offensive have raised the specter of McCarthyism and all the ugliness that it represented).

What is clear from these examples is that curriculum debates are hotly contested because they represent fundamental questions about the purposes of schooling. The transmission of knowledge, as we have suggested, is never objective or value neutral. Rather, it represents what particular interest groups believe students should know. Because there is little agreement about this, it is no surprise that there is significant conflict over the content of the curriculum. We have also suggested that the shaping of the curriculum is a complex process with many groups having input; but if there is one dominant group in this process, it is professional educators whose expertise enables them to justify their claims. However, professional educators are not a cohesive interest group, so many of the most heated curriculum debates involve disagreements within this group about the nature and purpose of the curriculum.

The Sociology of the Curriculum

Sociologists of curriculum have focused on not only what is taught but why it is taught. As we have mentioned, sociologists of curriculum reject the objectivist notion that curriculum is value neutral; rather, they view it as a reflection of particular interests within a society. Additionally, sociologists believe that the school curriculum includes both what is formally included as the subject matter to be learned—the formal curriculum—as well as the informal or hidden curriculum. The hidden curriculum includes what is taught to students through implicit rules and messages, as well as through what is left out of the formal curriculum. For example, very few undergraduate or graduate students can list more than one nineteenth-century American feminist. In fact, many do not know that there was a feminist movement in the nineteenth century (for a complete discussion, see Leach, 1980). Why is this the case? We believe it is because the history of women has never been a part of the school curriculum. Certain ideas, people, and events are not part of the curriculum because those who formulate it do not deem them important enough. From the standpoint of the formal curriculum, this is a political and social statement; in terms of the hidden curriculum, students receive a message that these things are just not important, which ultimately is a powerful force in shaping human consciousness. The sociology of curriculum, as the following discussion will illuminate, is concerned with both the formal and informal curriculum.

The sociology of the curriculum concentrates on the function of what is taught in schools and its relationship to the role of schools within society. As we stated in Chapter 4, functionalist and conflict theories of school and society differ about the roles of schools in U.S. society. Functionalists believe the role of the schools is to integrate children into the existing social order—a social order that is based on consensus and agreement. Conflict theorists believe that the role of schools is to reproduce the existing social order—a social order that represents the dominant groups in society. Based on these differences, the two theories have different perspectives on the school curriculum.

Functionalists argue that the school curriculum represents the codification of the knowledge that students need to become competent members of society. From this perspective, the curriculum transmits to students the cultural heritage required for a cohesive social system. Thus, the role of the curriculum is to give students the knowledge, language, and values to ensure social stability, for without a shared common culture social order is not possible.

The general functionalist theory, derived by the work of Emile Durkheim (1962, 1938/1977) in the late nineteenth and early twentieth centuries, was concerned with the role of schools in combating the social and moral breakdown initiated by modernization. As the processes of industrialization, secularization, and urbanization weakened the bonds between people and the rituals that traditionally gave people a sense of community, Durkheim argued that the schools had to teach students to fit into the less cohesive modern world.

Modern functionalist theory, developed in the United States through the works of Talcott Parsons (1959) and Robert Dreeben (1968), stressed the role of the schools in preparing students for the increasingly complex roles required in a modern society. This society, according to functionalists, is a democratic, meritocratic, and expert society (Hurn, 1993, pp. 44–47) and the school curriculum is designed to enable students to function within this type of society. According to Hurn (1993, pp. 193–194), functionalists believe that in the twentieth century, the curriculum had to change to meet the new requirements of the modern world. In this respect, the schools began to move away from the teaching of isolated facts through memorization to the general task of teaching students how to learn. Thus, for functionalists, the specific content of the curriculum, such as history or literature, is less important than the role of schools in teaching students how to learn—a skill vital in an increasingly technocratic society.

In addition to teaching general cognitive skills, functionalists believe that schools teach the general values and norms essential to a modern society. According to Parsons (1959) and Dreeben (1968), modern society is one where individuals are rewarded based on achievement and competence. This meritocratic system is reflected in the way schools operate, with the norm of universalism (that people are treated according to universal principles of evaluation) rather than particularism (that people are treated according to individual characteristics, such as family background, personality, etc.) the basis for evaluation.

Finally, functionalists believe that schools teach students the values that are essential to a modern society. According to this theory, modern society is a more cosmopolitan and tolerant one than traditional society, and schools teach students to respect others, to respect differences, and to base their opinions on knowledge rather than tradition. Such attitudes are necessary in a society where innovation and change are the foundation of technological development, and schools teach students these vitally important things. In summary, the functionalist theory is a positive view of the role of the schools and suggests that what schools teach are the general norms, values, and knowledge required for the maintenance and development of modern society.

According to conflict theorists, who provide a far more radical view of the roles of schools in society, the functionalist perspective of what is taught in schools is more a reflection of ideology than empirical reality. Conflict theorists do not believe that schools teach liberal values and attitudes such as tolerance and respect. Rather, they believe that schools' hidden curriculum teaches the attitudes and behaviors required in the workplace and that the formal curriculum represents the dominant cultural interests in society.

As we pointed out in Chapter 4, Neo-Marxists, such as Bowles and Gintis (1976), believe that the hidden curriculum of the school teaches the character traits, behaviors, and attitudes needed in the capitalist economy. According to their correspondence theory, school organization and processes reflect the social needs of the economic division of labor, with the schools preparing students to fit into the economic order. From this perspective, the hidden curriculum differentially prepares students from different social class backgrounds with the type of personality traits required in the workplace. For example, working-class children attend working-class schools where the values of conformity, punctuality, and obedience to authority are relayed through the hidden curriculum; middle-class children attend middle-class schools where the hidden curriculum is more likely to teach the values of initiative and individual autonomy; upper-class children attend elite private schools where the hidden curriculum rewards independence, creativity, and leadership. Thus, working-class students are prepared for working class jobs, middle-class students are prepared for middle-class jobs, and upper-class students are prepared for leadership positions in the corporate and political arenas. Although, as we will argue later in this chapter, this view of schooling is far too neat and rational, there are significant social class-related differences between schools. We will also show that there are significant curriculum and pedagogical differences *within* schools and that these differences may be as important as the ones *between* different schools.

Whereas Neo-Marxists such as Bowles and Gintis emphasize the importance of the hidden curriculum in the shaping of values, other conflict theorists stress the effects of the formal and hidden curriculum on the reproduction of consciousness (Hurn, 1993, p. 197). According to these social reproduction theorists, such as Apple and Bourdieu, the role of the curriculum is to shape the way people think and in doing so to reproduce the dominant interests of society. Thus, for Apple (1978, 1979a, 1979b, 1982a, 1982b) the school curriculum represents the dominant class, cultural, and gender interests within society, and students internalize these interests as they go through schools. Bourdieu (1973) and Bourdieu and Passeron (1977) argued that the school curriculum represents a form of cultural capital, which separates different groups within the system of social stratification. This cultural capital symbolizes the "high culture" of the dominant groups within society as opposed to the popular culture of the masses.

Since the school system, according to conflict theorists, is highly stratified according to social class, and because students from different social class backgrounds learn different things in school, the cultural capital required for membership in the dominant groups is not universally learned but is acquired by children whose families already possess such knowledge. The system is not completely closed, however, as the system of curriculum tracking teaches at least some students in all secondary schools this high-status knowledge. The important point is that through the cultural capital transmitted through the school curriculum, the class differences in society are reflected not merely in terms of economic wealth and income but through cultural differences. Thus, through a subtle yet complex process, the schools transmit both a common body of knowledge to all students, usually at the elementary school level, and a stratified body of knowledge to students, usually at the secondary level. According to conflict theorists, this process allows for societal reproduction on one hand, and for class and cultural stratification on the other hand.

Hurn (1993, pp. 197–198) suggested that these forms of radical conflict theory are far more ideological than they are empirical. Although they point to a number of important functions of the curriculum, they do not provide sufficient evidence about the nature of the curriculum or curriculum change to support their assertions. Additionally, in arguing that school curriculum both reproduces the overall interests of the dominant groups in society by reflecting their interests and separates groups based on differential access to such a curriculum, the theory never fully explains how this is possible. If the school curriculum functions both as a means of societal reproduction and cultural separation, specifically how does it accomplish this Herculean task? Moreover, the theory needs to document empirically the ways in which the curriculum reproduces social stratification between dominant and subordinate groups by looking at the curriculum and teaching practices in different schools serving different groups. To date, this has not been accomplished sufficiently.

A different variety of conflict theory, which we discussed in Chapter 4, is the neo-Weberian conflict theory of Randall Collins. For Collins, both functionalist and Neo-Marxist conflict theory are far too rational. These theories, according to Collins (1979), posit too cohesive a link between the economy, the workplace, and the schools. If the role of the curriculum is truly to give students the knowledge and skills needed in the workplace, then how does one explain the relatively weak relationship between schooling and work-related skills? Collins has argued that most work skills are learned on the job, not in schools. Further, he has suggested that schools transmit a cultural currency (Hurn, 1993, pp. 198–199) to students through a credentialing process, and that the actual content of what is learned in schools is less relevant than the credential. Thus, it is not that the specific content of the curriculum is functionally related to the workplace, but it is that the credential given by schools reflects the ability of some groups to attain it and the failure of other groups to do so.

For Collins, the link between the school curriculum and the skills required in the workplace is very weak. Moreover, he has stated that the curriculum reflects the interests of various groups rather than one dominant group. If anything, the traditional school curriculum, with its emphasis on the liberal arts and sciences, reflects the cultural beliefs of those who shape the curriculum—the middle-class professional educators who have primary input into curricular matters. It is their cultural values that are represented in schools as much as the values of the upper class.

Finally, this view demonstrates that what is taught in schools must be understood as part of the larger process of cultural conflict and stratification, with school knowledge important not so much for its functional value but for its value in attaining access to specific occupations. It is this belief that the credential is related to occupational performance rather than the fact that it actually is that makes it so important. To the contrary, Collins has suggested that the actual knowledge and skills learned in acquiring a credential do not correlate highly with the actual requirements of most occupations. Therefore, Collins has provided a more cynical and skeptical view of what is taught in schools and has suggested that a more multidimensional view of conflict is required to understand the complexities of the curriculum.

Multicultural Education

The conflict perspective is illustrated nicely by the debates over multicultural education. Beginning in the 1980s, critics of the humanist curriculum argued that the traditional curriculum was Eurocentric and male dominated. They argued that the curriculum had to be transformed to represent the varied voices of the groups that make up the United States.

James Banks (1993; Banks & McGee Banks, 1995, 2009) has been the premier writer on multicultural education over the past three decades. Banks (Banks & McGee Banks, 1995) has made it clear that there is no one definition of multiculturalism and, more importantly, that multicultural approaches are by no means new, but must be traced back to the end of the nineteenth century. He has presented a typology of five dimensions of multiculturalism: content integration, knowledge construction, prejudice reduction, equity pedagogy, and empowering school culture.

Geneva Gay (1995) provided one of the best and most comprehensive discussions of multicultural curriculum theory available. Gay argued that "a high degree of consensus exists among multiculturalists on the major principles, concepts, concerns, and directions for changing educational institutions to make them more representative of and responsive to the cultural pluralism that exists in the United States and the world" (p. 40) and that "educational equity and excellence for all children in the United States are unattainable without the incorporation of cultural pluralism in all aspects of the educational process."

A related component of multicultural education is termed *culturally relevant pedagogy*. Proponents of culturally relevant pedagogy (Foster, 1995, pp. 570–581; Ladson-Billings, 1994, 2004) have described a number of characteristics of successful teachers of African-American students, including having high self-esteem and a high regard for others; seeing themselves as part of the community; believing that all students can succeed; helping students make connections between their community, national, and global identities; and seeing teaching as "pulling knowledge out" (Ladson-Billings, 1994, p. 34). Further, Ladson-Billings (1994, p. 55) described the social relations of cultural relevant pedagogy in the following way: (1) The teacher–student relationship is fluid, extending to interactions beyond the classroom and into the community; (2) the teacher demonstrates a connectedness with all students; (3) the teacher encourages a "community of learners"; and (4) the teacher encourages students to learn collaboratively. Students are expected to teach each other and be responsible for each other.

Conservative critics of multicultural education (see Sleeter, 1995, for an overview) argued that it threatened the foundation of Western civilization and the role of schooling in transmitting this culture. Even liberals such as historian Arthur Schlesinger, Jr. suggested that multicultural education might lead to the breakdown of social order (Schlesinger, 1992). Supporters of multicultural education also raised questions (Semel, 1996). If curriculum and pedagogy, as multiculturalists suggest, need to be culture centered to meet the needs of each group, how does one construct a truly multicultural curriculum out of the diverse and different needs of all the groups that make up this nation's society? If an Afrocentric curriculum is the appropriate culture-centered curriculum for African-Americans, do schools need separate, culture-specific curricula for Asian-Americans, Puerto-Ricans, Mexican-Americans, or White Americans (or for specific white ethnic groups, as well)? Based on their unique histories, problems, and cultures (Takaki, 1993, 1998a, 1998b), the more appropriate question seems to be: How does one revise and expand the curriculum to include multiple culture-centered approaches? If the goal of multiculturalism is rather to produce multiple, but separate, curricula, each tailored to specific groups, then educators may be in danger of what Schlesinger (1992) terms a "disuniting of America." The problem with the conservative critique of multiculturalism that argues for the superiority of the Western canon is that it calls for an either/or stance and assumes a unity that has never existed; however, many multiculturalists (Gordon, 1995; King, 1995) appear to call for the same either/or position (Eurocentric or Afrocentric). Given the diversity of ethnic, race, class, and gender groups in U.S. society, the problem of developing a multicultural curriculum that is both culture centered and not separatist remains one of the greatest challenges in education (see Semel, 1996, for a detailed analysis of multiculturalism).

Curriculum Theory and Practice: The Reconceptualization of Curriculum Studies

For most of the twentieth century, the field of curriculum studies was concerned with relating the study of curriculum to classroom practice. From the child-centered and social-reconstructionist strands of progressive education in the first half of the century (Semel & Sadovnik, 1999) to the professionalization of teacher education (Labaree, 1996), the subject of curriculum studies has often been more concerned with practice than theory and has viewed classroom practice within the narrow confines of schools. Beginning in the 1970s, critical curriculum theorists both in the United States and England questioned the assumptions of curriculum studies and argued that school knowledge represented the socially constructed interests of dominant groups in society (Apple, 1979a, 1992, 1993; Sadovnik, 1991a; Young, 1971).

From the 1970s onward, William Pinar has been the preeminent figure in the reconceptualization of curriculum studies into the field of curriculum theory (Kincheloe, 2010; Pinar, 1975, 1978a, 1978b, 1979, 1988; Pinar et al., 1995). Building on the critical curriculum theory of Apple and others, Pinar integrated both psychoanalytic and postmodern approaches to the curriculum. His approach called for the separation of theory and practice, rather than its traditional integration. Pinar suggested that this separation was necessary for curriculum theorists to have the necessary distance to understand the complex factors that affect practice. However, he also indicated that eventually theory and practice had to be reconnected. He also connected the personal (autobiographical) to the study of schools by relating experience to theory. By the 1990s, reconceptualized curriculum theory had become a dominant voice in the field, with its own national conference.

In the 1990s, amid the calls for teacher education reform that criticized university-based schools of education for failing to adequately connect theory to practice and involve education professors in school improvement (Holmes Group, 1995; Labaree, 1996; National Commission on Teaching and America's Future, 1996), curriculum theory came under fire. Wraga (1997, 1999) argued that the reconceptualization of curriculum studies into curriculum theory has resulted in a false dichotomy between theory and practice, eschewed the historic roles of universities from the 1862 Morrill Act (see Chapter 3) onward to provide practical knowledge for social policy, and created an elitism in education characteristic of the split in the sciences between pure and applied science. Wraga has called for the reestablishment of a Deweyan vision that educational theory must be tested in real-life schools (Wraga, 1999).

The Wraga–Pinar debate reflects much of the educational debate of the 1990s by reducing complex issues to either/or poles. As Dewey noted in *Experience and Education* (1938), both sides of either/ors are usually equally misinformed. Critical curriculum studies and reconceptualized curriculum theory have provided an important corrective to traditional approaches by demanding that scholars examine the social, political, and economic forces outside schools that affect classroom discourse and practice. These approaches have made important contributions to the knowledge of how schools contribute to social inequalities. However, curriculum theorists have often been so detached from the everyday life of teachers and students that they have had little impact on school reform and improvement. As we move deeper into the new millennium, the field of curriculum studies needs to integrate the rich findings of curriculum theory into a more pragmatic approach to school improvement. Such a vision is consistent with Dewey's pragmatism, which stressed the need to balance theory, research, and practice.

Pedagogic Practices: How the Curriculum is Taught

Thus far in this chapter, we have focused on what is taught in schools and why it is taught. As students, you are aware that how something is taught is as important as, and at times more important than, the content. On the most simplistic level, how something is taught is important to you because it can make the difference between learning the material or not learning it. Moreover, we have all sat in classes with teachers who certainly knew their subject matter but did not have the ability or teaching skills to convey it to the class. Conversely, the ability to teach something without the requisite knowledge of the subject matter is equally problematic. Thus, the relationship between curriculum, the content of education, and pedagogy (the process of teaching) is an interdependent one, with each being a necessary but insufficient part of the act of teaching.

On a more complex level, the process of teaching, like the curriculum, is not an objective skill agreed on by all practitioners; rather, it is also the subject of disagreements over what constitutes appropriate teaching practices. Additionally, sociologists of education (Bernstein, 1990; Sadovnik, 1991a) suggest that different pedagogic practices, like different curricula, are differentially offered to different groups of students, often based on class, racial, ethnic, and gender differences.

The Philosophy of Teaching: Differing Views on Pedagogic Practices

Philip Jackson, in his insightful book, *The Practice of Teaching* (1986), provided a thoughtful discussion of the philosophical dimensions of teaching. He suggested that there have been different views about teaching—some see it as an art or craft while others see it as a scientific enterprise with distinct and testable methodological principles. Although the scope of this chapter does not permit us to go into this in detail, this section will outline some of the salient features of the major philosophical viewpoints on teaching practices.

Jackson (1986, pp. 115–145) has distinguished between the two dominant traditions of teaching: the mimetic and the transformative. In Chapters 2, 3, and 5, we referred to progressive and traditional (conservative) models in U.S. education. Using these terms, the mimetic tradition loosely coincides with the traditional (conservative) model and the transformative with the progressive model.

The *mimetic* tradition is based on the viewpoint that the purpose of education is to transmit specific knowledge to students. Thus, the best method of doing this is through what is termed the *didactic method*, a method that commonly relies on the lecture or presentation as the main form of communication. At the heart of this tradition is the assumption that the educational process involves the relationship between the knower (the teacher) and the learner (the student), and that education is a process of transferring information from one to the other. Based on the belief that the student does not possess what the teacher has, the mimetic model stresses the importance of rational sequencing in the teaching process and assessment of the learning process (i.e., a clear statement of learning goals and a clear means to assess whether students have acquired them). The emphasis on measurable goals and objectives has become a central component of many teacher education programs, with the attempt to create a science of teaching often viewed as the key to improving educational achievement.

The *transformative* tradition rests on a different set of assumptions about the teaching and learning process. Although learning information makes the student different than he or she was before, this model defines the function of education more broadly and, according to some, more ambiguously. Simply put, proponents of this tradition believe that the purpose of education is to change the student in some meaningful way, including intellectually, creatively, spiritually, and emotionally. In contrast to the mimetic tradition, transformative educators do not see the transmission of knowledge as the only component of education and thus they provide a more multidimensional theory of teaching. Additionally, they reject the authoritarian relationship between teacher and student and argue instead that teaching and learning are inextricably linked.

Thus, the process of teaching involves not just the didactic transfer of information but the conversation between teacher and student in such a way that the student becomes an integral part of the learning process. Although the lecture may be used in this tradition, the dialectical method, which involves the use of questioning, is at the core of its methodology. Derived from the teaching methods of Socrates, as presented in the dialogues of Plato, and given philosophical grounding in the works of John Dewey, transformative educators believe that all teaching begins with the active participation of the student and results in some form of growth. Exactly what type of growth is desired varies with the specific goals of the classroom, but given the broader spectrum of goals outlined by transformative educators, it is more difficult to assess and measure educational outcomes. Moreover, the transformative tradition tends to reject the scientific model of teaching and instead views teaching as an artistic endeavor.

Dewey was somewhat ambiguous about what he believed to be the goals of education, saying that the goal of education was simply growth leading to more growth (Cremin, 1990, p. 125). However, the transformative tradition has often defined growth within a radical critique of the status quo. Critical theorists such as Freire (1972, 1977, 1978) and Giroux (1983a, 1983b, 1988, 1991), existential phenomenologists such as Greene (1978, 1988), and feminist theorists such as Belenky (Belenky et al., 1986), Laird (1989), and Martin (1987) believe that the purpose of education is to change human consciousness and in doing so begin to change society. These perspectives view teaching as a political activity; its goal is to transform students' minds as the first step in radical social transformation.

For example, feminist theorists (Macdonald & Macdonald, 1981; Miller, 1982; Mitrano, 1979) believe that traditional curriculum and pedagogy reproduce the dominant patriarchal relations of society and reinforce male domination. They teach competition and sexism, rather than cooperation and gender equality. Therefore, feminists suggest that a curriculum and pedagogy that teach caring and that are explicitly anti-sexist are required.

Critical theorists, who are political radicals, argue that traditional curriculum and pedagogy reproduce the consciousness required in a competitive, capitalist society. They suggest that a critical pedagogy is required—one that enables students to critique the dominant ideologies of society and that is explicitly concerned with democratic and egalitarian principles. Thus, for the radical wing of the transformative tradition, growth leading to more growth is unacceptable, as the definition of growth is left at the level of the individual student. What is necessary, they argue, is individual growth that leads to social change. It should be noted also that these contemporary educational theories are examples of the social meliorist tradition outlined earlier in this chapter.

A major difference between the mimetic (traditional) and transformative (progressive) models of teaching relates to the question of authority relations in the classroom. Given the fact that the traditional model views the teacher as the knowledgeable authority in the classroom, traditional classrooms usually have explicit authority relations, with teachers in charge and students in a subservient position. The lesson is usually teacher directed, with students speaking when spoken to and in response to direct questions. The progressive model usually has less authoritarian authority relations in the classroom, with authority internalized within the student rather than in direct response to the teachers' higher authority. Although there are differences in authority, they are often less explicitly structured. Additionally, students usually have more input in their education and the classroom is often more child centered than teacher directed.

It is important to point out that these two models of teaching are ideal types, and that most classrooms are neither totally one nor totally the other. Most teachers combine different methods of teaching and most classrooms are neither totally authoritarian nor totally unstructured. Nonetheless, most classrooms, schools, and teachers lean in one direction or the other, based on philosophical and sociological factors. On a philosophical level, the belief in one model over the other is an essential determinant of classroom practice; on a sociological level, the use of different models appears to correlate with class differences.

For example, Bernstein's (1990) work on pedagogic practices has indicated that the looser authority relations of what he calls invisible pedagogy (usually found in progressive education) are found in schools with middle- and upper middle-class populations; the more authoritarian relations of what he calls visible pedagogy (usually found in traditional education) are found in schools with poor and working-class populations as well as in schools with upper-class populations. Although the poor and the working class seem to receive the same form of pedagogic practices, they receive a very different form of curriculum from the upper class, with the upper class receiving a classical humanist curriculum and the poor and working class receiving a social efficiency curriculum (that often is vocationally based). Bernstein argued that these class differences in pedagogic practices are the result of the different functions of schooling for different groups.

The important point here is that different teaching practices are not the result of philosophical preferences only, nor are they randomly distributed between schools in a nonrational manner. They are also related to sociological factors and may be important in understanding differences in academic achievement between groups. We will explore this in more detail in our discussion of the stratification of the curriculum and again in Chapter 9, when we discuss explanations of unequal educational achievement among different groups.

The Stratification of the Curriculum

As we have noted, the social efficiency curriculum has been the dominant model in U.S. public education since the 1920s. From this period onward, U.S. schools offered a stratified curriculum to students, with some students receiving an academic curriculum and others receiving a vocational or general curriculum. Curriculum stratification (i.e., the division of the curriculum), usually at the secondary school level, is not the only form of differentiation in U.S. schools. Ability grouping, or the separation of students into groups based on putative ability (usually based on standardized tests), is another important form of stratification. Ability grouping begins at the elementary school level with reading and mathematics groups within the same classroom, and is often extended in the upper elementary and middle school levels with separate classes with the same curriculum but different ability levels. These ability groups are often directly related to high school curriculum tracks (different curricula and different abilities) or ability groups (similar curricula and different abilities).

It is important to note that ability grouping and curriculum tracking are related aspects of the curriculum stratification system. Students, from elementary school through college, may be separated according to ability, curriculum, or both. For example, there are a number of different ways that schools organize the curriculum. First, some schools require all students to learn the same curriculum and therefore group students without regard to ability (heterogeneous grouping). Second, other schools require all students to learn the same curriculum and thus group students based on ability (homogeneous grouping). Third, other schools stratify students based on both ability and the curriculum, with high-ability students at the secondary level enrolled in an academic curriculum and low-ability students enrolled in a vocational or general curriculum. Finally, although these differences are found within schools, there are also important differences between schools, both public and private, in terms of their curriculum and pedagogy.

These differences between schools are often based on the social class differences of the students who attend them. They are found at all levels of education through the university, where the U.S. system provides different types of postsecondary education based on both curriculum and ability (e.g., from vocational education and liberal arts education at the community colleges, to liberal arts education at selective elite private colleges and universities, to variations of both at other public and private colleges and universities).

The factors affecting ability group and/or curricula track placement, as well as the outcomes of such placement, have been the subject of considerable debate in the sociology of education. For example, the degree to which track placement is based on meritocratic criteria and actually reflect ability—or the degree to which it is based on nonmeritocratic criteria such as race, class, and gender—are important empirical questions. Additionally, the effects of such placement on the life chances and educational careers of groups of students are likewise crucial to understanding the relationship between schooling and inequalities. These issues will be explored in detail in Chapter 9, which discusses explanations of educational inequality. At this point it is important to understand that U.S. schools are stratified by curriculum and ability, and these differences are reflected both between schools at all levels (e.g., differences between public and private schools at all levels, and differences between public schools at all levels) and within schools through tracking and ability grouping. Further, it is important to understand why such practices exist.

The rationales for curriculum tracking and ability grouping are complex, as they speak to some of the most fundamental questions concerning teaching and learning. First, should all students learn the same things or should different groups of students learn different things, depending on their needs, interests, and future plans? Second, is there a common body of knowledge that all students, regardless of their future plans, should learn? Third, if all students should learn the same things, at least for a part of their education, should they learn them in heterogeneous groups or homogeneous ability groups? That is, given individual differences in ability, can students of different abilities learn the same material at the same pace, without some students falling behind or others being held back? Or is it more effective to teach students of different abilities at different paces in order to ensure that they all eventually learn the same material?

Debates about these questions have been central to U.S. education since the 1920s. In terms of the curriculum, the dominant social efficiency model has accepted the view that all students should not be required to take the same curriculum and that the secondary school curriculum should meet the different aspirations of different groups of students. In terms of ability grouping, the separation of students into homogeneous ability groups, beginning at the elementary level, has been a salient feature of U.S. education from about the same time (e.g., see Oakes, 1985). Moreover, there is often a strong relationship between elementary school ability grouping and secondary school track placement (Hurn, 1993; Oakes, 1985, 2005).

According to Oakes (1985, 2005), ability grouping and tracking have been based on four rationales. The first is that students learn more effectively in homogeneous groups, and that students with different abilities require different and separate schooling. The second is that "slower" students develop a more positive self-image if they do not have to compete with "brighter" students. The third is that placement procedures accurately reflect students' academic abilities and prior accomplishments. The last rationale is that homogeneous groups are easier to manage and teach. Oakes argued that each of these are myths that cannot be supported by empirical evidence and that ability grouping and curriculum tracking have unfairly limited the lives of students from lower socioeconomic backgrounds who are far more likely to be placed in lower tracks. In Chapter 9, we will review the evidence on the effects of these processes; for now, it is important to understand that they have been significant organizational processes in the stratification of curriculum and pedagogy.

The Effects of the Curriculum: What is Learned in Schools?

Thus far in this chapter, we have discussed the organization of the curriculum and its effect on what is taught in schools. It is important to note, however, that what is taught in schools is not necessarily equivalent to what is learned in schools. Much of the discussion about curriculum assumes that the curriculum is important precisely because it affects student consciousness, values, and so on. This is true only to the extent that the school curriculum is actually internalized by students; if it is not (i.e., if the students do not actually learn what is taught or what is in the curriculum), then the claim that schooling transmits important knowledge to students and that it has important social functions may be more ideological than real.

Hurn (1993, pp. 199–201) pointed out that there are a number of methodological problems in studying school effects, in general, and what students learn cognitively and noncognitively, in particular. First, it is difficult to separate school effects from more general processes of childhood and adolescent development. To what extent the increased knowledge of children as they get older is due to schooling and to what extent it is due to developmental patterns and maturation is difficult to ascertain. Second, it is difficult to separate the effects of schooling from other variables, including social class and cultural factors. For example, one may be able to ascertain that students with more education have more academic knowledge than those with lower levels of education or that they may have more liberal political values. However, it is not easy to demonstrate that these differences have been caused by the independent effects of schooling rather than the effects of social class or cultural differences external to the processes of schooling.

Despite these difficulties, some things are known about the effects of schooling that suggest that schools have some important effects on students. First, the evidence indicates that students who have higher levels of educational attainment do know more about school subjects than those with lower levels of attainment. Research on school effects (Hurn, 1993, pp. 201–204) suggests that schooling does increase knowledge; that there is a strong correlation between formal schooling and tests of cognitive skills, such as reasoning, mathematics, and so on; and that evidence from the United States and other societies (Hurn, 1993, pp. 206–216) shows that schools have powerful effects on cognitive development. This evidence suggests that the cynical view of conflict theorists such as Collins (that little is really learned in school and that schooling is mostly a credentialing process) is not fully supported by empirical evidence. This does not refute Collins's claim that school knowledge is not necessary for the workplace (this is a different question), but it does demonstrate that schools do teach things to students (whether it is valuable or not is as much an ideological as it is an empirical question).

A second issue related to the effects of schooling regards the effects of different schools and different tracks within schools. This is a very controversial question, with proponents of the effective school movement arguing that there are specific school characteristics that correlate highly with learning. At the same time, however, there is evidence (Hurn, 1993) to suggest that school characteristics, independent of other factors such as the social class background of students, make little difference in student learning.

Although we will review these disagreements more fully in Chapter 9 in our discussion of education and inequality, it is important to note here that some research on curriculum tracking does provide an important piece of the puzzle. If students in different curriculum tracks within the same school—or more importantly, within different ability groups with similar curricula within the same school—have substantially different educational experiences and this results in vastly different educational learning outcomes, then one may conclude that schooling does have important effects. Oakes's (1985) research on tracking and ability grouping suggested such a process. Although we will suggest in Chapter 9 that these findings are not universally accepted (as it is difficult to rule out the independent effects of outside factors such as family), they do provide some support for the argument that schools affect different groups of students in significantly different ways.

Another important aspect of what students learn in school concerns the noncognitive effects of schooling. Since both functionalists (Dreeben, 1968) and conflict theorists (Bowles & Gintis, 1976) believe that schools teach important societal values and beliefs to students (albeit they disagree about whose values and what they are), it is important to empirically document the actual effects in this area. The empirical evidence is incomplete and inconclusive, but there are some conclusions that may be drawn. First, there is some evidence (Hurn, 1993, p. 205) that increased levels of education lead to greater tolerance, greater openness, and less authoritarianism. Further, the evidence does not support the radical view that schools in capitalist societies teach conformity, docility, and obedience to authority as the only values; the effects of schooling are more complicated. Finally, given the multiple influences on values, including the role of the family and the media, it is difficult to isolate the independent role of schooling. Hurn (1993, p. 218) has suggested:

> Students in contemporary society are exposed to a wide variety of *competing values and ideals* both within schools and in the wider environment, and many of these implicit and explicit messages cancel each other out. Thus although *particular* and *unusual* schools may have quite powerful effects on some students, schooling in *general* cannot be said to have enduring or important effects on one set of attitudes and values rather than another.

Although we agree that the effects of schooling on values and attitudes has been exaggerated by both functionalists and Neo-Marxists, the fact that some schools do have powerful effects on student attitudes, that students in different curriculum tracks are often taught and learn different attitudes, and that students with more education have different attitudes and values does suggest that schools do have some effects on students. That it is difficult, as Hurn points out, to disentangle these effects from other societal institutions demonstrates the complex relationship between schooling and other educating institutions; it does not suggest that schooling is unimportant.

Conclusion

This chapter has discussed the content and process of schooling: curriculum and pedagogy. We have suggested that curriculum and pedagogy are not objective phenomena, but rather must be understood within the context of their sociological, philosophical, political, and historical roots. The curriculum represents what particular groups think is important and, by omission, what they believe is not important. What is included and excluded is often the subject of debate and controversy. Teachers too often are excluded from such decisions, but, as we argued in Chapter 1, you, as teachers, must be part of these debates. Only through an understanding of the complex issues involved can you become active and critical curriculum makers rather than passive reproducers of a curriculum into which you have no input.

Most importantly, we have pointed out that what is taught and how it is taught are complex matters with profound consequences, both for individuals and society. Although there are differences of opinion concerning the effects of curriculum organization and pedagogic practices, it is evident that differences in these areas are not random; they affect different groups of students in different ways. In the next chapters (8 and 9), we will explore the broader question of schooling and inequality, and examine how both factors within the schools, such as curriculum and pedagogy, as well as outside the school, such as family, neighborhood, economics, and other variables, are related to unequal educational attainment and achievement.

The following articles examine issues relating to curriculum and pedagogy. The first article, "The Politics of a National Curriculum," written by curriculum theorist Michael W. Apple, examines the politics of curriculum through an analysis of a national curriculum. Apple argues that the curriculum represents the dominant interests in society, and therefore curriculum decisions are always political and conflictual. Although Apple is not necessarily against a national curriculum, he points out that its proponents represent a particular curriculum ideology.

The second article, "The Mimetic and the Transformative: Alternative Outlooks on Teaching," written by educational theorist and researcher Philip W. Jackson, compares two different models of teaching: the mimetic and the transformative. Through an examination of their basic premises and methods, Jackson demonstrates how each model has been a significant part of the way teachers teach.

The third article, "The Silenced Dialogue: Power and Pedagogy in Educating Other People's Children," written by educator Lisa D. Delpit, analyzes the concept of *culturally relevant pedagogy*, and questions whether one form of pedagogic practice is appropriate for all children.

The Politics of a National Curriculum

Michael W. Apple

Introduction

Education is deeply implicated in the politics of culture. Its curriculum is never simply a neutral assemblage of knowledge, somehow appearing in the texts and classrooms of a nation. It is always part of a *selective tradition*, and is someone's selection, some group's vision of legitimate knowledge. It is produced out of the cultural, political, and economic conflicts, tensions, and compromises that organize and disorganize a society. As I argue in *Ideology and Curriculum* (Apple 1990) and *Official Knowledge* (Apple

1993), the decision to define some groups' knowledge as the most legitimate, as official, while other groups' knowledge hardly sees the light of day, says something extremely important about who has power in a society.

Consider social studies texts that continue to speak of the "Dark Ages" rather than using the historically more accurate and much less racist phrase "the age of African and Asian Ascendancy." Or consider books that treat Rosa Parks as merely a naive African-American woman who was simply too tired to go to the back of the bus rather than discussing her training in organized civil disobedience at the Highlander Folk School. The realization that teaching, especially at the elementary school level, has in large part been defined as women's work—with its accompanying struggles over autonomy, pay, respect, and deskilling—also documents the connections between curriculum and teaching and the history of gender politics (Apple 1988b). Thus, whether we like it or not, differential power intrudes into the very heart of curriculum, teaching, and evaluation. What *counts* as knowledge, the ways in which knowledge is organized, who is empowered to teach it, what counts as an appropriate display of having learned it, and—just as critically—who is allowed to ask and answer all of these questions are part and parcel of how dominance and subordination are reproduced and altered in this society (Bernstein 1977; Apple 1988a). There is, then, always a *politics* of official knowledge, a politics that embodies conflict over what some regard as simply neutral descriptions of the world and what others regard as elite conceptions that empower some groups while disempowering others.

Speaking in general about how elite culture, habits, and tastes function, Pierre Bourdieu (1984, p. 7) puts it this way:

> The denial of lower, coarse, vulgar, venal, servile—in a word, natural—enjoyment, which constitutes the sacred sphere of culture, implies an affirmation of the superiority of those who can be satisfied with the sublimated, refined, disinterested, gratuitous, distinguished pleasures forever closed to the profane. That is why art and cultural consumption are predisposed, consciously and deliberatively or not, to fulfill a social function of legitimating social difference.

As he goes on to say, these cultural forms, "through the economic and social conditions which they presuppose . . . are bound up with the systems of dispositions (habitus) characteristic of different classes and class fractions" (Bourdieu 1984, pp. 5–6). Thus, cultural form and content function as markers of class (Bourdieu 1984, p. 2). The granting of sole legitimacy to such a system of culture through its incorporation

within the official centralized curriculum, then, creates a situation in which the markers of taste become the markers of people. The school becomes a class school.

The contemporary tradition of scholarship and activism has been based on exactly these insights: the complex relationships between economic capital and cultural capital; the role of the school in reproducing and challenging the multitude of unequal relations of power (which go well beyond class, of course), and the roles that content and organization of the curriculum, pedagogy, and evaluation all play.

It is exactly now that these kinds of issues must be considered most seriously. This is a period—which we can call the *conservative restoration*—when conflict over the politics of official knowledge is severe. At stake is the very idea of public education and a curriculum that responds to the cultures and histories of large and growing segments of the American population. Even with a "moderate" Democratic administration now in Washington, many of this administration's own commitments embody the tendencies addressed below.

I intend to instantiate these arguments through an analysis of the proposals for a national curriculum and national testing. But in order to understand these issues, we must think *relationally*, and connect these proposals to the larger program of the conservative restoration. I intend to argue that behind the educational justification for a national curriculum and national testing is a dangerous ideological attack, the effects of which will be truly damaging to those who already have the most to lose. I shall first present a few interpretive cautions. Then I shall analyze the general project of the rightist agenda. Third, I shall show the connections between the national curriculum and national testing and the increasing focus on privatization and "choice" plans. And, finally, I want to discuss the pattern of differential benefits that will likely result.

The Question of a National Curriculum

Where should those of us who count ourselves a part of the long progressive tradition in education stand in relationship to the call for a national curriculum?

At the outset, I wish to make clear that I am not opposed in principle to a national curriculum. Nor am I opposed in principle to the idea or practice of testing. Rather, I wish to provide a more conjunctural set of arguments based on my claim that at this time—given the balance of social forces—there are very real dangers which are important to recognize. I shall confine myself largely to the negative case here, and my task is to raise serious questions about the implications of these developments in a time of conservative triumphalism.

We are not the only nation where a largely rightist coalition has put such proposals on the educational agenda. In England, a national curriculum, first introduced by the Thatcher government, is now mostly in place. It consists of "core and foundation subjects" such as mathematics, science, technology, history, art, music, physical education, and a modern foreign language. Working groups to determine the standard goals, "attainment targets," and content in each subject have already brought forth their results. This curriculum is accompanied by a national system of achievement testing—one that is both expensive and time-consuming—for all students in state-run schools at the ages of seven, eleven, fourteen, and sixteen (Whitty 1992, p. 24).

The assumption in many quarters in the United States is that we must follow nations such as Britain and especially Japan or we shall be left behind. Yet it is crucial that we understand that we *already* have a national curriculum, which is determined by the complicated nexus of state textbook adoption policies and the market in textbook publishing (Apple 1988b; Apple and Christian-Smith 1991). Thus, we have to ask whether a national curriculum—one that will undoubtedly be linked to a system of national goals and nationally standardized instruments of evaluation—is *better* than an equally widespread but somewhat more covert national curriculum established by textbook adoption states such as California and Texas, which control 20 to 30 percent of the market in textbooks (Apple 1993). Whether or not such a covert national curriculum already exists, however, there is a growing feeling that standardized national curricular goals and guidelines are essential to "raise standards" and to hold schools accountable for their students' achievement.

We can concede that many people representing an array of educational and political positions are involved in the call for higher standards, more rigorous curricula at a national level, and a system of national testing. Yet we must ask the question: which group is in the leadership of these "reform" efforts? This leads to another, broader question: who will benefit or lose as a result of all this? I contend that, unfortunately, rightist groups are setting the political agenda in education and that, in general, the same pattern of benefits that has characterized nearly all areas of social policy—in which the top 20 percent of the population reap 80 percent of the benefits (Apple 1989; Danziger and Weinberg 1986; Burtless 1990)—will be reproduced here.

We need to be very cautious of the genetic fallacy, the assumption that *because* a policy or a practice originates within a distasteful position it is fundamentally determined, in all its aspects, by its origination within that tradition. Take Edward Thorndike, one of the founders of educational psychology in the United States, for instance. The fact that his social beliefs were often repugnant—as evidenced by his participation in the popular eugenics movement and his notions of racial, gender, and class hierarchies—does not necessarily destroy every aspect of his research on learning. While I am not at all a supporter of this paradigm of research (its epistemological and social implications continue to demand major criticism),[1] this requires a different kind of argument than one based on origin. (Indeed, one can find some progressive educators turning to Thorndike for support for some of their claims about what needed to be transformed in our curriculum and pedagogy.)

It is not only those who are identified with the rightist project who argue for a national curriculum. Others who have historically been identified with a more liberal agenda have attempted to make a case for it (Smith, O'Day, and Cohen 1990).

Smith, O'Day, and Cohen suggest a positive, if cautionary, vision for a national curriculum. A national curriculum would involve the invention of new examinations, a technically, conceptually, and politically difficult task. It would require the teaching of more rigorous content and thus would require teachers to engage in more demanding and exciting work. Teachers and administrators, therefore, would have to "deepen their knowledge of academic subjects and change their conceptions of knowledge itself." Teaching and learning would have to be seen as "more active and inventive." Teachers, administrators, and students would need "to become more thoughtful, collaborative, and participatory" (Smith, O'Day, and Cohen 1990, p. 46).

In Smith, O'Day, and Cohen's (1990) words:

> Conversion to a national curriculum could only succeed if the work of conversion were conceived and undertaken as a grand, cooperative learning venture. Such an enterprise would fail miserably if it were conceived and organized chiefly as a technical process of developing new exams and materials and then "disseminating" or implementing them. (p. 46)

And they go on to say:

> A worthwhile, effective national curriculum would also require the creation of much new social and intellectual connective tissue. For instance, the content and pedagogy of teacher education would have to be closely related to the content of and pedagogy of the schools' curriculum. The content and pedagogy of examinations would have to be tied to those of the curriculum and teacher education. Such connections do not now exist, (p. 46)

The authors conclude that such a revitalized system, one in which such coordination would be built, "will not be easy, quick, or cheap," especially if it is to preserve variety and initiative. "If Americans continue to want educational reform on the cheap, a national curriculum would be a mistake" (Smith, O'Day, and Cohen 1990, p. 46). I could not agree more with this last point.

Yet they do not sufficiently recognize that much of what they fear is already taking place in the very linkage they call for. Even more importantly, what they do not pay sufficient attention to—the connections between a national curriculum and national testing and the larger rightist agenda—constitutes an even greater danger. It is this I wish to focus on.

Between Neoconservatism and Neoliberalism

Conservatism by its very name announces one interpretation of its agenda: it conserves. Other interpretations are possible, of course. One could say, somewhat more wryly, that conservatism believes that nothing should be done for the first time (Honderich 1990, p. 1). Yet in many ways, in the current situation, this is inaccurate. For with the Right now in ascendancy in many nations, we are witnessing a much more activist project. Conservative politics now are very much the politics of alteration—not always, but clearly the idea of "Do nothing for the first time" is not a sufficient explanation of what is happening either in education or elsewhere (Honderich 1990, p. 4).

Conservatism has in fact meant different things at different times and places. At times it involves defensive actions; at other times it involves taking the initiative against the status quo (Honderich 1990, p. 15). Today we are witnessing both.

Thus, it is important to set out the larger social context in which the current politics of official knowledge operates. There has been a breakdown in the accord that guided a good deal of educational policy since World War II. Powerful groups within government and the economy and within "authoritarian populist" social movements have been able to redefine —often in very retrogressive ways—the terms of debate in education, social welfare, and other areas of social policy. What education is *for* is being transformed (Apple 1993). No longer is education seen as part of a social alliance which combines many "minority"[2] groups, women, teachers, community activists, progressive legislators and government officials, and others who act together to propose (limited) social democratic policies for schools (e.g., expanding educational opportunities, limited attempts at equalizing outcomes, developing special programs in bilingual and multicultural education, and so on). A new alliance has been formed, one that has increasing power in educational and social policy. This new power bloc combines neoliberal elements of business with the New Right and with neoconservative intellectuals. Its interests are less in increasing the life opportunities of women, people of color, and labor than in providing the educational conditions believed necessary both for increasing international competitiveness, profit, and discipline and for returning us to a romanticized past of the "ideal" home, family, and school (Apple 1993).

The power of this alliance can be seen in a number of educational policies and proposals: (1) programs for voucher plans and tax credits to make schools operate like the thoroughly idealized free-market economy; (2) the movement at national and state levels to "raise standards" and mandate both teacher and student "competencies" and basic curricular goals and knowledge, increasingly through the implementation of statewide and national testing; (3) the increasingly effective attacks on the school curriculum for its antifamily and anti-free enterprise "bias," its secular humanism, its lack of patriotism, and its supposed neglect of the knowledge and values of the "Western tradition" and of "real knowledge"; and (4) the growing pressure to make the perceived needs of business and industry into the primary goals of the school (Apple 1988b; Apple 1993).

In essence, the new alliance in favor of this conservative restoration has integrated education into a wider set of ideological commitments. The objectives in education are the same as those which serve as a guide to its economic and social welfare goals. These include the expansion of the "free market," the drastic reduction of government responsibility for social needs (though the Clinton Administration intends to mediate this in not very extensive—and not very expensive—ways), the reinforcement of intensely competitive structures of mobility, the

lowering of people's expectations for economic security, and the popularization of what is clearly a form of Social Darwinist thinking (Bastian et al. 1986).

As I have argued at length elsewhere, the political Right in the United States has been very successful in mobilizing support *against* the educational system and its employees, often exporting the crisis in the economy onto the schools. Thus, one of its major achievements has been to shift the blame for unemployment and underemployment, for the loss of economic competitiveness, and for the supposed breakdown of traditional values and standards in the family, education, and paid and unpaid workplaces from the economic, cultural, and social policies and effects of dominant groups to the school and other public agencies. "Public" now is the center of all evil; "private" is the center of all that is good (Apple 1985).

In essence, then, four trends have characterized the conservative restoration in both the United States and Britain—privatization, centralization, vocationalization, and differentiation (Green 1991, p. 27). These trends are actually largely the results of differences within the most powerful wings of this alliance—neoliberalism and neoconservatism.

Neoliberalism has a vision of the weak state. A society that lets the "invisible hand" of the free market guide all aspects of its forms of social interaction is seen as both efficient and democratic. On the other hand, neoconservatism is guided by a vision of the strong state in certain areas, especially over the politics of the body and gender and race relations, over standards, values, and conduct, and over what kind of knowledge should be passed on to future generations (Hunter 1988).[3] These two positions do not easily sit side by side in the conservative coalition.

Thus, the rightist movement is contradictory. Is there not something paradoxical about linking all of the feelings of loss and nostalgia to the unpredictability of the market, "in replacing loss by sheer flux"? (Johnson 1991a, p. 40).

The contradiction between neoconservative and neoliberal elements in the rightist coalition are "solved" through a policy of what Roger Dale has called *conservative modernization*. Such a policy is engaged in

> simultaneously "freeing" individuals for economic purposes while controlling them for social purposes; indeed, in so far as economic "freedom" increases inequalities, it is likely to increase the need for social control. A "small, strong state" limits the range of its activities by transferring to the market, which it defends and legitimizes, as much welfare [and other activities] as possible. In education, the new reliance on competition and choice is not all pervasive; instead, "what is intended is a dual system, polarized between . . . market schools and minimum schools." (quoted in Edwards, Gewirtz, and Whitty forthcoming, p. 22)

That is, there will be a relatively less regulated and increasingly privatized sector for the children of the better-off. For the rest—whose economic status and racial composition will be thoroughly predictable—the schools will be tightly controlled and policed and will continue to be underfunded and unlinked to decent paid employment.

One of the major effects of the combination of marketization and the strong state is "to remove educational policies from public debate." That is, the choice is left up to individual parents and "the hidden hand of unintended consequences does the rest." In the process, the very idea of education being part of a *public* political sphere in which its means and ends are publicly debated atrophies (Education Group II 1991, p. 268).

There are major differences between democratic attempts at enhancing people's rights over the policies and practices of schooling and the neoliberal emphasis on marketization and privatization. The goal of the former is to *extend politics*, to "revivify democratic practice by devising ways of enhancing public discussion, debate, and negotiation." It is based inherently on a vision of democracy as an educative practice. The latter, on the other hand, seeks to *contain politics*. It wants to *reduce all politics to economics*, to an ethic of "choice" and "consumption" (Johnson 1991a, p. 68). The world in essence becomes a vast supermarket.

Enlarging the private sector so that buying and selling—in a word, competition—is the dominant ethic of society involves a set of closely related propositions. This position assumes that more individuals are motivated to work harder under these conditions. After all, we "already know" that public servants are inefficient and slothful, while private enterprises are efficient and energetic. It assumes that self-interest and competitiveness are the engines of creativity. More knowledge and more experimentation are created and used to alter what we have now. In the process, less waste is created. Supply and demand remain in a kind of equilibrium. A more efficient machine is thus created, one which minimizes administrative costs and ultimately distributes resources more widely (Honderich 1990, p. 104).

This ethic is not meant to benefit simply the privileged few. However, it is the equivalent of saying that you have the right to climb the north face of the Eiger or scale Mount Everest, provided, of course, that you are very good at mountain climbing and have the necessary institutional and financial resources (Honderich 1990, pp. 99–100).

Thus, in a conservative society, access to a society's private resources (and remember, the attempt is to make nearly *all* of society's resources private) is largely dependent on one's ability to pay. And this is dependent on one's being a person of an *entrepreneurial or efficiently acquisitive class type*. On the other hand, society's public resources (that rapidly decreasing segment) are dependent on need (Honderich 1990, p. 89). In a conservative society, the former is to be maximized, the latter is to be minimized.

However, the conservatism of the New Right does not merely depend in large portion on a particular view of human nature—the view of human nature as primarily self-interested. It has gone further; it has set out to degrade human nature, to force all people to conform to what at first could only be claimed to be true. Unfortunately, in no small measure it has succeeded. Perhaps blinded by their own absolutist and reductive vision of what it means to be human, many of our political leaders do not seem to be capable of recognizing what they have done. They have set out, aggressively, to drag down the character of a people (Honderich 1990, p. 81), while at the same time attacking the poor and the disenfranchised for their supposed lack of values and character.

Curriculum, Testing, and a Common Culture

As Whitty reminds us, what is striking about the rightist coalition's policies is its capacity to connect the neoconservative emphasis on traditional knowledge and values, authority, standards, and national identity with the neoliberal emphasis on the extension of market-driven principles (also embraced by Clinton) into all areas of society (Whitty 1992, p. 25). Thus, a national curriculum—coupled with rigorous national standards and a system of testing that is performance driven—is able at one and the same time to be aimed at "modernization" of the curriculum and the efficient "production" of better "human capital" *and* represent a nostalgic yearning for a romanticized past (Whitty 1992, p. 25). When tied to a program of market-driven policies such as voucher and choice plans, such a national system of standards, testing, and curriculum—while perhaps internally inconsistent—is an ideal compromise within the rightist coalition.

But one could still ask, won't a national curriculum coupled with a system of national achievement testing contradict in practice the concomitant emphasis on privatization and school choice? Can it really simultaneously achieve both? I maintain that this apparent contradiction may not be as substantial as one might expect. One long-term aim of powerful elements within the conservative coalition is not necessarily to transfer power from the local level to the center, although for some neoconservatives who favor a strong state in the area of morality, values, and standards, this may indeed be the case. Rather, these elements would prefer to decentralize such power altogether and redistribute it according to market forces, thus tacitly disempowering those who already have less power while employing a rhetoric of empowering the consumer. In part, both a

national curriculum and national testing can be seen as "necessary concessions in pursuit of this long term aim" (Green 1991, p. 29).

In a time of a loss of legitimacy in government and a crisis in educational authority, the government must be seen to be doing something about raising educational standards. After all, this is exactly what it promises to offer to "consumers" of education. This is why a national curriculum is crucial. Its major value does not lie in its supposed encouragement of standardized goals and content and of levels of achievement in what are considered the most important subject areas. This concern with achievement, of course, should not be totally dismissed. However, the major role of a national curriculum is rather in providing the framework within which national testing can function. It enables the establishment of a procedure that can supposedly give consumers "quality tags" on schools so that "free market forces" can operate to their fullest extent. If we are to have a free market in education in which the consumer is presented with an attractive range of choices, both a national curriculum and especially national testing then act as a "state watchdog committee" to control the "worst excesses" of the market (Green 1991, p. 29).[4]

However, let us be honest about our own educational history here. Even with the supposed emphasis of some people on student portfolios and other more flexible forms of evaluation, there is no evidence at all to support the idea that what will ultimately be installed—even if only because of time and expense—will be anything other than a system of mass standardized paper-and-pencil tests.

Yet we must also be clear about the social function of such a proposal. A national curriculum may be seen as a device for accountability that will help us establish benchmarks so that parents can evaluate schools. But it also puts into motion a system in which children themselves will be ranked and ordered as never before. One of its primary roles will be to act as "a mechanism for differentiating children more rigidly against fixed norms, *the social meanings and derivation of which are not available for scrutiny*" (Johnson 1991a, p. 79).

Thus, while the proponents of a national curriculum may see it as a means to create social cohesion and to give all of us the capacity to improve our schools by measuring them against objective criteria, the effects will be the reverse. The criteria may seem objective, but the results will not be, given existing differences in resources and class and race segregation. Rather than cultural and social cohesion, differences between "us" and the "others" will be generated even more strongly, and the attendant social antagonisms and cultural and economic destruction will worsen.

Richard Johnson helps us understand the social processes at work here.

> This nostalgia for "cohesion" is interesting, but the great delusion is that all pupils—black and white, working class, poor, and middle class, boys and girls—will receive the curriculum in the same way. Actually, it will be read in different ways, according to how pupils are placed in social relationships and culture. A common curriculum, in a heterogeneous society, is not a recipe for "cohesion," but for resistance and the renewal of divisions. Since it always rests on cultural foundations of its own, it will put pupils in their places, not according to "ability," but according to how their cultural communities rank along the criteria taken as the "standard." A curriculum which does not "explain itself," is not ironical or self-critical, will always have this effect. (Johnson 1991a, pp. 79–80)

These are significant points, especially the call for all curricula to *explain themselves*. In complex societies like ours, which are riven with differential power, the only kind of cohesion that is possible is one in which we overtly recognize differences and inequalities. The curriculum then should not be presented as "objective." Rather, it must constantly *subjectify* itself. That is, it must "acknowledge its own roots" in the culture, history, and social interests out of which it arose. It will accordingly neither homogenize this culture, history, and social interest, nor will it homogenize the students. The "same treatment" by sex, race and ethnicity, or class is not the same at all. A democratic curriculum and pedagogy must begin with a recognition of "the different social positionings and cultural repertoires in the classrooms, and the power relations between them." Thus, if we are concerned with "really equal treatment"—as I think we must be—we must base a curriculum on a recognition of those differences that empower and disempower our students in identifiable ways (Johnson 1991a, p. 80; Ellsworth 1989).

Foucault reminds us that if you wish to understand how power works, you should examine the margins, look at the knowledge, self-understandings, and struggles of those whom powerful groups in this society have cast off as "the other" (Best and Kellner 1991, pp. 34–75). The New Right and its allies have created entire groups of "others"—people of color, women who refuse to accept external control of their lives and bodies, gays and lesbians, the poor (and the list could go on). It is in the recognition of these differences that curriculum dialogue can occur. Such a national dialogue should begin with the concrete and public exploration of how we are differently positioned in society and culture. What the New Right embargoes–the knowledge of the margins, of how culture and power are indissolubly linked—becomes a set of indispensable resources for this task (Johnson 1991b, p. 320).

The proposed national curriculum of course would recognize some of these differences. But, as Linda Christian-Smith and I argue in *The Politics of the Textbook*, the national curriculum serves both to partly acknowledge difference and at the same time to recuperate it within the supposed consensus that exists about what we should teach (Apple and Christian-Smith 1991; see also Apple 1993). It is part of an attempt to recreate hegemonic power that has been partly fractured by social movements.

The very idea of a common culture upon which a national curriculum—as defined by neoconservatives—is to be built is itself a form of cultural politics. In the immense linguistic, cultural, and religious diversity that makes up the constant creativity and flux in which we live, it is the cultural policy of the Right to override such diversity. Thinking it is reinstituting a common culture, it is instead *inventing* one, in much the same way as E. D. Hirsch (1987) has tried to do in his self-parody of what it means to be literate (Johnson 1991b, p. 319). A uniform culture never truly existed in the United States, only a selective version, an invented tradition that is reinstalled (though in different forms) in times of economic crisis and a crisis in authority relations, both of which threaten the hegemony of the culturally and economically dominant.

The expansion of voices in the curriculum and the vehement responses of the Right become crucial here. Multicultural and antiracist curricula present challenges to the program of the New Right, challenges that go to the core of their vision. In a largely monocultural national curriculum (which deals with diversity by centering the always ideological "we" and usually then simply mentioning "the contributions" of people of color, women, and "others"), the maintenance of existing hierarchies of what counts as official knowledge, the revivifying of traditional Western standards and values, the return to a "disciplined" (and one could say largely masculine) pedagogy, and so on, are paramount. A threat to any of these becomes a threat to the entire worldview of the Right (Johnson 1991a, p. 51; Rose 1988).

The idea of a common culture—in the guise of the romanticized Western tradition of the neoconservatives (or even as expressed in the longings of some socialists)—does not give enough thought, then, to the immense cultural heterogeneity of a society that draws its cultural traditions from all over the world. The task of defending public education as *public*, as deserving of widespread support "across an extremely diverse and deeply divided people, involves a lot more than restoration" (Education Group II 1991, p. x).

The debate in England is similar. A national curriculum is seen by the Right as essential to prevent relativism. For most of its proponents, a common curriculum must transmit both the common culture and the high culture that has grown out of it. Anything else will result in incoherence, no culture, merely a "void." Thus, a national culture is "defined in exclusive,

nostalgic, and frequently racist terms" (Johnson 1991a, p. 71).

Richard Johnson's (1991a) analysis documents its social logic:

> In formulations like these, culture is thought of as a homogeneous way of life or tradition, not as a sphere of difference, relationships, or power. No recognition is given to the real diversity of social orientations and cultures within a given nation-state or people. Yet a selective version of a national culture is installed as an absolute condition for any social identity at all. The borrowing, mixing and fusion of elements from different cultural systems, a commonplace everyday practice in societies like [ours], is unthinkable within this framework, or is seen as a kind of cultural misrule that will produce nothing more than a void. So the "choices" are between . . . a national culture or no culture at all. (p. 71)

The racial subtext here is perhaps below the surface but is still present in significant ways.[5]

The national curriculum is a mechanism for the political control of knowledge (Johnson 1991a, p. 82). Once it is established, there will be little chance of turning back. It may be modified by the conflicts that its content generates, but it is in its very establishment that its politics lies. Only by recognizing its ultimate logic of false consensus and, especially, its undoubted hardening in the future as it becomes linked to a massive system of national testing can we fully understand this. When this probable future is connected to the other parts of the rightist agenda—marketization and privatization—there is reason to make us pause, especially given the increasingly powerful conservative gains at local, regional, and state levels (Apple 1993).

Who Benefits?

Since leadership in such efforts to "reform" our educational system and its curriculum, teaching, and evaluative practices is largely exercised by the rightist coalition, we need always to ask, "Whose reforms are these?" and "Who benefits?"

A system of national curricula and national testing cannot help but ratify and exacerbate gender, race, and class differences in the absence of sufficient resources both human and material. Thus, when the fiscal crisis in most of our urban areas is so severe that classes are being held in gymnasiums and hallways, when many schools do not have enough funds to stay open for the full 180 days a year, when buildings are disintegrating before our very eyes (Apple 1993), when in some cities three classrooms must share one set of textbooks at the elementary level (Kozol 1991)—I could go on—it is simply a flight of fantasy to assume that more standardized testing and national curriculum guidelines are the answer. With the destruction of the economic infrastructure of these same cities through capital flight, with youth unemployment at nearly 75 percent in many of them, with almost nonexistent health care, with lives that are often devoid of hope for meaningful mobility because of what might simply be called the pornography of poverty, to assume that establishing curricular benchmarks based on problematic cultural visions and more rigorous testing will do more than affix labels to poor students in a way that is seemingly more neutral is to totally misunderstand the situation. It will lead to more blame being placed on students and poor parents and especially to the schools that they attend. It will also be very expensive. Enter voucher plans with even wider public approval.

Basil Bernstein's analysis of the complexities of this situation and of its ultimate results is more than a little useful here. He says, "the pedagogic practices of the new vocationalism [neoliberalism] and those of the old autonomy of knowledge [neoconservatism] represent a conflict between different elitist ideologies, one based on the class hierarchy of the market and the other based on the hierarchy of knowledge and its class supports" (Bernstein 1990, p. 63). Whatever the oppositions between market- and knowledge-oriented pedagogic and curricular practices, present racial, gender, and class-based inequalities are likely to be reproduced (Bernstein 1990, p. 64). What he calls an "autonomous visible pedagogy"—one that relies on overt standards and highly structured models of teaching and evaluation—is justified by referring to its intrinsic worthiness. The value of the acquisition of say, the Western tradition, lies in its foundational status for "all we hold dear" and by the norms and dispositions that it instills in the students. "Its arrogance lies in its claim to moral high ground and to the superiority of its culture, its indifference to its own stratification consequences, its conceit in its lack of relation to anything other than itself, its self-referential abstracted autonomy" (Bernstein 1990, p. 87).

Its supposed opposite—one based on the knowledge, skills, and dispositions "required" by business and industry and one that seeks to transform schooling around market principles—is actually a much more complex ideological construction:

> It incorporates some of the criticism of the autonomous visible pedagogy . . . criticism of the failure of the urban school, of the passivity and inferior status [given to] parents, of the boredom of . . . pupils and their consequent disruptions of and resistance to irrelevant curricula, of assessment procedures which itemize relative failure rather than the positive strength of the acquirer. But it assimilates these criticisms into a new discourse: a new pedagogic Janus. . . . The explicit commitment to greater choice by parents . . . is not a celebration of participatory democracy, but a thin cover for the old stratification of schools and curricula. (Bernstein 1990, p. 87)

Are Bernstein's conclusions correct? Will the combination of national curricula, testing, and privatization actually lead away from democratic processes and outcomes? Here we must look not to Japan (where many people unfortunately have urged us to look) but to Britain, where this combination of proposals is much more advanced.

In Britain, there is now considerable evidence that the overall effects of the various market-oriented policies introduced by the rightist government are *not* genuine pluralism or the "interrupting [of] traditional modes of social reproduction." Far from this. They may instead largely provide "a legitimating gloss for the perpetuation of long-standing forms of structured inequality" (Whitty 1991, pp. 20–21). The fact that one of its major effects has been the disempowering and deskilling of large numbers of teachers is not inconsequential either (Apple 1993).

Going further, Edwards, Gewirtz, and Whitty have come to similar conclusions. In essence, the rightist preoccupation with "escape routes" diverts attention from the effects of such policies on those (probably the majority) who will be left behind (Edwards, Gewirtz, and Whitty forthcoming, p. 23).

Thus, it is indeed possible—actually probable—that market-oriented approaches in education (even when coupled with a strong state over a system of national curriculum and testing) will exacerbate already existing and widespread class and race divisions. Freedom and choice in the new educational market will be for those who can afford them. "Diversity" in schooling will simply be a more polite word for the condition of educational apartheid (Green 1991, p. 30; see also Karp 1992 and Lowe 1992).

Afterthoughts by Way of Conclusion

I have been more than a little negative in my appraisal here. I have argued that the politics of official knowledge—in this case surrounding proposals for a national curriculum and for national testing—cannot be fully understood in an isolated way. A national curriculum and national testing needs to be situated within larger ideological dynamics in which we are seeing an attempt by a new hegemonic bloc to transform our very ideas of what education is. This transformation involves a major shift—one that Dewey would have shuddered at—in which democracy becomes an economic, not a political, concept and where the idea of the public good withers at its very roots.

But perhaps I have been too negative. Perhaps there are good reasons to support national curricula and national testing even as currently constituted precisely *because* of the power of the rightist coalition.

It is possible, for example, to argue that only by establishing a national curriculum and national testing can we stop the fragmentation that will accompany the neoliberal portion of the rightist project. Only such a system would protect the very idea of a public school, would protect teachers' unions which in a privatized and marketized system would lose much of their power, would protect poor children and children of color from the vicissitudes of the market. After all, it is the free market that created the poverty and destruction of community that they are experiencing in the first place.

It is also possible to argue, as Geoff Whitty has in the British case, that the very fact of a national curriculum encourages both the formation of intense public debate about what knowledge should be declared official and the creation of progressive coalitions against such state-sponsored definitions of legitimate knowledge.[6] It could be the vehicle for the return of the political which the Right so wishes to evacuate from our public discourse and which the efficiency experts wish to make into merely a technical concern.

Thus, it is quite possible that the establishment of a national curriculum could have the effect of unifying oppositional and oppressed groups. Given the fragmented nature of progressive educational movements today, and given a system of school financing and governance that forces groups to focus largely on the local or state level, one function of a national curriculum could be the coalescence of groups around a common agenda. A national movement for a more democratic vision of school reform could be the result.

In many ways—and I am quite serious here—we owe principled conservatives (and there are many) a debt of gratitude. It is their realization that curriculum issues are not only about techniques that has helped to stimulate the current debate. When many women, people of color, and labor organizations fought for decades to have society recognize the selective tradition in official knowledge, these movements were often (though not always) silenced, ignored, or recuperated into dominant discourses (Apple 1993; Apple and Christian-Smith 1991). The power of the Right—in its contradictory attempt to establish a national common culture, to challenge what is now taught, and to make that culture part of a vast supermarket of choices and thus to purge cultural politics from our sensibilities—has now made it impossible for the politics of official knowledge to be ignored.

Should we then support a national curriculum and national testing to keep total privatization and marketization at bay? Under current conditions, I do not think it is worth the risk—not only because of its extensive destructive potential in the long and short run but also because I think it misconstrues and reifies the issues of a common curriculum and a common culture.

Here I must repeat the arguments I made in the second edition of *Ideology and Curriculum* (Apple 1990). The current call to return to a common culture in which all students are to be given the values of a specific group—usually the dominant group—does not in my mind concern a common culture at all. Such an approach hardly scratches the surface of the political and educational issues involved. A common culture can never be the general extension to everyone of what a minority means and believes. Rather, and crucially, it requires not the stipulation of the facts, concepts, skills, and values that make us all "culturally literate," but the creation of the conditions necessary for all people to participate in the creation and recreation of meanings and values. It requires a democratic process in which all people–not simply those who are the intellectual guardians of the Western tradition—can be involved in the deliberation over what is important. This necessitates the removal of the very real material obstacles—unequal power, wealth, time for reflection—that stand in the way of such participation (Williams 1989, pp. 35–36). As Raymond Williams (1989) so perceptively puts it:

> The idea of a common culture is in no sense the idea of a simply consenting, and certainly not of a merely-conforming society. [It involves] a common determination of meanings by all the people, acting sometimes as individuals, sometimes as groups, in a process which has no

particular end, and which can never be supposed at any time to have finally realized itself, to have become complete. In this common process, the only absolute will be the keeping of the channels and institutions of communication clear so that all may contribute, and be helped to contribute, (pp. 37–38)

In speaking of a common culture, then, we should not be talking of something uniform, something to which we all conform. Instead what we should be asking is precisely, for that free, contributive and common *process* of participation in the creation of meanings and values. It is the very blockage of that process in our institutions that must concern all of us.

Our current language speaks to how this process is being defined during the conservative restoration. Instead of people who participate in the struggle to build and rebuild our educational, cultural, political, and economic relations, we are defined as consumers (of that "particularly acquisitive class type"). This is truly an extraordinary concept, for it sees people as either stomachs or furnaces. We use and use up. We don't create—someone else does that. This is disturbing enough in general, but in education it is truly disabling. Leave it to the guardians of tradition, the efficiency and accountability experts, the holders of "real knowledge," or to the Christopher Whittles of this world who have given us commercial television in the classroom and intend to franchise "schools of choice" for the generation of profit (Apple 1993). Yet we leave it to these people at great risk, especially to those students who are already economically and culturally disenfranchised by our dominant institutions.

As I noted at the outset, we live in a society with identifiable winners and losers. In the future we may say that the losers made poor "consumer choices" and that's the way markets operate. But is this society really only one vast market?

As Whitty reminds us, in a time when so many people have found out from their daily experiences that the supposed "grand narratives" of progress are deeply flawed, is it appropriate to return to yet another grand narrative, the market? (Whitty 1992). The results of this narrative are visible every day in the destruction of our communities and environment, in the increasing racism of society, in the faces and bodies of our children, who see the future and turn away.

Many people are able to disassociate themselves from these realities. There is almost a pathological distancing among the affluent (Kozol 1991). Yet how can one not be morally outraged at the growing gap between rich and poor, the persistence of hunger and homelessness, the deadly absence of medical care, the degradations of poverty. If this were the (always self-critical and constantly subjectifying) centerpiece of a national curriculum (but then how could it be tested cheaply and efficiently, and how could the Right control its ends and means?), perhaps such a curriculum would be worthwhile. But until such a time, we can take a rightist slogan made popular in another context and apply it to their educational agenda —"Just say no."

Notes

A draft of this chapter was presented as the John Dewey Lecture, jointly sponsored by the John Dewey Society and the American Educational Research Association, San Francisco, April 1992. I would like to thank Geoff Whitty, Roger Dale, James Beane, and the Friday Seminar at the University of Wisconsin, Madison, for their important suggestions and criticism. An extended version will appear in *Teachers College Record*.

1. See, e.g., Gould (1981). Feminist criticisms and reconstructions of science are essential to this task. See, for example, Haraway (1989), Harding and Barr (1987), Tuana (1981), and Harding (1991).
2. I put the word "minority" in quotation marks here to remind us that the vast majority of the world's population is composed of persons of color. It would be wholly salutary for our ideas about culture and education to bear this fact in mind.

3. Neoliberalism doesn't ignore the idea of a strong state, but it wants to limit it to specific areas (e.g., defense of markets).
4. I am making a "functional," not necessarily an "intentional," claim here. See Liston (1988). For an interesting discussion of how such testing programs might actually work against more democratic efforts at school reform, see Darling-Hammond (1992).
5. For a more complete analysis of racial subtexts in our policies and practices, see Omi and Winant (1986).
6. Geoff Whitty, personal communication. Andy Green, in the English context, argues as well that there are merits in having a broadly defined national curriculum but goes on to say that this makes it even more essential that individual schools have a serious degree of control over its implementation, "not least so that it provides a check against the use of education by the state as a means of promoting a particular ideology" (Green 1991, p. 22).

References

Apple, M. W. 1985. *Education and Power*. New York: Routledge.

——. 1988a. Social Crisis and Curriculum Accords. *Educational Theory* 38: 191–201.

——. 1988b. *Teachers and Texts: A Political Economy of Class and Gender Relations in Education*. New York: Routledge.

——. 1989. American Realities: Poverty, Economy, and Education. In *Dropouts from School*, ed. Lois Weis, Eleanor Farrar, and Hugh Petrie, 205–223. Albany: State University of New York Press.

——. 1990. *Ideology and Curriculum*. 2d. ed. New York: Routledge.

——. 1993. *Official Knowledge: Democratic Education in a Conservative Age*. New York: Routledge.

Apple, M. W., and L. Christian-Smith, eds. 1991. *The Politics of the Textbook*. New York: Routledge.

Bastian, A., N. Fruchter, M. Gittell, C. Greer, and K. Haskins. 1986. *Choosing Equality*. Philadelphia: Temple University Press.

Bernstein, B. 1977. *Class, Codes and Control*. Vol. 3. New York: Routledge.

——. 1990. *The Structuring of Pedagogic Discourse*. New York: Routledge.

Best, S., and D. Kellner. 1991. *Postmodern Theory: Critical Interrogations*. London: Macmillan.

Bourdieu, P. 1984. *Distinction*. Cambridge: Harvard University Press.

Burtless, G., ed. 1990. *A Future of Lousy Jobs?* Washington, DC: Brookings Institution.

Danziger, S., and D. Weinberg, eds. 1986. *Fighting Poverty*. Cambridge: Harvard University Press.

Darling-Hammond, L. 1992. Bush's Testing Plan Undercuts School Reforms. *Rethinking Schools* 6 (March/April): 18.

Education Group II, eds. 1991. *Education Limited*. London: Unwin Hyman.

Edwards, T., S. Gewirtz, and G. Whitty. Forthcoming. Whose Choice of Schools? In *Sociological Perspectives on Contemporary Educational Reforms*, ed. Madeleine Arnot and Len Barton. London: Triangle Books.

Ellsworth, E. 1989. Why Doesn't This Feel Empowering? *Harvard Educational Review* 59: 297–324.

Gould, S. J. 1981. *The Mismeasure of Man*. New York: Norton.

Green, A. 1991. The Peculiarities of English Education. In *Education Limited*, ed. Education Group II, 6–30. London: Unwin Hyman.

Haraway, D. 1989. *Primate Visions*. New York: Routledge.

Harding, S. 1991. *Whose Science, Whose Knowledge?* Ithaca: Cornell University Press.

Harding, S., and J. Barr, eds. 1987. *Sex and Scientific Inquiry*. Chicago: University of Chicago Press.

Hirsch, E. O. Jr. 1987. *Cultural Literacy*. New York: Vintage.

Honderich, T. 1990. *Conservatism*. Boulder, CO: Westview Press.

Hunter, A. 1988. *Children in the Service of Conservatism*. Madison: University of Wisconsin Law School, Institute for Legal Studies.

Johnson, R. 1991a. A New Road to Serfdom. In *Education Limited*, ed. Education Group II, 31–86. London: Unwin Hyman.

——. 1991b. Ten Theses on a Monday Morning. In *Education Limited*, ed. Education Group II, 306–321. London: Unwin Hyman.

Karp, S. 1992. Massachusetts "Choice" Plan Undercuts Poor Districts. *Rethinking Schools* 6 (March/April): 4.

Kozol, J. 1991. *Savage Inequalities*. New York: Crown.

Liston, D. 1988. *Capitalist Schools*. New York: Routledge.

Lowe, R. 1992. The Illusion of "Choice." *Rethinking Schools* 6 (March/April): 1, 21–23.

Omi, M., and H. Winant. 1986. *Racial Formation in the United States*. New York: Routledge.

Rose, S. 1988. *Keeping Them Out of the Hands of Satan*. New York: Routledge.

Smith, M., J. O'Day, and D. Cohen. 1990. National Curriculum, American Style: What Might It Look Like. *American Educator* 14: 10–17, 40–47.

Tuana, N., ed. 1989. *Feminism and Science*. Bloomington: Indiana University Press.

Whitty, G. 1991. Recent Education Reform: Is It a Postmodern Phenomenon? Paper presented at the conference on Reproduction, Social Inequality, and Resistance, University of Bielefeld, Germany.

——. 1992. *Education, Economy, and National Culture*. Milton Keynes, England: Open University Press.

Williams, R. 1989. *Resources of Hope*. New York: Verso.

The Mimetic and the Transformative

Alternative Outlooks on Teaching

Philip W. Jackson

The Greek sophist Protagoras allegedly claimed that on every subject two opposite statements could be made, each as defensible as the other. Whether or not he was right in a universal sense is something for logicians and rhetoricians to decide. However, insofar as the affairs of everyday life are concerned, he seems to have hit upon a fundamental truth, for we encounter daily all manner of "opposite statements," each with its share of supporters and critics.

As might be expected, education as a field of study is no exception to the rule. There too, differing outlooks, poles apart at first glance, are as common as elsewhere. Who, for example, is unfamiliar with the many verbal exchanges that have taken place over the years between "traditional" educators on the one side and their "progressive" opponents on the other, debates in which the merits of "child-centered" practices are pitted against those considered more "subject-centered"?

This [reading] introduces a dichotomy that encompasses the differences just named as well as others less familiar, though it is not usually talked about in the terms I will employ here. Indeed, the names of the two outlooks to be discussed have been purposely chosen so as to be *un*familiar to most followers of today's educational discussions and debates. My reason for this is not to introduce novelty for its own sake, much less to add glitter by using a pair of fancy terms. Instead, it is to avoid becoming prematurely embroiled in the well-known controversies associated with phrases like "child-centered" and "subject-centered," controversies that too often degenerate into mud-slinging contests which reduce the terms themselves to little more than slogans and epithets. A similar fate may well await the pair of terms to be introduced here. But for the time being the fact that they are rather new, or at least newly employed within an educational context, should prevent that.

In brief, I contend in this [reading] that two distinguishably different ways of thinking about education and of translating that thought into practice undergird most of the differences of opinion that have circulated within educational circles over the past two or three centuries. Framed within an argument, which is how they are usually encountered, each of these two outlooks seeks to legitimate its own vision of how education should be conducted. It does so by promoting certain goals and practices, making them seem proper and just, while ignoring others or calling them into question.

These dichotomous orientations are not the exact opposites of which Protagoras spoke, though they are often presented that way by people propounding one or the other. How they *are* related to each other is a question I will consider in some detail in the second half of this [reading]. For now, however, it will suffice to call their relationship enigmatic. Most of the time their challengers and defenders are depicted at swords' points, but there is a perspective from which the two outlooks appear complementary and interdependent. Indeed, there are angles of vision from which what originally seemed to be two diametrically opposed orientations suddenly appear to be one.

What shall we name these two points of view? As the chapter title already reveals, I recommend

they be called the "mimetic" and the "transformative." I also propose we think of them not simply as two viewpoints on educational matters but as two traditions within the domain of educational thought and practice. Why *traditions?* Because each has a long and respectable history going back at least several hundred years and possibly beyond. Also, each is more than an intellectual argument. Each provokes feelings of partisanship and loyalty toward a particular point of view; each also entails commitment to a set of related practices. In short, each comprises what might be called (following Wittgenstein[1]) a "form of life," a relatively coherent and unified way of thinking, feeling, and acting within a particular domain— in this instance, the sphere of education. The term "traditions" stands for that complexity. Its use reminds us that each outlook stretches back in time, and that each has a "lived" dimension that makes it something much more than a polemical argument.

The Mimetic Tradition

We turn to the "mimetic" tradition first not because it is any older or any more important than the one called "transformative," but principally because it is the easier of the two to describe. In addition, it is closer to what most people today seem to think education is all about. Thus, presenting it first has the advantage of beginning with the more familiar and moving to the less familiar. Third, it is more harmonious with all that is thought of as "scientific" and "rigorous" within education than is its competitor. To all who rank that pair of adjectives highly, as I reservedly do myself, therein lies an additional reason for putting it first.

This tradition is named "mimetic" (the root term is the Greek word *mimesis*, from which we get "mime" and "mimic") because it gives a central place to the transmission of factual and procedural knowledge from one person to another, through an essentially *imitative* process. If I had to substitute another equally unfamiliar word in its place, with which to engage in educational debate, I would choose "epistemic"—yet another derived from the Greek, this from *episteme*, meaning knowledge. The first term stresses the *process* by which knowledge is commonly transmitted, the second puts its emphasis on the *content* of the transaction. Thus we have the "mimetic" or the "epistemic" tradition; I prefer the former if for no other reason than that it places the emphasis where I believe it belongs, on the importance of *method* within this tradition.

The conception of knowledge at the heart of the mimetic tradition is familiar to most of us, though its properties may not always be fully understood even by teachers committed to this outlook on teaching. For this reason it seems essential to say something about its properties.

First of all, knowledge of a "mimetic" variety, whose transmission entails mimetic procedures, is by definition identifiable in advance of its transmission. This makes it secondhand knowledge, so to speak, not in the pejorative sense of that term, but simply in that it has to have belonged to someone first before it can belong to anyone else. In short, it is knowledge "presented" to a learner, rather than "discovered" by him or her.[2]

Such knowledge can be "passed" from one person to another or from a text to a person; we can thus see it as "detachable" from persons *per se*, in two ways. It is detachable in the first place in that it can be preserved in books and films and the like, so that it can "outlive" all who originally possessed it. It is detachable, secondly, in the sense that it can be forgotten by those who once knew it. Though it can be "possessed," it can also be "dispossessed" through memory loss. Moreover, it can be "unpossessed" in the sense of never having been "possessed" in the first place. A correlate of its detachability is that it can be "shown" or displayed by its possessor, a condition that partially accounts for our occasional reference to it as "objective" knowledge.

A crucial property of mimetic knowledge is its reproducibility. It is this property that allows us to say it is "transmitted" from teacher to student or from text to student. Yet when we speak of it that way we usually have in mind a very special kind of process. It does not entail handing over a bundle of some sort as in an actual "exchange"

or "giving." Rather, it is more like the transmission of a spoken message from one person to another or the spread of bacteria from a cold-sufferer to a new victim. In all such instances both parties wind up possessing what was formerly possessed by only one of them. What has been transmitted has actually been "mirrored" or "reproduced" without its ever having been relinquished in the process.

The knowledge involved in all transmissions within the mimetic tradition has an additional property worth noting: It can be judged right or wrong, accurate or inaccurate, correct or incorrect on the basis of a comparison with the teacher's own knowledge or with some other model as found in a textbook or other instructional materials. Not only do judgments of this sort yield a measure of the success of teaching within this tradition, they also are the chief criterion by which learning is measured.

My final remark about knowledge as conceived within the mimetic tradition may already be obvious from what has been said. It is that mimetic knowledge is by no means limited to "bookish" learning, knowledge expressible in words alone. Though much of it takes that form, it also includes the acquisition of physical and motor skills, knowledge to be *performed* in one way or another, usually without any verbal accompaniment whatsoever. "Knowing that" and "knowing how" is the way the distinction is sometimes expressed.[3]

Here then are the central epistemological assumptions associated with the mimetic tradition. The key idea is that some kind of knowledge or skill can be doubly possessed, first by the teacher alone (or the writer of the textbook or the computer program), then by his or her student. In more epigrammatic terms, the slogan for this tradition might well be: "What the teacher (or textbook or computer) knows, that shall the student come to know."

How might the goal of this tradition be achieved? In essence, the procedure for transmitting mimetic knowledge consists of five steps, the fourth of which divides in two alternate routes, "a" or "b," dependent on the presence or absence of student error. The series is as follows:

Step One: *Test*. Some form of inquiry, either formal or informal, is initiated to discover whether the student(s) in question already knows the material or can perform the skill in question. This step is properly omitted if the student's lack of knowledge or skill can be safely assumed.

Step Two: *Present*. Finding the student ignorant of what is to be learned, or assuming him or her to be so, the teacher "presents" the material, either discursively—with or without the support of visual aids—or by modeling or demonstrating a skillful performance or some aspect thereof.

Step Three: *Perform/Evaluate*. The student, who presumably has been attentive during the presentation, is invited or required to repeat what he or she has just witnessed, read, or heard. The teacher (or some surrogate device, such as a test scoring machine) monitors the student's performance, making a judgment and sometimes generating a numerical tally of its accuracy or correctness.

Step Four (A): (Correct performance) *Reward/Fix*. Discovering the performance to be reasonably accurate (within limits usually set in advance), the teacher (or surrogate device) comments favorably on what the student has done and, when deemed necessary, prescribes one or more repetitions in order to habituate or "fix" the material in the student's repertoire of things known or skills mastered.

Step Four (B): (Incorrect performance) *Enter Remedial Loop*. Discovering the student's performance to be wrong (again within limits usually established in advance), the teacher (or surrogate) initiates a remedial procedure designed to correct the error in question. Commonly this procedure begins with a diagnosis of the student's difficulty followed by the selection of an appropriate corrective strategy.

Step Five: *Advance*. After the unit of knowledge or skill has been "fixed" (all appropriate corrections having been made and drills undertaken), the teacher and student advance to the next unit of "fresh" instruction, returning to Step One, if deemed necessary by the teacher, and repeating the moves in sequential order. The sequence of steps is repeated until the student has mastered all the prescribed knowledge or until all efforts to attain a prescribed level of mastery have been exhausted.

In skeletal form, this is the way instruction proceeds within the mimetic tradition. Readers familiar with cybernetic models will readily recognize the five steps outlined as an instance of what is commonly referred to as a "feedback loop" mechanism, an algorithmic device equipped with "internal guidance circuitry."[4]

Which teachers teach this way? Almost all do so on occasion, yet not all spend an equal amount of time at it. Some teachers work within the mimetic tradition only on weekends, figuratively speaking, about as often as a "do-it-yourself-er" might wield a hammer or turn a wrench. Others employ the same techniques routinely on a day-to-day basis, as might a professional carpenter or mechanic.

Which do which? That question will be treated at some length later in this [reading], where I will take up the relationship between the two traditions. For now it will suffice to observe in passing what is perhaps obvious, that teachers intent upon the transmission of factual information, plus those seeking to teach specific psychomotor skills, would more likely use mimetic procedures than would those whose conception of teaching involved educational goals less clearly epistemic in nature.

What might the latter category of goals include? To answer that question we must turn to the second of the two dominant outlooks within educational thought and practice, which I have chosen to call:

The Transformative Tradition

The adjective "transformative" describes what this tradition deems successful teaching to be capable of accomplishing: a transformation of one kind or another in the person being taught—a qualitative change often of dramatic proportion, a metamorphosis, so to speak. Such changes would include all those traits of character and of personality most highly prized by the society at large (aside from those having to do solely with the possession of knowledge *per se*). They also would include the eradication or remediation of a corresponding set of undesirable traits. In either case, the transformations aimed for within this tradition are typically conceived of as being more deeply integrated and ingrained within the psychological makeup of the student—and therefore as perhaps more enduring—than are those sought within the mimetic or epistemic outlook, whose dominant metaphor is one of "adding on" to what already exists (new knowledge, new skills, etc.) rather than modifying the would-be learner in some more fundamental way.

What traits and qualities have teachers working within the transformative tradition sought to modify? Our answer depends on when and where we look. Several centuries ago, for example, when the mission of schools was primarily religious, what was being sought was nothing other than students' salvation through preparing them for Bible reading and other religiously oriented activities. Such remains the goal of much religious instruction today, though the form of its expression may have changed somewhat.

Over the years, as schooling became more widespread and more secular in orientation, educators began to abandon the goal of piety *per se*, and focused instead upon effecting "transformation" of character, morals, and virtue. Many continue to speak that way today, though it is more common to name "attitudes," "values," and "interests" as the psychological traits many of today's teachers seek to modify.

However one describes the changes sought within the transformative tradition, it is interesting that this undertaking is usually treated as more exalted or noble than the more mimetic type of teaching. Why this should be so is not readily apparent, but the different degrees of seriousness attached to the two traditions are apparent in the metaphors associated with each of them.

As I have already said, within the mimetic tradition knowledge is conceived of as something akin to material goods. Like a person materially wealthy, the possessor of knowledge may be considered "richer" than his ignorant neighbor. Yet, like the materially rich and poor, the two remain fundamentally equal as human beings. This metaphor of knowledge as coins in one's purse is consonant with the concomitant belief that it is "detachable" from its owner, capable of being "shown," "lost," and so forth. A related metaphor, one often used to lampoon the mimetic tradition, depicts the learner as a kind of vessel into which knowledge is "poured" or "stored." What is important about all such metaphors is that the vessel in question remains essentially unchanged, with or without its "contents."

The root image within the transformative tradition is entirely different. It is much closer to that of a potter working with clay than it is to someone using the potter's handiwork as a container for whatever contents such a vessel might hold. The potter, as we know, not only leaves her imprint on the vessel itself in the form of a signature of some kind, she actually molds and shapes the object as she creates it. All who later work with the finished product have a different relationship to it entirely. They may fill it or empty it to their hearts' content. They may even break it if they wish. But all such actions accept the object in question as a "given," something whose essence is fundamentally sacrosanct.

The metaphor of teacher-as-artist or teacher-as-creator gives the transformative tradition an air of profundity and drama, perhaps even spirituality, that is largely lacking within the mimetic tradition, whose root metaphor of mere addition of knowledge or skill is much more prosaic. But metaphors, as we know, are mere figures of speech. No matter how flattering they might be, they don't tell us whether such flattery is deserved. They leave us to ask whether teachers working within the transformative tradition actually succeed in doing what they and others sometimes boast they can do. And that's not all they leave unanswered. Beyond the question of whether transformative changes due to pedagogical interventions really occur at all there awaits the more practical question of *how* they happen. What do teachers do to bring them about? As we might guess, it is easier to answer the former question than the latter.

Fictional accounts of teachers who have had enduring effects on their students of the kind celebrated within the transformative tradition are familiar enough to be the stock in trade of the pedagogical novel. *Goodbye, Mr. Chips* and *The Prime of Miss Jean Brodie*[5] are but two of such works that come to mind most readily. Each exemplifies a teacher who has a profoundly transformative influence on his or her students. But what of real life? Do teachers *there* make a difference of the same magnitude as do the fictional Chipses and Brodies?

An answer to that question which I find quite convincing is contained in a study undertaken by Anne Kuehnle, a student of mine a few years back. In preparation for her term paper in a course on the analysis of teaching, work which later became the basis of her master's thesis, Kuehnle distributed questionnaires to 150 friends and neighbors in her hometown of Elmhurst, Illinois; she asked them to write a paragraph or two about the teachers they remembered most vividly. The results were striking. Not only did most respondents comply enthusiastically with the request, their descriptions yielded literally scores of vignettes showing the transformative tradition in action. Here are but three of them, chosen almost at random.

> He moved the learning process from himself to us and equipped us to study independently. We were able to see such mundane concepts as money supply, price mechanism, supply and demand, all around us. We became interested. We actually talked economics after class! In Eckstein's class I became aware that I was there to evaluate, not ingest, concepts. I began to discriminate . . .

She was, to me, a glimpse of the world beyond school and my little town of 800 people. She was beautiful, vivacious, witty, and had a truly brilliant mind. Her energy knew no limit —she took on all the high school English classes, class plays, yearbook, began interpretive reading and declamatory contests, started a library in the town, and on and on. *She* was our town's cultural center.

His dedication rubbed off on nearly all of us. I was once required to write him a 12-page report, and I handed in an 84-page research project. I always felt he deserved more than the minimum.[6]

These three examples are quite representative of the protocols quoted throughout Kuehnle's report. So if we can trust what so many of her respondents told us—and I am inclined to do so, for had I been asked I would have responded much as they did—there seems no shortage of testimonial evidence to support the conclusion that at least some teachers do indeed modify character, instill values, shape attitudes, generate new interests, and succeed in "transforming," profoundly and enduringly, at least some of the students in their charge. The question now becomes: How do they do it? How are such beneficial outcomes accomplished?

As most teachers will readily testify, the answer to that question will disappoint all who seek overnight to become like the teachers described in Kuehnle's report. It seems there *are* no formulas for accomplishing these most impressive if not miraculous feats of pedagogical skill. There are neither simple instructions for the neophyte nor complicated ones for the seasoned teacher. There is not even an epigram or two to keep in mind as guides for how to proceed, nothing analogous to the ancient "advice" that tells us to feed a cold and starve a fever.

And yet that last point is not quite as accurate as were the two that came before it. For if we look carefully at what such teachers do and listen to what others say about their influence, we begin to see that they *do* have some characteristic ways of working after all, "modes of operation" that, even if they can't be reduced to recipes and formulas, are worth noting all the same. The three of these modes most readily identifiable seem to me to be:

1. *Personal modeling.* Of the many attributes associated with transformative teaching, the most crucial ones seem to concern the

teacher as a person. For it is essential to success within that tradition that teachers who are trying to bring about transformative changes personify the very qualities they seek to engender in their students. To the best of their ability they must be living exemplars of certain virtues or values or attitudes. The fulfillment of that requirement achieves its apex in great historical figures, like Socrates and Christ, who epitomize such a personal model; but most teachers already know that no attitude, interest, or value can be taught except by the teacher who himself or herself believes in, cares for, or cherishes whatever it is that he or she holds out for emulation.

2. *"Soft" suasion.* Among teachers working toward transformative ends, the "showing" and "telling" so central to the mimetic tradition (actions contained in Step Two: *Present* of the methodological paradigm outlined above) are replaced by less emphatic assertions and by an altogether milder form of pedagogical authority. The teaching style is rather more forensic and rhetorical than it is one of proof and demonstration. Often the authority of the teacher is so diminished by the introduction of a questioning mode within this tradition that there occurs a kind of role reversal, almost as though the student were teaching the teacher. This shift makes the transformative teacher look humbler than his or her mimetic counterpart, but it is by no means clear that such an appearance is a trustworthy indicator of the teacher's true temperament.

3. *Use of narrative.* Within the transformative tradition "stories" of one kind or another, which would include parables, myths, and other forms of narrative, play a large role. Why this should be so is not immediately clear, but it becomes so as we consider what is common to the transformations that the schools seek to effect. The common element, it turns out, is their moral nature. Virtues, character traits, interests, attitudes, values—as educational goals all of them fall within the moral realm of the "right" or

"proper" or "just." Now when we ask about the function or purpose of narrative, one answer (some might say the only one) is: to moralize.[7] Narratives present us with stories about how to live (or how not to live) our lives. Again, Socrates and Christ come readily to mind as exemplars of the teacher-as-storyteller as well as the teacher about whom stories are told.

The examples of Socrates and Christ as both transformative models and as storytellers help us to realize that differences in the conception of teaching within the two traditions go far beyond the question of what shall be taught and how it shall be done. They extend to the psychological and epistemological relationship between the teacher and his or her students.

Within the mimetic tradition the teacher occupies the role of expert in two distinct ways. He or she supposedly is in command of a specifiable body of knowledge or set of skills whose properties we have already commented upon. Such knowledge constitutes what we might call *substantive* expertise. At the same time the teacher is thought to possess the know-how whereby a significant portion of his or her substantive knowledge may be "transmitted" to students. The latter body of knowledge, whose paradigmatic contours have also been sketched, constitutes what we might call the teacher's *methodological* expertise. The students, by way of contrast, might be described as doubly ignorant. They neither know what the teacher knows, substantively speaking, nor do they know how to teach it in methodological terms. This dual condition of ignorance places them below the teacher epistemologically no matter where they stand regarding other social attributes and statuses.

Within the transformative tradition, the superiority of the teacher's knowledge, whether substantive or methodological, is not nearly so clear-cut. Nor is the teacher's status in general vis-à-vis his or her students. Instead, the overall relationship between the two is often vexingly ambiguous if not downright upsetting to some students; it can even become so at times to teachers themselves. Nowhere are many of these ambiguities portrayed more dramatically than in the early Socratic dialogues of Plato.[8] In the person of Socrates we witness perhaps the most famous of all transformative teachers in action. He is also a teacher whose actions are often as puzzling as they are edifying.

Does Socrates know more than his students? Well of course he does, says commonsense, why else would so many seek him out for advice and confront him with the most profound of questions? Yet, as we know, Socrates rarely if ever answers the questions he is asked, often professing to know less about the answer than does the questioner himself. Is he feigning ignorance when he behaves that way? It is not always easy to tell, as we can gather from the frequent expressions of puzzlement on the part of those conversing with him. And what about his method? How canny is he as a teacher? Does he really know what he is doing every step of the way or is he more or less bumbling along much of the time, never quite sure of where he is going or of how to get there? Again, it is hard to say for sure. There are times when he seems completely in control of the situation, but other times when he seems utterly confused about what to say or do next; he even goes so far as to say so. Finally, what shall we make of the social relationship between Socrates and his fellow Athenians? Where do they stand in relation to each other? That too is a difficult question to answer definitively. Certainly he was greatly revered by many of his followers—Plato, of course, chief among them. But he was just as obviously envied by some and actively disliked by others.

A fuller treatment of the complexities and ambiguities of the Socratic method is beyond the scope of this work.[9] However, the little I have already said should make the point that ambiguities like those in the Socratic dialogues are common to the transformative tradition within teaching wherever it may be found. They are so because all such teachers are engaged in what is fundamentally *a moral undertaking* much like that of Socrates, whether they acknowledge it or not. Moreover, it is also *a philosophic* undertaking. That too is not always recognized by those actually engaged in such an enterprise.

What does it mean to speak of transformative teaching in these terms? In what sense is it either a moral or a philosophic undertaking? It is moral in that it seeks moral ends. Teachers working within the transformative tradition are actually trying to bring about changes in their students (and possibly in themselves as well) that make them better persons, not simply more knowledgeable or more skillful, but better in the sense of being closer to what humans are capable of becoming—more virtuous, fuller participants in an evolving moral order.

It is philosophic in that it employs philosophical means. No matter how else they might describe their actions, teachers working within the transformative tradition seek to change their students (and possibly themselves as well) by means neither didactic nor dogmatic. Instead, they use discussion, demonstration, argumentation. Armed only with the tools of reason, the transformative teacher seeks to accomplish what can be attained in no other way. Here is how one student of the process describes its operation within philosophy proper.

> We have discovered philosophy to be the sum total of those universal rational truths that become clear only through reflection. To philosophize, then, is simply to isolate these rational truths with our intellect and to express them in general judgments. . . .

The teacher who seriously wishes to impart philosophical insight can aim only at teaching the art of philosophising. He can do no more than show his students how to undertake, each for himself, the laborious regress that alone affords insight into basic principles. If there is such a thing at all as instruction in philosophy, it can only be instruction in doing one's own thinking; more precisely, in the independent practice of the art of abstraction.[10]

Another commentator on the same subject sums up the difference by referring to himself as "a philosopher, not an expert." "The latter," he goes on to explain, "knows what he knows and what he does not know: the former does not. One concludes, the other questions—two very different language games."[11]

But talk of teachers being engaged in a moral and philosophic enterprise has its difficulties. For one thing, it sounds rather pretentious, especially when we consider some of the more mundane aspects of the average teacher's work—the routines of giving assignments, grading papers, taking attendance, keeping order in the classroom, and so on. Little of such activity deserves to be called either moral or philosophical. Moreover, teachers themselves do not seem to talk that way about what they do. Least of all do those who do it best, like Socrates.

The way out of these difficulties is to deny neither the moral and philosophical dimensions of teaching nor the prosaic nature of much that teachers actually do. Rather it requires that we acknowledge the compatibility of both viewpoints, seeing them as complementary rather than mutually exclusive. In short, nothing save a kind of conceptual narrow-mindedness keeps us from a vision of teaching as both a noble and a prosaic undertaking. Erasmus approached that insight several centuries ago when he remarked that "In the opinion of fools [teaching] is a humble task, but in fact it is the noblest of occupations."[12] Had he been a trifle more charitable he might have added that the fools were not totally wrong. Their trouble was that they were only half right.

Teachers themselves often overlook the moral dimensions of their work, but that failing must be treated as a problem to be solved, rather than as evidence of the amorality of teaching itself. There is no doubt that one can teach without giving thought to the transformative significance of what he or she is doing. But whether it should be so performed is another question entirely. Moreover, though the teacher may pay no attention whatsoever to such matters, we must ask if they are thereby eliminated as a class of outcomes. The well-known phenomenon of *unintended consequences*, sometimes referred to as "incidental learnings" when they take place within the context of a classroom, leads us to suspect that the delivery of moral messages and actions of transformative significance may often take place whether the teacher intends them to or not. Indeed, it is far more interesting to ask whether such outcomes are inevitable, which is equivalent to asking whether all teachers are ultimately working within the transformative tradition whether they realize it or not.

From "The Mimetic and the Transformative" in *The Practice of Teaching* by Philip W. Jackson (New York: Teachers College Press, 1986). Reprinted by permission.

Notes

1. Ludwig Wittgenstein, *Philosophical Investigations* (Oxford: Basil Blackwell, 1968), p. 9e.
2. Aristotle once remarked that "All instruction given or received by way of argument proceeds from pre-existent knowledge." (*Posterior Analytic*, Book, I, 71a). By this he meant that we must begin with major and minor premises whose truth is beyond dispute before we can move to a novel conclusion. This is not quite the same as claiming that all knowledge is secondhand, but it does call attention to how much of the "known" is properly described as having been "transmitted" or "passed along" to students from teachers or teacher surrogates, such as textbooks or computers.
3. For a well-known discussion of that distinction, see Gilbert Ryle, *The Concept of Mind* (New York: Barnes and Noble, 1949).
4. See, for example, G. A. Miller, E. Galanter, and K. H. Pribham, *Plans and the Structure of Behavior* (New York: Holt, 1960).
5. James Hilton, *Goodbye Mr. Chips* (Boston: Little, Brown and Co., 1934) and Muriel Spark, *The Prime of Miss Jean Brodie* (Philadelphia: Lippincott, 1961).
6. Anne Kuehnle, "Teachers remembered," unpublished master's thesis, University of Chicago, June 1984.
7. See Hayden White, "The value of narrativity in the representation of reality," in W. J. T. Mitchell (ed.), *On Narrative* (Chicago: University of Chicago Press, 1981), 1–24. Also, John Gardner, *On Moral Fiction* (New York: Basic Books, 1978). Gardner points out that "the effect of great fiction is to temper real experience, modify prejudice, humanize" (p. 114).
8. See Edith Hamilton and Huntington Cairns (eds.), *The Collected Dialogues of Plato* (Princeton, New Jersey: Princeton University Press, 1961). See especially the *Charmides, Laches, Euthydemus, Protagoras, Gorgias,* and *Meno.*
9. For a fuller treatment of these and other ambiguities having to do with Socrates' teaching style see Gregory Vlastos, "Introduction: The paradox of Socrates," in Gregory Vlastos (ed.), *The Philosophy of Socrates* (Notre Dame, Indiana:

University of Notre Dame Press, 1980), 1–21. Several other essays in that volume treat specialized aspects of the subject, such as Socrates' use of the technique of *elenchus*. See also, W. K. C. Guthrie, *Socrates* (Cambridge: Cambridge University Press, 1971), especially "The ignorance of Socrates," pp. 122–129. Also, Gerasimos Xenophon Santas, *Socrates* (Boston: Routledge & Kegan Paul, 1979). An unusually enlightening essay on the Socratic method is contained in

Leonard Nelson, *Socratic Method and Critical Philosophy* (New York: Dover Publications, 1965), 1–40.

10. Nelson, *Socratic Method*, 10–11.
11. Jean-Francois Lvotard, *The Postmodern Condition: A Report on Knowledge* (Minneapolis: University of Minnesota Press, 1984), xxv.
12. Claude M. Fuess and Emory S. Basford (eds.), *Unseen Harvests: A Treasury of Teaching* (New York: Macmillan, 1947), v.

The Silenced Dialogue

Power and Pedagogy in Educating Other People's Children

Lisa D. Delpit

A black male graduate student who is also a special education teacher in a predominantly black community is talking about his experiences in predominantly white university classes:

> There comes a moment in every class where we have to discuss "The Black Issue" and what's appropriate education for black children. I tell you, I'm tired of arguing with those white people, because they won't listen. Well, I don't know if they really don't listen or if they just don't believe you. It seems like if you can't quote Vygotsky or something, then you don't have any validity to speak about your *own* kids. Anyway, I'm not bothering with it anymore, now I'm just in it for a grade.

A black woman teacher in a multicultural urban elementary school is talking about her experiences in discussions with her predominantly white fellow teachers about how they should organize reading instruction to best serve students of color:

> When you're talking to white people they still want it to be their way. You can try to talk to them and give them examples, but they're so headstrong, they think they know what's best for *everybody*, for *everybody's* children. They won't listen; white folks are going to do what they want to do *anyway*.
>
> It's really hard. They just don't listen well. No, they listen, but they don't *hear*—you know how your mama used to say you listen to the radio, but you *hear* your mother? Well they don't *hear* me.
>
> So I just try to shut them out so I can hold my temper. You can only beat your head against a brick wall for so long before you draw blood. If I try to stop arguing with them I can't help myself from getting angry. Then I end up walking around praying all day "Please Lord, remove the bile I feel for these people so I can sleep tonight." It's funny, but it can become a cancer, a sore.
>
> So, I shut them out. I go back to my own little cubby, my classroom, and I try to teach the way I know will work, no matter what those folk say. And when I get black kids, I just try to undo the damage they did.
>
> I'm not going to let any man, woman, or child drive me crazy—white folks will try to do that to you if you let them. You just have to stop talking to them, that's what I do. I just keep smiling, but I won't talk to them.

A soft-spoken Native Alaskan woman in her forties is a student in the Education Department of the University of Alaska. One day she storms into a black professor's office and very uncharacteristically slams the door. She plops down in a chair and, still fuming, says, "Please tell those people, just don't help us anymore! I give up. I won't talk to them again!"

And finally, a black woman principal who is also a doctoral student at a well-known university on the West Coast is talking about her university experiences, particularly about when a professor lectures on issues concerning educating black children:

> If you try to suggest that's not quite the way it is, they get defensive, then you get defensive, then they'll start reciting research.
>
> I try to give them my experiences, to explain. They just look and nod. The more I try to explain, they just look and nod, just keep looking and nodding. They don't really hear me.
>
> Then, when it's time for class to be over, the professor tells me to come to his office to talk more. So I go. He asks for more examples of what I'm talking about, and he looks and nods while I give them. Then he says that that's just *my* experience. It doesn't really apply to most black people.
>
> It becomes futile because they think they know everything about everybody. What you have to say about your life, your children, doesn't mean anything. They don't really want to hear what you have to say. They wear blinders and earplugs. They only want to go on research they've read that other white people have written.
>
> It just doesn't make any sense to keep talking to them.

Thus was the first half of the title of this text born: "The Silenced Dialogue." One of the tragedies in this field of education is that scenarios such as these are enacted daily around the country. The saddest element is that the individuals that the black and Native Alaskan educators speak of in these statements are seldom aware that the dialogue *has* been silenced. Most likely the white educators believe that their colleagues of color did, in the end, agree with their logic. After all, they stopped disagreeing, didn't they?

I have collected these statements since completing a recently published article, a somewhat autobiographical account entitled "Skills and Other Dilemmas of a Progressive Black Educator," in which I discuss my perspective as a product of a skills-oriented approach to writing and as a teacher of process-oriented approaches.[1] I described the estrangement that I and many teachers of color feel from the progressive movement when writing process advocates dismiss us as too "skills oriented." I ended the article suggesting that it was incumbent upon writing process advocates, or indeed, advocates of any progressive movement, to enter into dialogue with teachers of color, who may not share their enthusiasm about so-called new, liberal, or progressive ideas.

In response to this article, which presented no research data and did not even cite a reference, I received numerous calls and letters from teachers, professors, and even state school personnel from around the country, both black and white. All of the white respondents, except one, have wished to talk more about the question of skills versus process approaches—to support or reject what they perceive to be my position. On the other hand, *all* of the nonwhite respondents have spoken passionately on being left out of the dialogue about how best to educate children of color.

How can such complete communication blocks exist when both parties truly believe they have the same aims? How can the bitterness and resentment expressed by the educators of color be drained so that the sores can heal? What can be done?

I believe the answer to these questions lies in ethnographic analysis, that is, in identifying and giving voice to alternative worldviews. Thus, I will attempt to address the concerns raised by white and black respondents to my article "Skills and Other Dilemmas." My charge here is not to determine the best instructional methodology; I believe that the actual practice of good teachers of all colors typically incorporates a range of pedagogical orientations. Rather, I suggest that the differing perspectives on the debate over "skills" versus "process" approaches can lead to an understanding of the alienation and miscommunication, and thereby to an understanding of the "silenced dialogue."

In thinking through these issues, I have found what I believe to be a connecting and complex theme: what I have come to call "the culture of power." There are five aspects of power I would like to propose as given for this presentation:

1. Issues of power are enacted in classrooms.
2. There are codes or rules for participating in power; that is, there is a "culture of power."
3. The rules of the culture of power are a reflection of the rules of the culture of those who have power.
4. If you are not already a participant in the culture of power, being told explicitly the rules of that culture makes acquiring power easier.
5. Those with power are frequently least aware of—or least willing to acknowledge—its existence. Those with less power are often most aware of its existence.

The first three are by now basic tenets in the literature of the sociology of education, but the last two have seldom been addressed. The following discussion will explicate these aspects of power and their relevance to the schism between liberal educational movements and that of non-white, non-middle-class teachers and communities.[2]

1. *Issues of power are enacted in classrooms.* These issues include: the power of the teacher over the students; the power of the publishers of textbooks and of the developers of the curriculum to determine the view of the world presented; the power of the state in enforcing compulsory schooling; and the power of an individual or group to determine another's intelligence or "normalcy." Finally, if schooling prepares people for jobs, and the kind of job a person has determines her or his economic status and, therefore, power, then schooling is immediately related to that power.

2. *There are codes or rules for participating in power; that is, there is a "culture of power."* The codes or rules I'm speaking of relate to linguistic forms, communicative strategies, and presentation of self; that is, ways of talking, ways of writing, ways of dressing, and ways of interacting.

3. *The rules of the culture of power are a reflection of the rules of the culture of those who have power.* This means that success in institutions—schools, workplaces, and so on—is predicated upon acquisition of the culture of those who are in power. Children from middle-class homes tend to do better in school than those from nonmiddle-class homes because the culture of the school is based on the culture of the upper and middle classes—of those in power. The upper and middle classes send their children to school with all the accoutrements of the culture of power; children from other kinds of families operate within perfectly wonderful and viable cultures but not cultures that carry the codes or rules of power.

4. *If you are not already a participant in the culture of power, being told explicitly the rules of that culture makes acquiring power easier.* In my work within and between diverse cultures, I have come to conclude that members of any culture transmit information implicitly to co-members. However, when implicit codes are attempted across cultures, communication frequently breaks down. Each cultural group is left saying, "Why don't those people say what they mean?" as well as, "What's wrong with them, why don't they understand?"

Anyone who has had to enter new cultures, especially to accomplish a specific task, will know of what I speak. When I lived in several Papua New Guinea villages for extended periods to collect data, and when I go to Alaskan villages for work with Native Alaskan communities, I have found it unquestionably easier, psychologically and pragmatically, when some kind soul has directly informed me about such matters as appropriate dress, interactional styles, embedded meanings, and taboo words or actions. I contend that it is much the same for anyone seeking to learn the rules of the culture of power. Unless one has the leisure of a lifetime of "immersion" to learn them, explicit presentation makes learning immeasurably easier.

And now, to the fifth and last premise:

5. *Those with power are frequently least aware of—or least willing to acknowledge—its existence. Those with less power are often most aware of its existence.* For many who consider themselves members of liberal or radical camps, acknowledging personal power and admitting participation in the culture of power is distinctly uncomfortable. On the other hand, those who are less powerful in any situation are most likely to recognize the power variable most acutely. My guess is that the white colleagues and instructors of those previously quoted did not perceive themselves to have power over the nonwhite speakers. However, either by virtue of their position, their numbers, or their access to that particular code of power of calling upon research to validate one's position, the white educators had the authority to establish what was to be considered "truth" regardless of the opinions of the people of color, and the latter were well aware of that fact.

A related phenomenon is that liberals (and here I am using the term "liberal" to refer to those whose beliefs include striving for a society based upon maximum individual freedom and autonomy) seem to act under the assumption that to make any rules or expectations explicit is to act against liberal principles, to limit the freedom and autonomy of those subjected to the explicitness.

I thank Fred Erickson for a comment that led me to look again at a tape by John Gumperz on cultural dissonance in cross-cultural interactions.[3] One of the episodes showed an East Indian interviewing for a job with an all-white committee. The interview was a complete failure, even though several of the interviewers appeared to really want to help the applicant. As the interview rolled steadily downhill, these "helpers" became more and more indirect in their questioning, which exacerbated the problems the applicant had in performing appropriately. Operating from a different cultural perspective, he got fewer and fewer clear clues as to what was expected of him, which ultimately resulted in his failure to secure the position.

I contend that as the applicant showed less and less aptitude for handling the interview, the power differential became ever more evident to the interviewers. The "helpful" interviewers, unwilling to acknowledge themselves as having power over the applicant, became more and more uncomfortable. Their indirectness was an attempt to lessen the power differential and their discomfort by lessening the power-revealing explicitness of their questions and comments.

When acknowledging and expressing power, one tends towards explicitness (as in yelling at your ten-year-old, "Turn that radio down!"). When deemphasizing power, there is a move toward indirect communication. Therefore, in the interview setting, those who sought to help, to express their egalitarianism with the East Indian applicant, became more and more indirect—and less and less helpful—in their questions and comments.

In literacy instruction, explicitness might be equated with direct instruction. Perhaps the ultimate expression of explicitness and direct instruction in the primary classroom is Distar. This reading program is based on a behaviorist model in which reading is taught through the direct instruction of phonics generalizations and blending. The teacher's role is to maintain the full attention of the group by continuous questioning, eye contact, finger snaps, hand claps, and other gestures, and by eliciting choral responses and initiating some sort of award system.

When the program was introduced, it arrived with a flurry of research data that "proved" that all children—even those who were "culturally deprived"—could learn to read using this method. Soon there was a strong response, first from academics and later from many classroom teachers, stating that the program was terrible. What I find particularly interesting, however, is that the primary issue of the conflict over Distar has not been over its instructional efficacy—usually the students did learn to read—but the expression of explicit power in the classroom. The liberal educators opposed the methods—the direct instruction, the explicit control exhibited by the teacher. As a matter of fact, it was not unusual (even now) to hear of the program spoken of as "fascist."

I am not an advocate of Distar, but I will return to some of the issues that the program, and direct instruction in general, raises in understanding the differences between progressive white educators and educators of color.

To explore those differences, I would like to present several statements typical of those made with the best of intentions by middle-class liberal educators. To the surprise of the speakers, it is not unusual for such content to be met by vocal opposition or stony silence from people of color. My attempt here is to examine the underlying assumptions of both camps.

"I want the same thing for everyone else's children as I want for mine."

To provide schooling for everyone's children that reflects liberal, middle-class values and aspirations is to ensure the maintenance of the status quo, to ensure that power, the culture of power, remains in the hands of those who already have it. Some children come to school with more accoutrements of the culture of power already in place—"cultural capital," as some critical theorists refer to it[4]—some with less. Many liberal educators hold that the primary goal for education is for children to become autonomous, to develop fully who they are in the classroom setting without having arbitrary, outside standards forced upon them. This is a very reasonable goal for people whose children are already participants in the culture of power and who have already internalized its codes.

But parents who don't function within that culture often want something else. It's not that they disagree with the former aim, it's just that they want something more. They want to ensure that the school provides their

children with discourse patterns, interactional styles, and spoken and written language codes that will allow them success in the larger society.

It was the lack of attention to this concern that created such a negative outcry in the black community when well-intentioned white liberal educators introduced "dialect readers." These were seen as a plot to prevent the schools from teaching the linguistic aspects of the culture of power, thus dooming black children to a permanent outsider caste. As one parent demanded, "My kids know how to be black—you all teach them how to be successful in the white man's world."

Several black teachers have said to me recently that as much as they'd like to believe otherwise, they cannot help but conclude that many of the "progressive" educational strategies imposed by liberals upon black and poor children could only be based on a desire to ensure that the liberals' children get sole access to the dwindling pool of American jobs. Some have added that the liberal educators believe themselves to be operating with good intentions, but that these good intentions are only conscious delusions about their unconscious true motives. One of the black anthropologist John Gwaltney's informants in *Drylongso* reflects this perspective with her tongue-in-cheek observation that the biggest difference between black folks and white folks is that black folks *know* when they're lying!

Let me try to clarify how this might work in literacy instruction. A few years ago I worked on an analysis of two popular reading programs, Distar and a progressive program that focused on higher-level critical thinking skills. In one of the first lessons of the progressive program, the children are introduced to the names of the letters *m* and *e*. In the same lesson they are then taught the sound made by each of the letters, how to write each of the letters, and that when the two are blended together they produce the word *me*.

As an experienced first-grade teacher, I am convinced that a child needs to be familiar with a significant number of these concepts to be able to assimilate so much new knowledge in one sitting. By contrast, Distar presents the same information in about forty lessons.

I would not argue for the pace of Distar lessons—such a slow pace would only bore most kids—but what happened in the other lesson is that it merely provided an opportunity for those who already knew the content to exhibit that they knew it, or at most perhaps to build one new concept onto what was already known. This meant that the child who did not come to school already primed with what was to be presented would be labeled as needing "remedial" instruction from day one; indeed, this determination would be made before he or she was ever taught. In fact, Distar was "successful" because it actually *taught* new information to children who had not already acquired it at home. Although the more progressive system was ideal for some children, for others it was a disaster.

I do not advocate a simplistic "basic skills" approach for children outside of the culture of power. It would be (and has been) tragic to operate as if these children were incapable of critical and higher-order thinking and reasoning. Rather, I suggest that schools must provide these children the content that other families from a different cultural orientation provide at home. This does not mean separating children according to family background, but instead, ensuring that each classroom incorporate strategies appropriate for all the children in its confines.

And I do not advocate that it is the school's job to attempt to change the homes of poor and nonwhite children to match the homes of those in the culture of power. That may indeed be a form of cultural genocide. I have frequently heard schools call poor parents "uncaring" when parents respond to the school's urging, saying, "But that's the school's job." What the school personnel fail to understand is that if the parents were members of the culture of power and lived by its rules and codes, then they would transmit those codes to their children. In fact, they transmit another culture that children must learn at home in order to survive in their communities.

"Child-centered, whole language, and process approaches are, needed in order to allow a democratic state of free, autonomous, empowered adults, and because research has shown that children learn best through these methods."

People of color are, in general, skeptical of research as a determiner of our fates. Academic research has, after all, found us genetically inferior, culturally deprived, and verbally deficient. But beyond that general caveat, and despite my or others' personal preferences, there is little research data supporting the major tenets of process approaches over other forms of literacy instruction, and virtually no evidence that such approaches are more efficacious for children of color.[5]

Although the problem is not necessarily inherent in the method, in some instances adherents of process approaches to writing create situations in which students ultimately find themselves held accountable for knowing a set of rules about which no one has ever directly informed them. Teachers do students no service to suggest, even implicitly, that "product" is not important. In this country, students will be judged on their product regardless of the process they utilized to achieve it. And that product, based as it is on the specific codes of a particular culture, is more readily produced when the directives of how to produce it are made explicit.

If such explicitness is not provided to students, what it feels like to people who are old enough to judge is that there are secrets being kept, that time is being wasted, that the teacher is abdicating his or her duty to teach. A doctoral student of my acquaintance was assigned to a writing class to hone his writing skills. The student was placed in the section led by a white professor who utilized a process approach, consisting primarily of having the students write essays and then assemble into groups to edit each other's papers. That procedure infuriated this particular student. He had many angry encounters with the teacher about what she was doing. In his words:

> I didn't feel she was teaching us anything. She wanted us to correct each other's papers and we were there to learn from her. She didn't teach anything, absolutely nothing.
>
> Maybe they're trying to learn what black folks knew all the time. We understand how to

improvise, how to express ourselves coercively. When I'm in a classroom, I'm not looking for that, I'm looking for structure, the more formal language.

Now my buddy was in [a] black teacher's class. And that lady was very good. She went through and explained and defined each part of the structure. This [white] teacher didn't get along with that black teacher. She said that she didn't agree with her methods. But I don't think that white teacher *had* any methods.

When I told this gentleman that what the teacher was doing was called a process method of teaching writing, his response was, "Well, at least now I know that she *thought* she was doing *something*. I thought she was just a fool who couldn't teach and didn't want to try."

This sense of being cheated can be so strong that the student may be completely turned off to the educational system. Amanda Branscombe, an accomplished white teacher, recently wrote a letter discussing her work with working-class black and white students at a community college in Alabama. She had given these students my "Skills and Other Dilemmas" article to read and discuss, and wrote that her students really understood and identified with what I was saying. To quote her letter:

> One young man said that he had dropped out of high school because he failed the exit exam. He noted that he had then passed the GED without a problem after three weeks of prep. He said that his high school English teacher claimed to use a process approach, but what she really did was hide behind fancy words to give herself permission to do nothing in the classroom.

The students I have spoken of seem to be saying that the teacher has denied them access to herself as the source of knowledge necessary to learn the forms they need to succeed. Again, I tentatively attribute the problem to teachers' resistance to exhibiting power in the classroom. Somehow, to exhibit one's personal power as expert source is viewed as disempowering one's students.

Two qualifiers are necessary, however. The teacher cannot be the only expert in the classroom. To deny students their own expert knowledge *is* to disempower them. Amanda Branscombe, when she was working with black high school students classified as "slow learners," had the students analyze rap songs to discover their underlying patterns. The students became the experts in explaining to the teacher the rules for creating a new rap song. The teacher then used the patterns the students identified as a base to begin an explanation of the structure of grammar, and then of Shakepeare's plays. Both student and teacher are expert at what they know best.

The second qualifier is that merely adopting direct instruction is not the answer. Actual writing for real audiences and real purposes is a vital element in helping students to understand that they have an important voice in their own learning processes. E. V. Siddle examines the results of various kinds of interventions in a primarily process-oriented writing class for black students.[6] Based on readers' blind assessments, she found that the intervention that produced the most positive changes in the students' writing was a "mini-lesson" consisting of direct instruction about some standard writing convention. But what produced the *second* highest number of positive changes was a subsequent student-centered conference with the teacher. (Peer conferencing in this group of black students who were not members of the culture of power produced the least number of changes in students' writing. However, the classroom teacher maintained—and I concur—that such activities are necessary to introduce the elements of "real audience" into the task, along with more teacher-directed strategies.)

"It's really a shame but she (that black teacher upstairs) seems to be so authoritarian, so focused on skills and so teacher directed. Those poor kids never seem to be allowed to really express their creativity. (And she even yells at them.)"

This statement directly concerns the display of power and authority in the classroom. One way to understand the difference in perspective between black teachers and their progressive colleagues on this issue is to explore culturally influenced oral interactions.

In *Ways with Words*, Shirley Brice Heath quotes the verbal directives given by the middle-class "townspeople" teachers:[7]

- "Is this where the scissors belong?"
- "You want to do your best work today."

By contrast, many black teachers are more likely to say:

- "Put those scissors on that shelf."
- "Put your name on the papers and make sure to get the right answer for each question."

Is one oral style more authoritarian than another?

Other researchers have identified differences in middle-class and working-class speech to children. Snow and others, for example, report that working-class mothers use more directives to their children than do middle- and upper-class parents.[8] Middle-class parents are likely to give the directive to a child to take his bath as, "Isn't it time for your bath?" Even though the utterance is couched as a question, both child and adult understand it as a directive. The child may respond with "Aw, Mom, can't I wait until . . . ," but whether or not negotiation is attempted, both conversants understand the intent of the utterance.

By contrast, a black mother, in whose house I was recently a guest, said to her eight-year-old son, "Boy, get your rusty behind in that bathtub." Now, I happen to know that this woman loves her son as much as any mother, but she would never have posed the directive to her son to take a bath in the form of a question. Were she to ask, "Would you like to take your bath now?" she would not have been issuing a directive but offering a true alternative. Consequently, as Heath suggests, upon entering school the child from such a family may not understand the indirect statement of the teacher as a direct command. Both white and black working-class children in the communities Heath studied "had

difficulty interpreting these indirect requests for adherence to an unstated set of rules."[9]

But those veiled commands are commands nonetheless, representing true power, and with true consequences for disobedience. If veiled commands are ignored, the child will be labeled a behavior problem and possibly officially classified as behavior disordered. In other words, the attempt by the teacher to reduce an exhibition of power by expressing herself in indirect terms may remove the very explicitness that the child needs to understand the rules of the new classroom culture.

A black elementary school principal in Fairbanks, Alaska, reported to me that she has a lot of difficulty with black children who are placed in some white teachers' classrooms. The teachers often send the children to the office for disobeying teacher directives. Their parents are frequently called in for conferences. The parents' response to the teacher is usually the same. "They do what I say; if you just *tell* them what to do, they'll do it. I tell them at home that they have to listen to what you say." And so, does not the power still exist? Its veiled nature only makes it more difficult for some children to respond appropriately, but that in no way mitigates its existence.

I don't mean to imply, however, that the only time the black child disobeys the teacher is when he or she misunderstands the request for certain behavior. There are other factors that may produce such behavior. Black children expect an authority figure to act with authority. When the teacher instead acts as a "chum," the message sent is that this adult has no authority, and the children react accordingly. One reason that is so, is that black people often view issues of power and authority differently than people from mainstream middle-class backgrounds.[10] Many people of color expect authority to be earned by personal efforts and exhibited by personal characteristics. In other words, "the authoritative person gets to be a teacher because she is authoritative." Some members of middle-class cultures, by contrast, expect one to achieve authority by the acquisition of an authoritative role. That is, "the teacher is the authority because she is the teacher."

In the first instance, because authority is earned, the teacher must consistently prove the characteristics that give her authority. These characteristics may vary across cultures, but in the black community they tend to cluster around several abilities. The authoritative teacher can control the class through exhibition of personal power; establishes meaningful interpersonal relationships that garner student respect; exhibits a strong belief that all students can learn; establishes a standard of achievement and "pushes" the students to achieve that standard; and holds the attention of the students by incorporating interactional features of black communicative style in his or her teaching.

By contrast, the teacher whose authority is vested in the role has many more options of behavior at her disposal. For instance, she does not need to express any sense of personal power because her authority does not come from anything she herself does or says. Hence, the power she actually holds may be veiled in such questions/commands as "Would you like to sit down now?" If the children in her class understand authority as she does, it is mutually agreed upon that they are to obey her no matter how indirect, soft-spoken, or unassuming she may be. Her indirectness and soft-spokenness may indeed be, as I suggested earlier, an attempt to reduce the implication of overt power in order to establish a more egalitarian and nonauthoritarian classroom atmosphere.

If the children operate under another notion of authority, however, then there is trouble. The black child may perceive the middle-class teacher as weak, ineffectual, and incapable of taking on the role of being the teacher; therefore, there is no need to follow her directives. In her dissertation, Michelle Foster quotes one young black man describing such a teacher:

> She is boring, boring. She could do something creative. Instead she just stands there. She can't control the class, doesn't know how to control the class. She asked me what she was doing wrong. I told her she just stands there like she's meditating. I told her she could be mediating for all I know. She says that we're supposed to know what to do. I told her I don't know

nothin' unless she tells me. She just can't control the class. I hope we don't have her next semester.[11]

But of course the teacher may not view the problem as residing in herself but in the student, and the child may once again become the behavior-disordered black boy in special education.

What characteristics do black students attribute to the good teacher? Again, Foster's dissertation provides a quotation that supports my experience with black students. A young black man is discussing a former teacher with a group of friends:

> We had fun in her class, but she was mean. I can remember she used to say, "Tell me what's in the story, Wayne." She pushed, she used to get on me and push me to know. She made us learn. We had to get in the books. There was this tall guy and he tried to take her on, but she was in charge of that class and she didn't let anyone run her. I still have this book we used in her class. It has a bunch of stories in it. I just read one on Coca-Cola again the other day.[12]

To clarify, this student was *proud* of the teacher's "meanness," an attribute he seemed to describe as the ability to run the class and pushing and expecting students to learn. Now, does the liberal perspective of the negatively authoritarian black teacher really hold up? I suggest that although all "explicit" black teachers are not also good teachers, there are different attitudes in different cultural groups about which characteristics make for a good teacher. Thus, it is impossible to create a model for the good teacher without taking issues of culture and community context into account.

And now to the final comment I present for examination:

> *"Children have the right to their own language, their own culture. We must fight cultural hegemony and fight the system by insisting that children be allowed to express themselves in their own language style. It is not they, the children, who must change,*

but the schools. To push children to do anything else is repressive and reactionary."

A statement such as this originally inspired me to write the "Skills and Other Dilemmas" article. It was first written as a letter to a colleague in response to a situation that had developed in our department. I was teaching a senior-level teacher education course. Students were asked to prepare a written autobiographical document for the class that would also be shared with their placement school prior to their student teaching.

One student, a talented young Native American woman, submitted a paper in which the ideas were lost because of technical problems—from spelling to sentence structure to paragraph structure. Removing her name, I duplicated the paper for a discussion with some faculty members. I had hoped to initiate a discussion about what we could do to ensure that our students did not reach the senior level without getting assistance in technical writing skills when they needed them.

I was amazed at the response. Some faculty implied that the student should never have been allowed into the teacher education program. Others, some of the more progressive minded, suggested that I was attempting to function as gatekeeper by raising the issue, and had internalized repressive and disempowering forces of the power elite to suggest that something was wrong with a Native American student just because she had another style of writing. With few exceptions, I found myself alone in arguing against both camps.

No, this student should not have been denied entry to the program. To deny her entry under the notion of upholding standards is to blame the victim for the crime. We cannot justifiably enlist exclusionary standards when the reason this student lacked the skills demanded was poor teaching at best and institutionalized racism at worst.

However, to bring this student into the program and pass her through without attending to obvious deficits in the codes needed for her to function effectively as a teacher is equally criminal—for though we may assuage our own consciences for not participating in victim blaming, she will surely be accused and convicted

as soon as she leaves the university. As Native Alaskans were quick to tell me, and as I understood through my own experience in the black community, not only would she not be hired as a teacher, but those who did not hire her would make the (false) assumption that the university was putting out only incompetent Natives and that they should stop looking seriously at any Native applicants. A white applicant who exhibits problems is an individual with problems. A person of color who exhibits problems immediately becomes a representative of her cultural group.

No, either stance is criminal. The answer is to *accept* students but also to take responsibility to *teach* them. I decided to talk to the student and found out she had recognized that she needed some assistance in the technical aspects of writing soon after she entered the university as a freshman. She had gone to various members of the education faculty and received the same two kinds of responses I met with four years later: faculty members told her either that she should not even attempt to be a teacher, or that it didn't matter and that she shouldn't worry about such trivial issues. In her desperation, she had found a helpful professor in the English Department, but he left the university when she was in her sophomore year.

We sat down together, worked out a plan for attending to specific areas of writing competence, and set up regular meetings. I stressed to her the need to use her own learning process as insight into how best to teach her future students those "skills" that her own schooling had failed to teach her. I gave her some explicit rules to follow in some areas; for others, we devised various kinds of journals that, along with readings about the structure of the language, allowed her to find her own insights into how the language worked. All that happened two years ago, and the young woman is now successfully teaching. What the experience led me to understand is that pretending that gatekeeping points don't exist is to ensure that many students will not pass through them.

Now you may have inferred that I believe that because there is a culture of power, everyone should learn the codes to participate in it, and that is how the world should be. Actually, nothing could be further from the truth. I believe in a diversity of style, and I believe the world will be diminished if cultural diversity is ever obliterated. Further, I believe strongly, as do my liberal colleagues, that each cultural group should have the right to maintain its own language style. When I speak, therefore, of the culture of power, I don't speak of how I wish things to be but of how they are.

I further believe that to act as if power does not exist is to ensure that the power status quo remains the same. To imply to children or adults (but of course the adults won't believe you anyway) that it doesn't matter how you talk or how you write is to ensure their ultimate failure. I prefer to be honest with my students. I tell them that their language and cultural style is unique and wonderful but that there is a political power game that is also being played, and if they want to be in on that game there are certain games that they too must play.

But don't think that I let the onus of change rest entirely with the students. I am also involved in political work both inside and outside of the educational system, and that political work demands that I place myself to influence as many gatekeeping points as possible. And it is there that I agitate for change, pushing gatekeepers to open their doors to a variety of styles and codes. What I'm saying, however, is that I do not believe that political change toward diversity can be effected from the bottom up, as do some of my colleagues. They seem to believe that if we accept and encourage diversity within classrooms of children, then diversity will automatically be accepted at gatekeeping points.

I believe that will never happen. What will happen is that the students who reach the gatekeeping points—like Amanda Branscombe's student who dropped out of high school because he failed his exit exam—will understand that they have been lied to and will react accordingly. No, I am certain that if we are truly to effect societal change, we cannot do so from the bottom up, but we must push and agitate from the top down. And in the meantime, we must take the responsibility to *teach*, to provide for students who do not already possess them, the additional codes of power.[13]

But I also do not believe that we should teach students to passively adopt an alternate code. They must be encouraged to understand the value of the code they already possess as well as to understand the power realities in this country. Otherwise they will be unable to work to change these realities. And how does one do that?

Martha Demientieff, a masterful Native Alaskan teacher of Athabaskan Indian students, tells me that her students, who live in a small, isolated, rural village of less than two hundred people, are not aware that there are different codes in English. She takes their writing and analyzes it for features of what has been referred to by Alaskan linguists as "Village English," and then covers half a bulletin board with words or phrases from the students' writing, which she labels "Our Heritage Language." On the other half of the bulletin board she puts the equivalent statements in "Standard English," which she labels "Formal English."

She and the students spend a long time on the "Heritage English" section, savoring the words, discussing the nuances. She tells the students, "That's the way we say things. Doesn't it feel good? Isn't it the absolute best way of getting that idea across?" Then she turns to the other side of the board. She tells the students that there are people, not like those in the village, who judge others by the way they talk or write.

> We listen to the way people talk, not to judge them, but to tell what part of the river they come from. These other people are not like that. They think everybody needs to talk like them. Unlike us, they have a hard time hearing what people say if they don't talk exactly like them. Their way of talking and writing is called "Formal English."
>
> We have to feel a little sorry for them because they have only one way to talk. We're going to learn two ways to say things. Isn't that better? One way will be our Heritage way. The other will be Formal English. Then, when we go to get jobs, we'll be able to talk like those people who only know and can only really listen to one way. Maybe after we get the jobs we can help them to learn how it feels to have another language, like ours, that feels so good. We'll talk like them when we have to, but we'll always know our way is best.

Martha then does all sorts of activities with the notions of Formal and Heritage or informal English. She tells the students,

> In the village, everyone speaks informally most of the time unless there's a potlatch or something. You don't think about it, you don't worry about following any rules—it's sort of like how you eat food at a picnic—nobody pays attention to whether you use your fingers or a fork, and it feels *so* good. Now, Formal English is more like a formal dinner. There are rules to follow about where the knife and fork belong, about where people sit, about how you eat. That can be really nice, too, because it's nice to dress up sometimes.

The students then prepare a formal dinner in the class, for which they dress up and set a big table with fancy tablecloths, china, silverware. They speak only Formal English at this meal. Then they prepare a picnic where only informal English is allowed.

She also contrasts the "wordy" academic way of saying things with the metaphoric style of Athabaskan. The students discuss how book language always uses more words, but in Heritage language, the shorter way of saying something is always better. Students then write papers in the academic way, discussing with Martha and with each other whether they believe they've said enough to sound like a book. Finally, students further reduce the message to a "saying" brief enough to go on the front of a T-shirt, and the sayings are put on little paper T-shirts that the students cut out and hang throughout the room. Sometimes the students reduce other authors' wordy texts to their essential meanings as well.

The following transcript provides another example. It is from a conversation between a black teacher and a Southern black high school student named Joey, who is a speaker of Black English. The teacher believes it very important to discuss openly and honestly the issues of language diversity and power. She has begun the discussion by giving the student a children's book written in Black English to read.

TEACHER: What do you think about that book?
JOEY: I think it's nice.

TEACHER: Why?
JOEY: I don't know. It just told about a black family, that's all.
TEACHER: Was it difficult to read?
JOEY: No.
TEACHER: Was the text different from what you have seen in other books?
JOEY: Yeah. The writing was.
TEACHER: How?
JOEY: It uses more of a southern-like accent in this book.
TEACHER: Uhm-hmm. Do you think that's good or bad?
JOEY: Well, uh, I don't think it's good for people down this-a-way, cause that's the way they grow up talking anyway. They ought to get the right way to talk.
TEACHER: Oh. So you think it's wrong to talk like that?
JOEY: Well . . . {Laughs}
TEACHER: Hard question, huh?
JOEY: Uhm-hmm, that's a hard question. But I think they shouldn't make books like that.
TEACHER: Why?
JOEY: Because they are not using the right way to talk and in school they take off for that, and li'l chirren grow up talking like that and reading like that so they might think that's right, and all the time they getting bad grades in school, talking like that and writing like that.
TEACHER: Do you think they should be getting bad grades for talking like that?
JOEY: {Pauses, answers very slowly} No . . . no.
TEACHER: So you don't think that it matters whether you talk one way or another?
JOEY: No, not long as you understood.
TEACHER: Uhm-hmm. Well, that's a hard question for me to answer, too. It's, ah, that's a question that's come up in a lot of schools now as to whether they should correct children who speak the way we speak all the time. Cause when we're talking to each other we talk like that even though we might not talk like than when we get into other situations, and who's to say whether it's—
JOEY: {Interrupting} Right or wrong.
TEACHER: Yeah.
JOEY: Maybe they ought to come up with another kind of . . . maybe Black English or

something. A course in Black English. Maybe Black folks would be good in that cause people talk, I mean black people talk like that, so . . . but I guess there's a right way and wrong way to talk, you know, not regarding what race. I don't know.

TEACHER: But who decided what's right or wrong?

JOEY: Well that's true . . . I guess white people did. {Laughter. End of tape.}

Notice how throughout the conversation Joey's consciousness has been raised by thinking about codes of language. This teacher further advocates having students interview various personnel officers in actual workplaces about their attitudes toward divergent styles in oral and written language. Students begin to understand how arbitrary language standards are, but also how politically charged they are. They compare various pieces written in different styles, discuss the impact of different styles on the message by making translations and back translations across styles, and discuss the history, apparent purpose, and contextual appropriateness of each of the technical writing rules presented by their teacher. *And* they practice writing different forms to different audiences based on rules appropriate for each audience. Such a program not only "teaches" standard linguistic forms, but also explores aspects of power as exhibited through linguistic forms.

Tony Burgess, in a study of secondary writing in England by Britton, Burgess, Martin, McLeod, and Rosen, suggests that we should not teach "iron conventions . . . imposed without rationale or grounding in communicative intent," but "critical and ultimately cultural awareness."[14] Courtney Cazden calls for a two-pronged approach:

1. Continuous opportunities for writers to participate in some authentic bit of the unending conversation . . . thereby becoming part of a vital community of talkers and writers in a particular domain, and

2. Periodic, temporary focus on conventions of form, taught as cultural conventions expected in a particular community.[15]

Just so that there is no confusion about what Cazden means by a focus on conventions of form, or about what I mean by "skills," let me stress that neither of us is speaking of page after page of "skill sheets" creating compound words or identifying nouns and adverbs, but rather about helping students gain a useful knowledge of the conventions of print while engaging in real and useful communicative activities. Kay Rowe Grubis, a junior high school teacher in a multicultural school, makes lists of certain technical rules for her eighth graders' review and then gives them papers from a third grade to "correct." The students not only have to correct other students' work, but also tell them why they have changed or questioned aspects of the writing.

A village teacher, Howard Cloud, teaches his high school students the conventions of formal letter writing and the formulation of careful questions in the context of issues surrounding the amendment of the Alaska Land Claims Settlement Act. Native Alaskan leaders hold differing views on this issue, critical to the future of local sovereignty and land rights. The students compose letters to leaders who reside in different areas of the state seeking their perspectives, set up audioconference calls for interview/debate sessions, and, finally, develop a videotape to present the differing views.

To summarize, I suggest that students must be *taught* the codes needed to participate fully in the mainstream of American life, not by being forced to attend to hollow, inane, decontextualized subskills, but rather within the context of meaningful communicative endeavors; that they must be allowed the resource of the teacher's expert knowledge, while being helped to acknowledge their own "expertness" as well; and that even while students are assisted in learning the culture of power, they must also be helped to learn about the arbitrariness of those codes and about the power relationships they represent.

I am also suggesting that appropriate education for poor children and children of color can only be devised in consultation with adults who share their culture. Black parents, teachers of color, and members of poor communities must be allowed to participate fully in the discussion of what kind of instruction is in their children's best interest. Good liberal intentions are not enough. In an insightful 1975 study entitled "Racism without Racists: Institutional Racism in Urban Schools," Massey, Scott, and Dornbusch found that under the pressures of teaching, and with all intentions of "being nice," teachers had essentially stopped attempting to reach black children.[16] In their words: "We have shown that oppression can arise out of warmth, friendliness, and concern. Paternalism and a lack of challenging standards are creating a distorted system of evaluation in the schools." Educators must open themselves to, and allow themselves to be affected by, these alternative voices.

In conclusion, I am proposing a resolution for the skills/process debate. In short, the debate is fallacious; the dichotomy is false. The issue is really an illusion created initially not by teachers but by academics whose worldview demands the creation of categorical divisions—not for the purpose of better teaching, but for the goal of easier analysis. As I have been reminded by many teachers since the publication of my article, those who are most skillful at educating black and poor children do not allow themselves to be placed in "skills" or "process" boxes. They understand the need for both approaches, the need to help students establish their own voices, and to coach those voices to produce notes that will be heard clearly in the larger society.

The dilemma is not really in the debate over instructional methodology, but rather in communicating across cultures and in addressing the more fundamental issue of power, of whose voice gets to be heard in determining what is best for poor children and children of color. Will black teachers and parents continue to be silenced by the very forces that claim to "give voice" to our children? Such an outcome would be tragic, for both groups truly have something to say to one another. As a result of careful listening to alternative points of view, I have myself come to a viable synthesis of perspectives. But both sides do need to be able to listen, and I contend that it is those with the most power, those in the majority, who must take the greater responsibility for initiating the process.

To do so takes a very special kind of listening, listening that requires not only open eyes and ears, but open hearts and minds. We do not really see through our eyes or hear through our ears, but through our beliefs. To put our beliefs on hold is to cease to exist as ourselves for a moment—and that is not easy. It is painful as well, because it means turning yourself inside out, giving up your own sense of who you are, and being willing to see yourself in the unflattering light of another's angry gaze. It is not easy, but it is the only way to learn what it might feel like to be someone else and the only way to start the dialogue.

There are several guidelines. We must keep the perspective that people are experts on their own lives. There are certainly aspects of the outside world of which they may not be aware, but they can be the only authentic chroniclers of their own experience. We must not be too quick to deny their interpretations, or accuse them of "false consciousness." We must believe that people are rational beings, and therefore always act rationally. We may not understand their rationales, but that in no way militates against the existence of these rationales or reduces our responsibility to attempt to apprehend them. And finally, we must learn to be vulnerable enough to allow our world to turn upside down in order to allow the realities of others to edge themselves into our consciousness. In other words, we must become ethnographers in the true sense.

Teachers are in an ideal position to play this role, to attempt to get all of the issues on the table in order to initiate true dialogue. This can only be done, however, by seeking out those whose perspectives may differ most, by learning to give their words complete attention, by understanding one's own power, even if that power stems merely from being in the majority, by being unafraid to raise questions about discrimination and voicelessness with people of color, and to listen, no, to *hear* what they say. I suggest that the results of such interactions may be the most powerful and enpowering coalescence yet seen in the educational realm—for *all* teachers and for *all* the students they teach.

From Lisa D. Delpit, "The Silenced Dialogue: Power and Pedagogy in Educating Other People's Children," *Harvard Educational Review*, 58:3

Notes

1. See chapter 1 of this [original] volume, "Skills and Other Dilemmas of a Progressive Black Educator."
2. Such a discussion, limited as it is by space constraints, must treat the intersection of class and race somewhat simplistically. For the sake of clarity, however, let me define a few terms: "black" is used herein to refer to those who share some or all aspects of "core black culture" (see John Gwaltney, *Drylongso*, New York: The New Press, 1993), that is, the mainstream of black America—neither those who have entered the ranks of the bourgeoisie nor those who are participants in the disenfranchised underworld. "Middle-class" is used broadly to refer to the predominantly white American "mainstream." There are, of course, nonwhite people who also fit into this category; at issue is their cultural identification, not necessarily the color of their skin. (I must add that there are other nonwhite people, as well as poor white people, who have indicated to me that their perspectives are similar to those attributed herein to black people.)
3. *Multicultural Britain: "Crosstalk,"* National Centre of Industrial Language Training, Commission for Racial Equality, London, England, John Twitchin, producer.
4. See, for example, M. W. Apple, *Ideology and Curriculum* (Boston: Routledge and Kegan Paul, 1979).
5. See E. V. Siddle, "A Critical Assessment of the Natural Process Approach to Teaching Writing," unpublished qualifying paper, Harvard University, 1986.
6. See E. V. Siddle, "The Effect of Intervention Strategies on the Revisions Ninth Graders Make in a Narrative Essay," unpublished doctoral dissertation, Harvard University, 1988.
7. Shirley Brice Heath, *Ways with Words* (Cambridge, Eng.: Cambridge University Press, 1983), p. 280.
8. C.E. Snow, A. Arlman-Rup, Y. Hassing, J. Josbe, J. Joosten, and J. Vorster, "Mother's Speech in Three Social Classes," *Journal of Psycholinguistic Research* 5(1976), pp. 1–20.
9. Heath, *Ways with Words*, p. 280.
10. I would like to thank Michelle Foster, who is presently planning a more in-depth treatment of the subject, for her astute clarification of the idea.
11. Michelle Foster, "'It's Cookin Now': An Ethnographic Study of the Teaching Style of a Successful Black Teacher in a White Community College," unpublished doctoral dissertation, Harvard University, 1987, pp. 67–68.
12. Ibid., p. 68.
13. B. Bernstein makes a similar point when he proposes that different educational frames cannot be successfully institutionalized in the lower levels of education until there are fundamental changes at the postsecondary levels (see "Class and Pedagogies: Visible and Invisible," in B. Bernstein, *Class, Codes, and Control*, vol. 3 [Boston: Routledge and Kegan Paul, 1975]).
14. I. Britton, T. Burgess, N. Martin, A. McLeod, and H. Rosen, *The Development of Writing Abilities* (London: Macmillan Education for the Schools Council, and Urbana, Ill.: National Council of Teachers of English, 1975/1977), p. 54.
15. Ibid., p. 20.
16. G.C. Massey, M.V. Scott, and S.M. Dornbusch, "Racism without Racists: Institutional Racism in Urban Schools," *The Black Scholar* 73 (1975), pp. 2–11.

8 Equality of Opportunity and Educational Outcomes

The evolution of the U.S. education system is a story that is profoundly moving because it is a narrative of struggle. From the founding of the Republic, there has been a deep belief on the part of the American people in equality of opportunity. Echoing throughout the Declaration of Independence and the Constitution of the United States are the voices of people who demand to be treated with respect, dignity, and equality. From its inception, public education has been conceived of as a social vehicle for minimizing the importance of class and wealth as a determinant of who shall get ahead. Before the word *meritocracy* was invented, Americans believed that hard work, thrift, and a little bit of luck should determine who receives the economic and social benefits that the society has to offer. To some degree, education has helped to make this dream come true. Yet, there is an underside to this story. The United States has only been partially successful in developing an educational system that is truly meritocratic and just.

In this chapter, we examine this belief in equal opportunity in the context of the social realities of life in the United States. We ask very fundamental questions: To what degree do schools mitigate the significance of such ascriptive characteristics as class, race, and gender in determining who shall receive the benefits of education? Do differences between schools make a difference in who gets ahead? What is the relationship between education and economic outcomes? And last, is it reasonable to characterize the U.S. educational system as meritocratic, or does the educational system simply reproduce existing social and economic inequalities?

In 1842, Horace Mann said, "Education, then, beyond all other devices of human origin, is the great equalizer of the conditions of men—the balance wheel of the social machinery" (Walker, Kozma, & Green, 1989, p. 133). From the viewpoint of the year 2000, can one say with certainty that Horace Mann's dream has become a reality? The answer to this question requires empirical investigation. To determine the relationship between education and equality is a complex intellectual task. Interpreting these facts is also complex. Perhaps you remember from Chapter 2 our discussion of the four fundamental points of view: conservative, neo-liberal, liberal, and radical. Nowhere are the differences between these three groups more clearly drawn than in their rivaling interpretations of the empirical facts concerning the degree of equality in the United States. There is, so to speak, a set of calculations that could be called life arithmetic. But there is also a set of interpretations that accompany this arithmetic that are shaded by the shadow of ideology. We do not, nor could we, definitively resolve these debates. However, based on the data that are available, we would be less than candid if we did not admit that, to our way of thinking, U.S. society is deeply stratified by class, race, and gender. These forms of stratification negatively impact on the mobility of certain individuals and groups. Throughout the 1980s, the emphasis on educational reform focused on competition and excellence. In a society that is increasingly multicultural, we believe that reform must also focus on cooperation and equity.

Calculating Educational and Life Outcomes

Most people are aware that society is stratified—there are rich people, poor people, and people in between. People are discriminated against on the basis of gender and race. Curiously, the significance of these issues is often muted by public perceptions that in the United States, individuals, through their own efforts, can overcome the effects of stratification—that is, educational and social mobility are matters of individual life experiences. Although it is true that certain individuals do become upwardly mobile because of their success in business or because they possess an unusual talent, the stark fact is that the overwhelming number of individuals will remain in the social class into which they were born. Social stratification is a structural characteristic of societies. Human differences do not cause social stratification; social stratification causes human differences.

Sociologist Daniel Rossides (1976, p. 15) defined *social stratification* as follows:

> Social stratification is a hierarchical configuration of families (and in industrial societies in recent decades, unrelated individuals) who have differential access to whatever is of value in the society at a given point and over time, primarily because of social, not biopsychological, variables.

He went on to point out that "a full system of social stratification emerges only when parents can see to it that their children inherit or acquire a social level equal or superior to their own regardless of innate ability" (p. 16). In other words, parents attempt to roll the dice of life chances in favor of their children so that they may be successful in terms of material comfort, security, personal fulfillment, and occupation.

Rossides (1976) described three basic forms of social stratification. *Caste stratification* occurs in agrarian societies where social level is defined in terms of some strict ascriptive criteria such as race and/or religious worth. *Estate stratification* occurs in agrarian societies where social level is defined in terms of the hierarchy of family worth. *Class stratification* occurs in industrial societies that define social level in terms of a hierarchy of differential achievement by individuals, especially in economic pursuits. Within each one of these major forms of stratification there can be other hierarchies (i.e., patriarchal distinctions between men and women), and the three major forms of stratification can overlap within any given society. For example, in the United States, individuals can experience caste stratification because of their race, while simultaneously experiencing class stratification because of their occupation and lack of property.

With this discussion as a prelude, one can begin to look at the United States in terms of social stratification. There can be little doubt that the population of the United States is stratified by class. Very briefly, approximately 1–3 percent of Americans are members of the upper class, approximately 15 percent of Americans are upper middle class, another 25 percent belong to the lower middle class, 40 percent are working class, and 20 percent belong to what has been called the underclass. Each of these classes have a somewhat different relationship to the economy. The upper class derives most of its wealth through the possession of property; the upper middle class is essentially a professional and managerial class; the lower middle class are likely to be semi-professionals such as school teachers and small business owners; the working class derive their income directly from their labor and are often paid an hourly wage; and the underclass are marginal to the economy and are often extremely poor.

In the last 30 years, the upper and upper middle classes in the United States have become increasingly wealthy while the other classes have experienced a relative decline in terms of their economic security and income. In fact, the United States is the most unequal industrial country in terms of the distribution of income. According to Phillips (1990, p. 11), "America's top 420,000 households alone accounted for 26.9 percent of U.S. family net worth—in essence, 26.9 percent of the nation's wealth. The top 10 percent of households, meanwhile, controlled approximately 68 percent." In 1988, approximately 1.3 million Americans were millionaires, which is double the number of millionaires in 1980. In 1953, there were only 27,000 millionaires in the United States. It was not since the latter part of the nineteenth century that the United States has experienced such an upsurge of wealth into the upper classes. In 1999, the number of millionaires dramatically increased, with over 400,000 in New York City alone (Koch, 1999). Moreover, during the 1990s, as the number of millionaires skyrocketed, due, in part, to an incredible rise in the stock market (especially Internet stocks), the number of poor also increased (Wilson, 1999). In 2011, the Occupy Wall Street movement brought the issue of income inequality into the public spotlight, as protestors banded around the slogan "We are the 99 percent." Occupy Wall Street continues to impact discourse on disparities in wealth in the United States.

Again, according to Phillips (1990), the "downside of the American dream" is that individuals in the lower middle class, the working class, and the underclass have suffered a decline in terms of their incomes when income is adjusted for inflation. To cite one example, in 1972, weekly per worker income was $366. In 1987, the weekly per worker income was $312, when adjusted for inflation. These data indicate that when calculating the effects of class in determining an individual's or group's life arithmetic, one must not fail to take into account the increasing significance of class. These inequalities increased in the 1990s and at the beginning of the twenty-first century, with the top decile of income earners experiencing significant gains in income and wealth, and the bottom decile experiencing significant declines (Andersen, 1999; Anyon, 2005a; Wilson, 1999). These inequalities of income and wealth have widened over the past decade and are at the crux of philosophical disagreements between the Democratic and Republican parties, the former believing that such huge differences are economically and socially unjustifiable and contrary to the American ethos of equity, and the latter believing that they are the earned rewards of hard work and necessary for economic investment and growth (for an analysis of these gaps, see Duncan and Murnane, 2011).

Clearly, connecting the linkages between class and other forms of stratification and educational outcomes is extremely complex. In Chapter 4, we presented Persell's model for analyzing the relationship of what she called "the societal structure of dominance" and educational outcomes. By analyzing the relationship between the societal, institutional, interactional, and intrapsychic levels, you can see that there is a set of interrelated social and school variables that create the context for the production of educational outcomes. In brief, economic and political resources directly influence the selectivity of schools and the authority structures within schools, which, in turn, influence the climate of expectations and patterns of interactions within schools.

To illustrate these relationships, imagine a public school located in a wealthy white suburb and a public school located in an urban neighborhood. The suburban school will differ significantly from the urban school in terms of its resources, its ability to monitor students' progress, its discipline, its climate of expectations, and its culture. In effect, the suburban school is similar to a private school in that it can provide better educational opportunities for its students than the urban school, which has very few resources and educates students who come to school with few advantages.

Sociologists of education have studied the relationship between education and mobility in great detail. Sometimes the study of mobility is referred to as the *status-attainment process*. Summarizing this literature is virtually impossible since there is no consensus about how much education influences attainment. Clearly, the number of years of education an individual possesses is directly linked to occupation and income. For example, individuals who attain managerial and professional statuses are very likely to have a bachelor's degree from college and to have attended some graduate school. Laborers and individuals in the service fields are, on average, likely to have a high school diploma. In terms of wages, individuals without a high school diploma are paid, on average, $421 per week for their work, whereas individuals who possess a college degree are paid approximately $1,089 per week for their labor (U.S. Bureau of the Census, 2012).

To complicate matters further, other forms of stratification also influence income. In 2009, a man age 25 or over with a college degree earned $72,868 a year on average, whereas a woman with the same educational qualifications earned $44,078 a year. If minorities and nonminorities are compared in terms of how much they earn, one discovers that, as in the case of gender, nonminority individuals earn considerably more money than do minority individuals (U.S. Bureau of the Census, 2012).

Shortly, we will discuss the effects of race and gender on educational attainment, but for now, the central point to be made is that there is a relationship between education and attainment, although it is certainly not an open contest, as was alleged by Turner (1960) some 45 years ago. You may recall from Chapter 4 that we discussed the work of Rosenbaum (1976), who suggested that educational mobility was similar to what he called "tournament selection." In this form of competition, winners are allowed to proceed to the next round and losers are dropped. Some students are eliminated, but "winning" students must still continue to compete. Unfortunately, from the point of view of equality of opportunity, this tournament is not played on a truly level field. Privilege can tilt the field to the advantage of whites, males, and the wealthy. The empirical results of this tilting are discussed next.

Class

Students in different social classes have different kinds of educational experiences. There are several factors that can influence these class-based experiences. For instance, education is extremely expensive. The longer a student stays in school, the more likely he or she needs parental financial support. Obviously, this situation favors wealthier families. Families from the upper class and the middle class are also more likely to expect their children to finish school, whereas working-class and underclass families often have lower levels of expectation for their children. From a cultural point of view, schools represent the values of the middle and upper classes.

Studies show that the number of books in a family's home is related to the academic achievement of its children. Middle and upper middle-class children are more likely to speak "standard" English. Clearly, the ability to use this standard English is an educational asset. Teachers have been found to think more highly of middle-class and upper middle-class children than they do of working-class and underclass children because working-class and underclass children do not speak middle-class English. This phenomenon leads to labeling children, ostensibly according to their abilities, but covertly according to their social class backgrounds. Also, data show that peer groups have a significant influence on students' attitudes toward learning. In a school that enrolls many middle-class students, there is a high likelihood that more emphasis is placed on high academic achievement than in a school where there are few middle-class children.

It is little wonder, then, that class is directly related to achievement and to educational attainment; there is a direct correlation between parental income and children's performance on achievement tests, as well as placement in ability groups and curriculum track in high school. Study after study shows that class is related to achievement on reading tests and basic skills tests. Children from working-class and underclass families are more likely to underachieve, drop out, and resist the curriculum of the school. In terms of going on to college, there is little doubt that the higher an individual's social class, the more likely he or she is to enroll in college and to receive a degree. The more elite the college, the more likely the college is to enroll upper-class and upper middle-class students. In sum, social class and level of educational attainment are highly correlated. This finding represents a challenge to those who believe in equality of opportunity.

Race

Despite the Civil Rights legislation of the 1960s, U.S. society is still highly stratified by race. An individual's race has a direct impact on how much education he or she is likely to achieve. Among

16–24 year-olds, for instance, 5.2 percent of white students drop out of school, whereas 9.3 percent of African-American students and 17.6 percent of Hispanic-American students are likely to drop out of school. Among 17-year-olds, 89 percent of white students will be able to read at the intermediate level, which includes the ability to search for specific information, interrelate ideas, and make generalizations about literature, science, and social studies materials. However, 66 percent of African-American students have reached that level of reading proficiency and 70 percent of Hispanic-American students are reading at the intermediate level (U.S. Department of Education, National Center for Education Statistics, 2003). It is not surprising, therefore, that these lower levels of proficiency are reflected by the fact that minorities have, on average, lower SAT scores than white students. As you know, there is a direct link between SAT scores and admission to college. There is also a link between SAT scores and being awarded scholarships for study in postsecondary institutions.

That race is related to educational outcomes is undeniable, although, given the nature of U.S. society, it is extremely difficult to separate race from class. In a society as segregated as that in the United States, it is not surprising that minority students receive fewer and inferior educational opportunities than white students. Explanations as to why minorities underachieve compared to whites vary. But, at one level, the answer is not terribly complex. Minorities do not receive the same educational opportunities as whites, and their rewards for educational attainment are significantly less.

Gender

Historically, an individual's gender was directly related to his or her educational attainment. Even though women are often rated as being better students than men, in the past they were less likely to attain the same level of education. Today, females are less likely to drop out of school than males, and are more likely to have a higher level of reading proficiency than males. The same is true for writing. The one area that males outperform females is in mathematics proficiency. There are numerous explanations as to why males do better than females in mathematics, the most convincing of which is related to the behavior of classroom teachers who tend to assume that females will not do as well as males in mathematics. Overall, males are more likely to score higher on the SATs than females. It should be added that more women are now attending post-secondary institutions than men, although it is true that many of the postsecondary institutions that women attend are less academically and socially prestigious than those postsecondary institutions attended by men (Persell, Catsambis, & Cookson, 1992).

In the last 20 years, gender differences between men and women, in terms of educational attainment, have been reduced. Recent data from the United States, the United Kingdom, Canada, and Australia indicate that not only have girls caught up to boys in almost all measures of academic achievement, policy makers are now discovering the "boy problem" (Arnot, David, & Weiner, 1999; Datnow & Hubbard, 2002; Riordan, 1999). Liberals argue that these increases demonstrate the success of educational reforms aimed at improving achievement; conservatives argue that the decline in male achievement and attainment is a result of the "feminizing" of the classroom. There are still significant advantages for men when competing for the most prestigious academic prizes, however. Whether men receive preferential treatment within schools is an issue that will be discussed in the next chapter. There is little doubt that society discriminates against women occupationally and socially. Given this, one might wonder about the relationship between educational attainment and occupational attainment for women. Are these two forms of attainment highly correlated or, in fact, is there only a weak relationship between educational attainment and occupational attainment for women?

Educational Achievement and Attainment of African-American, Hispanic-American, and Women Students

The academic achievement of students from different backgrounds is an important aspect of sociological research on education. The National Center for Education Statistics publishes yearly statistical reports, including *The Condition of Education*, which provides important statistical data on a variety of educational issues. The following discussion and data rely heavily on *The Condition of Education, 2012* (2012).

Figures 8.1 through 8.4 (pp. 345–349) indicate these achievement gaps among whites, blacks, and Hispanics; they also show that achievement goes up in relation to parental level of education. Figures 8.5 through 8.6 (pp. 350–352) indicate the achievement gaps with respect to gender. Females achieve at higher levels in reading at ages 9, 13, and 17; females achieve at slightly higher levels in mathematics at age 9 and at lower levels at ages 13 and 17; and females achieve at lower levels in science at ages 9, 13, and 17.

From 1973 to 1986, the gaps in reading and mathematics between 13-year-old African-Americans and Hispanics and whites narrowed and then increased from 1986 to 1999; for 17-year-olds, the gaps in reading and mathematics narrowed until 1988 and then increased from 1988 to 1999. These gaps have remained relatively constant through 2008 (National Assessment of Educational Progress, 2009). Females have outperformed males in reading since 1973 and males have out-performed females in mathematics and science since 1973.

Although the achievement gaps have decreased since the 1970s, a closer examination reveals that much of the progress occurred until 1988. Since then, the gaps have widened or remained steady. According to data reported by the Education Trust (2004b), the gaps between African-Americans and Hispanics on one hand, and whites on the other have increased in reading and mathematics since 1988 (see Figures 8.7 through 8.10 on pages 353–354). This has occurred despite federal legislation aimed at reducing these gaps, including Goals 2000 and NCLB. There appear to be a number of explanations for these trends, including the significant effects of early federal policies in the 1960s and 1970s, including programs such as Head Start and the long-term effects of the crack cocaine epidemic of the 1980s, with many minority and poor children born addicted to cocaine and showing cognitive deficits in the 1990s.

The rationale for preschool programs such as Head Start or the mandate in New Jersey under Abbott v. Burke for free preschool for all 3- and 4-year-olds in the low-income, urban districts, is that these gaps begin well before kindergarten (Lynch, 2004/2005). Figures 8.11 and 8.12 (pp. 355 and 356) illustrate that blacks enter kindergarten with lower reading and mathematics skills than whites. These differences persist at all income levels, and will be discussed further in Chapter 9.

Text continues on page 357.

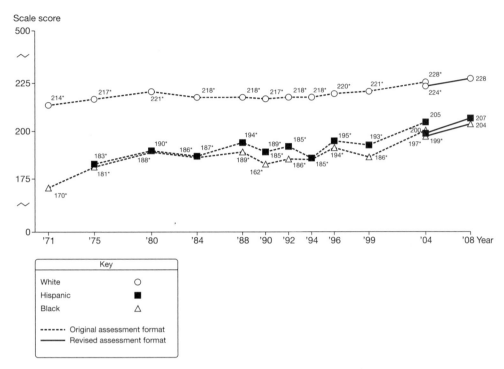

Figure 8.1a Trends in NAEP Average Reading Scale Scores for 9-Year-Old Students by Race/Ethnicity.

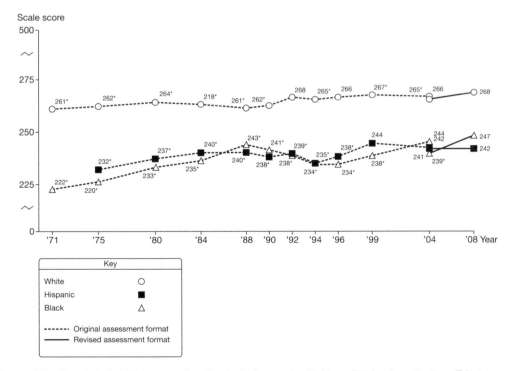

Figure 8.1b Trends in NAEP Average Reading Scale Scores for 13-Year-Old Students by Race/Ethnicity.

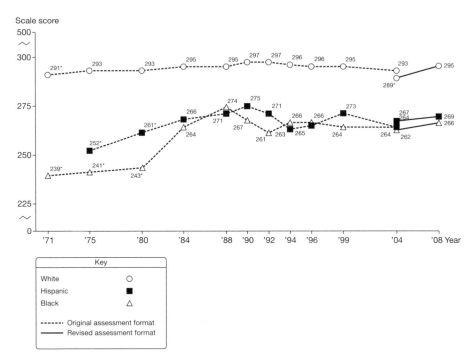

Figure 8.1c Trends in NAEP Average Reading Scale Scores for 17-Year-Old Students by Race/Ethnicity.

* Significantly different from 1999.
Source: National Center for Education Statistics, National Assessment of Educational Progress, 2008 Long-Term Trend Assessment.

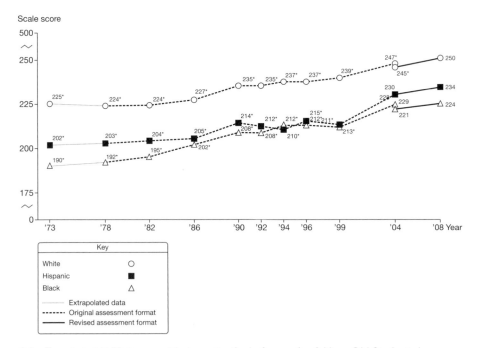

Figures 8.2a Trends in NAEP Average Mathematics Scale Scores for 9-Year-Old Students by Race/Ethnicity.

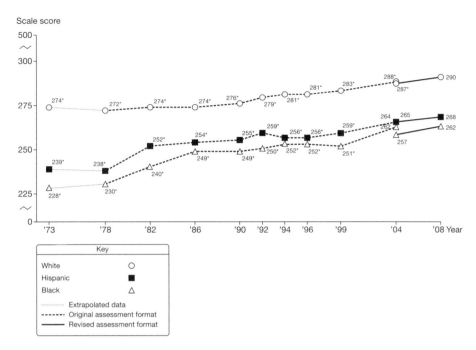

Figure 8.2b Trends in NAEP Average Mathematics Scale Scores for 13-Year-Old Students by Race/Ethnicity.

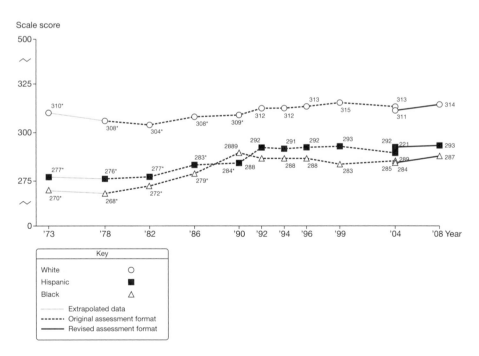

Figure 8.2c Trends in NAEP Average Mathematics Scale Scores for 17-Year-Old Students by Race/Ethnicity.

* Significantly different from 1999.
Source: National Center for Education Statistics, National Assessment of Educational Progress (NAEP), 2008 Long-Term Trend Assessment.

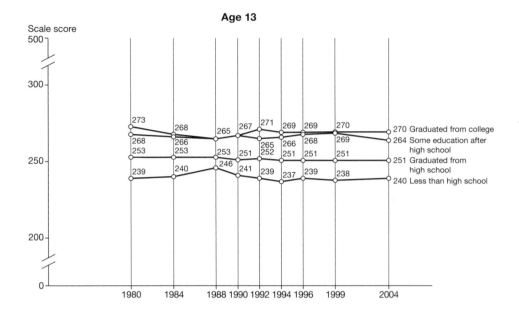

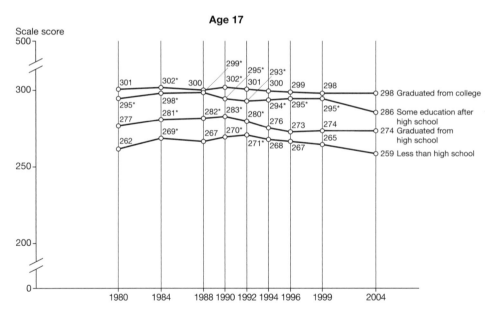

Figure 8.3 Trends in NAEP Average Reading Scale Scores by Parents' Highest Level of Education.

* Significantly different from 1999.
Source: National Center for Education Statistics, National Assessment of Educational Progress (NAEP), 2004 Long-Term Trend Assessment.

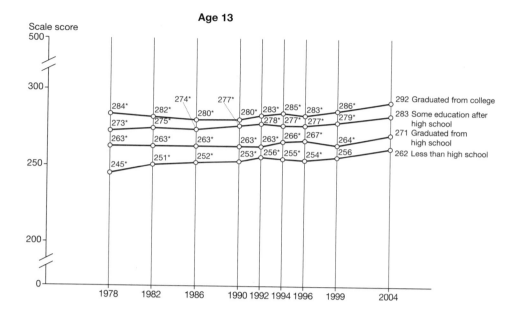

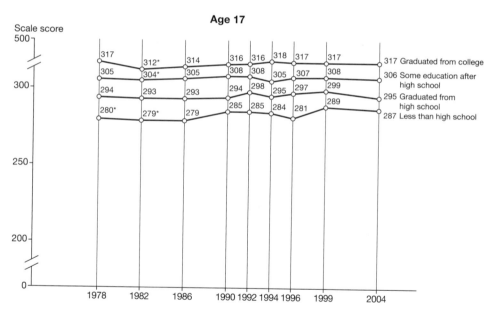

Figure 8.4 Trends in NAEP Average Mathematics Scale Scores by Parents' Highest Level of Education.

* Significantly different from 1999.
Source: National Center for Education Statistics, National Assessment of Educational Progress (NAEP), 2004 Long-Term Trend Assessment.

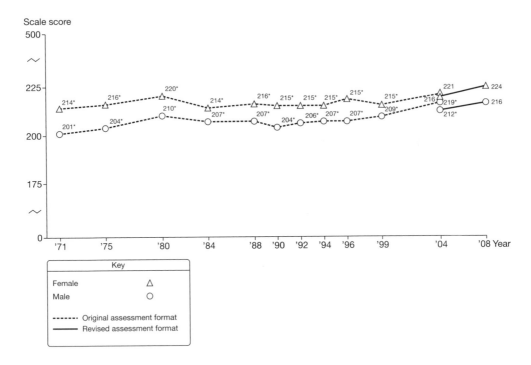

Figure 8.5a Trends in NAEP Average Reading Scale Scores for 9-Year-Old Students by Gender.

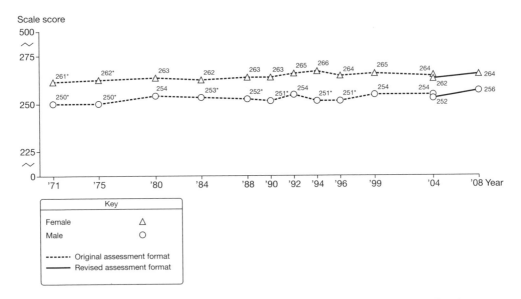

Figure 8.5b Trends in NAEP Average Reading Scale Scores for 13-Year-Old Students by Gender.

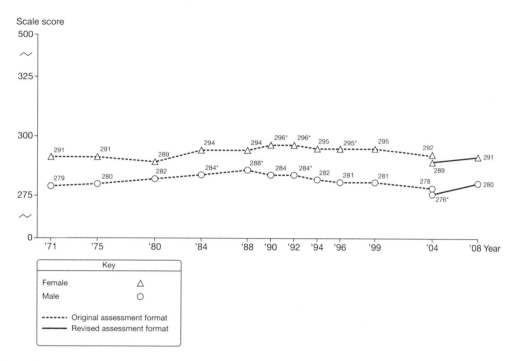

Figure 8.5c Trends in NAEP Average Reading Scale Scores for 17-Year-Old Students by Gender.

* Significantly different from 1999.
Source: National Center for Education Statistics, National Assessment of Educational Progress (NAEP), 2008 Long-Term Trend Assessment.

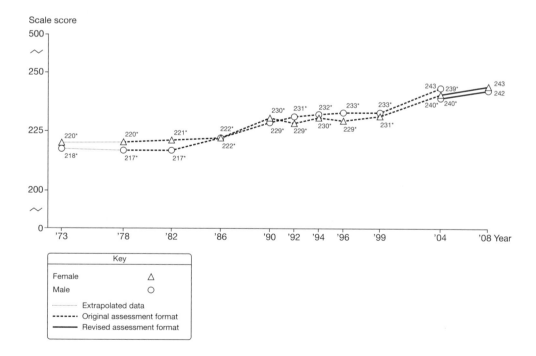

Figure 8.6a Trends in NAEP Average Mathematics Scale Scores for 9-Year-Old Students by Gender.

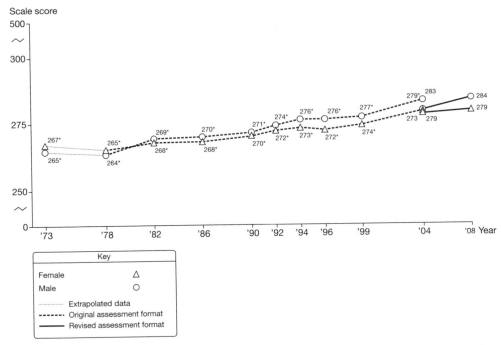

Figures 8.6b Trends in NAEP Average Mathematics Scale Scores for 13-Year-Old Students by Gender.

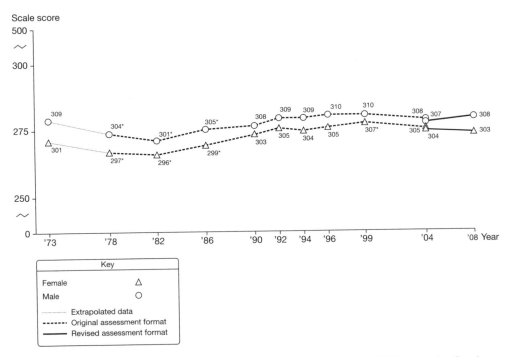

Figure 8.6c Trends in NAEP Average Mathematics Scale Scores for 17-Year-Old Students by Gender.

* Significantly different from 1999.
Source: National Center for Education Statistics, National Assessment of Educational Progress (NAEP), 2008 Long-Term Trend Assessment.

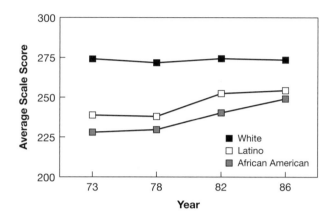

Figure 8.7 Gaps Narrow 1973–86, NAEP Math Scores, 13-year-olds.

Source: U.S. Department of Education, National Center for Education Statistics. *NAEP 1999, Trends in Academic Progress.* Washington, DC: U.S. Department of Education, August 2000, p. 108.

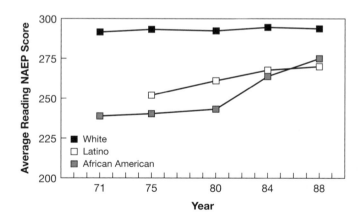

Figure 8.8 Gaps Narrow 1970–88, NAEP Reading, 17-year-olds.

Source: U.S. Department of Education, National Center for Education Statistics. *NAEP 1999 Trends in Academic Progress.* Washington, DC: U.S. Department of Education, August 2000, p. 107.

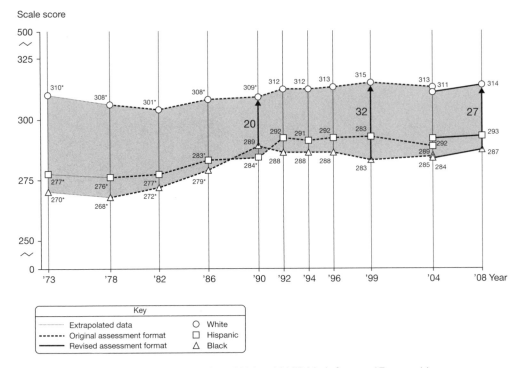

Figure 8.9 Gaps Narrow, Then Hold Steady or Widen: NAEP Math Scores, 17-year-olds.

Source: U.S. Department of Education, National Center for Education Statistics. *NAEP 2008.*

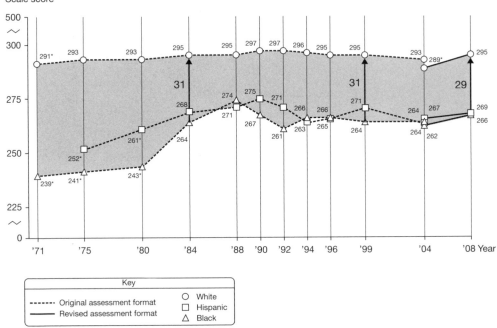

Figure 8.10 After 1988, Gaps Mostly Widen: NAEP Reading, 17-year-olds.

Source: U.S. Department of Education, National Center for Education Statistics. *NAEP 2008*

A. Reading Skills at Start of Kindergarten

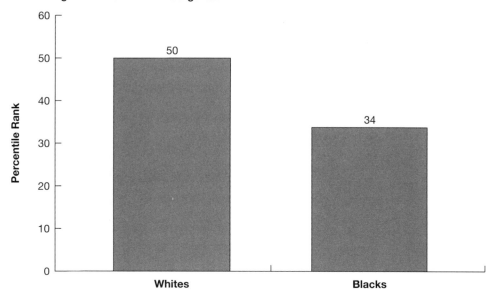

B. Reading Skills on Entering Kindergarten by Race and Socioeconomic Status

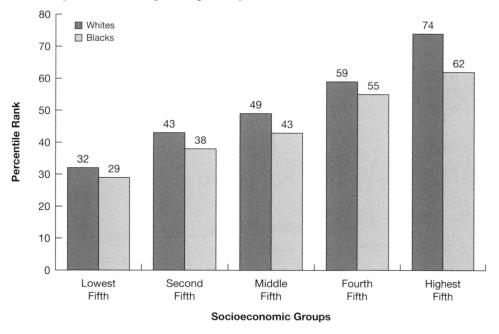

Figure 8.11 Kindergarten Reading Skills.

Note: The reading performance of black students has been normalized to the reading performance of white students.

Source: Lee and Burkam (2002).

A. Mathematics Skills at Start of Kindergarten

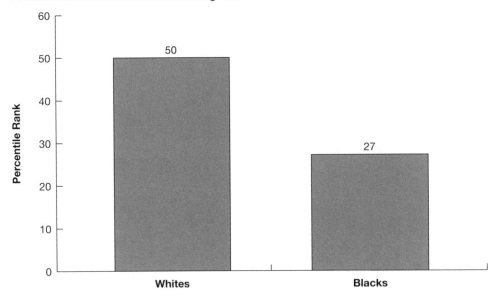

B. Mathematics Skills on Entering Kindergarten by Race and Socioeconomic Status

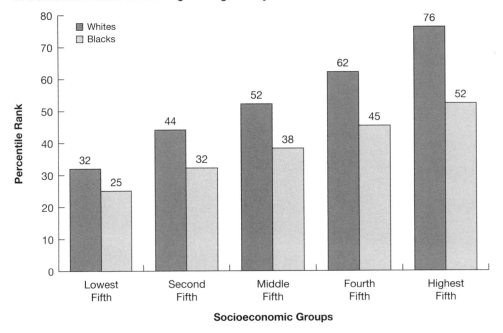

Figure 8.12 Kindergarten Mathematics Skills.

Note: The mathematics performance of black students has been normalized to the mathematics performance of white students.

Source: Lee and Burkam (2002).

Attainment

These gaps in achievement are reflected in attainment gaps among groups. For persons of both sexes 25 years old or older, 92.1 percent of whites graduated from high school and 33.3 percent received a bachelor's degree; 84 percent of African-Americans graduated from high school and 19.9 percent received a bachelor's degree; 88.8 percent of Asian-Americans graduated from high school and 52.4 percent received a bachelor's degree; 62.7 percent of Hispanic-Americans graduated from high school and 13.9 percent received a bachelor's degree. Also, 86.6 percent of males graduated from high school and 30.1 percent received a bachelor's degree; 87.6 percent of females graduated from high school and 29.8 percent received a bachelor's degree (U.S. Bureau of the Census, 2012).

The Scholastic Aptitude Test (SAT) has become the unofficial college entrance examination in the United States. Begun as a utopian experiment to create a meritocratic aristocracy of talent in the 1930s by Henry Chauncey, the president of the newly founded Educational Testing Service (ETS), and Harvard president James Bryant Conant, by the 1990s, the SAT became a high-stakes test that appeared to serve the affluent and white at the expense of the poor and nonwhite (Lemann, 1999). Rather than providing a fair, meritocratic process giving the best and brightest, regardless of family background, a chance to attain the Jeffersonian ideal of mobility, the examination has advantaged the already advantaged, with some exceptions. *The Digest of Educational Statistics* (U.S. Department of Education, National Center for Education Statistics, 2002) indicates that white students outperform all other students, with the exception of Asian-American students; and male students continue to outperform female students. Lemann (1999) in his history of the SAT, argues that in part through the use of private preparation services such as Stanley Kaplan and Princeton Review, affluent families have managed to use the SATs to their advantage. The case of Asian-Americans, however, provides an important exception—one that will be explored in the next chapter.

These data indicate that despite improvements by minority students, African-American and Hispanic-American students still lag behind white students in educational achievement and attainment. Female students, however, outperform male students in most categories, with the exception of mathematics and science, where they have made some gains. The problem, however, with these data is that *The Condition of Education* does not include measures of socioeconomic status and social class background in order to provide similar analyses of the relationship between social class and educational achievement and attainment. More importantly, these data do not control for the independent effects of social class with respect to racial, ethnic, and gender differences—that is, to what degree do race, ethnic, and gender differences begin to disappear when social class is controlled? Much research indicates that social class is strongly and independently related to educational attainment and achievement (Bowles & Gintis, 1976; Hurn, 1993; Riordan, 1997). Recent data from *The Digest of Educational Statistics* (U.S. Department of Education, National Center for Education Statistics, 1997a) support this relationship. For example, although the *Digest* does not control for income or social class, it does have measures of parental level of education, which is one indicator of socioeconomic status. Using this measure, we see that reading proficiency is both highly correlated with race, ethnicity, and parental level of education, with higher level of education predicting higher reading proficiency.

The significant sociological question is how to explain the reasons why these differences exist and persist. As the following section and Chapter 9 indicate, race, ethnicity, and socioeconomic levels are also highly correlated with curriculum track placement, with working-class and minority students more likely to be in lower tracks, and white and affluent students more likely to be in higher tracks. In addition (see Figures 8.13 to 8.18 on pages 358–363), low-income and minority students are more likely to have less challenging curricula, less likely to be in advanced placement classes, more likely to have underqualified and less experienced teachers, more likely

Text continues on page 364.

A. Percentage of High School Graduates with Substantial Credits in Academic Courses, 1982 and 2005

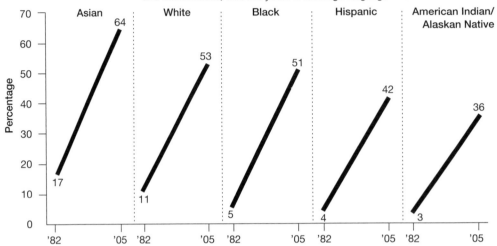

B. Distribution of Advanced Placement Examinations Compared with the Distribution of the High School Population, by Race/Ethnicity, 2010

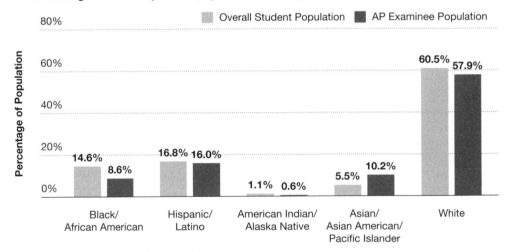

Note: Because some AP exam takers identify themselves as "Other" for race/ethnicity or do not provide race/ethnicity, the "AP Examinee Population" in this figure only represents 93.2%.

Figure 8.13 Rigor of Curriculum.

Source for 8.13A: National Center for Education Statistics, *Digest of Education Statistics 2010,* Table 161. Original data from National Center for Education Statistics, *High School Transcript Study.*

Source for 8.13B: College Board, *The 7th Annual AP Report to the Nation,* February 2011.

A. Percentage of Secondary-Level Core Academic Courses Taught by a Teacher With Neither Certification Nor Major, 2007–2008

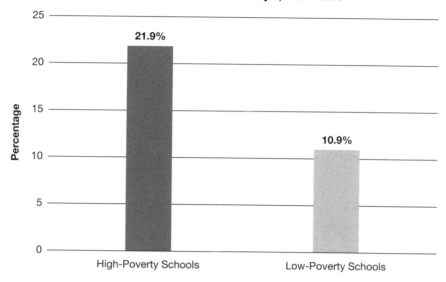

B. Percentage of Eighth Graders Whose Math Teachers Lack Certification in Middle/Junior High School or in Secondary School Mathematics, by Race/Ethnicity and Poverty, 1996–2000

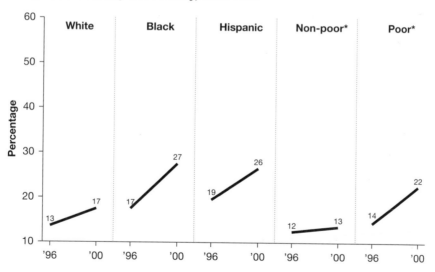

Figure 8.14 Teacher Preparation.

* As measured by whether eligible for free/reduced lunch.

Source for 8.14A: Sarah Almy and Christina Theokas, *High-Poverty Schools Continue to Have Fewer In-Field Teachers,* Education Trust, November 2010.

Source for 8.14B: http://nces.ed.gov/nationsreportcard/naepdata

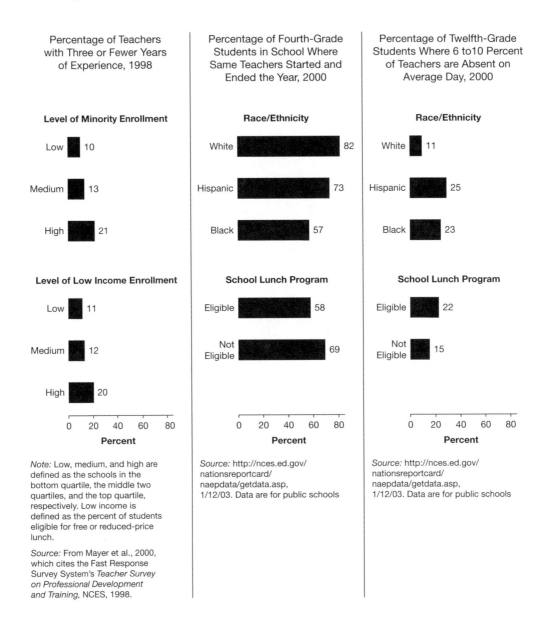

Percentage of Teachers with Three or Fewer Years of Experience, 1998

Level of Minority Enrollment

Low — 10
Medium — 13
High — 21

Level of Low Income Enrollment

Low — 11
Medium — 12
High — 20

0   20   40   60   80
Percent

Note: Low, medium, and high are defined as the schools in the bottom quartile, the middle two quartiles, and the top quartile, respectively. Low income is defined as the percent of students eligible for free or reduced-price lunch.

Source: From Mayer et al., 2000, which cites the Fast Response Survey System's *Teacher Survey on Professional Development and Training,* NCES, 1998.

Percentage of Fourth-Grade Students in School Where Same Teachers Started and Ended the Year, 2000

Race/Ethnicity

White — 82
Hispanic — 73
Black — 57

School Lunch Program

Eligible — 58
Not Eligible — 69

0   20   40   60   80
Percent

Source: http://nces.ed.gov/ nationsreportcard/ naepdata/getdata.asp, 1/12/03. Data are for public schools

Percentage of Twelfth-Grade Students Where 6 to10 Percent of Teachers are Absent on Average Day, 2000

Race/Ethnicity

White — 11
Hispanic — 25
Black — 23

School Lunch Program

Eligible — 22
Not Eligible — 15

0   20   40   60   80
Percent

Source: http://nces.ed.gov/ nationsreportcard/ naepdata/getdata.asp, 1/12/03. Data are for public schools

Figure 8.15 Teacher Experience and Attendance.

By the Percent of Minority Students

By the Percent of Students Eligible for School Lunch Program

By the Percent of Students with Limited-English Proficiency

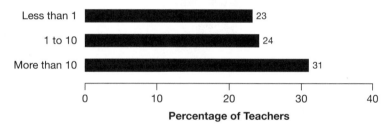

Figure 8.16 Percentage of Teachers with Classes of 25 or More Students, 1999–2000.

*In classes with less than 10 percent minority students, 22 percent of the teachers have 25 or more students in their classes.

Source: National Center for Education Statistics, *School and Staffing Survey (SASS)*, 1999–2000.

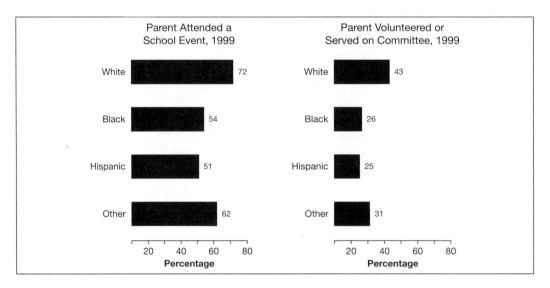

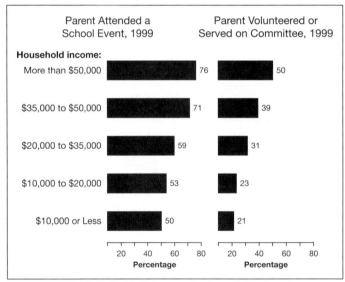

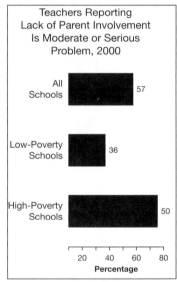

Figure 8.17 Parent Participation.

Sources: Child Trends Data Base (original source—NCES, *The Condition of Education, 2001)* and *Education Week*, "Quality Counts," 2003, p. 62.

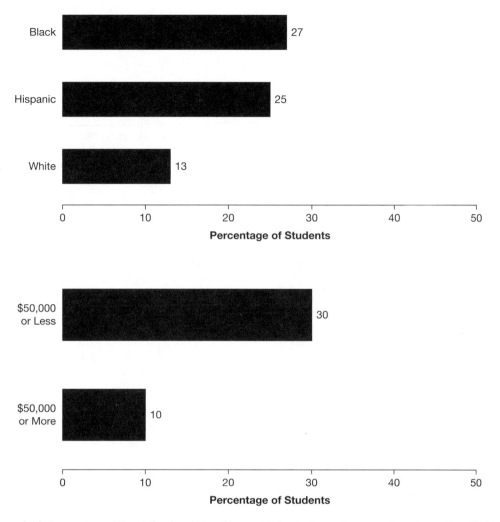

Figure 8.18 Percentage of Third-Graders Who Changed Schools Three Times or More Since First Grade, by Race/Ethnicity and Income, 1990–1991.

Source: U.S. General Accounting Office, *Elementary School Children: Many Change Schools Frequently, Harming Their Education*, February 1994, pp. 27–28. Percentages for race/ethnicity are interpolated from bar chart.

to be in larger classes, more likely to change schools, and less likely to have their parents participate in school activities than affluent and white students (Barton, 2003, 2004). In the next chapter, we will explore various explanations of these educational inequalities more fully.

Students with Special Needs

The field of special education has mirrored the debates about equality of educational opportunity and the concern with the appropriate placement of students with special educational needs. Beginning in the late 1960s, parents of children with special needs (including physical and learning disabilities) began to put pressure on the educational system to serve their children more appropriately and effectively. Arguing that their children were often treated as invisible and not given appropriate services, or in some cases excluded entirely from schools, parent groups demanded legislation to ensure that their children receive an appropriate and adequate education (Budoff, 1975; Gartner & Lipsky, 1987; Milofsky, 1974; Weatherly & Lipsky, 1977).

In 1975, Congress passed the Education of All Handicapped Children Law (EHA) (PL 94–142), which included six basic principles: (1) the right of access to public education programs; (2) the individualization of services; (3) the principle of "least restrictive environment"; (4) the scope of broadened services to be provided by the schools and a set of procedures for determining them; (5) the general guidelines for identifying disability; and (6) the principles of primary state and local responsibilities (Gartner & Lipsky, 1987 in Hehir & Latus, 1992, p. 126). The purpose of the law was to guarantee that children with special needs were properly identified and placed in appropriate classes, defined as the "least restrictive environment." This meant that students should be placed in specially designated classes if they required such a placement and in regular classes with assistance, if they could function in the mainstream. The law was reauthorized in 1996 as the Individuals with Disabilities Education Act (IDEA).

By the mid-1980s, the efficacy of the law became a critical issue for policy makers and advocates of the disabled. Critics (Biklen, 1985; Gartner & Lipsky, 1987; Lytle, 1988) argued that despite its good intentions, the law produced adverse effects, such as the over-identification of students with handicapping conditions, the failure of special education students to make it back into the mainstream, and the overrepresentation of minority students in special education classes. Defenders (Singer & Butler, 1987) countered that, despite some problems, the EHA provided significant increases in the quality of services for children with disabilities.

In the late 1980s, critics of special education pushed the *regular education initiative (REI)*, which called for mainstreaming children with disabilities into regular classes. The REI called for *inclusion* of almost all children into the mainstream, which many critics argued would result in chaos and the inability to educate mainstream children effectively. Proponents of REI argued that democratic principles require that all students be educated together and that special education placement had not proven effective for most students (Gartner & Lipsky, 1987; Lilly, 1986; Pugach & Lilly, 1984; Reynolds, Wang, & Walberg, 1987; Stainback & Stainback, 1989). Critics of REI (Kaufman, 1989) countered that inclusion of the majority of students with special needs was unfair to both "regular" and special students, neither of whom would be served effectively. They indicated that special education reform should ensure that the "least restrictive environment" principle of the EHA be more fully implemented.

Skrtic (1991), in a comprehensive essay in *Harvard Educational Review*, analyzed the relationship between the organizational structure of public education and the bureaucratization of special education since 1975. Arguing that the organizational procedures of special education had resulted in a system that was often concerned more with its own perpetuation than with the needs of students, Skrtic argued for reform of the entire system to ensure proper placement and education. Skrtic placed the special education system in the larger context of educational bureaucracy and suggested that it needed to be understood as part of the more general system of testing and track-ing. He concluded that special education be reformed within a democratic overhaul of public education.

Today, the field of special education remains in conflict. The field of disability studies has emerged to challenge convention theories in the field (Davis, 2010). Disability studies theorists argue that handicapping conditions are for the most part socially constucted and although there may be cognitive differences at the polar ends, the vast majority of chidren labelled as handicapped can be better served in mainstream settings. Criticism, especially from the growing fields of neuro and cognitive sciences, argue that there are real cognitive differences among children and that students often need separate special education placement (for an overview, see Patten & Campbell, 2011). Nowhere is this better illustrated than in the cases of hyperactive deficit and attention disorder (HDAD) and autism spectrum disorders. Disability studies proponents argue that the increase in the number of children with these disorders is a consequence of over-labeling; neuro and cognitive scientists argue that it is the result of better testing and diagnosis (for an overview of the field, see Hehir, 2005).

Thus, the controversies over REI and EHA continue. As we move ahead in the twenty-first century, it is imperative that educational researchers provide empirical evidence to inform placement decisions. It is clear that far too many students have been labeled and placed into special education classes and that, for many, these classes have resulted in lifetime sentences that have limited their educational opportunities. It is also clear that minority students have been overrepresented in special education placements. However, it is not clear that all students with special needs will benefit from inclusion, nor that students in the mainstream will not be harmed academically from wholesale mainstreaming. What is needed is a flexible system that provides appropriate placements for students with special needs: an inclusion class for those who can function within it and a special class for students whose needs require a separate placement. Unfortunately, too often the politics of special education has been more important than the needs of children. As you will see in Chapter 9, this has been true of tracking in general.

Conclusion

In this section, we have examined the relationship between social stratification and educational outcomes. We have made a strong case that the ideal of equal opportunity is somewhat tarnished by the reality that an individual's origin has a significant impact on his or her destination. Education is related to mobility, but this relationship is made complex by the fact that education cannot erase the effects of inequality. Class and race, in particular, continue to haunt the egalitarian ideal that all children should be treated equally. Thinking in terms of life arithmetic, one might say that in the equation of educational outcomes, who you are is almost as significant a factor as what you know. Critics of this position might argue that effective schools can make a difference in terms of providing equality of opportunity. In the next section, we examine the issue of whether school differences have a significant impact on educational outcomes.

School Differences and Educational Outcomes

There is now a great controversy as to whether differences between schools lead to significant differences in terms of student outcomes. This may surprise you. After all, it seems only common sense that the better the school, the greater its positive impact on students. A deep faith in the power of education to overcome ignorance and inequality virtually requires one to believe that there is a close and powerful relationship between the characteristics of schools and their effects on students. Untangling this issue is a complex intellectual challenge.

The essential problem can be stated as follows: To what degree can student outcomes, whether they be cognitive or affective, be attributed directly to the organizational characteristics of schools? How can family influences, maturation, and peer influences be separated from the organizational influences of schools on students? Obviously, this is not an either/or proposition—hence, the complexity of the problem. This problem is compounded by the fact that schools have direct and indirect effects on students' lives. For example, one direct effect is the amount of cognitive growth that can be attributed to years of schooling. Indirect effects are more difficult to measure but, nonetheless, are significant because they relate to the social consequences of having attended certain types of schools. Thus, the graduate of a socially elite private school may have gone to school the same number of years as the graduate of an inner-city public school, but the social marketability of their degrees is quite different. The higher the social status of a school, the more likely the school will be able to increase the social statuses of its graduates. Considering what is known about the class system, this should not be totally surprising, even though it may be somewhat repugnant. This issue was raised briefly in Chapter 4, when we discussed the difference between educational amount and educational route.

There are two major rivaling hypotheses concerning the relationship between school characteristics and student outcomes. The first hypothesis states that there is a strong, positive correlation between school quality and student achievement. Curiously, conservatives, liberals, and radicals all seem to subscribe to this hypothesis. Conservatives and liberals see this positive correlation as an expression of meritocracy, whereas radicals see this correlation as an expression of oppression. The second hypothesis is not popular in the educational community or with the public at large. This hypothesis states that there is a very weak relationship between school characteristics and student outcomes. That is, the organizational characteristics of schools are not strong enough to undo the cognitive and social consequences of class background. In other words, degrees simply credentialize students; the actual content of what they have learned is not terribly significant (Meyer, 1977; Collins, 1975). Testing these rivaling hypotheses is a demanding empirical task.

In this section, we examine the issues raised by the preceding rivaling hypotheses. Not all of the evidence is in; therefore, hard-and-fast conclusions cannot be drawn. But the debate is significant because in the balance lie significant policy decisions.

The Coleman Study (1966)

If you were to pick up almost any textbook on education, you would most likely read that differences among schools account for a variety of student outcomes. Almost everybody in education and in the public at large is committed to the civil religion that education is meritocratic and transformative. Most educational reform movements rest on this assumption. To say that differences among schools do not really matter that much in terms of student cognitive outcomes is close to civil heresy. Up until the 1960s, no one really challenged the assumption that school characteristics were extremely important in determining student outcomes. It seemed common sense that the more books a school had and the more degrees the teachers had, the more the students would learn.

With the advent of computers, large-scale survey analysis became possible by the mid-1960s. Researchers could collect huge amounts of national data and analyze the data relatively rapidly. On the forefront of this type of research was the sociologist James Coleman. During this period, Coleman received an extremely large grant to study the relationship between the organizational characteristics of schools and student achievement. The motivation behind this grant was to demonstrate that African American students and white students had fundamentally different schooling experiences. It was hoped by policy makers that Coleman's study would provide the rationale for federally funding those schools that were primarily attended by minority students.

The results of Coleman's study were shocking because what he found, in essence, was that the organizational differences between schools were not particularly important in determining student outcomes when compared to the differences in student-body compositions between schools. On average, students who attended schools that were predominantly middle class were more likely to do better on tests of achievement than students who attended school where middle-class students were not a majority. Peer group association could be more important than the number of books in the library. It should not surprise you at this point that Coleman's findings caused a tremendous controversy. After all, if differences among schools are only weakly related to student outcomes, what did this say about the power of education to overcome inequalities?

Responses to Coleman: Round One

There were two major responses to Coleman's findings. On one hand, other sociologists examined and reexamined Coleman's data. On the other hand, a group of minority scholars, led by Ron Edmonds of Harvard University, set about the task of defining those characteristics of schools that made them effective. Edmonds argued strongly that all students could learn and that differences between schools had a significant impact on student learning. We will discuss in some depth the "effective school" movement in Chapters 9 and 10.

Within the sociological community, the debate concerning Coleman's findings produced a number of studies that, when all the dust settled, more or less substantiated what Coleman and his colleagues had found. Despite the nation's best intentions, differences among schools are not powerful predictors of differences in student outcomes. After an extensive review of the literature, McDill (1978, p. 2) concluded:

> In the past twelve years a body of empirical knowledge has accumulated, beginning with the *Equality of Educational Opportunity* survey (Coleman et al., 1966), and based on both cross-sectional and longitudinal studies, which unequivocally indicates that, overall, between school differences in any measurable attribute of institutions are only modestly related to a variety of outcome variables.

In other words, where an individual goes to school has little effect on his or her cognitive growth or educational mobility. This seems to be a case where the data and common sense separate. Can it be true that the characteristics of an academically elite school are relatively insignificant in terms of student outcomes? Clearly, the implications of these findings would lead one to believe that the road to equality of opportunity does not go through the schoolhouse door. The political nature of these findings was explosive. After all, if student-body composition has such a major effect on student learning, then the policy implication is clearly that poor students should go to school with middle-class students in order to equalize their educational opportunities. This assumption was the foundation that justifies busing students between schools and between school districts.

During the 1970s, this debate continued and some researchers began to examine the effects of magnet schools on student learning, arguing that schools that were innovative, learner centered, and mission driven could make a difference in what students learned and how they learned it. These studies were intriguing and provided a ray of research hope for those optimists who still believed in the efficacy of education to provide equal opportunities for all children. Still, from a research point of view, these findings were not terribly convincing. At this point, James Coleman and his colleagues at the University of Chicago reentered the debate.

The Coleman Study (1982)

In 1982, James Coleman, Thomas Hoffer, and Sally Kilgore published *High School Achievement: Public, Catholic, and Private Schools Compared*. Like the first Coleman report, this book set off a firestorm of controversy. Coleman and his associates found that when they compared the average test scores of public school and private school sophomores, there was not one subject in which public school students scored higher than private school students. In reading, vocabulary, mathematics, science, civics, and writing tests, private school students outperformed public school students sometimes by a wide margin. Coleman and his associates (1982, p. 177) concluded:

> In the examination of effects on achievement, statistical controls on family background are introduced, in order to control on those background characteristics that are most related to achievement. The achievement differences between the private sectors and the public sector are reduced (more for other private schools than for Catholic schools) but differences remain.

In other words, differences among schools do make a difference. The Coleman findings of 1966 were challenged by the Coleman findings of 1982. Coleman and his colleagues argued that private schools were more effective learning environments than public schools because they place more emphasis on academic activities and because private schools enforce discipline in a way that is consistent with student achievement. In short, private schools demand more from their students than do public schools. As in 1966, the more recent Coleman findings were challenged by a number of sociologists and other scholars. And, as in 1966, Coleman's findings essentially withstood the criticisms leveled at them. However, the interpretations of these findings are still a matter of debate.

Responses to Coleman: Round Two

The debate over the *High School Achievement* findings has centered on the interpretations attached to the magnitude of the findings. What Coleman and his associates saw as significant, others saw as nearly insignificant. For example, Jencks (1985) used Coleman's findings to compute the estimated yearly average achievement gain by public and Catholic school students. He estimated that the annual increment attributable to Catholic schooling was tiny. To put it simply, the differences that do exist between public and Catholic schools are statistically significant, but in terms of significant differences in learning, the results are negligible. The interpretation was echoed by Alexander and Pallas (1983, p. 122):

> What then of Coleman, Hoffer, Kilgore's claim that Catholic schools are educationally superior to public schools? If trivial advantage is what they mean by such a claim, then we suppose we would have to agree. But judged against reasonable benchmarks, there is little basis for this conclusion.

Subsequent studies that have compared public and private schools have also found that private schools seem to "do it better," particularly for low-income students (Chubb & Moe, 1990; Bryk, Lee, & Holland, 1993). The same criticisms that have been directed at Coleman and his colleagues, however, can be directed at Chubb and Moe. Yes, private schools seem to have certain organizational characteristics that are related to student outcomes, but are these relationships as significant as some researchers claim? This debate is not resolved, and one can expect that more research and more controversy will surface. For example, a recent article by Baker and Riordan argued that Catholic schools in the 1990s have become more elite, belying the argument that they are modern common schools (Bryk, Lee, & Holland, 1993; Greeley, 1982). In a scathing response, sociologist and priest Andrew Greeley argued that Baker and Riordan's evidence ignores the past two decades of findings that support a democratic view of Catholic schools. It appears that there is evidence to support parts of both views. Catholic schools seem to advantage low-income minority students, especially in urban areas. However, they are also becoming more elite and like suburban public schools. Given this trend, it will be interesting to see if they continue to serve the poor.

Responses to Coleman: Coleman Round Three

More than forty years after the publication of Coleman's *Equality of Educational Opportunity*, Geoffrey Borman and Maritza Dowling applied the most sophisticated statistical tools to evaluate educational data in a similar manner as Coleman had done in 1966. Borman and Dowling's findings partially confirm both Coleman's original data from 1966 and his 1982 study. According to Borman and Dowling (2010, p. 1202):

> Formal decomposition of the variance attributable to individual background and the social composition of the schools suggests that going to a high-poverty school or a highly segregated African American school has a profound effect on a student's achievement outcomes, above and beyond the effect of individual poverty or minority status. Specifically, both the racial/ethnic and social class composition of a student's school are 1 3/4 times more important than a student's individual race/ethnicity or social class for understanding educational outcomes.

In other words, where an individual goes to school is often related to her race and socioeconomic background, but the racial and socioeconomic composition of a school has a greater effect on student achievement than an individual's race and class. Borman and Dowling, similar to Coleman in his 1966 study, argue that race and class are predictors of academic success. However, Borman and Dowling break from Coleman's 1966 argument that schools don't matter. Instead, Borman and Dowling argue that school segregation based on race and socioeconomic status and within school interactions dominated by middle-class values are largely responsible for gaps in student achievement. Borman and Dowling's study concludes that education reform must focus on eliminating the high level of segregation that remains in the United States' education system and that schools must bring an end to tracking systems and biases that favor white and middle-class students.

Conclusion

Do school differences make a difference in terms of student outcomes? At this point, probably the best answer to this question is a highly qualified and realistic yes. Schools that are less bureaucratic and more academically oriented are better learning environments for students. But, and this is a big *but*, these findings should not be interpreted to mean that private schools are substantially superior to public schools and therefore the public system should be privatized. On a related note, if people think of school organizations and student outcomes within the class structure, it is quite likely that differences among schools matter for middle-class children because they are the beneficiaries of the meritocratic scramble for educational advantage. For very wealthy students, the schools they attend bear almost no relationship to the money they will inherit, and for very poor students, their economic and social disadvantages are so profound that schools have little hope of altering their life chances.

The relationship between social class, race, and achievement is a complex one. Although higher social class is correlated with higher achievement, the degree to which this is due to factors inside or outside schools is the subject of significant research.

Tables 8.1 and 8.2 (about Long Island, New York) and Figures 8.19 through 8.26 (about New Jersey, pages 370–375) present a simple and at the same time complex view of equality of educational opportunity and educational inequalities. First, these data suggest that although funding is important, the socioeconomic level of communities is the most powerful explanation of unequal performance, often independent of funding. Second, they indicate that because race is so strongly correlated with socioeconomic level, race is also strongly associated with achievement, but not always independent of social class. Third, although schools with lower socioeconomic levels clearly have lower academic achievement, there are enough examples of schools (Ann Street, North Star Academy Charter School, and Robert Trent Academy Charter School, all in Newark,

Table 8.1 School Wealth, Funding, and Achievement in Nassau County, Long Island, Eastern Suburbs of New York City (Funding Figures Are for the 2010–2011 School Year; Regents Data Are for the 2010–2011 School Year)

Contiguous Districts[1]	District Wealth Ratio[2]	Spending per Student (General Education, Excluding Special Education)	% Pass Integrated Algebra Regents[3]	% Regents Diploma	% Graduates of 4-Year Colleges	% Graduates of 2-Year Colleges
Freeport	0.688	$13,385	65%	79%	28%	27%
Baldwin	0.990	$12,035	81%	92%	53%	40%
Roosevelt	0.578	$12,689	48%	42%	26%	32%
Bellmore-Merrick	1.248	$12,259	96%	97%	73%	24%
Carle Place	1.551	$14,703	95%	92%	67%	30%
East Williston	2.370	$15,859	98%	95%	84%	13%
Hempstead	0.507	$13,695	52%	63%	40%	26%
Garden City	2.593	$12,703	98%	98%	89%	9%
Glen Cove	2.017	$13,639	77%	93%	51%	39%
North Shore	2.341	$16,727	90%	96%	80%	14%

[1] The grouped districts border each other.

[2] District wealth ratio compares each district's wealth to the state average, which is defined as 1.0. Wealthier districts have a ratio higher than 1.0, while poorer districts are below 1.0.

[3] Regents examinations are statewide tests in New York State required to graduate from high school. State standards require that all students take and pass five regents examinations in order to graduate.

Notes on School Districts

Freeport is a racially-mixed community on the South Shore of Long Island, which is lower middle to middle class. Baldwin is a majority white community contiguous to Freeport, which is middle class.

Roosevelt is a predominantly African American community in the middle of Nassau County on Long Island, which is predominantly poor and lower middle class. The Roosevelt School District was taken over by the New York State Education Department in the mid-1990s due to poor academic performance and is currently being managed by the State Education Department. Bellmore-Merrick is a predominately white community contiguous to Roosevelt. It is a central secondary school district, with feeder elementary schools from Bellmore and Merrick. Its three high schools serve a population that ranges from lower middle class to upper middle class.

Carle Place is a predominantly white middle-class community on the middle of Nassau County. East Williston is a predominantly white upper middle-class district contiguous (north) of Carle Place.

Hempstead is a predominantly African American community, which ranges from poor to middle class. Garden City is a predominantly white upper middle-class community contiguous (immediately northwest) of Hempstead.

Glen Cove is a mixed-racial community on the North Shore of Nassau County (Long Island), which ranges from lower middle class to upper middle-class. North Shore is a predominantely white, upper middle-class community contiguous (southeast) of Glen Cove.

Source: New York State Department of Education, as cited in "School by School Report Card" (2011).

Table 8.2 School Wealth, Funding, and Achievement on Long Island (Nassau and Suffolk Counties) by Social Class and Race

	District Wealth Ratio	Spending per Student 2010–2011 (General Education, Excluding Special Education)	% Pass English Regents (2010–2011)	% Regents Diploma (2010–2011)	% Graduates to 4-Year Colleges (2010–2011)	% Graduates to 2-Year Colleges (2010–2011)
North Shore Districts (>80% White and Asian; High SES)						
Great Neck	3.358	$15,575	97%	96%	86%	10%
Jericho	3.031	$16,556	97%	99%	90%	6%
Locust Valley	5.011	$16,127	94%	99%	83%	11%
Manhasset	3.974	$14,722	98%	97%	91%	4%
Roslyn	2.510	$14,767	98%[1]	97%	90%	6%
"Urban"-like Suburban Districts (>80% African American or Hispanic; Low SES)						
Hempstead	0.507	$13,695	52%	63%	40%	26%
Roosevelt	0.578	$12,689	48%	42%	26%	32%
Uniondale	0.854	$16,237	68%	87%	39%	41%

Note: The North Shore of Long Island is considered the metropolitan area's *gold coast*, made famous in F. Scott Fitzgerald's *The Great Gatsby*. The term *"urban"-like suburban districts* is used to describe districts that are demographically similar to the urban districts described in Kozol's *Savage Inequalities*, as well as to illustrate that these inequalities are not limited to urban-suburban differences, but are found within suburbs, as well. As we noted in Chapter 1, rural schools often mirror the problems found in many urban schools. See Singer (1999) for a detailed analysis of Long Island school districts and educational inequality.

Source: New York State Department of Education, as cited in "School by School Report Card" (2011).

New Jersey) to suggest that schools have the ability to overcome the external nonschool factors and make a significant difference (see Figures 8.21 through 8.26 on pages 373–375).

New Jersey's public schools and public charter schools provide excellent examples. Newark (under state takeover since 1995), all other low-income urban Abbott districts, and the I and J highest wealth districts illustrate the relationship among race, ethnicity, social class, and academic achievement. As a result of New Jersey's Abbott v. Burke decision that has mandated that the states high-need, low-income urban districts are funded at the average of the state's highest socioeconomic districts, New Jersey's urban Abbott districts receive more money than all but the highest-income districts. As these data indicate (see Figures 8.19 and 8.20 on page 372), even with equal spending, students in low-income districts still perform at significantly lower levels, although there have been significant improvements, especially at the fourth-grade level (Education Law Center, 2005). However, in Newark, there are sometimes significant achievement differences among schools with similar socioeconomic, race, and ethnic characteristics, with some schools having high achievement and others much lower achievement. This is true for both public and charter schools (Barr, 2004a, 2004b). At the high school level, the major differences are between selective magnet schools, where students are admitted based on test scores, and comprehensive schools, where all students are admitted. However, the achievement scores of a number of nonselective schools in Newark that are at or above the state, district, and districts with similar socioeconomic level (District Factor Groups DFG) average (Figures 8.21 through 8.26 on pages 373–375) demonstrate that schools can make a difference independent of the social class, race, and ethnicity of their students (New Jersey Assessment of Knowledge and Skills, 2011). In the final analysis, in New Jersey—ranked by the Education Trust (www.edtrust.org) as one of the most equitable states with respect to funding of low-income schools—social class, race, and ethnicity remain powerful predictors of academic success. The complex intersection among social class, race, and ethnicity, as well as how school and nonschool factors affect achievement, are the subject of the next chapter.

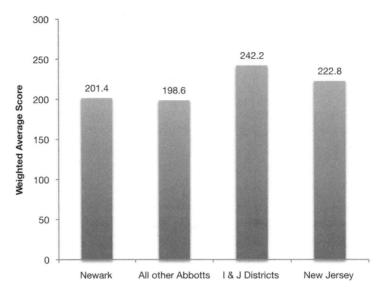

Figure 8.19 High School Proficiency Assessment (HSPA) Math Average Scores by District Grouping, 2010–2011.

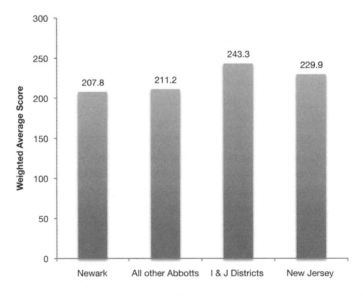

Figure 8.20 High School Proficiency Assessment (HSPA) Language Arts Learning Average Scores by District Grouping, 2010–2011.

School Segregation

As we noted in Chapter 4, schools have become increasingly segregated over the past two decades. The Harvard Civil Rights Project (www.civilrightsproject.harvard.edu) provides data on the racial and ethnic composition of school districts throughout the United States. Research indicates that, despite the fact that schools are less segregated than 40 years ago, the degree of racial and ethnic segregation is increasing.

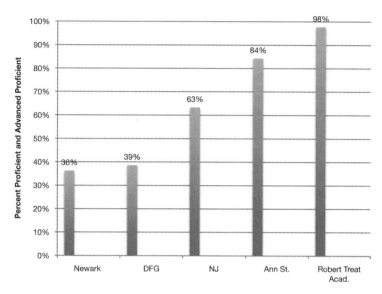

Figure 8.21 Grade Four New Jersey Assessment of Skills and Knowledge (NJASK4) 2010–2011: Language Arts Literacy.

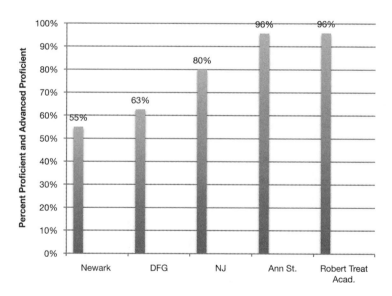

Figure 8.22 Grade Four New Jersey Assessment of Skills and Knowledge (NJASK4) 2010–2011: Math.

Although there is disagreement about the effects of integration on achievement, there is considerable evidence that students in highly segregated schools have lower achievement and graduation rates and that minority students in integrated schools have higher levels of achievement (Orfield & Lee, 2004, pp. 24–25; UCLA Civil Rights Project, 2012; Wells, Duran, & White, 2008). Even though there was widespread dissatisfaction with busing for desegregation, there is evidence that students attending integrated schools received educational and social benefits.

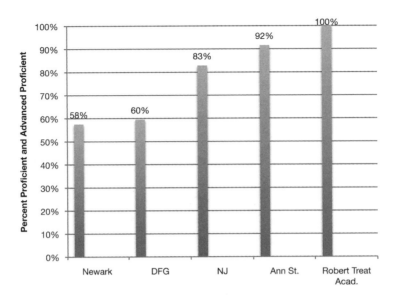

Figure 8.23 Grade Eight New Jersey Assessment of Skills and Knowledge (NJASK8) 2010–2011: Language Arts Literacy.

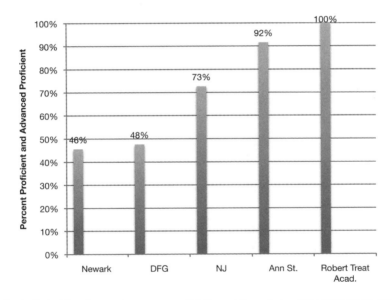

Figure 8.24 Grade Eight New Jersey Assessment of Skills and Knowledge (NJASK8) 2010–2011: Math.

In a study of students who attended desegregated high schools in the early 1980s in five cities— Austin, Texas; Charlotte, North Carolina; Montclair, New Jersey; Pasadena, California; and Topeka, Kansas—20 years after their graduation, Wells et al. (2008) found that the majority of these students looked back favorably at their experiences, despite the difficulties of being the ones to integrate formerly segregated schools. Moreover, the majority of both whites and blacks stated that they now live in segregated neighborhoods and that their children attend more segregated schools than they did.

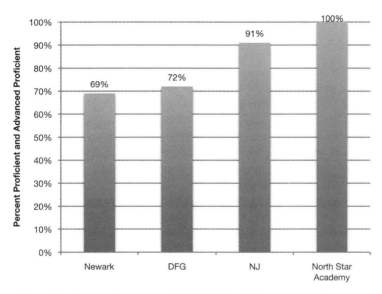

Figure 8.25 High School Proficiency Assessment (HSPA) 2010–2011: Language Arts Literacy.

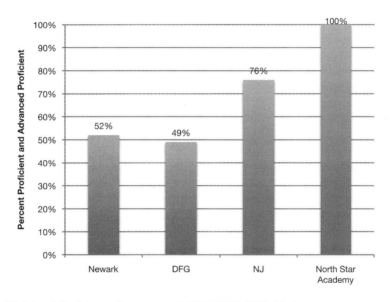

Figure 8.26 High School Proficiency Assessment (HSPA) 2010–2011: Math.

Educational Attainment and Economic Achievement

As we saw earlier, college graduates are likely to earn higher salaries than high school graduates, and it should be noted here that high school graduates are likely to be paid more per hour than people who have not graduated from high school. Jencks and colleagues (1979, p. 230) wrote:

> The best readily observable predictor of a young man's eventual status or earnings is the amount of schooling he has had. This could be because schooling is an arbitrary rationing devise for allocating scarce jobs; or because schooling imparts skills, knowledge, or attitudes that employers value; or because schooling alters men's aspirations.

That education is related to employment and economic achievement is undeniable. In 1987, for instance, a man 25 years or older, with three to five years of high school, was likely to earn roughly $22,000 a year. From then on, each increment in educational attainment (four years of high school, one to three years of college, four years of college, and five years or more of college) is associated with higher income. In 1987, for example, a man with five years or more of college was likely to earn $45,000 a year. The same pattern holds true for women, only for each level of educational attainment, they earn roughly $10,000 less a year than men. Looking at the relationship between educational attainment and economic achievement in another light, one can see is a strong inverse relationship between unemployment and educational attainment. That is, the more highly educated an individual is, the more unlikely it is that he or she will be unemployed. As the labor market creates more high-skill jobs and fewer manufacturing jobs, the economic value of a college education will become even more pronounced.

From our previous discussion, you are aware of the fact that educational attainment alone does not explain economic achievement. Class background is a powerful predictor of economic achievement. The higher an individual's class background, the more likely he or she is to earn more money than individuals from other classes. Moreover, the higher the prestige of the occupation, the more likely it is to be filled with people with relatively high academic credentials. In surveys of occupational prestige, the professions are consistently rated to be more prestigious than other occupations, and to become a professional usually requires a great deal of education.

Not withstanding this discussion, it is not clear what it is about education that makes it so economically valuable. Jencks and associates (1979) posed three possible explanations for the close relationship between educational attainment and economic achievement. It could be that education is simply a sorting device. That is, educational credentials signal to employers the market value of a prospective employee, with little reference to what the employee actually knows. Another possible explanation for why education is related to economic achievement is that educated people actually know something that is valuable to employers. The employer hires the individual with more education because he or she is more expert. The third explanation that Jencks offered concerning the relationship between education and economic achievement is that there is an interaction between years of schooling and aspirations. That is, motivated people stay in school and staying in school motivates people to achieve. There is, among some people, a hunger for education that far exceeds the rational need for a marketplace credential. After all, most college professors make relatively small amounts of money when compared to their years of education. Some people simply enjoy learning.

Sociologists have tested these rivaling explanations. Collins (1971), for instance, asked employers why they hired college graduates for managerial jobs. Did employers actually inquire into what prospective employees knew? Was there a test of potential employees' expertise? Or was it simply the credential that seemed to matter in the decision-making process? You may remember our discussion of the differences between functional and conflict theorists in Chapter 2. Collins was testing the relative efficacy of these two theories. If employers made employment decisions based on what prospective employees knew, this would substantiate the functionalist perspective because it would support the argument that the amount of schooling was a reliable index for expertise. On the other hand, if employers made employment decisions simply on the basis of a prospective employee's paper credentials, then this would be an argument for the conflict perspective. In effect, employers would be hiring individuals based on the social status of possessing a credential, rather than on the individuals' knowledge and expertise.

Collins found that, on balance, the conflict perspective was supported. Employers seldom even knew what prospective employees had studied in school, nor did they consider such knowledge to be particularly relevant in making their employment decisions. A businessman who saw education primarily as an initial screening devise said:

Industry places a high value on the college degree, not because it is convinced that four years of schooling insure that individuals acquire maturity and technical competence, but rather because it provides an initial point of division between those more trained and those less trained; those better motivated and those less motivated; those with more social experience and those with less. (cited in Persell, 1977, p. 159)

In his book *Education and Jobs: The Great Training Robbery* (1970), Ivar Berg found that years of schooling are generally related (and sometimes negatively related) to job performance ratings. That is, his findings were very similar to those of Collins: Education counts but mostly as a social credential and not as an academic indicator of presumed expertise. Berg (1970, p. 185) wrote:

Educational credentials have become the new property in America. Our nation, which has attempted to make the transmission of real and personal property difficult, has contrived to replace it with an inheritable set of values concerning degrees and diplomas which will most certainly reinforce the formidable class barriers that remain, even without the right within families to pass benefits from parents to their children.

It seems that, from the available evidence, one can conclude that although educational attainment is directly related to economic achievement, the reason for this relationship has very little to do with technical competence but a great deal to do with social acceptability. These findings may surprise you—even shock you. Nobody maintains that the intrinsic value of an education is of no economic or social value. What is being said is that in a class system, educational credentials are valuable assets in the great status race, above and beyond their intrinsic intellectual value.

Education and Inequality: Mobility or Reproduction?

In this chapter, we have put to the test the American belief in equality of educational opportunity and found that this belief is based partly on reality and partly on blind faith. The amount of education an individual receives is directly related to his or her life chances. But life chances are also directly related to where an individual is located in the class structure. Life chances are also directly related to race and, to a somewhat lesser degree, gender. Organizational characteristics of schools do have a slight impact on student outcomes such as achievement, but these differences are quite small. The larger truth is that differences between the organizational characteristics of schools only marginally affect the life chances of students, especially if social class is held constant. Although educational credentials are good predictors of economic achievement, the reason for this relationship has less to do with the amount of learning that has taken place than it has to do with the power of credentials to send social signals of respectability.

From this account, it should be clear that although education provides a method of economic and social mobility, in the main, education reproduces the existing class structure. Marxist scholars, such as Bowles and Gintis (1976), have argued that there is a direct correspondence between the class system and the educational system. Although we do not subscribe to a deterministic or mechanical view of the relationship between school and society, it does appear that educational opportunities are closely related to one's social class position and that, for the overwhelming majority of people, there is little likelihood that their educational credentials will lift them out of their social class of origin.

The issues that have been raised in this chapter are so fundamental and so related to the concept of democracy that they will continue to shape U.S. educational policy for the foreseeable future. The passionate belief of Americans that education can resolve economic and social problems will be put to the test in the years ahead. Although one's heart wants to believe that, through education, the United States can achieve equality of opportunity, one's head must remain skeptical. The empirical evidence indicates that the United States is a long way away from achieving equal educational opportunity.

In this chapter, we have touched on many important issues regarding the relationship between education, occupation, and the reproduction of social inequalities. We include three articles that highlight some of the issues that have been discussed in this chapter. The first article, "Class and the Classroom: Even the Best Schools Can't Close the Race Achievement Gap," written by journalist Richard Rothstein, analyzes the black–white achievement gap and the limits and possibilities of schools in reducing them.

The second article, "Chartering and Bartering: Elite Education and Social Reproduction," written by sociologists Caroline Hodges Persell and Peter W. Cookson, Jr., illuminates the relationship between college counselors in elite U.S. boarding schools and U.S. colleges and universities that are academically selective. This article documents the process by which informal personal relationships bind institutions together. These relationships have little or nothing to do with the maintenance of a meritocracy but have a great deal to do with the transmission of privilege.

The third article, "College-for-All: Do Students Understand What College Demands?," written by sociologist James E. Rosenbaum, provides an analysis of the opposite side of U.S. education than the one explored by Persell and Cookson. Rosenbaum examines the effects of the "college-for-all" ideology, which states that college education is a right for everyone, especially for disadvantaged students. This ideology discourages students from working hard in high school and leaves many unable to handle the demands of a college education, often resulting in failure and dropping out.

Class and the Classroom

Even the Best Schools Can't Close the Race Achievement Gap

Richard Rothstein

The achievement gap between poor and middle-class black and white children is widely recognized as our most important educational challenge. But we prevent ourselves from solving it because of a commonplace belief that poverty and race can't "cause" low achievement and that therefore schools must be failing to teach disadvantaged children adequately. After all, we see many highly successful students from lower-class backgrounds. Their success seems to prove that social class cannot be what impedes most disadvantaged students.

Yet the success of some lower-class students proves nothing about the power of schools to close the achievement gap. In every social group, there are low achievers and high achievers alike. On average, the achievement of low-income students is below the average achievement of middle-class students, but there are always some middle-class students who achieve below typical low-income levels. Similarly, some low-income students achieve above typical middle-class levels. Demography is not destiny, but students' family characteristics are a powerful influence on their relative average achievement.

Widely repeated accounts of schools that somehow elicit consistently high achievement from lower-class children almost always turn out, upon examination, to be flawed. In some cases, these "schools that beat the odds" are highly selective, enrolling only the most able or most motivated lower-class children. In other cases, they are not truly lower-class schools—for example, a school enrolling children who qualify for subsidized lunches because their parents are graduate students living on low stipends. In other cases, such schools define high achievement at such a low level that all students can reach it, despite big gaps that remain at more meaningful levels.

It seems plausible that if some children can defy the demographic odds, all children can, but that belief reflects a reasoning whose naiveté we easily recognize in other policy areas. In human affairs where multiple causation is typical, causes are not disproved by exceptions. Tobacco firms once claimed that smoking does not cause cancer because some people smoke without getting cancer. We now consider such reasoning specious. We do not suggest that alcoholism does not cause child or spousal abuse because not all alcoholics are abusers. We understand that because no single cause is rigidly deterministic, some people can smoke or drink to excess without harm. But we also understand that, on average, these behaviors are dangerous. Yet despite such understanding, quite sophisticated people often proclaim that the success of some poor children proves that social disadvantage does not cause low achievement.

Partly, our confusion stems from failing to examine the concrete ways that social class actually affects learning. Describing these may help to make their influence more obvious—and may make it more obvious why the achievement gap can be substantially narrowed only when school improvement is combined with social and economic reform.

The Reading Gap

Consider how parents of different social classes tend to raise children. Young children of educated parents are read to more consistently and are encouraged to read more to themselves when they are older. Most children whose parents have college degrees are read to daily before they begin kindergarten, but few children whose parents have only a high school diploma or less benefit from daily reading. And, white children are more likely than black children to be read to in their prekindergarten years.

A 5-year-old who enters school recognizing some words and who has turned the pages of many stories will be easier to teach than one who has rarely held a book. The second child can be taught, but with equally high expectations and effective teaching, the first will be more likely to pass an age-appropriate reading test than the second. So the achievement gap begins.

If a society with such differences wants all children, irrespective of social class, to have the same chance to achieve academic goals, it should find ways to help lower-class children enter school having the same familiarity with books as middle-class children have. This requires rethinking the institutional settings in which we provide early childhood care, beginning in infancy.

Some people acknowledge the impact of such differences but find it hard to accept that good schools should have so difficult a time overcoming them. This would be easier to understand if Americans had a broader international perspective on education. Class backgrounds influence relative achievement everywhere. The inability of schools to overcome the disadvantage of less-literate homes is not a peculiar American failure but a universal reality. The number of books in students' homes, for example, consistently predicts their test scores in almost every country. Turkish immigrant students suffer from an achievement gap in Germany, as do Algerians in France, as do Caribbean, African, Pakistani, and Bangladeshi pupils in Great Britain, and as do Okinawans and low-caste Buraku in Japan.

An international reading survey of 15-year-olds, conducted in 2000, found a strong relationship in almost every nation between parental occupation and student literacy. The gap between the literacy of children of the highest-status workers (such as doctors, professors, and lawyers) and the lowest-status workers (such as waiters and waitresses, taxi drivers, and mechanics) was even greater in Germany and the United Kingdom than it was in the United States.

After reviewing these results, a U.S. Department of Education summary concluded that "most participating countries do not differ significantly from the United States in terms of the strength of the relationship between socio-economic status and literacy in any subject." Remarkably, the department published this conclusion at the same time that it was guiding a bill through Congress—the No Child Left Behind Act—that demanded every school in the nation abolish social class differences in achievement within 12 years.

Urging less-educated parents to read to children can't fully compensate for differences in school readiness. Children who see parents read to solve their own problems or for entertainment are more likely to want to read themselves. Parents who bring reading material home from work demonstrate by example to children that reading is not a segmented burden but a seamless activity that bridges work and leisure. Parents who read to children but don't read for themselves send a different message.

How parents read to children is as important as whether they do, and an extensive literature confirms that more educated parents read aloud differently. When working-class parents read aloud, they are more likely to tell children to pay attention without interruptions or to sound out words or name letters. When they ask children about a story, the questions are more likely to be factual, asking for names of objects or memory of events.

Parents who are more literate are more likely to ask questions that are creative, interpretive, or connective, such as, "What do you think will happen next?" "Does that remind you of what we did yesterday?" Middle-class parents are more likely to read aloud to have fun, to start conversations, or as an entree to the world outside. Their children learn that reading is enjoyable and are more motivated to read in school.

The Conversation Gap

There are stark class differences not only in how parents read but in how they converse.

Explaining events in the broader world to children at the dinner table, for example, may have as much of an influence on test scores as early reading itself. Through such conversations, children develop vocabularies and become familiar with contexts for reading in school. Educated parents are more likely to engage in such talk and to begin it with infants and toddlers, conducting pretend conversations long before infants can understand the language.

Typically, middle-class parents ask infants about their needs, then provide answers for the children. ("Are you ready for a nap now? Yes, you are, aren't you?") Instructions are more likely to be given indirectly: "You don't want to make so much noise, do you?" This kind of instruction is really an invitation for a child to work through the reasoning behind an order and to internalize it. Middle-class parents implicitly begin academic instruction for infants with such indirect guidance.

Yet such instruction is quite different from what policy-makers nowadays consider "academic" for young children: explicit training in letter and number recognition, letter-sound correspondence, and so on. Such drill in basic skills can be helpful but is unlikely to close the social class gap in learning.

Soon after middle-class children become verbal, their parents typically draw them into adult conversations so the children can practice expressing their own opinions. Being included in adult conversations this early develops a sense of entitlement in children; they feel comfortable addressing adults as equals and without deference. Children who ask for reasons, rather than accepting assertions on adult authority, develop intellectual skills upon which later academic success in school will rely. Certainly, some lower-class children have such skills and some middle-class children lack them. But, on average, a sense of entitlement is based on one's social class.

Parents whose professional occupations entail authority and responsibility typically believe more strongly that they can affect their environments and solve problems. At work, they explore alternatives and negotiate compromises. They naturally express these personality traits at home when they design activities in which children figure out solutions for themselves. Even the youngest middle-class children practice traits that make academic success more likely when they negotiate what to wear or to eat. When middle-class parents give orders, the parents are more likely to explain why the rules are reasonable.

But parents whose jobs entail following orders or doing routine tasks show less sense of efficacy. They are less likely to encourage their children to negotiate over clothing or food and more likely to instruct them by giving directions without extended discussion. Following orders, after all, is how they themselves behave at work. Their children are also more likely to be fatalistic about obstacles they face, in and out of school.

Middle-class children's self-assurance is enhanced in after-school activities that sometimes require large fees for enrollment and almost always require parents to have enough free time and resources to provide transportation. Organized sports, music, drama, and dance programs build self-confidence and discipline in middle-class children. Lower-class parents find the fees for such activities more daunting, and transportation may also be more of a problem. Organized athletic and artistic activities may not be available in their neighborhoods, so lower-class children's sports are more informal and less confidence-building, with less opportunity to learn teamwork and self-discipline. For children with greater self-confidence, unfamiliar school challenges can be exciting. These children, who are more likely to be from middle-class homes, are more likely to succeed than those who are less self-confident.

Homework exacerbates academic differences between these two groups of children because middle-class parents are more likely to help with homework. Yet homework would increase the achievement gap even if all parents were able to assist. Parents from different social classes supervise homework differently. Consistent with overall patterns of language use, middle-class parents—especially those whose own occupational habits require problem solving—are more likely to assist by posing questions that break large problems down into smaller ones and that

help children figure out correct answers. Lower-class parents are more likely to guide children with direct instructions. Children from both classes may go to school with completed homework, but middle-class children are more likely to gain in intellectual power from the exercise than lower-class children.

Twenty years ago, Betty Hart and Todd Risley, two researchers from the University of Kansas, visited families from different social classes to monitor the conversations between parents and toddlers. Hart and Risley found that, on average, professional parents spoke more than 2,000 words per hour to their children, working-class parents spoke about 1,300, and welfare mothers spoke about 600. So by age 3, the children of professionals had vocabularies that were nearly 50 percent greater than those of working-class children and twice as large as those of welfare children.

Deficits like these cannot be made up by schools alone, no matter how high the teachers' expectations. For all children to achieve the same goals, the less advantaged would have to enter school with verbal fluency that is similar to the fluency of middle-class children.

The Kansas researchers also tracked how often parents verbally encouraged children's behavior and how often they reprimanded their children. Toddlers of professionals got an average of six encouragements per reprimand. Working-class children had two. For welfare children, the ratio was reversed—an average of one encouragement for two reprimands. Children whose initiative was encouraged from a very early age are more likely, on average, to take responsibility for their own learning.

The Role Model Gap

Social class differences in role modeling also make an achievement gap almost inevitable. Not surprisingly, middle-class professional parents tend to associate with, and be friends with, similarly educated professionals. Working-class parents have fewer professional friends. If parents and their friends perform jobs requiring little academic skill, their children's images of their own futures are influenced. On average, these children must struggle harder to motivate themselves to achieve than children who assume, on the basis of their parents' social circle, that the only roles are doctor, lawyer, teacher, social worker, manager, administrator, or businessperson.

Even disadvantaged children usually say they plan to attend college. College has become such a broad rhetorical goal that black eighth-graders tell surveyors they expect to earn college degrees as often as white eighth-graders do. But despite these intentions, fewer black than white eighth-graders actually graduate from high school four years later; fewer enroll in college the following year; and fewer still persist to get bachelor's degrees.

This discrepancy is not due simply to the cost of college. A bigger reason is that while disadvantaged students say they plan to go to college, they don't feel as much parental, community, or peer pressure to take the courses or to get the grades they need to become more attractive to college admission offices. Lower-class parents say they expect children to get good grades, but they are less likely to enforce these expectations, for example with rewards or punishments. Teachers and counselors can stress doing well in school to lower-class children, but such lessons compete with children's own self-images, formed early in life and reinforced daily at home.

As John Ogbu and others have noted, a culture of underachievement may help explain why even middle-class black children often don't do as well in school as white children from seemingly similar socioeconomic backgrounds. On average, middle-class black students don't study as hard as white middle-class students and blacks are more disruptive in class than whites from similar income strata.

This culture of underachievement is easier to understand than to cure. Throughout American history, many black students who excelled in school were not rewarded for that effort in the labor market. Many black college graduates could find work only as servants or Pullman car porters or, in white-collar fields, as assistants to less-qualified whites. Many Americans believe that these practices have disappeared and that blacks

and whites with similar test scores now have similar earnings and occupational status. But labor market discrimination continues to be a significant obstacle—especially for black males with high school educations.

Evidence for this comes from employment discrimination cases, such as the prominent 1996 case in which Texaco settled for a payment of $176 million to black employees after taped conversations of executives revealed pervasive racist attitudes, presumably not restricted to executives of this corporation alone. Other evidence comes from studies that find black workers with darker complexions have less success in the labor market than those with identical education, age, and criminal records but lighter complexions.

Still more evidence comes from studies in which blacks and whites with similar qualifications are sent to apply for job vacancies; the whites are typically more successful than the blacks. In one recent study where young, well-groomed, and articulate black and white college graduates, posing as high school graduates with identical qualifications, submitted applications for entry-level jobs, the applications of whites with criminal records got positive responses more often than the applications of blacks with no criminal records.

So the expectation of black students that their academic efforts will be less rewarded than the efforts of their white peers is rational for the majority of black students who do not expect to complete college. Some will reduce their academic efforts as a result. We can say that they should not do so and, instead, should redouble their efforts in response to the greater obstacles they face. But as long as racial discrimination persists, the average achievement of black students will be lower than the average achievement of whites, simply because many blacks (especially males) who see that academic effort has less of a payoff will respond rationally by reducing their effort.

The Health and Housing Gaps

Despite these big race and social class differences in child rearing, role modeling, labor market experiences, and cultural characteristics, the lower achievement of lower-class students is not caused by these differences alone. Just as important are differences in the actual social and economic conditions of children.

Overall, lower-income children are in poorer health. They have poorer vision, partly because of prenatal conditions and partly because, even as toddlers, they watch too much television, so their eyes are poorly trained. Trying to read, their eyes may wander or have difficulty tracking print or focusing. A good part of the over-identification of learning disabilities for lower-class children may well be attributable to undiagnosed vision problems that could be easily treated by optometrists and for which special education placement then should be unnecessary.

Lower-class children have poorer oral hygiene, more lead poisoning, more asthma, poorer nutrition, less-adequate pediatric care, more exposure to smoke, and a host of other health problems. Because of less-adequate dental care, for example, they are more likely to have toothaches and resulting discomfort that affects concentration.

Because low-income children live in communities where landlords use high-sulfur home heating oil and where diesel trucks frequently pass en route to industrial and commercial sites, they are more likely to suffer from asthma, leading to more absences from school and, when they do attend, drowsiness from lying awake at night, wheezing. Recent surveys in Chicago and in New York City's Harlem community found one of every four children suffering from asthma, a rate six times as great as that for all children.

In addition, there are fewer primary-care physicians in low-income communities, where the physician-to-population ratio is less than a third the rate in middle-class communities. For that reason, disadvantaged children—even those with health insurance—are more likely to miss school for relatively minor problems, such as common ear infections, for which middle-class children are treated promptly.

Each of these well-documented social class differences in health is likely to have a palpable effect on academic achievement; combined, their influence is probably huge.

The growing unaffordability of adequate housing for low-income families also affects achievement. Children whose families have difficulty finding stable housing are more likely to be mobile, and student mobility is an important cause of failing student performance. A 1994 government report found that 30 percent of the poorest children had attended at least three different schools by third grade, while only 10 percent of middle-class children had done so. Black children were more than twice as likely as white children to change schools this often. It is hard to imagine how teachers, no matter how well trained, can be as effective for children who move in and out of their classrooms as they can be for those who attend regularly.

Differences in wealth are also likely to be important determinants of achievement, but these are usually overlooked because most analysts focus only on annual family income to indicate disadvantage. This makes it hard to understand why black students, on average, score lower than whites whose family incomes are the same. It is easier to understand this pattern when we recognize that children can have similar family incomes but be of different economic classes. In any given year, black families with low income are likely to have been poor for longer than white families with similar income in that year.

White families are also likely to own far more assets that support their children's achievement than are black families at the same income level, partly because black middle-class parents are more likely to be the first generation in their families to have middle-class status. Although the median black family income is about two-thirds the median income of white families, the assets of black families are still only 12 percent those of whites. Among other things, this difference means that, among white and black families with the same middle-class incomes, the whites are more likely to have savings for college. This makes white children's college aspirations more practical, and therefore more commonplace.

Narrowing the Gaps

If we properly identify the actual social class characteristics that produce differences in average achievement, we should be able to design policies that narrow the achievement gap. Certainly, improvement of instructional practices is among these, but a focus on school reform alone is bound to be frustrating and ultimately unsuccessful. To work, school improvement must combine with policies that narrow the social and economic differences between children. Where these differences cannot easily be narrowed, school should be redefined to cover more of the early childhood, after-school, and summer times, when the disparate influences of families and communities are now most powerful.

Because the gap is already huge at age 3, the most important new investment should no doubt be in early childhood programs. Pre-kindergarten classes for 4-year-olds are needed, but they barely begin to address the problem. The quality of early childhood programs is as important as the existence of such programs themselves. Too many low-income children are parked before television sets in low-quality day-care settings. To narrow the gap, care for infants and toddlers should be provided by adults who can create the kind of intellectual environment that is typically experienced by middle-class infants and toddlers. This requires professional caregivers and low child-adult ratios.

After-school and summer experiences for lower-class children, similar to programs middle-class children take for granted, would also be needed to narrow the gap. This does not mean remedial programs where lower-class children get added drill in math and reading. Certainly, remediation should be part of an adequate after-school and summer program, but only a part. The advantage that middle-class children gain after school and in summer comes from the self-confidence they acquire and the awareness of the world outside that they develop through organized athletics, dance, drama, museum visits, recreational reading, and other activities that develop inquisitiveness, creativity, self-discipline, and organizational skills. After-school and summer programs can be expected to narrow the achievement gap only by attempting to duplicate such experiences.

Provision of health-care services to lower-class children and their families is also required to narrow the achievement gap. Some health services are relatively inexpensive, such as school vision and dental clinics. A full array of health services will cost more, but it cannot be avoided if we truly intend to raise the achievement of lower-class children.

The connection between social and economic disadvantage and an academic achievement gap has long been well known. Most educators, however, have avoided the obvious implication: Improving lower-class children's learning requires ameliorating the social and economic conditions of their lives. School board members—who are often the officials with the closest ties to public opinion—cannot afford to remain silent about the connection between school improvement and social reform. Calling attention to this link is not to make excuses for poor school performance. It is only to be honest about the social support schools require if they are to fulfill the public's expectation that the achievement gap will disappear.

From Richard Rothstein, "Class and the Classroom: Even the Best Schools Can't Close the Race Achievement Gap," *American School Board Journal*, 191, no. 10, October 2004. Reprinted by permission.

Chartering and Bartering

Elite Education and Social Reproduction

Caroline Hodges Persell and Peter W. Cookson, Jr.

The continuation of power and privilege has been the subject of intense sociological debate. One recurring question is whether the system of mobility is open or whether relationships of power and privilege are reproduced from one generation to the next. If reproduction occurs, is it the reproduction of certain powerful and privileged families or groups (cf. Robinson, 1984)? Or, does it involve the reproduction of a structure of power and privilege which allows for replacement of some members with new recruits while preserving the structure?

The role of education in these processes has been the subject of much dispute. Researchers in the status attainment tradition stress the importance for mobility of the knowledge and skills acquired through education thereby emphasizing the meritocratic and open basis for mobility (e.g., Alexander and Eckland, 1975; Alexander et al., 1975; Blau and Duncan, 1967; Haller and Portes, 1973; Otto and Haller, 1979; Kerckhoff, 1984; Sewell et al., 1969, 1970; Wilson and Portes, 1975). On the other hand, theorists such as Bowles and Gintis (1976) suggest education inculcates certain non-cognitive personality traits which serve to reproduce the social relations within a class structure; thus they put more emphasis on non-meritocratic features in the educational process.

Collins (1979) also deals with non-meritocratic aspects when he suggests that educational institutions develop and fortify status groups, and that differently valued educational credentials protect desired market positions such as those of the professions. In a related vein, Meyer (1977) notes that certain organizational "charters" serve as "selection criteria" in an educational or occupational marketplace. Meyer defines "charter" as "the social definition of the products of [an] organization" (Meyer, 1970: 577). Charters do not need to be recognized formally or legally to operate in social life. If they

exist, they would create structural limitations within a presumably open market by making some people eligible for certain sets of rights that are denied to other people.

Social observers have long noted that one particular set of schools is central to the reproduction and solidarity of a national upper class, specifically elite secondary boarding schools (Baltzell, 1958, 1964; Domhoff, 1967, 1970, 1983; Mills, 1956). As well as preparing their students for socially desirable colleges and universities, traditionally, such schools have been thought to build social networks among upper class scions from various regions, leading to adult business deals and marriages. Although less than one percent of the American population attends such schools, that one percent represents a strategic segment of American life that is seldom directly studied. Recently, Useem and Karabel (1984) reported that graduates of 14 elite boarding schools were much more likely than non-graduates to become part of the "inner circle" of Fortune 500 business leaders. This evidence suggests that elite schools may play a role in class reproduction.

Few researchers have gained direct access to these schools to study social processes bearing on social reproduction. The research reported here represents the first systematic study of elite secondary boarding schools and their social relations with another important institution, namely colleges and universities.

The results of this research illustrate Collins' view that stratification involves networks of "persons making bargains and threats . . . [and that] the key resource of powerful individuals is their ability to impress and manipulate a network of social contacts" (1979: 26). If such were the case, we would expect to find that upper class institutions actively develop social networks for the purpose of advancing the interests of their constituencies.

By focusing on the processes of social reproduction rather than individual attributes or the results of intergenerational mobility, our research differs from the approaches taken in both the status attainment and status allocation literature. Status attainment models focus on individual attributes and achievements, and allocation models examine structural supports or barriers to social mobility; yet neither approach explores the underlying processes. Status attainment models assume the existence of a relatively open contest system, while reproduction and allocation models stress that selection criteria and structural barriers create inequalities, limiting opportunities for one group while favoring another (Kerckhoff, 1976, 1984). Neither attainment nor allocation models show how class reproduction, selection criteria, or structural opportunities and impediments operate in practice.

Considerable evidence supports the view that structural limitations operate in the labor market (e.g., Beck et al., 1978; Bibb and Form, 1977; Stolzenberg, 1975) but, with the exception of tracking, little evidence has been found that similar structural limitations exist in education. Tracking systems create structural impediments in an open model of educational attainment (Oakes, 1985; Persell, 1977; Rosenbaum, 1976, 1980), although not all research supports this conclusion (e.g., Alexander et al., 1978; Heyns, 1974).

In this [reading] we suggest that there is an additional structural limitation in the key transition from high school to college. We explore the possibility that special organizational "charters" exist for certain secondary schools and that a process of "bartering" occurs between representatives of selected secondary schools and some college admissions officers. These processes have not been clearly identified by prior research on education and stratification, although there has been some previous research which leads in this direction.

Empirical Literature

Researchers of various orientations concur that differences between schools seem to have little bearing on student attainment (Averch et al., 1972; Jencks et al., 1972; Meyer, 1970, 1977). Indeed, Meyer (1977) suggests the most puzzling paradox in the sociology of American education is that while schools differ in structure and resources, they vary little in their effects because all secondary schools are assumed to have similar "charters." Meyer believes that no American high school is specially chartered by selective colleges in the way, for instance, that certain British Public Schools have been chartered by Oxford and Cambridge Universities. Instead, he suggests that "all American high schools have similar status rights, (and therefore) variations in their effects should be small" (Meyer, 1977: 60).

Kamens (1977: 217–218), on the other hand, argues that "schools symbolically redefine people and make them eligible for membership in societal categories to which specific sets of rights are assigned." The work of Alexander and Eckland (1977) is consistent with this view. These researchers found that students who attended high schools where the social status of the student body was high also attended selective colleges at a greater rate than did students at other high schools, even when individual student academic ability and family background were held constant (Alexander and Eckland, 1977). Their research and other work finding a relationship between curricular track placement and college attendance (Alexander et al., 1978; Alexander and McDill, 1976; Jaffe and Adams, 1970; Rosenbaum, 1976, 1980) suggest that differences between schools may affect stratification outcomes.

Research has shown that graduation from a private school is related to attending a four-year (rather than a two-year) college (Falsey and Heyns, 1984), attending a highly selective college (Hammack and Cookson, 1980), and earning higher income in adult life (Lewis and Wanner, 1979). Moreover, Cookson (1981) found that graduates of private boarding schools attended more selective colleges than did their public school counterparts, even when family background and Scholastic Aptitude Test (SAT) scores were held constant. Furthermore, some private colleges acknowledge the distinctive nature of certain secondary schools. Klitgaard (1985: Table 2.2) reports that students from private secondary schools generally had an advantage for admission to Harvard over public school graduates, even when their academic ratings were comparable. Karen (1985) notes that applications to Harvard from certain private boarding schools were placed in special colored dockets, or folders, to set them apart from other applications. Thus, they were considered as a distinct group. Not only did Harvard acknowledge the special status of certain schools by color-coding their applicants' folders, attendance at one of those schools provided an advantage for acceptance, even when parental background, grades, SATs, and other characteristics were controlled (Karen, 1985).

Networks and the Transmission of Privilege

For these reasons we believe it is worth investigating whether certain secondary schools have special organizational charters, at least in relation to certain colleges. If they do, the question arises, how do organizational charters operate? Network analysts suggest that "the pattern of ties in a network provides significant opportunities and constraints because it affects the relative access of people and institutions to such resources as information, wealth and power" (Wellman, 1981: 3). Furthermore, "because of their structural location, members of a social system differ greatly in their access to these resources" (Wellman, 1981: 30). Moreover, network analysts have suggested that class-structured networks work to preserve upper class ideology, consciousness, and life style (see for example Laumann, 1966: 132–36).

We expect that colleges and secondary schools have much closer ties than has previously been documented. Close networks of personal relationships between officials at certain private schools and some elite colleges transform what is for many students a relatively standardized, bureaucratic procedure into a process of negotiation. As a result, they are able to communicate more vital information about their respective needs, giving selected secondary school students an inside track to gaining acceptance to desired colleges. We call this process "bartering."

Sample and Data

Baltzell (1958, 1964) noted the importance of elite secondary boarding schools for upper class solidarity. However, he was careful to distinguish between those boarding schools that were truly socially elite and those that had historically served somewhat less affluent and less powerful families. He indicates that there is a core group of eastern Protestant schools that "set the pace and bore the brunt of criticism received by private schools for their so-called 'snobbish,' 'undemocratic' and even 'un-American' values" (Baltzell, 1958: 307–308). These 16 schools are: Phillips (Andover) Academy (MA), Phillips Exeter Academy (NH), St. Paul's School (NH), St. Mark's School (MA), Groton School (MA), St. George's School (RI), Kent School (CT), The Taft School (CT), The Hotchkiss School (CT), Choate Rosemary Hall (CT), Middlesex School (MA), Deerfield Academy (MA), The Lawrenceville School (NJ), The Hill School (PA), The Episcopal High School (VA), and Woodberry Forest School (VA). We refer to the schools on Baltzell's list as the "select 16."[1]

In 1982 and 1983, we visited a representative sample of 12 of the select 16 schools. These 12 schools reflect the geographic distribution of the select 16 schools. In this time period we also visited 30 other "leading" secondary boarding schools drawn from the 1981 Handbook of Private Schools' list of 289 "leading" secondary boarding schools. This sample is representative of leading secondary boarding schools nationally in location, religious affiliation, size, and the sex composition of the student body. These schools are organizationally similar to the select 16 schools in offering only a college preparatory curriculum, in being incorporated as non-profit organizations, in their faculty/student ratios, and in the percent of boarders who receive financial aid. They differ somewhat with respect to sex composition, average size, the sex of their heads, and number of advanced placement courses (see Table 8.3). However, the key difference between the select 16 schools and the other "leading" schools is that the former are more socially elite than the latter. For instance, in one of the select 16 boarding schools in 1982, 40 percent of the current students' parents were listed in Social Register.[2]

Table 8.3 Comparison of Population and Two Samples of Boarding Schools

	Total Population (N = 289)	Other Boarding School Sample (N = 30)	Select 16 Sample (N = 12)
Percent with college preparatory curriculum	100	100	100
Percent with no religious affiliation	65	70	67
Percent incorporated, not-for-profit	83	90	83
Average faculty/ student ratio	0.17	0.15	0.15
Average percent of boarders aided	15	16	18
Percent of schools which are all-boys	28	17	33
Percent of schools which are all-girls	17	28	0
Percent coeducational schools	55	55	67
Percent with male heads	92	73	100
Average number of advanced courses	3.5	4.8	6.7
Average size	311	322	612

Note: Computed from data published in the *Handbook of Private Schools* (1981).

All 42 schools were visited by one or both of the authors. Visits lasted between one and five days and included interviews with administrators, teachers and students. Most relevant to this study were the lengthy interviews with the schools' college advisors. These interviews explored all aspects of the college counseling process, including the nature and content of the advisors' relationships with admissions officers at various colleges. At a representative sample of six of the select 16 schools and a representative sample of 13 of the other "leading" schools a questionnaire was administered to seniors during our visits.[3] The questionnaire contained more than 50 items and included questions on parental education, occupation, income, number of books in the home, family travel, educational legacies as well as many questions on boarding school life and how students felt about their experiences in school. Overall, student survey and school record data were collected on 687 seniors from the six select 16 schools and 658 seniors from other leading schools. Although not every piece of data was available for every student, we did obtain 578 complete cases from six select 16 schools and 457 cases from ten leading schools.[4] School record data included student grade point averages, Scholastic Aptitude Test (SAT) scores, class rank, names of colleges to which students applied, names of colleges to which students were accepted, and names of colleges students will attend. This material was supplied by the schools after the seniors graduated, in the summer or fall of 1982 and 1983. With this population actual enrollment matches school reports with high reliability. The record data have been linked with questionnaire data from the seniors and with various characteristics of the college. The colleges students planned to attend, were coded as to academic selectivity, Ivy League, and other characteristics not analyzed here.[5]

Chartering

Historical evidence shows that the select 16 schools have had special charters in relation to Ivy League colleges in general, and Harvard, Yale, and Princeton in particular. In the 1930s and 1940s, two-thirds of all graduates of 12 of the select 16 boarding schools attended Harvard, Yale, or Princeton (Karabel, 1984). But, by 1973, this share had slipped noticeably to an average of 21 percent, although the rate of acceptance between schools ranged from 51 percent to 8 percent (Cookson and Persell, 1978: Table 8.4). In the last half century, then, the proportion of select 16 school graduates who attended Harvard, Yale or Princeton dropped substantially.

This decrease was paralleled by an increase in the competition for admission to Ivy League colleges. According to several college advisors at select 16 boarding schools, 90 percent of all applicants to Harvard in the 1940s were accepted as were about half of those in the early 1950s. In 1982, the national acceptance rate for the eight Ivy League schools was 26 percent, although it was 20 percent or less at Harvard, Yale and Princeton (*National College Data Bank*, 1984).

The pattern of Ivy League college admissions has changed during this time. Ivy League colleges have begun to admit more public school graduates. Before World War II at Princeton, for example, about 80 percent of the entering freshmen came from private secondary schools (Blumberg and Paul, 1975: 70). In 1982, 34 percent of the freshman class at Harvard, 40 percent of Yale freshmen, and 40 percent of Princeton freshmen were from nonpublic high schools (*National College Data Bank*, 1984).

This shift in college admissions policy, combined with increased financial aid and an inflationary trend in higher education that puts increased emphasis on which college one attends, contributes to the large number of applications to certain colleges nationally. Thus, while in the past decade the number of college age students has declined, the number of students applying to Ivy League colleges has increased (Mackay-Smith, 1985; Maeroff, 1984; Winerip, 1984).

In view of these historical changes, is there any evidence that the select 16 schools still retain special charters in relation to college admissions? When four pools of applications to the Ivy League colleges are compared, the acceptance rate is highest at select 16 schools, followed by a highly selective public high school, other leading boarding schools, and finally the entire national pool of applications (Table 8.4).[6]

While we do not have comparable background data on all the applicants from these various pools, we do know that the students in the highly selective public high school have among the highest academic qualifications in the country.[7] Their combined SAT scores, for example, average at least 150 points higher than those of students at the leading boarding schools. On that basis they might be expected to do considerably better than applicants from

boarding schools: which they do at some colleges but not at Harvard, Yale or Princeton.

The most revealing insights into the operation of special charters, however, are provided by a comparison between select 16 boarding schools and other leading boarding schools—the most similar schools and the ones on which we have the most detailed data.

Students from select 16 schools apply to somewhat different colleges than do students from other leading boarding schools. Select 16 school students were much more likely to apply to one or more of the eight Ivy League and at least one of the other highly selective colleges than were students from other leading boarding schools (Table 8.5). Among those who applied, select 16 students were more likely to be accepted than were students from other boarding schools, and, if accepted, they were slightly more likely to attend.

Before we can conclude that these differences are due to a school charter, we need to control for parental SES[8] and student SAT scores.[9] This analysis is shown in Table 8.6. One striking finding here is the high rate of success enjoyed by boarding school students in general. At least one-third and as many as 92 percent of the students in each cell of Table 8.6 are accepted. Given that the average freshman combined SAT score is more than 1175 at these colleges and universities, it is particularly notable that such a large proportion of those with combined SAT scores of 1050 or less are accepted.

In general, high SAT scores increase chances of acceptance, but the relationship is somewhat attenuated under certain conditions. Students with low SAT scores are more likely to be accepted at highly selective colleges if they have higher SES backgrounds, especially if they attend a select 16 school. These students seem to have relatively high "floors" placed under them, since two thirds of those from select 16 schools and more than half of those from other schools were accepted by one of the most selective colleges.[10]

The most successful ones of all are relatively low SES students with the highest SATs attending select 16 schools—92 percent of whom were accepted. Students from relatively

Table 8.4 Percent of Applications That Were Accepted at Ivy League Colleges from Four Pools of Applications

College Name	Select 16 Boarding Schools[1] (1982–83)	Other Leading Boarding Schools[2] (1982–83)	Selective Public High School[3] (1984)	National Group of Applicants[4] (1982)
Brown University				
Percent accepted	35	20	28	22
Number of applications	95	45	114	11,854
Columbia University				
Percent accepted	66	29	32	41
Number of applications	35	7	170	3,650
Cornell University				
Percent accepted	57	36	55	31
Number of applications	65	25	112	17,927
Dartmouth College				
Percent accepted	41	21	41	22
Number of applications	79	33	37	8,313
Harvard University				
Percent accepted	38	28	20	17
Number of applications	104	29	127	13,341
Princeton University				
Percent accepted	40	28	18	18
Number of applications	103	40	109	11,804
University of Pennsylvania				
Percent accepted	45	32	33	36
Number of applications	40	19	167	11,000
Yale University				
Percent accepted	40	32	15	20
Number of applications	92	25	124	11,023
Overall percent accepted	42	27	30	26
Total number of applications	613	223	960	88,912

Notes:
[1] Based on school record data on applications of 578 seniors.
[2] Based on school record data on the applications of 457 seniors.
[3] Based on data published in the school newspaper.
[4] Based on data published in the *National College Data Bank* (1984).

Table 8.5 Boarding School Students' College Application, Chances of Acceptance, and Plans to Attend

	Ivy League Colleges % (N)	Highly Selective Colleges % (N)
A. Percent of boarding school samples who applied		
Select 16 boarding schools	61 (353)	87 (502)
Other leading boarding schools	28 (129)	61 (279)
B. Percent of applicants who were accepted		
Select 16 boarding schools	54 (191)	84 (420)
Other leading boarding schools	36 (47)	64 (178)
C. Percent of acceptees who plan to attend		
Select 16 boarding schools	79 (151)	81 (340)
Other leading boarding schools	53 (25)	77 (137)

Table 8.6 Percent of Students Who Applied to the Most Highly Selective Colleges Who Were Accepted, SAT Scores, SES, and School Type Held Constant

| | Student Combined SAT Scores | | | | | |
| | High (1580–1220) | | Medium (1216–1060) | | Low (1050–540) | |
Student Socio-economic Status	Select 16 Schools %(N)	Other Leading Boarding Schools % (N)	Select 16 Schools % (N)	Other Leading Boarding Schools %(N)	Select 16 Schools % (N)	Other Leading Boarding Schools % (N)
High	87 (93)	70 (33)	80 (73)	64 (36)	65 (34)	53 (30)
Medium	89 (100)	71 (28)	85 (66)	76 (46)	44 (18)	35 (51)
Low	92 (72)	72 (25)	78 (51)	69 (32)	55 (33)	33 (49)

Note: Based on student questionnaires and school record data on 1035 seniors for whom complete data were available.

modest backgrounds appear to receive a "knighting effect" by attending a select 16 school. Thus, select 16 schools provide mobility for some individuals from relatively less privileged backgrounds. To a considerable degree all students with high SATs, regardless of their SES, appear to be "turbo-charged" by attending a select 16 school compared to their counterparts at other leading schools.

At every level of SATs and SES, students' chances of acceptance increase if they attend a select 16 school. Such a finding is consistent with the argument that a chartering effect continues to operate among elite educational institutions. The historical shifts toward admitting more public school students on the part of Ivy League colleges and the increased competition for entry, described above, have meant that more effort has been required on the part of select 16 schools to retain an advantage for their students. We believe that certain private boarding schools have buttressed their charters by an increasingly active bartering operation.

Bartering

Normally, we do not think of the college admissions process as an arena for bartering. It is assumed that colleges simply choose students according to their own criteria and needs. Few students and no high schools are thought to have any special "leverage" in admissions decisions. Our research revealed, however, that select 16

boarding schools—perhaps because of their perennial supply of academically able and affluent students—can negotiate admissions cases with colleges. The colleges are aware that select 16 schools attract excellent college prospects and devote considerable attention to maintaining close relationships with these schools, especially through the college admissions officers. Secondary school college advisors actively "market" their students within a context of tremendous parental pressure and increasing competition for admission to elite colleges.

Select 16 College Advisors and Ivy League Admissions Directors: The Old School Tie

Of the 11 select 16 school college advisors on whom data were available, 10 were graduates of Harvard, Yale, or Princeton. Of the 23 other leading boarding school college advisors on whom data were available, only three were Ivy League graduates, and none of them was from Harvard, Yale, or Princeton. College advisors are overwhelmingly white men. At the select 16 schools only one (an acting director) was a woman, and at other schools five were women. Some college advisors have previously worked as college admissions officers. Their educational and social similarity to college admissions officers may facilitate the creation of social ties and the sharing of useful information. Research shows that the exchange of ideas most frequently occurs between people who share certain social attributes (Rogers and Kincaid, 1981).

College advisors at select 16 schools tend to have long tenures—15 or more years is not unusual. On the other hand, college advisors at other schools are more likely to have assumed the job recently. A college advisor at one select 16 school stressed the "importance of continuity on both sides of the relationship." Thus, it is not surprising that select 16 schools hold on to their college advisors.

Select 16 college advisors have close social relationships with each other and with elite college admissions officers that are cemented through numerous face-to-face meetings each year. All of the select 16 schools are on the east coast, whereas only 70 percent of the other leading boarding schools are in that region. However, even those leading boarding schools on the east coast lack the close relationships with colleges that characterize the select 16 schools. Thus, geography alone does not explain these relationships.

The college advisors at most of the boarding schools we studied have personally visited a number of colleges around the country. Boarding schools often provide college advisors with summer support for systematic visits, and a number of geographically removed colleges offer attractive incentives, or fully paid trips to their region (e.g., Southern California). These trips often take place during bitter New England winters, and include elegant food and lodging as well as a chance to see colleges and meet admissions officers.

However, the college advisors at select 16 schools are likely to have visited far more schools (several mentioned that they had personally visited 60 or 70 schools) than college advisors at other schools (some of whom had not visited any). They are also much more likely to visit regularly the most selective and prestigious colleges.[11]

Numerous college admissions officers also travel to these boarding schools to interview students and meet the college advisors. The select 16 schools have more college admissions officers visit than do other schools: more than 100 in any given academic year is not unusual.

College advisors have drinks and dinner with selected admissions officers, who often stay overnight on campus. As one college advisor noted, "We get to establish a personal relationship with each other." Moreover, Ivy League colleges bring students from select 16 schools to their campus to visit for weekends.

By knowing each other personally, college advisors and admissions officers "develop a relationship of trust," so that they can evaluate the source as well as the content of phone calls and letters. We observed phone calls between college advisors and admissions officers when we were in their offices. Several college advisors mentioned, "It helps to know personally the individual you are speaking or writing to," and one college advisor at a select 16 school said, "I have built up a track record with the private colleges over the years."

Virtually all of the select 16 school college advisors indicated that in the spring—before colleges have finished making their admissions decisions—they take their application files and drive to elite colleges to discuss "their list." They often sit in on the admissions deliberations while they are there. In contrast, the other schools' college advisors generally did not make such trips. Such actions suggest the existence of strong social networks between select 16 school college advisors and elite college admissions officers.

How the System Works: "Fine Tuning" the Admissions Process

Bartering implies a reciprocal relationship, and select 16 schools and elite colleges have a well-developed system of information exchange. Both sides have learned to cooperate to their mutual benefit. College advisors try to provide admissions officers with as much information about their students as possible to help justify the acceptance of a particular applicant. Select 16 schools have institutionalized this process more than other schools. The most professional operation we found was in a select 16 school where about half the graduating class goes to Harvard, Yale or Princeton. There, the college advisor interviews the entire faculty on each member of the senior class. He tape records all their comments and has them transcribed. This produces a "huge confidential dossier which gives a very good sense of where each student is." In addition, housemasters and coaches write reports. Then the college advisor interviews each senior, dictating notes after each interview. After assimilating all of these comments on each student, the college advisor writes his letter of recommendation, which he is able to pack with corroborative details illustrating a candidate's strengths. The thoroughness, thought, and care that goes into this process insures that anything and everything positive that could be said about a student is included, thereby maximizing his or her chances for a favorable reception at a college.[12]

Information also flows from colleges to the secondary schools. By sitting in on the admissions process at colleges like Harvard, Princeton, and Yale, select 16 school college advisors say they "see the wealth and breadth of the applicant pool." They get a first-hand view of the competition their students face. They also obtain a sense of how a college "puts its class together," which helps them to learn strategies for putting forward their own applicants.

By observing and participating in the admissions process, select 16 school college advisors gain an insider's view of a college's selection process. This insider's knowledge is reflected in the specific figures select 16 advisors mentioned in our conversations with them. One select 16 school college advisor said that a student has "two and one half times as good a chance for admission to Harvard if his father went there than if he did not." Another said, "while 22 percent in general are admitted to Ivy League colleges, 45 percent of legacies are admitted to Ivy League colleges." In both cases, they mentioned a specific, quantified statement about how being a legacy affected their students' admissions probabilities.[13] Similarly, several select 16 school college advisors mentioned the percentages of the freshman class at Harvard and Yale that were from public and private schools, and one even mentioned how those percentages have changed since 1957. College advisors at other schools do not lace their conversations with as many specific figures nor do they belong to the special organization that some of the select 16 schools have formed to share information and strategies.

The special interest group these schools have formed is able to negotiate with the colleges to their students' advantage. For instance, the college advisors explained that select 16 school students face greater competition than the average high school student and carry a more rigorous course load.[14] Therefore, this group persuaded the colleges that their students should not receive an absolute class rank, but simply an indication of where the students stand by decile or quintile. Colleges may then put such students in a "not ranked" category or report the decile or quintile rank. No entering student from such a secondary school is clearly labeled as the bottom person in the class. To our knowledge, only select 16 schools have made this arrangement.

Armed with an insider's knowledge of a college's desires, select 16 school college advisors seek to present colleges with the most appropriate candidates. As one select 16 school college advisor said, "I try to shape up different applicant pools for different colleges," a process that has several components. First, college advisors try to screen out hopeless prospects, or as one tactfully phrased it, "I try to discourage unproductive leads." This is not always easy because, as one said, "Certain dreams die hard." College advisors in other schools were more likely to say that they never told students where they should or should not apply.

One select 16 school requires students to write a "trial college essay" that helps the college advisor ascertain "what kind of a student this is." From the essay he can tell how well students write, determine whether they follow through and do what they need to do on time, and learn something about their personal and family background. With faculty and student comments in hand, college advisors can begin to assemble their applicant pools. One thing they always want to learn is which college is a student's first choice, and why. This is useful information when bartering with colleges.

Some college advisors are quite frank when bartering, for example, the select 16 college advisor who stressed, "I am candid about a student to the colleges, something that is not true at a lot of schools where they take an advocacy position in relation to their students. . . . We don't sell damaged goods to the colleges." College advisors at other schools did not define their role as one of weeding out candidates prior to presenting them to colleges, although they may do this as well. It would seem then that part of the gate-keeping process of admission to college is occurring in select 16 secondary schools. College advisors, particularly those with long tenures at select 16 schools, seem quite aware of the importance of maintaining long-term credibility with colleges, since credibility influences how effectively they can work for their school in the future.

While the children of certain big donors (so-called "development cases") may be counseled with special care, in general the college advisors have organizational concerns that are more important than the fate of a particular student. Several select 16 school college advisors spoke with scorn about parents who see a rejection as the "first step in the negotiation." Such parents threaten to disrupt a delicate network of social relationships that link elite institutions over a considerable time span.

At the same time, college advisors try to do everything they can to help their students jump the admissions hurdle. One select 16 school college advisor said:

> I don't see our students as having an advantage (in college admissions). We have to make the situation unequal. We do this by writing full summary reports on the students, by reviewing the applicants with the colleges several times during the year, and by traveling to the top six colleges in the spring. . . . [Those visits] are an advocacy proceeding on the side of the students. The colleges make their best decisions on our students and those from [another select 16 school] because they have the most information on these students.

Another select 16 college advisor said. "We want to be sure they are reading the applications of our students fairly, and we lobby for our students." A third select 16 college advisor made a similar statement, "When I drive to the [Ivy League] colleges, I give them a reading on our applicants. I let them know if I think they are making a mistake. There is a lobbying component here."

Select 16 college advisors do not stop with simply asking elite college admissions officers to reconsider a decision, however. They try to barter, and the colleges show they are open to this possibility when the college admissions officer says, "Let's talk about your group." One select 16 college advisor said he stresses to colleges that if his school recommends some-one and he or she is accepted, that student will come. While not all colleges heed this warranty, some do.

One select 16 college advisor said, "It is getting harder than it used to be to say to an admissions officer, 'take a chance on this one,' especially at Harvard which now has so many more applications." But it is significant that he did not say that it was impossible. If all else fails in a negotiation, a select 16 college advisor said, "we lobby for the college to make him their absolute first choice on the waiting list." Such a compromise represents a chance for both parties to save face.

Most public high school counselors are at a distinct disadvantage in the bartering process because they are not part of the interpersonal network, do not have strategic information, and are thus unable to lobby effectively for their students. One select 16 advisor told us about a counselor from the Midwest who came to an Ivy League college to sit in on the admissions committee decision for his truly outstanding candidate—SATs in the 700s, top in his class, class president, and star athlete. The select 16 college advisor was also there, lobbying on behalf of his candidate—a nice undistinguished fellow (in the words of his advisor, "A good kid") with SATs in the 500s, middle of his class, average athlete, and no strong signs of leadership. After hearing both the counselors, the Ivy League college chose the candidate from the select 16 school. The outraged public school counselor walked out in disgust. Afterwards, the Ivy League college admissions officer said to the select 16 college advisor, "We may not be able to have these open meetings anymore." Even in the unusual case where a public school counselor did everything that a select 16 boarding school college advisor did, it was not enough to secure the applicant's admission. Despite the competitive environment that currently surrounds admission to elite colleges, the admissions officers apparently listen more closely to advisors from select 16 boarding schools than to public school counselors.

Conclusions and Implications

The graduates of certain private schools are at a distinct advantage when it comes to admission to highly selective colleges because of the special charters and highly developed social networks these schools possess. Of course, other factors are operating as well. Parental wealth (which is not fully tapped by a measure of SES based on education, occupation, and income), preference for the children of alumni, Advanced Placement (AP) coursework, sports ability especially in such scarce areas as ice hockey, crew or squash, and many other factors also influence the process of college admission. Elite boarding schools are part of a larger process whereby more privileged members of society transmit their advantages to their children. Attendance at a select 16 boarding school signals admissions committees that an applicant may have certain valuable educational and social characteristics.

Significantly, neither the families nor the secondary schools leave the college admissions process to chance or to formal bureaucratic procedures. Instead, they use personal connections to smooth the process, and there is reason to believe that those efforts affect the outcomes. The "knighting effect" of select 16 schools helps a few low SES, high SAT students gain admission to highly selective colleges, evidence of sponsored mobility for a few worthy youngsters of relatively humble origins. Our findings are consistent with Kamens' (1974) suggestion that certain schools make their students eligible for special social rights. Furthermore, the interaction between social background, SATs, and select 16 school attendance suggests that both individual ability and socially structured advantages operate in the school-college transition.

These results illustrate Collins' (1979) view that stratified systems are maintained through the manipulation of social contacts. They show one way that networks and stratification processes are interconnected. College access is only one aspect of the larger phenomenon of elite maintenance and reproduction. Elite boarding schools no doubt contribute as well to the social contacts and marriage markets of their graduates. What this instance shows is that reproduction is not a simple process. It involves family and group reproduction as well as some structural replacement with carefully screened new members. There is active personal intervention in what is publicly represented as a meritocratic and open competition. The internal processes and external networks described here operate to construct class privileges as well as to transmit class advantages, thereby helping to reproduce structured stratification within society.

If this example is generalizable, we would expect that economically and culturally advantaged groups might regularly find or create specially chartered organizations and brokers with well-developed networks to help them successfully traverse critical junctures in their social histories. Such key switching points include the transition from secondary school to college, admission to an elite graduate or professional school, obtaining the right job, finding a mentor, gaining a medical residency at a choice hospital (Hall, 1947, 1948, 1949) getting a book manuscript published (Coser et al., 1982), having one's paintings exhibited at an art gallery or museum, obtaining a theatrical agent, having one's business considered for venture capital or bank support (Rogers and Larsen, 1984), being offered membership in an exclusive social club, or being asked to serve on a corporate or other board of directors (Useem, 1984).

In all of these instances, many qualified individuals seek desired, but scarce, social and/or economic opportunities. Truly open competition for highly desired outcomes leaves privileged groups vulnerable. Because the socially desired positions are finite at any given moment, processes that give an advantage to the members of certain groups work to limit the opportunities of individuals from other groups.[15] In these ways, dominant groups enhance their chances, at the same time that a few worthy newcomers are advanced, a process which serves to reproduce and legitimate a structure of social inequality.

Notes

We wish to thank E. Digby Baltzell, Steven Brint, Kevin Dougherty, Eliot Freidson, Kathleen Gerson, David Greenberg, Wolf Heydebrand, Herbert Menzel, John Meyer, Karen Miller, Richard R. Peterson, Edwin Schur, Susan Shapiro, Beth Stevens, and a number of anonymous reviewers for their thoughtful reactions to this paper.

1. Others besides Baltzell have developed lists of elite private schools, including Baird (1977), Domhoff (1967, 1970, 1983), and McLachlan (1970).
2. We were not able to compute the percent of students in *Social Register* for every school because most schools do not publish the names of their students. Hence, we were not able to look their families up in *Social Register*. We do know that less than .000265 percent of American families are listed in *Social Register*. See Levine (1980) for an historical discussion of the social backgrounds of students at several of the select 16 schools.
3. We asked to give the student questionnaires at nine of the 12 select 16 schools and six of those nine schools agreed. At the other leading schools, we asked to give the questionnaires at 15 and 13 schools agreed.
4. Three leading schools did not supply the college data.
5. Following Astin et al. (1981: 7), we measured selectivity with the average SAT scores of the entering freshmen.
6. The entire national applicant pool includes the relatively more successful subgroups within it. If they were excluded, the national acceptance rate would be even lower.
7. Students admitted to this selective public high school must be recommended by their junior high school to take a competitive entrance exam, where they must score very well. The school was among the top five in the nation with respect to the number of National Merit Scholarships won by its students, and each year a number of students in the school win Westinghouse science prizes. This school was selected for purposes of comparison here because academically it is considered to be among the very top public schools in the nation. However, it does not have the social prestige of the select 16 boarding schools.
8. SES was measured by combining father's education, father's occupation, and family income into a composite SES score. These SES scores were then standardized for this population, and each student received a single standardized SES score.
9. The combined verbal and mathematics scores were used.
10. We performed separate analyses for boys and girls to see if sex was related to admission to a highly selective college when type of boarding school, SATs, and SES were held constant, and generally it was not. Girls who attend either select 16 or other leading boarding schools do as well: or better in their admission to college as do their male counterparts, with the single exception of girls at select 16 schools in the top third on their SATs and SES. In that particular group, 92 percent of the boys but only 77 percent of the girls were accepted at the most highly selective colleges. Since that is the only exception, boys and girls are discussed together in the text of the paper.
11. Our field visits and interviews with college advisors at two highly selective public high schools and three open admissions public high schools show that college advisors at even the most selective public high schools generally do not personally know the admissions officers at colleges, particularly at the most selective and Ivy League colleges, nor do they talk with them over the phone or in person prior to their admissions decisions.
12. Such a procedure requires considerable financial and personnel resources. Select 16 schools have more capital intensive and professional office services supporting their college admissions endeavor than otherschools. Most of them have word processors, considerable professional staff, and ample secretarial and clerical help.
13. We did not ask students what colleges their parents attended so we could not control for college legacy in our analysis. Future research on the admissions process should do so.
14. One way select 16 schools establish their reputations as rigorous schools is through the numbers of their students who succeed on the Advanced Placement (AP) Exams given by the College Entrance Examination Board. Compared to other secondary schools, select 16 schools offer larger numbers of advanced courses (Table 8.3), encourage more students to take them, coach students very effectively on how to take the test, and maintain contacts with the people who design

and read AP exams so that they know what is expected and can guide students accordingly. (See Cookson and Persell, 1985, for more discussion of these processes.) Other schools are much less likely than select 16 ones to have teachers who have graded AP exams or to know people who have helped to write the tests.

15. See Parkin (1979) for a discussion of social closure as exclusion and usurpation.

References

Alexander, Karl L., Martha Cook and Edward L. McDill 1978 "Curriculum tracking and educational stratification: some further evidence." American Sociological Review 43:47–66.

Alexander, Karl L. and Bruce K. Eckland 1975 "Contextual effects in the high school attainment process." American Sociological Review 40: 402–16.

—— 1977 "High school context and college selectivity: institutional constraints in educational stratification." Social Forces 56:166–88.

Alexander, Karl L., Bruce K. Eckland and Larry J. Griffin 1975 "The Wisconsin model of socio-economic achievement: a replication." American Journal of Sociology 81:324–42.

Alexander, Karl L. and Edward L. McDill 1976 "Selection and allocation within schools: some causes and consequences of curriculum placement." American Sociological Review 41:963–80.

Astin, Alexander W., Margo R. King, and Gerald T. Richardson 1981 The American Freshman: National Norms for Fall 1981. Los Angeles: Laboratory for Research in Higher Education, University of California.

Averch, Harvey A., Steven J. Carroll, Theodore S. Donaldson, Herbert J. Kiesling, and John Pincus 1972 How Effective is Schooling? A Critical Review and Synthesis of Research Findings. Santa Monica, CA: The Rand Corporation.

Baird, Leonard L. 1977 The Elite Schools. Lexington, MA: Lexington Books.

Baltzell, E. Digby 1958 Philadelphia Gentlemen. New York: Free Press.

——1964 The Protestant Establishment. New York: Random House.

Beck, E. M., Patrick M. Horan, and Charles M. Tolbert II 1978 "Stratification in a dual economy." American Sociological Review 43:704–20.

Bibb, Robert C. and William Form 1977 "The effects of industrial, occupational and sex stratification on wages in blue-collar markets." Social Forces 55:974–96.

Blau, Peter and Otis D. Duncan 1967 The American Occupational Structure. New York: Wiley.

Blumberg, Paul M. and P. W. Paul 1975 "Continuities and discontinuities in upper-class marriages." Journal of Marriage and the Family 37:63–77.

Bowles, Samuel and Herbert Gintis 1976 Schooling in Capitalist America. New York: Basic Books.

Collins, Randall 1979 The Credential Society. New York: Academic Press.

Cookson, Peter Willis, Jr. 1981 "Private secondary boarding school and public suburban high school graduation: an analysis of college attendance plans." Unpublished Ph.D. dissertation, New York University.

Cookson, Peter W., Jr. and Caroline Hodges Persell 1978 "Social structure and educational programs: a comparison of elite boarding schools and public education in the United States." Paper presented at the annual meeting of the American Sociological Association, San Francisco.

—— 1985 Preparing for Power: America's Elite Boarding Schools. New York: Basic Books.

Coser, Lewis A., Charles Kadushin, and Walter W. Powell 1982 Books: The Culture & Commerce of Publishing. New York: Basic Books.

Domhoff, G. William 1967 Who Rules America? Engle-wood Cliffs: Prentice-Hall.

—— 1970 The Higher Circles. New York: Vintage.

—— 1983 Who Rules America Now? Englewood Cliffs: Prentice-Hall.

Falsey, Barbara and Barbara Heyns 1984 "The college channel: private and public schools reconsidered." Sociology of Education 57:111–22.

Hall, Oswald 1946 "The informal organization of the medical profession." Canadian Journal of Economics and Political Science 12:30–41.

—— 1948 "The stages of a medical career." American Journal of Sociology 53:327–36.

—— 1949 "Types of medical career." American Journal of Sociology 55:243–53.

Haller, Archibald O. and Alejandro Portes 1973 "Status attainment processes." Sociology of Education 46:51–91.

Hammack, Floyd M. and Peter W. Cookson, Jr. 1980 "Colleges attended by graduates of elite secondary schools." The Educational Forum 44:483–90.

Handbook of Private Schools 1981 Boston: Porter Sargent Publishers, Inc.

Heyns, Barbara 1974 "Social selection and stratification within schools." American Journal of Sociology 79:1434–51.

Jaffe, Abraham and Walter Adams 1970 "Academic and socio-economic factors related to entrance and retention at two- and four-year colleges in the late 1960s." New York: Bureau of Applied Social Research, Columbia University.

Jencks, Christopher, Marshall Smith, Henry Acland, Mary Jo Bane, David Cohen, Herbert Gintis, Barbara Heyns, and Stephan Michelson 1972 Inequality. New York: Basic Books.

Kamens, David 1974 "Colleges and elite formation: the case of prestigious American colleges." Sociology of Education 47:354–78.

—— 1977 "Legitimating myths and educational organization: the relationship between organizational ideology and formal structure." American Sociological Review 42:208–19.

Karabel, Jerome 1984 "Status-group struggle, organizational interests, and the limits of institutional autonomy: the transformation of Harvard, Yale, and Princeton 1918–1940." Theory and Society 13:1–40.

Karen, David 1985 "Who gets into Harvard? Selection and exclusion." Unpublished Ph.D. dissertation. Department of Sociology, Harvard University.

Kerckhoff, Alan C. 1976 "The status attainment process: socialization or allocation?" Social Forces 55:368–81.

—— 1984 "The current state or social mobility research." Sociology Quarterly 25:139–53.

Klitgaard, Robert 1985 Choosing Elites. New York: Basic Books.

Laumann, Edward O. 1966 Prestige and Association in an Urban Community: An Analysis of an Urban Stratification System. Indianapolis: Bobbs-Merrill.

Levine, Steven B. 1980 "The rise of American boarding schools and the development of a national upper class." Social Problems 28:63–94.

Lewis, Lionel S. and Richard A. Wanner 1979 "Private schooling and the status attainment process." Sociology of Education 52:99–112.

Mackay-Smith, Anne 1985 "Admissions crunch: top colleges remain awash in applicants despite a smaller pool." Wall Street Journal (April 2):1,14.

Maeroff, Gene I. 1984 "Top Eastern colleges report unusual rise in applications." New York Times (February 21):A1,C10.

McLachlan, James 1970 American Boarding Schools: A Historical Study. New York: Charles Scribner's Sons.

Meyer, John 1970 "The charter: Conditions of diffuse socialization in school." Pp. 564–78 in W. Richard Scott (ed.), Social Processes and Social Structure. New York: Holt, Rinehart.

—— 1977 "Education as an institution." American Journal of Sociology 83:55–77.

Mills, C. Wright 1956 The Power Elite. London: Oxford University Press.

National College Data Bank 1984 Princeton: Peterson's Guides, Inc.

Oakes, Jeannie 1985 Keeping Track: How Schools Structure Inequality. New Haven: Yale University Press.

Otto, Luther B. and Archibald O. Haller 1979 "Evidence for a social psychological view of the status attainment process: four studies compared." Social Forces 57:887–914.

Parkin, Frank 1979 Marxism Class Theory: A Bourgeois Critique. New York: Columbia University Press.

Persell, Caroline Hodges 1977 Education and Inequality. New York: The Free Press.

Robinson, Robert V. 1984 "Reproducing class relations in industrial capitalism." American Sociological Review 49:182–96.

Rogers, Everett M. and D. Lawrence Kincaid 1981 Communications Networks: Toward a New Paradigm for Research. New York: The Free Press.

Rogers, Everett M. and Judith K. Larsen 1984 Silicon Valley Fever: The Growth of High-Tech Culture. New York: Basic Books.

Rosenbaum, James E. 1976 Making Inequality: The Hidden Curriculum of High School Tracking. New York: Wiley.

—— 1980 "Track misperceptions and frustrated college plans: an analysis of the effects of tracks and track perceptions in the national longitudinal survey." Sociology of Education 53:74–88.

Sewell, William H., Archibald O. Haller, and Alejandro Portes 1969 "The educational and early occupational attainment process." American Sociological Review 34:82–91.

Sewell, William H., Archibald O. Haller, and George W. Ohlendorf 1970 "The educational and early occupational status achievement process: Replication and revision." American Sociological Review 35:1014–27.

Social Register 1984 New York: Social Register Association.

Stolzenberg, Ross M. 1975 "Occupations labor markets and the process of wage attainment." American Sociological Review 40:645–65.

Useem, Michael 1984 The Inner Circle: Large Corporations and the Rise of Business Political Activity in the U.S. and U.K. New York: Oxford University Press.

Wellman, Barry 1981 "Network analysis from method and metaphor to theory and substance." Working Paper Series 1B, Structural Analysis Programme, University of Toronto.

Wilson, Kenneth L. and Alejandro Portes 1975 "The Educational attainment process: Results from a national sample." American Journal of Sociology 81:343–63.

Winerip, Michael 1984 "Hot colleges and how they get that way." New York Times Magazine. (November 18):68ff.

College-for-All

Do Students Understand What College Demands?[3]

James E. Rosenbaum

Sociology has long tried to discover the ways disadvantaged backgrounds harm youth. While human capital theory in economics attributes such problems to deficiencies in individuals' ability or motivation, sociology looks at the ways societal factors block opportunity. However, reality is likely to be more complex. Societal factors do sometimes pose explicit barriers; but explicit barriers are relatively ineffective because they are so obviously unjust, readily seen, and easily attacked. Ambiguous opportunities and unclear requirements may be far more important in blocking mobility than explicit barriers (Cicourel and Kitsuse, 1963; Rosenbaum, 1978, 1989). Clark (1960) showed that the ambiguous mission of community colleges seemed to offer access to four-year colleges when, in fact, these institutions "cooled out" aspirations as students gradually realized that college was not appropriate for their abilities.

In the decades since Clark's study, community colleges have grown enormously. While four-year college enrollment roughly doubled between 1960 and 1990, public community college enrollment increased five-fold in the same period—from 200,000 to over 1,000,000 (U.S. Department of Health, Education, and Welfare, 1992, Table 169). In turn, college opportunities have dramatically increased. While 45.1% of high school graduates entered some postsecondary institution in 1960, over 62% did in 1993. Moreover, community colleges initiated open-admissions policies and remedial courses to reduce the academic barriers to college; and the Associate of Arts (AA) degree has increased in value in the labor market so that students do not need a BA to get an economic benefit from attending community college (Brint and Karabel, 1989; Grubb, 1992, 1993, 1995). Community colleges have increased access to an economically valued degree.

Have these changes created an easy route to college success, or do they merely confuse students so that they fail to prepare themselves appropriately? Studies since Clark's have continued to find substantial college attrition (Grubb, 1989) and have focussed on the factors that redirect students' plans (Karabel, 1986). Yet, rather than focus on the cooling-out process in community colleges, one must rememberthat "cooling out" is just the institutional mechanism for dealing with failure–not the original cause.

Clark took the term "cooling out" from Goffman's (1952) analysis of confidence swindles. The key to a swindle is to give "marks" confidence that they will gain a valuable reward at very little cost and then lure them to an "easy success" strategy. That is why a "mark" willingly hands over something of value to a swindler, and people pay for "snake oil" remedies that offer high expectations for a small price. Marks only realize that their expectations were mistaken at a later time, after the person who encouraged the expectation is no longer present.

This paper contends that the high level of community-college dropout arises because high schools offer vague promises of open opportunity for college but fail to specify the actual requirements for successful degree completion. Like Goffman's confidence schemes, students are promised college for very little effort. Lured by the prospect of easy success, students choose easy curricula and low efforts. Just as some high schools implicitly offer students an undemanding curriculum in return for nondisruptive behavior (Sedlak, Wheeler, Pullin, and Cusick, 1986), many high schools enlist students' cooperation by telling them that college is the only respectable goal and that it is easily attainable by all. Rather than community college failure arising from an overt barrier in community colleges, the seeds of failure in community colleges may arise much earlier—when youth are still in high school.

In the current era, many high schools encourage the "college-for-all" norm which states that all students can and should attend college but which fails to tell students what they must do to attain this goal (Rosenbaum, Miller, and Krei, 1996). The college-for-all norm (CFA) is a variant of "the contest mobility norm" which says that opportunity for upward mobility should always stay open (Turner, 1960). This norm encourages youth to retain ambitions of advancement as long as possible, but it ignores barriers that limit youths' careers (Rosenbaum, 1975, 1976, 1986).

Americans are rightly proud of the CFA norm. It discourages schools from tracking students prematurely, and it encourages high expectations in youth. It argues for better instruction in schools, especially schools serving low-income youth. Without this norm, society might give up on raising the educational achievement of the most disadvantaged youth.

While it is not meant to be deceptive, the CFA norm can inadvertently encourage a deception that hurts many youth, including the disadvantaged youth it is meant to help. The CFA norm encourages all students to plan on college regardless of their past achievement. To avoid discouraging students, the CFA norm avoids focussing on requirements; but, in the process, it fails to tell students what steps they should take and does not warn them when their low achievements make their college plans unlikely to be attained. While such encouragement helps younger children, it may mislead students in their later years of high school.

Thus, while 70.9% of high school seniors in the class of 1982 planned to get college degrees, half of 12th-grade students lacked basic 9th-grade math and verbal skills (Murnane and Levy, 1997), and only about half of college entrants completed a college degree (Resnick and Wirt, 1996). The completion rate from two-year colleges is even worse. For the 1980 graduates enrolled full time in two-year public colleges in October 1980, less than 40% (38.8%) completed any degree (AA or higher) by 1986, and the rates were only 15.2% for the substantial numbers

(about 25%) who were enrolled part time (U.S. Department of Health, Education, and Welfare, 1992, Table 287). Students rarely attain their college plans. For the 1980 graduates who planned less than four years of college (but more than a certificate), less than 20% (19.9%) attained a college degree (AA or higher) in the next six years (U.S. Department of Health, Education, and Welfare, 1992, Table 286).

This has not always been true. The dropout rate from public two-year colleges increased sharply after 1972 (49.6% in 1980 vs. 36.0% in 1972, Grubb, 1989, Table 2). One reason for these disappointing outcomes is that school officials do not warn students about potential problems. Rather than acting as gatekeepers as they did in earlier decades (Rosenbaum, 1976), guidance counselors now urge all students to attend college but rarely warn poorly prepared students that they will have difficulty completing a degree (Rosenbaum, Miller, and Krei, 1996). Rather than hurting students by posing obstacles to their plans, counselors may now be hurting students by not informing them of potential obstacles they will face later on.

Contrary to Karabel's (1986) interpretation of community colleges as institutions which mislead students, Goffman's model suggests that deception is earlier, more subtle, and often in a different location. Indeed, "marks" go along with a swindle because their hopes are initially "heated up" to unrealistic expectations, and "cooling out" is only done late in the process. Thus, rather than focus on the "cooling out" process, one needs to examine why youth have unrealistically high expectations—the precipitating conditions for why "cooling out" is required.

This paper asserts that information is central to this process. If high school students are informed that they are poorly prepared for community college, they can either increase their efforts to prepare themselves or revise their plans to be more realistic. In either case, "cooling out" is unneeded, and youths' plans will be less likely to fail.

High schools probably do not intentionally deceive students. Rather, many schools have well-intentioned practices of raising students' expectations; but these practices may have unintended consequences. High schools encourage college plans for all students, even poorly achieving students whose subsequent failure is highly predictable even before they enter community colleges. Yet, students do not anticipate their probable failure, and they do not take actions to prepare themselves for their goals.

Such a mechanism is more subtle than the one Karabel describes. Poor information allows many students to have high hopes, to use their high school experiences poorly, and thus to seem to be personally responsible for their failures—in precisely the way that human capital theory describes. By the time students enter community college, their eventual outcomes are largely determined. Community colleges cannot be blamed for the poor preparation of their entrants. Yet, the high schools which poorly convey information about requirements are not a visible target. Indeed, they are praised for encouraging students to have "high expectations."

The above description suggests that students' perceptions of college requirements are key to their efforts in high school and to their college attainments. It can be posed as a model with several elements:

1. Many seniors believe they can attain college plans with low high school achievement.
2. Students with these beliefs, including college-bound students, exert little effort in high school.
3. Such beliefs are partly correct—students can enter college even if they have low achievement.
4. High school achievement predicts degree completion, but students' plans do not anticipate this relationship.
5. High school achievement predicts much of the lower attainment and disappointed plans of disadvantaged students.
6. Students with low high school achievement get less economic payoff for college degrees.

This paper takes these contentions as hypotheses and presents analyses to test them empirically.

The analyses support these hypotheses and pose serious challenges to current practices. This paper concludes that shielding high school seniors from the realities of college demands and allowing them to hold unrealistic plans is not a kindness. It is a deception which prevents students from taking actions to improve their achievement or to revise their plans and make better use of high school. Students with unrealistic plans should be so informed. They should be encouraged to increase their efforts or to develop backup plans and preparation.

Data and Methods

This report is based on three kinds of data. First, students' perceptions are described using detailed interviews of a nonrandom sample of high school seniors in two high schools. Second, students' views are systematically analyzed using a survey administered to a random sample of 2,091 seniors classes in 12 high schools across the Chicago metropolitan area during 1992–94. The schools and sample are diverse in ethnicity and SES backgrounds and are described in detail elsewhere (Rosenbaum and Roy, 1996).

Third, students' outcomes are assessed using the recent release of the 12-year follow-up of the High School and Beyond 1980 sophomores (National Center for Educational Statistics, 1983). This national sample was first surveyed in 1980 (when respondents were sophomores) and subsequently resurveyed in 1982, 1984, 1986, and 1992. Of the original 14,825 sophomores in 1980, the survey obtained responses from 95.1% in 1982 (n = 14,102), and 85.3% in 1992 (n = 12,640). This survey provides a unique opportunity for a long-term study of the determinants of educational attainments. This paper studies the outcomes for the individuals responding in both the 1982 and 1992 surveys.

Many Seniors Believe They Can Attain College Plans with Low High School Achievement

Economic theory is a good model of our rational common sense assumptions. For instance, human capital theory explains students' achievement using two factors: students' inherent capabilities and their efforts to invest in themselves. The theory says students will invest in themselves and exert effort in school because they know there is a societal payoff.

While it is widely assumed that students believe that school efforts have a payoff, this assumption is rarely examined. Do students believe that school effort and achievement are relevant and helpful in improving their future careers? Of course teachers tell this to students, but it is clearly in teachers' own self-interest to convince students of their own importance. As parents and teachers often notice, one of the less convenient aspects of adolescence is the cognitive capacity that enables them to doubt what they are told.

Stinchcombe (1965) hypothesized that many students believed that school was not relevant to their future careers and that students' school efforts were determined, not only by their internal motivation, but also by their perceptions of schools' future relevance. While economists assume that incentives exist and are seen, Stinchcombe suggests this may not be true for work-bound students. Unfortunately, while Stinchcombe provided an intriguing model, his small sample and bivariate analyses (on a card sorter in the precomputer age) were too simple for a convincing test.

To examine these ideas, a nonrandom sample of 50 students was interviewed about how they thought about the relevance of school. Consistent with the dictum, "the more things change, the more they stay the same," these interviews in 1993 found similar sentiments to those Stinchcombe found 30 years previously. Many students reported that school was not relevant to their future careers. Yet something had changed. While Stinchcombe found that only work-bound students expressed these beliefs in 1960, these sentiments were also expressed by college-bound students in 1993. Many students who planned to attend college reported that high school achievement was not relevant to their future careers. Their comments suggested that the vast expansion of community colleges over the past 30 years contributed to their views. One student noted, "High school doesn't really matter . . . , because . . . junior college is not such a big deal to get into" (#42). Another said, "If you could apply yourself [in junior college], you'd get better grades" [regardless of how you did in high school] (#27). Many students agreed with the student who saw the "two-year college as another chance for someone who's messed up in high school" (#39). This second chance was also viewed as making high school effort less relevant. As one student said in explaining why he does not try hard in high school, "I think college is much more important than high school" (#16).

To examine Stinchcombe's hypotheses more systematically, survey items were constructed which reflected two aspects of individuals' perceptions of schools' relevance: whether students believed that high school education had relevance for their future success (hereafter "future relevance") and whether students believed that there was no penalty if they had poor school performance (hereafter "no penalty" attitude). The first variable refers to students' belief that high school can help their future careers; the second refers to beliefs that bad school performance (even if possibly relevant) is not necessarily a barrier to attaining their future careers.[1]

Surveys were recently administered to 2,091 high school seniors enrolled in 12 city and suburban high schools in a large, Midwestern metropolitan area. Just as Stinchcombe found, the survey found that many students doubted school's future relevance. This was not only true for work-bound students. Almost as many college-bound students held such beliefs. On five-point scales ranging from "strongly agree" to "strongly disagree," our analyses found that 30–40% of students did not agree with such statements as, "My courses give me useful preparation I'll need in life" (39.3% for whole sample, for college-bound respondents, 37.2%), "School teaches me valuable skills" (29.7%, college 28.2%), and "Getting a good job depends on how well you do at school" (36.6%, college 36.5%). We summed to create a scale for "future relevance."

Similar patterns appear for items concerned with lack of penalty for poor high school grades. Almost 46% of students agree with the item

"Even if I do not work hard in high school, I can still make my future plans come true" (45.9%, college 44.3%). While educators want students to believe that students with bad grades rarely get college degrees or good jobs, many students disagree with the first point (regarding graduation from two-year colleges, 40.7% for whole sample, college 41.2%) and almost as many disagree with the second (getting good jobs after high school, 37.9%, college 32.9%). Most surprisingly, despite many campaigns against dropping out of high school, over 40% of seniors do not disagree with the statement "People can do OK even if they drop out of high school" (43.7%, college 40.8%). Apparently, many students see no penalty to their planned careers if they do not have high school diplomas, good grades, and work hard in school. We summed these latter items to create a scale for "no penalty."

The two scales of "future relevance" and "no penalty" are correlated, but the correlation is far from perfect (r = .30). Students who plan to get a college degree have a somewhat higher sense of schools' "future relevance," and a lesser sense that there is "no penalty" if they do poorly in high school, than students without college plans, but the difference is small (about 1/3 of a standard deviation). Moreover, these beliefs vary substantially within such groups, and the variation is similar within both groups (standard deviations of .61–.65).

Students with These Beliefs Exert Little Effort in High School

While there is nothing wrong with students having optimistic hopes, we would be concerned if students responded to these beliefs by reducing their efforts. This section examines: what factors may determine future relevance and no penalty beliefs, what factors may determine students' school efforts, and whether these beliefs mediate the potential influence of other factors on students' school efforts and may have independent influences on students' school efforts.

The antecedents of future relevance and no penalty beliefs are first examined. The survey asked three or more items relating to locus of control, parent support, teacher help, school help, peer pro-school influences, and peer anti-school (rebellion) influences. Items were factor analyzed and scales were constructed. All had alpha coefficients over .70. The survey also asked about respondents' race, ethnicity, parents' education and occupation, and gender (for details, see Rosenbaum and Roy, 1996).

First, OLS regression analyses show that both future relevance and no-penalty are strongly explained by parent support for school, teacher help, and personal locus of control. Peers and low-SES studies also have significant coefficients but gender and being Black do not (Table 8.7, columns 1 and 2).

Second, we examine the antecedents of students' school effort. Effort is measured by a scale combining students' reports of their behaviors (how much time they spend on homework) and three other items: I just do enough to pass my classes, I try to do my best in school, I only work in school if I'm worried about failing (each coded on a five-point scale from "strongly agree" to "strongly disagree").

As in previous research (Kandel and Lesser, 1972), these analyses find that students' school efforts are explained by parent, peer, and school variables (Table 8.7, column 3). Males and having low-SES have negative coefficients, but ethnicity has no influence. Students' locus of control has a large and significant effect.

However, when future relevance and no-penalty are added to the analysis, we find that they mediate much of the potential influence of parents, school help, teacher help, and locus of control and reduce the negative coefficient of SES to nonsignificance. In contrast, their addition has relatively little effect on the influence of the two peer variables (see column 4). After controlling for other factors, future relevance and no-penalty also have significant independent effects on effort (standardized coefficients of .155 for future relevance, –.145 for "no penalty," column 4). Thus, these beliefs have significant and independent associations with effort, perhaps indicating strong effects in reducing students' school efforts.

These findings have implications for theory and practice. Theoretically, this study supports Stinchcombe's hypothesis. Students vary in whether they see school as relevant to their future lives, and this variable is strongly associated with their school efforts. In addition, this study identifies a second measure—the "no penalty" belief—and shows that both beliefs have significant, independent relationships with school effort.

These results imply that some youth have misread the American emphasis on opportunity. While Americans want society to provide "second chances" to youth, Stevenson and Stigler (1992) warn that youth might misinterpret this to mean that school failures never matter and effort is not needed. This study finds that many youth see little penalty to avoiding school work and little payoff to high school, and these beliefs may justify their poor effort in high school.

Of course, it is possible that causality goes in the other direction—that individuals rationalize their poor effort by denying future relevance.

However, these views, whether beliefs or rationalizations, are held by 40% of students so they are not just the problems of a few individuals. Indeed, since guidance counselors do not challenge these beliefs, part of the problem arises from school practices (Rosenbaum, Miller, and Krei, 1996). Even if these views arise as rationalizations, they are not effectively challenged by schools and represent misconceptions that encourage a continuing cycle of further low effort.

Students Can Enter College Even if They Have Low Achievement

Are students wrong when they say school achievement is not relevant to their futures? Community colleges are frequently seen as "second chance" institutions for those who have done poorly before, offering open admissions, low tuition, and remedial courses. In some community college departments, remedial courses may be 40% of the courses offered. Over 40% of freshmen at public two-year colleges take

Table 8.7 Determinants of Future Relevance, No Penalty, and Effort (Standardized Coefficients)

	Future Rel.	No Penalty	Effort (Step 1)	Effort (Step 2)
Parental support for school	.1702**	−.2786**	.2795**	.2128**
Rebellious peers	−.0576*	.0943**	−.1369**	−.1143**
Pro-school peers	.0949**	−.0217	.1157**	.0979**
Locus of control	.1253**	−.1655**	.2060**	.1627**
Female	−.0411	−.0149	.1051**	.1094**
Low SES	−.0439*	.0828**	−.0554*	−.0366
Black	.0344	−.0202	.0006	−.0076
Hispanic	.0526*	−.0391	−.0370	−.0510*
Asian	.0660**	−.0030	−.0043	−.0149
Teacher help	.2822**	.0510*	.0893**	.0530*
School help	.1310**	−.0441	.0564**	.0300
Future relevance				.1550**
No penalty belief				−.1448**
R-squared (adjusted)	.2446	.1710	.2947	.3393

n = 2.091, * = p < .05, ** = p < .01

one or more years of remedial coursework just to acquire the same skills they did not learn in high school (National Center for Educational Statistics, 1995).

Although sociologists have produced extensive research showing that grades are strongly related to college attendance (e.g., Kerckhoff and Campbell 1977; Porter, 1974), much of this research is based on studies from the 1960s and 1970s. Yet, college admissions have changed a great deal since 1960. As noted, the five-fold growth of community colleges has dramatically increased opportunities to go to college, and fewer students are likely to face barriers to access to college.

Moreover, community colleges have initiated open-admissions policies and remedial courses to reduce the academic barriers to college. In the past, college admission standards compelled lower-achieving students to confront their unrealistic college plans. While college admission standards were a severe barrier to college for low-achieving students in 1960, admission standards are now practically nonexistent in community colleges. For example, Illinois high school graduates can attend a community college even if they have Ds and no college-prep courses (after age 21, even a diploma is not required). In addition, a full array of remedial courses have been devised to provide high-school-level curricula in the community colleges in order to improve students' chances of success (Brint and Karabel, 1989; Dougherty, 1994; Grubb and Kalman, 1994). Open admissions policies and remedial courses have removed some academic barriers to college entrance.

Are students correct in the belief that high school performance is not relevant to their educational outcomes? The High School and Beyond data indicate that poor high school performance does not prevent college attendance. Even students with low grades (Cs or lower) can attend college. Indeed, 27% of students enrolling in two-year colleges had low grades in high school. That is only slightly less than the proportion of students with low grades who did not enroll in any postsecondary education (30%). Obviously, low grades are not a barrier to enrolling in two-year colleges.

College-bound students who think high school effort is irrelevant to their future plans are partly correct—high school grades are not an obstacle to enrollment in two-year colleges.

High School Achievement Predicts Degree Completion, but Students' Plans Do Not Anticipate This Relationship

Having found that many students believe high school achievement is not relevant and, indeed, that many students with low grades can enter two-year colleges, one must wonder whether these students are correct that high school achievement is not relevant to college attainment. Or do these beliefs lead students to make plans which they will be unable to realize? This section of the paper addresses these questions with simple percentages, and the next section uses multivariate analyses.

These analyses emphasize grades because all students know their grades, so students could use this knowledge if they chose to do so. But do they choose to do so? Because most people have had a few teachers who gave arbitrary or unfair grades, grades are often dismissed as erroneous and irrelevant. Yet, knowledge of scale construction suggests that averaging grades eliminates random idiosyncrasies and might make grade averages a meaningful indicator. This section examines whether students' cumulative grade point averages in high school predict college outcomes.

Our analyses of the High School and Beyond data find that many students with college plans fail to attain college degrees, and high school grades strongly predict which students fail at their college plans. Of the 12,475 seniors with complete information on plans, grades, and educational attainment, 8,795 (70.5%) planned to get a college degree (AA or higher) in their senior year in high school. Many seniors (4,103 of the 12,475) had low grades (Cs or lower), yet 50.8% of those with low grades still planned to get a college degree (n = 2,086).

However, low grades have a strong impact on actual educational attainment. Among all seniors with college plans, 40.3% succeed in getting a college degree (AA or higher) in the

10 years after high school (Table 8.8a). By comparison, low high school grades cut students' chances in half—only 19.6% of seniors with low grades attained their college plans.

Of all the seniors planning to get a BA or higher (n = 5,528), 49.5% succeed in getting that degree (Table 8.8b). However, students with As have a 70.7% chance of getting as BA or higher, and those with Bs have a 46.6% chance. Students planning BAs who have a C average or less (n = 916) achieve BA degrees at less than half the rate of all students with BA plans (49.5% – 20.5%). It might also be noted that 73% of those with poor grades do little homework—less than an hour per week, and low homework time decreases their BA chances to only 11%.

Since the AA is a shorter and perhaps easier degree than a BA, one might expect that students planning to get AA degrees are more likely to be successful. That is not the case. Seniors who plan to get an AA degree succeed less often than those planning a BA. Of the 3,267 seniors who plan to get an AA degree, only 23.9% succeed in getting a college degree (AA or higher) in the next 10 years; and of those with low grades (Cs or lower), only 12.6% do

(Table 8.8c). The success rates are even lower for those with low grades who did little homework (n = 248; p = 8%). Recall that these tables report students' college-degree outcomes, based only on their high school grades, and giving youth 10 years to attain any college degree (AA or higher).

Why do over half of seniors with low grades believe they can attain college degrees? Perhaps "social promotion" practices in high schools, which automatically promote students each year to the next grade regardless of their achievement, may encourage this belief. Similarly, open admissions at community colleges may contribute to this belief. Seeing these two practices, which award attainments without requiring academic achievement, students may infer a similar view of college degrees—as an award for putting in time that does not require academic achievement. This may also suggest that students view school as a credentialing process rather than a human-capital-building process.

Ironically, although colleges offering AA degrees are more accessible than BA colleges to students with low grades, the AA degree is not necessarily more available to them. Students with AA plans have lower success rates than

Table 8.8 Percentage of Seniors with College Plans Who Complete College Degrees within 10 Years

Table 8.8a. Percentage of Seniors with College Plans (AA or higher) Who Complete at Least an AA

Average high school grades	As	Bs	Cs or lower	Total
Percent attaining AA or higher	69.5	43.2	19.6	40.3
N	2007	4702	2086	8795

Table 8.8b. Percentage of Seniors with BA Plans Who Succeed in Completing at Least a BA Degree

Average high school grades	As	Bs	Cs or lower	Total
Percent attaining BA or higher	70.7	46.6	20.5	49.5
N	1668	2944	916	5528

Table 8.8c. Percentage of Seniors with AA Plans Who Succeed in Completing at an AA

Average high school grades	As	Bs	Cs or lower	Total
Percent attaining AA or higher	46.6	27.1	12.6	23.9
N	339	1758	1170	3267

Note: The data displayed represent 1992 degree attainment figures for "High School and Beyond" respondents who were seniors in 1982.

students with BA plans, both because students with AA plans are twice as likely to have low grades and because their chances of getting the degree are very slim if they have low grades (12.6%). Multivariate analyses indicate that grades and homework time explain most of this differential success rate between those with BA and AA plans (Rosenbaum and Miller, 1998).

Newspaper stories sometimes report that students who got As in high school actually lack the academic skills to do well in college. This may explain our findings that only half (49.5%) of students with As in high school complete an AA degree or higher (although low SES seems to be more important than low test scores in explaining these failures). Yet, newspapers rarely consider the other issue, that students with Cs in high school have very little chance of completing a college degree, and their plans do not seem to recognize these risks.

In sum, many students report that they plan to get a college degree even though they have poor academic achievement. Yet, in fact, low grades predict much lower chances of attaining a degree. Within the High School and Beyond data, over 80% of students with low grades who planned to get a college degree failed to do so, and the failures were even greater for those planning an AA degree. Even without making any causal inferences, the strong predictive power of high school grades is important—it tells seniors how to place their bets. While students are correct that they can enter a college with low grades, they are usually mistaken in thinking that they can complete the degree. Their poor success rates make these outcomes a real long shot, not something students should be counting on.

High School Achievement Predicts Much of the Lower Attainment and Disappointed Plans of Disadvantaged Students

While the strong predictive power of high school grades tells seniors how to place their bets, do grades really predict educational attainment after controlling for other factors? If students want to raise their chances, they need to know whether to focus on improving grades,

homework time, or track placement; and they may be worried that their future attainment is predestined by their social background (SES, ethnicity, gender) or intelligence (as test scores are sometimes interpreted). Policy makers also need to know to what extent grades or other factors predict the lower outcomes and disappointed plans of disadvantaged students.

Regression analysis is a good way to examine these issues. It allows researchers to look at simple gross associations between background characteristics and attainment and then to examine the mediating and independent predicting power of other factors such as high school achievement. We ran a series of OLS regressions on the High School and Beyond cohort who graduated in 1982 and were followed through 1992. The survey had 8,969 respondents who provided information for all variables in our model.

Our basic analyses made use of five dependent variables: students' cumulative grade point averages (Grades), tested achievement (Test), homework time (HW), educational plans (EdPlan), and educational attainment (EdYears). The first four were based on information gathered in the students' senior year, 1982; educational attainment constituted the number of years of students' educational attainments in 1992. Our independent variables included social background variables (Black, Hispanic, female, and a cumulative index of parents' SES computed in the High School and Beyond file), region of the U.S. (South, West, and Northeast regions, with the Midwest as the comparison), and school variables (private school, general, and vocational tracks, with college track as the comparison). Subsequent analyses concerned with plans and educational attainment added grade point average, tested achievement, and homework time as additional independent variables.

These analyses revealed several effects. First, Blacks, Hispanics, and low-SES students have lower grades and achievement test scores (Table 8.9, columns 1 and 3). If these coefficients indicate influences, they are partly mediated by track and private schools (columns 2 and 4). But even after controls are entered, Blacks,

Table 8.9 Regression Analyses for the Predictions of Grades, Tests, Homework, Educational Plans and Attainment

	1 Grades	2 Grades	3 Test	4 Test	5 HW	6 HW	7 EdPlan	8 EdPlan	9 EdPlan	10 EdYears	11 EdYears	12 EdYears
SES	.207*	.163*	.368*	.295*	.223*	.164*	.450*	.378*	.240*	.386*	.324*	.201*
Black	−.141*	−.150*	−.212*	−.202*	.055*	.060*	.096*	.094*	.159*	−.023*	−.026*	.050*
Hispanic	−.110*	−.115*	−.201*	−.187*	−.007	.002	−.013	−.008	.060*	−.059*	−.045*	.024*
Female	.178*	.176*	−.037*	−.041*	.179*	.174*	.035*	.031*	−.014	.013	.007	−.040*
South		.020		−.055*		−.060*		−.014*	.012		−.023*	−.008
West		.047*		−.007		−.017		.014	.013		−.058*	−.064*
NE		−.073*		.037*		.002		−.015	−.017		.038*	.045*
Private		−.021		.059*		.092*		.061*	.028*		.075*	.056*
Vocational		−.164		−.221*		−.119*		−.206*	−.098*		−.176*	−.075*
General		−.173		−.178*		−.172*		−.211*	−.104*		−.184*	−.085*
Test					.288*				.236*			
GPA									.126*			.221*
HW									.200*			.105*
R2(adj)%	12.2	16.1	27.2	33.5	7.8	12.1	19.6	25.3	41.2	16.5	22.1	36.3
n	8969	8969	8969	8969	8969	8969	8969	8969	8969	8969	8969	8969

Note: Standardized coefficients are presented. * = p < .05

Hispanics, and low SES youth have lower grades and test scores.

Second, SES and being Black are associated with homework time, although in different directions (column 5), and the SES relationship is only partly diminished after controls are entered (column 6). While low-SES youth spend less time on homework than high-SES youth, Blacks spend significantly more time on homework than Whites (Hispanics spend about the same as Whites). Despite potential concerns because homework time is self-reported, Fordham and Ogbu's (1986) findings would predict that Blacks would underreport school effort (to avoid being seen as "acting White"), and these analyses find the opposite (Fordham and Ogbu's prediction was also not supported in Cook and Ludwig's, 1997, analysis). If homework time turns out to be an important predictor of educational attainment, then it may account for problems of low-SES students but is not likely to do so for Blacks.

Third, low-SES youth have lower educational plans, but Blacks have higher plans than Whites (column 7). These results remain after controls are entered for track and private schools (column 8). The SES relationship declines after controlling for grades, tests, and homework time, but the positive association for Blacks increases (column 9). Blacks have even higher plans than others with similar achievement, as previous research has noted (Jencks et al., 1972).

Fourth, Black, Hispanic, and low-SES youth have lower educational attainment (column 10). These relationships are only slightly altered after controls for track and private schools (column 11). However, these relationships are largely mediated by grades, test scores, and homework time. Indeed, when grades, test scores, and homework time are added to the analysis, the SES relationship declines substantially (from .324 to .201), although it remains statistically significant and the Black and Hispanic coefficients actually reverse and become significantly positive (column 12). Thus, students' grades, homework time, and tested achievement explain a significant part of the lower attainment of low-SES students, and Black and Hispanic students have higher attainments than Whites with similar achievement.

Finally, by adding seniors' plans to the regression, the analyses can discover which high school information predicts the disappointing attainments of disadvantaged students many years later (see Table 8.10). Since a few students (8.4%) attained more than they planned, they are removed from the analyses in Table 8.10, leaving 8,117 students in the analyses.[2] As a result Table 8.10 shows the factors predicting which students' attainments fall short of their plans—explaining discrepancies between the 31.5% of students who attained their senior-year plans and the 60.1% who attained one or more years less than they planned. The analyses found that low-SES, Black, and Hispanic students had significantly lower attainments than they had planned (Table 8.10, column 1). However, when variables for school achievement and effort were added, the ethnic variables became insignificant and the SES coefficient became smaller (Table 8.10, column 3). Apparently, the disappointments of Black and Hispanic students are entirely predictable from their lower achievement and effort in high school.

Indeed, students' plans do not take sufficient account of their achievement. Over 58% (.142/.244) of the relationship between test scores and attainment and 78% (.173/.221) of the relationship between grades and attainment remain after controlling for plans (Table 8.10, columns 2 and 3). Less than half of these relationships are mediated by plans. Thus, consistent with the cross-tabular analyses (displayed in Table 8.8), we conclude that, even after controls, seniors' college plans vastly underestimate how much their grades and test scores predict their ultimate educational outcomes.

It is noteworthy that the female coefficient on educational attainment, which is virtually zero in the early regressions (Table 8.9, column 10), becomes significantly negative after controlling

for achievement (column 12). Apparently, women have roughly the same educational attainments as males, but their attainments are still below what they would be if their previous achievement were the only determinant. Females have higher grades and homework time than males (but slightly lower test scores, see Table 8.9, columns 1–6), so there should be some concern about why their attainments are lower than their achievement would predict.

Finally, while the above analyses look at simple additive effects of ethnicity, one might still wonder if some of the factors in our model have different coefficients for Blacks and Whites. One indication of bias is when Blacks get less benefit from their achievements than Whites. In the 1970s, Porter (1974) found that Blacks received less gain in educational attainment from their high school grades than did Whites. Our regression analyses for educational attainment run separately for Whites and Blacks find that grades have about the same coefficients for both (Table 8.10, columns 4 and 6—betas .224 and .214), and the same is true for test scores (.228 and .227) but slightly larger coefficients for Whites than for Blacks (.114 vs .071) when it comes to homework.[3] Thus, Blacks get roughly the same gain in attainment for increases in their test scores and grades as Whites, although they get slightly less gain for increases in their homework time. Apparently, the old pattern of discrimination in which Blacks got lower attainment benefits for increasing their grades is no longer the case. Indeed, SES, test scores, and grades are somewhat stronger predictors of attainment for Blacks than for Whites (Table 8.10, columns 5 and 7).

In sum, these results indicate that SES, ethnicity, private schools, and track are related to attainment; but grades, test scores, and homework time also have effects which tend to mediate much of the relationship between disadvantaged backgrounds and attainment. However, there are indications that many students do not realize how much high school achievement predicts future attainment. While all students probably know their grades, their plans underestimate the extent that their grades predict their later attainment—and this is true

Table 8.10 Regression Analyses for the Predictions of Educational Attainment: All Students, Whites and Blacks

	Whites 1 EdYears	Blacks 2 EdYears	3 EdYears	4 EdYears	5 EdYears	6 EdYears	7 EdYears
SES	.154*	.211*	.127*	.213*	.113*	.225*	.190*
Black	−.072*	.050*	−.008				
Hispanic	−.035*	.032*	.011				
Female	.002	−.032*	−.025*	−.048*	−.031*	.055*	.024
South	−.006	.002	−.002	−.002	−.003	−.073	−.076*
West	−.060*	−.059*	−.064*	−.066*	−.069*	−.040	−.037
NE	.041*	.041*	.046*	.046*	.052*	.012	.011
Private	.031*	.045*	.031*	.047*	.033*	.019	.008
Vocational	−.083*	−.083*	−.044*	−.089*	−.047*	−.012	.000
General	−.089*	−.093*	−.052*	−.097*	−.052*	−.044	−.024
Test		.244*	.142*	.227*	.118*	.228*	.175*
Grades		.221*	.173*	.214*	.170*	.224*	.196*
HW		.119*	.050*	.114*	.040*	.071*	.043
Plans	.483*		.354*		.383*		.201*
R2(adj)%	40.3	38.3	45.4	38.1	46.0	27.2	30.0
n	8117	8117	8117	5014	5014	996	996

Note: Standardized coefficients are presented. * = p < .05. Analyses based on cases where EdYears is less than or equal to EdPlans.

for both Black and White students. Indeed, grades are the single best predictor of the ways attainment falls short of plans, and this predictability is somewhat larger for Blacks than for Whites. If students could focus on changing one set of attributes in high school to make their plans come true, they should improve those associated with their grades.[4,5]

Thus, these analyses suggest that students are overly complacent about the ease of getting a college degree. Many students have plans that have little chance of succeeding because their plans underestimate the relationship between high school achievement and later attainment. This is particularly true for Blacks, Hispanics, and low-SES students whose attainments fall short of their plans. These disappointments are largely predicted by their high school achievements (Table 8.10, columns 1 and 3). It seems likely that these students might work harder if they realized the future relevance of their high school achievement.

Students with Low High School Achievement Get Less Economic Payoff to College Degrees

Despite these odds, some students with low high school grades get college degrees. Do they get the same earnings payoff from college as students with better grades? While Murnane, Willett, and Levy (1995) have shown additive wage payoffs of educational attainment and achievement (measured by test scores), the present analyses examine whether college degrees have lower payoffs for those with lower achievement, which is operationalized by high school grades since it more clearly indicates achievement (rather than ability) and is known by all students. The above model is used to explain the 1991 earnings of the same High School and Beyond cohort, adding dummy variables for educational attainment (AA representing those who had received the AA but no higher; BA representing those who had earned the BA but no higher degree; and MA representing those who had earned an MA or higher degrees). By taking the log of annual earnings as the dependent variable, unstandardized coefficients can be interpreted as percentage increases in earnings, so these tables report unstandardized coefficients. Thus, in the first step of the analysis, the High School and Beyond data indicate that youth who earn AA and BA degrees report 10.1% and 14.5% higher earnings, respectively, than those without a degree (Table 8.11, column 1).

Table 8.11 Regression Analyses for the Predictions of Earnings

	Ln (Earnings)	Ln (Earnings)
SES	.101*	.101*
Black	.040	.041
Hispanic	.026	.025
Female	−.299*	−.299*
South	−.032*	−.032*
West	−.036	−.036
NE	.097*	.099*
Private	.043*	.045*
Vocational	−.030	−.031
General	−.027	−.026
Test	.003*	.003*
Grades	.034*	.025*
HW	−.004	−.004
AA	.101*	.155*
BA	.145*	.166*
MA	.096*	−.112*
AALoGPA		−.227*
BALoGPA	−.123*	
MALoGPA		.022
c	9.657	9.695
R2 (adj.) %	13.2	13.5

Note: Nonstandardized coefficients are presented. * = p < .05, N = 8,413

To see if students with low grades get the same benefits from those degrees, these analyses create a new dummy variable (AA-LoGPA) for people who got an AA degree and had low grades in high school (AA-LoGPA equals 1 if a person has an AA degree and high school grades of C or lower, 0 otherwise), and similar variables for BALoGPA and MA-LoGPA. Adding these three variables into the regression, the analyses find that youth who had low high school grades got less earnings advantage for their college degrees (Table 8.11, column 2). To figure the payoff to BAs for students with Cs, the coefficients for BA and BA-LoGPA are added, so the payoff to a BA degree is 4.3% (.166 − .123 = .043), and the payoff to an AA degree is −7.2%, less than if they had not gotten the degree (.155 − .227 = −.072). While the average student gets strong earnings benefits from BA and AA degrees, students with low grades get much smaller earnings benefits from a BA degree and lower earnings from an AA degree than from no degree.[6] Previous studies have found that poor grades predict lower earnings for young adults who have only a high school diploma (Miller, 1997; Rosenbaum, Miller, and Roy, 1996). These results indicate that low grades also substantially reduce the payoffs to college degrees (cf. also Rosenbaum and Miller, 1998).

Conclusion

These analyses help elucidate the problem of disadvantaged youth. Simple gross analyses find that low-SES, Black, and Hispanic students have lower educational attainment. However, the SES coefficient declines, and the ethnic disadvantages actually reverse and become advantages when achievement variables are entered. Thus, Blacks and Hispanics have significantly higher educational attainment than Whites with the same level of high school achievement. In addition, high school grades and test scores predict many of the cases where disadvantaged youth have lower attainment than they had planned.

Looking at these results, some might blame disadvantaged youth for their failures; but another interpretation is more plausible.

Students' plans are what they think they can expect in the future, and their plans are likely to influence their high school efforts. In finding that students' plans do not take sufficient account of the influence of grades on their ultimate educational attainment, one can infer that students do not realize how much high school achievement affects their actual prospects. This is consistent with the future relevance and "no penalty" beliefs noted earlier. These results may indicate that schools fail to provide clear information to these youth which is consistent with what is known about counselors' advising practices (Rosenbaum, Miller, and Krei, 1996).

What is the harm in letting students have "high expectations"? Perhaps these plans are just dreams that make students a little happier and do them little harm. As noted, guidance counselors say they do not want to disappoint young people and so they encourage all students to attend college, even students with low achievement.

Consistent with this interpretation, Manski (1989) has proposed that many youth begin community college as an "experiment," a low-cost way to discover whether they can make it in college. But is it really low cost? Manski analyzes the process from the viewpoint of a student who is already in a community college, noting that his analysis does not consider students before they enter college.

However, there are opportunity costs to any decision, and this "experiment" has some large opportunity costs to students while they are still in high school. Should students with more than an 80% chance of failing at college place *all* their bets on their college experiment? Or would it be prudent for such students to hedge their college bets?

A first opportunity cost of the college-for-all norm is that students' high expectations may inadvertently encourage them to see high school as irrelevant and thus to make poor use of high school. Our interviews and survey of high school seniors indicate that 40% of students with college plans believe that high school is irrelevant. Postponing the key test for whether one is "college-bound" until after high school may inadvertently tell students that high school achievement is not important.

A second opportunity cost of the college-for-all norm is that it may lead to a lack of effort. Human capital theory posits that people invest effort in improving their capabilities if they believe better outcomes will result. But if they believe they can get the same outcomes without added effort, they will not make the effort. If students realize that their low high school grades will be associated with blocked college plans, they might increase their efforts in high school. Yet High School and Beyond data indicate that a large majority (78.0%) of poorly achieving high school students with college plans do less than an hour a day of homework, and many (25.3%) do less than an hour in a whole week. These High School and Beyond students exert little effort, even though they have low grades (which predict an 80% failure rate). Moreover, guidance counselors let these students hold unrealistic plans because they wish to encourage "high expectations" and "second chances" (Rosenbaum, Miller, and Krei, 1996). Students are not told what level of high school achievement is needed to succeed in community college, and they are lulled into a complacency that leaves them unprepared for getting college degrees.

The third opportunity cost of the college-for-all norm is that students with little prospect for getting a college degree will fail to get vocational training. Encouraging poorly achieving students to delay their work preparation until they see the results of their college "experiment" makes it likely that they will make poor use of vocational preparation in high school, which has been shown to improve earnings (Campbell, Basinger, Dauner, and Parks, 1986; Kang and Bishop, 1986; Rosenbaum, 1996). Indeed, students with poor grades are less likely to be in vocational courses if they have college plans than if they are not planning college (Rosenbaum, unpublished analyses), and many students with low probability of success in college have no backup plans or training. Similarly, many public schools (such as those in Chicago) have reduced or ended their vocational programs because they expect all students to delay their vocational decisions until they get to college.

Although Manski did not consider it, there is an even more inexpensive experiment to help students infer their readiness for college—high school. If the CFA norm did not focus so much on getting everyone into college, then high schools could tell students their realistic chances of attaining college degrees. If students realized that high school achievement is the first "experiment," and this "experiment" has strong predictive power, then students with poor grades would either revise their plans downwards, or they might try to correct bad habits that lead to poor achievements.

Protecting students' high expectations when they are unwarranted is not a kindness; it is a deception. Failing to challenge students to examine the plausibility of their college plans has serious opportunity costs—it prevents them from seeing the importance of high school, it prevents them from taking the additional efforts that might make their plans more likely to come true, and it prevents them from preparing for alternative outcomes. When some seniors have high school records that make their college plans highly likely to fail, schools' protection of their "high expectations" is not a kind gesture. It looks a lot more like the confidence scheme that Goffman describes, distracting the "mark" from taking other constructive actions.

Unfortunately, students understand very well the *short-term* consequences of their high school efforts—they are minor. But they assume that this means that high school achievement and effort are irrelevant and that there will be no penalty if they do badly in high school. They believe they can postpone their efforts until they get into college, and their plans will work out fine.

Students' misperceptions may arise from their limited knowledge about older cohorts. High school students can see the college enrollment of last year's seniors more easily than the college completion of much older students, and they can more easily identify with the students a year older than themselves who enter college than with the 28-year-olds who never finished the degree. As a result, perceptions are likely to be distorted. Students easily perceive college enrollment, for which high school

achievements are irrelevant, but they have difficulty seeing college completion, for which high school achievements are highly relevant. Under such circumstances, students' perceptions will not improve unless policy action is taken.

Policy Implications

The community college system and its open admissions policies are rightfully a source of pride. They have created new opportunities for large numbers of youth. However, open admissions may inadvertently contribute to students' complacency. Students with low grades may not realize that they have very poor prospects of getting a degree or earnings benefits from that degree.

High schools are partly responsible for such delusions. Our research suggests that high school guidance counselors believe that open admission means that they do not have to discourage students' college expectations. They believe that "high expectations" should be encouraged, and they report that they get complaints from parents and principals if they try to discourage unrealistically high plans (Rosenbaum, Miller, and Krei, 1996). Counselors' practices may help explain why students hold these views.

While policy has focussed on opening college admissions, it has not devoted similar effort to providing clear information about community colleges (Orfield, 1997; Paul, 1997, Rosenbaum, Miller, and Krei, 1997). Indeed, many schools push the college-for-all (CFA) norm, which lulls students into a complacency, which ultimately is unwarranted. High school grades could inform students about their likelihood of attaining a college degree, but this fact is hidden from students' awareness, and perhaps even teachers' and counselors' awareness.

To return to Goffman's model, the CFA norm is highly misleading and does great harm to youth. It offers big promises to students without warning that few low-achieving students will get a college degree. Indeed, it leaves many youth worse off than before, keeping them in the dark about actual requirements so they fail to take suitable actions to prepare themselves to accomplish their plans. It also harms youth as they waste time, energy, and money on a college experience they are ill prepared to handle and that is likely to lead to failure, low self-esteem, and misused opportunities in high school. While high school counselors brag about their college enrollment rates, students will blame themselves for the failure that they did not anticipate but which was highly predictable.

The CFA norm also has big impact on policies and practices in schools. An example can be seen in the Chicago public schools in the early 1990s when Superintendent Argie Johnson urged all of the city's high schools to stress college goals. She closed or withdrew resources from many vocational programs. Even the famous Chicago Vocational School began stressing that its goal was no longer vocational, but college. Meanwhile, the Chicago schools had low achievement levels, many of their graduates lacked the academic skills needed to take college-credit courses in the city college, and the degree completion rates at the city colleges were very low. The superintendent's urging that more students attend college was politically popular because it fit the CFA norm. It stressed "high expectations," but it may have led to increased failure.

This is not to urge that one abandon "high expectations" entirely or scrap open admissions policies. But three other reforms are warranted.

First, high schools should provide more complete information on community college success rates as a function of students' grades, test scores, and homework time. This could be aided by a universally recognized test of achievement (not aptitude or intelligence), either statewide (such as Illinois's IGAP achievement test) or national (such as Clinton's proposal for national proficiency examinations). Even if such tests are not available, grades can be used. While the grades from individual teachers are highly imperfect, grade point averages have strong predictive power. Schools and society should be stressing their importance to students. Students need to realize that "open admissions" does not mean that high school achievement is irrelevant.

Second, linkages between high schools and colleges may help improve high school students' understanding of college requirements. By seeing

that many college students must repeat high school classes, high school students will learn that they can work hard now, or next year they can repeat the same class and pay tuition for it. Several recent reforms seek to improve coordination of high school and college programs which may help students see the future relevance of their current courses (e.g., tech-prep, 2 + 2 programs, and career academies; see Berryman and Bailey, 1992; Stern, Finkelstein, Stone, Latting, and Dornsife, 1995).

Finally, students must be prepared for backup career options if their college plans are unlikely to succeed. While schools can encourage all students to aim for college, this should not be an excuse to cut vocational programs. Research indicates that after controls for test scores, vocational education graduates are 10–15% more likely to be in the labor force and are paid 8–9% more than graduates of academic programs (Campbell et al., 1986; Kang and Bishop, 1986; Rosenbaum, 1996).[7] Even if students plan to attend community college, low success rates at these colleges suggest that backup plans would be prudent, particularly for students with low grades. Over 80% of such students fail to get a degree and lose time, tuition, and self-confidence in the process. After they drop out of college, they enter the labor market without the vocational skills or preparation that they might have gotten if they had not been taken in by the college-for-all rhetoric.

Notes

1. Somewhat similar beliefs have been shown to influence students' achievements (Mickelson, 1990); but since achievement is influenced by many factors besides motivation, this study has chosen to focus on the determinants of effort (cf. also Steinberg, 1996, for an excellent overview).

2. Since one would not be concerned about the disappointment of very high plans, analyses were also run using recoded versions of plans and attainments in which values higher than BA were recoded to be the same as BA = 16. This recode does not alter results very much so those results are not reported.

3. Similar results are obtained on the full sample of 8,969 individuals not shown here.

4. What determines grades? Bowles and Gintis (1976) have suggested noncognitive components

which are not supported in some other studies (Bills, 1983; Rosenbaum and Kariya, 1989, 1991). Miller and Rosenbaum (1998) pursue this question in greater detail.

5. Logit analyses were also run to see the determinants of who got AA or higher versus the high school graduates who got less than an AA. Using the same independent variables as the regression, the results indicate virtually the same conclusions as the above linear regression: grades, test scores, and homework all have significant influences, with grades having the largest influence. Grades have even larger influence than test scores in explaining disappointed plans. Similar findings occur in explaining who got BA or higher, although the grade influence is even greater. These tables are not reported because the results are virtually the same as those reported here.

6. Youth who did not complete high school are removed from this analysis so the constant represents all youth with high school diplomas but no college degrees. Note that the Malogpa coefficient is not significant and only 22 (4%) of MA students had low high school grades.

7. Kane and Rouse (1995) find that students get some economic benefit from the college credits they earn, even if they do not complete college degrees. However, these benefits may depend on whether the courses were vocational and in particular fields (Grubb, 1995). If the economic benefits of college courses (without a degree) arise from the vocational preparation they offer, then vocational courses in high schools or nondegree programs could possibly provide similar benefits. It is possible that the economic value of isolated college credits comes because individuals seek specific job-relevant courses, perhaps because of a job they already hold or one they know is available. Employers in some fields (tool and die, machining, etc.) require employees to obtain a few specific courses but not a certificate or degree (Rosenbaum and Binder, 1996).

Moreover, for many students, the economic benefits of some colleges are negligible. Kane and Rouse (1995, p. 602) found that "40% [of two-year college dropouts] completed fewer than a semester's worth of credits" and a large number completed none, so the economic benefits of college entry were minimal for these students. Given that most of these students probably expected to get college degrees, they surely got much less academic and economic benefit from college than they anticipated and experienced relatively large psychological costs.

I am grateful to Tom Bailey, Regina Deil, Maureen Hallinan, Jens Ludwig, Aaron Pallas, Shazia Miller, and Bruce Biddle for thoughtful comments on earlier drafts of this paper. Support for this work was provided by the Spencer Foundation, the Community College Research Center at Columbia University, and the Institute for Policy Research at Northwestern University. Of course, the opinions expressed here are solely those of the author. Correspondence concerning this article should be sent to James E. Rosenbaum, Institute for Policy Research and School of Education and Social Policy, Northwestern University, 2040 Sheridan Road, Evanston, IL 60208 U.S.A. Tel: 847–491–3795; Fax: 847–491–9916; E-mail:J-Rosenbaum@nwu.edu

From *Social Psychology of Education, 2* (1): 55–80, 1997, "College for All: Do Students Understand What College Demands?" by James E. Rosenbaum, © 1997 Springer Science and Business Media. Reprinted with kind permission from Springer Science and Business Media.

References

Berryman, Susan E. and Bailey, Thomas R. (1992). *The double helix: Education and the economy.* New York: Teachers College Press.

Bills, David (1983). Social reproduction and the Bowles-Gintis thesis of a correspondence between school and work settings. *Research in sociology of education and socialization.* Greenwood, CT: JAI.

Bowles, Samuel and Gintis, Herbert (1976). *Schooling in capitalist America.* New York: Basic Books.

Brint, Steven and Karabel, Jerome (1989). *The diverted dream.* New York: Oxford University Press.

Campbell, Paul B., Basinger, K. S., Dauner, M. B., and Parks, M. A. (1986). *Outcomes of vocational education.* Columbus, OH: Ohio State University, National Center for Research in Vocational Education.

Cicourel, Aaron V. and Kitsuse, John I. (1963). *The educational decision-makers.* Indianapolis: Bobbs Merrill.

Clark, Burton (1960). The "cooling out" function in higher education. *American Journal of Sociology, 65,* 569–576.

Cook, Philip J. and Ludwig, Jens (1997). Weighing the burden of "acting White": Are there race differences in attitudes toward education? *Journal of Policy Analysis and Management, 16*(2), 256–278.

Dougherty, Kevin J. (1994). *The contradictory college.* Albany, NY: SUNY Press.

Fordham, Signithia and Ogbu, John (1986). Black students' school success: Coping with the burden of "acting White." *The Urban Review, 18*(3), 176–206.

Goffman, Erving (1952, November). Cooling the mark out: Some aspects of adaptation to failure. *Psychiatry, 15,* 451–463.

Grubb, W. Norton (1989). Dropouts, spells of time, and credits in postsecondary education. *Economics of Education Review, 8*(1), 49–67.

Grubb, W. Norton (1992). Postsecondary education and the sub-baccalaureate labor market. *Economics of Education Review, 11*(3), 225–248.

Grubb, W. Norton (1993). The varied economic returns of postsecondary education. *Journal of Human Resources, 28*(2), 265–282.

Grubb, W. Norton (1995). Response to comment. *Journal of Human Resources, 30*(1), 222–228.

Grubb, W. Norton and Kalman, Judy (1994, November). Relearning to earn. *American Journal of Education, 103,* 54–93.

Jencks, Christopher L., Smith, Smith, Acland, Henry, Bane, Mary Jo, Cohen, David K., Gintis, Herbert, Heyns, Barbara, and Michaelson, Stephan (1972). *Inequality.* New York: Basic Books.

Kandel, Denise and Lesser, Gerald (1972). *Youth in two worlds: United States and Denmark.* New York: Jossey-Bass.

Kane, Thomas and Rouse, Cecilia E. (1995). Labor-market returns to two- and four-year college. *American Economic Review, 85*(3), 600–614.

Kans, Suk and Bishop, John (1986). The effect of curriculum on labor market success. *Journal of Industrial Teacher Education,* 133–148.

Karabel, Jerome (1986). Community colleges and social stratification in the 1980s. In L.S. Zwerling (Ed.), *The community college and its critics.* San Francisco: Jossey-Bass, pp. 13–30.

Kerckhoff, Alan C. and Campbell, Richard T. (1977). Black-White differences in the educational attainment process. *Sociology of Education, 50*(1), 15–27.

Manski, Charles F. (1989). Schooling as experimentation. *Economics of Education Review, 8*(4), 305–312.

Mickelson, Roslyn. (1990, January). The attitude-achievement paradox among Black adolescents. *Sociology of Education, 63,* 44–61.

Miller, Shazia (1997). *Shortcut: High school grades as a signal of human capital.* Paper presented at the annual meeting of the American Sociological Association, Toronto.

Miller, Shazia and Rosenbaum, James (1998). *What do grades mean?* Unpublished manuscript, Northwestern University, Institute for Policy Research.

Murnane, Richard, Willett, John B., and Levy, Frank (1995). The growing importance of cognitive skills in wage determination. *Review of Economics and Statistics, 77*(2), 251–266.

Murnane, Richard and Levy, Frank (1997). *Teaching the new basic skills.* New York: The Free Press.

National Center for Educational Statistics. (1983). *High school and beyond: 1980 senior cohort first follow-up (1982): Datafile user's manual.* Chicago: National Opinion Research Center.

National Center for Educational Statistics (1983). *High school and beyond: Data file user's manual.* Chicago: National Opinion Research Center.

National Center for Educational Statistics (1995). *Remedial education at higher education institutions.* Washington, DC: U.S. Department of Education.

Orfield, Gary (1997). Going to work: Weak preparation, little help. In Kenneth K. Wong (Ed.), *Advances in educational policy* (Vol. 3). Greenwood, CT: JAI Press, pp. 3–32.

Paul, Faith (1997). Negotiated identities and academic program choice. In Kenneth K. Wong (Ed.), *Advances in educational policy* (Vol. 3). Greenwood, CT: JAI Press, pp. 53–78.

Porter, James N. (1974, June). Race, socialization and mobility in educational and early occupational attainment. *American Sociological Review, 39,* 303–316.

Resnick, Lauren B. and Wirt, John G. (1996). The changing workplace. In Lauren B. Resnick and John G. Wirt (Eds.), *Linking school and work.* San Francisco: Jossey Bass, pp. 1–22.

Rosenbaum, James E. (1975). The stratification of socialization processes. *American Sociological Review, 40*(1), 48–54.

Rosenbaum, James E. (1976). *Making inequality.* New York: Wiley.

Rosenbaum, James E. (1978). The structure of opportunity in school. *Social Forces, 57,* 236–256.

Rosenbaum, James E. (1986). Institutional career structures and the social construction of ability. In G. Richardson (Ed.), *Handbook of theory and research for the sociology of education.* Westport, CT: Greenwood Press, pp. 139–171.

Rosenbaum, James E. (1989). Organizational career systems and employee misperceptions. In Michael Arthur, Douglas T. Hall, and Barbara Lawrence (Eds.), *Handbook of career theory.* New York: Cambridge University Press, pp. 329–353.

Rosenbaum, James E. (1996, Summer). Policy uses of research on the high school-to-work transition. *Sociology of Education,* Summer, pp. 102–122.

Rosenbaum, James E. and Kariya, Takehiko (1989). From high school to work: Market and institutional mechanisms in Japan. *American Journal of Sociology, 94*(6), 1334–1365.

Rosenbaum, James E. and Kariya, Takehiko (1991). Do school achievements affect the early jobs of high school graduates in the United States and Japan? *Sociology of Education*, 64, 78–95.

Rosenbaum, James E. and Binder, Amy (1997, January). Do employers really need more educated youth? *Sociology of Education*, 70, 68–85.

Rosenbaum, James E. and Miller, Shazia (1998). The earnings payoff to college degrees for youth with poor high school achievement. *Unpublished manuscript, Northwestern University, Institute for Policy Research.

Rosenbaum, James E., Miller, Shazia, and Krei, Melinda (1996, August). Gatekeeping in an era of more open gates. *American Journal of Education*, 104, 257–279.

Rosenbaum, James E., Miller, Shazia, and Krei, Melinda (1997). What role should counselors have? In Kenneth K. Wong (Ed.), *Advances in educational policy* (Vol. 3). Greenwood, CT: JAI Press, pp. 79–92.

Rosenbaum, James E. and Roy, Kevin (1996, April). Trajectories for success in the transition from school to work. Paper presented at the annual meeting of the American Educational Research Association, New York.

Rosenbaum, James E., Miller, Shazia, and Roy, Kevin (1996, August). Long-term effects of high school grades and job placements. Paper presented at the annual meeting of the American Sociological Association, New York.

Sedlak, Michael W., Wheeler, Christopher W., Pullin, Diane C, and Cusick, Phillip A. (1986). *Selling students short*. New York: Teachers College Press.

Steinberg, Lawrence (1996). *Beyond the classroom*. New York: Simon and Shuster.

Stern, David, Finkelstein, Neal, Stone, James, Latting, John, and Dornsife, Carolyn (1995). *School to work: Research on programs in the United States*. Washington and London: Falmer Press.

Stevenson, Harold W., and Stigler, James W. (1992). *The learning gap*. New York: Simon and Shuster.

Stinchcombe, Arthur L. (1965). *Rebellion in a high school*. Chicago: Quadrangle.

Turner, Ralph (1960). Sponsored and contest mobility and the school system. *American Sociological Review*, 25, 855–867.

U.S. Department of Health, Education, and Welfare (1992). *Digest of educational statistics*. Washington, DC: U.S. Government Printing Office.

9 Explanations of Educational Inequality

In Chapter 8, we explored unequal educational outcomes among various groups in U.S. society. The data suggest that there are significant differences in educational achievement and attainment based on social class, race, gender, and other ascriptive characteristics. Further, such unequal outcomes call into question the country's ideology of equality of educational opportunity and the ethos that schooling provides an important mechanism for social mobility. Although the data indicate that there has been mobility for individuals and that schooling has become increasingly tied to the labor market as a credentialing process, they do not support the democratic-liberal faith that schooling provides mobility for entire groups. In fact, the data indicate that the relationship between family background and economic outcomes has been fairly consistent, with family background exerting a powerful effect on both educational achievement and attainment, and economic outcomes.

Given the persistent inequalities of educational outcomes—especially those based on race, class, and gender (although, as we noted in the previous chapter, social class remains the most powerful factor in explaining educational inequalities)—the next step is to explain these unequal outcomes of the schooling process. In a society that is at least ideologically committed to the eradication of educational inequality, why do these differences continue to persist, often in the face of explicit social policies aimed at their elimination?

In this chapter, we will review the complex explanations of the problem. As you will see, there are numerous conflicting theories of educational inequality. We will present an overview of each and then offer our own multidimensional approach to understanding this most difficult situation. Let us note at the outset that there are no simple explanations and no simple solutions, despite experts' claims to the contrary. More often than not, the literature on educational inequality is filled with ideological explanations devoid of evidence. It is incumbent, however, to sift through the polemics and examine the research in order to reach reasonable conclusions. Given the complexity of the problem, this is no easy task; given the enormity and gravity of the problem, there is no choice but to continue to attempt to solve it.

Explanations of Unequal Educational Achievement

The two major sociological theories of education provide a general understanding of the problem, although from very different directions. Both theories are also concerned about the existence of profound and persistent inequalities, albeit from different vantage points. Functionalists believe that the role of schools is to provide a fair and meritocratic selection process for sorting out the best and brightest individuals, regardless of family background. The functionalist vision of a just society is one where individual talent and hard work based on universal principles of evaluation are more important than ascriptive characteristics based on particularistic methods of evaluation.

Functionalists expect that the schooling process will produce unequal results, but these results ought to be based on individual differences between students, not on group differences. Thus, although there is a persistent relationship between family background and educational outcomes, this does not in and of itself mean that the system fails to provide equality of opportunity. It is possible that even with equality of opportunity there could be these patterns of unequal results, although most functionalists would agree that this is highly unlikely. Therefore, functionalists believe that unequal educational outcomes are the result, in part, of unequal educational opportunities. Thus, for functionalists, it is imperative to understand the sources of educational inequality so as to ensure the elimination of structural barriers to educational success and to provide all groups a fair chance to compete in the educational marketplace. This perspective has been the foundation of liberal educational policy in the United States since the 1960s.

Conflict theorists are not in the least bit surprised by the data. Given that conflict theorists believe that the role of schooling is to reproduce rather than eliminate inequality, the fact that educational outcomes are to a large degree based on family background is fully consistent with this perspective. Nonetheless, conflict theorists are also concerned with inequality and its eradication. Whereas functionalists focus on the attempts to provide equality of opportunity and to ensure a meritocratic system, conflict theorists are concerned with both equality of opportunity and results. That is, conflict theorists, who usually fall into the more radical political category, do not believe that equality of opportunity is a sufficient goal.

A system that could guarantee equitable and fair treatment to all would not necessarily produce equal results, as individual differences (rather than group differences) would still play an important role in creating significant inequalities. Although most radicals do not believe that complete equality of results is possible or even desirable, they do want to reduce significantly the degree of educational, social, and economic inequalities. Thus, conflict theorists call for more radical measures to reduce inequality; also, they are far more skeptical than functionalists that the problem can be solved.

Despite these differences, both functionalists and conflict theorists agree that understanding educational inequality is a difficult task. Further, it is clear that the third sociological approach, interactionist theory, is necessary to grasp fully the problem. Interactionism suggests that one must understand how people within institutions such as families and schools interact on a daily basis in order to comprehend the factors explaining academic success and failure. Thus, in addition to studying empirical data on school outcomes, which often explains what happens, one must also look into the lives and worlds of families and schools in order to understand why it happens. Many of the research studies of educational inequality that are discussed in this chapter use an interactionist approach based on fieldwork in order to examine what goes on in families and schools.

The next step is to explain race-, class-, and gender-based inequalities of educational attainment and achievement. Researchers have posed two different sets of explanations. The first is centered on factors outside of the school, such as the family, the community, the culture of the group, the peer group, and the individual student. These explanations are often termed *student-centered* (Dougherty & Hammack, 1990, p. 334) or *extra-school* (Hurn, 1993, p. 161) *explanations*. The second is centered on factors within the school, such as teachers and teaching methods, curriculum, ability grouping and curriculum tracking, school climate, and teacher expectations. These explanations are often termed *school-centered* (Dougherty & Hammack, 1990, p. 334) or *within-school* (Hurn, 1993, p. 162) *explanations*.

Although there is merit in both approaches, the dichotomy between what are inexorably linked spheres is somewhat shortsighted. As Hurn (1993, pp. 161–162) has pointed out, functionalists tend to support extra-school explanations because these provide support for the view that the schooling process is somewhat meritocratic and that educational inequalities are caused by factors outside the schooling process. Conflict theorists, although not denying the deleterious impact of extra-school factors such as poverty, believe that schools play an important role in reproducing the problems. The attempt to pigeon-hole the explanation into one explanatory system denies the connection between schooling and other societal institutions.

We prefer a more multidimensional approach, such as the one outlined by Persell (1977), which argues that educational inequality is the product of the relationship between societal, institutional, interactional, and intrapsychic variables. Thus, in order to understand education and inequality, one must explore not only what goes on within society and its institutions (such as the family and the school), but also the connections between them and their effects on individuals and groups. In the following sections, we outline the major student-centered and school-centered explanations and then propose a more multidimensional synthesis of these explanations.

Before we begin, it is important to discuss briefly the interconnection between race, class, gender, and ethnicity. As we noted in Chapter 8, individuals have more than one ascriptive status. For example, in terms of gender, men and women belong to different social classes and races, and come from different ethnic groups. In terms of race and ethnicity, members of different racial and ethnic groups may belong to different socioeconomic classes. Thus, there are differences in educational attainment and achievement between working-class and middle-class women or men, between working-class and middle-class blacks or whites, and between different ethnic groups based on social class position.

Sociological research on educational outcomes attempts to separate the independent effects of these variables, although their relationship is often difficult to distinguish. It is clear, however, that although gender, race, and ethnicity have independent effects, and that women, African-Americans, and other ethnic groups are often negatively affected by societal and school processes, social class background has the most powerful effect on educational achievement and attainment. This is not to say that women or African-Americans as groups may not be disadvantaged in schools, independent of social class background; only that social class appears to be the more powerful explanatory variable in explaining educational attainment and achievement.

On one hand, given the powerful relationship between social class and educational attainment and achievement, much of the sociological research on educational outcomes has focused on class issues. On the other hand, given the significant relationship between social class and race, the problems of African-Americans' achievement, and the important political movements aimed at ameliorating conditions of African-American poverty and improving African-American educational performance, this research has also focused on the relationship between race and education. In the following sections, we do not treat issues of race and class separately. Rather, we look at research that sometimes examines race as a separate category, sometimes looks at class as a separate category, and sometimes looks at them together. The following discussion assumes that groups that do not fare well in school do so because of their subordinate position in society, with race, class, gender, and ethnicity important components of a group's position. As the bulk of research concentrates on race and class, the following discussion concentrates on these studies.

We are not implying that gender and ethnicity are unimportant. A growing body of literature is interested in the educational performance of different ethnic groups, including Asians, Italians, Latinos, and others (Doran & Weffer, 1992; Lomawaima, 1995; Nieto, 1995; Pang, 1995; Wong-Fillmore & Valdez, 1986). Additionally, the problems faced by students whose first language is not English are increasingly the subject of educational research (Hakuta & Garcia, 1989; Nieto, 1995; Pang, 1995; Thornburg & Karp, 1992; Wong-Fillmore & Valdez, 1986). The following discussions of student-centered and school-centered explanations, although not directly related to particular ethnic groups, assume that the student- and school-related processes that affect working-class and black students also affect other ethnic groups in a similar manner.

The research on gender and education is crucial for understanding how schooling affects particular groups (American Association of University Women, 1992; Arnot, 2012). Unlike the research on ethnicity, this research cannot be easily subsumed under the student- or school-centered rubric. As we noted in Chapter 8, although there are some differences in the educational attainment and achievement of men and women, these differences are less than those based on race and class. Women do better in the humanities and men do better in math and science. However, the key difference is not in education but rather in economic outcomes, with women, despite somewhat equal levels of education, doing significantly less well economically. Part of the reason for this is related to labor-market issues and gender discrimination in the workplace. Some of it is due to the different occupational choices made by men and women, with traditionally female positions rewarded less well than those occupied by men. Why women select different career paths, many of which pay less well than those selected by men, is an important question. It can be examined through the research on gender and education, which looks specifically at the ways schools socialize men and women differently.

Whereas much of the research on education and inequality focuses on the cognitive outcomes of schooling and concentrates on educational attainment and achievement, research on gender and education also focuses on the noncognitive outcomes of schooling. Thus, this research looks at the ways in which schooling affects the manner in which men and women come to view themselves, their roles, and society. Feminist scholarship on schooling examines questions of unequal opportunity for women, the differential socialization processes for boys and girls in schools, and the ways in which the hidden curriculum unequally affects women. Although feminists argue that these differential socialization patterns begin in the family and that girls bring cultural differences to the school, the bulk of educational research focuses on school-related processes. Hence, in the subsequent discussions of student-centered and school-centered explanations, we discuss gender inequalities under the school-centered rubric.

Student-Centered Explanations

In the 1960s, sociologists of education interested in educational inequality often worked from a set of liberal political and policy assumptions about why students from lower socioeconomic backgrounds often did less well in school than students from higher socioeconomic backgrounds. The conventional wisdom of the time suggested that economically disadvantaged students attended inferior schools—schools that spent less money on each student, schools that spent less money on materials and extracurricular activities, and schools that had inferior teachers. The argument continued that if school differences and financing were responsible for the problem, then the solution was simply to pump resources and money into schools with children from lower socioeconomic backgrounds.

A number of research studies in the 1960s and 1970s demonstrated, however, that the conventional liberal wisdom was far too simplistic and that solutions were far more complex. Coleman and colleagues (1966), in *Equality of Educational Opportunity*, commonly referred to as the Coleman Report, argued that school differences were not the most significant explanatory variable for the lower educational achievement of working-class and nonwhite students. Rather, the report suggested that it was the differences among the groups of students that had a greater impact on educational performance. Additionally, research by Jencks and colleagues (1972) indicated that the differences between schools in privileged areas and in economically disadvantaged areas had been exaggerated. Moreover, where significant differences did exist, they did not sufficiently explain the inequalities of educational performance.

This research suggested that there were far more significant differences in academic performance among students in the same school than among students in different schools. This latter finding on what is termed *within-school differences* (as opposed to *between-school differences*) does not rule out the possibility that schools affect educational inequality, as it is possible that differences in the school such as ability grouping and curriculum tracking may explain these differences. Nevertheless, the research by Coleman and by Jencks cast doubt on the claim that differences between schools explained the performance gap among students from different socioeconomic or racial backgrounds. We will return to the question of school differences later in this chapter, but for now, it is important to discuss the consequences of these findings.

If school differences and financing did not explain unequal educational performance, then perhaps the schools themselves were not the most important factor. Based on the Coleman Report, educational researchers and policy makers concluded that the reason students from lower socioeconomic backgrounds did less well in school had more to do with the students themselves, their families, their neighborhood and communities, their culture, and perhaps even their genetic makeup. These student-centered explanations became dominant in the 1960s and 1970s, and are still highly controversial and politically charged.

Genetic Differences

The most controversial student-centered explanation is the genetic or biological argument. From a sociological and anthropological perspective, biological explanations of human behavior are viewed as limited because social scientists believe that environmental and social factors are largely responsible for human behavior. Recent advances in the understanding of mental illnesses such as schizophrenia, however, suggest that there may be biochemical and genetic causes. This research indicates that although social and psychological factors are crucial, biological factors cannot be ruled out entirely. Having said this, the question remains as to whether there is evidence to support the argument that differences in school performance among groups of students are due to genetic differences among these groups, particularly in intelligence.

The argument that unequal educational performance by working-class and non-white students is due to genetic differences in intelligence was offered by psychologist Arthur Jensen in a highly controversial article in the *Harvard Educational Review* (1969). Jensen indicated that compensatory programs (i.e., programs aimed at improving the educational performance of disadvantaged students) were doomed to failure because they were aimed at changing social and environmental factors, when the root of the problem was biological. Jensen, based on sophisticated statistical analyses, argued that African-Americans, genetically, are less intelligent than whites and therefore do less well in school, where intelligence is an important component of educational success. Given these data and his conclusions, Jensen was pessimistic about the likelihood that the academic performance of African-Americans could be substantially improved.

Hurn (1993, pp. 142–152) provided a detailed and balanced assessment of the IQ controversy. Given the sensitivity of the subject, more often than not, the debate about Jensen's work consisted of polemical attacks accusing him of being a racist and dismissed his claim that there is a biological basis of intelligence, rather than carefully considering his arguments. Hurn demonstrated through a careful analysis of Jensen's thesis that although there is evidence that a genetic component to human intelligence exists, and that although a small percentage of the social class differences in intelligence may be attributed to genetic factors, the most significant factor affecting intelligence is social. Moreover, he argued that there is no persuasive evidence that social class and racial differences in intelligence are due to genetic factors. Additionally, Hurn and others have indicated that these differences in intelligence are due in part to the cultural bias of IQ test questions, the conditions under which they are given, and cultural and family differences (Bowles & Gintis, 1976, Chapter 4; Kamin, 1974; Persell, 1977, pp. 58–75). In the 1990s, the genetic argument reemerged with the publication of *The Bell Curve* (1994) by Richard Herrnstein and Charles Murray. This book presented many of the same arguments made in the 1960s by Jensen and was greeted with similar criticism (Kincheloe, Steinberg, & Gressom, 1996).

Given the weakness of the genetic argument, how does one explain unequal educational performance by working-class and nonwhite students? As we stated earlier, as a result of the Coleman and Jencks studies, researchers looked to the family and the culture of the students for answers. Cultural deprivation and cultural difference theories have been two related approaches. Although these theories are more widely accepted by social scientists, because they view social and cultural factors as essential, they have been no less controversial.

Cultural Deprivation Theories

In light of the Coleman Report's findings that school differences and resources did not adequately explain unequal performance by working-class and nonwhite students, some educational researchers argued that these students came to school without the requisite intellectual and social skills necessary for school success. Cultural deprivation theory, popularized in the 1960s, suggests that working-class and nonwhite families often lack the cultural resources, such as books and other educational stimuli, and thus arrive at school at a significant disadvantage.

Moreover, drawing on the thesis advanced by anthropologist Oscar Lewis (1966) about poverty in Mexico, cultural deprivation theorists assert that the poor have a deprived culture—one that lacks the value system of middle-class culture. According to this perspective, middle-class culture values hard work and initiative, the delay of immediate gratification for future reward, and the importance of schooling as a means to future success. The culture of poverty eschews delayed gratification for immediate reward, rejects hard work and initiative as a means to success, and does not view schooling as the means to social mobility. According to cultural deprivation theorists such as Deutsch (1964), this deprivation results in educationally disadvantaged students who achieve poorly because they have not been raised to acquire the skills and dispositions required for satisfactory academic achievement (Dougherty & Hammack, 1990, p. 341).

Based on this etiology, policy makers sought to develop programs aimed not at the schools but rather at the family environment of working-class and nonwhite students. Compensatory education programs such as Project Head Start—a preschool intervention program for educationally and economically disadvantaged students—are based on the assumption that because of the cultural and familial deprivation faced by poor students, the schools must provide an environment that makes up for lost time. If these students are not prepared for school at home, then it is the role of the preschool to provide the necessary foundation for learning. Further, programs such as Head Start attempt to involve parents in their children's schooling and to help them develop parenting and literacy skills necessary for their children's academic development.

Cultural deprivation theory was attacked vociferously in the 1960s and 1970s by social scientists who believed it to be paternalistic at best and racist at worst. Critics argue that it removes the responsibility for school success and failure from schools and teachers, and places it on families. Further, they suggest that it blames the victims of poverty for the effects of poverty rather than placing the blame squarely where it belongs: on the social and economic processes that produce poverty (Baratz & Baratz, 1970; Dougherty & Hammack, 1990, p. 341; Ryan, 1971).

Another criticism of cultural deprivation theory concerned the relative failure of many of the compensatory education programs that were based on its assumptions about why disadvantaged children have lower levels of achievement than more advantaged children. Although Project Head Start has received mixed evaluations (with early findings somewhat negative and later research providing more positive results; cf. Weikert & Schweinhart, 1984), compensatory programs, as a whole, have not improved significantly the academic performance of disadvantaged students. Given these criticisms and the weakness of the geneticist argument, a third student-centered explanation emerged: cultural difference theory.

Cultural Difference Theories

Cultural difference theorists agree that there are cultural and family differences between working-class and nonwhite students, and white middle-class students. Working-class and nonwhite students may indeed arrive at school with different cultural dispositions and without the skills and attitudes required by the schools. This is not due to deficiencies in their home life but rather to being part of an oppressed minority. The key difference in this perspective is that although cultural difference theorists acknowledge the impact of student differences, they do not blame working-class and nonwhite families for educational problems. Rather, they attribute cultural differences to social forces such as poverty, racism, discrimination, and unequal life chances.

There are a number of different varieties of cultural difference theory. First, researchers such as anthropologist John Ogbu (1978, 1979, 1987) argue that African-American children do less well in school because they adapt to their oppressed position in the class and caste structure. Ogbu argued that there is a "job ceiling" for African-Americans in the United States, as there is for similar caste-like minorities in other countries, and that African-American families and schools socialize their children to deal with their inferior life chances rather than encourage them to internalize those values and skills necessary for positions that will not be open to them. Although this is a complex, and at times a hidden, process, the results are lower educational attainment and performance.

Ogbu's later work (Fordham & Ogbu, 1986) suggests that school success requires that African-American students deny their own cultural identities and accept the dominant culture of the schools, which is a white middle-class model. African-American students thus have the "burden of acting white" in order to succeed (Fordham, 1997). This explanation, as we will see later in this chapter, rejects the argument that school-centered explanations are unimportant, and proposes the interaction of school and student variables to explain educational achievement. The view that there are cultural differences between the culture of the school and the culture of working-class and non-white students has resulted in calls for changes in school curriculum and pedagogy to more adequately represent the cultures of minority children. As we stated in Chapter 7, the demand for multicultural curricula is rooted in the belief that the schools need to reflect the cultures of all the students who attend, not just the culture of dominant social groups.

Ogbu's macrosociological perspective is similar to those of Bowles and Gintis (1976), whose correspondence theory suggests that working-class students adapt to the unequal aspects of the class structure, and to Bourdieu and Passeron (1977) and Bernstein (1977), whose theories point out the ways in which class and cultural differences are reflected in the schools. Bernstein, in particular, has often been accused of being a cultural deprivation theorist because of his theory that working-class students in England have a different language and communication code, which disadvantages them in the schools. Bernstein (1990) has consistently denied that working-class language is deficient. Rather, he has stated that cultural and class differences are a product of an unequal economic system and that the schools reward middle-class communication codes, not working-class codes. This viewpoint is a complex one, as it sees educational inequality as a product of the relationships between the economic system, the family, and the schools, with cultural differences turned into deficits by the schooling process. As with Ogbu's theories, Bernstein's theory insists on looking at the schools as sources of educational inequality, not just the culture or families of working-class students.

Bourdieu's concepts of social and cultural capital are also important in understanding how cultural differences affect educational inequality (Swartz, 1997). More affluent families give their children access to cultural capital (e.g., visits to museums, concerts, travel, etc.) and social capital (e.g., networks for access to educational resources, college admissions, parental involvement, etc.). Although Bourdieu recognizes that economic capital (income and wealth) are still paramount in providing affluent families with an educational advantage, social and cultural capital are more subtle ways that social class advantages reproduce educational inequalities. Lareau (1989, 2003, 2011) uses Bourdieu's concepts to examine social class differences in child rearing, and the relationship between family and schools. Lareau argues that working-class families use a natural growth model of child rearing in which children are encouraged to be independent and play on their own. Middle-class families use a model of concerted cultivation in which children's time is rigidly planned by their parents and where formal classes and activities are utilized to enhance their class advantages.

Ogbu's research also examines the relationship between language and educational achievement among low-income, inner-city African-American students (Ogbu, 1999). Based on an extensive ethnographic study of a low-income community in Oakland, California, Ogbu documents the tensions between the standard English required for school success and the "slang-English" (Black English) used in the community. Consistent with Bernstein's analysis of restricted (working-class) and elaborated (middle-class) codes, Ogbu argues that although African-American students and parents believe it is important that schools teach standard English for educational and occupational mobility, they are ambivalent about its use within the community. Such ambivalence results in difficulties in using standard English and is an important factor in explaining educational inequalities for these students.

Just as Bernstein does not see British working-class language as inferior, Ogbu does not see African-American linguistic codes as culturally deficient. Black English is a different dialect that is defined as deficient by the dominant linguistic codes of schooling and society. The question is how low-income African-American students can be successfully bidialectic—that is, be able to use standard English for academic and occupational mobility, and not feel they are committing cultural or racial suicide. The film *Educating Rita* illustrates this problem for a British working-class woman who enrolls in the Open University. Eventually, she must choose between continuing her education or losing her husband, who rejects her new use of middle-class codes. Ultimately, she leaves her husband and working-class community and attains academic success. The question is: Is the price of losing one's culture too high a price to pay?

Ogbu's article appeared after the Oakland School District's 1996 Ebonics (Black English) controversy. The Oakland School Board voted (and subsequently rescinded) a policy to teach Ebonics as a second language as a way of promoting standard English language literacy. The policy resulted in a national controversy in which many African-American leaders, including Jesse Jackson, stressed the importance of standard English. Ogbu's work demonstrates that the issue is far more complex than telling low-income African-American students to simply learn standard English. Rather, linguistic codes are at the heart of unequal power relations between dominant and subordinate groups and represent one's definition of cultural identity. Clearly, standard English is necessary for academic and occupational success; internalizing and acting on this is a more difficult social psychological problem.

Ogbu's last book, completed shortly before his death in 2003, examined the persistence of the black–white achievement gap in middle and upper middle-class communities. Asked by the African-American parents in Shaker Heights, Ohio, to help them understand why their children were performing at lower levels than their white classmates, Ogbu spent a year studying the community and its schools. He concluded that although there were school-based reasons for unequal achievement, especially the underrepresentation of African-American students in honors and advanced placement classes and their overrepresentation in regular classes, the main reasons had to do with student, parental, and community cultures. African-American students studied less, watched more television, and had lower aspirations than their white classmates. They were also more likely to be affected by an anti-school culture and received less pressure from their parents to excel in school. Ogbu did not discount school factors, but argued that they are related to powerful cultural differences (Ogbu, 2003). Tyson's research, however, does not fully support Ogbu's findings. In her studies of integrated schools in North Carolina, she found mixed evidence of the burden of acting white and more importantly found that black students were more negatively affected by race-based tracking in the schools rather than cultural or racial attitudes learned at home or in their communities (Tyson, 2011; Tyson et al. 2005).

A second type of cultural difference theory sees working-class and nonwhite students as resisting the dominant culture of the schools. From this point of view, these students reject the white middle-class culture of academic success and embrace a different, often antischool culture—one that is opposed to the culture of schooling as it currently exists. Research by Willis (1981) on working-class boys in England shows that these students explicitly reject middle-class values and enthusiastically embrace a working-class culture, which eschews the values of schooling. They consciously reject schooling and resist academic success. This resistance results in dropping out of school and into the world of work—that is, the world of the factory floor, which they romanticize as the proper place for men.

A study of suburban life in the New York–New Jersey metropolitan area (Gaines, 1991) documents the antischool culture of working-class suburban adolescents, for whom heavy metal, rock and roll music, and "souped-up" automobiles are the symbols of adolescent culture, with the academic life of schooling consciously rejected and scorned. According to this type of cultural difference theory, these cultural norms are not inferior to middle-class norms, only different. Thus, the fact that society and its schools demand middle-class cultural norms places these students at a distinct disadvantage. Cultural difference theorists, such as Ogbu, suggest that subordinate groups often see little reason to embrace the culture of schooling, as they do not believe it will have value for them. Given the labor market barriers to these groups, Ogbu has argued that this type of resistance may, in fact, be a form of cultural adaptation to the realities of economic life.

The problem with cultural difference theory, according to Hurn (1993, pp. 154–155), is that it is too culturally relativistic. That is, in its insistence that all cultures are equally valid, and that all values and norms are acceptable in the context of the culture that generated them, cultural difference theorists too often deny cultural problems and dysfunction. Although it is fair to acknowledge that cultural deprivation theorists are often ethnocentric and biased, and that the culture of schooling often alienates students from working-class and nonwhite families, it is apparent that cultural patterns may negatively affect school performance. That these patterns are often caused by social and economic forces does not eliminate them, nor reduce their negative impact on academic achievement. As Hurn (1993, p. 154) stated:

> The claim that lower-class environments are not deficient in their provision of resources for intellectual growth but reflect differential valuations of ideal family forms is also problematic. While we may grant some of the characterizations of lower-class family life as pathological are ethnocentric and insensitive to cultural differences, much research has shown that poverty and unemployment make it extremely difficult for lower-class families to maintain relationships *they define* as satisfactory. Among poor black families, for example, over 50% of the households are headed by women, and illegitimacy rates exceed 60 percent. There is little evidence that blacks regard such families as desirable, and indeed there is increasing evidence that in the 1980s the black community began to define this situation as a crisis in the black family. The causes of that crisis undoubtedly lie in the legacy of discrimination and in poverty and unemployment. But it is hard to deny that the instability of family life in many lower-class black households makes for an unpropitious environment for the development of intellectual skills.

Lemann (1991), in his journalistic history of the black migration from the Mississippi Delta to Chicago in the post-World War II years, chronicled the cycles of poverty, hopelessness, and despair that mark life in the public housing projects of Chicago. Although he argued that economic transformations and conditions are the root causes of poverty, and that racism and discrimination exacerbate the problems, he nonetheless pointed out that the culture of the projects—with their rampant violence, drug abuse, and hopelessness—are part of the problem. Although it is important not to blame the poor for their situation and to understand that what Lemann described is a result of poverty, it is equally important to acknowledge that such life-styles should not be celebrated as "resistance." Rather, as Lemann noted, public policy must simultaneously address the elimination of the social and economic conditions responsible for poverty and the behaviors that serve to reproduce it.

In Chapter 8, we presented data on the academic success of Asian-American students. Recent political decisions in California to eliminate affirmative action in college admissions to state universities and to end bilingual education have placed Asian-American achievement in a national spotlight. With respect to bilingual education, why do Asian-Americans do better than other students whose first language is not English? With respect to affirmative action, ending affirmative action in California has resulted in a significant increase in the percentage of Asian-Americans attending the state's flagship institutions such as Berkeley and UCLA, with over 60 percent of Berkeley's first-year classes now comprised of Asian-Americans; and a subsequent decline in the percentage of African-American and Hispanic-American students (Orfield & Miller, 1998; UCLA Civil Rights Project, 2012). Sociologists disagree about the causes of Asian-American academic success. One explanation is that as voluntary immigrants (Ogbu, 1999), Asian-Americans come to the United States willing to adapt to the dominant culture in order to succeed. Another explanation is that a large number of Asian-Americans come from the educated middle classes of their native countries and already possess the skills and dispositions necessary for academic success. A third is that Asian-Americans possess family values that place enormous emphasis on educational achievement and have high expectations for their children.

Critics of cultural theories argue that blaming poor people for their problems is "blaming the victim" (Ryan, 1971). They argue that poor people suffer dramatically from the ravages of poverty, which affects their academic performance. Richard Rothstein (2004b) argues that poor people suffer from significant health problems, including high rates of asthma, exposure to lead paint, smoking and alcohol use, poor vision and nutrition, lower birth weight, and inadequate health care. These poverty-related health problems can have significant effects on academic achievement. For example, exposure to lead paint or to smoking, alcohol, or drugs can lower IQ and limit cognitive development. Rothstein argues that investments in improving the health of low-income children will significantly reduce the achievement gaps based on income. Although some may see this explanation as cultural deprivation theory in reverse, it is difficult to ignore the relationship between family beliefs in the importance of academic success and Asian-American academic achievement. Lew (2005a, 2005b, 2005c), however, argues that the "model minority" explanation of Asian-American student success overlooks the variation among these students. According to Lew, there are significant numbers of failing Asian-American students. Successful Asian-American students are more likely to come from more affluent families and to make use of social capital, including community networks that help them navigate the academic world. Stanton-Salazar's (2001) research on Mexican-American students supports the importance of social capital for immigrant students.

It is important to transcend the often emotional and political arguments that accompany discussions of cultural deprivation and differences. Too often, those who point to the negative impact of cultural differences on academic achievement are accused of class and racial bias, when such ethnocentrism is not part of their analysis. Clearly, the poor should not be blamed for their problems, as the causes of poverty are more social and economic than they are cultural. Neither should the cultural differences related to school success and failure be denied. The key is to move past the ideological and to eliminate the social and educational barriers to school success for working-class and nonwhite students. Perhaps more importantly, one must recognize that unequal educational achievement cannot be explained by looking at students and their families alone; one must also look at the schools themselves.

School-Centered Explanations

Earlier in this chapter, we reviewed the early research of Coleman and Jencks on the relationship between school quality and resources, and unequal academic attainment. Although their research questioned the conventional wisdom that between-school differences are the key factor in explaining differences in student performance between groups, it did not exclude the possibility that schools have significant effects on students. Although Coleman's early work concluded that student differences were more important than school differences, a conclusion that his subsequent work on public and private schools rejects (Coleman, Hoffer, & Kilgore, 1982; Coleman & Hoffer, 1987), and Jencks concluded that school effects were minimal, both researchers found that there are significant within-school differences that suggested schools may indeed make a difference.

For example, how does one explain differences in academic performance among groups of students within the same school? A completely individualistic explanation states that these differences are the result of individual differences in intelligence or initiative. Another student-centered explanation sees these differences as the result of student differences prior to entering school. School-centered explanations, however, suggest that school processes are central to understanding unequal educational performance. In the 1980s, educational researchers examined carefully the myriad processes within schools that explain the sources of unequal academic achievement. This school-centered research focused on both between- and within-school processes.

School Financing

Jonathan Kozol (1991), in his muckraking book *Savage Inequalities*, compared public schools in affluent suburbs with public schools in poor inner cities. He documented the vast differences in funding between affluent and poor districts, and called for equalization in school financing. In Chapter 8, we presented recent data on differences in funding between affluent and poor school districts. As these data indicated, in 2009–2010, significant differences between affluent suburban and poorer urban districts remain, with New York City schools receiving less than $21,000 per student and affluent Long Island schools receiving over $25,000 per student (see Table 9.1). These differences have remained consistent in most states through 2012, with the exception of a number of states, including Delaware, Kentucky, Massachusetts, Minnesota, and New Jersey. In order to comprehend why these inequalities exist, it is important to understand the way in which public schools are financed in the United States.

Public schools are financed through a combination of revenues from local, state, and federal sources. However, the majority of funds come from state and local taxes, with local property taxes a significant source. Property taxes are based on the value of property in local communities and therefore is a proportional tax. Since property values are significantly higher in more affluent communities, these communities are able to raise significantly more money for schools through this form of taxation than poorer communities with lower property values. Additionally, since families in more affluent communities have higher incomes, they pay proportionately less of their incomes for their higher school taxes.

Thus, more affluent communities are able to provide more per-pupil spending than poorer districts, often at a proportionately less burdensome rate than in poorer communities. This unequal funding has been the subject of considerable legal attack by communities that argue that funding based on local property taxes is discriminatory under the Equal Protection Clause of the Fourteenth Amendment and that it denies equality of opportunity.

In Serrano v. Priest (1971), the California Supreme Court ruled the system of unequal school financing between wealthy and poor districts unconstitutional. It did not, however, declare the use of property taxes for school funding illegal. Five other state courts (in Arizona, Minnesota,

New Jersey, Texas, and Wyoming) rendered similar rulings within the next year. However, in 1973, the U.S. Supreme Court in San Antonio (Texas) Independent School District v. Rodriguez reversed a lower-court ruling and upheld the use of local property taxes as the basis for school funding. In a 5–4 opinion, the Court ruled that this method of funding, although unjust, was not unconstitutional. Justice Thurgood Marshall, in a dissenting opinion, stated that the decision represented a move away from a commitment to equality of opportunity (Johnson, 1991, p. 308).

Table 9.1 School Funding in New York City and Selected Long Island Districts: 2009–2010 School Year

District	Wealth Ratio (higher = more wealth)	Spending per Pupil (Including Special Education Students)
New York City (Bronx, King's, New York, Queen's, and Richmond Counties)	1.019	$ 20,756
Nassau County		
Baldwin	1.047	$21,357
Bellmore-Merrick	1.262	$19,434
East Williston	2.564	$26,927
Franklin Square	1.199	$15,590
Freeport	0.740	$20,841
Garden City	2.587	$22,750
Hempstead	0.538	$21,860
Long Beach	2.203	$30,074
Malverne	1.387	$26,146
Manhasset	4.340	$27,840
New Hyde Park	1.383	$18,396
Oyster Bay	5.451	$29,969
Roosevelt	0.575	$25,757
Roslyn	2.573	$25,476
Suffolk County		
Amagansett	25.378	$43,638
Amityville	1.224	$26,616
Central Islip	0.648	$26,550
Copiague	0.750	$19,419
Hauppauge	1.668	$21,855
Huntington	1.910	$23,024
Miller Place	1.044	$19,370
Northport	1.905	$22,658
Quogue	22.341	$35,387
Rocky Point	0.808	$17,582
South Huntington	1.289	$21,365
Shoreham-Wading River	1.349	$20,925
West Islip	1.000	$18,592
Wyandanch	0.446	$25,712

Note: Nassau County is directly east of New York City's borough of Queens and stretches approximately 30 miles to the Suffolk County border. Nassau County includes the wealthy *Gold Coast* made famous by F. Scott Fitzgerald in the *Great Gatsby;* Jones Beach, planned by famous planner Robert Moses; Levittown, one of the first planned communities built for GIs returning from WWII; Roosevelt Field, one of the first and still among the largest shopping malls in the country; and Mitchell Field, the departure site of Charles Lindberg's historic cross-Atlantic flight. The county has communities of great wealth, great poverty, and many middle-income communities. Although western Suffolk County is suburban, it becomes more rural the further east you go. It has numerous farms and vineyards, as well as the famous beach resort areas of Fire Island and the Hamptons. It, too, has communities of great wealth, great poverty, and many middle-income communities. For a more detailed analysis, see Singer (1999).

Source: New York State Department of Education, as cited in "Fiscal Profile Reporting System" (2012). www.oms.nysed.gov/faru/Profiles/profiles_cover.html

Although the Supreme Court decision has made it unlikely that the federal government will intervene in local financing of public schools, individual states have taken on the responsibility of attempting to decrease inequalities in school financing. The Kentucky, Texas, Arkansas, California, Connecticut, Montana, New Jersey, New York, Washington, West Virginia, and Wyoming state courts have ruled against their states' system of school financing. The Kentucky decision called for a shift to state funding of schools to ensure equality of educational opportunity. In Abbott v. Burke (1990), the New Jersey Supreme Court ruled that the funding differences between rich and poor districts was unconstitutional. This resulted in the Quality Education Act (QEA), which was implemented (Anyon, 1997; Firestone, Goertz, & Natriello, 1997). As a result of Abbott V (1998), New Jersey's 31 urban districts receive the highest per-pupil funding anywhere in the country (> $15,000 per student). Although Abott has been replaced by the state's new funding formula, SFRA, the urban districts still receive at or above the average of the state's wealthiest districts. In the future, it appears that more states will begin to use state funding to close the gap between rich and poor districts. The use of foundation state aid programs, which seeks to make sure all districts receive a minimum standard of funding, with more state aid going to poorer districts in order to enable poorer districts to meet this minimum level, is one way of providing equality of opportunity. Although wealthier districts are still able to go above this minimum by taxing themselves at higher rates through property taxes, the use of foundation aid programs, at the very least, attempts to guarantee that all districts have the minimum necessary to provide a quality education (Johnson, 1991, pp. 314–320).

The use of federal aid to equalize school funding is a controversial issue. Proponents argue that such aid has occurred historically, as in the Elementary and Secondary Education Act of 1965. They also argue that it is the fairest and most progressive system of school financing, as it would guarantee equality of opportunity regardless of residence. Advocates of a federal system of financing, such as Kozol (1991), believe that schools should be financed through federal income taxes. Critics, however, believe that, under the Tenth Amendment to the Constitution, education is a state and local matter, and that federal financing would threaten local decision-making.

It is clear that the present reliance on local property taxes and state aid has not reduced inequalities of financing. Thus, children from lower socioeconomic backgrounds do not receive equality of opportunity, at least in terms of funding. Although, as we note in the next sections, differences in academic achievement among students from different social classes cannot be understood in terms of funding alone, there is a moral as well as educational question at issue. Even if, as some researchers suggest (e.g., see Jencks et al., 1972), equalization of funding would not reduce inequalities of achievement among groups, is it fair that some students have significantly more money spent on them than others?

Critics of school financing believe equalization is a moral imperative, but there is not widespread agreement on this matter. For example, when New York Governor Mario Cuomo, faced with severe budgetary shortfalls during the recession in 1991, cut state aid to education more severely in affluent suburbs than in poorer cities, such as New York City, the hue and cry in the suburbs was extraordinary. Affluent suburban districts—faced with dramatic reductions in state aid, which resulted in teacher layoffs and cutbacks in services—argued that such proportionate cutbacks threatened their ability to maintain their academic excellence. Governor Cuomo responded that state aid should be cut in districts spending sometimes over twice as much per pupil than in city districts. Thus, the question of funding is not a moral issue alone; it is a political issue, as different communities struggle to give their children what they consider the best possible education. In doing so, however, critics maintain that affluent communities continue to defend their advantages over poorer communities. In 2004, New York state's highest court mandated an additional $5.6 billion for the New York City public schools in its ruling in the decade-long Campaign for Fiscal Equity lawsuit. Today, although the legislature agreed to more adequately fund New York City's schools, budget crises have prevented the state from fully implementing the formula. In the same year, Governor Arnold Schwarzenegger settled the Williams v. State of California case by agreeing to set new state standards to ensure an adequate education to all the state's children.

Although the question of the morality of unequal school financing is an important one, its effect on unequal achievement is equally important. There is disagreement over the extent to which school financing affects unequal academic achievement, but it is clear that school factors other than financing have an important impact on achievement. Nonetheless, there is increasing evidence that school financing matters (Baker & Welner, 2010, 2011; Firestone, Goertz, & Natriello, 1997; Hedges, Laine, & Greenwald, 1994; Rebell, 2009).

The broad-based mandates of Abbott V, in New Jersey, including in all 31 poor urban districts (Abbott districts), resulted in the following: (1) parity funding equal to the state's highest wealth districts; (2) full-day preschool for all 3- and 4-year-olds; (3) comprehensive whole school reform; (4) supplemental funding for school health and other student needs; and (5) a multi-billion-dollar school facilities and construction plan. However, under SFRA many of these reforms have been discontinued. New Jersey's school achievement results under Abbott demonstrated improvements in the Abbott districts at the fourth-grade level. Some of these are surely a result of the Abbott reforms. Although improvements were slower at the higher grades, there is evidence to suggest that similar improvements might follow if the state continues its historic commitment to its poorest children. Under SFRA, this is less than clear.

Effective School Research

The findings of Coleman and Jencks that differences in school resources and quality do not adequately explain between-school differences in academic achievement was viewed by teachers as a mixed blessing. On one hand, if student differences are more important than school differences, then teachers cannot be blamed for the lower academic performance of nonwhite and working-class students. On the other hand, if schools' effects are not significant, then schools and, more specifically, teachers can do little to make a positive difference. Although Jencks's admonition that societal change was necessary to improve schools may have made teachers feel less directly responsible for problems that were often beyond their control, it also left teachers with a sense of hopelessness that there was little, if anything, they could do to improve schooling from inside the schools. Critics of the student-centered findings went further. They argued that this research took the responsibility away from schools and teachers, and placed it on communities and families. Common sense, they believed, suggested that there were differences between good and bad schools, and between good and incompetent teachers. These differences certainly had to have some effects on students. The difficult empirical task, however, is to untangle the ways in which school processes affect student learning.

The concern with unequal educational performance of nonwhite and working-class students is at the heart of such inquiry. The finding that within-school differences are as or more significant than between-school differences raised questions about the common-sense argument that students from lower socioeconomic backgrounds do poorly simply because they attend inferior schools. Ronald Edmonds (1979a), an African-American former school superintendent and Harvard professor, suggested that comparing schools in different socioeconomic communities was only part of the puzzle. He argued that researchers needed to compare schools within lower socioeconomic communities as well. If all schools in such neighborhoods produce low educational outcomes, and these lower outcomes could not be explained in terms of school differences in comparison to schools in higher socioeconomic communities, then the student-centered findings could be supported. Conversely, if there are significant differences in student performance between schools within lower socioeconomic neighborhoods, then there have to be school effects. That is, how is it possible that homogeneous groups of students (i.e., in terms of race and socioeconomic class) in a lower socioeconomic community perform differently depending on the school that they attend? Student-centered explanations would suggest that the factors outside the schools that affect nonwhite and working-class students are the same in different schools within the same neighborhood. Thus, if students from the same racial and socioeconomic backgrounds attending different schools within the same community perform at significantly different rates, then something within the schools themselves must be affecting student performance.

Based on this logic, Edmonds and other effective school researchers (Austin & Garber, 1985; Brookover et al., 1979) examined schools that produced unusually positive academic results given what would be expected, based on the socioeconomic composition of the school and/or schools that are unusually effective in general. *The effective school literature*, as it is termed, suggests that there are characteristics of unusually effective schools that help to explain why their students achieve academically. These characteristics include the following (Stedman, 1987):

- A climate of high expectations for students by teachers and administrators.
- Strong and effective leadership by a principal or school head.
- Accountability processes for students and teachers.
- The monitoring of student learning.
- A high degree of instructional time on task, where teachers spend a great deal of their time teaching and students spend a great deal of their time learning.
- Flexibility for teachers and administrators to experiment and adapt to new situations and problems.

These phenomena are more likely to be found in effective schools than ineffective ones, independent of the demographic composition of the students in the school. Given the differences between students in schools in lower and higher socioeconomic neighborhoods, these findings may suggest that there are a higher number of schools with these characteristics in higher socioeconomic communities. Or, given the extra-school factors in these neighborhoods, it is easier for schools in higher socioeconomic communities to develop such characteristics within their schools. More importantly, these findings suggest that there are things that schools can do to positively affect student achievement in lower socioeconomic communities (Thernstrom & Thernstrom, 2003; The Education Trust, 2004a).

The effective school research suggests that there are school-centered processes that help to explain unequal educational achievement by different groups of students. It supports the later work of Coleman and his colleagues (Coleman, Hoffer, & Kilgore, 1982; Coleman & Hoffer, 1987) that argues that Catholic schools produce significantly better levels of academic achievement because of their more rigorous academic curriculum and higher academic expectations. Ironically, Coleman has thus moved full circle from his earlier work, which stated that students—not schools—were the most significant explanatory variable, to his recent work, which states that schools make a significant difference independent of the students who attend. Critics of Coleman's recent work (see Chapter 8), however, suggest that he has insufficiently controlled for student and parental effects and that such extra-school differences may be more important than the differences between public and Catholic schools. What these ongoing debates indicate is that school and student effects cannot be isolated and that the interaction between these factors must be addressed more completely. We will return to this point later in this chapter.

Although the effective school literature has attracted much support from policy makers and is often cited in the educational reform literature as the key to school improvement (Stedman, 1987), the road from research to implementation is not a clear one. The effective school researchers do not provide clear findings on implementation, nor do they provide answers to how effective schools are created. Additionally, some critics of the effective school movement argue that its definition of effective schools is based on narrow and traditional measures of academic achievement, such as standardized test scores, and that such a perspective defines educational success from a traditional back-to-basics perspective. Such a view may result in school reform that emphasizes success on standardized tests, and overlooks other nontraditional and progressive measures of school success, which may emphasize artistic, creative, and noncognitive goals as well (cf. Cuban, 1983; Dougherty & Hammack, 1990, p. 339; Stedman, 1985, 1987). In order to respond to these criticisms, effective school researchers are attempting to replicate their findings in numerous schools (New Jersey Assessment of Knowledge and Skills, 2011).

Between-School Differences: Curriculum and Pedagogic Practices

The effective school research points to how differences in what is often termed *school climates* affect academic performance. Much of this research looked at differences between schools in inner-city, lower socioeconomic neighborhoods in order to demonstrate that schools can make a difference in these communities. Although there are problems with the research, most researchers agree that its findings support the argument that schools do affect educational outcomes, at times, independent of extra-school factors.

Nonetheless, one is still faced with the task of explaining why a larger proportion of students who attend schools in higher socioeconomic communities achieve well in school. Is it because a larger proportion of schools in these communities have school climates conducive to positive academic achievement? This is a difficult question and the data are insufficient to support unequivocally such a claim. A number of theorists, however, argue that there are significant differences between the culture and climate of schools in lower socioeconomic and higher socioeconomic communities.

Bernstein (1990), examining the situation in England, suggested that schools in working-class neighborhoods are far more likely to have authoritarian and teacher-directed pedagogic practices, and to have a vocationally or social efficiency curriculum at the secondary level. Schools in middle-class communities are more likely to have less authoritarian and more student-centered pedagogic practices and to have a humanistic liberal arts college preparatory curriculum at the secondary level. Upper-class students are more likely to attend elite private (in England, they are called *public schools*) schools, with authoritarian pedagogic practices and a classical-humanistic college preparatory curriculum at the secondary level. Bernstein's theory is similar to Bowles and Gintis's view that the type of schooling corresponds to the social class of students in a particular school, with such differences a vehicle for socializing students from different social class backgrounds to their different places in society. Anyon's (1980) research on U.S. schools supports these findings.

Although Bernstein's work is theoretical and needs further empirical support, especially as it relates to U.S. education, there is a growing research literature that supports the existence of class-based school differences. Rist's (1970, 1973) work on urban schools, Fine's (1991) ethnography of urban school dropouts, MacLeod's (1995) description of urban schooling, Cookson and Persell's (1985) analysis of elite boarding schools, Powell, Farrar, and Cohen's (1985) descriptions of U.S. secondary schools, and Lightfoot's (1983) portraits of urban, suburban, and elite high schools all document important class-related differences in school climate, curriculum, and pedagogic practices. Moreover, journalistic portraits—including Freedman's (1990) description of a New York City high school, Kidder's (1989) discussion of a Massachusetts elementary school, and Sachar's (1991) portrait of a New York City middle school—further support the existence of these differences.

What this research does not explain is why these differences exist and precisely how they affect the different academic achievement of their students. Do schools reflect differences in student cultures that exist prior to entry into school, thus supporting student-centered explanations? Or do students respond to the different curricula, pedagogic practices, and expectations that exist in different types of schools? Finally, is there sufficient evidence to support the argument that differences in academic achievement are caused by the differences in curricula, pedagogic practices, and expectations in the different schools? These are important questions. Unfortunately, there is conflicting evidence concerning these overall conclusions. There is, however, reason to conclude that these school differences are part of the complex explanation of unequal educational achievement.

For example, a high school student at a "select 16" boarding school, such as Groton, St. Paul's, Hotchkiss, or Andover (for a complete list of the select 16, see Cookson & Persell, 1985), attends a school with a large campus in a bucolic country-like setting. His or her parents pay a hefty tuition (over $40,000 with room and board per year) to support small class size, extracurricular activities, the latest in technological and curricular innovations, and support services, including counseling, tutoring, and college advisement. A high school student in an upper middle-class suburb attends a school with many of these features, although he or she lives at home, not at school. His or her parents pay high taxes to support the level of funding necessary to provide these types of services. A high school student in a poor urban neighborhood attends a school that is often overcrowded, with large classes, a student/counselor ratio of sometimes 400 to 1, and without the latest in technology and curricula innovations.

In his book *Savage Inequalities* (1991), Jonathan Kozol portrayed these significant differences in per-student spending between suburban and urban schools. Cookson, Persell, and Catsambis (1992) documented the achievement differences between boarding schools, private day and parochial schools, and public schools. Although sociologists of education differ as to whether these achievement differences are caused by school differences, independent of student background factors, school differences must play a significant role.

The 17-year-old sitting on the ninth green on the Hotchkiss Golf Course, looking at the fall foliage on the rolling hills of Connecticut, sees a very different set of possibilities than the 17-year-old sitting in the schoolyard at Seward Park High School in New York City (the subject of Freedman's book *Small Victories*). Of course, these different life chances begin with their different class backgrounds, but their different school environments teach them to dream a different set of dreams. Research on the relationship between schooling and life expectations (Cicourel & Kitsuse, 1963; MacLeod, 1995; Ogbu, 1978; Rosenbaum, 1976) suggests that schooling can elevate or limit student aspirations about the future. It seems obvious that these two students receive very different sets of aspirations from their schooling—aspirations that more often than not translate into educational achievement, college choices, and eventual occupational destinations. Whether schooling is the causal factor is beside the point—that it is part of the process seems evident.

Within-School Differences: Curriculum and Ability Grouping

As we have stated, not only are there significant differences in educational achievement between schools but within schools, as well. The fact that different groups of students in the same schools perform very differently suggests that there may be school characteristics affecting these outcomes. As we argued in Chapter 7, ability grouping and curriculum grouping (often referred to as *tracking by ability* or *curriculum tracking*) is an important organizational component of U.S. schooling.

At the elementary school level, students are divided into reading groups and separate classes based on teacher recommendations, standardized test scores, and sometimes ascriptive characteristics such as race, class, or gender. For the most part, elementary students receive a similar curriculum in these different groups, but it may be taught at a different pace, or the teachers in the various groups may have different expectations for the different students. At the secondary school level, students are divided both by ability and curriculum, with different groups of students often receiving considerably different types of education within the same school.

There is considerable debate among educators and researchers about the necessity, effects, and efficacy of tracking. From a functionalist perspective, tracking is viewed as an important mechanism by which students are separated based on ability and to ensure that the "best and brightest" receive the type of education required to prepare them for society's most essential positions. For functionalists, the important thing is to ensure that track placement is fair and meritocratic—that is, based on ability and hard work rather than ascriptive variables. Conflict theorists, conversely, suggest that tracking is a mechanism for separating groups, often based on ascriptive characteristics, and that it is an important mechanism in reproducing inequalities.

Debates concerning the pedagogical necessity of ability and curriculum grouping abound. Many teachers and administrators argue that heterogeneous groups are far more difficult to teach and result in teaching to the middle. This results in losing those with lower abilities and boring those with higher abilities. Critics of tracking (Oakes, 1985; Sadovnik, 1991b) suggest that homogeneous grouping results in unequal education for different groups, with differences in academic outcomes often due to the differences in school climate, expectations, pedagogic practices, and curriculum between tracks.

Echoing this view, Albert Shanker (1991) stated that education in the United States assumes that students in the lower tracks are not capable of doing academic work and thus schools do not offer them an academically challenging curriculum. When these students do not perform well on examinations measuring their skills and knowledge, it confirms those expectations. The problem, Shanker suggested, is that students cannot learn what they have not been taught. Further, he pointed out that these students are capable of far more than teachers realize, and suggested that if teachers demanded and expected more, students would meet the raised expectations. Hallinan (1994b) argued that although tracking does produce inequalities based on curriculum differences, it need not do this. She suggested that tracks with equally demanding curriculum need not produce such negative results.

Much of the debate concerning tracking is emotional and ideological. Moreover, proponents of each view often lack sound empirical evidence to support their claims. It is important, then, to explore what the research states about ability and curriculum grouping by asking four important questions. First, is there evidence to support the claim that there are significant differences between tracks? Second, are there significant differences in educational attainment by students in different tracks? Third, are track placements based on discriminatory practices founded on ascriptive characteristics or are they founded on meritocratic selection mechanisms? Fourth, do the differences in the tracks explain the differences in academic attainment between tracks?

With respect to differences between tracks, many researchers (Braddock, 1990a, 1990b; Catsambis, 1994; Dougherty, 1996; Gamoran, 1987, 1993; Grant, 2011; Lucas, 1999; Oakes, 1985, 1990; Oakes, Gamoran, & Page, 1992; Sadovnik, 1991b; Tyson, 2011) stated that there are significant differences in the curricula and pedagogic practices of secondary school curriculum groups. Oakes (1985, 2005) suggested that the lower tracks are far more likely to have didactic, teacher-directed practices, with rote learning and fact-based evaluation. Higher tracks are more likely to have more dialectical, student-centered practices, with discussion and thinking-based evaluation. These differences hold even when the tracks are based on ability rather than curriculum (i.e., when students in different ability tracks learn the same material, it is usually taught in a very different manner in the lower tracks). When the tracking is based on different curricula, students in different curriculum groups receive essentially different educations within the same school.

With respect to the effects of tracking and track placement, tracking has a significant effect on educational attainment at both the elementary and secondary levels. Although the effects appear to be larger for elementary school ability grouping than for high school tracking, most researchers agree that tracking affects educational attainment and achievement, independent of student characteristics (Alexander & Cook, 1982; Catsambis, 1994; Dougherty, 1996; Oakes, 1985, 1990, 1994b). Additionally, track placement is associated with student race and social characteristics, with working-class and nonwhite students more likely to be assigned to lower tracks (Alexander & Cook, 1982; Dreeben & Gamoran, 1986; Hallinan, 1984; Oakes, Gamoran, & Page, 1992; Rosenbaum, 1980a, 1980b). There is insufficient evidence, however, to prove that track placement is based on discriminatory rather than meritocratic practices.

Although some researchers (Oakes, 1985, 2005) argue that the race and social class-based composition of tracks is evidence of discrimination, Hurn (1993, pp. 165–167) has contended that high school tracking placement, as well as its effects, is a far more complex process. He suggested that the evidence on track placement and outcomes is mixed, but that, on the whole, track placement is based more on previous ability and aspirations than on discriminatory practices. Although this may suggest that student characteristics prior to schooling or to high school placement are important factors, it also suggests that ability is an important part of high school track assignment. Hurn pointed out, however, that high school track placement may be dependent on elementary school processes, including ability grouping and teacher expectations, which may be far less meritocratic.

Research on the self-fulfilling prophecy of teacher expectations (Rist, 1970; Rosenthal & Jacobson, 1968) and of elementary school ability groups and reading groups (Eder, 1981; Felmlee & Eder, 1983; McDermott, 1977) point to the impact of teacher expectations and ability grouping on student aspirations and achievement at the elementary school level. Persell (1977), in her review of the teacher expectations literature, argued that teacher perceptions of students and their abilities have an impact on what is taught, how it is taught, and, ultimately, student performance. Although more research is needed to determine clearly the extent to which these different expectations are based on ascriptive rather than meritocratic factors, there is reason to believe that such processes are not entirely meritocratic (Rist, 1970).

Finally, research indicates that differences in tracks help to explain the variation in academic achievement of students in different tracks. Some researchers argue that discrepancies in the amount of instruction are responsible for these differences (Barr & Dreeben, 1983; Dreeben & Gamoran, 1986); others point to differences in the quality of instruction (McDermott, 1977; Oakes, 1985, 2005; Persell, 1977); still others point to both (Allensworth, Montgomery, & Lee, 2009, Riegle-Crumb & Grodsky, 2010; Lucas, 1999; Spade, Columba, & Vanfossen, 1997; Tyson, 2011). It seems clear that differences in the curriculum and pedagogic practices between tracks are partly responsible for the diverse academic achievement of students in different tracks. Given that more working-class and nonwhite students are placed in the lower tracks, it is evident that such school-related practices have a significant effect on their lower academic achievement. What is not entirely clear is the degree to which such placement is unfair and discriminatory or meritocratically based on ability or on characteristics such as ability and aspirations brought by students to the school. This brings you full circle to the question of student-centered versus school-centered explanations. As we have noted, neither one, by itself, is sufficient to explain unequal educational performance. What is needed is a more integrated and multidimensional approach.

Gender and Schooling

In October 1991, during the confirmation hearing of Supreme Court Justice nominee Clarence Thomas, Anita Hill, a law professor at the University of Oklahoma, charged that Judge Thomas sexually harassed her when he was her supervisor at the Department of Education and later at the EEOC (the Equal Employment Opportunity Commission). The charges and subsequent Senate

Judiciary Committee hearings on the allegations pointed to significant differences between how men and women see the world. When the all-male, 14-member committee originally voted to pass the nomination on to the Senate without investigating Professor Hill's charges, women throughout the country were outraged, charging that "men just don't get it" (meaning that they do not take sexual harassment seriously). This episode pointed to a much larger question: If men and women see the world differently, why does this occur? Feminist scholarship on gender differences, in general, and gender and schooling, in particular, has concentrated on this issue.

Although the feminist movement in the United States dates back at least to the mid-nineteenth century (cf. Leach, 1980), the second wave of feminism began in the 1960s. Influenced by the French feminist Simone de Beauvoir (1952) and reacting to the narrowly defined gender roles of the 1950s, feminists in the 1960s and 1970s—including Betty Friedan, Gloria Steinem, Ellen Willis, Germaine Greer, and Kate Millett—challenged the view that biology is destiny. Vivian Gornick (1987) in her poignant essay "The Next Great Moment in History Is Theirs," argued that differences between men and women are cultural, not biological, and that women deserve equality in the public and private spheres of life (the family and the workplace). Thus, the feminist movement challenged unequal treatment of women in all aspects of society and worked actively to change both attitudes and laws that limited the life chances of women.

Feminist scholarship on schooling has attempted to understand the ways in which the schools limit the educational and life chances of women. It has focused on achievement differences (Fennema, 1974; Sadker & Sadker, 1985), on women and school administration (Shakeshaft, 1986, 1987), on the history of coeducation (Tyack & Hansot, 1990), on the relationship between pedagogy and attitudes and knowledge (Belenky et al., 1986), and other related issues. A significant aspect of this literature concerns gender differences in how men and women see the world, their cultural causes, and the role of schools in perpetuating or eliminating them.

Carol Gilligan, a psychologist at Harvard's Graduate School of Education, has been one of the most influential feminist scholars working in the area of gender differences. In her book, *In a Different Voice* (1982), she criticized the view asserted by the psychologist Lawrence Kohlberg that there is a developmental hierarchy in moral decision-making. Kohlberg placed a justice orientation to moral reasoning (based on universal principles) on a higher plane than a caring orientation (based on interpersonal feelings). Gilligan argued that women are more likely to adopt a caring orientation, in part because they are socialized to do so, and that Kohlberg's hierarchical categories judged women unfairly. She continued that women do reason in a different voice and that this female voice as an important component of the human experience should not be devalued. Gilligan's work pointed to the differences and their relation to gender socialization and how society rewards men for "male" behavior and negatively affects women for "female" behavior.

Gilligan's work has been extremely controversial among feminists. Many scholars have adopted her concept of caring as a part of female psychology and argue that the schools devalue connectedness and caring in favor of male behaviors such as competition (Martin, 1987; Noddings, 1984). Many feminists argue that schools should revise their curricula and pedagogic practices to emphasize caring and connectedness (Belenky et al., 1986; Laird, 1989). Other feminists (Epstein, 1990) are troubled by the conservative implications of Gilligan's work, which they argue reinforces traditional gender differences by attributing behaviors as typically female and male. The argument that women are more caring and connected, and men more competitive and intellectual, may reproduce sexist stereotypes that historically justified the domestic roles of women. These feminists believe that traditional male and female characteristics are part of the full range of human possibilities, and that schools should socialize both boys and girls to be caring and connected.

Despite these differences, feminists agree that schooling often limits the educational opportunities and life chances of women in a number of ways. For example, boys and girls are socialized differently through a variety of school processes. First, curriculum materials portray men's and women's roles often in stereotypical and traditional ways (Hitchcock & Tompkins, 1987). Second, the traditional curriculum, according to Bennett and LeCompte (1990) "silences women" by omitting significant aspects of women's history and women's lives from discussion. As with other groups calling for multicultural curriculum, feminists call for a more gender-fair curriculum. Third, the hidden curriculum reinforces traditional gender roles and expectations through classroom organization, instructional practices, and classroom interactions (Bennett & LeCompte, 1990, pp. 234–237). For example, research demonstrates that males dominate classroom discussion (Brophy & Good, 1970; Martin, 1972) and receive more attention from teachers (LaFrance, 1985; Lippitt & Gold, 1959; Sikes, 1971), and that teachers are more likely to assist males with a task but to actually do the task for female students (Sadker & Sadker, 1985).

A fourth way that schooling often limits the educational opportunities and life chances of women is that the organization of schools reinforces gender roles and gender inequality. For example, the fact that women are far more likely to teach elementary grades and men secondary grades gives the message to children that women teach children and men teach ideas. The fact that men are far more likely to be administrators, despite recent advances in this area, reinforces the view that men hold positions of authority. Although some research on single-sex and coeducation indicates that females do better in single-sex schools (Datnow & Hubbard, 2002; Shakeshaft, 1987; Tyack & Hansot, 1990) and are given more leadership opportunities in women's colleges (Miller-Bernal, 1993, 2000; Miller-Bernal and Poulson, 2006), recent research does not support the conclusion that females do better in single-sex schools (American Association of University Women, 1998; Datnow & Hubbard, 2002; Shmurak, 1998), with the exception of females from lower socioeconomic backgrounds (Riordan, 1994, 1998). Nonetheless, legal scholar Rosemary Salomone (2003) argues that although "the research as a whole does not refute or support single-sex schooling . . . voluntary single-sex schooling is a legally acceptable option, especially for disadvantaged children" (*Publishers Weekly*, 2003). These unequal processes help to explain both gender differences in attitudes and academic achievement.

Given the role that schools play in reproducing gender inequalities, feminists argue that school organization, curriculum, and pedagogic practices need to be changed to address more adequately the needs of females. For example, Gilligan's study of the Emma Willard School (Gilligan et al., 1990), a private girls school in Troy, New York, concludes that by adolescence, girls receive an education that devalues their inner voice and limits their opportunities. That this occurs in a single-sex school devoted to the education of females suggests that females face more significant problems of educational opportunity in coeducational institutions.

Interestingly, research in Great Britain (Arnot, 2002, 2012; Arnot, David, & Weiner, 1999; Arnot & Dillabough, 2000) and the United States (American Association of University Women, 1998; Riordan, 1999) indicates that the gender gap in achievement has diminished greatly, if not disappeared. In both countries, females outperform males in almost all academic areas (with the exception of secondary chemistry and physics) and females have higher high school graduation rates and higher levels of college attendance and graduation, and boys are significantly overrepresented in special education classes. In both countries, educational policy makers have begun to analyze the "boy problem" in order to understand the reasons that boys have begun to lag behind girls.

Do Schools Reproduce Inequality?

The research on educational inequality, as you have read, is quite complex and perplexing. There is a significant difference of opinion as to the role of the school in affecting student performance, with school-centered explanations stressing the role of schools and student-centered explanations stressing the importance of what students bring to school. Additionally, the research is conflicting concerning the central hypotheses of functionalism and conflict theory. Some researchers believe that the schools unfairly perpetuate social inequalities and thus confirm conflict theorists' belief that schools advantage the dominant groups in society. Other researchers believe that there is insufficient evidence to support much of conflict theory, at least in regard to school processes, and that some of the evidence supports the functionalist view that school selection processes are meritocratic (Hurn, 1993).

How does one reconcile these apparent contradictions? First, we suggest that school-centered and student-centered explanations are not diametrically opposed, but rather need to be incorporated into a multidimensional theory of education and inequality. Second, we suggest that although there is evidence to support some of the functionalists' hypotheses, on the whole, there is more evidence to support conflict theorists' claim that schools help to reproduce inequality. Schools are only part of this process, and must be seen within the context of a larger set of institutional forces affecting social stratification.

Persell's (1977) model for understanding education and inequality, presented in Chapter 4, outlines the relationship between four levels of sociological analysis: the societal level, the institutional level, the interactional level, and the intrapsychic level. The social stratification system, at the societal level, produces structures of domination and societal level ideologies. The structures of domination affect the institutions within a society, including the family, the schools, the churches and synagogues, the media, and others. The important point is that different social groups, based on their position in the societal hierarchy, have different institutional experiences, and are affected in different ways by the social structure. Thus, families from lower socioeconomic backgrounds face different problems and have different life chances than families from higher socioeconomic backgrounds. Much of the student-centered literature focuses on these processes. Children from different classes also attend different types of schools, which often vary in terms of school climate, quality, and outcomes. Much of the school-centered literature focuses on these processes.

The relationships between families and schools at the institutional level, and what goes on within schools at the interactional levels, are not isolated from each other but are dialectically intertwined. Clearly, students from lower socioeconomic backgrounds face significantly different problems in their communities due to factors such as racism, poverty, and other societal and institutional processes. To argue whether they are different or deficient is beside the point; that they negatively impact on children is the point. Children from lower socioeconomic backgrounds thus have significantly lower life chances before they enter schools. Once they enter, they often attend schools that are inferior and have significantly less funding, and encounter school processes that limit their educational chances. That the evidence does not overwhelmingly support the view that school funding and climate are independently responsible for their lower achievement does not eliminate these as part of the problem. It only means that there are other nonschool variables that also affect educational performance. It is clear that at the intrapsychic level, students from different social class backgrounds leave school with different educational outcomes, both cognitive (in terms of learning) and noncognitive (in terms of values and self-esteem). Research on within- and between-school differences demonstrates how school processes may affect such outcomes.

Student-centered theories suggest that these unequal outcomes are the result of differences at the societal and institutional levels, but that families and communities are more important than schools. School-centered theories stress the importance of schooling in reproducing inequality. Persell's (1977) model suggests that society, communities, families, and schools cannot be separated from each other. Societal forces unequally affect families and schools. The result is a complex process through which students from lower socioeconomic backgrounds have lower levels of educational attainment and achievement.

Research that attempts to connect the four levels of sociological analysis is needed to more clearly understand the role of schooling in the reproduction of inequality. Studies by Annette Lareau (1989, 2003, 2011) on social class differences in the relationship between family and school documents the importance of both family and schools. She also demonstrates how the differences in schooling for working-class and middle-class students are an important factor in unequal outcomes. Using Bourdieu's concept of cultural capital (the cultural symbols and resources a group has), Lareau demonstrated that those with cultural capital have significant advantages in the schooling process. More ethnographic research of this type—which explores the processes within schools, families, and communities, and their relationship to educational outcomes—is needed.

Do schools reproduce inequality? Based on the evidence reviewed in this chapter, our conclusion is they do not, solely by themselves. Schools are part of a larger complex process in which social inequalities are transmitted across generations. Although there is evidence of social mobility for individuals through schooling and of a degree of meritocracy within schools, there is insufficient evidence to support the functionalist argument that schools are a means for the meritocratic selection of individuals based on talent and hard work. Rather, there is more powerful evidence to support the conflict view that schools are part of the process through which dominant groups maintain their advantages.

The first of the articles below, "It's Not 'a Black Thing': Understanding the Burden of Acting White and Other Dilemmas of High Achievement", written by sociologists Karolyn Tyson, William Darity, and Domini Castellino, analyzes the effects of tracking on African-American students in integrated schools in the context of the burden of acting white thesis.

The second article, "Gender Inequalities in Education," written by sociologists Claudia Buchmann, Thomas A. DiPrete, and Anne McDaniel, provides an overview of the social science evidence on gender inequalities in education.

The third article, "From Social Ties to Social Capital: Class Differences in the Relations Between Schools and Parent Networks," written by sociologists Erin McNamara Horvat, Elliot B. Weininger, and Annette Lareau, analyzes the relationship between family and school. They argue that middle-class parents, who possess more social capital than working-class parents, have distinct advantages in advancing their children's educational achievement. The authors explore how each group of families interacts with their children's schools, and conclude that family differences between working-class and middle-class parents are part of the reason why middle-class children are more successful in school.

The fourth article, "A Black Student's Reflection on Public and Private Schools," written by Imani Perry, provides a poignant analysis of an African-American student's struggle with issues of race and schooling. Written when she was a high school student, Perry discusses the differences between her education at both public and private schools, and the miseducation of African-Americans in U.S. society. She went on to complete a J.D. and Ph.D., and is currently a Professor of African-American Studies at Princeton University.

It's Not "a Black Thing"

Understanding the Burden of Acting White and Other Dilemmas of High Achievement

Karolyn Tyson, William Darity, Jr., and Domini R. Castellino

Almost 20 years have passed since Fordham and Ogbu (1986) published the article, Black Students' School Success: Coping with the "Burden of Acting White." Yet it remains among the most influential publications addressing the academic underachievement of black students and the black–white achievement gap. Social scientists have produced little empirical evidence to substantiate the claim that an "oppositional peer culture" or a "burden of acting white" is pervasive in the black community, or that either explains the underachievement of black students or some part of the black-white achievement gap. Still, there is strong public belief in these assertions. Indeed, as we found in this study, the acting white theory significantly influences how schools address problems related to black underachievement, which, in turn, helps to determine whether these solutions ultimately can be effective. Thus, further assessment of this hypothesis is a critical step toward understanding and addressing the problem of the black–white achievement gap.

In this article, we review the burden of acting white hypothesis, describe the current debate, and use interview data from eight secondary schools in North Carolina to assess the hypothesis. We find that a burden of acting white exists for some black students, but that it is not prevalent among the group. None of the black middle-school informants reported discussions or expressed any concern about acting white related to academic behavior or performance, and only a small minority of the older informants did so. Moreover, high-achieving black students across the sample schools were not deterred from taking advanced courses or striving to do well because they feared accusations of acting white or other teasing. Equally interesting, in some schools, high achieving white students

experienced a similar but more pervasive "burden" of high achievement. That is, both black and white high-achieving students sometimes encounter forms of hostility from lower-achieving peers.

This study contributes to the current debate on the burden of acting white hypothesis in several important ways. First, few qualitative studies addressing this hypothesis have focused on more than one or two schools. We gathered qualitative data from students and staff at eight secondary schools. The multisite design permitted greater attention to the potential influence of contextual aspects of schools. Second, the in-depth nature of the interviews allowed us to probe more deeply and specifically into issues related to a burden of acting white, including particular academic behaviors and decisions, factors that large-scale surveys generally do not capture. In particular, our focus on the decisions students make with regard to the academic level of the courses they take (e.g., electing honors versus regular classes) is unique. Finally, we attempted to distinguish a burden of acting white from other more generic dilemmas of high achievement. We argue that the burden of acting white cannot be attributed specifically to black culture. Rather, it appears to develop in some schools under certain conditions that seem to contribute to animosity between high- and low-achieving students within or between racial and socioeconomic groups. This may help to explain the mixed research findings regarding the existence of an oppositional peer culture or a burden of acting white among black students. For example, studies by Ainsworth-Damell and Downey (1998), Downey and Ainsworth-Damell (2002), Ferguson (2001), and Kao, Tienda, and Schneider (1996) have discounted the oppositional culture hypothesis. Similarly,

Cook and Ludwig (1998) found no support for the related burden of acting white hypothesis. Conversely, Farkas, Lleras, and Maczuga (2002) and Steinberg, Dornbusch, and Brown (1992) claimed to find evidence of an oppositional culture among black students. Yet researchers generally have not paid attention to the process by which all students absorb and interpret various messages from their school environments. In particular, experiencing and witnessing inequality within schools may foster the type of animosity evidenced in the oppositional attitudes of teenagers toward school.

The "Burden of Acting White" Hypothesis

Among black Americans, the term "acting white" is used in reference to blacks who use language or ways of speaking; display attitudes, behaviors, or preferences; or engage in activities considered to be white cultural norms (Bergin and Cooks 2002; McArdle and Young 1970; Neal-Barnett 2001; Perry 2002; Tatum 1997). Although understandings of what comprises acting white may vary (by region, social class, or age, for example), some understandings remain remarkably constant (e.g., listening to heavy metal music is almost always considered a "white" preference). The term also has come to be used with respect to indicators of academic performance and success (Bergin and Cooks 2002; Neal-Barnett 2001). For example, using focus groups to understand how black teenagers define "acting white," Neal-Barnett (2001:82) reported that the list of items the students identified included "being in honors or advance placement classes," in addition to "speaking Standard English, dressing in clothes from the Gap or Abercrombie and Fitch rather than Tommy Hilfiger and FUBU, [and] wearing shorts in the winter."

Fordham and Ogbu (1986), drawing on Fordham's qualitative study of one predominantly black urban high school and the narratives of eight academically capable black students, posited that acting white was part of a larger oppositional peer culture constructed by black Americans in response to their history

of enslavement, and the discrimination and persistent inequality they face (including discriminatory treatment in the labor market). The oppositional identity was said to be "part of a cultural orientation toward schooling which exists within the minority community" (p. 183). Academic achievement is not valued in the community because it is perceived as conforming to standard norms of success among white Americans (see Spencer et al. 2003 for a counterargument). Moreover, it does not pay off for blacks as it does for others. Consequently, black students striving for academic success have their cultural authenticity as blacks called into question and are accused of acting white.

Fordham and Ogbu (1986) claimed that the choice between representing an authentic "black" self and striving for academic success creates a "burden of acting white" and contributes to the relatively low academic performance of black students (for examples of similar assertions, see Herbert 2003; McWhorter 2000; Wasonga and Christman 2003; Weissert 1999). However, the findings did not show that any informant in the original study related accusations of "acting white" directly to academic achievement, or ever used the term.

Empirical Assessments of the Hypothesis

Only within the past 10 years have the main propositions of the oppositional culture thesis, including "the burden of acting white," been examined empirically. Two high-profile studies (Ainsworth-Damell and Downey 1998; Cook and Ludwig 1998), both using data from the National Educational Longitudinal Study (NELS), found little evidence of either an oppositional culture or a burden of acting white among black adolescents. For example, Ainsworth-Darnell and Downey's (1998) analysis of NELS data showed that blacks actually had more pro-school attitudes than whites, and Cook and Ludwig (1998) reported finding little difference between black and white adolescents in the degree to which they valued academic achievement. The results of the latter study also suggested that there were more social benefits than costs to high academic achievement for black students.

Another more recent analysis of survey data from schools in Shaker Heights, Ohio, also found little evidence of a black adolescent peer culture oppositional to achievement (Ferguson 2001). Ferguson found that black and white students with similar family background characteristics were not very different in terms of their satisfaction with school, interest in their studies, or opposition to achievement (2001:387). Qualitative studies (2003; Carter forthcoming; Tyson 2002), too, have failed to substantiate the acting white and oppositional culture hypotheses.[1] Yet, there is empirical evidence consistent with some of Fordham and Ogbu's (1986) claims (Bergin and Cooks 2002; Ford and Harris 1996; Mickelson and Velasco forthcoming; Steinberg et al. 1992). Neal Barnett's (2001) focus groups with black adolescents showed that high-achieving black students often encounter charges of acting white, and some respond in ways that undermine their academic performance. In Horvat and Lewis' (2003) study of two urban high schools, one racially diverse and one predominantly black, two of eight high-achieving participants reported being accused of acting white. Only in one instance, however, was the charge clearly in response to academic behaviors, as opposed to speech or other behaviors. In that case, the student attended the racially diverse school (43 percent white, 16 percent black, and 41 percent other).

In a survey of black fifth- and sixth-grade students at an all-black, low-income school, Ford and Harris (1996) found that half of the sample knew students who were teased for academic achievement, 26 percent reported being rejected when they made good grades, and 16 percent reported not having as many friends when they achieved. However, because reference to acting white was not included in the survey and the sample was all black, it is not clear whether these peer-related achievement problems were peculiar to black students. On the surface, the reported behaviors appeared to be indistinguishable from the general culture of mediocrity that "shuns academic excellence," which a number of studies have reported among students of all ethnicities

(Coleman 1961; Cookson and Persell 1985; Steinberg 1996). The latter explanation would be consistent with the reports of Cook and Ludwig (1998), Ainsworth-Darnell and Downey (1998), and Ferguson (2001), all of whom found black and white students sharing similar attitudes toward school.

Fordham and Ogbu (1986) used quotes from eight students to describe how a burden of acting white undermines blacks' academic performance. Their informants said they attempted to downplay or camouflage their ability using such strategies as being the class clown, being involved in athletics, or doing just enough to get by. The participants in Horvat and Lewis' (2003) study also attempted to camouflage and downplay their achievements in the presence of lower-achieving peers. However, students in virtually all racial and ethnic groups confront similar dilemmas with respect to high academic achievement, and they also tend to use similar strategies (Cookson and Persell 1985; Kinney 1993; Steinberg 1996). As Coleman (1961) showed long ago, the problem most high schools face is that learning and achievement are not what matter most to adolescents. Popularity and looking good are the top concerns, and doing well in school does not do much for popularity. Dilemmas of high achievement are neither new nor unique to African Americans, yet many researchers have not carefully separated the effects of being a teenager from those of race, gender, and class.

The experience of being ridiculed because of high achievement is not identical in nature for all groups. As described earlier, some issues are peculiar to black students. However, to claim that a distinctive burden of high achievement exists for black students, we must be able to distinguish between the typical culture of mediocrity found among students from all racial and ethnic groups i.e., general oppositionality) and a peer culture among blacks that specifically racializes and devalues achievement and achievement-related behaviors. This important distinction has been missed in other studies (Ford and Harris 1996; Fordham and Ogbu 1986; Horvat and Lewis 2003).

Finally, in some cases, findings regarding the link between black achievement and acting white or an oppositional culture may reflect methodological problems. Farkas et al. (2002) reported that "very good" black females in high minority schools were more likely to be put down by peers than were other students. The authors interpreted this as evidence of an oppositional peer culture among black students. Downey and Ainsworth-Darnell (2002), however, identified methodological flaws in the study and argued that the data of Farkas et al. (2002) show an oppositional peer culture among about 4 percent of blacks in the sample, a figure too small to explain the black–white achievement gap. Again, we argue that all dilemmas of high achievement are not properly defined as a burden of acting white.

Differences in methodological approaches are important, but they do not fully explain the conflicting results reported in the literature. Key questions remain. Do high-achieving black students experience a burden of high achievement distinct from that experienced by other adolescents? Are black students concerned about excelling academically because of a belief that academic striving and high achievement is antithetical to black cultural authenticity, or that it may be perceived as such by others and therefore negatively sanctioned?

We provide answers by drawing on data from a larger study investigating North Carolina public schools. Specifically, we evaluate the evidence for a burden of acting white in light of the following premises. To claim a burden of acting white, two primary conditions must be present: ridicule or criticism directed toward black students must be racialized *and* it must be specifically connected to academic behaviors (rather than behaviors such as dress or speech), decisions, or performance. However, even if those two conditions are met, the burden of acting white cannot be implicated in the black–white achievement gap unless such peer criticisms are demonstrably part of the local school culture (i.e., widespread) and shown to affect black students' academic behaviors (e.g., withholding of effort) or decisions (e.g., electing not to take high-ability courses). Similarly, the burden of acting white cannot be implicated in the black–white achievement gap if the criticisms directed toward high-achieving black students are no more significant than those directed toward high-achieving students in general.

Data and Methods

In 2000–2001, we undertook a study for the North Carolina Department of Public Instruction (NCDPI) examining the underrepresentation of minority students in rigorous courses (advance placement [AP] and honors) and programs (academically and intellectually gifted [AIG] and academically gifted [AG]) in public schools throughout the state.[2] The NCDPI study provided an opportunity to address the claims advanced by the burden of acting white hypothesis. However, these data were not collected exclusively or specifically for that purpose.

Sampling Schools

We used data collected annually by the NCDPI from all public schools to assess the extent of minority underrepresentation in rigorous courses and programs statewide. For each school, we developed a Disparity Index to calculate the ratio of the percentage of minority students in advanced courses and programs relative to the percentage of minority students enrolled in the school. We then measured underrepresentation of minority students in the AP and honors courses that most North Carolina high schools offer. Next, in cooperation with the NCDPI staff, we designed a survey to assess the programs and courses available at each school, the criteria for enrollment, and the processes for identification. Elementary/middle school surveys gathered current (2000–2001) data on gifted programs and enrollment by race and gender. High school surveys gathered data on advanced curricular offerings, but not enrollment.[3] The surveys were completed by principals, assistant principals, or school counselors.

For a more detailed analysis, we selected a subsample of 11 schools from the total sample of schools returning surveys and interviewed students, teachers, counselors, and principals at these schools. Our goal in the design of the original study was not to generate a representative sample of schools. We deliberately included some schools that over- and underrepresented minority students in advanced courses and programs to learn more about the factors that might affect minority access to and participation in more challenging curricula. We also sought some diversity in the subsample in terms of school socioeconomic status, racial composition, and urbanicity.[4] Because of our particular interest in the high school placement process, in which students presumably have a choice in the courses they take, we selected a larger number of high schools than middle schools. Finally, in the current analysis, we excluded the three elementary schools because we found that students at that level were dealing with slightly different issues. For example, as others have noted (Spencer 1984; Tyson 2002), race was not a salient category for the grade school children we interviewed. Table 9.2 presents descriptive information for each of the eight schools we discuss. The generalizability of our findings is limited by the small number of schools. The shortage of suburban schools in the sample prevented a more thorough analysis of the influence exerted by locale effects.

The Schools and Advanced Curricula Offerings

For this analysis,[5] we focus on the presence of black students, rather than all minorities, in rigorous courses and programs. As shown in Table 9.3, black students were underrepresented in the gifted program at one middle school (Jackson) and well represented at the other middle school (Kilbom).[6] Both schools also offered accelerated classes in math (pre-algebra in seventh grade and algebra in eighth grade) and language arts, open to any qualified student. Kilborn Middle School also offered AP courses, for which students received high school credit.

Across the high schools, black students were underrepresented in all but 2 of 19 AP courses

Table 9.2 Selected Characteristics of Schools, 1999–2000

	Middle schools		High schools					
	Jackson	Kilborn	Avery	Banaker	Clearview	Dalton	East	Franklin
Student race								
Black %	50	10	13	88	60	39	27	54
White %	49	87	85	8	38	60	71	30
Other %	2	2	2	4	2	2	2	16
Principal[a]	WM	WM	WM	BM	BM	WM	WM	WF
Lunch %[b]	37	48	8	12	38	28	17	43
School size	798	659	987	1,038	1,139	1,725	2,015	1,443
White income, $	56,226	39,152	43,204	66,940	43,489	48,648	55,602	43,531
Black income, $	27,203	26,483	32,057	39,287	26,960	27,362	28,266	28,993
Locale	Suburb	Rural	Rural	Urban	Rural	Rural	Urban	Urban

Notes: Percentages do not total 100 due to rounding. Data for 2000–2001 are similar in most cases and identical in others (e.g., middle school figures are identical for both years). White and black incomes are of those living in school county. WM = white male; BM = black male; WF = white female.

a Race and gender of school principal.

b Percent of lunches that are free or reduced priced.

and 1 of 13 honors courses under consideration (Table 9.3), although in a few cases, the ratio approached parity. Dalton High School showed the most severe underrepresentation of black students in both AP and honors courses. A general pattern of underrepresentation state-wide limited our ability to select a more varied subsample of schools. However, one school (Banaker High School) showed a black majority in each of the courses studied. Most schools offered an average of 6 AP courses per year, but Avery High School offered just 3 and Banaker offered 10. Banaker also offered an International Baccalaureate (IB) program that provides in prep classes, which are less exclusive than honors or AP courses.[7]

Sampling Informants

Although we were required to work with school officials to identify students, the characteristics of our sample mirrored the student population of the schools as a whole, with only minor exceptions. Specifically, the achievement, and in two cases, the grade level, mix at the schools was more limited than in the student population. For example, all the student participants at Kilborn Middle School were 8th graders, and 12 of the 14 participants at Franklin High School were 11th graders. Our informants also tended to be higher-achieving students, particularly the white students (Table 9.4).

Few of the 36 white secondary school informants reported earning grades lower than C. Only one earned grades below D, and a larger proportion of whites reported that they were academically gifted.[8] The black informant group was more diverse, with a mix of high-achieving and average students. Overall, there were few low-achieving students in the group. This is not a limitation because the theory we are assessing was developed with reference to the experiences of academically capable students, half (4) of whom were high achievers. Furthermore, we had 40 black participants attending eight different schools, whereas Fordham and Ogbu (1986) studied the experiences of eight black students attending one school.

Interviews

A team of three or four black female interviewers spent one day at each school conducting interviews. We interviewed a total of 85 secondary school students (Table 9.4): 40 black, 36 white, and 9 other students of color (this

Table 9.3 Disparity in Percent of Black Student Enrollment in High Ability Courses and Programs 1999–2000

	Middle schools		High schools					
Percent black	Jackson	Kilborn	Avery	Banaker	Clearview	Dalton	East	Franklin
Student body	50	10	13	88	60	39	27	54
Academically gifted	9	11	NA	NA	NA	NA	NA	NA
AP Biology	NA	NA	25	64	12	0	17	NA
AP English	NA	NA	9	75	0	7	12	46
AP Calculus	NA	NA	NA	65	17	0	40	50
AP History	NA	NA	5	84	NA	9	10	40
Honors Biology	NA	NA	NA	NA	NA	NA	23	NA
Honors English	NA	NA	3	83	27	6	12	46
Honors History	NA	NA	0	89	30	12	11	42

Notes: The percent black in each school remains the same in 2000–2001 and in most cases the pattern of results is not significantly different. Data for 2000–2001 are available from first author upon request. AP = advanced placement; NA = not applicable or not offered.

Table 9.4 Selected Characteristics of Informants by Race and Gender

Black	White	Hispanic	Native	American	Asian	Female	Total
Students[a]	40	36	3	1	5	52 (61%)	85
MS	9	12	1	0	2	14 (58%)	24
HS	31	24	2	1	3	38 (62%)	61
Previous gifted identification	22	25	1	1	1	35 (70%)	so
Ever taken AP (HS only)	15	13	1	0	2	22 (71%)	31
Ever taken Honors (HS only)[b]	11	8	0	0	0	11 (58%)	19
Mother's education[c]							
Less than HS		1	0	0	0		
HS	11	11	0	0	3		
Some college	4	2	0	0	0		
Technical/vocational	3	1	0	0	0		
AA degree	6	3	0	0	0		
BA/BS degree	13	13	2	1	1		
Advanced degree	1	3	0	0	0		
School personnel	20	45	0	2	0	44 (66%)	67
Teachers	10	30	0		0	28 (68%)	41
Counselors	7	6	0		0	13 (93%)	14
Administrators	3	9	0	0	0	3 (25%)	12

Note: Data are shown as number (n) with exception indicated. MS = middle school; HS = high school; AP = advanced placement.

a Data are based on school's identification of a mix of white and minority students enrolled in different courses.
b This count does not include students who have ever taken AP.
c Information on mother's education is more complete than that on father's education.

report focuses on the black and white students only). The duration of the interviews was 45 to 75 minutes. Eight students requested not to be tape-recorded. The remaining interviews were taped and transcribed.

The interviews were semistructured. We asked students a standard set of questions addressing their grades; which courses they were taking; how they made these choices; their attitudes toward school, learning, achievement, peers, and teachers; and other related aspects of the school experience. We posed questions to students regarding their own, their friends', and their peers' reactions to high- and low-achieving students and placement in rigorous courses and programs, issues at the center of the acting white phenomenon. Because the NCDPI study did not contain individual-level socioeconomic status data, we also collected information from students on parent education and employment (Appendix Tables AI and A2 provide this data for each informant quoted).[9]

School staff self-selected into the study on the basis of their availability the day of our visit. At each school, we interviewed principals, counselors, and teachers. At the eight secondary schools, 67 adults were interviewed (Table 9.4) about the selection of courses and programs offered by the school, student placement and course selection processes, student attitudes toward particular courses and achievement, perceptions of and expectations for students, and efforts to increase the participation of minority and low-income students in rigorous courses and programs.

Data Analysis

We used two methods of textual analysis: manual and computer-based (ATLAS) approaches. Two research assistants and one of the authors read the transcripts and coded interviews for factors such as perceptions of students in particular courses and programs, self-perceptions, friends' encouragement and support for academic endeavors, friend and peer response to achievement, and self-reported reasons why students took particular classes. Coders individually summarized each interview in terms of these factors and highlighted the corresponding dialogue. They summarized the interviews by race and school and included quotes that best illustrated each interpretative point. The three coders agreed on almost all interpretations and generally chose the same quotes to illustrate particular points. We then identified the dominant patterns across the interviews.

The qualitative software program ATLAS helped us uncover the process by which a burden of acting white emerges by capturing the achievement and related social experiences of students, their understanding of those experiences, and the context in which they occurred. The analysis focuses on students' own accounts and interpretations of their behavior, experiences, and decisions. For an alternative viewpoint, we also include excerpts from our interviews with school staff.

Results

We begin by addressing the achievement orientation of black students as assessed through their course selection decisions.[10] Then we address the nature of black adolescents' peer culture with regard to academic striving and achievement, assessed through the experiences of high achievers. Finally, we address similarities and differences between black and white adolescent peer cultures related to achievement.

Black Adolescent Achievement Orientation

Contrary to the notion that black students do not value academic achievement, we found an expressed desire to do well academically among all informants. In explaining their course choices, students' responses overwhelmingly centered on how they thought they would fare in the class, including whether they thought they were academically prepared, how willing they were to take on the anticipated amount or level of work, and whether they were likely to earn a good grade. The following statement highlights this trend:

> As far as the honors class, don't take it unless you absolutely have to. *[laughs]* I wouldn't advise that. It's not it will bring your grade point average down, just taking it will bring anybody's grade point average down. [Whitney, black female senior at Avery High School]

Many black students opted out of advanced classes, but none reported doing so because of concerns about negative peer reactions to achievement, even when they encountered such reactions.

Each middle school offered a gifted program and accelerated classes for qualified students. We asked students whether they participated in these courses and programs and whether they had a desire to do so. Shandra, a black female seventh grade student at Jackson Middle School, gave the following response when asked if she wanted to be in the gifted program, which is one of the most visible, and as far as students are concerned, unequivocal signs of superior ability: "Well, not really, because I'm lazy and you have to do more projects and stuff, but besides the projects, yes." Although Shandra had not been invited to participate, she was not opposed to being in the gifted program, so long as it did not entail more work for her. Shandra reported earning As and Bs, and was enrolled in the seventh grade pre-algebra class, so there was no evidence that she was averse to academic success. Another black student at Jackson Middle School, Les, reported dropping out of the gifted program "because, like, some of the things, I couldn't get it." Consequently, Les decided to "start back on general–on the basics." He also opted to take general math instead of pre-algebra. Les's grades (which included Cs and an F) were not as good as those earned by most of the other black informants. His decision to avoid the advanced classes appears to have been motivated more by his doubts about his ability to master the course materials than by an unwillingness to work hard.

Marc, another seventh-grade black male at Jackson Middle School, pushed for an opportunity to participate in the gifted program:

Interviewer: So who recommended you in sixth grade to take the test again?

Marc: Nobody. It was my choice . . . I went, um, to ask them to take the test again. 'Cause I figured if nobody asked me, then I would never be in AG, so, I decided to take the test over again. I decided that, I guess if I didn't take the test in sixth grade then I wouldn't have another chance to take it again.

Marc said he took the IQ and achievement tests to hold himself "to a higher standard." At the same time, however, he elected not to take pre-algebra because, as he put it, "I have trouble with the work I have now." Opting into the gifted program but out of other advanced courses suggests that Marc may have been interested mainly in the gifted label. If holding himself to a higher standard had been his first priority, it seems likely he would have accepted the challenge of taking pre-algebra. Yet, his seeking the opportunity to participate in the gifted program indicates that, like the other black informants, Marc was comfortable striving for academic success and being perceived as smart.

The narratives of the black high school students, though similar to those of their younger counterparts, were more often tied to concerns about the future, including getting into a "good college" and getting a "good job." Thus, although the desire to do well was clear, what that meant varied for individuals. For some black adolescents, doing well included taking higher-level courses to improve college options, grade point averages, or both:

James: Almost every, every class that was honors that I could take, I took. [black male senior at Clearview High School]

Interviewer: And how did that come to be?

James: Well it started out with I just wanted to achieve, wanted to excel. I want to go to college. I wanted to go to Chapel Hill [University of North Carolina], so I knew that I had to achieve, so I decided, okay, I will start taking honors classes and they will help me out.

Interviewer: When your mom and dad were helping you pick out classes and you decided to do this IB program, did you have any reason to take the classes?

Tyler: I wanted to stay ahead academically, you know, having a, have an edge on the competition. You know, I wanted to make sure I would be prepared for college. [black male junior at Banaker High School]

Interviewer: Okay, and in, now that you've been in high school, why did you choose to take the honors and AP classes?

Tamela: Well I'm, I mean, I like challenges. You know what I'm sayin'? I don't like to take just somethin' that I could get by on, or whatever. And I also wanted to have some honors and AP courses under my belt depending on which college I'm gonna apply to. [black female junior at Dalton High School]

These comments are at odds with theories positing that black students learn ambivalence toward academic achievement in their communities (Fordham and Ogbu 1986).[11] Concerns of black students about getting into the college of their choice and doing well once there are not consistent with a fear of academic striving.

For other black students, particularly the lower-achieving informants, doing well did not require taking advanced courses. The goal was to get good grades, regardless of the class level.

Interviewer: Why have you chosen the ones [classes] that you have?

Paul: They're easier . . . *[laughs]* [black male junior at Avery High School]

Interviewer: Do you like being in those college prep classes?

Paul: Yes ma'am.

Interviewer: Why? What do you like about it?

Paul: Everything. I mean—I mean I can do honors, but I don't know if I could be working that hard. I'd probably slack off. So I just take regular college prep.

Interviewer: Now where do the black kids fit into these groups [of students who take honors or regular classes-athletes, those considered popular or smart, or those who dress awkward], into these groups that you just described? Are they a group on their own; are they mostly what group?

Jessica: I mean, they could fit in either [honors or regular classes] group. I don't know, but I think they're more likely, say [in] regular classes. [black female senior at Clearview High School]

Interviewer: How come?

Jessica: I don't know. Maybe they feel they can't do it or something. The people that I'm around, that's the way they feel. They wouldn't be able to make the grade in the class to pass.

Black adolescents appeared to be more afraid of failure than of success. Average and lower-achieving students also had a desire to do well in school, and for some, avoiding advanced classes was one strategy to ensure that they would. A concern with poor academic performance is the opposite of what might be expected in a peer culture that demeans academic achievement. Indeed, as Fordham and Ogbu (1986:196) noted, doing poorly is one way for students to "minimize the stress" of being perceived as a high achiever. Yet our informants and the peers they described were more concerned about low than high achievement. No interviewee said or implied that reluctance to enroll in advanced courses on their part was connected to an oppositional peer culture. Rather, reluctance was connected to students' self-perceptions of ability.

Black Adolescent Peer Culture and High Achievement

None of the black informants at Avery, Franklin, Banaker, East, or Clearview high schools reported problems with black peers related to high achievement. Some welcomed public recognition of their achievement, and even sought it, as did the students Mickelson and

Velasco (forthcoming) studied. At these schools, black students reported receiving support for academic accomplishments and striving, especially among friends, just as the black females did in the study of Horvat and Lewis (2003). Our black informants at Clearview High School, all of whom were enrolled in advanced courses, insisted that excelling academically was not a problem and said that they did not feel any pressure to underachieve, even when they were the "only one" in a particular advanced course. The comments of their peers and friends mostly concerned the difficulty of the advanced courses.

Interviewer: How do you think students in this school react to you personally and the AP group generally with respect to your being involved in the program?

James: That's a wide variety of reactions. It ranges from "Man, I can't believe you're taking this, this is really hard. Why are you messing with it in your senior year? You should be relaxing" to "Oh man, you are taking that? You must be smart," and stuff. And that kind of thing. [black male senior at Clearview High School]

Interviewer: What do other students in the school say about, you know, taking honors courses, or anything. Does there seem to be any sort of um, you know, pressure not to take honors courses or AP courses?

Hakim: On some courses, I think, there might not, I mean, there might be some pressure on with "Oh man, that's just too hard." You know. "You might fail this." [black male junior at Clearview High School]

No ambivalence about achievement is evident in these statements. Instead of other blacks sanctioning them for academic striving, peers and friends in their comments give mostly cautions about the difficulty of the advanced courses. We found a similar pattern at other schools.

At Banaker, the predominantly black high school, one APIIB teacher reported that her regular instruction students "looked up to" the IB students because they "appreciated" the fact that the IB courses were tough, and "admired" the students who were able to meet the challenges of the program. Banaker students, especially, dismissed any suggestion that as high-achieving black students, they were ostracized by their peers.

Interviewer: Did your friends have any reaction to you being in the IB program or at any time during elementary and junior high?

Tyler: Not really, not any negative reactions. You know, they always, you know, say, "You're so smart," stuff like that, whatever. I don't think any had animosity towards me. [black male junior at Banaker High School]

Interviewer: Did your friends have any other types of reactions to you taking these classes?

Michelle: They thought I was crazy for taking, [laughs] especially taking like the AP class, and plus honors classes. They thought I was crazy. And it was like, "Well, I just gotta handle it." But they were pretty much supportive. [black female senior at Banaker High School]

Interviewer: Have your friends had any reaction to you being in these classes?

Kimmi: Well, you know how your friends do. They just feel like, "We know you're going to take the honors classes or something." And they'll be like, "Don't let yourself go down (in the rankings), because we know you got to be third, fourth, or do something." And they'll try to be like, "Yeah, you got the highest grade" or something. But not anything like, "You're a nerd." Nothing stupid like that. [black female junior at Banaker High School]

High-achieving students appeared to enjoy a certain level of respect among their friends at Banaker High School, where informants also flatly denied that acting white was an issue.

Interviewer: Have you ever heard anybody in this school accuse anybody else of acting white, or anything like that?

Ernest: No. [black male senior at Banaker High School] *Interviewer:* No? *Ernest:* Hunh-uh.

We pressed the black informants on the question of peer and friend response to achievement to be sure that we were not missing some part of their experience. Many found these questions somewhat amusing, because achievement simply was not an issue.

Interviewer: And here, do you get any sort of reaction from any of your friends about being in the honors classes?

Zora: No. [black female junior at Avery High School]

Interviewer: Not at all? Nobody ever says anything?

Zora: No. [laughs]

Interviewer: Okay, how about–

Zora: Because a lot of them take them too. So, I mean, we don't talk about it.

Interviewer: Right. Okay, how about students just around the school, not necessarily the people you hang out with, but people who are just kind of walking in the hall . . .

Zora: Naw. [laughs a little]

Interviewer: Nothing? Why do you keep laughing?

Zora: It's just funny, I mean, we don't talk about that.

Interviewer: How do your friends-how do your friends react to your being in college prep and not honors classes?

Paul: We never talk about it. [black male junior at Avery High School]

Interviewer: Okay. And how do you feel about them being, you know, those who are in the honors–

Paul: We never talk about it.

That some black students did not discuss their academic pursuits and achievements with friends is not surprising. Steinberg (1996) reported similar findings for a diverse sample of students. Furthermore, in interviews with school personnel we found support for the claims of Avery High School students that high achievement was not a problem for blacks at their school. For example, a new assistant principal (a black woman) commented that she had not seen as much peer pressure to underperform among minority students at Avery as she had seen at her previous school:

I was really impressed, last year, the first time report cards went out and many of the minority students . . . walked up to me and said, "Ms. H, look at my report card," and saw As. That was a different experience.

In some schools, however, black students expressed concern over racial isolation in advanced classes, supporting Ferguson's (2001:352) assumption that "honors and AP courses may be socially isolating for black students" and Mickelson and Velasco's (forthcoming) findings in a study of high-achieving black students in the Charlotte-Mecklenberg School system in North Carolina. This was the case for our informants at the two middle schools and at Dalton High School in particular. Crystal, the only minority student in her eighth-grade gifted class at Jackson Middle School, found isolation from peers of similar background troubling. When asked whether she hung out with her gifted classmates outside class, Crystal responded, "Only a couple," adding that she did not "get along" with some of them "at all." She called these students "the other group . . . the preps" and noted that "some can be snotty at times." According to Crystal, the preps are "rich people," "white," and "they, like, live in the Winston neighborhood."

> This sense of standing apart from the dominant population in advanced courses, especially a population perceived as arrogant, causes peculiar discomfort for some students. The other two black informants in the gifted program at Jackson Middle School had one another for company in the seventh-grade gifted class. Neither expressed any concerns about feeling different, isolated, or left out.

At Kilborn Middle School, Pelham, a black male, indicated that he had no problem being labeled as gifted, but as one of only two blacks in his gifted classes, he felt "a little bit odd being there" when the topic of one class was slavery. Elaborating, he said, "I don't know—it's like, you know, everybody looking at me, or something like that, if it's, you know, slavery." Pelham's discomfort with particular topics in the predominantly white advanced classes is not unlike that expressed by black adolescents in other studies

(Hemmings 1996; Mickelson and Velasco forthcoming; Tatum 1997). Interestingly, however, Pelham's and Crystal's discomfort did not deter them from being in the gifted program.

High-achieving black students at Dalton High School also persisted in advanced classes although they encountered similar problems of isolation. Note the similarity between the following description of students in the advanced classes at Dalton High School and that of Crystal's peers in the gifted classes at Jackson Middle School mentioned earlier:

Tamela: You have the snooty people, who only want to talk with you if you live in Eden Terrace, or if you like— [black female junior at Dalton High School]
Interviewer: What is Eden Terrace?
Tamela: That's like the little preppy tow—, suburb—
Interviewer: Uh-huh, and is that predominantly–
Tamela: Yes, it is. It's predominantly white. They have a lot of teachers, a lot of prominent people in the community that live out there, so—I mean, if you live in Eden Terrace, and if you make a certain amount of money, or whatever, you're in their little clique group, or whatever.

Tamela went on to explain that her classmates did things to offend her and to question her presence in the advanced classes. She reported getting "certain vibes" from some of the white girls (whom she described as "really snobby"), indicating that they did not want her in the classes (e.g., they "make little gestures and snicker" when Tamela gets "a higher test grade than them"). Interestingly, having been classmates since middle school, neither removed the racial boundary between the white students and Tamela nor erased their questions about her ability.

A Burden of Acting White

Dalton High School's high-achieving black students contended with more than social isolation. This rural school with more than 1,700 students was the only school in which we found evidence of a burden of acting white with respect to achievement. Sociologically, this case is significant because, as Buroway (1991) has argued, as an exception to the pattern found at the other seven schools, it can provide important theoretical insight that may improve the theory as a whole.

Both students and school personnel mentioned oppositional attitudes among blacks. Teachers, principals, and counselors repeatedly traced the underrepresentation of minority students in the school's advanced courses to aspects of an oppositional culture among minority students. Some adults noted that it is not "cool for minority students to be smart," and that black students are "embarrassed" about their ability. Others maintained that black students "don't place a high value on education," and that males, especially, are "averse to success" because it constitutes "betraying their brothers." Thus, to address the problem of minority underrepresentation in advanced courses, the school sought to ease high-achieving black students' isolation in the courses and insulate them from the criticisms of their peers by establishing a club for these students to come together.

Our two black student informants confirmed the presence of an oppositional culture, and particularly a burden of acting white, at Dalton High School. Our interviewees, one senior and one junior, were high-achieving females enrolled in honors and AP courses. Both had been accused of acting white by their black peers because of their academic behaviors.[12] We emphasize these cases to acknowledge that this experience is real, and as many journalistic accounts attest (see, for example, the *New York Times* series "How Race Is Lived in America," June to July 2000), it can be extremely difficult and painful for some.

Interviewer: Okay, do your friends have any reaction to you being in the AP and honors courses?
Tamela: Oh man, they—a lot of people, well my good friends that are, that are in my honors English class, most of them, we take almost the same kinda course loads so, I mean, we support each other. And then I have some other black friends that say that I'm too smart, I'm trying to act white, or whatever, because I'm in such hard classes. [black female junior at Dalton High School]

Tamela did not seem upset by these remarks. She continued to hang out with some of the same students who accused her of acting white. The other student, Alicia (black female senior at Dalton High School), experienced harsher treatment and reacted more strongly. She recalled being called "white girl" and "Oreo" by fellow blacks in middle school after she had been placed in an accelerated class with only whites. She described that period as "hell." Alicia's middle-class background, which differed from Tamela's more modest socioeconomic status, further distinguished her from the many black students at Dalton High School who lived in nearby housing projects.[13] It also may have contributed to how Alicia's white peers perceived her. She quoted one white female as saying, "Alicia, you're not black—you speak correct English, you take honors courses. You're not what I picture as black." High-achieving black students in other research (Tatum 1997) report similar incidents.

A black counselor at Dalton High School recalled that a few years earlier her daughter "was the only black on the principal's list" and often "the only black in the core courses." At the principal's request, the counselor had conducted a survey of minority students and found that many were concerned about social and racial isolation in advanced courses:

> They did not like being in honors courses because often they were the only ones . . . Also, some of the kids felt that if they were in these honors classes, that there appears, the black kids look at them as if they were acting white, not recognizing that you could be smart and black. A lot of white kids looked at them, basically, "You're not supposed to be smart and black, so why are you here?"

An important and often overlooked consequence of the underrepresentation experienced by minorities in advanced classes is the perpetuation among both blacks and whites of stereotypes about black intellectual ability and the value of education in the black community.

Stark underrepresentation in honors and AP classes also leaves high-achieving black students vulnerable to being perceived as arrogant by their peers. As Alicia put it, "I've had to deal with things from other black students, black students who see that I am smart; they seem to think that I think I'm better than them." Her conscious efforts to avoid "com[ing] off like I think I'm better than other people" were undermined by the visual disparity of her presence in advanced classes, leaving Alicia feeling frustrated and angry:

> I think when you walk by a door and see one or two spots [blacks] in a class, I think that's when you start perceiving, "Oh, they must be stuck up, rich preppy people." The problem comes from society because it is ingrained in us that blacks must act, speak, dress a certain way and if you deviate from those expected norms your blackness is questioned. I question it myself I'm being denounced and rejected by blacks and that's ridiculous . . . I've changed so much since ninth grade. I came in here timid because I am black, and I was the only black person in my honors classes.

For some students, the visual image of racial patterns of academic placement may mean little. For others, however, it may be a constant reminder of the cultural system of white superiority, prompting ideas that link whiteness with certain academic behaviors. Thus, the threat posed to black students by such stereotypes can extend beyond the test-taking situation that Steele (1997) described. Alicia found her most basic self-understandings called into question:

> If you make all As, you're white. If you're not coming in here with Cs and Ds and Fs, then something's wrong with you. You don't have a life—that's what it was. They thought I didn't do anything else but study . . . You are called a betrayer of your race, and then you start questioning your blackness as I did. And I was like, "Well, what *is* wrong with me?"

Although Dalton High School was the only school at which informants explicitly linked academic achievement to accusations of acting white, one student at Jackson Middle School, located in a suburb of a county with a relatively large gap in black–white median income, discussed acting white with regard to other, nonacademic behaviors. This important distinction is clear in the following exchange.

Interviewer: What about different racial groups in this school? Are there, is it integrated, do black and white students hang out together all the time, or are they more separate? How does that work?

Marc: Most of the time, but a lot of the black people think that they're better than the white people, or vice versa. Or the black people will always pick on the white people about what they do [inaudible], and if you're black and you act like you're white, then they would hold it against you. The black people would not like you as much . . . Well if you're black and you act like you're—you do stuff that the white people do, then, then, like skateboarding and stuff like that, then they say that you're white and that you, I don't know how to really say it, they just say that you're really white and that you don't care about everybody else that's black. And stuff like that. Like if you surf or if you talk differently, like "dude" or something like that. 'Cause sometimes I say that. [black male, seventh grade at Jackson Middle School]

Interviewer: Okay. So do black students tease you sometimes?

Marc: Sometimes.

Interviewer: Are there other things besides skateboarding or surfing that are labeled as white?

Marc: Mm, just about everything that black people don't do. Like if it's not associated with, like—I'm not talking about with the school—but drugs or shooting or something like that, then it's considered black.

Interviewer: What about AG?

Marc: AG is really mixed up. I mean, most of the people in AG that I know of are white. I'm one of the few black people that are in AG.

Interviewer: Okay. So, does anybody say, "You're in AG, you're white, you act white"?

Marc: No.

Interviewer: They don't associate that, only when you say "dude" and talk about surfing?

Marc: Yeah, stuff like that.

In the schools we studied, a burden of acting white was not pervasive in black peer groups. Black students sometimes were teased for achievement or for being smart, but that teasing was not usually racialized, and therefore was no different from the typical teasing (i.e., general oppositionality) other high-achieving students experience. Moreover, as the following quotations from black and white students illustrate, some of our informants perceived much of this teasing as harmless, and most downplayed its importance.

Interviewer: What kind of reaction did your friends have about you being in this (IB) program? You said most of your friends are in it, right?

Barbara: Yeah. But like people that were my friends before I came here and stuff, are like, "Oh, she's a smart girl now." And like, when someone needs help, everyone comes to me and like, "I know you know how to do this, cause you're in IB." And every—a lot of people joke about it and stuff. [black female sophomore at Banaker High School]

Interviewer: How do your friends react to your being in this program (honors and AP)?

Lila: They're like, "Geesh, what's wrong with you?" *[laughs]* I don't know. They make fun of me a lot for my grade point average. They call me by the number instead of my name. But, I don't know, it's a lot of playful joking. [white female junior at Avery High School]

Ned: If they know you are in honors or AG, they think you are a genius. People see you in different ways, mostly it's a good way, but they also see you as limited in scope, like someone that does nothing but study all day long. [white male junior at Franklin High School]

Maggie: There were like five of us in the [gifted] class, and then in my [gifted] math class there was about ten, it doubled for math,

but it was like I felt kind of left out from everybody else, and people would like, be like "You guys are too smart, y'all smarty-pants." And it kind of got better like in the eighth grade because a lot more people came into the AG program . . . and in high school it's like more accepted and it's okay to be in honors, but in fifth grade it was kind of like a funny thing. [white female junior at Avery High School]

Clearly, among both whites and blacks, perceptions of high-achieving students are not entirely positive. Nor is the experience of the white high achiever always positive. Comments such as "What's wrong with you?" "Limited in scope," "kind of a funny thing," and "felt kind of left out" highlight the negative side of being perceived as "too smart" and are consistent with other research findings. Thus, contrary to the implications of the burden of acting white and oppositional peer culture hypotheses—that white students generally have superior standards for academic achievement and are embedded in peer groups that support and encourage academic striving—the experiences described by some of our white informants indicate the presence of a much less achievement-oriented academic culture. Our findings are consistent with those of other studies showing black and white students differing little in the degree to which they value academic achievement (Cook and Ludwig 1998; Ferguson 2001).

Hannah, a white female senior at Clearview High School, described a particularly egregious form of ridicule she experienced from white peers. Explaining that some girls at her school did not like her or her friends because they were "smart" and played sports, Hannah reported that one girl taunted her by saying, "I used to have a friend like you who was perfect. She killed herself . . . It just got to be too much for her; she was number one in her class too; she played volleyball and everything and she ended up killing herself." We asked if she thought a lot of people saw her as "perfect":

Hannah: No, because I'm wild.

Interviewer: Wild, how?

Hannah: I don't try to act, it's like I still want to be [Hannah], I don't try to be like arrogant and everything in front of everybody else, like I'll be the first one to declare, "I'm going to write on this desk," or "I'm stupid," I don't try that arrogance.

Hannah's strategy of acting "wild" is similar to tactics described by black students in Fordham and Ogbu's (1986) article. Hannah did not say she acted wild specifically to camouflage her achievement, but she acknowledged that this behavior deflected attention from her achievement and reminded people that she was not "perfect."

A Burden of High Achievement Among Whites

Hannah's narrative uncovers a pattern of deepseated animosity between higher- and lower-achieving students in some schools, especially when the former group is perceived to be socially or economically advantaged. We found the most striking cases of such animosity at Clearview High School and Kilborn Middle School. Evidence of similar animosity also was present at East High School and Dalton High School. All but East High School have relatively large percentages of students eligible for free or reduced-priced lunches, and are located in rural areas. We found no animosity toward higher-achieving students at Banaker or Franklin high schools. At Franklin, school staff emphasized that most students came from similar, modest backgrounds (Table 9.2). One white teacher, when asked to explain why minority students at Franklin were well represented in advanced courses (Table 9.3), offered the following opinion:

> Well, you know, we're from a very low-wealth county and, uh, it's not, the wealth is not, the whites don't have all the money. It's just as many poor whites as there are poor blacks or poor Indians. We're all in the same boat together. So in some areas it may be a racial, socioeconomic breakdown to it; it's not here. We don't really have an upper class.

At Dalton High School, few white students mentioned animosity between high and low achievers, but that omission may reflect the fact that all white informants were high achieving and, with the exception of one, Lexie, all were socioeconomically advantaged (e.g., parents had at least a four-year degree). Lexie, whose parents had no more than a high school education, had experiences in the advanced classes similar to those Tamela and Crystal described. Lexie felt alienated from her AP classmates and did not socialize with them, apparently because, beginning in middle school, the social class differences between them created a boundary. "I was the rejected alien, the one in the corner," she told us, and she continued to view her peers as not "approachable." The group boundaries drawn between students in middle school carried over to high school. Even as a senior, Lexie continued to maintain distance from her more privileged peers.[14]

Socioeconomically disadvantaged whites at Clearview High School told similar tales.[15] For example, Ingrid, whose parents held working-class jobs, explained why she was "not close to" fellow AP students:

> We have like, out here we have like the high spots [unclear], I guess you would say, the ones that were well brought up with the wealthy parents and things like that. And then we have the middle class and their parents work for what they get, they work hard and everything, but they're just not as well off, and then we have like the low class, the ones that have hardly nothing and things like that. I would say, I'm not being judgmental, not trying to be, but the majority of the smarter kids taking the honors courses are the well-off kids, because I think a lot of them are pressured into it maybe by their parents. [white female senior at Clearview High School]

Ingrid noted that "the low-class" students in advanced classes sometimes were ridiculed for trying to be like the high-status "well-off" students:

Interviewer: And would they [lower class students] typically be in honors classes?

Ingrid: Most of them aren't. Now you have some of them that are really smart and that are [sounds like imitate] and they get picked on for it because they don't look as nice as some of the other ones do.

Interviewer: Who picks on them?

Ingrid: Different people, not necessarily the people actually in the class with them but the other people saying, "I don't know why you're in there, you're not smart enough, you're not like them."

Interviewer: So they get picked on for being in the honors classes?

Ingrid: I guess for, because other people can look at them like they're trying to be like them, but you know you can't be.

The unmistakable similarity between this account and the "burden" Fordham and Ogbu described as peculiar to black students suggests that the composition of advanced courses may encourage the development of these attitudes and help breed animosity.

Visible social status disparity in track placement appears to affect how students perceive those classes and the students who take them, as other research also shows (Mickelson and Velasco forthcoming; Tatum 1997). Sennett and Cobb's (1972:82) work on the sources of social class injury in schools discusses this sorting process among younger students:

> In the Watson school, by the time the children are ten or eleven the split between the many and the few who are expected to "make something of themselves" is out in the open; the aloofness developing in the second grade has become open hostility by the sixth . . . What has happened, then, is that these children have directed their anger at their schoolmates who are rewarded as individuals rather than at the institution which is withholding recognition of them.

Among the older students in our sample schools, hostility directed toward wealthy higher-achieving students usually marked them as snobs. For instance, a white student at East High School told us about a friend in advanced geometry who, she said,

> really didn't want to be in the advanced class because she didn't want to be categorized as one of the snobs. Because a lot of people in advanced geometry or the advanced classes are—this is kind of weird to put this—but they're kind of rich and they really are snobs. [Anna Beth, white female sophomore at East High School]

This perception of snobbery led some parents to veto their children's participation in gifted programs. Ingrid's mother, for example, would not let her participate in her elementary school's gifted programs: "She said that she didn't want me to think I was better than other kids." Ingrid explained:

> [Now] I understand why she did that . . . [A] lot of the students, some of the smarter ones, think that they're a lot better than the other ones that have learning problems and things . . . They just exclude you from them as far as like everybody has their own little clique, and they're like, "Well, we're the smarter people and the other people are dumb"; kind of thing. [white female senior at Clearview High School]

Interviews at Kilborn Middle School revealed similar resistance to gifted placement among low-income whites. According to school staff, parents in the rural farming town where the middle school is located sometimes refused to have their children tested for admittance into the gifted program because "they don't want their kids to feel like they're better than anybody else." The principal reported hearing this from parents "all the time." A teacher who mentioned this attitude among parents added that it came mostly from low-income parents. The teacher, who believed that low-income parents' academic expectations were low, cited this and the fact that parents did not want their kids identified as smart as possible explanations for low income children's underrepresentation in Kilborn's gifted program.

White student interviewees at Kilborn Middle School identified a "high and mighty" attitude (evidenced by "acting like you are better than everyone else") among students taking accelerated classes. Words like "snobby," "snooty," and "snotty," as well as comments about students who think they are "better than [others]" came up often in descriptions of high-achieving students, especially those perceived as "rich." Joey, a white male eighth grade student whose parents were high school graduates, told us he thought some of his classmates in the AP classes were "kind of snobby" and explained that these students' "parents have high up jobs, and they-they are high-up people." Adam, a white male eighth grade student from a working-class family, who is taking advanced classes, concurred, noting that some of his classmates "act like they are better than you in some ways."

We asked Sarah, a white female student at Kilborn Middle School who was not taking advanced classes, whether the students who had been in the gifted program of her elementary school were the same people currently enrolled in AP classes. Her response—"I really don't know because they're more of the preppier people; I don't hang out with the preppy people"—shows the distance between the "haves" and the "have nots" at the school. Sarah added that some of the AP students "are just snobbish" and noted the arrogance of the "preps."

Interviewer: Okay. Well, tell me about the different groups of kids at the school.
Sarah: Okay. There are people like me—just try and stay away from-we're not really, we're not the rich, rich people, you know, just like the normal, average kid, I guess you could say. And then we have preps, as we call kids who think they're better than everyone else because they have more money or whatever.

Students in the advanced classes at Kilborn Middle School also faced ridicule. According to Linda, a white female in the eighth grade gifted program at Kilborn Middle School, AP students are "put down by others . . . because they're smart," and are teased "about just the way they look or something." Carrie, also in the gifted program, reported that students are embarrassed to be known as smart:

Carrie: I think—they don't—some people don't like to be known as smart. I don't know why, but that's just how they feel. [white female, eighth grade at Kilborn Middle School]
Interviewer: Are these people that you're thinking of, are they in fact "smart," or are they people who are not—who don't think of themselves as smart?
Carrie: They are smart. They are really smart and they can be—like a bunch of people chose not to be in that class, because they didn't—they just didn't want to be known as one of the smart kids, I guess. I don't know. Which, I mean, I just don't see—there's nothing wrong with it. It's something to be proud of.
Interviewer: Is there—do you perceive that there's a stigma attached to being smart in this school?
Carrie: I don't—a bunch of people think there is, but there's not, really. I mean, there used to be. Like in elementary school, people that were smart, they'd get beat up a lot. [chuckles] . . . Well, not really with girls. With boys. The, like, the puny, smart guys got picked on all the time.

Although Carrie insisted that she was proud to be in the gifted program, she admitted that when she was in the third grade, she had at first not wanted to be in the program "because I thought my friends might not be my friends anymore . . . I just thought that they might be embarrassed to hang out with me, because I would be one of the dorks."

The sense that students enrolled in the accelerated classes were arrogant may partly explain why these students were ridiculed by others, and why being smart might be burdensome in some schools. At Kilborn Middle School, where nearly half of the student body received free or reduced-priced lunches, and where the accelerated classes were perceived as dominated by the "rich people," low-status students seemed to turn academic striving and smartness on its head, a process of inverted social closure, demeaning what they once publicly valued. To the extent that students value smartness, its uneven distribution is problematic. Studies investigating what happens when students are not able to realize the goal of academic success have found that some students construct subcultures that reject, at least outwardly, the school's values and assessments (Sennett and Cobb 1972; Stinchcombe 1964). Subsequently, these students seek ways to earn respect and esteem that do not depend on the school's valuation. Our findings show a similar pattern. Some groups of students—in this case, low achievers, earn respect and esteem at the expense of others—in this case, high achievers.

Discussion and Conclusion

This study assessed the burden of acting white hypothesis. Our interviews revealed ambivalence toward achievement among black students at just one of eight secondary schools. Contrary to the burden of acting white hypothesis the black students in this study who avoided advanced courses did so for fear of not doing well academically. Their decision to opt out was motivated by their own concern that they might not be able to handle the amount or level of work required, and that their grades might suffer. With few exceptions (e.g., Spencer et al. 2003), researchers have not considered that black adolescents, like other students, need to feel competent, and that they work to preserve a positive self-concept.

Racialized ridiculing of high-achieving black students was evident for only 2 of 40 black adolescents, both of whom attended the same school.[16] A similarly designed study with a larger sample of schools, including more with characteristics similar to Dalton High School's (e.g., racially mixed, large black–white income and placement gaps) would likely have shown more evidence of a burden of acting white for black students. Significantly, however, despite the real pain and frustration allegations of acting white may cause, it did not deter our informants from enrolling in advanced courses or striving for academic success. Thus, our data

provide little evidence to suggest, as Fordham and Ogbu (1986) claimed, that a burden of acting white is a "major reason" why black students do poorly in school and a key contributor to the achievement gap.

In constructing the theory of a burden of acting white, Fordham and Ogbu (1986) overlooked important similarities between the experiences of their informants and those of white students. Indeed, the narratives of black and white students at the eight schools in our study suggest that a burden of high achievement (either racialized or class-based oppositionality) may be a common experience in some schools in which high-status groups are perceived to be privileged in placement and achievement. Our results support Blau's (2003:54) assumption that "the racial composition of a school's body of retained students and low-status students sends a signal to all students in the school," because when socioeconomically advantaged students appear to be overrepresented in advanced courses, we also find a pattern of animosity directed at that group.

We do not have data on the social class composition of courses to substantiate the students' views that "rich" students dominated the higher-level courses, but many studies on tracking confirm their perception that these students have an unfair advantage in course placement (Gamoran 1992; Gamoran and Mare 1989; Hallinan 1994; Lucas 1999; Oakes 1985). Moreover, given that "situations defined as real are real in their consequences," it seems likely that some students may choose lower-level academic classes, in which they can expect the comfort of being among peers of similar background, rather than advanced courses, in which they may anticipate feeling socially isolated or conspicuous in their difference. Some students also seem especially concerned to avoid being perceived as exhibiting the arrogance of privilege.

The charge of acting white directed toward black students striving for academic success involves much more than opposition to white cultural norms. In a society characterized by patterns of race and class privilege, the charge of acting white is loaded with the resentment (misdirected) of the less privileged toward the few individuals among them who receive the coveted rewards bestowed by those in power. Where black students do possess oppositional attitudes, this orientation is not likely to arise merely from their having been born black. Rather, oppositional attitudes appear to be connected to everyday experiences of inequality in placement and achievement. Mickelson and Velasco (forthcoming) came to a similar conclusion in their study of high-achieving black students. For black adolescents, academic achievement can become yet another characteristic delineating the boundaries of whiteness —a conspicuous marker similar to "wearing shorts in the winter."

We found a similar process among low-status whites. Class distinctions provided a way for them to understand their relative underachievement while maintaining a sense of dignity and respect in the face of disparate outcomes. For low-income white students, patterns of placement and achievement can become another indicator of social class, marking the boundary between the "haves" and the "have nots." Most problematic for whites, similar to that for blacks who faced a burden of acting white, was the perception that the low-status student was attempting to assume the characteristics of the "other," especially an air of superiority or arrogance.

Inconsistencies in research findings related to an oppositional peer culture among black students become more understandable once the importance of context is recognized. Thus, we speculate that a focus on school structures rather than culture may produce greater insight and more consistent results. As we found in the current study, the degree of inequality and how it is perceived by students varies across schools. The combination of particular factors (e.g., percentage of student body receiving free or reduced-priced lunches and the gap in black–white median income in the area) appears to affect how students perceive inequality. The patterns identified in this study suggest that institutional structures may shape how culture is enacted in school in response to a burden of high achievement among black students, whether it

manifests itself in opposition to white norms or— as is common to most adolescents—as concern about being perceived as arrogant, a "dork," or a "nerd." Students in all racial and ethnic groups confront similar dilemmas of high academic achievement, and they also tend to use similar strategies of downplaying achievement (Harter 1990; Kinney 1993; Steinberg 1996). Thus, we join Mary Patillo-McCoy (1999:208) in concluding that "radical systemic changes, not the reorganization of people's cultural beliefs," are the solution to oppositional peer cultures in schools. Patterns of social inequality reproduced and affirmed in tracking exacerbate the well-documented antiachievement ethos among America's youth.

Our study suggests that there are three distinct types of oppositionality to high achievement. The first is a general oppositionality, in which peer taunts take the form of labels such as "nerd," "dork," or "brainiac," and may cross racial and class lines. The second type, which is the form we set out to detect and explain in this study, is racialized oppositionality, in which peer taunts directed at black high achievers by other blacks include labels such as "Oreo" or the charge of "acting white." The third type, also found in this study, is class-based (intraracial) oppositionality, in which peer taunts include "snooty" and charges of persons acting "high and mighty" or like they are better than others.[17]

The second type is more likely to be part of the local school culture of schools in which socioeconomic status differences between blacks and whites are stark and perceived as corresponding to patterns of placement and achievement. Similarly, the third type of oppositionality is more likely to be part of the local school culture of schools in which socioeconomic status differences among whites are stark and perceived as corresponding to patterns of placement and achievement.[18] Further research is needed to further refine and test these hypotheses.

Commonplace notions concerning the burden of acting white have captured the sociological imagination. Yet, surprisingly, sociologists have not paid enough attention to similarities in the daily experiences of black and white students in schools. Designing studies that provide greater detail on students' experiences will allow researchers to identify the nuances that distinguish a burden of acting white from other more generic problems of high achievement that confront the average teenager. The empirical foundation underlying the burden of acting white thesis is fragile at best. Until we recognize that these processes generalize beyond one specific group, we will continue to go astray in our efforts to understand the black–white achievement gap.

Appendix

Table A.1 Demographic Information on Student Informants Quoted

Schools	Student informant	Grade	Race	Gender
Jackson Middle School	Crystal	8	Black	Female
	Les	7	Black	Male
	Marc	7	Black	Male
	Shandra	7	Black	Female
Kilborn Middle School	Adam	8	White	Male
	Carrie	8	White	Female
	Joey	8	White	Male
	Linda	8	White	Female
	Pelham	8	Black	Male
	Sarah	8	White	Female
Avery High School	Lila	11	White	Female
	Maggie	11	White	Female
	Paul	11	Black	Male
	Whitney	12	Black	Female
	Zora	11	Black	Female
Banaker High School	Barbara	10	Black	Female
	Ernest	12	Black	Male
	Kimmi	11	Black	Female
	Michelle	12	Black	Female
	Tyler	12	Black	Male
Clearview High School	Hakim	11	Black	Male
	Hannah	12	White	Female
	Ingrid	12	White	Female
	James	12	Black	Male
	Jessica	12	Black	Female
Dalton High School	Alicia	12	Black	Female
	Lexie	12	White	Female
	Tamela	11	Black	Female
East High School	Anna Beth	10	White	Female
Franklin High School	Ned	11	White	Male

Note: To ensure anonymity, the names of all schools and informants have been changed.

Table A.2 Demographic Information on Students' Parents

Schools	Student	Mother		Father	
		Education	Employment	Education	Employment
Middle Schools					
	Crystal	AD	Administrator	HS	Factory Worker
Jackson	Les	HS	Food Service	NA	NA
	Marc	Less Than HS	Teacher	DK	Construction Worker
	Shandra	BA	Teacher	NA	NA
	Adam	HS	Nonemployed	HS	Plumber
Kilborn	Carrie	BA	Educator	BA	Stock Broker
	Joey	HS	Self-employed	HS	Manufacturing Position
	Linda	DK	Nonemployed	BA	Manager
	Pelham	DK	Assistant Principal	HS	Magistrate
	Sarah	Less Than HS	Sample Person	NA	NA
High Schools					
Avery	Lila	HS	Homemaker	Some College	Quality Assurance Position
Position	Maggie	HS	Secretary	HS	Express Courier
	Paul	Some College	Secretary	Some College	Butcher
	Whitney	Some College	Nursing Assistant	Some College	Service Position
	Zora	BA	Accounts Payable	BA	Contractor
	Barbara	BA	Dietician	DK	Service Position
Banaker	Ernest	Some College	Computers	NA	NA
	Kimmi	BA	Teacher	BA	Laboratory Scientist
	Michelle	HS	Machine Operator	Tech/Voc	Unemployed
	Tyler	BA	Teacher	AD	Statistician
Clearview	Hakim	HS	Machine Operator	Tech/Voc	Truck Driver
	Hannah	BA	Teacher	NA	NA
	Ingrid	Some College	Textile	Less than HS	Carpenter
	James	HS	Mill Manager	HS	Construction
	Jessica	AA	Film Technician	NA	NA
Dalton	Alicia	AA	Self-employed	BA	Community College Administrator
	Lexie	HS	Lead Agent	HS	Coordinator
	Tamela	AA	Nonemployed	NA	NA East
	Anna lileth	HS	Secretary	HS	Manager
Franklin	Ned	AA	Assistant Teacher	AA	Manager

Note: To ensure anonymity, the names of all schools and informants have been changed. AD = advanced degree; HS = high school; Tech/Voc = technical/vocational.

• DK = informant doesn't know; NA = not applicable (informant lives in single-parent home and has no contact with other parent).

Notes

1. Akom's research site was a 98 percent black urban high school. Carter's study used interview and survey data from black and Latino/a adolescents, ages 13–20 years, in a low-income urban community. Tyson studied two all-black elementary schools.

2. Individual schools use either "academically gifted" (AG) or "academically and intellectually gifted" (AIG), so we use both terms in this study according to which was used by a particular school or informant.

3. We received 866 (47%) completed elementary/middle school surveys and 231 (52%) completed high school surveys. These mail-in rates are higher than average for school surveys (U.S. Department of Education 1997).

4. School socioeconomic status is determined by participation in free or reduced-priced lunch programs.

5. To ensure anonymity, the names of all schools and informants have been changed.

6. Data for 1999–2000 were used to assess the minority presence in rigorous courses in high school and to select the subsample of schools. The figures for most courses in 2000–2001 were not significantly different. However, we use the 1999–2000 figures in this report (Table 9.3) because it takes time for attitudes to form, and the attitudes we assess in the interviews likely developed from recent rather than current experiences.

7. At Avery High School, the standard courses, which generally do not have grade point average (GPA) enrollment requirements and have not been or most courses in 2000–2001 were not significantly different. However, we use the 1999–2000 figures in this report (Table 9.3) because it takes time for attitudes to form, and the attitudes we assess in the interviews likely developed from recent rather than current experiences weighted, are called "college prep."

8. We asked principals to distribute consent forms to a mix of minority and white students at different grade levels, some enrolled in regular academic courses only and some enrolled in advanced courses. School staff may have selected higher-achieving students (possibly to have only their "good" students participate), or higher-achieving students may have been more likely than others to return consent forms agreeing to participation in the study.

9. Parent educational and occupational data for all the participants are available from the first author upon request.

10. Note that these decisions are not unconstrained. Students' ability to select advanced classes is, at least in part, a cumulative effect of past curricular experiences.

11. There was no clear pattern with respect to students' family background and their course level. See Appendix, Table A2.

12. We do not know whether Dalton High School's high-achieving black males encountered the same problems, but we did observe that some attended a meeting of the school club for high-achieving black students.

13. According to students' reports, blacks at Dalton High School were noticeably less well off than whites.

14. Another white informant at Dalton High School indicated that because she was "smart" her friends thought "I think I'm better than them." She did not refer to status group distinctions, however, nor did the white informant at Avery High School who described an almost identical situation.

15. Socioeconomic data by race for the schools were not available, but our interviews with black students at Clearview High School showed less perception of class differences between blacks and whites than found at Dalton High School (where we interviewed far fewer black students). Intraracially, however, the interviews showed more animosity among white students at Clearview tied to a greater perception of class differences among that group.

16. We found evidence of a burden of acting white in another study we conducted involving 65 high-achieving black students at 19 high schools. However, it was not widespread, and the school context mattered. For example, preliminary analyses identified about ten cases in which students reported encountering racialized oppositionality. All were cases of students attending racially mixed schools, and almost all the students were isolated from other blacks in advanced classes. Few of these students were in schools in which an oppositional culture was embedded, however.

17. The accusation of acting as if you are "better than" others usually is linked to charges of acting white as well. Among blacks, class-based condemnations may also include the label "bourgie."

18. Our data suggest that school locale (e.g., urban, rural) also may be significant, but it is not clear how or why. Moreover, other research (including our own and that of Mickelson and Velasco [forthcoming]) shows that a burden of acting white exists for black students in urban schools. It seems likely that certain combinations of school factors can create a "perfect storm" effect, producing a burden of acting white for some students.

Karolyn Tyson is Assistant Professor of Sociology at the University of North Carolina at Chapel Hill. She is interested in understanding how schooling practices and context, developmental processes, and culture affect academic engagement and outcomes, particularly among black students. Her current research centers on local samples of students in elementary through high school, relying heavily on ethnographic and interview data.

William Darity, Jr., is the Cary C. Boshamer Professor of Economics at the University of North Carolina at Chapel Hill. His research interests include racial and ethnic economic inequality, North–South models of trade and growth, interpreting Mr. Keynes, the economics of the Atlantic slave trade, and the social psychological effects of exposure to unemployment. He has published more than 100 articles in professional journals and authored or edited 7 books.

Domini R. Castellino is a Research Scientist at the Center for Child and Family Policy at Duke University. She is a developmental psychologist specializing in the family processes involved in scholastic and achievement outcomes for youth. Her research interests include post-high school transitions, adolescent academic achievement, career development, and high-achieving African American youth.

References

Ainsworth-Darnell, James W. and Douglas B. Downey. 1998. "Assessing the Oppositional Culture Explanation for Racial/Ethnic Differences in School Performance." *American Sociological Review* 63:536–53.

Akom, A. A. 2003. "Reexamining Resistance as Oppositional Behavior: The Nation of Islam and the Creation of a Black Achievement Ideology." *Sociology of Education* 76:305–25.

Bergin, David and Helen Cooks. 2002. "High School Students of Color Talk About Accusations of 'Acting White'." *The Urban Review* 34:113–34.

Blau, Judith R. 2003. *Race in the Schools: Perpetuating White Dominance?* Boulder, CO: Lynne Rienner Publishers.

Burawoy, Michael. 1991. *Ethnography Unbound: Power and Resistance in the Modern Metropolis.* Berkeley, CA: University of California Press.

Carter, Prudence. Forthcoming. *Not in the "White" Way: Identity, Culture and Achievement of Low Income African American and Latino Students.* New York: Oxford University Press.

Coleman, James. 1961. *The Adolescent Society: The Social Life of the Teenager and Its Impact on Education.* New York: The Free Press of Glencoe.

Cook, Philip J. and Jens Ludwig. 1998. "The Burden of Acting White: Do Black Adolescents Disparage Academic Achievement." Pp. 375–400 in *The Black-White Test Score Gap*, edited by Christopher Jencks and Meredith Phillips. Washington, DC: Brookings Institution Press.

Cookson, Peter W. and Caroline Hodges Persell. 1985. *Preparing for Power: Americas Elite Boarding Schools.* New York: Basic Books.

Downey, Douglas B. and James W. Ainsworth Darnell. 2002. "The Search for Oppositional Culture among Black Students." *American Sociological Review* 61:156–64.

Farkas, George, Christy Lleras, and Steve Maczuga. 2002. "Does Oppositional Culture Exist in Minority and Poverty Peer Groups?" *American Sociological Review* 67:148–55.

Ferguson, Ronald. 2001. "A Diagnostic Analysis of Black-White GPA Disparities in Shaker Heights, Ohio." Pp. 347–414 in *Brookings Papers on Education Policy 2001*, edited by Diane Ravitch. Washington, DC: Brookings Institution Press.

Ford, Donna Y. and J. John Harris. 1996. "Perceptions and Attitudes of Black Students toward School, Achievement, and Other Educational Variables." *Child Development* 67:1141–52.

Fordham, Signithia and John U. Ogbu. 1986. "Black Students' School Success: Coping with the 'Burden of Acting White'." *The Urban Review* 18: 176–206.

Gamoran, Adam. 1992. "Access to Excellence: Assignment to Honors English Classes in the Transition from Middle to High School." *Educational Evaluation and Policy Analysis* 14:185–204.

Gamoran, Adam and Robert D. Mare. 1989. "Secondary School Tracking and Educational Inequality: Compensation, Reinforcement or Neutrality?" *American Journal of Sociology* 94: 1146–83.

Hallinan, Maureen T. 1994. "Tracking: From Theory to Practice." *Sociology of Education* 67:79–91.

Harter, Susan. 1990. "Self and Identity Development." Pp. 352–87 in *At the Threshold: The Developing Adolescent*, edited by S. S. Feldman and G. R. Elliott. Cambridge, MA: Harvard University Press.

Hemmings, Annette. 1996. "Conflicting Images? Being Black and a Model High School Student." *Anthropology and Education Quarterly* 27:20–50.

Herbert, Bob. 2003. "Breaking Away." *New York Times*, July 10, p. 23. Retrieved July 10, 2003 (http://www.nytimes.com/2003/07/10/opinion/10HERB.html?ex=1058871290&ei=1&en=elae41358bf07ale).

Horvat, Erin McNamara and Kristine Lewis. 2003. "Reassessing the 'Burden of Acting White': The Importance of Peer Groups in Managing Academic Success." *Sociology of Education* 76:265–80.

Kao, Grace, Marta Tienda, and Barbara Schneider. 1996. "Racial and Ethnic Variation in Academic Performance." *Research in Sociology of Education and Socialization* 11:263–97.

Kinney, David A. 1993. "From Nerds to Normals: The Recovery of Identity among Adolescents from Middle to High School." *Sociology of Education* 66:21–40.

Lucas, Samuel. 1999. *Tracking Inequality: Stratification and Mobility in American Schools.* New York: Teachers College Press.

McArdle, Clare and Nancy Young. 1970. "Classroom Discussion of Racial Identity or How Can We Make It Without 'Acting White'." *American Journal of Orthopsychiatry* 41:135–41.

McWhorter, John. 2000. *Losing the Race: Self Sabotage in Black America.* New York: The Free Press.

Mickelson, Roslyn and Anne Velasco. Forthcoming. "Bring it On! Diverse Responses to 'Acting White' Among Academically Able Black Adolescents." In *Beyond Acting White: Reassessments and New Directions in Research on Black Students and School Success,* edited by Erin McNamara Horvat and Carla O'Connor. New York: Rowman and Littlefield.

Neal-Barnett, Angela. 2001. "Being Black: New Thoughts on the Old Phenomenon of Acting White." Pp. 75–87 in *Forging Links: African American Children: Clinical Developmental Perspectives,* edited by A. Neal-Barnett, J. M. Contreras, and K. A. Kerns. Westport, CT: Praeger.

New York Times. 2002. "How Race Is Lived in America." June 4–July 16. Retrieved March 26, 2005 (www.nytimes.com/library/national/race).

Oakes, Jeannie. 1985. *Keeping Track: How Schools Structure Inequality.* New Haven, CT: Yale University Press.

Pattillo-McCoy, Mary. 1999. *Black Picket Fences: Privilege and Peril among the Black Middle Class.* Chicago, IL: University of Chicago Press.

Perry, Pamela. 2002. *Shades of White: White Kids and Racial Identities in High School.* Durham, NC: Duke University Press.

Sennett, Richard and Jonathan Cobb. 1972. *The Hidden Injuries of Class.* New York: Vintage Books.

Spencer, Margaret Beale. 1984. "Black Children's Race Awareness, Racial Attitudes, and Self Concept: A Reinterpretation." *Journal of Child Psychology and Psychiatry* 25:433–41.

Spencer, Margaret Beale, William Cross, Vinay Harpalani, and Tyhesha Goss. 2003. "Historical and Developmental Perspectives on Black Academic Achievement: Debunking the 'Acting White' Myth and Posing New Directions for Research." Pp. 273–304 in *Surmounting All Odds: Education, Opportunity, and Society in the New Millennium,* edited by C. C. Yeakey and R. D. Henderson. Greenwich, CT: Information Age Publishers.

Steele, Claude M. 1997. "A Threat in the Air: How Stereotypes Shape Intellectual Identity and Performance." *American Psychologist* 52: 613–29.

Steinberg, Laurence. 1996. *Beyond the Classroom: Why School Reform Has Failed and What Parents Need To Do.* New York: Simon and Schuster.

Steinberg, Laurence, Sanford M. Dornbusch, and Bradford B. Brown. 1992. "Ethnic Differences in Adolescent Achievement: An Ecological Perspective." *American Psychologist* 47:723–29.

Stinchcombe, Arthur. 1964. *Rebellion in a High School.* Chicago, IL: Quadrangle Books.

Tatum, Beverly Daniel. 1997. *"Why Are All the Black Kids Sitting Together in the Cafeteria?" And Other Conversations about Race.* New York: Basic Books.

Tyson, Karolyn. 2002. "Weighing in: Elementary-Age Students and the Debate on Attitudes toward School among Black Students." *Social Forces* 80:1157–89.

U.S. Department of Education. 1997. "Improving the Mail Return Rates of SASS Surveys: A Review of the Literature," Working Paper No. 97–18, by Cornette Cole, Randall Palmer, and Dennis Schwanz. Washington, DC: National Center for Education Statistics.

Wasonga, Teresa and Dana Christman. 2003. "Perceptions and Construction of Meaning of Urban High School Experiences among African American University Students: A Focus Group Approach." *Education and Urban Society* 35: 181–201.

Weissert, Will. 1999. "Report Cites Racial Gap in Student Performance." *Chronicle of Higher Education,* October 29, vol. XLVI(10), A4.

Gender Inequalities in Education

Claudia Buchmann, Thomas A. DiPrete, and Anne McDaniel

Introduction

Just over a decade ago, Jacobs (1996, p. 156) noted that the literature on gender inequalities in education "often treats all aspects of education as disadvantaging women." This assessment is less valid today, as much research now examines the ways in which girls and women are advantaged in some aspects of education, as well as those in which they continue to trail boys and men. Although girls have long gotten better grades in school than boys, most researchers brushed aside this point because women did not translate their better performance into higher levels of educational attainment relative to men (Mickelson 1989). But as women have come to far outnumber men among new college graduates in most industrialized societies, new questions about gender inequalities in education have emerged.

This article provides a selective, cross-disciplinary review of the literature on gender inequalities in educational performance and attainment from early childhood to young adulthood. We map the terrain of current gender inequalities for a wide range of educational indicators, we discuss the theoretical perspectives that have been used or could prove useful for explaining these inequalities, and we suggest how future research could advance understanding of the complex nature of differences between males' and females' educational experiences.

Most research assumes that individuals progress through the educational system in a sequential mode and that early school experiences set the stage for those that follow (Pallas 2003). Research also tends to be bifurcated between that focused on educational outcomes and experiences during childhood and adolescence (corresponding with primary and secondary school) and that focused on educational attainment and higher education. Following these tendencies, we structure this review into three sections. In the first, we assess the current state of knowledge regarding gender inequalities in primary and secondary school, from children's earliest experiences with formal schooling, as they enter kindergarten through the end of compulsory schooling, which in most industrialized societies is the end of secondary school. This section focuses on educational achievement, as much of the literature on gender differences during childhood and adolescence attends to performance differences between girls and boys. Of course, performance in elementary and secondary school is linked to the level of schooling one ultimately attains. The second section provides an empirical overview of gender inequalities in young adulthood and beyond in terms of educational attainment, including high school completion, enrollment in postsecondary education, college completion, and graduate and professional school experiences. The pathways that individuals take from high school to college and the completion of a college degree vary greatly (Goldrick-Rab 2006). Within this apparently endless variation, however, there are gendered patterns that demand examination. In the third and final section, we offer several fruitful directions for future research.

Because we focus on formal schooling bounded by entry into kindergarten through completion of college, we do not consider research on gender differences in very early childhood and preschool (see Kraft & Nickel 1995 for a review) or continuing and adult education (Jacobs & Stoner-Eby 1998, Jacobs & King 2002). We focus on U.S.-based research but incorporate literature from other industrialized countries and cross-national research where noteworthy. Patterns of gender inequalities in developing societies are quite different from those in most industrialized societies, and space limitations preclude us from considering this important topic here (but see King & Hill 1993, Buchmann & Hannum 2001).

From Kindergarten through High School

In the United States, most children start formal schooling at age 5, but approximately 10% of children begin kindergarten a year later. Parents decide when their children begin school and, along with teachers, determine whether children are promoted to the next grade.

Delayed entry into kindergarten, or academic redshirting, is more common among boys and among children from families of high socio-economic status (SES) (Graue & DiPerna 2000). Nationally representative data from the Early Childhood Longitudinal Study of the Kindergarten Cohort (ECLS-K) indicate that boys comprise about 60% of the children with delayed kindergarten entry and 66% of those who repeat kindergarten (Malone et al. 2006). Boys are also more likely than girls to be retained a grade or more during elementary school (Alexander et al. 2003, Entwisle et al. 2007).

These differences in early school trajectories are important to bear in mind when comparing boys and girls in terms of their academic performance. In age-based comparisons, girls will have attained a slightly higher average grade level than boys. In grade-based comparisons, most common in research, boys will be slightly older on average than girls. The matter is made even more confusing owing to the different developmental trajectories of girls and boys, with girls tending to mature more quickly than boys (Tanner 1978, Gullo & Burton 1992). One could argue that comparisons using chronological age ignore sex differences in maturational tempo and result in comparing more mature girls to less mature boys (Eaton & Yu 1989), yet these complexities are infrequently considered in the literature.

Gender Differences in Academic Performance

Many researchers, educators, and politicians regard academic performance as the bottom line in K–12 education. From parent–teacher associations meetings to the national No Child Left Behind Act, the question "how are our children doing?" is usually addressed with data from standardized tests and other uniform assessments or grades and report cards. When the question turns to "who is doing better, girls or boys?" the answer depends on the age of students being compared and whether grades or test scores are used. The two measures capture different elements of academic performance and ability, as is evident by the generalization that males tend to obtain higher scores on standardized tests, whereas females tend to get higher grades (Duckworth & Seligman 2006). Most of the literature on academic performance focuses on adolescents, but the recent availability of data for younger children (such as the ECLS-K) has stimulated research on performance earlier in childhood.

Test scores. Gender differences in test scores have been the subject of much research for many decades. Maccoby & Jacklin's (1974) important book *The Psychology of Sex Differences* provided a comprehensive analysis of more than 1600 studies in the areas of achievement, personality, and social relations and served to stimulate much interest and new research on gender differences in achievement in particular. Despite the large literature in this area (see Willingham & Cole 1997 for a review), disagreement remains on several fronts, including when in the life course gender differences in math performance emerge (Leahey & Guo 2001), whether males are more variable than females on measures of achievement (Willingham & Cole 1997), and whether sex differences in test scores are declining over time. Some researchers argue that gender gaps in test scores have narrowed in recent decades (Feingold 1988, Hyde et al. 1990), but on the basis of their meta-analysis of test results for writing, math, and science, Hedges & Nowell (1995) conclude that gender gaps in test scores have remained relatively stable over the past 30 years.

Results from various national and international large-scale assessments indicate that boys have higher test scores in mathematics and girls have higher test scores in reading (Baker & Jones 1993, Beller & Gafni 1996, Nowell & Hedges 1998, Gallagher & Kaufman 2005, Marks 2007), but there is considerable cross-national variation in the size of these gaps (A.M. Penner, unpublished observations). There is also a life course component to gender differences in test scores; research consistently finds generally similar performance of girls and boys in mathematics and reading in the early grades and a growing male advantage in math scores and growing female advantage in reading scores as they move through school (Maccoby & Jacklin 1974, Willingham & Cole 1997). These gender-based performance differences persist in standardized tests, such as the SAT, used in higher education admissions, although they tend be small and the distributions of male and female scores overlap substantially (Hyde 2005, Kobrin et al. 2007). Inferring gender differences in math and verbal abilities from gender differences in SAT scores is problematic because the sample of SAT test takers is not representative of the general population and because more females than males take the SAT, so the sample of males is more highly selected (Spelke 2005).

Some evidence suggests that gender gaps in test scores are more pronounced among low-income children (Hinshaw 1992), but results are not definitive. For example, Entwisle et al. (2007) find that although girls and boys start first grade with similar reading scores, a female-favorable gap in reading emerges by fifth grade, but only for children from economically disadvantaged families; boys and girls from middle- and upper-class families had very similar reading scores. Conversely, with nationally representative data, T.A. DiPrete & J. Booher-Jennings (unpublished observations) find that girls have higher reading scores than boys across all levels of SES.

Grades and behaviors related to school success. Girls have long obtained higher grades in school than boys. Even in the 1950s and 1960s girls earned higher grades than boys and had higher class standing in high school (Alexander & Eckland 1974, Alexander & McDill 1976, Mickelson 1989). Today, from kindergarten through high school and even in college, girls get better grades in all major subjects, including math and science (Perkins et al. 2004).

As early as kindergarten, girls have more advanced reading skills than boys (West et al. 2000, Tach & Farkas 2006), and boys continue to have more problems with reading in elementary school (Trzesniewski et al. 2006).

Boys are overrepresented in populations with reading disabilities, antisocial behavior, mental retardation, attention disorders, dyslexia, stuttering, and delayed speech (Halpern 1997, Muter 2003, Rutter et al. 2004). Moffitt et al. (2001) find that males are at higher risk for antisocial behavior that is neurodevelopmental in origin, but for antisocial behavior that originates in the context of social relationships, gender differences are negligible. Trzesniewski et al. (2006) demonstrate that antisocial behavior and reading difficulties go hand in hand for boys; antisocial behavior leads to poor reading skills and vice versa. Emotional and behavioral problems early in childhood also contribute to educational outcomes later in life, such as the likelihood of repeating a grade in secondary school, completing high school, and enrolling in college (Shanahan 2000, McLeod & Kaiser 2004).

Girls also have advantages in social skills and classroom behavior. Analyses of ECLS-K data find that as early as kindergarten, "boys display more developmental disabilities, more disruptive conduct in class and less positive orientations to learning activities" (Zill & West 2001). For example, according to parent and teacher reports, twice as many boys as girls have difficulty paying attention in kindergarten, and girls more often demonstrate persistence in completing tasks and an eagerness to learn. These advantages in orientation to learning and other social skills grow during the early elementary school years and plausibly account for a portion of the more rapid reading gains that girls achieve during this period (T.A DiPrete & J. Booher-Jennings, unpublished observations). During adolescence, high school teachers consistently rate girls as putting forth more effort and as being less disruptive than boys (Downey & Vogt Yuan 2005). Adolescent girls also possess higher levels of other noncognitive skills such as attentiveness and organizational skills (Farkas et al. 1990, Jacob 2002), self-discipline (Silverman

2003, Duckworth & Seligman 2006), leadership qualities, and interest in school, all of which facilitate academic success (Rosenbaum 2001). These gender differences in noncognitive skills may be central in explaining why boys get higher test scores in some domains but girls generally get higher grades. Farkas et al. (1990) show that teachers' judgments of students' noncognitive characteristics are powerful determinants of course grades even when cognitive performances are controlled.

Finally, in areas where females once lagged behind males in the rigor of their high school coursework, they now outpace males. Until recently, girls trailed boys in the number and intensity of the mathematics courses they took. Now boys and girls take equally demanding math classes in high school (Catsambis 2005), and girls get better grades in those classes (Gallagher & Kaufman 2005). Female high school graduates are more likely to have taken biology and chemistry courses than males (Xie & Shauman 2003). Girls have also come to outpace boys in the number of college preparatory courses and Advanced Placement examinations they take (Bae et al. 2000, Freeman 2004). Girls are more involved in extracurricular activities, with the notable exception of participation on athletic teams (Bae et al. 2000), and they participate in more cultural activities within and outside of school (Dumais 2002). All these advantages are related to academic success in high school, to the likelihood of enrolling in college, and to ultimate educational attainment, as we discuss in detail below.

Explaining Gender Gaps from Kindergarten to High School

In the search for explanations of gender inequalities, sociological research tends to ignore biological differences and focus solely on social and economic factors (Huber 2008, this volume). As Halpern and colleagues (2005, p. 53) point out: "Opponents of the idea that biology has contributed even a small part to male and female differences are quick to label biological explanations as sexist . . . [but] biological hypotheses are not necessarily sexist. There does not have to be

a 'smarter sex' with a 'better biology' to conclude that there are biological origins to any cognitive ability." Some sex differences in some cognitive tasks are well established. Spelke (2005, p. 953) summarizes the nuanced patterns of cognitive differences as follows: "Girls and women tend to excel on tests of verbal fluency, arithmetic calculation, and memory for the spatial locations of objects. Boys and men tend to excel on tests of verbal analogies, mathematical word problems, and memory for the geometric configuration of an environment." Nonetheless, compared to larger, more reliable sex differences in measures of motor behavior, sexuality, and aggression, differences in cognition are small, leading Spelke (2005) to conclude that males and females have equal aptitude for mathematics and science.

Larger sex differences in performance on complex quantitative tasks emerge during or after elementary school and grow larger with age, making it "difficult to tease apart the biological and social factors that produce them" (Spelke 2005, p. 953). Indeed, much evidence indicates that intrinsic capacities and environmental experiences play interrelated roles in the complex process of learning (Dehaene 1997, Spelke & Newport 1998, Halpern 2000). Research that focuses exclusively on social and environmental factors provides an incomplete picture of the complex nature of gender differences in educational performance. For example, T.A. DiPrete & J. Booher-Jennings (unpublished observations) show that the standard set of socioeconomic and demographic variables cannot explain gender differences in social development in kindergarten. There are also longstanding questions of how traditional gender stereotypes and norms influence students' perceptions of their own abilities and the socialization of girls and boys within their families and schools. One interesting line of research regarding the relevance of stereotypes examines the relationship between stereotype threat, or the fear of conforming to stereotypes about a subgroup to which one belongs, and women's poorer performance on math tests. Steele and colleagues argue that because of conventional notions that men outperform women on standardized tests, especially in mathematics, women experience a heightened anxiety during test taking that interferes with their test performance (Steele 1997, Spencer et al. 1999).

Of course, many aspects of one's family of origin are integrally related to both educational performance and attainment. Aside from the potential role of family background and educationally relevant resources, which we discuss in greater detail below, some studies find differences in parental involvement depending on the gender of the child. Stevenson & Baker (1987) found that parents are more involved in school activities with sons and more involved in home activities with daughters; as children grow older, parental involvement with boys declines, but their involvement with girls remains constant. On the one hand, Muller (1998) finds that parental involvement in children's schooling is not gender specific and further speculates that parental involvement may serve to counteract gender stereotypes about math and science as male domains. On the other hand, Entwisle et al. (2007) maintain that the large growth in the gender reading score gap between first and fifth grade among low-income students is due in part to parents' lower reading expectations of boys. Similarly, Mandara (2006) proposes that certain parenting styles, such as those lacking an authoritative component, exacerbate gender differences in education among African Americans. The empirical basis for these claims is questionable for the simple reason that parenting styles and parental expectations may be responsive to the personalities and behavior of children, and thus may be consequences as well as causes of gender differences. Research designs for measuring the causal influence of parental behavior on children uncontaminated by the responsiveness of parental behavior to the characteristics of their children are rare in this literature.

Studies of gender gaps in educational performance have also looked to teachers and the environments within schools and classrooms for possible explanations. In the past, girls and boys were often placed in different tracks in high school (Hallinan & Sorensen 1987, Entwisle

et al. 1994), but today, as noted above, girls' and boys' course taking patterns are more similar. The female advantage in grades is not due to females taking easier courses in high school (Leonard & Jiang 1999) or college (Buchmann & DiPrete 2006).

There is an ongoing, contentious debate regarding whether teachers systematically favor one gender over the other, though the identity of the putative "victim" gender has changed over time. Research based on classroom observation in the early 1990s talked about "how schools shortchange girls," with teachers calling on and praising boys more often than girls (Am. Assoc. Univ. Women 1992, Sadker & Sadker 1994) only to be followed more recently by arguments that schools favor girls and contribute to a "war against boys" (Sommers 2000).

The empirical evidence of whether and how teachers' gender plays a role in causing gender differences in educational outcomes is inconclusive. Some large-scale studies find that males perform no better when taught by male teachers than by female teachers (Sokal et al. 2007). In contrast, Dee (2005, 2006) finds that having a female teacher instead of a male teacher in the subjects of science, social studies, and English in middle school raises the achievement of girls and lowers the achievement of boys, producing an overall gender gap of 8% of a standard deviation (Dee 2006, p. 70). It is unclear whether these effects arise from gender bias in teaching or whether they demonstrate that the effectiveness of instruction is partly a matter of fit and that students learn more on average from teachers of the same gender. Moreover, because the students in Dee's sample were not randomly assigned to teachers, male students with low performance may have been assigned to male teachers as a strategy for improving their performance (Sokal et al. 2007).

From High School to College

One of the most striking features in the terrain of higher education in recent years is the growing gender gap in college enrollment and completion. Young women consistently outperform their male peers in high school graduation. The proportion of both men and women enrolling in college has increased since the 1970s, but the increase for women has been much more substantial. Trend statistics in the United States also reflect a striking reversal of a gender gap in college completion that once favored males. In 1960, 65% of all bachelor degrees were awarded to men. Women continued to lag behind men in college graduation rates until 1982 when they reached parity with men. From 1982 onward the percentage of bachelor's degrees awarded to women continued to climb such that by 2005 women received 58% of all bachelor's degrees (Snyder & Dillow 2007) and comprised 57% of all college students. The U.S. Department of Education predicts the "new" female-favorable gaps in college enrollment and completion will continue to widen over the next decade. The probability of completing college is contingent on many factors, including the likelihood of finishing high school, the timing of the transition to college, the type of college attended, and the course of study in college. A growing body of research demonstrates that women now gain an advantage over men from most of these contingencies.

We limit our discussion to gender inequalities in the quantity of education received, or what Charles & Bradley (2002) have termed the vertical dimension of educational stratification. Gender differences in fields of specialization (major) and type of institution (elite versus nonelite, public versus private) represent distinctions in the type of education received within a given level of education, or the horizontal dimension of segregation. Although women outnumber men overall in their college attendance and graduation rates, we still need to consider questions regarding differences in the college experiences of men and women. Despite their greater numerical representation, are women concentrated in less prestigious institutions and in less well-remunerated fields of study? Or are their growing numbers accompanied by advances into more lucrative occupations? Gerber & Cheung (2008) address these questions in detail in their review of gender differences in horizontal stratification.

The Transition from High School to College

In the United States, completing high school is the first step to gaining access to postsecondary education. Many youth are excluded from the pool of eligible college students because they have not completed high school. The "status dropout rate" reflects the percentage of 16- to 24-year-olds who are not enrolled in high school and who have not earned a high school diploma or a Certificate of General Educational Development (GED). Since 1990, the status dropout rate of females has been lower than that of males. During the 1990s, male and female dropout rates appeared to converge, but since 1996 female dropout rates have declined further, and the gap has widened again. In 2005, almost 11% of males age 16 to 24 were dropouts, compared to 8% of females (Snyder & Dillow 2007). Dropout rates vary substantially by ethnic group, but the male disadvantage holds for all major groups. In 2005, male dropout rates for whites, blacks, and Hispanics were 6%, 12%, and 26%, respectively, compared with 5%, 9%, and 18%, respectively, for females of the same groups (Snyder & Dillow 2007). Among high school graduates, more males than females acquire a GED, which is an indicator of a lower level of college preparedness than a high school diploma (S. Dynarski, unpublished observations).

Students who enroll in college directly after high school have higher rates of overall college enrollment, persistence in college, and graduation (Bozick & DeLuca 2005, Horn & Premo 1995). Although men used to be more likely than women to enroll in college directly after high school, since 1996 males are substantially more likely than females to delay enrollment in college. Of those who enrolled in college in the year 2000, 60% of men compared to 66% of women enrolled immediately after high school (Freeman 2004). The female advantage in immediate college enrollment holds for all SES groups, although it is smaller for those of high SES backgrounds (King 2000, Bozick & DeLuca 2005).

Completing College

Women currently earn 58% percent of all bachelor's degrees awarded in the United States (Snyder & Dillow 2007). The female advantage in degree completion exists for all racial groups, but there are important variations by race and ethnicity in the size of the gap. It is largest for blacks, but it is also large for Hispanics and Native Americans. Women earn 66% of all bachelor's degrees awarded to blacks; the figures are 61% for Hispanics, 60% for Native Americans, 55% for Asians, and 57% for whites (Snyder & Dillow 2007). Note that the especially large gender gap for blacks does not constitute a reversal but, rather, a continuation of a long female-favorable trend. As early as 1954, when the great majority of black college students were enrolled in historically black colleges and universities (HBCUs), women comprised 58% of students enrolled in HBCUs. When the Census Bureau began tracking bachelor's degrees by race and gender in 1974, women earned 57% of all degrees awarded to blacks (*Journal of Blacks in Higher Education* 1999, p. 7).

Beyond the United States, higher proportions of females than males currently attain tertiary education in most European countries as well as in Australia, Canada, and New Zealand. Among the 30 member nations of the Organisation for Economic Cooperation and Development (OECD), the once prevalent male advantage in college completion has disappeared in all but four countries—Switzerland, Turkey, Japan, and Korea (OECD 2006).

In the United States, one major reason that women earn more degrees than men is their lower rate of dropout, once enrolled (Buchmann & DiPrete 2006). Women also earn their degrees more quickly. Freeman (2004) found that 66% of women who enrolled in college in 1995–1996 had completed a bachelor's degree by 2001, compared with only 59% of men. Men were more likely to have no degree or not to be enrolled, but they were also more likely still to be enrolled in a bachelor's degree program than women. Whereas 50% of black and Hispanic women had completed a bachelor's degree in this period, only 37% of black men and 43% of Hispanic men had done so.

Finally, women have made substantial gains in earning graduate and professional degrees. In 1970, women earned 40% of master's degrees and a mere 14% of doctoral degrees. Currently, women are more likely than men to attend graduate school; they earn 59% of master's degrees and 49% of doctoral degrees (Snyder & Dillow 2007). Similar trends have occurred within professional degrees. In 1970, women earned 5% of law degrees, 8% of medical degrees, and 1% of dentistry degrees (Freeman 2004). Currently, women earn 49% of law degrees, 47% of medical degrees, and 44% of dentistry degrees (Snyder & Dillow 2007).

Explaining Gender Gaps in Higher Education

The reversal from a male advantage to a female one in college enrollment and completion is an important topic of study both in its own right and because of its potential impacts on labor markets, marriage markets, family formation, and other arenas. Clearly, understanding the nature, causes, and consequences of the changing gender gaps in higher education is an important task for social scientists. This section focuses on individual and institutional explanations for the rising female advantage in higher education. In addition to discussing the findings of research in this emerging area, we discuss other plausible explanations, some of which have not been assessed empirically to date but have been topics of speculation in the popular press.

Individual-Level Factors

Status attainment and rational choice perspectives primarily focus on family and individual-level explanations for variations in postsecondary enrollment. Status attainment theory examines access to resources, broadly defined, related to attending and completing college. Rational choice perspectives consider how incentives and constraints shape individuals' decisions regarding whether to attain higher education. Individuals for whom benefits exceed costs, including opportunity costs, should be most likely to attain a college degree (but see Beattie 2002). These perspectives overlap, and both are useful for advancing our understanding of gender disparities in transitions into and out of higher education.

Family resources. Research in sociology, much of it in the status attainment tradition (Blau & Duncan 1967, Jencks 1972), and economics (Leibowitz 1977, Becker 1991) demonstrates the importance of parental education and other family-related resources for an individual's educational attainment. Resources related to family background exert their influence at each level of educational attainment, partly through academic performance and partly through educational transitions, given performance. Financial capital; social capital; access to role models, mentors, and information; individual attitudes (especially aspirations); and prior academic performance are also important determinants of inequalities in educational attainment. These resources, which are amassed from family, neighborhood, and school environments, explain in part ethnic and racial differences in educational attainment; children of different races and ethnicities come from families, neighborhoods, and schools with different average levels of resources. Girls and boys, however, are not segregated by family or neighborhood, and in the United States they are generally not segregated by school. Resources may be an important part of the explanation for the historical male advantage in educational attainment, but that explanation concerns the process by which environmentally available resources differentially flow to one gender or another. Moreover, with gender inequality changing so rapidly, it is likely that gender-specific flows of resources have changed considerably over the past 50 years; therefore, we must treat the results of published research in this area as historically contingent.

Even when girls and boys share the same household, family resources need not be equally distributed across sons and daughters. For example, socialization arguments emphasize the importance of role modeling, such that children model their parents as they form their own educational and occupational aspirations and attainment. Some scholars argue that role modeling is sex specific; girls look more to their mothers and boys more to their fathers as they develop their educational and occupational aspirations (Rosen & Aneshensel 1978). According to this perspective, after controlling for the overall educational level of the parents, daughters should do relatively better in households with a better-educated mother than in households with a better-educated father, and sons should be affected more negatively than daughters by the absence of a father in the home.

Buchmann & DiPrete (2006) find that the relationship between family background and college completion has changed for men and women over the second half of the twentieth century. In cohorts born before the mid-1960s, the gender gap favoring males was small or nonexistent, and daughters were able to reach parity with sons only in the minority of families with two college-educated parents. Parents with a high school education or less appeared to favor sons over daughters, and the gender gap in college completion favoring males was largest among these less-educated families. For cohorts born after the mid-1960s, the male advantage declined and even reversed in households with less-educated parents or those with an absent father. This change produced a situation in which the female advantage emerged first among families with absent or less-educated fathers. It remains largest among these families, but has gradually extended to all family types. These findings offer little support for gender role socialization; instead Buchmann & DiPrete (2006) argue that the pattern reflects a growing vulnerability of sons of less-educated or absent fathers.

Academic performance. The gender differences in academic performance and behaviors during high school discussed above are likely related to the female advantage in college enrollment and completion, but research has not sorted out all the mechanisms that link performance in high school with college outcomes. Perhaps females' higher aspirations to attend college explain, in part, their greater performance in high school. In 1980, more male than female high school seniors (60% versus 54%) expected to graduate from a four-year college, but by 2001 the trend had reversed, with 82% of female high school seniors expecting a four-year degree, compared with 76% of male high school seniors (Freeman 2004, p. 66). The reversal of the gender gap in educational expectations from one favoring males to one favoring females is not limited to the United States; in nearly all OECD member countries, young women are more likely to expect to attend college than are their male counterparts (Buchmann & Dalton 2002, McDaniel 2007).

At the same time, females' higher educational aspirations and higher college graduation rates likely stem from the female advantage in academic performance that develops over the educational career. Some research finds that the female-favorable gap in postsecondary enrollment is due in part to young women's better grades and tests scores and the greater number of math and science courses they take in high school (Goldin et al. 2006, Cho 2007) as well as their tendency to spend more time on homework and avoid disciplinary problems (Jacob 2002) relative to their male counterparts. Gender differences in high school behaviors also lay the foundation for women's better academic performance in college, which in turn plays a large role in producing the female advantage in college completion (Buchmann & DiPrete 2006).

Incentives and returns to college. Individuals' knowledge of the returns to a college degree also play an important role in their decisions regarding how much education to acquire. One plausible reason for the rising rates of women's college enrollment and completion is that the returns to college have been rising more for women than for men. Research finds that whereas women's wage returns to higher education have increased, male returns have increased even more rapidly, owing to declining opportunities for high-wage, male-dominated manufacturing jobs for high school educated workers (Averett & Burton 1996, Charles & Luoh 2003, Perna 2003). But DiPrete & Buchmann (2006) argue that wage returns comprise too narrow a basis for evaluating the relative returns to higher

education for men and women. They assess whether the growing female advantage in college completion is related to changes in the returns to higher education for women and men in terms of earnings, the probability of getting married and staying married, the family standard of living, and insurance against poverty. Via a trend analysis of the value of higher education for each of these outcomes measured against the baseline value of a high school education, they find that standard-of-living and insurance-against-poverty returns to higher education have risen faster for women than for men. Thus, it is plausible that the female-favorable trend in college completion may derive at least in part from responses to gender-specific changes in the value of higher education.

DiPrete & Buchmann (2006) show that the total returns to a college degree have also risen for men, albeit not as rapidly as for women. In addition to the well-known rising return to education in the labor market for men, the earnings value of a spouse for men has grown with both the rising female earnings and the increasing financial vulnerability of men to divorce (McManus & DiPrete 2001). Arguably, one puzzling aspect of the reversal of the gender gap in college completion is the slow pace of growth in men's rates of college completion in the face of rising returns to college for men. Research suggests a socialization-based disadvantage for males that is relatively stronger in families with low-educated or absent fathers (Buchmann & DiPrete 2006). But whether this disadvantage plays out through a lack of knowledge about the value of postsecondary education and the way to convert it into labor market success, through a lower priority placed on education relative to other short-term goals, or through some other mechanism is not yet clear.

Institutional Factors

Beyond the factors that shape individuals' resources and incentives to attain a college education, institutional-level factors also shape gendered patterns of college access and success. These include sociocultural changes in gender roles and expectations about life course trajectories for women and men. Shifts in the structure of the labor market such as declining discrimination against women and changes in occupational sex segregation also impact individual incentives to attend college, as do changes in institutions of higher education themselves, such as the growth of community colleges, the rising costs of higher education, and changes in financial aid regulations. We also need to consider the role of the military, which may compete with higher education for young adults, especially young men, in shaping gender-specific patterns of participation in higher education.

Gender-role attitudes. In the United States, there have been large changes in gender-role attitudes in recent decades, with the clear trend of declining numbers of Americans expressing support for traditional gender roles and far greater numbers expressing more egalitarian views (Brewster & Padavic 2000, Brooks & Bolzendahl 2004). Recent research finds support for a causal relationship between gender-role attitudes and subsequent behaviors and attitudes as diverse as childbearing (Kaufman 2000), voting behavior (Brooks 2000), and marital satisfaction (Amato & Booth 1995). Changes in gender-role attitudes are also related to the growing college attendance of young women, but in complex ways and coupled with other factors (DiPrete & Buchmann 2006, Goldin 2006). Goldin et al. (2006) show that young women's rising expectations for future employment encouraged them to attend and complete college, but the increase in the median age of first marriage among college students in recent decades also played a role. Although women's growing rates of college completion and graduate/professional education likely contributed to the rising median age of first marriage, the later age of first marriage also probably reinforced the trend in college completion; as women married later, they could take college more seriously and form their identities before getting married and having a family. The access to reliable contraception in the form of the birth control pill positively impacted women's college attendance and a host of related factors, including their age of first marriage, professional labor force participation, and age of first birth (Goldin & Katz 2002, Goldin 2006).

Labor markets. Between the 1970s and 1990s the gender wage gap declined, and women with high levels of human capital (in terms of education and labor force experience) saw the greatest increase in their wages (Spain & Bianchi 1996, Morris & Western 1999). Moreover, research indicates that returns to labor force experience increased by a larger amount for women than for men during this period (Blau & Kahn 1997) owing to rising levels of women's human capital, but also owing to the passage and enforcement of antidiscrimination laws (Goldin 2006). Occupational sex segregation also fell between 1970 and 1990, although the rate of decline slowed in the second decade (Morris & Western 1999). This meant that more women entered prestigious and often better-paid positions in occupational sectors such as law, business, and the sciences (Goldin 2006). All these changes in the labor market impacted women's decisions to attend college and are related to women's rapidly rising rates of college enrollment and completion from the 1980s onward.

Educational institutions. Changes in higher education institutions also may have altered the access or pathways to college in gender-specific ways. The second half of the twentieth century witnessed the dramatic expansion first of the four-year college system and then of the community college system. If community college serves as a springboard to enrollment and graduation from four-year college, the expansion of the community college system may have been responsible, in part, for the female-favorable trend in college completion. But Buchmann & DiPrete (2006) find that although women enroll in two-year colleges at a slightly higher rate than men, the female advantage in two-year college attendance has little impact on their advantage in four-year college completion.

Other major changes in higher education have been the rising cost of tuition, declining levels of grant-based financial aid, and increases in student loans (Alon 2007). Cursory evidence suggests that women and men receive similar levels of financial support from their families (Jacobs 1999), but it is possible that changes in financial aid or the increasing costs of college are affecting men and women differently. Some recent research indicates that women are more responsive than men to programs that decrease college costs (Seftor & Turner 2002; S. Dynarksi, unpublished observations), suggesting that policies aimed at making college more afford-able will exacerbate the female advantage in college enrollment. This is an important topic for further research.

Military service. To what degree does the mili-tary compete with higher education for young adults, especially young men? The U.S. military recruits about 200,000 enlisted personnel each year, almost all of whom are high school graduates. The size of the military has remained stable in the past 20 years; since 1975 it has comprised less than 1% of the total population. In 2007, active duty personnel comprised almost 1.4 million people, 85% of whom were men (U.S. Dep. Defense 2007). The enlisted popu-lation is disproportionately young, with more than 50% under the age of 25, so it is possible that military service competes with college as a destination for young adults, and especially young men. But decisions to enlist in the mili-tary and to enroll in college need not be mutually exclusive. Many of the young people who enlist after high school cite the educational benefits available to them to get a college edu-cation either during or after their military service as a primary motivation to enlist (Kleykamp 2006). Thus, for some, military service may make enrolling in college possible, albeit at a later point in life. Moreover, of the 20,000 officers commissioned by the armed forces each year, nearly all are college graduates, and about 40% received their commission through participa-tion in a university's Reserve Officer Training Program (ROTC) (Segal & Segal 2004, p. 8). For this group, military enlistment occurs after completing college.

On the whole, men who serve in the military receive less education than those who do not serve. Among high school graduates, veterans serving during the peacetime cold war period were less likely to attain a college education than were nonveterans at all levels of SES (MacLean 2005). This difference held even among those who reported plans to attend college. It is possible that merely delaying college enrollment reduces the likelihood of attending or completing college, perhaps owing to a sense that one has become "too old" for college, or perhaps because serious romantic involvement is more likely as one ages (Hogan 1981). It is not known whether military service reduces the likelihood of attaining a college degree or whether the military differen-tially selects young people who are less committed to postsecondary education (MacLean & Elder 2007). MacLean's (2005) findings are at least consistent with the idea that military service competes with higher education for young men. To the best of our knowledge, no research has examined the relationship between military service and educational attainment for women or whether the effects of military service found in the past remain the same for military personnel today. These are important questions for future research.

Directions for Future Research

Gender inequalities in education have seen much change, with young women gaining advantages over young men in ways that could not have been anticipated just two decades ago. The future promises to bring more change than stability. Throughout this review we have highlighted some important questions for future research: How should research appropriately account for the different developmental trajec-tories of girls and boys when comparing their performance? Have gender differences in test scores declined over time? How can research examine the influences of parents' and teachers' perceptions and behaviors on children, when these perceptions and behaviors are them-selves shaped by children's personalities and behaviors? Why are young men less likely to enroll in college immediately after graduating high school? Why have men's rates of college completion not kept pace with the rising returns to college for men? Do changes in college costs and the availability of financial aid affect men and women differently?

In addition to research designed to answer these questions, we believe there are three research agendas that would prove useful in advancing our understanding of gender inequalities in education.

1. Research needs to examine gender inequalities in education early in the life course: female-favorable trends in college enrollment and completion are likely due, in part, to gender differences in earlier behaviors and experiences. Recent important advances in biology, genetics, psychology, neuroscience, and other arenas (Kimura 1999, Halpern 2000, Cahill 2005, Spelke 2005) that shed light on gender differences in cognitive development and skills as well as noncognitive abilities in early childhood. Sociologists would do well to become more educated about these advances, or they risk becoming increasingly irrelevant in the important public and scholarly debates about the intersection of biological and social factors related to gender differences that emerge early in childhood and gender differences more generally (Freese et al. 2003).

Data from new longitudinal surveys such as the ECLS-B, ECLS-K, and National Children's Study, some of which gather data on biological as well as psychosocial environmental factors, will enable researchers to advance knowledge on gender differences in development, cognition, and a wide range of other factors in the next decade. Sociologists' nearly exclusive focus on the social and economic determinants of behavior may change as an interdisciplinary group of scholars increasingly attends to the potential importance of gene-environment interactions and interactions between the social environment and a variety of psychobiological systems (Adam et al. 2007). More than ever, the study of gender differences in early childhood must be an interdisciplinary enterprise, with connected efforts in sociology, psychology, biology, neuroscience, genetics, and other disciplines.

2. There is a great need for research on how the structure and practices of schooling relate to gender differences in educational outcomes. For example, the National Association for Single-Sex Public Education reports that, as of April 2006, at least 223 public schools in the United States were offering gender-separate educational opportunities, up from just 4 in 1998. Most of these cases involved single-sex classrooms within coeducational schools, but 44 were wholly single-sex schools (Dee 2006). This rise in single-sex schooling may be developing in response to public concerns about boys' poor academic performance that have gained attention on magazine covers (e.g., "The Problem With Boys" *Newsweek* 2006) and best-selling books like *Raising Cain: Protecting the Emotional Lives of Boys* (Kindlon & Thompson 2000). Single-sex schooling may be a reasonable policy response to the underperformance of boys, but to implement such massive changes without empirically based assessments of the consequences of such changes is short-sighted. For example, recent research by Wong et al. (2002) on Hong Kong schools found that girls do better in single-sex classrooms whereas boys do better in mixed-sex classrooms. Other research shows that the performance of both boys and girls improves when the proportion of female students in the classroom increases (Hoxby 2000, Lavy & Schlosser 2007). These studies suggest that an increase in single-sex schooling could exacerbate rather than ameliorate the relative underachievement of boys.

3. Future research must investigate gender differences by race, ethnicity, SES, and immigrant status. Such research should attend to vulnerable segments of the population and to males who may be at particular risk for poor performance and low educational attainment. A rare example of such work is Lopez's (2003) ethno-graphic study of 66 low-income, second generation Dominican, West Indian, and Haitian young adults who grew up in New York City during the 1970s–1990s. Through her interviews, Lopez finds that gendered norms within families, including strong social controls and responsibilities for daughters and more

independence and lax regulations for sons, can put sons and daughters on very different educational pathways. Other important evidence on how gender differences may be conditioned by race and SES comes from the work of Entwisle et al. (2007), who find that the gender gap in reading at the start of elementary school is larger for children from disadvantaged backgrounds relative to middle-class children. These studies should serve as exemplars for future research that examines how gender intersects with race, ethnicity, class, and immigrant statuses in creating complex inequalities in educational experiences and outcomes. Many of women's and girls' historical disadvantages in education have not only disappeared in the United States and other industrialized countries, they reversed. Old paradigms of comprehending gender differences in education as solely due to widespread obstacles to females' achievement no longer help guide research. A new frontier for research lies in understanding the developmental, cognitive, and environmental sources of males' and females' educational outcomes. In sum, we have much to learn about the nature, causes, and consequences of the changing gender gaps in education across the life course. This rapidly shifting terrain of gender inequalities raises important questions for researchers, policy makers, and educators who want to understand how to improve the educational performance and attainment of all youth—males and females alike—and for educational institutions striving to respond to the needs of their students. Clearly, much work remains to be done.

Disclosure Statement

The authors are not aware of any biases that might be perceived as affecting the objectivity of this review.

Literature Cited

Adam E, Klimes-Dougan B, Gunnar MR. 2007. Social regulation of the adrenocortical response to stress in infants, children, and adolescents: implications for psychopathology and education. In *Human Behavior, Learning, and the Developing Brain: Atypical Development*, ed. D Coch, G Dawson, KW Fischer, pp. 264–304. New York: Guilford. 2nd ed.

Alexander KL, Eckland BK. 1974. Sex differences in the educational attainment process. *Am. Sociol. Rev.* 39(5):668–82

Alexander KL, Entwisle DR, Dauber SL. 2003. *On the Success of Failure: A Reassessment of the Effects of Retention in the Primary School Grades.* Cambridge, UK: Cambridge Univ. Press

Alexander KL, McDill E. 1976. Selection and allocation within schools: some causes and consequences of curriculum placement. *Am. Sociol. Rev.* 41(6):963–80

Alon S. 2007. The influence of financial aid in leveling group differences in graduating from elite institutions. *Econ. Educ. Rev.* 26(3):296–311

Amato PR, Booth A. 1995. Changes in gender role attitudes and perceived marital quality. *Am. Sociol. Rev.* 60(1):58–66

Am. Assoc. Univ. Women. 1992. *How Schools Shortchange Girls.* Washington, DC: AAUW & Natl. Educ. Assoc.

Averett S, Burton ML. 1996. College attendance and the college wage premium: differences by gender. *Econ. Educ. Rev.* 15(1):37–49

Bae Y, Choy S, Geddes C, Sable J, Snyder T. 2000. *Trends in Educational Equity of Girls and Women.* Washington, DC: Natl. Cent. Educ. Stat.

Baker DP, Jones DP. 1993. Creating gender equality: cross-national gender stratification and mathematical performance. *Sociol. Educ.* 66(2):91–103

Beattie IR. 2002. Are all adolescent econometricians created equal? Race, class, and gender differences in college enrollment. *Sociol. Educ.* 75(1):19–43

Becker G. 1991. *A Treatise on the Family.* Cambridge, MA: Harvard Univ. Press

Beller M, Gafni N. 1996. The 1991 international assessment of educational progress in mathematics and sciences: the gender differences perspective. *J. Educ. Psych.* 88(2):365–77

Blau FD, Kahn LM. 1997. Swimming upstream: trends in the gender wage differential in the 1980s. *J. Lab. Econ.* 15(1):1–42

Blau PM, Duncan OD. 1967. *The American Occupation Structure.* New York: John Wiley

Bozick R, DeLuca S. 2005. Better late than never? Delayed enrollment in the high school to college transition. *Soc. Forces* 84(1):527–50

Brewster K, Padavic I. 2000. Change in gender-ideology, 1977–1996: the contributions of intra-cohort change and population turnover. *J. Marr. Fam.* 62(2):477–87

Brooks C. 2000. Civil rights liberalism and the suppression of a Republican political realignment in the United States, 1972 to 1996. *Am. Sociol. Rev.* 65(4):483–505

Brooks C, Bolzendahl C. 2004. The transformation of US gender role attitudes: cohort replacement, social-structural change and ideological learning. *Soc. Sci. Res.* 33(1):106–133

Buchmann C, Dalton B. 2002. Interpersonal influences and educational aspirations in 12 countries: the importance of institutional context. *Sociol. Educ.* 75(2):99–122

Buchmann C, DiPrete TA. 2006. The growing female advantage in college completion: the role of family background and academic achievement. *Am. Sociol. Rev.* 71(4):515–41

Buchmann C, Hannum E. 2001. Education and stratification in developing countries: a review of theories and research. *Annu. Rev. Sociol.* 27: 77–102

Cahill L. 2005. His brain, her brain. *Sci. Am.* 292 (5):40–47

Catsambis S. 2005. The gender gap in mathematics: merely a step function? See Gallagher & Kaufman 2005, pp. 220–45

Charles KK, Luoh MC. 2003. Gender differences in completed schooling. *Rev. Econ. Stat.* 85(3): 559–77

Charles M, Bradley K. 2002. Equal but separate? A cross-national study of sex segregation in higher education. *Am. Sociol. Rev.* 67(4):573–99

Cho D. 2007. The role of high school performance in explaining women's rising college enrollment. *Econ. Educ. Rev.* 26(4):450–62

Dee T. 2005. A teacher like me: does race, ethnicity or gender matter? *Am. Econ. Rev.* 95(2):158–65

Dee T. 2006. The why chromosome: how a teacher's gender affects boys and girls. *Educ. Next* Fall:69–75

Dehaene S. 1997. *The Number Sense: How the Mind Creates Mathematics.* Oxford: Oxford Univ. Press

DiPrete TA, Buchmann C. 2006. Gender-specific trends in the values of education and the emerging gender gap in college completion. *Demography* 43(1):1–24

Downey DB, Vogt Yuan AS. 2005. Sex differences in school performance during high school: puzzling patterns and possible explanations. *Sociol. Q.* 46(2):299–321

Duckworth AL, Seligman MEP. 2006. Self-discipline gives girls the edge: gender in self-discipline, grades, and achievement test scores. *J. Educ. Psychol.* 98(1):198–208

Dumais SA. 2002. Cultural capital, gender, and school success: the role of habitus. *Sociol. Educ.* 75(1): 44–68

Eaton WO, Yu AP. 1989. Are sex differences in child motor activity level a function of sex differences in maturational status? *Child Dev.* 60(4):1005–11

Entwisle DR, Alexander KL, Olson LS. 1994. The gender gap in math: its possible origins in neighborhood effects. *Am. Sociol. Rev.* 59(6):822–38

Entwisle DR, Alexander KL, Olson LS. 2007. Early schooling: the handicap of being poor and male. *Sociol. Educ.* 80(2):114–38

Farkas G, Grobe RP, Sheehan D, Shuan Y. 1990. Cultural resources and school success: gender, ethnicity, and poverty groups within an urban school district. *Am. Sociol. Rev.* 55(1):127–42

Feingold A. 1988. Cognitive gender differences are disappearing. *Am. Psychol.* 43(2):95–103

Freeman CE. 2004. *Trends in Educational Equity for Girls and Women.* Washington, DC: Natl. Cent. Educ. Stat.

Freese J, Li JA, Wade LD. 2003. The potential relevances of biology to social inquiry. *Annu. Rev. Sociol.* 29:233–56

Gallagher AM, Kaufman JC, ed. 2005. *Gender Differences in Mathematics: An Integrative Psychological Approach.* Cambridge, UK: Cambridge Univ. Press

Gerber T, Cheung SY. 2008. Horizontal stratification in postsecondary education: forms, explanations, and implications. *Annu. Rev. Sociol.* 34:299–318

Goldin C. 2006. The quiet revolution that transformed women's employment, education, and family. *Am. Econ. Rev.* 96(2):1–21

Goldin C, Katz LF. 2002. The power of the pill: oral contraceptives and women's career and marriage decisions. *J. Polit. Econ.* 110(4):730–70

Goldin C, Katz LF, Kuziemko I. 2006. The homecoming of American college women: the reversal of the college gender gap. *J. Econ. Perspect.* 20(4): 133–56

Goldrick-Rab S. 2006. Following their every move: an investigation of social class differences in college pathways. *Sociol. Educ.* 79(1):61–79

Graue ME, DiPerna J. 2000. Redshirting and early retention: who gets the "gift of time" and what are its outcomes? *Am. Educ. Res. J.* 37(2):509–34

Gullo DF, Burton CB. 1992. Age of entry, preschool experience, and sex as antecedents of academic readiness in kindergarten. *Early Childhood Res. Q.* 7(2):175–86

Hallinan MT, Sorensen AB. 1987. Ability grouping and sex differences in mathematics achievement. *Sociol. Educ.* 60(2):63–72

Halpern DF. 1997. Sex differences in intelligence: implications for education. *Am. Psychol.* 52(10): 1091–1102

Halpern DF. 2000. *Sex Differences in Cognitive Ability.* Hillsdale, NJ: Lawrence Erlbaum

Halpern DF, Wai J, Saw A. 2005. A psychobiosocial model: why females are sometimes greater than and sometimes less than males in math achievement. See Gallagher & Kaufman 2005, pp. 48–72

Hedges LV, Nowell A. 1995. Sex differences in mental test scores, variability, and numbers of high-scoring individuals. *Science* 269(5220):41–45

Hinshaw SP. 1992. Externalizing behavior problems and academic underachievement in childhood and adolescence: causal relationships and underlying mechanisms. *Psychol. Bull.* 111(1):127–55

Hogan DP. 1981. *Transitions and Social Change: The Early Lives of American Men.* New York: Academic

Horn LJ, Premo MD. 1995. *Profile of Undergraduates in US Postsecondary Education Institutions: 1992–93, with an Essay on Undergraduates at Risk.* Washington, DC: Natl. Cent. Educ. Stat.

Hoxby C. 2000. *Peer effects in the classroom: learning from gender and race variation.* NBER Work. Pap. 7867, Natl. Bur. Econ. Res., Cambridge, MA

Huber JN. 2008. Reproductive biology, technology, and gender inequality: an autobiographical essay. *Annu. Rev. Sociol.* 34:1–13

Hyde JS. 2005. The gender similarities hypothesis. *Am. Psychol.* 60(6):581–92

Hyde JS, Fennema E, Ryan M, Frost LA, Hopp C. 1990. Gender comparisons of mathematics attitudes and affect: a meta-analysis. *Psychol. Women Q.* 14(3):299–342

Jacob BA. 2002. Where the boys aren't: noncognitive skills, returns to school and the gender gap in higher education. *Econ. Educ. Rev.* 21:589–98

Jacobs JA. 1996. Gender inequality and higher education. *Annu. Rev. Sociol.* 22:153–85

Jacobs JA. 1999. Gender and the stratification of colleges. *J. High. Educ.* 70(2):161–87

Jacobs JA, King RB. 2002. Age and college completion: a life-history analysis of women aged 15–44. *Sociol. Educ.* 75(3):211–30

Jacobs JA, Stoner-Eby S. 1998. Adult enrollment and educational attainment. *Ann. Am. Acad. Polit. Soc. Sci.* 559(1):91–108

Jencks C. 1972. *Inequality: A Reassessment of the Effect of Family and Schooling in America.* New York: Basic Books

J. Blacks Higher Educ. 1999. Special report: college degree awards: the ominous gender gap in African American higher education. *J. Blacks Higher Educ.* 23:6–9

Kaufman G. 2000. Do gender role attitudes matter? Family formation and dissolution among traditional and egalitarian men and women. *J. Fam. Issues* 21(1):128–44

Kimura D. 1999. *Sex and Cognition.* Cambridge, MA: MIT Press

Kindlon D, Thompson M. 2000. *Raising Cain: Protecting the Emotional Life of Boys.* New York: Ballantine

King EM, Hill MA. 1993. *Women's Education in Developing Countries: Barriers, Benefits, and Policies.* Baltimore, MD: Johns Hopkins Univ. Press

King J. 2000. *Gender Equity in Higher Education.* Washington, DC: Am. Counc. Educ.

Kleykamp MA. 2006. College, jobs, or the military? Enlistment during a time of war. *Soc. Sci. Q.* 87(2):272–90

Kobrin JL, Sathy V, Shaw EJ. 2007. *A Historical View of Subgroup Performance Differences on the SAT Reasoning Test.* New York: College Board

Kraft RH, Nickel LD. 1995. Sex-related differences in cognition: development during early childhood. *Learn. Individ. Diff.* 7(3):249–71

Lavy V, Schlosser A. 2007. *Mechanisms and impacts of gender peer effects at school.* NBER Work. Pap. 13292, Natl. Bur. Econ. Res., Cambridge, MA

Leahey E, Guo G. 2001. Gender differences in mathematical trajectories. *Soc. Forces* 80(2):713–32

Leibowitz A. 1977. Parental inputs and children's achievement. *J. Hum. Res.* 12(2):242–51

Leonard DK, Jiang J. 1999. Gender bias and the college predictions of the SATs: a cry of despair. *Res. Higher Ed.* 40(4):375–407

Lopez N. 2003. *Hopeful Girls, Troubled Boys: Race and Gender Disparity in Urban Education.* New York: Routledge

Maccoby EE, Jacklin CN. 1974. *The Psychology of Sex Differences.* Palo Alto, CA: Stanford Univ. Press

MacLean A. 2005. Lessons from the cold war: military service and college education. *Sociol. Educ.* 78(3):250–66

MacLean A, Elder GH. 2007. Military service in the life course. *Annu. Rev. Sociol.* 33:175–96

Malone LM, West J, Denton KF, Park J. 2006. *The Early Reading and Mathematics Achievement of Children Who Repeated Kindergarten or Who Began School a Year Late.* Washington, DC: Natl. Cent. Educ. Stat.

Mandara J. 2006. The impact of family functioning on African American males' academic achievement: a review and clarification of the empirical literature. *Teacher's Coll. Rec.* 108(2):206–23

Marks GN. 2007. Accounting for the gender gap in reading and mathematics: evidence from 31 countries. *Oxford Rev. Educ.* 34(1):1–21

McDaniel AE. 2007. *Gender gaps in educational and occupational expectations across 30 industrialized countries: a study of similarities and differences.* Master's thesis, The Ohio State Univ.

McLeod JD, Kaiser K. 2004. Childhood emotional and behavioral problems and educational attainment. *Am. Sociol. Rev.* 69(5):636–58

McManus P, DiPrete TA. 2001. Losers and winners: the financial consequences of divorce for men. *Am. Sociol. Rev.* 66(2):246–68

Mickelson RA. 1989. Why does Jane read and write so well? The anomaly of women's achievement. *Sociol. Educ.* 62(1):47–63

Moffitt TE, Caspi A, Rutter M, Silva PA. 2001. *Sex Differences in Antisocial Behavior: Conduct Disorder, Delinquency, and Violence in the Dunedin Longitudinal Study.* Cambridge, UK: Cambridge Univ. Press

Morris M, Western B. 1999. Inequality in earnings at the close of the twentieth century. *Annu. Rev. Sociol.* 25:623–57

Muller C. 1998. Gender differences in parental involvement and adolescents' mathematics achievement. *Sociol. Educ.* 71(3):336–56

Muter V. 2003. *Early Reading Development and Dyslexia*. London: Whurr

Nowell A, Hedges LV. 1998. Trends in gender differences in academic achievement from 1960 to 1994: an analysis of differences in mean, variance, and extreme scores. *Sex Roles* 39(1–2):21–43

OECD. 2006. *Education at a Glance: OECD Indicators 2006*. Paris: OECD

Pallas AM. 2003. Educational transitions, trajectories and pathways. In *Handbook of the Life Course*, ed. JT Mortimer, MJ Shanahan, 8:165–84. New York: Kluwer Acad.

Perkins R, Kleiner B, Roey S, Brown J. 2004. *The High School Transcript Study: A Decade of Change in Curricula and Achievement, 1990–2000*. Washington, DC: Natl. Cent. Educ. Stat.

Perna LW. 2003. The private benefits of higher education: an examination of the earnings premium. *Res. Higher Educ.* 44(4):451–72

Rosen BC, Aneshensel CS. 1978. Sex differences in the educational-occupational expectation process. *Soc. Forces* 57(1):164–86

Rosenbaum J. 2001. *Beyond College for All: Career Paths for the Forgotten Half*. New York: Russell Sage

Rutter M, Caspi A, Fergusson D, Horwood J, Goodman R, et al. 2004. Sex differences in developmental reading disability. *JAMA* 291:2007–12

Sadker M, Sadker D. 1994. *Failing at Fairness: How America's Schools Cheat Girls*. New York: Maxwell Macmillan

Seftor N, Turner S. 2002. Back to school: federal student aid policy and adult college enrollment. *J. Hum. Res.* 37(2):336–52

Segal DR, Segal MW. 2004. America's military population. *Popul. Bull.* 59(4):1–40. www. prb.org/ Source/ACF1396.pdf

Shanahan MJ. 2000. Pathways to adulthood in changing societies: variability and mechanisms in life course perspective. *Annu. Rev. Sociol.* 26:667–92

Silverman IW. 2003. Gender differences in delay of gratification: a meta-analysis. *Sex Roles* 49(9–10): 451–63

Snyder TD, Dillow SA. 2007. *Digest of Educational Statistics 2006*. Washington, DC: Natl. Cent. Educ. Stat.

Sokal L, Katz H, Chaszewski L, Wojick C. 2007. Good-bye, Mr. Chips: male teacher shortages and boys' reading achievement. *Sex Roles* 56(9–10): 651–59

Sommers CH. 2000. *The War Against Boys: How Misguided Feminism Is Harming our Young Men*. New York: Touchstone

Spain D, Bianchi SM. 1996. *Balancing Act: Motherhood, Marriage and Employment among American Women*. New York: Russell Sage

Spelke ES. 2005. Sex differences in intrinsic aptitude for mathematics and science? A critical review. *Am. Psychol.* 60(9):950–58

Spelke ES, Newport E. 1998. Nativism, empiricism and the development of knowledge. In *Handbook of Child Psychology. Vol. 1: Theoretical Models of Human Development*, ed. W Damon, RM Lerner, pp. 275–340. New York: Wiley

Spencer SJ, Steele CM, Quinn DM. 1999. Stereotype threat and women's math performance. *J. Exp. Soc. Psychol.* 35(1):4–28

Steele CM. 1997. A threat in the air: how stereotypes shape intellectual identity and performance. *Am. Psychol.* 52(6):613–29

Stevenson DL, Baker DP. 1987. The family-school relation and the child's school performance. *Child Dev.* 58(5):1348–57

Tach LM, Farkas G. 2006. Learning-related behaviors, cognitive skills, and ability grouping when schooling begins. *Soc. Sci. Res.* 35(4):1048–79

Tanner JM. 1978. *Foetus into Man: Physical Growth from Conception to Maturity*. Cambridge, MA: Harvard Univ. Press

Trzesniewski KH, Moffitt TE, Caspi A, Taylor A, Maughan B. 2006. Revisiting the association between reading achievement and antisocial behavior: new evidence of an environmental explanation from a twin study. *Child Dev.* 77(1): 72–88

U.S. Dep. Defense. 2006. *Population Representation in the Military Services, Fiscal Year 2005*. Washington, DC: USGPO

West J, Denton K, Reaney L. 2000. *The Kindergarten Year: Findings from the Early Childhood Longitudinal Study*. Washington, DC: Natl. Cent. Educ. Stat.

Willingham WW, Cole SE. 1997. *Gender and Fair Assessment*. Mahwah, NJ: Lawrence Erlbaum

Wong KC, Lam YR, Ho LM. 2002. The effects of schooling on gender differences. *Brit. Educ. Res. J.* 28(6):827–43

Xie Y, Shauman KA. 2003. *Women in Science: Career Processes and Outcomes*. Cambridge, MA: Harvard Univ. Press

Zill N, West J. 2001. *Entering Kindergarten: A Portrait of American Children When They Begin School: Findings from the Condition of Education 2000*. Washington, DC: Natl. Cent. Educ. Stat.

From Social Ties to Social Capital

Class Differences in the Relations Between Schools and Parent Networks

Erin McNamara Horvat, Elliot B. Weininger, and Annette Lareau

The concept of social capital has undergone a meteoric rise to prominence over the last 15 years, as even a brief search of publication databases throughout the social sciences will document. Moreover, above and beyond its prominence in various subspecialties of sociology, political science, and neighboring disciplines, the concept's reach now extends into more distant fields such as public health (Hawe & Schiell, 2000; Morrow, 1999, 2000) and public housing research (Lang & Hornburg, 1998); it has also been placed on the agenda in various policy debates (see, for example, Woolcock, 1998).

This prominence is clearly reflected in educational research. James Coleman (1988, 1990) and Pierre Bourdieu (1986), the figures most frequently credited with theoretical development of the notion of social capital, both displayed an abiding interest in the sociology of education, thus ensuring that the concept would make itself known in that field of inquiry.[1] Nevertheless, in the context of educational research, studies elevating the concept of social capital to a prominent position have exhibited a restricted methodological scope, primarily using quantitative techniques. We argue that ethnography can make an important contribution by providing insights into the underlying actions that produce or expend social capital, thereby complementing quantitative research.

We take as our point of departure one of the most frequently invoked kinds of social capital—that of parental networks—to examine its impact on children's schooling. Using a large ethnographic dataset, we describe variations in the architecture of such networks. We also examine how they facilitate particular actions affecting children's school experiences. In doing so, we are particularly interested in assessing how

social capital comes into play when problematic issues arise at school. Our data suggest that there are important class-specific differences in the architecture of parental networks and, associated with this, in parents' capacity to effectively intervene in school matters. On the basis of this result, we suggest certain reformulations that may render the concept of social capital more useful in the context of educational research.

In what follows, we first briefly review the various conceptions of social capital that have animated educational research. After a short discussion of methodology, we demonstrate that parental networks vary across class categories. Our findings imply that the form of "intergenerational closure" identified by Coleman (1998, 1990) as one of the paradigmatic instances of educationally relevant social capital—network ties connecting parents of school peers—is primarily a middle-class phenomenon. In the case of working-class and poor families, by contrast, closure is organized predominantly along kinship lines. The data further indicate that the presence of professionals in parental networks is substantially more prevalent in the middle class. We follow with a discussion of how problems at school are dealt with by middle-class parents, on the one hand, and by poor and working-class parents, on the other, focusing on the manner in which these networks may play a role. Here we show that the resources that are made available to middle-class parents through their networks affect various aspects of their children's schooling, including teacher behavior, track placement, and program participation. We conclude by arguing that in the educational context, social capital may be just as likely to function as a mechanism that facilitates the intergenerational transmission of advantage as one that ameliorates its effects.

Social Capital and Education

Use of the term "social capital" has been plagued by conceptual murkiness. The "foundational" statements in the social capital literature—primarily those of Coleman (1988, 1990) and Bourdieu (1986)—were relatively brief and imprecise, leaving subsequent researchers free to develop discrepant meanings of the same term. Moreover, as Portes (1998) noted in a review, some of the most widely cited uses of the concept—including those of Coleman (1988, 1990) and Putnam (1996)—failed to distinguish adequately between the constitutive elements of social capital, the various manners in which it can be put to use, and the manifold consequences it brings about. The upshot of this, Portes argued, was analyses that often did not live up to their explanatory ambitions, punctuated from time to time by tautological declarations or equations that did little more than attach new labels to familiar variables.

Consequently, the most recent research has devoted considerable attention to the development of a theoretically clarified, broadly oriented, and analytically rigorous conceptualization of social capital (Lin, 2001; Portes, 1998; Portes & Sensenbrenner, 1993; Woolcock, 1998). However, with occasional exceptions (discussed later), educational research has not been involved in this conceptual work. Instead, studies of the (hypothesized) importance and role of social capital in educational contexts have proceeded largely on the basis of examples provided by Coleman (1988, 1990) and, in particular, examples of intergenerational closure (networks connecting the parents of school peers) and parent-child relations (and more specifically, parental involvement in children's schooling). In the case of intergenerational closure, social capital is understood in terms of a set of social relations that enables the reciprocal monitoring of children by the parents of peers, thereby increasing adherence to behavioral norms that are presumed to affect school performance. In the case of parent-child relations, social capital denotes the intensity—construed affectively or normatively—with which parents undertake behaviors that contribute to their children's schooling, such as studying together.

(See Dika & Singh, 2002, for a review of educational research on social capital.) The outcomes of studies proceeding from these definitions have not, by and large, triggered theoretical reconsideration of the notion of social capital.[2]

The majority of studies examining social capital in school settings have used quantitative methodologies to address outcomes such as test scores and grades, study habits, or high school dropout patterns and college attendance. The results have been less than decisive. Taking up the question of familial social capital, Goyette and Conchas (in press) reported modest effects for a parent-child interaction index on the amount of time devoted to homework among Mexican and Vietnamese youth. Likewise, Smith, Beaulieu, and Seraphine (1995)—using indicators such as maternal employment, number of siblings, and (self-reported) parental monitoring practices—have registered associations between familial social capital and the likelihood of college attendance; however, these associations were partially contingent on location (i.e., urban, suburban, town, or rural residency). Using different data and measures, McNeal (1999) found that familial social capital is only efficacious in keeping children from dropping out of high school in combination with high socioeconomic status—that is, when parents have a high income, education, and/or occupational prestige.[3]

The literature on intergenerational closure (that is, networks connecting parents of school peers) has been even more mixed. Both Muller (1995) and Carbonaro (1998) reported effects on mathematics achievement; the latter study also discerned an impact on high school dropout rates. However, Morgan and Sørensen (1999) subsequently presented data implying that the results for mathematics were spurious, a claim Carbonaro (1999) assented to. Muller and Ellison (2001) have also reported a modest negative effect on class cutting. In contrast, however, Goyette and Conchas (in press) found no association between a Colemanesque measure of closure and time devoted to homework among Mexican or Vietnamese youth. It is interesting that Teachman, Paasch, and Carver (1997), taking up the subject of high school dropout rates, discerned a significant interaction between income and a measure of whether parents know the parents of their child's friends.[4] The work of Stanton-Salazar (1997) and Stanton-Salazar and Dornbusch (1995) constitutes something of an exception to the literature because it moves away from the general orientation toward Coleman's theoretical premises. Drawing on Bourdieu, Stanton-Salazar renders central class and race differences in the architecture and function of interpersonal networks: "[W]hereas working class community and networks are organized on the basis of scarcity and conservation, the cosmopolitan networks constructed by middle-class members are oriented toward maximizing individual (and group) access to the mainstream marketplace" (1997, p. 4). Indeed, Stanton-Salazar insists on the stratified character of social networks strongly enough to define social capital in terms of the "degree and quality of middle-class forms of social support" transmitted through social ties (1997, p. 5). From this perspective, social capital is largely implicated in the reproduction of stratification—an argument that finds at least provisional support in the quantitative studies (mentioned earlier) that exhibit a positive effect for social capital only in combination with an indicator of social position.

The institutional conditions under which schooling occurs generally fall outside the scope of the studies just discussed. Others, however, take a more critical edge. Some of these highlight resources that low-income families provide for their children but which go unrecognized by school officials. Delgado-Gaitan (1992), for example, in a study of six Mexican-American families, finds that neither resources inside the home, such as parents assisting with homework, and resources outside the home, such as parents procuring information from co-workers on how to manage a problem at their child's school, are presently not recognized in the school. Similarly, Villanueva (1996), in a study of three generations of Latino families, stresses the "wisdom" of grandparents who are not formally educated yet provide important lessons to children and grandchildren. The work of both Delgado-

Gaitan and Villanueva thus highlights the important role played by the school in selectively legitimating family resources.

In a related vein, Mehan and his colleagues (1996) studied an untracking effort in San Diego called Advancement Via Individual Determination (AVID), in which a sample of underperforming minority students was placed in a special class and provided with additional support services (i.e., help in procuring college applications, visiting campuses, and negotiating the application process). Mehan and his colleagues argue that if social and cultural capital can be inculcated and activated by institutional agents, then schools need not merely be reproducers of class cultures but can assist in transformation (see also Moll, Amanti, Neff, & Gonzales, 1992). Similarly, Valenzuela (1999) reported that the recent immigrants in her study of Latino students in a Texas high school had higher levels of social capital than their U.S.-born counterparts, but also found that the social capital held by these students was no match for the exclusionary tracking practices of the school. Thus, although this work is useful in directing us to consider the strengths to be found in low-income immigrant families and communities, the fact remains that the school has an independent and critical role in deciding crucial aspects of children's educational advancement. In this context, the literature suggests that the social networks accessible by working-class and poor families are less valuable than those of middle-class families for negotiating the particular institutional environment formed by the school.

In this article we approach social capital in terms of the emergent consensus (Lin, 2001; Portes, 1998; Stanton-Salazar, 1997) that the concept must be taken to refer to the material and immaterial resources that individuals and families are able to access through their social ties. In contrast to Stanton-Salazar, whose work focuses primarily on the network ties that profitably connect students with key institutional agents such as teachers and guidance counselors, we return to one of the "canonical" implementations of the concept of social capital by asking whether informal parental networks differ by class in their basic architecture and whether parents differ in how they put their network ties to use in resolving problems with schools to secure advantageous outcomes for their children.[5] In particular, we take up the question of whether and how social capital can enable certain actors to *contest* the judgments or behavior of agents who occupy positions of institutional authority—in this case, educators and school officials. On the basis of our results, we subsequently return to questions of theory, arguing that, consistent with the work of Lin (2001) in particular, it is necessary to give a central place to the theme of *inequality* in efforts to re-conceptualize social capital.

Data and Method

The findings reported here are based on interviews with and observations of 88 third-and fourth-grade children and their families. The interviews were carried out in phases as part of a larger study that intensively examined children's lives both in and out of school. The study was designed to provide an in-depth comparison of parents' relationships with schools as well as other institutions, including health care and organized leisure activities such as organized sports, Brownies, and Boy Scouts. Third and fourth graders were selected because at that stage parents are still heavily involved in children's lives, yet children also begin to display some autonomy regarding their leisure time. All names used in this article are pseudonyms.

The third author of this article, a White middle-class woman, began the study by locating a pool of children in a third-grade classroom in the Mid-western university community of Lawrenceville (population approximately 25,000). She conducted participant observations and in-depth interviews at Quigley school, a mixed-race and mixed-class environment. In conducting the interviews she was assisted by a Black graduate student. In addition, she observed children in out-of-class activities such as sporting events. These data were collected in 1989–1990. After a move to a large Northeastern city, the third author continued data collection. Here, because of residential segregation, schools tended to be homogeneous by race and class. In the end,

she settled for including a predominantly White suburban school with some Black middle-class families in it (Swan) and a city school in a White workingclass neighborhood (Lower Richmond) that drew a number of poor Black families from an adjacent housing project.[6] These data were collected from 1993 to 1995. During data collection in the Northeast, a mixed-race and mixed-gender team of graduate students assisted the third author.[7] The third author conducted almost all of the classroom observations and was assisted by the team for the interviews and observations of school and community events. Thus the study was organized around classrooms in three different schools: Quigley, Swan, and Lower Richmond (see Table 9.5). It was primarily from these classrooms that the families were recruited. It is important to note that the project was conceived of as a single study. Although the data collection spanned multiple sites over a relatively long period of time, the same core interview protocol was used throughout (with modest additions and deletions), and the sampling techniques remained consistent. Most important, the research questions and aims of the study remained fundamentally the same for the duration of the project.

In all three schools, observations included both in-class and out-of-classroom activities. The classroom observations included routine classroom activities and lessons. Researchers also observed parent-teacher conferences, PTA meetings, and special events such as graduation, school fairs, book fairs, Back-to-School Night, and classroom celebrations of Halloween and Valentine's Day. During these informal school activities, visible differences in the density of the parental networks were observed. As in Lareau's 2000 study showing that middle-class parents were more connected to one another and to the school, the middle-class parents observed for this study were involved in the life of the school (for example, they ran the book fair and school fair) and connected to one another. The parents at Lower Richmond did not know each other. On Back-to-School Night the classroom was quiet before the start of the program. Few greetings were exchanged among parents. The reverse was true at Swan. Before the beginning of the formal

Table 9.5 Summary of School Characteristics

School characteristic	Quigley	Lower Richmond	Swan
Type of school and grades served	Public 1–3	Public K–5	Public K–5
Number of students enrolled	200	475	450
Racial composition of student body	52% White[a] 44% Black 3% Asian 1% Hispanic	54% White 44% Black 1% Asian 1% Hispanic	90% White[b] 8% Black 2% Asian
Percentage of school population eligible for free lunch	40%	64%	n/a[c]
Surrounding area	Midwestern university town	Residentially stable, White working-class neighborhood close to a Black poor area in a large Northeastern city	Predominantly White, suburban middle-class area in a large Northeastern city

Note. n/a = not applicable.

a The ethnic breakdown is for the entire school district, which included four elementary schools, one junior high school, and one high school. The elementary schools were racially balanced.

b Estimated by the researcher on the basis of conversations with the principal.

c The school did not offer a free lunch program.

program on Back-to-School Night the room was alive with parents' conversations about children's organized activities. The room was noisy. In addition, parent-run school events at Swan were more elaborate. For example, the school fair at Swan had more booths and fancier rides than the fair at Lower Richmond. Following up on the patterns observed at the schools, the third author and her assistants carried out interviews—averaging about 2 hours each—with 137 parents or guardians of the various children. It is these data, in particular, that we draw on here.

The families in each school were allocated to class categories on the basis of criteria widely used in contemporary sociology (e.g., Wright, 1997; Zipp & Plutzer, 1996), although the relatively small number of cases precluded highly differentiated schemes similar to those developed for quantitative class analysis. On the basis of detailed information concerning respondents' jobs, we grouped some families in the middle-class category in which at least one adult was employed in an occupation that entailed some kind of managerial (as opposed to merely

supervisory) authority or presupposed some type of highly credentialed skill.[8] Correlatively, families in which adult members' jobs did not exhibit either of those attributes were grouped in the working-class category. We broke with the tendency of most sociological studies of class, however, by adding a category for "the poor" to our data, under which were grouped families for whom government assistance, rather than participation in the labor market, constituted the primary means of subsistence. Our reason for doing so was that one of our schools included a substantial number of children from such families, and their exclusion would have been arbitrary. To select interviewees, students at each school were grouped by race and social class. Then every third student was selected and a letter was sent home explaining the study and requesting one interview each with the mother and the father (the parents were interviewed separately). In these classrooms (which ranged from 26 to 30 students) more than 90% of the parents agreed to participate. The classrooms did not, however, yield sufficient numbers of children in some key categories (i.e., middle-class

Black children and poor White children). These children were recruited elsewhere.[9]

As was indicated earlier, most of the families in the study were recruited from three schools. Given the significant impact of school culture and norms on the behavior of students and families, it is reasonable to question whether our results are due to school effects. That is, it could be argued that some of the class effects that we report are actually the result of differences between the schools. Because of the high degree of class homogeneity in the schools from which most of our sample was drawn, it is difficult to put this concern to rest. Thus, although our results clearly point to the power of the middle-class parents to harness social capital in their interactions with schools, this finding could also be affected by the school context. Further research that samples students from a wide selection of school settings is needed to disentangle these effects.

Although social class is the central focus of this article, the roles of race and family structure are worthy of comment. Briefly, we found comparable social class patterns interwoven across race boundaries; we consider the role of race later in the article. Similarly, reflecting a national pattern, we found social-class differences to be interwoven with differences in family structure (see Table 9.6). Middle-class children were far more likely to come from two-parent households. In the sample of 36 middle-class children, only three came from single-parent

families. Although some of the poor children had regular contact with their fathers, none resided together. The working-class families had a mixed family structure with both two-parent and single-parent households. Although family structure is not the focus of this article, it may be confounded with the class differences we report.

Results: Class Differences in the Architecture and Mobilization of Networks

We proceed by first examining class differences in the shape or architecture of familial networks. We show that for middle-class families, webs of social ties tend to be woven through children's lives and especially through the organized activities they participate in, as well as through informal contacts with educators and other professionals. By contrast, the social networks of working-class and poor families tend to be rooted in and around kinship groups; ties to other parents and to professionals are considerably less common. We subsequently examine how these differences come into play when families encounter problems with the school. Here we demonstrate that middle-class parents, largely as a result of their network ties, have considerably greater resources at their disposal when it comes to dealing with such problems than do their working-class and poor counterparts. We detail the ways—both individual and collective—that they put them to use. Finally, we discuss

Table 9.6 Family Structure, by Race and Class

Social Class	Intact, two-parent, original family		Blended family[a]		Single-parent family		Family run by grandparent or guardian	
	Black	White	Black	White	Black	White	Black	White
Middle-class	13	17	2	1	3	0	0	0
Working-class	6 Black 6 White 1 Bi-racial		0	1	3	5	2	2
Poor	0	3	0	0	12	9	2	0

a "Blended families" include single- and two-parent households where a parent has remarried or there are other live-in adults who are romantically attached.

some alternative ways that social networks can affect families' daily lives.

Network Patterns

Parental networks, our data suggest, differ dramatically by social class. We demonstrate this through an examination of children's participation in organized activities, the existence of ties between parents of school peers, parental ties to professionals, and frequency of contact with kin. Here we rely on quantified tabulations of our interview data as well as on ethnographic interpretation. We make no claim that the tabulations can serve as the basis for inferences to corresponding populations; we use them merely as a convenient method for summarizing our findings.[10]

The role of children's organized activities in determining the shape of parents' networks was striking in our data. In families of all classes, informal connections between parents, when they existed, were largely generated and sustained through children's out-of-school activities. Typical was a White middle-class mother's response when asked how she knew another parent: "Our kids are the same age and PTA. They did similar activities, ballet, and all that together." The father of a White middle-class girl described how his children's school relationships and activities have shaped the family's social life: "Oh, yeah, I mean, between school and sports and scouts . . . those three things, you know, we've gotten maybe closer to some other families whose children are on the same routine than we would have otherwise." Another father of a middle-class White boy provided this account of how he knows some of the family's friends:

> Uh, Hingham are through soccer and Nadine's mother is through pre-school; Crowley's Dad goes to our church but he's in our department and we socialize with them; and Pete Hughes through athletics and Meadows through athletics and Nichols through athletics.

Working-class and poor families also tended to make connections with other parents through their children's activities. In a typical response, a working-class White mother reported how she knows a particular parent: "I know her from just bein' in Brownies." Parents used the significant amount of time spent waiting and watching at children's activities to get to know other parents. Here Ms. Logan, the aunt and guardian of a working-class White boy, described the typical process: "We would go and watch the game and that way you get to know some of the parents a little bit better. If you know some of the parents anyway, it gives you some time to visit and interact with them." Despite the importance of organized children's activities in fostering and sustaining parental networks for members of all classes, there were substantial differences in the rates at which children participated in these activities. Middle-class children enrolled at significantly higher levels than their working-class or poor counterparts. As indicated in Table 9.7, middle-class children participated in just under five organized activities on average, whereas working-class children participated in just under three, and poor children participated in just under two. Given that children's activities are a central pathway for the formation and maintenance of parental connections, these differences suggest that in at least one important arena, middle-class parents have greater opportunity to forge such connections.

As has been noted, much of the literature on social capital focuses on the issue of ties between the parents of school peers. These ties figured prominently in the informal social connections that were forged as a result of children's participation in organized activities. Thus our data imply that the type of social closure that is central to Colemanesque accounts of social capital is considerably more common in the middle class. In the interviews, parents were presented with a list of all of the children in their child's class and asked to identify those whose parents they would recognize and chat with if they ran into them in the grocery store. As Table 9.8 indicates, middle-class parents reported that they would likely recognize and chat with a parent of seven classmates, on average, as compared with only

Table 9.7 Average Number of Child's Organized Activities, by Class

Organized activities	Middle-class	Working-class	Poor
Number of organized activities	4.9	2.5	1.5
Items with missing data[a]	2.5	3.0	2.0
N	36	26	26

Note. This table is based on information provided by each child's primary caregiver. Organized activities included Brownies or Cub Scouts, music lessons, team sports (soccer, Little League, etc.), nonteam sports (gymnastics, karate, etc.), Tot Tumbling, dance lessons (ballet, tap dance, etc.), religious classes, choir, art classes, and any activity offered through a recreational center that required formal enrollment.

a Not every respondent was asked about all of the activities that were eventually coded (although each was asked if his or her child participated in any activities not explicitly mentioned).

three for working-class parents. Hence, on the basis of our data it would appear that, among families of 8- to 10-year-old children, this indicator of social capital is not independent of social class.

However, the differences characterizing familial networks went beyond those pertaining to ties between parents of school peers. In another key area—acquaintance with various sorts of professionals—a similar pattern was apparent. This is highlighted in Table 9.9. The data imply that middle-class parents are far more likely to include professionals in their interpersonal networks than are working-class and poor parents. Thus almost all of the middle-class parents in our study reported that they knew a teacher, in contrast to less than half of the working-class parents and about a third of the poor parents. Analogously, two thirds of middle-class parents reported that they knew a lawyer,

Table 9.8 Average Number of Child's School Peers Whose Parent(s) Were Known to Respondent, by Class

Peers	Middle-class	Working-class
Number of peers whose parent(s) were known to respondent	6.8	3.0
N	21	19

Note. This table is based on information provided by each child's primary caregiver. The "poor" group is excluded because most poor White families had to be recruited from outside the schools being studied. Because we did not have extensive information about such schools, we did not ask the same questions of respondents whose children attended them. The study included 36 middle-class families and 26 working-class families. Lower numbers are reported here as a result of missing data.

Table 9.9 Proportion of Children Whose Parents/Guardians Knew Professionals, by Class

Type of professional	Middle-class	Working-class	Poor
Teacher	93.5%	47.6%	33.3%
Psychologist	48.4%	19.0%	8.7%
Lawyer	67.7%	35.0%	13.6%
Doctor	70.4%	15.0%	18.2%
N	27–31	20–21	22–24

Note. This table is based on information provided by each child's primary caregiver. The study included 36 middle-class families, 26 working-class families, and 26 poor families. Lower numbers are reported here as a result of missing data.

in contrast to a third of the working-class parents and only 14% of the poor families. The results for acquaintance with a doctor and a psychologist are similar: Despite some variation in the size of the working class–poor gap, middle-class families are always far more likely than all others to include professionals in their networks. To be sure, such a finding is not wholly surprising, given that a substantial proportion of the respondents in the middle-class category are themselves professionals. Nevertheless, as we demonstrate in the next section, professionals of various sorts can serve as a key resource for resolving some of the problems that crop up in the course of a child's schooling.

If the working-class and poor parents did not exhibit extensive ties to other parents or to professionals, what were the defining characteristics of their interpersonal networks? To be sure, parents in working-class families—like their middle-class counterparts—enjoyed friendships with co-workers; and members of all classes often counted neighbors among their close friends.[11] This being said, for both the working-class and poor families in our sample, the primary source of network ties was kinship. Indeed, the informal social life of family members frequently revolved around contact with relatives. This was in marked contrast to middle-class families, whose relatives often did not live in close geographic proximity and whose contacts with relatives were more likely to take the form of occasional events (e.g., holiday get-togethers). Table 9.10 includes two measures of the importance of kinship ties in the lives of working-class and poor families. Although the measures are imprecise, they indicate that frequent contact with a parent was considerably more common among working-class and poor respondents and that frequent contact with any extended family member was at least somewhat more common.[12] Also worthy of emphasis—a factor for which we lack a quantitative summary, however—was the prominence of relatives in the everyday lives of working-class and poor children: A great deal of leisure time was devoted to informal play with cousins of varying ages. The fact that the extended family played such an important role in the life of both children and adults in these families carries an interesting implication: The children were often enmeshed in a form of intergenerational closure; however, it was not one that was generated by school-centered networks.

Having examined the network "profiles" of families located in different social classes, we now take up the question of how parents' social capital may affect their children's school experiences. We address this issue through an analysis of situations in which parents may feel compelled

Table 9.10 Frequency of Parents'/Guardians' Contact with Extended Family Members, by Class

Contact with extended family	Middle-class	Working-class	Poor
Saw mother at least five times per year[a]	52.2%	87.5%	83.3%
N	23	16	12
Saw an extended family member at least five times per year[b]	63.6%	80.0%	69.2%
N	33	20	26

Note. This table is based on information provided by each child's primary caregiver. The study included 36 middle-class families, 26 working-class families, and 26 poor families. Lower numbers are reported here partly as a result of missing data.

a When a respondent reported a mother who was deceased, he or she was excluded from this calculation. There were 5 such cases among the middle-class families, 3 among the working-class families, and 10 among the poor families.

b These figures are based on the respondent's contact with the extended family member whom he or she saw most frequently. For the working-class and poor families, the rates on this variable are lower than the measure of contact with the mother because cases in which the mother was reported deceased are included here.

to intervene in their children's schooling. Our data imply that middle-class networks frequently make available various resources that parents can (and do) use to deal with such situations, thereby attaining a desired outcome for their children. For example, when confronted with inappropriate behavior on the part of a teacher, parents' ties to other parents often enabled them to function as "guardian angels," descending on the school en masse and quickly bringing about change. In contrast, working-class and poor parents inevitably responded to such situations in a purely individualized fashion. Likewise, middle-class parents' networks provided resources that made it possible to customize their children's educational careers in important ways—for example, by contesting a placement decision or obtaining additional resources for a learning-disabled child. In contrast, working-class and poor parents, lacking these resources, were considerably less likely to dispute the school's authority.

Responding to Inappropriate Teacher Behavior

In the schools that we studied, teachers occasionally acted inappropriately, either by losing their temper with a student and yelling or by striking or pushing a student. Middle-class parents responded in a very different fashion to these incidents than did working-class and poor parents. Middle-class parents mobilized resources to respond collectively. By contrast, in working-class and poor families, these incidents were treated as the behavior of an individual teacher with a student and were addressed at the individual level. Although kinship networks were often aware of the difficulty, other parents in the school community were not.

The case of Garrett Tallinger, a White middle-class boy, provides an example. In the course of what was supposed to be a noncompetitive football game, a dispute broke out with the physical education teacher over whether Garrett had scored a touchdown. According to Garrett's mother,

Carl [the teacher] evidently pushed Garrett away, I mean, he just lost it. He just didn't want these kids in this big argument with him. And he must have thrown down the football, but it bounced up and hit one of the kids. Although one of the kids said he just threw it right at him. [He] pushed Garrett, picked up another kid, I mean, one of the kids, he picked [him] up and threw him down, sent the girls inside, apologized evidently, who knows, . . . and kept the boys out. But it really frightened the kids. It frightened the girls, because they were very upset, when they got to class. Carl went in, apologized to the girls. . . . He apologized on the spot and then left. The school. This was the last period of the day. But the boys were really shaken. Well, some of the boys.

Ms. Tallinger did not learn about these events from her son. Instead, she returned home that day to find a slew of phone messages already awaiting her:

I had come home with this major traffic jam . . ., walk in the door, Garrett's in the basement, . . . and I had all these phone messages, Georgia Finley, Midge Bartlett, Rick's mother. [Before I could even say hello to the children I got another phone call.] Sarah says, "Have you talked to Garrett?" I said, "No." I could tell by her tone of voice. She said, "Well . . .," and then she proceeded to tell me that Don [her son] was practically bruised. . . . At this point, I still hadn't talked to Garrett.

By then members of the school board were getting calls. The parental network facilitated a quick and collective response. The teacher and the principal called the Tallingers that weekend. There was a meeting with the parents the following Tuesday. The teacher was suspended for a week.

In stark contrast, working-class and poor families handled these same types of incidents in a more individual fashion. In the following example, the live-in boyfriend of the mother of Wendy Driver, a White working-class girl, describes what occurred after a school bus driver pushed Wendy. Their intervention was restricted to the individual level; only the family, principal, and bus driver were involved:

> The bus driver pushed her back into her seat and we feel that the bus driver has slips that he fills out. If the kids are not behaving, he's supposed to fill them out and turn them in and then let the school handle it, not touch the children. That's not what he's there for. So we went up. Well, I went up. I was off that day. And I took her up and spoke to one of the counselors and she said that the principal wasn't in yet, so I said OK and I let her go to class and I came home. I went back up when the principal came in and I sat down and I talked to the principal. She seemed like a real nice person. She said she'll see what's going on. He is supposed to fill out slips and not touch students. So ever since then, she hasn't come home and said anything about the bus driver touching her.

In a similar, though more serious, example, a poor Black girl had her hair pulled by a teacher. The girl's aunt (also her guardian) responded by writing the teacher a "very nasty note." When asked to relay what the note said, she replied:

> I told him you put your damn hands on my daughter's head one more fuckin' time and I'll be there to fuck you up, period. Keep your hands off her. You don't have to pull her hair because she's not doing anything that bad. I know Kadija. Kadija don't do nothin'—she said somebody was messin' with her. You keep your hands off her, so I had no more problems out of him for the whole year [laughs].

In both cases, only immediate family members undertook the intervention. Although both actions were successful in the sense that they prevented future misbehavior, neither, to the best of our knowledge, resulted in formal disciplinary sanctions on the order of the one brought about by the Tallingers and their acquaintances.

In addition, among many working-class and poor parents there was knowledge that teachers would "hit kids" from time to time. For instance, Ms. Yanelli, a White working-class mother, had "heard" this:

> Well, I heard that Mr. Tier hits kids. And, uh, do you believe that? I don't know. I mean, there's talk in the neighborhood and I thought, what do you mean, he hits kids? He wouldn't get away with that so I kind of didn't believe it. And I asked Billy about it and he said once in a while he'll give him a noggin on the head, you know.

Nevertheless, despite this information, she liked the teacher because her son liked him:

> But, I really like Mr. Tier. He got Billy real interested this year and that means a lot to me because in Ms. Green's class he would daze out, just daze out, and that was our problem last year. . . . But he was so excited about having Mr. Tier this year he came home and said, I've got the best teacher in the whole school.

Our observations confirm that, on occasion, school officials or teachers would manhandle a student, by shoving or vigorously shaking him or her, or twisting an arm. Thus events that created an explosion of collective outrage among middle-class families tended to generate isolated anger or even resigned acceptance within working-class and poor families.[13]

Customizing Children's School Careers

Special Services

One very clear difference between the working-class and poor families and the middle-class families was in the way that parents handled any special educational needs their child might have. Whether the issue was a possible learning disability or inclusion in a "gifted" program, middle-class parents were much more proactive about the (perceived) educational needs of their children. Mobilizing network members to provide testing and gather information was the norm when a family was presented with a problem of this sort. Parents routinely talked about discussing these types of issues with family and friends who were in the field of education. For example, the mother of Melanie Handlon, a White middle-class girl, tapped into her networks when the school suggested that Melanie might have a learning disability.

> Well, [the school] decided at the end of last year that they didn't think [testing] was necessary. She had improved in all of her subjects. And now when this year started they again suggested that we have her tested, and we are going to do it this year. Uh, I've been watching and observing her. My sister-in-law, who is a teacher, has been watching her and observing her. We don't see any of the classic things that, you know, they diagnose for learning disabilities.

A similar process took place in the case of children potentially eligible for inclusion in a gifted program. In the case of the Marshalls, a middle-class Black family, we can again see how a parent collected information through network ties and then used it to secure the desired outcome for her daughter. Stacey Marshall had applied for admittance to the gifted program but had scored slightly below the minimum threshold on the entrance exam. She subsequently enrolled in a school activity called Problem Solving that was run by the teacher who administered the gifted program. Encountering Ms. Marshall in the hall one afternoon, the teacher declared, "You really should get her tested. She's an extremely bright child." After discussing the matter with her husband, Ms. Marshall determined that they should "scrape together the money" (about $200) to have Stacey tested by a private psychologist. In the following excerpt Ms. Marshall details her use of community contacts to locate a psychologist:

> I found out about Terry Hoffman [the psychologist] from . . . a White friend of mine . . . whose son had been at the same . . . school with [Stacey's older sister]. They live in a different school district and, as it turns out, they had gone through the same thing with her son. Her son had not made the screening test at his elementary school. And June [the mother] is very, um, . . . aggressive and assertive and she kinda hit the roof. You know, "Well wha'd'ya mean?" If you don't make it, you can challenge it. And she decided, "I'm takin' Drew [her son]

some place else." And she had found this Terry Hoffman.

Networks were pivotal both in making the decision to have Stacey tested and in locating a psychologist to conduct the testing. Stacey was tested by Dr. Hoffman and scored high enough that her parents were able to push to have her admitted to the gifted program.

Also interesting in this respect is the case of Marcus Baldwin, a Black middle-class boy. Two months into his third-grade year, Ms. Baldwin heard from his teacher that "he wasn't learning anything, wasn't makin' any gains." The teacher and the counselor called a conference to deliver this information, in which they said that they thought Marcus had "serious delays." The educators proposed testing him for learning disabilities. Ms. Baldwin was upset that it had taken them so long to notify her. Drawing on her extensive professional networks, she decided to have him evaluated herself:

> I'm in the field of mental health so I know psychologists. I have a Master's in clinical [psychology]. . . . I've done almost everything. I've worked all the settings: community mental health, school, residential, . . . all of that, individual . . . therapy, group therapy, testing. I—I've done it all. So I got a psychologist to evaluate him. It was someone I know that I have worked with in the past. We were in the same organization. . . . He was a school psychologist, certified school psychologist.

Ms. Baldwin was able to use the assessment provided by her colleague to challenge the educators' conclusions:

> He evaluated him and Marcus tested out above-average intelligence. Well what's goin' on? So, we had a big conference: the principal, the teacher, [the psychologist] came—presented the test, everything. And then they're like: We have to figure out what's—what has happened. If you've got a kid who has above-average intelligence and the performance is—is totally different: Where are things?

Thus Ms. Baldwin's network ties provided her with the leverage that allowed her to contest the school officials' view of her child's abilities.

In contrast, working-class and poor families rarely used network ties to try to intervene in placement processes or to dispute assessments —whether the families were sanguine about the results or not. They did not, by and large, mobilize networks to challenge gatekeepers in schools. Indeed, some parents were wary of contact with professionals and also felt that they should be able to "handle it themselves." This sentiment is apparent in the response provided by Ms. Nelson, a Black working-class mother, when asked whether she and her husband would take their child to a counselor or psychologist:

> Well, there's nothing wrong with them [counselors and psychologists]— if you can't do it, you go find somebody else. If you can't handle it. But I shouldn't have to go somewhere. I don't send mine anywhere else when I can deal with the situation or we can deal with the situation.

In combination with the fact that their networks included so few professionals, this ethos rendered working-class and poor parents highly dependent on the school in the area of assessment and considerably more deferential than their middle-class counterparts in matters pertaining to placement. In one example, Wendy Driver, a White girl from a working-class family, was unable to read by fourth grade. Her mother was very concerned but felt that she could depend on the school to advise her on a course of action:

> I think they just want to keep it in the school [for] now, and when they get to a point where they can't figure out what it is, . . . then I guess they'll send me somewhere else. . . . So I figured I'd wait until the first report card to see what they'd say and then take it from there.

Nor did she have any idea what she might do to address the issue herself:

> I wouldn't even know where to start going. On the radio there was something for children having problems reading and this and that call

and I suggested it to a couple different people and they were like, wait a second, it's only to get you there and you'll end up paying an arm and a leg. So I said to my mom, no, I'm going to wait until the first report card and go up and talk to them up there [at the school].

Whereas Ms. Baldwin could and did turn to colleagues for information, Ms. Driver's source of information was a radio advertisement. Later in the year, Ms. Driver knew that the teachers disagreed about how to proceed with her daughter. At a conference the fourth-grade teacher recommended retention, but the reading specialist argued that Wendy should be promoted. Ms. Driver felt incapable of adjudicating between them and ultimately left the decision to the school, on the grounds that she "[didn't] want to jump into anything and find out that it's the wrong thing."

Requesting a Teacher

Middle-class parents also used their networks to exert control over another critical aspect of their children's educational lives: selection of a teacher.[14] In the course of our interviews, parents were asked if they had ever requested a particular teacher for their child. As can be seen in Table 9.11, the results indicate that the middle-class parents were more than twice as likely to have made such a request as the working-class parents.[15]

Table 9.11 Proportion of Parents/Guardians Who Requested a Teacher, By Class

Parental requests	Middle-class	Working-class
Requested a teacher	34.4%	15.8%
N	32	19

Note. This table is based on information provided by each child's primary caregiver. The poor group is excluded because most poor White families had to be recruited from outside the schools being studied. Because we did not have extensive information about those schools, we did not ask the same questions about the school experiences of respondents whose children attended them. The study included 36 middle-class families and 26 working-class families. Lower numbers are reported here as a result of missing data.

To know which teacher to request, these middle-class parents used their connections with other parents and with professional educators. The following response from Mr. Conner, the father of a middle-class White boy, provides another example of the importance of professional connections:

> I don't think I [sought out such information] specifically. My wife probably did—she's more involved in the whole educational process. She's been a teacher, and she probably takes a much more active role researching about school, talking to other parents, finding out about teachers for the upcoming year, and requesting a teacher for the next year.

This remark reveals a general middle-class orientation toward the quasistrategic customization of children's school careers ("the whole educational process")—that is, a careful scrutiny of potential opportunities to "improve," "correct," and render more "fulfilling" their children's school experience. (Also typical is the fact that the majority of the actual work is done by the mother.)

Informal conversations with other parents that touched on the subject of teachers often took place at school events or at community events such as church functions or children's activities. When asked where she gathered information on prospective teachers, Ms. Hughes, a White middle-class mother who had made many such requests, replied, "Oh, from parents—just out on the soccer field or, you know, you kind of scout around." Ms. Irving, the mother of a Black middle-class girl, offered the following account:

> Well, I have several friends who are teachers in the school district. And I have several friends that have kids who go to the school. . . . So you talk to someone who has an older kid who had her [the teacher]. What did you think of her, ya know? And usually when you do that you go, you talk to someone whose child had the same learning ability. Or whose child you would like to see [your child] do as well as. I've done that

before. I've asked people, you know, What do you think of her? Or just in talking to people. . . . You hear about other teachers, just in associating with other parents.

Thus Ms. Irving not only perceived a need to gather information that could be useful in improving her child's school experience but also exhibited a deft awareness of the variable relevance of information provided by various sources. An analogous sensitivity is apparent in the remarks of Ms. McNamara, a middle-class White mother who also described teacher selection in strategic terms: "I try to not request very often. . . . Because if you do . . . it's like, you get ignored. It's better to, like, save your ammunition for when you really need it."

In contrast, working-class and poor parents tended to accept the luck of the draw in their children's teacher assignments. This attitude presumably was due, at least in part, to the distinct character of their interpersonal networks, which typically lacked the type of contacts used by their middle-class counterparts for gathering the information that fueled teacher requests. Nevertheless, even when working-class and poor parents did have more or less compelling information regarding a teacher, they were much less likely to make a request. Rather, if they heard about an undesirable teacher at the bus stop, grocery store, or laundromat, they simply "hoped" that their child would avoid him or her. As Ms. Doerr, a Black working-class mother, put it:

> What's her name for next year? I sure hope she don't get her. What's her name, Ms. Worthingham or something like this, she's a fourthgrade teacher. I've heard horrible things about her. . . . It seems that she's not very friendly and she doesn't like children at all. In fact, I've been told that she's a real redneck.

Indeed, it appeared that many working-class and poor parents assumed that they had neither the capacity nor the right to intervene in such matters under the gatekeepers' jurisdiction.

Contesting the Curriculum

The occasional furors that erupted over curricular issues gave rise to processes similar to those that we have already examined. Middle-class parents, for example, shared concerns about aspects of the curriculum with other parents.

Thus when her child's school decided to hold an AIDS awareness week, Ms. Hopewell, the mother of a middle-class White girl, brought the matter before the PTA, arguing that it was inappropriate for young children and instigating a wide-ranging discussion. Although no consensus emerged among the parents, the school decided to send home formal notification of the program, offering parents the opportunity to hold their child out if they wished.

The full range of resources that middle-class parents have at their disposal becomes apparent in the case of the Kaplans, a middle-class Jewish family. In early fall, their son's class began practicing for the winter holiday program. The Kaplans were offended by a Christian song that the choir teacher had selected (as part of a multicultural holiday program) that included the lyrics "come let us bow and worship Him now." They were offended not for religious reasons but because they felt the lyrics blurred the distinction between church and state. Ms. Kaplan complained to the choir teacher, but the teacher felt that the song was in keeping with the overall diversity of the holiday program. Ms. Kaplan then went to the principal. Although usually highly attuned to parents' concerns, the principal sided with the choir teacher in this instance.

Mr. and Ms. Kaplan first attempted to mobilize other parents. They circulated a petition but found some parents unsupportive and unwilling to sign. They also wrote a letter on their own to the district superintendent, triggering a districtwide policy review. The offending song was removed from the holiday program. (The principal was "counseled" on issues of sensitivity as well.) The Kaplans were satisfied with this outcome but found that it had strained their relationships with some of the other parents. It is important to note that, in the process of contesting the school's authority, they did not expend all of the resources at their disposal. An old college friend of Ms. Kaplan's, who happened to work for a major television network on a national show, called to say hello in the middle of the drama. The friend offered to send down a camera crew to do a story; Ms. Kaplan declined, preferring to hold that option in reserve.

Alternative Network Functions

Our discussion thus far has presented an image of working-class and poor networks that verges on privation: Lacking extensive ties both to other parents in their child's school and to professionals, we have suggested, these parents tend to handle the problematic situations that arise in the course of their children's schooling on a purely individual basis, if they don't concede authority to the school altogether. Nevertheless, we do not wish to create the impression that working-class and poor familial networks are irrelevant. What is striking about our dataset is precisely the fact that these networks appear to offer working-class and poor families so little purchase on matters pertaining to schooling. They do, however, fulfill important functions in other areas of daily life, a point that we detail briefly in this section.

As noted earlier, working-class and poor families had stronger ties with kin than did middle-class families. These networks typically were dense, and much leisure time was spent with immediate and extended family members. Kinship ties also played a crucial role in enabling parents to deal with various exigencies, such as transportation to and from work. Here Ms. Connor, a White working-class mother, discusses the routine contact she has with her family:

Ms. Connor: [My parents] live on Spring Lane, which is a 5-minute drive from here. . . . If we ever need anything he [my father] can get to us. My brother lives up the street. I have another brother that lives down the street. I have a sister that lives over a few streets, and my twin sister lives around the corner from my parents, so we are all within 5 minutes of each other.

Q: And how often would you guess that you see your parents?

Ms. Connor: Every day. My father takes me to work every day.

Q: He drives you to work?

Ms. Connor: Yeah. He was driving me when I was working two jobs. Now I've been walking the kids to the bus stop. It's off and on, off and on. So when I'm not working two jobs I'm with the kids, and when I am working two jobs he drives me so I can get there quicker.

Later in the interview she described her close relationship with her mother and her sisters:

> Oh, we go to the laundromat, shopping, we spend every single holiday together and all the preparations for the holidays together. We have our Easter egg dyes—all of us; and one year I had 12 kids and four sets of parents and all kinds of dye and we dyed 15 dozen eggs, and Christmas time we do all the malls and see Santa Claus. . . . We're always together, inseparable.

In addition to transportation, extended family members frequently provided childcare, emotional support, and, at times, financial assistance. Thus Ms. Yanelli typically relied on her mother when her son had half days at school:

> Well, uh, I'll start throwing hints like 2 weeks before. I'll say to my mom, There's only a half day next week, or I'll give her my car. She doesn't have a car so she'll get the car and she'll do it. But as soon as the school year starts, I'm like, all these half days are gonna kill me. I just hate to ask people for anything. I'm sure they would do it but I just don't like to ask them to do it. They've got their own lives.

To be sure, the vagaries of residential location affected these dynamics: Working-class and poor families in our dataset were more likely than their middle-class counterparts to live in close proximity to kin. However, insofar as it is possible for us to separate objective issues of location from subjective ones, those families also appeared substantially more likely to consider extended kin to be an integral part of their daily lives—Ms. Yanelli's fierce sense of familial independence includes her mother—unlike middle-class families, for whom contact with relatives was reserved for "events" (e.g., holidays).

It is interesting that working-class and poor respondents did recognize the impact that "connections" could have. Needless to say, however, the connections at issue were not the psychologists and television producers that middle-class families would call on in times of need. This fact becomes palpably clear in the case of Ms. Grover, the mother of a poor White boy:

Ms. Grover: Yeah, my mom works at, at, um, House of Bargains, so she gets me a discount on their clothes, the smaller kids' clothes. And I can wear the clothes from there.

Q: Good connection there.

Ms. Grover: Yeah, it's always a good to have people connected.

For working-class and poor families, network ties had little relevance to the enhancement of schooling. Instead, they served primarily to alleviate problems stemming from economic necessity: transportation and childcare, clothing and money.

The Role of Race

Although we found that social class was most prominent in shaping the architecture and function of networks, race also played a role. In other analyses not reported here, the third author provides a detailed analysis of the ways in which race is interwoven with class (Lareau, 2003). Briefly, she argues that the largest differences in the organization of children's daily lives—including familial networks and styles of interaction with institutional representatives—are across lines of class, not race. The analysis indicates that middle-class families, Black and White, have far more in common with each other than they do with working-class and poor families of either race. As others have noted, Black middle-class parents express concern about their children experiencing racial discrimination in the wider world, particularly when they come into contact with institutions (Cose, 1995; Hochschild, 1995; Tatum, 1987). Black middle-class parents also take stock of the racial balance of many of their children's activities, for example by working hard to ensure that their son or daughter is never the only Black child participating in an event. Nevertheless, aspects of everyday life such as time use, social networks, and strategies for interacting with institutions that were exhibited by middle-class Black families were extremely similar, and in many ways indistinguishable, from those of their White counterparts. Moreover, a similar cross-racial pattern was found in the case of working-class and poor families. Below, we elaborate on the social-class similarities across race groups in three areas: children's organized activities, kin visits, and interventions with teachers in school.

As we illustrated earlier, one of the most important conduits for parental networks was children's activities. In comparing Black and White children's activities, we found very little difference by race. The cases of Alexander Williams, a Black middle-class boy, and Garrett Tallinger, a White middle-class boy, exemplify the similarities we found. Garret Tallinger is the oldest of three boys in his family. Both of his parents are professionals. His activities (apart from those he engages in as a part of school) include soccer team, traveling soccer team, basketball team, summer basketball team, swim team, and piano. The list of activities for Alexander Williams is strikingly similar. Alexander's parents also both work in professional positions. He is an only child. Outside school, Alexander is involved in soccer team, basketball team, community choir, church choir, Sunday school, and piano. The parents of both boys spend considerable time ferrying them to and from these activities, and during the study each boy found sometimes that the schedule for one of his activities overlapped or conflicted with another.[16] There were also indications in our data that Black parents tended to know other Black parents, in particular, when attending racially diverse organized activities and in school settings. These parents sometimes discussed

racial issues together, including, for example, the need for more Black teachers in the school district. Still, with the exception of church, the activities that the middle-class Black children in this sample participated in were racially integrated. In these activities, we observed middle-class Black and White mothers chatting together. Overall, middle-class children (Black and White) participated in many more organized activities than did their working-class and poor counterparts. These activities broadened parents' networks.

Similarly, in terms of contact with kin, we found a pattern that was characterized by distinct social class differences across race. Both Black and White middle-class families spent less time with kin than did working-class and poor families of both races. Typically, extended family lived far away, requiring significant travel and making visits time-intensive and infrequent. For example, Ms. Hopewell, a White middle-class mother with five children, drove 10 hours for an annual vacation with her husband's family, stating, "It's really the only time they get to see their cousins, which is why we want to kind of do it. The cousins get along famously." Similarly, a Black middle-class couple, Mr. and Mrs. Irving, did not have any relatives within 50 miles. They saw relatives only once a year. Mr. and Mrs. Williams, a Black middle-class couple, had to fly to see their relatives; they saw them three times per year but spoke on the phone more often. Even in middle-class families where kin lived in the same city, however, visits were less frequent than in working-class and poor families, Black and White. For example, the Whatleys, a middle-class Black family, lived across town (20 minutes by car) from aunts, uncles, and cousins on both sides of their family and yet saw them only on special occasions. As Ms. Whatley noted, "Most of our families live [across town] so we have very little contact just because of distance, you know, face-to-face. Except for holidays, special occasions or running down there, but it's not like a weekly thing." By contrast, for White and Black working-class and poor families in the study, extended kin were generally present in their daily lives. A White working-class mother, Ms. Yanelli, spoke on the phone with "all of my family" every day. A Black poor mother took care of her sister's children while her sister was between residences. It was hard to overestimate the importance of kin in the lives of working-class and poor families in this study.

In addition, middle-class parents of both races tended to intervene on their children's behalf in similar ways. As detailed above, we found that middle-class Black and White parents took steps on their children's behalf that we did not observe with working-class and poor parents. Ms. Baldwin, a Black middle-class mother activated an arsenal of resources when her son developed academic problems in third grade. Similarly, Mrs. Handlon, a White middle-class mother, hired a tutor when her daughter had learning problems. As we have reported elsewhere (Lareau, in press), Black mothers had more work in their childrearing tasks than did their White counterparts because, in addition to the generic shepherding of their children through schools and other institutions, they were vigilant about the possibility of racial discrimination and insensitivity on the part of officials, a concern that White parents were spared. Nevertheless, the general pattern of intervention in schooling was apparent in both Black and White homes.

It is important to note that the children whom we studied were relatively young. We expect that the role of race looms larger as children age, as peer groups become more segregated, and as individuals face racial pressures in dating and marital selection (Tatum, 1987). Racial discrimination was also part of the lived experience of these families: They lived in racially segregated neighborhoods, Black fathers experienced slights and insults as they encountered Whites in public settings, and many of the Black parents noted racial difficulties in their work lives. Black parents also wanted their children to have a positive Black identity; many attended Black churches. Thus race was undoubtedly salient in the lives of the families. However, in the aspects that we studied, particularly the organization of children's schedules and the propensity for parents to intervene in schooling, Black and White parents exhibited very similar patterns of behavior. In sum, within this limited, nonrandom sample, the racial differences in parents' childrearing practices were minimal.

Discussion

For this article we have used an ethnographic dataset, composed of extensive information on the families of 88 children, to examine the nature of parental networks and their impact on schooling. Our aim has been to describe variation in the architecture of social networks and to explore class differences in the mobilization or activation of network ties by parents in school settings. Given our methodology, systematic outcomes are hard to measure; however, our data do point to several important findings regarding the shape of the networks, their function in school settings, and the theoretical implications for social capital theory.

We find that Coleman's (1988, 1990) school-based "intergenerational closure"—that is, networks that link parents of school peers—is primarily a middle-class phenomenon. Moreover, these networks appear to form, at least in part, as a result of children's participation in organized activities, which is itself far more frequent in the middle-class. In contrast, working-class and poor families exhibit a form of intergenerational closure that is often circumscribed or delimited by kinship (see Fischer, 1982). In general, the social networks that we observed among working-class and poor families did not include ties to school or children's activity-based contacts.

We also find that the parental networks of middle-class families are far more likely to include professionals of various sorts than are those of their working-class and poor counterparts. Moreover, parental networks tend to be homogeneous with respect to class, in the sense that middle-class networks do not encompass working-class or poor parents, and working-class and poor networks do not encompass middle-class parents; in other words, informal networks tend to be "homophilous" (Lin, 2001). This network homogeneity is generally unrecognized in the tradition of social capital research stemming from Coleman (1988, 1990).

And although it is to some degree a function of school homogeneity, we believe it extends beyond that.

These network differences are clearly associated with differences in the way that problems with the school are handled. Working-class and poor parents tend to undertake individual responses and do not receive much concrete support through their networks in doing so. By contrast, middle-class parents sometimes react collectively; at other times they act individually but maintain the possibility of collective involvement in reserve. In yet other instances, middle-class parents draw on ties to individuals unconnected with the school who can provide the information, expertise, or authority necessary to compel the school to follow a preferred course of action. In short, both the architecture of parental networks and their use vis-à-vis the school vary dramatically by class.

Parents must decide how to handle the various problems, small or large, that inevitably crop up in the course of their children's schooling, as well as whether to try to intercede in the school's routine practices. To be sure, our data do not enable us to establish unequivocally whether the types of interventions we have documented tend to cumulate and whether they thereby have definite consequences for educational outcomes. Nevertheless, even if forms of parental involvement such as teacher requests are judged unlikely to dramatically affect children's educational attainment, interventions in issues such as teacher behavior, track placement, and program participation are a different matter. Indeed, Lucas (1999) has described a contemporary tracking regime in which placements in different subject areas are uncoupled from one another, resulting in an increase in the significance of parental interventions as determinants of tracking location (see also Baker & Stevenson, 1986; Lareau, 2000; Useem, 1992). Thus, although we lack longitudinal data, there is good reason to suspect that the forms of parental behavior that we have documented are relevant to student outcomes.

What do these findings suggest for future research examining social capital in educational settings? The most comprehensive general theory of social capital produced to date is that of Lin (2001), and it is largely against the background of this theory that our results can best be understood. From our perspective, Lin's fundamental insight (consistent with Bourdieu, 1986, before him) is that a theory of social capital that focuses on the resources that are transferred or pooled through social networks must necessarily include the social-structural location of the actors involved in its purview. This implies that any such theory is simultaneously a theory of inequality in social capital (see Lin 2001 [esp. pp. 243–249], 2000). Thus, the working-class and poor parents we observed and spoke with were often able to draw on their networks for crucial forms of assistance. In particular, childcare needs were frequently satisfied through the support of extended family members; from time to time, financial needs could also be met through kin networks. Nevertheless, important though they undoubtedly were for the lives of the children in working-class and poor families, these resources were both qualitatively and quantitatively distinct from those that were pooled or transferred through middle-class networks. Educational researchers who draw on the social capital concept would thus do well to specify the nature and social distribution of the resources that are identified by means of this concept.

The reorientation of much of the social capital literature that is implied by this viewpoint can be briefly illustrated. In their analysis of high school dropout rates, Teachman et al. (1997) demonstrate the existence of significant interactions between family income and (school-centered) intergenerational closure. They view this result as a partial confirmation of Coleman's (1988) hypothesis "that the production of human capital in subsequent generations occurs when social capital allows the financial and human capital of parents to influence children" (Teachman et al., p. 1354). In contrast, we tend toward the opposite interpretation of their data: The efficacy of parental networks and parental school involvement should be viewed as conditional upon the presence of other forms of capital.[17]

Nevertheless, although we are inclined to view our results through the lens of a network-centered theory of social capital, our data do not fully lend themselves to the conceptual vocabulary on which this theory typically draws. To a large extent, the empirical research accompanying the development of the theory has revolved around the study of occupational mobility. In this research tradition, certain aspects of network ties have frequently been foregrounded, including the presence of strong versus weak ties and the preponderance of dense versus "bridging" ties (Lin 1999, 2000, 2001; see also Bian, 1997). These concepts do not map onto our ethnographic data particularly well. To take just one example, the connections forged between parents at children's organized activities were often weak, involving no more than intermittent encounters on the sidelines of a soccer field. In some cases, however, when the children of two families participated in activities together over the course of many years—or when they participated in multiple activities simultaneously—parents forged extremely strong ties, replete with frequent social interactions that were independent of the children's activities. On the basis of our dataset, we are unable to identify any clear patterns in the middle-class group that would account for the observed efficacy of informal networks in these terms.

Nevertheless, we believe that our findings can inform social capital theory in interesting ways. Parental interventions in schooling represent, in effect, an assertion of power in an institutional arena where parents are formally endowed with only a restricted authority. In many of the examples provided here, parents were able to mobilize sufficient network resources to essentially trump the authority that school officials wielded on the basis of their institutional positions. Their success indicates not merely an instrumental use of social capital but a quasi-conflictual one. The theme of conflict remains relatively undeveloped in the social capital literature, and we hope to see it pursued further.[18]

In undertaking to criticize a substantial portion of the educational research on social capital, we do not wish to overstep the bounds of what can reasonably be argued on the basis of the analysis that we have presented. It is thus prudent to note the most important limitations of our study. This means, in the first place, recalling the usual caveats concerning qualitative research (e.g., its limited generalizability) as well as the fact that we lack longitudinal data on the families that we studied. Also worth mentioning is a limitation created by the sample design—namely, the absence of immigrants. Immigrants have loomed large in the literature on social capital and entrepreneurship (see the discussions in Portes, 1998; Portes & Sensenbrenner, 1993), and there is a growing body of literature on immigrant experiences in the American Southwest (Delgado-Gaitan, 1992, 2001; Mehan et al., 1996; Villanueva, 1996). In addition, the nature of our data does not enable us to cleanly partition effects attributable to social class from school effects (although this ambiguity is, to some extent, grounded "in reality," because the composition of school populations is rarely independent of students' class background). Last, and most important, our article focuses on young children and their families. This focus stands in contrast to the majority of the literature, which—using quantitative datasets such as NELS—follows children from middle school to high school and college. Indeed, the whole question of whether and how particular forms of social capital are tied to the life course of the child remains unexplored in the literature, the present article included.

With these caveats in mind, we would nevertheless like to draw a more general lesson from our investigation. Throughout the wider literature, theorists and researchers have often ascribed an excessively palliative character to social capital, rendering it, in extreme cases, the foundational condition of a well-functioning democracy and an efficient market. In these accounts, some of which have also been influential in educational research, differences in power and in other resources recede into the background (except, that is, in studies that view social capital as an independent corrective to such differences). In contrast, consistent with Lin (2001) and Stanton-Salazar (1997), we would emphasize that although various resources that flow through parental networks (for example, the capacity for reciprocal monitoring of children) are class-neutral, a wide variety are not. Moreover, whereas certain resources that are relevant in the educational context, such as information, may vary with a family's class position, others, such as economic and cultural capital, are in fact constitutive of it (at least in Bourdieu's [1984, pp. 101–125] framework). This implies that researchers drawing on the social capital concept cannot be content to treat "social ties" as a generic good. To the contrary, especially when individuals or families must contend with institutional agents, social capital is frequently deployed to overcome resistance. In such situations (and, we suspect, in many others), it is not the simple fact of network connections that is significant, but rather the quantity and quality of the resources that are accessed through them—vis-à-vis the particular institutional setting. In our view it is only once such efficacy has been established empirically that the designation of social ties as a "capital" is warranted.

Notes

An earlier version of this article was presented at the annual meeting of the American Educational Research Association, New Orleans, April 2002. Annette Lareau gratefully acknowledges the financial support of the Spencer Foundation. We thank Nikki Johnson for her research assistance and the anonymous reviewers for their many helpful suggestions. All errors are the responsibility of the authors. Please direct correspondence to Erin McNamara Horvat, Urban Education Program, 264 Ritter Hall, Temple University, Philadelphia, PA 19122.

1. Indeed, the inclusion in the National Education Longitudinal Survey of questions [intended to allow for testing of hypotheses drawing on Coleman's (1988, 1990) account of social capital reflects well the importance ascribed to the concept in the field of educational research.
2. It is important to note the theoretical foundations underlying the conceptions of social capital and how they implicate the actions of both families and schools. In our work, we find the theoretical perspective of Pierre Bourdieu to be particularly useful in understanding the dynamic between schools and families. Bourdieu has produced a vast body of work, which is accompanied by a large and growing secondary literature that explains and extends his ideas. Readers who would like to explore Bourdieu's work in this area are directed to consult Bourdieu (1977, 1984, 1986, 1990, 1994) as well as Bourdieu and Passeron (1977), Bourdieu and Wacquant (1992), and the secondary works by Calhoun, LiPuma, and Postone (1993), Robbins (1991), and Swartz (1997). Bourdieu's notion of social capital is part of a larger framework that uses the concepts of *habitus*, *field*, and *symbolic violence*, as well as various forms of capital (economic, cultural, social, and symbolic). Social capital can be conceived of as the set of valuable connections of an individual. Unlike Coleman, Bourdieu recognizes the unequal value of various network ties. In the school setting, the ties that are valuable are by-and-large middle-class. Bourdieu (Bourdieu & Passeron, 1977) and others (Bernstein, 1974; McLaren, 1998; Mehan et al., 1996; Stanton-Salazar, 1997) have argued that schools are essentially middle-class institutions that reward middle-class behaviors. That is, the behaviors that most easily map onto the expectations of teachers and others at school are those that are most likely to be rewarded. In the realm of social capital, the connections or parental networks that are the most valued in school settings are those that provide leverage in this middle-class environment. Parent's connections to middle-class professionals thus provide them with valuable capital in the school setting.
3. Valenzuela and Dornbusch (1994) report an interesting, positive association between familism —understood in terms of culturally specific phenomena of proximity to, contact with, and emotional affinity with adult kin—and school grades among Mexican students. Valenzuela and Dornbusch proffer an account based on Coleman's notion of social capital. But once again, it turns out that social capital is efficacious only in combination with an indicator of social position —in this case, parental education (Valenzuela & Dornbusch, 1994, pp. 30–31).
4. We leave out of this discussion works, such as Bankston and Zhou (1995), that use alternative conceptions of social capital (in this case, subjective identification with an ethnic community).
5. Because it focuses so exclusively on membership in voluntary organizations, the tradition of social capital research established by Putnam (2000) ends up excluding a variety of forms and instances of social capital from its purview—that is, precisely those in which the transfer or sharing of resources occurs on an informal basis. We thank an anonymous reviewer for drawing our attention to this implication of our research.
6. This is approach to data collection does in fact echo the general pattern of class segregation in the nation (Massey & Denton, 1993) but did result in a limitation to the study. It is impossible to know

if parents would have behaved differently had they resided in a community that was different in terms of class.

7. The first and second authors were not part of the data collection team, coming to the project only after it had been completed. Their participation was therefore limited to analysis of the data.

8. The schools from which we recruited the families included very few children of employers or self-employed workers, rendering moot the perennial question of whether these categories belong to the middle-class

9. District statistics indicated that a vast a majority of the White and Black children were on school lunch, from which we surmised that they were poor. Interviews, however, revealed that most of the White families had unreported income that boosted them out of the poverty level. As a result, we needed to recruit additional White poor families. These families were generally recruited by using flyers in social service offices and posting flyers on telephone poles in another neighborhood; as an incentive, these White poor families were paid ($25 per interview). No other families were paid for interviews. But we did bring a pie with us to all of the other interviews, and we followed up (for the entire sample) with a hand-written thank you note. A number of the Black middle-class families, again where the schools did not provide sufficient number of cases to fill this category, were recruited through informal networks.

10. The tabulations suffer from certain problems, further implying that they should be read with caution. In particular, all of the tabulations are beset (with varying degrees of severity) by missing data, usually as a result of time constraints on interviews. In addition, in some tabulations it was impossible to include figures for the poor group. The reason, as explained above, is that all of the poor White families were recruited from schools other than those on which the study was focused, thus entailing changes in the questions posed by the interviewer.

11. Nevertheless, it should be pointed out that, among all classes, these friendships tended to be relatively class homogenous.

12. We do not include any measures of contact with the respondent's father because a substantial proportion of interviewees (especially in the poor category) reported growing up without a father present.

13. In our sample, working-class and poor parents were themselves considerably more likely to use corporal punishment in disciplining their children.

14. An extensive literature highlights the importance of teacher quality in enhancing student outcomes. See, for example, Darling-Hammond (2000) and Haycock (1998).

15. Here again we were unable to tabulate responses for the poor group (see note 5).

16. We do not subdivide the results in Table 9.7 by race because cell sizes become very small.

17. From our theoretical vantage point, the income-closure interaction might be expected on the grounds that, within the confines the given model, income may serve as an indicator of quantitative and qualitative differences in the potential effectiveness or "value" of parental network ties. This expectation would rest on the assumption that income functions reasonably well as a proxy for the resources (economic, cultural, and symbolic) that network partners make available—or in our preferred vocabulary, the assumption that networks are relatively class-homogeneous. Of course, in the case of school-based intergenerational closure, this assumption is true simply as a matter of definition to the extent that the school itself is class-homogeneous.

18. The question also arises here of whether school reforms might attenuate the pervasive advantage that accrues to middle-class families on the basis of their social capital. In this respect, Mehan et al. (1996) and Noguera (2001) have reported some suggestive results, and Stanton-Salazar (1997) has provided a compelling theoretical account of just what an alternative arrangement would have to look like. However, Stanton-Salazar (1997, pp. 17–21) also carefully details the institutional and organizational barriers to such an arrangement and does so with enough force to temper optimism.

References

Baker, D. P., & Stevenson, D. L. (1986). Mothers' strategies for children's school achievement: Managing the transition to high school. *Sociology of Education, 59,* 156–166.

Bankston, C. L., & Zhou, M. (1995). Effects of minority-language literacy on the academic achievement of Vietnamese youths in New Orleans. *Sociology of Education, 68,* 1–17.

Bernstein, B. (1974). *Class, codes and control: Theoretical studies towards a sociology of language.* New York: Schocken Books.

Bian, Y. (1997). Bringing strong ties back in: Indirect ties, network bridges, and job searches in China. *American Sociological Review, 62,* 366–385.

Bourdieu, P. (1977). *Outline of a theory of practice* (R. Nice, Trans.). Cambridge, UK: Cambridge University Press.

Bourdieu, P. (1984). *Distinction: A social critique of the judgment of taste* (R. Nice, Trans.). Cambridge, MA: Harvard University Press.

Bourdieu, P. (1986). The forms of capital. In J. G. Richardson (Ed.), *Handbook of theory and research for the sociology of education* (pp. 241–258). New York: Greenwood Press.

Bourdieu, P. (1990). *The logic of practice* (R. Nice, Trans.). Stanford, CA: Stanford University Press.

Bourdieu, P. (1994). *Language and symbolic power* (G. Raymond & M. Adamson, Trans.). Cambridge, MA: Harvard University Press.

Bourdieu, P., & Passeron, J. (1977). *Reproduction in education society and culture* (R. Nice, Trans.). Thousand Oaks, CA: Sage.

Bourdieu, P., & Wacquant, L. J. D. (1992). *An invitation to reflexive sociology.* Chicago: University of Chicago Press.

Calhoun, C., LiPuma, E., & Postone, M. (Eds.). (1993). *Bourdieu: Critical perspectives.* Chicago: University of Chicago Press.

Carbonaro, W. J. (1998). A little help from my friends' parents: Intergenerational closure and educational outcomes. *Sociology of Education, 71,* 295–313.

Carbonaro, W. J. (1999). Opening the debate on closure and schooling outcomes. *American Sociological Review, 64,* 682–686.

Coleman, J. S. (1988). Social capital and the creation of human capital. *American Journal of Sociology, 94* (Suppl.), S95–S120.

Coleman, J. S. (1990). *Foundations of social theory.* Cambridge, MA, and London: Harvard University Press.

Cose, Ellis. (1995). *The rage of a privileged class.* New York: HarperPerennial.

Delgado-Gaitan, C. (1992). School matters in the Mexican-American home: Socializing children to education. *American Educational Research Journal, 29,* 495–513.

Delgado-Gaitan, C. (2001). *The power of community: Mobilizing for family and schooling.* New York: Rowman & Littlefield.

Darling-Hammond, L. (2000). Teacher quality and student achievement: A review of state policy evidence. *Education Policy Analysis Archives, 8.* Available at http://olam.ed.asu.edu/epaa/v8n1/

Dika, S. L., & Singh, K. (2002). Applications of social capital in educational literature: A critical synthesis. *Review of Educational Research, 72,* 31–60.

Fischer, C. S. (1982). *To dwell among friends: Personal networks in town and city.* Chicago: University of Chicago Press.

Goyette, K. A., & Conchas, G. Q. (in press). Should families be praised or blamed? A look at the relative influences of family and non-family social capital on Vietnamese and Mexican Americans' study habits. In B. Fuller & E. Hannum (Eds.), *Research in the sociology of education: Vol. 13. Schooling and social capital in diverse cultures.* Oxford, UK: Elsevier.

Hawe, P., & Schiell, A. (2000). Social capital and health promotion: A review. *Social Science and Medicine, 51,* 871–885.

Haycock, K. (1998). Good teaching matters . . . a lot. *OAH Magazine of History, 13,* 61–63.

Hochschild, J. l. (1995). *Facing up to the American dream: Race, class, and the soul of the nation.* Princeton, NJ: Princeton University Press.

Lang, R. E., & S. P. Hornburg. (1998). What is social capital and why is it important to public policy? *Housing Policy Debate, 9,* 1–16.

Lareau, A. (2000). *Home advantage: Social class and parental intervention in elementary education.* Lanham, MD: Rowman & Littlefield.

Lareau, A. (2002). Invisible inequality: Social class and childrearing in Black families and White families. *American Sociological Review, 67,* 747–776.

Lareau, A. (2003). *Unequal childhoods: Class, race, and family life.* Berkeley, CA: University of California Press.

Lin, N. (1999). Social networks and status attainment. *Annual Review of Sociology, 25,* 467–487.

Lin, N. (2000). Inequality in social capital. *Contemporary Sociology, 29,* 785–795.

Lin, N. (2001). *Social capital: A theory of social structure and action.* Cambridge, UK: Cambridge University Press.

Lucas, S. R. (1999). *Tracking inequality: Stratification and mobility in American high schools.* New York and London: Teachers College Press.

Massey, D. S., & Denton, N. (1993). *American apartheid: Segregation and the making of the underclass.* Cambridge, MA: Harvard University Press.

McLaren, P. (1998). *Life in schools: An introduction to critical pedagogy in the foundations of education.* New York: Longman.

McNeal, R. B. (1999). Parental involvement as social capital: Differential effectiveness on science achievement, truancy, and dropping out. *Social Forces, 78,* 117–144.

Mehan, H., Villanueva, I., Hubbard, L., & Lintz, A. (1996). *Constructing school success: The consequences of untracking low-achieving students.* New York and Cambridge, UK: Cambridge University Press.

Moll, L. C., Amanti, C., Neff, D., & Gonzalez, N. (1992). Funds of knowledge for teaching: Using a qualitative approach to connect to homes and classrooms. *Theory Into Practice, 31,* 132–141.

Morgan, S. L., & Sørensen, A. B. (1999). Parental networks, social closure, and mathematics learning: A test of Coleman's social capital explanation of school effects. *American Sociological Review, 64,* 661–681.

Morrow, V. (1999). Conceptualizing social capital in relation to the well-being of children and young people: A critical review. *Sociological Review, 47,* 744–766.

Morrow, V. (2000). "Dirty looks" and "trampy places" in young people's accounts of community and neighborhood: Implications for health inequalities. *Critical Public Health, 10,* 141–153.

Muller, C. (1995). Parental ties to the school and community and mathematics achievement. In Peter W. Cookson, Jr., & Barbara Schneider (Eds.), *Transforming schools* (pp. 57–79). New York and London: Garland Publishing.

Muller, C., & Ellison, C. G. (2001). Religious involvement, social capital, and adolescents' academic progress: Evidence from the national education longitudinal study of 1988. *Sociological Focus, 34*, 155–183.

Noguera, P. (2001). Racial politics and the elusive quest for excellence and equity in education. *Education and Urban Society, 34*, 18–24.

Portes, A. (1998). Social capital: Its origins and applications in modern sociology. *Annual Review of Sociology, 24*, 1–24.

Portes, A., & Sensenbrenner, J. (1993). Embeddedness and immigration: Notes on the social determinants of economic action. *American Journal of Sociology, 98*, 1320–1350.

Putnam, R. D. (1996). The strange disappearance of civic America. *The American Prospect, 24*, 34–48.

Putnam, R. D. (2000). *Bowling alone: The collapse and revival of American community.* New York: Simon & Schuster.

Robbins, D. (1991). *The work of Pierre Bourdieu.* Boulder, CO: Westview Press.

Smith, M. H., Beaulieu, L. J., & Seraphine, A. (1995). Social capital, place of residence, and college attendance. *Rural Sociology, 60*, 363–380.

Stanton-Salazar, R. (1997). A social capital framework for understanding the socialization of racial minority children and youths. *Harvard Educational Review, 67*, 1–40.

Stanton-Salazar, R., & Dornbusch, S. M. (1995). Social capital and the reproduction of inequality: Information networks among Mexican-origin high school students. *Sociology of Education, 68*, 116–135.

Swartz, D. (1997). *Culture and power: The sociology of Pierre Bourdieu.* Chicago: University of Chicago Press.

Tatum, B. D. (1987). *Assimilation blues: Black families in a White community.* New York: Greenwood Press.

Teachman, J. D., Paasch, K., & Carver, K. (1997). Social capital and the generation of human capital. *Social Forces, 75*, 1343–1359.

Useem, E. (1992). Middle schools and math groups: Parents' involvement in children's placement. *Sociology of Education, 65*, 263–279.

Valenzuela, A. (1999). *Subtractive schooling: U.S.–Mexican youth and the politics of schooling.* New York: State University of New York Press.

Valenzuela, A., & Dornbusch, S. M. (1994). Familism and social capital in the academic achievement of Mexican origin and Anglo adolescents. *Social Science Quarterly, 75*, 18–36.

Villanueva, I. (1996). Change in the educational life of Chicano families across three generations. *Education and Urban Society, 29*, 13–34.

Woolcock, M. (1998). Social capital and economic development: Toward a theoretical synthesis and policy framework. *Theory and Society, 27*, 151–208.

Wright, E. O. (1997). *Class counts: Comparative studies in class analysis.* Cambridge, UK: Cambridge University Press.

Zipp, J. F., & Plutzer, E. (1996). Wives and husbands: Social class, gender, and class identification in the U.S. *Sociology, 30*, 235–252.

A Black Student's Reflection on Public and Private Schools

Imani Perry

My name is Imani Perry. I am a fifteen-year-old Black female who has experienced both private and public education. These experiences have led me to believe there are significant differences between the two types of education that deserve to be acknowledged and resolved by society as a whole.

After ten years in private schools I made the decision to attend a public school. I left because I felt isolated as a person of color. I yearned to have a large, strong Black community be a part of my development. I believed that I would find such a community in the public high school of my city, which is a fairly urban school with approximately 2,600 students, 20 percent of whom are Black.

Despite the fact that I had never been in a traditional public school environment, when I decided to go to one I had certain expectations about the teaching. I assumed that the teaching philosophy would be similar to that of the private schools I had attended. I expected that any teaching differences that did exist would be limited to less sophisticated reading, or a less intense work load. As I quickly learned, the differences were more substantial.

I believe the differences I found in the teaching between the private and public schools that I attended would best be illustrated by several examples of what I encountered. My initial realization of this difference began with an argument I had with a math teacher over a point value on a test. I felt that he should give partial credit for problems with computational errors rather than procedural errors or conceptual misunderstanding. I presented this point to the math teacher, who responded by saying math is computation and the theories and concepts of math are only used to compute. I was astonished by this statement. Coming from a school where the teachers' stated goal for freshman math was to begin to teach you how to become a "theoretical mathematician," my entire perception of math was different. Perhaps that emphasis of theoretical math was also extreme; nevertheless, I believe that a good math teacher believes that computation in math should be used to assist in the organization of theories. Computation is a necessary but not sufficient step toward math knowledge. I felt this teacher was probably the product of schooling that did not emphasize the artistic qualities of math. While I could sympathize with his position, I felt that all I loved about math—new ideas, discussing unproved theorems, and developing personal procedures—was being ignored. I withdrew from this course only to find the ideological differences emerged again in my advanced English class at the public school, particularly in essay writing.

In this class, once we wrote a paper—mind you, with no assistance from the teacher—the process ended. We did not discuss papers, receive constructive criticism, or improve them through rewriting. Despite the fact that there was no proofreading assistance offered, 10 percent of the grade was taken off for sentence errors. It seemed as if the teacher assumed we no longer needed to continue developing our writing skills.

These examples illustrate my belief that my learning environment had changed from a place where thought and theory were emphasized to a place where form and precision were emphasized. The teaching system at the public school appears to assume that at some point in our education, learning and thinking are no longer important. Schooling in this situation becomes devoted to making things look correct. This is in sharp contrast to my private schools, where proper form was something I learned was necessary, but secondary in importance to the content and organization of what is produced.

Because of this difference in the concept of teaching and learning, there is also a difference in what and who teachers consider intelligence. The teaching at the public school has less to do with thinking and processing ideas, and more to do with precision and detail in appearance. Therefore, students who are considered intelligent by the public school faculty possess different skills than those at the private schools I have attended. In the public school a student is considered intelligent if he or she is well-behaved and hard working. The ability to grasp a subject in its entirety—from theory to practice—is not valued.

For example, in the fall of 1987 there was an academic contest, where my school was competing against other public schools. All the teachers I encountered were very enthusiastic about it. The students who were selected to participate were raised on a pedestal. These students, most of whom were clean-cut and apparently straight-laced, were to serve as our models of very intelligent students. They were drilled in formulas, book plots, and other information for several days a week. It seemed as if the teachers were not concerned with whether the students digested the depth of these subjects and resources as long as the students completed all the reading, memorized the facts, and could repeat the information. The contest was more a demonstration of a memory function than anything else. In my opinion there is nothing wrong with such a contest, but it should be recognized for what it is and is not. One thing it is not is a true measure of knowledge and ability. This was never recognized by the school.

Another example of how a different view of intelligence is manifested in this public school is the school's view of two students whom I know. I will identify them as Student A and Student B. Student B is an intellectual. She reads, is analytical in her discussions and is knowledgeable. Student A is very precise with his homework, answers the patronizing questions the teachers ask ("What color was the horse?" "Black with a white spot!" "Correct!"), and is very "all-American" in behavior and appearance. Student A is considered more intelligent at this public school because he displays skills that are considered signs of intelligence at this school. The intelligence criteria at this school are more related to superficial qualities such as appearance, knowing facts, etc., rather than the intellectual qualities that student B possesses. Student B displays an ability to learn and write in creative and analytical formats. I left a school where the criterion for intelligence was the student's thought process resulting from the information, for a school where the information was the measure of intelligence.

In reflecting on schooling it is important to realize that all people, including teachers, have biases based on the physical appearances of other people. On the train most people are more likely to sit next to the clean-shaven Harvard freshman than next to the Mohawked, multiple-earringed punk-rocker. In teachers, however, these biases should diminish as they begin to know a student. Unfortunately, in the public school there is an absence of teacher-student contact. Because of this lack of contact there are no criteria by which intelligence can be determined, besides grades, appearance, and behavior. As I mentioned before, the grading system at this school often reflects one's ability to memorize and not one's thinking and analytical abilities. Moreover, since people are biased in their acceptance of different appearances, students who look different are judged differently. The only way they can make up for this difference is to be "well behaved," and, as I will mention later, the definition of well-behaved is arbitrary.

All these issues I have discussed have very negative effects for students from minority groups, more specifically the Black and Hispanic youths who make up a large percentage of most urban schools. It is those Black and Hispanic students who retain strong cultural characteristics in their personalities who are most negatively acted by teachers' emphasis on behavior, appearance, and respect for authority.

Public schools' emphasis on the teaching of form merely trains students for low-powered or menial jobs that do not require analytical thought. It is evident when most students are discussing what they intend to be that their goals are most often focused toward areas and professions about which they have some idea or knowledge. If in class you've never spoken about how language and colloquialisms are reflections of the society you are studying, you definitely will not be thinking of being a linguist. And if you are only asked to type a paper summarizing the book, rather than writing an analysis of it, the primary skill shown is typing. This should not be the main skill which is emphasized.

The neglect of intellectual development also occurs in higher-level classes, but at least the resources, books, etc., available to students are not altogether lacking in intellectual value. Occasionally these resources will have depth and content, be philosophical, or insightful. But in lower-level classes, where minority students are most often found and where bad textbooks are used without outside resources, the reading has less content, and the point of reading is to perfect reading skills, not to broaden thinking skills or gain knowledge of how the subject is currently affecting us. It is often not possible to broaden your thinking skills or knowledge with the books used in lower-level classes, which are more often stripped of any content. In an upper-level class, if you have a parent who wants you to know the subject in depth, and to think about it, it is possible to do that detached from the school environment, because the subject matter may have content, or have some meaning beyond the words. My high-level sophomore English class read *Moby Dick* as an outside reading. We didn't discuss the symbolism or religious qualities of it, but I am aware of them because I read critical essays and discussed them with my mother. If one is reading a book which has been stripped of meaningful content, it is not helpful to do outside research, because it is lacking in meaning.

Many students from minority groups are being trained only in form and not in creative ways of thinking. This I believe causes disenchantment among students. Upper-class students are not as affected, because of their social class, and their "social responsibility" to be achievers. This is especially true of upper-class students in a public school whose social-class peers are in private schools. But instead of striving to be true learners, they quickly learn how to be good students by being well-behaved. What well-behaved means is always taking the teacher's word as absolute truth and never questioning the teacher's authority. This definition of well-behaved is of course culturally based and can be in opposition to cultures of Black and Hispanic students.

In Black and Hispanic cultures, respect and obedience come and develop with the relationship. Rather than being automatic, respect must be earned. For example, one will occasionally hear a Black child say to a stranger, "You can't tell me what to do, you're not my mother." But at the same time, often one will see Black kids following the orders and rules of an adult friend of the family, whom they would under no circumstances disrespect. In addition, in Black and Hispanic cultures it appears that adult and child cultures are more integrated than those of other ethnic groups. For example, parties in the Hispanic community will often have an age range from toddler to elderly. Children are often present in the conversation and socializing of adults and are not treated as separate, as they may be in other cultures.

When this relationship is not made between teacher and student, it is not an acceptable educational situation, because the Black and Hispanic students are now expected to respect someone in a different manner than their culture has socialized them to. Often students are not aware of the fact that the demands being placed on them by the relationship conflict with those of their culture. They then show signs of what a teacher views as a lack of the respect that he/she deserves. The student might feel it is just a sign that they do not know the teacher and have no obligation to him or her. Many times I have seen a dumbstruck student of color sent to detention; when asked what he or she did, the student will seriously say that he or she has no idea; perhaps that he or she sucked his or her teeth in dismay, or something of that sort.

Black and Hispanic students have less of a chance at building strong relationships with any teachers because their appearance and behavior may be considered offensive to the middle-class White teachers. These students show signs of what White teachers, and some teachers of color, consider disrespect, and they do not get the nurturing relationships that develop respect and dedication. They are considered less intelligent, as can be seen in the proportion of Blacks and Hispanics in lower-level as opposed to upper-level classes. There is less of a teacher-student contact with "underachievers," because they are guided into peer tutoring programs. Perhaps this is understandable, because the teachers have less of a vested interest in the achievement of students that are not of their community, or have less of an idea of how to educate them. Public school teachers are no longer part of the same community as the majority of their students. The sad part of the situation is that many students believe that this type of teaching is what academic learning is all about. They have not had the opportunity to experience alternative ways of teaching and learning. From my experience in public school, it appears that many minority students will never be recognized as capable of analytical and critical thinking.

In the beginning of this article I spoke about my decision to leave my private school because of feeling isolated. After three months at a large urban public school I found myself equally isolated—intellectually as well as racially. My thinking process has gradually affected my opinions and character. I am in upper-level classes in which there are barely any kids of color, except Asians. Black and Hispanic students have been filtered down into lower-level classes. Most of the students I meet are kind, interesting people whom I like and respect. However, because the environment of the school is one in which ideas are not valued or fostered, I find it difficult to discuss issues with them, because my thoughtfulness has flourished, while others have been denied an opportunity to explore their intellectual development. I am now at a point of deciding which isolation is worse, cultural/racial or intellectual-opinion-based and slightly racial. This is a decision many Black students who have attended private schools at some time are wrestling to make, a decision that will affect their development, knowledge, and viewpoint of education, and their relationships to educators—those supposed possessors of greater knowledge than themselves.

Afterword

Since the writing of this article I have returned to a private school with the feeling that one's educational development is too much to sacrifice. I now attend a private high school with a strong unified Black community, as well as academic merit. Even though I did not remain at the urban public school, I valued my experience there, mostly because through it I learned one of the most blatant forms of oppression and inequity for lower-class students in American society, and I appreciate the opportunities with which I have been blessed.

10 Educational Reform and School Improvement

In Chapter 2, we presented conservative, liberal, radical, and neoliberal perspectives on educational problems. Throughout this book, we have examined a number of educational problems from the foundations perspective. This chapter looks at the most significant educational problems and the role of teachers and schools in solving them. To what extent do teachers and schools make a difference? To what degree can they make a difference? Most importantly, to what extent are teachers and schools limited in their ability to solve educational and social problems without significant changes outside the schools?

In Chapter 1, we related the stories of two teachers. The first, memorialized by the late *New York Times* education writer Fred Hechinger, was a beloved teacher who made a significant impact on the lives of her students. The second, a veteran teacher in an urban school district, retired from teaching because of the difficult problems she faced. We asked to what extent do the structural problems faced by teachers limit their ability to affect meaningful change and, conversely, to what degree do talented, enthusiastic, and excellent teachers have the ability to affect educational change in spite of the significant problems that they face. Although there is no easy answer to this question, it is clear that teachers work within social and organizational environments that indeed have profound effects on them and often limit their ability to affect meaningful change. It is also clear that teachers can and do make a difference, often in spite of what may seem like intractable problems.

Thus, although teachers can and do make a difference, the research indicates that solutions to educational problems cannot rely on the talent, energy, and hard work of teachers alone, but must reform the social and organizational conditions of schooling (Sizer, 1992). Before we examine ways in which educational reforms have attempted to do this, let us first look at some examples of how individual teachers make a difference.

Effective Teachers

Jessica Siegel taught high school English and journalism at Seward Park High School, on New York City's lower east side, for ten years. Samuel Freedman's *Small Victories* (1990) poignantly chronicles Jessica's struggles, triumphs, and defeats as she attempted to teach her students, most of them poor and immigrants, to value an education and to make their dreams a reality. Teaching in a neighborhood long a haven for immigrants and their children—first for East European Jews and Italians at the turn of the twentieth century, and now for Asians, Dominicans, and other Latinos—Jessica battles against the effects of poverty, drugs, gangs, homelessness, family violence and abuse, and language difficulties to give her students an opportunity to succeed in school and in life.

As the advisor to the Seward Park student newspaper, she uses journalism as a vehicle to involve students in the learning experience. Freedman captures the daily struggles, the long hours, and the selfless dedication of a teacher committed to making a difference in the lives of her students. He also captures the bureaucratic nonsense, the petty collegial jealousies, the social problems, and the school conditions that make success difficult, if not impossible. Jessica encourages students to go to college, she helps them with their applications, and she even drives them to college interviews. For every student she helps succeed and who gets into college, there are many others with talent and dreams who do not graduate.

After ten years of heroic and successful teaching, Jessica decides to leave teaching and return to her first career as a journalist. In part, she leaves because she wants to be a journalist; in part, she leaves because to be a successful teacher required too much personal sacrifice, with too little reward. Freedman's book portrays the limits and possibilities of good teaching—that teachers like Jessica make an important difference, but that without reform of schools, teachers like Jessica may leave teaching. In her review of the book, Johnson (1991, p. 184) stated:

> Freedman leaves us with admiration for Jessica Siegel, respect for many of her colleagues, compassion for her students, anger at a seemingly impersonal school bureaucracy, and remorse for a society that values cash more than children. . . . Yet it is clear that much more can be done to support exemplary teachers like Jessica Siegel. The moral of *Small Victories* is sobering and unequivocal: If we do not change schools to support good teaching, many good teachers will leave schools.

The film *Stand and Deliver* chronicles the work of Jaime Escalante at Garfield High School in East Los Angeles, a poor neighborhood of African-Americans, Mexican-Americans, and other Latino-Americans. Jaime Escalante refuses to accept the stereotype that students from low-income neighborhoods cannot succeed at high-level academic work. He came to Garfield as a computer teacher after a successful career as a computer analyst in the corporate world and immediately instituted an Advanced Placement (AP) Calculus program, despite the objections of the chairperson of the Mathematics Department, a woman who did not want to set the students up for failure.

Stand and Deliver portrays the heroic efforts of Jaime Escalante to teach his student advanced mathematics. He demonstrates what positive expectations can do and how hard work and dedication on the part of teachers and students can often overcome the pernicious effects of poverty, racism, and social problems. Despite a shortage of materials, the accusation of the Educational Testing Service (ETS) that his students cheated on the AP test (according to ETS, because they had many of the same wrong answers; according to Jaime Escalante, because they did too well for students from their backgrounds), and numerous personal hurdles that students had to overcome, all 18 students passed the AP examination the first year of the program. Within four years, over 85 students passed the AP calculus examination.

The film demonstrates a number of important points. First, a talented and dedicated teacher can make a difference. Second, if teachers expect all students to learn and excel, they can and do. Third, it is possible to institutionalize the effective teaching of one teacher into an overall school philosophy, as Garfield High School had to do in order to serve as many students as it now does. Despite these positive lessons, however, there has been a tendency to romanticize the work of Jaime Escalante, or worse to use his success as an example that all that is necessary to improve schools in low-income neighborhoods is to raise expectations. The fact is that although Jaime Escalante did make a difference, students at schools like Garfield High School still have significantly fewer opportunities than students at more affluent high schools. Furthermore, teachers like Jaime Escalante cannot eliminate the negative effects of poverty and other social problems.

These two stories of wonderful teachers can be supplemented by your own recollections of wonderful teachers who have influenced your lives. Unfortunately, they can also be countered by your own stories of terrible teachers and ineffective schools. Our point in telling these stories is to indicate that, as teachers, you can make a difference. However, they also demonstrate that wonderful teachers alone cannot ameliorate societal and school problems, and that wonderful teachers in ineffective schools are severely limited in what they can accomplish. In addition, although there are significant numbers of excellent teachers and the majority of teachers are effective, conservatives and neo-liberals maintain that there still are too many ineffective ones and that it is far too difficult to get them out of the system. However, the foundations perspective enlightens one to the importance of changing structures, not just individuals, if the educational system is to improve. For the past three decades, there have been a number of significant reform efforts aimed at doing just this. The following section explores some of these efforts.

Educational Reform from the 1980s to 2012

The 1980s and 1990s and into the twenty-first century were periods of significant debate and reform in U.S. education. Beginning in 1983, with the National Commission on Educational Excellence's report *A Nation at Risk*, government leaders, educational reformers, teacher organizations, administrators, and various other interest groups attempted to improve the quality of U.S. schools. Although the decades included two specific waves of reform, the first beginning in 1983 and the second in 1985 and continuing through 2012, the period must be understood as a conservative response to the progressive reforms of the 1960s and 1970s, if not the entire progressive agenda of the twentieth century.

In the 1980s, the major reform actors shifted from the federal to the state to the local levels. In the 1990s and 2000s, President Clinton's Goals 2000, President Bush's No Child Left Behind (NCLB), and President Obama's Race to the Top (RTT) placed the federal government back at the forefront of educational policy. From the outset, the federal government, through the Department of Education, attempted to balance its ideological belief that education is not a federal governmental matter, with its commitment to providing the impetus for change. First, through its influential report, *A Nation at Risk*, written during the tenure of Secretary Terrel Bell, and second, through his successor William Bennett's use of his office as a "bully pulpit," the U.S. Department of Education played a significant role in keeping the pressure on states and localities to improve educational outcomes, which for Secretary Bennett defined the goals of educational reform. Finally, NCLB and RTT placed accountability at the forefront of reforms aimed at reducing the achievement gap.

The educational reforms from the 1980s to today consisted of two waves of reform (Bacharach, 1990; Passow, 1989). The first wave, marked by the reports of the early and mid-1980s, and the educational initiatives directly responding to them, were concerned primarily with the issues of accountability and achievement (Dougherty, 1990, p. 3). Responding to the call for increased academic achievement, many states increased graduation requirements, toughened curriculum mandates, and increased the use of standardized test scores to measure student achievement.

By the mid to late 1980s, however, it became increasingly clear that such top-down reform would be ineffective in dealing with the schools' myriad problems. Although raising achievement standards for students and implementing accountability measures for evaluating teachers had some positive effects, many (including the National Governors Association, which took a leading role in reform) believed that educational reform had to do more than provide changes in evaluation procedures. The second wave of reform, then, was targeted at the structure and processes of the schools themselves, placing far more control in the hands of local schools, teachers, and communities. Whereas the first wave was highly centralized at the state level, the second wave was more decentralized to the local and school levels. What they had in common, however, was what the Governors Conference emphasized as the "triple theme of achievement, assessment, and accountability" (Bacharach, 1990, p. 8). By the mid-1990s, however, the first and second waves began to overlap, with top-down federal and state mandates defining the goals and standards of education, but leaving it to local districts to implement them.

Despite the second wave's insistence that locally based reforms were central to success, many critics (including teacher organizations and unions) argued that the reforms were highly bureaucratic and aimed primarily at assessment procedures. Significant reforms, they suggested, had to emphasize both changes within schools, and changes that involved teachers, students, and parents as part of the reform process, not merely as objects of it. From the latter part of the 1980s through the end of the 1990s, reforms that emphasized teacher empowerment, school-based management, and school choice, charter schools, and tuition vouchers became the most important ones under consideration.

To summarize, the first wave of reform reports stressed the need for increased educational excellence though increased educational standards and a reversal of the rising tide of mediocrity. Passow (1989, p. 16) stated the following themes as essential to the first wave of educational reform:

1. The need to attain the twin goals of excellence and equity.
2. The need to clarify educational goals, unburdening schools from responsibilities they cannot or should not fill.
3. The need to develop a common core curriculum (not unlike the standard college-bound curriculum) with few or no electives, little or no curricular differentiation, but only pedagogical differentiation.
4. The need to eliminate tracking programs so that students could tackle the common core courses in a common curriculum in different ways.
5. The need for major changes in vocational education: in the student populations served, the curricula provided, and the sites of such education if offered.
6. The need for education to teach about technology, including computer literacy, and to become involved in the technological revolution.
7. The need to "increase both the duration and intensity of academic learning," lengthening the school day and the school year.
8. The need to recruit, train, and retain more academically able teachers, to improve the quality of teaching, and to upgrade the professional working life of teachers.
9. The need to redefine the principal's role and put the "principal squarely in charge of educational quality in each school."
10. The need to forge new partnerships between corporations, business, and the schools.

Typifying the second wave of educational reform were the recommendations of the State Governor's Conference. Governor Lamar Alexander, in *Time for Results: The Governor's 1991 Report on Education* (1986), summarized the Governor's Association's year-long analysis of a variety of issues, including teaching, leadership and management, parental involvement and choice, readiness, technology, school facilities, and college quality, with (among others) the following recommendations:

1. Now is the time to work out a fair, affordable Career Ladder salary system that recognizes real differences in function, competence, and performance of teachers.
2. States should create leadership programs for school leaders.
3. Parents should have more choice in the public schools their children attend.
4. The nation—and the states and local districts—need report cards about results, and about what students know and can do.
5. School districts and schools that do not make the grade should be declared bankrupt, taken over by the state, and reorganized.
6. It makes no sense to keep closed half a year the school buildings in which America has invested a quarter of a trillion dollars while we are undereducated and overcrowded.

7. States should work with four- and five-year-olds from poor families to help them get ready for school and decrease the chances that they will drop out later.
8. Better use of technologies through proper planning and training for use of videodiscs, computers, and robotics is an important way to give teachers more time to teach.
9. States should insist that colleges assess what students actually learn while in college. (Cited in Passow, 1989, p. 23)

During both waves of educational reform, a number of programs and initiatives received considerable attention. Among these are school choice, charter schools, tuition vouchers, school-business partnerships, privatization, school-to-work programs, school-based management, reform of teacher education, the effective school movement, state intervention in local districts, and school finance litigation.

Federal Involvement in Education

By the early 1990s, it was still unclear as to whether school reforms would begin to produce some of the improvements they promised. In 1990, President G.H.W. Bush—with the support of the National Governors Association—announced six national goals for U.S. education:

1. Goal 1: By the year 2000, all children will start school ready to learn.
2. Goal 2: By the year 2000, the high school graduation rate will increase to at least 90 percent.
3. Goal 3: By the year 2000, American students will leave grades 4, 8, and 12, having demonstrated competency in challenging subject matter, including English, mathematics, science, history, and geography, and every school in America will ensure that all students learn to use their minds well, so they may be prepared for responsible citizenship, further learning, and productive employment in our modern economy.
4. Goal 4: By the year 2000, U.S. students will be first in the world in mathematics and science achievement.
5. Goal 5: By the year 2000, every adult American will be literate and will possess the skills necessary to compete in a global economy and exercise the rights and responsibilities of citizenship.
6. Goal 6: By the year 2000, every school in America will be free of drugs and violence and will offer a disciplined environment conducive to learning. ("Text of Statement of Goals Adopted by the Governors," 1990, pp. 16–17)

Until 1993, President Bush's educational reform proposal America 2000, based on these national goals, was in the implementation stage. America 2000 built on four related themes:

1. creating better and more accountable schools for today's students;
2. creating a New Generation of American schools for tomorrow's students;
3. transforming America into a nation of students; and
4. making our communities places where learning will happen. (America 2000, 1991)

Within each of the objectives, America 2000 proposed a number of specific goals:

Creating better and more accountable schools for today's students:

1. World Class Standards in Five Core Subjects (English, mathematics, science, history, and geography).
2. A system of voluntary national examinations.

3. Schools as the site of reform.
4. Providing and promoting school choice.
5. Promoting outstanding leadership by teachers and principals.

Creating a new generation of American Schools for tomorrow's students:

1. The development of Research and Development teams, funded by the business community, to develop these schools.
2. The creation of at least 535 New American Schools that "break the mold" of existing school designs.
3. The development of leadership at all levels, federal, state, and local.
4. The commitment of families and children devoted to learning.

Transforming America into a nation of students:

1. Strengthening the nation's education effort for yesterday's students, today's workers.
2. Establishing standards for job skills and knowledge.
3. Creating business and community skill clinics.
4. Enhancing job training opportunities.
5. Mobilizing a "nation of students," by transforming a "Nation at Risk" into a "Nation of Students."

Making our communities places where learning will happen:

1. Developing greater parental involvement.
2. Enhancing program effectiveness for children and communities.

When President Clinton was elected in November 1992, he already had a great deal of experience as an educational reformer. As Governor of Arkansas, he led a statewide campaign for teacher accountability, higher academic standards for students, and public school choice. In the late 1980s, he was Chair of the National Governors Association and led the governors in establishing a national agenda for educational improvement. As president, Clinton promised to revitalize education and pay close attention to issues of equity and community service. To this end, he initiated legislation for national service and legislation that would make college student loans easier to obtain and at a lower interest level. His Goals 2000 bill formally recognized the national goals and provided a framework for what is referred to as "systemic" reform. *Systemic reform* is the coordination of reform efforts at the local, state, and federal levels. It is top-down support for bottom-up reform. An important component to systemic reform is the creation of national standards; panels of experts are currently creating content standards, performance standards, and new forms of assessment. A key issue in the development of national standards is the degree to which government is responsible for providing students with equal opportunities to learn if they are to be held to high standards. The reauthorization of the Elementary and Secondary Education Act provided an opportunity for the Clinton administration to fulfill its promise for greater education equity because the ESEA is the federal government's largest compensatory education program.

Goals 2000: Building on a Decade of Reform

Goals 2000 was a direct outgrowth of the state-led education reform agenda of the 1980s, which included increasing high school graduation requirements, particularly in math and science, instituting statewide testing programs, offering more Advanced Placement courses, promoting the use of technology in the classroom, and instituting new teacher evaluation programs.

Unlike the piecemeal approach favored during the Reagan–Bush years, the systemic approach to educational reform was comprehensive and focused on coordinating state policy with restructured governance. The objective of systemic reform was to create coherent educational policy. Systemic reform gave the Clinton educational agenda a set of organizing principles that were unique in U.S. educational history. Supporters of systemic reform like to describe it as "top-down support for bottom-up reform." By creating a coherent plan for reform, the Clinton administration had been unusually successful in winning bipartisan support prior to the November 1994 elections. This support resulted in the passage of several bills, including Direct Government Student Loans, National Service, the Safe Schools Act, the reauthorization of the Office of Educational Research and Improvement, the School-to-Work Opportunities Act of 1994, the Improving America's Schools Act of 1993, and the overall reauthorization of the Elementary and Secondary Education Act.

The key intellectual element of the administration's effort was Goals 2000. This law provides the framework of reform that shaped the educational ethos of the Clinton administration. Title I codified the original six National Education Goals concerning school readiness, school completion, student academic achievement, leadership in math and science, adult literacy, and safe and drug-free schools, and added two new goals related to parental participation and professional development. Title II established the National Education Goals Panel, which built public support for the goals, reported on the nation's progress on meeting the goals, and reviewed the voluntary national content, student performance, and voluntary learning standards. Title III provided a state grant program to support, accelerate, and sustain state and local education improvement efforts. Title IV established a new program to create parent information and resource centers. Title V created a National Skills Board to serve as a catalyst in stimulating the development and adoption of a voluntary national system of occupational skills standards. Rather than see the federal government as an educational safety net, the authors of Goals 2000 saw the federal government, despite the rhetoric of volunteerism, as crafting, shaping, and, to some degree, controlling education throughout the 50 states. There can be little doubt that issues of school autonomy and authority have been dramatically altered by the passage of the bill.

Borman and colleagues (1996) provided a comprehensive sociological analysis of Goals 2000 in the following areas: (1) systemic reform; (2) national standards for content and performance; (3) opportunity-to-learn standards; (4) school-to-work standards; (5) school, parent, and community support; (6) professional development; (7) safe, disciplined, and drug-free schools; and (8) implications of the Goals 2000 legislation. The authors indicated that although there have been some significant gains in each of the areas, Goals 2000 is insufficient to provide significant systemic reform of U.S. schools. As sociologists of education, the authors concluded that systemic reform requires significant reforms outside of the educational context, which federal legislation has not mandated.

The bulk of educational reforms with respect to standards and assessments were initiated at the state level. By the end of the decade, 48 states had tested their students, 40 states had standards in all core subjects, and many states had increased standards for teachers ("Text of Statement of Goals Adopted by the Governors," 1999, p. 5). Assessments to measure achievement continue to be controversial (pp. 11, 15–17). What is clear is that the 1990s became defined as the decade of standards, often imposed top-down by federal mandates and state initiatives. While the educational reforms implemented by President Clinton are significant, we believe that genuine reform must include issues of teacher empowerment, diversity, and creating schools that are communities. In the final section, we will propose a more systematic approach to educational reform.

No Child Left Behind

The No Child Left Behind Act is a landmark and controversial piece of legislation that had far-reaching consequences for education in the United States. Already there is talk of spreading similar accountability efforts to higher education in the next reauthorization of the Higher Education Act. And, of course, state governments have been busily pushing accountability requirements for K–12 and higher education for years now. No Child Left Behind was the centerpiece of President George W. Bush's educational policy. A logical progression of the standards movement initiated in 1983 by *A Nation at Risk* and in federal legislation under Presidents G.H.W. Bush (America 2000) and W.J. Clinton (Goals 2000), NCLB was the most comprehensive federal legislation governing state and local educational policies in U.S. history.

No Child Left Behind represented a logical extension of a standards movement that tossed the left's critique of U.S. education back on itself. Based on the critique that U.S. education has historically underserved low-income and minority children through curriculum tracking, poor instruction, and low-quality teachers in urban schools, NCLB mandates the uniform standards for all students in order to reduce and eventually eliminate the social class and race achievement gap by 2014.

The key components of NCLB are:

- Annual testing is required of students in grades 3 through 8 in reading and math plus at least one test in grades 10 through 12; science testing to follow. Graduation rates are used as a secondary indicator for high schools.
- States and districts are required to report school-by-school data on student test performance, broken out by whether the student is African-American, Hispanic-American, Native American, Asian-American, white non-Hispanic, special education, limited English proficiency (LEP), and/or low income.
- States must set adequate yearly progress (AYP) goals for each school. In order to meet AYP, not only must each subgroup make progress in each year in each grade in each subject, but there must also be 95 percent participation of each subgroup as well. The increments in AYP should be arranged so that 100 percent of students reach proficiency by 2014.
- Schools that don't meet AYP for two years are labeled "In Need of Improvement" (INOI). Initially, this means that schools must offer students the option to go to another public school and/or to receive federally funded tutoring. Funds would also be made available for teacher professional development. In the absence of meeting future AYP targets, schools would be subject to "restructuring" (firing teachers and principal; state takeover; private company takeover; etc.).
- Schools must have "highly qualified" teachers for the "core academic subjects" (English, reading or language arts, math, science, foreign languages, civics and government, economics, arts, history and geography) by 2005–2006.

Advocates of NCLB, including progressive organizations such as the Education Trust, argue that its annual testing and disaggregation requirements will force states to ensure that low-income students who continue to lag far behind higher income students will meet the same standards, and thus reduce the achievement gap by 2014. Critics from both the academic and political worlds argue that however noble the goal of eliminating the achievement gap, NCLB does not provide sufficient funds to improve failing schools and, more importantly, is heavy on punishment and light on building school capacity. Liberal and radical critics argue that NCLB fails to acknowledge the social and economic foundation of unequal schooling and is a backdoor to the implementation of publicly funded school vouchers and the dismantling of public education in the United States. Finally, assessment experts argue that since the types of tests and definitions of adequate yearly progress vary by state, there is no uniform definition of "proficiency," and since the assessments evaluate schools rather than students, schools with high mobility rates are punished for such a high turnover, most of the time outside of their control. In addition, because the assessments are based on a zero-sum definition of proficiency rather than a value-added one, schools whose students show significant progress but are still below proficiency are labeled as failures rather than rewarded for their progress (Sadovnik et al., 2008).

Although NCLB was scheduled to be reauthorized in 2008, this had not happened in 2012. Under the Obama Administration, however, the U.S. Department of Education issued waivers to many states if they met criteria under Race to the Top, including its teacher and school accountability, charter school, and school improvement requirements.

Race to the Top

Shortly after taking office, President Barack Obama established the Race to the Top Fund through the historic American Recovery and Reinvestment Act of 2009. The primary goal of this initiative was to aid states in meeting the various components of NCLB. The initial legislation provided $4.35 billion for a competitive grant program that awards states for improving student outcomes and closing achievment gaps by developing plans in the following four education reform areas:

1. Adopting standards and assessments that prepare students to succeed in college and the workplace and to compete in the global economy.
2. Building data systems that measure student growth and success and inform teachers and principals about how they can improve instruction.
3. Recruiting, developing, rewarding, and retaining effective teachers and principals, especially where they are needed most.
4. Turning around our lowest-achieving schools.

In 2010, the federal government reviewed grant applications and awarded funds to Delaware and Tennessee during the first phase of the program and an additional nine states plus the District of Columbia during the second phase of the program. Following these initial grants, the federal government awarded grants to another seven states at the end of 2011. In order to receive Race to the Top funds, states needed to submit applications demonstrating their progress towards implementing the four education reforms outlined above. The federal government then scored applications based on a publicized rubric. Out of a possible 500 points, states could receive 40 points for expanding the use of charter schools, 40 points for adopting the national Common Core Standards, and 58 points for developing new teacher and principal evaluation tools. Largely in response to the competition for grants from the Race to the Top Fund, many states quickly adopted the Common Core Standards, expanded the number of charter schools, and developed new principal and teacher evaluation tools. Some 45 states now utilize the national Common Core Standards to guide instruction. These standards primarily focus on English Language Arts Instruction and Mathematics Instruction. The impact of changes resulting from Race to the Top remains to be understood, but it is clear that President Obama's Race to the Top Fund has had a tremendous impact on the direction of education reform.

Supporters of Race to the Top contend that the grants will aid states as they work to meet the NCLB mandates, improve student outomes, and eliminate the achievement gaps. Despite President Obama's Race to the Top program and its focus on aiding states to meet NCLB requirments, the administation recently initiated a NCLB waiver program. The federal government now grants NCLB waivers exempting states from certain NCLB requirements in exchange for commitments to further reform efforts. Of the 18 states to receive Race to the Top grants,

14 have already been awarded NCLB waivers. Critics of NCLB, Race to the Top, and NCLB waivers, such as Diane Ravitch, argue that all of these reform efforts will remain ineffective. Ravitch notes that NCLB and Race to the Top rely too heavily on standardized testing and the expansion of school choice through charter schools and that these reforms have not demonstrated any significant degree of success in improving acheivement (Ravitch, 2010).

Approaches to Reform

Over the past decade, two different approaches to urban school reform have developed. The first is the neo-liberal approach, represented by the Education Equity Project, which stresses the independent power of schools in eliminating the achievement gap for low-income students. The second, represented by the Broader Bolder Approach, stresses that school level reform alone is necessary but insufficient, and that societal and community level reforms are necessary. Much of the political debate over urban educational reform has been ideological and often with no reliance on empirical evidence. The importance of sociological theory and research is to provide more objective, empirical evidence to inform these debates.

In creating the Education Equality Project (EEP), Joel Klein, Chancellor of the New York City Public Schools and Reverend Al Sharpton seek to eliminate the achievement gap by "working to create an effective school for every child." To create effective schools, the EEP works to ensure that every school has a highly effective teacher and principal; to create system-wide accountability; to empower parents, as well as to encourage them to demand more from their schools and from themselves; and to constantly focus on what will be the best decision for students (EEP website). In their effort to do this, it may require "ruffling union feathers," as the group believes that to eliminate the achievement gap, failing teachers and principals should not be protected (Toppo, 2008).

The second is supported by most liberals and radicals, and represented by the societal/community-based approach of the Broader Bolder Approach founded by Pedro Noguera and Helen Ladd and based on the works of Jean Anyon, Richard Rothstein and others who argue that schools are limited institutions for eradicating the effect of poverty and its effects on children. In Anyon's radical approach, "an all-out attack on poverty and racial isolation that by necessity will affect not only the poor, but the more affluent as well, will be necessary in order to remove the barriers that currently stand in the way of urban educational change" (1997, p. 13). The economic and social differences between races and classes affects academic achievement at all levels from prenatal, to early childhood, to their overall health, welfare, and living environment (Rothstein, 2004b).

There are, for example, inequalities that can occur to children even before they are born. Mothers with low socioeconomic status, and to some extent the low socioeconomic status of the father, are associated with low birth weight babies and with infant mortality (Fiscella & Williams, 2004). Twice as many African-American children are born with a low birth weight than white children, and children of low birth weight typically have lower IQ scores, mild learning disabilities, and attention disorders (Hoffman, Llaga, & Snyder, 2003; Hack, Klein, & Taylor, 1995). Children of low-income families have greater risks of death from infectious diseases (ID) and sudden infant death syndrome (SIDS), higher rates of child abuse, higher rates of exposure to lead poisoning and smokers, higher rates of asthma, greater incidents of developmental delay and learning disabilities, and more exposure to violence and drug trafficking (Fiscella & Williams, 2004).

Minority and lower class children have more vision, hearing, and oral health problems than white children, which can affect their ability to focus and learn during school. For example, twice as many poor children have severe vision impairments, which is more likely to interfere with their academic work (Starfield, 1982). In many cases there is a failure then to diagnose the problem due to the lack of adequate healthcare, available doctors, and time available for parents to take their children to the doctor. Physicians serving low socioeconomic patients have greater logistical and financial burdens, greater problems communicating because of differences in language, culture, and health literacy, and a lack of resources to deal with all of these problems (Fiscella & Williams, 2004). Children who receive normal optometric services have been shown to improve in reading beyond their normal growth for their age (Rothstein, 2004b).

Within the home environment, there are inequalities that can indirectly affect a child's ability to learn. Asthma can also be triggered by factors in the home environment such as dust, mold, and cockroaches. This is important to consider when developing health policies because asthma is the biggest cause of chronic school absence and also leads to low socioeconomic children being over-classified for special education (Corburn, Osleeb, & Porter, 2006).

There also are neighborhood health and environmental factors that influence an individual and the community's ability to be healthy. Typically, there is a disparity in the number of health facilities, with fewer facilities being located in high poverty neighborhoods (Komaromy et al., 1996). There are also fewer quality grocery stores, exercise facilities, parks and recreation spaces. Therefore, "[F]ully closing the black–white achievement gap is both desirable and feasible, but will first require social and economic reforms that would result in distributing black and white students equally between the social classes" (Rothstein, 2004b, p. 18). To do that, the federal government needs to aim reforms at the entire urban system as a whole, initiating economic and social reforms for all citizens (Anyon, 1997).

The Coleman Report (1966) highlighted the importance of neighborhood and social class variables on education. Integrating social classes can lead to improvements in educational achievement (Wells & Crain, 1991). Constructing new social and economic policies that address family, community, and neighborhood inequities, such as increasing the poverty line, fully funding affordable housing programs, providing rental subsidies, providing assistance to families to find units in nicer neighborhoods, enforcing fair housing laws, building more mixed-income housing, and changing local zoning laws that prevent public housing from being built in better neighborhoods, will help to eliminate the neighborhood differences between groups in the United States and ultimately equalize and improve the educational level of our society as a whole.

School-Based Reforms

School Choice, Charter Schools, and Tuition Vouchers

During the 1980s and 1990s, many educational researchers and policy analysts indicated that most public schools were failing in terms of student achievement, discipline, and morality. At the same period, some researchers were investigating private schools and concluding that they were more effective learning environments than public schools. Private schools were reputed to be accountable, efficient, and safe. Moreover, the work of Coleman, Hoffer, and Kilgore (1982) seemed to prove that private school students learned more than their public school counterparts. Other research on magnet schools (schools with special curricula and student bodies) seemed to indicate that public schools that operated independently of the public school bureaucracy were happier, healthier, and more academically productive than zone schools where students were required to attend based on their residence.

As the 1980s came to a close, some researchers reasoned that magnet schools and private schools were superior to neighborhood public schools because schools of choice reflected the desires and needs of their constituents and were thus sensitive to change. For several decades, the idea of school choice had been on the fringes of the educational policy world in the form of voucher proposals. Essentially, voucher proponents argued that if families, rather than schools, were funded, it would allow for greater parental choice and participation. Moreover, by voting with their dollars, parents would reward good schools and punish bad schools. A voucher system, in effect, would deregulate the public school system. That a voucher system might also privatize the public school system was a muted issue.

By the late 1980s, however, school choice was at the forefront of the educational reform movement. Presidents Reagan and Bush supported choice and one influential White House report enumerated a number of reasons why choice was the right reform for the times (Paulu, 1989). In essence, choice was a panacea that was nonbureaucratic, inexpensive, and fundamentally egalitarian because it allowed market forces to shape school policy rather than subjecting educators to the heavy hand of the educational bureaucracy. A very influential book by John E. Chubb and Terry M. Moe, *Politics, Markets, and America's Schools* (1990), seemed to provide empirical evidence that unregulated school choice policies, in and of themselves, would produce a structural reform in U.S. education.

Congressional support for greater school choice was expressed in a bill that was passed by the House of Representatives in the summer of 1990, which, among other things, provided direct federal support for open enrollment experiments. Needless to say, all this political activity stirred up a great deal of controversy and confusion. Choice is controversial because it is deeply political and rests on a set of assumptions about educational marketplaces and private schools that are questionable. It is confusing because choice is a rubric that covers a wide variety of policies that are quite different, except that they include an element of student and parental choice. Next, we briefly touch on some of the major types of school choice plans that have been recently implemented in the United States (see Cookson, 1994, for a complete discussion).

Intersectional choice plans include public and private schools. For example, the cities of Milwaukee and Cleveland provided tuition vouchers to students who attended private neighborhood schools. The inclusion of private schools in choice plans stirred a great deal of debate among policy makers because there are fundamental issues of constitutionality and equity inherent in any public policy that transfers funds from the public sector to the private sector. In the United States, there is a constitutionally protected division between Church and State that forbids the establishment of any state religion and thus forbids State support of any particular religion. Because an overwhelming number of private schools in the United States are religiously affiliated, this issue is critical. However, in 2002, the U.S. Supreme Court in Zelman v. Simmons-Harris ruled that the Cleveland voucher program did not violate the First Amendment separation of Church and State, making future voucher programs more likely. Additionally, equity issues arise from the fact that some private schools are believed to contribute to the maintenance of social inequalities. The most elite secondary schools in the United States, for instance, are private. A public policy that would transfer funds to these schools would clearly raise issues of equal educational opportunity.

Intrasectional school choice policies include only public schools. States, such as Minnesota, permit students to attend school in any public school district in the state, so long as the nonresident school district is willing, has space, and the transfer does not upset racial balance. Statewide choice plans, such as Minnesota's, have been adopted by a number of other states. Most choice plans, however, are more limited geographically. The most common form of intrasectional choice plans permit students to attend schools outside of their community school district. These interdistrict choice plans commonly allow urban students to cross district lines and attend suburban schools and vice versa. In St. Louis, for example, minority students from the inner city are able to attend suburban schools that are located in relatively affluent white neighborhoods. In theory, students from the suburbs are supposed to be drawn into the inner city by some outstanding magnet schools, but, in fact, only a handful of white students have traveled into the inner city to attend school.

Intradistrict choice plans refer to any option available to students within a given public school district. These options range from a choice of curriculum within a particular school to allowing students to attend any school in the district. One particular intradistrict choice plan that has gained a great deal of recognition is *controlled choice*. In this type of plan, students choose a school anywhere in a district or within some zones within a district. The key to this policy is that student choices are not allowed to upset racial balances. In effect, some students may not be able to enroll in their first-choice schools if it would mean increased districtwide racial segregation. Often, other factors are also taken into consideration, such as whether an applicant has a sibling already in his or her school of choice. There are several successful controlled choice districts in the United States, including Cambridge (Massachusetts), Montclair (New Jersey), and District 4 located in the borough of Manhattan in New York City. District 4 also allows students outside its boundaries to attend schools within the district, thus combining intradistrict and interdistrict features.

Boston initiated a controlled choice plan that may serve as a test of whether these types of plans can be successfully implemented on a citywide basis. According to Charles L. Glenn, executive director of the Office of Educational Equity in the Massachusetts Department of Education, the choice plan in Boston appears to be operationally successful, although "vulnerable schools" (i.e., those with declining student populations) need extra assistance to remain open and to provide services to the students who attend them. According to Glenn (1991, p. 43), "Public school choice will not produce overnight miracles, and the Boston experience—like that of Soviet-bloc economies—shows how very difficult it can be to reform an entrenched institution with a monopoly position and a tradition of top-down decision making."

Throughout the 1990s, public school choice, tuition vouchers for private schools, and charter schools (schools that are publicly funded by state charters but independent of many school district mandates) have been key educational reforms. Powers and Cookson (1999) summarized the available evidence on school choice and concluded that (1) market-driven choice programs increase stratification within school districts; (2) choice programs increase the educational opportunities for minority students, who, without these programs, would be limited to their neighborhood public schools; (3) choice parents tend to be more involved in their children's education; (4) choice parents tend to be more satisfied with their children's education; and (5) there is disagreement among researchers about the effect of choice on student achievement. For example, using the same data on Milwaukee Parental Choice Program (MPCP), Witte, 1996; Witte, Sterr, and Thorn, 1995; Witte et al., 1994 argued that the effect of choice has been inconsistent; Greene and Peterson (1996) argued that MPCP has resulted in significant achievement gains; and Rouse's (2002) findings are in the middle.

Beginning with the publication of Chubb and Moe's *Politics, Markets and Schools* (1990), school choice advocates have pushed for the introduction of free markets into K–12 public education. Arguing that public education is dominated by a public bureaucracy dominated by teacher unions, choice advocates believe that only through the introduction of market competition will public schools, especially in urban areas, be forced to improve.

Charter Schools

Passage of the first state-legislated charter law in Minnesota in 1991 has spawned enactment of charter laws in 41 states, as well as the District of Columbia and Puerto Rico. The movement has produced nearly 3,700 charter schools serving 1,076,964 students nationwide (The Center for Education Reform (CER) website, October 2005). Demand for charter schools remains high, as evidenced by the 70 percent of charter schools with waiting lists for admission (RPP International, 1998, 1999, 2000, 2001; Fabricant & Fine, 2012).

States are responding to this demand by authorizing more charters and amending charter laws to accommodate the desire for growth, while other states without charter laws consider their enactment (CER, 2003; Finn, Manno, & Vanourek, 2000; RPP International, 1998, 1999, 2000,

2001). Charter schools are public schools that are free from many of the regulations applied to traditional public schools, and in return are held accountable for student performance. In essence, they "swap red tape for results" (*New York Times*, 10/1/89), also referred to as an "autonomy for-accountability" trade within the movement. The "charter" itself is a performance contract that details the school's mission, program, goals, students served, methods of assessment, and ways to measure success. It is a formal, legal document between those who establish and run a school ("operators") and the public body that authorizes and monitors such schools ("authorizers"). Charter schools are, in theory, autonomous. They produce the results in the ways they think best, for charter schools are self-governing institutions with wide control over their own curriculum, instruction, staffing, budget, internal organization, calendar, etc. (Finn et al., 2000).

As a public school, a charter school is paid for with tax dollars (no tuition charges) and must be open to all students in the school district. And whereas charter schools can be started by virtually anyone (teachers, parents, nonprofit agencies, for-profit organizations, community members, etc.), charters are supposed to demonstrate results to the public agencies that review and approve their charter, as well as monitor and audit their progress. Authorization may be handled by a single agency, such as the state Department of Education in New Jersey. Or a state may have multiple authorizing agencies, including local school boards, community colleges, state colleges and universities (Hill et al., 2001). Accountability is a critical component of the charter movement; if a charter school fails to meet the provisions of its charter, it can lose its funding and be forced to shut its doors.

Proponents of charter schools have long argued that they provide a more effective and efficient alternative for low-income children, especially in urban areas. Often tied to the school choice and voucher movements, advocates believe that, freed from the bureaucratic constraints of traditional urban public schools, charter schools will provide a better education at a lower cost. However, in 2004 the American Federation of Teachers, long a skeptic, if not an opponent, of charter schools, issued a statistical report that found that district public schools outperformed charter schools nationally (Nelson, Rosenberg, & Van Meter, 2004). Immediately following its release, a group of education researchers, some long associated with the school choice and voucher movement, were signatories to a full-page advertisement in the *New York Times*, condemning the AFT study for sloppy research, arguing that the study failed to control sufficiently for student background variables, used one year of data rather than multi-year data sets, and did not measure the value-added effects of charter schools on their students, many of whom came to charters far below state proficiency levels (*New York Times*, 2004).

In 2006, the National Center for Educational Statistics released its report on charter schools, whose study design satisfied some of the criteria for acceptable research outlined in the *Times* advertisement and concluded that after controlling for student demographic characteristics, students in traditional public schools had higher overall achievement in fourth grade reading and mathematics. These differences were not statistically significant for charter schools affiliated with a public school district, while unaffiliated charter schools scored significantly lower than traditional public schools (Braun et al., 2006). These findings were confirmed by a recent comparison of achievement in public, private and charter schools (Lubienski & Lubienski, 2006).

Charter school advocates (see Center for Education Reform, 2005), however, argue that charter schools often admit students who have not performed well in public schools and that it takes time for charter schools to have an impact. Given the lack of statewide student level data, however, the Department of Education and Lubienski studies could not examine the value added effects of district and charter schools when controlling for student background factors. Hoxby (2004b), a leading proponent of charter schools and school choice, released studies that compared charter schools nationally with their neighboring district schools (as a way for controlling for student background factors and comparing them to the schools where the charter school students would have remained if they did not have choice) and of students on waiting lists for charter schools who remained in the neighboring district schools. Both studies indicated that students in charter schools had higher achievement than those who remained in the neighboring district schools, even after controlling for student background variables. Miron and Nelson (2001, 2002) argue that we still do not know enough about student achievement in charter schools and often do not have the type of data needed to effectively evaluate charter school performance. In 2009, The Center for Research on Educational Outcomes (CREDO, 2009a) at Stanford released its national charter school report, which indicated that there were wide variations in the quality of charter schools in the United States and that on the whole charter school students performed below district public school students (Center for Research on Educational Outcomes, 2009). At the same time, Hoxby (2009) issued a report on New York City charter schools showing that students in the charter schools outperformed students in NYC district schools, controlling for a variety of variables, including family background. Additionally, she issued a critique of the CREDO study, which resulted in a series of written debates between CREDO and Hoxby (see CREDO website, 2009a: http://credo.stanford.edu/ for these).

Vouchers

In the 1990s, a number of states, including Wisconsin, Ohio and Florida implemented school voucher programs, all of which were challenged in state courts for violating the separation of Church and State. In 2002, the U.S. Supreme Court in Zelman v. Simmons-Harris ruled that the Cleveland, Ohio, voucher program did not violate the establishment clause of the First Amendment. Specifically, that because the vouchers went directly to families rather than to religious schools and because they could be used in either religious or secular private schools, the voucher program did not violate the constitutional prohibition against public money being used for religious purposes.

Following this decision, many policy experts believed that there would be widespread adoption of new voucher programs. Although Washington, D.C. adopted a voucher program in 2004, there has not been a significant increase in new programs. In 2006, the Florida Supreme Court ruled that its voucher program violated the state's constitution for a uniform system of public education. However, since then the Florida Opportunity Scholarship Program has been modified to meet the Court's ruling, and it now serves low-income and special needs students for the purposes of providing equal education. Nevertheless, there continues to be considerable debate nationally about the use of public funds for sending children to private schools as well as whether the evidence supports the claims of voucher advocates about their effects.

Voucher advocates argue that school choice will have three important educational impacts. First, it will provide low-income parents with the same choices as middle-class parents and lead to increased parental satisfaction with their children's schools. Second, given the absence of the large educational bureaucracy of urban school systems, charter and voucher schools will provide better learning environments for low-income students and result in higher student achievement. Third, due to the competitive market effects of competition from charter and voucher schools, urban public schools will be forced to improve or close their doors. This will result in higher student achievement in urban public schools.

Over the past decade there has been considerable controversy over whether the empirical evidence supports the claims of choice advocates, particularly with respect to the voucher programs in Milwaukee and Cleveland. Witte and colleagues (1995) found that voucher students did not significantly perform better in either math or reading, compared to students who attend public schools, when controlling for socioeconomic status, race and ethnicity (Witte et al., 1995). Instead, he found statistical significance for the negative effects of attending choice schools on reading scores in the second year of the program, 1991–1992 (Carnoy, 2001). Greene and colleagues (Greene et al., 1996) found that those students who applied and won vouchers made significant gains in both math and reading compared to those students who applied to vouchers but ended up in public schools (Greene et al., 1996). Rouse (1998) compared annual gains for a larger sample of voucher students with both general Milwaukee public school students and students who applied for vouchers but did not enter the program. She found a gain of only 1.5 to 2.3 percentile points per year in math for voucher students, but no statistically significant differences in reading scores. Although her research methods overcame some of the limitations of Greene's methods, some argue that her study was still limited in selection bias and accounting for the possibility of other factors, such as students' families and home practices that would have contributed to math score gains (Fuller et al., 1996; Hess, 2002).

In 1995, Wisconsin ended its assessment of the Milwaukee voucher program and since then there is little data available for analyzing the effects of the program on student achievement. Van Dunk and Dickman (2003) argue that the data required for a systematic accountability for the Milwaukee program does not exist and until it does, choice advocates and critics do not have the evidence necessary to support their claims.

The Ohio State Department of Education commissioned Metcalf (1998) and Metcalf et al. (1999, 2001, 2003) to study the voucher program. He found that there was no significant difference in achievement between voucher students and their public school peers, when controlling for socioeconomic backgrounds and other background variables. After four years of longitudinal research, Metcalf et al. (2004) provide some cautionary observations, including that operational procedures are crucial, that parents cite safety, academic quality and classroom order as the main reasons for parental choice, that public and private school classrooms are similar, and overall conclusions about voucher effects are elusive.

Hoxby (2000a, 2001) found that competition leads to higher test scores and lower costs of neighboring public school systems. Hoxby (2001) argues that test scores from Milwaukee public schools subject to voucher and charter school competition increased more rapidly compared to test scores of similar schools elsewhere in Wisconsin that did not face school-choice competition.

Voucher advocates cite a growing body of literature that shows how voucher programs increase student achievement, empower low-income families, increase parental satisfaction rate, improve public education through competition, and offer a more cost-effective method for financing schools. School choice and voucher advocates claim that low-income and minority students will increase their academic achievement at private and parochial schools because they will not be confined to low-performing neighborhood schools but rather will be free to select more effective schools. With this freedom of choice, the parents will increase their satisfaction rate and involvement with their children's schooling.

Proponents also argue that by injecting market competition into the education system, low-performing urban schools will be forced to deliver higher quality education at a lower cost. And schools that are clearly not producing positive effects or operate at a high cost, will simply be put out of "business." That is, private schools supported by public funds actually do a better job than public schools, as well as improve the quality of public schools by introducing competition among low-performing public schools.

Critics of voucher programs argue that proponents' claims have underlying assumptions, limited methods of analysis, drain resources from public schools, and cause further inequality of education. They argue that there simply is not enough evidence to validate the claims made by proponents. In some cases, they point to contradicting evidence. For instance, the critics argue that there is no conclusive evidence that learning opportunities at private and parochial schools actually lead to higher test scores. As far as parental satisfaction rate, there is a limited understanding of the relationship between parental satisfaction rate and higher student achievement.

Ladd (2002), in a balanced and exhaustive review of the literature, concludes that,

> Contrary to the claims of many voucher advocates, widespread use of school vouchers is not likely to generate substantial gains in the productivity of the U.S. K–12 education system . . . The challenge for policymakers is to find ways to expand parental choices without excessively privileging the interests of individual families over the social interests that justify the funding of K–12 education.

Clearly, there is disagreement about whether school choice will lead to the revitalization of public education in the United States. It may well be that choice is a method of school improvement, but cannot by itself resolve many of the fundamental problems associated with public education. Moreover, choice plans usually involve complex and volatile issues of constitutionality, equity, and feasibility. For instance, how will already impoverished school districts pay for the increased transportation costs required by many choice plans? In sum, there is evidence that school choice can lead to improvement in individual schools, but there is little convincing evidence that choice will result in the overall improvement of U.S. education.

School–Business Partnerships

During the 1980s, business leaders became increasingly concerned that the nation's schools were not producing the kinds of graduates necessary for a revitalization of the U.S. economy. Several school-business partnerships were formed, the most notable of which was the Boston Compact begun in 1982. These partnerships have been formed in other cities. For instance, in 1991, the Committee to Support Philadelphia Public Schools pledged management assistance and training to the Philadelphia School District to restructure and implement a site-based management plan. In return, the city promised that by 1995 it would raise the test scores of its graduates and improve grade promotion rates. Other school-business partnerships include scholarships for poor students to attend college and programs where businesses "adopt" a school.

However, despite the considerable publicity that surrounds these partnerships, the fact is that in the 1980s, only 1.5 percent of corporate giving was to public primary and secondary public schools (Reich, 1991, p. 43). In fact, corporate and business support for public schools has fallen dramatically since the 1970s.

Over the past decade, however, a group of foundations and entrepeneurs have contributed significantly to educational reform efforts, most often of the neo-liberal variety. For example, the Walton Foundation has funded charter schools and voucher initiatives. The Bill and Melinda Gates Foundation has contributed hundreds of million dollars to small schools and more recently to teacher effectiveness. And what Diane Ravitch (2010) and Barbara Miner (2010) have termed the "billionaires boys club" have contributed significant amounts to a number of neo-liberal reforms. One such example is the $100 million contributed by Facebook founder Mark Zuckerberg to improve education in Newark, New Jersey.

School–business partnerships have attracted considerable media attention, but there is little convincing evidence that they have significantly improved schools or that, as a means of reform, school–business partnerships will address the fundamental problems facing U.S. education. Whether or not the new entrpeneurs or the education minded foundations will have more of an effect waits to be seen.

Privatization

From the 1990s, the traditional distinction between public and private education became blurred, with private education companies increasingly becoming involved in public education in a variety of ways. First, for-profit companies, such as the Edison Company, took over the management of failing schools and districts. The Philadelphia Public Schools, taken over by the state of Pennsylvania in 2003 due to low student achievement, hired for-profit companies, including Edison, as well as local universities, including Penn and Temple to manage its schools. Second, for-profit companies, such as Kaplan and Sylvan Learning Centers, have the majority of contracts for supplemental tutoring under NCLB. It is too early to assess the efficacy of such privatization, but it is clear that corporations see the multi-billion-dollar education industry as a lucrative market. In 2012, Philadelphia, New Orleans, and other cities, portfolio models of education have replaced traditional school districts, with schools operated by a combination of providers, including traditional district schools, charter schools, and schools operated by for-profit Educational Management Organizations (EMO). Bulkley, Henig, and Levin (2010) concluded that the success of these types of reforms has been mixed.

School-to-Work Programs

In the 1990s, school–business partnerships became incorporated into school-to-work programs. Their intent was to extend what had been a vocational emphasis to non-college-bound students regarding skills necessary for successful employment and to stress the importance of work-based learning.

On May 4, 1994, President Bill Clinton signed the School-to-Work Opportunities Act of 1994. This law provided seed money to states and local partnerships of business, labor, government, education, and community organizations to develop school-to-work systems. The law did not create a new program, but allowed states and their partners to bring together efforts at education reform, worker preparation, and economic development to create a system—a system to prepare youth for the high-wage, high-skill careers of today's and tomorrow's global economy.

Using federal seed money, states and their partnerships were encouraged to design the school-to-work system that made the most sense for them. While these systems were different from state to state, each was supposed to provide every U.S. student with the following:

- Relevant education, allowing students to explore different careers and see what skills are required in their working environment.
- Skills, obtained from structured training and work-based learning experiences, including necessary skills of a particular career as demonstrated in a working environment.
- Valued credentials, establishing industry-standard benchmarks and developing education and training standards that ensure that proper education is received for each career.

Every state and locally created school-to-work system had to contain three core elements: (1) school-based learning (classroom instruction based on high academic and business-defined occupational skill standards); (2) work-based learning (career exploration, work experience, structured training and mentoring at job sites); and (3) connecting activities (courses integrating classroom and on-the-job instruction, matching students with participating employers, training of mentors, and the building of other bridges between school and work).

Although the school-to-work programs were well intentioned, researchers (Charner, 1996; Mortimer, 1996) have suggested that these programs often failed to fulfill their promise. The U.S. system of vocational education remains a "second-class" educational track, which often does not equip students with a sound liberal arts foundation and is not adequately connected to career opportunities. Unlike other nations, such as Japan and Germany, U.S. students who do not wish to go on to postsecondary education are not given adequate career paths.

Teacher Education

The emergence and development of teacher education as an educational problem was a response to the initial debates concerning the failure of the schools (Labaree, 1992a, 1992b, 1996). If the schools were not working properly, then teachers and teaching—perhaps the most important piece in the puzzle—had to be looked at critically. In addition, teacher organizations such as the National Education Association (NEA) and the American Federation of Teachers (AFT), fearing the scapegoating of their members, took an active role in raising the debate as the opportunity to both recognize and improve the problematic conditions under which, from their perspective, most of their members work.

Finally, if teachers and teaching were indeed part of the problem, then perhaps the education and training of teachers was a good starting point for analysis. Thus, teacher education, and schools and colleges of education, long the object of critical scrutiny within universities, became the subject of intensive national investigation. By 1986, at least five major reports (by the National Commission on Excellence in Teacher Education, the California Commission on the Teaching Profession, the Holmes Group, the Southern Regional Education Board, and the Carnegie Report of the Task Force on Teaching as a Profession) outlined major problems in teacher education and the professional lives of teachers, and proposed a large-scale overhaul of the system that prepares teachers. Although the reports differed in some respects, there was widespread agreement about the nature of the problem. The debate revolved around three major points:

1. The perceived lack of rigor and intellectual demands in teacher education programs.
2. The need to attract and retain competent teacher candidates.
3. The necessity to reorganize the academic and professional components of teacher education programs at both the baccalaureate and post-baccalaureate levels. (Teacher Education Project, 1986)

Although all five reports contributed to the ongoing discussions, the Carnegie and Holmes reports attracted the most public response and became symbolic of the teacher education reform movement. (Perhaps this was because they represented two of the major interest groups in teacher education—in the case of Carnegie, major political and educational leaders, and for Holmes, the Deans of Education from the major research universities.) Therefore, this section will analyze the Carnegie and Holmes reports as representative of the current attempts to improve the training of teachers (see Labaree, 1992a and 1992b for a detailed discussion).

The Carnegie Report, entitled *A Nation Prepared: Teachers for the 21st Century* (1986) and prepared by its Task Force on Teaching as a Profession (including representatives from corporations, the NEA and AFT, school journalists and administrators, legislators, the Governor of New Jersey, and a Dean of Education of a major research university), focused on the necessity of educational quality for a competitive U.S. economy and the value of education in a democratic political system. Building on the critique offered by *A Nation at Risk*, the Carnegie Report suggested that improvements in teacher education were necessary preconditions for improvements in education.

In addition to this underlying democratic-liberal model of education, the report argued that the decline in traditional low-wage jobs in the U.S. economy and the corresponding increase in high-technology and service positions would require the schools to better prepare its students for this "new" economic reality. In this regard, also, the Carnegie Report stressed the centrality of better prepared teachers to meet the challenges of the twenty-first century. Echoing this political-economic perspective, the report stated:

> If our standard of living is to be maintained, if the growth of a permanent underclass is to be averted, if democracy is to function effectively [in the twenty-first] century, our schools must graduate the vast

majority of their students with achievement levels long thought possible for only the privileged few. The American mass education system, designed in the early part of the century for a mass production economy, will not succeed unless it not only raises but redefines the essential standards of excellence and strives to make quality and equality of opportunity compatible with each other. (1986, p. 3)

In order to accomplish these democratic-liberal goals, the Carnegie Report (1986, p. 3) called for "sweeping changes in educational policy," which would include the restructuring of schools and the teaching profession, the elimination of the undergraduate education major, the recruitment of minorities into the teaching profession, and the increase of standards in teacher education and in teaching.

The Holmes Group, on the other hand, avoided explicit political–economic goals, but focused on the relationship between university-based teacher education, the professional lives of teachers, and the structure of the schools themselves. Arguing that their role as teacher-educators gave a unique and also perhaps subjective perception of these issues, the Holmes Report, entitled *Tomorrow's Teachers* (1986), outlined a set of five goals and proposals for the improvement of teacher education. Michael Sedlak, one of the original coauthors of the report, introduced his brief summary of the document by stressing that "the Holmes Group is dedicated not just to the improvement of teacher education but to the construction of a genuine profession of teaching" (1987, p. 315). The goals of the report included raising the intellectual soundness of teacher education, creating career ladders for teachers, developing entry-level requirements into the profession, linking schools of education at the university level to schools, and improving schools for students and teachers.

In two subsequent reports, *Tomorrow's Schools* (1990) and *Tomorrow's Schools of Education* (1995), the Holmes Group advocated systemic changes in professional development and radically altering schools of education with an emphasis on school–university partnerships and professional development schools (PDS). Critics of the Holmes Group (Labaree, 1992a, 1992b, 1996) argued that its proposals represented a "disabling vision" for schools of education, as they limit their roles to teacher education only, while deemphasizing their other important roles in research and education in broader societal and psychological contexts.

Despite differences in tone and some minor differences in emphasis, both the Carnegie and Holmes Reports focus on the same general concerns:

1. They agree that overall problems in education cannot be solved without corresponding changes in teacher education.
2. Teacher education programs must be upgraded in terms of their intellectual rigor and focus, their need to emphasize the liberal arts, their need to eliminate undergraduate teacher education programs and, like other professions (i.e., psychology, social work, law, medicine), move professional training and certification to the graduate level.
3. Rigorous standards of entry into the profession must be implemented, and systematic examinations to monitor such entry must be developed.
4. University teacher education programs and schools must be connected in a more systematic and cooperative manner.
5. Career ladders that recognize differences in knowledge, skill, and commitment must be created for teachers.
6. Necessary changes must be made in the schools and the professional lives of teachers in order to attract and retain the most competent candidates for the profession.

John Goodlad, in *Teachers for Our Nation's Schools* (1990), proposed a radical transformation of the way teachers are prepared, requiring an overhaul of university-based teacher preparation.

Echoing many of the recommendations of the Carnegie Commission and the Holmes Group on school-university cooperation, Goodlad stressed the importance of rewarding teacher-educators for their work, rather than relegating them, as is currently the case, to the bottom rung of the university status hierarchy.

In the 1990s, teacher education and professionalization continued to be significant issues. Talbert (1996) argued that both teacher education and professional development programs have been inadequate for equipping prospective teachers and teachers to fulfill their myriad responsibilities. Most teachers receive one-shot professional development workshops that have little effect on their performance. She argued that long-term systemic professional development is needed.

As head of the National Commission on Teaching and America's Future, Linda Darling-Hammond (1996b) has been one of the recent leaders of the teacher education reform. The commission report indicated that the criticisms presented by the Carnegie and Holmes reports in the 1980s had not been adequately addressed. It pointed out that "school reform cannot succeed unless it focuses on creating the conditions in which teachers can teach, and teach well" (p. vi), and it identified the following barriers to improving teacher education development: (1) low expectations for student performance, (2) unenforced standards for teachers, (3) major flaws in teacher preparation, (4) slipshod teacher recruitment, (5) inadequate induction for beginning teachers, (6) lack of professional development and rewards for knowledge and skill, and (7) schools that are structured for failure rather than success. Therefore, the Commission recommended the following:

1. Get serious about standards, for both students and teachers.
2. Reinvent teacher preparation and professional development.
3. Fix teacher recruitment and put qualified teachers in every classroom.
4. Encourage and reward teacher knowledge and skill.
5. Create schools that are organized for student and teacher success. (National Commission on Teaching and America's Future, 1996, pp. vi–vii)

Representative of the second wave of educational reforms, the effective school movement's recommendations, as well as those of the Carnegie, Holmes, and National Commission on Teaching and America's Future reports, emphasized the processes of teaching and learning, the school environment, and especially the need to improve the professional lives and status of teachers.

Since the 1990s, a number of alternatives to traditional university-based teacher education emerged, such as Teach for America (TFA) and the New Teacher Project (NTP). These programs sought to recruit high-performing college graduates for immediate entry into underserved urban and rural schools. Rather than these prospective teachers having to complete a traditional multi-year university-based program, they complete instead a summer student teaching program and are immediately placed in underserved schools. TFA, founded in the 1990s by Wendy Kopp, based on her Princeton senior thesis, has become the largest alternative teacher education program in the U.S. It recruits the "best and brightest" from elite colleges and universities, and requires that they teach for a minimum of two years in an urban or rural school. NTP has contracts with numerous cities to provide a more rapid route to the classroom. In New York City, the New York City Teaching Fellows Program provides an alternate route, similar to TFA, for teacher candidates to enter the city's schools without completing traditional teacher education requirements. An alternate route program has existed in New Jersey since the 1980s, but is less selective than the other programs. Proponents of these programs argue that traditional university teacher education programs have lower performing students compared to the general student population and lack rigor. Critics of these programs argue that no other profession would permit its practitioners to enter the field without training and because many of these programs, especially TFA, only require two years of service, the attrition rate is very high (Darling-Hammond, 2010). Proponents argue that the attrition rate for traditionally prepared teachers is also significantly high. Both agree that the key is whether or not there is a difference between each group in their effect on their student learning. To date, the evidence is not conclusive (Boyd et al., 2010).

Teacher Quality

What is clear is that how to recruit and retain high quality teachers is among the most important problems in American education. NCLB's requirement that all schools have highly qualified teachers in every classroom highlighted the problem of unqualified teachers in urban schools. But whereas most teachers meet the highly qualified standards of NCLB, the data indicate that significant numbers of classrooms staffed by teachers who are not highly qualified in the particular subject they teach. This is the result of the practice called out-of-field teaching—teachers being assigned to teach subjects which do not match their training or education. This is a crucial practice because highly qualified teachers actually may become highly unqualified in that circumstance.

At the secondary school level, about one fifth of classes in each of the core academic subjects (math, science, English, social studies) are taught by teachers who do not hold a teaching certificate in the subject taught. The data also show that urban schools—especially low-income ones—have more out-of-field teaching than others. Urban schools with high levels of minority students also typically have a larger percentage of novice teachers (The Education Trust, 2010a, from Schools and Staffing Survey, 2003–2004).

Ingersoll (1999, 2003, 2004) asserts that problems in staffing urban schools have less to do with teacher shortages and more with organizational issues inside schools. Principals often find it easier to hire unqualified teachers than qualified ones, and the absence of status and professionalism, and poor working conditions in teaching leads to high dropout rates in the first five years of teaching. Therefore, urban districts are constantly replacing teachers on an ongoing basis, which has significant consequences since it takes years to become an expert teacher. Rates of teacher attrition and misassignment are more prevalent in urban and high poverty schools (Ingersoll, 1999, 2003, 2004).

Ingersoll's research suggests that programs aimed at solving urban school staffing problems at the supply level through alternative teacher education programs such as Teach for America, the New York City Teaching Fellows Program and New Jersey's Alternative Certification Program (all of which allow college graduates with majors in their teaching field to enter teaching without traditional certification through a college teacher education program) fail to address the organizational problems within schools that are responsible for high turnover rates (Ingersoll, 2004).

Recently, school improvement reformers have stressed the existence of teacher tenure and seniority based transfers and layoff provisions in union contracts as a primary factor in preventing an improvement of teacher quality. A number of provisions in the Race to the Top funding and new contracts like the one in Washington, D.C. have addressed some of these issues.

The Effective School Movement

In response to A Nation at Risk and other reports criticizing the effectiveness of U.S. public schools, the school effectiveness movement emerged and suggested that there were characteristics in good schools that could be used as models for improving educational effectiveness. The late Ron Edmonds, one of the early leaders of this movement, argued that educational reform and improvement must consider problems of both equity and quality. Based on Edmonds's work on effective schools for disadvantaged students (Edmonds, 1979a), research on school effectiveness sought to identify the characteristics of effective schools (Brookover et al., 1979, 1982).

The school effectiveness research points out five key factors that define successful schools: (1) high expectations for all students, and staff acceptance of responsibility for student learning; (2) instructional leadership on the part of the principal; (3) a safe and orderly environment conducive to learning; (4) a clear and focused mission concerning instructional goals shared by the staff; and (5) frequent monitoring of student progress (Gartner & Lipsky, 1987, p. 389).

Based on this research, educational policy makers focused on how to build the capacity in districts, schools, and classrooms to improve student achievement and to reduce the achievement gaps. Research suggests that districts have a specific role to play in assisting schools to build the necessary capacity to improve student achievement. Districts can assist schools in developing organizational/structural and instructional capacity. Research provides advice to districts about how they can build organizational capacity, and suggests a focus on the following five dimensions:

1. vision and leadership;
2. collective commitment and cultural norms;
3. knowledge or access to knowledge;
4. organizational structures and management;
5. resources. (Goertz, Floden, & O'Day, 1995, p. 3)

Research also argues that the reform process itself is instrumental in building capacity, and indicates four strategies for building the capacity for standards-based reforms:

1. articulating a reform vision;
2. providing instructional guidelines;
3. restructuring governance and organizational structures;
4. establishing evaluation and accountability mechanisms. (Goertz et al., 1995, p. 4)

In other words, it is incumbent on districts to do the following:

- Assist schools in using achievement data as a baseline for targeted improvement.
- Provide districtwide professional development aimed at improving teacher knowledge and skills.
- Help schools align their curriculum and instruction to state learning standards and assessments.
- Target those students and schools with the most need for districtwide help.

Efforts aimed at capacity building must start with a vision of what an effective school should look like. After all, it is at the school level—more than at the district—that student achievement is most directly impacted. There is general agreement in the research conducted on the effective practices of high-performing, high-poverty schools. These schools (American Federation of Teachers, 1998, 1999; American Institutes for Research, 1999; Carter, 2000; Connell, 1999; Haycock, 1999; Johnson et al., 1999; Lein et al., 1997; U.S. Department of Education, 1998, 2001):

- Set high standards and develop curriculum and assessment tools based on those standards.
- Hold teachers and school administrators accountable for student performance and meeting goals.
- Create a safe and orderly academic environment.
- Employ teachers who are experienced and qualified to teach their subject matter and have access to quality professional development and school administrators who are committed to education.

- Encourage parental and community involvement.
- Enjoy administrative flexibility in making decisions involving curriculum, personnel, and school budgets.

Research from the U.S. Department of Education, National Center for Education Statistics (2000b), summarized the key components of school quality as follows:

- Teacher quality and experience, including the academic skills of teachers, teachers who are teaching in their field of preparation, teacher experience, professional development.
- Classroom climate, including course content and alignment with learning standards, technology, class size, pedagogy.
- School context, including school leadership, goals, professional community, discipline, academic environment.

In order to be more specific about school capacity, it is useful to look at what the research says about the characteristics of effective schools and classrooms, and also about effective teachers. The characteristics described encompass structural issues, broad school and classroom-culture issues, and specific instructional issues.

The National Center for Educational Statistics (U.S. Department of Education, 2000b) concluded that there are five characteristics of effective schools that have a positive effect on student learning:

1. School leadership that provides direction, guidance, and support.
2. School goals that are clearly identified, communicated, and enacted.
3. A school faculty that collectively takes responsibility for student learning.
4. School discipline that establishes an orderly atmosphere conducive to learning.
5. School academic organization and climate that challenges and supports students toward higher achievement. (p. 36)

At the level of the classroom, research indicates that a variety of factors—including course content, pedagogy, technology and class size—have an impact on student achievement. However, without effective teachers, these factors mean little. Research indicates that at the classroom level, effective instructional practices, implemented by knowledgeable teachers, are a prerequisite for school improvement (Darling-Hammond et al., 2005).

Research reveals a lot about the characteristics of effective teachers. What this research means on a practical level is that the state must partner with districts and schools to build an infrastructure that will increase the likelihood that every teacher possesses the characteristics listed below. According to the research, the most qualified teachers possess the following characteristics (Ingersoll, 2003):

- Strong academic skills.
- Teaching within the individual's field of expertise—having an equivalent of a major in the field.
- At least three years' teaching experience.
- Participation in high-quality professional development programs.

Class size is another component of effective schools, especially for low-income students. A Tennessee class size study provides important evidence on the value of small classes (Krueger, 1998; Mosteller, 1995; Sanders & Rivers, 1996). Based on a random assignment experiment, this study indicated that there were significant achievement gains made by students in the smaller classes, when controlling for all other factors. Further, the greatest gains were made by black students in the early grades. Further studies confirmed that the largest gains were made by black, disadvantaged students (Achilles, 1996; Finn, J. D., 1998; Grissmer, Flanagan, & Williamson, 1998; Hanuschek, 1998; Krueger, 1998; Mosteller, Light, & Sachs, 1996; U.S. Department of Education, 1998). A report by the U.S. Department of Education, National Center for Educational Statistics (2000b) suggests that reductions in class size have the potential for helping all students in the primary grades (U.S. Department of Education, 2000b, p. 35). Based on the Tennessee evidence, it appears that for disadvantaged students the gains are especially strong. Beginning in the 1990s, a number of nonprofit organizations developed models for school improvement, based on the research evidence on effective schools. These include Success for All, a highly structured and scripted program founded by Robert Slavin at Johns Hopkins University; Accelerated Schools, a program that provides rigorous curriculum for students at risk, founded by Henry Levin at Stanford and now at Teachers College, Columbia University; the Coalition of Essential Schools, a progressive school reform program, founded by Theodore Sizer at Brown University; a capacity-building model founded by the Hudson Institute; the Comer School Development Program, a program based on school–family partnerships, founded by James Comer at Yale Medical Schools; Core Knowledge, a program based on "traditional" core knowledge, founded by E.D. Hirsch at the University of Virginia; and America's Choice, a program based on standards and assessments, aligned instructional systems, focus on literacy and mathematics, leadership, and professional learning communities, founded by the National Center for Education and the Economy (for a complete list, see www.nwrel.org/scpd/catalog/modellist.asp).

Federal funds were available for comprehensive school reform programs in low-income schools. However, the programs had to demonstrate that the school reform program integrated all eleven of the components outlined in the Comprehensive School Reform (CSR) Program Guidance (www.csrclearinghouse.org/index.cgi?l=csr_ program_components):

1. Proven methods and strategies based on scientifically based research.
2. Comprehensive design.
3. Professional development.
4. Measurable goals and benchmarks.
5. Support within the school.
6. Support for teachers and principals.
7. Parental and community involvement.
8. External technical support and assistance.
9. Annual evaluation.
10. Coordination of resources.
11. Strategies that improve academic achievement—The program must meet one of the following requirements:

    a. the program has been found, through scientifically based research, to significantly improve the academic achievement of participating students;

    or

    b. the program has been found to have strong evidence that it will significantly improve the academic achievement of participating children.

The evidence on the success of these programs has been the subject of considerable debate, particularly Success for All (SFA). Pogrow (1996, 1999, 2000) has argued that SFA has not significantly improved its schools, whereas Slavin (1997a, 1997b, 1999) has argued that there is considerable scientific evidence to demonstrate his program's effectiveness. More recent research by the American Institutes for Research (Aladjem et al., 2002) demonstrates differences in effectiveness among 24 programs, but also indicates that many programs improve low-income schools. A 2004 study by the Consortium on Policy Research in Education (May, Supovitz, & Perda, 2004) showed significant achievement gains in schools using America's Choice in Rochester, New York. Borman, Hewes, Overman and Brown (2003) have provided a meta-analysis of the studies on the effects of CSR and conclude that comprehensive school reforms have the potential for improving schools and reducing the achievement gaps.

The evidence suggests that these types of reforms have the potential for improving low-income, high-minority schools. The Education Trust (2010a) provided examples of many high-performing, low-income, high-minority schools. Further, it argued that there are some districts (e.g., Aldine and El Paso, Texas) and some states (e.g., Delaware, Illinois, Massachusetts, North Carolina, and Texas) that have significantly reduced the race, ethnic, and social class achievement gaps through the types of educational policies outlined in this chapter. However, sometimes such reforms fail to improve consistently failing schools and more drastic action is taken.

Societal, Community, Economic, and Political Reforms

State Intervention and Mayoral Control in Local School Districts*

For several decades at least, school accountability has been a prominent issue on the national education scene. Accountability has taken many forms, often involving state regulation or oversight. It has included state certification of school personnel and of school districts; statewide testing and assessment of pupils; state monitoring of local fiscal, management, and educational practices; local districts reporting to the state; state dissemination of report cards and other district- and school-specific information to the public; and state intervention in the operation of local districts when problems were identified and solutions were determined to be beyond the local capacity.

Virtually all state accountability systems focus on rewards and sanctions. State policy makers increasingly are directing their attention to how to reward schools and districts that perform well and how to sanction those that do not. As of 2000, 38 states had some form of rewards or sanctions in place: 8 states rewarded school districts, 20 rewarded schools, 29 imposed sanctions on school districts, and 32 imposed sanctions on schools. Three states (Delaware, Oklahoma, and Texas) did all four. For an excellent description and analysis of the accountability structures in each state, see CPRE (Consortium for Policy Research on Education), *State Assessment & Accountability Systems: 50 State Profiles* (2000).

Some systems include school or district takeover as ultimate accountability measures. As of 2000, 23 states have enacted statutes authorizing their state education agencies to take control of school districts from local authorities: Alabama, Arkansas, California, Connecticut, Illinois, Iowa, Maryland, Massachusetts, Michigan, Mississippi, Missouri, New Jersey, New Mexico, New York, North Carolina, Ohio, Oklahoma, Pennsylvania, Rhode Island, South Carolina, Tennessee, Texas, and West Virginia. Most of those statutes provide for a succession of increasingly severe sanctions imposed on underperforming districts, leading to takeover as a last resort, whereas some provide only for takeover; some indicate a preference for assistance to local boards and administrators, again with takeover a last resort; and still others indicate no such preference. Most

---

* This section is adapted from P. Tractenberg, M. Holzer, G. Miller, A. R. Sadovnik, and B. Liss (2002), Developing a Plan for Reestablishing Local Control in the State-Operated School Districts. Newark, NJ: Institute on Education Law and Policy, Rutgers University (http://ielp.rutgers.edu/projects/qsac).

provide for systems of assessment or accreditation of schools and districts statewide, whereas others target a single troubled school district. As to the basis for takeover, most statutes authorize action on the basis of poor academic performance; others refer to district governance and management as well as academics. Most provide for replacement of administrative personnel with a state-appointed administrator, and some provide for a "receiver," or transfer of control to municipal officials, or annexation into a neighboring school district.

In short, there appears to be no standard method of imposing or implementing state control of local school districts, and there appears to be no standard method of returning control to local authorities. The experience with state takeovers is still relatively limited and fragmentary, but it has led to some perceived advantages and disadvantages. Among the advantages are the following:

- Takeover is, in appropriate cases, a necessary expression of a state's constitutional responsibility for public education.
- Properly done, takeover can provide a good opportunity for state and local decision makers to combine resources and knowledge to improve children's learning.
- Takeover can allow a competent executive staff to guide an uninterrupted and effective implementation of school improvement efforts.
- Takeover can help create a healthy environment in which the local community can address a school district's problems.
- Takeover can make possible more radical changes in low-performing school districts than the customary regimen.
- Takeover, by its relatively extreme and dramatic nature, can put school boards throughout the state on notice that personal agendas, nepotism, and public bickering can have severe consequences.
- If the state carefully collects and analyzes pupil achievement and other data in state-operated districts and schools, it can lead to improvements in statewide accountability efforts.

The perceived disadvantages of state takeover include the following:

- Takeover may be seen as a thinly veiled attempt to reduce local control over schools and to increase state authority over school districts, especially if state government is dominated by one political party and urban districts by another.
- The very concept of state takeover suggests that some local communities lack the capacity to operate effective public schools, and that the state has ready answers and personnel capable of turning around poor performance of the most educationally disadvantaged students.
- State takeover might place poorly prepared state-selected officials in charge, with little possibility of any meaningful change occurring in the classroom.
- Takeover tends to rely on narrow learning measures (i.e., standardized test scores) as the primary criterion for takeover decisions.
- No matter what triggers takeover, it usually focuses, at least initially, on cleaning up petty corruption and incompetent administration and does not get at the root problems impeding the learning of disadvantaged students in urban school districts.
- By fostering a negative image of school board members, administrators, teachers, students, and parents in urban districts, takeover tends to undermine their self-esteem and capacity to improve their performance.
- Takeover that largely supplants local responsibility for the schools inevitably leads to frictions and confrontations between state and local officials that slow the overhaul of management practices, drain resources from educational reforms, and reinforce community resentments.

There is very little research on the effects of state takeovers. For the most part, the studies suggest that takeover has yielded more gains in central office activities than in classroom instructional practices. Illustratively, state takeovers are credited with the following:

- Reducing nepotism within a school district's decision-making process.
- Improving a school district's administrative and fiscal management practices.
- Removing the threat of teachers' strikes within a school district.
- Upgrading the physical condition of schools.
- Implementing innovative programs within a school district, such as small schools programs and cooperative arrangements between schools and social service agencies.

Unfortunately, however, the limited research suggests that under state takeover, student achievement gains often have fallen short of expectations.

Nevertheless, several states, including California, Connecticut, Kentucky, and West Virginia, have intervention schemes that have resulted in improvements in failing school districts. What they have in common is their focus on improving the local school district's capacity to correct its own problems and to operate a successful educational program. Both the literature and the reported experience of states that have the highest rated state intervention programs suggest that local capacity building must be the cornerstone of successful state involvement. New Jersey, which took over its three largest school districts—Jersey City in 1987, Paterson in 1991, and Newark in 1995—has been less successful, with all three districts still under state control (Tractenberg et al., 2002). Unlike New Jersey, where a command-and-control approach did little to improve failing districts, California's approach in the Compton Unified School District provides an example of how state intervention may be successful. Through the County Office Fiscal Crisis and Management Assistance Team's (FCMAT) capacity-building approach, the Compton District was returned to local control in four years. Currently, FCMAT is working in the Oakland School District, which was taken over by the state in 2004.

The types of reforms, including state intervention, cost money, and low-income, high-minority schools often have significantly less money to spend, despite the availability of federal Title 1 funds. These funding disparities have been the subject of considerable legal actions.

A popular reform implemented over the past decade is mayoral control of urban districts. Similar to state takeover, mayoral control has been a favored neo-liberal reform, with urban mayors and business leaders arguing that centralizing governance into the mayor's office is more effective and efficient than traditional elected school boards. Proponents argue that mayoral control eliminates corruption, leads to effective and efficient management and budgets, increases student achievement, and reduces the political battles endemic to elected school boards (Moscovitch et al., 2010). Critics argue that it has not increased achievement significantly, is undemocratic, and has reduced community and parental involvement (Moscovitch et al., 2010).

The evidence on mayoral control is mixed. Wong et al. (2007) found that mayoral control resulted in modest improvements in student achievement. However, Henig (2009) found that non-mayoral cities had greater improvements. Moscovitch et al. in their study of nine cities with varying degrees of mayoral control (Baltimore, Boston, Chicago, Cleveland, Detroit, Hartford, New York, Philadelphia, and Washington, D.C.) found that although there were achievement gains in most of the cities, it was impossible to attribute them causally to mayoral control. In addition, they found improvements in a number of areas, including efficiency and stability. The authors conclude that their study supports Viteritti's position that governance structure "is not a solution, it is an enabler . . . creat[ing] possibilities for the kind of bold leadership needed to turn around failing school districts" (Viteritti, 2009). Good governance is necessary but not sufficient for meaningful educational reform, and mayoral control is not the only form of good governance.

"Given the benefits we have seen in the nine cities, mayoral control should be one of a number of options available, as long as parental and community input and involvement are not stifled as they have been in some cities" (Moscovitch et al., 2010, p. 120).

School Finance Reforms

Following the Supreme Court's 1973 decision in Rodriguez v. San Antonio, which declared there is no constitutional right to an equal education, school finance equity and adequacy advocates litigated at the state level. Even before Rodriguez, Robinson v. Cahill was filed in 1970 against the state of New Jersey, citing discrimination in funding for some school districts, which prosecutors believed was creating disparities in urban students' education by failing to provide all students with a "thorough and efficient" education, as guaranteed under the New Jersey State Constitution. Although the State enacted an income tax in accordance with the ruling of this case in 1973, the program was never fully funded. By 1980, more evidence had been accumulated regarding the inequality of education in urban areas and the Education Law Center filed Abbott v. Burke, on behalf of several urban school districts also due to a violation of the "thorough and efficient" clause.

The court ruled in 1990, stating that more funding was needed to serve the children in the poorer school districts. In order to provide a "thorough and efficient education" in urban districts, funding was equalized between urban and suburban school districts. It was also determined that extra funding was to be distributed to provide additional programs in order to eliminate disadvantages within poorer school districts.

In 1998, the state was required to implement a package of supplemental programs, including preschool, as well as a plan to renovate urban school facilities. Abbott V implemented additional entitlements for urban schools, including whole school reform, full day kindergarten, preschool for all 3- and 4-year-olds, a comprehensively managed and funded facilities program to correct code violations; a plan to eliminate overcrowding, and to provide adequate space for all educational programs at Abbott schools.

Other supplemental programs included social services, increased security, a technology alternative education, school-to-work, after-school, and summer-school programs (Education Law Center, 2010; Yaffe, 2007). What made Abbott different from other school finance decisions is that, in addition to equalizing funding, the court recognized that factors outside schools had to be addressed as well. Its requirement for the funding of mandatory preschool and supplemental services illustrated this approach.

In 2009, the New Jersey Supreme Court ruled as constitutional a new funding formula, SFRA, that eliminated the Abbott remedies and implemented a formula for allocating funding to all districts based on student needs. According to the state, this "money follows the child" approach would more equitable distribute funding to all "at-risk" children in the state, including in its rural and lower income urban rim districts. The Education Law Center in its legal challenge argued that the new formula would take necessary funding away from the urban districts. School finance researchers are currently studying the law's effects.

Other states, including Kentucky, Massachusetts, and New York, had similar litigation. In 1993, New York state began its own 16-year battle for equity in education. A group of concerned parents and advocates banded together under the non-profit group called the Campaign for Fiscal Equity (CFE) to challenge the state to provide a "sound basic" education for all students that prepares them to participate in society. A "sound basic education" was defined according to Justice DeGrasse as "high school graduates [who] must be able to evaluate complex issues that may arise in jury service or voting and they must also be able to obtain and hold competitive employment" (CFE). In CFE v. State of New York, the State Supreme Court found the state school funding formula to be unconstitutional in 2001. Following a series of appeals, the state was ordered to provide New York City public schools with additional funding for their annual operating budget. CFE continues its advocacy work to ensure that the implementation of reforms and distribution of money is meeting the needs of the lowest performing students in the schools with the highest need.

Although all of these educational reforms have demonstrated the potential to improve schools for low-income and minority children, especially in urban areas, by themselves they are limited in reducing the achievement gaps (Anyon, 2005; Rothstein, 2004b; Sadovnik, 2011b; Tractenberg et al., 2004) unless they also address the factors outside of schools responsible for educational inequalities. In addition to school-based programs, such as early childhood programs, summer programs, and after-school programs, Rothstein (2004b, pp. 129–150) calls for economic programs to reduce income inequality and to create stable and affordable housing, and the expansion of school-community clinics to provide health care and counseling. He also warns that although school finance suits are necessary to ensure that all children receive an adequate education, without addressing the economic forces outside of schools they will not be sufficient. Rothstein, a liberal, and Anyon, a radical, both conclude that school reform is necessary but insufficient to reduce the achievement gaps without broader social and economic policies aimed at addressing the pernicious effect of poverty.

Full Service and Community Schools

Another way to attack education inequity is to examine and plan to educate not only the whole child, but also the whole community. Dryfoos's model of full service schools (Dryfoos, 1994, 2005), Canada's Harlem Children's Zone (Tough, 2008), and Newark's Broader Bolder Approach, are three models of community-based reforms. Full service schools focus on meeting students' and their families educational, physical, psychological, and social needs in a coordinated and collaborative fashion between school and community services (Dryfoos, 1994, 2005). In this model, schools service as community centers within neighborhoods that are open extended hours to provide a multitude of services such as adult education, health clinics, recreation facilities, after-school programs, mental health services, drug and alcohol programs, job placement and training programs, and tutoring services.

Specifically designed to target and improve at-risk neighborhoods, full-service schools aim to prevent problems, as well as to support them. Whereas this model supports Anyon's (1997) argument to repair the larger social and economic problems of society as a means of improving public education, there is no evidence that full-service schools affect student achievement.

Harlem Children's Zone

Growing up in the South Bronx and an-all black community on Long Island didn't prepare Geoffrey Canada for the academic and social challenges he faced at Bowdoin College in Maine. As a result, he wanted to ensure that other African-American children were prepared. The aspect of Canada's approach that is unique compared to other philosophies from boarding schools, charities, and social service agencies, is that he wants to leave children where they are, simultaneously changing them and their neighborhood, instead of removing them from the neighborhood (Tough, 2008).

Canada hopes that children can positively "contaminate" Harlem, NY; he said that

> when you've got most of the kids in a neighborhood involved in high-quality programs, you begin to change the cultural context of that neighborhood. If you are surrounded by people who are always talking about going to college, you're going to end up thinking, "Hey, maybe this is something I could

do, too." You can't help but get contaminated by the idea. It just seeps into your pores, and you don't even know that you've caught the virus (Tough, 2008).

It is more common for educated parents to read to their children when they are younger, as well as to encourage them to read more independently when they are older (Bianchi & Robinson, 1997; Hofferth & Sandberg, 2001). White parents typically spend more time educating their child at home than black parents, so African-American children often are behind from the beginning of the school process (Rothstein, 2004a). Black children are more likely than white children to watch television for longer periods of time (Rothstein, 2004a). Providing quality early childhood education helps minority and low-income children to be successful, rather than further behind, when they begin formal schooling.

As a result, Canada provides programs for parents in Harlem before their children are even born in attempt to infuse all knowledge that middle-class parents know they should do for their fetuses and infants in a "sensitive way." Participants of "Baby College" are recruited from every corner of Harlem to participate in the program, where instructors of color teach them how to have academic conversations with your children, as well as how to provide them with a healthy home environment and acceptable forms of discipline. Baby College even purchases items that parents need and cannot afford for their homes.

Canada expresses hope that all parents will pass along the "Harry Potter values" to their children in order for them to be as academically successful. Canada's formula, along with an extended school day and tutoring for at-risk students paid off in 2007 when a significant number of his middle-school students improved their state test results to meet grade level requirements in math and reading, and the middle school earned an "A" on the New York City Department of Education school report card evaluation process.

In Newark, Pedro Noguera is implementing the Broader Bolder Approach as a pilot program in six K–8 feeder schools into Central High School, in one of the lowest income communities in Newark, the ward of the 1967 Newark riots.

Although supporters laud reforms such as the Harlem Children's Zone and "no excuses" schools, the ones in the KIPP (Knowledge as Power Program) as evidence of the positive effects of high expectations and strong discipline on student achievement, critics point to their cultural deficit model and highly disciplinarian processes as problematic, although at the same time praising their impact (Sadovnik et al., 2008).

Connecting School, Community, and Societal Reforms

Research conducted over a 20-year period by the Consortium for Chicago School Research at the University of Chicago demonstrates that a combination of school, community, and societal level reforms are necessary to reduce the achievement gap (Bryk et al., 2010). Their research argues that successful school reform must be based on a number of essential supports, including:

1. leadership as the driver for change;
2. parent–community ties;
3. professional capacity;
4. student-centered learning climate;
5. instructional guidance.

Nonetheless, they demonstrate that these supports are most needed and difficult to implement in the highest poverty schools and that educational reforms must include policies aimed at the amelioration of the effects of poverty.

To summarize, educational reform in the United States from the 1980s to 2012 has emphasized the excellence side of the excellence and equity equation. Although federal, state, and local reforms have resulted in some improvement in achievement, critics (Berliner & Biddle, 1995) have pointed out that the U.S. educational system was never as problematic as its conservative critics suggested. They suggest that the real problem in U.S. education has been, and continues to be, that it works exceptionally well for children from higher socioeconomic backgrounds and exceptionally poorly for those from lower socioeconomic backgrounds. Despite the efforts of school choice and charter school programs to address these inequalities, particularly those in urban schools, the available evidence does not overwhelmingly support the claims of their advocates for a reduction in educational inequality. As the nation moves further into the new millennium, educational equity needs to continue to be on the front burner of educational reform.

In her 2010 book, *The Flat World and Education: How America's Commitment to Equity Will Determine Our Future*, Linda Darling-Hammond outlines five key elements needed to reform education. These elements of reform are based on a sound review of data on the U.S. education system and evidence from education reforms around the world. Darling-Hammond's five elements include:

1. meaningful learning goals;
2. intelligent, reciprocal accountability systems;
3. equitable and adequate resources;
4. strong professional standards and supports; and
5. schools organized for student and teacher learning.

In addition to building these five elements into the U.S. education system, Darling-Hammond notes that our society must provide for the basic needs of all children so that they are able to focus their attention on their academic work instead of on survival. Like many others, Darling-Hammond concludes that the U.S. education system will continue to fail many of its students at great cost to society as a whole if it does not equalize access to educational opportunity and support meaningful learning (Darling-Hammond, 2010).

A Theory of Educational Problems and Reforms

In Chapters 1 and 2, we examined a number of pressing educational problems and the ways in which conservatives, liberals, neo-liberals, and radicals defined and approached them. Throughout the book, we have looked at how anthropologists, historians, philosophers, political scientists, sociologists, and educators have analyzed a variety of issues and problems.

For the past decade, the dominant political definition of educational problems has been a conservative one, with the crisis in education defined in terms of the decline of standards and authority, and the putative mediocrity of U.S. schools and students. From the *Nation at Risk* report in 1983 through President Clinton's educational reform proposal Goals 2000 in 1994, G.W. Bush's No Child Left Behind, and President Obama's Race to the Top, the question of how to improve schools has centered on definitions of academic excellence. Although we certainly believe there is some merit to the conservative claims about the need to raise standards for all U.S. students, the preoccupation with excellence has unfortunately obscured other significant educational problems, most particularly those related to issues of equity. Despite NCLB's emphasis on reducing the achievement gaps, equity still has been less important than raising standards.

Furthermore, the emphasis on standards has defined educational problems narrowly, looking primarily on the intellectual and skills function of schooling to the exclusion of the social and psychological functions. Schools, in addition to teaching children skills and knowledge, also should provide students from all backgrounds the opportunity to succeed in U.S. society, as well as to develop their individual potential. The Deweyan conception that schools should have integrative, developmental, and egalitarian functions has been lost in the past decade, with the latter two almost fully overlooked.

Thus, school improvement ought to be aimed at all three aspects of schooling. In the *integrative realm*, schools do need to improve their effectiveness in teaching basic skills and knowledge. Although the conservative claim that the decline in educational standards is the cause of U.S. economic decline is overstated, the nation's students too often graduate from high school without the requisite skills or knowledge for postsecondary education. In part, this is due to the erosion of the academic function of schooling in the twentieth century and the belief that all students cannot handle an academically rigorous curriculum. On one hand, to the extent that curriculum tracking and ability grouping has limited access to an academic curriculum to working class and nonwhite students, the erosion of standards has been significantly undemocratic. On the other hand, since academic standards and performance appear to have declined across social class, race, gender, and ethnic lines, the problem of mediocrity is a problem for U.S. education in general.

Where we part company with conservatives is with regard to their preoccupation with standards as the most significant educational problem and with their emphasis on academic standards as either ends in themselves or as they relate to technological and economic imperatives. The reason a society should want a literate and skilled citizenry is not just because these traits are necessary for the economic system. They are also, as Dewey argued, the cornerstone of a democracy, where intelligent and informed citizens take an active role in their community. Thus, education is not an end in and of itself but is instrumental in the life of a democratic society.

In the *developmental realm*, schools need to become more humane institutions where students develop as complete human beings. The conservative emphasis on academic standards and the life of the mind is too shortsighted. Although the life of the mind is important, so too is the life of the heart. Schools need to emphasize, as well, values such as caring, compassion, and cooperation, as feminist educators have correctly pointed out (Laird, 1989; Noddings, 1984). Moreover, schools ought to be places that nurture the creative and spiritual (spiritual need not connote religious) lives of children and enable them to develop a thirst for active learning and creative endeavor. In far too many of this nation's schools, student creativity and imagination is stifled rather than developed.

What is wrong with U.S. schools in this regard is not new. It has been the subject of criticism from Dewey's progressive call for child-centered schools that would emphasize community and development, to the romantic progressive critiques of schooling in the 1960s as authoritarian and stifling, to current calls for educational reform from a variety of individuals and groups. All of these emphasize the need to create schools to educate children in all aspects of life—the social, psychological, emotional, moral, and creative—not just the intellectual. These efforts have included feminist educators with their concern with caring and cooperation, holistic educators with their concern for creative and spiritual dimensions, radical educators with their concern with transformative and liberating dimensions, and progressive educators with their concern for community, democracy, and the need to connect students' lives to the curriculum. These educators encompass both the liberal and radical political spectrum, and continue to define educational problems more broadly than do conservatives and neo-liberals, and to define solutions that are aimed at making schools places where children want to be.

Perhaps the most overlooked aspect of schooling during the past decades of conservative and neo-liberal ascendancy has been the *egalitarian realm* of schooling. Although many of the reports on the crisis in education have stressed the need to balance equity and excellence, the role of schooling in providing equality of opportunity and possibilities for social mobility have often taken a backseat. As we argued in Chapters 8 and 9, inequalities of educational opportunity and achievement have remained persistent problems. Jonathan Kozol, in his book *Savage Inequalities* (1991), pointed to the profound inequalities in funding between schools in poor urban areas and affluent suburban districts. In a muckraking style, Kozol placed the issue of equity back on the nation's front burner and demonstrated how current conditions belie the democratic and egalitarian ethos of U.S. schooling.

In a report on Kozol's book, *Time Magazine* (October 14, 1991) chronicled the political controversies over unequal funding of public schools based on property taxes. Although many child advocacy groups have called for the elimination of property taxes in educational financing because they are an advantage to affluent neighborhoods with higher property values, there is often strong opposition from parents in affluent neighborhoods against a "Robin Hood" plan, which would redistribute funds from affluent to poor districts. Kozol, who is interviewed in the article, stated that it is not that affluent parents do not care in the abstract about poor children, but that in the concrete they care more about giving their own children the best education they can afford. They believe that their tax dollars should support their own schools and that redistribution would lead to across-the-board mediocrity.

Although these conflicts point to the sharp divisions and perhaps ambivalence Americans feel about equity issues, they also point out the difficulty of ameliorating problems of educational inequality. Nonetheless, the fact seems clear that in the twenty-first century, the divisions between rich and poor and in the schooling they receive is becoming more glaring than ever. The solutions to these problems will not be easy, and certainly cannot be addressed through school reform alone, but it is apparent that the issue of equity must be on the front burner. Thus, efforts at school improvement must consider equity issues as central to their agenda.

What we are suggesting is that educational reform needs to be aimed at creating schools that teach students the basic skills and knowledge necessary in a technological society—where students have the opportunity to develop their emotional, spiritual, moral, and creative lives; where concern and respect for others is a guiding principle; where caring, cooperation, and community are stressed; where students from different social classes, races, genders, and ethnic groups have equality of opportunity; and where inequalities of class, race, gender, and ethnicity are substantially reduced. These goals, which have been the cornerstone of progressive education for almost a century, are goals that progressives (both liberals and radicals) have too often felt obliged to apologize for, as they have been viewed as either politically naive or Utopian. They are neither, although they certainly will be difficult to achieve.

At the beginning of this chapter, we discussed some effective teachers and suggested that effective teaching is necessary but not sufficient to solve educational problems. Without reforms aimed at societal problems, many educational dilemmas will remain unsolved. At the school level, unless schools are restructured to support good teaching and learning, teachers will continue to swim upstream against the current of school improvement.

There are, however, examples of schools that succeeded. Central Park East Secondary School (CPESS) was a school in East Harlem, which was part of the Center for Collaborative Education (CCE) in New York City. The Center consists of elementary, middle, and high schools, and is affiliated with the Coalition for Essential Schools. CPESS was a progressive urban public secondary school that subscribed to the CCE's 12 principles of education:

1. Schools that are small and personalized in size.
2. A unified course of study for all students.
3. A focus on helping young people use their minds well.
4. An in-depth, interdisciplinary curriculum respectful of the diverse heritages that encompass U.S. society.
5. Active learning with student-as-worker/student-as-citizen and teacher-as-coach.

6. Student evaluation by performance-based assessment methods.
7. A school tone of unanxious expectation, trust, and decency.
8. Family involvement, trust, and respect.
9. Collaborative decision-making and governance.
10. Choice.
11. Racial, ethnic, economic, and intellectual diversity.
12. Budget allocations targeting time for collective planning.

Under the leadership of Deborah Meier until the late 1990s, and a committed and talented faculty, CPESS provided an alternative to the failing comprehensive high schools for urban students. Fine (1991) used CPESS to demonstrate the possibilities for change and described it "as an example of what can be" (p. 215). Unfortunately, after Meier's departure the school went downhill and eventually was closed (Semel & Sadovnik, 2008). Nonetheless, many of its successful features are now part of the small schools movement operated by New Visions for Public Schools in New York City and funded by the Gates Foundation, which has shown promise and other small schools throughout the United States (Arristia & Hoffman, 2012).

David Berliner and Bruce Biddle (1995, pp. 282–336), two eminent educational researchers, outlined 10 principles toward the improvement of education consistent with our views of educational reform:

1. Schooling in the United States can be improved by according parents more dignity and their children more hope.
2. Schooling in the United States can be improved by making certain that all schools have funds needed to provide a decent education for their students. This will require more fairness in school funding.
3. Schooling in the United States can be improved by reducing the size of the nation's largest schools.
4. Schooling in the United States can be improved by enlarging the goals of the curricula. This will require thoughtful learning environments where the emphasis is on skills needed for membership in a democratic society.
5. Schooling in the United States can be improved by adopting innovative teaching methods that serve enlarged curricular aims.
6. Schooling in the United States can be improved by adjusting the content of the curriculum. This will require deemphasizing the tie between schooling and employment and by expanding curricula tied to the productive use of leisure.
7. Schooling in the United States can be improved by rethinking and redesigning the system for evaluating student achievement.
8. Schooling in the United States can be improved by changing the ways in which schools manage heterogeneity. This change will mean abandoning the age-graded classroom and finding alternatives for ability groups and tracks.
9. Schooling in the United States can be improved by strengthening the ties between communities and their schools. Such ties can be promoted through programs that encourage more active roles for parents, more contacts between parents and teachers, and expanded visions for the responsibilities of schools.
10. Schooling in the United States can be improved by strengthening the professional status of teachers and other educators. In *Sacred Trust: A Children's Education Bill of Rights* (2011), Peter Cookson argues that every child in the United States should have equal access to a high-quality education.

Cookson outlines the following 10 basic education rights that the United States should guarantee to all children:

1. The right to a neighborhood public school or a public school of choice that is funded for excellence.
2. The right to physical and emotional health and safety.
3. The right to have his or her heritage, background, and religious differences honored, incorporated in study, and celebrated in the culture of the school.
4. The right to develop individual learning styles and strategies to the greatest extent possible.
5. The right to an excellent and dedicated teacher.
6. The right to a school leader with vision and educational expertise.
7. The right to a curriculum based on relevance, depth, and flexibility.
8. The right of access to the most powerful educational technologies.
9. The right to fair, relevant, and learner-based evaluations.
10. The right to complete high school.

These rights are essential for every child to have equality of educational opportunity and to reduce significantly the achievement gaps.

We began this book with the conviction that the foundations perspective (i.e., the use of the politics, history, sociology, and philosophy of education) is an important tool in understanding and solving educational problems. Throughout the book, through text and readings, we have provided an analysis of many educational problems and a look at some of the proposed solutions. We end it with the conviction that teachers can make a difference, that schools can and must be restructured, and that the types of reforms discussed here are possible. They will not happen, however, unless people make them happen. School improvement is thus a political act. As prospective teachers and teachers, you must be a part of the ongoing struggle to improve this nation's schools. As Maxine Greene (1988, p. 23) stated:

> [I am] not the first to try to reawaken the consciousness of possibility . . . or to seek a vision of education that brings together the need for wide-awakeness with the hunger for community, the desire to know with the wish to understand, the desire to feel with the passion to see. I am aware of the ambivalences with respect to equality and justice as well. Fundamentally, perhaps, I am conscious of the tragic dimension in every human life. Tragedy, however, discloses and challenges; often it provides images of men and women on the verge. We may have reached a moment in our history when teaching and learning, if they are to happen meaningfully, must happen on the verge. Confronting a void, confronting nothingness, we may be able to empower the young to create and re-create a common world—and, in cherishing it, in renewing it, discover what it signifies to be free.

We believe that as teachers, you will have the opportunity to contribute to the improvement of this nation's schools. As we have attempted to indicate throughout this book, solutions to educational problems are by no means easy, as the problems are complex and multidimensional. Teachers alone will not solve these problems. However, they must be part of the solution. We encourage you to accept the challenge.

The following articles examine issues relating to educational reform and school improvement. The first article, "A Few Thoughts on Making This Work," by educational researcher Frederick Hess, argues that many of today's educational reforms are doomed to fail because they have not altered fundamentally the nature of American public education.

The second article, "Education and Poverty: Confronting the Evidence," by social scientist Helen F. Ladd, argues that educational reforms aimed at reducing the achievement gap are doomed to fail unless there are corrsponding policies to reduce poverty.

A Few Thoughts on Making This Work

Frederick M. Hess

Perhaps the greatest idea that America has given the world is the idea of education for all. The world is entitled to know whether this idea means that everybody can be educated, or only that everybody must go to school.

(Robert Hutchins, former president of the University of Chicago, 1951)

Insanity: doing the same thing over and over again and expecting different results.

(Albert Einstein)

The notion that in 2040, busloads of twelve-year-olds will be boarding a bus at 7:30 a.m. for a ride to a comprehensive school building where they would bend over texts and notebooks from 8 until 3 now makes about as much sense as expecting that those same students will be delivering rubber-banded newspapers to their neighbors by bike or heading to the public library so that they can track down resources through the card catalogue. The seismic shifts in society and culture are well under way, shaping the interests, behavior, and even the dating habits of today's students. The question is whether we will harness new opportunities and tame them to serve our educational needs. If we do not, we will not stop the gradual changes under way. But we will ensure that, like previous waves of reform, new efforts are the work of opportunists and tinkerers working at the margins.

Rethinking today's arrangements starts not by embracing this or that new measure, but by revisiting our notions of what schooling is and should look like. Schools look the way they do because of long-ago agendas, inertia, and efforts to meet the challenges of earlier eras. Tackling today's challenges starts by asking what it is we hope to accomplish, and then reimagining schooling to suit those purposes. In pursuing this "unbundling" of the schoolhouse, it is useful to think along two dimensions. One is rethinking the structure of schooling: how schools are governed, what teaching entails, how to configure the school day, and so forth. The second dimension involves rethinking the content of schooling: what students learn, when they learn it, how curricula are sequenced, and so forth. An easy way to understand the distinction is to recognize that a virtual school in which students are taught entirely by online instructors has obviously overhauled the structure of schooling, but is probably still using a scope and sequence of learning that reflects the norms in local brick-and-mortar schools. Unbundling that second, content dimension requires not just rethinking the governance or delivery of schooling, but envisioning ways to use new tools to customize instruction to the needs, strengths, and interests of individual students.

Unbundling means regarding schools not as self-contained boxes that have to meet every need for every child, but as one option among many—with many schools also serving as brokers of instructional services, coordinating stand-alone providers to deliver instruction and support under their roofs. Music teachers in the community might provide instruction in lieu of the school's music program, or a district might turn its foreign language instruction over to a contractor that handles faculty and online support.

One eye-opening example of how this might all work is provided by the fascinating School of One experiment in New York City. The School of One, created by the New York City Department of Education in partnership with for-profit provider Wireless Generation, starts from the presumption that new technologies mean we no longer have to teach classes of twenty-five students the same thing at the same time. Rather, it should be possible to customize what a student learns each day based on what she has already mastered and needs to learn, to do so with an eye toward the ways in which that student learns best, and to do so in a way that maximizes the efficient use of school resources. The School of One manages this feat (currently, just for middle school math) by collecting data on which learning objectives students have mastered and how they like to learn, and then assigning them each day to appropriate lessons.

On a given day, depending on the content in question, a student might learn in a large group, from a tutor, in a small group, using a computer simulation, or any number of other ways. A student's mastery of each learning objective is gauged using an assessment, and students aren't sent on to the next objective until they've learned the present one. Rather than one teacher having to shepherd twenty-five students through the curriculum from start to finish, teachers can now swap lessons and focus on those they teach best—while advanced students can move more rapidly and lagging students can get extra instruction. The result allows students to move at their own pace, teachers to concentrate on teaching to their strengths, teacher aides to provide targeted support, students to spend more time learning in the manner they like best, and makes it harder for kids to get lost in the shuffle. Am I suggesting that the School of One is "the answer" or the wave of the future? Of course not. But it does provide a powerful example of how unbundling can give us leave to start using tools and talent in smarter ways.

Even if we wished it were otherwise, financial pressures, a changing labor market, new technologies, and the inadequacy of our old model means that schooling will inexorably change. Our choice is not whether change will come, but the pace and manner in which it comes. Making change work for our ends requires not an eager new orthodoxy but a commitment to unshackle ourselves from entrenched debates, outdated arrangements, and misplaced fears. It requires getting past the desire for mushy, a-bit-of-this-and-a-bit-of-that consensus and by addressing legitimate concerns about whether a less constricting world of schooling might aggravate social stratification or yield to profiteering. And it requires approaching questions of talent, financing, technology, and coordination in a manner that can provide essential support and quality control.

Getting Past the Search for "Middle Ground"

In a 2009 *New York Times* book review essay entitled "Dreams of Better Schools," Andrew Delbanco discussed two recent books, one by left-leaning education professor, veteran educator, and standards critic Mike Rose and another by E. D. Hirsch, the Core Knowledge champion and prominent critic of education schools whom we encountered in chapter 5.[1] On the surface, the two books appear to be resolutely anchored in the stale debates of recent decades. In *Why School?*, Rose frets that excessive testing and standardization stifles learning; in *The Making of Americans*, Hirsch worries that romantics like Rose are dismissive of curriculum and content.

But looking further, Delbanco suggested that both volumes "get a lot of things right," especially in flagging "universal education for citizenship as indispensable for democracy," in Rose's concession that some testing can be useful, and in Hirsch's willingness "to end the standoff between left and right" Delbanco concluded, "If there is to be progress in the schools, we need more of this kind of moderation. Otherwise we will remain caught between the usual warring parties: pro-teacher-union versus anti-union groups; those who favor mayoral control against those who prefer community control. . . . The disputes have gotten tired, and Hirsch and Rose know it. Almost in spite of themselves, they give hints of a middle ground."

The problem with Delbanco's reflexive plea for "middle ground" solutions is that this comfortable, appealing mantra too often summons new orthodoxies rather than questioning the old. The problem with seeking middle ground between champions and critics of the teacher unions, mayoral control, or standardized testing is that the easiest way to compromise is by leaving the old regularities intact and sprinkling in a handful of new resources, programs, and initiatives. Lord knows there's nothing wrong with centrism and moderation. But, over time, we have seen middle-ground, centrist solutions such as teacher "career ladders" and magnet schools plopped atop existing systems that remain unchanged, only to amount to one more fad. Emancipatory reform is not about finding a middle way but about stripping away old routines, rules, and habits of mind to create new room for educators and problem solvers to do profoundly better.

Getting Past "Whole School" Improvement

Today, we ask school systems to tackle a vast array of responsibilities, making it difficult for them to do anything particularly well. Schools are expected to hire faculty who can provide instruction for the diverse needs of English language learners, special needs students, and gifted students; to provide students with physical education, extracurricular supervision, counseling, and other services; and to excel at all of this. Once upon a time, when most industrial enterprises adopted the same organizational logic and for the same reasons, this arrangement seemed sensible enough. Now, however, it is an anachronistic burden on educators in a century where providers can offer specialized services across geographic boundaries and where even such trivial products as cell-phone plans can be intensively customized.

The "whole school" expectation makes it harder to specialize or focus on particular needs. Even if their expertise is in designing curricula for middle school math or helping ELL students master English or recruiting and training alternative educators, new providers find themselves struggling to launch new schools and tackling everything from facilities to information systems. No one suggested that Amazon creator Jeff Bezos travel around the country shilling his new plan to sell books and music online to already established stores until he found a taker. Nor was he told that the only way for his plan to be taken seriously was if he would agree to also launch a chain of brick-and-mortar stores that could do everything Barnes & Noble and Borders already did, but better. This would be a recipe for stagnation; yet, in schooling, it stands as the norm.

Finding a new path requires shifting from a world where public officials provide access to "a school" to one where their aim is ensuring that all students benefit from schooling that serves their needs. This entails abandoning the industrial model where each school aspires to be a self-contained provider of manifold services. Today, because we regard each school in this manner, we speak of educational choice as the ability of families to choose school A rather than school B. Such options are relevant only to a limited slice of the population; many families may be less interested in shuffling their child among schools than in merely helping her obtain better math instruction, more convenient and intensive tutoring, or richer instruction in the arts. Indeed, providers like Tutor.com or Smarthinking can provide families with tutoring in a variety of subjects, twenty-four hours a day. For many middle-class families, the more relevant choice may be not the option to switch schools but the ability to tap school spending to purchase one-on-one instruction in biology or chemistry in lieu of enrolling their child in this or that school-offered elective.

Allowing broader choices among approved providers means that students will increasingly benefit from various providers—either within the schoolhouse or without. Is it possible that today's schools, states, and districts can do this?

In theory, of course it is. But the reality is that established organizations have enormous difficulty taking advantage of new tools or technologies that would require the dismantling of entrenched routines, pecking orders, expectations, and rules.

Getting Past Geography

From the tribe to the village to the nation-state, political communities have always been defined by geographic space. For most of human history, such an arrangement was sensible and, really, inevitable. Organizing schools and school districts thusly was a no-brainer for Common School and Progressive reformers, who made geography an organizing principle in everything from attendance zones to district governance. At the same time, while we've historically organized communities spatially, alternatives have always existed. Private groups like the Masons or the Catholic Church have formed communities, chosen officials, and governed themselves across great distances and formal lines of governance.

Today, advances in communications have given rise to new, virtual communities. However, even communities as seemingly decentralized and nonhierarchical as Wikipedia have tempered their initial laissez-faire instincts and, over time, developed governance structures to protect against abuse and to police quality. The growth of national and international networks in education and schooling means the question is not whether they will exist but whether it is possible to devise meaningful governance beyond what is hard-wired into existing geographical units.

The nature of contemporary technology and transportation, however, is that they lessen the significance of geography and physical space. Virtual communities among those with similar interests are now commonplace; two decades ago they belonged to the realm of science fiction. Rather than seeking dates at the local bar, singles searching for romance and a life partner turn to online dating services. One can now routinely travel from New York to Beijing in less time than it took a nineteenth-century educator to travel from New York to Chicago. Clearly, a growing share of complex transactions that once depended on face-to-face relationships with local professionals can be completed online, even as the reality of modern air travel can allow a data maven to sit down with educators in Baltimore, Boston, and Buffalo in the space of a single day. Yet, even as these revolutionary developments have triggered seismic shifts outside of schooling in finance, trade, industry, and culture, educational debates regarding school choice, governance, and instruction remain rooted in arrangements that are shaped primarily by geography.

Much of schooling obviously can and should always be organized spatially. For those disturbed by all this talk of technology and virtual communities, it's useful to note that personal interaction will always be a vital part of schooling, especially for younger children or those lacking strong adult figures in their lives. But, keep in mind how much socializing (e.g., Facebook), matchmaking (e.g., eHarmony), and professional networking (e.g., LinkedIn) have migrated online in the past decade. In the same way, many tasks central to teaching and learning, such as lecturing, tutoring, and assessment, might be pursued more powerfully (and certainly more cost-effectively, more conveniently, and in a more customized fashion) through Web-based technologies.

Addressing Concerns About Segregation and Stratification

Even if we free ourselves from some of these mental traps, legitimate questions emerge as soon as we start rethinking the organizations of schooling and teaching. Skeptics fear that alternative schooling arrangements that allow this kind of heterogeneity will lead to self-selection or other forms of stratification. This is a concern that resonates in an age marked by concerns about home-grown terrorists and stark political divides between "red" and "blue" America. I'd argue that the problem is far less worrisome that many might imagine—and that legitimate concerns can be addressed through smart policies that still allow for institutional redesign.

Social divides are a subject of real concern, but there is dreadfully little reason to believe that traditional school districts with their catch-all facilities and millions of conventionally employed teachers are particularly good at combating these tensions. In 2008, the U.S. Department of Education reported that 70 percent of white students attend schools that are at least 75 percent white; while other research shows that, in industrial states, over half of all black children attend school that are over 90 percent minority.[2]

The vast majority of families already exercise school choice, with more than 50 percent doing so by choosing their residence partly in order to choose a school.[3] Those are families that can afford to do so by buying homes in communities known to have good schools. In other words, as Milton Friedman surmised a half century ago, when school assignment and quality is bundled in with one's housing purchase, we create strong incentives for the affluent to self-segregate while fostering stratification and isolating the dis-advantaged.[4] The familiar machinery of school districts, attendance zones, and "whole-school" provision reinforces these patterns and streng-thens this dynamic.

There is a simple reason that suburban families and the affluent don't clamor for school choice: they already have chosen their school and are reasonably satisfied with it. Generally satisfied with but not necessarily delighted by the schooling they receive, the affluent have routinely supplemented their children's school-ing with tutors, college consultants, and musical instruction. This allows them to privately address any concerns.

Ultimately, vague concerns about stratifica-tion or segregation should not be a reason to cling to the status quo, or to reject it. Public funding, monitoring, and accountability can be designed to address such concerns. If the fear is that providers will shortchange low-income children or those with special needs, weighted funding formulas can direct more dollars to those who serve them. Such systems are up and running in districts like Houston and Seattle. Eligibility for some programs can be reserved for the less affluent, as with the Milwaukee Parental Choice Program, or for children in persistently low-performing schools, as with Florida's voucher program. Such solutions are a matter of program design, about which reasonable people can disagree. But it is ultimately more fruitful to debate such policies in terms of potential costs and benefits than by suggesting that some of the options are somehow illegitimate or intrinsically dubious.

Addressing Concerns About Quality Control

Opening up state-run, bureaucratically managed systems to a variety of new providers also creates obvious concerns that new providers will manipulate circumstances for their own advantage. I obviously have little sympathy for claims that "nontraditional" providers (for-profit or nonprofit) are darkening the previously pristine world of schooling with the stain of self-interest. American education has long been dominated by unions, neighborhood groups, and administrators as self-interested and greedy as anybody in the private sector. That said, any call to shift from state-operated schools ruled by familiar patterns must wrestle with the poten-tially adverse consequences of self-interested sellers and quick-buck artists.

Just as is true today, some for-profit and non-profit operators will be self-promoters out to make a buck, and others will be little more than snake oil salesmen. Even if these constituted only a tiny handful of providers—and they represent much more than that—it would be necessary to safeguard children and taxpayers against un-acceptable behaviors. The ink was scarcely dry on the No Child Left Behind Act before its provision allowing federal funds to pay for private-tutoring providers yielded large numbers of dubious operations. A world that welcomes more such activity must do a far better job ensuring that money is spent wisely and well, and that providers are accountable for delivering good value at a good price.

In the long run, whether children and taxpayers benefit depends on the wiles of buyers at least as much as on the scruples of would-be sellers. The biggest problem we face today, in policing the quality of charter schooling or NCLB tutoring, is that so many of today's buyers are inept. For instance, the vast majority of charter school authorizers are traditional school districts for whom this is a peripheral responsibility of modest import. Most of today's buyers are themselves creatures of the status quo. They are mostly state and district officials, and sometimes school leaders, with scant experience at gauging value-for-money. They're only sporadically accountable for the wisdom or efficacy of their purchasing decisions. They're not rewarded for cost savings or dinged for failing to deliver. Addressing the quality-control challenge begins by ensuring that those charged with approving and overseeing providers take that work seriously and have the expertise and resources to do it well. Some of today's best charter school authorizers, and especially the criteria sketched out by the National Association of Charter School Authorizers, offer some terrific guidance on this score.

When it comes to promoting quality and accountability in a more dynamic system, there are three particular cautions worth keeping in mind. The first is that public education involves public funds and therefore necessarily invites appropriate public oversight. The second is that markets work as intended only when consumers have access to good and useful information. The third is that where there is so much fragmentation or ambiguity that costs and benefits are hard to judge, and where the opportunities for chicanery are real requiring providers to be approved in some fashion can make sense.

In practice, policing against the waste of public funds will require empowering district and school leaders to be more vigilant procurers of services and then holding them accountable for their results. At the same time, allowing providers to deliver instruction or other services to families will call for some kind of "approved provider" list. The intuition is simple; the mechanics of how this might be approved less so. When public funds support schools or service providers that aren't state-operated—as they do today in the case of charter schools, publicly funded vouchers in Milwaukee or Florida, or tutors operating under the No Child Left Behind Act's "supplemental service" provision—there is

a need to determine who should be eligible. This requires establishing criteria governing finances, operations, and performance. It also means deciding how much freedom operators will have and how closely they will be monitored. Finally, it entails deciding what conditions or performance outcomes will be expected if providers are to retain their eligibility.

None of this is novel or needs to be created whole-cloth. These same determinations are made routinely in fields like health care, when insurers decide on lists of eligible providers. The Department of Defense and the Environmental Protection Agency, just like any state and local government, have processes for tackling these challenges. The need is to thoughtfully translate these models to schooling in ways that respect the challenges at hand.

If the aim of emancipating our schools is, in part, to move past the false faith in uniform provision, it is important to craft metrics that reflect the instruction or service they are providing. An insistence on uniform metrics implies a uniformity of provision. This means the performance measures that might be contemplated for providers of music instruction can and should be quite different from those that provide reading. The need is not for new one-size-fits-all federal or state rules, but for states, communities, and third parties to design systems that promote transparency and accountability without imposing new orthodoxies.

As families gain more leeway to steer public dollars to providers other than district schools, the public has a right to insist that providers meet reasonable conditions. Exactly what those conditions should look like is the kind of crucial conversation that we have not yet embarked upon. The degree to which those regulatory conditions ought to be primarily fiduciary, as with government contracting; to be based on professional qualifications, as in medicine; or to be based upon measured performance will depend on context and will have to ultimately be resolved through experimentation and trial and error. None of this is self-executing. Public officials still need to play a crucial role, but it will be increasingly as monitors and decreasingly as monopolistic operators.

The Talent Challenge

It's often said that teachers deserve to be paid like rock stars. Of course, if Bruce Springsteen or Beyonce weren't allowed to sell albums and could only perform for audiences of twenty or twenty-five fans at a time, they'd be paid like teachers. The riches enjoyed by rock stars are a consequence of their ability to entertain audiences of 20,000 or more while selling their music to millions. It is the tools and technologies that extend their reach that make this possible. Supported by teams of assistants, equipment specialists, agents, bookers, and handlers, the musicians themselves are actually the face of complex organizations that have learned to leverage modern tools. Drawing from this example, the most obvious opportunities ahead for making similar gains in schooling are those that take advantage of rethinking careerism, specialization, and how new providers might augment schoolhouse instruction.

Rather than try to convince today's twenty-two-year-olds to enter—and remain in—teaching, we might do better if we rethink the profession with an eye to the contemporary talent pool. There is enormous interest in teaching among talented college graduates, but not necessarily as a lifelong vocation. This is not surprising, as the Bureau of Labor Statistics has reported that the typical college graduate today holds six jobs by the age of thirty-two.[5] Mid-career professionals also express a great deal of interest in teaching—but don't necessarily want to abandon their current careers, have little stomach for teacher training programs (even those of the "alternative" variety), and may be more interested in teaching a few hours a day, or a week, than in becoming "teachers."

The realities of the modern labor market argue for freeing ourselves from the expectation that teaching should necessarily be a full-time, careerist endeavor. One approach is being pioneered by Boston-based Citizen Schools, which recruits adults from a wide variety of occupations to design apprenticeship after-school experiences for middle school kids. Internships, work-based learning, and service-learning opportunities would seem an integral component of many redesigned high schools, all of which happily can expose students to other adults who care about what they are doing and can provide low-stakes mentoring and career advice. Such avenues suggest exploring the potential of relying upon a smaller, more selective, specialized and professionalized core of tenured careerists, supplemented by more support staff in the schools and a much wider array of adults who help to support student learning outside the schoolhouse walls.

Today, our aim is to find 3.3 million teachers who have completed roughly similar training in order to fill 3.3 million broadly similar roles. Instead, just as registered nurses and thoracic surgeons work side by side in an operating room, we might envision schools where the exquisitely trained work alongside those with more rote preparation. And, just as in a hospital, we might have no difficulty recognizing that one has a skill set that is scarcer and required more training than another, and alter duties and compensation accordingly. Rather than hire them in the same fashion or envision their roles as different rungs on a career ladder, we might comfortably recognize that they are on distinctive tracks. Such a step would not require that we find 3.3 million equally skilled teachers, but instead allow us to focus on seeking a much smaller body of highly skilled teachers and *then* an army of other educators who could complement them in a variety of roles.

Specialization inside schools mirrors the opportunities to do the same outside the schoolhouse. The familiar staffing model requires schools with many classrooms, each featuring a teacher working face-to-face with a particular group of students. This "people-everywhere" strategy was a natural for the Romans or America's founders, but we have devised some new tools in the past few decades. People-everywhere is expensive, does little to leverage the strengths or expertise of individual instructors, and limits the available talent pool in a given locale to the educators who will live there. Why not take a page from Washington, D.C. –based Smarthinking, which uses tutors with advanced degrees in the United States and a number of other nations to provide intensive instruction to students, twenty-four hours a day, seven days a week, and in about two dozen subjects?

The Techology Challenge

Quantum leaps in productivity are always about using new advances in technology and management to render skilled employees more productive. Unfortunately, our approach to schooling has long reflected the admonition written into the Elementary and Secondary Education Act of 1965: "supplement, not supplant."[6] Technology has not been used to allow educators to slough off rote duties and focus on what they do best or to allow schools and systems to shuck unnecessary personnel.

Schooling has proceeded under the assumption that each year requires as many people—or more—as it did the year before, and technology is regarded as a perpetually "second-best" option. Consequently, new technological delivery is generally treated as an unattractive alternative rather than a lever that can help transform. Technology has persistently disappointed as film projectors, televisions, computers, and the Internet have largely served as a series of expensive baubles shoveled into otherwise unchanged schools and classrooms,[7] but this should come as no surprise. Harvard Business School professor Clay Christensen has argued that the instinctive response of any established organization when innovations emerge is to cram them into the existing model in order to do the familiar a little bit better. He has consequently advised, "The way to implement an innovation so that it will transform an organization is to implement it disruptively."[8] Harnessing the power of Web-based instruction and other new tools is only possible if they begin to displace, and not merely augment, traditional routines.

Substituting technology for laborious tasks can remake schooling by shifting away from the traditional shape of the schoolhouse and school district in a number of scenarios. For example, allowing graduate students in Boston or New York to tutor students in rural communities requires Web-based communication to match students in need with instructional expertise—wherever that expertise can be found. Finding ways for highly skilled teachers to instruct hundreds (or even thousands) of children at once requires staffing and instructional strategies that rethink how teaching talent is used. Enabling

school "systems" to operate networks of similar schools that are dotted across multiple communities requires a new concept of what constitutes a school district. Of course, none of these benefits come easily.

The Financing Challenge

The existing school funding model grew haphazardly from its localist origins. The earliest schools in colonial America were funded by local sources. Over time, the state took on an increasing role in supplementing these funds. In the early twentieth century, local dollars still accounted for the vast majority of spending, but by century's end, the state and local share was a rough split—with most state aid intended to help equalize disparities in funding due to intrastate variations in local wealth. Meanwhile, the federal government first got substantially involved in school spending in the 1960s, with most of its dollars going to support low-income students and a slew of categorical programs. Today, Uncle Sam accounts for about one-tenth of the nation's $600 billion in K–12 spending. Most of this money is tied up in district salaries and in formulas that allocate staff to schools based on class size and staffing formulas.

All of this is intended to provide schools to all children and to provide a more equitable distribution of dollars. This system, with its emphasis on enrollment, funding categories, and intricate formulas and rules, is hostile to efforts to rethink staffing or schooling. As I write, the cutting edge of finance reform is thought to be efforts to make sure that poor schools get their fair share and to adjust funding so that dollars more accurately follow the students. This approach to weighted student funding is certainly an improvement over traditional funding models, but it still envisions nothing more than the government's funneling of a block of money to a school for each child who attends.

Other models, more similar to a flex-spending account, promise to create more opportunities to help families secure the instruction and services they need—whether that involves academic tutoring or musical training, whether virtual or live. One place to look for an example of empowered consumer spending that could be applied to education is health savings accounts. Health savings accounts (HSAs) are one option in the world of health insurance designed to give individuals greater control over their money. Created in 2003, HSAs allow individuals to pay for qualified medical expenses.[9] Individuals wind up with greater control over medical care purchases and greater incentives to shop around for better care and to save for future health costs.

Applied to education, such an approach would allow families to be free to procure services from an array of approved providers with some or all of their child's school funding. A given family could procure music instruction from tutor X, athletic involvement from program Y, and academic services from school Z. A family would have an allotment of money to be spent on a child's schooling, and those dollars could be steered to approved providers in a variety of ways, depending on the child's needs.

Allowing families to redirect the money they save from one educational need to another can create incentives to think about costs and benefits more carefully. Currently, families have no reason to know or to care if a district reading program costs $1,000 per student or $4,000 per student. Consequently, there's a natural bias toward time and labor-intensive programs, as these seem "better" to parents than alternatives. Such parental preferences make it harder for school and district leaders to employ more cost-effective alternatives, and give them less incentive to seek out such options. Empowering parents to contemplate costs as well as benefits means that some will likely do so, and it can offer educators new opportunities to make smart decisions.

A crucial hindrance to our ability to rethink schooling is inattention to cost-effectiveness. In most of the world, we think about improvement as a matter of delivering more bang for the buck. In schooling, however, accountability and performance is judged almost entirely in terms of test scores and graduation rates—with remarkably little attention to how much it costs a school, district, or program to deliver those. Indeed, there's subtle (and sometimes not so subtle) pressure—from advocacy groups and federal policies—for states and districts to spend more money each year. Finding new efficiencies is more likely to raise eyebrows or pass unnoticed than to gain plaudits. All of this tends to stifle efforts to rethink the delivery of schooling and to discourage educators from finding more efficient ways to tap talent and technology. In a world of tighter budgets, an easy first step is for states and districts to start reporting cost per pupil as part of their accountability systems—and to recognize schools and districts which are both effective and cost-effective.

The Coordination Challenge

A century ago, the dominant challenge for providers of goods or services was often just getting their offerings to people. The ability to coordinate and deliver merchandise was the defining characteristic of Sears & Roebuck. Today, new transportation, communication, and management tools mean that coordination and delivery can be pretty readily outsourced—enabling providers to focus on quality. In schooling, however, the pressure on each school and district to deliver a raft of services to an array of students with various needs means there's a need to invest enormous time and energy in coordinating delivery before turning to quality. Obviously, importing a math provider to hire and train the math teachers charged with providing middle school algebra pose new challenges, as does giving families more leeway to purchase tutoring from approved providers with public funds, but it's very possible that these challenges will prove more tractable than will the question of how a-little-bit-of-everything institutions can excel.

If a family prefers having their son taught by a team of face-to-face or online tutors in lieu of a traditional school—either because local school choices are mediocre or because of the child's particular needs or gifts—there are obvious challenges relating to scheduling and quality control. Let's presume that the cost of the two options is the same. (If the unconventional option were less, it would raise interesting questions about how to reward the family's decision and what to do with the balance;

if more, the state would presumably impose restrictions).

In such a case, there is a natural niche for aggregators who can schedule and certify the quality of various instructors. The reality is that very, very few families will have the time, energy, or resources to assemble a crew of four or six tutors—electronic or otherwise. So, aggregators who can recommend tutors and approaches, based upon student need and family preferences, will prove essential and will need to be accountable for their handiwork. This is a role, of course, that some existing schools or school districts might find themselves well suited to provide.

Indeed, some communities will find it advisable to retain much of the structure of systems and schools as we know them today, at least for a long stretch to come. In those locales where much of the old infrastructure is retained, the coordination of many services would be a matter of system and school leaders bringing in new providers to supplement or replace offerings, or to provide new choices. Families would lean on the familiar school and system to judge of ferings, with their decisions focused on choosing between program offerings or the decision of whether to access some services (such as arts instruction, tutoring or support, or enrichment opportunities) outside the traditional school-house. One consequence of releasing schooling from the old strictures is that it gives these established actors new opportunities to seize upon their strengths in new ways.

What Lies Ahead

Freeing up and unbundling schooling is less about forcing change than enabling it. If affluent communities are reluctant to exploit new oppor-tunities, so be it; reinvention is hard enough when pursued by the committed. Systems that work passably well in those communities that attract great teachers and serve advantaged families ought not be forcibly dismantled. But for communities worst-served by the status quo, emancipatory reform could offer a much-needed alternative.

At times, I may seem to belittle those who have built the system of schooling that we have inherited. That's not my intention. Despite some quirks and questionable calls, they bequeathed us a rich heritage—a national system of staffed, funded facilities and an infrastructure of training programs, assessments, and state and local governance agencies. Ideally, this legacy should leave America enviably positioned for the twenty-first century, a time when prosperity and power will rest heavily upon learning and education. We spent more than three centuries building out a system of universal K–12 education that now encompasses rich and poor, white and black. We have a mighty infrastruc-ture of facilities, transportation, technology, and institutions for training educators. We have millions of credentialed teachers and a vast network of school districts and funding mechanisms.

It would be a shame indeed if our seeming advantages ultimately hindered us. Yet that appears only too possible. For our vast edifice of schooling also has an enormous appetite for resources: dollars, people, and energy that are poured into programs, curricula, and professional development carried out within the confines of the status quo. We are allowing systems and schools to claim their $600 billion a year, and then fuel reinvention—whether it involves pay systems, training, school design, or technology—with dollars sprinkled around the edges. Redesign requires freeing up the dollars and talent and energy that state, local, and federal government pump into K–12 schooling day in and day out.

Because ascendant international compet-itors like India and China did not mirror our enormous investment in erecting school systems in the nineteenth and twentieth centuries, they find themselves today with a far less developed educational infrastructure. By clinging so fiercely to what we've built, however, we risk allowing nations less wedded to aged designs to slingshot past us. Having never made the investments in schools and teachers that we did in the pre-industrial and industrial eras, they find themselves free to erect policies and institutions particularly geared to the tools and challenges of this century. It would be a bitter irony indeed if our inability to leave behind anachronistic routines and stale habits of mind meant that the achievements of the Common Schoolers and Progressives that fueled American success in the twentieth century were to hold us back in the twenty-first. We have the power to take another road, if we find the strength to free ourselves from the heavy hand of the past. The choice that lies before us is whether or not to do so.

Notes

1. Andrew Delbanco, "Dreams of Better Schools," *New York Review of Books* 56 (2009), www.nybooks.com/articles/23377?, accessed May 5, 2010.
2. Jeanne H. Ballantine and Joan Z. Spade, *Schools and Society: A Sociological Approach to Education* (Thousand Oaks, CA: Sage, 2008), 280.
3. Caroline Hoxby, "If Families Matter Most, Where Do Schools Come In?" in *A Primer on America's Schools*, ed. Terry Moe (Stanford, CA: Hoover Institution Press, 2001), 104.
4. Milton Friedman, "The Role of Government in Education," in *Economics and the Public Interest*, ed. Robert A. Solo (New Brunswick, NJ: Rutgers University Press, 1955).
5. Bureau of Labor Statistics, "Number of Jobs Held, Labor Market Activity, and Earnings Growth among the Youngest Baby Boomers: Results from a Longitudinal Survey," Bureau of Labor Statistics, June 27, 2008, www.bls.gov/news.release/pdf/nlsoy.pdf, accessed May 5, 2010.
6. U.S. Department of Education, "Supplement Not Supplant Provision of Title III of the ESEA" (Washington, DC: U.S. Department of Education), www2.ed.gov/programs/sfgp/supplefinal attach2.pdf, accessed May 5, 2010.
7. Larry Cuban, *Oversold and Underused: Computers in the Classroom* (Cambridge, MA: Harvard University Press, 2003).
8. Clayton M. Christensen and Michael B. Horn, "How Do We Transform Our Schools?" *Education Next* 8 (Summer 2008), http://educationnext.org/how-do-we-transform-our-schools/, accessed May 28, 2010.
9. U.S. Treasury, "Health Savings Accounts (HSAs)," www.ustreas.gov/offices/public-affairs/hsa/, accessed on May 5, 2010.

Education and Poverty

Confronting the Evidence

Helen F. Ladd

Evidence-based policy making. That is the rallying cry for policy researchers like many of us and also for many policy makers, including the Obama administration itself. Providing a forum for researchers to present and discuss policy relevant research that can provide the evidence needed for better policy making is one of the major functions of this Association.

Policy relevant evidence often comes from careful studies of specific policy interventions such as job training or negative income tax programs and is based on random control trials or other forms of rigorous quantitative and qualitative analysis. Many of you in the audience today have made major methodological and substantive contributions through research of this type in a range of policy areas.

I want to focus today on the policy importance of evidence of a broader type – a type that does not require any sophisticated modeling. And I will do so in the context of my main field of policy research, education policy.

Historically, this country prided itself on its outstanding education system, which educated a higher proportion of its population to more advanced levels than most other countries. The Sputnik challenge from Russia in the late 1950s and the publication of *A Nation at Risk* (1983) during the Reagan years, however, highlighted significant concerns about the quality of the U.S. education system. Concerns today are based on average test scores of U.S. students that are middling compared to those of other nations, on U.S. graduation rates that once were well above those of most other countries but now have been overtaken by rising rates in other countries, and on abysmal educational attainment and test score performance of many disadvantaged students, especially those in urban centers. These patterns and trends, as well as recent widely publicized documentaries including for example, *Waiting for Superman*, have convinced many people that our education system is in crisis.[1]

During the decades following *A Nation at Risk*, U.S. education policy makers responded to the perceived crisis in a variety of ways such as creating ambitious national goals and promoting standards based reform. Of interest here are the policy initiatives of the past decade, which include school accountability in the form of the federal No Child Left Behind Act, test-based approaches to evaluate teachers, and promotion of expanded parental choice, charter schools, and competition.

I will argue today that these current policy initiatives are misguided because they either deny or set to the side a basic body of evidence documenting that students from disadvantaged households on average perform less well in school than those from more advantaged families. Because they do not directly address the educational challenges experienced by disadvantaged students, these policy strategies have contributed little—and are not likely to contribute much in the future—to raising overall student achievement or to reducing achievement and educational attainment gaps between advantaged and disadvantaged students. Moreover, such policies have the potential to do serious harm.

Addressing the educational challenges faced by children from disadvantaged families will require a broader and bolder approach to education policy than the recent efforts to reform schools. It will also require a more ambitious research agenda—one that APPAM researchers—not just those of us who typically focus our research on education policy but also researchers in a wide range of social policy issues—are in a good position to advance.

Evidence on the Relationship Between Family Background and Educational Outcomes

Study after study has demonstrated that children from disadvantaged households perform less well in school on average than those from more advantaged households. This empirical relationship shows up in studies using observations at the levels of the individual student, the school, the district, the state, the country. The studies use different measures of family socioeconomic status (SES): income related measures such as family income or poverty; education level of the parents, particularly of the mother; and in some contexts occupation type of the parents or employment status. Studies based on U.S. administrative data often measure SES quite crudely, using eligibility for free and reduced price lunch, for example, as a proxy for low family income, and using student race as a proxy for a variety of hard to measure characteristics. Studies based on longitudinal surveys often include far richer measures of family background. Regardless of the measures used and the sophistication of the methods, similar patterns emerge.

I start with differences in test scores between U.S. students whose families have high and low socio-economic status as measured by family income. The best research on income-based achievement gaps appears in a recent study by Sean Reardon for which he compiled test scores for school-aged children and family income from a large number of U.S. based nationally representative surveys over a 55 year period. By standardizing income differentials and achievement levels to make them comparable over time, he was able to estimate the trend in reading and math test scores gaps between the children in the 90th and the 10th income percentiles. As shown by the rising line in Figure 10.1 for reading gaps, the results are striking. The figure shows that, when first measured in the early 1940s, the gap in reading achievement between children from high and low income families was about 0.60 standard deviations. It subsequently more than doubled to 1.25 standard deviations by 2000.[2]

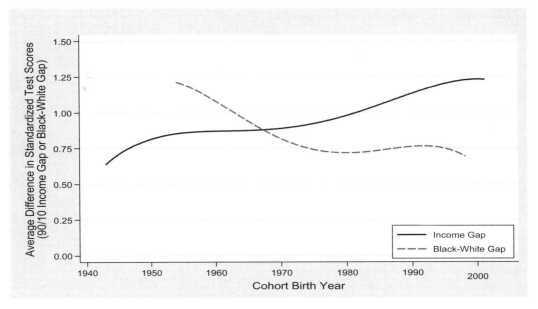

Figure 10.1 Simplified version of graph in Sean Reardon, Ch. 5 in G. Duncan and R. Murnane, Whither Opportunity? Rising Inequality and the Uncertain Life Chances of Low Income Children (New York, Russell Sage, 2011).

These income-based achievement gaps are large. To put them in perspective, consider the black–white test score gap as measured by the National Assessment of Education Progress (NAEP) for 13-year-olds, depicted by the dashed line in Figure 10.1.[3] That gap was about 1 standard deviation in the 1970s, then fell to about 0.50 during the 1980s where it has remained relatively constant. As a result, the achievement gap between children from high and low income families is now far larger than the gap between black and white children.

People can disagree about whether the relationship between family income, or broader measures of SES, on the one hand and educational outcomes on the other is correlational or causal. For example, it may be that factors correlated with low income such as poor child health or single parent family structures account for the relationship rather than income itself.

Further, people may disagree about the extent to which schools and school policies contribute to the low achievement of children from low SES households. At this point, I simply want to draw attention to the correlation. Later I will say more

about the mechanisms through which low SES may translate into low academic performance.

Suffice it to say at this point that research documents a variety of symptoms of low SES that are relevant for children's subsequent educational outcomes. These include, for example, poor health, limited access to home environments with rich language and experiences, low birth weight, limited access to high quality pre-school opportunities, less participation in many activities in the summer and after school that middle class families take for granted, and more movement in and out of schools because of the way the housing market operates for low income families. Differences in outcomes between high and low SES families may also reflect the preferences and behaviors of families and teachers. Compared to low SES families, for example, middle and upper class families are better positioned to work the education system to their advantage by assuring that their children attend the best schools and get the best teachers, and they are more likely to invest in out-of-school activities that improve school outcomes such as tutoring programs, camps and traveling.[4]

The preferences and behaviors of teachers are also a contributing factor in that many teachers with strong credentials tend to be reluctant to teach in schools with large concentrations of disadvantaged students than in schools with more advantaged students (Jackson, 2009 and Clotfelter, Ladd and Vigdor, 2011).

The logical implication of the low achievement of poor children relative to their better off counterparts is that average test scores are likely to be lower in schools, districts or states with high proportions of poor children, all else held constant, than in those with fewer poor children. Figure 10.2 illustrates this negative relationship between child poverty and test scores across U.S. states in 2009, with 8th grade reading scores in Figure 10.2a and 8th grade math scores in Figure 10.2b. The achievement scores in these graphs are from the National Assessment of Educational Progress (NAEP) and are based on random samples of students in each state while state poverty rates are from the American Community Survey.

Of course, not all else is constant. Among other things that differ across states is the quality of the states' education systems. Test scores in Massachusetts, for example, far exceed their predicted levels given the state's 12 percent child poverty rate, presumably in part because the state implemented in 1998 an aggressive and

comprehensive education reform strategy that included support for young children. In contrast, test scores in California, are well below those predicted for its 20 percent poverty rate, presumably in part because of its long history of limiting spending on education. Moreover, other factors may also contribute to the patterns. Massachusetts, for example, has a highly educated parental population, and California has a large immigrant population. Nonetheless the overall negative relationship between the child poverty rate and student performance in both graphs is clear.

Consistent with the graphs, a simple bivariate regression of state test scores and state poverty rates indicates that a full 40 percent of the variation in reading scores and 46 percent of the variation in math scores is associated with variation across states in child poverty rates. The addition of one other explanatory variable related to family background, the percent of children who are members of minority groups, increases the explanatory power of the relationship to about 50 percent in reading and 51 percent in math. Clearly the mix of family backgrounds is highly correlated with patterns of student achievement across states.

Stronger evidence that child poverty itself may be causally linked to educational outcomes, especially for math, is shown in Table 10.1.

Table 10.1 Within-State Changes in NAEP Test Scores (Standardized) as a Function of Within-State Changes in the Child Poverty Rate

	4th grade		8th grade	
	Reading	Math	Reading	Math
Child poverty rate (%)	−0.023*	−0.030***	−0.030**	−0.030***
	(0.012)	(0.011)	(0.012)	(0.010)
Constant	0.402*	0.514	0.523	0.518
	(0.209)	(0.194)	(0.205)	(0.0177)
State fixed effects?	Yes	Yes	Yes	Yes
Observations	282	240	277	239
R-squared	0.908	0.932	(0.917)	(0.944)

Sample is NAEP test scores (standardized across states) for years 1998, 2002, 2003, 2005, 2007, 2009 for reading and for years 2000, 2003, 2005, 2007, and 2009 for math. Calculations by the author.

Notes: * From PISA, 2010. Absolute scale across countries, approximated as percent of students more than 1 standard deviation below the mean ** Percent of students with income less than 50 percent of median income within the country. *** UNICEF scale 2010. Recalculated by the author to eliminate the education component (scale = 1 to 6)

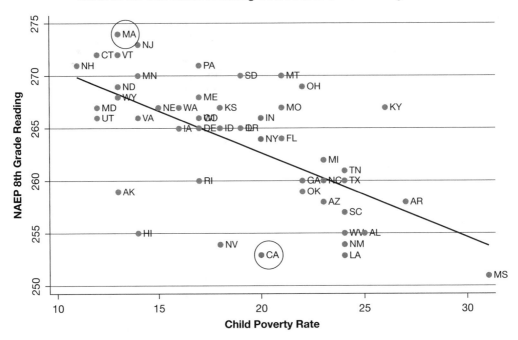

Figure 10.2a State NAEP 8th grade reading scores and child poverty rate, 2009.

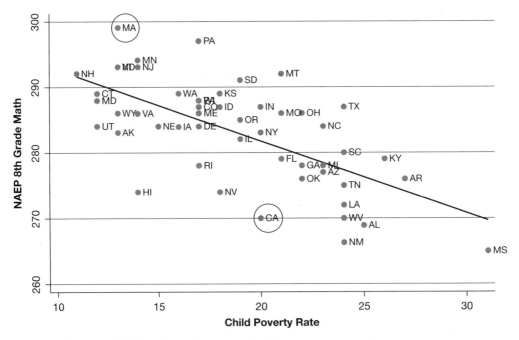

Figure 10.2b State NAEP 8th grade math scores and child poverty rate, 2009.

The estimates reported here are based on data from six administrations of the NAEP during the past 10–12 years and are based on panel regression models with state fixed effects.[5] The outcome variables are 4th and 8th grade NAEP reading and math scores standardized across states. The state fixed effects control for time-invariant characteristics of a state such as its population mix and historical commitment to education that could well affect educational outcomes and that might be correlated with state poverty rates. Consistent with the view that child poverty adversely affects student achievement, the negative coefficients on the poverty rate variables demonstrate that increases in child poverty rates during the last 10 years translated into reductions in average test scores.

A strong correlation between student achievement and family background shows up as well in the international data for developed countries. The pattern emerges for comparisons both within and across countries. I focus here on test scores from the Programme for International Student Assessment (PISA) managed by the Organization for Economic Co-Operation and Development (OECD). To facilitate comparisons across developed countries of children from similar backgrounds, the OECD has constructed a measure of the economic, cultural, and social status (ESCS) of the families of all children tested. This measure incorporates information on the household's occupational status, the parents' education level, and, as a proxy for the family's income or wealth, household possessions.[6] This measure is comparable to what we in the U.S. would call socio-economic status and is an absolute scale that allows one to compare students with similar family backgrounds across countries.

Figure 10.3 displays student performance of 15 year olds in reading by ESCS percentile for the U.S. and each of the 13 countries whose students scored higher on average than U.S. students in 2009. The reported scores on the vertical axis are standardized as of 2000 to have a mean of 500 and a standard deviation of 100.

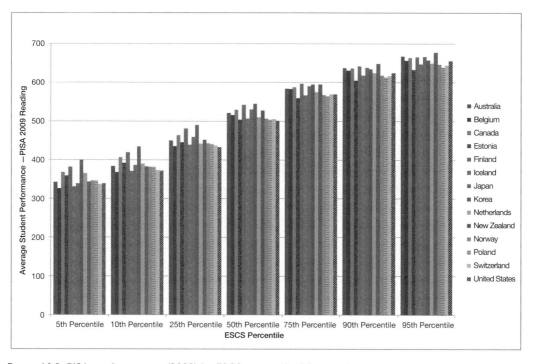

Figure 10.3 PISA reading scores (2009) by ESCS percentile, 14 countries.

The figure shows strong positive correlations between family ESCS and student performance in all 14 countries. Average test scores for students in the 5th percentile across all the countries are about 350, far below the average of about 660 for students in the 95th percentile, and the test scores rise monotonically both overall and within each country. Even in countries such as Korea, Finland and Canada that are typically viewed as having high performing education systems, the patterns hold: achievement levels of the low ESCS children fall far short of those of their more advantaged counterparts.

Compared to other countries, Finland and South Korea appear to have the most success with their very low ESCS students. This relative success largely reflects each country's strong commitment to education and to equal educational opportunity. In Finland, this commitment is rooted in the country's Lutheran heritage and the recognition that an educated population is the country's most valuable resource (Sahlberg, 2011). In South Korea, the country's historical ties to Confucianism and current efforts to expand the economy lead parents in all ESCS groups to put tremendous pressure on their children to succeed in school (Ahn, 2011).[7] But even in those countries, large differences emerge between students from low and high ESCS families.

The performance of U.S. students (see the bars at the far right in each set) follows the same pattern as the other 13 countries. Notably, however, U.S. students in families with ESCS below the median perform particularly badly relative to their low-ESCS peers in other countries while U.S. students from more advantaged backgrounds perform reasonably well by international standards. That is, the largest shortfalls in performance among U.S. students are concentrated among those with relatively low ESCS. These shortfalls suggest there is room for the U.S. to do better by its disadvantaged students.

As was true across U.S. states, these within-country patterns imply that countries with high proportions of low ESCS students are likely to have lower overall test scores than countries in which incomes are distributed more equally. The data in Table 10.2 illustrate some cross country patterns by comparing the U.S. to three high performing countries: Finland, Canada and the Netherlands. The first two columns show that U.S. 15-year-olds score at lower levels on average than their counterparts in the other countries on both reading and math tests. The following three columns show that this lower average performance is not surprising in light of the significantly greater disadvantage of children in the U.S. relative to the other three countries.

As shown in the third column, the percentage of students living in low ESCS families (defined by the OECD as those more than one standard deviation below the mean) in the U.S., is more than 2½ times that in Finland and Canada

Table 10.2 PISA Test Scores, and Child Context, Selected Countries

	PISA reading 2009	PISA math 2009	Students with low ESCS (%)*	Children living in poor homes (%)**	Child well being (UNICEF scale (1–6, high is better)***
US	**500**	**487**	**10.4**	**20.6**	**2**
Finland	536	541	3.9	4.2	5
Canada	524	527	3.7	15.1	3
The Netherlands	508	526	6.5	11.5	6

Notes: * From PISA, 2010. Absolute scale across countries, approximated as percent of students more than 1 standard deviation below the mean ** Percent of students with income less than 50 percent of median income within the country. *** UNICEF scale 2010. Recalculated by the author to eliminate the education component (scale = 1 to 6) and 50 percent more than in The Netherlands. In contrast to the ESCS measure, which is based on an absolute scale across countries, the poverty measure in the following column is country specific and refers to the percent of students who live in households with income less than 50 percent of the country's median income. According to this measure, more than 1 in 5 children in the U.S. live in poverty, far more than the 1 in 25 in Finland, 1 in 7 in Canada and 1 in 9 in the Netherlands. The final column denotes the material and health well-being of children as measured by UNICEF. The highest score of 6 for the Netherlands on this measure denotes that the country was above average among 24 countries in terms of both the material and health well-being of its children, and the lowest score of 2 for the U.S. means that it was below average on both measures.[8]

The patterns are fully consistent with the view that the low average test scores of U.S. students largely reflect our extremely high poverty rate and our relative lack of attention to the overall well-being of our children.

This pattern emerges in a more systematic manner from a large number of empirical studies based on international test score data such as Trends in Math International Mathematics and Study (TIMMS) and earlier versions of PISA, as ably summarized by Hanushek and Woessman (2010). In particular, cross country studies estimated at both the country level and the student level find strong associations between students' socio-economic backgrounds and their educational achievement (Hanushek and Woessman, 2010, p. 16 and Table 6). Moreover, the studies document that these associations with educational outcomes are far stronger than those for school resources.

My reading of the patterns in the table, as buttressed by the evidence from the larger and more systematic empirical studies, is that it would be difficult, if not impossible, for the U.S. to replicate the success of higher scoring countries such as Finland, Canada and the Netherlands by focusing on school reform alone, and that is especially true for school reform that pays little attention to meeting the social needs of disadvantaged children.

I find it useful to summarize the basic point that I am making here with the following simple functional relationship:

$$\text{Educational outcomes} = f(\text{public school quality, context}).$$

Public school quality refers to the quality of a specific school or of a larger unit depending on whether the analysis refers to individual schools, school districts, states, or countries. Context refers here to the socioeconomic backgrounds of the students, as well as cultural considerations, including the commitment level of families to the education of their children (as I highlighted above with reference to Finland and Korea) and the success of the country in meeting the non-education needs of children (as I highlighted with reference to the Netherlands). According to this formulation, low educational outcomes could well reflect the low quality of the public schools, or they could reflect an adverse educational context, or some combination of both. Within a single country, the SES background of the children's families is likely to be the most important component of context.

Defining and measuring what I have labeled "public school quality" raises a complex set of conceptual and empirical issues that Susanna Loeb and I have addressed elsewhere (Ladd and Loeb, forthcoming). Two points about the concept as I am using it in this formulation are worth noting. First, because context matters, educational outcomes alone—even far richer and more comprehensive measures than the student test scores now being used in the U.S.—cannot serve as an appropriate proxy for school quality. To serve that role, at a minimum they would need to be adjusted for the relevant educational context of the school, district, or state.

Second, it may be helpful to think of public school quality as the direct output of the education system, where the system includes the managerial input of state and local education policy makers, school-level inputs such as teachers and principals, and educational resources such as technology, facilities, and instructional materials. School quality may differ across schools or jurisdictions because of differences in both the quantity and quality of inputs as well as in the effectiveness with which they are used. Because of the complexity of the concept, it is difficult to measure public school quality in practice, and is probably best done through some combination of cost-adjusted resources and direct observation (Ladd and Loeb, forthcoming).

The functional relationship highlights that while education policy makers have direct control over school quality, they have less control over educational outcomes because of the role that context—and particularly the family background of the students—plays in shaping educational outcomes.

Possible Policy Responses to this Evidence

I now turn to the potential policy responses to the empirical correlation between educational outcomes and educational context. Policy responses depend in part on the policy goals. Throughout the rest of my talk, I will assume there are two interrelated goals: one is to increase average educational outcomes, and the other is to reduce skills and attainment gaps between advantaged and disadvantaged students. Raising average achievement or performance levels is often justified in terms of the need to prepare graduates for a knowledge-based society and the desire to make sure U.S. workers remain competitive with their international counterparts for future jobs. Perhaps even more important, a well-educated populace is essential for a functioning democracy and for the nurturing of a culturally rich and innovative society. Reducing achievement gaps recognizes the importance of education to the life chances of individuals and the fact that the U.S. as a whole has a stake in assuring that all citizens can participate fully in the economic and political life of the country. Of course policies that closed gaps by raising the achievement of disadvantaged students with no decline in the achievement of advantaged students would also raise average achievement.

I. Reduce the Incidence of Poverty or Low SES

One logical policy response to the correlations I have been describing would be to pursue policies to reduce the incidence of poverty or other contributors to low SES. That might be done, for example, through macro-economic policies designed to reduce unemployment, cash assistance programs for poor families, tax credits for low wage workers, or an all-out assault "war on poverty" as pursued by Lyndon Johnson in the 1960s. This approach would appear to be a particularly desirable policy response in the present period given the current high unemployment rates and also the dramatic increase in income inequality in this country since the early 1970s. In the three decades after 1970, the coefficient of variation in family income increased by 40 percent (Campbell et al., 2008, Table 3.1). Moreover by 2010 the poverty rate had risen to 15.1 percent, its highest level since 1993, and the child poverty rate had risen to 21 percent.

Inattention to these inequalities is likely to lead to even greater achievement gaps in the future. Moreover, many considerations that extend well beyond the realm of education policy make a compelling case for the country take strong steps to reduce income inequality.[9]

Nonetheless, I do not dwell on this policy response here. The main reason is that such a policy thrust is not in the cards, at least in the near term. With the budget crises at the national and state levels, and the strong political power of conservative groups, no one with significant political power is actively pushing the strategy of reducing poverty and income inequality at this time. Nor are they likely to do so in the immediate future, unless the current protests in New York City and elsewhere succeed in putting the issue of income inequality back on the policy agenda.[10]

A second reason for not dwelling on this policy response, regardless of how desirable it may be, it that any serious effort to reduce poverty and to equalize incomes will take a long time, and the country cannot wait that long to address the educational needs of the current generation of children.

I note, however, that past efforts to address poverty and socioeconomic inequalities appear to have played some role in reducing achievement gaps, especially those between black children who are disproportionately represented among low income families and white children who tend to come from more affluent families. In combination with other policies including civil rights initiatives, for example, anti-poverty programs during the 1960s appear to have contributed to some of the significant reduction in the black white test score gaps during the 1960s and early 1970s. But, as I said before, I am not optimistic that such policies will be revived in the current political environment.

2. Deny the Power of the Correlation and Expect Schools Alone to Offset any Adverse Effects of the Educational Context

An alternative policy response is for education policy makers simply to deny the correlation between education outcomes and family background or other relevant elements of the context. Policy makers can deny the correlation by setting the same high achievement and attainment expectations for all students and requiring all schools to meet the proficiency standard, regardless of the mix of students in the school. In other words, schools serving large proportions of low SES students that failed to fully offset the adverse family contexts of their students would be labeled as failing schools. That is, in fact, what our current federal policy, No Child Left Behind (NCLB), does. The starting point under NCLB is similar achievement standards for all children.

Specifically, it requires that all children meet grade-specific proficiency standards, as measured by test scores, by the year 2013/14, with the proviso that the proficiency standards can differ by state. Because many children, and especially those from disadvantaged backgrounds, started out well below the achievement standards, the legislation required states to set year-by-year goals for the schools that would move all students to proficiency by the deadline. Of course, even if we set aside the role of family background, the goal of 100 percent proficiency is absurd unless the proficiency levels are set so low as to be meaningless. The reason is that it ignores the normal distribution of talent among individual students. But my focus here is on how the legislation in practice denies the power of the correlation between family background and student achievement for groups of students.

Under NCLB, each school must meet the same standard, regardless of whether it serves low or high SES students and must do so for all relevant subgroups within the school defined by income, minority status and LEP status. Interestingly, NCLB policy explicitly acknowledges that some groups of students are likely to perform at lower levels than others, which is fully consistent with the correlations I have been talking about. But NCLB acknowledges those differences only to make sure that the schools do not ignore the disadvantaged students. In fact, the policy is clearly based on the presumption that the schools themselves can and should offset any educational disadvantages those children bring to the classroom. In this sense NCLB denies the correlation between family background and student achievement.

Possible Rationales for Denial

Why might policy makers have chosen to deny the correlation? I can think of at least four reasons.

One possibility is that policy makers believe that schools themselves *should* offset the effects of low SES. This normative view might reflect in part the historical observation that schooling has often served as the route to prosperity and social mobility. This normative view may also reflect the increasing importance of education to an individual's life chances. Data clearly show, for example, that the earnings of workers with low levels of education have been level or even falling in recent years for a combination of demographic, technological and institutional reasons, while the earnings of those with a college degree have risen, which implies a significant increase in the returns to education (Golden and Katz, 2008).

This normative perspective suggests that it would be inappropriate—and even immoral—to let schools off the hook simply because they serve large concentrations of children who face greater educational challenges than other children. It does not, however, confront the difference between what might be desirable from a normative perspective and what is feasible in practice.

A second possible rationale for policy makers to deny the correlation between low SES and educational outcomes is that they simply do not want to set lower expectations for some groups of children than for others, or to engage in what President George W. Bush referred to as the "soft bigotry of low expectations"(Noe, 2004). The fear here is that if they set lower outcome goals for some schools than for other schools it will become a self-fulfilling prophecy.

Sending a signal that some children are less able to learn than others would be inconsistent with the basic tenet of the standards based reform movement. As articulated by O'Day and Smith in their well-known 1993 paper, the standards movement starts from the premise that, while it may take some children longer than others, all children can learn to high and ambitious standards. Of course, for that learning to occur, the conditions must be right. In the effort to translate their views into policy, supporters of standards based reform paid attention to part of the required conditions by calling for "opportunity to learn" (OTL) standards (Ravitch, 1995). These OTL standards were intended to make sure that all children would have access to the quality teaching necessary for them to learn, but still implicitly assumed that schools alone could address the challenges of low SES children. In any case, the high resource costs of implementing OTL standards made them a political nonstarter.[11]

Though understandable and also commendable in some ways, this reluctance even to suggest that some children face educational challenges that schools alone may not be able to address signifies a denial of the basic correlations between family background and student achievement. Simply wanting something to be true does not make it so.

A third possible rationale for denying the correlation is the evidence that some schools appear to have successfully achieved high academic results for large concentrations of children from disadvantaged family contexts. The argument is that if some schools can "beat the odds," it is reasonable to expect all schools to do so. Included among the "successful" schools are various charter schools, including the highly touted Knowledge is Power Program (KIPP) schools, as well as specific schools operated by charismatic leaders.

One must be careful about this argument for a number of reasons. One is that a close look at the data shows that many of the schools cited as being successful in fact met the success criterion only in a few grades or in a single year (Rothstein, 2004a, ch. 2). Another is that to the extent that the success of some of the schools is attributable to their success in attracting low SES students from the high end of the ability or motivation distribution, it cannot be scaled up to the larger system. Yet some schools, such as many charter schools in Boston and (possibly many) of the KIPP schools, undoubtedly have successfully found a way to educate low SES children to high levels (Angrist & al, 2011, Mathematica, 2010). At best, however, such success can be generalized only to children with the types of motivated parents that apply to such schools. Also the charter schools that have beaten the odds, and especially the KIPP schools, typically have significant extra funding from philanthropic sources that permit them to do things that have not generally been viewed as feasible within the traditional public schools, such as offering longer school days, Saturday classes, and longer school year and requiring teachers to teach longer hours.

That some individual schools have raised achievement levels for children from disadvantaged families is undoubtedly a good thing, at least for the children who attend such schools. At the same time, believing that one can simply extrapolate from these few success stories to the system as a whole requires a willful denial of the basic empirical relationship between SES and educational achievement.

A fourth potential rationale for denying the correlation is more nefarious. This rationale is the desire to discredit schools and generate pressure for greater privatization of the education system. The requirement under NCLB that all schools meet the same high standards for all their students inevitably will lead either to large numbers of failing schools or to dramatic lowering of state standards. Both outcomes serve to discredit the public education system and lend support to arguments that the system itself is failing and needs to be changed in major ways. The importance of this rationale for denying the correlation and supporting NCLB in its current form is hard to gauge, but my guess it that it played some role, at least among some policy makers.[12]

Evaluation of NCLB

Regardless of the potentially laudable intentions of some of NCLB's advocates, their rationales for denying the contribution of family background to educational outcomes are flawed. Since NCLB is built on this sort of denial, it a deeply flawed policy. The evidence on NCLB, briefly summarized here, supports this assertion.

The evidence suggests that NCLB has not succeeded in raising student test scores, as measured by the nation's report card, the National Assessment of Educational Progress, by anywhere near the desired amounts (Dee and Jacobs, 2011). At best it has raised the average math scores of 4th graders by a small amount, with somewhat larger effects for disadvantaged students at that level. The effects on 8th grade math scores may be positive but are not clear, and no effects emerge for reading scores at either the 4th or 8th grade levels.

At the same time NCLB has generated a range undesirable side effects—including large numbers of failing schools,[13] narrowing of the curriculum, low morale among teachers who are facing pressure to achieve goals that they cannot meet, and, as has become abundantly clear in recent months by the cheating scandals in Atlanta and elsewhere, significant amounts of cheating by teachers under extreme pressure to raise student test scores.

In recognition of these failures of NCLB, an increasing number of policy makers are

acknowledging that it would be desirable to shift away from the absolute standard to some form of value added measure of school effectiveness. I have more to say about that approach in the next section.

3. Set the Context Aside and Focus on Improving School Quality by Reducing Inefficiencies

An alternative policy response to the correlation between context and educational outcomes is for education policy makers to set contextual considerations aside on the ground that they can do little to change them. Thus, while policy makers might well be aware of the importance of family background and other relevant aspects of the context, they choose to ignore that aspect of the educational challenge and to focus their attention exclusively on making schools themselves work better, something over which they have direct control. Although this approach is preferable to the approach of outright denial, it is likely neither to raise overall achievement, nor to reduce achievement gaps very much, and could do serious harm.

In practice—but not by necessity because school quality could also be improved by investing more resources in education—this policy response in recent years has started from the perception that the U.S. education system is rife with inefficiencies and that the inefficiencies can be eliminating by better use of information and incentives. The intent is to get better outcomes with few or no new resources. This strategy could potentially also reduce achievement gaps if the policy reduced inefficiencies more in the high poverty schools relative to the low poverty schools.

NCLB, itself, has been justified in part by this logic. Lack of adequate parental monitoring of schools, argue some, means that external monitoring and incentives are needed to induce schools to work harder to meet governmental goals. By measuring, reporting and, in many cases, attaching positive consequences to strong performance and negative consequences to weak school performance, policy makers provide incentives for schools and school districts to focus attention of what is being measured and to work either harder or "smarter."

Two other strategies currently on the policy agenda fit into this policy response category of reducing inefficiencies. One is the use of student test scores for evaluating teachers for high stakes purposes and the other is governance changes in the form of charter schools and vouchers to promote competition and innovation.

Test-Based Evaluation of Teachers

Research suggests that individual teachers are the most important *school related* factor affecting student achievement and that there is wide variation in quality among teachers, both across and within schools.[14] Moreover, the data show that it is extremely hard to fire teachers. Based on this research, many policy makers are convinced that the use of student test scores for the purposes of evaluating teachers will improve school quality by reducing the disparities in teacher quality within and across schools.[15]

The good news here is that policy makers are increasingly accepting the idea that when using student test scores for the purposes of evaluating teachers, it makes more sense to use some form of value added measure rather than the raw test scores. Because value added measures take into account the achievement levels that children bring to the classroom, the measures isolate, at least in principle, the contributions of specific teachers to student learning. In this sense, policy makers are explicitly recognizing that some students start the year less well prepared than others, and they are acknowledging that individual teachers should not be held responsible for achievement differences that are outside their control.

By attaching stakes to these value added measures, education policy makers hope to incent existing teachers to work harder toward the goal of raising student achievement, to provide objective information to school leaders designed to make it easier for them to remove ineffective teachers, and to attract a new brand of teachers to the profession, teachers who are less interested in job security and more interested in being rewarded for good performance.

The attention to value added, however, does nothing by itself to help teachers address the educational challenges that disadvantaged children bring to the classroom. In that sense it ignores the correlation between family background and student performance. Even if it were true that value added models generated valid and reliable measures of teacher effectiveness (which extensive research shows they generally do not) this focus on teacher effectiveness at best pushes teachers to work hard toward the goal of raising student test scores, with no attention paid to other academic and non-academic needs of children that may impede their ability to learn (Baker et al., 2010). As a consequence, while this policy focus could potentially improve some educational outcomes, it will do so only if the policy diagnosis of rampant inefficiency is correct. To the extent that policy makers are misreading the situation and attributing educational shortfalls—especially those in high poverty schools—to production inefficiencies rather than to context, the strategy is not likely to be very effective, and could do some serious harm. How much good it does in practice is an empirical question.

The best U.S. evidence to date indicates that providing financial incentives for teachers to raise test scores does not lead to the desired results. In a recent experiment in which randomly assigned math teachers in grades 5–8 in Nashville were offered large bonuses for raising their students' test scores, for example, no differences emerged in the test scores of those teacher offered the incentive and those in the control group (Springer et al., 2010).[16]

More generally, the focus on test based evaluation of teachers provides incentives for them to narrow the curriculum to the tested subjects of math and reading, and to direct teacher attention to basic skills away from student reasoning skills. In addition, statistical problems of bias and unreliability can lead to unfair and arbitrary treatment of teachers, which in turn lowers morale and reduces the appeal of teaching as a profession (Baker et al., 2010).

I am not suggesting that existing methods for evaluating and developing teachers are adequate. Instead, my point is that evaluations that place heavy weight on student test scores are likely to do more harm than good because they start from the assumption that teachers are shirking rather than the assumption that they need support and constructive counseling. Peer assistance and review programs that combine support with accountability appear to be a more promising alternative to the current system.[17]

Governance Changes Designed to Promote Efficiency

Also high on the school reform agenda of those seeking more efficient schools are governance changes in the form of charter schools and voucher programs. Charter schools are publically funded schools operated by nonprofit or private companies that have significantly more autonomy than the traditional public schools. Voucher programs provide financial support for families to send their children to private schools. I focus here on charter schools because of their greater prevalence relative to voucher funded private schools and because the Obama administration has been actively pushing states to expand charter schools.

To the extent that charter schools are intended to provide new—and better—schooling options for disadvantaged children, they would appear to be addressing the educational challenges of disadvantaged students. And indeed some charter schools are doing that. As I mentioned earlier, a few charter schools appear to be doing a good job of promoting academic success among children from disadvantaged families, albeit often with the help of substantial additional resources from private philanthropists or from charismatic leaders.

Despite these highly touted successes, charter school reform effort as a whole is more appropriately viewed as a governance change that ignores the educational challenges facing disadvantaged children than a reform that targets those challenges directly. I say that for several reasons. One is that many states are increasingly justifying the expansion of charter schools on the ground that they will provide necessary competition to the traditional public sector, which is viewed by many reformers as

bureaucratic and excessively beholden to unions. The competitive pressure from charter schools, it is hoped, will force traditional schools to use their resources more efficiently. Thus, a major justification for charter schools is similar to that for the test-based evaluation of teachers, namely that inefficiency is a significant cause of the poor average performance of U.S. students relative to other countries.

In addition, there is little reason to believe that governance changes alone will lead schools to address in a systematic way the challenges facing disadvantaged students. In the absence of significant additional external financial and programmatic support, charter schools serving disadvantaged students are likely to be no more successful in raising achievement levels than their traditional public school counterparts and indeed may be less so given the challenges in running a school and the large concentrations of disadvantaged students found in some charter schools. Consistent with this prediction, the evidence suggests that on average charter schools are either less effective or no more successful than traditional public schools, although some studies suggest that they may generate some positive achievement gains for low income students (CREDO, 2009, Gleason et al., 2010). The patterns were particularly dramatic in my 2007 study of charter schools in North Carolina with Robert Bifulco, where we found that the students in charter schools serving large proportions of minority students exhibited even greater adverse effects on student achievement than students in charter schools serving more middle class students (Bifulco and Ladd, 2007). Thus, there is little evidence that charter schools in practice are providing better schooling options on average for disadvantaged children. Indeed the movement could be harming the options for some children by draining funds from the traditional public schools that continue to serve the bulk of disadvantaged students.

This discussion should not be interpreted as an argument either for or against charter schools. My own personal view is they have a role to play in any overall education system, but that role should be limited to the fringe of the system (Fiske and Ladd, 2001). The main point is that governance changes of this type do little in a systematic way to improve outcomes for disadvantaged children. At the same time, policy makers can learn from the success stories. One central lesson from the KIPP schools for example seems to be that some disadvantaged children thrive on longer school days, a clear focus on goals, a no-excuses culture and more parental involvement (Angrist et al., 2011).

4. Directly Address the Educational Challenges Faced by Low SES Children

A fourth policy response to the correlation between family background and student outcomes is for education policy makers to work with other agencies and community groups to pursue strategies specifically designed to reduce the adverse impact of low SES on educational outcomes—both for the low SES children themselves and for other children. Such an approach, in my view, must be an essential component of any serious effort to reduce achievement gaps and to raise student achievement. Instead of denying or ignoring the context, this approach specifically acknowledges and confronts the evidence in a serious manner by addressing the symptoms or correlates of poverty that directly impede student learning.

Here is where policy researchers, and especially APPAM researchers, have a large role to play. Many of you have done, and are currently doing, excellent research along these lines. I particularly commend the research in the new Russell Sage volume edited by Greg Duncan and Richard Murnane, entitled *Whither Opportunity? Rising Inequality and the Uncertain Life Chances of Low-Income Children*. The papers in this book document the many mechanisms through which rising income inequality in this country widens the educational gap between low and higher income children.

But there is much more work to be done, particularly by teams of interdisciplinary researchers who pay close attention to local context, address topics that do not fit neatly into clearly defined policy silos, and address the very real political and organizational constraints that typically limit the purview of educational

decision making. I outline here two central components of this policy approach, addressing the education-related challenges facing low SES children and assuring that all children have access to high quality schooling.

Addressing the Education-Related Challenges of Low SES Children

The observation that low SES is highly predictive of poor educational outcomes by itself provides little guidance for education policy makers who have little or no control over the backgrounds of the students, at least in the aggregate, within a community. To address those challenges, policy makers need to understand the mechanisms through which low SES translates into educational gaps.

Fortunately, we already know a lot about those mechanisms. Research reviewed by Janet Currie, for example, documents a clear link between child poverty and poor health outcomes and how many of those poor health outcomes translate into low cognitive outcomes (Currie, 2009). Other researchers have documented how an impoverished early childhood limits access to language and problem solving skills and to variation in experiences that serve as the basic springboard for future learning. In addition, family poverty and low SES during the school years translates into limited access to books and computers at home or to activities away from home in "novel" places (Phillips, 2011). Family poverty during the school years is also typically associated with significant residential movement as families struggle to find stable housing arrangements. Such movement is disruptive not only for the children who move in and out of schools, but also for the other children in schools with high proportions of mobile students (Raudenbush et al., 2011). Children in low income families also experience far more learning loss during the summer than do their peers from more affluent families.

The policy implications of these patterns are straightforward at one level, but difficult to implement effectively in practice. Those difficulties reflect the absence of simple solutions that apply to all situations, the high costs of some quality programs, the need for government agencies and community groups to work together, and the difficulties of taking programs to scale.

I provide examples of three types of policy interventions here.

Early Childhood and Pre-School Programs

Already on the national and state policy agendas are efforts to compensate for impoverished early childhood experiences with early childhood and pre-school programs. Rigorous evaluations of a few intensive, high quality programs, such as the Carolina Abecedarian and the High Hope/Perry PreSchool Project, demonstrate strong positive effects on program participants that persist into adulthood (Mervis, 2011), but the path from small randomized controlled trials to public policy is not straightforward (Gormley, 2011). Although many positive outcomes also emerge from evaluations of the federal Head Start and Early Head Start programs and various state programs, the results from studies of these larger and less intense programs are somewhat mixed (Barnett, 2011).

Moreover, missing from most of the existing studies is attention to the broader effects of programs when implemented at scale and evaluation of effects on all groups of children in a community, not just the participants. My own recent work with my Duke colleagues, Kenneth Dodge and Clara Muschkin, which relies on data from all births in North Carolina for multiple birth cohorts linked to third grade test scores begins to fill that gap. We examine the community wide effects of two highly touted North Carolina programs, one focused on the early years of childhood, and the other on four year olds and find that both programs generate moderately large positive effects on third grade outcomes for both programs. But our work is still in an early stage and applies to only one state. Moreover, it represents only one small part of a much larger research agenda, one that must also include attention to the best ways to assure quality services. Of major concern going forward is that the severity of state budget crises may undercut the programmatic gains that have been made in recent years.

School-Based Health Clinics and Social Services

Many other countries are far ahead of the U.S. in addressing the health and developmental needs of their children. In Finland, for example, all children are required to have health examinations at ages two and five. These examinations assess the child's developmental level as well as physical health, and the records follow the children into school. In this way, schools and parents can address the developmental needs of children early. School welfare teams composed of school nurses, social welfare counselors and teachers meet on a regular basis to discuss and address the challenges of individual children. The Finns take pride in the fact that they identify close to a third of their children in the early years of schooling as needing special services, and that the proportion needing special attention declines as children progress through school.[18]

The situation differs in the U.S. Assuring that all children have access to health insurance has been on the policy agenda in recent years, but access to insurance alone does little to assure that children obtain the heath care they need to thrive in school. A more direct approach, now being implemented in some places, is to set up health clinics in the schools serving large proportions of disadvantaged students or at a minimum to assure that all children have easy access to clinics. These health clinics can provide routine and preventative care, provide services to children with acute health problems in a timely manner, monitor children's health in a systematic way as they progress through school, and can address basic dental and vision problems that might otherwise impede children's learning. Strict confidentiality requirements related to medical records makes it difficult to examine the effects of such clinics on individual participants, but it would be useful for researchers and practitioners to work together to experiment with and to evaluate efforts of this type (see Peterson et al., 2004 for a summary of existing research and its limitations).

Children's learning can be impeded not only by poor physical health. It can also be impeded by poor mental health and depression caused by problems at home, including domestic abuse, divorce, alcoholism, depressed parents, and work related stress, problems that require attention from social service agencies. In some cases, children get the help they need through existing agencies. But many others may suffer in silence in ways that keep them from functioning effectively in the classroom. A logical policy response is to provide mental health and social welfare counselors in schools, especially in schools with large concentrations of disadvantaged children who are least likely to have access to the resources they need to deal with their challenges. A 2000 comprehensive review of the literature on school based mental health services concluded that many provided positive benefits but that most evaluations ignored or underemphasized school-relevant outcomes (Rones and Hoagwood, 2000).

I applaud the recent efforts of researchers to measure the effects of mental health counselors in elementary schools and I would strongly support more research of this type. In a recent study, for example, Randall Reback (2010) used cross-state differences in state policies to document that elementary school students in states with more aggressive school counselor policies were associated with greater test scores gains and that the polices were causally linked to teachers' perceptions of school climate. In addition, Carrell and Hoekstra (2010) find large effects on student test scores from the presence of counselors in elementary schools, with the effects identified by within school variation over time in access to services. Much as it distresses me to acknowledge the current cutbacks in school nurses and counselors associated with budget pressures in many states, I note that such cutbacks could provide opportunities for researchers to examine the effects of removing the supports.

After-School and Summer Programs

American children typically spend very little time in school. On a typical school day, most children spend less than half their non-sleeping hours in school and over the course of the year they spend fewer than half of all days in school.

This short time in school puts low SES children at a significant learning disadvantage relative to their more advantaged peers whose parents are often able to provide them a rich set of opportunities for learning outside of school, whether that be after school, on weekends or during the summer. The rising gap in incomes has been accompanied by a rising gap in the amount high and low income families spend on out-of-school enrichment activities such as music lessons, travel and summer camps.[19] These activities matter not only because they are enriching in their own right but also because they provide experiential background useful for learning as children progress through school.

Many other countries have been far more aggressive than the U.S. in equalizing these opportunities through extended school hours, after school and summer programs and extended year programs. Many Dutch schools have been converted into community schools, for example, with a variety of enrichment activities after school hours. The Koreans go to the (undesirable, in my view) extreme of keeping all high school students in school late into the evening specifically to keep middle class families from taking advantage of evening hours to put their children in extra tutoring programs. Within the U.S. some charter schools, and particularly the KIPP schools, have pursued the strategy of a longer school day, week and year, and many non-profit groups are now supporting after school programs.

The evidence on the effectiveness of after school programs and summer schools is somewhat mixed (Cooper et al., 2000). As is true for many of the programs mentioned here, the quality and nature of the program matter. Research shows for example that marginally expanding in-school time without improving how that time is used does not improve learning. At the same time, some high intensity summer programs have generated academic gains in high poverty areas, and some low cost reading programs have reduced summer reading loss (Jacob and Lefgren 2004; Allington et al., 2010). Clearly much more experimentation and research would be useful.

Providing High Quality Schools for Disadvantaged Students

It does little or no good for policy makers to address the out-of-school challenges of disadvantaged children, however, if the schools those children attend are low quality. Researchers have shown, for example, that one reason for the more rapid fading of Head Start benefits for black than for white participants is that the black children ended up in lower quality elementary schools than their white counterparts (see overview in Currie, 2001). Thus a central component of any policy agenda designed to address the needs of children from disadvantaged families is to assure that the schools such children attend are high quality.

To achieve that end, policy makers must assure, first, that children in schools serving large proportions of disadvantaged students have access to high quality teachers, principals, supports for students, and other resources and, second, that the schools are held accountable for the quality of their internal processes and practices. At the risk of being criticized by some groups within the education policy community for daring to suggest that it is time for education policy makers to end their obsession with test-based outcome measures of school quality and to shift the focus to the quality of inputs and school processes, that is exactly what I am proposing here.

Assuring Quality Inputs

Research studies consistently document that high poverty schools typically have teachers with lower qualifications along many dimensions than schools with more advantaged students. My own work with Duke colleagues clearly demonstrate that pattern for North Carolina schools, with particularly large discrepancies in teacher credentials across high and low poverty middle schools, with the same patterns emerging for school principals (Clotfelter et al., 2007). Further, ambitious work by Heather Hill and colleagues show that math teachers in high poverty schools have lower math knowledge for teaching (based on a measure that is distinct from math content knowledge or degrees) than

their counterparts in more advantaged schools (Hill, 2007).

The policy challenge is to find ways to even out the distribution of teacher and principal quality across schools. Although it may be tempting to attribute the current maldistribution largely to the provisions of union contracts, that is a mistake. One need only observe that patterns emerge not only in unionized states but also in non-union states such as North Carolina. Research shows that teacher preferences play a fundamental role in the uneven distribution; although not all teachers are reluctant to teach in high poverty or high minority schools, many apparently are (Jackson, 2009; Clotfelter et al., 2011). Hence, the challenge is to find ways to make schools serving disadvantaged children more attractive to high quality teachers than they currently are. Education policy makers can do so by implementing school assignment policies designed to balance the socio-economic and/or racial mix of students across schools; making sure that high poverty schools have strong school leadership and the support services such as nurses and social workers required for teachers to be successfully with their students; and by using financial incentives to attract and retain teachers in schools with large proportions of challenging-to-educate children. Because states and districts are responsible for the quality of these inputs, they are the ones, not the schools themselves, who should be held accountable for any shortfalls.

Holding Schools Accountable

At the same time, individual schools also should be held accountable, but only for things that are under their control. Specifically, they should be held accountable for the internal policies and practices that help to produce a far broader set of educational outcomes than student achievement alone as measured by test scores. Schools might be held accountable, for example, for providing a safe and supportive school environment and a climate that promotes respect among children and teachers; for tracking the individual developmental needs of all the children they serve and for implementing strategies to address those needs; and for delivering the curriculum in a coherent manner that engages students as partners in the learning process and appropriately pushes them all to the limits of their abilities.

Clearly, accountability of this type is a far cry from the punitive test-based accountability that we now have in this country. One starting point for this new form of accountability would be the school inspectorates that are common in many countries around the world. My own research on education review offices or inspectorates in New Zealand and the Netherlands suggests that there is no one perfect model or even a single best model that could or should be directly transferred to the U.S. (Ladd, 2010). Nonetheless, I believe that it is time for the U.S. to start experimenting with an inspectorate approach that involves human judgment and, if well implemented, has the potential to provide useful and constructive guidance to individual schools on how they can become more effective (Ladd, 2007.)

Even in a more positive and constructive accountability system along these lines, student tests would continue to play a role. An expanded version of the National Assessment of Educational Progress that covered more subjects would permit states to determine the areas in which they are doing well or poorly relative to national norms (Rothstein et al., 2008). And at the school level, teachers would continue to give tests and other assessment for the purposes of diagnosing the strengths and weaknesses of their students. One of the things schools would be held accountable for would be their procedures for measuring student learning, and for their systems for responding to those results, including making sure the children get the social services they need to succeed. The point is that school quality would be defined in terms of how well schools are operated with the goal of meeting the educational needs of all their children.[20]

Such a shift would move us away from a failed and punitive test-based accountability system that does not work in favor of an approach that has the potential to be far more constructive and also more consistent with the broad set of aspirations we have for our public education system.

Conclusion

Such bolder and broader strategies designed to address the educational needs of low income children will cost money, could be complex and undoubtedly will need to differ from place to place depending on the local context. Because many of the policies must be tailored to the local context, state and local communities will have to play a major role.

The most productive step for the federal government in the short run would be to eliminate No Child Left Behind. The logic of my argument this afternoon is that in its place the federal government should implement strategies designed to help state and local governments address in a more constructive and positive manner the educational needs of low SES children and to assure that poor children have equal access to quality schools. Ideally, the longer run agenda should also include a major effort to reduce child poverty.

More research is needed both on the mechanisms such as poor physical and health, limited out of school opportunities, and family stress through which poverty adversely affects student learning, and on the programs and combinations of strategies best suited to address these challenges. Because these strategies are likely to require action by multiple governmental agencies and to cut across a number of policy areas, I invite those of you who work in the interrelated areas of education and social policy to engage with others who focus on organizations and management in this important endeavor to reduce the impact of poverty and low socio-economic status on educational outcomes.

Notes

1. Not everyone agrees that the system is in crisis. See, for example, the critique of this view by Berliner and Biddle (1995).
2. The figure is a simplified version of graph 5.3 in Reardon, 2011. The trend line is estimated based on the income based achievement gaps calculated from the 12 nationally representative studies that include data on reading scores for school age children and information on family income. The fitted regressions line is weighted by the inverse of the sampling variance of each estimate. The

figure for math is similar (see figure 5.4 in Reardon, 2011).

3. The estimated black-white gap trend line is based on all the available black white gap information that is available in NAEP long term trends for 13 year olds and Main NAEP for eighth graders, with the latter adjusted for age differences. The line can be interpreted at the trend in the gap for 13 year olds. See footnote 6 in Reardon, 2011.

4. See Duncan and Murnane (2011) and the articles therein for detailed empirical analysis of many of these mechanisms.

5. The years included in the analysis differ somewhat between reading and math regressions because of slight differences in when the tests were administered. The child poverty rates from 2002 to the present are from the American Community Survey and those for 2000 are from the Census. The 1998 reading scores by state are matched with state child poverty rates for 2000.

6. The index is based on the following variables: the international socio-economic index of occupational status of the father or mother, whichever is higher; the level of education of the father or mother, whichever is higher, converted into years of schooling; and an index of home possessions, which is based on student reports of access to education related possessions such as desks, computers and books, and availability of items such as such as televisions, cars, and cellular phones. The index is standardized to a mean of zero for the population of students in OECD countries, with each country given equal weight. A score of -1.0 on this index means that the student is more disadvantaged than five-sixths of the students in the average OECD country (OECD, Volume II, 2010, p. 29).

7. Moreover, to keep advantaged families from gaining an advantage by putting their children in "cram" schools for additional tutoring, the government requires most high school students to remain in school until 10:00 or 11:00 each weekday night and to attend school every second Saturday. These behaviors impose large societal costs in that Korean children have little time to interact with their families and to pursue non-school activities. (Based on visits to Korean schools by the author in June, 2011.)

8. The UNICEF overall measure of child wellbeing also includes educational well-being. I deleted the educational wellbeing component for this analysis to focus on the non-education components of child wellbeing (UNICEF, 2010).

9. See, for example, the arguments for why greater equality makes societies stronger in Wilkinson and Pickett (2009).

10. This is a reference to the Occupy Wall Street protests that were occurring in New York City and that were spreading to other cities at the time this talk was written.

11. Discussion with Diane Ravitch, October 4, 2011.

12. Consistent with this perspective in a slightly different context is the response of Chester Finn (a former chair and member of the National Assessment Governing Board) to concerns about the high proficiency cut scores proposed for the National Assessment of Educational Progress. The realism of the cut scores was less important, he argued, than of demonstrating that many students were failing in order to send a signal to the nation about the urgency of improving education (reported in Rothstein et al., 2008, p. 62.)

13. Tracking reports show 38 percent of schools nationwide and more than half of the schools in 12 states and DC are currently not meeting the annual requirements of the NCLB legislation. The percentage of failing schools differs across states with the toughness of the state's proficiency standards. Moreover, with no change in the law or without the new waiver policy recently enacted by the Obama administration, the percentages of failing schools are likely to increase significantly in the next few states because many states backloaded the increases required to meet the 2014 goals (CEP, 2011).

14. In fact, while the evidence suggests that teachers may be more important than small class sizes, It is worth noting that no studies compare the impact of teachers to a variety of other inputs such as principal quality or the coherence of the curriculum. (See Rothstein www.epi.org/publication/ib286/

15. At least one prominent education researcher has argued that replacing the 5 to 10 percent of the weakest teachers would generate outcomes for U.S. students that are similar to those in Finland or Canada (Hanushek, 2010).

16. Other rigorous studies with more positive results are based on experiments in other countries and, for a variety of reasons, may not be directly relevant to the U.S. For a full discussion, see National Research Council, 2011.

17. See, for example, the reports produced by The Project on the Next Generation of Teachers at the Harvard Graduate School of Education (http://gse.harvard.edu/~ngt/. Also see study by Kane et al., 2010.

18. Presentation by Finnish National Board of Education to a North Carolina Delegation of Educators, September 26, 2011).

19. The spending gap between families in the top and bottom family income quintiles was approximately $2,700 in the early 1970s (in 2008 dollars) and rose to $7,500 by 2004–06 (Kaushal, Magnuson, and Waldfogel, 2011).

20. A model accountability system along these lines has been proposed by the Campaign for a Broader, Bolder Approach to Education (Boldeapproach.org).

References

Allington, R.L., et al. (2010). Addressing Summer Reading Setback Among Economically Disadvantaged Elementary Students. Reading Psychology, 31, 411–427.

Ahn, Byong Man (2011). Education in South Korea: National Treasure or National Headache? Invited speech for the annual conference of the Association for Education Finance and Policy, Seattle, WA.

Angrist, J.D., Pathak, P.A., & Walters, C.R. (2011). Explaining Charter School Effectiveness. National Bureau for Economic Research, Working Paper No. 17332, Cambridge, MA (August).

Baker, E.L, Barton, P.E. Darling-Hammond, L., Haertel, E., Ladd, H.F., Linn, R.L. Ravitch. D. Rothstein, R., Shavelson, R.J. & Shepard, L.A. Problems with the use of student test scores to evealuate teachers." Economic Policy Institute Briefing Paper #278. (www.epi.org/page/-/pdf/bp278.pdf)

Barnett, W. S. (August 19, 2011). Effectiveness of Early Educational Intervention. Science, 333, 975–978.

Berliner, D. C. & Biddle, B.J. (1995). The Manufactured Crisis: Myths, Fraud, and the Attack on America's Public Schools. Cambridge, MA: Perseus Books Group.

Bifulco, R. & Ladd, H.F. (2007). School Choice, Racial Segregation and Test Score Gaps: Evidence from North Carolina's Charter School Program. Journal of Policy Analysis and Management, 26, 31–56.

Campbell, M.E., Haveman, R., Wildhagen, T. & Wolfe, B.L. (2008). Income Inequality and Racial Gaps in Test Scores. In K. Magnuson & J. Waldfogel, eds. Steady Gains and Stalled Progress: Inequality and the Black–White Test Score Gap. New York: Russell Sage Foundation.

Carrell, S. E. & Hoekstra, M. (2010). Are School Counselors a Cost-Effective Education Input? (working paper www.edon.ucdavid/scarrell/counselors_input. pdf).

Center on Education Policy (CEP) (2011). Update with 2009–10 Data and Five-Year Trend. How Many Schools Have Not Made Adequate Yearly Progress? Washington, D.C.: Center on Education Progress.

Clotfelter, C.T., Ladd, H.F., Vigdor, J.L. & Wheeler, J. (2007). High Poverty Schools and the Distribution of Teachers and Principals. North Carolina Law Review, 85, 1345–1380.

Clotfelter, C.T., Ladd, H.F., & Vigdor, J.L. (2011). Teacher Mobility, School Segregation, and Pay-Based Policies to Level the Playing Field. Education Finance and Policy, 6, 399–438.

Cooper, H., Charlton, K., Valentine, J.C., Muhlenbruck, L. & Borman, G.D. (2000). Making the Most of Summer School: A Meta-Analytic and Narrative Review. Monographs of the Society for Research in Child Development, 65, 1–127.

Currie, J. (2001). Early Childhood Education Programs. Journal of Economic Perspectives. Bol. 15, 32, pp. 213–230.

Currie, J. (2009). Healthy, Wealthy, and Wise: Socioeconomic Status, Poor Health in Childhood, and Human Capital Development. Journal of Economic Literature, 47, 87–122.

Dee, T. & Jacobs, B. (2011). The Impact of No Child Left Behind on Student Achievement. Journal of Policy Analysis and Management, 30, 418–446.

Duncan, G. & Murnane, R. (2011). Whither Opportunity? Rising Inequality and the Uncertain Life Chances of Low-Income Children. New York: Russell Sage.

Fiske, E. & Ladd, H.F. (2001). Lessons from New Zealand. In P.E. Peterson & D.E. Campbell (eds), Charters, Vouchers, and Public Education (pp. 59–79). Washington, D.C.: Brookings Institution Press.

Gleason, P., Clark M., Tuttle C.C, & Dwoyer E. (2010). The Evaluation of Charter School Impacts: Final Report, (NCEE 2010–4030). Washington, DC: National Center for Education Evaluation and Regional Assistance, Institute of Education Sciences, U.S. Department of Education.

Goldin, C. D. & Katz, L. F. (2008). The Race Between Education and Technology. Cambridge, MA: Harvard University Press.

Gormley, W. T., Jr. (2011). From science to policy in early childhood education. Science, 333, 978–981.

Hanushek, E. (2010). The Economic Value of Higher Teacher Quality, National Bureau of Economic Research, Paper no. 16606 (December).

Hanushek & Woessman (2010). The Economics of International Differences in Educational Achievement. NBER working paper 15949. www.Nber.org/papers/w15949.

Hill, H.C. (2007). Mathematical Knowledge of Middle School Teachers: Implications for the No Child Left Behind Policy Initiative. Educational Evaluation and Policy Analysis, 29, 2, 95–114.

Jackson, C. K. (2009). Student Demographics, Teacher Sorting, and Teacher Quality: Evidence from the End of School Desegregation. The Journal of Labor Economics, 27, 213–256.

Jacob, B.A. & Lefgren, L. (2004). Remedial Education and Student Achievement: A Regression-Discontinuity Analysis. The Review of Economics and Statistics, 86, 226–244.

Kaushal, N., Mangnuson, K. & Waldfogel, J. (2011). How is Family Income Related to Investments in Childrens Learning? In G. Duncan and R. Murnane (eds), Whither Opportunity? Rising Income Inequality and the Uncertain Life Chances of Low-Income Children. New York: Russell Sage Foundation.

Kim, J.S. & White, T.G. (2011). Solving the problem of summer reading loss. Phi Delta Kappan, 92, 64–67.

Ladd, H.F. & Loeb, S. (forthcoming). The Challenges of Measuring School Quality: Implications for Educational Equity. In D. Allen & R. Reich, Education, Democracy and Justice. Chicago: University of Chicago Press.

Ladd, H.F. (2010). Education Inspectorate Systems in New Zealand and the Netherlands. Education Finance and Policy, 5, 378–392.

Ladd, H.F. (2007). Holding Schools Accountable Revisited. APPAM – Spencer Foundation Lecture (Available at www.APPAM.org under awards).

Ladd, H. F., Muschkin, C. & Dodge. (2011). From Birth to School: Early Childhood Programs and Third Grade Outcomes in North Carolina. Paper presented at the fall 2011 meetings of the Association for Public Policy Analysis and Management. Washington, D.C.

Lear, J.G. (2007) Health at School: A Hidden Health Care System Emerges from the Shadows. Health Affairs, 26, 2, 409–419.

Mervis, J. (August 19, 2011). Giving children a head start is possible – But it's not easy. Science, 333(6045), 956–957.

National Research Council (NRC) (2011). Incentives and Test-Based Accountability in Education. Committee on Incentives and Test-Based Accountability in Public Education, M. Hout and S.W. Elliotts (eds). Board on Testing and Assessment, Division of Behavioral and Social Sciences and Education. Washington, DC: The National Academies Press.

Noe, C. (2004). Bush Decries Democrats' Soft Bigrotry of Low Expectations. NewsMax.com. January 9.

OECD (2010). PISA 2009 Results: Overcoming Social Background – Equity in Learning Opportunities and Outcomes, volume II. Paris: Organization for Economic Co-operation and Development.

Raudenbush, S.W., Jean, M. & Art, M. (2011). Year-by-year and Cumulative Impacts of Attending a High-Mobility Elementary School on children's Mathematics Achievement in Chicago, 1995 to 2005. In Duncan, G. and Murnane, R. (eds) Whither Opportunity? Rising Inequality and the Uncertain Life Chances of Low-Income Children. New York City: Russell Sage, 359–376.

Ravitch, D. (1995). National Standards in American Education: A Citizen's Guide. Washington, D.C.: Brookings Institution.

Raymond, M. (2009), Multiple Choice: Charter School Performance in 16 States. Stanford, CA: Center for Research on Education Outcomes, Stanford University.

Reardon, S. (2011). The Widening Achievement Gap Between the Rich and the Poor: New Evidence and Possible Explanations. In G.J. Duncan and R.J. Murnane (eds), Whither Opportunity?: Rising Inequality, Schools and Children's Life Chances. New York, Russell Sage, 91–116.

Reback, R. (2010). Schools' Mental Health Services and Young Children's Emotions, Behavior and Learning. Journal of Policy Analysis and Management, 29(4).

Rones, M. & Hoagwood, K. (2000). School-Based Mental Health Services: A Research Review. Clinical Child and Family Psychology Review, 3, 223–241.

Rothstein, R. (2004). Class and Schools: Using Social, Economic and Educational Reform to Close the Black-White Achievement Gap. New York: Teachers' College.

Rothstein, R. Jacobsen, R. & Wilder, T. (2008). Grading Education: Getting Accountabililty Right, Washington, D.C. and New York, New York: Economic Policy Institute and Teachers College Press.

Sahlberg, P. (2011). Finnish Lessons: What can the world learn from educational change in Finland? New York: Teachers' College Press.

Smith, M.S. & O'Day, J.A. (1993). School Reform and Equal Opportunity: An Introduction to the Education Symposium. Stanford Law & Policy Review, 10, 15–20.

Springer, M., Ballou, D., Hamilton, L., Le, V., Lockwood, J.R., McCafffrey, D. Pepper, M. & Stecher, B. (2010). Teacher Pay for Performance: Experimental Evidence from the Project on Incentives in Teaching. Nashville, TN: National Center on Performance Incentives at Vanderbilt University. (www.performanceincentives.org)

Tuttle, C.C., Teh, B., Nichols-Barrer, I., Gill, B.P. & Gleason, P. (2010). Student Characteristics and Achievement in 22 KIPP Middle Schools. Mathematica Policy Research, Washington, D.C., Retrieved from www.mathematicampr.com/publications/pdfs/education/kipp_fnlrpt.pdf.

UNICEF (2010). The Children Left Behind: A league table of inequality in child well-being in the world's rich countries. Innocenti Report Card 9. Florence: Innocenti Research Center.

Wilkinson, R. & Pickett, K. The Spirit Level: Why Greater Equality Makes Societies Stronger. New York: Bloomsbury Press.

Appendix

Suggested Resources

Research Literatures

ERIC can be searched online to find research and reflections on a wide variety of educational topics: www.eric.ed.gov

Jstor: www.jstor.org (found at college and university libraries that subscribe.) Jstor contains electronic versions of journal articles more than several years old in such journals as Sociology of Education, American Journal of Sociology, American Sociological Review, and others.

National Library of Education: www.ed.gov/NLE/index.html

Online Journals and/or Abstracts

Anthropology and Education Quarterly: www.aaanet.org/cae/aeq
Black Issues in Higher Education: www.blackissues.com
Chronicle of Higher Education: chronicle.com
Education Week: edweek.org
Educational Leadership: www.ascd.org/cms/index.cfm
Harvard Education Letter: www.edletter.org
Harvard Education Review: www.gse.harvard.edu/~hepg/her.html
Rethinking Schools: www.rethinkingschools.org
Teachers College Record at www.tcrecord.org
Sociological Research Online is at: www.socresonline.org.uk

Online News Sources

Boston Globe: www.boston.com
LA Times: www.latimes.com
New York Times: www.nytimes.com
Library of Congress: www.loc.gov
New York Public Library: www.nypl.org

Professional Associations

Association of School Administrators: www.aasa.org
American Educational Research Association: www.aera.net
American Sociological Association (ASA): www.asanet.org
Sociology of Education Section: www.asanet.org/sections/educat.html
Association for Supervision and Curriculum Development: www.ascd.org
Council for Aid to Education: www.cae.org
Council of Chief State School Officers: www.ccsso.org
Council of Great City Schools: www.cgcs.org
Education Commission of the States: www.ecs.org
National Library of Education: www.ed.gov/NLE/

From Caroline Hodges Persell and Floyd M. Hammack, "Internet Resources: How Instructors Are Using the World Wide Web in Teaching the Sociology of Education." A section within *Teaching the Sociology of Education: A Resource Manual*, 6th ed. (Washington DC: American Sociological Association, 2004). Reprinted by permission.

National Board for Professional Teaching Standards: www.nbpts.org
National Education Association: www.nea.org
Sociology of Education Section, ASA: www.asanet.org/soe

Research Organizations

AACTE Education Policy Clearinghouse: www.edpolicy.org
Center for Social Organization of Schools: www.csos.jhu.edu
Consortium for Policy Research in Education: www.upenn.edu/gse/cpre
National Center for Research in Vocational Education: vocserve.berkeley.edu

National Research and Development Centers

National Science Foundation: www.nsf.gov
Office of Educational Research and Improvement: www.ed.gov/offices/OERI/index.html
Office of Postsecondary Education: www.ed.gov/about/offices/list/ope/index.html
RAND Organization: www.rand.org
U.S. Department of Education: www.ed.gov/index.jsp
White House Briefing Room, Education: www.whitehouse.gov/fsbr/education.html

Educational Reform Organizations and Information

Achieve: www.achieve.org/achieve/achievestart.nsf?opendatabase
AVID: www.avidcenter.org
Center on School, Family, and Community Partnerships: www.csos.jhu.edu/p2000/center.html
Coalition for Essential Schools: www.essentialschools.org
Comer School Development Program: http://info.med.yale.edu/comer
Edison Schools: www.edisonproject.com
New American Schools Network: www.naschools.org
Public Education Network: www.publiceducation.org
Success for All: www.successforall.net

Testing: Test Preparation and Tutoring Organizations

ACT: www.act.org
Educational Testing Service (ETS): www.ets.org
Kaplan: www.kaplan.com
Kumon: www.kumon.com
National Assessment of Student Progress (Nation's Report Card):
    http://nces.ed.gov/nationsreportcard/site/home.asp
Princeton Review: www.princetonreview.com
Psychological Corporation: www.tpc-international.com
Sylvan Associates: www.sylvanlearning.com

Higher Education Resources

American Association of Colleges and Universities: www.aacu-edu.org
American Association of Community Colleges: www.aacc.nche.edu
Association for Institutional Research: www.airweb.org
Association for the Study of Higher Education: www.ashe.ws
Community College Web: www.mcli.dist.maricopa.edu/cc
Educause (formerly Educom and CAUSE): www.educause.net
Fund for the Improvement of Postsecondary Education: www.ed.gove/about/offices/list/ope/fipse
Higher Education Resource Hub: www.higher-ed.org
League for Innovation in the Community College: www.league.org

National Center for Postsecondary Improvement: www.stanford.edu/group/ncpi/index.html
National Center for Public Policy and Higher Education: www.highereducation.org
Review of Higher Education: www.press.jhu.edu/journals/review_of_higher_education; also try
    http://muse.jhu.edu/journals/rhe
Society for College and University Planning: www.scup.org
Western Interstate Commission on Higher Education: www.wiche.edu

International Materials

Digest of Educational Statistics: International Comparisons:
    http://nces.ed.gov/programs/digest/d03/list_tables4.asp#c6
International Association for Social Science Information Service & Technology: www.iassistdata.org
International Bureau of Education: www.ibe.unesco.org
International Education Links: http://nces.ed.gov/partners/inernat.asp
Swedish Social Science Data Service: www.ssd.gu.se/enghome.html
UNESCO: www.unesco.org

Data

Country and Data Book: www.census.gov/statab/www/ccdb.html
General Social Survey (GSS) is available on-line, and simple analyses may be conducted on-line at:
    www.webapp.icpsr.umich.edu/cocoon/ICPSR-SERIES/00028.xml
National Center for Educational Statistics (NCES): http://nces.ed.gov
NCES Encyclopedia of Education Statistics: http://nces.ed.gov/edstats
NCES Surveys: http://nces.ed.gov/surveys
Roper Center for Public Policy Research: www.ropercenter.uconn.edu
State Education Report Cards: http://measuringup2000.highereducation.org
U.S. Census Bureau, Home Page: http://census.gov

Teaching Resources*

Common Core State Standards Initiative: www.corestandards.org
Federal Resources for Educational Excellence: http://free.ed.gov/
Library of Congress' Teaching Resources Page: www.loc.gov/teachers
PBS Resources for the Classroom: www.pbs.org/teachers

Professional Associations for Teachers*

American Federation of Teachers: www.aft.org
National Board for Professional Teaching Standards: www.nbpts.org
National Education Association: www.nea.org
For a comprehensive list of subject-specific teacher organizations, see www.unm.edu/~jka/sts/proforg.html

---

* Additional resources gathered by Ryan Coughlan.

Permissions

References

Abowitz, K. & Karabe, R. (2010). Charter schooling and democratic justice. *Educational Policy, 24,* 534–558.

Achilles, C. M. (1996). Response to Eric Hanushek: Students achieve more in smaller classes. *Educational Leadership, 76.*

Achinstein, B., Ogawa, R., Sexton, D., & Freitas, C. (2010). Retaining teachers of color: A pressing problem and a potential strategy for "hard-to-staff" schools. *Review of Educational Research, 80*(1), 71–107.

Addi-Raccah, A. & Ayalon, H. (2008). From high school to higher education: Curricular policy and postsecondary enrollment in Israel. *Educational Evaluation and Policy Analysis, 30,* 31–50.

Adler, M. (1982). *The paideia proposal: An educational manifesto.* New York: Macmillan.

Adler, M. (1990). *Reforming education: The opening of the American mind.* New York: Macmillan.

Aladjem, D., Shive, J., Fast, E. F., Herman, R., Borman, K., Katzenmeyer, W., Hess, M., & Hoffer, T. (2002). *A large-scale mixed-methods approach to studying comprehensive school reform* (available from the American Institutes for Research, 1000 Thomas Jefferson Street, NW, Washington, DC 20007).

Albjerg, P. G. (1974). *Community and class in American education, 1865–1918.* New York: John Wiley.

Alexandar, L. (1986). Chairman's summary. In *Time for results: The governor's 1991 report on education.* National Governors Association Center for Policy Research and Analysis. Washington, DC: National Governors Association.

Alexander, K., Bozick, R., & Entwise, D. (2008). Warming up, cooling out, or holding steady? Persistence and change in educational expectations after high school. *Sociology of Education, 81,* 371–396.

Alexander, K. & Cook, M. (1982). Curriculum and course-work. *American Sociological Review, 47,* 626–640.

Alexander, K. & Pallas, A. M. (1983). Private schools and public policy: New evidence on cognitive achievement in public and private schools. *Sociology of Education, 56,* 170–182.

Alexander, K. A., Entwisle, D. R., & Dauber, S. L. (1994). *On the success of failure: A reassessment of the effects of retention in the primary grades.* New York: Cambridge University Press.

Allan, E. (2010). *Policy discourses, gender and education: Constructing women's status.* New York: Routledge

Allen, W. R. (1988). Black students in U.S. higher education: Toward improved access, adjustment and achievement. *Urban Review, 20,* 165–188.

Allen, W. R. (1992). The color of success: African American college student outcomes at predominantly white and historically Black public colleges and universities. *Harvard Educational Review, 62,* 26–44.

Allen, W. R., Epps, E. G., & Haniff, N. Z. (1991). *College in Black and White: African American students in predominantly White and historically Black public universities.* Albany: State University of New York Press.

Allensworth, E., Nomi, T., Montgomery, N., & Lee, V. (2009). College preparatory curriculum for all: Academic consequences of requiring algebra and English I for ninth graders in Chicago. *Educational Evaluation and Policy Analysis, 31,* 367–391.

Allison, C. (1998). *Teachers for the new South.* New York: Peter Lang.

Almy, S., & Theokas, C. (2010). *Not prepared for class: High-poverty schools continue to have fewer in-field teachers.* Washington, DC: The Education Trust.

Altbach, P. G., Kelly, G. P., Petrie, H. G., & Weis, L. (Eds.). (1991). *Textbooks in American society: Politics, policy, and pedagogy.* Albany: State University of New York Press.

Althusser, L. (1971). Ideology and ideological state apparatuses. In *Lenin and philosophy and other essays.* New York: Monthly Review Press.

America 2000. (1991). Washington, DC: The White House.

American Association of University Women. (1992). *How schools shortchange girls.* Washington, DC: AAUW Educational Foundation and National Education Association.

American Association of University Women. (1998). *Separated by sex: A critical look at single-sex education for girls.* Washington, DC: AAUW Foundation.

American Federation of Teachers. (1998). *Building on the best, learning from what works: Six promising school-wide reform programs*. Washington, DC: Author.

American Federation of Teachers. (1999). *Improving low-performing high schools: Ideas & promising programs for high schools*. Washington, DC: Author.

American Institutes for Research. (1999). *An educator's guide to schoolwide reform*.

Amidon, E. J. & Flanders, N. A. (1971). *The role of the teacher in the classroom*. Minneapolis, MN: Paul S. Amidon and Associates.

Ancess, J. & Wichterle Ort, S. (1999). *How the coalition campus schools have re-imagined high school: Seven years later*. New York: The National Center for Restructuring Education, Schools, and Teaching, Teachers College, Columbia University.

Andersen, J. (1988). *The education of blacks in the south, 1860–1935*. Chapel Hill, NC: University of North Carolina Press.

Andersen, M. L. (1999). Restructuring for whom? Race, class, gender and the ideology of invisibility. Presidential Address, *Eastern Sociological Society*, March 5, Boston.

Antler, J. (1987). *Lucy Sprague Mitchell: The making of a modern woman*. New Haven, CT: Yale University Press.

Antler, J. & Biklen, S. K. (Eds.). (1990). *Changing education: Women as radicals and conservators*. Albany, NY: State University of New York Press.

Anyon, J. (1980). Social class and the hidden curriculum of work. *Journal of Education, 162*, 67–92.

Anyon, J. (1983). Workers, labor and economic history, and textbook content. In M. W. Apple & L. Weis (Eds.), *Ideology and practice in schooling* (pp. 37–60). Philadelphia, PA: Temple University Press.

Anyon, J. (1994a). The retreat of marxism and socialist feminism: Postmodern theories in education. *Curriculum Inquiry, 24*, 115–134.

Anyon, J. (1994b). Teacher development and reform in an inner city school. *Teachers College Record, 96*(1), 14–31.

Anyon, J. (1995a). Educational reform, theoretical categories, and the urban context. *Access: Critical Perspectives and Policy Studies in Education, 14*(1), 1–11.

Anyon, J. (1995b). Inner city school reform: Toward useful theory. *Urban Education, 30*(1), 56–70.

Anyon, J. (1997). *Ghetto schooling: A political economy of urban educational reform*. New York: Teachers College Press.

Anyon, J. (2005a). *Radical possibilities: Public policy urban education and a new social movement*. New York: Routledge.

Anyon, J. (2005b). What "counts" as educational policy? Notes toward a new paradigm. *Harvard Educational Review, 75*(1), 65–88.

Anyon, J. (2009). Progressive social movements and educational equity. *Educational Policy, 23*, 194–215.

Anyon, J. (2011). *Marx and education*. New York: Routledge.

Apple, M. W. (1978). Ideology, reproduction, and educational reform. *Comparative Educational Review, 22*(3), 367–387.

Apple, M. W. (1979a). *Ideology and curriculum*. Boston, MA: Routledge & Kegan Paul.

Apple, M. W. (1979b). The other side of the hidden curriculum: Correspondence theories and the labor process. *Journal of Education, 162*, 7–66.

Apple, M. W. (1982a). *Cultural and economic reproduction in education*. Boston, MA: Routledge & Kegan Paul.

Apple, M. W. (1982b). *Education and power*. Boston, MA: Routledge & Kegan Paul.

Apple, M. W. (1990). What reform talk does: Creating new inequalities. In S. Bacharach (Ed.), *Educational reform: Making sense of it all* (pp. 155–164). Boston, MA: Allyn & Bacon.

Apple, M. W. (1992). The text and cultural politics. *Educational Researcher, 21*(7), 4–11, 19.

Apple, M. W. (1993). *Official knowledge: Democratic education in a conservative age*. New York: Routledge.

Apple, M. W. (2004). Creating difference: Neo-liberalism, neo-conservatism and the politics of education reform. *Educational Policy, 18*, 12–44.

Apple, M. (2009). Is racism in education an accident? *Educational Policy, 23*, 651–659.

Apple, M. W. (2009). *Global crises, social justice, and education*. New York: Routledge.

Apple, M. W. & Christian-Smith, L. K. (Eds.). (1991). *The politics of the textbook*. London: Routledge.

Apple, M. W., Ball, S. J., & Armando Gandin, L. (2009). *The Routledge international handbook of the sociology of education*. New York: Routledge.

Archer, M. S. (1979). *Social origins of educational systems*. Beverly Hills, CA: Sage.

Aries, P. (1962). *Centuries of childhood: A social history of family life*. New York: Vintage Books.

Aristotle. (1943). *Politics*. New York: Modern Library.

Armor, D. (1995). *Forced justice: School desegregation and the law*. New York: Oxford University Press.

Arnot, M. (2002). *Reproducing gender: Selected critical essays on educational theory and feminist politics*. London: Falmer.

Arnot, M. (2008). *Educating the gendered citizen: Sociological engagements with national and global agendas*. Oxford: Routledge.

Arnot, M. (2012). *Gender and education*. New York: Routledge.

Arnot, M., David, M., & Weiner, G. (1999). *Closing the gender gap: Postwar education and social change*. Cambridge: Polity.

Arnot, M. & Dillabough, J. (2000) *Challenging democracy: International perspectives on gender, education and citizenship*. New York: Routledge.

Arnot, M. & Weiler, K. (Eds.). (1993). *Feminism and social justice in education*. London: Falmer.

Arnove, R. F., Altbach, P. G., & Kelly, G. P. (Eds.). (1992). *Emergent issues in education: Comparative perspectives*. Albany, NY: State University of New York Press.

Aronowitz, S. (1987/1988). Postmodernism and politics. *Social Text, 18*, 94–114.

Aronowitz, S. & Giroux, H. (1985). *Education under siege*. South Hadley, MA: Bergin and Garvey.

Aronowitz, S. & Giroux, H. (1991). *Postmodern education: Politics, culture and social criticism*. Minneapolis, MN: University of Minnesota Press.

Arons, S. (1986). *Compelling belief: The culture of American schooling*. Amherst, MA: University of Massachusetts Press.

Arrastia, L. & Hoffman, M. (2012). *Starting up: Critical lessons from 10 new schools*. New York: Teachers College Press.

Arsen, D., et al. (1999). *School choice policies in Michigan: The rules matter*. Education Policy Center at Michigan State University. www.epc.msu.edu/publications/ rules/summary.pdf.

Arthur, J. & Shapiro, A. (Eds.). (1995). *Culture wars: Multiculturalism and the politics of difference*. Boulder, CO: Westview Press.

Arum, R. & LaFree, G. (2008). Educational attainment, teacher–student ratios, and the risk of adult incarceration among U.S. birth cohorts since 1910. *Sociology of Education, 81*, 397–421.

Atkinson, P. (1981). Bernstein's structuralism. *Educational Analysis, 3*, 85–96.

Atkinson, P. (1985). *Language, structure and reproduction: An introduction to the sociology of Basil Bernstein*. London: Methuen.

Atkinson, P., Davies, B., & Delamont, S. (1995). *Discourse and reproduction: Essays in honor of Basil Bernstein*. Cresskill, NJ: Hampton Press.

Attewell, P. (2001) The winner-take-all high school: Organizational adaptations to educational stratification. *Sociology of Education, 74*, 267–296.

Attewell, P. (2001). Comment: The first and second digital divides. *Sociology of Education, 74*, 252–259.

Attewell, P. & Thurston, D. (2008). Raising the bar: Curricular intensity and academic performance. *Educational Evaluation and Policy Analysis, 30*, 51–71.

Attewell, P. & Lavin, D. (2008). *Passing the torch: Does higher education for the disadvantaged pay off across the generations?* Russell Sage Foundation.

Austin, G. R. (Ed.). (1982). *The rise and fall of national test scores*. New York: Academic Press.

Austin, G. R. & Garber, H. (Eds.). (1985). *Research on exemplary schools*. Orlando, FL: Academic Press.

Ayalon, H., Grodsky, E., Gamoran, A., & Yogev, A. (2008). Diversification and inequality in higher education: A comparison of Israel and the United States. *Sociology of Education, 81*(3), 211–241.

Bacharach, S. (1990). *Educational reform: Making sense of it all*. Boston, MA: Allyn & Bacon.

Bailyn, B. (1960). *Education in the forming of American society*. Chapel Hill, NC: University of North Carolina Press.

Baker, B. (2010a). School finance 101. Retrieved December 23, 2010 from http://schoolfinance101.wordpress.com/slide-and-data-library/

Baker, B. (2011). School finance 101. Retrieved June 8, 2012 from http://schoolfinance101.wordpress.com/slide-and-data-library/

Baker, B. & Elmer, D. (2009). The politics of off-the-shelf school finance reform. *Educational Policy, 23*, 66–105.

Baker, B. D. & Ramsey, M. J. (2010) What we don't know can't hurt us? Evaluating the equity consequences of the assumption of uniform distribution of needs in Census Based special education funding. *Journal of Education Finance, 35*(3), 245–275.

Baker, B. D. & Welner, K. G. (2010) Premature celebrations: The persistence of inter-district funding disparities. Education Policy Analysis Archives. http://epaa.asu.edu/ojs/article/viewFile/718/831

Baker, B. D. & Welner, K. (2011) School finance and courts: Does reform matter, and how can we tell? *Teachers College Record, 113*(11), 2374–2414.

Baker, D. P. (1992). The politics of American catholic school expansion, 1870–1930. In B. Fuller & R. Rubinson (Eds.), *The political construction of education* (pp. 189–206). New York: Praeger.

Baker, D. P. (1993). Compared to Japan, the U.S. is a low achiever . . . really: New evidence and comment on Westbury. *Educational Researcher, 22*, 18–26.

Baker, D. P. (1994). In comparative isolation: Why comparative research has so little influence on American sociology of education. In A. M. Pallas (Ed.), *Research in sociology of education and socialization* (Vol. 10) (pp. 53–70). Greenwich, CT: JAI Press.

Baker, D. P. & LeTendre, G. K. (2006). *National differences, global similarities*. Palo Alto, CA: Stanford.

Baker, D. P. & Riordan, C. (1998, September). The "eliting" of the common American Catholic school and national education crisis. *Phi Delta Kappan*, pp. 16–23.

Baker, D. P. & Smith, T. (1997). Three trends in the condition of education in the United States. *Teachers College Record, 99*(1), 14–18.

Baker, D. P. & Stevenson, D. L. (1986). Mothers' strategies for children's school achievement: Managing the transition to high school. *Sociology of Education*, 59, 156–166.

Baker, D. P. & Stevenson, D. L. (1991). State control of the curriculum and classroom instruction. *Comparative Education Review*, 64, 1–10.

Baker, D. P., Ethnington, C., Sosniak, L., & Westbury, I. (Eds.). (1992). *In search of more effective mathematics education: Evidence from the Second International Mathematics Study*. Norwood, NJ: Ablex.

Banks, J. A. (1988). *Multiethnic education: Theory and practice* (2nd ed.). Boston, MA: Allyn & Bacon.

Banks, J. A. (1993). Multicultural education: Historical development, dimensions, and practice. In L. Darling-Hammond (Ed.), *Review of research in education* (pp. 3–49). Washington, DC: American Educational Research Association.

Banks, J. A. & McGee Banks, C. (1995). *Handbook of research on multicultural education*. New York: Macmillan.

Banks, J. & McGee Banks, C. (2009). *Multicultural education: Issues and perspectives*. Hoboken, NJ: Wiley.

Baratz, S. S. & Baratz, J. C. (1970). Early childhood intervention: The social science base of institutional racism. *Harvard Educational Review*, 40, 29–50.

Barber, B. (1992). *An aristocracy of everyone: The politics of education and the future of America*. New York: Ballantine.

Barone, C. (2011). Some things never change: Gender segregation in higher education across eight nations and three decades. *Sociology of Education*, 84, 157–176.

Barr, J. (2004a). *A statistical portrait of New Jersey's schools*. Newark, NJ: Cornwall Center for Metropolitan Studies.

Barr, J. (2004b). *A statistical portrait of Newark's schools*. Newark, NJ: Cornwall Center for Metropolitan Studies.

Barr, R. & Dreeben, R. (1983). *How schools work*. Chicago: University of Chicago Press.

Bartlett, L. & Johnson, L. (2010). The evolution of new teacher induction policy: Support, specificity, and autonomy. *Educational Policy*, 24, 847–871.

Barton, A., Tan, E., & Rivet, A. (2008). Creating hybrid spaces for engaging school science among urban middle school girls. *American Educational Research Journal*, 45, 68–103.

Barton, P. (2003). *Parsing the achievement gap*. Princeton, NJ: Educational Testing Service.

Barton, P. (2004, November). Why does the gap still persist? *Educational Leadership*, 8–13.

Bastian, A., Fruchter, N., Gittell, M., Greer, C., & Haskins, K. (1985). *Choosing equality: The case for democratic schooling*. Philadelphia, PA: Temple University Press.

Baudrillard, J. (1981). *For a critique of the political economy of the sign* (C. Levin, Trans.). St. Louis, MO: Telos Press.

Baudrillard, J. (1984). The precession of simulacra. In B. Wallis (Ed.), *Art after modernism: Rethinking representation* (pp. 213–281). Boston, MA: David Godine.

Bayles, E. (1966). *Pragmatism in education*. New York: Harper and Row.

Beauboeuf, T. & Augustine, D. S. (1996). *Facing racism in education*. Cambridge, MA: Harvard University Press.

Beauvoir, Simone de. (1952). *The second sex* (1st American ed.). New York: Knopf.

Becker, G. (1964). *Human capital*. New York: National Bureau of Economic Research.

Becker, H. S. (1952). Social-class variations in the teacher-pupil relationship. *Journal of Educational Sociology*, 25, 451–465.

Beineke, J. (1998). *There were giants in the land: The life of William Heard Kilpatrick*. New York: Peter Lang.

Belenky, M. F., Clinchy, B. M., Goldberger, N. R., & Tarule, J. M. (1986). *Women's ways of knowing: The development of self, voice, and mind*. New York: Basic Books.

Belfield, C. R. & Levin, H. M. (2001a). *The effects of competition on educational outcomes: A review of US evidence*. National Center for the Study of Privatization in Education, Columbia University. Available at http://ncspe.org.

Belfield, C. R. (2001b). *Tuition tax credits: What do we know so far?* National Center for the Study of Privatization in Education, Columbia University. Available at http://ncspe.org.

Belfield, C. R., & Levin, H. M. (2002). The effects of competition between schools on educational outcomes: A review for the United States, 72. *Review of Education Research*, 279.

Belfield, C. & Levin, H. (2007). *The price we pay: Economic and social consequences of inadequate education*. Washington, DC: Brookings.

Bell, D. (Ed.). (1980). *Shades of brown: New perspectives on school desegregation*. New York: Teachers College Press.

Bennett, K. P. & LeCompte, M. D. (1990). *How schools work*. New York: Longman.

Bennett, P. & Lutz, A. (2009). How African American is the net black advantage? Differences in college attendance among immigrant Blacks, native Blacks, and Whites. *Sociology of Education*, 82, 70–100.

Bennett, W. (1984). *To reclaim a legacy*. Washington, DC: National Endowment for the Humanities.

Bennett, W. (1988). *James Madison High School*. Washington, DC: U.S. Office of Education.

Bensman, D. (2000). *Central park east and its graduates: Learning by heart*. New York: Teachers College Press.

Benson, L., Harkavy, I. R., & Puckett, J. L. (2007). *Dewey's dream: universities and democracies in an age of education reform: civil society, public schools, and democratic citizenship.* Philadelphia, PA: Temple University Press.

Berends, M., Bodilly, S., & Kirby, S. (2002). Looking back over a decade of whole-school reform: The experience of new American schools. *Phi Delta Kappan, 84*(2), 168–175.

Berends, M., Goldring, E., Stein, M., & Cravens, X. (2007). *Instructional conditions in charter schools and students' mathematic achievement gains.* Nashville, TN Center on School Choice, Vanderbilt University, Peabody College: National

Berends, M., Springer, M. G., & Walberg, H. J. (2007). *Charter school outcomes.* New York: Routledge.

Berends, M., Lucas, S., & Penaloza, R. (2008). How changes in families and schools are related to trends in black–white test scores. *Sociology of Education, 81*, 313–344.

Berg, I. (1970). *Education and jobs: The great training robbery.* New York: Praeger.

Berger, P. L. & Luckmann, T. (1967). *The social construction of reality: A treatise in the sociology of knowledge.* New York: Anchor Books.

Berliner, D. & Biddle, B. (1995). *The manufactured crisis.* New York: Longman.

Berman, P. & Chambliss, D. (2000). *Readiness of low-performing schools for comprehensive reform.* Washington, DC: RPP International.

Bernstein, B. (1973a). *Class, codes, and control* (Vol. 1). London: Paladin.

Bernstein, B. (1973b). *Class, codes, and control* (Vol. 2). London: Routledge & Kegan Paul.

Bernstein, B. (1977). *Class, codes, and control* (Vol. 3). London: Routledge & Kegan Paul.

Bernstein, B. (1990). *The structuring of pedagogic discourse: Volume IV: Class, codes and control.* London: Routledge.

Bernstein, B. (1996). *Pedagogy, symbolic control and identity: Theory, research, and critique.* London: Taylor & Francis.

Best, R. (1983). *We've all got scars.* Bloomington, IN: Indiana University Press.

Bestor, A. (1953). *Educational wastelands.* Urbana, IL: University of Illinois Press.

Bianchi, S. & Robinson, J. (1997). What did you do today? Children's use of time, family composition, and the acquisition of social capital. *Journal of Marriage and the Family, 59*, 332–344.

Biddle, B., Good, T., & Goodson, I. (Eds.). (1996). *International handbook of teachers and teaching.* Amsterdam: Kluwer Academic Publishers.

Bidwell, C. (1965). The school as a formal organization. In J. G. March (Ed.), *Handbook of organizations* (pp. 994–1003). Chicago: Rand McNally.

Bidwell, C. E., Plank, S., & Muller, C. (1996). Peer social networks and adolescent career development. In A. C. Kerckhoff (Ed.), *Generating social stratification: Toward a new generation of research.* Denver, CO: Westview Press.

Bifulco, R., Cobb, C. D., & Bell, C. (2009). Can interdistrict choice boost student achievement? The case of Connecticut's interdistrict magnet school program. *Educational Evaluation and Policy Analysis, 31*, 323–345

Biklen, D. (1985). *Advancing the complete school: Strategies for effective mainstreaming.* New York: Columbia University Press.

Binder, A. J. (2000). Why do some curricular challenges work while others do not? The case of three afrocentric challenges. *Sociology of Education, 73*, 69–91.

Blau, P. & Duncan, O. D. (1967). *The American occupational structure.* New York: Wiley.

Bloom, A. (1987). *The closing of the American mind.* New York: Simon & Schuster.

Bloomfield Cucchiara, M. & McNamara Horvat, E. (2009). Perils and promises: Middle-class parental involvement in urban schools. *American Educational Research Journal, 46*, 974–1004.

Blount, J. (1998). *Destined to rule the schools: Women and the superintendency.* Albany, NY: State University of New York Press.

Bluestone, B. & Harrison, B. (1982). *The de-industrialization of America.* New York: Basic Books.

Bobbitt-Zeher, D. (2007). The gender income gap and the role of education. *Sociology of Education, 80*(1), 1–22.

Boli, J. & Ramirez, F. O. (1986). World culture and the institutional development of mass education. In J. G. Richardson (Ed.), *Handbook of theory and research in the sociology of education* (pp. 65–90). Westport, CT: Greenwood Press.

Boli, J., Ramirez, F. O., & Meyer, J. W. (1985). Exploring the origins and expansion of mass education. *Comparative Education Review, 29*, 145–170.

Bolivar, J. & Chrispeels, J. (2011). Enhancing parent leadership through building social and intellectual capital. *American Educational Research Journal, 48*, 4–38.

Bond, L. A., Roeber, E., & Braskamp, D. C. (1994). *The status of statewide student assessment programs in the United States.* Washington, DC: Council of Chief State School Officers.

Booth, A. & Dunn, J. (Eds.). (1995). *Family-school links: How do they affect educational outcomes?* Hillsdale, NJ: Erlbaum.

Borman, G. D. & Dowling, N. M. (2008). Teacher attrition and retention: A meta-analytic and narrative review of the research. *Review of Educational Research, 78*(3), 367–409.

Borman, G. & Dowling, M. (2010). Schools and inequality: A multilevel analysis of Coleman's equality of educational opportunity data. *Teachers College Record, 112*(5), 1–2. www.tcrecord.org ID Number: 15664, Date Accessed: 1/31/2010.

Borman, G., Hewes, G., Overman, L., & Brown, S. (2003). Comprehensive school reform and student achievement: A meta-analysis. *Review of Educational Research, 73*(2), 125–230.

Borman, K. (1992). *The first "real" job: A study of young workers*. Albany, NY: State University of New York Press.

Borman, K. & Spring, J. (1984). *Schools in central cities*. New York: Longman.

Borman, K., Cookson, P. W., Jr., Sadovnik, A. R., & Spade, J. Z. (1996). *Implementing educational reform: Sociological perspectives on educational policy*. Norwood, NJ: Ablex.

Borman, K. and Associates. (2005). *Meaningful urban education reform: Confronting the learning crisis in mathematics and science*. Albany, NY: SUNY Press

Borman, K., Tyson, W., & Halperin, R. (2010). *Becoming an engineer in public universities: Pathways for women and minorities*. New York: Palgrave Macmillan.

Boudon, R. (1974). *Education, opportunity, and social inequality: Changing prospects in Western society*. New York: Wiley.

Bourdieu, P. (1973). Cultural reproduction and social reproduction. In R. Brown (Ed.), *Knowledge, education, and cultural change* (pp. 71–112). London: Tavistock Publications.

Bourdieu, P. (1984). *Distinction: A social critique of the judgment of taste*. Cambridge, MA: Harvard University Press.

Bourdieu, P. & Passeron, J.-C. (1977). *Reproduction: In education, society, and culture*. Beverly Hills, CA: Sage.

Bowder, D. (Ed.). (1982). *Who was who in the Greek world?* Oxford: Phaedon Press.

Bowen, W. G. & Bok, D. (1998). *The shape of the river: Long-term consequences of considering race in college and university admissions*. Princeton, NJ: Princeton University Press.

Bowles, S. (1977). Unequal education and the reproduction of the social division of labor. In J. Karabel & A. H. Halsey (Eds.), *Power and ideology in education* (pp. 137–152). New York: Oxford University Press.

Bowles, S. & Gintis, H. (1976). *Schooling in capitalist America: Educational reform and the contradictions of economic life*. New York: Basic Books.

Bowles, S. & Gintis, H. (1986). *Democracy and capitalism*. New York: Basic Books.

Boyd, D., Grossman, P., Hammemess, K., Lankford, R., Loeb, S., McDonald, M., Reininger, M., Ronfeldt, M., & Wyckoff, J. (2008). Surveying the landscape of teacher education in New York City: Constrained variation and the challenge of innovation. *Educational Evaluation and Policy Analysis, 30*, 319–343.

Boyd, D., Grossman, P., Lankford, H., Loeb, S., & Wyckoff, J. (2009). Teacher preparation and student achievement. *Educational Evaluation and Policy Analysis, 31*, 441–462.

Boyer, E. (1983). *High school*. New York: Harper and Row.

Boyer, E. (1990). The new agenda for the nation's schools. In S. Bacharach (Ed.), *Education reform: Making sense of it all* (pp. 30–38). Boston, MA: Allyn & Bacon.

Bracey, G. (1991). Why can't they be like we were? *Phi Delta Kappan, 72*, 106–121.

Braddock, J. H., II. (1990a). *Tracking: Implications for student race-ethnic subgroups*. Baltimore, MD: Johns Hopkins University, Center for Research on Effective Schooling for Disadvantaged Students.

Braddock, J. H., II. (1990b). Tracking the middle grades: National patterns of grouping for instruction. *Phi Delta Kappan, 71*, 445–449.

Braddock, J. H., II, & Dawkins, M. P. (1993). Ability grouping, aspirations, and attainments: Evidence from the national educational longitudinal study of 1988. *Journal of Negro Education, 62*, 324–336.

Braddock, J. H., II, & McPartland, J. M. (1990). Alternatives to tracking. *Educational Leadership, 47*(1), 76–79.

Braddock, J. H., II, & McPartland, J. M. (1992). *More effective education for disadvantaged students: A conceptual framework on learning environments and student motivation*. Baltimore, MD: Johns Hopkins University, Center for Research on Effective Schooling for Disadvantaged Students.

Bradley Commission. (1988). *Building a history curriculum*. Washington, DC: Educational Excellence Network.

Brameld, T. (1956). *Toward a reconstructed philosophy of education*. New York: Holt, Rinehart and Winston.

Braun, H., Jenkins, F., & Grigg, W. (2006). *A closer look at charter schools using hierarchical linear modeling*. Washington, DC: U.S. Department of Education, National Center for Education Statistics.

Brint, S. (1998). *Schools and societies*. Thousand Oaks, CA: Pine Forge Press.

Brint, S. (2006). *Schools and societies* (2nd ed.). Stanford, CA: Stanford University Press.

Brint, S. & Karabel, J. (1989). *The diverted dream: Community colleges and the promise of educational opportunity in America, 1900–1985*. New York: Oxford University Press.

Bronfennbrenner, U. (1970). *Two worlds of childhood: U.S. and U.S.S.R.* New York: Russell Sage Foundation.

Brookover, W., et al. (1979). *School social systems and student achievement: Schools can make a difference.* New York: Praeger.

Brookover, W., et al. (1982). *Creating effective schools: An inservice program for enhancing school learning climate and achievement.* Holmes Beach, FL: Learning Publications.

Brophy, J. E. & Good, T. L. (1970). Teachers' communication of differential expectations for children's classroom performance: Some behavioral data. *Journal of Educational Psychology, 61,* 365–374.

Brown, D. K. (1995). *Degrees of control: A sociology of educational expansion and occupational credentialism.* New York: Teachers College Press.

Brown, L. & Gilligan, C. (1992). *Meeting at the crossroads: Women's psychology and girls' development.* Cambridge, MA: Harvard University Press.

Bryk, A. S., Easton, J. Q., Kerbow, D., Rollow, S. G., & Sebring, P. A. (1993). *A view from the elementary schools: The state of reform in Chicago.* Chicago, IL: Consortium on Chicago School Research.

Bryk, A. S., Lee, V. E., & Holland, P. B. (1993). *Catholic schools and the common good.* Cambridge, MA: Harvard University Press.

Bryk, A. S., et al. (2010). *Organizing schools for improvement: Lessons from Chicago.* Chicago, IL: University of Chicago Press.

Buchmann, C. (2009). Gender inequalities in the transition to college. *Teachers College Record, 111*(10), 2320–2346.

Buchmann, C., DiPrete, T., & McDaniel, A. (2008). Gender inequalities in education. *The Annual Review of Sociology, 34,* 319–337.

Budoff, M. (1975). Engendering change in special education practices. *Harvard Educational Review, 45*(4). In T. Hehir & T. Latus (Eds.). (1992). *Special education at the century's end: Evolution of theory and practice since 1970* (pp. 69–88). Cambridge, MA: Harvard Educational Review.

Bulkley, K. & Fisher J. (2002). *A decade of charter schools: From theory to practice.* Consortium for Policy Research in Education. Available at www.cpre.org.

Bulkley, K. E., Henig, J. R., & Levin, H. M. (2010). *Between public and private: Politics, governance, and the new portfolio models for urban school reform.* Cambridge, MA: Harvard Education Press.

Bulkley, K. & Wohlstetter (Eds.). (2004). *Taking account of charter schools: What's happened and what's next.* New York: Teachers College Press.

Bulman R. C. & Kirp, D. L. (1999). The shifting politics of school choice. In Sugarman, S. D., & Kemerer, F. R. (Eds.), *School choice and social controversy: Politics, policy and law.* (pp. 36–67). Brookings Institution Press.

Burbules, N. & Rice, S. (1991). Dialogue across differences: Continuing the conversation. *Harvard Educational Review, 67*(4), 393–416.

Burbules, N. & Rice, S. (1992). Can we be heard? A reply to Leach. *Harvard Educational Review, 62*(2), 264–271.

Burris, B. (1983a). *No room at the top.* New York: Praeger.

Burris, V. (1983b, August). The social and political consequences of overeducation. *American Sociological Review, 48,* 454–467.

Buss, W. G. (1999). Teachers, teachers' unions, and school choice. In S. D. Sugarman & F. R. Kemerer (Eds.), *School choice and social controversy: Politics, policy and law* (pp. 300–331). Washington, DC: Brookings Institution Press.

Button, W. H. & Provenzano, E. E. (1989). *History of education and culture in America.* Englewood Cliffs, NJ: Prentice-Hall.

Butts, R. F. (1978). *Public education in the United States: From revolution to reform.* New York: Holt, Rinehart and Winston.

Butts, R. F. & Cremin, L. A. (1953). *A history of education in American culture.* New York: Holt.

Callahan, R. E. (1962). *Education and the cult of efficiency.* Chicago, IL: University of Chicago Press.

Campaign for Fiscal Equity. A brief history of the lawsuit. www.cfequity.org/static.php?page=history oflawsuit&category=resources. Accessed October 1, 2012.

Canada, K. & Pringle, R. (1995). The role of gender in college classroom interactions: A social context approach. *Sociology of Education, 68*(3), 161–186.

Carl, J. (1994). Parental choice as national policy in England and the United States. *Comparative Education Review, 38*(3), 294–322.

Carnegie Task Force on Teaching as a Profession. (1986). *A nation prepared: Teachers for the 21st century.* Washington, DC: Carnegie Forum on Education and the Economy.

Carnoy, M. (1974). *Education as cultural imperialism.* New York: McKay.

Carnoy, M. (Ed.). (1975). *Schooling in a corporate society.* New York: McKay.

Carnoy, M. (2001). *School vouchers: Examining the evidence.* Washington, DC: Economic Policy Institute.

Carnoy, M. & Levin, H. (Eds.). (1976). *The limits of educational reform.* New York: Longman.

Carnoy, M. & Levin, H. (1985). *Schooling and work in the democratic state.* Stanford, CA: Stanford University Press.

Carnoy, M., Jacobsen, R., Mishel, L., & Rothstein, R. (2005). *The charter school dust-up: Examining the evidence on enrollment and achievement.* New York: Teachers College Press.

Cannata, M. (2011). The role of social networks in the teacher job search process. *The Elementary School Journal, 111*(3), 477–500.

Carbonaro, W. & Covay, E. (2010). School sector and student achievement in the era of standards based reforms. *Sociology of Education, 83,* 160–182.

Carpenter, P. (1985). Single-sex schooling and girls' academic achievements. *Australian and New Zealand Journal of Sociology, 21*, 456–472.

Carpenter, P. & Hayden, M. (1987). Girls' academic achievements: Single-sex versus coeducational schools in Australia. *Sociology of Education, 60*, 156–167.

Carter, S. M. (2000). *No excuses: Lessons from 21 high-performing, high-poverty schools.* Washington, DC: The Heritage Foundation.

Catsambis, S. (1994). The path to math: Gender and racial-ethnic differences in mathematics participation from middle school to high school. *Sociology of Education, 67*, 199–215.

Catsambis, S., Jordan, W. J., & McPartland, J. M. (1994). *Effects of program and course tracking on high school students' behaviors, attitudes, and aspirations.* Baltimore, MD: Johns Hopkins University, Center for Social Organization of Schools.

Cavallo, D. (1981). *Muscles and morals: Organized playgrounds and urban reform, 1880–1920.* Philadelphia, PA: University of Pennsylvania Press.

Cavallo, D. (1999). *A fiction of the past: The sixties in America history.* New York: St. Martin's Press.

Center for Education Reform. (2005). *About charter schools.* Retrieved April 6, 2006 from www.edreform.com/charterschools/

Center for Policy Research on Education (CPRE). (2000). *Assessment and accountability systems: 50 state profiles.* Philadelphia, PA: CPRE, University of Pennsylvania.

Center for Research on Educational Outcomes (CREDO) (2009a). National Charter School Study. Palo Alto, CA: Stanford. http://credo.stanford.edu/ Accessed December 25, 2009.

Center for Research on Educational Outcomes (CREDO) (2009b). The Hoxby-CREDO debates. Palo Alto, CA: Stanford. Posted on http://credo.stanford.edu/ Accessed August 18, 2010.

Center on Education Policy. (2004). *From the capital to the classroom: Year 2 of the No Child Left Behind Act.* www.cep.dc.org/displayDocument.cfm?DocumentID=299. Accessed October 1, 2012.

Center on Organization and Restructuring of Schools. (1995). *Bibliography on school restructuring.* Madison, WI: University of Wisconsin-Madison, Wisconsin Center for Education Research.

Chabbot, C. & Ramirez, F. O. (2000). Development and education. In M. T. Hallinan (Ed.), *Handbook of sociology of education.* New York: Kluwer, 2000.

Chall, J. S., Jacobs, V. A., & Baldwin, L. E. (1990). *The reading crisis: Why poor children fall behind.* Cambridge, MA: Harvard University Press.

Chambliss, J. J. (Ed.). (1996). *Philosophy of education: An encyclopedia.* New York: Garland.

Charner, I. (1996). School-to-work opportunities: Prospects and challenges. In K. Borman, P. W. Cookson, Jr., A. R. Sadovnik, & J. Z. Spade (Eds.), *Implementing educational reform: Sociological perspectives on educational policy* (pp. 139–170). Norwood, NJ: Ablex.

Chenoworth, K. (2009). *How it's being done: Urgent lessons from unexpected schools.* Harvard Education Press.

Cherryholmes, C. (1988). *Power and criticism: Post-structural investigations in education.* New York: Teachers College Press.

Childs, J. L. (1931). *Education and the philosophy of experimentalism.* New York: Century.

Chubb, J. E. (2003). Real choice. In Paul E. Peterson (Ed.), *Our schools our future . . . Are we still at risk?* (pp. 329–362), Stanford, CA: Hoover Institution.

Chubb, J. E. & Moe, T. M. (1990). *Politics, markets, and America's schools.* Washington, DC: Brookings Institution.

Chudgar, A. and Luschei, T. F. (2009). National income, income inequality, and the importance of schools: A hierarchical cross-national comparison. *American Educational Research Journal, 46*, 626–658.

Cicourel, A. V. & Kitsuse, J. I. (1963). *The educational decision-makers.* New York: Bobbs-Merrill.

The Civil Rights Project, Harvard University. (2002). *The impact of racial and ethnic diversity on educational outcomes: Cambridge, MA School District,* www.civilrightsproject.harvard.edu/research/diversity/cambridge_diversity.php. Accessed October 1, 2012.

Clark, B. (1962). *Educating the expert society.* San Francisco, CA: Chandler.

Clark, R. (1983). *Family life and school achievement: Why poor black children succeed or fail.* Chicago, IL: University of Chicago Press.

Coburn, C. E. & Russell, J. L. (2008). District policy and teachers' social networks. *Educational Evaluation and Policy Analysis, 30*, 203–235.

Cochran, M. (2011). International perspectives on early childhood education. *Educational Policy, 25*, 65–91.

Cochran-Smith, M., Shakman, K., Jong, C., Terrell, D. G., Barnatt, J., & McQuillan, P. (2009). Good and just teaching: The case for social justice in teacher education. *American Journal of Education, 115*(3), 347.

Cohen, D., Raudenbush, S., & Ball, D. (2001). Resources, instruction, and research. In R. Boruch & F. Mosteller (Eds.), *Evidence matters: Randomized trials in education research.* Washington, DC: The Brookings Institution.

Cohen, D. K. (1995). What standards for national standards? *Phi Delta Kappan, 76*, 751–757.

Cohen, D. K., McLaughlin, M. W., & Talbert, J. E. (Eds.). (1993). *Teaching for understanding: Challenges for policy and practice.* San Francisco, CA: Jossey-Bass.

Cohen, E. G. (1994a). *Designing groupwork: Strategies for the heterogeneous classroom.* New York: Teachers College Press.

Cohen, E. G. (1994b). Restructuring the classroom: Conditions for productive small groups. *Review of Educational Research, 64,* 1–35.

Cohen, E. G., Lotan, R., & Leechor, C. (1989). Can classrooms learn? *Sociology of Education, 62,* 75–94.

Coleman, J. S. (1961). *The adolescent society.* Glencoe, IL: The Free Press.

Coleman, J. S. (1965). *Adolescents and the schools.* New York: Basic Books.

Coleman, J. S. (1990). *Foundations of social theory.* Cambridge, MA: The Belknap Press of Harvard University Press.

Coleman, J. S., et al. (1966). *Equality of educational opportunity.* Washington, DC: U.S. Government Printing Office.

Coleman, J. S. & Hoffer, T. (1987). *Public and private schools: The impact of communities.* New York: Basic Books.

Coleman, J., Hoffer, T., & Kilgore, S. (1982). *High school achievement: Public, catholic, and private schools compared.* New York: Basic Books.

Collegeboard. (2012). 8th Annual AP Report to the Nation. New York.

Collins, R. (1971). Functional and conflict theories of educational opportunity. *Harvard Educational Review, 38,* 7–32.

Collins, R. (1975). *Conflict sociology: Toward an explanatory science.* New York: Academic Press.

Collins, R. (1979). *The credential society.* New York: Academic Press.

Comer, J. (1988). Educating poor minority children. *Scientific American, 259*(5), 42–48.

Comer, J. (1996). *Rallying the whole village: The Comer process for reforming education.* New York: Teachers College Press.

Comer, J. (1993). The Yale school development program: Process, outcomes and policy implications. *Urban Education, 28,* 166–199.

Comer, J. & Haynes, N. M. (1991). Parent involvement in schools: An ecological approach. *Elementary School Journal, 91,* 271–277.

Conley, D. (2001). Capital for college: Parental assets and postsecondary schooling. *Sociology of Education, 74,* 59–71.

Connell, N. (1999). *Beating the odds: High-achieving elementary schools in high-poverty neighborhoods.* New York: Educational Priorities Panel.

Connell, R. W. (1993). Disruptions: Improper masculinities and schooling. In L. Weis & M. Fine (Eds.), *Beyond silenced voices* (pp. 191–208). Albany, NY: State University of New York Press.

Consoletti, A. (2012). Charter School Laws Across the States 2012. Center for Education Reform.

Cook, T. (2002). Randomized experiments in education: Why are they so rare? *Educational Evaluation and Policy Analysis, 24*(3), 175–200.

Cookson, P. W., Jr. (1989). United States of America: Contours of continuity and controversy in private schools. In G. Walford (Ed.), *Private schools in ten countries: Policy and practice.* London: Routledge.

Cookson, P. W., Jr. (1991). Politics, markets, and America's schools: A review. *Teacher College Record, 93,* 156–160.

Cookson, P. W., Jr. (1992). *The choice controversy.* Newbury Park, CA: Corwin Press.

Cookson, P. W., Jr. (1994). *School choice: The struggle for the soul of American education.* New Haven, CT: Yale University Press.

Cookson, P. W., Jr. (1995, Spring). Goals 2000: Framework for the new educational federalism. *Teachers College Record, 96*(3), 405–417.

Cookson, P. W., Jr. (2011). *Sacred trust: A children's education bill of rights.* Thousand Oaks, CA: Corwin.

Cookson, P. W., Jr. & Persell, C. H. (1985). *Preparing for power: America's elite boarding schools.* New York: Basic Books.

Cookson, P. W., Jr., Persell, C. H., & Catsambis, S. (1992). Differential asset conversion: Class and gendered pathways to selective colleges. *Sociology of Education, 65,* 208–225.

Cookson, P. W., Jr., Sadovnik, A. R., & Semel, S. F. (Eds.). (1992). *International handbook of educational reform.* Westport, CT: Greenwood Press.

Coons, J. E. (2001). Rescuing school choice from its friends. *America, 7,* 185.

Cooper, R. & Jordan, W. (2003). Cultural issues in comprehensive school reform. *Urban Education, 38*(4), 380–397.

Corburn, J., Osleeb J., & Porter, M. (2006). Urban asthma and the neighborhood environment in New York City, *Health Place, 12,* 167–179.

Corwin, R. (1970). *Militant professionalism: A study of organizational conflict in high schools.* New York: Appleton-Century-Crofts.

Counts, G. S. (1932). *Dare the schools build a new social order?* New York: John Day.

Cowen, J. (2010). Who chooses, who refuses? Learning more from students who decline private school vouchers. *Working Paper,* University of Kentucky.

Cremin, L. A. (1961). *The transformation of the school.* New York: Vintage Books.

Cremin, L. A. (1972). *American education: The colonial experience, 1607–1783.* New York: Harper and Row.

Cremin, L. A. (1977). *Traditions of American education.* New York: Basic Books.

Cremin, L. A. (1980). *American education: The national experience, 1783–1876.* New York: Harper and Row.

Cremin, L. A. (1988). *American education: The metropolitan experience, 1876–1980.* New York: Harper and Row.

Cremin, L. A. (1990). *Popular education and its discontents.* New York: Harper and Row.

Cronin, J. (2011). *Reforming Boston schools, 1930–2006: Overcoming corruption and racial segregation*. New York: Palgrave.

Crosnoe, R. & Cooper, C. (2010). Economically disadvantaged children's transitions into elementary school: Linking family processes, school contexts, and educational policy. *American Educational Research Journal, 47*, 258–291.

Cross, C. T. (2004). *Political education: National policy comes of age*. New York: Teachers College Press.

Crul, M. & Holdaway, J. (2009). Children of immigrants in schools in New York and Amsterdam: The factors shaping attainment. *Teachers College Record, 111*(6), 1476–1507.

Cuban, L. (1983, June). Effective schools: A friendly but cautionary note. *Phi Delta Kappan, 64*, 695–696.

Cuban, L. (1984). *How teachers taught: Constancy and change in American classrooms, 1890–1980*. New York: Longman.

Cuban, L. (1990a). Reforming again, again, and again. *Educational Researcher, 19*(1), 3–13.

Cuban, L. (1990b). Why do some reforms persist? In S. Bacharach (Ed.), *Education reform: Making sense of it all*. Boston, MA: Allyn & Bacon.

Cuban, L. (2010). *As good as it gets: What school reform brought to Austin*. Cambridge, MA: Harvard University Press.

Cubberly, E. P. (1934). *Public education in the United States: A study and interpretation of American educational history*. Boston, MA: Houghton Mifflin.

Cucchiara, M. & Horvat, E. (2009). Perlis and promises: Middle-class parental involvement in urban schools. *American Educational Research Journal, 46*, 943–973.

Cuffaro, H. K. (1995). *Experimenting with the world*. New York: Teachers College Press.

Cummins, J. (1993). Empowering minority students: A framework for intervention. In L. Weis & M. Fine (Eds.), *Beyond silenced voices: Class, race, and gender in United States schools* (pp. 101–118). Albany, NY: State University of New York Press.

Curti, M. (1959/1971). *The social ideas of American educators*. Totowa, NJ: Littlefield, Adams & Company.

Cusick, P. A. (1983). *The egalitarian ideal and the American high school*. New York: Longman.

D'Souza, D. (1991). *Illiberal education: The politics of race and sex on campus*. New York: The Free Press.

Dahl, R. A. (1961). *Who governs?* New Haven, CT: Yale University Press.

Darling-Hammond, L. (1984). *Beyond the commission reports: The coming crisis in teaching*. Santa Monica, CA: Rand.

Darling-Hammond, L. (1992). *Standards of practice for learner-centered schools*. New York: National Center for Restructuring Schools and Teaching.

Darling-Hammond, L. (1996a). The right to learn and the advancement of teaching: Research, policy, and practice for democratic education. *Peabody Journal of Education, 67*(3), 123–154.

Darling-Hammond, L. (1996b). Restructuring schools for high performance. In S. Fuhrman & J. O'Day (Eds.), *Rewards and reforms: Creating educational incentives that work* (pp. 144–194). San Francisco, CA: Jossey-Bass.

Darling-Hammond, L. (1997). *The right to learn: A blueprint for creating schools that work*. San Francisco, CA: Jossey-Bass.

Darling-Hammond, L. (2004). Inequality and the right to learn: Access to qualified teachers in California's public schools. *Teachers College Record, 106*(10), 1936–1966.

Darling-Hammond, L. (2010). *The flat world and education: How America's commitment to equity will determine our future*. New York: Teachers College Press.

Darling-Hammond, L. with Bransford, J. (Eds.). (2005). *Preparing teachers for a changing world: What teachers should learn and be able to do*. San Francisco, CA: Jossey-Bass.

Darling-Hammond, L. with Snowden, J. (Eds.). (2005). *A good teacher in every classroom: Preparing the highly qualified teachers our children deserve*. San Francisco, CA: Jossey-Bass.

Darling-Hammond, L., Ancess, J., & Falk, B. (1995). *Authentic assessment in action: Studies of schools and students at work*. New York: Teachers College Press.

Darling-Hammond, L., Berry, B., & Thoreson, A. (2001). Does teacher certification matter? Evaluating the evidence. *Educational Evaluation and Policy Analysis, 23* (1), 57–77.

Darling-Hammond, L., Holtzman, D. J., Gatlin, S. J., & Vasquez-Helig, J. V. (2005). *Does teacher preparation matter? Evidence about teacher certification, Teach for America, and teacher effectiveness*. Palo Alto, CA: Stanford University. Downloaded from www.schooldesign.net/binaries/(teachercert.pdf on May 27, 2005.

Darwin, C. (1982). *On the origin of the species*. New York: Penguin. (Original work published 1859)

Datnow, A., & Hubbard, L. (2002). *Gender in policy and practice*. New York: Routledge/Falmer.

Datnow, A., & Stringfield, S. (2000). Working together for reliable school reform. *Journal of Education for Students Placed at Risk, 5*(1&2), 183–204.

Datnow, A., Borman, G., Stringfield, S., Overman, L., & Castellano, M. (2003). Comprehensive school reform in culturally and linguistically diverse contexts: Implementation and outcomes from a four-year study. *Educational Evaluation and Policy Analysis, 25*(2), 25–54.

Dauber, S. L., & Epstein, J. L. (1993). Parents' attitudes and practices of involvement in inner-city elementary and middle schools. In N. Chavkin (Ed.), *Families and schools in a pluralistic society* (pp. 53–71). Albany, NY: State University of New York Press.

Davies, S. (1995). Leaps of faith: Shifting currents in critical sociology of education. *American Journal of Sociology, 100*(6), 1448–1478.

Davies, S. and Quirke. L. (2007). The impact of sector on school organizations: The logics of markets and institutions. *Sociology of Education, 80*(1), 66–89.

Davis, L. J. (2010). *The disability studies reader.* New York: Routledge.

de Beauvoir, S. (1989). *The second sex.* New York: Random House. (Original work published 1952).

Debray-Pelot, E. & McGuinn, P. (2009). The new politics of education: Analyzing the federal education policy landscape in the post-nclb era. *Educational Policy, 23*, 15–42.

Decker, P., Mayer, D. P., & Glazerman, S. (2004). *The effects of Teach for America on students: Evidence from a national evaluation.* Princeton, NJ: Mathematica.

Delamont, S. (1983). *Interaction in the classroom.* London: Routledge.

Delamont, S. (1989). *Knowledgeable women: Structuralism and the reproduction of elites.* New York: Routledge & Kegan Paul.

Delamont, S. (1990). *Sex roles and the school* (2nd ed.). London: Routledge.

Delamont, S. (1991). The hit list and other horror stories. *Sociological Review, 39*(2), 238–259.

DelFattore, J. (1992). *What Johnny shouldn't read: Textbook censorship in America.* New Haven, CT: Yale University Press.

Delpit, L. (1995). *Other people's children.* New York: The New Press.

Derrida, J. (1981). *Positions.* Chicago, IL: University of Chicago Press.

Derrida, J. (1982). *Of grammatology.* Baltimore, MD: Johns Hopkins University Press.

Deutsch, M., and Associates (1964). *The disadvantaged child.* New York: Basic Books.

Dewey, J. (1897). My pedagogic creed. In M. S. Dworkin (Ed.), *Dewey on education* (pp. 19–32). New York: Teachers College Press.

Dewey, J. (1899). The school and society. In M. S. Dworkin (Ed.), *Dewey on education* (pp. 33–90). New York: Teachers College Press.

Dewey, J. (1902). The child and the curriculum. In M. S. Dworkin (Ed.), *Dewey on education* (pp. 91–111). New York: Teachers College Press.

Dewey, J. (1916). *Democracy and education: An introduction to the philosophy of education.* New York: Macmillan.

Dewey, J. (1927/1984). *The public and its problems.* In *John Dewey: The later works. Vol. 2: 1925–1927.* Carbondale and Edwardsville: Southern Illinois University Press. (Original work published 1927).

Dewey, J. (1938). *Experience and education.* New York: Macmillan.

Diamond, J. B. (2007). Where the rubber meets the road: Rethinking the connection between high-stakes testing policy and classroom instruction. *Sociology of Education, 80*(4), 285–313.

Dillabough, J., McLeod, J., & Mills, M. (2010). *Troubling gender in education.* New York: Routledge.

DiMaggio, P. (1982, April). Cultural capital and school success: The impact of status culture participation on the grades of U.S. high school students. *American Sociological Review, 47*, 189–201.

DiMaggio, P., & Mohr, J. (1984). Cultural capital, educational attainment, and marital selection. *American Journal of Sociology, 90*(6), 1231–1261.

Dobbie, W. & Fryer, R. (2011). Are high-quality schools enough to increase achievement among the poor? Evidence from the Harlem Children's Zone. *American Economic Journal*, 158–187.

Domhoff, G. W. (1967). *Who rules America?* Englewood Cliffs, NJ: Prentice-Hall.

Domhoff, G. W. (1983). *Who rules America now?* Englewood Cliffs, NJ: Prentice-Hall.

Domina, T., Conley, A., & Farkas, G. (2011). The link between educational expectations and effort in the college-for-all era. *Sociology of Education, 84*, 93–112.

Domina, T., Conley, A., & Farkas, G. (2011). The case for dreaming big. *Sociology of Education, 84*, 118–121.

Donaldson, M. & Johnson, S. (2010). The price of misassignment: The role of teaching assignments in teach for America teachers' exit from low-income schools and the teaching profession. *Educational Evaluation and Policy Analysis, 32*, 299–323.

Doran, B. & Weffer, W. (1992). Immigrant aspirations, high school process and academic outcomes. *American Education Research Journal, 29*(1), 163–181.

Dougherty, J., Harrelson, J., Maloney, L., Murphy, D., Smith, R., Snow, M., & Zannoni, D. (2009). School choice in suburbia: Test scores, race, and housing markets. *American Journal of Education, 115*, 523–548.

Dougherty, K. (1987, April). The effects of community colleges: Aid or hindrance to socioeconomic attainment? *Sociology of Education, 60*, 86–103.

Dougherty, K. (1988, Summer). Educational policymaking and the relative autonomy of the state: The case of occupational education in the community college. *Sociological Forum, 3*, 400–432.

Dougherty, K. (1990). *Quality, equality, and politics: The political sources of the current school reform wave*. Paper presented at the Annual Meeting of the American Sociological Association.

Dougherty, K. (1994). *The contradictory college: The conflicting origins, impacts, and futures of the community college*. Albany, NY: State University of New York Press.

Dougherty, K. (1996). Opportunity-to-learn standards: A sociological critique. *Sociology of Education*, Extra Issue (Special Issue on Sociology and Educational Policy: Bringing Scholarship and Practice Together), 40–65.

Dougherty, K. & Hammack, F. (1990). *Education and society*. New York: Harcourt Brace Jovanovich.

Dougherty, K. & Sostre, L. (1992). Minerva and the market: The sources of the movement for school choice. *Educational Policy*, 6, 160–179.

Downey, D. B. (2008). Black/white differences in school performance: The oppositional culture explanation. *Annual Review of Sociology*, *34*, 107–126.

Downey, D., Ainsworth, J., & Qian, Z. (2009). Rethinking the attitude-achievement paradox among blacks. *Sociology of Education*, 82, 1–19.

Downey, D. B., von Hippel, P., & Broh, B. (2004). Are schools the great equalizer? Cognitive inequality during the summer months and the school year. *American Sociological Review*, 69, 613–635.

Downey, D., Hippel, P., & Hughes, M. (2008). Are "failing" schools really failing? Using seasonal comparison to evaluate school effectiveness. *Sociology of Education*, 81, 242–270.

Dreeben, R. (1968). *On what is learned in school*. Boston, CA: Addison-Wesley.

Dreeben, R. (1994). The sociology of education: Its development in the United States. *Research in Sociology of Education and Socialization*, 10.

Dreeben, R. & Gamoran, A. (1986). Race, instruction, and learning. *American Sociological Review*, *51*, 660–669.

Dronkers, J. & Robert, P. (2008). Differences in scholastic achievement of public, private government-dependent, and private independent schools: A cross-national analysis. *Educational Policy*, 22, 541–577.

Dryfoos, J. G. (1994). *Full service schools: A revolution in health and social services for children, youth, and families*. San Francisco, CA: Jossey-Bass.

Dryfoos, J. (1998). *Full service schools: A revolution in health and social services for children, youth, and families*. San Francisco, CA: Jossey-Bass.

Dryfoos, J. G., Quinn, J., & Barkin, C. (2005). *Community schools in action: lessons from a decade of practice*. Oxford ; New York: Oxford University Press.

Du Bois, W. E. B. (1935). Does the negro need separate schools? *Journal of Negro Education, 4*, 328–335.

Dumais, S. A. (2002). Cultural capital, gender, and school success: The role of habitus. *Sociology of Education*, 77, 44–68.

Duncan, G. & Murnane, R. (2011). *Whither opportunity?: Rising inequality, schools, and children's life chances*. New York: Russell Sage Foundation.

Durkheim, E. (1947). *The division of labor in society*. Glencoe, IL: The Free Press. (Original work published 1893).

Durkheim, E. (1954). *The elementary forms of religious life*. Glencoe, IL: The Free Press. (Original work published 1915).

Durkheim, E. (1956). *Education and sociology* (S. D. Fox, Trans.). New York: The Free Press.

Durkheim, E. (1962). *Moral education: A study of the theory and application of the sociology of education*. New York: The Free Press.

Durkheim, E. (1965). *The elementary forms of the religious life*. New York: The Free Press.

Durkheim, E. (1938/1977). *The evolution of educational thought* (P. Collins, Trans.). London: Routledge & Kegan Paul. (Original work published 1938).

Dworkin, A. G. (1985). *When teachers give up: Teacher burnout, teacher turnover, and their impact on children*. Austin, TX: Hogg Foundation for Mental Health and Texas Press.

Dworkin, A. G. (1987). *Teacher burnout in the public schools: Structural causes and consequences for children*. Albany, NY: State University of New York Press.

Dworkin, A. G., Haney, C. A., Dworkin, R. J., & Telschow, R. L. (1990). Stress and illness behavior among urban public school teachers. *Educational Administration Quarterly*, 26, 59–71.

Dworkin, M. S. (Ed.). (1959). *Dewey on education*. New York: Teachers College Press.

Eder, D. (1981, July). Ability grouping as a self-fulfilling prophecy: A micro-analysis of teacher-student interaction. *Sociology of Education*, 54, 151–162.

Eder, D. (1995). *School talk*. New Brunswick, NJ: Rutgers University Press.

Eder, D. & Parker, S. (1987). The cultural reproduction of gender: The effect of extracurricular activities on peer-group culture. *Sociology of Education*, 60, 200–213.

Edmonds, R. (1979a). Effective schools for the urban poor. *Educational Leadership*, *37*(1), 5–24.

Edmonds, R. (1979b, March-April). Some schools work and more can. *Social Policy*, 28–32.

Edmonds, R. (1982). Programs of school improvement: An overview. *Educational Leadership*, 40, 4–11.

Education Commission of the States. (1983). *Action for excellence: A comprehensive plan to improve our nation's schools*. Denver, CO: Author. (ERIC ED 235 588).

Education Commission of the States. (2004). *ECS report to the nation: State implementation of No Child Left Behind.* Denver, CO: Education Commission of the States.

Education Equality Project. (2010). *What We Stand For: Our Mission.* www.educationequalityproject. org/what_we_stand_for/our_mission. Accessed April 1, 2010.

Education Law Center. (1996). *Wiping out disadvantages: The programs and services needed to supplement regular education for poor school children.* Newark, NJ: Author.

Education Law Center. (1998). *Transforming teaching and learning in special needs districts.* Newark, NJ: Education Law Center.

Education Law Center. (2005). *Abbott indicators report.* Newark, NJ: Education Law Center.

Education Law Center. (2010). *History of Abbott.* www.edlawcenter.org/ELCPublic/AbbottvBurke/ AbbottHistory.htm. Accessed April 1, 2010.

Education Trust. (1998). *Good teaching matters: How well-qualified teachers can close the gap.* Washington, DC: Author.

Education Trust. (2003). *Telling the whole truth (or not) about highly qualified teachers:* New state data. Washington, DC: Author.

Education Trust. (2004a). *Education watch: The nation.* Washington, DC: Author.

Education Trust. (2004b). *Education watch: Achievement gap summary tables.* Washington, DC: Author.

Education Trust. (2005). *Increasing achievement and closing gaps between groups.* Washington DC: Author. www.2.edtrust.org/EdTrust/Product+ Catalog/recent+ presentations.htm. Accessed June 2, 2005.

Education Trust. (2007). *It's being done: Academic success in unexpected schools.* Washington, D.C.: The Education Trust.

Education Trust. (2009). *How it's being done: Urgent lessons from unexpected schools.* Washington, DC: The Education Trust.

Education Trust. (2009). *Education watch: National report.* Washington, DC

Education Trust (2010a). *Education watch: The nation.* Washington, DC: The Education Trust.

Education Trust. (2010b). *Education watch: Achievement gap summary tables.* Washington, DC: The Education Trust.

Education Trust. (2010c). *Achievement in America: How are we doing? What comes next?* Washington, DC: The Education Trust, www.edtrust.org/dc/ resources/presentations. Accessed April 1, 2010.

Education Trust. (2010d). *Close the hidden funding gaps in our schools.* Washington, DC: The Education Trust, www.edtrust.org/dc/publication/close-the-hidden-funding-gaps-in-our-schools. Accessed April 1, 2010.

Education Week. (2000). *Lessons of a century: A nation's schools comes of age.* Bethesda, MD: Author.

Education Week. (2005). No small change: Targeting money toward student performance. Quality counts, 2005. Bethesda, MD: *Education Week, 24,* 17.

Educational Priorities Panel. (1987). *A teacher for the apple: Why New York City can't staff its schools.* New York: Author.

Egan, K. (1992). Review of *The unschooled mind: How children think and how schools should teach,* by Howard Gardner. *Teachers College Record, 94*(2), 397–406.

Eisenmann, L. (1998). *Historical dictionary of women's education.* Westport, CT: Greenwood Press.

Eisner, E. W. (1995). Standards for American schools: Help or hindrance? *Phi Delta Kappan, 78,* 758–764.

Ellsworth, E. (1989). Why doesn't this feel empowering? Working through the repressive myths of critical pedagogy. *Harvard Educational Review, 59*(3), 297–324.

Elmore, R. F. (1990). *Reconstructing schools: The next generation of educational reform.* San Francisco, CA: Jossey-Bass.

Elmore, R. F. (1993). School decentralization: Who gains? Who loses? In J. Hannaway & M. Carnoy (Eds.), *Decentralization and school improvement: Can we fulfill the promise?* San Francisco, CA: Jossey-Bass.

Elmore, R. F. (1994a). *Educational renewal: Better teachers, better schools.* San Francisco, CA: Jossey-Bass.

Elmore, R. F. (1994b, December). Thoughts on program equity: Productivity and incentives for performance in education. *Educational Policy, 8*(4), 453–459.

Elmore, R. F. (2004). *School reform from the inside out: Policy, practices and performance.* Cambridge, MA: Harvard.

Ensminger, M. E. & Slusarcick, A. L. (1992). Paths to high school graduation or dropout: A longitudinal study of a first-grade cohort. *Sociology of Education, 65,* 95–113.

Entwisle, D. R. & Alexander, K. (1992). Summer setback: Race, poverty, school composition, a mathematics achievement in the first 2 years of school. *American Sociological Review, 57,* 72–84.

Entwisle, D. R., Alexander, K., & Gordon, L. S. (1997). *Children, schools and inequality.* Boulder, CO: Westview.

Entwisle, D. R., Alexander, K. L., & Olson, L. S. (2007). Early schooling: The handicap of being poor and male. *Sociology of Education, 80*(2), April 2007, 114–138.

Epstein, C. F. (1990). *Deceptive distinctions: Sex, gender and the social order.* New Haven, CT: Yale University Press.

Epstein, J. (2001). *School, family and community partnerships: Preparing educators and improving schools.* Boulder, CO: Westview.

Epstein, J. L. (1986). Parents' reactions to teacher practices of parent involvement. *The Elementary School Journal, 86,* 277–294.

Epstein, J. L. (1987). Toward a theory of family-school connections: Teacher practices and parent involvement. In K. Hurrelmann, F. Kaufmann, & F. Losel (Eds.), *Social intervention: Potential and constraints* (pp. 121–136). New York: DeGruyter.

Epstein, J. L. (1990). School and family connections: Theory, research, and implications for integrating sociologies of education and family. In D. Unger & M. Sussman (Eds.), *Families in community settings: Interdisciplinary perspectives* (pp. 99–126). New York: Haworth Press.

Epstein, J. L. (1991a). Effects on student achievement of teacher practices of parent involvement. In S. Silvern (Ed.), *Advances in reading/language research, Vol. 5. Literacy through family, community and school interaction.* Greenwich, CT: JAI Press.

Epstein, J. L. (1991b, January). Paths to partnership: What we can learn from federal, state, district, and school initiatives. *Phi Delta Kappan, 72*(5), 344–349.

Epstein, J. L. (1992). School and family partnerships. In M. Alkin (Ed.), *Encyclopedia of educational research* (6th ed.) (pp. 1139–1151). New York: Macmillan.

Epstein, J. L. (1995). School/family/community partnerships: Caring for the children we share. *Phi Delta Kappan, 76,* 701–712.

Epstein, J. L., Sanders, M. G., Simon, B. S., Salinas, K. C, Jansorn, N. R., & Van Voorhis, F. L. (2002). *School, family, and community partnerships: Your handbook for action* (2nd ed.). Thousand Oaks, CA: Corwin.

Erickson, D. (1986). Choice and private schools: Dynamics of supply and demand. In D. C. Levy (Ed.), *Private education: Studies in choice and public policy* (pp. 82–109). New York: Oxford University Press.

Erickson, F. (1987). Transformation and school success: The politics and culture of educational achievement. *Anthropology and Education Quarterly, 18*(4).

Erlichson B. A., Goertz, M., & Turnbull, B. (1999). *Implementing whole school reform in New Jersey: Year one in the first cohort.* New Brunswick, NJ: Center for Government Services, Rutgers University.

Erlichson, B. A. & Goertz, M. (2001). *Implementing whole school reform in New Jersey: Year two.* New Brunswick, NJ: Center for Government Services, Rutgers University.

Fabricant, M. & Fine, M. (2012) *Charter schools and the corporate makeover of public education.* New York: Teachers College Press.

Farkas, G., Grobe, R. P., Sheehan, D., & Shuan, Y. (1990). Cultural resources and school success: Gender, ethnicity, and poverty groups within an urban school district. *American Sociological Review, 55,* 127–142.

Fashola, O. S. & Slavin, R. E. (1998). Schoolwide reform models: What works? *Phi Delta Kappan, 370.*

Featherman, D. L. & Hauser, R. M. (1978). *Opportunity and change.* New York: Academic Press.

Feinberg, W. (1996). Affirmative action and beyond: A case for a backward-looking gender and race-based policy. *Teachers College Record, 97,* 362–399.

Felmlee, D. & Eder, D. (1983, April). Contextual effects in the classroom: The impact of ability groups on student attention. *Sociology of Education, 56,* 77–78.

Fennema, E. (1974). Mathematics learning and the sexes: A review. *Journal for Research in Mathematics Education, 5,* 126–139.

Fennema, E. & Leder, G. (1990). *Mathematics and gender.* New York: Teachers College Press.

Ferguson, R. (2007). *Toward excellence with equity: An emerging vision for closing the achievement gap.* Cambridge, MA: Harvard Education Press.

Fine, M. (1986). Why urban adolescents drop into and out of public high school. *Teachers College Record, 87,* 393–409.

Fine, M. (1988). Sexuality, schooling and adolescent females. *Harvard Educational Review, 58*(1), 29–53.

Fine, M. (1991). *Framing dropouts: Notes on the politics of an urban public high school.* Albany, NY: State University of New York Press.

Fine, M. (1993). [Ap]parent involvement: Reflections on parents, power, and urban public schools. *Teachers College Record, 94,* 682–708.

Fine, M. (Ed.). (1994). *Chartering urban school reform.* New York: Teachers College Press.

Finkelstein, B. (1989). *Governing the young: Teacher behavior in popular primary schools in 19th century United States.* London: Falmer Press.

Finkelstein, B. (1992). Education historians as mythmakers. In G. Grant (Ed.), *Review of research education* (pp. 255–297). Washington, DC: American Educational Research Association.

Finn, C. (1989). Presentation at *Forum on National Standards.* Teachers College, Columbia University.

Finn, C. E., Manno, B. V., & Vanourek, G. (2000). *Charter schools in action.* Princeton, NJ: Princeton University Press.

Finn, J. D. (1998). *Class size and students at risk: What is known? What is next?* U.S. Department of Education. Washington, DC: Office of Educational Research and Improvement.

Finnigan, K. S. & Gross, B. (2007). Do accountability policy sanctions influence teacher motivation? Lessons From Chicago's low-performing schools. *American Educational Research Journal, 44,* 594–630.

Firestone, W. A., Goertz, M. E., & Natriello, G. (1997). *From cashbox to classroom: The struggle for fiscal reform and educational change in New Jersey.* New York: Teachers College Press.

Fiscella, K. & Williams, D. R. (2004). Health disparities based on socioeconomic inequities: Implications for urban health care. *Academic Medicine, 79,* 1139–1147.

Fishman, S. & McCarthy, L. (1998). *John Dewey and the challenge of classroom practice.* New York: Teachers College Press.

FitzGerald, F. (1979). *America revised: History schoolbooks in the twentieth century.* Boston, MA: Little, Brown.

Fletcher, J. M. & Tienda, M. (2009). High school classmates and college success. *Sociology of Education, 82*(4), 287–314.

Fordham, S. (1997). *Blacked out: Dilemmas of race, identity, and success at Capital High.* Chicago, IL: University of Chicago Press.

Fordham, S. & Ogbu, J. (1986). Black students' school success: Coping with the "burden" of "acting white." *The Urban Review, 18*(3), 176–206.

Forsey, M., Davies, S., & Walford, G. (Eds.) (2008). *The globalisation of school choice?* London: Symposium Books.

Foster, M. (1995). African-American teachers and culturally relevant pedagogy. In J. A. Banks & C. McGee Banks (Eds.), *Handbook of research on multicultural education* (pp. 570–581). New York: Macmillan.

Frankenberg, E. & Lee, C. (2002). *Race in American public schools: Rapidly resegregating school districts.* Cambridge, MA: The Civil Rights Project, Harvard University Press.

Frankenberg, E. & Lee, C. (2003). *Charter schools and race: A lost opportunity for integrated education,* Cambridge, MA: The Civil Rights Project, Harvard University Press, www.epaa.asu.edu/ojs/article/view/260/386. Accessed October 1, 2012.

Frankenberg, E., Lee, C., & Orfield, G. (2003). *A multiracial society with segregated schools: Are we losing the dream?* Cambridge, MA: The Civil Rights Project, Harvard University Press.

Frankenberg, E. & Orfield, G. (2007). *Lessons in integration: realizing the promise of racial diversity in American schools.* Charlottesville, VA: University of Virginia Press.

Franklin, B. M. (1995). *From backwardness to at risk: Childhood learning difficulties and the contradictions of school reform.* Albany, NY: State University of New York Press.

Freedman, S. G. (1990). *Small victories.* New York: Harper-Collins.

Freeman, R. (1976). *The overeducated American.* New York: Academic Press.

Freire, P. (1972). *Pedagogy of the oppressed.* New York: Herder and Herder.

Freire, P. (1977). *Education for critical consciousness.* New York: Seabury Press.

Freire, P. (1978). *Pedagogy in process.* New York: Seabury Press.

Freire, P. (1985). *The politics of education.* South Hadley, MA: Bergin and Garvey.

Freire, P. (1987). *A pedagogy for liberation.* South Hadley, MA: Bergin and Garvey.

Fruchter, N. (2007). *Urban schools, public will.* New York: Teachers College Press.

Fullan, M. G. & Stiegelbauer, S. (1991). *The new meaning of educational change.* New York: Teachers College Press.

Fuller, B. (2000). *Inside charter schools.* Cambridge, MA: Harvard University Press.

Fuller, B. & Rubinson, R. (Eds.). (1992). *The political construction of education: The state, school expansion, and economic change.* New York: Praeger.

Fuller, B., Elmore, R., & Orfield, G. (Eds.). (1996). *School choice: The cultural logic of families, the political rationality of schools. Who chooses? Who loses? Culture institutions and the unequal effects of school choice.* New York: Teachers College Press.

Furlong, J., Cochran-Smith, M., & Brennan, M. (2011). *Policy and politics in teacher education.* New York: Routledge.

Furstenberg, F. & Hughes, M. E. (1995). Social capital and successful development among at-risk youth. *Journal of Marriage and the Family, 57,* 580–592.

Futrell, M. H. (1990). Redefining national security: New directions for education reform. In S. Bacharach (Ed.), *Education reform: Making sense of it all* (pp. 259–268). Boston, MA: Allyn & Bacon.

Gaines, D. (1991). *Teenage wasteland: Suburbia's dead end kids.* New York: Pantheon.

Gamarnikow, E. & Green, T. (1999). Developing social capital: Dilemmas, possibilities and limitations in education. In A. Hayton (Ed.), *Tackling disaffection and social exclusion* (pp. 46–64). London: Kogan Page.

Gamoran, A. (1986). Instructional and institutional effects of ability groupings. *Sociology of Education, 59,* 185–198.

Gamoran, A. (1987). The stratification of high school learning opportunities. *Sociology of Education, 60,* 135–155.

Gamoran, A. (1993). Alternative uses of ability grouping in secondary schools: Can we bring high-quality instruction to low-ability classes? *American Journal of Education, 101,* 1–22.

Gamoran, A. (1996a). Curriculum standardization and equality of opportunity in Scottish secondary education, 1984–1990. *Sociology of Education, 29,* 1–21.

Gamoran, A. (1996b). Student achievement in public magnet, public comprehensive, and private city high schools. *Educational Evaluation and Policy Analysis.*

Gamoran, A. (2001). American schooling and education inequality: A forecast for the 21st century. *Sociology of Education, 74*, Extra Issue, 135–153.

Gamoran, A. (2003). *Transforming teaching in math and science: How schools and districts can support change.* Sociology of Education Series, New York: Teachers College Press.

Gamoran, A. & Berends, M. (1987). The effects of stratification in secondary schools: A synthesis of survey and ethnographic research. *Review of Educational Research, 57*, 415–437.

Gamoran, A. & Dreeben, R. (1986). Coupling and control in educational organizations. *Administrative Science Quarterly, 31*, 612–632.

Gamoran, A. & Mare, R. D. (1989). Secondary school tracking and educational inequality: Compensation, reinforcement, or neutrality? *American Journal of Sociology, 94*(5), 1146–1183.

Gamoran, A., Nystand, M., Berends, M., & LePore, P. (1995). An organizational analysis of the effects of ability grouping. *American Educational Research Journal, 32*, 59–87.

Garcia, D. (2008). The impact of school choice on racial segregation in charter schools. *Educational Policy, 22*, 805–853.

Gardner, H. (1989). *To open minds: Chinese clues to the dilemma of contemporary education.* New York: Basic Books.

Gardner, H. (1991). *The unschooled mind: How children think and how schools should teach.* New York: Basic Books.

Gardner, H. (1992). A response. *Teachers College Record, 94*(2), 407–413.

Garet, M., Porter, A., Desimone, L., Birman, B., & Yoon, K. (2001). What makes professional development effective? Results from a national sample of teachers. *American Educational Research Journal, 38*(4), 915–945.

Garraty, J. A. (1985). *A short history of the American nation, Vol. B—Since 1865.* New York: Harper and Row.

Gartner, A. & Lipsky, D. K. (1987). Beyond special education: Toward a quality system for all students. *Harvard Educational Review, 57*, 367–395.

Gay, G. (1995). Curriculum theory and multicultural education. In J. A. Banks & C. McGee Banks (Eds.), *Handbook of research on multicultural education* (pp. 25–43). New York: Macmillan.

Gay, P. (Ed.). (1964). *John Locke on education.* New York: Teachers College Bureau of Publications.

Gewertz, C. (2005). A level playing field. *Education Week, 24*, 17, 41–45, 47–48.

Gibson, M. & Ogbu, J. (1992). *Minority status and schooling: A comparative study of immigrants and involuntary minorities.* New York: Garland.

Giddens, A. (1998). *The third way.* Cambridge, MA: Polity.

Gill, B., Timpane, P. M., Ross, K. E., Brewer, D. J., & Booker, K. (2001). *Rhetoric vs. reality; What we know and what we need to know about vouchers and charter schools.* Santa Monica: RAND Corporation.

Gillborn, D. (2008). *Racism and education: Coincidence or conspiracy?* Oxford: Routledge.

Gilligan, C. (1982). *In a different voice.* Cambridge, MA: Harvard University Press.

Gilligan, C., Lyons, N., & Hanmer, T. (1990). *Making connections: The relational worlds of adolescent girls at Emma Willard School.* Cambridge, MA: Harvard University Press.

Giroux, H. (1981). *Ideology, culture and the process of schooling.* Philadelphia, PA: Temple University Press.

Giroux, H. (1983a). Theories of reproduction and resistance in the new sociology of education. *Harvard Educational Review, 53*, 257–293.

Giroux, H. (1983b). *Theory and resistance in education.* South Hadley, MA: Bergin and Garvey.

Giroux, H. (1988). *Teachers as intellectuals.* Granby, MA: Bergin and Garvey.

Giroux, H. (1991). *Postmodernism, feminism, and cultural politics: Redrawing educational boundaries.* Albany, NY: State University of New York Press.

Glenn, C. L. (1991). Will Boston be the proof of the choice pudding? *Educational Leadership, 48*, 41–43.

Goertz, G., Floden, R., & O'Day. (1995). *Building capacity for education reform.* Consortium for Policy Research Education (CPRE) Policy Briefs. Philadelphia, PA: University of Pennsylvania, (pp. 1–10).

Goertz, M. (2009). Standards-based reform: Lessons from the past, directions for the future. In K. Wong & R. Rothman (Eds.) *Clio at the table: Using history to inform and improve education policy* (pp. 107–123). New York: Peter Lang Publishing.

Goldrick-Rab, S. & Pfeffer, F.T. (2009). Beyond access: Explaining socioeconomic differences in college transfer. *Sociology of Education, 82*(2), 101–125.

Goldsmith, P. (2011). Coleman revisited: School segregation, peers and frog ponds. *American Educational Research Journal, 48*, 508–535.

Goodlad, J. I. (1979). *What schools are for.* Bloomington, IN: Phi Delta Kappa.

Goodlad, J. I. (1984). *A place called school: Prospects for the future.* New York: McGraw-Hill.

Goodlad, J. I. (1990). *Teachers for our nation's schools.* San Francisco, CA: Jossey-Bass.

Goodlad, J. I. (1991, November). Why we need a complete redesign of teacher education. *Educational Leadership, 49*, 7–10.

Goodson, I. (1993). *School subjects and curriculum change* (3rd ed.). London: Falmer Press.

Goodwin, R. K. & Kemerer, F. R. (2002). *School choice tradeoffs: Liberty, equity & diversity*. Austin, TX: University of Texas Press.

Gordon, B. (1995). Knowledge construction, competing theories, and education. In J. A. Banks & C. McGee Banks (Eds.), *Handbook of research on multicultural education* (pp. 184–199). New York: Macmillan.

Gordon, D. (1977). *Problems in political economy: An urban perspective*. Boston, MA: D. C. Heath.

Gore, J. (1993). *The struggle for pedagogies: Critical and feminist discourses as regimes of truth*. New York: Routledge.

Gornick, V. (1987). The next great moment in history is theirs. In A. R. Sadovnik et al. (Eds.), *Exploring society* (pp. 260–266). New York: Harper and Row.

Goslin, D. (1965). *The school in contemporary society*. Atlanta, GA: Scott, Foresman.

Government Accounting Office. *No Child Left Behind Act: Improvements needed in education's process for tracking states' implementation of key provisions*. www.gao.gov/cgi-bin/getrpt?GAO-04-734. Accessed October 1, 2012.

Grant, G. (1988). *The world we created at Hamilton High*. Cambridge, MA: Harvard University Press.

Grant, G. (2009). *Hope and despair in the American city: Why there are no bad schools in Raleigh*. Cambridge, MA: Harvard University Press.

Grant, G. (2011). *Hope and despair in the American city: Why there are no bad schools in Raleigh*. Cambridge, MA: Harvard Education Press.

Grant, L., Horan, P. M., & Watts-Warren, B. (1994). Theoretical diversity in the analysis of gender and education. *Research in Socialization of Education and Socialization, 10*, 71–110.

Greeley, A. M. (1982). *Catholic schools and minority students*. New Brunswick, NJ: Transaction Books.

Greeley, A. M. (1998, September). The so-called failure of Catholic schools. *Phi Delta Kappan*, pp. 24–25.

Greene, J. & Peterson, P. (1996). *Methodological issues in evaluation research: The Milwaukee school choice program*. Occasional Paper 96–4. Cambridge, MA: Harvard University Program in Educational Policy and Governance.

Greene, J. P., Peterson, P. E., Du, J., Boeger, L., & Frazier, C. L. (1996). *The effectiveness of school choice in Milwaukee: A secondary analysis of data from the program's evaluation*. Occasional Paper 96–3. Cambridge, MA: Harvard University, Program in Educational Policy and Governance

Greene, J. P., Peterson, P. E., & Du, J. (1999, January). Effectiveness of school choice: The Milwaukee experiment. *Education and Urban Society, 31*(2), 190–213.

Greene, M. (1973). *Teacher as stranger: Educational philosophy for the modern age*. Belmont, CA: Wadsworth.

Greene, M. (1978). *Landscapes of learning*. New York: Teachers College Press.

Greene, M. (1988). *The dialectic of freedom*. New York: Teachers College Press.

Greene, M. (1989). The question of standards. *Teachers College Record, 94*, 9–14.

Greene, M. (1993). The passions of pluralism: Multiculturalism and the expanding community. *Educational Researcher, 22*(1), 13–18.

Greer, C. (1973). *The great school legend*. New York: Viking Press.

Grissmer, D., Flanagan, A., & Williamson, S. (1998). Why did the Black-White score gap narrow in the 1970s and 1980s? In C. Jencks & M. Phillips (Eds.), *The black/white test score gap*. Washington, DC: Brookings Institution Press.

Grissmer, D. W., Flanagan, A., Kawata, J. H., & Williamson, S. (2000). *Improving student achievement: What NAEP state test scores tell us*. Santa Monica: RAND Corporation.

Grodsky, E., Warren, J., & Kalogrides, D. (2009). State high school exit examinations and NAEP long-term trends in reading and mathematics. *Educational Policy, 23*, 615–650.

Gross, B., Booker, K., & Goldhaber, D. (2009). Boosting student achievement: The effect of comprehensive school reform on student achievement. *Educational Evaluation and Policy Analysis, 31*, 111–128.

Guarino, C. M., Santibanez, L., & Daley, G. A. (2006). Teacher recruitment and retention: A review of the recent empirical literature. *Review of Educational Research, 76*(2),173–208.

Gutek, G. (1991). *An historical introduction to American education* (2nd ed.). Prospect Heights, IL: Waveland Press.

Guthrie, W. K. (1969). *A history of Greek philosophy, Volume 3, Part 2: Socrates*. Cambridge: Cambridge University Press.

Gutmann, A. (1987). *Democratic education*. Princeton, NJ: Princeton University Press.

Haberman, M. (2005). Teacher burnout in black and white. *The New Educator, 1*(3), 153–175.

Habermas, J. (1979). *Communication and the evolution of society*. Boston, MA: Beacon Press.

Habermas, J. (1981). Modernity versus postmodernity. *New German Critique, 8*(1), 3–18.

Habermas, J. (1982). The entwinement of myth and enlightenment. *New German Critique, 9*(3), 13–30.

Habermas, J. (1983). Modernity: An incomplete project. In H. Foster (Ed.), *The anti-aesthetic: Essays on postmodern culture* (pp. 3–16). Seattle, DC: Bay Press.

Habermas, J. (1987). *The philosophical discourse of modernity* (F. Lawrence, Trans.). Cambridge, MA: MIT Press.

Hack, M., Klein, N., & Taylor, G. (1995). Long-term developmental outcomes of low birth weight infants. *The Future of Children, 5*(1), 176–196.

Hacker, A. (1992). *Two nations: Black and white, separate, hostile, unequal.* New York: Scribners.

Hakuta, K. & Garcia, E. (1989). Bilingualism and education. *American Psychologist, 53,* 374–379.

Hallinan, M. T. (1984). Summary and implications. In P. Peterson, L. C. Wilkinson, & M. Hallinan (Eds.), *The social context of instruction* (pp. 229–240). New York: Academic Press.

Hallinan, M. T. (1987). Ability grouping and student learning. In M. T. Hallinan (Ed.), *The social organization of schools: New conceptualizations of the learning process* (pp. 41–69). New York: Plenum.

Hallinan, M. T. (1990). The effects of ability grouping in secondary schools: A response to Slavin's Best-Evidence Synthesis. *Review of Educational Research, 60,* 501–504.

Hallinan, M. T. (1994a). Tracking: From theory to practice. *Sociology of Education, 67,* 79–84.

Hallinan, M. T. (1994b). School differences in tracking effects on achievement. *Social Forces, 72,* 799–820.

Hallinan, M. T. (2001). Sociological perspectives on Black-White inequalities in American schooling. *Sociology of Education, 74,* Extra Issue, 50–70.

Hallinan, M. (2008). Teacher influences on students' attachment to school. *Sociology of Education, 81,* 271–283.

Hallinan, M. T. (Ed.). (2000). *Handbook of sociology of education.* New York: Kluwer.

Hammack, F. M. (1986). Large school systems: Dropout reports: An analysis of definitions, procedures and findings. *Teachers College Record, 87,* 324–342.

Hammack, F. (Ed.). (2004). *The comprehensive high school today.* New York: Teachers College Press.

Hammack, F. (2010). Paths to legislation or litigation for educational privilege: New York and San Francisco compared. *American Journal of Education, 116*(3), 371–395.

Hannaway, J. & Carnoy, M. (1993). *Decentralization and school improvement: Can we fulfill the promise?* San Francisco, CA: Jossey-Bass.

Hanushek, E. A. (1994). *Making schools work: Improving performance and controlling costs.* Washington, DC: The Brookings Institution.

Hanushek, E. A. (1998). *The evidence on class size.* Rochester, NY: University of Rochester, W. Allen Wallis Institute of Political Economy.

Harris, A. L. & Robinson, K. (2007). Schooling behaviors or prior skills? A cautionary tale of omitted variable bias within oppositional culture theory. *Sociology of Education, 80*(2), 139–157.

Harvard Civil Rights Project. (2004). www.civilrights project. harvard.edu.

Harvey, D. (1989). *The condition of postmodernity: An inquiry into the origins of cultural change.* Cambridge, MA: Basil Blackwell.

Hatch, T. (2002). When improvement programs collide. *Phi Delta Kappan, 83*(8), 626–634, 639.

Hauser, R. & Featherman, D. (1976). Equality of schooling: Trends and prospects. *Sociology of Education, 49,* 99–119.

Haycock, K. (1999). *Dispelling the myth: High poverty schools exceeding expectations.* Washington, DC: The Education Trust.

Haynes, N. & Comer, J. P. (1993). The Yale school development program: Process, outcomes, and policy implications. *Urban Education, 28,* 166–199.

Hayton, A. (Ed.). (1999). *Tackling disaffection and social exclusion.* London: Kogan Page.

Hechinger, F. (1987, November 10). Gift of a great teacher. *New York Times.*

Heck, S. F. & Williams, C. R. (1984). *The complex roles of the teacher: An ecological perspective.* New York: Teachers College Press.

Hedges, L. V., Laine, R. D., & Greenwald, R. (1994). Does money matter? A meta-analysis of studies of the effects of differential school inputs on student outcomes. *Educational Researcher, 23,* 5–14.

Hehir, T. (2005). *New directions in special education: Eliminating ableism in policy and practice.* Cambridge, MA: Harvard Education Press.

Hehir, T. & Latus, T. (1992). *Special education at the century's end: Evolution of theory and practice since 1970.* Cambridge, MA: Harvard Educational Review.

Heller, J. (1985). *Catch 22.* New York: Dell.

Henig, J. (1994). *Rethinking school choice: Limits of the market metaphor.* Princeton, NJ: Princeton University Press.

Henig, J. R. (1995). *Rethinking school choice: Limits of the market metaphor.* Princeton, NJ: Princeton University Press.

Henig, J. (2009). Mayoral control: What we can and cannot learn from other cities. In J. Viteritti (Ed.), *When mayors take charge: School governance in the city* (pp. 19–45). Washington, DC: Brookings Institution Press.

Henig, J. (2009). Politicization of evidence: Lessons for an informed democracy. *Educational Policy, 23,* 137–160.

Henig, J. & Stone, C. (2008). Rethinking school reform: The distractions of dogma and the potential for a new politics of progressive pragmatism. *American Journal of Education, 114*(3), 191–218.

Henig, J. R. & Sugarman, S. D. (1999). The nature and extent of school choice. In S. Sugarman & F. R. Kemerer (Eds.), *School choice and social controversy: Politics, policy and law* (pp. 13–35). Washington, DC: Brookings Institution Press.

Herman, M. (2009). The black-white-other achievement gap: Testing theories of academic performance among multiracial and monoracial adolescents. *Sociology of Education, 82,* 20–46.

Herman, R., Aladjem, D., McMahon, P., O'Malley, A., Quinones, S., & Woodruff, D. (1999). *An educators' guide to schoolwide reform.* Washington, DC: American Institutes for Research.

Herrnstein, R. J. (1973). *IQ in the meritocracy*. Boston, MA: Little, Brown.

Herrnstein, R. J. & Murray, C. (1994). *The bell curve: Intelligence and class structure in American life*. New York: The Free Press.

Hess, F. M. (2002). *Revolution at the margins: The impact of competition on urban school systems*. Washington, DC: Brookings Institution Press.

Hess, F. (2008). Looking for leadership: Assessing the case for mayoral control of urban school systems. *American Journal of Education, 114*, 219–246.

Hess, F. (2010). *The same thing all over again: How school reformers get stuck in yesterday's ideas*. Cambridge, MA: Harvard University Press.

Hess, F. M. (Ed.). (2005). *Urban school reform: Lessons from San Diego*. Cambridge, MA: Harvard University Press.

Hess, F. M., Rotherham, A. J., & Walsh, K. (2004). *A qualified teacher in every classroom? Appraising old answers and new ideas*. Cambridge, MA: Harvard University Press.

Hess, G. A., Jr. (1991). *School restructuring, Chicago style*. Newbury Park, CA: Corwin Press.

Hess, G. A., Jr. (1994). Introduction: School-based management as a vehicle for school reform. *Education and Urban Society, 26*, 203–219.

Hess, G. A., Jr. (1995). *Restructuring urban schools: A Chicago perspective*. New York: Teachers College Press.

Heubert, J. P. & Hauser, R. M. (1999). *High stakes: Testing for tracking, promotion, and graduation*. Washington, DC: National Academy Press.

Heyns, B. (1978). *Summer learning and the effects of schooling*. New York: Academic Press.

Hibel, J., Farkas, G., & Morgan, P. (2010). Who is placed into special education? *Sociology of Education, 83*, 333–345.

Hildebrand, J. (1998, May 4). Winners, losers in a money game. *Newsday*, A5, A26–A27.

Hill, P. T. (2005). Assessing student performance in charter schools: Why studies often clash and answers remain elusive. *Education Week, 24*(18), 33, 44.

Hill, P. T. & Bonan, J. (1991). *Decentralization and accountability in public education*. Santa Monica, CA: Rand.

Hill, P. T., Campbell, C., & Harvey, J. (2000). *It takes a city: Getting serious about urban school reform*. Washington, DC: Brookings Institution Press.

Hill, P., Lake, R., Celio, M. B., Campbell, C., Herdman, P., & Bulkley, K. (2001). *A study of charter school accountability*. Jessup, MD: U.S. Department of Educational Research and Improvement.

Hirsch, E. D., Jr. (1987). *Cultural literacy*. Boston, MA: Houghton Mifflin.

Hirsch, E. D., Jr. (1988). *Cultural literacy: What every American needs to know*. New York: Random House.

Hitchcock, M. E. & Tompkins, G. E. (1987). Are basal reading textbooks still sexist? *The Reading Teacher, 41*, 288–292.

Hochschild, J. (1984). *The new American dilemma: Liberal democracy and school desegregation*. New Haven, CT: Yale University Press.

Hochschild, J. (1986). *What's fair? American beliefs about distributive justice*. Cambridge, MA: Harvard University Press.

Hochschild, J. (1995). *Facing up to the American dream: Race, class and the soul of the nation*. Princeton, NJ: Princeton University Press.

Hodgkinson, H. (1985). *All one system: Demographics of education, kindergarten through graduate school*. Washington, DC: Institute for Educational Leadership.

Hodgkinson, H. (1991, September). Reform versus reality. *Phi Delta Kappan*, 9–16.

Hoffer, T. (1992). Middle school ability grouping and student achievement in science and mathematics. *Educational Evaluation and Policy Analysis, 14*, 205–227.

Hoffer, T., Greeley, A. M., & Coleman, J. S. (1985, April). Achievement growth in public and Catholic schools. *Sociology of Education, 58*, 74–97.

Hofferth, S. & Sandberg, J. (2001). How American children spend their time. *Journal of Marriage and the Family, 63*, 295–308.

Hoffman, K., Llaga, C., & Snyder, T. (2003). *Status and trends in the education of Blacks*. Washington, DC: U.S. Department of Education, National Center for Education Statistics.

Hofstadter, R. (1966). *Anti-intellectualism in American life*. New York: Rand.

Hogan, D. J. (1978). Education and the making of the Chicago working class, 1880–1930. *History of Education Quarterly, 18*, 227–270.

Hogan, D. J. (1985). *Class and reform: School and society in Chicago, 1880–1930*. Philadelphia, PA: University of Pennsylvania Press.

Holmes Group. (1986). *Tomorrow's teachers*. East Lansing, MI: Author.

Holmes Group. (1990). *Tomorrow's schools*. East Lansing, MI: Author.

Holmes Group. (1995). *Tomorrow's schools of education*. East Lansing, MI: Author.

Honig, B. (1990). The key to reform: Sustaining and expanding upon initial success. In S. Bacharach (Ed.), *Education reform: Making sense of it all* (pp. 52–56). Boston, MA: Allyn & Bacon.

Honig, M. (2009). No small thing: School district central office bureaucracies and the implementation of new small autonomous schools initiatives. *American Educational Research Journal, 46*, 387–422.

Hopper, E. (1971). Stratification, education and mobility in industrial societies. In E. Hopper (Ed.), *Readings in the theory of educational systems*. London: Hutchinson.

Horn, J. & Miron, G. (2002a). *Evaluation of Connecticut charter schools and the charter school initiative: Final report.* Kalamazoo, MI: Evaluation Center Western Michigan University.

Horn, J. & Miron, G. (2002b). *An evaluation of the Michigan charter school initiative: performance, accountability, and impact.* Kalamazoo, MI: Evaluation Center Western Michigan University. www.wmich.edu/evalctr. Accessed October 1, 2012.

Horowitz, H. L. (1984). *Alma mater: Design and experience in the women's colleges from their nineteenth century beginnings to the 1930s.* New York: Knopf. (Second edition published by University of Massachusetts Press in 1993).

Horvat, E. M. (2003). Reassessing the "Burden of 'Acting White'": The importance of peer groups in managing academic success. *Sociology of Education*, 76, 265–280.

Howell, W. G. & Peterson, P. E. (2002). *The education gap: Vouchers and urban schools.* Washington, DC: Brookings Institution Press.

Hoxby, C. M. (2000a). Does competition among public schools benefit students and taxpayers? *American Economic Review*, 90, 5.

Hoxby, C. M. (2000b). The effects of class size on student achievement: New evidence from population variation. *Quarterly Journal of Economics*, 115, 4.

Hoxby, C. M. (2001). All school finance equalizations are not created equal. *Quarterly Journal of Economics*, 116, 4.

Hoxby, C. M. (2004a). A straightforward comparison of charter schools and regular public schools in the United States. HIER Working Paper. www.wacharterschools.org/learn/studies/hoxbyallcharters.pdf. Accessed October 1, 2012.

Hoxby, C. M. (2004b). Achievement in charter schools and regular public schools in the United States: Understanding the differences. HIER Working Paper. www.vanderbilt.edu/schoolchoice/downloads/papers/hoxby2004.pdf. Accessed October 1, 2012.

Hoxby, C. M. (2009). The New York City charter school evaluation project. Cambridge, MA: National Bureau of Economic Research. www.nber.org/~schools/charterschoolseval. Accessed December 12, 2009.

Hoxby, C. M. & Rockoff, J. (2004). The impact of charter schools on student achievement. HIER Working Paper. http://post.economics.harvard.edu/faculty/ hoxby/papers.html.

Hubbard, L., Stein, M. K., & Mehan, H. (2006). *Reform as learning: When school reform collides with school culture and community politics.* New York: Routledge.

Hunter, M. (1982). *Mastery teaching.* El Segundo, CA: TIP Publications.

Hurn, C. J. (1993). *The limits and possibilities of schooling* (3rd ed.). Boston, MA: Allyn & Bacon.

Hursh, D. (2007). Assessing No Child Left Behind and the rise of neoliberal education policies. *American Educational Research Journal*, 44, 493–518.

Illich, I. (1970). *Deschooling society.* New York: Harper and Row.

Ingersoll, R. (1999). The problem of underqualified teachers in American secondary schools. *Educational Researcher*, 28, 26–37.

Ingersoll, R. (2001). Teacher turnover and teacher shortages. *American Educational Research Journal*, 38(3), 499–534.

Ingersoll, R. (2003). *Who controls teachers' work?: Power and accountability in America's schools.* Cambridge, MA: Harvard University Press.

Ingersoll, R. (2004). Why some schools have more under-qualified teachers than others. In Diane Ravitch (Ed.), *Brookings papers on education policy*. Washington, DC: Brookings Institution Press.

Ingersoll, R. M. (1994). Organizational control in secondary schools. *Harvard Educational Review*, 64, 150–172.

Ingersoll, R. & Perda, D. (2010). Is the supply of mathematics and science teachers sufficient? *American Educational Research Journal*, 47, 563–594.

Inkeles, A. (1979). National differences in scholastic performance. *Comparative Education Review*, 23, 386–407.

Institute on Education Law and Policy (2009). *Pockets of Educational Excellence.* Newark: Rutgers University. http://ielp.rutgers.edu/docs/poe.final.pdf. Accessed January 17, 2011.

Jackson, P. (1968). *Life in classrooms.* New York: Holt, Rinehart and Winston.

Jackson, P. (1986). *The practice of teaching.* New York: Teachers College Press.

Jackson, P. (1997). *John Dewey and the lessons of art.* New Haven, CT: Yale University Press.

Jacob, B. (2007). The challenges of staffing urban schools with effective teachers. *The Future of Children*, 17(1), 129–153.

Jacobs, J. A. (1995). Gender and academic specialties: Trends among recipients of college degrees in the 1980s. *Sociology of Education*, 68, 81–98.

James, M. (Ed.). (1995). *Social reconstruction through education: The philosophy, history, and curricula of a radical ideal.* Norwood, NJ: Ablex.

James, M. (2005). *The conspiracy of the good: Civil rights and the struggle for community in two American cities, 1875–2000.* New York: Peter Lang.

James, W. (1978). *Varieties of religious experience.* New York: Norton.

Jameson, F. (1982). Postmodernism and consumer society. In H. Foster (Ed.), *The anti-aesthetic: Essays on post-modern culture* (pp. 11–125). Seattle, DC: Bay Press.

Jencks, C. (1985). How much do high school students learn? *Sociology of Education, 58*, 128–135.

Jencks, C. (1987). *What is post-modernism?* New York: St. Martin's.

Jencks, C. (1992). *Rethinking social policy: Race, poverty, and the underclass.* New York: Harper Perennial.

Jencks, C., Bartlett, S., Corcoran, M., Crouse, J., Eaglesfield, D., Jackson, G., McClelland, K., Mueser, P., Olneck, M., Schwartz, J., Ward, S., & Williams, J. (1979). *Who gets ahead?* New York: Basic Books.

Jencks, C., Smith, M., Acland, H., Bane, M. J., Cohen, D., Gintis, H., Heyns, B., & Michelson, S. (1972). *Inequality.* New York: Basic Books.

Jennings, J. (2010). School choice or schools' choice?: Managing in an era of accountability. *Sociology of Education, 83*, 227–247.

Jennings, J. & DiPrete, T. (2010). Teacher effects on social and behavioral skills in early elementary school. *Sociology of Education, 83*, 135–159.

Jensen, A. (1969). How much can we boost I.Q. and scholastic achievement? *Harvard Educational Review, 39*, 1–23.

Jeynes, W. (2008). What we should and should not learn from the Japanese and other East Asian education systems. *Educational Policy, 22*, 900–927.

Johnson, J. (1991). *Introduction to the foundations of American education* (8th ed.). Boston, MA: Allyn & Bacon.

Johnson, J. F., Jr., & Asera, R. (Eds.) (1999). *Hope for urban education: A study of nine high-performing, high-poverty, urban elementary schools.* Austin, TX: The Charles A. Dana Center, The University of Texas at Austin.

Johnson, S. M. (1990). *Teachers at work: Achieving success in our schools.* New York: Basic Books.

Johnson, S. M. (1991). Review of *Small victories* by Samuel G. Freedman. *Teachers College Record, 93*(1), 180–184.

Johnson, S. M. & Project on the Next Generation of Teachers. (2004). *Finders and keepers: Helping new teachers survive and thrive in our schools* (1st ed.). San Francisco, CA: Jossey-Bass.

Johnson, W. R. (1987). Empowering practitioners: Holmes, Carnegie, and the lessons of history. *History of Education Quarterly, 27*, 221–240.

Johnson, W. R. (1989). Teachers and teacher training in the twentieth century. In D. Warren (Ed.), *American teachers: Histories of a profession at work* (pp. 237–256). New York: Macmillan.

Kaestle, C. F. (1973). *The evolution of an urban school system.* Cambridge, MA: Harvard University Press.

Kaestle, C. F. (1983). *Pillars of the republic: Common schools and American society, 1780–1860.* New York: Hill & Wang.

Kaestle, C. F. (1991). *Literacy in the United States: Readers and reading since 1800.* New Haven, CT: Yale University Press.

Kaestle, C. F. & Vinovskis, M. A. (1978). From apron strings to ABCs: Parents, children and schooling in nineteenth-century America. In J. Demos & S. S. Boocock (Eds.), *Turning points: Historical and sociological essays on the family* (pp. 39–80). Chicago, IL: University of Chicago Press.

Kaestle, C. F. & Vinovskis, M. A. (1980). *Education and social change in nineteenth-century Massachusetts.* New York: Basic Books.

Kafka, J. (2008). "Sitting on a tinderbox": Racial conflict, teacher discretion, and the centralization of disciplinary authority. *American Journal of Education, 114*, 247–270.

Kahlenberg, R. (2001). *All together now: Creating middle-class schools through public school choice.* Washington, DC: Brookings Institution Press.

Kahne, J., Sporte, S., De La Torre, M., & Easton, J. (2008). Small high schools on a larger scale: The impact of school conversions in. *Educational Evaluation and Policy Analysis, 30*, 281–315.

Kamens, D. H. (2009). The expanding polity: Theorizing the links between expanded higher education and the new politics of the post 1970s. *American Journal of Education, 116*(1), 99–124.

Kamin, L. (1974). *The science and politics of I.Q.* Potomac, MD: Erlbaum.

Kaminsky, J. (1992). A pre-history of educational philosophy in the United States: 1861–1914. *Harvard Educational Review, 62*(2), 179–198.

Kantor, H. & Brenzel, B. (1992). Urban education and the truly disadvantaged: The historical roots of the contemporary crisis, 1945–1990. *Teachers College Record, 94*(2), 278–314.

Karabel, J. (1972). Community colleges and social stratification. *Harvard Educational Review, 42*, 521–562.

Karabel, J. & Halsey, A. H. (Eds.). (1977). *Power and ideology in education.* New York: Oxford University Press.

Karen, D. (1990). Toward a political-organizational model of gatekeeping: The case of elite colleges. *Sociology of Education, 63*, 227–240.

Karen, D. (1991a). Achievement and ascription in admission to an elite college: A political-organizational analysis. *Sociological Forum, 6*, 349–380.

Karen, D. (1991b). Politics of race, class, and gender: Access to higher education in the United States, 1960–1986. *American Journal of Education, 99*, 208–237.

Karen, D. (2002). Changes in access to higher education in the United States: 1980–1992. *Sociology of Education, 75*, 191–210.

Karier, C. (Ed.). (1976). *Shaping the American educational state.* New York: Free Press.

Karier, C., Violas, P., & Spring, J. (1973). *Roots of crisis: American education in the twentieth century.* New York: Rand McNally.

Katz, J. (1988). Unpublished commentary on New York City education.

Katz, M. B. (1968). *The irony of early school reform: Educational innovation in mid-nineteenth-century Massachusetts.* Cambridge, MA: Harvard University Press.

Katz, M. B. (1971a). *Class, bureaucracy, and schools: The illusion of educational change in America.* New York: Praeger.

Katz, M. B. (1971b). *School reform, past and present.* Boston, MA: Little, Brown.

Katz, M. B. (1987). *Reconstructing American education.* Cambridge, MA: Harvard University Press.

Katz, M. B. (1990). *The undeserving poor: From the war on poverty to the war on welfare.* New York: Pantheon Books.

Katzman, L., Gandhi, A. G., Harbour, W. S., & LaRock, J. D. (Eds.). (2005). *Special education for a new century.* Cambridge, MA: Harvard University Press.

Katznelson, I. & Weir, M. (1985). *Schooling for all.* New York: Basic Books.

Kaufman, J. M. (1989). The regular-education initiative as Reagan-Bush education policy: A trickle-down theory of the hard to teach. *Journal of Special Education, 23*(3), 256–278.

Keddie, N. (1971). Classroom knowledge. In M. F. D. Young (Ed.), *Knowledge and control.* London: Collier.

Kelly, G. P. (1992). Women and higher education reforms: Expansion without equality. In P. W. Cookson, A. R. Sadovnik, & S. F. Semel (Eds.), *International handbook of educational reform* (pp. 545–559). Westport, CT: Greenwood Press.

Kelly, S. (2008). What types of students' effort are rewarded with high marks? *Sociology of Education, 81,* 32–52.

Kelly, S. (2009). The black-white gap in mathematics course taking. *Sociology of Education, 82,* 47–69.

Kelly, S. & Price, H. (2011). The correlates of tracking policy: Opportunity hoarding, status competition or a technical-functional explanation? *American Educational Research Journal, 48,* 560–585.

Kennedy, M. M. (2005). *Inside teaching: How classroom life undermines reform.* Cambridge, MA: Harvard University Press.

Kerckhoff, A. C. (1986). The effects of ability grouping. *American Sociological Review, 51,* 842–858.

Kerckhoff, A. C. (1993). *Diverging pathways: Social structure and career deflections.* New York: Cambridge University Press.

Kerckhoff, A. C. (2001). Education and social stratification process in comparative perspective. *Sociology of Education, 74,* Extra Issue, 3–18.

Kerckhoff, A. C. & Everett, D. D. (1986). Sponsored and contest education pathways in Great Britain and the United States. In A. C. Kerckhoff (Ed.), *Research in sociology of education and socialization* (Vol. 6) (pp. 133–163). Greenwich, CT: JAI Press.

Kesey, K. (1977). *One flew over the cuckoo's nest.* New York: Penguin.

Khalil, D. (2012). *Who teaches where? Evidence from a mixed methods study of teacher candidates' preference for an urban school setting.* Newark, NJ: Rutgers University Press.

Kidder, T. (1989). *Among schoolchildren.* Boston, MA: Houghton Mifflin.

Kilgore, S. (1991). The organizational context of tracking in schools. *American Sociological Review, 56,* 189–203.

Kimball, R. (1990). *Tenured radicals: How politics has corrupted higher education.* New York: Harper and Row.

Kincheloe, J. (2010). *Knowledge and critical pedagogy: An introduction.* New York: Springer.

Kincheloe, J. & Steinberg, S. (Eds.). (1998). *Unauthorized methods: Strategies for critical teaching.* New York: Routledge.

Kincheloe, J., Steinberg, S., & Gressom, A. (1996). *Measured lies: The bell curve examined.* New York: St. Martin's.

King, J. E. (1995). Culture-centered knowledge: Black studies, curriculum transformation, and social action. In J. A. Banks & C. McGee Banks (Eds.), *Handbook of research on multicultural education* (pp. 265–290). New York: Macmillan.

Kingston, P. W. (1986, Fall). Theory at risk: Accounting for the excellence movement. *Sociological Forum, 1,* 632–656.

Kingston, P. W. (2001). The unfulfilled promise of cultural capital theory. *Sociology of Education, 74,* Extra Issue, 88–99.

Kirp, D. L. (1982). *Just schools: The idea of racial equality in American education.* Berkeley, CA: University of California Press.

Kirst, M. W. (1984). *Who controls our schools?* New York: W. H. Freeman.

Kitto, H. D. F. (1951). *The Greeks.* New York: Penguin.

Kliebard, H. M. (1986). *The struggle for the American curriculum: 1893–1958.* Boston, MA: Routledge & Kegan Paul.

Kluger, R. (1975). *Simple justice: The history of Brown v. Board of Education and black America's struggle for equality.* New York: Knopf.

Koch, E. (1999, December 3). Just arresting homeless is fruitless. *Newsday,* p. A57.

Kohl, H. (1967). *36 children.* New York: New American Library.

Komaromy, M., Grumbach, K., Drake, M., Vranizan, K., Lurie, N., Keane, D., & Bindman, A. B. (1996).

The role of black and hispanic physicians in providing health care for underserved populations, *The New England Journal of Medicine, 334*, 1305–1310.

Kommarovsky, M. (1985). *Women in college*. New York: Basic Books.

Konstantopoulos, S. & Chung, V. (2009). What are the long-term effects of small classes on the achievement gap? Evidence from the lasting benefits study. *American Journal of Education, 116*, 1–30.

Kozol, J. (1967). *Death at an early age*. New York: Houghton Mifflin.

Kozol, J. (1986). *Illiterate America*. New York: New American Library.

Kozol, J. (1991). *Savage inequalities*. New York: Crown.

Kraushaar, O. F. (1972). *American nonpublic schools: Patterns of diversity*. Baltimore, MD: Johns Hopkins University Press.

Krueger, A. B. (1998). *Experimental estimates of education production functions*. Princeton, NJ: Princeton University Industrial Relations Section.

Kurlaender, M. & Ma, J. (2003). *Educational benefits of racially and ethnically diverse schools*. Cambridge, MA: The Civil Rights Project, Harvard University.

Kurlaender, M. & Yun, J. (2003). *Fifty years after Brown: New evidence on the impact of school racial composition on student outcomes*. Cambridge, MA: The Civil Rights Project, Harvard University.

Labaree, D. F. (1986). Curriculum, credentials, and the middle class: A case study of a nineteenth-century high school. *Sociology of Education, 59*, 42–57.

Labaree, D. F. (1988). *The making of an American high school: The credentials market and the Central High School of Philadelphia, 1838–1939*. New Haven, CT: Yale University Press.

Labaree, D. F. (1992a). Doing good, doing science: The Holmes group reports and the rhetorics of educational reform. *Teachers College Record, 93*(4), 628–640.

Labaree, D. F. (1992b). Power, knowledge, and the rationalization of teaching: A genealogy of the movement to professionalize teaching. *Harvard Educational Review, 62*(2), 123–155.

Labaree, D. F. (1996). A disabling vision: Rhetoric and reality in tomorrow's schools of education. *Teachers College Record, 97*(2), 166–205.

Labaree, D. F. (1997). *How to succeed in school without really learning: The credential race in American education*. New Haven, CT: Yale University Press.

Labaree, D. F. & Pallas, A. M. (1996). Dire straits: The narrow vision of the Holmes Group. *Educational Researcher, 25*(5), 25–28.

Labov, W. (1970). The logic of non-standard English. In F. Williams (Ed.), *Language and poverty* (pp. 153–189). Chicago, IL: Markham.

Ladd, H. (2011). Teachers' perceptions of their working conditions: How predictive of planned and actual teacher movement? *Educational Evaluation and Policy Analysis, 33*, 235–261.

Ladd, H. F. (2002). *Market-based reforms in urban education*. Washington, DC: Economic Policy Institute.

Ladd, H. F. & Fiske, E. B. (2003). The uneven playing field of school choice: Evidence from New Zealand. *Journal of Policy Analysis & Management, 43*.

Ladson-Billings, G. (1994). *The dreamkeepers*. San Francisco, CA: Jossey-Bass.

Ladson-Billings, G. (2004). Landing on the wrong note: The price we paid for Brown. *Educational Researcher, 33*(7), 3–13.

LaFrance, M. (1985). The school of hard knocks: Nonverbal sexism in the classroom. *Theory Into Practice, 24*, 40–44.

Lagemann, E. C. (1979). *A generation of women: Education in the lives of progressive reformers*. Cambridge, MA: Harvard University Press.

Lagemann, E. C. (1989). *The politics of knowledge: The Carnegie Corporation, philanthropy, and public policy*. Hanover, NH: University Press of New England.

Laird, S. (1989). Reforming "Women's true profession": A case for "feminist pedagogy" in teacher education? *Harvard Educational Review, 58*(4), 449–463.

Lareau, A. (1989). *Home advantage: Social class and parental intervention in elementary education*. London: Falmer.

Lareau, A. (2003). *Unequal childhood: Class, race and family life*. Los Angeles, CA: University of California Press.

Lareau, A. (2011). *Unequal childhoods: class, race, and family life, second edition with an update a decade later*. Berkeley, CA.: University of California Press.

Lareau, A. & Horvat, E. M. (1999). Moments of social inclusion and exclusion: Race, class, and cultural capital in family-school relationships. *Sociology of Education, 72*, 37–53.

Lasch, C. (1983). *The culture of narcissism*. New York: Norton.

Lather, P. (1991). *Getting smart: Feminist research and pedagogy within the postmodern*. New York: Routledge.

Lauen, D. L. (2007). Contextual Explanations of School Choice. *Sociology of Education, 80*(3) 179–209.

Lauen, D. L. (2008). The false promises of school choice in NCLB. In A. R. Sadovnik, J. A. O' Day, G. Bohrnstedt, & K. Borman (Eds.), *No Child Left Behind and the reduction of the achievement gap: Sociological perspectives on federal educational policy*. New York: Routledge.

Lauen, D. (2009). To choose or not to choose: High school choice and graduation in Chicago. *Educational Evaluation and Policy Analysis, 31*, 179–199.

Lavin, D., Alba, R., & Silberstein, R. (1981). *Right versus privilege: The open admissions experiment at the City University of New York.* New York: The Free Press.

Lavin, D. & Hyllegard, D. (1996). *Changing the odds: Open admissions and the life chances of the disadvantaged.* New Haven, CT: Yale University Press.

Leach, M. (1992). Can we talk? A response to Burbules and Rice. *Harvard Educational Review, 62*(2), 257–263.

Leach, W. (1980). *True love and perfect union: The feminist reform of sex and society.* New York: Basic Books.

LeCompte, M. D. (1987). The cultural context of dropping out: Why remedial programs don't solve the problems. *Education and Urban Society, 19,* 232–249.

LeCompte, M. D. & Dworkin, A. G. (1991). *Giving up on school: Student dropouts and teacher burnouts.* Newbury Park, CA: Corwin.

Lee, C. D. & Slaughter-Defoe, D. T. (1995). Historical and sociocultural influences on African American education. In J. A. Banks & C. McGee Banks (Eds.), *Handbook of research on multicultural education* (pp. 348–371). New York: Macmillan.

Lee, G. (1961). *Crusade against ignorance: Thomas Jefferson on education.* New York: Teachers College Press.

Lee, V. E. (1985). *Access to higher education: The experience of Blacks, Hispanics, and low socio-economic status Whites.* Washington, DC: Division of Policy Analysis and Research, American Council on Education.

Lee, V. E. & Burkham, D. (2002). *Inequality at the starting gate: Social background differences in achievement as children begin school.* Washington, DC: Economic Policy Institute.

Lee, V. E. & Bryk, A. (1986). Effects of single-sex and co-educational high schools on achievement, attitudes, behaviors, and sex differences. *Journal of Educational Psychology, 78,* 381–395.

Lee, V. E. & Bryk, A. (1988). Curriculum tracking as mediating the social distribution of high school achievement. *Sociology of Education, 61,* 78–94.

Lee, V. E. & Bryk, A. (1989). A multilevel model of the social distribution of high school achievement. *Sociology of Education, 62,* 172–192.

Lee, V. E. & Croninger, R. G. (1994). The relative importance of home and school in the development of literacy skills for middle-grade students. *American Journal of Education, 102*(2), 286–329.

Lee, V. E. & Frank, K. A. (1990). Students' characteristics that facilitate the transfer from two-year to four-year colleges. *Sociology of Education, 63,* 178–193.

Lee, V. E., Croninger, R. G., & Smith, J. B. (1994). Parental choice of schools and social stratification in education: The paradox of Detroit. *Educational Evaluation and Policy Analysis, 16*(4), 434–457.

Lee, V. E., Dedrick, R. F., & Smith, J. B. (1991). The effect of the social organization of schools on teachers' self-efficacy and satisfaction. *Sociology of Education, 64,* 190–208.

Lee, V. E., Mackie-Lewis, C., & Marks, H. M. (1993). Persistence to the baccalaureate degree for students who transfer from community college. *American Journal of Education, 120,* 80–114.

Lee, V. E., Marks, H. M., & Byrd, T. (1994). Sexism in single-sex and coeducational independent secondary school classrooms. *Sociology of Education, 67,* 92–120.

Lee, V. E. & Smith, J. B. (1995, October). Effects of high school restructuring and size on gains in achievement for early secondary school students. *Sociology of Education, 68*(4), 241–270.

Lee, V.L. & Ready, D. (2006). *Schools within schools: Possibilities and pitfalls of high school reform.* New York: Teachers College Press.

Lein, L., Johnson, J. F., Jr., & Ragland, M. (1997). *Successful Texas schoolwide programs.* Austin, TX: The Charles A. Dana Center, The University of Texas at Austin.

Legters, N. E., Balfanz, R., Jordan, W. J., & McPartland, J. M. (2002). *Comprehensive reform for urban high school.* New York: Teachers College Press.

Lemann, N. (1991). *The promised land.* New York: Vintage.

Lemann, N. (1999). *The big test: The secret history of the American meritocracy.* New York: Farrar, Straus and Giroux.

Lesko, N. (1988). *Symbolizing society: Stories, rites, and structure in a catholic high school.* New York: Falmer Press.

Lesko, N. (2001). *Act your age! A cultural construction of adolescence.* New York: Routledge.

Lever, J. & Schwartz, P. (1971). *Women at Yale: Liberating a college campus.* Indianapolis: Bobbs-Merrill.

Levine, D. U. & Havighurst, R. J. (1989). *Society and education* (7th ed.). Boston, MA: Allyn & Bacon.

Levinson, D., Cookson, P. W., Jr., & Sadovnik, A. R. (2000). *Encyclopedia of the sociology of education.* New York: Falmer.

Levinson, D. L., Cookson, P. W., Jr., & Sadovnik, A. R. (2002). *Encyclopedia of education and sociology.* New York: Routledge.

Lew, J. (2005a). *Success and failure of Asian American youths in urban schools: A case of second-generation Korean Americans.* New York: Teachers College Press.

Lew, J. (2005b). The other story of model minorities: Korean American high school dropouts in urban context. *Anthropology and Education Quarterly, 35*(3), 303–323.

Lew, J. (2005c). *Success and failure among 1.5 and second-generation Korean American youths in urban schools: Significance of social class and school context.* New York: Teachers College Press.

Lewis, A. (2003). *Race in the schoolyard: Negotiating the color line in classrooms and communities.* New Brunswick, NJ: Rutgers University Press.

Lewis, C. (1995). *Educating mind and heart: Rethinking the roots of Japanese education.* London: Cambridge University Press.

Lewis, D. & Nakagawa, K. (1995). *Race and educational reform in the American metropolis: A study of school decentralization.* Albany, NY: State University of New York Press.

Lewis, J. F. (1995). Saying no to vouchers: What is the price of democracy? *National Association of Secondary School Principals Bulletin, 79*, 41–51.

Lewis, O. (1966). The culture of poverty. *Scientific American, 215*, 19–25.

Lieberman, A. (Ed.). (1988). *Building a professional culture in schools.* New York: Teachers College Press.

Lieberman, A. (Ed.). (1995). *The work of restructuring schools: Building from the ground up.* New York: Teachers College Press.

Lieberman, A. & Miller, L. (1984). The social realities of teaching. In A. Lieberman & L. Miller (Eds.), *Teachers, their world, and their work.* Alexandria, VA: Association for Supervision and Curriculum Development.

Lieberman, A., Darling-Hammond, L., & Zuckerman, D. (1991, August). *Early lessons in restructuring schools.* New York: National Center for Restructuring Education, Schools, and Teaching.

Lightfoot, S. L. (1978). *Worlds apart.* New York: Basic Books.

Lightfoot, S. L. (1983). *The good high school.* New York: Basic Books.

Lilly, M. S. (1986, March). The relationship between general and special education. *Counterpoint, 6*(1), 10.

Lipman, P. (1998). *Race, class and power in school restructuring.* New York: State University of New York Press.

Lipman, P. (2003). *High stakes education: Inequality, globalization, and urban school reform.* New York: Routledge.

Lipman, P. (2011). *The new political economy of urban education: Neoliberalism, race, and the right to the City.* New York: Routledge.

Lippitt, R. & Gold, M. (1959). Classroom social structure as a mental health problem. *Journal of Social Issues, 15*, 40–49.

Little, J. W. (1990). Conditions of professional development in secondary schools. In M. W. McLaughlin, J. E. Talbert, & N. Bascia (Eds.), *The contexts of teaching in secondary schools: Teachers realities* (pp. 187–223). New York: Teachers College Press.

Little, J. W. (1992). *Two worlds: Vocational and academic teachers in comprehensive high schools.* Berkeley, CA: National Center for Research in Vocational Education, University of California at Berkeley.

Little, J. W. (1993a). Professional community in comprehensive high schools: The two worlds of academic and vocational teachers. In J. W. Little & M. W. McLaughlin (Eds.), *Teachers work: Individuals, colleagues, and contexts* (pp. 137–163). New York: Teachers College Press.

Little, J. W. (1993b, Summer). Teachers' professional development in a climate of educational reform. *Education Evaluation and Policy Analysis, 15*(2), 129–151.

Liu, E., Rosenstein, J. G., Swan, A. E., & Khalil, D. (2008a). When districts encounter teacher shortages: The challenges of recruiting and retaining mathematics teachers in urban districts. *Leadership and Policy in Schools, 7*(3), 296–323.

Lleras, C. (2008). Race, racial concentration, and the dynamics of educational inequality across urban and suburban schools. *American Educational Research Journal, 45*, 886–912.

Lleras, C. & Rangel, C. (2009). Ability grouping practices in elementary school and African American/Hispanic achievement. *American Journal of Education, 115*(2), 279–304.

Lloyd, S. M. (1987). *The Putney school: A progressive experiment.* New Haven, CT: Yale University Press.

Loewen, J. W. (1995). *Lies my teacher told me.* New York: New Press.

Lomawaima, K. T. (1995). Educating Native Americans. In J. A. Banks & C. McGee Banks (Eds.), *Handbook of research on multicultural education* (pp. 331–347). New York: Macmillan.

Long, B. T. & Kurlaender, M. (2009). Do Community Colleges Provide a Viable Pathway to a Baccalaureate Degree? *Educational Evaluation and Policy Analysis, 31*, 30–53.

Long, M. C. & Tienda, M. (2008). Winners and losers: Changes in Texas University admissions post-Hopwood. *Educational Evaluation and Policy Analysis, 30*, 255–280.

Lortie, D. (1975). *School teacher: A sociological study.* Chicago, IL: University of Chicago Press.

Losen, D. & Orfield, G. (Eds.). (2002). *Racial inequity in special education.* Cambridge, MA: Harvard Education Publishing Group.

Lubienski, C. (2001). Redefining "public" education: Charter schools, common schools, and the rhetoric of reform. *Teachers College Record, 103*(4), 634–666.

Lubienski, C. (2003). Innovation in education markets: Theory and evidence on the impact of competition and choice in charter schools. *American Educational Research Journal, 40*(2), 394–443.

Lubienski, C. (2005). Public schools in marketized environments: Shifting incentives and unintended consequences of competition-based educational reforms. *American Journal of Education*, *111*(4), 464–486.

Lubienski, C. (2005). School choice as a civil right: District responses to competition and equal educational opportunity. *Equity & Excellence in Education*, 38(4), 331–341.

Lubienski, C. & Lubienski, S. T. (2006). Charter schools, academic achievement and NCLB. *Journal of School Choice*, 1(3), 55–62.

Lubienski, C. & Weitzel, P. (2010). The Charter school experiment: Expectations, evidence, and implications. Cambridge, MA: Harvard Education Press.

Lubienski, C., Weitzel, P., & Lubienski, S. T. (2009). Is there a "consensus" on school choice and achievement? Advocacy research and the emerging political economy of knowledge production. *Educational Policy*, 23(1), 161–193.

Lubienski, S. T. & Lubienski, C. (2006). School sector and academic achievement: A multi-level analysis of NAEP mathematics data. *American Educational Research Journal*, 43(4), 651–698.

Lubienski, S., Lubienski, C., & Crane, C. (2008). Achievement differences and school type: The role of school climate, teacher certification, and instruction. *American Journal of Education*, 115, 97–138.

Lucas, S. R. (1999). *Tracking inequality: Stratification and mobility in American high schools*. New York: Teachers College Press.

Lucas, S. R. (2001). Race, class, and tournament track mobility. *Sociology of Education*, 74, 139–156.

Lucas, S. R. (2002). Sociodemographic diversity, correlated achievement, and de facto tracking. *Sociology of Education*, 75, 328–348.

Lugg, C. & Robinson, M. (2009). Religion, advocacy coalitions, and the politics of U.S. public schooling. *Educational Policy*, 23, 242–266.

Lukas, J. A. (1986). *Common ground*. New York: Vintage Books.

Luke, A. (1988). *Literacy, textbooks, and ideology*. London: Falmer Press.

Luke, C. & Jennifer, G. (Eds.). (1992). *Feminisms and critical pedagogy*. New York: Routledge.

Lynch, R. G. (2004/2005, Winter). Preschool pays: High-quality education would save billions. *American Educator*, 26–35.

Lyotard, J. F. (1984). *The postmodern condition* (G. Bennington & B. Massumi, Trans.). Minneapolis, MN: University of Minnesota Press.

Lytle, J. H. (1988). Is special education serving minority students? A response to Singer and Butler. *Harvard Educational Review*, 58(1). In T. Hehir & T. Latus (1992). *Special education at the century's end: Evolution of theory and practice since 1970*

(pp. 191–197). Cambridge, MA: Harvard Educational Review.

Macdonald, J. & Macdonald, S. (1981). Gender values and curriculum. *Journal of Curriculum Theorizing*, 3(1), 299–304.

Macedo, D. (1990). *Literacies of power: What Americans are not allowed to know*. Boulder, CO: Westview.

MacInnes, G. (1999). *Kids who pick the wrong parents and other victims of voucher schemes*. New York: The Century Foundation.

MacLeod, J. (1995). *Ain't no makin' it: Aspirations and attainment in a low income neighborhood* (2nd ed.). Boulder, CO: Westview.

Maedus, G. & Clarke, M. (2001). The adverse impact of high-stakes testing on minority students: Evidence from one hundred years of test data. In G. Orfield & M. L. Kornhaber (Eds.), *Raising standards or raising barriers: Inequality and high-Stakes testing in public education* (pp. 85–106). New York: The Century Foundation Press.

Maeroff, G. I. (1988). *The empowerment of teachers: Overcoming the crisis of confidence*. New York: Teachers College Press.

Maher, F. & Tetrault, M. T. (1994). *The feminist classroom*. New York: Basic Books.

Maher, F. & Tetrault, M. K. (2006). *Diversity and privilege in the Academy*. New York: Routledge.

Maier, A. (2012). Doing good and doing well: Credentialism and Teach for America. *Journal of Teacher Education*, 63(10), 10–22.

Maier, A. & Youngs, P. (2009). Teacher preparation programs and teacher labor markets: How social capital may help explain teachers' career choices. *Journal of Teacher Education*, 60(4), 393–407.

Male, G. A. (1992). Educational reform in France. In P. W. Cookson, Jr., A. Sadovnik, & S. Semel (Eds.), *International handbook of educational reform*. Westport, CT: Greenwood Press.

Malone, D. & Rauch, B. (1960). *Empire for liberty*. New York: Appleton-Century-Crofts.

Mangino, W. (2009). The downside of social closure: Brokerage, parental influence, and delinquency among African American boys. *Sociology of Education*, 82, 147–172.

Mannheim, K. (1936). *Ideology and Utopia: An introduction to the sociology of knowledge*. New York: Harcourt, Brace & World.

Mannheim, K. (1952). *Essays on the sociology of knowledge*. New York: Oxford University Press.

Marsh, H. W. (1989a). The effects of attending single-sex and coeducational high schools on achievement, attitudes, behaviors and on sex differences. *Journal of Educational Psychology*, 81, 70–85.

Marsh, H. W. (1989b). Effects of attending single-sex and coeducational high schools: A response to Lee and Bryk. *Journal of Educational Psychology*, 81, 651–653.

Marsh, H. W. (1991). Public, catholic single-sex, and catholic coeducational high schools: Their effects on achievement, affect, and behaviors. *American Journal of Education, 99*, 320–356.

Martin, J. R. (1987). Reforming teacher education, rethinking liberal education. *Teachers College Record, 88*, 406–409.

Martin, R. (1972). Student sex and behavior as determinants of the type and frequency of teacher-student contacts. *Journal of School Psychology, 10*, 339–347.

Martin-Kniep, G. & Kniep, W. M. (1992). Alternative assessment: Essential, not sufficient for systematic change. *Holistic Education Review, 9*(4), 4–13.

Marx, K. (1844/1964). *The economic and philosophical manuscripts of 1844*. New York: International Publishers.

Marx, K. (1867/1967). *Das Kapital, Volume I*. New York: International Publishers.

Marx, K. (1893/1967). *Das Kapital, Volume II*. New York: International Publishers.

Marx, K. (1894/1967). *Das Kapital, Volume III*. New York: International Publishers.

Marx, K. (1852/1963). *The eighteenth brumaire of Louis Bonaparte*. New York: International Publishing Company.

Marx, K. (1847/1971). *The poverty of philosophy*. New York: International Publishers.

Marx, K. & Engels, F. (1846/1947). *The German ideology*. New York: International Publishers.

Marx, K. & Engels, F. (1848/1983). *The communist manifesto*. New York: International Publishers.

Massell, D. & Fuhrman, S., with Kirst, M., Odden, A., Wohlstetter, P., Carver, C., & Yee, G. (1994). *Ten years of state education reform, 1983–1993: Overview with four case studies*. New Brunswick, NJ: Consortium for Policy Research in Education.

Massell, D. & Goertz, M. (1999). *Local strategies for building capacity: The district role in supporting instructional reform*. Philadelphia, PN: CPRE, University of Pennsylvania.

Massey, D. & Denton, N. A. (1993). *American apartheid: Segregation and the making of the underclass*. Cambridge, MA: Harvard University Press.

Mattingly, D., Prislin, R., McKenzie, T., Rodriquez, J., & Kayzar, B. (2002). Evaluating evaluations: The case of parent involvement programs. *Review of Educational Research, 72*(4), 549–576.

May, H., Supovitz, J., & Perda. (2004). *A longitudinal study of the impact of America's Choice on student performance in Rochester, New York, 1998–2003*. Consortium for Policy Research on Education. Philadelphia, PN: University of Pennsylvania.

Mazzeo, C. (2001). Frameworks of state: Assessment policy in historical perspective. *Teachers College Record, 103*(3), 367–397.

McCarthy, C. (1993). Beyond the poverty of theory in race relations: Nonsynchrony and social difference in education. In L. Weis & M. Fine (Eds.), *Beyond silenced voices: Class, race and gender in United States schools* (pp. 325–346). Albany, NY: State University of New York Press.

McCarthy, C. & Critcheloe, W. (Eds.). (1993). *Race, identity and representation in education*. New York and London: Routledge.

McCulloch, G. (2011). *The struggle for the history of education*. New York and London: Routledge.

McDermott, R. P. (1977). Social relations as contexts for learning. *Harvard Educational Review, 47*, 198–213.

McDermott, R. P. & Varenne, H. (1995). Culture as disability. *Anthropology and Education Quarterly, 26*(3), 324–348.

McDill, E. (1978). *An updated answer to the question: Do schools make a difference?* Paper presented at the National Institute of Education: International Conference on School Organization and Effect, San Diego, CA.

McLaren, P. (1989). *Life in schools*. New York: Longman.

McLaren, P. (1991). Schooling and the postmodern body: Critical pedagogy and the politics of enfleshment. In H. Giroux (Ed.), *Postmodernism, feminism, and cultural politics: Redrawing educational boundaries* (pp. 144–173). Albany, NY: State University of New York Press.

McLaren, P. (1995). *Critical pedagogy and predatory culture: Oppositional politics in a postmodern era*. London and New York: Routledge.

McLaren, P. & Hammer, R. (1989). Critical pedagogy and the postmodern challenge: Toward a critical postmodernist pedagogy of liberation. *Educational Foundations, 3*(3), 29–62.

McLaughlin, M., Artiles, A., & Pullin, D. (2001). Challenges for the transformation of special education in the 21st century: Rethinking culture in school reform. *Journal of Special Education Leadership, 14*(2), 51–62.

McLaughlin, M. & Talbert, J. (2003). *Reforming districts: How districts support school reform*. Seattle, WA: Center for the Study of Teaching and Policy.

McLaughlin, M. W. & Little, J. W. (Eds.). (1993). *Teachers work: Individuals, colleagues, and contexts*. New York: Teachers College Press.

McLaughlin, M. W. & Talbert, J. E. (1993a). *Contexts that matter for teaching and learning*. Stanford, CA: Center for Research on the Context of Secondary School Teaching.

McLaughlin, M. W. & Talbert, J. E. (1993b). How the world of students and teachers challenges policy coherence. In S. H. Fuhrman (Ed.), *Designing coherent education policy: Improving the system*. San Francisco, CA: Jossey-Bass.

McNeal, R. B., Jr. (1995). Extracurricular activities and high school dropouts. *Sociology of Education*, 68, 62–81.

McNeil, L. M. (1986). *Contradictions of control: School structure and school knowledge*. New York: Routledge.

McNeil, L. M. (1988a). Contradictions of control, Part I: Administrators and teachers. *Phi Delta Kappan*, 69(5), 333–339.

McNeil, L. M. (1988b). Contradictions of control, Part II: Teachers, students and curriculum. *Phi Delta Kappan*, 69(6), 432–438.

McNeil, L. M. (1988c). Contradictions of control, Part III: Contradictions of reform. *Phi Delta Kappan*, 69(7), 478–485.

McNeil, L. M. (1988d). *Contradictions of control: School structure and school knowledge*. New York: Routledge.

McNeil, L. M. (2000). *Contradictions of school reform: Educational costs of standardized testing*. New York: Routledge.

Mehan, H., Villanueva, I., Hubbard, L., & Lintz, A. (1996). *Constructing school success: The consequences of un-tracking low achieving students*. Cambridge: Cambridge University Press.

Meier, D. (1995). *The power of their ideas*. Boston, MA: Beacon.

Melguizo, T. (2010). Are students of color more likely to graduate from college if they attend more selective institutions?: Evidence from a cohort of recipients and nonrecipients of the gates millennium scholarship program. *Educational Evaluation and Policy Analysis*, 32, 249–272.

Metcalf, K. K. (1998). *Evaluation of the Cleveland scholarship program: Second year report 1997–98*. Bloomington, IN: Indiana Center for Evaluation, Indiana University.

Metcalf, K. K. (1999). *Evaluation of the Cleveland scholarship & tutoring grant program 1996–1999*. Bloomington, IN: Indiana Center for Evaluation, Indiana University.

Metcalf, K. K., West, S. D., Legan, N. A., Paul, K. M., & Boone, W. J. (2001). *Cleveland scholarship program evaluation 1998–2000*. Bloomington, IN: Indiana Center for Evaluation, Indiana University.

Metcalf, K. K., West, S. D., Legan, N. A., Paul, K. M., & Boone, W. J. (2003). *Evaluation of the Cleveland scholarship and tutoring program 1998–2001*. Bloomington, IN: Indiana Center for Evaluation, Indiana University.

Metcalf, K. K., et. al. (2004). *Evaluation of the Cleveland scholarship and tutoring program 1998–2002*. Bloomington, IN: Indiana Center for Evaluation, Indiana University.

Metz, M. H. (1978). *Classrooms and corridors: The crisis of authority in desegregated secondary schools*. Berkeley, CA: University of California Press.

Metz, M. H. (1986). *Different by design: The context and character of three magnet schools*. New York: Routledge & Kegan Paul.

Metz, M. H. (1990). How social class differences shape teachers' work. In M. McLaughlin, J. Talbert, & N. Bascia (Eds.), *The contexts of teaching in secondary schools: Teachers' realities* (pp. 40–107). New York: Teachers College Press.

Meyer, J. W. (1977, July). The effects of education as an institution. *American Journal of Sociology*, 83, 55–77.

Meyer, J. W. & Rowan, B. (1977). The structure of educational organizations. In M. Meyer & Associates (Eds.), *Environments and organizations* (pp. 78–109). San Francisco, CA: Jossey-Bass.

Meyer, J. W. & Rowan, B. (1978). Institutionalized organizations: Formal structure as myth and ceremony. *American Journal of Sociology*, 83, 340–363.

Meyer, J. W., Kamens, D., Benavot, A., Cha, Y. K., & Wong, S. Y. (1992). *School knowledge for the masses: World models and national primary curriculum categories in the twentieth century*. London: Falmer.

Meyer, J. W., Ramirez, F. O., Rubinson, R., & Boli, J. (1977). The world educational revolution, 1950–1970. *Sociology of Education*, 50, 242–258.

Meyer, J. W., Tyack, D., Nagel, J., & Gordon, A. (1979). Public education as nation-building in America. *American Journal of Sociology*, 85, 591–613.

Mickelson, R. A. (1990). The attitude-achievement paradox among black adolescents. *Sociology of Education*, 63, 44–61.

Mickelson, R. A. (1999). International business machinations: A case study of corporate involvement in local educational reform. *Teachers College Record*, 100(3), 476–512.

Mickelson, R. A. (2002). Subverting Swann: First and second generation segregation in the Charlotte-Mecklenburg schools. *American Education Research Journal*, 38(2), 215–252.

Mickelson, R. A. (2003). Gender Bourdieu, and the anomaly of women's achievement redux. *Sociology of Education*, 75, 373–375.

Mickelson, R. A. (2008). Twenty-first century social science on school racial diversity and educational outcomes. *Ohio State Law Journal*, 69, 1173–1227.

Mickelson, R. A. & Ray, C. A. (1994). Fear of falling from grace: The middle class, downward mobility, and school desegregation. *Research in Sociology of Education and Socialization*, 10, 207–238.

Mickelson, R. A., Ray, C. A., & Smith, S. S. (1993). The growth machine and the politics of urban educational reform: The case of Charlotte, North Carolina. In N. Stromquist (Ed.), *Education in the urban context*. New York: Praeger.

Miles, K. H. (2000). *Money matters: Rethinking school district spending to support Comprehensive School*

Reform. Arlington, VA: New American Schools Issue Brief.

Miller, J. (1982). Feminist pedagogy: The sound of silence breaking. *Journal of Curriculum Theorizing*, 4, 5–11.

Miller, L. & Smith, S. (2011). Did the no child left behind act miss the mark? Assessing the potential benefits from an accountability system for early childhood education. *Educational Policy*, 25, 193–214.

Miller-Bernal, L. (1980). Comment on Tidball's women's colleges and women's achievers revisited. *Signs*, 6, 342–345.

Miller-Bernal, L. (1989). College experiences and sex-role attitudes: Does a women's college make a difference? *Youth and Society*, 20, 363–387.

Miller-Bernal, L. (1993). Single sex versus coeducational environments: A comparison of women students' experiences at four colleges. *American Journal of Education*, 102(1), 23–54.

Miller-Bernal, L. (2000). *Separate by degree: Women students' experiences in single-sex and coeducational colleges*. New York: Peter Lang.

Miller-Bernal, L. & Poulson, S. (2004). *Going coed: Coeducation at formerly men's college, 1950–2000*. Nashville, TN: Vanderbilt University Press.

Miller-Bernal, L. & Poulson, S. (2005). *Going coed: Coeducation at formerly women's colleges*. Nashville, TN: Vanderbilt University Press.

Miller-Bernal, L. & Poulson, S. L. (2006). *Challenged by coeducation : Women's colleges since the 1960s* (1st ed.). Nashville, TN: Vanderbilt University Press.

Mills, C. W. (1956). *The power elite*. New York: Oxford University Press.

Mills, C. W. (1959). *The sociological imagination*. New York: Oxford University Press.

Milofsky, C. (1974). Why special education isn't special. *Harvard Educational Review*, 44(4). In T. Hehir & T. Latus. (1992). *Special education at the century's end: Evolution of theory and practice since 1970* (pp. 47–68). Cambridge, MA: Harvard Educational Review.

Miner, B. (2010). The ultimate superpower: Supersized dollars driving Waiting For Superman agenda. Rethinking Schools, Not Waiting for Superman website. www.notwaitingforsuperman.org/Articles/20101020.MinerUltimateSuperpower?action=download&upname=TheUltimateSuperpower_Miner.pdf. Accessed January 17, 2011.

Mirel, J. E. (1993). *The rise and fall of an urban school system: Detroit, 1907–81*. Ann Arbor, MI: University of Michigan Press.

Miron, G. & Nelson, C. (2001). *Autonomy in exchange for accountability: An initial study of Pennsylvania charter schools—Executive summary*. Kalamazoo, MI: The Evaluation Center, Western Michigan University. www.wmich.edu/evalctr. Accessed October 1, 2012.

Miron, G. & Nelson, C. (2002). *What's public about charter schools? Lessons learned about choice and accountability*. Thousand Oaks, CA: Corwin Press.

Miron, G. & Nelson, C. (2004). Student academic achievement in charter schools: What we know and why we know so little. In K. Bulkley & Wohlstetter (Eds.), *Taking account of charter schools: What's happened and what's next* (pp. 161–175). New York: Teachers College Press

Miron, G., Evergreen, S., & Urschel, J. (2008). *The impact of school choice reforms on student achievement*. Boulder and Tempe: Education and the Public Interest Center & Education Policy Research Unit. http://nepc.colorado.edu/files/CHOICE-10-Miron-FINAL-withapp22.pdf. Accessed January 20, 2011.

Mitrano, B. (1979). Feminist theology and curriculum theory. *Journal of Curriculum Studies*, 2, 211–220.

Mitter, W. (1992). Germany. In P. W. Cookson, Jr., A. R. Sadovnik, & S. F. Semel (Eds.), *International handbook of educational reform* (pp. 209–228). Westport, CT: Greenwood Press.

Moe, T. M. (2001). *Schools, vouchers, and the American public*. Washington, DC: Brookings Institution Press.

Montt, G. (2011). Cross-national differences in educational achievement inequality. *Sociology of Education*, 84, 49–68.

Moore, R., Arnot, M., Beck, J., & Daniels, H. (2010). *Knowledge, power and educational reform: Applying the sociology of Basil Bernstein*. Oxford: Routledge.

Morgan, S. L. & Todd, J. J. (2009). Intergenerational closure and academic achievement in high school: A new evaluation of Coleman's conjecture. *Sociology of Education*, 82(3), 267–285.

Morris, V. C. (1966). *Existentialism in education*. New York: Harper and Row.

Mortenson, T. (1997). Research seminar on public policy analysis of opportunity for post secondary education. Education Trust website, www.edtrust.org. Accessed May 25, 2005.

Mortimer, J. T. (1996). A sociological perspective on school-to-work opportunities: Response and rejoinder. In K. Borman, P. W. Cookson, Jr., A. R. Sadovnik, & J. Z. Spade (Eds.), *Implementing educational reform: Sociological perspectives on educational policy* (pp. 171–184). Norwood, NJ: Ablex.

Mortimore, P. & Whitty, G. (1999). School improvement: A remedy for social exclusion. In A. Hayton (Ed.), *Tackling disaffection and social exclusion* (pp. 80–94). London: Kogan Page.

Moscovitch, R., Sadovnik, A. R., Barr, J. M., Davidson, T., Moore, T. L., Powell, R., Tractenberg, P. L., Wagman, E., & Zha, P. (2010). *Governance and urban school improvement: Lessons for New Jersey from nine cities*. Rutgers, NJ: Institute on Education Law and Policy.

Mosteller, F. (1995). The Tennessee study of class size in the early grades. *The Future of Children, 5*(2), 113–127.

Mosteller, F., Light, R. J., & Sachs, J. A. (1996). Sustained inquiry in education: Lessons from skill grouping and class size. *Harvard Education Review, 66*(4), 797–842.

Mosteller, F. & Moynihan, D. P. (1972). *On equality of educational opportunity.* New York: Vintage Books.

Muller, C. (1993). Parent involvement and academic achievement: An analysis of family resources available to the child. In B. Schneider & J. S. Coleman (Eds.), *Parents, their children, and schools* (pp. 77–114). Boulder, CO: Westview Press.

Muller, C. & Kerbow, D. (1993). Parent involvement in the home, school, and community. In B. Schneider & J. S. Coleman (Eds.), *Parents, their children, and schools* (pp. 13–42). Boulder, CO: Westview Press.

Murphy, J. (1991). *Restructuring schools: Capturing and assessing the phenomena.* New York: Teachers College Press.

Murphy, J. & Hallinger, P. (1993). *Restructuring schooling: Learning from ongoing efforts.* Newbury Park, CA: Corwin.

Murphy, J. & Louis, K. S. (1994). *Reshaping the principalship: Insights from transformational reform efforts.* Thousand Oaks, CA: Corwin.

Murray, C. (1989). *In pursuit of happiness and good government.* New York: Touchstone Books.

Muse, I. (n.d). One-teacher schools in America. *Teacher Educator, 33,* 141.

Myrdal, G. (1944). *An American dilemma.* New York: Harper and Ruthers.

Nasir, N., McLaughlin, M., & Jones, A. (2009). What does it mean to be African American? Constructions of race and academic identity in an urban public high school. *American Educational Research Journal, 46,* 73–114.

Nassaw, D. (1979). *Schooled to order.* New York: Oxford University Press.

National Center for History in the Schools. (1994). *National standards for United States history: Exploring the American experience.* Los Angeles: Author.

National Center for Educational Statistics. (1997). *Monitoring school quality: An indicators report.* Washington, DC: U.S. Department of Education, Office of Educational Research.

National Commission on Excellence in Education. (1983). *A nation at risk.* Washington, DC: U.S. Government Printing Office.

National Commission on Social Studies in Schools. (1989). *Charting a course: Social studies for the 21st century.* Washington, DC: Author.

National Commission on Teaching and America's Future. (1996). *What matters most: Teaching for America's future.* New York: Author.

National Council for the Social Studies. (1994). *Expectations of excellence: Curriculum standards for social studies.* Washington, DC: Author.

National Council of Teachers of Mathematics. (1989). *Curriculum and evaluation standards for school mathematics.* Reston, VA: Author.

National Education Goals Panel. (1988). *Restructuring the education system.* Washington, DC: Author.

National Education Goals Panel. (1989). *Restructuring in progress.* Washington, DC: Author.

National Education Goals Panel. (1991). *Measuring progress toward the national education goals.* Washington, DC: Author.

National Working Commission on Choice in K-12 Education. (2003). *School choice: Doing it the right way makes a difference.* Washington, DC: The Brookings Institution, available at www.brookings.edu/gs/brown/ 20031116schoolchoicereport.pdf.

Natriello, G. (Ed.). (1986). *School dropouts: Patterns and policies.* New York: Teachers College Press.

Natriello, G. (Ed.). (1997). The state of American education: Special section. *Teachers College Record, 99*(1), 9–72.

Natriello, G., McDill, E., & Pallas, A. (1990). *Schooling disadvantaged students: Racing against catastrophe.* New York: Teachers College Press.

Neckerman, K. (2006). Schools betrayed: Roots of failure in inner-city education. Chicago, IL: University of Chicago Press.

Neil, R., Farley-Ripple, E., & Bymes, V. (2009). The effect of teacher certification on middle grades and achievement in an urban district. *Educational Policy, 23,* 732–760.

Neill, A. S. (1960). *Summerhill.* New York: Holt.

Nelson, F. H., Rosenberg, B., & Van Meter, N. (2004). *Charter school achievement on the 2003 National Assessment of Educational Progress.* Boulder, CO: National Education Policy Center.

Network of Progressive Educators. (1991). Statement of principles. *Pathways, 7*(2), 3.

New Jersey Assessment of Knowledge and Skills. (2011). Trenton: New Jersey Department of Education.

New Jersey Department of Education. (2004). School report cards. www.state.nj.us/education. Accessed December 18, 2004.

New York City Board of Education. (1989). *Human relations task force: Final report.* New York: Author.

New York City Department of Education. (2003). Student achievement reports. www.nycenet.edu. Accessed September 18, 2004.

New York State Board of Regents. (1998). *Teachers prepared. The Regents report on teacher education in New York state.* Albany, NY: New York State Department of Education.

New York State Council on Children and Families. (2012). Kids' well-being indicators clearinghouse. www.nyskwic.org. Accessed October 1, 2012.

New York State Board of Regents. (1999). *Teaching to higher standards*. Albany, NY: New York State Department of Education.

New York State Department of Education. (2004). School report cards. www.nysed.gov. Accessed January 30, 2005.

Newberg, N. A. & Cohen, B. J. (1991). *The Southwest Philadelphia educational complex: Report on a pilot project to create and manage a cluster of schools based on feeder patterns*. Philadelphia, PA: Graduate School of Education, University of Pennsylvania.

Nieto, S. (1995). A history of the education of Puerto Rican students in U.S. mainland schools: "Losers," "outsiders," or "leaders." In J. A. Banks & C. McGee Banks (Eds.), *Handbook of research on multicultural education* (pp. 388–411). New York: Macmillan.

Noddings, N. (1984). *Caring: A feminine approach to ethics and moral education*. Berkeley, CA: University of California Press.

Noddings, N. (1995). *Philosophy of education*. Boulder, CO: Westview.

Noguera, P. A. (2003). *City schools and the American dream: Reclaiming the promise of public education*. New York: Teachers College Press.

Noguera, P. A. (2004) Social capital and the education of immigrant students: Categories and generalizations. *Sociology of Education, 77*, 180–184.

O'Day, J. A. (2002). Complexity, accountability, and school improvement. *Harvard Educational Review, 72*(3), 293–329.

O'Day, J. & Bitter, C. (2003). *Evaluation study of the immediate intervention/underperforming schools program and the high achieving/improving schools program of the P.S. Accountability Act of 1999*. Palo Alto, CA: American Institutes for Research.

O'Day, J. A. & Smith, M. S. (1992). Systemic reform and equal educational opportunity. In S. H. Fuhrman (Ed.), *Designing coherent education policy* (pp. 250–312). San Francisco, CA: Jossey-Bass.

O'Day, J., Bitter, C. & Gomez, L. (2011). *Education reform in New York City*. Harvard Education Press.

Oakes, J. (1985). *Keeping track: How schools structure inequality*. New Haven, CT: Yale University Press.

Oakes, J. (1990). *Multiplying inequalities: The effects of race, social class, and tracking on opportunities to learn math and science*. Santa Monica, CA: Rand.

Oakes, J. (1994a). *Opportunity to learn: Can standards-based reform be equity-based reform?* Paper presented for Effects of New Standards and Assessment on High Risk Students and Disadvantaged Schools, a research forum for the New Standards Project, Harvard University, Cambridge, MA.

Oakes, J. (1994b). More than misapplied technology: A normative and political response to Hallinan. *Sociology of Education, 67*, 84–89.

Oakes, J. (2004). Investigating the claims in *Williams v. the State of California*: An unconstitutional denial of education's basic tools. *Teachers College Record, 106*(10), 1889–1906.

Oakes, J. (2005). *Keeping track*. New Haven, CT: Yale University Press.

Oakes, J., Gamoran, A., & Page, R. N. (1992). Curriculum differentiation: Opportunities, outcomes, and meanings. In P. W. Jackson (Ed.), *Handbook of research on curriculum* (pp. 570–608). New York: Macmillan.

Oakes, J. & Guiton, G. (1995). Matchmaking: The dynamics of high school tracking decisions. *American Educational Research Journal, 32*, 3–33.

Oakes, J. & Saunders, M. (2008). *Beyond tracking: Multiple pathways to college, career, and civic participation*. Cambridge, MA: Harvard Education Press.

Odden, A. (2000). The costs of sustaining educational change through comprehensive school reform. *Phi Delta Kappan, 81*(6), 433–438.

Odden, A., Picus, L., & Goetz, M. (2010). A 50-state strategy to achieve school finance adequacy. *Educational Policy, 24*, 628–654.

Ogbu, J. (1978). *Minority education and caste*. New York: Academic Press.

Ogbu, J. (1979). Social stratification and the socialization of competence. *Anthropology and Education Quarterly, 10*(1).

Ogbu, J. (1987). Variability in minority school performance: A problem in search of an explanation. *Anthropology and Education Quarterly, 18*, 312–334.

Ogbu, J. U. (1992). Low school performance as adaptation: The case of blacks in Stockton, California. In M. A. Gibson & J. U. Ogbu (Eds.), *Minority status and schooling: A comparative study of immigrants and involuntary minorities* (pp. 249–285). New York: Garland.

Ogbu, J. U. (1999, Summer). Beyond language: Ebonics, proper English, and identity in a Black-American speech community. *American Educational Research Journal, 36*(2), 147–184.

Ogbu, J. (2003). *Black Americans students in an affluent suburb: A study of academic disengagement*. Mahwah, NJ: Erlbaum.

Olneck, M. R. (1993). Terms of inclusion: Has multiculturalism redefined equality in American education? *American Journal of Education, 101*, 234–260.

Olneck, M. R. (2009). What have immigrants wanted from American schools? What do they want now?: Historical and contemporary perspectives on immigrants, language, and American schooling. *American Journal of Education, 115*(3), 379–406.

Olsen, B. & Sexton, D. (2009). Threat rigidity, school reform, and how teachers view their work inside current education policy contexts. *American Educational Research Journal, 46*, 9–44.

Olsen, L. (1999). Researchers rate whole-school reform models. *Education Week*, 14.

Orfield, G. (1992). Money, equity, and college access. *Harvard Educational Review, 62*, 337–372.

Orfield, G. (2004). *Dropouts in America: Confronting the graduate rate crisis*. Cambridge, MA: Harvard University Press.

Orfield, G. & Ashkinaze, C. (1991). *The closing door: Conservative policy and black opportunity*. Chicago, IL: University of Chicago Press.

Orfield, G. & Eaton, S. (1996). *Dismantling desegregation: The quiet reversal of Brown v. Board of Education*. New York: New Press.

Orfield, G. & Lee, C. (2002). *Why segregation matters: Poverty and educational inequality*. Cambridge, MA: The Civil Rights Project, Harvard University Press.

Orfield, G. & Lee, J. (2004). *Brown at 50: King's dream or Plessy's nightmare?* http://civilrightsproject. ucla.edu/research/k-12-education/integration-and-diversity/brown-at-50-king2019s-dream-or-plessy 2019s-nightmare/orfield-brown-50-2004.pdf. Accessed October 1, 2012.

Orfield, G. & Miller, E. (1998). *Chilling admissions: The affirmative action crisis and the search for alternatives*. Cambridge, MA: Harvard Education Publishing Group.

Orfield, G. & Yun, J. T. (1999). Resegregation in American schools. Cambridge, MA: The Civil Rights Project, Harvard University, http://civilrights project.ucla.edu/research/k-12-education/integration-and-diversity/resegregation-in-american-schools/ orfield-resegregation-in-american-schools-1999.pdf. Accessed October 1, 2012.

Owens, A. (2010). Neighborhoods and schools as competing and reinforcing contexts for educational attainment. *Sociology of Education, 83*(4), 287–311.

Ozmon, H. A. & Craver, S. M. (1990). *Philosophical foundations of education*. Columbus, OH: Merrill.

Page, A. L. & Clelland, D. A. (1978, September). The Kanawha County textbook controversy. *Social Forces, 57*, 265–281.

Page, R. N. (1991). *Lower track classrooms: A curricular and cultural perspective*. New York: Teachers College Press.

Page, R. N. & Valli, L. (Eds.). (1990). *Curriculum differentiation: Interpretive studies in U.S. secondary schools*. Albany, NY: State University of New York Press.

Pallas, A. M., Entwisle, D. R., Alexander, K. L., & Cadigan, D. (1987). Children who do exceptionally well in first grade. *Sociology of Education, 60*, 257–271.

Pallas, A. M., Entwisle, D. R., Alexander, K. L., & Stluka, M. F. (1994). Ability group effects: Instructional, social, or institutional. *Sociology of Education, 67*, 27–46.

Palmieri, P. (1987). From republican motherhood to race suicide: Arguments on the higher education of women in the United States, 1820–1920. In C. Lasser (Ed.), *Educating men and women together* (pp. 49–66). Champaign-Urbana, IL: University of Illinois Press.

Palmieri, P. (1995). *In Adamless Eden*. New Haven, CT: Yale University Press.

Pang, V. O. (1995). Asian Pacific American students: A diverse and complex population. In J. A. Banks & C. McGee Banks (Eds.), *Handbook of research on multicultural education* (pp. 412–424). New York: Macmillan.

Pankratz, R. S. & Petrosko, J. M. (Eds.) (2000). *All children can learn: Lessons from the Kentucky reform experience*. San Francisco, CA: Jossey-Bass.

Park, H., Byun, S., & Kim, K. (2011). Parental involvement and students' cognitive outcomes in Korea: Focusing on private tutoring. *Sociology of Education, 84*, 3–22.

Parsons, T. (1959). The school class as a social system. *Harvard Educational Review, 29*, 297–318.

Passow, A. H. (1989). Present and future directions in school reform. In T. Sergiovanni & J. Moore (Eds.), *Schooling for tomorrow* (pp. 13–39). Boston, MA: Allyn & Bacon.

Passow, A. H., Noah, H. J., Eckstein, M. A., & Mallea, J. R. (1976). *The national case study: An empirical comparative study of education in twenty-one countries*. New York: Wiley.

Paterson, L. & Iannelli, C. (2007). Social class and educational attainment: A comparative study of England, Wales, and Scotland. *Sociology of Education, 80*(4), 330–358.

Patten, K. E. & Campbell, S. R. (2011). *Educational neuroscience*. Malden, MA: Wiley-Blackwell.

Patterson, J. T. (2002). *Brown v. Board of Education: A civil rights milestone and its troubled legacy*. New York: Oxford.

Paulu, N. (1989). *Improving schools and empowering parents: Choice in American education*. Washington, DC: U.S. Government Printing Office.

Payne, C. (2008). *So much reform, so little change: The persistence of failure in urban schools*. Cambridge, MA: Harvard Education Press.

Perez-Pena, R. (2012). At CUNY, stricter admissions bring ethnic shift, *New York Times*. Retrieved from www.nytimes.com/2012/05/23/nyregion/at-cunys-top-colleges-black-and-hispanic-freshmen-enrollments-drop.html?ref=cityuniversityofnewyork. Accessed October 1, 2012.

Perkinson, H. (1995). *The imperfect panacea: American faith in education, 1865–1968*. New York: McGraw-Hill.

Perlmann, J. (1988). *Ethnic differences: Schooling and social structure among the Irish, Italians, Jews, and Blacks in an American city, 1880–1935*. New York: Cambridge University Press.

Perlstein, D. (2004). *Justice, justice: School politics and the eclipse of liberalism*. New York: Peter Lang.

Persell, C. H. (1977). *Education and inequality*. New York: The Free Press.

Persell, C. H. (1990). *Understanding society*. New York: HarperCollins.

Persell, C. H. & Cookson, P. W., Jr. (1982). *The effective principal in action*. Reston, VA: National Association of Secondary Principals.

Persell, C. H., Catsambis, S., & Cookson, P. W., Jr. (1992). Family background, school type, and college attendance: A conjoint system of cultural capital transmission. *Journal of Research on Adolescence, 2*, 1–23.

Peshkin, A. (1986). *God's choice: The total world of a fundamentalist Christian school*. Chicago, IL: University of Chicago Press.

Peters, R. S. (1965). *Ethics and education*. London: Allen and Unwin.

Peters, R. S. (Ed.). (1973). *The philosophy of education*. London: Oxford University Press.

Phillips, K. P. (1990). *The politics of rich and poor: Wealth and the American electorate in the Reagan aftermath*. New York: Random House.

Pickering, W. F. & Walford, G. (1998). *Durkheim on education*. London: Routledge.

Pickering, W. S. F. (2009). *Durkheim: Essays on morals and education*. New York: Routledge.

Picus, L. (1995). *Does money matter in education? A policy-maker's guide*. Selected Papers in School Finance. Washington, DC: National Center for Education Statistics.

Pinar, W. F. (1975). Currere: Toward reconceptualization. In W. F. Pinar (Ed.), *Curriculum theorizing: The reconceptualists* (pp. 396–414). Berkeley, CA: McCutchan.

Pinar, W. F. (1978a). Notes on the curriculum field 1978. *Educational Researcher, 7*(8), 5–12.

Pinar, W. F. (1978b). The reconceptualization of curriculum studies. *Journal of Curriculum Studies, 10*(3), 205–214.

Pinar, W. F. (1979). What is reconceptualization? *The Journal of Curriculum Theorizing, 1*, 93–104.

Pinar, W. F. (Ed.). (1988). *Contemporary curriculum discourses*. Scottsdale, AZ: Gorsuch Scarisbrick.

Pinar, W. F., Reynolds, W. M., Slattery, P., & Taubman, P. M. (1995). *Understanding curriculum*. New York: Peter Lang.

Pincus, F. L. (1980). The false promise of community colleges. *Harvard Educational Review, 50*, 332–360.

Pincus, F. L. (1985). From equity to excellence: The rebirth of educational conservatism. In B. Gross & R. Gross (Eds.), *The great school debate* (pp. 329–344). New York: Simon and Schuster.

Pink, W. & Noblit, G. W. (Eds.). (1995). *Continuity and contradiction: The futures of the sociology of education*. Creskill, NJ: Hampton Press.

Plank, S., DeLuca, S., & Estacion, A. (2008). High school dropout and the role of career and technical education: A survival analysis of surviving high school. *Sociology of Education, 81*, 371–396.

Plato. (1945). *Republic*. New York: Oxford University Press.

Plato. (1971). *Meno*. New York: Macmillan.

Plato. (1986). *The dialogues of Plato*. New York: Bantam.

Pogrow, S. (1996). Reforming the wannabe reformers: Why education reforms almost always end up making things worse. *Phi Delta Kappan, 77*(10), 656–663.

Pogrow, S. (1999). Rejoinder: Consistent large gains and high levels of achievement are the best measures of program quality: Pogrow responds to Slavin. *Educational Researcher, 28*(8), 24–31.

Pogrow, S. (2000). The unsubstantiated Success of Success For All. *Phi Delta Kappan. 81*(8), 596–600.

Porter, A. C., Polikoff, M. S., & Smithson, J. (2009). Is there a de facto national intended curriculum? Evidence From state content standards. *Educational Evaluation and Policy Analysis, 31*, 238–268.

Powell, A. G., Farrar, E., & Cohen, D. K. (1985). *The shopping mall high school*. Boston, MA: Houghton Mifflin.

Power, S., Warren, S., Gillborn, D., Clark, A., Thomas, S., & Coate, K. (2001). *Education in deprived areas*. London: Institute of Education University of London.

Powers, J. (2009). *Charter schools: From reform imagery to reform reality*. New York: Palgrave.

Powers, J. M., & Cookson, P. W., Jr. (1999). School choice as a political movement. *Educational Policy, 13*(1,2), 104–122.

Pratt, C. (1924). *Experimental practice in the city and country school*. New York: E. P. Dutton.

Publishers Weekly. (2003). Review of Rosemary Salomone, *Same, different, equal: Rethinking single-sex schooling*. New York: Publishers Weekly, Reed Business Information.

Pugach, M. & Lilly, M. S. (1984). Reconceptualizing support services for classroom teachers: Implications for teacher education. *Journal of Teacher Education, 35*(5), 48–55.

Quality counts, 1999. (1999, January 11). *Education Week, 28*(17).

Ramirez, F. O. & Boli, J. (1987a). Global patterns of educational institutionalization. In G. M. Thomas et al. (Eds.), *Institutional structure: Constituting state, society, and the individual*. Newbury Park, CA: Sage.

Ramirez, F. O. & Boli, J. (1987b, January). The political construction of mass schooling: European origins and worldwide institutionalization. *Sociology of Education, 60*, 15.

Ravitch, D. (1974). *The great school wars, New York City, 1805–1973: A history of the public schools as battlefield of social change.* New York: Basic Books.

Ravitch, D. (1977). *The revisionists revised.* New York: Basic Books.

Ravitch, D. (1983). *The troubled crusade.* New York: Basic Books.

Ravitch, D. (1985). *The schools we deserve.* New York: Basic Books.

Ravitch, D. (1989). *Multiculturalism in the curriculum.* Presentation to the Manhattan Institute.

Ravitch, D. (1994). *Personal communication.* New York: Author.

Ravitch, D. (2000). *Left back: A century of failed school reforms.* New York: Simon & Schuster.

Ravitch, D. (2010). The death and life of the great American school system. New York: Basic Books.

Ravitch, D. & Finn, C. E. (1987). *What do our seventeen year olds know?* New York: Basic Books.

Ray, C. A. & Mickelson, R. A. (1993). Restructured students for restructured work: The economy, school reform, and noncollegebound youth. *Sociology of Education, 66,* 1–23.

Ready, D. (2010). Socioeconomic disadvantage, school attendance, and early cognitive development: The differential effects of school exposure. *Sociology of Education, 83,* 271–286.

Ready, D. G., Lee, V. E., & Welner, K. (2004). Educational equity and social structure: School size, overcrowding, and school-within-schools. *Teachers College Record, 106*(10), 1989–2014.

Ream, R. & Palardy, G. (2008). Reexamining social class differences in the availability and the educational utility of parental social capital. *American Educational Research Journal, 45,* 274–318.

Ream, R. & Rumberger, R. (2008). Student engagement, peer social capital, and school dropout among Mexican American and non-Latino white students. *Sociology of Education, 81,* 109–139.

Reardon, S. F. (2001). Suburban racial change and suburban school segregation: 1987–96. *Sociology of Education, 74,* 79–101.

Reardon, S. F. (2011) The widening academic achievement gap between the rich and the poor: New evidence and possible explanations. In R. Murnane & G. Duncan (Eds.), *Whither opportunity? Rising inequality and the uncertain life chances of low-income children,* New York: Russell Sage Foundation, 2011.

Reardon, S. F. & Bischoff, K. (2011). Income inequality and income segregation. *AJS American Journal of Sociology, 116*(4), 1092–1153.

Reardon, S. & Bischoff, K. (2011) More unequal and more separate: Growth in the residential segregation of families by income, 1970–2009. *US2010 Project.*

Reardon, S. & Bischoff, K. (Forthcoming). Income inequality and income segregation. *American Journal of Sociology.*

Reardon, S. & Rhodes, K. (Forthcoming). *The effects of socioeconomic school integration plans on racial school desegregation.* In E. Frankenberg, E. DeBray-Pelot, & G. Orfield (Eds.), *Legal and policy options for racially integrated education in the South and the nation,* Chapel Hill, NC: University of North Carolina Press.

Reardon, S., Arshan, N., Atteberry, A., & Kurlaender, M. (2010). Effects of failing a high school exit exam on course taking, achievement and persistence, and graduation. *Educational Evaluation and Policy Analysis, 32,* 498–520.

Reardon, S., Grewal, E., Kalogrides, D., & Greenberg, E. (Forthcoming). Brown fades: The end of court-ordered school desegregation and the resegregation of American public schools. *Journal of Policy Analysis and Management.*

Rebell, M. A. (2009). *Courts and kids: Pursuing educational equity through the state courts.* Chicago, IL: University of Chicago Press.

Reese, W. J. (1986). *Power and the promise of school reform: Grassroots movements during the progressive era.* Boston, MA: Routledge & Kegan Paul.

Reese, W. J. (1995). *The origins of the American high school.* New Haven, CT: Yale University Press.

Reich, R. B. (1990). Education and the next economy. In S. Bacharach (Ed.), *Education reform: Making sense of it all* (pp. 194–212). Boston, MA: Allyn & Bacon.

Reich, R. B. (1991, January 20). Succession of the successful. *The New York Times Magazine,* pp. 42–45.

Renzulli, L., Parrott, H., & Beattie, I. (2011). Racial mismatch and school type: Teacher satisfaction and retention in charter and traditional public schools. *Sociology of Education, 84,* 23–48.

Reynolds, M. C., Wang, M. C., & Walberg, H. J. (1987). The necessary restructuring of special and general education. *Exceptional Children, 53*(5), 391–398.

Riegle-Crumb, C. & Grodsky, E. (2010). Racial-ethnic differences at the intersection of math course-taking and achievement. *Sociology of Education, 83,* 248–270.

Riehl, C. (2001). Bridges to the future: Contributions of qualitative research to the sociology of education. *Sociology of Education, 74,* Extra Issue, 115–134.

Riordan, C. (1985). Public and catholic schooling: The effects of gender context policy. *American Journal of Education, 93,* 518–540.

Riordan, C. (1990). *Girls and boys in school: Together or separate?* New York: Teachers College Press.

Riordan, C. (1992). Single- and mixed-gender colleges for women: Educational, attitudinal, and occupational outcomes. *Review of Higher Education, 15,* 327–346.

Riordan, C. (1994). Single-gender schools: Outcomes for African and Hispanic Americans. *Research in Sociology of Education and Socialization, 10*(1994): 177–205.

Riordan, C. (1997). *Equality and achievement: An introduction to the sociology of education.* New York: Longman.

Riordan, C. (1998). The future of single-sex schools: In *Separated by sex: A critical look at single-sex education for girls* (pp. 53–62). Washington, DC: AAUW Foundation.

Riordan, C. (1999, November 17). The silent gender gap. *Education Week.*

Rist, R. C. (1970). Student social class and teacher expectations: The self-fulfilling prophecy in ghetto education. *Harvard Educational Review, 40,* 411–451.

Rist, R. C. (1973). *The urban school: A factory for failure.* Cambridge, MA: MIT Press.

Rizvi, F. & Lingard, B. (2009). *Globalizing education policy.* New York: Routledge.

Rodriguez, L. (2008). Teachers know you can do more: Understanding how school culture of success affects urban high school students. *Educational Policy, 22,* 758–780.

Roeber, E. D. (2003). *Assessment models for No Child Left Behind.* Washington, DC: Education Commission of the States, www.ecs.org/html/Document.asp?chouseid=4009. Accessed October 1, 2012.

Rofes, E. & Stulberg, L. (2006). *The emancipatory promise of charter schools.* Albany, NY: SUNY Press.

Rogers, D. (1968). *110 Livingston Street: Politics and bureaucracy in the New York City schools.* New York: Random House.

Rorty, R. (1980). *Philosophy and the mirror of nature.* Princeton, NJ: Princeton University Press.

Rosenbaum, J. E. (1976). *Making inequality: The hidden curriculum of high school tracking.* New York: Wiley.

Rosenbaum, J. E. (1980a). Social implications of educational grouping. In D. Berliner (Ed.), *Review of research in education* (pp. 361–401). Washington, DC: American Educational Research Association.

Rosenbaum, J. E. (1980b). Track misperceptions and frustrated college plans. *Sociology of Education, 53,* 74–87.

Rosenbaum, J. E. (1998). College-for-all: Do students understand what college demands? *Social Psychology of Education, 2,* 50–85.

Rosenbaum, J. E. (2001). *Beyond college for all: Career paths for the forgotten half.* New York: Russell Sage Foundation.

Rosenbaum, J. (2011). The complexities of college for all: Beyond fairy-tale dreams. *Sociology of Education, 84,* 113–117.

Rosenbaum, J. & Deil-Amen, R. (2006). *After admission: From college access to college success* (with Regina). New York: Russell Sage Foundation.

Rosenbaum, J. E. & Jones, S. A. (1995). Creating linkages in the high school-to-work transition: Vocational teachers' networks. In M. Hallinan (Ed.), *Making schools work.* New York: Plenum.

Rosenbaum, J. E., Stern, D., Hamilton, M. A., Hamilton, S. F., Berryman, S. E., & Kazis, R. (1992). *Youth apprenticeship in America: Guidelines for building an effective system.* Washington, DC: William T. Grant Foundation Commission on Youth and America's Future.

Rosenthal, R. & Jacobson, L. (1968). *Pygmalion in the classroom.* New York: Holt, Rinehart and Winston.

Rossi, R. & Stringfield, S. (1995). What we must do for students placed at risk. *Phi Delta Kappan, 77,* 73–76.

Rossides, D. W. (1976). *The American class system: An introduction to social stratification.* New York: Houghton Mifflin.

Rothstein, R. (2000). Equalizing resources on behalf of disadvantaged children. In R. D. Kahlenberg (Ed.), *A notion at risk: Preserving public education as an engine for social mobility* (pp. 21–92). New York: The Century Foundation Press.

Rothstein, R. (2004a). Class and the classroom. *American School Board Journal,* 17–21.

Rothstein, R. (2004b). *Class and schools: Using social, economic, and educational reform to close the Black-White achievement gap.* New York: Teachers College Press.

Rothstein, R. (2010). How to fix our schools: It's more complicated, and more work, than the Klein-Rhee "Manifesto" wants you to believe. *The Education Digest, 76*(6), 32–37.

Rouse, C. E. (1998). Private vouchers and student achievement: An evaluation of the Milwaukee Parental Choice Program. *Quarterly Journal of Economics, 113*(2), 533–602.

Rouse, C. E. (2002). Private vouchers and student achievement: More evidence from the Milwaukee parental choice program. Working paper No. 396, Industrial Relations Section, Princeton, University, Princeton, NJ.

Rousseau, J. J. (1979). *Emile* (A. Bloom, Trans.). New York: Basic Books.

Rowan, B. & Miracle, A. (1983). Systems of ability grouping and the stratification of achievement in elementary school. *Sociology of Education, 56,* 133–144.

RPP International. (1998). *The state of charter schools 1998.* Washington, DC: U.S. Department of Education, Office of Educational Research and Improvement.

RPP International. (1999). *The state of charter schools 1999.* Washington, DC: U.S. Department of Education, Office of Educational Research and Improvement.

RPP International. (2000). *The state of charter schools 2000.* Washington, DC: U.S. Department of Education, Office of Educational Research and Improvement.

RPP International. (2001). *Challenge and opportunity: The impact of charter schools on school districts.* Washington, DC: U.S. Department of Education, Office of Educational Research and Improvement.

Rubinson, R. (1986). Class formation, politics and institutions: Schooling in the United States. *American Journal of Sociology, 92,* 519–548.

Rumberger, R. W. & Gandara, P. (2004). Seeking equity in the education of California's English learners. *Teachers College Record, 106*(10), 2032–2056.

Rury, J. L. (1991). *Education and women's work: Female schooling and the division of labor in urban America, 1870–1930.* Albany, NY: State University of New York Press.

Rury, J. L. & Mirel, J. E. (1997). The political economy of urban education. In M. Apple (Ed.), *Review of Research in Education, 22* (pp. 49–110). Washington, DC: AERA.

Rury, J. & Saatcioglu, A. (2011). Suburban advantage: Opportunity hoarding and secondary attainment in the postwar metropolitan north. *American Journal of Education, 117*(3), 307–342.

Russell, B. (1926). *Education and the good life.* New York: Boni and Liveright.

Rust, V. (1991). Postmodernism and its comparative education implications. *Comparative Education Review, 35*(4), 610–626.

Rutgers School of Law. Supreme Court Syllabus. *Raymond Abbott et al. v. Fred G. Burke et al.* (A-155-97). http://njlaw.rutgers.edu/collections/courts/supreme/a-155-97.opn.html. Accessed October 1, 2012.

Rutledge, S., Harris, D., & Ingle, W. (2010). How principals "bridge and buffer" the new demands of teacher quality and accountability: A mixed-methods analysis of teacher hiring. *American Journal of Education, 116*(2), 211–242.

Rutter, M., Maughan, B., Mortimore, P., & Ouston, J. (1979). *Fifteen thousand hours.* London: Open Books.

Ryan, J. E. & Heise, M. (2002). *The political economy of school choice. Yale Law Journal, 111,* 2043.

Ryan, W. (1971). *Blaming the victim.* New York: Random House.

Sachar, E. (1991). *Shut up and let the lady teach.* New York: Poseidon Press.

Sadker, M. & Sadker, D. (1985, March). Sexism in the schoolroom of the '80's. *Psychology Today,* 54–57.

Sadker, M. & Sadker, D. (1994). *Failing at fairness: How America's schools cheat girls.* New York: Scribners.

Sadovnik, A. R. (1991a). Basil Bernstein's theory of pedagogic practice: A structuralist approach. *Sociology of Education, 64*(1), 48–63.

Sadovnik, A. R. (1991b). Derailing high school tracking: One beginning. *Pathways, 7*(2), 4–8.

Sadovnik, A. R. (1994). *Equity and excellence in higher education.* New York: Peter Lang.

Sadovnik, A. R. (Ed.). (1995a). *Knowledge and pedagogy: The sociology of Basil Bernstein.* Norwood, NJ: Ablex.

Sadovnik, A. R. (1995b). Postmodernism and the sociology of education: Closing the gap between theory, research and practice. In W. Pink & G. Noblit (Eds.), *Continuity and contradiction: The futures of the sociology of education* (pp. 309–326). Creskill, NJ: Hampton Press.

Sadovnik, A. R. (2008). Schools, social class and youth: A Bernsteinian analysis. In L. Weis, *The way class works* (pp. 315–329). New York: Routledge.

Sadovnik, A. R. (2011a). *Sociology of education: A critical reader (Second Edition).* New York: Routledge.

Sadovnik, A. R. (2011b). *Waiting for school reform: Charter schools as the latest imperfect panacea.* New York: Teachers College Record.

Sadovnik, A. R. & Semel, S. F. (Eds.). (2002). *Founding mothers and others: Women educational leaders during the progressive era.* New York: Palgrave.

Sadovnik, A. R., Persell, C., Baumann, E., & Mitchell, R., Jr. (1987). *Exploring society.* New York: Harper and Row.

Sadovnik, A. R., O'Day, J., Borhnstedt, G., & Borman, K. (Eds.). (2008). *No child left behind and the reduction of the achievement gap: Sociological perspectives on federal educational policy.* New York: Routledge.

Sahlberg, P. (2010) *Finnish lessons: What can we learn from education change on Finland.* New York: Teachers College Press.

Salomone, R. (2003). *Same, different, equal: Rethinking single-sex schooling.* New Haven, CT: Yale University Press.

Sanders, M. (1996). *School-family-community partnerships and the academic achievement of African-American urban adolescents.* Center Report. Baltimore, MD: Center for Research on the Education of Students Placed at Risk, Johns Hopkins University.

Sanders, M. (2009). Collaborating for change: How an urban school district and a community-based organization support and sustain school, family, and community partnerships. *Teachers College Record, 111*(7), 1693–1712.

Sanders, W. L. & Rivers, J. C. (1996). *Cumulative and residual effects of teachers on future student academic achievement.* Knoxville, TN: University of Tennessee Value-Added Research and Assessment Center.

Sanjek, R. (1998). *The future of us all.* Ithaca, NY: Cornell University Press.

Sarason, S. B. (1982). *The culture of the school and the problem of change*. Boston, MA: Allyn & Bacon.

Sartre, J. P. (1974). *Existentialism and human emotions*. New York: Philosophical Library.

Scarr, S. & Weinberg, R. A. (1978). The influence of "family background" on intellectual attainment. *American Sociological Review, 43*, 674–692.

Scheffler, I. (1960). *The language of education*. Springfield, IL: Charles Thomas.

Schlesinger, A. M., Jr. (1992). *The disuniting of America*. New York: Norton.

Schaub, M. (2010). Parenting for cognitive development from 1950 to 2000: The institutionalization of mass education and the social construction of parenting in the United States. *Sociology of Education, 83*, 46–66.

Schneider, B. & Bryk, A. (1996). *Social trust: A moral resource for school improvement*. Chicago, IL: Center for School Improvement.

Schneider, B. & Coleman, J. S. (1993). *Parents, their children, and schools*. Boulder, CO: Westview Press.

Schneider, B., Schiller, K. S., & Coleman, J. S. (1995). *Public school choice: Some evidence from the National Education Longitudinal Study of 1988*. Chicago, IL: University of Chicago, Center for the Study of the Economy and the State, Working Paper Series No. 113.

Schön, D. A. (1983). *The reflective practitioner: How professionals think in action*. New York: Basic Books.

School by school report card: The state's second yearly look at Long Island's districts. (1998, March 15). *Newsday*, pp. H1–H11.

School choice: A guide to picking a public school in New York City. (1998). *Newsday*, special reprint.

Schorr, L. B. & Schorr, D. (1989). *Within our reach: Breaking the cycle of disadvantage*. New York: Doubleday.

Schwartz, F. (1981). Supporting or subverting learning: Peer group patterns in four tracked schools. *Anthropology and Education Quarterly, 12*, 99–121.

Schwartz, H. (2010). *Housing policy is school policy: Economically integrative housing promotes academic success in Montgomery County, Maryland*. New York: The Century Foundation.

Scott, J. (2009). The politics of venture philanthropy in charter school policy and advocacy. *Educational Policy, 23*, 106–136.

Scott, J., Lubienski, C., & DeBray-Pelot, E. (2009). The politics of advocacy in education. *Educational Policy, 23*, 3–14.

Sedlak, M. (1987). Tomorrow's teachers: The essential arguments of the Holmes Group Report. *Teachers College Record, 88*(3), 314–325.

Seller, M. & Weis, L. (1997). *Beyond black and white: New voices in U.S. schools*. Albany, NY: State University of New York Press.

Semel, S. F. (1992). *The Dalton School: The transformation of a progressive school*. New York: Peter Lang.

Semel, S. F. (1996). Yes, but . . .: Multiculturalism and the reduction of educational inequality. *Teachers College Record, 98*(1), 153–177.

Semel, S. F. & Sadovnik, A. R. (1995, Summer). Lessons from the past: Individualism and community in three progressive schools. *Peabody Journal of Education, 70*(4), 56–85.

Semel, S. F. & Sadovnik, A. R. (1998). Durkheim, Dewey, and progressive education: Individualism and community in the history of American education. In W. F. Pickering & G. Walford (Eds.), *Durkheim on education*. London: Routledge.

Semel, S. F. & Sadovnik, A. R. (1999). *Schools of tomorrow, schools of today: What happened to progressive education?* New York: Peter Lang.

Semel, S. F. & Sadovnik, A. R. (2008). Small schools and the history of education: Lessons from the history of progressive education. *Teachers College Record, 110*(9), 1774–1771.

Sewall, G. (1991). Common culture and multiculture. *Social Studies Review, 7*.

Sewell, W. & Hauser, R. M. (1974). *Education, occupation, and earnings*. New York: Academic Press.

Sewell, W. & Hauser, R. M. (1976). Causes and consequences of higher education: Modes of the status attainment process. In W. H. Sewell, R. M. Hauser, & D. L. Featherman (Eds.), *Schooling and achievement in American society*. New York: Academic Press.

Sexton, P. C. (1961). *Education and income*. New York: Viking.

Shakeshaft, C. (1986). A gender at risk. *Phi Delta Kappan, 67*, 449–503.

Shakeshaft, C. (1987). *Women in educational administration*. Newbury Park, CA: Sage.

Shanker, A. (1991, October). Lecture at Adelphi University.

Shavit, Y. & Blossfeld, H. P. (Eds.). (1993). *Persistent inequalilty: Changing educational attainment in thirteen countries*. Boulder, CO: Westview Press.

Sherman, J. (1994). *The condition of education in rural schools*. U.S. Department of Education. Washington, DC: Federal Printing Office.

Shmurak, C. B. (1998). *Voices of hope: Adolescent girls of single-sex and coeducational schools*. New York: Peter Lang.

Sikes, J. (1971). *Differential behavior of male and female teachers with male and female students*. Unpublished Doctoral Dissertation, University of Texas, Austin.

Silberman, C. (1969). *Crisis in the classroom*. New York: Random House.

Simon, B. S. (2004). High school outreach and family involvement. *Social Psychology of Education, 7*, 185–209.

Singer, A. (1999). American apartheid: Race and the politics of school finance on Long Island, N.Y. *Equity and Excellence in Education, 32*(3), 25–36.

Singer, J. D. & Butler, J. A. (1987). The education for all handicapped children act: Schools as agents of social reform. *Harvard Educational Review, 57*(2). In T. Hehir & T. Latus (1992). *Special education at the century's end: Evolution of theory and practice since 1970* (pp. 159–190). Cambridge, MA: Harvard Educational Review.

Siskin, L. S. (1991). Departments as different worlds: Subject subcultures in secondary schools. *Educational Administration Quarterly, 27*(2), 134–160.

Siskin, L. S. (1994). *Realms of knowledge: Academic departments in secondary schools*. London: Falmer.

Siskin, L. S. & Little, J. W. (Eds.). (1995). *The subjects in question: Departmental organization and the high school*. New York: Teachers College Press.

Sizer, T. R. (1984). *Horace's compromise: The dilemma of the American high school*. Boston, MA: Houghton Mifflin.

Sizer, T. R. (1985). *Horace's compromise: The dilemma of the American high school* (2nd ed.) Boston, MA: Houghton Mifflin.

Sizer, T. R. (1992). *Horace's school: Redesigning the American high school*. Boston, MA: Houghton Mifflin.

Sizer, T. R. (1996). *Horace's hope*. Boston, MA: Houghton Mifflin.

Skerrett, A. & Hargreaves, A. (2008). Student diversity and secondary school change in a context of increasingly standardized reform. *American Educational Research Journal, 45*, 913–945.

Skinner, B. F. (1971). *Beyond freedom and dignity*. New York: Bantam.

Skocpol, T. (1995). *Social policy in the United States*. Princeton, NJ: Princeton University Press.

Skrtic, T. (1991). The special education paradox: Equity as a way to excellence. *Harvard Educational Review, 61*(2). In T. Hehir & T. Latus (1992). *Special education at the century's end: Evolution of theory and practice since 1970* (pp. 203–272). Cambridge, MA: Harvard Educational Review.

Slavin, R. E. (1983a). *Cooperative learning*. New York: Longman.

Slavin, R. E. (1983b). When does cooperative learning increase student achievement? *Psychological Bulletin, 94*, 429–445.

Slavin, R. E. (1987). Ability grouping and student achievement in elementary schools: A best evidence synthesis. *Review of Educational Research, 57*, 293–336.

Slavin, R. E. (1988, September). Synthesis of research on grouping in elementary and secondary schools. *Educational Leadership, 46*, 67–77.

Slavin, R. E. (1990a). Achievement effects of ability grouping in secondary schools: A best-evidence synthesis. *Review of Educational Research, 60*, 471–500.

Slavin, R. E. (1990b). *Cooperative learning: Theory, research and practice*. Englewood Cliffs, NJ: Prentice-Hall.

Slavin, R. E. (1991). Are cooperative learning and untracking harmful to the gifted? *Educational Leadership, 48*(6), 68–71.

Slavin, R. E. (1997a). Design competitions: A proposal for a new federal role in educational research and development. *Educational Researcher, 26*(1), 22–28.

Slavin, R. E. (1997b). Rejoinder: Design competitions and expert panels: Similar objectives, very different paths, *Educational Researcher, 26*(6), 21–22.

Slavin, R. E. (1999). Rejoinder: yes, control groups are essential in program evaluation: A response to Pogrow. *Educational Researcher, 28*(3), 36–38.

Sleeter, C. (1995). An analysis of the critiques of multicultural education. In J. A. Banks & C. McGee Banks (Eds.), *Handbook of research on multicultural education* (pp. 81–94). New York: Macmillan.

Smerdon, B. A. & Borman, K. M. (2009). *Saving America's high schools*. Washington, DC: The Urban Institute Press.

Sohoni, D. & Saporito, S. (2009). Mapping school segregation: Using GIS to explore racial segregation between schools and their corresponding attendance areas. *Journal of Education, 115*, 569–600.

Solomon, B. M. (1985). *In the company of educated women*. New Haven, CT: Yale University Press.

Soltis, J. (Ed.). (1981). *Philosophy and education*. Eightieth Yearbook of the National Society for the Study of Education, Part I. Chicago, IL: National Society for the Study of Education.

Sowell, T. (1977, March 27). New light on the black I.Q. controversy. *New York Times Magazine*, pp. 56–63.

Spade, J. Z., Columba, L., & Vanfossen, B. E. (1997). Thinking in mathematics and science: Courses and course-selection procedures. *Sociology of Education, 70*(2), 108–127.

Spillane, J. (1998). State policy and the non-monolithic nature of the local school district: Organizational and professional considerations. *American Educational Research Journal, 35*(1), 33–63.

Spillane J. & Thompson, C. (1997). Reconstructing conceptions of local capacity: The local education agency's capacity for ambitious instructional reform. *Educational Evaluation and Policy Analysis, 19*(2), 185–203.

Spring, J. (1972). *Education and the rise of the corporate state*. Boston, MA: Beacon Press.

Spring, J. (1986). *The American school: 1642–1985*. New York: Longman.

Spring, J. (1989). *American education* (4th ed.). New York: Longman.

Spring, J. (2010). *The politics of American education.* New York: Routledge.

Stainback, S. & Stainback, W. (1989). Integration of students with mild and moderate handicaps. In D. K. Lipsky & A. Gartner (Eds.), *Beyond special education: Quality education for all* (pp. 41–52). Baltimore, MD: Paul H. Brookes.

Stanton-Salazar, R. (2001). *Manufacturing hope and despair: The school and kin support networks of U.S. Mexican youth.* New York: Teachers College Press.

Stanton-Salazar, R. D. & Dornbusch, S. M. (1995). Social capital and the reproduction of inequality: Information networks among Mexican-origin high school students. *Sociology of Education,* 68(2), 116–135.

Starfield, Barbara. (1982). Child health and socioeconomic status, *American Journal of Public Health,* 72, 532–534.

Stedman, L. C. (1985). A new look at the effective schools literature. *Urban Education,* 20, 295–326.

Stedman, L. C. (1987). It's time we changed the effective schools formula. *Phi Delta Kappan,* 69, 215–224.

Stein, M. K. & Coburn, C. E. (2008). Architectures for learning: A comparative analysis of two urban school districts. *American Journal of Education,* 114, 583–626.

Steinberg, S. & Kincheloe, J. (1998). *Changing multiculturalism.* London: Open University Press.

Sternberg, R. (2008). Increasing academic excellence and enhancing diversity are compatible goals. *Educational Policy,* 22, 487–514.

Stevens, F. I. (1993a). Applying an opportunity-to-learn conceptual framework to the investigation of the effects of teaching practices via secondary analysis of multiple case study summary data. *Journal of Negro Education,* 62, 232–248.

Stevens, F. I. (1993b). *Opportunity to learn: Issues of equity for poor and minority students.* Washington, DC: National Center for Education Statistics.

Stevens, F. I. (1993c). Opportunity to learn and other social contextual issues: Addressing the low academic achievement of African American students. *Journal of Negro Education,* 62, 227–231.

Stevenson, D. & Baker, D. (1991). State control of the curriculum and classroom instruction. *Sociology of Education,* 64, 1–10.

Stevenson, D. L., Schiller, K. S., & Schneider, B. (1994). Sequences of opportunities for learning. *Sociology of Education,* 67, 184–198.

Stinchcombe, A. (1964). *Rebellion in a high school.* Chicago, IL: Quadrangle Books.

Stodolsky, S. S. (1993). A framework for subject matter comparisons in high schools. *Teaching and Teacher Education,* 9, 333–346.

Strain, J. P. (1975). Idealism: A clarification of an educational philosophy. *Educational Theory,* 25, 263–271.

Stringfield, S., Ross, S., & Smith, L. (Eds.) (1996). *Bold plans for school restructuring: The New American Schools designs.* Hillsdale, NJ: Erlbaum.

Suad Nasir, N., McLaughlin, M. W., & Jones, A. (2009). What does it mean to be African American? Constructions of race and academic identity in an urban public high school. *American Educational Research Journal,* 46, 73–114.

Suarez-Orozco, M. & Qin-Hilliard, D. (Eds.). (2004). *Globalization: Culture and education in the new millennium.* Berkeley, CA: University of California Press.

Sugarman, S. D. (1999). School choice and public funding. In S. D. Sugarman & F. R. Kemerer (Eds.), *School choice and social controversy: Politics, policy and law* (pp. 111, 139). Washington, DC: Brookings Institution Press.

Supovitz, J. & May, H. (2003). *The relationship between teacher implementation of America's choice and student learning in Plainfield, New Jersey.* Philadelphia, PA: Consortium for Policy Research in Education.

Swartz, D. (1997). *Culture and power: The sociology of Pierre Bourdieu.* Chicago, IL: University of Chicago Press.

Swidler, A. (1979). *Organizations without authority: Dilemmas of social control in free schools.* Cambridge, MA: Harvard University Press.

Takaki, R. (1993). *A different mirror: A history of multicultural America.* Boston, MA: Little, Brown.

Takaki, R. (1998a). *A larger memory: A history of our diversity, with voices.* Boston, MA: Little, Brown.

Takaki, R. (1998b). *Strangers from a different shore: A history of Asian Americans.* Boston, MA: Back Bay.

Talbert, J. E. (1992). *New strategies for developing our nation's teacher force and ancillary staff with a special emphasis on implications for Chapter 1.* Paper commissioned by the U.S. Department of Education.

Talbert, J. E. (1993). Constructing a schoolwide professional community: The negotiated order of a performing arts school. In J. W. Little & M. W. McLaughlin (Eds.), *Teachers' work: Individuals, colleagues, and contexts* (pp. 164–184). New York: Teachers College Press.

Talbert, J. E. (1995). Boundaries of teachers' professional communities in U.S. high schools: Power and precariousness of the subject department. In L. S. Siskin & J. W. Little (Eds.), *The subjects in question: Departmental organization and the high school* (pp. 68–94). New York: Teachers College Press.

Talbert, J. E. (1996). Primacy and promise of professional development in the nation's reform agenda: Sociological views. In K. Borman, P. W. Cookson, Jr., A. R. Sadovnik, & J. Z. Spade (Eds.), *Implementing educational reform: Sociological perspectives on educational policy* (pp. 283–312). Westport, CT: Ablex.

Talbert, J. E. & McLaughlin, M. W. (1994, February). Teacher professionalism in local school context. *American Journal of Education, 102,* 123–153.

Tamir, E. (2008). Theorizing the politics of educational reform: The case of New Jersey's alternate route to teacher certification. *American Journal of Education, 115*(1), 65–95.

Task Force on the Common School. (2002). *Divided we fail: Coming together through public school choice.* New York: The Century Foundation.

Taylor, G. (2009), Choice, competition, and segregation in a United Kingdom urban education market. *American Journal of Education, 115*(4), 549–568.

Teacher Education Project. (1986). *A compilation of the major recommendations of teacher education.* Washington, DC: National Educational Project.

Teachers College Record. (1979, Winter). *81*(2), 127–248.

Teske, P. & Schneider, M. (2001). What research can tell policymakers about school choice. *Journal of Policy Analysis & Management, 20,* 609.

Text of statement of goals adopted by the governors. (1990, March 7). *Education Week, 9,* 16–17.

Thernstrom, A. & Thernstrom, S. (2003). *No excuses: Closing the racial gap in learning.* New York: Simon and Schuster.

Thomas, K. J. & Staiger, D. O. (2003). Unintended consequences of racial subgroup rules. In P. E. Peterson & M. R. West (Eds.), *No child left behind? The politics and practice of accountability.* Washington, DC: Brookings Institution Press.

Thornburg, D. & Karp, K. S. (1992). Lessons learned: Mathematics + science + higher order thinking second language learning =? *Journal of Language Minority Students, 10,* 159–184.

Thorne, B. (1993). *Gender play: Girls and boys in school.* New Brunswick, NJ: Rutgers University Press.

Tidball, E. (1973). Perspectives on academic women and affirmative action. *Journal of Higher Education, 54,* 130–135.

Tidball, E. (1980). Women's colleges and women's achievers revisited. *Signs, 5,* 504–517.

Tidball, E. (1985). Baccalaureate origins of entrants into American medical schools. *Journal of Higher Education, 56,* 385–402.

Tidball, E. (1986). Baccalaureate origins of recent natural science doctorates. *Journal of Higher Education, 57,* 606–620.

Tidball, M. E., Tidball, C. S., Smith, D. G., & Wolf-Wendel, L. E. (1999). *Taking women seriously: Lessons and legacies for educating the majority.* Phoenix, AZ: American Council on Education/Onyx Press.

Time Magazine. Do poor kids deserve poor schools? (1991, October 14), pp. 60–61.

Toenjes, L. A., Dworkin, A. G., Lorence, J., & Hill, A. N. (2002). High-stakes testing, accountability, and student achievement in Texas and Houston. In J. E. Chubb & T. Loveless (Eds.), *Bridging the achievement gap* (pp. 109–130). Washington, DC: The Brookings Institution.

Toppo, Greg. (June 11, 2008). Sharpton, education plan may tear union ties, *USA Today.* www.usatoday.com/news/education/2008-06-11-race-equality_N.htm. Accessed April 2, 2010.

Tough, Paul. (2008). *Whatever it takes: Geoffrey Canada's quest to change Harlem and America.* New York: Houghton Mifflin Company.

Torres, C. A. (2008). *Education and neoliberal globalization.* New York: Routledge.

Tractenberg, P., Holzer, M., Miller, G., & Sadovnik, A. (2002). *Developing a plan for reestablishing local control in the state-operated districts.* Newark, NJ: Institute on Education Law and Policy, Rutgers University. www.ielp/rutgers.edu. Accessed October 1, 2012.

Tractenberg, P., Sadovnik, A., & Liss, B. (2004). *Tough choices: An informed discussion of school choice.* Newark, NJ: Institute on Education Law and Policy, Rutgers University. www.ielp/rutgers.edu.

Tractenberg, P., Liss, B., Moscovitch, R., & Sadovnik, A. R. (2006). Don't forget the schools: Legal considerations for tax reform. Institute on Education Law and Policy, Rutgers University

Traub, J. (1994). *City on a hill: Testing the American dream at City College.* Reading, MA: Addison-Wesley.

Trow, M. (1961). The second transformation of American secondary education. *International Journal of Comparative Sociology, 2,* 144–166. In Karabel, J. & Halsey, A. H. (Eds.), *Power and ideology in education* (pp. 105–118). New York: Oxford University Press, 1977.

Trueba, H., Jacobs, L., & Kirton, E. (1990). *Cultural conflict and adaptation: The case of Hmong children in American society.* New York: Falmer.

Turner, R. H. (1960, October). Sponsored and contest mobility and the school system. *American Sociological Review, 25,* 855–867.

Tushnet, M. (1994). *Making civil rights law: Thurgood Marshall and the supreme court, 1936–1961.* New York: Oxford University Press.

Twentieth Century Fund Task Force on Federal Elementary and Secondary Education Policy. (1983). *Making the grade.* New York: Author. (ERIC ED 233 112).

Tyack, D. (1974). *The one best system.* Cambridge, MA: Harvard University Press.

Tyack, D. (1990). Restructuring in historical perspective: Tinkering toward utopia. *Teachers College Record, 92,* 170–191.

Tyack, D. & Cuban, L. (1995). *Tinkering toward utopia: A century of public school reform*. Cambridge, MA: Harvard University Press.

Tyack, D. & Hansot, E. (1982). *Managers of virtue: Public school leadership in America, 1820–1980*. New York: Basic Books.

Tyack, D. & Hansot, E. (1990). *Learning together: A history of coeducation in American public schools*. New Haven, CT: Yale University Press.

Tyson, K. (2003). Notes from the back of the room: Problems and paradoxes in the schooling of young Black students. *Sociology of Education, 76*, 326–343.

Tyson, K. (2011). *Integration interrupted: Tracking, black students, and acting white after Brown*. New York: Oxford University Press.

Tyson, K., Darity, W., & Castellino, D. (2005). It's not "a Black thing": Understanding the burden of acting White and other dilemmas of high achievement. *American Sociological Review, 70*(4) (Aug.), 582–605.

UCLA Civil Rights Project. (2012). http://civilrights project.ucla.edu. Accessed October 1, 2012.

U.S. Bureau of the Census. (1998). *Statistical abstract of the United States, 1998*. Washington, DC: Government Printing Office.

U.S. Bureau of the Census. (2003a). *Current populations reports*. Washington, DC: Author.

U.S. Bureau of the Census. (2003b). *Annual demographic survey*. Washington, DC: Author.

U.S. Bureau of the Census. (2012). Current Population Reports. Washington, DC.

U.S. Department of Education, National Center for Education Statistics. (1989a). *The condition of education, 1989 edition*. Washington, DC: Government Printing Office.

U.S. Department of Education, National Center for Education Statistics. (1989b). *The digest of education statistics, 1989*. Washington, DC: Government Printing Office.

U.S. Department of Education, National Center for Education Statistics. (1996). *NAEP 1994 trends in academic progress*. Washington, DC: Author.

U.S. Department of Education, National Center for Education Statistics. (1997a). *The digest of educational statistics*. Washington, DC: Author.

U.S. Department of Education, National Center for Education Statistics. (1997b). *Pursuing excellence: A study of U.S. fourth grade mathematics and science achievement in international context*. Washington, DC: Author.

U.S. Department of Education, National Center for Education Statistics. (1998). *The condition of education, 1998 edition*. Washington, DC: Author.

U.S. Department of Education, National Center for Education Statistics. (2006). *The digest of education statistics*. Washington, DC.

U.S. Department of Education, National Center for Education Statistics. (2012a). *The condition of education*. Washington, DC.

U.S. Department of Education, National Center for Education Statistics. (2012b). *NAEP trial urban district assessment*, http://nationsreportcard.gov/tuda.asp. Accessed October 1, 2012.

U.S. Department of Education, National Center for Education Statistics, Office of Educational Research and Improvement. (1994). *School-to-work: What does research say about it?* Washington, DC: Author.

U.S. Department of Education, National Center for Education Statistics, Office of Educational Research and Improvement. (1998a). *Tools for schools: School reform models supported by the National Institute on the Education of At-Risk Students*. Washington, DC: Author.

U.S. Department of Education, National Center for Education Statistics, Office of Educational Research and Improvement. (2000b). *Monitoring school quality: An Indicators Report* (NCES 2001–030). Washington, DC: Author.

U.S. Department of Education, National Center for Education Statistics, Office of the Under Secretary and Office of Elementary and Secondary Education. (2000a). *The digest of educational statistics*. Washington, DC: Author.

U.S. Department of Education, National Center for Education Statistics, Office of the Under Secretary and Office of Elementary and Secondary Education. (2001). *First annual school improvement report: Executive order on actions for turning around low-performing schools*. Washington, DC: Author.

U.S. Department of Education, National Center for Educational Statistics, Office of the Under Secretary and Office of Elementary and Secondary Education. (2002). *The digest of educational statistics*. Washington DC: Author.

U.S. Department of Education, National Center for Educational Statistics, Office of the Under Secretary and Office of Elementary and Secondary Education. (2003). *The digest of educational statistics*. Washington DC: Author.

U.S. Department of Education, National Center for Educational Statistics, Office of the Under Secretary and Office of Elementary and Secondary Education. (2004). *The condition of education: National assessment of educational progress*. Washington, DC: Author.

U.S. Department of Education, National Center for Education Statistics, Office of the Under Secretary and Office of Elementary and Secondary Education. (2004). *Parental involvement, Title 1, Part A: Non-regulatory guidance*. Washington DC: Author.

U.S. Department of Education, National Center for Educational Statistics, Office of the Under

Secretary and Office of Elementary and Secondary Education. (2009). *The condition of education: National assessment of educational progress.* Washington, DC: Author.

U.S. Department of Education, National Center for Education Statistics, Office of the Under Secretary and Office of Elementary and Secondary Education. (2010). *The digest of education statistics.* Washington, DC: Author.

U.S. Department of Education, National Center for Education Statistics, Office of the Under Secretary and Office of Elementary and Secondary Education. (2012). *The digest of education statistics.* Washington, DC: Author.

U.S. Department of Education, Office of Planning and Evaluation. (1998). *Turning around low-performing schools: A guide for state and local leaders.* Washington, DC: Author.

Useem, E. L. (1991). Student selection into course selection sequences in mathematics: The impact of parent involvement and school policies. *Journal of Research on Adolescence, 1,* 231–250.

Useem, E. L. (1992a). Getting on the fast track in mathematics: School organizational influences on math track assignment. *American Journal of Education, 100*(3), 325–353.

Useem, E. L. (1992b). Middle schools and math groups: Parents' involvement in children's placement. *Sociology of Education, 65,* 263–279.

Useem, E. L. (1994). *Renewing schools: A report on the Cluster Initiative in Philadelphia.* Philadelphia, PA: PATHS/ PRISM: The Philadelphia Partnership for Education.

Valentine, C. A. (1968). *Culture and poverty: Critique and counter proposals.* Chicago, IL: University of Chicago Press.

Valentine, C. A. (1975). Deficit, difference and bicultural models of Afro-American behavior. In Challenging the myths: The schools, the blacks and the poor. *Harvard Educational Review* (Reprint Series No. 5), 1–21.

Valenzuela, A. (1999). *Subtractive schooling: U.S. Mexican Youth and the politics of caring.* Albany, NY: SUNY Press.

Vandenberg, D. (1971). *Being and education: An essay in existential phenomenology.* Englewood Cliffs, NJ: Prentice-Hall.

Van Dunk, E. & Dickman, E. (2003). *School choice and the question of accountability.* New Haven, CT: Yale University Press.

Vanfossen, B. E., Jones, J. D., & Spade, J. Z. (1987). Curriculum tracking and status maintenance. *Sociology of Education, 60,* 104–122.

Van Hook, J. (2002). Immigration and African American educational opportunity: The transformation of minority schools. *Sociology of Education, 75,* 169–189.

Van Voorhis, F. L. (2003). Interactive homework in middle school: Effects on family involvement and students' science achievement. *Journal of Educational Research, 96*(9), 323–339.

Velez, W. (1989). Why Hispanic students fail: Factors affecting attrition in high schools. In J. H. Ballantine (Ed.), *Schools and society: A unified reader* (2nd ed.). Palo Alto, CA: Mayfield.

Vergari, S. (2002). *The charter school landscape,* University of Pittsburgh Press.

Verstegen, D. (1993). Financing education reform: "Where did all the money go?" *Journal of Education Finance, 19,* 1–35.

Verstegen, D. & McGuire, C. K. (1991). The dialectic of reform. *Educational Policy, 5,* 386–411.

Viadero, D. (1999). Who's in, who's out. *Education Week,* 12.

Vinovskis, M. A. (1995). *Education, society, and economic opportunity: A historical perspective on persistent issues.* New Haven, CT: Yale University Press.

Viteritti, J. P. (1999). *Choosing equality.* Washington, DC: Brookings Institution Press.

Viteritti, J. P. (Ed.). (2009). *When mayors take charge: School governance in the city.* Washington, DC: Brookings Institution Press.

Walford, G. (1992a). Educational choice and equity in Great Britain. *Educational Policy, 6,* 123–381.

Walford, G. (1992b). Educational reform in Great Britain. In P. W. Cookson, Jr., A. R. Sadovnik, & S. Semel (Eds.), *International handbook of educational reform.* Westport, CT: Greenwood Press.

Walford, G. (1999). Educational reform in England and Wales. In D. L. Levinson, P. W. Cookson, Jr., & A. R. Sadovnik (Eds.), *Encyclopedia of sociology and education.* New York: Garland.

Walker, J. H., Kozma, E. J., & Green, R. P., Jr. (1989). *American education: Foundations and policy.* St. Paul, MN: West.

Waller, W. (1965). *The sociology of teaching.* New York: Wiley.

Walters, P. B. (2001). Educational access and the State: Historical continuities and discontinuities in racial inequality in American education. *Sociology of Education, 74,* Extra Issue, 35–45.

Warren, R., Grodsky, E., & Lee, J. (2008). State high school exit examinations and postsecondary labor market outcomes. *Sociology of Education, 81,* 77–107.

Wasley, P. (1994). *Stirring the chalkdust: Tales of teachers changing classroom practice.* New York: Teachers College Press.

Weakliem, D., McQuillan, J., & Schauer, T. (1995). Toward meritocracy? Changing social-class differences in intellectual ability. *Sociology of Education, 68,* 271–287.

Weatherly, R. A. & Lipsky, M. (1977). Street-level bureaucrats and institutional innovation: Implementing special education reform. *Harvard*

Educational Review, 47(2). In T. Hehir & T. Latus (1992). *Special education at the century's end: Evolution of theory and practice since 1970* (pp. 89–119). Cambridge, MA: Harvard Educational Review.

Weber, M. (1976). Types of authority. In L. A. Coser & B. Rosenberg (Eds.), *Sociological theory: A book of readings*. New York: Macmillan.

Wechsler, H. S. (2001). *Access to success in the urban high school: The middle college movement*. New York: Teachers College Press.

Wehlege, G. G. & Smith, G. A. (1992). Building new programs for students at risk. In F. M. Newmann (Ed.), *Student engagement and achievement in American secondary schools* (pp. 92–118). New York: Teachers College Press.

Weikert, D. & Schweinhart, L. J. (1984). *Changed lives: The effects of the Perry Preschool Program on youths through age 19*. Ypsilanti, MI: High Scope.

Weiler, K. (1988). *Women teaching for change*. South Hadley, MA: Bergin and Garvey.

Weiler, K. (1998). *Country schoolwomen: Teaching in rural California, 1850–1950*. Palo Alto, CA: Stanford University Press.

Weir, M., Orloff, A., & Skocpol, T. (1988). *The politics of social policy in the United States*. Princeton, NJ: Princeton University Press.

Weis, L. (1985). *Between two worlds: Black students in an urban community college*. Boston, MA: Routledge & Kegan Paul.

Weis, L. (Ed.). (1988). *Class, race and gender in American education*. Albany, NY: State University of New York Press.

Weis, L. (1992). *Working class without work*. Albany, NY: State University of New York Press.

Weis, L. (1993). White male working-class youth: An exploration of relative privilege and loss. In L. Weis & M. Fine (Eds.), *Beyond silenced voices* (pp. 237–258). Albany, NY: State University of New York Press.

Weis, L. (2004). *Class reunion: The remaking of the American white working class*. New York: Routledge.

Wells, A. S. (1991). Choice in education: Examining the evidence on equity. A symposium on politics, markets, and America's schools. *Teachers College Record, 93*(1), 137–155.

Wells, A. S. (1993a). The sociology of school choice: Why some win and others lose in the educational marketplace. In E. Rassell & R. Rothstein (Eds.), *School choice: Examining the evidence*. Washington, DC: The Economic Policy Institute.

Wells, A. S. (1993b). *Time to choose: America at the crossroads of school choice policy*. New York: Hill and Wang.

Wells, A. S. (1995). Reexamining social science research on school desegregation: Long- versus short-term effects. *Teachers College Record, 96*, 691–706.

Wells, A. S. (1996). African-American students' view of school choice. In B. Fuller, R. Elmore, & G. Orfield (Eds.), *School choice: The cultural logic of families, the political rationality of schools. Who chooses? Who loses? Culture institutions and the unequal effects of school choice*. New York: Teachers College Press.

Wells, A. S. & Crain, R. L. (1992). Do parents choose school quality or school status? A sociological theory of free market education. In P. W. Cookson, Jr. (Ed.), *The choice controversy* (pp. 65–82). Newbury Park, CA: Corwin Press.

Wells, A. S. & Crain, R. L. (1999). *Stepping over the color line: African American students in White suburban schools*. New Haven, CT: Yale.

Wells, A. S. & Serna, I. (1996). The politics of culture: Understanding local political resistance to detracking in racially mixed schools. *Harvard Educational Review, 66*, 93–118.

Wells, A. S., Artiles, L., Carnochan, S., Cooper, C, Grutzik, C., Holme, J., Lopez, A., Scott, J., Slayton, J., & Vasudeva, A. (1998). *Beyond the rhetoric of charter school reform: A study of ten California districts*. Los Angeles, CA: University of California, Los Angeles.

Wells, A. S., Holme, J. J., Tijerina Revilla, A., & Atanda, A. K. (2004). How desegregation changed us: The effects of racially mixed schools on students and society: A study of desegregated high schools and their class of 1980 graduates. www.tc.columbia.edu/faculty/documents.htm?facid=asw86. Forthcoming in *In search of Brown*, Harvard University Press, 2005.

Wells, A. S., Duran, J., & White, T. (2008). Refusing to leave desegregation behind: From graduates of racially diverse schools to the Supreme Court. *Teachers College Record, 110*(12), 2532–2570.

Wells, A. S., Holme, J. J., Revilla, A. J., & Atanda, A. K. (2008). *Both sides now: The story of school desegregation's graduates*. Berkeley, CA: University of California Press.

Wells, A. S., Baldridge, B., Duran, J., Lofton, R., Roda, A., Warner, M., White, T., & Czreskowski, C. (2009). *Why boundaries matter: A study of five separate and unequal Long Island school districts*. New York: Teachers College, Columbia University, Center for Understanding Race and Education.

Wenglinsky, H. (1997). How money matters: The effect of school district spending on academic achievement. *Sociology of Education, 70*, 221–237.

Westbrook, R. B. (1991). *John Dewey and American democracy*. Ithaca, NY: Cornell University Press.

Wexler, P. (1976). *The sociology of education: Beyond equality*. Indianapolis, IN: Bobbs-Merrill.

Wexler, P. (1987). *Social analysis of education*. London: Routledge & Kegan Paul.

Wexler, P. (1992). *Becoming somebody*. London: Falmer.

Wexler, P. (1996). *Holy sparks: Social theory, education, and religion.* New York: St. Martin's.

Wexler, P. (2007). *Symbolic movement: Critique and spirituality in sociology of education.* Rotterdam, Netherlands: Sense Publishers.

Wexler, P. (2008). *Social theory in education primer.* New York: Peter Lang.

White, M. (1987). *The Japanese educational challenge.* New York: The Free Press.

Whitehead, A. N. (1957). *The aims of education and other essays.* New York: The Free Press.

Whitty, G. (1985). *Sociology and school knowledge.* London: Methuen.

Whitty, G. (1997). Creating quasimarkets in education: A review of recent research on parental choice and school autonomy in three countries. *Review of Research in Education, 22,* 3–48.

Whitty, G. & Power, S. (2000). Marketization and privatization in mass education systems. *International Journal of Educational Development, 20.*

William T. Grant Foundation Commission on Work, Family, and Citizenship. (1988). *The forgotten half: Pathways to success for America's youth and young families.* Washington, DC: William T. Grant Foundation.

Willis, P. (1981). *Learning to labor: How working class kids get working class jobs.* New York: Columbia University Press.

Wilson, W. J. (1987). *The truly disadvantaged: The inner city, the underclass, and public policy.* Chicago, IL: University of Chicago Press.

Wilson, W. J. (1995). *When work disappears.* Cambridge, MA: Harvard University Press.

Wilson, W. J. (1998). The role of the environment in the Black-White test score gap. In C. Jencks & M. Phillips (Eds.), *The Black-White test score gap* (pp. 501–510). Washington, DC: Brookings Institution Press.

Wilson, W. J. (1999, March 6). Rising inequality and the case for multiracial coalition politics. Keynote address, Eastern Sociological Society, Boston.

Wirt, F. & Kirst, M. (1972). *Political and social foundations of education.* Berkeley, CA: McCutchan.

Wirt, F. & Kirst, M. (1982). *Schools in conflict.* San Francisco, CA: McCutchan.

Witte, J. (1990). Choice and control: An analytical overview. In W. H. Clune & J. F. Witte (Eds.), *Choice and control in American education, Volume 1: The theory of choice and control in American education.* New York: Falmer.

Witte, J. (1996). Who benefits from the Milwaukee choice program. In B. Fuller, R. F. Elmore, & G. Orfield (Eds.), *Who chooses? Who loses? Culture institutions and the unequal effects of school choice* (pp. 118–137). New York: Teachers College Press.

Witte, J. (2000). *The Market approach to education.* Princeton, NJ: Princeton University Press.

Witte, J. & Walsh, D. J. (1990). A systematic test of the effective schools model. *Educational Evaluation and Policy Analysis, 12,* 188–212.

Witte, J., Thorn, C. A., Pritchard, K. M., & Claiborn, M. (1994). *Fourth-year report: Milwaukee parental choice program.* Department of Political Science and the Robert LaFollette Institute of Public Affairs, University of Wisconsin-Madison.

Witte, J., Sterr, T. D., & Thorn, C. A. (1995). *Fifth-year report: Milwaukee parental choice program.* Department of Political Science and the Robert LaFollette Institute of Public affairs, University of Wisconsin-Madison.

Wohlstetter, P., Malloy, C., Chau, D., & Polhemus, J. (2003). Improving schools through networks: A new approach to urban school reform. *Educational Policy, 17*(4), 399–430.

Wolk, R. (1998). Strategies for fixing failing public schools. *Education Week Supplement,* 43.

Wong, K. K., Shen, F. X., Anagnostopoulous, D., & Rutledge, S. (2007). *The education mayor: Improving America's schools.* Washington, DC: Georgetown University Press.

Wong, S. L. (1991). Evaluating the content of textbooks: Public interests and professional authority. *Sociology of Education, 64*(1), 11–18.

Wong-Fillmore, L. & Valdez, C. (1986). Teaching bilingual children. In M. Wittrock (Ed.), *Handbook of research on teaching* (3rd ed.). New York: Macmillan.

Woolfolk, A. E. (1990). *Educational psychology* (4th ed.). Boston, MA: Allyn & Bacon.

Wraga, W. G. (1997). Patterns of interdisciplinary curriculum organization and professional knowledge of the curriculum field. *Journal of Curriculum and Supervision, 12*(2), 98–117.

Wraga, W. G. (1999). "Extracting sun-beams out of cucumbers": The retreat from practice in reconceptualized curriculum studies. *Educational Researcher, 28*(1), 4–13.

Wright, L. B. (1957). *The cultural life of the American colonies.* New York: Harper & Brothers.

Wright, R. (1969). *Native son.* New York: Harper and Row.

Wrigley, J. (1982). *Class, politics and public schools: Chicago, 1900–1950.* New Brunswick, NJ: Rutgers University Press.

Wrigley, J. (Ed.). (1992). *Education and gender equality.* London: Falmer.

Yaffe, Deborah. (2007). *Other people's children: The battle for justice and equality in New Jersey's schools.* New Brunswick, NJ: Rutgers University Press.

Yamamoto, Y. & Brinton, M. (2010). Cultural capital in East Asian educational systems: The case of Japan. *Sociology of Education, 83,* 67–83.

Yeomans, E. (1979). *The Shady Hill School: The first fifty years.* Cambridge, MA: Windflower Press.

Young, M. (1958). *The rise of the meritocracy, 1870–2033: An essay on education and equality.* London: Thames and Hudson.

Young, M. F. D. (1971). *Knowledge and control: New directions for the sociology of education.* London: Collier-Macmillan.

Young, M. F. D. (2007). *Bringing knowledge back in: From social constructivism to social realism in the sociology of education.* Oxford: Routledge.

Zajda, J. I. (1980). *Education in the U.S.S.R.* New York: Pergamon.

Zavadsky, H. (2009). Bringing school reform to scale: Five award winning urban districts. Cambridge, MA: Harvard Education Press.

Zeichner, K. M. (2009). *Teacher education and the struggle for social justice.* New York: Routledge.

Zelman v. Simmons-Harris, 122 S.Ct. 2460 (2002).

Zigler, E. & Muenchow, S. (1992). *Head Start: The inside story of America's most successful educational experiment.* New York: Basic Books.

Zigler, E. & Styfco, S. (1993). *Head Start and beyond: A national plan for extended childhood intervention.* New Haven, CT: Yale University Press.

Zigler, E. & Valentine, J. (Eds.). (1979). *Project Head Start: A legacy of the war on poverty.* New York: The Free Press.

Zweigenhaft, R. L. & Domhoff, G. W. (1991). *Blacks in the white establishment? A study of race and class in America.* New Haven, CT: Yale University Press.

Index

Also of Interest...

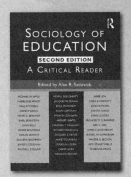

Sociology of Education: A Critical Reader, Second Edition.

Edited by Alan R. Sadovnik

PB ISBN: 978-0-415-80370-0

This comprehensive and bestselling Reader examines the most pressing topics in sociology and education while exposing students to examples of sociological research on schools.

Foundations of Education: The Essential Texts

Edited by Susan F. Semel

PB ISBN: 978-0-415-80625-1

This volume contains substantial selections from those works widely regarded as central to the development of the Foundations field, helping aspiring teachers interpret the craft of teaching within the historical, philosophical, cultural, and social contexts of education.

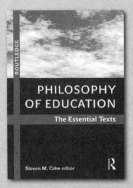

Philosophy of Education: The Essential Texts

Edited by Steven M. Cahn

PB ISBN: 978-0-415-99440-8

This anthology is organized around ten of the most widely taught and read classic philosophers of education. From Plato to John Dewey, this book offers the "essential texts" that lay the foundation for education students' course of study.